The Manual to Online Public Records

The Researcher's Tool to Online Resources
of Public Records and Public Information

4th Edition

By Sankey & Hetherington

©2017 by Facts on Demand Press
BRB Publications, Inc
PO Box 27869
Tempe, AZ 85285
800-929-3811
www.brbpublications.com

Facts
ON DEMAND
◘ **PRESS**

The Manual to Online Public Records

The Researcher's Tool to Online Resources of Public Records and Public Information
Fourth Edition

©2017 By BRB Publications, Inc.
PO Box 27869 • Tempe, AZ 85285 • 800.929.3811
ISBN13: 978-1-889150-62-8

Text written by: Michael L. Sankey and Cynthia Hetherington
Government Sites Sections Complied by: Michael Sankey and BRB Publications, Inc.
Selected Editing by: Mark Hodgson
Cover Design by: Robin Fox & Associates

Cataloging-in-Publication Data
(Provided by Quality Books, Inc.)
     Sankey, Michael L., 1949- author.
          The manual to online public records : the
     researcher's tool to online resources of public records
     and public information / by Sankey & Hetherington. --
     4th edition.
          pages cm
          First edition gives Hetherington first on title page;
     Sankey has primary responsibility for the work overall.
          ISBN 978-1-889150-62-8

          1. Electronic public records--United States--
     Directories. 2. Public records--United States--
     Directories. 3. Internet research.   I. Hetherington,
     Cynthia, author. II. Title. III. Title: Online public
     records.

     JK468.P76S36 2017   025.06'973
                              QBI16-900031

Table of Contents

Recorded Documents, Judgments, and Liens (includes UCC filings); Securities and Securities Dealers; Sexual Offender Registries; Tax Assessor and Collector Records; Telephone Numbers; Trademarks & Service Marks; Unclaimed Funds; Vital Records (includes SSA Death Index and Obituaries); Voter Registration; Workers' Compensation; World Wide Web

Advantages Online Public Record Vendors Provide; Types of Publuc Record Vendors; Vendors and Privacy Concerns; Beware of Instant Web-Based Background Checks; Where to Find a Vendor; Resource Lists of Selected Vendors By Topic

51 state chapters with profiles of these online record providers: major state agencies, occupational licensing boards, state and local courts, assessors and recorders

Federal Court Structure; How Federal Trial Court Case Records are Organized; Case Assignments and Court Locations: Electronic Access - CM/ECF and PACER: Bankruptcy Records and the Multi-Court Voice Case Information Syatem (McVCIS); Federal Court Record Searching Hints; What to do When Record Search Results Do Not Include Identifiers; Obtaining Closed Case Files and the Federal Records Centers; Other Federal Courts;

The Read Me Page

The depth and scope of information that exists online about people, businesses, and places is staggering. These cyber trails record major events in people's lives – from birth to the first car and house, to death, wills, and probate. Add to this the paths of social networks and search engines that reflect an abundance of willingly shared personal information. It is no wonder that today's society treats public record information as a commodity.

With literally thousands of public record and public information sources accessible on the web by anyone, how do you know which sites are useful and which ones are fluff? As most of us know, just because something is on the internet doesn't make it true. What should be taken into consideration when you evaluate the information they offer?

This manual is designed to provide facts and procedures that you can use to improve your business and record searching. These pages will help you to more effectively find and compile information on both individuals and businesses. More importantly, this book will provide the skills needed to evaluate the reliability and accuracy of web sources.

How to Use This Book to Your Advantage

The chapters in *The Manual to Online Public Records* will lead you to many, many diverse and accurate sources of records. A brief review of how this content flows will make it easier for you to find specific material you need. Below are short summaries of each chapter with explanations on their applications.

The Manual to Online Public Records will guide you to many, many sources of records. Use the following outline to more easily find the specific information that you need.

Chapter 1 - Online Public Record Fundamentals and Site Evaluation Techniques

This chapter is strongly recommended if you are new to using public records. And if you consider yourself a public records guru, certain sections, such as the one describing evaluation techniques, might be especially valuable to you.

Chapter 2 - Using Search Engines to Your Advantage.

While most anyone can do a Google search; knowing how to the conduct more advanced searches will save time and reap better results.

Chapter 3 - Using Social Media Sites to Your Advantage

Keeping abreast of web and technology developments requires vigilance. Using social media sites to investigate or research people and events is a science. With a focus on Facebook, Twitter and LinkedIn, this chapter examines search techniques, shortcuts, and investigating tools.

Chapter 4 - Record Searching From A tTru Z

The chapter includes key record types examined in alphabetical order, from Archives to Worker's Compensation. Each record type is packed with unique resources and how-to-search tips.

Chapter 5 - Selected Vendors

Tips on finding vendors are provided, along with a select list of data aggregators sorted by the type of records they provide.

Chapter 6 - Online Sites Offered by States and Counties

Comprising the bulk of this publication, this chapter examines on a state-by-state and in an easy to use format the online offerings from state and local governments. Free online access and fee-based systems are indicated, all within the type or category of records available.

Chapter 7 - How to Obtain Records From the Federal Court System

This chapter explains how the Federal Court System works, what data is available electronically, and how to access case files stored at the Federal Archives.

Some Straight Talk

How many of these six statements about public record searching do you believe are true?

1. It's all free online. Why should I have to pay for it?

2. I can find all the information I need using Google.

3. Certain record types may be available to the public in one state, but not in another.

4. To do a criminal record search, all I need is an online national database; I don't need to go to the courthouse.

5. I do background checks for employers, but I am not governed by the Fair Credit Reporting Act because I do not provide credit reports.

6. To do comprehensive public record searching online, all I need is my $29 membership web account that lets me search 35,000+ databases of public records.

Only statement #3 is true. The other five statements represent beliefs often held by those looking for easy ways to find public records. If you practice due diligence when using public records for decision-making, you probably knew that only #3 is true.

Whether or not you use public records for decision-making on the job, or even if you are a casual record searcher, this book will likely help you and perhaps even change the way you conduct your searches.

Cynthia Hetherington & Michael Sankey

# Chapter 1

Online Public Record Fundamentals and Site Evaluation Techniques

This chapter has two sections that describe basic terminology, resources, and processes that will hopefully enable the reader to get the most out of this book.

- **Part One** examines the two primary sources of public records and key concepts that are critical to know when searching for public records.
- **Part Two** examines how to analyze the accuracy and value of an online site.

But first let's take a quick look at the type of information one may find online when looking for public records.

The Types of Data You Will Find Online

Effective use of online records requires an understanding of how the following *types* of information differ.

Public Records

Public records are records of incidents or actions filed or recorded with a government agency for the purpose of notifying others – the public – about the matter. For example, deeds are recorded in order to keep track of property owners. Mortgages are recorded to indicate liens on the property. Prospective buyers and lenders search these records to verify ownership and determine if the property is subject to liens or easements. These records are public; anyone requiring details about your property may review or copy these documents.

Public Information

Telephone book listings is an example of **public information**; that is, information that you freely provide to facilitate the flow of commercial and private communications. Another example is information placed on social network sites such as Facebook or LinkedIn. And when you sign up for the discount card at the local grocery store you have made information about yourself publicly available to entities purchasing marketing lists.

Knowing the difference between public records and public information will help you understand some of the differences between online sites and how they gather their data.

Personal Information

The question of whether personal information should be made available online, and by whom and to whom goes well beyond the focus of this book. Suffice it to say that **personal information** may be found in either public records or in public information. To a limited extent, such information will remain private unless it is disclosed to some outside entity that could make it public.

Viewable personal identifiers on public records are necessary for identification and/or to match public records to the correct individual.

Part One: Where to Find Public Records

Online access to public records comes in several varieties and packages, but searching really boils down to two primary resources:

    A. Government Agency Sources

    B. Private Sector Record Vendors.

A. Searching Government Agency Sources

Five important truths apply to searching online public records online of government agencies—

1. More than 25% of state and county government agencies do not provide public records online.

2. Government sites can be free or fee- based; the latter generally being more robust.

3. Most government public record websites that are free to search contain no personal identifiers beyond names.

4. Often the searchable and viewable information found online is limited to name indexes and summary data rather than document images. Most access sites – especially those that are free – permit the former and not the latter. While online portals can be a quick path to viewable or downloadable record data, they often are merely conduits to view a record index. To view the actual records, one must usually place an order to receive document images.

5. Accessibility to government records varies by jurisdiction. Just because records are accessible in your state or county, do not assume the same accessibility exists in the next county or state.

Keep these truths in mind and your searches will lead to better results.

The Accessibility Paradox

Truth #5 above, often referred to as the *accessibility paradox*, adds to the challenge of accessing government records.

A category of records may be severely restricted and withheld from the public in one state, while entirely available in another. This is particularly true for criminal histories, motor vehicle records, and non-certified vital records. Keep this in mind as your public record searching takes you from state-to-state and county-to-county.

Record Indexing and the Importance of Identifiers

Record index is used often throughout this book. A record index points to a location or file number where documents, such as recordings, case files, deeds, and articles of incorporation are kept. If a record is about a court case, the index is a summary of the proceedings. If you are searching at an unfamiliar location, then an understanding of how the index is presented one of first items you need to check. A public record index can be electronic, but also can exist on-site on card files, in books, on microfiche, etc. AA public record index can be in an electronic file, on an on-site card file, in a book, or on microfiche, etc. A record index can be organized in a variety of ways – by name, by year, by case or file number, or by name and year. Depending on the type of public record, an alpha index could be by plaintiff and/or defendant, by grantor and/or grantee, by address, or by year, etc.

Remember that the *primary search that government agencies provide* is often *a search of the index*. If someone says that they can view a certain number of county court records online, they are likely referring to an index summary of records, rather than all the files and pages contained within a case history.

Identifiers on Records

The lack of identifiers displayed when searching online is a significant problem for employers such as financial institutions that require a high level of accuracy. The existence of any possible erroneous information must be checked by a manual search to insure the proper identity of the subject. Even then, identifiers may be removed.

Government agencies that offer online access on a fee or subscription basis – usually to pre-approved requesters – are more apt to disclose personal identifiers (such as date of birth) than the free access sites. Very few provide social security numbers, and those that do usually mask the first five digits. Some sites even hide the birth month and day and only provide the birth year. For example, most U.S. District Court and Bankruptcy Court PACER search systems provide little (sometimes only the last four digits of social security numbers and no date of birth) or no personal identifiers, thus making reliable "name searches" nearly impossible.

What If the Index Doesn't Have Matching Identifiers?

You will often find that an online index of records at government agencies does not contain a personal identifier. In that situation, one must search for personal identifiers within the record file itself or in associated paperwork.

For example, let us say you are searching for a record on Joe B. Cool with a DOB of 01/01/1985. And let us say the search yields an index showing a possible record match of J Cool with no DOB, and another possible match with a Joseph Cool with a partial DOB match. The next step is to examine the two files to determine if the files contain matching personal identifiers. When utmost accuracy is required, common names may require the viewing of dozens of files.

The Redaction Trend

Redaction is simply removing or hiding certain elements within a record or the record index. In recent years, a number of government agencies have been redacting personal information for both the index and the actual records.

In some cases, however, the costs of redacting potentially sensitive information is forcing government agencies to simply block public access to their records. Balancing privacy concerns with the benefits of shared information is an ongoing challenge that will continue to affect policies related to public record searches.

About Record Fees and Charges

Fees and other charges for public records result from transactions or the delivery of services (time, salaries, supplies, etc.) to record, store, and track these events. Although public records may be free of charge to view, they are not necessarily free of charge when provided as file copies. Fees can also be expected if government personnel must perform onsite searches.

Fees commonly charged at government agencies – whether searching is performed online or on site – include: copy fees (to make copies of documents); search fees (for clerical personnel to search for the record); certification fees (to certify a document as being accurate and coming from the particular agency); and fees to expedite (to place you at the "front of the line").

Subscription Accounts or Pay as You Order

Payment for records from both government sites and vendor sites is usually done through a subscription account or pay as you go using a credit card.

Subscription accounts are common, and many agencies, such as state motor vehicle agencies, only provide online record access to pre-approved, high-volume, ongoing accounts. Typically, this contractual access involves fees and a specified, minimum amount of usage.

A number of the online agencies profiled in Chapter 6 provide access to information on a pay-as-you-go basis, often requiring a credit card payment. Some agencies offer a glimpse of the index or docket, but will charge a fee for the record copy. Some allow the record to be printed on the spot, while others will only mail it.

Fees can, and do, vary widely between jurisdictions - even for the same record type. Copy fees vary from $.10 to $10 per page, while search fees range from under a dollar to as much as $65.

BRB's online Public Record Research System (PRRS found at www.brbpublications.com) relates the specific fees involved with all record access methods for more than 22,000 government agencies.

B. Searching Private Sector Sources - Record Vendors

Selecting the right record vendor for your particular search requires a systematic approach that identifies the types of vendors available and knowing how they work with clients. Before signing up with every potential online vendor that catches your eye, try to narrow your search to the type of vendor most suitable for your record needs. The many specialized vendors that are mentioned throughout this book can be categorized as follows:

- **Distributors**   (data aggregators with proprietary databases)
- **Gateways**   (instantaneous electronic access from direct sources or distributors)
- **Search Firms**   (professional search services using direct sources and all other vendors)
- **Verification Firms**   (employment screening and tenant screening firms)
- **Record Retrievers**   (onsite record researchers and document retrievers)

About Distributors and Gateways

Distributors

Distributors, generally, are automated public record dealers who combine public sources of bulk data and/or online access to develop their own in-house database products. Sometimes called *data aggregators*, they collect or buy public record information from government repositories. They may also purchase and hold records from other distributors or from public information vendors, like phone companies, and then combine the content in useful ways. Many distributors use data extraction which is often referred to as *screen scraping*. (See the article by John Kloos on Data Extraction starting on the next page.)

The hundreds of data distributors in the U.S can often be categorized as follows:

1. Vertical distributors, which collect multiple data types on a local or regional basis
2. Horizontal distributors which collect single-purpose types of information, on a regional or national basis
3. Vertical and Horizontal distributors which perform both of the above functions

An example of a Vertical distributor is iDocket.com, a Texas-based company that offers online access to records from more than 300 courts in Texas.

An example of a Horizontal Distributor is Aristotle (www.aristotle.com). Aristotle purchases voter registration records nationwide and sells customized, authorized lists to political candidates and political parties.

An example of a distributor that is both vertical and horizontal is LexisNexis (www.lexisnexis.com), a multi-service company that offers access to many and varied nationwide databases for a variety of clients. A key point is when a database vendor sells purchases data from a government agency, the vendor is bound by any existing restriction or disclosure laws attached to the data by the originating government repository. These access restrictions can range from zero for recorded documents or level three sexual predators, to severe for voter registrations or vehicle ownership.

Gateways

Gateways are similar to distributors, but they do not warehouse records – they merely provide a sophisticated method to electronically access existing databases from other locations or hosts.

Gateways therefore provide clients with automated electronic access to 1) multiple proprietary database vendors or 2) government agency online systems. Gateways provide one-stop shopping for multiple geographic areas and/or categories of information. Gateways are very prominent on the Internet, advertising access to records for many different purposes.

Many gateways exist per a contractual relationship with a government agency and a chosen vendor. For example over thirty states provide online access to driving records using the National Information Consortium (www.nicusa.com). Details of these access points are described in Chapter 6.

Gateways may use multiple sources and may also use extraction.

Companies can be both distributors and gateways. For example, a number of online database companies are both primary distributors of corporate information and also gateways to real estate information from other primary distributors.

Search Firms

Firm that provide public record search and document retrieval services are prominent on the web. They obtain the records by either using distributors or gateways, or by going directly to government agencies. Their services are not always online-oriented since not all records are online, and because copies of documents must often be obtained. Search firm often have built their own network of on-site specialists, (see Record Retrievers below). Therefore search firms often combine online proficiency with document retrieval expertise. Search firms sometimes to focus on one geographic region – like New England – or one specific types of public record information – like criminal records. There are literally hundreds of search firms in the U.S.

Search firms often provide services not only on an ongoing basis to businesses and clients, but also to the general consumer market.

Verification Firms

Verification firms provide services to employers and businesses when the search subject has given consent for the verification. An example of a verification firm is one that provides access to, and use of, certain public records provided by pre-employment and tenant screening firms. For these firms, activities are subject to provisions in the Fair Credit Reporting Act (FCRA). Verification firms that use information provided by motor vehicle records, likewise, are governed by the Drivers Privacy Protection Act (DPPA).

Since verification firms generally perform services for clients who have first received consent from the subject, they do not warehouse or collect data to be resold. The service provided by a pre-employment screening company is often called a background screen or a background report. Their service should not be confused with 'an investigation' as provided by private investigators (see below) or with search firms that provide general public record searches.

There are over 1,000 pre-employment screening firms in the U.S., not counting the many private investigators who also offer screening. This number also does not include the many online consumer sites or consumer links that offer broad, but limited, instant background checks on people.

About Private Investigation Agencies

Private investigators and agencies often provide record retrieval services (see below) or search firm services (see above). In fact the principal and/or employees of a search firms or verification firms often have a state-issued private investigators license.

Since private investigators research and analyze information about legal, financial, and personal matters, they often use results from public record searches within the final reports they provide to clients. Purposes include investigating or verify a subject's background, find missing persons, or investigating cyber-crimes.

Record Retrievers

A different vendor somewhat similar to a search firm is known as a *local document retriever* or simply, a *record retriever*. Retrievers are hands-on researchers for hire who visit government agencies in-person. The 500+ members of the Public Record Retriever Network (PRRN) are listed by state and counties served at www.PRRN.us. This organization establishes industry standards for the retrieval of public record documents, and members operate under a Code of Professional Conduct. The use of record retrievers can be especially productive in jurisdictions where online access is not available.

Web Data Extraction & Screen Scraping Technology

An old concept with a new application is being used by a number of vendors today. This technology is called web data extraction, but the name currently in vogue is *Screen Scraping*.

Web Data Extraction, or Screen Scraping, is described in the following informative article written by Mr. John Kloos, President of BackChecked LLC, Phoenix, AZ www.backchecked.com. Mr. Kloos is well known within the background screening industry. He has served on the Board of Directors of the National Association of Professional Background Screeners and is a frequent speaker on industry topics. We sincerely thank Mr. Kloos for allowing us to reprint his article.

Web Data Extraction (a.k.a. Screen Scraping) and Online Public Records

by John Kloos

As soon as the first public records became available online in the late 1990's you can be sure that somewhere some computer programmer started thinking about a way to automate the process of searching them. After all, what's better than not having to go to the court house? How about not having to manually enter the search parameters into the various court websites? Instead, let a computer program do the grunt work!

Fast forward to today and we find that many large public records research companies are taking full advantage of this opportunity, utilizing a process known as *Web Data Extraction*. Although it may have become commonplace, it is still important to understand exactly what it is and how it works, especially if your understanding of the research process is anchored in the 1980's.

Let's start with the technology that makes it possible.

Web Data Extraction – What is it?

In the public records research marketplace, this technology is often referred to as *Screen Scraping*. In fact, *Screen Scraping* is a term dating to the 1960's when programmers wrote processes to read or "scrape" text from computer terminals so that it could be used by other programs. *Web Data Extraction* is a much more sophisticated technology that incorporates the automated scheduling, extraction, filtering, transformation and transmission of targeted data available via the Internet. To say that a well-deployed *Web Data Extraction* system is performing *Screen Scraping* is like calling a modern refrigerator an ice box.

An example of a relatively simple *Web Data Extraction* application is the free service Google provides for repeatedly searching news articles on a specific topic. Because I am in the Background Screening Industry, I use Google to conduct a daily search for articles that include the phrase "background check." Every morning, I am greeted with an email that lists new articles, complete with links to each one. Nice.

An example of a more complex *Web Data Extraction* application would be collecting competitive data in your marketplace. Are there any new announcements by your competitors? What new products are they selling? What's available in their on-line catalogues? Are their prices changing? Have they formed any new partnerships? Are there any newcomers to the industry? Obviously, the technology behind this type of application is much more sophisticated than the *Google News* search mentioned above.

With the shear amount of information available via the Internet, it's no surprise that a large number of off-the-shelf *Web Data Extraction* tools are now available at a very reasonable cost. Both start-up and industry veterans in the public records research market now utilize these platforms. Others have developed custom systems. The benefits are obvious: reduced costs and shorter turn-around times. But, what are the risks?

Web Data Extraction in Online Public Records Research

The first factor to consider in Public Records Research is that the stakes can be high. Consider the consequences of missing data while conducting competitive analysis compared to the ramifications of missing a felony record while doing a background check. This is likely the main reason that the public records industry was relatively slow to adopt this new technology-- the established comfort level with direct human involvement, even when a search was conducted on-line.

Another reality to consider is that state and county jurisdictions are not necessarily pleased that *Web Data Extraction* technology is being used to search records on websites that were designed and implemented to serve humans. In addition to the fear that their sites may be overloaded by technology that is much faster than the typical human's ability to point and click, there is a legitimate concern that public records will be systematically extracted and used to populate commercial databases.

In an effort to thwart *Web Data Extraction* systems, many government agencies have equipped their sites with a challenge-response test, known as a CAPTCHA. Coined in 2000 by a group from Carnegie Mellon University, this acronym stands for "Completely Automated Public Turing test to tell Computers and Humans Apart." It works by presenting the user with a purposely distorted image that contains letters and/or numbers. In order to gain access to the desired data, the characters must be re-entered by the user. Of course, as with almost any roadblock they encounter, smart programmers have found ways to beat the CAPTCHA test, resulting in a back and forth battle that is sure to continue far into the future.

All such controversy aside, it is certain that the use of *Web Data Extraction* systems will continue to expand. The economics are simply too compelling to believe otherwise. Consider what would happen if you were to hold a contest between a well-implemented Web Data Extraction system and a well-rested human record retriever. The task: perform 1,000 searches on a county website that provides full online access. The end results should be identical. However, the *Web Data Extraction* system is going to finish the job in less than an hour. It won't get tired. It won't make an error while copying results. It won't get distracted by a phone call. And it won't call you to complain that it can't be expected to search every possible variation of Mickey Johannes MacDougal.

This does not mean to suggest the days of the human Record Retriever are finished. Not all records are available online nor is there any guarantee that you will be able to find a *Web Data Extraction* system that meets your standards.

Evaluating Public Record Providers Who Utilize Web Data Extraction Systems

If you routinely rely on third party providers to conduct public records research, you will eventually encounter a provider that employs *Web Data Extraction* for at least some jurisdictions. In this case, there a few key questions to ask.

1. Does the provider have the proper domain expertise in public records research?

Even the brightest computer programmers are unlikely to develop a good system if there is no one to educate them and provide detailed requirements and quality assurance tests. It's important that experienced public records researchers have provided this expertise and that they have remained involved in on-going development.

2. Does the provider keep current with changes at the jurisdictions being searched?

Unlike with system interfaces developed between cooperative partners, county and state jurisdictions are under no obligation to inform operators of a *Web Data Extraction* system that a change has been made to their site. It's important that the provider constantly monitor government sites for changes that can affect the outcome of a search.

3. Is the provider committed to monitoring and complying with the legal restrictions contained on each site?

Although they may be providing public records, each jurisdiction maintains its own policies regarding use of their public data. These policies are presented in text format for examination by a human. The provider must be aware of these policies and commit to remaining compliant.

4. Does the provider have a comprehensive test plan to ensure that results from automated activity are equal to that of a human researcher?

To maintain confidence that it is working properly, any automated system needs to be tested on a continuous basis. Since the cost of running test searches is low in an automated system, beware of a provider who is unwilling to accommodate tests against known results on a regular basis.

Conclusion

Although very controversial just a few years ago, *Web Data Extraction* has become mainstream. Most of the larger public research providers are utilizing the technology in some way, melding it with legacy systems that support traditional methods. Furthermore, new providers have emerged in the past few years, specializing in the technology, providing service in only those jurisdiction where *Web Data Extraction* can be counted on to get the complete job done.

Still, *Web Data Extraction* in the public records market is not so mature that you should take it for granted. Make sure it's right for your particular needs. It can also be valuable to demonstrate your knowledge of the technology, whenever contacting new vendors or reviewing current providers.

Know the Difference Between Consumer and Professional Vendor Sites

The Internet is filled with web pages offering low-cost deals claiming to have access to the most records. How do you differentiate between these public record web stores, and how do you know which site is going to give you the best overall search or service?

First, remember that there are websites that specialize in providing services to consumers, and others that specialize in providing ongoing services to professionals. It is important to remember the advantages and disadvantages of each.

About Consumer-Oriented Sites

Consumer sites are great for finding personal information such as telephone numbers or addresses of old friends and family members. Sometimes these sites are referred to as People Search websites and are usually categorized as either distributors or gateways. One-stop shops certainly have advantages as a quick way to find low-cost public records information about someone, such as a neighbor, or a person dating a relative. Often these providers search multiple free sites at the same time, and charge a "membership fee" for the convenience. And some of these sites offer links to free public information as a draw to sell searches to consumers. Other consumer sites include their own proprietary data with other public data in a specialized search. The amount of free data provided is often related to how aggressively their SEO (Search Engine Optimization) is structured.

Consumer sites can be useful if their limitations are kept in mind. One example of an excellent people search site is PeopleSmart.com, which offers recommendations and recourse when desired records can not be found online..

In general, consumer sites are rarely used by professionals who require a deeper due diligence when searching public records. Limitations of consumer sites often include issues of comprehensiveness, timeliness, legal compliance, and searching techniques. When using these sites, ask yourself questions like "How old is this data that is purported to be updated frequently?" Also, beware of misleading statements in marketing material. For example, there are few truly national databases, because many government agencies do not sell records to vendors. In fact, some agencies are precluded from doing so because they are not yet computerized.

 SEARCH TIP As you will learn in Chapter 6, if 25% of courts' felony records are not online, then how accurate is a so-called instant national criminal check?

To be candid, this book is filled with references to professional sites and largely ignores consumer sites. For example, the recommended sites and vendors listed in Chapter 4 are included because their services and expertise are specific to the topics covered within the chapter. The vendor list at the end of this chapter is certainly not exhaustive, but the vendors were selected because the types of records they provide are more closely related to the many of the public records profiled throughout this book.

About Professional-Oriented Search Sites

Like consumer sites, professional sites can be Distributors or Gateways. What separates the *consumer site users* from *professional site users* is often the purpose of the record search and level of due diligence required. Using data sources that are timely and authentic is a must when performing a full-scale background check, a pre-employment background screen, or an asset and lien search.

Finding professional search sites is not always easy. A Google search on *driving records* or *driving record check* will find many service companies, but will probably not yield the industry icons. The fact is, there is a limited number of driving record vendors who offer high-volume pricing with national coverage, because these vendors limit their services to specific clientele, such as the insurance or trucking industries or pre-employment screening companies. These vendors do not show up prominently in search engine results and you won't often see Google ads posted by them. A Google search will, however, yield plenty of vendors looking to sell to those with an occasional need.

Part 2 – How to Evaluate the Accuracy and Value of Online Content

This section presents ways to improve your analysis of public record searching. If you are a professional and the use of public records is important to your operation, determining the value of the searchable content is crucial.

Everyone is trying to either save a buck or gain an edge over the competition; hence, finding the best online resources is an imperative. The information provided herein is meant to help you provide better service to your clients and possibly save you money. And, as a bonus, the recommendations and cautions will help minimize your exposure to litigation.

Are the Correct Questions Being Asked?

Habitual questions often asked about using an online site are:

- "How much does it cost?"
- "Is the data current?"

But the questions that really need to be asked and answered are:

- "Is 'x' a primary source or a secondary source?"
- "Is an online search of 'x' equivalent to an onsite search? "

Sure, you can ask a colleague for a recommendation about an online site. But you likely will not find full scale information, either for a colleague or from a on a post on a social media site or list serve. The reality is firms who have taken the time to fully analyze online sites are not going to give their analysis away freely. The data is much too valuable.

The Three Keys to Evaluation

There are three primary consideration areas when evaluating searchable record content for your needs—

1. **Search Mechanics**
2. **The Viewable Data**
3. **The Severity of the Disclosure**

1. Analyze the Search Mechanics

Check the Name Field Logistics

How does the search work when searching by name? Are there wild cards? How do you handle a search when the record could be under the name of Tom or Thomas? Will the use of a middle initial help? One of the easiest and quickest ways to find answers is to look for a *"Help Me"* or "Searching Tips" section. They are not always evident, and even if available, are often ignored. Impatient researchers not wanting to be bogged done by reading instructions will eventually run into trouble.

Another common problem in the name field is the manner in which business names are shown. If searching for records on *The ABC Company*, do you search under both "The…" and "ABC…"?

Consider testing the site using prior searches that were successful. In this way you can experiment with different search parameters and note the results.

Searchable by All Involved Parties?

Let's say you are looking for liens or civil litigation facts on a subject. Using a free online search of a government database, you perform your search and find no hits, and report to your client there is no record on file. But what if you were not aware the records for this particular database source is only searchable by the first name entered on the list of defendants, even when there are multiple parties involved? Perhaps this sounds a bit far-fetched, but unfortunately this situation is far from uncommon. New York, for example, offers a free statewide search of the civil index which reportedly operates in this manner.

It is therefore recommended that you use previously completed searches that contain multiple parties and re-search by all party names. Determine for yourself whether or not a site's searchable index includes all the names or parties

Use of the DOB Field

Are you looking for leads on the whereabouts of someone - or are you preparing a report that will be submitted to an attorney which could be used in court? Can you get by with just the name and year of birth?

If the DOB is critical to your search and it is available as a search component on the search site you are using or evaluating, great. But try the same search without entering data in the DOB field and see what results are now produced. Consider the possibility that more records under the same subject name could be found. And in the process you may even find a missing middle initial or an address that previously had not surfaced.

The reality is that the DOB appears inconsistently on records or in the index of certain types of databases. This is especially true for civil court case records. To find the DOB of a common name, you may need to pull and examine the full case file or call the involved attorney, as that may be the only way to verify that the record you found belongs to the subject of your search.

Redaction can also change the outcome when using a DOB in a search. In Wyoming, for example, a State Rule effective January 1, 2011 directed redaction of the birth day and birth month on public record pleadings and exhibits filed at the courts. From that date forward, the courts created two copies of each document – one public copy that is redacted, and one non-public copy that contains the full DOB and social security number. It is important to note that some Wyoming court judges have directed their courts to redact partial identifiers on **all** prior cases filed, and not just those filed since 01/01/11. How would you know this if you were using an uninformed consumer vendor site?

Can You Search Using Multiple Case Types or Case Date Fields?

Much like searching all involved parties, these are key components of a search site that need to be tested if you want to use the site for serious research. The site may have a drop-down box, but you cannot always rely on the "all" choice. Therefore, it is a good idea to test with known cases and see if there are any anomalies or patterns that surface.

Will the Search Subject be Notified?

Some states require that the subject be informed when certain types of inquiries are made, including identifying the requester. This is especially important if your inquiry is confidential or if the subject's discovery of the search could lead to any embarrassment. Requests for driving records in North Dakota, for example, and criminal records from the AOCFastCheck system in Kentucky, both require that subjects be informed of the inquiry.

2. Analyze the Viewable Data

How Far Back Does the Search Go?

Obviously it is beneficial to know the record retention period, or "throughput" – how far back records are maintained. A case in point. Let's say you are hired to do a seven-year search on a subject in a number of geographic locations. You assume all of your sources go back that far, but, unbeknownst to you, one of them only goes back five years. If the record search connected research involving litigation or background, and incomplete data is used, are you prepared for the possible legal action that you or your client could face?

It is surprising how many sites do NOT inform users of record throughput, and this is even true for certain state judicial sites.

With a little effort, however, you can often find the throughput listed on a site and it is well worth the effort to do so. Chapter 6 provides examples where the throughput varies widely from county to county on a state's judiciary online site. (Check out Indiana, Kansas, and North Dakota.)

This is an important factor which helps determine if an online resource should be used only as a secondary or supplemental search, as opposed to a primary search source.

How Current is the Data?

Knowing how current the information is is crucial, and any explanation of timeliness that doesn't provide clear and concise dates is inadequate. A vendor may claim it updated a record index last week, but what if this data still reflects a sixty-day delay or data entry backlog? If there is an investigation of an incident in progress by an occupational licensing board, will your online resource show the latest results?

This so-called "update gap" is common in state criminal agencies such as the State Police or Department of Public Safety, which receive and hold case information received from the courts. (See the Criminal Record Repository section in Chapter 4 for some eye-opening statistics from a recent U.S. Department of Justice Study.)

Why take chances? Make sure the level of due diligence you require matches the results of the search you perform.

Confirm the Sources and Geographic Boundaries of the Search

Look for disclosure statements confirming the sources of the database you are searching. If the site belongs to a vendor, look for verification regarding the completeness of the data. Judging the reliability of a database requires knowing the system's data boundaries.

Statewide or Partial State or Single County

If you are using a state government public records site, confirm whether the search is for statewide or county data. And if statewide, verify that all counties are reporting for a specific date.

As you will see in Chapter 6, thirty-two states provide some type of centralized online access to court records information. Unfortunately, as records for Arizona and Arkansas reflect, not all of these sites are all-inclusive wherein an online search is equivalent to searching each county court in-person. If a vendor is supplying you with an "instant criminal record search" in Arizona, you better look again and verify the geographic coverage. Don't make assumptions about this important matter.

Countywide or Single County Agency

The same cautions described above are required when conducting searches within counties (or parishes, etc.). Records within geographic regions are not necessarily co-mingled or organized in ways that we assume. This is especially true for upper and lower courts. In Virginia, for example, one online system exists for Circuit (upper) Courts, and another for the District (lower) Courts. In Ohio, the upper court (Court of Common Pleas) has a countywide system online, while the lower courts (Municipal Courts) are not included.

As another example of unpredictable geographic organization of data, consider property-related records in New Hampshire. The recording offices are Register of Deeds (for real estate) and Town/City Clerk (for farm-related UCCs). To complicate matters, Grafton, Hillsborough, Merrimack, Strafford, and Sullivan are names for both a town/city and a county.   And the following unincorporated towns do not have a Town Clerk, so all liens are registered at the corresponding county: Cambridge (Coos), Dicksville (Coos), Green's Grant (Coos), Hale's Location (Carroll), Millsfield (Coos), and Wentworth's Location (Coos).

As should now be obvious, the utmost care is necessary when searching for records in an unfamiliar state or county.

Heed the Adage "Garbage In and Garbage Out"

As reliable as some sites are, and though they may pass your tests with flying colors, the fact remains that many public records are created by humans who manually enter data. A certain number of errors and typos, such as missed characters or transposed digits or letters, are a given.

Understand the pluses and minuses of a site and make use of *wild cards* to enhance the value of your search results.

3. Analyze the Disclaimer

Does the site you are using have a bias or purpose that is inconsistent with your intent? Many government websites that offer access to online records specify caveats, limitations, disclosure restrictions, as well as statements that the data should be used for informational purposes only. A common reaction is often "yeah, so what?"

But consider the site's disclaimer in relationship to your due diligence needs. Is the disclaimer merely a "CYA" courtesy warning, or should this site truly not be used as a primary search site? What if you provide research to an attorney and you use a statewide civil records site in South Dakota which prohibits the use of the site if the data is resold? Any possible exposure there?

Below is an example of a disclaimer on a Rhode Island site at http://courtconnect.courts.state.ri.us.

> "This website is provided as an informational service only and does not constitute and should not be relied upon as an official record and/or schedule of the court. Since the full date of birth and other personally identifying information is not included in this service, the information contained herein shall not be relied upon to confirm a person's identity or a person's criminal record for any purpose including, but not limited to, background checks or employment."

In other words this site should not be used for background checks. Sites with such disclaimers should be considered as supplemental or secondary sources only, especially if you are performing searches that require strict due diligence. Using a web source with such a disclaimer for a criminal record search likely will not comply with the Federal Fair Credit Reporting Act, which regulates pre-employment screening.

Putting it Altogether

Everyone is not going to have the same criteria or due diligence needs. Therefore, use the following checklist as a general guide for determining what is going to work best for your operation.

✓ Analyze Your Product/Service Requirements

Begin by making a couple of lists, which include:

1. Products or services that you have promised your clients.
2. Evaluation categories mentioned previously that carry any degree of importance to you. Differentiate those that are mandatory to your needs from those that are supplemental.

You can even take this a step further: Create a matrix spreadsheet and assign point values based on level of importance. Compare this analysis to the level of service or coverage you have promised to your clientele. What level of due diligence is your client expecting? Have you allocated enough costs (time and fees) in a search to properly do the job?

✓ Monitor Your Core Sites

Keeping track of offerings of online sites is like herding cats. As the saying goes - the only constant in life is change, and those changes can be good or bad. Sites often add more content or more search criteria, and they can take content away. And new sites are always popping up. For example here at BRB Publications, in 2016 we added or modified over 2,500 of the listed links to our list of free government search sites.

The point is, after you create your own analysis matrix and list of core sites, do not park and sit on your analysis for two years.

✓ Make a Statement Describing Your *Best Practices*

Formulate a description of the ideal online source and the necessary components that they must offer for you to consider them a primary resource. What components, or lack thereof, lead to classifying a site as being secondary? Do you have a similar best practice statement provided to clients about your online research process, or do you merely state something to the effect that we do the best we can?

Below are four questions to ask yourself about your own best practices. Your answers will offer insight into your current online research procedures.

- How Do You Measure Value?
- Do You Cut Corners and, if so, Where?
- Do You Monitor or Evaluate Sites?
- How Will your Results Hold Up in Court?

Hopefully, this chapter has provided some insight into analyzing record searching procedures. The next two chapters will put you on the road to becoming an expert when using of search engines, social networks, and media sites.

# Chapter 2

Using Traditional Search Engines for Locating Public Information

This chapter examines the creative searching features and offerings provided by search engines. Using these advanced techniques greatly enhances the searching of public information.

Note the next chapter examines how to use search engines to find social network users and content.

Inside This Chapter:

- The Reliance on Search Engines
- Getting the Most Out of Google
- Other Useful Google Tools
- Other Worthy Search Engines
- Using eBay.com
- Craigslist Searching
- SearchTempest.com & Claz.org
- Bing.com
- Zoominfo.com
- Wayback Machine on Archive.org
- Summary

The Reliance on Search Engines

The Internet has come a long way since the days of command line searching through services like Gopher, Veronica, Jughead, and Archie. Now familiar with Google, Bing and other popular engines, there was a time when a Google search used an "or" for more than one-word search as in a search for *George Washington* would produce pages with *George* and other pages with *Washington* listed in them. So accustomed to this magical resource have we become, that the ability to retain knowledge and apply critical thinking have been trumped by asking Siri, or running a search off your phone for a quick answer.

Researchers rely on search engines to search Internet content (webpages, blogs, news, etc.) for specified keywords and then return a list of those webpages where the keywords were found. Answers can be found instantly with almost zero effort. However, the simplicity in using these easy tools often takes away from the technologically superior searches that can be conducted and reap richer results. Many users will plug in a word or phrase and hit the "Search" button without much thought as to running a smarter search. Some will take advantage of adding quotes around phrases or common expressions, but most just type and go. Also missed are the other search tools created by these services such as mapping, news, videos, etc.

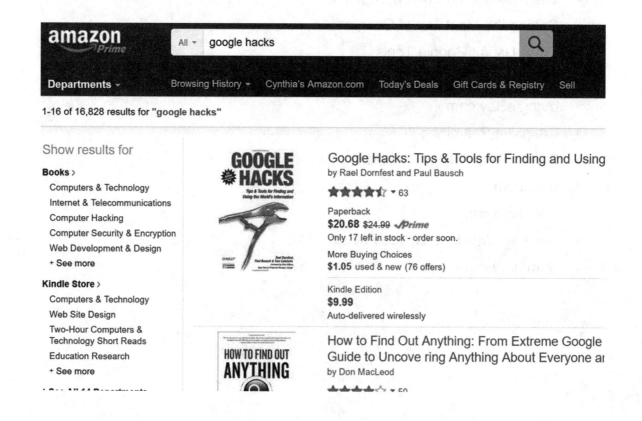

Among the earliest engines developed are Yahoo.com, Altavista.com, and Google.com. There are several online resources that excel in helping you understand the history of these engines as well as learn more about their functionality, how they rank pages, how to use these resources to their best ability, and what else is on the horizon in the searcher's world. Amazon (above) offers over sixteen thousand titles searching "google hacks" in their online bookstore. The gurus Gary Price (the Invisible Web and author) and Chris Sherman (founder of Searchenginewatch.com), and look for Ran Hock's (author of four editions of *The Extreme Searcher's Internet Handbook,)* which is a handy resource for any new searcher, for more information. The balance of this chapter examines the advanced search features of those search engines with the most robust and useful offerings for expertly searching public information.

Getting the Most Out of Google

As the market-share leader of free search tools on the Internet, Google certainly gets a good deal of use. However, it is probably one of the most poorly used online resources available. There are numerous enhancements that go well beyond merely pushing words through and clicking "Google Search" or "I'm Feeling Lucky." An accomplished investigator should know how to use Google's advanced-search features, operators, and how to take advantage of its advanced search feature settings and preferences settings.

Using Google's Preferred Results

For example, one way to save a lot of time and not miss vital hits is to set the *Number of Results* from 10 (the default) to 100. (This is also recommended for other search engines.)

To do this, go to the first screen of Google.com, click on Settings, which is in the right corner of the page or upper right-hand corner (sometimes looks like a sprocket), and then slide down to Results per page. Here you see a choice to slide the choice from 10 to 100. Slide that bar to 100 and click the Save button at the bottom of the page. Then every time you use Google, it will give you 100 results per page. You may have to change Google Instant Predictions to Never show Instant Results first.

Google Instant predictions

When should we show you results as you type?

○ Only when my computer is fast enough

○ Always show Instant results

◉ Never show Instant results

Results per page

10	20	30	40	50		100

Faster   Slower

The *Settings* option also allows you to specify the default tolerance for "safe searching filtering." Google's *SafeSearch* blocks webpages containing explicit sexual content from appearing in search results. The filter option allows you to Turn on *SafeSearch* by checking the box offered. For investigations I recommend that you uncheck that box, and not filter your searches. A great deal of valuable investigative content is sitting on websites which host profane material. (Please leave *SafeSearch* turned on if children or anyone sensitive to objectionable material).

The *Preferences* option (see *Settings*) also allows you to specify the default tolerance for "safe searching filtering." Google's *SafeSearch* blocks webpages containing explicit sexual content from appearing in search results. The filter options are:

- Use strict filtering (filter both explicit text and explicit images)
- Use moderate filtering (filter explicit images only—default behavior)
- Do not filter my search results

Google Operators

Using Google operators will smarten a search and enable you to find the right link faster. Look in the first column in the table below for the bolded characters known as operators. They help define or "narrow" a search.

This Search	Operator	Google Finds Pages Containing ...
cooking Italian	None	Both the words cooking and Italian but not together or in order
vegetarian **OR** vegan	**OR**	Information on vegetarian or vegan
"Can I get a witness"	""	The exact phrase "Can I get a witness"
Henry +8 Great Britain	+	Information about Henry the Eighth (8), weeding out other kings of Great Britain
automobiles ~glossary	~	Glossaries about automobiles as well as dictionaries, lists of terms, terminology, etc.
salsa -dance	-	The word "salsa" but NOT the word "dance" (note the space before the hyphen)
salsa-dancer	-	All forms of the term, whether spelled as a single word, a phrase, or hyphenated (note the lack of a space)
define:congo	**define:**	Definitions of the word "congo" from the Web
site:virtuallibrarian.com	**site:**	Searches only one website for expression, in this case virtuallibrarian.com
filetype:doc	**filetype:**	Find documents of the specified type, in this case MS Word documents
link:virtuallibrarian.com	**link:**	Find linked pages, i.e. show pages that point to the URL

Also available on Google are the common mathematical operators you would use on your computer. The following symbols between any two numbers will automatically perform a math function.

Symbol Function

+ Addition

- Subtraction

* Multiplication

/ Division

Other *Advanced Google Operators* can be located through the *Advanced Search Page* or performed right in the search box.

Google operators can also be **combined**. Follow the example below:

site:hp.com filetype:pdf "5010 LaserJet" printer FAQ

This search is directed to the Hewlett Packard website; looking for Adobe Acrobat PDF file of Frequently Asked Questions file regarding the 5010 LaserJet printer.

A great resource for search help for beginners to experts is www.googleguide.com. There are dozens more operators and search techniques to use.

Proximity Searching

When an **asterisk "*"** is used between words or expressions, Google offers a very effective proximity searching feature. Used between two expressions, proximity will return results that are within 15 words of each other.

For example, a search for "**cynthia hetherington**" investigator returned 2,010 matches in Google.

Whereas, the search "**cynthia hetherington**" * investigator resulted in 22 matches.

Hence, the expression "**cynthia hetherington**" did appear on the same web page as "investigator" 2,010 times, but it only occurred in close proximity to "investigator" 22 times out of the 2,010 matches.

What is Cynthia Hetherington used a secondary or middle name though? You can search within the quotes multiple name variations such as "**cynthia * hetherington**" and the name variations such as,

Cynthia L Hetherington

Cynthia R Hetherington

Cynthia Pixie president of Stix Hetherington

The mentioned results all manage to keep cynthia *within 15 words* of Hetherington

This will generate a larger search number than "cynthia Hetherington" which only permits for a space between the two names.

To really take advantage of this search try adding your extended search terms coupled with another * next such as: "cynthia * hetherington" * investigator (note that you can only run two * so long as one of the expressions and * is in quotes)

Common Phrase Searching

For English language searches, consider the common colloquialisms people use in everyday language. With email, text messaging, and other basic device communications, writing has turned into an extension of speaking. People no longer think about what they are writing; as far as grammar is concerned, they tend to write like they speak. Thus shorthand and common expressions are found. Below are common expressions used to create phrase searching.

- I hate XXX (my job, my mom, my school, my employer)

- Better than XXX (<restaurant>, <product>, <any proper noun>)

- I love XXX (my job, my mom, my school, my employer)

- XXX was the nicest (<geography/location>, <company or person>)
- XXX was the worst
- XXX was off the charts
- XXX was off the hook
- XXX was off the map
- XXX was such a jerk/babe/<expletive>
- XXX was so hot/stupid/boring

An example search in Google for "Better than Disney" returned hits such as:

- Is Disney Land better than Disney World?
- Nick [Nickelodeon's children's network] is slightly better than Disney

Be inventive and consider how you would describe a similar topic, then run your search in the same style using quotes to contain the phrases.

Other Useful Google Tools

Beyond Web searching, Google also offers image searching, news searching, books, maps, products, translations, documents, calendars, etc. as shown in the screen below. We will review how to use three of the more useful Google tools for record searching.

Google Alerts

Google Alerts are one of the handiest tools that Google offers. Google Alerts sends emails automatically when there are new Google results for your submitted list of search terms. The results are culled from Google News, Web, Blogs, Video, and Groups.

The easiest way to get to the Alerts feature in Google is simply at Google.com/alerts. Type in your search query – such as a proper name, expression or phrase search. Be sure to use Google Operators described earlier in order to filter and smarten your search results.

You can set up your alert to email you: 1) as it happens or 2) once a day or 3) once a week. You can also use the "Result Type" pull down menu to select what types of sources you want Google to use when creating the alerts. The image on the right below indicates the choices.

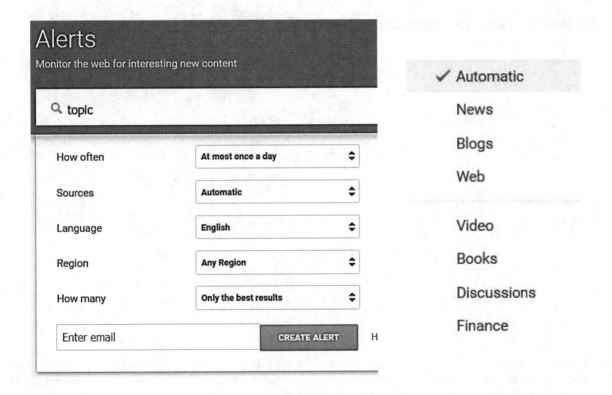

To get the most out of Google Alerts, it is recommended to make your search as effective as possible and to choose from Sources Automatic (everything) and How many should be All results.

Google Images

Image searching in Google can return a host of interesting results. Using the same type of text search queries, the *Advanced Image Searching* offers limiters by image type; such as black and white, color, drawing, and has a search feature for finding just faces and just news content.

The *Faces* only feature is helpful at narrowing down large result matches, and the *News Content* feature is terrific considering the image search takes place only within media and press oriented websites.

Normally, news and media searches are conducted on databases such as LexisNexis or Factiva, where images have been stripped out of the stories.

The screen image on the next page indicates the many search possibilities and parameters that Google Images offers.

You can also "Search by image" by selecting the small camera in the in the images.Google search box. From here you either paste your image URL or upload the photo from your desktop. Google will look for images that are exactly the same, similar or holding the same content (i.e. filename, tagged name).

Search by image   ✕

Search Google with an image instead of text.

Paste image URL ⑦ | Upload an image

[   ]   Search by image

Google Maps

Google Maps is a great tool that is quite useful beyond the well-known *driving directions* and the *Where Is* features. To become acquainted, search an area with familiarity to see the variety of tools that go beyond directions of East to West.

Google has been photographing the street views of every avenue, street and bi-way for almost a decade. Conveniently from your desk you can view an address as it appeared recently and from 2007, such as the following for the World Trade Center in NY City. In 2007 there was no building, and as of the last photo taken in 2014, it is NY's largest skyscraper.

World Trade Center 2007

World Trade Center 2014

Google MyMaps

To truly personalize and take the best advantage of the mapping resources, login to your Gmail or Google+ account and set Google.com/mymaps account. The *My Maps* tab offers tools that allow you to customize your own searches and really "z in" on certain geographical aspects of the geography.

The image below shows how a search can be narrowed to show real estate listings, user contributed photos (with Picasa V Album or Panoramio), and places of interest. The distance measurement tool is handy when trying to establish the len between two points on the map and has various measurement methods offered. For example, the distance betw Minneapolis and St. Paul Minnesota is 8.73084 mi or 128.052 football fields, 13.1711 верста, 281.019 pools, etc.

Other Worthy Search Engines

Other traditional search engines with valuable searching features for public information research include—

- Ask.com
- Bing.com
- Yahoo.com

Using eBay

Ebay and its partner Paypal offer over a decade's worth of information on their users.

Using the eBay site as a research tool often leads to a treasure trove of information about a subject.

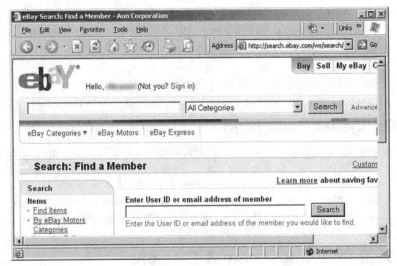

Here is how to search by a person's name, email address, or best of all, the first half of an email address, which is very likely also the person's username, on eBay.

- Go to *Advanced Search* from the homepage, upper right-hand corner
- Choose *Find a Member* from the left-hand column
- Type in the first half of the person's personal email address. For example, for crazybird@gmail.com, type "crazybird"

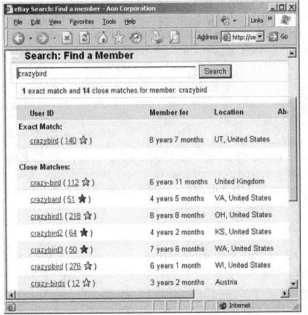

The results screen shows one perfect match for "crazybird" in Utah. This person has held this account with eBay.com for over eight years.

Note: Remember to take into account that this could be a mismatch, especially if the name is a common one like "baseballfan" or "nascarfanatic."

If you think you have a match to your person, visit the person's online profile on eBay and read EVERYTHING they have on their page. Insight can be developed by looking at the items they've bought and sold and by reviewing all comments made to and by the individual.

Once you gather comments, click over to the *Feedback Profile* for the individual. Down the right-hand side are a few selectable items under *Member Quick Links*. Look at *View ID History* to see if the member changed an ID in eBay in the past ten years. You can also *Add to Favorite Sellers* to be alerted when that person places new items for sale on eBay.

Craigslist Searching

The site craigslist.org is an online emporium *or* a flea market, depending on your perspective. The large want-ad listings include products, garage-sale items, rental properties, houses for sale, services, and personal ads. The catch to correctly searching Craigslist is its geographic restriction. If you are interested in items in San Francisco, that is the only geographic location you should search under; example is http://sfbay.craigslist.org. Craigslist will *not* allow you to search multiple jurisdictions at once. To expand your search, you have to specify Northern California or name another area. Or you can use SearchTempest.com.

SearchTempest.com & Claz.org

Tired of hunting around Craigslist for your suspect's posts, stolen goods, or to see if your hard-to-find sports memorabilia is anywhere to be found? Craigslist itself does not offer a way to search across broad geographic areas. Lo and behold a search engine to the rescue: Searchtempest. Also Claz.org for all the other auction sites like Backpages.com and Reachoo.com.

For Searchtempest, you search by distance (in miles) to a zip code, pick multiple cities, type of sale, and if you want eBay, oodle and Amazon results. A search on *'Dukes of Hazard' from New Jersey* brought up results as far as Monterey Bay, California. Of course, one of the key reasons to search within eBay or Craigslist is not only to find your Dukes of Hazard memorabilia – but to discern if your subject is using auction Web sites and services with a unique user account.

Once you have conducted your search, an added bonus to SearchTempest is that if your search is something you want to be alerted about future sales of, click on the RSS option in the upper right hand corner named "Feeds For This Search." An OPML file will be created which you can drag into your email browser, and it will create a folder marked with the title of your search. Anytime a sale matching your original criteria appears through Searchtempest.com, your RSS inbox will show a new message.

Claz.org reaches into the auction sites that Searchtempest leaves behind, hence the two complement each other well. Especially as Claz covers Backpage.com, a popular site for advertising stolen goods, black market products and is rife with human trafficking.

Claz also offers alerting services via RSS, similar to Searchtempest. After your initial search, at the bottom of the results page are two buttons for RSS and Save this Search. Choose RSS and then choose which tool to readh from. I recommend Microsoft Outlook, as it is encumbered into the same email system most investigative professionals are using. Choose *Subscribe Now* and your email should open up. You will see a Folder under RSS Feeds folder in Outlook. Every time a new entry goes in there, you will get the update in your email.

Bing.com

Introduced by Microsoft, Bing is the latest search engine to take on the formidable pace-setters Google and Yahoo. Bing focuses on four key areas: shopping, local, travel, and health.

A number of features and benefits of this new search engine are reviewed below. It is worth mentioning that Bing's interface is rather pleasant with a photo backdrop, which is fine on a computer with no bandwidth issues. However, large image files are always a burden when you are strictly looking for content, not bells and whistles. Bing's PDA version – accessible by Blackberry, iPhone, and similar devices – opens with a plain-text screen.

Bing Search Features and Settings

Go straight to *Preferences* in the right-hand corner and change the settings for *Results* from 10 to 50 (the highest number). The search box can contain up to 150 characters, including spaces. The standard stop words ("a," "the," "and," etc.) can be included in your search if they're used in quoted phrases, e.g., "The Di Vinci Code."

One odd feature was the increase of results when searching with quotes against a name. A search without quotes on **Cynthia Hetherington** returned 45,500 results, whereas a search with the quotes returned 2,850 results.

Although the algorithm is not clear, it is possible Bing uses a proximity command as a default when searching one or more expressions. This would make sense to limit bad results such as a document that lists "Cynthia Nixon" at the top of the webpage and "Hetherington Smith LLP" six pages later. A nice feature brought back to use in database searching is the Boolean terms "or" and "not." By default, search engines tend to assume the "and" (e.g., chocolate "and" cake), and the "not," which can also be represented as a "−" (minus) in the query. Although the "or" (represented as "|") gets a little lost in the advanced features, it is good to see Bing highlighting this little-used but resourceful feature.

Bing has brought back parentheses to allow you to combine expressions to be included or not. This is great for intelligence investigators who suffer due to popular names flooding their results. For example, **Bill Gates** returns 24 million hits. Add **(Gates Foundation)** to the search and you are limited to 700,000 results. If you subtract (or **NOT Gates Foundation**), the results jump back up, but the results will be significantly less than the original 24 million.

On the right-hand side of the results page, if you mouse over the returned links, you will see your search expression as it appears within the context of the website that was found. Other links offered on that page are also revealed.

Zoominfo

Another great source for free searching is Zoominfo.com. Information is collated from websites that the Zoominfo's software *bots* – also known as intelligent agents – have captured and matched to a particular person or company. You can search by company, person, or industry. This is truly one of the most useful specialist search engines on the Internet. You can locate an abundance of *who's who* straight from Zoominfo. Keep in mind though that this information is being generated from other websites and needs to be verified.

Searching begins by finding the *Find Contacts* on the home page in order to bring you to the free search tool. Then searching on Cynthia's name, Zoominfo produces what looks like a resume with business experience, association connections, education credentials, and photos in some cases.

Two other search tricks to locating names that are viewable in Zoominfo are:

1. Conduct a Google search such as site:Zoominfo.com "cynthia Hetherington"
2. Type out the name in the address bar as so: www.zoominfo.com/people/cynthia/hetherington

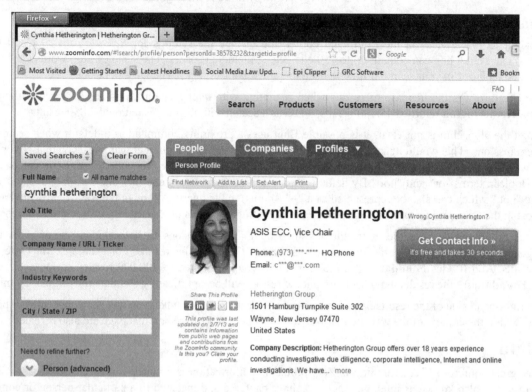

The information found in the left-hand column is produced from the web matches Zoominfo agents found on the right-hand side. These articles, website matches, and directory listings all are assembled into the resume-like profile you see above.

Keep in mind that when searching by a personal name, there may be several matches in the results list. Be sure to look at each one because Zoominfo.com may not connect the dots between two profiles and merely list the names separately. For example, Cynthia Hetherington has twelve separate line entries including some listed as Cindy Hetherington. Look at each line item to insure that you do not miss any important or random information on your subject.

One problem when using Zoominfo is attempting to look up a very common name. There will be thousands of results. The best approach is to search a common name in the *advance search section* and narrow results down by combining name and company name.

Wayback Machine on Archive.org

The mission of Archive.org is "...to help preserve those artifacts and create an Internet library for researchers, historians, and scholars. The Archive collaborates with institutions including the Library of Congress and the Smithsonian."

Archive.org offers researchers and historians a view of a website as captured by the Wayback Machine on a specific date. A web address is entered into the search parameter creating a results page. In the case of http://www.data2know.com, this website has been continually archived since August 18, 2000 and as recently as April 1, 2016.

From January 1, 1996 to April 1, 2016, the Wayback Machine recorded the website http://www.data2know.com in the following years:

The circled dates of the calendar shown on the screen capture to follow denote that a change occurred on the www.data2know.com website.

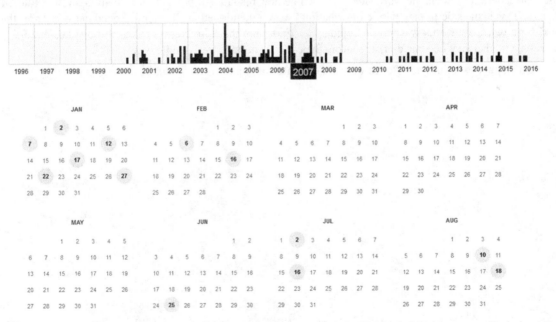

The correct date that the website was captured is in the web address. Wayback Machine records their captures as follows:

http://web.archive.org/web/YYYYMMDDhhmmss/www.website.com/index.html

The phrase "YYYYMMDDhhmmss" is equal to the "year month date hour minute second." Hence, in http://web.archive.org/web/20050403055101/www.data2know.com/index.html the code 20050403055101 equals the exact date and time of April 3, 2005 5:51:01 AM

Summary

As this is our fourth edition of the Manual to Online Public Records, nothing in general would be a new phenomenon to many seasoned online searchers. Still websites continue to develop new avenues for researchers to explore and keep up with the bevy of information on individuals' activities and antics. Online information is now expected to be available 24 hours a day, and it needs to be free and easy to find to the average consumer. The quintillion options offered by any one query to Google, who only gives back one or two valuable links, is staggering.

Yet, commercial Internet is now greater than twenty years old. With that length of age attributed to it, user histories have been stored for just as long. Hence eBay transactions from 1996 are still accessible. Google.com searches from its earliest days are stored in logs somewhere. Services like Zoominfo and Archive.org are preserving websites long gone from their servers.

To uncover valuable information, it takes imagination and creative searching along with the ability to know where these services are, what they cover, and how long they have been around to uncover valuable information.

With this abundance of historical information on the Web, an individual's online activity can easily, though lightly, be researched. Couple the online profile that is developed through these searches with any press releases and media found through online news channels and a public records search, as outlined in the rest of this book, and it will result in enough information for a very robust profile.

The *now* generation –social network sites – is a whole new resource of potential information and is explored in the next chapter. This is the side of the "Public Information" search mentioned in Chapter 1. Social networks are 'the best of the best' for a researcher. This is where individuals post not only their preferences, likes and dislikes, hobbies, sports, and interests, but also they become diarists sharing their life stories in a very public way.

The next chapter examines how "once what was private and inane" is now "public and the new reality."

Chapter 3

Researching Social Networks

Dictionary.com defines social network as a noun to mean two things:

"1. a network of friends, colleagues, and other personal contacts:

Strong social networks can encourage healthy behaviors.

2. Digital Technology in the form of (a) an online community of people with a common interest who use a website or other technologies to communicate with each other and share information, resources, etc.: a business-oriented social network. Or (b) a website or online service that facilitates this communication."

Inside This Chapter:

- The Quest for Public Exposure
- Facebook
- Pinterest
- Instagram
- Linkedin
- Twitter
- Flickr
- Myspace
- Live Video Broadcasting
- Using Search Engines to Find Social Network Users and Information
- Using Search Engines to Find Content
- Emoji Searches
- Summary

The Quest for Public Exposure

Social networks are a representation of Web 2.0 programming. Developers have created a way for end users, regardless of their ability, to tailor an environment to share stories through text, sound, and pictures.

Popular social networking sites known as weblogs (**blogs** for short), such as Twitter.com and Facebook.com, have opened up the Web to individuals who want to participate on the Internet but do not have the technical knowhow, time, money to create a website.

Blogs allow for simple input, storage, and are easily searchable. A blog about Italian cooking could be created for free in minutes. Once available, the author selects certain keywords, known as tags, to help draw traffic to their blog. These keywords are updated as the blog grows; so, for instance, specific restaurants can be named, recipes, points of interest, or *whatever* subject the author wants to focus on.

Other social network tools like Youtube.com or Flickr.com are video and photo sites. They allow users to express themselves by uploading imagery and sharing whatever they feel like with the world. These services also encourage tagging (labeling or indexing) the photo or video in order to make it searchable. For example, photos of the San Diego Zoo would be tagged with 'San Diego' and 'zoo' thereby creating fast links for anyone using a search tool to look for either topic.

In comparison, a webpage is fully index-able, but there is nothing really guiding the reader to what the author wants to call attention to. Tags are focused and direct *versus* the hit or miss word match you get from full-page indexing. This is not to say that blogs are not indexed by the full page. Google and other traditional search engines still scan and index the full pages of blogs, but specialized engines like Icerocket.com and Technorati.com put the heavier emphasis on the tags indicated by the author, resulting in better search results.

As an investigative source, this is a super benefit for those who are looking for individuals based on a username, hobby, or location.

A Trick of the Trade

A convenient trick recommended by Cynthia is to go to gmail.com, hotmail.com, or yahoo.com and create an email account that you can use for registration on various social network sites. This email is referred to as your "throw away email account" because you are able to move through the various sites and services without exposing your actual everyday email account to spam or unwanted emails. In other words, when you are tired of it, throw it away.

To summarize, social networks use the latest web development programming to make the Internet more accessible for those who were otherwise technically challenged. Anyone can get involved by creating an account for themselves and communicating with the world in the form of a blog, or they can create an account with a video service or photo service in order to share images and videos.

Let's examine what is possible in what social networks offer and how they can be used for locating information about a person or topic.

Facebook

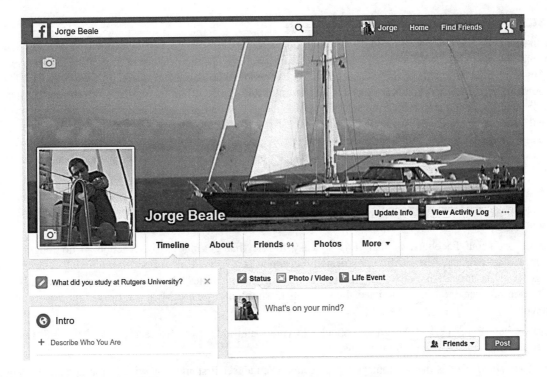

Even though there are thousands of social networks spanning corporate worlds, embedded in geographic regions, or focused in cultural norms to attract specific masses, Facebook.com is the go-to leader in social networking.

Facebook's latest statistics are astounding. According to Facebook Company Info (newsroom.fb.com/company-info) the top numbers, as of early 2016 are:

- 1.09 billion daily active users on average
- 989 million mobile daily active users on average
- 1.65 billion monthly active users
- 1.51 billion mobile monthly active users
- Approximately 84.2% of our daily active users are outside the US and Canada

Considering the earth current holds 7.4 billion people presently (worldometers.info/world-population) that gives Facebook a good grasp on the human population despite creed, color, borders or preferences.

That means hundreds of billions of people from all over the planet are logging in and sharing through Facebook their entire lives.

There are still several hundred million users who are only occasional participants in the service. It is no wonder every investigator wants to learn about using Facebook in their investigations. This issue will start by doing its best to help you understand the users and their perspective when using Facebook. Then we'll later discuss Facebook as an investigative tool, and finally we'll talk about the legal issues involved, terms of service, and common sense to investigating with this tool because even though there are a billion active inhabitants, it is still the Wild West of the Internet.

Understanding the Facebook User

Keep in mind the Web has been around for over a dozen years, and for most of that time, the only participants were those individuals who could create web pages, edit them, FTP them, and had a place to house them (i.e. www.mycompany.com). Maybe there were 10 out of 200 people who could and would do this regularly. The Web was their domain, and it was an exclusive club for programmers and geeks. Then the earlier blogs began to appear as social networks such as Xanga.com and Tribe.net, and soon enough the masses started getting wind and wanted to try it out. The real WOW came when Myspace.com hit the scene and "all those young people" started sharing information about their bands, schools, photos, and their antics. Sure enough, other blogs were out there for the more journalistic types, such as typepad.com and livejournal.com. In this zone people could contribute their thoughts and opinions, but not much else.

Here is where social networking stayed for a long time until Facebook arrived. It is a perfect marriage of blogging ideas, thoughts, and opinions, coupled with the ability upload photos, videos, reference other websites, and most importantly, find old friends.

The best part about Facebook is that it is so easy to use that getting into the action is no longer exclusive to programmers and geeks. Also, brilliant by design, Facebook is a very clean and non-intimidating Web presence so the older generations are not turned off by flashy images or blaring tunes jumping out at them suddenly. In a very Google'esqe manner, they have modeled their design in simplicity, where Myspace thrives on action and noise (i.e. Yahoo.com).

So here we have it. A perfect design that appeals to young and old, offers free access to friends and family, and will help people find their lost high school chums.

Ahh… *Facecrack!* This is the phenomenon that occurs when a user first signs on with their authentic credentials. They sit down for the first time and create an account; entering information like what books and movies they enjoy, marital status, and education and employment history. And this is where the little addiction to Facecrack starts.

Next thing you know, Facebook has aggregated all the other graduates from their high school and offered them up as people they should "friend" (which is now a verb, along with unfriending, in Webster's Dictionary). Given the natural curiosity of most folks, they start to friend these individuals if only to see how they aged. Next, the new user is posting status updates about their daily activities, uploading photos and videos, playing online games, and commenting on their friends' walls.

Investigating Techniques

The chief component of the Facecrack addict, and even the occasional Facebook user, is that they usually do not consider what they are writing on their walls and in their profiles to be an open source. When a participant updates their profile, in their mind's eye they see a specific entity reading that information. Usually this entity looks, smells, sounds, and acts just like themselves and their friends. They might not be aware that complete strangers, bosses, competitors, ex-lovers, and potentially future suitors might peek in on their updates. Even now, I just took a break, looked at my own Facebook profile, and saw one member advising everyone to turn on an afternoon soap opera, another telling everyone she's "taking Ruby to the vet," and others were either quoting historical phrases or lyrics or were complaining that it is only Thursday instead of the weekend. Nothing too offensive, however, I wonder if any of these self-confessors ever consider "what if my mother or boss could read this?" And that's the investigative key! They aren't asking those questions. They are blindly updating and informing the world of their activity, family updates, and photos, and it is up to the investigator to look and see if they can uncover any information from these profiles. Is it taking advantage of them? Not really. No one forced the user to open an account and broadcast their lives. Also, when the accounts are set up, they have the option to completely lock unknown parties out! Facebook is very clear on their privacy set ups.

Indeed, when Facebook offers someone an account, they are given the option to set passwords and permit only certain other users, friends, and networks into their profile. Originally, the default was to permit "friends and networks" to see a profile. When networks were originally set up with a profile, the user would add Central New Jersey, San Francisco Bay, or another regionally specific network to identify what area of the country they were most interested in and most likely from. If I were investigating them, I would make sure I was in the same regional network as they are. Then because of the "friends and networks" default, I could in most cases view their entire profile, including photos and wall posts.

Apparently this was not a great secret because the nice folks at Facebook caught on and quickly stopped allowing regional network selection, eliminating this way of viewing someone's profile without actually friending them.

The other method might not be a method so much as a tactic. When used wisely, it can return some rich gains, and by all means, has worked for me more times than not. However, when it does not work, it can either leave you hanging or have a backlash which can compromise your whole case. Try friending your target. This direct route is dangerous so consider this section like a mine-field and treat it with the same respect you would if you had to tread across said mine-field wearing a blindfold. In other words, here is the disclaimer, *do not try this if you are unsure of the outcome!*

Using an account created specifically for Facebook investigations (more on terms of service later), I have a profile that is not exactly as forthcoming as my own personal account. You can create variations on your own real account for learning purposes and see what I mean. Mine is for my dog, Java. Java has discussions, friends, and photos, but if you look for her in Facebook searches, you won't find much out there because she's pretty good at setting up her security preferences.

When we come to a person's profile we need to look into, the first thing I'll check is the photo. This little feature, which is always set to public unless they uncheck it, is a huge resource all by itself. Surveillance investigators can't help but love getting people's photos from Facebook. Second, do they have any fan pages listed? Are they a fan of In and Out Burger and Arbor Day Fund? Final thing to check is the friend's list. If the list is available (again this is normally defaulted to show friends), then I can scan the entire list and look for other associates I might be trying to develop or family members based on same last name.

After examining the list of friends for any known associates, matching family names to garner leads, I will then take a gander at how many friends this target has Using the following statistics, provided by Pew Research, we see most adults average approximately 150 friends. Consider the following:

- 39% of adult Facebook users have between 1 and 100 Facebook friends
- 23% have 101-250 friends
- 20% have 251-500 friends
- 15% have more than 500 friends

If the target of an investigation has more than 150 friends, or anything above 100 friends, they are probably not too discerning about whom they are friending. Anything above 200 friends and I'm considering that the user really isn't paying attention to the quality of friend they are letting in, but is just interested in clicking "accept" or trying to build some larger number of friends. Whatever the reason, we use the numbers as a cue.

If they are hovering at the lower end, I will start sending invitations to friend my target's friend list. Java's profile picture is of a cute dog with plush toy. She's hard to resist and often gets invited in without question. Even so, not everyone is gullible, so she'll eventually get questioned to which she will usually ignore that user and find another. Once Java has enough friends (10 or so) of my target, she'll then try to directly friend the target. The target user will see the invite, see that they have 10 friends in common, and (since it's man's nature to not be confrontational) will hopefully invite her in.

If my target has hundreds of friends, I don't bother with the extra friending. The user is not really checking who they are letting in so I go right for it.

On the other hand, if the user has less than 100 friends, or if they have ignored my friend requests, another measure is necessary. From the investigation I have to date, I try to find the hobbies, sports, and interests of the target, and try to pre-empt and predict what fan pages they might be part of. Indeed, I might have discerned their fan pages right away when I saw their initial profile, so I'll use this. I join their fan pages. No, by being in the same fan network I cannot view their profile, but it will give credibility when I try to friend them. What I am doing is morphing my profile to match the target's profile so I become appealing and someone they want to connect to.

What if they have very minimal information, a handful of friends, and seem intimidating to even approach? Then I don't bother. They are probably not using Facebook as much as I think and aren't worth the effort to try to read their wall. If you do attempt to friend a target with little activity, they might catch on that you are not a friendly friend but more of an investigative one, or a nuisance, depending on the situation.

Using Sense and Caution

This brings us to the common sense step. Just because people are using Facebook, does not mean they are spilling their secrets, exchanging intellectual property, or talking about their finances openly. Most of the discussions we've seen over the years remind me of coffee shop chatter. People who are mildly comfortable with each other exchange the day's events, some pleasantries, some flirtations, and the occasional political flare-up. They discuss sports, cheer their teams, swap vacation pictures, and cajole their neighbors. If a tragedy has occurred, you'll see them reaching out for support.

Finally, and most importantly, Facebook continues to change its privacy settings. The default is now open source versus the closed source it used to be. So before you go through any of these methods, first and foremost check the person's profile to see if it is even locked down. You might be surprised that what you thought would be an insurmountable task to see what they are writing about, turns out to be a few mouse clicks away!

In closing I want to talk about the terms of service. Facebook is an amazing application that hosts a seventh of the world population every day in active users. You can imagine the security troubles, breeches, and nuisances they see on an hourly basis. They do their best with setting policies for privacy, making the users responsible for their own network security settings, and putting in place a clear set of terms.

As with most software applications, very few users actually read the terms of service before jumping in and hardly realize that the terms change often, even after they have signed on and agreed to them. Yet the terms of service are very clear about creating false profiles under Section 4, ("You will not provide any false personal information on Facebook, or create an account for anyone other than you without permission."), and in the law enforcement guidelines sent out, they are equally clear that if they identify a false profile for the purpose of an investigation, they will remove it.

Of course, you will see hundreds of pages of fictional characters and dead celebs who all have active Facebook accounts. Look up Julia Child and you'll see she's Facebook-ing from the grave. Zephoria online marketing study stated that 83 million accounts on Facebook were false accounts. (zephoria.com/top-15-valuable-facebook-statistics)

Pinterest

Pinterest.com is a digital bulletin board for cool and interesting things. Users find images they like and pin them to their own boards. Similar to a teenager's bedroom walls full of posters and rock show ticket stubs, a Pinterest.com user finds images, inspirational sayings, keepsakes, and other memorabilia and pins it to their Pinterest account. In 2012 Pinterest was growing by leaps and bounds, but it has since calmed down, and hosts loyal users who still visit and share their favorite things in this social setting.

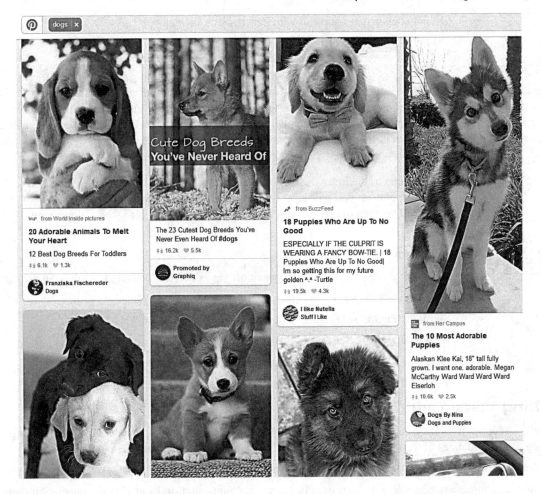

Investigator Takeaways

- If you know the username of the individual, try it after the pinterest.com/USERNAME
- If you don't know their username, go to Facebook.com or Twitter.com to find their username
- Once you are in their account, you can make an assessment of their likes and dislikes
- Often times a link to their Twitter and Facebook account is available
- Who they are following and who follows them is also available
- "Repins from" is not necessarily a friend

Notes to Users

To protect your own account follow these privacy settings which can be found under the Options section.

- Choose whether your profile page is available to search engines
- Go to Settings and turn on the "Prevent Search Engines from including your profile in their search results"

- Do not connect your account with Facebook or Twitter
- Do not use the same user id as Facebook or Twitter

Instagram

Instagram.com is a popular free online photo-sharing and social networking service that enables its users to take a picture, apply a digital filter to it, and share it on a variety of social networking services, including its own and other leading sites such as Facebook or Twitter. Users can add hashtags (the "#" sign in front of a word designating it to be a topic) to photos and make comments. Once the photo is uploaded others can make comments and like the photo.

Investigator Takeaways

- If you know the username of the individual, try it after the instagram.com/USERNAME
- If they are sharing their photos, you will get a firsthand account of personal information
- If they haven't set their account to private, you will see who they follow and who follows them

 KEY FACT   **Notes to Users**

In order to set any features, you need to work off your device. After logging into your account:

- Click on the sprocket in the upper right hand corner
- Scroll to "Photos are Private" and select ON
- Also review Share Settings in the same menu
- Here you will find Facebook, Twitter, and Tumblr, to name a few
- The site does not work well with older versions of Internet Explorer

Searching Instagram

By itself, Instagram from the desktop view will not give you a good investigative perspective. To possibly gain latitude and longitude coordinates of the photo, use an assortment of search tools such as Iconosquare and Websta.me.

Iconosquare

Log onto the Iconosquare.com site with your own Instagram account—sign-in located in the upper right-hand corner of the Web site—then begin searching by username, hashtag, or keyword. Search on the hashtag #partiedtillthecowscamehome (all one word). Your search should return the photo I uploaded. From the search results you will get my nickname, full name, and the tags I added to the photo, such as #nappingdog and #mybirthday. I have also tagged the photo with @*hetheringtongrp* so that it will show up on Twitter as well as Instagram.

The photo will have a timestamp indicating when the photo was taken, which is Unix time (for an explanation of Unix time, search on the phrase in your favorite search engine). After the photo's timestamp may appear a pencil icon with words such as Gingham, or X-Pro II, which indicate the filters used on the photo. Lastly, on the photo the word "somewhere" will appear with a small icon next to it; when clicked on, the icon will open a map below the photo indicating the location of where the photo was taken. If when taking the photo with a smartphone the user had turned off the location transfer on his/her phone, the space would be blank. Since Instagram is a social media tool, you will see that my friends Heart (Instagram's version of Facebook's Like) my photo—rather important to note because, since my Facebook account is locked down, Facebook users who are not my Facebook Friends cannot see my Facebook Friends list. However, since I shared my Instagram photo on Facebook and Twitter, Friends who Like my photo on Facebook will automatically Heart it on Instagram. Most people simply connect to Instagram—and other social media sites—with their Facebook or Twitter accounts, inextricably tying all their profiles into one login across the multiple media sites.

The crossover function allows the investigator to develop lists of associates that the investigator previously couldn't see due to Facebook security features.

Websta.me

Websta.me is an Instagram Web viewer and very similar to Iconosquare. Using Websta.me to view my photo will present a more accurate timestamp on the photo, indicating how many seconds, minutes, or days earlier the photo was posted. You can search by both hashtag (#) and user name. My own search on #partiedtillthecowscamehome did not turn up my own account. Do note that on Websta.me you can search by emoji, the tiny digital icons used to express emotions in social media. When searching by emoji, if the emoji are hashtagged (#emoji), you will see both those who posted with the emoji and those who put the emoji.

LinkedIn

LinkedIn.com is the professional social network, targeting adults who want to share and network their business experience. In reality, both adults and young people can register in any service, however the focus of LinkedIn is more concerned about professional networking than social networking.

An amazing amount of information is posted on LinkedIn pages. The obvious data that jumps out includes the name, location, and work position. Also discoverable items may include one's education, past employment, affiliations to associations, particular networking groups, and any posted recommendations.

Individuals can be quite revealing about themselves on Linkedin, and they offer up probably too much personal information. Below is the LinkedIn page for co-author Cynthia Hetherington.

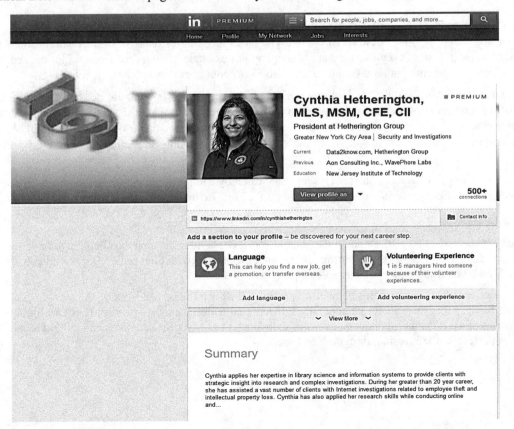

LinkedIn and Diploma Mills

An interesting background check search is a diploma mill search on Linkedin. Go to LinkedIn's *Advanced Search* and in the education section enter the known name of a college **Diploma Mill** such as **Almeda**. A Diploma Mill is a non-accredited school offering degrees for sale with little or no academic requirements (just money). For a few hundred dollars, Almeda grants 'degrees' based on one's life experiences. You will be amazed by the number of people (thousands) who tout their education credentials from Almeda on their Linkedin profile.

Twitter

In 144 characters or less you can blast your thoughts, opinions, and ideas – or absolute nonsense – to the world via Twitter.com. Although many are quick to discredit the value of Twitter for investigative uses, the truth is that this service is probably one of the best resources to arrive online since Google. When someone decides it is a good time to complain about their job, boss, or spouse, they might do this openly on Twitter. Perhaps a Tweet stems from an incident such as an accident or pandemonium erupting (perhaps due to workplace and school violence). Those tweets are all archived and searchable!

You can search directly in Twitter via search.twitter.com. What is key about Twitter? The content is real time – and so are search results. Potentially, you can find information posted within seconds. Also helpful is the ability to geo-locate Twitter posters based on tweets. You can look for mentions of wine tasting near Sonoma County with a search that looks like this >>>   #winetasting near:"sonoma county, ca" within:15mi

You can also use the advanced search (http://twitter.com/search-advanced) in Twitter to make it easier as well.

Flickr

Flickr.com, Photobucket.com, Picassa.com, Kodak.com, and similar online services offer great places to park digital images to share with the world. These services are a great idea for families that live in different locations who want to share images of the kids or of events as they are happening. For example, if Grandma lives in Florida, and the grandkids are in New York, the parents can send Grandma a link to Flickr.com after they celebrate a holiday.

However, Grandma is not the only one looking at these photos and many of them are not of kids at holidays. Anyone can find office workers at office parties taking snapshots of their cubes or office spaces and sharing way too much on the business side of what happens internally. Such a photo may demonstrate the desktop of a busy right handed (mouse position) working gal who is using Microsoft Outlook email and working on perhaps an office layout or marketing campaign.

The trick to searching in Flickr and other such sites is to search by company name, personal name, username (if known), and also add phrases like "at work" or "at school" or "on the job." Be imaginative.

Myspace

Myspace.com was one of the earliest and most popular social networking sites on the Web. Begun as a tool for local musicians to share songs, gig dates, and information about themselves with their fans, Myspace quickly took off as the go-to site for anyone who considers themselves hip.

Recommended searches are a person's name, the username, the town the person lives in, the school attended, or the employer's name. All of these items are generally self-reported within the user's profile. These profiles can be extremely revealing. It is amazing how many users abandoned their Myspace accounts, and left vitals and details about themselves perfect for the investigator to grab and use.

Live Video Broadcasting

Periscope, **Meerkat** and **Younow** all offer continuous live video broadcasting which puts the broadcaster in the seat to chat, share, lament, follow through on dares and video themselves performing these acts. Other phone to phone services also offer this such as Snapchat and Vine. All are searchable by name, nickname, cell phone number and #hashtags. At this writing the serious popular trend is amongst 20 and under year olds. However, as all social networks take off, they start with the young people and progress to their parents and more senior ages. Younow.com is a good starting point for those unfamiliar with broadcasting, as you do not need a password or account to just watch these videos. Unfortunately, people have done more harm than good for themselves, as these video feeds often project drunk driving, crime in action, over indulging, employees ignoring their work, and students ignoring their teachers. All this happens while the "fans" watch and comment, encouraging the broadcaster to continue the bad behavior.

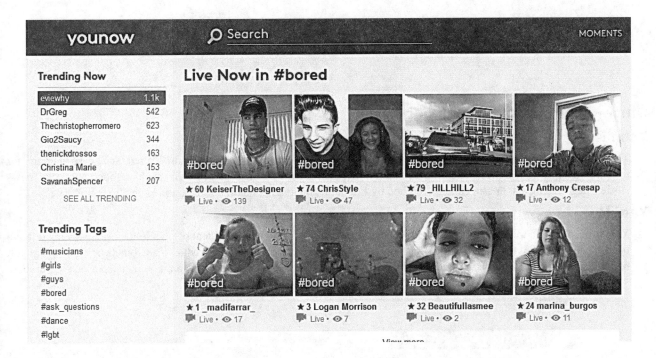

Using Search Engines to Find Social Network Users

Searching in social networks is twofold. You can search by content and you can search for username. Though Google is an excellent search tool for locating the actual social network profile, it is not very good for searching the posts and content within a social network site. Each of the following are located at ".com" unless otherwise stated.

Pipl

Considered the best search engine for user's social network accounts, Pipl.com has been the go-to source for investigators for several years. It can be searched by full name, nickname, email address, and even phone number. Though Pipl.com does not find every last social network site and location, its coverage is very thorough.

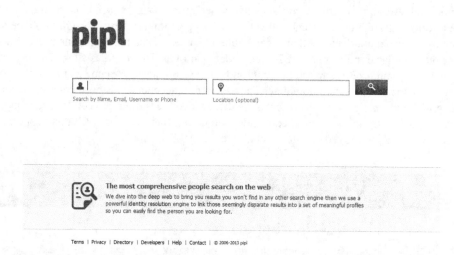

Other Recommended Search Engines

Yasni

Yasni is developed in Germany and therefore has a bit more European content, than United States, so it great for international profile searches. They like to break down their results by the type of media, such as social networks, news stories, negative media. Yasni can be searched by full name, nickname, email address, and even phone number.

Yatedo

Yatedo results tend to focus on professional social network sites, hence a good deal of profile material e seems to have been taken from LinkedIn and Spoke.com. A section is devoted to web matches which can sometimes pull a site you missed in the broader Google searches. Search Yatedo by full name, nickname, email address, and even phone number.

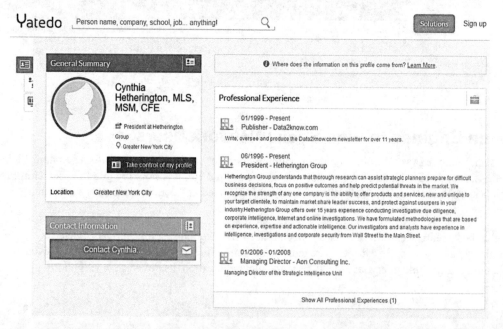

Namechk & Peekyou

If you have the subject's nickname already, these two sites are excellent for tracking down other social network accounts. Type in the known nickname and watch the sites that already have that name in use grey out, meaning your subject may actually be the person behind the account.

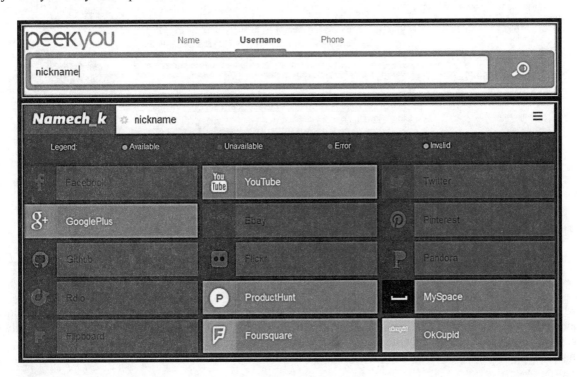

Socialmention

Socialmention.com digs through unique content and posts on social networks that do not run as popular as Facebook and Twitter, as it looks at blogs and microblog, such as Reddit. They organize information in several methods. There is the standard date/time or relevance results list, but Socialmention also offers several analytical features such as sentiment (putting posts into positive, negative, or neutral categories based on the linguistics of the post). Top keywords are also highlighted. The best feature of Socialmention is the ability to set up an RSS feed to your email service by choosing the RSS button on the right hand side of the screen. Searches you are interested in conducting often, for example a brand or company name, you can have sent to your RSS folder in your email server.

See the screen capture on the next page.

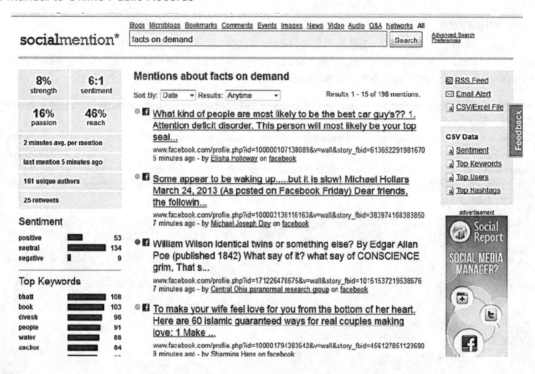

Keyword and username searches on social networks will vary based on the region of the world, culture of the individual or group and many other factors. To learn about new social networks or for locating social networks that focus on individual cultures, social groups, and country specific blogs – visit Wikipedia.org at http://en.wikipedia.org/wiki/List_of_social_networking_websites.

Emoji Searches

An overwhelming majority of social network posters are now writing with imagery. They are no longer limited to words alone but can convey a thousand words with one photo. The following images of detective, bomb and wink are intuitively understood by those reviewing them.

Detective   Bomb   Wink

Emoji characters are small images used to convey emotion. The standards organization, known officially as the Unicode Committee (unicode.org) is working to provide a unique encoding number for every character used on a computer. Yes, there exists a committee tasked with standardizing the variety of online smiley icons—and it has specific criteria for the selection process (*unicode.org/emoji/selection.html*). In 2016 Unicode 9.0 released seven new emoji.

The Unicode character for investigator is 1F575 – (aka Sleuth or Spy)

Tiny and new, the significance of the emoji can be easily overlooked, dismissed as silly, childish, nonsensical. Yet, a picture—even a tiny one—is worth a thousand words. Once you are onboard with these small images possibly being a key element in developing ongoing casework, you will learn to embrace searches using them—and yes, you can make a case using them. The difficult part will be for the seasoned investigator explaining his/her findings to the client: "Yes, we located the hidden assets based on both the money bag icon and the sail boat icon on his Facebook updates."

Unicode's dictionary of emoji can be found http://unicode.org/emoji/charts/full-emoji-list.html

Searching by Emoji

Classic icons, around for years now, are made up of keyboard characters arranged to represent an image. Consider the ubiquitous smiley face icon :-) made from keyboard characters—specifically, the colon, the dash, and the close paren. Those keyboard characters are searchable; they have Unicode and hexadecimal values from which the search development world can create combination searches. Now, you can search on emoji as well. This new kind of searching—image searching— can be quite profound and effective, for searching in the language in which digital natives converse is a necessary strategy in a social media investigator's approach.

Consider the following logic items:

- In English, my name is Cynthia.
- In Unicode, my name is U+ 0043 0079 006E 0074 0068 0069 0061.
- In English, my profession is Investigator.
- In Unicode, my profession is U+1F575.
- The on-screen representation of my Unicode profession is:
- In the above logic items, the items searchable online are my name (Cynthia), my profession (Investigator), and its image of the sleuth (or spy).

Where Can You Search for These Items?

Not in Google. However, there are a half dozen other locations for emoji searching.

Bing: The easiest emoji search tactic on Bing is from a cell phone because the emoji keyboard is built right into the cell phone's keyboard. Of course, a desktop can also be used for emoji searching. Use your mouse to grab the image, drop the image into a search box, and then select Search to view related results. It is also possible to search on a combination of emoji and words. For example, search on the icon for a police officer and the word nearest— nearest—to locate the nearest police officer; an assortment of answers closely matching the search query should appear. Bing started emoji searches in October, 2014 *(http://blogs.bing.com/search/2014/10/27/doyou-speak-emoji-bing-does)*.

Instagram: Log into Instagram.com and drop your image into the search query box, and then search on it; all Instagram posts with your image's hashtag (#) in the posts or comments will be displayed in your returned search results.

Emojipedia*:* An encyclopedia of emoji information, by searching a specific emoji, multiple versions of that image will be returned. Besides understanding the connotation of the image itself, emojipedia.org will let you know if an Apple iOS or LG Samsung or other device generated the image. Plug in an emoji and search Emojipedia's vast dictionary of images.

Emojifinder*:* Type a word or an emoji into emojifinder.com and it will show you the matching images and/or words that would appear—whether you recognize them or not.

Fileformat*:* A longtime ready reference source for technical coder questions, fileformat.com is the best for getting the historical and relevant resources of an emoji.

As social media applications, and their unique texting linguistics and vernacular, possibly turn our language from a statement, "I'm hungry; I would like a slice of pizza.", to a basic image representing the statement—in this case, a slice of pizza —we might predict the downfall of proper verbal communication. And yet, isn't language an ever-evolving thing? We Americans don't speak the Queen's English; many of us in modern times no longer use words such as fortnight. Language progressively changes with culture; as investigators, it is our responsibility to continuously stay on top of such changes. Fortunately for us, the technology world offers up effective search applications to assist with our research and locate these odd characters that now say a thousand words in one simple image.

Summary

In today's identity theft-aware environment, there are privacy advocates arguing for tighter controls on SSNs, personal identifiers, health and financial records, and any other piece of information that can be misused. The irony is while these advocates fight for discretion and privacy of an individual's personal information, that person is "out there" sharing even more than identifiers and addresses with the entire universe! Individuals, as we have seen through social networks, are living online. They rely on the Web to relay their stories, carry their message, and carve out a bit of themselves virtually to anyone everywhere who would log in.

As researchers, it is to our benefit to take advantage of these self-exposing persons and keep abreast of the latest social network developments in order to keep informed. From this point forward, there can only be more service offerings on the Web to take advantage of. Some good advice is to learn the resources outlined in this chapter and stay tuned to what is on the horizon.

Chapter 4

Record Searching From A Thru Z

This Chapter presents key record information topics in an alphabetical index. From *Archives* to *Worker's Compensation,* the resources covered herein represent a mix of searchable government sites and private company sites. Chapter 6 provides specific data found at the state, county, parish or local government levels including courts and recorder's offices.

Topics Covered In This Chapter:

- Archives
- Aviation Records
- Banks & Financial Institutions
- Business Entity Records
- Copyrights
- Court Records (includes civil, criminal, etc. records)
- Court Records on Judicial Statewide Systems
- Court Records of Native Americans
- Criminal Records at State Repositories
- Elections: Candidates, PACs, Lobbyists, and Voters
- Environmental Information
- Federal Agencies
- Federal Sanctions & Watch Lists
- Genealogy Resources
- GIS and Mapping
- Incarceration Records
- Internal Revenue Service (IRS) Records
- Media Resources
- Military Records

- Missing Persons
- Most Wanted Lists
- Motor Vehicle Records (includes drivers, vehicles, vessels, accident reports, etc.)
- Occupations & Licensing Boards
- Patents
- Privacy and Privacy Rights Resources
- Recalls, Products and Safety
- Recorded Documents, Judgments, and Liens (includes UCC filings)
- Securities and Securities Dealers
- Sexual Offender Registries
- Tax Assessor and Collector Records
- Telephone Numbers
- Trademarks & Service Marks
- Unclaimed Funds
- Vital Records (includes SSA Death Index and Obituaries)
- Voter Registration
- Workers' Compensation
- World Wide Web

Archives: Federal

The National Archives and Records Administration (NARA) at archives.gov is America's record keeper and it serves as the archival arm of the federal government. NARA not only preserves documents and materials related to the U.S., but also ensures people can access the information.

The National Archives Catalog at www.archives.gov/research/catalog is the online portal for searching. It provides access to data, digitized records, and selected series from Access to Archival Databases (AAD), over one million electronic records from the Electronic Records Archives (ERA), all of the web pages from Archives.gov, and all of the web pages from the Presidential Libraries. Another good starting point to search by topic is www.archives.gov/research/topics. To find all of the NARA locations and affiliated sites visit www.archives.gov/locations. Also see the Military Records section later in the chapter.

The Federal Record Centers, part of NARA, hold the closed case files from Federal U.S. District & Bankruptcy Courts. See Chapter 7 (Searching Federal Court Records) for the locations and information on how to obtain these cases files.

Archives: State

Every state has an Archives agency that collects and preserves historical government records, and makes them available for public use. The websites for the all states' Archives are found in the next chapter.

Aviation Records

Government Sources - U.S.

Besides information about regulations and policies, the **Federal Aviation Administration (FAA)** faa.gov provides searchable data about aircraft including registration and ownership, airports, air traffic, training and testing. The FAA site is the also the main government information center regarding certification for pilots and airmen. For example, the Aircraft Inquiry and database download is at http://registry.faa.gov/aircraftinquiry, the Airman Inquiry is at https://amsrvs.registry.faa.gov/airmeninquiry. Other searchable topics from the home page include current flight delay information nationwide and accident incident data.

The Federal National Transportation Safety Board (NTSB) ntsb.gov maintains an aviation accident database from 1962 forward about civil aviation accidents and selected incidents within the U.S., its territories and possessions, and in international waters. Six different online services are offered. One may search the database or even download the entire database. Preliminary reports are posted within days; final reports may take months before posted. Some information prior to 1993 is sketchy. See http://www.ntsb.gov/_layouts/ntsb.aviation/index.aspx.

Government Sources - Foreign

The Canadian government site to search Canadian Civil Aircraft Register and aircraft information is http://wwwapps.tc.gc.ca/saf-sec-sur/2/ccarcs-riacc/Menu.aspx.

For information about aircraft registration standards for participating countries see the **International Civil Aviation Organization** web page www.icao.int.

Private Sources

Below are recommended private information resource centers:

- Landings.com is an excellent news and overall reference resource.
- AirCharterGuide search services include charter operator ratings, see www.aircharterguide.com/Operators.
- GlobalAir has an extensive and useful Aviation Directory, see https://www.globalair.com/directories.

Banks & Financial Institutions

Office of the Comptroller of the Currency

The Office of the Comptroller of the Currency (OCC), a bureau of the U.S. Dept. of the Treasury, charters, regulates, and supervises all national banks and federal savings associations. The OCC also supervises federally chartered branches and agencies of foreign banks that may not be members of the Federal Reserve System. At the **Licensing** tab at www.occ.gov one can find lists of active banks and federal savings associations by name or by city and state.

The OCC has the statutory authority to take action against Institution-Affiliated Parties (IAPs) including:

- Officers, directors, and employees,
- A bank's controlling stockholders, agents, and certain other individuals.

Search **enforcement actions** for violations of laws, rules or regulations, unsafe or unsound practices, violations of final orders, etc., and for IAP breaches of fiduciary duty at http://apps.occ.gov/EASearch/.

Federal Deposit Insurance Corporation (FDIC)

The Federal Deposit Insurance Corporation (FDIC) insures deposits in banks and thrift institutions for at least $250,000 and identifies, monitors and addresses risks to the deposit insurance funds when a bank or thrift institution fails. The FDIC Institution Directory is found at https://www5.fdic.gov/idasp/advSearchLanding.asp. The FDIC has the statutory authority to take enforcement actions against the following entities —

- FDIC-insured state chartered banks that are not members of the Federal Reserve System
- FDIC-insured branches of foreign banks
- Officers, directors, employees, controlling shareholders, agents, and certain other categories of individuals (institution-affiliated parties) associated with such institutions

The FDIC **Enforcement Decisions and Orders** (ED&O) contains the full text of the formal enforcement actions against financial institutions that are regulated by the FDIC or against their affiliated parties. The ED&O is updated on a monthly basis. To view enforcement actions, go to https://www5.fdic.gov/EDO/index.html.

Federal Reserve Board

The Federal Reserve federalreserve.gov is the central bank of the U.S. As such it supervises and has the statutory authority to take formal enforcement actions against the following entities —

- State member banks
- Bank holding companies
- Non-bank subsidiaries of bank holding companies
- Edge and agreement corporations
- Branches and agencies of foreign banking organizations operating in the United States and their parent banks
- Officers, directors, employees, and certain other categories of individuals associated with the above banks, companies, and organizations (referred to as "institution-affiliated parties")

The Federal Reserve can take formal **enforcement actions** against the entities listed above for violations of laws, rules, or regulations, unsafe or unsound practices, breaches of fiduciary duty, and violations of final orders. Since August 1989, the Federal Reserve has made all final enforcement orders public. Search at www.federalreserve.gov/apps/enforcementactions/search.aspx.

The **National Information Center (NIC)**, part of the Federal Reserve System, is a central repository of data about banks and other institutions that the Federal Reserve has a supervisory, regulatory, or research interest. This includes both domestic and foreign banking organizations which operate in the U.S. The USBA Search allows one to search for an institution's current and non-current information by name and location. Those two sites above are accessible from the main site at www.ffiec.gov/nicpubweb/nicweb/NicHome.aspx.

National Credit Union Administration

The National Credit Union Administration (NCUA) ncua.gov is an independent federal agency that charters and supervises federal credit unions. The web page offers plenty of research and data access.

Business Entity Records

Businesses are formed in many shapes and sizes. They may be organized as corporation, limited liability companies, partnerships, limited liability partnerships, etc. They can be designated for-profit or not-for-profit. And they can be a public company (selling shares of ownership to the public) or non-public. This section covers a number of topics and categories related to business entity records. For extensive information on researching business entities - check out *The Guide to Online Due diligence Investigation* by Cynthia Hetherington.

Searching for Information on Publicly Owned (Traded) Companies

There are two important facts to know about finding information about publicly traded companies:

1. Publicly traded companies operating in the U.S. are required by federal law to register with the Securities and Exchange Commission (SEC).

2. If a publicly traded company does not meet certain thresholds, then it submits filings to a state regulatory securities agency instead of the SEC.

A registration statement, filed with the appropriate securities exchange or state regulators, discloses information on the management and financial condition of the entity, and describes how the proceeds of the offering will be used. Either the SEC or these state agencies monitor the registered companies for any irregularities or potential fraudulent behavior.

Note: This section examines first how to find information on publicly traded companies at the federal level, then how to find information at the state level on both public and privately held companies at the state level. This is followed by an analysis of key vendors who offer excellent reference data online in this subject area.

Federal Sources: The SEC and EDGAR

Publicly traded companies must inform the public the complete truth about their businesses' financial data. All non-exempt companies (see below), foreign and domestic, are required to file registration statements, periodic reports, and other forms with the U.S. Securities and Exchange Commission (SEC). Since May 6, 1996, these documents are filed electronically using EDGAR – the **E**lectronic **D**ata **G**athering **A**nalysis and **R**etrieval system. Thus, EDGAR is an extensive repository of U.S. corporation information available and anyone can access and download this information for free. The reports these publically traded entities must file include the following:

*   10-K – an annual financial report that includes audited year-end financial statements.
*   10-Q – a quarterly, unaudited report.
*   8K – a report detailing significant or unscheduled corporate changes or events.
*   Securities offering, trading registrations, and final prospectus.
*   DEF-14 – a definitive proxy statement offering director names, their compensation and position.

The list above is not inclusive. There are other miscellaneous reports filed, including those dealing with security holdings by institutions and insiders. Access to all of these documents provides a wealth of information.

The free record searching site to EDGAR's 21+ million records is www.sec.gov/edgar/searchedgar/webusers.htm.

A helpful *How To Guide* for searching publicly traded companies is at www.sec.gov/investor/pubs/edgarguide.htm.

The private sector has a number of vendors and data aggregators that offer access to EDGAR records. These vendors combine enhanced search tools with other added features with the basic EDGAR search.

The SEC also provides electronic access to its enforcement actions. For details, see the *Securities and Securities Dealers* section later in this chapter.

State Sources of Business Entity Records

In general, businesses that are not public companies are registered at the state level, usually with the office of the Secretary of State. The typical types of business entities that have records available at the state level include:

- Corporations (including Foreign and Non-Profit)
- Partnerships (Limited, Limited Liability, and General)
- Limited Liability Companies
- Franchises
- *Trade Names, Fictitious Names, Assumed Names

*Fictitious names and trade names can be registered at either the local (county or city) or state level, depending on the state's specifications.

Every state provides a business search tool on the web to find information on state-registered business entities. Usually these look-ups are free and include all business entities types, including non-profits. You will find these state web sites Also you may visit www.brbpublications.com to find all the states' links for free searches.

While most states have one central agency that oversees business entity records and filings, there are several exceptions.

- **Arizona** – The **Corporation Commission** oversees corporation and LLC records as well as foreign (out-of-state) corporations registered to do business in the state. The **Secretary of State** oversees all partnerships including LPs and LLPs; as well as trademarks, service marks, and trade names.
- **South Carolina** – The **Secretary of State Division of Business Filings** oversees corporation, LP, LLP, LLC, trademark and servicemark records. However, in general, entities are not required to disclose the names of directors, officers or members to the Secretary of State's Office. Business corporations must submit the names of directors on the Annual Report that are filed with the **Department of Revenue**.
- **Kansas** – The state of Kansas does not register sole proprietorship, d/b/a, assumed name, trade name or fictitious name entities.

State Regulatory Agencies and Blue Sky Laws

Every state has securities laws – often referred to as **Blue Sky Laws** – designed to protect investors against fraud. These laws, which do vary from state to state, typically require companies making small offerings to register these offerings before they can be sold in a particular state.

Records of the filings by companies registering under Blue Sky Laws, as well as any records of legal actions, are held by designated state regulatory securities agencies. These agencies oversee the licensing and regulation of securities broker-dealers, agents, investment advisers and investment adviser representatives, and financial planners. The agencies also protect investors against securities fraud by taking enforcement actions.

These records are open to the public and can be a great source of data when searching for assets, ownership records, or doing background investigations.

An excellent links list to all the state regulatory agencies home pages is found at the North American Securities Administrators Association web page at www.nasaa.org/about-us/contact-us/contact-your-regulator/.

Other Entity Types: Searching Non-Profits

Private foundations, charities, non-profits, churches, hospitals, schools, or publicly-supported organizations are subject to special considerations regarding federal taxes. These entities file different forms with the IRS and all must contribute detailed financial and member information, which can be a great asset for the online intelligence investigator.

The information regarding officers and the financials in a non-profit organization is completely transparent in the Form 990 - an annual report that certain federally tax exempt organizations must file with the IRS. Form 990 provides information on the filing organization's mission, programs, finances, and beyond. For example, on Part 8 of the Form all the trustees are listed, which can be a great investigative lead.

Searching these entities at the state level is much like searching the for-profits entities, but these online sources can actually provide added depth to investigators and researchers. Whether you are looking to reveal experts in the field, local interests to a region, or the financial participation of a particular foundation, these organizations can open a number of investigative leads. Finding the organizations or affiliations to which a person can give insight into that person's character. Categories can include religious, athletic, health, child focused, or specific-interest related. What is also good to know is there are several vendors who specialize in providing material and content about on non-profits. These firms are profiled later in this section.

Other Entity Types: Searching Franchise Records

Franchises are regulated by both the Federal Trade Commission (FTC) and by state regulatory agencies. (See *Blue Sky Laws* below.) If the franchise involves a public offering, then records may also be in the SEC database.

A key public record document associated with a franchise is the Uniform Franchise Offering Circular (UFOC). Usually this document may be obtained from a state agency or from a vendor, but not the FTC.

The International Franchise Association (IFA) franchise.org is a great resource of in-depth information about franchising and finding Franchise Members by topic or service.

Searching Business Entity Records

An initial search for a business entity's records usually starts with a record index. An index *hit* will lead to a document file number or images of documents. Most states provide a centralized index of all their registered business entities (corporations, partnerships, LLCs, LLPs, etc.) and usually this index is searchable online.

A good researcher must become familiar with the alphabetizing system in use, regardless if the search is on-site or online. For example, knowing the answers to the questions below can prove to be crucial to a search.

- How to search when a company name starts with the word *The*. Should you search for *The* ABC Company or search by ABC Company, *The* ?

- Know the procedure when a company name starts with a number. Is the number alphabetized as a word? Are listings with numbers found at the front or the end of the index?

- Watch for key words indicating name changes, former entities, or related companies. For example, if a company is known as YESS Embroidery and Screenprinting, it would be worthwhile to search for YESS Embroidery, YESS Screenprinting, YESS Screenprinting and Embroidery, The YESS Company, etc. Also, ascertain if the use of an "&" in place of the word "and" will modify the search results.

- Know the capacity for error and forgiving of typos. If you can pull an alphabetical index list, make sure that screenprinting is not listed as screnprinting [sic] or even screen printing, etc.

- Many large companies with offices or clients in multiple states will incorporate in Delaware or Nevada.

Information found in a registration file typically includes the date of registration, status, name and address of the registered agent and, sometimes, the names and addresses of officers, directors or principals. The registered agent is the person authorized to receive legal papers such as service of process. The registered agent can be a company attorney, a principal, or a designated third party who specializes in representing business entities.

The registration file can hold a myriad of other company documents. For example, a corporation registration file will typically include the articles of incorporation, annual reports, merger documents, name changes, and termination papers. Partnership and LLC filings may include similar documents with details such as how decisions are made, how profits are distributed, and names and addresses of all limited and general partners or owners. **Finding this material is a good way to find the affiliates of a search subject.**

All state agencies provide a **business name check** so that a new entity can make sure the name is not already used by an existing business entity. Many offer this service online. Performing a business name check is often a good way to find where a business is located and may lead to additional information about a business.

Checking to see if a company is currently registered and filings are current is called a **status check.** If an entity's registration is current and there are no problems, a document known as a Good Standing may be purchased. If available, articles of incorporation including amendments as well as copies of annual reports also may provide useful information about an entity or business owner. Know that corporate records may not be a good source for a business address because most states allow corporations to use a registered agent (third party) as their address for service of process.

Using a Company's Web Page as a Resource

Do not underestimate the usefulness of news stories, press releases, and other data displayed a company's website. The "About Us" section may accurately offer company history and ownership information. However, it is best to verify any company-produced literature. Given that investigators always verify their leads, take a look to see what is on the website that may offer clues.

Recommended Non-Government Resources

Of course every major stockbrokerage firm offers some free information on the web about publicly traded companies. Search engines Yahoo! and Google also provide in-depth data on publicly traded companies. Also, check out *The Motley Fool* at www.fool.com and the *Investors Business Daily* at www.investors.com. The site at www.annualreports.com provides access to annual reports.

Finding the ownership and records of private companies can be a difficult task. The entity may be registered at the state, but minimal public disclosure and required forms may be available.

Key analysis points to learn more about a company is to determine who the administration is, what type of financials can be obtained, how many locations there are, and in what type of industry it is involved. There are numerous online services to research both large and small corporations. The given for large companies is that *the bigger they are, the easier it is to gather information on them.* The tasking issues are discerning the volumes of data and deciding on what is valuable and current and what is not. Researching the target company by using online database vendors is a must. To the plus, there are a number of vendors who profile both public and private companies. Hoovers.com and Manta.com are different, but both provide excellent sites. Local Chambers of Commerce and Better Business Bureaus may be useful; to find their local offices go to www.worldchambers.com and www.bbb.org.

When the question comes down to "who owns whom?" two valuable resources for finding the ultimate parent of a company are recommended—

- The Directory of Corporate Affiliations at www.corporateaffiliations.com owned by LexisNexis.
- Dun & Bradstreet.

The next portion of this section takes an in-depth look at some of the most comprehensive vendors and vendor products.

ThomasNet

One of the most powerful resources for searching **industrial information, products and services** is ThomasNet (www.thomasnet.com). From the home page you can also link to worldwide industrial information from more than 700,000 suppliers worldwide.

Dun & Bradstreet

With more than 100 million companies in its database, Dun & Bradstreet is the largest international provider of business reports. Very small, one-man companies and very large, mega corporations are found in its international collection. Researchers and investigators often will find D&B is worth the starting subscription price of several thousand dollars. However, you can search for the address of a company for free. At www.dnb.com, see the *Company Search* box. This *Find a Company* search box extends to international searches.

Here are some practical reasons that illustrate the need to use D&B—

- Fraudulent companies often share fax numbers, even though they generate new phone numbers for business. **Always search for the fax!**

- Searching by the principal's name will often show former company interests or current company interests.

- Dun & Bradstreet automatically does Soundex searching. The name Bill will generate William hits.

- Address searches will show other companies listed at the same address, including mail drops and suspicious addresses.

If you cannot afford D&B directly, you can access their reports through one of B&B's resellers, such as Dialog, SkyMinder, LexisNexis and Bureau van Dijk. If you are a licensed investigator with Thomson Reuters CLEAR, TLO or Accurint, they resell D&B reports. However, keep in mind that direct service subscribers get much better pricing.

Kompass.com

Kompass, which originated in Switzerland, is now present in 70 countries with a very reasonably priced collection of information on more than 4.5 million companies globally. Subscribers can locate the executives of companies, obtain addresses, corporate structures, names of key figures, company turnover information, company descriptions, product names and services, trade and brand names, and location of branches. Free searches include the following topics—

- Region – Geographically locate all companies

- Products/Services – Type of product (i.e. clocks, telephones, hamburgers)

- Companies – Name of company

- Trade names – Name of product

- Executives – Search by person at the top

- Codes – NAICS, SIC and other government-related codes

SkyMinder.com

SkyMinder, an incredible aggregator of other corporate business and credit reports, supplies online credit and business information on more than 50 million companies in 230 countries. SkyMinder is also one of the best places to buy inexpensive D&B header reports. SkyMinder is a key resource used by many private investigators.

A complete source list for Skyminder and a free trial offer is found at www.skyminder.com/basic/info_sources.asp. The source list includes a note on how often the data is updated for each source.

Bureau van Dijk (BvDEP)

Because there is so much that Bureau van Dijk (www.bvdinfo.com/en-gb/home) has to offer, cataloging its many databases is difficult. With a unique name for each service, international databases, such as Orbis, Mint and Osiris, are teamed up with country-specific services like Ruslana (Russia), Sabi (Spain) and Jade (Japan).

Orbis is its flagship global company database with an emphasis on private company information, having 200 million private companies worldwide. With its descriptive information and company financials, Orbis displays extensive detail on items such as news, market research, ratings and country reports, scanned reports, ownership and mergers and acquisitions data.

Orbis provides several different reports for a company. You can view a summary report, a report that automatically compares a company to its peers or view more detailed reports that are taken from BvDEP's specialist products. More detailed information is available for listed companies, banks and insurance companies, and major private companies, more detailed information is available.

CLEAR – Thomson Reuters

CLEAR is a very strong investigative platform designed for professionals who need detailed record information about individuals and companies. Provided by Thomson Reuters, CLEAR has a vast collection of public records in their proprietary database.

CLEAR also provides other useful search tools including access to cell phone and utility data, as well as blogs, news and more from social network sites.

The CLEAR platform is especially helpful for corporate security, collections, insurance investigations, and for law enforcement and government personnel.

Visit https://clear.thomsonreuters.com/clear_home/index.jsp.

Vendor Resources for Searching Non-Profits and Foundations

GuideStar (www.guidestar.org) is a great starting point to find detailed financial information about non-profits. It also offers free access to basic information on 1.8 million tax-exempt organizations. Registration is required for users. GuideStar's fee-searching content includes searchable data from IRS Forms 990 and the IRS Business Master File, including comprehensive facts on employee compensation and grant activity.

Below are several other recommended organizations that are quite helpful for finding information on non-profits.

Capital Research Center (CRC) www.capitalresearch.org, established in 1984 to study non-profit organizations, provides a free database search of non-profits including associated activists and directors.

The Foundation Center is a unique national organization that serves as an authoritative source of information on foundation and corporate giving. See http://foundationcenter.org.

NOZA is advertised as the world's largest searchable database of charitable donors. They help subscribers find donations. See www.nozasearch.com.

Charity Navigator is an independent charity evaluator, with ongoing evaluations on over 8,000 worthy charities in the U.S. See www.charitynavigator.org.

Civil Court Records

See **Court Records** and **Court Records on Statewide Systems**

Copyrights

The United States Copyright Office administers the copyright system, see www.copyright.gov. The U.S., the Copyright Law (www.loc.gov/copyright/title17/) governs the use of these copyrighted: literary works; musical works including words; dramatic works including music; pantomimes and choreographic works; pictorial, graphic, and sculptural works; motion pictures and other audiovisual works; sound recordings; architectural work, but *not* titles, names, short phrases, and slogans; familiar symbols or designs; variations of typographic ornamentation, lettering, or coloring; mere listings of ingredients or contents; ideas; procedures; methods; systems; processes; concepts; principles; discoveries; devices; works of common property, nor containing no original authorship like calendars, rulers, and public lists or tables.

About Copyrights and Authorship

Since 1978, copyright protection exists from the time the work is created in fixed form and ordinarily given a term enduring for the author's life plus 70 years after. For works made for hire, and for anonymous and pseudonymous the duration of a copyright is 95 years from publication or 120 years from creation, whichever is shorter. The copyright for the work of authorship immediately becomes the property of the author who created the work. Only the author or those deriving their rights through the author can rightfully claim copyright. In the case of works made for hire, the employer and not the employee is considered the author.

Where to Search

A free search of the Library of Congress database is at www.copyright.gov/records/.

Search Canadian copyrights free at: http://strategis.ic.gc.ca/app/cipo/copyrights/displaySearch.do?language=eng.

Court Records

Court records are one of the most widely sought types of public record in the U.S. This section provides an in-depth review of how court records are maintained and search tips. Also see:

- **Court Records: State Judicial Systems** later in this chapter.
- **Criminal Records Section** later in this chapter.
- **Federal Court Records** in Chapter 7.
- The **individual state, county and local courts providing online access** are profiled in Chapter 6.

The extensive diversity of the courts and their record keeping systems can be overwhelming. Courts exist at four levels: federal, state, county (or parish), and local municipalities. And all four levels can be found within the same county.

Each state has its own court system, created by statutes or constitution to enforce state civil and criminal laws. Sometimes the terms *state court* and *county court* can be a source of confusion because state trial courts are located at county courthouses. Within this book the phrase *state courts* refers to the courts belonging to the state court systems; and *county courts* refers to those courts administered by county authority.

Local municipal courts can be managed by the local city, town or village government whose laws they enforce. Some lower level courts are called justice courts.

Courts at Parishes, Boroughs, and Certain Cities

In Louisiana the word Parish is equivalent to what is a county in another state. Alaska is organized by Boroughs. In Colorado, Missouri, and Virginia a city may have the same jurisdictional authority of a county.

Rather than continually restate these facts, please assume when the text is speaking of county courts that these other courts are included.

How State Courts Operate

Before searching an online index of court records you should first familiarize yourself with basic court structures and procedures. The general structure of all state court systems has four tiers:

1. Appellate courts
2. Intermediate appellate courts
3. General jurisdiction trial courts
4. Limited jurisdiction trial courts

The two highest levels, **appellate** and **intermediate appellate** courts, only hear cases on appeal from the trial courts. "Opinions" of these appellate courts are of particular interest to attorneys seeking legal precedents for newer cases. However, opinions can be useful to record searchers because they summarize facts about the case that will not show on an index or docket.

General jurisdiction trial courts oversee a full range of civil and criminal litigation, usually handling felonies and higher dollar civil cases. The general jurisdiction courts often serve as the appellate courts for cases appealed from limited jurisdiction courts and even from the local courts. Many court researchers refer to general jurisdiction courts as upper courts.

Limited jurisdiction trial courts come in several varieties. Many limited jurisdiction courts handle smaller civil claims (such as $15,000 or less), misdemeanors, and pretrial hearings for felonies. Localized municipal courts are also referred to as courts of limited jurisdiction. Many court researchers refer to limited jurisdiction courts as lower courts.

Some states, Iowa for instance, have consolidated their general and limited court structure into one combined court system. Other states, Maryland for example, have very distinct differences between upper and lower courts. In these states if you are performing a county search, each court must be separately searched.

Some courts – sometimes called special jurisdiction courts – have general jurisdiction but are limited to one type of litigation. An example is the Court of Claims in New York which only processes liability cases against the state.

About Municipal, Town, and Village Courts

Localized courts preside over city or town misdemeanors, infractions, and ordinance violations at the city, town or township level. Sometimes these courts may be known as justice courts. New York has 1,400 Town and Village Justice Courts generally handle misdemeanors, local ordinance violations, and traffic violations including DWIs.

In most states there is a distinction between state-supported courts and the local courts in terms of management, funding, and sharing of web pages.

The Online State Judicial Systems

 Every state has an administrative agency that oversees the upper three levels and, depending the type of court, the fourth level as well.

This agency is important because actually **more counties and courts are found online on systems managed by this agency, then managed by a local court.** For more information about searching these sites see the **Court Records on Statewide Judicial Systems** section later in this chapter.

Watch for Divisions and Name Variations

 The structure of the court system and the names used for courts often vary widely from state-to-state. Civil and criminal records may be handled by different divisions within a court or sometimes by completely different courts with different names. For example, in Tennessee the Chancery Court oversees civil cases but criminal cases are tried in Circuit Courts, except in districts with separate Criminal Courts as established by the state legislature. In Iowa the District Court is the highest trial court whereas in Michigan the District Court is a limited jurisdiction court.

How Courts Maintain Records

Case Numbering and Record Index

Each case is assigned a number and case record information is indexed using this number. Courts also, usually, cross reference the case number index to the names of the parties involved. Therefore, to find specific case file documents, you need to know the applicable case number or else you must perform a name search to find the case number.

The Docket Sheet – A Key Information Resource

Information from cover sheets and from documents filed as a case goes forward is recorded on the *docket sheet*. Thus the docket sheet, sometimes called a register of actions, is a running summary of a case history. Each action, such as motions, briefs, exhibits, etc., is recorded in chronological order. While docket sheets differ somewhat in format from court to court, the basic information contained on a docket sheet is consistent. Docket sheets will contain:

- Name of court, including location (division) and the judge assigned;
- Case number and case name;

- Names of all plaintiffs and defendants/debtors;

- Names and addresses of attorneys for the plaintiff or debtor;

- Nature and cause (e.g., statute) of action.

- Date and summary of all materials and motions filed in a case

- Case outcome (disposition)

Most courts enter the docket data into a computer system. Within a state or judicial district, the courts may be linked together via a single computer system.

What is Really Found Online

The primary search of court records is a search of the docket index. When someone tells you "I can view xxx county court records online," this person is most likely talking about viewing an index summary of records and not about viewing the actual case file document pages.

But docket sheets from cases closed before the advent of computerization may not be in the computer system. And in some locations all docket information is non-computerized. Media formats include microfilm, microfiche, index cards, and paper that may even be hand-written.

The Case Disposition

The term *disposition* is frequently used when discussing or searching court records. The case disposition refers to the final outcome of a case - such as a judgment in a civil matter or if a party is determined to be guilty in a criminal matter.

There are some cases where decisions were rendered, but the results are not recorded or the case file number is removed from the index. In certain situations, a judge can order the case file sealed or removed – expunged – from the public repository. Examples include if a defendant enters a diversion program (drug or family counseling), or a defendant makes restitution as part of a plea bargain; these cases may not be searchable. The only way to gain direct access to these types of case filings is through a subpoena. However, savvy researchers and investigators will sometimes search news media sources if need be.

Use of Identifiers and Redaction

Identifiers are important to record searching. They serve two different although related purposes.

1. The identifiers of the subject must be used to analyze a public record for the purpose of determining if the record is about that subject. Perhaps the records are indexed by the last name but also display either the full or partial DOB or perhaps the address or even a partial SSN. If so, a searcher having prior knowledge of the DOB or address or SSN will have a more accurate search result.

2. The identifiers act as an important safeguard for both the requesting party and the subject of the search. There is always the chance that the Harold Johnson on whom a given repository has a record is not the same Harold Johnson on whom a check has been requested. The possibility of a misidentification can be decreased substantially if other identifiers can match the individual to the record. Providing an identifier as simple as just the middle initial is likely to help identify the correct Harold Johnson.

The federal, state, and local agencies that maintain court record systems make substantial efforts to protect the public from identity theft and limit the disclosure of certain personal information such as Social Security Numbers, phone numbers, and addresses. Many agencies are now redacting personal information from their records.

Often the redaction will not apply to the DOB on the records. At least part of the DOB is necessary to determine the proper identity of someone who has a common name. There are plenty of news stories about how someone was denied a job because a background check was done and the wrong information was reported, wrong information pertaining to someone else with the same name. The balance of privacy interests versus public jeopardy goes beyond the purposes of this book. However, the key point here is to be aware of change and know that redactions can and will alter public record searching procedures.

The Types of Court Cases Found Online

Below is a summary of the types of court cases and records found at the state or local level. Note that bankruptcies are not found on this list because bankruptcy cases are filed at the federal level.

- **Civil Actions** - For money damages usually greater than $5,000. Also, some states have designated dollar amount thresholds for upper or lower (limited) civil courts. Most civil litigation involves torts or contract.
- **Small Claims** - Actions for minor money damages, generally under $5,000, no juries involved.
- **Criminal Felonies** - Generally defined as crimes punishable by one year or more of jail time. There can be multiple levels or classes.
- **Criminal Misdemeanors** - Generally defined as minor infractions with a fine and less than one year of jail time. Misdemeanors also have multiple levels or classes.
- **Probate** - Estate matters, settling the estate of a deceased person, resolving claims and distributing the decedent's property.
- **Eviction Actions** - Landlord/tenant actions, can also known as an unlawful detainer, forcible detainer, summary possession, or repossession.
- **Domestic Relations** – Sometimes known as *Family Law*, with authority over family disputes, divorces, dissolutions, child support or custody cases.
- **Juvenile** – Authority over cases involving individuals under a specified age, usually 18 years but sometimes 21.
- **Traffic** – May also have authority over municipal ordinances.
- **Specialty Courts** – Water, equity in fiduciary questions, tort, contracts, tax, etc.

More about Civil Court Cases

A civil case usually commences when a plaintiff files a complaint with a court against defendants. The defendants respond to the complaint with an answer. After this initial round, there may be literally hundreds of activities before the court issues a judgment. These activities can include revised complaints and their answers, motions of various kinds, discovery proceedings (including depositions) to establish the documentation and facts involved in the case. All of these activities are listed on a docket sheet, which may be a piece of paper or a computerized index.

Once a civil court issues a judgment, either party may appeal the ruling to an appellate division or court. In the case of a money judgment, the winning side can usually file it as a judgment lien with the county recorder. Appellate divisions usually deal only with legal issues and not the facts of the case.

One common problem when searching civil records is they often show very few, if any, personal identifiers on the index or case files. Sometimes extensive research is required to properly determine the identity of a person subject of a search.

About Judgments

When a judgment is rendered in court, the winning party usually files and records a lien notice (called an Abstract of Judgment in many states). Per DictionaryLaw.com, an Abstract of Judgment is defined as:

"...a written summary of a judgment which states how much money the losing party owes to the person who won the lawsuit (judgment creditor), the rate of interest to be paid on the judgment amount, court costs, and any specific orders that the losing party (judgment debtor) must obey, which abstract is acknowledged and stamped so that it can be recorded at the county recorder. The purpose of an abstract of judgment is to create a public record and create a lien or claim if necessary on any real estate owned or later acquired by the loser located in the county in which the abstract of judgment is recorded."

Judgments can be searched at the local or county level usually in the same index as real estate records. See the *Recorded Documents, Judgments, and Liens* section.

Searching Tip: Watch for Overlapping Jurisdictions

In some states, the general jurisdiction court and the limited jurisdiction court have overlapping dollar amounts for civil cases. That means a case could be filed in either court. Check both courts; never assume.

More about Criminal Court Cases

In a criminal case, the plaintiff is a government jurisdiction. The government brings the action against the defendant for violation of one or more of its statutes. The term disposition refers to the final outcome of a criminal court case. A disposition is an important piece of information on a criminal record or record index, along with the defendant's name, some type of personal identifier, the charge, and the case number. This is also a key term when legal use of records is governed by state laws and the federal FCRA (Fair Credit Reporting Act). The information that could be disclosed on a criminal record includes the arrest record, criminal charges, fines, sentencing and incarceration information.

Criminal court records are eventually submitted to a central repository controlled by a state agency such as the State Police or Department of Public Safety. See *Criminal Record Repositories* later in this chapter.

There is a huge difference on the record access procedures between the state repositories and the courts. Records maintained by the court are generally open to the public, but not all state criminal record repositories open their criminal records to the public.

Eight Tips for Searching Courts' Online Record Databases

1. Be Aware Not All Courts Are Online

A surprising number of courts do not have computerized record keeping. Per the latest statistics taken from the Public Record Research System (https://www.brbpublications.com/products/Prrs.aspx), 74.5% of civil courts and 71.45% of criminal courts provide online access to an historical docket index. Does this make you wonder about the so-called instant national background search?

2. Online Searching is Generally Limited to Docket Sheets

Most courts that offer online access limit the search to the docket sheet data - opposed to displaying case file images. But checking a courthouse's computer online docket index is the quickest way to find if case records exist online. Just be sure to check all name variations and spelling variations.

In general, case document images are rarely online, at least for free. Those courts that offer case images are usually subscription based and often require e-filing of documents. The reality is to obtain case documents one must go on-site.

3. Learn the Index and What Data is Viewable

All indices are different. For example, some of the questions you need to ask and to be answered are: How far back does the index go? Are all cases online? How current is the index - real time? With 24 hours? With 7 days? What identifiers are needed to search and are shown on results? Is the search countywide, or do other courts in the county need to be searched?

Most civil courts index records by both plaintiffs and defendants, but some courts only index by the defendant name. A plaintiff search can be useful to determine if someone is especially litigious.

4. Understand the Search Mechanics

Look for any help screens that may offer advice, such as the use of wildcards. If the search lets you input a partial name this will help you find records that may have name spelling variances. For civil cases, the usual reasonable requirement is a defendant (or plaintiff) name – full name if it is a common name – and the time frame to search – e.g., 2002-2017. For criminal cases, the court may require more identification, such as date of birth (DOB), to ascertain the correct individual.

5. Be Aware of Restricted Records

Courts have types of case records, such as juvenile and adoptions, which are not released without a court order. Records may also be sealed form view or expunged. The presiding judge often makes a determination of whether a particular record type is available to the public. Some criminal court records include the arresting officer's report. In some locations this information is regarded as public record, while in other locations the police report may be sealed.

6. Watch for Multiple Courts as Same Location

Do not assume a search is countywide. When the general jurisdiction and limited jurisdiction courts are in the same building and use the same support staff, yes...chances are the record databases are combined as well. But that does not necessarily mean you will receive a search of both databases. Check it out as you may need to do two searches.

7. Watch for Overlapping Jurisdictions on Civil Limits

In many states, the general jurisdiction court and the limited jurisdiction court have overlapping dollar amount limits for civil cases. That means cases filed within a certain dollar (such as between $15,000 and $25,000) can be filed in either court. Check both courts; never assume.

8. Look for the Lag Time

Depending on the level of due diligence needed, a good searcher needs to know what the time delay is for posting records. Is it a week or more or 24 hours, or in real time? This is important if the search is conducted in connection with high due diligence such as with litigation or hiring matters.

Court Records on Judicial Statewide Systems

The online court records obtainable from this venue are widespread, often free, and overall very worthwhile.

As mentioned previously, every state has a judicial branch that oversees that state's trial and appellate court system. The name of the agency will vary, but it is often known as the Administration Office of the Courts (AOC) or State Court Administrator' Office.

Knowing about this agency and their online services is important because thru the AOC more counties and courts are online than from the individual county-based systems. Consider these overall statistics about state judicial systems and the state courts at the county level, again from the Public Record Research System:

- 27 States Offer Online Access to Both Civil and Criminal Records Statewide
- 5 States Offer Online Access to Partial Statewide Access
- 5 States Offer Access to Only Online Civil Records Statewide
- 1 State Offers Access to Only Online Criminal Records Statewide
- 13 States Have Online Access to Neither

The specific states and sites with web access are profiled in Chapter 6.

These Systems are Not Created Equal - Know the State-by-State Variations

Online researchers must be aware that there are many nuances to these searches. The value of a *statewide* court search varies by state. Consider these evaluation points:

- **Pay or free or both?** While some of the free searches are good, the adage *you pay for what you get* can certainly apply here.

- **Is the search a statewide search?** All counties may not be on the system.

- **Is the throughput posted and is there uniformity?** For example, one county may have cases dating back for seven years, while another county may have only two years of history.

- **Are identifiers shown?** The lack of identifiers to properly identify a subject varies widely from state-to-state. A lack of is especially apparent on the free access search systems.

- And perhaps the most important evaluation point: **Is an online search equivalent to searching onsite?** The level of your due diligence and need for accuracy will determine if using an online site that is in reality a supplemental search is sufficient for your needs. This of course is true for ANY online site for ANY type of public record.

Court Records of Native Americans

Native American Tribes are indigenous, sovereign entities and are not governed by state or federal courts. Therefore court records pertaining to tribal matters or regarding incidents occurring on tribal land will not be found in the state or federal courts. But there is an excellent online resource about tribal court and law matters.

The Tribal Court Clearinghouse

Sponsored by the Tribal Institute, the Tribal Court Clearinghouse is a comprehensive website resource for American Indian and Alaska Native Nations, tribal justice systems, victim services providers, tribal service providers, and others involved in the improvement of justice in Indian country. The *Tribal Law* tab provides direct links to many resources including Tribal Courts, Tribal Court Decisions, and Law Enforcement resources. The Tribal Institute also does a great job of listing and describing the many federal government agencies and native organizations involved with Native Americans. This very useful site is found at www.tribal-institute.org/index.htm

Criminal Records at State Repositories

Editor's Note: This section is limited to a discussion to specific state criminal record database repositories. Additional information about criminal records or criminal related records is found at:

- **Court Records**
- **Court Records on Statewide Judicial Systems**
- **Incarceration Records**
- **Sexual Offender Registries**
- **Federal Agency Sanctions & Watch Lists**
- **Federal Courts (Chapter7)**

All states have a central repository of criminal records of individuals who have been subject to that state's criminal justice system. The repository is managed by a state law enforcement agency. The exact agency name varies from state-to-state, but is often called the State Police or the Department of Public Safety. Generally these repositories are designated as the state's Official Source for performing a background check. (This can be a problem if this is the only resource used, as you will be shown later.)

The information at the state repository is submitted by state, county, parish, and municipal courts as well as from local law enforcement. The forwarded information includes notations of arrests and charges, the disposition, and if from law enforcement agencies a set of fingerprints.

Criminal-related records exist in other state repositories including incarceration (prison) systems, sexual predator registries, and on federal government sanction and watch lists. These venues are examined elsewhere in this chapter. And there are vendors who collect and maintain proprietary databases of criminal record information gathered from as many of the above mentioned sources as possible.

Availability of Records to the Public Varies by State

In general, the criminal records are public when at the courts. But when the records are forwarded to the state repositories there are often restrictions placed on access by the general public. For example, per the Public Record Research System from BRB Publications, only 27 states release criminal records (name search) to the general public without consent of the subject, 17 states require a signed release from the subject, and 6 states require submission of fingerprints.

Detailed information about each state's online system is presented in Chapter 6.

Facts about Accuracy and Completeness, Especially When Fingerprints Not Submitted

Employers and state occupation licensing boards often depend on states' criminal record repositories as primary resources when performing a criminal record background check. However, these entities may not realize that a search of these record repositories may not be as accurate and complete as assumed, regardless if fingerprints are submitted.

There are three key reasons why the completeness, consistency, and accuracy of state criminal record repositories could be suspect—

1. Timeliness of Receiving Arrest and Disposition Data
2. Timeliness of Entering Arrest and Disposition Data into the Repository
3. Inability to Match Dispositions with Existing Arrest Records

The basis for these concerns is supported by documented facts provided by the U.S. Department of Justice (DOJ). Every two years the DOJ's Bureau of Justice Statistics releases an extensive Survey of State Criminal Record Repositories. The latest survey, released December 2015 and based on statistics complied as of Dec 31, 2014, is a 117-page document with 36 data tables. The survey is available at https://www.ncjrs.gov/pdffiles1/bjs/grants/249799.pdf.

Below are some eye-catching facts reflected from the current Survey:

- 8 states report 25% or more of all dispositions received could NOT be linked to the arrest/charge information in the state criminal record database. 14 states don't know how many dispositions they have that cannot be linked. (Table 8a)
- 20 states have over 3 million unprocessed or partially processed court dispositions, ranging from 200 in Michigan and North Dakota to over 1 million in Nevada. (Table 14)
- 11 states report at least a 50 day backlog between the time when a felony case is decided and when the record is entered in that state's criminal history database. 18 states do not know how long the delay is. (Table 14)

The statistics below is taken directly from this Survey.

State	% of Arrests in last 5 years that have final case dispositions recorded (Table 1)	Percentage of all dispositions received that could NOT be linked to a specific arrest record.	Average # of Days between occurrence of final felony court disposition and receipt of data by repository	Average # of Days between receipt of final felony court disposition and entry in state criminal database
AL	20%	unknown	1	nr
AK	91%	unknown	23	35

State	% of Arrests in last 5 years that have final case dispositions recorded (Table 1)	Percentage of all dispositions received that could NOT be linked to a specific arrest record.	Average # of Days between occurrence of final felony court disposition and receipt of data by repository	Average # of Days between receipt of final felony court disposition and entry in state criminal database
AR	79%	1%	21	1
AZ	66%	16%	16	2
CA	na	8%	nr	60
CO	34%	44%	0	0
CT	98%	15%	1	1
DE	96%	0%	1	1
DC	43%	nr	nr	nr
FL	66%	28%	28	1
GA	85%	0%	30	2
HI	89%	22%	9	0
IA	88%	2%	7	7
ID	39%	nr	1	1
IL	37%	3%	30	32
IN	43%	40%	nr	1
KS	41%	nr	nr	nr
KY	19%	18%	90	90
LA	na	14%	na	60
MA	na	nr	nr	nr
MD	95%	26%	10	0
ME	65%	unknown	15	0
MI	75%	11%	248	2,233
MN	nr	nr	<1	1
MO	70%	17%	507	2
MS	11%	nr	nr	2
MT	53%	5%	16	32
NC	72%	0%	12	0
ND	81%	nr	nr	0
NE	75%	0%	1	1
NH	83%	41%	nr	nr
NJ	83%	19%	nr	7
NM	20%	nr	nr	nr
NV	55%	44%	nr	nr
NY	88%	8%	1	1

State	% of Arrests in last 5 years that have final case dispositions recorded (Table 1)	Percentage of all dispositions received that could NOT be linked to a specific arrest record.	Average # of Days between occurrence of final felony court disposition and receipt of data by repository	Average # of Days between receipt of final felony court disposition and entry in state criminal database
OH	40%	47%	na	na
OK	34%	nr	30	30
OR	78%	12%	na	100
PA	62%	26%	nr	1
RI	na	0%	5	5
SC	na	unknown	16	1
SD	na	nr	nr	nr
TN	75%	2%	30	nr
TX	92%	2%	30	1
UT	72%	19%	0	0
VA	89%	21%	14	14
VT	88%	5%	60	60
WA	94%	3%	7	5
WI	83%	8%	nr	nr
WV	na	2%	nr	nr
WY	82%	3%	60	2

Please don't misunderstand the message here – there are certainly good reasons for performing a search of a state repository record database. A statewide search covers a wider geographic range than a county search. And a state search is certainly less expensive than a separate search of each county. Many states do have strong database systems. But for proper due diligence for performing a criminal record search, using a state search AND a county search of criminal records AND a search from a vendor's proprietary database should be considered. This is extremely critical for employers making hiring decisions in states with legislative limitations on using criminal records without dispositions or using misdemeanor records.

Universal Background Checks

This phrase - Universal Background Check - has morphed from a nonsensical term to a new addition in Wikipedia primarily because of all the hubbub and political maneuvering over checking people buying guns at gun shows and other private sales.

A politician who is calling for a Universal Background Check merely demonstrates a lack of knowledge about the subject matter and is simply jumping on the bandwagon of using the newly coined phrase.

I wonder how Beldar Conehead would define a Universal Background Check? His definition of a Ford Lincoln Mercury Sable was spot on.

A personal conveyance named after its inventor, an assassinated ruler, a character from Greco-Roman myth, and a small furry mammal.

I suspect Beldar would define a Universal Background Check along these lines:

An examination to see if someone's name is listed in a federally administered incomplete and mistake filled database that is populated by data from non-federal sources which are often reported voluntarily and inconsistently, often have a huge backlog of records not yet entered, and often contain partial records that cannot be matched to the original existing partial record.

Beldar's definition is supported by the U.S. Department of Justice as per the above mentioned DOJ Study.

If politicians and the news media want to define these checks in a broad and inaccurate manner regardless of which side of the NRA side of the fence they sit, there is no stopping them. We just have to read and cringe.

Death Records

See the **Vital Records** section for information regarding death records, the Social Security Administration' Death Index, and about obituary records. Also see **Genealogy Records** section.

Elections: Candidates, PACs, Lobbyists, and Voters

Numerous federal, state, and local public records associated with the election process and many of these records are viewable online.

Voter Registration

Voting registration records are public record sources of the voting history, the addresses, and sometimes telephone numbers of individual voters. Every state has a central election agency or commission and all have a central repository of voter information collected from the local level agencies per federal mandate HAVA (Help America Vote Act of 2002, Public Law 107-252).[1]

In general, voter registration records are publicly accessible at the local level and not so accessibly at the state level. Roughly 2/3's of states will only release voter registration information to those with a political or research purpose. Political purposes include purchase by political parties or candidates to solicit votes.

As shown in Chapter 6, only a handful of states offer an online search of a voter's status. A few public record vendors offer online access to their proprietary database of voter records. Perhaps the best known vendor is Aristotle.com. Record data released generally includes name, address and telephone numbers, unless specifically blocked by the registrant. We believe all states and local agencies block the release of Social Security Numbers.

Campaign Finance and Disclosure

Candidates for state and local office are subject to the campaign finance laws. Once a candidate raises, receives or expends more than designated threshold in a year, the candidate is required to register and report from whom the funds are raised. That same is true for committees working on behalf of political parties or candidate or for specific political measures. All of this information is public record and it is generally found online.

PACs: Political Action Committee

A Political Action Committee (PAC) raises money in the support of (or against) political candidates, legislation and ballot items. PACs often represent businesses large or small, or special interest groups such as unions or the NRA, etc. PACs must register at the state or federal level, depending on the purpose of the PAC, and follow pre-set guidelines. Since PACs are a matter of public record, the registration information and donations are searchable by the public. State PAC online resources are usually with the same agency that oversees elections, but sometimes PACs are managed by a totally different state agency as shown in Chapter 6. Federal level sites are covered later within this section.

---

[1] South Dakota is exempt from HAVA.

Lobbyists

Lobbyists are individuals paid to communicate with public office holders in order to influence government decisions. As with PACs, lobbyists must be registered at the government level where they are trying to influence votes. The registration of lobbyists is a matter of public record.

In some states lobbyists are registered with the same agency that oversees elections, in other the lobbyist records are with a different agency, such as an agency that oversees ethics of legislative-related people and entities. The resources for online access to lobbyist data are shown in Chapter 6 within the appropriate section.

Federal Agency Resources

Federal Election Commission (FEC)

The Federal Election Commission (FEC) administers and enforces the Federal Election Campaign Act (FECA), which is the statute that governs the financing of federal elections. To locate information about the political donations go to the Federal Election Commission's website at www.fec.gov. The site provides some excellent search tools under the *Campaign Finance Disclosure Portal*. Also, try the *Search* tab for your favorite celebrity name

Internal Revenue Service

The IRS monitors what can be deducted as donations to a PAC or by a PAC. On the web page one can search by name of employer for all electronic and paper submissions of Form 8871 Political Organization Notice of Section 527 Status, and Form 8872 Political Organization Report of Contributions and Expenditures. Also searchable from this site are the paper submissions of Form 990 Return of Organizations Exempt from Income Tax - the form filed by many public charities and other exempt organizations. See http://forms.irs.gov/app/pod/basicSearch/search?execution=e2s1.

Lobbyists & Laws

Lobbyists must register with the Senate to disclose who hired them, how much they are paid, what issues or bills they are lobbying on behalf, and the federal agencies they are contacting. There is no search web page of registered lobbyists. To research laws, click on the *Public Disclosure* tab at www.senate.gov.

The Office of the Clerk for the U.S. House of Representatives site at http://lobbyingdisclosure.house.gov offers information about lobbying at the House and a search of Past Contribution Filings.

Agent for a Foreign Principal for Political Reasons

The Foreign Agents Registration Act (FARA) requires individuals acting as agents of foreign principals in a political or quasi-political capacity to make periodic public disclosure of their relationship with the foreign principal, as well as activities, receipts and disbursements in support of those activities. Many searching features are provided at www.fara.gov.

Four Private Sector Resources

1. OpenSecrets.org is an extremely useful site. Per their web page "...is the nation's premier research group tracking money in U.S. politics and its effect on elections and public policy. Nonpartisan, independent and nonprofit, the organization aims to create a more educated voter, an involved citizenry and a more transparent and responsive government."

2. Another recommended site is FollowTheMoney.org which is maintained by the National Institute on Money in State Politics. The Institute provides a searchable database with substantive profiles on candidates and issues, insightful reports and reliable data for all 50 states. This excellent web page also has many, many other database searches available on a subscription basis only.

3. Also, a great searchable directory of lobbying firms is found at LobbyData.com. Search by name, the agency involved or by issue.

4. The **Vote Smart** site at www.votesmart.org/index.htm tracks many facts about candidates including campaign contributions; however, data may be lacking for local politicians. The site includes voting records and evaluations by special interest groups.

Environmental Information

Many environmental public records held by the government rest at two locations: the **Environmental Protection Agency** and the **National Library of Medicine**. The content to follow looks at each agency and public records associated with health hazards. At the end of this section, be sure to check out **Scorecard**, a pollution information site.

Environmental Protection Agency (EPA)

The EPA's Environmental Facts Warehouse at www.epa.gov/enviro is an excellent starting place to search for environmental information related to locations. There are nine *Topic Searches*, each with the ability to find data by Zip Code, or by city and state.

Below are descriptions of more useful search sites and features provided by the EPA.

- EnviroMapper combines interactive maps and aerial photography to display various types of environmental information, including air releases, drinking water, toxic releases, hazardous wastes, water discharge permits, and Superfund sites. The site creates maps at the national, state, and county levels that can be linked to environmental text reports. Go to www.epa.gov/emefdata/em4ef.home.

- The EPA's Office of Enforcement and Compliance Assurance (OECA) works with EPA regional offices, state governments, tribal governments and other federal agencies on compliance with the nation's environmental laws. Two useful starting pages are offered. The Compliance Home is https://www.epa.gov/compliance. The Enforcement home at https://www.epa.gov/enforcement is a great starting point for enforcement cases and settlements.

- OECA also offers online access to its database called Enforcement & Compliance History Online (ECHO). Search the database for inspection, violation, enforcement action, and penalty information about compliance and enforcement information on approximately 800,000 regulated facilities. ECHO can be found at https://echo.epa.gov/. For a web search of cases and settlements go to http://cfpub.epa.gov/compliance/cases.

- Federal law requires facilities in certain industries which manufacture, process, or use significant amounts of toxic chemicals, to report annually on their releases of these chemicals to the EPA Toxics Release Inventory Program. *Superfund sites* are those throughout the United States and its territories which contain substances that are either designated as hazardous under the Comprehensive Environmental Response, Compensation and Liability Act (CERCLA), or identified as such under other laws. For information about the Superfund sites on the National Priorities List, email superfund.docket@epa.gov. Superfund sites are at https://www.epa.gov/superfund. Search EPA Records of Decisions (ROD) at https://www.epa.gov/superfund/search-superfund-decision-documents.

National Library of Medicine (NLM)

Household Products Database

This resource indicates the chemical ingredients found in household products and who manufactures specific brands. The database contains information on over 7,000 products. Email tehip@teh.nlm.nih.gov or visit http://householdproducts.nlm.nih.gov.

TOXMAP

TOXMAP (http://toxmap.nlm.nih.gov/toxmap/) is a Geographic Information System (GIS) using maps of the U.S. to help users visually explore data from the EPA's Toxics Release Inventory (TRI) (https://www.epa.gov/toxics-release-inventory-tri-program /) and Superfund Programs. EJSCREEN is a mapping tool at https://www.epa.gov/ejscreen that combines environmental and demographic indicators in maps and reports. Users can search the system by chemical name, chemical name fragment, and/or location (such as city, state, or ZIP code). TOXMAP also overlays map data such as U.S. Census population information, income figures from the Bureau of Economic Analysis, and health data from the National Cancer Institute (www.cancer.gov) and the National Center for Health Statistics (www.cdc.gov/nchs).

TOXNET

TOXNET, the Toxicology Data Network, provides multiple databases on toxicology, hazardous chemicals, environmental health, and toxic releases. The free access at http://toxnet.nlm.nih.gov provides easy searching to a great many databases.

Tox Town

This interactive web page is a great source of non-technical descriptions of chemicals, assorted links to selected, authoritative chemical information, and lists everyday locations where one might find toxic chemicals. Visit https://toxtown.nlm.nih.gov.

Private Sector Sites

One can find a variety of informative whistle blower sites on the web, usually supported by a law firms. Below are two non-attorney firm organizations worthy of mention.

Scorecard

Scorecard is a very popular, non-government web resource for information about pollution problems and toxic chemicals. Per their web page, one may learn about the pollution problems in community and learn who is responsible. See which geographic areas and companies have the worst pollution records. Visit http://scorecard.goodguide.com/.

Oceana

Oceana is the largest international organization dealing with on ocean conservation. Their scientists work closely with teams of economists, lawyers and advocates to achieve conservation results for the oceans. See http://oceana.org.

Federal Agencies

The two best starting points to find onlien information about federal agencies are mentioned below.

USA.Gov

This is a terrific online tool for government records because it is the U.S.A. Government's search engine. Over 100 different online functions that can be performed via this government interface, from opting out of direct marketing databases to locating zip codes. If you want to file a complaint against a government agency or take a virtual White House tour, it is probably available online through links on usa.gov.

The Government Printing Office

At the Government Printing Office, located at gpo.gov, one can search for a publication by name, author, keyword or subject. A search for *Public Records* as a Subject will return a number of matches. These are not necessarily online and waiting for you to click and grab, however many are. Actually, this site will tell you which government depository library has a hard copy physically on the shelf or if it can be acquired through your local library.

The government spends billions of dollars every year on industry analysis, medical trials, land management studies, etcetera. Always consider a government document when conducting any form of research. If it can be studied, the government has a report on it! These reports are significantly cheaper (often free!) compared to expensive market-research reports.

Federal Sanctions & Watch Lists

This section examines public record databases of individuals and companies that have sanctions, violations, enforcement actions, or warnings initiated against them by one of these federal government departments. To find enforcement actions taken by the Federal Reserve, see the *Banks & Financial Institutions* Section. To find enforcement action involving stocks and securities see the *Securities and Securities Dealers* Section.

Consolidated Screening List of Eleven Databases

The web page at http://export.gov/ecr/eg_main_023148.asp has links to eleven lists of parties for which the United States Government maintains restrictions on certain exports, re-exports or transfers of items. From this page one can also download a consolidated CSV file of all eleven lists. The eleven database lists are described below.

From the Commerce Department, Bureau of Industry and Security (BIS)

1. Denied Persons List

The Denied Persons List contains Individuals and entities that have been denied export privileges. The List is meant to prevent the illegal export of dual-use items before they occur and to investigate and assist in the prosecution of violators of the Export Administration Regulations.

2. Unverified List

This list of parties includes names and countries of foreign persons are whom BIS has been unable to verify in some manner in prior transaction or could not conduct a pre-license check ("PLC") or a post-shipment verification ("PSV") for reasons outside of the U.S. Government's control.

3. Entity List

The Entity List is a list of parties whose presence in a transaction can trigger a license requirement under the Export Administration Regulations. The original purpose was to inform the public of entities whose activities imposed a risk of diverting exported and re-exported items into programs related to weapons of mass destruction. Now the list includes those with any license requirements imposed on the transaction by other provisions of the Export Administration Regulations. The list specifies the license requirements that apply to each listed party.

From the Department of State:

4. Nonproliferation Sanctions List

This shows parties who have been sanctioned under various statutes per the Bureau of International Security. Note webpage is updated as appropriate, but the Federal Register is the only official and complete listing of nonproliferation sanctions determinations.

5. AECA Debarred List

Per the Directorate of Defense Trade Controls, this displays entities and individuals prohibited from participating directly or indirectly in the export of defense articles, including technical data and defense services. Pursuant to the Arms Export Control Act (AECA) and the International Traffic in Arms Regulations (ITAR), the AECA Debarred List includes persons convicted in court of violating or conspiring to violate the AECA and subject to "statutory debarment" or persons established to have violated the AECA in an administrative proceeding and subject to "administrative debarment."

From the Department of the Treasury:

6. Specially Designated Nationals (SDN) List

Per the Office of Foreign Assets Control, the **Specially Designated Nationals List** shows parties who may be prohibited from export transactions based on OFAC regulations.

7. Foreign Sanctions Evaders List

Foreign individuals and entities determined to have violated, attempted to violate, conspired to violate, or caused a violation of U.S. sanctions on Syria or Iran, as well as foreign persons who have facilitated deceptive transactions for or on behalf of persons subject to U.S. Sanctions. Transactions by U.S. persons or within the United States involving Foreign Sanctions Evaders (FSEs) are prohibited.

8. Sectoral Sanctions Identifications (SSI) List:

Individuals operating in sectors of the Russian economy with whom U.S. persons are prohibited from transacting in, providing financing for, or dealing in debt with a maturity of longer than 90 days.

9. Palestinian Legislative Council (PLC) List:

Individuals of the PLC who were elected on the party slate of Hamas, or any other Foreign Terrorist Organization (FTO), Specially Designed Terrorist (SDT), or Specially Designated Global Terrorist (SDGT).

10. The List of Foreign Financial Institutions Subject to Part 561:

The Part 561 List includes the names of foreign financial Institutions that are subject to sanctions, certain prohibitions, or strict conditions before a U.S. company may do business with them.

11. Non-SDN Iranian Sanctions Act List (NS-ISA):

The ISA List includes persons determined to have made certain investments in Iran's energy sector or to have engaged in certain activities relating to Iran's refined petroleum sector. Their names do not appear on the Specially Designated Nationals or Blocked Persons (SDN) List, and their property and/or interests in property are not blocked, pursuant to this action.

FDA – Food & Drug Administration

The FDA regulates scientific studies designed to develop evidence to support the safety and effectiveness of investigational drugs (human and animal), biological products, and medical devices. Physicians and other qualified experts ("clinical investigators") who conduct these studies are required to comply with applicable statutes and regulations intended to ensure the integrity of clinical data on which product approvals are based and, for investigations involving human subjects, to help protect the rights, safety, and welfare of these subjects.

FDA Enforcement Report Index – Recalls, Market Withdrawals, and Safety Alerts

The FDA Enforcement Report, published weekly, contains information on actions taken in connection with agency regulatory activities. Data includes Recalls and Field Corrections, Injunctions, Seizures, Indictments, Prosecutions, and Dispositions. Pending Recalls and Archived Enforcement Reports going back to 2010 can be found at the agency's web page at www.fda.gov/Safety/Recalls/EnforcementReports/default.htm.

Visit www.fda.gov/Safety/Recalls/default.htm for the most significant recalls, market withdrawals and safety alerts of products; all listed are based on the extent of distribution and the degree of health risk.

Debarment List

The FDA maintains a list at www.fda.gov/ICECI/EnforcementActions/FDADebarmentList/default.htm of individuals and entities that are prohibited from introducing any type of food, drug, cosmetics or associated devices into interstate commerce.

Disqualified or Restricted Clinical Investigator List

A disqualified or totally restricted clinical investigator is not eligible to receive investigational drugs, biologics, or devices. Some clinical investigators have agreed to certain restrictions with respect to their conduct of clinical investigations. See www.fda.gov/ICECI/EnforcementActions/ucm321308.htm

GSA – Government Services

Excluded Party List

The Excluded Parties List System (EPLS) contains information on individuals and firms excluded by various Federal government agencies from receiving federal contracts or federally approved subcontracts and from certain types of federal financial and non-financial assistance and benefits. Note that individual agencies are responsible for their data.

EPLS is now provided by the System for Award Management (SAM), which combined federal procurement systems and the Catalog of Federal Domestic Assistance into one new system. See www.sam.gov/portal/public/SAM/

Note: The SAM web page also provides search capabilities for other databases, as outlined later in this section.

Human Health Services, Department of

Excluded Individuals/Entities (LEIE)

The LEIE maintained by the Office of Inspector General (OIG) for the Department of Human Health Services is a list of currently excluded parties. The exclusions are based on convictions for program-related fraud and patient abuse, licensing board actions, and default on Health Education Assistance Loans. The searchable database is found at http://exclusions.oig.hhs.gov/. A downloadable version is at https://oig.hhs.gov/exclusions/exclusions_list.asp.

Justice Department

There are a number of Divisions within the Justice Department that maintain news articles, stories, records lists, and most wanted lists that can be very useful for research and investigation purposes.

Bureau of Alcohol, Tobacco, Firearms and Explosives

Below are two online resources:

- Federal Firearms License Validator - https://www.atfonline.gov/fflezcheck
- ATF Most Wanted List - www.atf.gov/most-wanted

Bureau of Investigation (FBI)

The FBI's Most Wanted Site at www.fbi.gov/wanted/wanted_by_the_fbi contains numerous lists to search, including kidnappings, missing persons, unknown bank robbers, and others.

Drug Enforcement Administration (DEA)

Search DEA fugitives at www.justice.gov/dea/fugitives.shtml by major metro areas. Also, major international fugitives and captured fugitives are found here.

Labor Department: Labor and Labor Unions

The Office of Labor-Management Standards (OLMS) in the U.S. Department of Labor is the Federal agency responsible for administering and enforcing most provisions of the Labor-Management Reporting and Disclosure Act of 1959, as amended (LMRDA). Note that OLMS does not have jurisdiction over unions representing solely state, county, or municipal employees. OLMS responsibilities include:

- Public Disclosure of Reports
- Compliance Audits
- Investigations
- Education and Compliance Assistance

The OLMS Internet Public Disclosure Room web page www.dol.gov/olms/regs/compliance/rrlo/lmrda.htm enables users to view and print reports filed by unions, union officers and employees, employers, and labor relations consultants.

Occupational Safety & Health Administration (OSHA)

The purpose of the Occupational Safety & Health Administration (OSHA) is to insure employee safety and health in the U.S. by setting and enforcing standards in the workplace. OSHA partners with the states for inspections and enforcements along with education programs, technical assistance and consultation programs.

There are a number of searchable OSHA databases at https://www.osha.gov. For example, search by establishment name for information on over 3 million inspections conducted since 1972 at https://www.osha.gov/oshstats/index.html. You can also search by the North American Industry Classification Code (NAIC) or the Standard Industrial Classification Code (SIC).

Another useful search is the Accident Investigation database at https://www.osha.gov/pls/imis/accidentsearch.html. This database contains abstracts dating back to 1984 and injury data dating back to 1972.

Small Business Administration (SBA)

The SBA maintains a database of Dynamic Small Business (DSBS) that, while primarily self-certified, does indicate certifications relating to 8(a) Business Development, HUBZone or Small Disadvantaged Business status. Visit http://dsbs.sba.gov/dsbs/search/dsp_dsbs.cfm.

To find woman-owned, veteran-owned, and service disabled veteran-owned specific profiles in this same SBA database go to the Quick Market Search screen at http://dsbs.sba.gov/dsbs/search/dsp_quicksearch.cfm.

Treasury Department

Federal Contractor & Vendor Eligibility Sites

An avenue of public record data sometimes overlooked is the individuals and businesses licensing to do business with the U.S. government. Below are two resources from this agency.

1. Central Contractor Registration (CCR)

The Central Contractor Registration (CCR) registers all companies and individuals that sell services and products to, or apply for assistance from, the federal government. The 450,000+ registrants at CCR are searchable online using a DUNS number, company name, or other criteria.

CCR is now provided by the System for Award Management (SAM), which is combining federal procurement systems and the Catalog of Federal Domestic Assistance into one new system.   See https://www.sam.gov/portal/public/SAM.

2. Online Representations and Certifications Application (ORCA)

The ORCA system allows contractors to enter company data regarding certification needed on federal contracts. This is a publicly accessible database, but it does require the subject's DUNS number.

ORCA is now provided by the System for Award Management (SAM) as described above.

Genealogy Resources

(Also see the **Vital Records Section**.)

Perhaps the most well-known resource of genealogical information is the Church of Jesus Christ of Latter-day Saints (Mormon Church). The Church has been actively gathering and preserving genealogical records worldwide for over 100 years. One may access genealogy records on-site at churches across the nation and on foreign soil. The genealogy site is familysearch.org.

There are several other, huge genealogical sites that have collected public record information along with historical documents from various sources. Below are a few recommended sites and starting points for genealogy record searching, presented in alphabetical order.

- Archives.com provides access to over 1 billion historical records.
- Cyndi's List at www.cyndislist.com has cross-referenced and categorized numerous links.
- Ancestry.com is a well-known site with a variety of comprehensive resources. Their brands include AncestryDNA, AncestryProGenealogists, Family Tree Maker, Fold3 and Newspapers.com
- The National Genealogical Society in Arlington, VA www.ngsgenealogy.org.

GIS and Mapping

GIS is the acronym used for Geographic Information System. Commonly associated with maps, GIS data can be displayed in a variety of product types with many associated uses. GIS can link and layer data attributes to specific criteria, such as addresses to people or parcels to building. GIS property details are used by the assessing offices at the county or municipality level for taxation and real estate associated matters.

Although they may appear intimidating, GIS mapping websites maintained by these government offices usually have a search mechanism for finding parcels, addresses, and sometimes, but not always, property owner names. A GIS website's search feature is not always displayed prominently, but many local assessor sites provide this service.

Find many GIS searching sites at the local level in Chapter 6.

A private site that does an excellent job of maintaining local links is www.netronline.com.

Incarceration Records

Incarceration records are criminal-related records of inmates housed or formerly housed at jails and prisons.

Prisons records refer to inmates held in state prisons and federal prisons. The details found in prison records vary widely by location and content. Of course those convicted of federal crimes are place in a federal prison, those for a state crime in a state prison.

Since jails are usually found at the local level and hold a variety of inmates, *jail records* are often a mix of persons with misdemeanor sentences and persons being held until transport to a state of federal facility. Jails records are probably the least useful to professional record searchers.

Federal Prison System

The Federal Bureau of Prisons web page offers a searchable Inmate Locator and a Facility Locator at www.bop.gov. The Inmate Locator contains records on inmates incarcerated or released from 1982 to present.

State Prison Systems

Each state has a government agency that manages the corrections departments and prisons. These agencies consider the inmate records to be public and will process information requests. Most states offer online inmate locators or look-ups but the level of information available varies widely from state to state. The searchable state sites are listed in Chapter 6.

Vendor Resources

Private companies are great resources for information and search links to state prison systems.

- An excellent website devoted to information about prisons and corrections facilities "…with the most comprehensive database of vendor intelligence in corrections…" is the Corrections Connection (www.corrections.com).

- VINELink.com, by Appriss Inc., is the online resource of VINE (Victim Information and Notification Everyday), the National Victim Notification Network. The primary objective of this site is to help crime victims obtain timely and reliable information about criminal cases and the custody status of offenders. From the map page a user can search for offenders in practically every state in the U.S. by name or identification number. As you will see in Chapter 6, many state incarcerations agencies offer links on their web pages to VINELink.

Also, check out www.theinmatelocator.com and inmatesplus.com. Plus the free public record links list sites (such www.brbpublications.com and http://publicrecords.searchsystems.net) offer a wealth of searching links.

Internal Revenue Service (IRS) Records

Most IRS records are not public – there is only a handful of record types that may be accessed.

Charitable Organizations

Exempt Organizations Select Check is an online search tool that allows users to select an exempt organization and check certain information about its federal tax status and filings. See www.irs.gov/Charities-&-Non-Profits/Exempt-Organizations-Select-Check.

Seized Property

Check what the IRS is auctioning at www.ustreas.gov/auctions/irs.

Verification of Income

The Income Verification Express Service (IVES) program is used by mortgage lenders and others within the financial community to confirm the income of a borrower during the processing of a loan application. The written consent of the taxpayer is required. These approved entities may obtain a full return or just the income informational info (the W-2). Visit https://www.irs.gov/individuals/ives-enrollment-procedures.

https://www.theworknumber.com is a private company service for obtaining proof of employment or income. The site is owned by Equifax.

Liens

See the **Recorded Documents, Judgments, and Liens** section.

Media Resources

The media is an often overlooked resource for finding clues to public records and public record trails. Researching 24-hour news outlets, press releases, company announcements, trade journals and magazines is a great way to find many leads. Below are some research sources and tips that should prove helpful. Also keep in mind that although many resources are online, a good starting point is often the local library.

News Journalism

Links to thousands of newspapers, radio and TV stations, magazines, and foreign outlets are found at two excellent web pages: www.editorandpublisher.com and www.newslink.org.

A web page specializing in magazine stories is www.highbeam.com.

Without a doubt the leading trade association for journalists is the **Investigative Reporters & Editors, Inc**. This organization promotes high standards while providing educational services to reporters, editors and others interested in investigative journalism. Visit the IRE web page at www.ire.org.

CNN provides a web page to obtain transcripts of broadcasts. Visit http://transcripts.cnn.com/TRANSCRIPTS/.

Back Issues in Print

The United States Book Exchange is a non-profit organization which supplies back issues of scholarly periodicals, trade journals, popular magazines and other serials to libraries worldwide. Visit them at www.usbe.com.

Another good resource for finding locations and stores selling back issues of a magazine is presented at www.trussel.com/books/magdeal.htm.

Other Web Resources

Fee-Based Resources

One of the advantages of the fee-based resources is the length of time stories are kept available. Depending on the service, some vendors maintain comprehensive data dating back 40 years or more. The following entities are highly recommended by Cynthia Hetherington:

- EBSCO (www.ebsco.com)
- Factiva from Dow Jones (www.dowjones.com/products/product-factiva/)
- InfoTrac (www.infotrac.com)
- ProQuest (www.proquest.com)

Free Resources

Websites that offer free access to news stories usually allow searching by either topic or by location. Here are four sites excellent for investigations.

These sites are organized **by topic**.

- Newspaper Archive (www.newspaperarchive.com). Use their seven-day free trial to see if this works for you.
- Google News (https://news.google.com/). Offers current news (within 30 days) and is an excellent source for local news with approximately 50,000 news sources worldwide.

These sites are organized **by location**.

- NewsLibrary.com enables a search by location and by available news on a specific topic.
- ThePaperBoy.com includes national and international locations.

Military Records

National Personnel Records Center (NPRC)

Military service records are kept by the National Personnel Records Center (NPRC) which is under the jurisdiction of the National Archives and Records Administration.

Recent military service and medical records are **not online**. The type of information released to the general public is dependent upon the veteran's authorization. However, most veterans and their next-of-kin can obtain free copies of their DD Form 214 (Report of Separation) and other records in several ways. Another key form used when searching military records is form SF-180 (or a signed release). See www.archives.gov/veterans/military-service-records.

Military Branches - Internet Sources

The Official Sites include—

www.army.mil	U.S. Army
www.af.mil	U.S. Air Force
www.navy.mil	U.S. Navy
www.marines.mil	U.S. Marine Corps
www.nationalguard	Army National Guard
www.ang.af.mil	Air National Guard
www.uscg.mil/default.asp	U.S. Coast Guard

National Gravesite Locator

The Nationwide Gravesite Locator maintained by the U.S. Department of Veterans Affairs includes burial records from many sources. Go to http://gravelocator.cem.va.gov.

Missing Persons

A links list of missing persons compiled by state agencies is free at www.ancestorhunt.com/missing-persons.htm. The privately operated Doe Network lists international missing persons and unidentified victims at www.doenetwork.org.

Most Wanted Lists

Many federal agencies (and some international agencies) have a web page with a Most Wanted List often with name searching capabilities. A web page with links to lists maintained by the FBI, U.S. Marshall, the Bureau of Alcohol, Tobacco, and Firearms (ATF), The Drug Enforcement Administration (DEA), and even the U.S. Postal Service is found at www.usa.gov/Citizen/Topics/MostWanted.shtml. View the FBI Kidnapping and Missing Persons Investigations web page free at www.fbi.gov/wanted/kidnap.

A quick way to find each state's Most Wanted Lists is at www.ancestorhunt.com/most-wanted-criminals-and-fugitives.htm.

Where available, County Sheriff websites often provide data on County Most Wanted individuals. These same sheriff websites may include missing persons, sexual predators, warrants, arrests, DUIs and other types of local pages as a public service.

Motor Vehicle Records

Motor vehicle records are essential decision-making tools used by many industries, particularly insurance companies, trucking firms, employers, lenders, and private investigators. In general, motor vehicle records can be made public only if personal information is not disclosed and depending on the type of record and the laws of a particular state.

The types of records characterized as motor vehicle records include—

- Driving history (sometimes known as an MVR)
- Driver license status
- Accident report
- Traffic ticket

- Vehicle registration and status
- Vehicle title (ownership), title history, liens
- Vessel title, title history, liens
- VIN – Vehicle Identification Number

In general, the databases for each of these record types are maintained by state agencies, but in some jurisdictions a local agency is empowered to process record requests.

 KEY FACT

Four Critical Guidance Tips

Before we cover motor vehicle record searching procedures and online access, there are four important rules to consider regarding these records—

1. There is NO national, all inclusive database of motor vehicle records.

2. Each state maintains its own separate database(s) of licensed drivers, vehicle registrations, vehicle ownership, accident reports, and other associated records.

3. Sometimes there are different state agencies within a state that manage separate record system. For example, in Texas driver licensing and driver records are governed by the Department of Public Safety, but vehicle ownership and registration is governed by the Department of Motor Vehicles.

4. The federal **Driver's Privacy Protection Act (DPPA)** sets specific standards when personal information can be included on a record, dependent upon the purpose of the record request. Certain defined personal information can only be revealed to requesters who have a permissible use as defined by DPPA. All states comply with DPPA. A copy of DPPA is found www.mvrdecoder.com.

Driving Records

A driving record is a historical index of a driver's moving violation convictions, accidents, and license sanctions. Depending on the state's record reporting procedure, an MVR can show activity anywhere from 3 years to a lifetime.

A driving record is often referred to as an **MVR.** The acronym MVR comes from the phrase "Motor Vehicle Record" or "Moving Violation Records." However, state motor vehicle agencies do not always refer to a driving record as an MVR; they may consider this term to mean a vehicle record. So if talking to someone at a state motor vehicle department about their records, be sure to be very clear on what you want or what you mean.

Personal information found on a driving record may include the licensee's address, height, weight, date of birth. As a rule, Social Security Numbers and medical information are always redacted and never released to record requesters. As mentioned, the release of Personal Information (PI) on motor vehicle records is governed by the DPPA, based on the premise if there is a permissible use or if the consent of the subject is given, then PI is released.

As mentioned, all states are in compliance with DPPA; however, some states have stricter policies than DPPA and will not release certain elements of personal information regardless if the requester has a permissible use.

About Online Access

All states offer online access to driving records, but there are many caveats. To receive DPPA-compliant records, the requester must qualified, be pre-approved, and often there is a minimum daily or monthly order level. If the requester is not DPPA-Compliant, certain states offer record access, but records are *sanitized* – meaning without personal information included.

Electronic access methods vary widely depending upon how orders are grouped or submitted, and by the media type. States may provide via interactive processing (results of a record request is shown immediately), or electronic batch processing (usually using FTP - File Transfer Protocol - technology), or both.

The License Status Report

A status report – essentially the top or header portion of a driving record – can sometimes be obtained as a separate record. The license status report generally indicates three important pieces of information:

1. The type or class of license issued which in turn tells what types of vehicles (commercial, non-commercial, motorcycle) can be operated. Different commercial license classes regulate the size or weight of the vehicle licensed to be driven.

2. Any special conditions placed on the license holder. These permissions and limitations are known as endorsements and restrictions. A typical restriction is a requirement to have *corrective lenses* when driving. Another example is a CDL license may have an endorsement that regulates if hazardous material can be hauled.

3. If the license is valid or under suspension or revocation.

A handful of states offer online status checks. Some are free and some are for a fee, as indicated in Chapter 6.

Accident or Crash Reports

Note many states use the term *crash reports* and will bristle if you use the term accident reports.

There are usually two types of accident records for each incident – the reports filed by the citizens involved and the reports prepared by the investigating officers. Copies of a citizen's accident report are not usually available to the public and are not reviewed herein. The profiles in Chapter 6 refer to reports prepared by the investigating officer.

A good rule of thumb is that accident records must be obtained from the agency that investigated the incident. A second rule of thumb is if this agency (that investigates the accident) is part of the same agency that holds driving records, then DPPA guidelines are followed with regards to honoring record requests.

Typical information found on an accident report includes drivers' addresses and license numbers as well as a description of the incident. Only a handful of states offer online access to accident reports.

Vehicle Records

There are many similarities between accessing driving records and accessing vehicle records, especially if records are administered by the same agency that handles driver records. Regardless of which agency oversees vehicle recordkeeping, record access is affected by DPPA as described for driving records. However, not every state offers online access. A few states offer status checks, as indicated. All of the online access sites are found in Chapter 6.

Normally the following categories of vehicle records are available:

*   Ownership and title
*   Registration and license plate data
*   Vehicle identification numbers (VINs)
*   Liens

Ownership and title records of vehicles can generally be obtained as either a current record or as a historical record showing all previous owners. Title data can indicate if a vehicle was at one time a junk vehicle, if the vehicle was once a subject of title washing (meaning previously branded as a salvage or flood-damaged vehicle) or even if the vehicle was previously a government owned vehicle.

Registration data is usually limited to the current year. Searches of license plates, to find the registered owner of a vehicle is not a public record search, there must be a disclosed permissible use.

Liens generally are part of the title record, but know that in some states the liens on vehicles are recorded at the county or at the Secretary of State's Office where UCCs are filed.

The same description above holds true for **vessel records** if the vessels are administered by the same motor vehicle agency. When watercraft and watercraft records are governed by a different government agency, the access policies are usually not governed by DPPA. In these states certain records may be more open to access, but generally access is governed by administrative rules or even by statute.

Per DPPA, vehicle record data that includes personal identifiers is never sold for marketing purposes.

About the VIN

VIN stands for Vehicle Identification Number. This number is internationally recognized as way to identify an individual vehicle, like a serial number. When buying a used vehicle, many people and dealers check the history of a vehicle from a vendor to help make an informed decision about the quality and value of the vehicle and the VIN is the key identifier used. Vehicles have a metal plate stamped with unique VIN located somewhere on the dashboard or door, but the VIN may also be found attached to other locations on the vehicle.

A VIN consists of 17 characters (vehicles manufactured before 1981 may have fewer characters) in a highly coded but strict format structure. A code table that shows all the possible meanings for each position is a very extensive document, and it changes frequently. Web resources to decode a VIN include:

- www.autocheck.com
- www.cardetective.com
- https://www.decodethis.com/

Vessels Records

Vessels and watercraft that weigh more than five tons are registered with the U.S. Coast Guard, www.st.nmfs.noaa.gov/st1/CoastGuard. Another handy location to search for larger vessels, or to search by lien or title, is the Coast Guard's National Vessel Documentation Center found at www.uscg.mil/hq/cg5/nvdc/.

Smaller vessels, usually those for pleasure or sport, are registered through a state motor vehicle department or a state environmental agency such as a Fish & Game Department. Usually but not always the same state agency that administers vehicle records also administers vessel records. In some states vessel records are controlled by an entirely different state government department or division.

The types of vessel records available from state agencies are very similar, with different terms used sometimes for the registration or plate type data. Not all states title watercraft, and those that do generally only require titles if the vessel is over a certain length or motorized or both. Similar requirements may be imposed when registration is mandatory. Also, in some states the liens on vehicles are recorded at the county or at the Secretary of State's Office where UCCs are filed.

All of the states' online access sites are found in Chapter 6.

For in-depth, detailed information about each state's procedures regarding all types of motor vehicle records, see The MVR Access and Decoder Digest. [2]

---

[2] Published annually by BRB Publications, www.brbpublications.com

Occupations & Licensing Boards

The process of regulating people who have professional occupations and businesses which required licenses is intended to protect the public from fraud and the unqualified. Information about these people and entities is often (but not always) a matter of public record and is often found online.

Types of Agencies Involved

Professional Occupations can be registered, certified, or licensed. In general there are three types of regulatory agencies involved in this process.

1. Private Entities

A certification body is a private association that has set the licensing or certification standards for many professions. The issuance of professional licenses can be based on completion of the requirements of professional associations. An example is the American Institute of Certified Public Accountants, which sets the standards for becoming a Certified Public Accountant (CPA). It does not license as CPA in a state (see below).

In addition, there are many professional designations issued by associations that are not recognized as official licenses by government, but are of interest to the professionals within an industry. For example, the initials CFE indicate an individual is a Certified Fraud Examiner and has met the minimum requirements for that title from the Association of Certified Fraud Examiners.

To find other resources that may oversee credentialing, see the *Trade Associations* section later in this chapter.

2. State Agencies

A state agency can administer the registration, certification, and occupational licensing of an individual intending to offer specified products or services in the designated area. If registration alone is required, there may not be a certification status showing that the person has met minimum requirements. Using the CPA example above, the New York State Education Department, Office of the Professions oversees the preparation, licensure, and practice of its CPAs.

Businesses may also fall under the administration of state entity, per statute. For example, a state may require business registration for an entity to do business or offer specified products or services in a designated area, such as registering a liquor license. Some business license agencies require testing or a background check. Others merely charge a fee after a cursory review of the application.

Often the state agencies are referred to as **licensing boards**. Sometimes many, many boards are under the direction of one specific branch of regulatory government. An example is health care related vocations.

3. Local Entities

Local county and municipal government agencies may require business registrations and permits in order for companies to operate (construction, signage, sell hot dogs on a street corner, etc.) within their borders. If you must check on local registrations and permits, call the offices at both the county (try the county recording office) and municipal level (try city hall) to find out what type of registrations may be required for the person or business you are investigating. Several of the free links lists sites will connect you to online searching sites when available.

Widespread Online Access

Per the BRB Publications database of occupational licensing boards, there are over 8,400 individual job titles or businesses that are administered for licensing, registration or certification by nearly 2,000 different state entities. **Some level of online searching exists for name verifications and even enforcement actions on over 65% of the occupations or businesses.**

The online sites are listed in Chapter 6.

What Information May Be Available

An agency may be willing to release part or all of the following—

- Field of Certification
- Status of License/Certificate
- Date License/Certificate if Issued
- Date License/Certificate if Expired
- Current or Most Recent Employer
- Social Security Number
- Address of Subject
- Complaints, Violations or Disciplinary Actions

The Council on Licensure, Enforcement, and Regulation (CLEAR)

An excellent organizational resource for entities or individuals involved in the licensing, non-voluntary certification or registration of hundreds of regulated occupations is the Council on Licensure, Enforcement, and Regulation (CLEAR) See www.clearhq.org.

Patents

United States Patent and Trademark Office

Most patent applications filed on or after November 29, 2000 will be published 18 months after the filing date of the application. Otherwise, all patent applications withheld until the patent is issued or the application is published. After the application has been published, the public may request a copy of the application file. After the patent is issued, the Office file containing the application and all correspondence leading up to issuance of the patent is made available in the Files Information Unit for inspection by anyone, and copies of these files may be purchased.

Search the United States Patent and Trademark office (USPTO) databases at www.uspto.gov/patents/process/search. Also for full-text patent information on U.S. patents granted since 1976 and full-page images since 1790 see http://patft.uspto.gov. Note that the text-searchable patent database begins with patents granted since 1976. Patents issued from 1790 through 1975 are searchable only by patent number, issue date, and current US classifications. Also, be aware neither assignment changes nor address changes recorded at the USPTO are reflected in the patent full-text or the patent full-page images.

The Patent Application Information Retrieval (PAIR) system provides a filing status check of a patent application. Actually a number of different searches from PAIR are accessible from the home page above. The site also permits third parties to obtain information on published applications on issued patents, status of maintenance fee payments, and if a re-issue application or re-examination request has been filed.

Private Resources

The World Intellectual Property Organization (WIPO), www.wipo.int/portal/en/index.html, is a specialized agency of the United Nations dedicated to promoting the effective use and protection of intellectual property worldwide. WIPO offers an international patent search at the site.

Also, check out www.intellogist.com/wiki/Compare:Patent_Search_System (a unique site that lists and compares patent search systems), www.freepatentsonline.com, and www.patentgenius.com.

Privacy and Privacy Rights Resources

Do Not Call & Opt Out Sites of Note

Listed below are several of the most effective organizations that assist the public to remove their names and addresses from marketing list organizations—

- National Do Not Call Registry - https://www.donotcall.gov
- Optout Prescreen.com - https://www.optoutprescreen.com/?rf=t
  (To opt-out or opt-in for offers of credit or insurance)
- Direct Marketing Association Email Opt Out - https://dmachoice.thedma.org/
- Report Unsolicited Faxes - http://transition.fcc.gov/eb/tcd/ufax.html

Privacy Rights Advocates

There are a number of organizations who specialize in representing the privacy interests of the consumer. You will find that some of these groups are extremely one-sided in their approach to many issues and view all vendors as data aggregators who cause harm by violating the privacy rights of unsuspecting individuals. However, there are organizations with a balanced view. They do understand the legitimacy of information requests from businesses based on with permissible use or permission or per statute, but at the same time are vibrant watchdogs monitoring that the information is used correctly. These listed are thought of very highly for their excellent programs to help individuals who have privacy concerns or have been wronged.

Privacy Rights Clearinghouse

This non-profit organization provides a myriad of information for consumers about privacy topics and is a strong voice for consumer advocacy issue. The web page at www.privacyrights.org displays excellent information on many topics. The organization also acknowledges the importance of balancing privacy implications with legitimate protection needs for the public good.

Privacy Rights publishes a list of "data brokers" at https://www.privacyrights.org/online-information-brokers-list. The majority of the 240+ entities listed provide "consumer site" services.

World Privacy Forum

This is another top organization with plenty of informative data on their web page. They specialize, among other topics, in protecting medical information. https://www.worldprivacyforum.org/

PrivacyExchange

PrivacyExchange.org, produced by The Center for Social & Legal Research, is an excellent and informative global information resource. www.privacyexchange.org

Electronic Privacy Information Center - EPIC

EPIC is a public interest research center in Washington, DC. EPIC was established in 1994 to focus public attention on emerging privacy and civil liberties issues and to protect privacy, freedom of expression, and democratic values in the information age. https://www.epic.org

Recalls, Products and Safety

Six federal agencies with very different jurisdictions together created www.recalls.gov. Searching is arranged by these topics: boats, consumer products, cosmetics, environment, food, medicine, and motor vehicle. Various search capabilities are offered. You can do a name search or use the tabs to find lists of recalls by product type.

See www.recalls.gov/nhtsa.html, a useful government site dedicated to vehicle recall issues site.

The FDA is very involved with product recalls and withdrawals and safety alerts. The site at www.fda.gov is home to many search services and search options.

Another great resource is the U.S. Consumer Product Safety Commission site at www.cpsc.gov.

Real Estate Records

See the **Recorded Documents, Judgments and Liens** section below.

Recorded Documents, Judgments, and Liens

Recorded documents, judgments and liens are among the most popular types of public records sought online. This data can show proof of ownership (deed to your house) or show when an asset is used as collateral for a loan (mortgage on your house). Finding recorded documents and lien notices is a necessity to making informed business-related decisions and these documents lead to a virtual treasure trove of data. Private investigators and attorneys research liens and recorded documents when doing an *Asset Lien* search because a lien search will often lead to finding other liens which in turn could lead to finding other assets.

The function of searching liens and recorded documents in the U.S. public record is truly an art because there are over 4,000 locations in the U.S. where one may file a lien notice or record a document. The locations can be at any of three levels: local municipality, county or parish, or state agency. These jurisdictions maintain indices to these recorded documents. Some government agencies maintain an overall index of all recorded documents and liens notices, while others maintain a series of separate indices within the same office. In other words, a researcher must know the particular index to search for a particular record. A good searcher knows to search ALL the indices.

The publicly recorded documents most often accessed are generally related to:

- Real Estate Transactions
- Uniform Commercial Code (UCC) Filings
- Judgments
- Other Liens (including federal and state tax liens, mechanics liens, etc.)

That does not imply that other records such as vital records, voter registration rolls, and fictitious names are inconsequential – far from it. Before examining each of theses documents types, let's first look at some essential facts related to searching these documents.

The Difference Between Personal Property and Real Property

An important first distinction when searching recorded public records is to know the difference between personal property and real property. This is because documents related to real property generally are recorded in different locations than personal property records.

Personal Property   Includes items such as bank accounts, vehicles, jewelry, computers, etc. This property can be collateral or consumer goods. Often when personal property is given as collateral, the lender will secure the loan by filing a **Uniform Commercial Code (UCC)** financing statement on the asset.

Real property   Involves real estate related assets such as homes, apartment building, land, etc. A **mortgage** is an example of a recorded document that secures the associated loan to finance real property.

Types of Liens and Security Interests

Liens - With or Without Consent

A lien is a lawful claim or right against property or funds for payment of a debt or for services rendered. There are two types of liens that are recorded: those **with consent (voluntary)** or **without consent (involuntary)**.

Examples of liens placed with the consent of an asset holder include mortgages, loans on car and vessels, and Uniform Commercial Code filings on business assets such as equipment or accounts receivable.

Examples of liens placed without the consent of an asset holder include federal and state tax liens, mechanic's liens, and liens filed on assets as the result of judgments issued by courts.

The Grantor-Grantee Index

Perhaps the most commonly used term to describe an index of recorded documents at a county/parish/city/town recorder's office is the **Grantor-Granter Index**.

The Grantor is the party that is a transferring title or some type of interest that involves a recording. The Grantee is the party that is the recipient of the title, interest or document. For example, if you purchase or re-finance real estate and borrow money from a bank, an instrument called a mortgage or deed of trust is generally involved. You, the borrower, are the Grantor since you granting the bank or lender a lien on the property. The lender or bank is recorded as the Grantee since it is the recipient of the interest in the property as collateral for the loan. Sometimes the Grantor-Grantee Index is known as the Forward-Reverse or Direct-Indirect Index.

About Judgments

When a judgment is rendered in court, the winning party usually files and records a lien notice (called an *Abstract of Judgment* in many states) against real estate owned by the defendant or party against whom the judgment is given. Sometimes judgments can be used to garnish wages or can be placed on bank accounts. If the loser of the judgment does not pay the judgment voluntarily then the winner of the judgment can force a sheriff's sale to collect money.

Judgments can be searched at the local or county level usually in the same index as real estate records. Many times judgments are bought and sold as commodities. An *Assignment of Judgment* is the transfer of the title and interest in a judgment from one person to another person.

The Search Location Problem

Keeping state laws variations and filing locations straight is a major challenge to the professional public record searching specialist. Where to search for recorded documents and property liens can be a perplexing puzzle. Just because a mailing address is Schenectady NY doesn't mean the property is located in Schenectady County. The property could be physically located in neighboring Albany County. **The fact is over 8,000 of the 45,000 or so ZIP Codes cross county lines.** Having access to an enhanced ZIP Code/place name/county locator product is a must. Finding involuntary liens—such as federal and state tax liens—and UCC filings can be even harder.

So, unless you know exactly where the real or personal property is located, and you are certain that everyone else who has filed or recorded liens also knows where to go, you may have a problem. You may have to search more than one county, town, city (or even state) to find the property or liens you need to know about. But knowing about the County Rule helps.

In most states, transactions are recorded at one designated recording office in the county where the property is located. But the key word in the last sentence is *most,* because there are exceptions. And if a researcher is not aware of the exceptions key mistakes can be made in filing or searching which could affect borrower and lenders in a very negative manner.

An excellent overview of important searching tips to have in hand when searching for liens and recorded documents is an article titled *The County Rule* written by the late Mr. Carl R. Ernst, founder of Ernst Publishing.[3] While this article was written some time ago, it is still very pertinent.

The County Rule by Carl R. Ernst

Where to search for recorded documents usually isn't a difficult problem to overcome in everyday practice. In most states, these transactions are recorded at one designated recording office in the county where the property is located.

We call this the "County Rule." It applies to types of public records such as real estate recordings, tax liens, Uniform Commercial Code (UCC) filings, vital records, and voter registration records. However, as with most government rules, there are a variety of exceptions which are summarized here.

The Exceptions

The five categories of exceptions to the County Rule (or Parish Rule, if searching in Louisiana) are listed below [Editor's Note: details for each state are listed in the State Profiles Section which follows.]—

Special Recording Districts (AK, HI)

Multiple Recording Offices (AL, AR, IA, KY, ME, MA, MS, TN)

Independent Cities (MD, MO, NV, VA)

Recording at the Municipal Level (CT, RI, VT)

Identical Names—Different Place (CT, IL, MA, NE, NH, PA, RI, VT, VA)

The Personal Property Problem and the Fifth Exception

The real estate recording system in the U.S. is self-auditing to the extent that you generally cannot record a document in the wrong recording office. However, many documents are rejected for recording because they are submitted to the wrong recording office. There are a number of reasons why this occurs, one of which is the overlap of filing locations for real estate and UCC.

Finding the right location of a related UCC filing is a different and much more difficult problem from finding a real estate recording. In the majority of states, the usual place to file a UCC financing statement is at the Secretary of State office—these are called central filing states. In the dual and local filing states, the place to file, in addition to the central filing office, is usually at the same office where your real estate documents are recorded. However, where there are identical place names referring to two different places, it becomes quite confusing, so hence, the fifth exemption.

Searching Real Estate Records

Every local entity (i.e. county, parish or town recorder of Deeds) records documents that transfer or encumber title. Many county, city, and parish government jurisdictions provide online access to indices of real estate records and

---

[3] Ernst Publishing publishes two extensive industry manuals - *The UCC Filing Guide* and *The Real Estate Recording Guide*. Visit www.ernstpublishing.com for more information.

recorded documents. Most sites are free if viewing an index, but an increasing number of government agencies will charge a fee to view or print an image or copy of a page within the file.

As with other types of public records, many investigators and researchers use these online resources as a pre-search or preliminary search, especially if dealing with an uncommon name.

Keep in mind there are a number of private companies who compile and maintain these records. Some offer free searching on the web as a way to drive users to their web pages. Some vendors offer bulk data for resale. Vendors are a very comprehensive resource to obtain electronic records.

There are a number of web pages that information on the property of specific homes (addresses). Check www.zillow.com, www.realtor.com, and www.trulia.com. For interactive map information, check out http://nationalmap.gov.

Types of Real Estate Recorded Documents Found Online

There many types of lien notices and recorded documents related to real estate files. Below are common names for documents that a public record researcher may find when searching real estate records. This list is certainly not all inclusive; there are many, many more. Also keep in mind that name variations will occur from state to state.

- **Deed of Trust or Mortgage of Deed of Trust** Generally a mortgage that secures a debt, and names three parties - the borrower (trustor), the beneficiary (lender), and the trustee who holds title to real property under the terms of a deed of trust.

- **Bill of Sale** A Bill of Sale will be recorded to show the transfer of most any kind of personal property.

- **Assignment of Deed of Trust** A transfer or sale of a Deed of Trust from the current lender (beneficiary) to a new beneficiary.

- **Abstract of Judgment** A court issued money judgment to secure payment to the creditor, usually creates a general lien on real property of the judgment debtor.

- **Declaration of Homestead** A document recorded by either a homeowner or head of household on their primary residence to protect his home from forced sale in satisfaction of certain types of creditors' claims.

- **Mechanic's Lien** A document recorded to create a lien in favor of persons contributing labor, material, supplies, etc., to a work of improvement upon real property.

- **Notice of Default** A notice to show that the borrower under a mortgage or deed of trust is behind in payments.

- **Notice of Lis Pendens** A notice that litigation is pending in court which may affect the title of the real estate involved.

- **Notice of Trustee's Sale** This document is recorded to notify the public of pending the foreclosure sale by the trust for non-payment or non-performance of the conditions of the deed of trust.

- **Power of Attorney** This document delegates the authority of an entity to an agent (attorney-in-fact) to allow this agent to act behalf of the entity in a designated capacity.

- **Quitclaim Deed** A form of deed that conveys or releases any interest that the grantor may have acquired in real property. Many times this type of deed is issued without title insurance.

- **Reconveyance** The instrument releases the loan that was a lien against real property. Can also be called a satisfaction of the loan or a release of lien or a release of mortgage.

- **Satisfaction of Mortgage** Release of the loan that was a lien against real property. This document may also be called a release of mortgage.

- **Subordination Agreement** This document is recorded when a current lender agrees to makes their encumbrance deed of trust beneath or junior to another loan. These loans are sometimes called seconds.

- **Trustee Deed in Lieu of Foreclosure** Document indicates the transfer of real property from the defaulting borrower to the beneficiary (lender) in lieu of foreclosure.

- **Trustee's Deed** A deed given by the trustee when the real property is sold under the power of sale in a deed of trust in a foreclosure proceeding.

- **Writ or Notice of Levy** A document to notify a party served with writ of execution that specific property is being taken to satisfy a debt.

Real Estate Records and the County Rule

Remember the earlier section on the County Rule? The second, third and fourth County Rules are very important to observe when searching real estate records in the states listed below.

- **Multiple Recording Offices.** In these states, some counties have more than one recording office; AL, AR, IA, KY, LA, ME, MA, MS, and TN.

- **Independent Cities.** Four states (MD, MO, NV, and VA) have independent cities that should be treated just as if they are counties. For example, St Louis City and St. Louis County are separate jurisdictions with separate sets of data.

- **Recording at the Municipal Level.** In CT, RI, and VT the recording jurisdiction is the town, not the county. The county clerk's office does not record documents.

Uniform Commercial Code

Uniform Commercial Code (UCC) filings are to personal property what mortgages are to real estate property. UCCs indicate where personal property, usually business related, is secured as collateral. A UCC recording allows potential lenders to be notified that certain assets of a debtor are already pledged to secure a loan or lease. Therefore, examining UCC filings is an excellent way to find many types of assets, security interests, and financiers.

Most state UCC websites provide a free search of the index. A few will permit free access to images, but most states charge a fee to access the full records, which usually involves a subscription service and registration, login, and password. Delaware is the only state that does not offer online access to an index of UCC records, except through certain contracted firms.

Chapter 6 gives the searchable web address for each state's central repository. Also, for specific links and updated information, visit the free public record searching sites found at www.brbpublications.com.

A number of private companies compile their own proprietary database of UCC and tax lien records or offer real time online services. Vendors are a very comprehensive resource to obtain electronic records over multiple jurisdictions, see Chapter 5.

UCC Searching Tips

Most UCC filings against businesses are found at the state where a business is organized, not where the collateral or chief executive offices are located. Most UCCs files against individuals are files in the state where the person resides. Therefore, you will need to know where a company is organized in order to know where to find recent UCC filings against it. (However federal tax liens are still generally filed where the chief executive office is located.)

The location to search UCC records changed dramatically in many states in July 2001 with the enactment of **Revised Article 9**. Prior to that date UCC documents were recorded either at a centralized state agency or at a local recording office. Since July 2001 all UCC documents are filed or recorded at a state level agency with the exception of certain real estate filings such as farm-related real estate (see Searching Real Estate Related UCC Collateral to follow).

Until June 30, 2001, liens on certain types of companies required dual filing (must file at BOTH locations) in some states, and records could be searched at BOTH locations. As of July 1, 2001, UCC filings other than those that go into real estate records were no longer filed at the local filing offices. According to the UCC Filing Guide (see www.ernstpublishing.com) less than 3% of UCC filings are done so at the local level.

Although there are significant variations among state statutes, the state level is now the best starting place to uncover liens filed against an individual or business, but it is not the only place to search. Strict due diligence may require a local search also, depending on the state, how many years back you wish to search, and the type of collateral. The best technique is to check both locales of records.

As a result of Revised Article 9 (Secured Transactions) of the Uniform Commercial Code, **the general rules for searching of UCC records** are as follows:

- Except in former local filing states, a search at the state level is adequate to locate all legally valid UCC records on a subject.
- Credit due diligence searching requires use of flexible search logic provided either by the state agency or private database vendors.
- Mortgage record searches will include any real estate related UCC filings.

Note that over the past several years, states' filing offices have been busy gaining legislative approval for implementing the additional amendments to Article 9. The changes went into effect July 1, 2013. These changes did not affect searching, but provided uniformity on how names are recorded on the filings.

Searching Real Estate-Related UCC Collateral Online

UCC financing statements applicable to real estate related collateral must be filed where real estate and mortgage records are kept, which is generally at the county level — except in Connecticut, Rhode Island, and Vermont where the Town/City Clerk maintains these records.

In general, the definition of real estate related UCC collateral is any property that in one form is attached to land, but that in another form is not attached. For the sake of simplicity, we can define the characteristics of two broad types of property that meet this definition:

1. Property that is initially attached to real property, but then is separated. Three specific types of collateral have this characteristic: minerals (including oil and gas), timber, and crops. These things are grown on or extracted from land. While they are on or in the ground they are thought of as real property, but once they are harvested or extracted they become personal property. Some states have a separate central filing system for crops.

2. Property that is initially personal property, but then is attached to land, is generally called fixtures. Equipment such as telephone systems or heavy industrial equipment permanently affixed to a building are examples of fixtures. It is important to realize that what is considered a fixture, like beauty, is in the eye of the beholder, since it is a somewhat vague definition.

UCC financing statements applicable to real estate related collateral must be filed where real estate and mortgage records are kept, which is generally at the county level — except in Connecticut, Rhode Island, and Vermont where the Town/City Clerk maintains these records.

Tax Liens

Tax liens are non-consensual liens placed by a government agency for non-payment of taxes. Of course the federal government and every state all impose taxes, such as sales, income, withholding, unemployment, and/or personal property. When these taxes go unpaid, the appropriate state agency can file a lien on the real or personal property of the subject.

Tax liens filed against individuals are frequently maintained at separate locations from those liens filed against businesses. For example, many number of states require liens filed against businesses to be filed at a central state location (i.e., Secretary of State's office) and liens against individuals to be filed at the county level (i.e., Recorder, Registrar of Deeds, Clerk of Court, etc.).

Searching Tips for Federal and State Tax Liens

Tax liens filed against individuals are frequently maintained at separate locations from those liens filed against businesses. For example, many number of states require liens filed against businesses to be filed at a central state location (i.e., Secretary of State's office) and liens against individuals to be filed at the county level (i.e., Recorder, Registrar of Deeds, Clerk of Court, etc.). So when searching tax liens, first and foremost one must realize there are actually four location possibilities in play:

1. Federal Tax Liens on Individuals

2. Federal Tax Liens on Businesses

3. State Tax Liens on Individuals

4. State Tax Liens on Businesses

Also, Federal tax liens are filed at the location of the taxpayer's principal address, which is not the same rule applied for UCC filings.

Therefore Federal tax liens will not necessarily be filed (recorded) at the same location/jurisdiction as a state tax lien.

These variances are shown in the *Recording Offices Summaries* section later in Chapter 6. In general, state tax liens on personal property will be found where UCCs are filed and tax liens on real property will be found where real property deeds are recorded, with few exceptions.

Another point to consider is that the IRS files their federal tax liens under the name of the taxpayer. But that name may be different than the name used on the filing papers when a business entity was registered.

Unsatisfied state and federal tax liens may be renewed if prescribed by individual state statutes. However, once satisfied, the time the record will remain in the repository before removal varies by jurisdiction. Many states will show a release of lien filing rather than deleting the original recording of the lien.

Other Types of Recorded Documents

There are numerous types of documents that can be recorded and are not related to real estate or personal property. Many of these documents are found at the same recording office that records real estate liens, and often times they appear in the same index. Mentioned below are several significant types.

Fictitious Names or Assumed Names

If a person operates a business not organized as a corporation, partnership, LLC, etc., under a name other his own, then it has a fictitious name. For example if Joe Cool is doing business as LowCost General Store, that business name must be registered. Depending on the state, this registration can take place at municipal, county or state. A fictitious name is also known as a **DBA** – meaning *Doing Business As*.

Forcible Detainer

A Forcible Detainer is a landlord's lien against a tenant's property for unpaid rent or damages. Sometimes the document is filed to essentially 'give notice.' If the tenant does not comply within a designated time period, the landlord can forcibly move the tenant's belongings off the property, usually with the assistance of local law enforcement.

Searching for evidence of a Forcible Detainer is part of the tenant screening process, which is governed by the federal Fair Credit Reporting Act (FCRA).

Vital Records

Birth certificates, death certificates, marriages licenses, and divorce decrees are often recorded at the local level and then forwarded to centralized state agency. These records may be available from both locations - local and state. Sometimes the local level is the only place to obtain a certified copy of a marriage or divorce action. Non-certified copies are often available online at the local level. See the *Vital Records Section* later in this chapter.

Wills

Many people record their Last Will and Testament at the local recorder's office. Some people confuse a probate court with this function. A probate court is not a recording office, but has records concerning decedents which include their wills (if any) and lists of assets.

Securities and Securities Dealers

Federal Level

While federal agencies oversee the regulatory and compliance issues which deal with publicly traded securities or with security dealers, there are several private entities with great authority as well. All of these agencies have the authority to investigate issues related to compliance or improprieties. Hence, these agencies are excellent resources to search for enforcement actions. Perhaps the most well-known government agency is the Securities and Exchange Commission (SEC).

SEC – Securities & Exchange Commission

The SEC oversees the participants in the securities world, including securities exchanges, securities brokers and dealers, investment advisors, and mutual funds. The SEC offers a number of useful online search sites through **EDGAR** at www.sec.gov/edgar/searchedgar/webusers.htm. See data presented earlier in this chapter under *Business Entity Records: Edgar and the SEC.*

Enforcement Actions: SEC-related enforcement actions are viewable online at www.sec.gov/divisions/enforce/enforceactions.shtml. These actions include civil lawsuits brought by the Commission in Federal court, administrative proceedings as instituted and/or settled, opinions issued by Administrative Law Judges in contested administrative proceedings, and opinions on appeals issued by the Commission on appeal of Initial Decisions or disciplinary decisions issued by self-regulatory organizations (e.g., NYSE or NASD).

Litigation Actions: The SEC page at www.sec.gov/litigation.shtml contains specific links to information on SEC enforcement actions including reports of investigations, trading suspensions, opinions issued by the Commission, briefs filed by SEC staff, trading suspensions, and notices concerning the creation of investors' claims funds in specific cases.

Financial Industry Regulatory Authority (FINRA)

Formerly the National Association of Securities Dealers (NASD), the Financial Industry Regulatory Authority (FINRA) is a resource to investigate brokers and brokerage firms. FINRA oversees over 4,700 brokerage firms, 167,000 branch offices, and more than 635,000 registered securities representatives. FINRA is probably the largest non-governmental regulator for all securities firms doing business in the U.S.

The website at www.finra.org offers *BrokerCheck®* which provides name searching of an individual or of a brokerage firm registered in FINRA. The user can download an eight-page Adobe Acrobat PDF file that outlines the subject's history, including employment. Brokerage firms are searchable for any disciplinary actions taken against a company, or brokers who are involved with arbitration awards, disciplinary, and regulatory events. Reach FINRA at 301-590-6500.

North American Securities Administrators Association (NASAA)

The North American Securities Administrators Association (NASAA) is devoted to investor protection. Members of NASAA are state securities regulators. They license firms and their agents, investigate violations of state and provincial law, file enforcement actions when appropriate, and educate the public about investment fraud. NASAA members also participate in multi-state enforcement actions and information sharing.

The NASAA web page (www.nasaa.org/) is a great resource of links to individual state, provincial, and territorial jurisdictions for securities laws, rules and regulations.

CRD and IARD

The Central Registration Depository (CRD) is a centralized filing system of licensed broker-dealers. The CRD was developed by state securities regulators, NASAA, FINRA, and the SEC. CRD reports are available through state regulatory authorities. CRD's computerized database contains the licensing and disciplinary histories on more than 650,000 securities professionals and 5,200 securities firms. IARD is the acronym for the Investment Advisor Registration Depository system is to investment advisers what the CRD is to broker-dealers.

More information and useful search links are located under the Industry Resources tab at the NASAA web page.

National Futures Association (NFA)

The National Futures Association (NFA) is a self-regulatory organization that safeguards the U.S. futures industry. The NFA web page offers name searching of individuals or firms. Results indicate any arbitration or regulatory action filed against any NFA listed individual or firm. Visit www.nfa.futures.org or call the Chicago headquarters at 312-781-1300.

Securities Class Action Clearinghouse

The Securities Class Action Clearinghouse provides detailed information relating to the prosecution, defense, and settlement of federal class action securities fraud litigation. The Clearinghouse maintains an index of than 40,600 complaints, briefs, filings, and other litigation-related materials. This content is maintained by the Stanford Law School and Cornerstone Research. Visit http://securities.stanford.edu.

State Level

Every state has its own securities laws – often referred to as **Blue Sky Laws** – designed to protect investors against fraud. The records of the filings by companies registering under the Blue Sky Laws, as well as any records of legal actions, are held by designated *state regulatory securities agencies*.

These state agencies also usually license and hold records of brokerage firms, their brokers, and investment adviser representatives doing business there.

Although these records are open to the public they are not generally found online. Those states with searchable online sites are shown in Chapter 6.

To find each state's address and web page, we suggest visiting the North American Securities Administrators Association (see above).

Sexual Offender Registries

Sexual offenses include aggravated sexual assault, sexual assault, aggravated criminal sexual contact, endangering the welfare of a child by engaging in sexual conduct, kidnapping, and false imprisonment. Under Megan's Law, sex offenders are classified in one of three levels or tiers based on the severity of their crime as follows: Tier 3 (high); Tier 2 (moderate); and Tier 1 (low).

Sex offenders must notify authorities of their whereabouts or when moving into a community.

Usually, the state agency that oversees the criminal record repository also administrates the Sexual Offender Registry (SOR) and offers a free search of registered sexual offenders who are living within the particular state. These state web pages are shown in Chapter 6.

The creation of the National Sexual Offender Registry (https://www.nsopw.gov) represents a coordinated effort by the Department of Justice and the state agencies hosting public sexual offender registries. The website has a national query to obtain information about sex offenders through a number of search options including name, Zip Code, county, and city or town. The site also has an excellent, detailed overview of each state's SOR policies and procedures.

Tax Assessor and Collector Records

In every county, parish, or local municipality there is an official – often called the Assessor – who is required by law to determine the value of all taxable property in a jurisdiction for property taxing purposes. This official publishes assessment reports and provides it to property owners with valuation notices. The official may also be known as the Auditor or Property Valuator.

Records of unpaid property taxes can be found in the office of the Treasurer or Tax Collector.

All of records are very public, very valuable, and often accessible online. Usually tax assessment records are searchable by name or by legal description (plat number), and not necessarily by the address.

There are several private sites that offer links lists to Tax Assessor offices. The site at www.pulawski.net is very easy to use and indicates when pages are last updated. Another excellent site specializing in listing tax assessors and recorder offices with web pages offering record searching capabilities is http://publicrecords.netronline.com. And the site at www.brbpublications.com provides address, phone number home page, and free searching links.

Chapter 6 shows the searchable web pages to several thousand assessor type sites.

Telephone Numbers

This section has two very distinctly different section parts, yet relevant to this topic.

Assignment of Area Codes - North American Numbering Plan (NANPA)

NANPA is the integrated telephone numbering plan serving the United States, its territories, and 18 other North American countries; Canada, Bermuda, Anguilla, Antigua & Barbuda, the Bahamas, Barbados, the British Virgin Islands, Cayman Islands, Dominica, Dominican Republic, Grenada, Jamaica, Montserrat, St. Kitts and Nevis, St. Lucia, St. Vincent and the Grenadines, Trinidad and Tobago, and Turks & Caicos.

While regulatory authorities in each participating country have plenary authority over numbering resources, the participating countries share numbering resources cooperatively. Thus NANPA holds overall responsibility for the administration of NANPA numbering resources, subject to directives from regulatory authorities in the countries that share participate in the NANP. See www.nanpa.com/index.html.

Key online searches include:

- **Area Code Maps** - Select a state and see area code boundaries.
- **Central Office Code Assignments** - Find out what codes are assigned or available for assignment in each geographic area code
- **Area Code Search** - Get information about individual area codes, including dialing plans and pointers to planning letters with split/overlay information.

Links to Yellow and White Pages and Directories

There are a number of web resources that provide name look-ups to find phone numbers. But the "problem" is some of sites take you through a search procedure then at the point of obtaining the phone number they attempt to charge a fee PLUS try to sell you other public record details about the person. We are purposely not recommending these commercial, consumer sites in this book. Below are several recommended search sites that do provide telephone numbers freely with a name search. The sites also offer a reverse phone look-up.

- www.superpages.com
- www.addresses.com
- www.anywho.com

Other very worthwhile vendor search tools include:

- Dun & Bradstreet's site at Hoover's (www.hoovers.com/) offers phone mailing-list services. Through various public records, news accounts, and telephone interviews, D&B has amassed a large amount of very specific contact information that can be purchased by the batch or in small doses. The lists are targeted for marketing purposes but investigators can use purchased lists to locate a target or subject by occupation, geography, or hobby.

- FoneFinder is a service tool providing the location and basic service provider for a telephone number. Search by the telephone number or by city or ZIP Code at www.fonefinder.net.

Trademarks & Service Marks

United States Patent and Trademark Office

The U.S. Patent and Trademark Office (USPTO) reviews trademark applications to determine if an applicant meets the requirements for federal registration. The USPTO does not decide who has the right to *use* a mark. Even without a registration, someone may still *use* any mark adopted to identify the source of goods and/or services. Once a registration is issued, it is up to the owner of a mark to enforce their rights in the mark based on ownership of a federal registration.

The Electronic Business Center offers trademark and status searching links at http://www.uspto.gov/trademark. There is no fee to search, but charges are incurred for certified copies.

To acquire trademark and/or service mark registration at the state level, applicants must file an application with the trademark office of the specific state in which protection is sought. The search sites are shown in Chapter 6.

Other Key Resources

- An astounding list of international trademark resources is found at www.ggmark.com/#International_Trademark_Law.

- A very extensive service for trademark searching, screening, and watching services is provided by **Thomson Compumark**. See http://trademarks.thomsonreuters.com.

- A rather comprehensive service for finding intellectual property and international trademark registries is www.ipmenu.org.

Unclaimed Funds

Unclaimed funds refers to money, stocks, bonds, dividends, utility deposits, vendor payments, gift certificates and insurance proceeds held by state or federal agencies who are looking for rightful owners.

Every state has an agency, sometimes called the Unclaimed Property Division, responsible for holding and returning these assets to the rightful owners. Nearly every one of these state agencies provides a link to find unclaimed monies. A link to each state's search site is provided Chapter 6 under the *Useful State Links* section.

National links list are easily found on the web.

- A great resource is the National Association of Unclaimed Property Administrators (NAUPA), a non-profit organization affiliated with the National Association of State Treasurers. Click on the map to find state sites. Another important feature that NAUPA offers is its list of various U.S. government agencies that hold unclaimed assets.

- At the ANUPA at www.unclaimed.org one may do national searches or find a profile of the state agency responsible for holding unclaimed funds, including a link to the state's free web search page.

- Another recommended vendor is Missing Money at www.missingmoney.com.

Uniform Commercial Code - UCC

See the **Recorded Documents and Liens Section**.

Vessels and Boats

See the **Motor Vehicle Records Section.**

Vital Records

(Also see the **Genealogy Resources Section** earlier in this chapter.)

Usually birth, death, marriage and divorce records can be searched at the local (county) level and/or at the state vital records office, which is usually part of a state health agency. Vital records are not necessarily public records. Many states place limitations, ranging from 50 to 100 years, before records are fully open. Therefore these newer records are not usually found online. In general, birth records are the most restrictive, death records the least restrictive, and marriage and divorce records somewhere in between. But the degree of restrictiveness may depend if a certified record is needed or if merely a computer printout will suffice. Certified copies of birth, death and marriage certificates can usually be obtained from the state agency; certified divorce certificates usually are obtained from the county or local entity.

Online ordering is often offered, usually from a vendor. State agencies that provide online ordering or host searchable databases of older records are listed in Chapter 6.

Recommended Vendors

There are several national vendors who specialize in providing vital records to clients, with a special emphasis on doing so on an expedited basis.

Perhaps the most well-known, one-stop shop is VitalChek.com, a LexisNexis company. VitalChek has relationships with nearly all the state vital record agencies and a number of local agencies. They offer a means to order and receive records in an expedited manner.

Another vendor with similar services is Vitalrec.com found at http://vitalrec.com. This web page provides some excellent links and good basic searching information about each state. The site has direct ties to Ancestry, a vendor specialized in genealogy records.

Another excellent site with a mixture of old and new records is www.archives.com. There is an annual subscription fee per year, but you have unlimited access to over 1 billion historical records.

Of course, the web abounds with marriage record sources, most of which are genealogy based.

Death Records & the Death Index of U.S. Social Security Administration

The Social Security Death Index (SSDI) contains the records of deceased persons who were assigned a SSN. Data is generated from the master death file of the U.S. Social Security Administration (SSA). The data is not searchable from a SSA site but a number of vendors purchase the data and make it available to the public.

Use Caution

Please note that the SSA does not have a death record for all persons. The SSA's Master Death File (DMF) used as a verification tool is good, but the absence of a particular person does not guarantee the person is alive. For example, effective November 1, 2011, the SSA no longer includes state death records in the DMF. Further, since the SSA no longer adds these entries, the SSA decided to remove 4.2 million existing state records from the DMF in November 2011. This removal represented a little over 4.7% of the entire database. One significant piece of information removed, coming from the state records data added to the DMF, was the last known residence (state, county) of a subject.

The law governing this action is found at www.ssa.gov/OP_Home/ssact/title02/0205.htm. Section 205(r) prohibits the SSA from disclosing state death records it receives, except in limited circumstances.

A good free search source is from an Ancestry.com site at http://search.ancestry.com/search/db.aspx?dbid=3693. Links to free search sites is found at http://genealogy.about.com/od/free_genealogy/a/ssdi.htm.

Obituaries

The database searches offered by Obituary Central at www.obitcentral.com include not only obituaries, but also cemetery searches. The data gets stronger as you go further back in time. The site shows many resources and other links of interest. News and media databases like LexisNexis, Factiva and Dialog are great resources for looking up obituaries going back 20 years.

Also, search obituaries at http://search.ancestry.com/oldsearch/obit/.

The Nationwide Gravesite Locator

The Nationwide Gravesite Locator is maintained by the U.S. Department of Veterans Affairs. The site includes burial records from many sources, see http://gravelocator.cem.va.gov/.

Voter Registration

See **Elections: Politics, Lobbyists, and Voters**

Workers' Compensation

Workers' compensation benefits are paid to people who have suffered an injury during the performance of their jobs. Every state has an agency that administrates workers' compensation cases and records; there is no national database.

A workers' compensation record of an incident may contain the date of the incident, employer, insurance company, type of injury, body part injured, time lost, and if there is a job-related disability. Obviously, these records are useful in background investigations and fraud cases. However, most records are considered to be confidential or at least certain portions of each case file are. They're usually only released to parties involved in a case or by subpoena. Generally what is considered public record by some states is limited to determining if a subject has filed a claim, and decisions, awards or orders in disputed cases.

Another piece of information about worker's compensation found perhaps more frequently online is the ability to do a status check of an employer - to determine if the employer has current coverage.

A handful of states will release some type of workers' compensation information online, the sites are indicated in Chapter 6.

Web Page Registry Public Records

There are plenty of useful resources with public information about web pages. A number of these sources report who owns a URL and how to contact them, the webmaster, the software, and even if an address has been blacklisted.

Search for a URL at http://whois.domaintools.com to find physical details about a website including meta description, registry creation and expiration dates, server details, webmaster contact info, and its all-important basic WhoIs record of the registrant.

InterNIC.net provides public information on domain names and other useful information on web topics such as viruses, IP address, website content, registries. Also InterNIC provides a simple WhoIs lookup.

Another good IP search site is ARIN at https://www.arin.net/resources/services/.

VeriSign.com provides a list of North American website registrars.

For an analytical profile of a website, visit http://nerdydata.com.

Other Recommended Web Page Resources and Tools

- The Internet Corporation for Assigned Names and Numbers (ICANN) is a network of inter-related sites who manage the naming system for the millions of internet sites. See https://www.icann.org.

- The Network Solutions WhoIs page at www.networksolutions.com/whois conveniently tells you if a name is available or not and under what suffix, also lets you search for expired domain names.

- An excellent tool for analyzing a website is the NetSolutions' WhoIs search at www.networksolutions.com/whois/index.jsp. Results include who owns or registered a site, the IP address, a screen capture of the home page, traffic ranking, more.

- To find out if anyone is imitating your site or stealing your content check out www.copyscape.com.

- Use the Xenu web check tool for reports on URLs and broken links. Go to http://home.snafu.de/tilman/xenulink.html and download the free Xenu's Link Sleuth. You can check the status of a list of URLs by posted a list on the site and Xenu will generate a report.

- To find the IP address (e.g. 200.100.100.80) you are using on your computer go to www.palserv.com/ipdisp.html or whatismyipaddress.com.

- To find information about an email address, check www.newultimates.com/email.

- Historical web pages can be found at the WayBack Machine at https://archive.org/.

- Another web searching resource is Search Engine Showdown at searchengineshowdown.com.

# Chapter 5

Selected Public Record Vendors

The purpose of this chapter is to familiarize you with the types of public record vendors in the business marketplace and to help you determine the right vendor for your record needs.

Before you sign-up for every interesting online consumer site that catches your eye, we suggest some key points and techniques in order to narrow your search to the type of site or vendor that best suits your needs.

If you have not done so already, please review the section in Chapter 1 called *Private Sector - Record Vendors*. This section, which starts on page 6, provides an excellent overview of the types of public record vendors that provide public records or public information. There is also significant material in the section titled *How to Evaluate the Accuracy and Worthiness of Online Content*. This text starts on page 12.

Advantages Online Public Record Vendors Provide

As previously explained, vendors must buy the data from the government agencies or from other vendors. So, what are the advantages of using a vendor instead of going direct to a government agency? There are many—

- One-stop shopping for many or all states or record types
- Speed of access - often instantaneously
- Experts on state compliance issues
- Help with reading or deciphering records
- Provide uniform record format
- Provide customized software to access and receive
- Understand the *how fast - how much* needs of clients

If you have not figured this out by now, let's be blunt. This book is filled with references to professional sites and largely ignores consumer sites. For example, the recommended sites and vendors listed in Chapter 4 are included because their services and expertise are specific to the topics covered within chapter. The vendor list at the end of this chapter is certainly not finite, but they were selected because the type of records they provide are closely connected with many of the public records profiled in the next chapter. It is not the purpose of this book to prove a lengthy list of consumer-oriented sites, per the definitions above.

Type of Public Record Vendors

As covered in Chapter 1, one can categorize a public record vendor as follows:

- **Distributors (data aggregators)**
- **Gateway**
- **Search Firm**
- **Verification Firm**
- **Record Retriever**

Also as covered in Chapter 1, online vendors' web pages can be classified as either

- **Consumer Sites**
- **Professional Sites**

So Why Do These Firms Appear in This Chapter?

There are two key facts about the firms appearing in this chapter:

1. Only Distributors (vendors with proprietary databases) or Gateways (vendors who instantly pass thru data from Distributers or government record sources.) are included.

2. For the most part, only vendors with *Professional Sites* are included.

Vendors and Privacy Concerns

Personal information is part of public records. Therefore personal information may also be found within the databases of distributors or often shown in the results presented by gateways. Of course the extent of the data displayed varies from state to state or county to county.

One problem that can surface is when the originating government source sells its data to a vendor, but later the government agency corrects or removes personal information. When the vendor is not notified of changes or does not update the content, then incorrect data on a person or subject would be reported.

Some vendors do offer consumers the chance to opt out or opt out the personal information in the vendor database. But if the data is removed, then there must also be a way to re-remove it the next time the database is updated from the originating agency.

For a more detailed discussion and excellent suggestions on other ways people can remove personal data or opt out, visit the web page for PrivacyRights.org.

Beware of Instant Web-Based Background Checks

There are many *consumer sites* offering to do background checks that sound a little too inviting. The reality is pre-employment screening firms, known as Consumer Reporting Agencies (CRAs), must abide by the provisions of the Federal Fair Credit Reporting Act (FCRA). In addition there are a myriad of state laws and compliance rules that go beyond the regulations imposed by FCRA. CRAs do have a web presence and do advertise their services. And yes, CRAs will use database criminal record vendors who provide very impressive supplemental yet useful data.

But there are many *consumer sites* advertising an instant, national background check for someone to learn about anyone's past. rarely do these site mention the FCRA. And since there is no true national database of criminal records and 25% of the felony courts are not online, the reality is the promotional wording these sites use is often very misleading.

So how do you determine if a web vendor is truly an FCRA-Complaint background screening service or a database distributer with a great marketing presence? If you find a site using any of the marketing schemes listed below, then a giant red flag should pop up in your mind and you need to take a closer look.

1. Charging membership fees for unlimited access to national background data

The most common type of site is charging a $29 to $35 fee for a one- to five-year membership term. Sites even offer an affiliate program where you set up your own site to sell memberships to others. But there is some benefit. These sites provide the ability to simultaneously search hundreds of free government sites at once; but there are no magic or special databases used. The membership fee is paying for a sophisticated hits or links to a series of free search pages belonging to others. Problems are currency of the data and how national is "national?"

2. Show endorsement by a phony or suspect trade association

Several of the suspect public records membership sites tout an endorsement from a national association of private investigators. Do a Google search on that association's name. Read the results. Some are phony.

3. Promote what amounts to non-FCRA compliant employment screening

Any public record professional will tell you that you cannot purchase a "background check" on a new hire for $15 and be truly protected from a negligent hiring lawsuit. Nor will the vendor likely be in compliance with the Federal Fair Credit Reporting Act (FCRA). You may be able to do quick record search from a couple web pages or court repository, or from a supplementary database vendor, but that does not equate to fulfilling the due diligence necessary in a professional pre-employment background check.

The bottom line is to use caution and common since if using one of these sites.

Where to Find a Vendor (Besides in This Book)

Using a Search Engine

This is a good way to find a consumer site vendor. These vendors thrive based on the strength of their SEO (Search Engine Optimization). Also, this is a good way to find many of the vertical-type vendors mentioned in Chapter 4. Picking a topic like Aviation or Unclaimed Funds will likely lead you to many of the entities mentioned in that chapter.

But this is not necessarily true for professional-oriented sites. If your business has a high volume need for a core state or county record such as court records, UCC fillings, or driving records, it is unlikely you will find the nation's leading vendors with a simple Google search.

Word of Mouth and Social Media

Reaching out to colleagues or networking on social media sites such as LinkedIn is a good way to find vendor alternatives.

Using a Trade Association Site

Trade Association websites often provide a wealth of information. They are useful for not only industry knowledge, but also for finding members plus entities with strong ties as vendors.

Here is a representative list of 90 national associations with strong ties to public records or public record searching. Poking around these sites is a good way to find vendors.

Acronym	Organization	Website
AAJ	American Association For Justice	https://www.justice.org/
AALL	American Assn of Law Librarians	www.aallnet.org
AAMVA	American Assn of Motor Vehicle Administrators	www.aamva.org
AAPL	American Assn of Professional Landmen	www.landman.org
ABA	American Bar Assn	www.americanbar.org/aba.html
ABA (2)	American Banking Assn	www.aba.com
ABFE	American Board of Forensic Examiners	www.acfei.com
ABI	American Bankruptcy Institute	www.aba.com
ABWA	American Business Women' Association	www.abwa.org
ACA	Assn of Collectors and Collection Professionals	www.acainternational.org
ACFE	Assn of Certified Fraud Examiners	www.acfe.com
AFIO	Assn of Former Intelligence Officers	www.afio.com
AICPA	American Institute of Certified Public Accountants	www.aicpa.org
AIIP	Assn of Independent Information Professionals	www.aiip.org
AIPLA	American Intellectual Property Law Assn	www.aipla.org
ALA	American Library Assn	www.ala.org

Acronym	Organization	Website
ALTA	American Land Title Assn	www.alta.org
AMA	American Management Assn	www.amanet.org
APA	American Psychological Assn	www.apa.org
APG	Assn of Professional Genealogists	https://www.apgen.org
ARELLO	Assn of Real Estate License Law Officials	https://www.arello.org
ASIS	American Society for Industrial Security	https://www.asisonline.org
ASLET	American Society of Law Enforcement Trainers	www.aslet.org
ASSE	American Society of Safety Engineers	www.asse.org
ATA	American Trucking Associations	www.trucking.org
CII	Council of Intl Investigators	www.cii2.org
DMA	Direct Marketing Assn	https://thedma.org/
EAA	Environmental Assessment Assn	www.eaa-assoc.org
EPIC	Evidence Photographers Intl Council	www.epic-photo.org
ESA	Electronic Security Association	www.alarm.org
FBINAA	FBI National Academy Assn	www.fbinaa.org
IAAI	Intl Assn of Arson Investigators	www.fire-investigators.org
IACREOT	Intl Assn of Clerks, Recorders, Election Officials and Treasurers	www.iacreot.com
IAHSS	Intl Assn of Healthcare Security & Safety	www.iahss.org
IALEIA	Intl Assn of Law Enforcement Intelligence Analysts	www.ialeia.org
IAoGO	Intl Association of Government Officials	www.nacrc.org
IIAA	Independent Insurance Agents of America	www.independentagent.com
INA	Intl Nanny Assn	http://nanny.org/
INOA	Narcotic Enforcement Officers Assn	http://neoa.org/
INTA	Intl Trademark Assn	www.inta.org
ION	Investigative Open Network	www.ioninc.com
IRE	Investigative Reporters and Editors	www.ire.org
IREM	Institute of Real Estate Management	www.irem.org
LES	Licensing Executive Society	www.lesusacanada.org
MBA	Mortgage Bankers Assn	https://www.mba.org
NACM	National Assn of Credit Managers	http://nacm.org/
NAFE	National Assn of Female Executives	www.nafe.com
NAFI	National Assn of Fire Investigators	www.nafi.org
NAHB	National Assn of Home Builders	www.nahb.org
NAHRO	National Assn of Housing & Redevelopment Officials	www.nahro.org
NALA	National Assn of Legal Assistants	https://www.nala.org/
NALFM	National Assn of Law Firm Marketers	www.legalmarketing.org
NALI	National Assn of Legal Investigators	www.nalionline.org
NALS	NALS...the Assn of Legal Professionals	www.nals.org
NALSC	National Assn of Legal Search Consultants	www.nalsc.org
NAMSS	National Assn of Medical Staff Svcs	www.namss.org
NAPBS	National Assn of Professional Background Screeners	www.napbs.com
NAPIA	National Assn of Public Insurance Adjustors	www.napia.com
NAPPS	National Assn of Professional Process Servers	http://napps.org

Acronym	Organization	Website
NAR	National Assn of Realtors	www.realtor.com
NAREIT	National Assn of Real Estate Investment Trusts	https://www.reit.com
NARPM	National Assn of Residential Property Managers	www.narpm.org
NASA	National Multifamily Resident Information Council	www.nmric.org
NASIR	Intl Assn of Security & Investigative Regulators	www.iasir.org
NAUPA	National Assn of Unclaimed Property Administrators	https://www.unclaimed.org/
NAWBO	National Assn of Women Business Owners	https://www.nawbo.org/
NCISS	National Council of Investigation & Security Services	www.nciss.org
NCRA	National Court Reporters Assn	www.ncra.org
NCRA	National Consumer Reporting Assn	www.ncrainc.org
NDIA	National Defender Investigator Assn	www.ndia.net
NFIB	National Federation of Independent Businesses	www.nfib.com
NFPA	National Federation of Paralegal Assns	www.paralegals.org
NGS	National Genealogical Society	www.ngsgenealogy.org
NHRA	National Human Resources Assn	www.humanresources.org/website/c/
NICB	National Insurance Crime Bureau	https://www.nicb.org
NLG	National Lawyers Guild	www.nlg.org
NPRRA	National Public Record Research Assn	www.nprra.org
NSA	National Sheriffs' Assn	www.sheriffs.org
PBUS	Professional Bail Agents of the United States	www.pbus.com
PIHRA	Professionals in Human Resources Assn	www.pihra.org
PRIA	Property Records Information Professionals Assn	www.pria.us
PRRN	Public Record Retriever Network	www.prrn.us
SCIP	Society of Competitive Intelligence Professionals	www.scip.org/
SFSA	Society of Former Special Agents of the FBI	www.socxfbi.org
SHRM	Society of Human Resources Management	https://www.shrm.org/
SIIA	Software & Information Industry Assn	www.siia.net
SILA	Society of Insurance License Administrators	www.sila.org
SLA	Special Libraries Assn	www.sla.org
USFN	America's Mortgage Banking Attorneys	www.usfn.org/
WAD	World Assn of Detectives	www.wad.net

Resource Lists of Selected Vendors

Of course there are many more public record vendors than the 135+ firms appearing in this section. The reason these particular companies were chosen is because they are either a Distributor (with a proprietary database) or a Gateway (a non-intervention instant link to government data).

Also, to find additional information and profiles on many more professional vendors and record searchers, go to https://www.brbpublications.com/SrchFirms/DistFirm.aspx.

Record Information Categories

This index consists of 12 Information Categories. The vendors are listed alphabetically within each category. Each listing includes the vendor's web address and the geographic coverage area in the U.S.

- Address/Location
- Bankruptcy
- Business Entity
- Criminal Information
- Driver and/or Vehicle
- Licenses/Registrations/Permits

- Property/Tax Assessor
- Real Estate Ownership
- Recorded Liens, UCCs, and Judgments
- Tenant History
- Vital Records
- Watercraft Records

These lists certainly are not all the Distributors and Gateways in the U.S., but what follows is a best efforts presentation of a representative group.

Bankruptcy

Vendors - Bankruptcy	Web Page	Region
Accurint- LexisNexis	www.accurint.com	US
Ameridex Information Systems	https://www.ameridex.com/	US
Aristotle International	http://aristotle.com/	US
Cambridge Statistical Research Associates	www.csrainc.com	US
Daily Report, The	www.thedailyreport.com	CA
DataQuick Property Finder	www.corelogic.com/solutions/property-information-analytic-solutions.aspx	US
Data-Trac.com	www.data-trac.com	US
DCS Information Systems	www.dcsinfosys.com/	US
Dun & Bradstreet	www.dnb.com	US
Equifax Credit Services	www.equifax.com/business/	US
Experian Credit Services	www.experian.com	US
Extrakt	http://extraktdata.com/	US
First American Data Tree	www.datatree.com/	US
Global Information Services	www.gisusdata.com/	US
Hoovers Inc	www.hoovers.com	US
Infogroup/infoUSA	https://www.infousa.com/	US
Infutor Dtata Soultions	www.infutor.com/	US
IRBsearch	www.irbsearch.com/	US
KnowX	https://www.knowx.com/index.jsp	US
Kompass USA Inc	http://us.kompass.com/	US
LocatePlus.com Inc	http://locateplus.com/	US
Martindale-Hubbell	www.martindale.com	US
Military Information Enterprises Inc	www.militaryusa.com	US
Motznik Information Services	https://www.motznik.com/	AK
National Background Data	https://www.nationalbackgrounddata.com/marketing/home.html	US
People Search - Intelius	https://www.intelius.com/	US
Plat System Services Inc	www.platsystems.com	MN, WI
Research Archives.com	www.researcharchives.com	US
SPIRIT Asset Protection, LLC	www.spiritassetprotection.com/	US
Tracers Information Specialists Inc	www.tracersinfo.com	US

Vendors - Bankruptcy	Web Page	Region
US SEARCH.com	www.ussearch.com/	US
Westlaw CLEAR	http://legalsolutions.thomsonreuters.com/law-products/support/clear	US

Business/Corporate Entity

Vendor	Web Page	Region
Accurint- LexisNexis	www.accurint.com	US
Accutrend Data Corporation	www.accutrend.com	US
Alacra	www.alacra.com	US
Attorneys Title Insurance Fund	https://www.thefund.com/default.aspx	FL
Background Information Services Inc.	www.bisi.com	CO
Better Business Bureau	www.bbb.org	US
Charles Jones Inc	https://www.charlesjones.com	US
CSC - Corporation Service Company	https://www.cscglobal.com/cscglobal/home/	US
DataQuick Property Finder	www.corelogic.com/solutions/property-information-analytic-solutions.aspx	US
Dun & Bradstreet	www.dnb.com	US
Fairchild Record Search Ltd	http://recordsearch.com/	US
GuideStar	www.guidestar.org/Home.aspx	US
Hoovers Inc	www.hoovers.com	US
Household Drivers Reports Inc (HDR Inc)	www.hdr.com	TX
Investigative Consultants Inc	www.icioffshore.com	US
IRBsearch	www.irbsearch.com/	US
KnowX	https://www.knowx.com/index.jsp	US
Kompass USA Inc	http://us.kompass.com/	US
LocatePlus.com Inc	http://locateplus.com/	US
Motznik Information Services	https://www.motznik.com/	AK
Record Information Services Inc	www.public-record.com	IL
Research Archives.com	www.researcharchives.com	US
SEAFAX Inc	https://www.seafax.com	US
Thomson Compumark	http://trademarks.thomsonreuters.com/	US
TLO Online Investigative Systems	www.tlo.com/	US
Tracers Information Specialists Inc	www.tracersinfo.com	US
US SEARCH.com	www.ussearch.com/	US
Westlaw CLEAR	http://legalsolutions.thomsonreuters.com/law-products/support/clear	US

Criminal Information

Vendor	Web Page	Region
Alacourt.com	https://v2.alacourt.com/	AL
Appriss Inc/VineLink	www.appriss.com/vine.html	US
Background Information Services Inc.	www.bisi.com	CO
Backgroundchecks.com	https://www.backgroundchecks.com/	US
CARCO Group	www.carcogroup.com/	US
Circuit Court Express	https://www.wvcircuitexpress.com/Default.aspx	WV
Connotate	www.connotate.com	US
CourtLink - LexisNexis	www.lexisnexis.com/en-us/products/courtlink-for-corporate-or-	US

Vendor	Web Page	Region
	professionals.page	
CourtSearch.com	https://www.courtsearch.com/	NC
Criminal Information Services Inc	www.criminalinfo.com	US
Daily Report, The	www.thedailyreport.com	CA
Data-Trac.com	www.data-trac.com	US
DCS Information Systems	www.dcsinfosys.com/	US
Doxpop	https://www.doxpop.com/prod/	IN
For The Record Inc	www.myftr.com	NC
For The Record Inc	www.myftr.com	VA
Global Information Services	www.gisusdata.com/	US
Household Drivers Reports Inc (HDR Inc)	www.hdr.com	TX
iDocket.com	www.idocket.com	TX
nnovative Data Solutions	www.knowthefacts.com/	US
IRBsearch	www.irbsearch.com/	US
Judici	www.judici.com	IL
KellPro Inc (ODCR)	www.kellpro.com	OK
KnowX	https://www.knowx.com/index.jsp	US
Mind Your Business Inc	www.mybinc.com/	NC
Motznik Information Services	https://www.motznik.com/	AK
National Background Data	https://www.nationalbackgrounddata.com/marketing/home.html	US
Publicdata.com	www.publicdata.com	US
Rapidcourt.com - NC Recordsonline.com	https://rapidcourt.com/	US
SJV & Associates LLC	www.sjvassoc.com	US
SPIRIT Asset Protection, LLC	www.spiritassetprotection.com/	US
TLO Online Investigative Systems	www.tlo.com/	US
Tracers Information Specialists Inc	www.tracersinfo.com	US
US SEARCH.com	www.ussearch.com/	US
Virtual Docket LLC	www.virtualdocket.com	DE
WestLaw Court Express	http://legalsolutions.thomsonreuters.com/law-products/support/court-express	US
XPOFACT	www.xpofact.com	MN

Driver and/or Vehicle Vital Records

Vendor	Web Page	Region
Accurint- LexisNexis	www.accurint.com	US
AutoDataDirect, Inc	www.add123.com	FL
CARCO Group	www.carcogroup.com/	US
CARFAX	www.carfax.com	US
Compass Driving Records	https://www.imvrs.com/	US
Confi-Chek	www.confi-chek.com	CA
Convergence Research Inc	https://www.convergenceresearch.com/	US
CourtSearch.com	https://www.courtsearch.com/	NC
Datalink Services Inc	https://www.imvrs.com/	US

Data-Trac.com	www.data-trac.com	US
DCS Information Systems	www.dcsinfosys.com/	TX
Explore Information Services	www.exploredata.com/	US
First InfoSource	https://secure.firstinfosource.com	MO
Global Information Services	www.gisusdata.com/	US
Household Drivers Reports Inc (HDR Inc)	www.hdr.com	TX
iiX (Insurance Information Exchange)	www.iix.com	US
IRBsearch	www.irbsearch.com/	US
Logan Registration Service Inc	https://www.loganreg.com/Welcome.aspx	US
National Background Data	https://www.nationalbackgrounddata.com/marketing/home.html	US
Records Research Inc	www.recordsresearch.com	US
SAMBA	www.sambasafety.com/	US
SJV & Associates LLC	www.sjvassoc.com	US
TR Information Services	www.fullsearch.com	US
Tracers Information Specialists Inc	www.tracersinfo.com	US
Westlaw CLEAR	http://legalsolutions.thomsonreuters.com/law-products/support/clear	US

Licenses/Registrations/Permits

Vendor	Web Page	Region
Accutrend Data Corporation	www.accutrend.com	US
Confi-Chek	www.confi-chek.com	US
Daily Report, The	www.thedailyreport.com	CA
E-Merges.com	www.emerges.com/	17 States
IRBsearch	www.irbsearch.com/	US
KnowX	https://www.knowx.com/index.jsp	US
Motznik Information Services	https://www.motznik.com/	AK
Publicdata.com	www.publicdata.com	US
Record Information Services Inc	www.public-record.com	IL
Thomson Compumark	http://trademarks.thomsonreuters.com/	US
Westlaw CLEAR	http://legalsolutions.thomsonreuters.com/law-products/support/clear	US

Property Tax/Assessor

Vendor	Web Page	Region
Alacourt.com	https://v2.alacourt.com/	AL
Avitar Associates of New England	www.avitarassociates.com/	NH
BS&A Software Records	https://is.bsasoftware.com/bsa.is/SelectUnit.aspx	MI
CountyAssessor.Info	www.countyassessor.info	OK
DataQuick Property Finder	www.corelogic.com/solutions/property-information-analytic-solutions.aspx	US
DataScout	www.datascoutpro.com	AR
Delta Computer Systems	www.deltacomputersystems.com/search.html	AL,MS
Guidepost - Beacon Portals	www.qpublic.net/	AR,IA,IN,MN,MO,SD
IQS-Info Quick Solution - SearchIQS	www.searchiqs.com/	CT,KY

Kentucky Land Records - KLR	www.kylandrecords.com/avail.php	KY
OKAssessor	http://oklahoma.usassessor.com/Shared/base/Home/Home.php	OK
Parcel Quest	www.parcelquest.com/pq-online/	CA
Patriot Properties	http://patriotproperties.com/	MA
TaxNetUSA	www.taxnetusa.com/	FL,TX
TaxRecords.com	www.taxrecords.com/	MD,NJ
True Automation	www.trueautomation.com/	TX
VamaNet	http://vamanet.com/cgi-bin/HOME	VA
VGSI - Vision Government Solutions, Inc.	www.vgsi.com/vision/Applications/ParcelData/Home.aspx	CT,MA,ME,NH.RI

Real Estate Ownership

Vendor	Web Page	Region
A-1 Abstracting and Research	www.a1abstracting.com/	IA
Accurint- LexisNexis	www.accurint.com	US
Apprentice Information Systems	www.arcountydata.com	AR
Attorneys Title Insurance Fund	https://www.thefund.com/default.aspx	FL
Canaan Title Solutions, LLC	www.parcelquest.com/pq-online/	ID,MT
Connecticut Land	https://connecticut-townclerks-records.com/User/Login.aspx	CT
County Recorder, The	www.thecountyrecorder.com	AZ,CO
Courthouse Retrieval System Inc	www.crsdata.net/main/	AL,NC,TN
CourthouseDirect.com	www.courthousedirect.com/	US
Daily Report, The	www.thedailyreport.com	CA
DataQuick Property Finder	www.corelogic.com/solutions/property-information-analytic-solutions.aspx	US
DataScout	www.datascoutpro.com	AR
DCS Information Systems	www.dcsinfosys.com/	US
Delta Computer Systems	www.deltacomputersystems.com/search.html	AL,MS
DigitalCourthouse	https://digitalcourthouse.com/default.asp	WV
eCCLIX.com	https://ecclix.com/	KY
eMapsPlus	http://emaps.emapsplus.com/	AL
Environmental Data Resources	http://edrnet.com/	US
eTitleSearch	www.etitlesearch.com	AR,TX
First American Data Tree	www.datatree.com/	US
Foreclosure Freesearch.com	www.foreclosurefreesearch.com	US
iDoc Market	https://idocmarket.com/Sites	MN,MT,TX,WY
Infocon Corporation	www.infoconcorporation.com	PA
infogroup/infoUSA.com - Am. Business Information	https://www.infousa.com/	US
IQS-Info Quick Solution - SearchIQS	www.searchiqs.com/	CT,KY
Kentucky Land Records - KLR	www.kylandrecords.com/avail.php	KY
KnowX	https://www.knowx.com/index.jsp	US
LocatePlus.com Inc	http://locateplus.com/	US
Metro Market Trends Inc	http://mmtinfo.com/	AL,FL

Vendor	Web Page	Region
Motznik Information Services	https://www.motznik.com/	AK
MyFloridaCounty.com	https://www.myfloridacounty.com/	FL
Parcel Quest	www.parcelquest.com/pq-online/	CA
People Search - Intelius	https://www.intelius.com/	US
Plat System Services Inc	www.platsystems.com	MN,WI
Public Data Corporation	www.pdcny.com	KY,NY
Real-info.com	www.real-info.com/index.asp	US
Realty Data Corp	www.realtydata.com	US
Record Information Services Inc	www.public-record.com	IL
Red Vision	www.redvision.com	AL,AZ,CA,CO,FL,MD,TX
SiteXdata.com	https://www.sitexdata.com/Home/RealEstate.aspx	US
SKLD Information Services LLC	www.skld.com	CO
Tapestry - Fidlar Technologies	https://tapestry.fidlar.com	AR,IL,IN,KS,MI,MN,WI
Texas Land Records	www.texaslandrecords.com	TX
TitleSearcher.com	www.titlesearcher.com	AR,NC,SC,TN
TitleX.com	www.titlex.net	TX
TLO Online Investigative Systems	www.tlo.com/	US
tnrealestate.com	www.tnrealestate.com	TN
Tracers Information Specialists Inc	www.tracersinfo.com	US
US SEARCH.com	www.ussearch.com/	US
US Title Search Network	www1.ustitlesearch.net/	TN
USLand Records.com	https://www.uslandrecords.com/ctlr/	17 States
Westlaw CLEAR	http://legalsolutions.thomsonreuters.com/law-products/support/clear	US

Recorded Liens, UCCs, and Judgments

Vendor	Web Page	Region
A-1 Abstracting and Research, LLC	www.a1abstracting.com/	IA
Accurint- LexisNexis	www.accurint.com	US
Alacourt.com	https://v2.alacourt.com/	AL
Attorneys Title Insurance Fund	https://www.thefund.com/default.aspx	FL
Background Information Services Inc.	www.bisi.com	CO
Banko®: LexisNexis	https://www.banko.com/app/bnk/main	US
Capitol Lien Records & Research Inc	https://www.capitollien.com/	US
Charles Jones Inc	https://www.charlesjones.com	DE,NJ,NY,PA
Circuit Court Express	https://www.wvcircuitexpress.com/Default.aspx	WV
Confi-Chek	www.confi-chek.com	CA
County Recorder, The	www.thecountyrecorder.com	AZ,CO
Court PC of Connecticut	http://courtpcofct.com	CT
CourthouseDirect.com	www.courthousedirect.com/	US
CourtLink - LexisNexis	www.lexisnexis.com/en-us/products/courtlink-for-corporate-or-professionals.page	US
CourtSearch.com	https://www.courtsearch.com/	NC

Vendor	Web Page	Region
CSC - Corporation Service Company	https://www.cscglobal.com/cscglobal/home/	US
Daily Report, The	www.thedailyreport.com	CA
Data-Trac.com	www.data-trac.com	US
Doxpop	https://www.doxpop.com/prod/	IN
Dun & Bradstreet	www.dnb.com	US
eCCLIX.com	https://ecclix.com/	KY
Equifax Credit Services	www.equifax.com/business/	US
Extrakt	http://extraktdata.com/	US
Fairchild Record Search Ltd	http://recordsearch.com/	US
iDoc Market	https://idocmarket.com/Sites	MN,MT,TX,WY
iDocket.com	www.idocket.com	TX
Infocon Corporation	www.infoconcorporation.com	PA
IQS - Info Quick Solutions	http://iqsworks.com/	CT,NY
IRBsearch	www.irbsearch.com/	US
Judici	www.judici.com	IL
KnowX	https://www.knowx.com/index.jsp	US
LANDEX	https://www.landex.com/	PA
LocatePlus.com Inc	http://locateplus.com/	US
Motznik Information Services	https://www.motznik.com/	AK
MyFloridaCounty.com	https://www.myfloridacounty.com/	FL
National Service Information	www.nsii.net	IN,KY,MI,OH
Nebraska Deeds Online	http://nebraskadeedsonline.us/	NE
Public Data Corporation	www.pdcny.com	KY,NY
Publicdata.com	www.publicdata.com	NY
Rapidcourt.com - NC Recordsonline.com	https://rapidcourt.com/	NC
Record Information Services Inc	www.public-record.com	IL
Red Vision	www.redvision.com	AZ,CA,FL,TX
Rental Research Services Inc	www.rentalresearch.com	MN,ND,WI
Search Network Ltd	www.searchnetworkltd.com/searchnetworkltd/	IA,KS
Tapestry - Fidlar Technologies	https://tapestry.fidlar.com	AR,IL,IN,KS,MI,MN,WI
Texas Land Records	www.texaslandrecords.com	TX
TexasFile	https://www.texasfile.com/	TX
TitleSearcher.com	www.titlesearcher.com	AR,NC,SC,TN
TLO Online Investigative Systems	www.tlo.com/	US
Tracers Information Specialists Inc	www.tracersinfo.com	US
Unisearch Inc	www.unisearch.com	CA,MC,OR,WA
US Land Records	https://www.uslandrecords.com	19 states
Virtual Docket LLC	www.virtualdocket.com	DE
WebRecon LLC	http://webrecon.com	US
Westlaw CLEAR	http://legalsolutions.thomsonreuters.com/law-products/support/clear	US

Tenant History

Vendor	Web page	Region
AIRS - American Information Research Services, Inc.	http://amer-info.com/	US
AmRent	https://www.amrent.com/	IL,TX,US
Contemporary Information Corp	https://www.cicreports.com/	US
Criminal Information Services Inc	www.criminalinfo.com	AZ,CA,ID,NV,OR,WA
Daily Report, The	www.thedailyreport.com	CA
Landlord Protection Agency	https://www.thelpa.com/lpa/	MN
Rental Research Inc	www.researchinc.net	WA
Rental Research Services Inc	www.rentalresearch.com	MN
TVS Tenant Verification Service Inc	https://www.tenantverification.com/	CA

Vital Records

Vendor	Web Page	Region
Ameridex Information Systems	https://www.ameridex.com/	US
Ancestry	www.ancestry.com	US
Cambridge Statistical Research Associates	www.csrainc.com	US
Daily Report, The	www.thedailyreport.com	CA
DCS Information Systems	www.dcsinfosys.com/	TX
Global Information Services	www.gisusdata.com/	US
Household Drivers Reports Inc (HDR Inc)	www.hdr.com	TX
Infocon Corporation	www.infoconcorporation.com	PA
Military Information Enterprises Inc	www.militaryusa.com	US
MyFloridaCounty.com	https://www.myfloridacounty.com/	FL
Red Vision	www.redvision.com	AZ,CA,FL,TX
TLO Online Investigative Systems	www.tlo.com/	US
Vital Records Information	http://vitalrec.com	US
VitalChek Network	https://www.vitalchek.com/	US

Reminder:

The reason these particular companies were chosen to appear is because they provide either a Proprietary Database or offer a non-intervention Gateway to the government public record categories shown in Chapter 6.

This is a best efforts presentation. Please keep in mind that the *Region* column primarily refers to online access from a gateway or proprietary database. These firms often offer additional services, including the ability to process requests to obtain records onsite or in-person in more states. .

Also, to find additional information and profiles on many more professional vendors and record searchers, go to https://www.brbpublications.com/SrchFirms/DistFirm.aspx.

State and Local Government Online Sources

Individual state chapters have been compiled into an easy to use format that details when records or record indices may be searched online.

Within each state's section, these four sub-chapter sections are presented in this order:

1. State Public Record Agencies
2. State Licensing and Regulatory Boards
3. County Courts
4. County Recorder, Assessor, & Other Sites of Note

Only agencies with online access are listed.

Be aware that some agencies provide both a pay and a free system.

Be sure to review the Structure and Online Access notes found at the beginning of each state's Courts and Recorder's Office sections. This is a good place to find out about statewide or multi-jurisdictional online systems. At the county (parish) level, if there is a statewide site that encompasses all county jurisdictions - look for a master section of text.

To save paper and the redundancy of displaying the same language for each county listing - a summary may be displayed at the beginning of that section.

One last tip...remember that just because records are maintained in a certain way in your state or county do not assume that any other county or state does things the same way.

> **Note:** The information found in this Chapter and in Chapter 7 is supplied by BRB Publications. While this data is current at press time, know that this data, especially web pages, will change over time.
>
> - For an updated list of the links for free record searches from these government agencies, visit www.brbpublications.com and click on the Free Public Record Searches link.
>
> - For those of you who need much more detailed information about the government agencies, BRB provides *The Public Record Research System (PRRS)*. To view details, go to the same web page and click on the Subscription Products link.

Alabama

Capital: Montgomery
          Montgomery County
Time Zone: CST
Population: 4,858,979,023
# of Counties: 67

Useful State Links

Website: **www.alabama.gov**
Governor: **http://governor.alabama.gov/**
Attorney General: **www.ago.state.al.us**
State Archives: **www.archives.state.al.us**
State Statutes and Codes: **http://alisondb.legislature.state.al.us/alison/CoAlogin.aspx**
Legislative Bill Search: **www.legislature.state.al.us**
Unclaimed Funds: **http://treasury.alabama.gov/unclaimed-property/**

State Public Record Agencies

Criminal Records

Alabama Bureau of Investigation, Attn: Identification Unit, http://dps.alabama.gov/Home/wfContent.aspx?ID=20&ID2=60&PLH1=plhSBI-IdentificationUnit This agency recommends that searchers contact http://background.alabama.gov/. This is a subscription service with a $25.00 search fee and a $75 annual fee. Employers using a CRA must be registered first and CRA must also be approved. This service also includes arrest only records and is in real-time. This site is considered to be the official search site for the state. A Sex Offender Registry and a Missing Persons search is offered at www.alea.gov/Home/.

Sexual Offender Registry

Alabama Bureau of Investigation/CIC, Sexual Offender Registry, https://app.alea.gov/Community/default.aspx Sex offender data and a felony fugitives list are available online at https://app.alea.gov/Community/wfSexOffenderSearch.aspx. Search by name, ZIP, city or county. Only data on adults is shown. Searches of missing persons and felony fugitives are also available from the home page.

Incarceration Records

Alabama Department of Corrections, Central Records Office, www.doc.alabama.gov/ Information on current inmates only is available online. Location, AIS number, physical identifiers, and projected release date are released. The database is updated weekly. Inmates sentenced as Youthful Offenders are not included in this search. The site, available from the home page, can be extremely slow to load.

Corporation, LP, LLC, LLP, Trade Names, Trademarks/Servicemarks

Secretary of State, Business Services Division, www.sos.alabama.gov/BusinessServices/BusinessEntities.aspx Search business entities free at www.sos.alabama.gov/vb/inquiry/inquiry.aspx?area=Business%20Entity. Search trademarks by applicant name or trademark number or description at www.sos.state.al.us/vb/inquiry/inquiry.aspx?area=Trademarks. Also, search UCC records, Notary Public records, Civil Law Notary records, City-County Lookup and Proposed Constitutional Amendments at www.sos.alabama.gov/GovtRecords/Default.aspx. Click on choice at left of page.

Uniform Commercial Code, Federal & State Tax Liens

UCC Division - SOS, UCC Records, www.sos.alabama.gov/BusinessServices/UCC.aspx There are online searches offered from the home page. Both a free, simple search and an advanced fee-based search are offered. The advanced search provides images, the free search does not. The free search offers access to the index by debtor name, or filing number. The advanced search is available to the public (credit card required) or to subscribers at a slightly lower feet. Search by name is $15.00 and $1.00 per page. Search by filing number for just $1.00 per page. Also there is a $9.75 electronic fee per transaction. Plus, non-subscribers must pay $4.50 fee and $.10 per page portal fee. Subscribers pay a $3.50 portal fee an no fee per page. For both searches, see http://arc-sos.state.al.us/cgi/uccname.mbr/input. *Other Options:* Bulk sale by CD for $1,500 plus $300 a week for updates. No images.

Vital Records Certificates

Center for Health Statistics, Record Services Division, www.adph.org/vitalrecords/ Online ordering is available from the webpage through a service provider www.vitalchek.com. This is considered expedited service. Check their sites for fees and turnaround times. *Other Options:* Index to records are available on microfilm for $40.00 per roll. There are 6 rolls of death records for 1908 through 1959. There are 11 rolls available for an index to marriage records for August 1936 to 1969. There is one microfilm roll of index for divorce records for 1950-59 available for $40.00.

Driver Records

Department of Public Safety, Driver Records-License Division, http://dps.alabama.gov/Home/wfContent.aspx?ID=30&PLH1=plhHome-DriverLicense Alabama.gov is designated the state's agent for online access of state driving records. A Subscriber Registration Agreement must be submitted. Both Alabama.gov and the Alabama DPS must approve all subscribers. There is a $95.00 annual administrative fee for accounts and the search fee is $9.75 per record. The driver license number is needed to search. The system is open 24 hours daily. Visit www.al.gov/subscriptions or call 866-353-3468.

Vehicle Ownership & Registration

Motor Vehicle Division - Records Unit, Alabama Dept. of Revenue, www.revenue.alabama.gov/motorvehicle/index.cfm Four subscription searches are offered: Registration search, Title search, VIN Check, and Abandoned Motor Vehicle data. All are $6.00 per search except Abandoned Motor Vehicle is $12.00. Ongoing users must access as approved, subscribers of Alabama Interactive - the NIC affiliate for the state. See www.al.gov/subscriptions. Subscribers also may be eligible to use other premium services such as obtaining a driving record, a vehicle VIN check, and a criminal record check, and for filing UCCs. *Other Options:* The MVD will only sell the complete database of vehicle registration and title information to vendors if the records are for permissible use. A signed contract is required.

Crash Reports

Alabama Law Enforcement Agency, Crash Records, www.alea.gov/Home/ Once the report has been identified and ordered, it is accessible online in a document format for seven days from the date of purchase. The fee for online purchase is $17.00 which includes a $2 processing fee above the $15.00 state fee. Visit https://www.alabamainteractive.org/dps_crash_report/welcome.action.

Voter Registration, Lobbyists, PACs

Secretary of State-Elections Division, PO Box 5616, www.alabamavotes.gov/ Download the PAC list at www.alabamavotes.gov/downloads/election/fcpa/paclist.pdf. Registered lobbyist list in Excel or PDF is downloadable at http://ethics.alabama.gov/news2.aspx *Other Options:* Bulk requests can be ordered from this office for voter data from all 67 counties. Call 334-242-7222 for fees and breakdowns of customized requests.

GED Certificates

Dept of Postsecondary Education, GED Testing program, https://www.accs.cc/index.cfm/adult-education/ged/ Third parties are routed to set up an account at: http://exchange.parchment.com/ged-receiver-registration-page. Parchment verifies that they are who they say they are so that they can place orders on behalf of students Parchment contacts the third party and provides training on the site for ordering. During this training any orders they have are placed. After this the third party can order on behalf of students. They still must upload a consent form for each student during the process. GED test takers can order duplicate copies of official GED transcripts and duplicate diplomas online at: www.gedtestingservice.com/testers/gedrequest-a-transcript.

Occupational Licensing Boards

These Health Center licenses are all searchable at http://dph1.adph.state.al.us/FacilitiesDirectory

Abortion/Reproductive Health Ctr	Hospital	Renal Disease Terminal Treatment Ctr
Ambulatory Surgery Ctr	Independent Clinical Labs	Residential Treatment Facilities
Assisted Living Facility Specialty Care	Mental Health Center	Rural Primary Care Hospital
Birthing Center	Nursing Home	Sleep Disorder Center
Cerebral Palsy Center	Organ Procurement Ctr	X-Ray (Portable) Supplier
Home Health Agency	Physiological Lab, Clinical	
Hospice	Rehabilitation Center	

The Rest:

Accountant Firm	www.asbpa.alabama.gov/findFirm.aspx
Accountant-CPA	www.asbpa.alabama.gov/findCPA.aspx
Anesthesiologist Assistant	www.albme.org/licenseesearch.html
Apprentices	www.fsb.alabama.gov/Licensees.aspx
Architect	www.boa.state.al.us/RosterSearch/Search.aspx
Athlete Agent (Registered)	www.sos.alabama.gov/vb/athleteagents/sasrch1.aspx
Attorney	https://www.alabar.org/for-the-public/find-a-member/
Audiologist	http://abespa.alabama.gov/licensees.aspx
Bank/Financial Institutions	http://216.226.177.103/loan_search.htm

Barber	https://alboc.glsuite.us/GLSuiteWeb/Clients/ALBOC/public/VerificationSearch.aspx
Beauty Shop/Salon/Booth Rental	https://alboc.glsuite.us/GLSuiteWeb/Clients/ALBOC/public/VerificationSearch.aspx
Check Casher	http://216.226.177.103/loan_search.htm
Chiropractor	http://chiro.state.al.us/searchlicensee.aspx?sm=c_d
Clinical Nurse Specialist	https://abn.alabama.gov/applications/LicenseLookup.aspx
Consumer Finance Company	http://216.226.177.103/loan_search.htm
Contractor, General/Subcontractor	http://genconbd.alabama.gov/DATABASE-SQL/roster.aspx
Cosmetic Studio	https://alboc.glsuite.us/GLSuiteWeb/Clients/ALBOC/public/VerificationSearch.aspx
Cosmetologist	https://alboc.glsuite.us/GLSuiteWeb/Clients/ALBOC/public/VerificationSearch.aspx
Cosmetologist/Esthetician/Manicurist/Mgr	https://alboc.glsuite.us/GLSuiteWeb/Clients/ALBOC/public/VerificationSearch.aspx
Counselor, Professional	www.abec.state.al.us/licensee.aspx
Counselor, Professional Disciplinary Actions	.www.abec.state.al.us/disciplinary.aspx
Dental Controlled Substance Permits	www.dentalboard.org/public/current-rosters/
Dentist, Dental Hygienist	www.dentalboard.org/public/current-rosters/
Dietitian/Nutritionist	www.boed.alabama.gov/licensee.aspx
Electrical Contractor	www.aecb.state.al.us/search.aspx
Electrician, Journeyman	www.aecb.state.al.us/search.aspx
Electrologist	https://alboc.glsuite.us/GLSuiteWeb/Clients/ALBOC/public/VerificationSearch.aspx
Embalmer	www.fsb.alabama.gov/Licensees.aspx
Emergency Medical Technician	www.adph.org/ems/Default.asp?id=5205
Engineer/Engineer in Training	www.bels.alabama.gov/Search.aspx
Esthetic'n Student/Instruct/Sch'l/Salon/Exam	.https://alboc.glsuite.us/GLSuiteWeb/Clients/ALBOC/public/VerificationSearch.aspx
Facilities	www.apob.alabama.gov/pages/directory.htm
Firefighter	www.alabamafirecollege.org/vertical-menu/forms-and-resources/certification-lookup/certification-search
Forester	http://asbrf.alabama.gov/vs2k5/rosterofforesters.aspx
Freight Forwarders	www.asdd.com/links_freight.html
Funeral Director	www.fsb.alabama.gov/Licensees.aspx
Funeral Service Establishments	www.fsb.alabama.gov/Licensees.aspx
Gas Fitter	http://pgfb.state.al.us/Inquiry.aspx
Geologist	www.algeobd.alabama.gov/
HazMat Service	http://adem.alabama.gov/programs/land/landforms/HWUOtran.pdf
Heating/Air Conditioning Contractor	http://hacr.alabama.gov/licensees/licensees.aspx
Home Builder	https://alhob.glsuite.us/GLSuiteweb/clients/alhob/public/LicenseeSearch.aspx
Home Inspector	www.inspectorseek.com/
Home Medical Equip Svcs Provider	www.homemed.state.al.us/Roster.aspx
Inland Ports	www.asdd.com/links_inlandports.html
Insurance Adjuster	https://sbs-al.naic.org/Lion-Web/jsp/sbsreports/AgentLookup.jsp
Insurance Agent/Broker/Producer	https://sbs-al.naic.org/Lion-Web/jsp/sbsreports/AgentLookup.jsp
Insurance Corp/Co/Partnership	https://sbs-al.naic.org/Lion-Web/jsp/sbsreports/CompanySearchLookup.jsp
Interior Designer	http://abrid.alabama.gov/find-a-designer/
Interpreter	www.albit.alabama.gov/search/Roster.aspx
Landscape Architect	www.abela.state.al.us/architects.html
Lead Abatement Contractor/Professional	www.adph.org/lead/
Lead Firm	www.adph.org/lead/
Lead Renovator Training Provider	www.adph.org/lead/
Legal/Dental Svc Representative	https://sbs-al.naic.org/Lion-Web/jsp/sbsreports/AgentLookup.jsp
Lender/Loan Source	http://216.226.177.103/loan_search.htm
Lobbyist, Archived Registered Lobbyist	http://ethics.alabama.gov/news2.aspx
Manicurist Salon/Sch'l/Student/Instruct'r/Exam	https://alboc.glsuite.us/GLSuiteWeb/Clients/ALBOC/public/VerificationSearch.aspx
Manufactured Housing Comm Inspectors	www.amhc.alabama.gov/inspectors.aspx
Marine Fumigation Services	www.asdd.com/links_fumigation.html
Marriage/Family Therapist Disciplinary Action	www.mft.state.al.us/discaction.aspx
Marriage/Family Therapist/Supervisor	www.mft.state.al.us/search.aspx
Massage Therapist	www.almtbd.state.al.us/licensee.aspx
Medical Gas Piper	http://pgfb.state.al.us/Inquiry.aspx

Midwife	https://abn.alabama.gov/applications/LicenseLookup.aspx
Mine Land Reclamation	www.osmre.gov/programs/aml.shtm
Mobile Home Set-up/Instal/Seller	www.amhc.alabama.gov/installers.aspx
Mobile Home/Modular Manufacturer	www.amhc.alabama.gov/manufacturers.aspx
Mortgage Broker	http://216.226.177.103/loan_search.htm
Motor Club Representative	https://sbs-al.naic.org/Lion-Web/jsp/sbsreports/AgentLookup.jsp
Notary Public	www.sos.state.al.us/vb/inquiry/inquiry.aspx?area=Notaries%20Public
Nurse Anesthetist, Practitioner	https://abn.alabama.gov/applications/LicenseLookup.aspx
Nurse-LPN/RN	https://abn.alabama.gov/applications/LicenseLookup.aspx
Nursing Disciplinary Action	https://abn.alabama.gov/applications/LicenseLookup.aspx
Nursing Home Administrator	www.alboenha.state.al.us/logon.html
Nutritionist	www.boed.alabama.gov/licensee.aspx
Occupational Therapist/Assistant	www.ot.alabama.gov/licensee.aspx
Optometrist	http://optometry.alabama.gov/Search.aspx
Orthotist	www.apob.alabama.gov/pages/directory.htm
Osteopathic Physician	www.albme.org/licenseesearch.html
Paramedic	www.adph.org/ems/Default.asp?id=5205
Pesticide Commercial Applicator/Dealer	http://agi.alabama.gov/ApplicatorSearch/commercial.aspx
Pesticide Private Applicator/Dealer	http://agi.alabama.gov/ApplicatorSearch/private.aspx
Pharmacist/Technician/Intern/Extern	www.albop.com/lookup.html
Pharmacy Store	www.albop.com/lookup.html
Physical Therapist Disciplinary Actions	www.pt.state.al.us/discipline.aspx
Physical Therapist/Assistant	www.pt.state.al.us/search.aspx
Physician/Medical Doctor/Assistant	www.albme.org/licenseesearch.html
Plumber	http://pgfb.state.al.us/Inquiry.aspx
Plumber/Gas Fitter Dosciplinary Actions	http://pgfb.state.al.us/DiscActions.aspx
Podiatrist	www.podiatryboard.alabama.gov/licensees.aspx
Polygraph Examiner Training Schools	www.polygraph.alabama.gov/Schools.htm
Pre-Need Sales Agent	https://sbs-al.naic.org/Lion-Web/jsp/sbsreports/AgentLookup.jsp
Private Investigator, Trainer	www.apib.alabama.gov/
Prosthetist	www.apob.alabama.gov/pages/directory.htm
Psychological Technician	www.psychology.state.al.us/licensee.aspx
Psychologist	www.psychology.state.al.us/licensee.aspx
Real Estate Agent/Broker	https://www.arello.com/
Real Estate Appraiser	http://reab.state.al.us/appraisers/searchform.asp
Scrap Tire Transporter/Processor	http://adem.alabama.gov/programs/land/landforms/ScrapTireProcessors2613.pdf
Securities Administrative Actions	www.asc.state.al.us/admin_action.aspx
Senior Volunteer, Medical	www.albme.org/licenseesearch.html
Shampoo Assistant	https://alboc.glsuite.us/GLSuiteWeb/Clients/ALBOC/public/VerificationSearch.aspx
Shipyard Services	www.asdd.com/links_shipyard.html
Social Worker Disciplinary Actions	www.abswe.state.al.us/discipline.aspx
Social Worker, Private Practice	www.abswe.state.al.us/search.aspx
Special Purpose License, Medical	www.albme.org/licenseesearch.html
Speech Pathologist	http://abespa.alabama.gov/licensees.aspx
Steamship Agencies	www.asdd.com/links_steamships.html
Stevedoring Companies	www.asdd.com/links_stevedoring.html
Surgeon/Assistant	www.albme.org/licenseesearch.html
Surplus Line Broker	https://sbs-al.naic.org/Lion-Web/jsp/sbsreports/AgentLookup.jsp
Surveyor, Land	www.bels.alabama.gov/Search.aspx
Teacher, Elementary School	https://tcert.alsde.edu/Portal/Public/Pages/SearchCerts.aspx
Transliterator	www.albit.alabama.gov/search/Roster.aspx
Trucking/Transport Companies	www.asdd.com/links_transport.html
Tug Services	www.asdd.com/links_tug.html
Warehousing Companies	www.asdd.com/links_warehousing.html

State and Local Courts

About Alabama Courts: **Circuit Courts** are the courts of general jurisdiction and exclusive jurisdiction on civil matters over $10,000. **District Courts** are the limited jurisdiction in civil matters. Civil cases between $3,000 and $10,000 may be concurrent and heard at either court, depending on local practice. Felony cases are heard by the Circuit Court, but note a misdemeanor committed with a felony can be tried with the felony. The Circuit Courts hear appeals for misdemeanors from the District Courts. Circuit and District courts are essentially combined at one location in all but eight larger counties. Barbour, Coffee, Jefferson, St. Clair, Talladega, and Tallapoosa Counties have two court locations within the county. Jefferson County (Birmingham), Madison (Huntsville), Marshall, and Tuscaloosa Counties have separate criminal divisions for Circuit Courts and/or District Courts. All counties have separate **Probate Courts**.

The web page for the Unified Judicial System is http://judicial.alabama.gov/

Appellate Courts: One may view Opinions at http://judicial.alabama.gov/supreme_opinions.cfm.

Online Court Access

Online Access is statewide, all courts participate in the system described below.

Online access is provided by a vendor designated by the courts. Records include criminal, civil, small claims, state traffic, domestic relations, and child support. The service is available ether as an 'on demand' system or by subscription. The system includes all active cases and disposed cases going back at least 10 years. Some courts have added cases going back as far as the late 1970's. One may email support@alacourtACCESS.com and ask for the dates when each county was automated. But know that some courts have added cases going back as far as the late 1970's. The information includes:

- Civil Cases - Circuit and District Courts
- Criminal Cases - Circuit and District Courts
- Domestic Relations & Child Support
- Traffic

- Outstanding Alias Warrants
- Trial Court Dockets
- Attorney Case Information

Below are descriptions of the various options available.

ON-DEMAND Access at https://pa.alacourt.com/default.aspx is for low volume users. A name search is $9.99 which includes details on one case; each additional case is $9.99. A case number search is $9.99. Images are $5.00 for the first 20 pages and $.50 per page each add'l. There is a case monitoring service offered as well; $29.99 for a Circuit Court case and $19.99 for a District Court case. To sign up visit https://pa.alacourt.com/default.aspx

The subscription service is found at https://v2.alacourt.com. There are two different types of subscriptions: Legal System and Background. There is a $150 set-up for either.

The Legal System is meant for attornies, bail bond companies, news media, and government agencies. The fee for a single user is $84 per month, 2 to 5 users is $104 per month, and 6+ users $134 per month. The Background subscription is meant for Commercial (background screening companies) and Internal (employers), each with a different priving package. For Internal, the fee is $150 per month for 100 searches, with each additional search charged $1.00. For Commercial, the fee is $225 per month for 100 searches with a $2.00 for ea add'l up to 1000 then $1.00 ea add'l. There is also a low volume choice for $100 per month for 10 searches and $5.00 ea add'l.

Not to be confusing but there are also Bulk Packages available for enterprise companies, fees vary from $.40 to $.60 a search for a minimum of 600 to 1,000. The web page provides the details.

Online County Sites Not Mentioned Above:
Baldwin County
Probate Court
Probate records are accessible at www.deltacomputersystems.com/al/al05/probatea.html.
Montgomery County
Probate Court
Probate and **marriage** index available free at www.mc-ala.org/ElectedOfficials/ProbateJudge/ProbateResources/Pages/ProbateRecordsSearch.aspx.
Morgan County
Probate Court
Search probate records at www.morgancountyprobate.com/online-records.aspx.

Recorders, Assessors, and Other Sites of Note

About Alabama Recording Offices: 67 counties, 71 recording offices. **The recording officer is the Judge of Probate.** Four counties have two recording offices- Barbour, Coffee, Jefferson, and St. Clair. Federal and state tax liens on personal property of businesses are filed with the Secretary of State. Other federal and state tax liens are filed with the County Judge of Probate.

About Tax Liens: Federal and state tax liens on personal property of businesses are filed with the Secretary of State. Other federal and state tax liens are filed with the County Judge of Probate.

Online Access

Recorded Documents

There is no statewide system for access to recorded documents, but approx. 23 counties offer online access to recorded documents. Some sites are subscription based.

Tax Assessor, Property, and GIS Data

You will find several vendors with these services.

- Access property assessment data for 9 counties at GIS-mapping and land database company eMapsPlus at http://emaps.emapsplus.com/.
- Access property assessment data free for 16 counties from Delta Computer Systems at www.deltacomputersystems.com/.

The Secretary of State's Lands and Trademarks Division offers free access to county-by-county tract books which reflect the original ownership of Alabama lands, see www.sos.state.al.us/GovtRecords/Land.aspx.

Unique Statewide Access

- Access to individual county lists of the Transcripts of Tax Delinquent Property is at http://revenue.alabama.gov/advalorem/transcript/. This site includes all counties.
- The Secretary of State's Lands and Trademarks Division offers free access to county-by-county tract books which reflect the original ownership of Alabama lands, see www.sos.state.al.us/GovtRecords/Land.aspx.

To avoid redundancy, since these statewide data sites are for every county, it is not included in the County Sites listed below.

County Sites:

Autauga County *Property, Taxation Records* Access the GIS-property info database and Tax Office free at http://emaps.emapsplus.com/standard/autaugacoal.html.

Baldwin County *Property, Taxation Records* Property tax data and property appraiser records at www.deltacomputersystems.com/search.html. Also, access to GIS/mapping for free at http://isv.kcsgis.com/al.baldwin_revenue/

Barbour County - Clayton Division *Property, Taxation Records* Access to GIS/mapping free at www.alabamagis.com/Barbour/.

Bibb County *Recorded Documents* www.bibbal.com/Default.asp?ID=158&pg=Probate+Office Subscription access to all recorded indices available, $25.00 signup fee, view images at $.75 each or less, print images $1.00 each. Data is same as appears on PAT. See http://sysconontine.com/?page_id=71.

Blount County *Property, Taxation Records* Public records available from the Revenue Commissioner's Office at www.blountrevenue.com/?page_id=28 includes property and assessment records. The county also offers a Search App for mobile devices. Property tax data and property appraiser records at www.deltacomputersystems.com/search.html.

Bullock County *Property, Taxation Records* Access to GIS/mapping for free at http://isv.kcsgis.com/al.bullock_revenue/.

Butler County *Property, Taxation Records* Access to GIS/mapping free at www.alabamagis.com/Butler/.

Calhoun County *Recorded Documents* www.calhouncounty.org/probate/index.html ubscription access to all recorded indices available, $25.00 signup fee, view images at $.75 each or less, print images $1.00 each. Data is same as appears on PAT. See http://sysconontine.com/?page_id=71.
Property, Taxation Records A personal property tax bill search is offered at http://gis.calhouncounty.org/PersonalProperty/.

Chambers County *Real Estate, UCC Records* www.chamberscountyal.gov/departments/circuit-clerk/probate/ Access real estate and UCC data online by subscription for $65.00 monthly fee. Records are live and go back 5 years. For info, call 334-864-4384.
Property, Taxation Records Access parcel data on the GIS-mapping site free at www.alabamagis.com/Chambers/.

Cherokee County *Property, Taxation Records*   Access to GIS/mapping for free at www.alabamagis.com/Cherokee/.

Chilton County *Property, Taxation Records*   Access to GIS/mapping free at www.alabamagis.com/Chilton/. Property tax data and property appraiser records at www.deltacomputersystems.com/search.html.

Choctaw County *Property, Taxation Records*   Access to GIS/mapping free at www.alabamagis.com/Choctaw/.

Clay County *Recorded Documents*   http://claycountyprobate.com/   Subscription access to all recorded indices available, $25.00 signup fee, view images at $.75 each or less, print images $1.00 each. Data is same as appears on PAT. See http://syscononline.com/?page_id=71.
Property, Taxation Records   Property tax data and property appraiser records at www.deltacomputersystems.com/. Also, access to property tax search and payment for free at http://claycountyprobate.com/taxes.

Cleburne County *Property, Taxation Records*   Access to GIS/mapping for a fee at www.alabamagis.com/Cleburne/. Must also install plug-in 'Flagship' before use.

Coffee County - Both Divisions *Recorded Documents*   Subscription access to all recorded indices available, $25.00 signup fee, view images at $.75 each or less, print images $.25 each. Data is same as appears on PAT. See http://syscononline.com/?page_id=71.
Property, Taxation Records   Search tax status by name at www.coffeecountyrevenue.com/search.aspx.

Colbert County *Recorded Documents*   www.colbertprobatejudge.org/   Subscription access to all recorded records indexes available, $25.00 signup fee, view images at $.75 each or less, print images $1.00 each. Data is same as appears on PAT. See http://syscononline.com/?page_id=71.
Property, Taxation Records   Property tax data and property appraiser records at www.deltacomputersystems.com/. Also, access to GIS/mapping free at http://isv.kcsgis.com/al.colbert_revenue/.

Conecuh County *Property, Taxation Records*   Access GIS/mapping free at www.alabamagis.com/conecuh/.

Coosa County *Property, Taxation Records*   Access GIS/mapping free at www.alabamagis.com/Coosa/disclaimer.cfm.

Covington County *Recorded Documents*   www.covingtonprobate.com/   Access to real property records through LMI (their provider), call 601-624-9633 for subscription info.
Property, Taxation Records   Access property tax records at www.alabamagis.com/covington/frameset.cfm.

Crenshaw County *Property, Taxation Records*   Also, access to tax search and pay for free at www.crenshawcountyalonline.com/RevenueCommissioner/TaxSearch/secondary.aspx?pageID=116.

Cullman County *Recorded Documents*   www.cullmancourts.org/probatecourt   Subscription access for $25.00 signup fee, 1st 50 pages-$.75 each, 51-100-$.50 each, view and print images $.50 each. Data is same as appears on PAT. See http://syscononline.com/?page_id=71.
Property, Taxation Records   Access the GIS-property info database and Tax Office free at http://cullmanrevenuecommissioner.com/. Also, access to GIS/mapping for free at http://isv.kcsgis.com/al.cullman/#/Home. Property tax data and property appraiser records at www.deltacomputersystems.com/.

Dale County *Recorded Documents*   www.dalecountyal.org/Departments/ProbateOffice.aspx   Subscription access to recorded record indices, $25.00 signup fee, view images at $.75 each or less, print images $1.00 each. Data is same as appears on PAT. See http://syscononline.com/?page_id=71.
Property, Taxation Records   Access to GIS/mapping free at www.alabamagis.com/dale/.

Dallas County *Property, Taxation Records*   Access the GIS-property info database and Tax Office free at http://emaps.emapsplus.com/standard/dallascoal.html. Also, access to tax record information free at www.dallascountyproperty-tags.com/taxes/default.aspx.

De Kalb County *Property, Taxation Records*   Property tax data and property appraiser records at www.deltacomputersystems.com/. Search records or property maps free at www.alabamagis.com/dekalb/.

Elmore County *Recorded Documents*   www.elmoreco.org/Default.asp?ID=157&pg=Probate+Office   Subscription access to all recorded indices available, $25.00 signup fee, view images at $.75 each or less, print images $1.00 each. Data is same as appears on PAT. See http://syscononline.com/?page_id=71.
Property, Taxation Records   Search property tax by name at www.elmorerevenuecommissioner.net/caportal_mainpage.aspx. Search personal property at www.elmorerevenuecommissioner.net/caportal_mainpage.aspx. Also, access to GIS/mapping for free at http://emaps.emapsplus.com/standard/elmorecoal.html.

Escambia County *Property, Taxation Records*   Property tax data and property appraiser records at www.deltacomputersystems.com/.

Etowah County *Recorded Documents*   http://etowahcounty.org/department/probate-court/   Access to parcel records free at http://isv.kcsgis.com/al.etowah/#/SearchOptions.
Property, Taxation Records   Property tax data and property appraiser records at www.deltacomputersystems.com/.

Fayette County *Property, Taxation Records*   Access parcel data on the GIS/mapping site free at www.alabamagis.com/Fayette/.

Franklin County *Recorded Documents* www.franklincountyal.org/index.html   Subscription access to all recorded indices available, $25.00 signup fee, view images at $.75 each or less, print images $.50 each. Data is same as appears on PAT. See http://syscononline.com/?page_id=71.
Property, Taxation Records   Access the GIS-property info database and Tax Office free at http://emaps.emapsplus.com/standard/franklincoal.html.

Geneva County *Recorded Documents* www.genevacounty.us/probate-judges.html   Subscription access to recorded record indices, $25.00 signup fee, view images at $.75 each or less, print images $1.00 each. Data is same as appears on PAT. See http://syscononline.com/?page_id=71.
Property, Taxation Records   Access to GIS/mapping free at www.alabamagis.com/Geneva/Frameset.cfm.

Henry County *Property, Taxation Records*   Access parcel data on the GIS-mapping site free at www.alabamagis.com/Henry/. Will work on certain mobile devices.

Houston County *Recorded Documents* http://houstoncountyprobate.org/   Subscription access to recorded record indices, $25.00 signup fee, view images at $.75 each or less, print images $.50 each. Data is same as appears on PAT. See http://syscononline.com/?page_id=71.
Property, Taxation Records   Access to property search for free at www.houstoncounty.org/revenue/search. Also, Access to GIS/mapping free at www.alabamagis.com/Houston/Frameset.cfm.

Jackson County *Recorded Documents*   Access to deeds and records free at www.deltacomputersystems.com/AL/AL39/DRLINKQUERYA.HTML.
Property, Taxation Records   Property tax data and property appraiser records at www.deltacomputersystems.com/. Also, access to property tax payments for free at www.jacksoncountyrevenue.com/PropertyTax.aspx#/.

Jefferson County - Bessemer Division *Recorded Documents* http://jeffcoprobatecourt.com/   Access to records for a fee at http://landmarkweb.jccal.org/landmarkweb. Copies are $2.00 per page.
Property, Taxation Records   The site at http://jeffcogis.jccal.org/jeffcomaps/Disclaimer.aspx provides free searches to tax appraisal data and maps. Search assessment data by name or parcel # or address.

Jefferson County - Birmingham Division *Recorded Documents*   Access to records for a onthly subscription fee of $100.00 unlimited or $2.00 per page, minimum $3.00 per document at . http://jeffconlinelandrecord.jccal.org/ailis/subscriptions.html.
Property, Taxation Records   The site at http://eringcapture.jccal.org/caportal/CAPortal_MainPage.aspx provides free searches to tax appraisal data. Also, access to GIS/mapping for free at http://jeffcogis.jccal.org/jeffcomaps/.

Lamar County *Property, Taxation Records*   Access to GIS/mapping free at www.alabamagis.com/Lamar/.

Lauderdale County *Recorded Documents* www.lauderdalecountyonline.com   Subscription access to all recorded indices available, $25.00 signup fee, view images at $.75 each or less, print images $1.00 each. Data is same as appears on PAT. See http://syscononline.com/?page_id=71.
Property, Taxation Records   Access to records search/GIS/mapping for free at http://isv.kcsgis.com/al.lauderdale_revenue/. Property tax data and property appraiser records at www.deltacomputersystems.com/.

Lawrence County *Property, Taxation Records*   Access the GIS-property info database free at http://isv.kcsgis.com/al.lawrence_revenue/. Also, access to property search at www.lawrencecountyrevenue.com/taxes?=property.

Lee County *Property, Taxation Records*   Property tax data and property appraiser records at www.deltacomputersystems.com/. Also, access parcel data on the GIS-mapping site free at www.alabamagis.com/lee/. Password required for full data.

Limestone County *Recorded Documents* http://limestonecounty-al.gov/departments/probate-judge/   Subscription access to all recorded indices available, $25.00 signup fee, view images at $.75 each or less, print images $.25 each. Data is same as appears on PAT. See http://syscononline.com/?page_id=71.
Property, Taxation Records   Access to records/mapping for free at www.limestonerevenue.net/caportal_mainpage.aspx.

Lowndes County *Property, Taxation Records*   Access to mapping for free at http://revenue.alabama.gov/advalorem/sections/mapping.cfm.

Macon County *Property, Taxation Records*   Free property record searches at www.maconcountyal.com/taxSearch?=revenue. Also, access the GIS-property info database and Tax Office free at http://emaps.emapsplus.com/standard/maconcoal.html. Also

Madison County *Recorded Documents* http://madisoncountyal.gov/departments/probate-judge   Access to the judge of probate's recording index is free at http://probate.co.madison.al.us/. Land records including images go back to 1971; marriage and military discharges back to 1976.
Property, Taxation Records   Property tax data and property appraiser records at www.deltacomputersystems.com/. Also, access to GIS/mapping for free at http://emaps.emapsplus.com/standard/madisoncoal.html.

Marion County *Property, Taxation Records*   Access to property record searches for free at https://marioncountyalabama.org/property.html#/WildfireSearch.

Marshall County *Recorded Documents*   Access to deeds by grantor/grantee free at www.deedlookup.org/.
Property, Taxation Records   Access property data free at www.landlookup.org/. Also, access records look-up or GIS/mapping for free at http://isv.kcsgis.com/al.marshall/#/Start. Property tax data and property appraiser records at www.deltacomputersystems.com/.

Mobile County *Recorded Documents*   http://probate.mobilecountyal.gov/default.asp   Access real property records back to 1984 and unclaimed property for free at http://probate.mobilecountyal.gov/recordssearch.asp. Two searches are available. For newer records (after 1983) one must register. Older records go back to 1813. Search marriage/probate records at https://roam.probate.mobilecountyal.gov/index.html. Must register to use.
Property, Taxation Records   Access real property and personal property tax records free at www.mobile-propertytaxal.com/bill_search.shtml. Also, City of Mobile property ownership data is free at http://maps.cityofmobile.org/gis/webmapping.aspx.

Monroe County *Recorded Documents*   www.monroecountyonline.com/probate/   Subscription access to all recorded indices available, $25.00 signup fee, view images at $.75 each or less, print images $1.00 each. Data is same as appears on PAT. See http://syscononline.com/?page_id=71.
Property, Taxation Records   Access to property tax for free at www.monroecountyonline.com/PropertyTaxSearch. Access to a list of Transcripts of Tax Delinquent Property is at http://revenue.alabama.gov/advalorem/transcript/.

Montgomery County *Recorded Documents*   www.mc-ala.org/ElectedOfficials/ProbateJudge/Pages/Default.aspx   Free access to records index found at www.mc-ala.org/ElectedOfficials/ProbateJudge/ProbateResources/Pages/ProbateRecordsSearch.aspx.
Property, Taxation Records   Access the property tax and assessment info using the left side choices at http://revco.mc-ala.org/.

Morgan County *Recorded Documents*   www.morgancountyprobate.com/   Access the index of recorded documents free at www.morgancountyprobate.com/online-records.aspx.
Property, Taxation Records   Property tax data and property appraiser records at www.deltacomputersystems.com/.

Perry County *Property, Taxation Records*   Access the GIS-property info database and Tax Office free at http://revenue.alabama.gov/advalorem/sections/mapping.cfm.

Pickens County *Property, Taxation Records*   Access parcel data on the GIS/mapping site free at www.alabamagis.com/Pickens/. Must download Mapguide Viewer Software first.

Pike County *Property, Taxation Records*   Access GIS/mapping property data free at www.alabamagis.com/Pike/. Also, access to property records free at www.pikerevenue.com/search.aspx?type=p.

Randolph County *Property, Taxation Records*   Access to property taxrecords for free at www.randolphcountyalabama.gov/. Click on Search & Pay Taxes. Also,

Russell County *Property, Taxation Records*   Access the GIS-property info database and Tax Office free at http://russellcountyrevenuecommissioner.com/search.aspx.

Shelby County *Recorded Documents, Notary Records*   https://www.shelbyal.com/index.aspx?nid=285   Access to the probate court recording data is free at http://probaterecords.shelbyal.com/. Marriage license is index only. No images.
Property, Taxation Records   Search property tax records free at http://probaterecords.shelbyal.com/.

St. Clair County *Property, Taxation Records*   Property tax data and property appraiser records at www.deltacomputersystems.com/AL/AL59/. View GIS at http://stclair.maps.arcgis.com/home/.

Sumter County *Property, Taxation Records*   Access to GIS/mapping free at www.alabamagis.com/Sumter/disclaimer.cfm.

Talladega County *Recorded Documents*   www.talladegacountyal.org/probate.htm   Subscription access to all recorded indices available, $25.00 signup fee, view images at $.75 each or less, print images $1.00 each. Data is same as appears on PAT. See http://syscononline.com/?page_id=71.

Tallapoosa County *Property, Taxation Records*   Access parcel data on the GIS-mapping site free at www.alabamagis.com/tallapoosa/. Password required for full data.

Tuscaloosa County *Probate Documents Records*   www.tuscco.com/government/departments/probate/   Access to probate records for a fee at https://probate.tuscco.com/ProbateRecords/. Must register.
Property, Taxation Records   Access to GIS/mapping for free at http://tuscaloosaal.mygisonline.com/.

Walker County *Recorded Documents*   www.walkercounty.com/   Subscription access to recorded indices, $25.00 signup fee, view images at $.75 each or less, print images $1.00 each. Data is same as appears on PAT. See http://syscononline.com/?page_id=71.
Property, Taxation Records   Access parcel data on the GIS-mapping site free at www.alabamagis.com/walker/. Must download Mapguide Viewer Software first. Password required for full data. Also, search, view and pay taxes at www.walkercountyrevenue.com/search.aspx.

Washington County *Property, Taxation Records*   Access the GIS-property info database and Tax Office free at www.alabamagis.com/Washington/.

Wilcox County *Property, Taxation Records*   Access to GIS/mapping free at www.alabamagis.com/Wilcoxgov/disclaimer.cfm.

Winston County *Recorded Documents*   www.winstoncountyprobate.org/   Subscription access to all recorded indices available, $25.00 signup fee, view images at $.75 each or less, print images $1.00 each. Data is same as appears on PAT. See http://syscononline.com/?page_id=71.
Property, Taxation Records   Access parcel data on the GIS-mapping site free at www.alabamagis.com/winston/. Must download Mapguide Viewer Software first. Password required for full data.

Alaska

Capital: Juneau
               Juneau Borough
Time Zone: AK (Alaska Standard Time)
Population: 738,432
# of Boroughs/Divisions: 23

Useful State Links

Website: **http://alaska.gov**
Governor: **http://archives.alaska.gov/**
Attorney General: **www.law.state.ak.us**
State Archives: **www.archives.state.ak.us**
State Statutes and Codes: **www.legis.state.ak.us/basis/folio.asp**
Legislative Bill Search: **www.legis.state.ak.us/basis/folio.asp**
Unclaimed Funds: **http://treasury.dor.alaska.gov/Unclaimed-Property.aspx**

State Public Record Agencies

Sexual Offender Registry

Department of Public Safety, Statewide Services Div-SOR Unit,   www.dps.alaska.gov/sorweb/Sorweb.aspx   The Alaska registry provides a single public website that sorts and provides registrant information by name, address, zip code, city name, registration status, or a total list. Name searching and geographic searching are both offered at http://dps.alaska.govsorweb/Search.aspx.

Incarceration Records

Alaska Department of Corrections, Research and Records,   www.correct.state.ak.us/   No online searching available from this agency, but it promotes a private company with a free search of DOC inmates and offenders at https://www.vinelink.com/vinelink/siteInfoAction.do?siteId=2001.

Corporation, LP, LLC, LLP, Trademarks/Servicemarks, Fictitious/Assumed Name

Corporation Section, Department of Commerce, Community & Econ Dev,   https://www.commerce.alaska.gov/web/cbpl/Corporations.aspx   At https://www.commerce.alaska.gov/CBP/Main/SearchInfo.aspx, search status information on corps, LLCs, LLP, LP (all both foreign and domestic), registered and reserved names. Search by entity name, registered agent name, or by officer name. From this site one may also download in CSV format tables of of corporations, business, and professional licensing databases.

Uniform Commercial Code

UCC Central File Systems Office, State Recorder's Office,   http://dnr.alaska.gov/ssd/recoff/UCC.cfm   One can search by debtor or secured party name, date, document number or document type at http://dnr.alaska.gov/ssd/recoff/searchUCC.cfm. There is no fee. Images of UCC document files/recorded from July 1, 2008 forward are available. Inactive UCCs (UCCs that are more than one year past their date of lapse) are purged from the database on an annual schedule. Not thatother recorded documents are available at http://dnr.alaska.gov/ssd/recoff/searchRO.cfm. Images of mining documents (Index Code MI, Document Type - Mining) and deed documents (Index Code D, Document Type - Deeds) recorded from January 1, 1973 forward are now available at http://dnr.alaska.gov/ssd/recoff/searchRO.cfm. Official certified copies must be requested and paid for through the recording district office where the plat was recorded. *Other Options:* CDs or FTPs of document images can be purchased from the State Recorder's Office (907-269-8878). Also this office provides a number of excellent searches at http://dnr.alaska.gov/ssd/recoff/searchRO.cfm.

Birth Certificates

Department of Health & Social Services, Bureau of Vital Statistics,   http://dhss.alaska.gov/dph/VitalStats/Pages/default.aspx   Records may be ordered online via a state-designated vendor at www.vitalchek.com. There are additional fees. Use of credit card required.

Death Records

Department of Health & Social Services, Bureau of Vital Statistics,   http://dhss.alaska.gov/dph/VitalStats/Pages/death/default.aspx   Records may be ordered online via a state-designated vendor at www.vitalchek.com. There are additional fees. Use of credit card required.   *Other Options:* Death certificate request form is found at http://dhss.alaska.gov/dph/VitalStats/Documents/death/death_form.pdf.

Marriage Certificates

Department of Health & Social Services, Bureau of Vital Statistics,   http://dhss.alaska.gov/dph/VitalStats/Pages/marriage/default.aspx   Records may be ordered online via a state-designated vendor at www.vitalchek.com. There are additional fees. Use of credit card required.   *Other Options:* The request form for Marriage licenses is found at http://dhss.alaska.gov/dph/VitalStats/Documents/marriage/marriage_form.pdf.

Divorce Records

Department of Health & Social Services, Bureau of Vital Statistics,   http://dhss.alaska.gov/dph/VitalStats/Pages/divorce/default.aspx   Records may be ordered online via a state-designated vendor at www.vitalchek.com. There are additional fees. Use of credit card required.   *Other Options:* Divorce Certificate Request form is found at http://dhss.alaska.gov/dph/VitalStats/Pages/divorce/default.aspx.

Workers' Compensation Records

Workers' Compensation,   http://labor.state.ak.us/wc/home.htm   Determine if an employer has coverage at https://www.ewccv.com/cvs/.

Driver Records

Division of Motor Vehicles, Attn: Research,   http://doa.alaska.gov/dmv/   Online access costs $10.00 per record. This is for pre-approved, ongoing requesters only. Note this is not a web-based system, requests are sent and received via email. Inquiries may be made at any time, 24 hours a day. Batch inquiries may call back within thirty minutes for responses. Search by the first four letters of driver's name, license number and date of birth.

Voter Registration, Campaign & Financial Disclosures

Division of Elections, PO Box 110017,   www.elections.alaska.gov   Search campaign disclosures records and lobbyist records at http://aws.state.ak.us/ApocReports/Home.aspx.   *Other Options:* The agency offers the complete voter registration database on CD-ROM for $21. Individual districts (there are 40) can be purchased on disk for $21.00 per district. Statewide lists are created every Friday.

GED Certificates

Dept of Labor - Employment Security Division, GED Program,   www.jobs.state.ak.us/abe/ged_req.htm   Records may be requested from https://www.diplomasender.com. A credit card is needed. Request must be ordered by the test taker. Employers and third parties must receive an email and/or Authentication Code from the test taker to then access the authorized documents. Turnaround time is 1-3 days.

Occupational Licensing Boards

Search these licenses at https://www.commerce.alaska.gov/cbp/Main/CBPLSearch.aspx?mode=Prof

Accountant-CPA	Dietitian/Nutritionist	Optician, Dispensing
Acupuncturist	Electrical Administrator	Optometrist
Anesthesia Permit, Dental	Engineer	Osteopathic Physician
Architect/Land Surveyors	Esthetician	Parenteral Sedation Permit (Dental)
Athletic Event Promoter	Funeral Director/Establishment	Pharmacist/Pharmacist Intern
Athletic Trainer	Geologist	Pharmacy/Technician
Audiologist/Hearing Aid Dealer	Hairdresser/Esthetician	Physical Therapist/Assistant
Barber	Hearing Aid Dealer	Psychologist/Psycholog'l Assistant
Barber Shop Owner/Sch'l/Instruc	Home Inspector	Real Estate Agent/Broker/Assoc
Big Game Guide/Hunting	Landscape Architect	Real Estate Appraiser
Guide/Assist/Transporter	Marriage & Family Therapist	Social Worker/Clinical
Chiropractor	Mechanical Administrator	Speech/Language Pathologist
Collection Agency/Operator	Mobile Home Dealer	Surveyor, Land
Concert Promoter	Mortician/Embalmer	Transporter, Game
Construction Contractor	Naturopathic Physician	Underground Storage Tank Worker/Contr
Contractor, Elect/Mech/Mining/Petrol	Nurse Anesthetist	Veterinarian/Veterinary Technician
Contractor, Residential	Nurse-RN/LPN/Nurses Aid	Alcohol Establishment
Cosmetologist/Hairdresser	Nursing Home Administrator	
Dentist/ Examiner/Dental Hygienist	Occupational Therapist/Assistant	

The Rest:

Aircraft-related Occupation .... www.faa.gov/licenses_certificates/airmen_certification/sport_pilot/
Alcohol Establishment .... https://www.commerce.alaska.gov/web/amco/ABCLicenseSearch.aspx
Approved Fingerprinters .... www.dps.alaska.gov/Statewide/background/fingerprinters.aspx
Attorney .... https://www.alaskabar.org/servlet/content/member_directory.html
Bail Bondsman.. https://sbs-ak.naic.org/Lion-Web/jsp/sbsreports/AgentLookup.jsp
Child Care Center.................................... www.muni.org/Departments/health/DirectServices/pages/child.aspx
Child Care Provider/Home........................ www.muni.org/Departments/health/DirectServices/pages/child.aspx
Concealed Handgun Permit .... www.dps.state.ak.us/Statewide/PermitsLicensing/
Independent Adjuster............................... https://sbs-ak.naic.org/Lion-Web/jsp/sbsreports/AgentLookup.jsp
Insurance Agent...................................... https://sbs-ak.naic.org/Lion-Web/jsp/sbsreports/AgentLookup.jsp
Insurance Company.................................. https://sbs-ak.naic.org/Lion-Web/jsp/sbsreports/CompanySearchLookup.jsp
Interior Designer Schools, Accredited .... http://abrid.alabama.gov/about-interior-design/schools-with-accredited-programs-in-alabama/
Lobbyist .... https://aws.state.ak.us/ApocReports/Lobbying/LobbyistDirectory.aspx
Notary Public .... http://aws.state.ak.us/NotaryDirectory/
Pesticide Applicator/Dealer .... www.kellysolutions.com/ak/
Pesticide Permit, Registration .... www.kellysolutions.com/ak/
Pilot, Aircraft .... http://registry.faa.gov/aircraftinquiry/NNum_Inquiry.aspx
Process Server .... www.dps.alaska.gov/statewide/PermitsLicensing/docs/CPSList.pdf
Reinsurance Intermediary Broker/Mgr....... https://sbs-ak.naic.org/Lion-Web/jsp/sbsreports/AgentLookup.jsp
School Administrator................................. https://education.alaska.gov/TeacherCertification/CertificationsSearch.cfm
School Special Service .... https://education.alaska.gov/TeacherCertification/CertificationsSearch.cfm
Septic Tank Installer .... http://dec.alaska.gov/water/wwdp/onsite/pdf/rptCurrentCI.pdf
Surplus Line Broker .... https://sbs-ak.naic.org/Lion-Web/jsp/sbsreports/AgentLookup.jsp
Teacher.. https://education.alaska.gov/TeacherCertification/CertificationsSearch.cfm
Viatical Settlement Broker .... https://sbs-ak.naic.org/Lion-Web/jsp/sbsreports/AgentLookup.jsp

State and Local Courts

About Alaska Courts: The **Superior Court** is the trial court of general jurisdiction. The Superior Court hears felony and civil cases generally involving $100,000 or more. The court also hears cases that involve children, cases about domestic relations matters, and estates or probate.

The **District Court** hears cases that involve state misdemeanors and violations of city and borough ordinances, first appearances and preliminary hearings in felony cases, record vital statistics (in some areas of the state), civil cases usually up to $100,000, but this can depend on the Authority of the Presiding Judge, small claims cases ($10,000 maximum), cases involving children on an emergency basis, domestic violence cases, and traffic. Also, some District Courts have made arrangements to have a judge travel to their court location and hear felony or upper limit civil cases. Thus the records are housed at this location. The court profiles indicate when this procedure is commonly used by a court.

Magistrate judges are judicial officers of the District Court. Their authority is more limited than the authority of a District Court. **Magistrate Judges hear** trials of municipal ordinance violations, state traffic infractions and other minor offenses. **Magistrates** are judicial officers of the District Courts. They preside in areas of the state where a fulltime district judge is not required and in metropolitan areas to help the workload of the District Court. They hear Small Claims cases which have a $10,000 limit. Small claims cases also can be up to $20,000 for wage claims brought by the Department of Labor.

The web page for the Alaska Court System is www.courts.alaska.gov.

Appellate Courts: The home page gives access to Appellate opinions. Also, the site at http://government.westlaw.com/akcases/ provides access to opinions of the Alaska Supreme Court and Alaska Court of Appeals.

About Court Online Access

Online Access is statewide, all courts participate in the system described below.

The case summary and docket information for Alaska trial courts is found on CourtView at www.courtrecords.alaska.gov/eservices/home.page.2. Records available include civil, criminal, traffic and wills. In general they are available since 1990, some court are scanning in older records. One may search by name, case number or ticket number, and give a date range on the DOB. Although all courts participate, the dates of the earliest available cases vary by court.

An excellent page with *how to use the system* features and if there are any recent cautions regarding the display of certain pieces of data and also access to e-filings is found at www.courts.alaska.gov/cvinfo.

Other Sites: None – no individual courts offer online access to court records.

Recorders, Assessors, and Other Sites of Note

About Alaska Recording Offices: The 23 Alaskan counties are called boroughs. However, real estate recording is done by technnically 34 Recording Districts per a system established at the time of the Gold Rush (1893-1916). Howvwer, in reality the Districts have consolidated and there are currently only 5 full time recording offices (Anchorage, Fairbanks, juneau, kenai, and Palmer) in the state. Some of the Districts are identical in geography to boroughs such as the Aleutian Islands, but other boroughs and districts overlap. Therefore, you need to know the recording district to which a given town or city is assigned. A helpful website is http://dnr.alaska.gov/ssd/recoff/findYourDistrict.htm

About Tax Liens: All state and federal tax liens are filed with the District Recorder.

Online Access

There are Several Statewide Online Access Resources

- The state's Recorder's Office at the Deptartment of Natural Resources provides a search site. Search recorded documents by many ways including name, date, doc #, doc type, plat, survey, free on the statewide system at http://dnr.alaska.gov/ssd/recoff/searchRO.cfm. Search entire state or by recording district, certian images back to June, 2001; index to 2000. Images of UCC document files/recorded from July 1, 2008 forward are available. The agency is working on a film converison wiith plans to display all images back to 1973.

- The Department of Natural Resources also prvides a search site for case information, land abstract data, and water rights. See http://dnr.alaska.gov/projects/las/.

- The Department of Natural Resources also has a search site for case file information land records, see http://dnr.alaska.gov/projects/las/.

Local Sites Other Than the Statewide Sites Mentioned Above:

Anchorage District *Property, Taxation Records*   Access appraisal data free at www.muni.org/pw/public.html.

Fairbanks District in Fairbanks North Star Borough *Property, Taxation Records*   Access to the Fairbanks North Star Borough property database is free online at http://old.co.fairbanks.ak.us/assessing/propsearch.aspx.

Juneau Recording District *Property, Taxation Records*   Access to City of Juneau Property Records database is free online at www.juneau.org/assessordata/sqlassessor.php.

Kenai District *Property, Taxation Records*   A parcel look-up is at http://ak-kenai-assessment.publicaccessnow.com/default.aspx. Search the AK DNR Land Information at http://dnr.alaska.gov/ssd/recoff/searchRO.cfm.

Palmer District in Matanuska-Susitna Borough *Property, Taxation Records*   Access borough property and property tax data free at www.matsugov.us/myproperty//

Arizona

Capital: Phoenix
              Maricopa County
Time Zone: MST
Population: 6,828,065
# of Counties: 15

Useful State Links

Website: **https://az.gov**
Governor: **http://azgovernor.gov/**
Attorney General: **https://www.azag.gov/**
State Archives: **www.lib.az.us/archives/**
State Statutes and Codes: **www.azleg.state.az.us/ArizonaRevisedStatutes.asp**
Legislative Bill Search: **www.azleg.state.az.us/Bills.asp**
Bill Monitoring: **http://alistrack.azleg.state.az.us/**
Unclaimed Funds: **www.azunclaimed.gov/**

Editor's Tip: Arizona is on Mountain Standard Time, but does not observe Daylight Savings Time rules. Thus, from the first Sunday in April to the last Sunday in October, nearly all Arizona locations will have the same clock time as Pacific Daylight Time, the same time as in California.

But there are exceptions. Some Arizona Indian Reservation offices may observe Daylight Savings Time. Notable is the Navajo Nation Indian Reservation in northeastern Arizona. This does not include the Hopi Indian Reservation, which is surrounded by the Navajos.

State Public Record Agencies

Sexual Offender Registry

Department of Public Safety, Sex Offender Compliance,   www.azdps.gov/Services/Sex_Offender/   Click on the Search the Sex Offender Registry tab at the home web page for Sex Offenders.   *Other Options:* A download of a list is available from the webpage for $25.00. See www.azdps.gov/Services/Sex_Offender/Downloads/.

Incarceration Records

Arizona Department of Corrections, Records Department,   https://corrections.az.gov/   For online search at https://corrections.az.gov/public-resources/inmate-datasearch, you must provide last name, first initial or ADC number. Any add'l identifiers are welcomed. Location, ADC number, physical identifiers and sentencing information are released. Inmates admitted and released from 1972 to 1985 may not be searchable on the web. Also available is ADC Fugitives - an alphabetical Inmate Datasearch listing of Absconders and Escapees from ADC.   *Other Options:* For a nominal fee, the Arizona Department of Corrections makes available on request copies of the inmate information contained on the ADC Website Inmate Datasearch in a WinZip file. See https://corrections.az.gov/request-copy-inmate-data-search-database

Corporation, LLC Records

Corporation Commission, Corporation Records,   www.azcc.gov/divisions/corporations/   eCorp allows you to find information about corporations and limited liability companies registered with the Arizona Corporation Commission. See http://ecorp.azcc.gov/ . Also, search Corp Commission's Securities Division Actions, Orders and Admin. Decisions pages at www.azcc.gov/divisions/securities/enforcement/.   *Other Options:* To purchase the database or in bulk, see www.azcc.gov/Divisions/Corporations/starpas1/rec2003.pdf. Call 602-364-4433.

Partnerships, LP, LLP, Trademarks/Servicemarks, Trade Names

Secretary of State, Trademarks/Tradenames/Limited Partnership Division, www.azsos.gov/business The website link at http://apps.azsos.gov/scripts/TNT_Search_engine.dll prvides a search for Registered Names, Trade Names, and Trademarks. Also available is the full Trade Name and Trademark index in data format. The Office of the Secretary of State, Business Services Division, provides the Non-Incorporated Registrations Index as a full DB or monthly files. Included with each single request is a complete listing of the registrations, associated filings, service of process agents and owners. See www.azsos.gov/services/public-information/database-purchasing.

Uniform Commercial Code, Federal & State Tax Liens

UCC Division, Secretary of State, www.azsos.gov/business/uniform-commercial-code-ucc The UCC record index can be searched for free at http://apps.azsos.gov/apps/ucc/search/. Searching can be done by debtor, secured party name, or file number. Images are available on records since 5/1994. SSNs have been redacted. Filings that exist before May 1994 have fiche locations at the bottom of the details page. *Other Options:* The agency offers five options of bulk database purchases. Requests must be in writing using their request form which can be downloaded from the web. See www.azsos.gov/services/public-information/database-purchasing.

Sales Tax Registrations

Revenue Department, Transaction (Sales) Tax Licenses and Registration, https://www.azdor.gov/ Verify a sales tax registration by tax license number online free at https://www.aztaxes.gov/LicenseVerification. Must be eight digits. Cannot search by company name.

Birth Certificates

Department of Health Services, AZ Office of Vital Records, www.azdhs.gov/licensing/vital-records/index.php#birth-certificates-home Records may be ordered online via www.vitalchek.com, a state-endorsed vendor. Images of birth certificates from 1887 to 1934 are available free online at http://genealogy.az.gov. Death certificates 1878-1959 are also available.

Death Records

Department of Health Services, AZ Office of Vital Records, www.azdhs.gov/licensing/vital-records/index.php#death-certificates-home Death certificate images 1878-1959 are available free online at http://genealogy.az.gov. Also available are images of birth certificates from 1887 to 1934. Records may be ordered online via vitalchek.com, a state-endorsed vendor.

Workers' Compensation Records

Industrial Commission of Arizona, Claims Division, www.azica.gov/ Claim records are not available online, but verify coverage by an employer at www.azica.gov/Homepage/HOME_NCCI_Redirect.aspx. One can also use a mobile app, see this page.

Driver Records

Motor Vehicle Division, Correspondence Unit, www.azdot.gov/mvd/index.asp Arizona's commercial online system (MVRRS) is interactive and batch and open 24 hours daily. Fee is $3.25 per record. This system is primarily for those requesters who qualify per DPPA. For more information call 602-712-7235. Interactive records have a fee of $6.00 (39-month) and $8.00 (5-year). This includes all portal fees. For more information about MVRRS, contact the Electronic Data Services Unit by email at eds@azdot.gov or call 602-712-7235. The site also permits licensed driver to view their own record. Fee is $3.00 and use of a credit card is required. Visit http://servicearizona.com/. Verify insurance information at https://servicearizona.com/webapp/insurance/. CDL holders and/or persons applying for a CDL may review the status of their CDL Medical Certification online at: www.azdot.gov/apps/cdl-medical-status-review.

Vehicle Ownership & Registration

Motor Vehicle Division - Director's Office, Record Services Section, www.azdot.gov/mvd/index.asp The Motor Vehicle Record Request System (MVRRS) is the single access point for electronic title and registration records. This is only for authorized users. There is a $3.00 portal fee added to the record search fee of $3.00, so the fee is $6.00. For more information contact the Electronic Data Services Units at 602-712-7235 or eds@azdot.gov. The MVD also offers access for vehicle owners to view and print their own title and registration records at https://servicearizona, fee is $3.00. See https://servicearizona.com/webapp/lienmvr/search?execution=e1s1 for a free lien status check. *Other Options:* Check the attorney general's stolen vehicle list free at https://theftaz.azag.gov/. Search by VIN of plate number.

Voter Registration, Campaign Finance, PAC, Lobbyists

Secretary of State, Election Services Office, www.azsos.gov/elections A search of candidates' campaign finance is found at http://apps.azsos.gov/apps/election/cfs/search/CandidateSearch.aspx. A multicandidate PAC list is found at http://apps.azsos.gov/apps/election/cfs/search/MulticandidatePac.aspx. A search of lobbyists is at www.azsos.gov/elections/lobbyists.

GED (HSEC) Transcripts

Department of Education, GED Testing - BIN #26, www.azed.gov/adultedservices/hse-transcripts/ The agency sends to a third-party vendor at https://www.nrspro.com/Unity/GED/123/Default.aspx. If the requester is a third party verifier and has the transcript number the verification takes 20 seconds. if the number is not known, the verification will take approx. 3 days.

Occupational Licensing Boards

Search these health-related licenses at www.azdhs.gov/licensing/index.php#azcarecheck

Ambulatory Surgical Ctr
Assisted Living Facility/Manager
Audiologist
Child Care
Clinic, Recovery Care
Clinic, Rural Health
Developmentally Disab'd Group Home
Group Home, Development Disabled
Group Home, Small
Health Clinic
Hearing Aid Dispenser

Home Health Agency
Hospice
Hospital
Infirmary
Juvenile Group Home
Long Term Care Facility
Medical Facility
Mentally Retarded Care Facility
Midwife Providers
Neuro Rehab Center
Out-Patient Physical Therapy

Out-Patient Surgical Center
Out-Patient Treatment Clinic
Recovery Center
Rehabilitation Agency
Renal Disease Facility
Speech Pathology
Speech-Language Pathologist
Treatment Clinic
X-Ray Supplier (Portable)

These licenses are all searchable at http://searchagriculture.az.gov/mastercontent/licsearch.aspx

Aerial Applicator, Pesticide
Agricultural Grower/Seller/Permit
Agricultural Lab
Agricultural Pest Control Advisor
Applicator, Pesticide, Private/Commercial

Feed Dealer/Wholesaler/Distribution, Commercial
Fertilizer Dealer/Distribution, Commercial
Fertilizer Product
Packer, Fruit/Vegetable
Pesticide Custom Applicator

Pesticide Distribution/Seller
Pesticide Registration
Pesticide Safety Trainer
Seed Dealer
Seed Labeler

The Rest:

Accountant-CPA/PA/Firm .... www.azaccountancy.gov/CPADirectory/CPASearch.aspx
Acupuncturist.. https://acupunctureboard.az.gov/consumer-information/directory
Acupuncturist School.................................... https://acupunctureboard.az.gov/continuing-education/acupuncture-schools
Adult Care Home Manager....................... www.aznciaboard.us/managers.html
Advance Fee Loan Broker.......................... http://azdfi.gov/Consumers/Licensees/default.asp
Aesthetician .... https://azboc.glsuite.us/glsuiteweb/Clients/AZBOC/Public/Verification/Search.aspx
Aesthetics Instructor.................................... https://azboc.glsuite.us/glsuiteweb/Clients/AZBOC/Public/Verification/Search.aspx
Air Pollution Source/Open Burning Permit http://legacy.azdeq.gov/databases/banksearch.html
Aircraft Dealer/Retail.................................... http://azdot.gov/mvd/professional-services/aircraft-services/forms
Aircraft Use Fuel Dealer/Mfg .... https://www.aztaxes.gov/Home
Amusement Park/Printing/Advertising .... https://www.aztaxes.gov/Home
Animal Crematory .... http://archivevetboard.az.gov/licdirnew/licenseeSearch.aspx
Appraisal Management Company .... https://boa.az.gov/directories/amc
Appraiser, Real Estate/Personal Property. https://www.aztaxes.gov/Home
Aquifer Protection Permit............................ http://legacy.azdeq.gov/databases/opcertsearch.html
Attorney .... www.azbar.org/FindaLawyer
Attorney Discipline .... www.azcourts.gov/attorneydiscipline/
Bank, State Chartered .... http://azdfi.gov/Consumers/Licensees/default.asp
Barber School/Instruction .... https://barberboard.az.gov/directories
Barber/Barber Shop.................................... https://barberboard.az.gov/directories
Behavior Analyst.. https://psychboard.az.gov/license/directory-search
Behavioral Health Emerg'y/Resi Svcs .... www.azdhs.gov/licensing/index.php#databases
Behavioral Outpatient Clinic/Rehab.......... www.azdhs.gov/licensing/index.php#databases
Bingo Operation.. https://www.aztaxes.gov/Home
Bondsman (Insurance) .... https://ptl.az.gov/app/doilookup/
Bone Densitometer Operator..................... https://ptl.az.gov/app/mrtbe/
Campground Memb'ship Broker/Seller...... http://services.azre.gov/publicdatabase/Default.aspx
Cannabis/Control'd Substance Dealer ...... https://www.aztaxes.gov/Home
Cemetery Broker/Salesperson .... http://services.azre.gov/publicdatabase/Default.aspx
Charity .... http://apps.azsos.gov/scripts/Charity_Search.dll
Charter School... www.ade.az.gov/charterschools/search/

Child Residential Home	www.azdhs.gov/licensing/index.php#databases
Chiropractor/Acupuncturist	https://chiroboard.az.gov/find-chiropractor
Clinical Laboratory	https://app.azdhs.gov/BFS/LABS/ELBIS/ArizonaCertifiedLabs/
Collection Agency	http://azdfi.gov/Consumers/Licensees/default.asp
Commercial Leasing	https://www.aztaxes.gov/Home
Concealed Weapon Permit	https://webapps.azdps.gov/public_inq/sgrd/ShowLicenseStatus.action
Condo/Timeshare Seller	http://services.azre.gov/publicdatabase/Default.aspx
Consumer Lender	http://azdfi.gov/Consumers/Licensees/default.asp
Contractor	www.azroc.gov/forms/contractorsearch.html
Cosmetologist/Nail Technician	https://azboc.glsuite.us/glsuiteweb/Clients/AZBOC/Public/Verification/Search.aspx
Cosmetology/Nail/School/Instructor	https://azboc.glsuite.us/glsuiteweb/Clients/AZBOC/Public/Verification/Search.aspx
Counselor, Professional	http://azbbhe.us/node/3
Court Reporter	www.azcourts.gov/cld/Court-Reporter-Certification-Program
Court Reporting Firm	www.azcourts.gov/cld/Court-Reporter-Certification-Program
Credit Union, State Chartered	http://azdfi.gov/Consumers/Licensees/default.asp
Day Care Establishment	http://hsapps.azdhs.gov/ls/sod/SearchProv.aspx?type=CC
Debt Management Company	http://azdfi.gov/Consumers/Licensees/default.asp
Defensive Driving Instructor	www.azcourts.gov/drive/School-and-Instructor-Certification-Information
Defensive Driving School	www.azcourts.gov/drive/School-and-Instructor-Certification-Information
Deferred Presentment Company	http://azdfi.gov/Consumers/Licensees/default.asp
Dental Office	https://dentalboard.az.gov/directory
Dentist/Assistant/Hygienist	https://dentalboard.az.gov/directory
Denturist/Denture Technologist	https://dentalboard.az.gov/directory
Detoxification Service	www.azdhs.gov/licensing/index.php#databases
Dispensing Naturopath	http://directorynd.az.gov/agency/pages/directorysearch.asp
Drug Mfg/Wholesaler	https://pharmacy.az.gov/license-permit-verification
Drug, Retail non-prescription	https://pharmacy.az.gov/license-permit-verification
Dry Well Registration	http://legacy.azdeq.gov/databases/drywellsearch.html
Environmental Laboratory	https://app.azdhs.gov/BFS/LABS/ELBIS/ArizonaCertifiedLabs/
Escrow Agent	http://azdfi.gov/Consumers/Licensees/default.asp
Family Day Care Home	www.azdhs.gov/licensing/index.php#databases
Fiduciary	www.azcourts.gov/Portals/26/fiduciary/1-14-2016FIDDIRECTORY.PDF
Funeral Pre-Need Trust Company	http://azdfi.gov/Consumers/Licensees/default.asp
Groundwater Pumping	http://legacy.azdeq.gov/databases/opcertsearch.html
Guidance Counselor	https://oacis.azed.gov/PublicOACIS/NormalPages/Educators.aspx
Health Screening Service	https://app.azdhs.gov/BFS/LABS/ELBIS/ArizonaCertifiedLabs/
Homeopathic Medical Assistant	www.azhomeopathbd.az.gov/asst_dir.asp
Homeopathic Physician	www.azhomeopathbd.az.gov/phy_dir.html
Insurance Producer	https://ptl.az.gov/app/doilookup/
Lake, Artificial	http://legacy.azdeq.gov/databases/opcertsearch.html
Laser Light Show	https://www.aztaxes.gov/Home
Legal Document Preparer	www.azcourts.gov/Portals/26/fiduciary/1-14-2016FIDDIRECTORY.PDF
Licensed ADHS Licensed Facilities	http://adhsgis.maps.arcgis.com/apps/OnePane/basicviewer/index.html
Liquor Producer/Whlse	www.azliquor.gov/query/query.cfm
Liquor Retail Co-Operative/Agent/Mgr	www.azliquor.gov/query/query.cfm
Lobbyist	http://apps.azsos.gov/scripts/Lobbyist_Search.dll
Lottery Retailer	https://www.arizonalottery.com/en/retailers/find-a-retailer
LPG Service Agency/Rep	www.ncwm.net/certificates
Mammography Technologist	https://ptl.az.gov/app/mrtbe/
Manufactured Home Dealer/Mfg	www.dfbls.az.gov/omh.aspx
Marriage & Family Therapist	http://azbbhe.us/node/3
Massage Therapy School	https://massagetherapy.az.gov/schools
MD Resident	www.azmd.gov/
Medical Gas Dist/Supplier	https://pharmacy.az.gov/license-permit-verification
Metrology Certification	www.ncwm.net/certificates

Midwife.. http://hsapps.azdhs.gov/ls/sod/SearchProv.aspx?type=MW
Mobile Home Dealer/Broker/Seller .... www.dfbls.az.gov/omh/licensing/salesperson.aspx
Mobile Home Installer/Mfg........................ www.dfbls.az.gov/omh.aspx
Money Transmitter.................................... http://azdfi.gov/Consumers/Licensees/default.asp
Mortgage Banker/BrokerCommercial .... http://azdfi.gov/Consumers/Licensees/default.asp
Motor Fuel Inspection .... www.ncwm.net/certificates
Motor Vehicle Dealer/Sales Finance .... http://azdfi.gov/Consumers/Licensees/default.asp
Naturopathic Medical Asst........................ http://directorynd.az.gov/agency/pages/directorysearch.asp
Naturopathic Physician............................. http://directorynd.az.gov/agency/pages/directorysearch.asp
Naturopatic Medical College, Accreditated https://nd.az.gov/resources/accredited-naturopathic-colleges
Notary Public .... http://apps.azsos.gov/apps/notary/search/Default.aspx
Nuclear Medicine Technologist .... https://ptl.az.gov/app/mrtbe/
Nurse-LPN/RN/Aide.................................. https://www.azbn.gov/services/license-verification/
Nursing - Imposter Alert............................ https://www.azbn.gov/discipline-complaints/imposters/
Nursing Care Inst Administrator .... www.aznciaboard.us/administrators.html
Occupational Therapist/Assistant.............. http://directoryot.az.gov/licensee_directory_new/
Optical Establishment............................... https://do.az.gov/directory
Optician.. https://do.az.gov/directory
Optometrist .... http://archiveoptometry.az.gov/directoryM.asp
Osteopathic Physician/Surgeon .... www.azdo.gov/GLSPages/DoctorSearch.aspx
Osteopathic Physician/Surgeon Actions.... www.azdo.gov/GLSPages/RecentActions.aspx
P&C Managing Agent, Life/Disability .... https://ptl.az.gov/app/doilookup/
Pesticide Applicator/Supv/Advisor............ http://opm.azda.gov/
Pesticide Company.................................. http://opm.azda.gov/
Pharmacist/Pharmacy Intern .... https://pharmacy.az.gov/license-permit-verification
Physical Therapist/Therapist Asst http://directoryptboard.az.gov/public1/pages/ptSearchEngineDrupal.asp
Physician/Medical Doctor/Assistant/Intern/Resident   www.azmd.gov/GLSPages/DoctorSearch.aspx
Physiotherapist .... https://chiroboard.az.gov/find-chiropractor
Pipeline .... https://www.aztaxes.gov/Home
Plant Operator .... http://legacy.azdeq.gov/databases/opcertsearch.html
Podiatrist... http://directorypodiatry.az.gov/drDir.htm
Political Action Committee .... http://apps.azsos.gov/apps/election/cfs/search/CandidateSearch.aspx
Post-Secondary Educ Institution .... http://archiveppse.az.gov/Licensee/LicenseeSearch.aspx
Post-Secondary Voc Program, Private...... http://archiveppse.az.gov/Licensee/LicenseeSearch.aspx
Premium Finance Company .... http://azdfi.gov/Consumers/Licensees/default.asp
Preschool/Headstart Facility..................... http://hsapps.azdhs.gov/ls/sod/SearchProv.aspx?type=CC
Private Investigator/Security Guard........... https://webapps.azdps.gov/public_inq/sgrd/ShowLicenseStatus.action
Process Server, Private............................. www.azcourts.gov/Portals/26/PPS/ProcessServers61316.pdf
Property Tax Agent................................... https://boa.az.gov/property-tax-agents
Psychologist.. https://psychboard.az.gov/license/directory-search
Radiation Handler/Machine .... https://ptl.az.gov/app/doilookup/
Radiologic Technologist .... https://ptl.az.gov/app/mrtbe/
Real Estate Agent/Broker/Sales............... http://services.azre.gov/publicdatabase/Default.aspx
Real Estate Appraiser............................... https://boa.az.gov/directories/appraiser
Real Estate Firm...................................... http://services.azre.gov/publicdatabase/Default.aspx
Real Estate School Instructor .... http://services.azre.gov/publicdatabase/Default.aspx
Rental of Personal Property .... https://www.aztaxes.gov/Home
Respiratory Therapist .... https://ptl.az.gov/app/rce/index.xhtml
Restaurant/Bar... https://www.aztaxes.gov/Home
Retail Sales Outlet................................... https://www.aztaxes.gov/Home
Risk Management Producers .... https://ptl.az.gov/app/doilookup/
Sales Finance Company .... http://azdfi.gov/Consumers/Licensees/default.asp
Savings and Loan, Chartered.................... http://azdfi.gov/Consumers/Licensees/default.asp
Scanner, Electronic System .... https://ctutools.azda.gov/dwm/pv/inspection_search.asp
School Bus Driver/Instructor..................... https://webapps.azdps.gov/public_inq/sgrd/ShowLicenseStatus.action

School Bus Transportation Provider	https://webapps.azdps.gov/public_inq/sgrd/ShowLicenseStatus.action
School Librarian/Library Aide	https://oacis.azed.gov/PublicOACIS/NormalPages/Educators.aspx
School Psychologist	https://oacis.azed.gov/PublicOACIS/NormalPages/Educators.aspx
Social Worker	http://azbbhe.us/node/3
Solar Energy Device	https://www.aztaxes.gov/Home
Substance Abuse Counselor	http://azbbhe.us/node/3
Surety	https://ptl.az.gov/app/doilookup/
Surplus Line Broker	https://ptl.az.gov/app/doilookup/
Teacher, Elem/Secondary/Special Ed	https://oacis.azed.gov/PublicOACIS/NormalPages/Educators.aspx
Telemarketing Firm	http://apps.azsos.gov/scripts/nph-TS_Search_engine.exe
Timbering	https://www.aztaxes.gov/Home
Timeshare Public Report/Condo Seller	http://services.azre.gov/publicdatabase/Default.aspx
Tobacco Product Distributor	https://www.aztaxes.gov/Home
Transporting/Towing Company	https://www.aztaxes.gov/Home
Travel Agent, Limited	https://ptl.az.gov/app/doilookup/
Trust Company	http://azdfi.gov/Consumers/Licensees/default.asp
Trust Div of Chartered Financial Inst	http://azdfi.gov/Consumers/Licensees/default.asp
Vendor	https://www.aztaxes.gov/Home
Veterinary Medicine/Surgery	http://archivevetboard.az.gov/licdirnew/licenseeSearch.aspx
Veterinary Premise (Hospital)	http://archivevetboard.az.gov/licdirnew/licenseeSearch.aspx
Veterinary Technician	http://archivevetboard.az.gov/licdirnew/licenseeSearch.aspx
Waste Water Collect'n/Treat't/Constr'n	http://legacy.azdeq.gov/databases/opcertsearch.html
Waste Water Facility Operator	http://legacy.azdeq.gov/databases/opcertsearch.html
Water Distribution System Operator	http://legacy.azdeq.gov/databases/opcertsearch.html
Water Quality Certification	http://legacy.azdeq.gov/databases/opcertsearch.html
Weighmaster, Public	www.ncwm.net/certificates
Weights/Measures Rep/Svc Agency	www.ncwm.net/certificates
Well Drilling Firm	www.azwater.gov/DrillersList/

State and Local Courts

About Arizona Courts: The **Superior Court** is the court of general jurisdiction and acts as an appellate court for Justice and Municipal courts. The Superior Court hears felony, misdemeanor (if not heard elsewhere), civil, property cases of $1,000 or more, eviction, probate, estate, divorce and naturalization issues.

Justice Courts oversee civil lawsuits where the amount in dispute is $10,000 or less, landlord and tenant controversies, small claims cases and a full range of civil and criminal traffic offenses, including DUIs. Justices of the peace also resolve other types of misdemeanor allegations (e.g. shoplifting, writing bad checks, violating restraining orders)

Municipal Courts may also be known as City or Magistrate Courts. These courts hear misdemeanor or civil traffic cases where no serious injuries occur as well as violations of city ordinances. They do not hear civil lawsuits between citizens.

Civil cases between $5,000 and $10,000 may be filed at either Justice Courts or Superior Courts. Preliminary felonies can be heard at either the Superior Court of Justice Courts, but not at the Municipal Courts. Justice Courts and Municipal Courts generally have separate jurisdiction based on case types as indicated in the text herein.
The web page for the Arizona Judicial Branch is www.azcourts.gov.

Appellate Courts: The page at www.azcourts.gov gives access to Appellate opinions and summaries.

About Court Online Access

There is no single source of statewide access but a near statewide system exists. However, the **Public Access to Court Case Information** online system provided by **Administrative Office of the Courts (AOC)** contains information about court cases for a **majority of the courts (153 of 180)** in Arizona. The system includes many Municipal Courts. But courts not covered include certain courts in the counties with the highest populations: Pima, Yavapai and Maricopa counties. Information provided includes detailed case information (i.e., case type, charges, filing and disposition dates), the parties in the case (not including victims and witnesses), and the court mailing address and location.

To perform searches, go to https://apps.supremecourt.az.gov/publicaccess/. Please note the site has a strong disclaimer which states in part "...not all cases from a participating court may be included....information should not be used as a substitute for a thorough background search of official public records..."

Local Ordinance Violations Removed from Online Arizona Court Records

Since 2015, local ordinance violations heard by the limited jurisdiction courts **(such as Muni Courts and Justice courts)** are no longer displayed on this online system and on the bulk data feeds. However, the cases will still show but without the local charge. Therefore, if there is a question about specific cases, the user must perform further research to verify the partial web information onsite against official court information filed at the court of record.

County Sites Not Part of the Site Mentioned Above:

Maricopa County

All Superior Courts   www.clerkofcourt.maricopa.gov/
Public access for both civil and criminal docket is free at www.superiorcourt.maricopa.gov/docket/index.asp. Case file docket can be printed. Family and probate case information can also be searched here. Search by first and last name, by business name.or by case #r. Case document images not shown.
All Justice Courts   http://justicecourts.maricopa.gov/Locations/index.aspx
Access court index free on the countywide site t http://justicecourts.maricopa.gov/FindACase/index.aspx. Can show incomplete dockets, also expired data.

Pima County

Superior Court   www.agave.cosc.pima.gov/
Civil: Online access to superior court records is free at www.agave.cosc.pima.gov/PublicDocs/. Search by name, business name, or by case number.
Pima County Consolidated Justice Court   www.jp.pima.gov/
Civil & Criminal: Online access is free at www.jp.pima.gov/casesearch/hmuver.aspx. You can search docket information for civil, criminal or traffic cases by name, docket or citation number. This site does not include the other Justice Courts in this county. This site does not include the other Justice Courts in this county. The system shows the month and year, but not day of birth. It costs $3.00 to obtain the complete DOB.

Yavapai County

Prescott Justice Court   http://courts.yavapai.us/prescottjc/
Access to City and Justice court docket indcesis free at http://71.216.160.127/csp/pcc/csp1.csp.

Recorders, Assessors, and Other Sites of Note

About Arizona Recording Offices: 15 counties, 16 recording offices (the Navajo Nation Recorder is the 16th office and covers northern parts of Apache and Navajo Counties). Recording officers are the County Recorder. Recordings are usually placed in a general Grantor/Grantee index. Federal and state tax liens on personal property of businesses are filed with the Secretary of State. Federal and state tax liens on individuals are filed with the County Recorder.

About Tax Liens: Federal and state tax liens on personal property of businesses are filed with the Secretary of State. Federal and state tax liens on individuals are filed with the County Recorder.

Online Access

All counties provide an online search to recorded documents and tax assessor information. The Navajo Nation does not provide online access. There is one notable vendor offering free access to county recorders' public documents for Apache, Cochise, Graham, Greenlee, LaPaz, Navajo, and Santa Cruz Counties. See www.thecountyrecorder.com.

County Sites:

Apache County   *Recorded Documents Records*   www.co.apache.az.us/Recorder/   Access to the recorder is free at www.thecountyrecorder.com/Disclaimer.aspx?jsEnabled=1. Index goes back to 1985. Images not online. Since January, 2014 the Recorder's Office returns the recorded Plats & Surveys to the Submitter and will not store the original document(s).
Property, Taxation Records   Access the assessor's property records for free at http://eagleweb.assessor.co.apache.az.us/assessor/web/. Also, the Treasurer's Office records are at www.co.apache.az.us/eagletreasurer/. Access assessor search page free at www.co.apache.az.us/parcelsearch/parcelsearch.aspx.

Cochise County   *Recorded Documents Records*   https://www.cochise.az.gov/recorder/home   Access the recorder office document search site free at www.thecountyrecorder.com/Disclaimer.aspx?jsEnabled=1. Index goes back to 1985.
Property, Taxation Records   Access the treasurer's back tax list free at https://www.cochise.az.gov/treasurer/back-tax-lien-information.. Also, access to GIS/mapping for free at https://www.cochise.az.gov/information-technology/gis.

Coconino County *Recorded Documents Records* www.coconino.az.gov/index.aspx?nid=319 Access the recorder system free at http://eaglerecorder.coconino.az.gov/recorder/web/. Documents are $1.00 to print; images back to 3/1999. Computer indexing from 1/1983 to present. For official or certified copies or inquiries on documents prior to 1983 please contact office at 928-679-7850 or 800-793-6181.
Property, Taxation Records Search assessor data at http://assessor.coconino.az.gov/assessor/web/. Also, access to parcel viewer free at https://gismaps.coconino.az.gov/parcelviewer/. Must register to create and print reports for properties free of charge.

Gila County *Recorded Documents Records* www.gilacountyaz.gov/government/recorder/index.php Access to grantor/grantee index from EagleWeb for free at http://recorder.gilacountyaz.gov/recorder/web/. Records back to 2/2/85.
Property, Taxation Records Search assessor property data and sales free at http://gis.gilacountyaz.gov/parcelweb/. Also, access to GIS/mapping free at www.gilacountyaz.gov/government/assessor/maps_and_record_surveys.php.

Graham County *Recorded Documents Records* www.graham.az.gov/county-recorder/ Access to recorder records is at www.thecountyrecorder.com/Disclaimer.aspx?jsEnabled=1. Index goes back to 1982, unofficial images go back to 1981.
Property, Taxation Records Access the assessor database of property and assessments free at http://72.165.8.69/PropertyInfo/ParcelSearch.aspx.

Greenlee County *Recorded Documents Records* www.co.greenlee.az.us/recorder/ Access to recorder records is free at www.thecountyrecorder.com/Disclaimer.aspx?jsEnabled=1. Indexes back to 1974, unofficial images back to 1974.
Property, Taxation Records Search treasurer's tax lien sale list free at www.co.greenlee.az.us/treasurer/taxlien.pdf.

La Paz County *Recorded Documents Records* www.co.la-paz.az.us/Recorder.html Access to the recorder documents at www.thecountyrecorder.com/Disclaimer.aspx?jsEnabled=1. Index back to 1984.
Property, Taxation Records Access to property records for free at http://publicrecords.lapazassessor.com/assessor/web/.

Maricopa County *Recorded Documents Records* http://recorder.maricopa.gov Access to images of documents for free at http://recorder.maricopa.gov/recdocdata/.
Property, Taxation Records Assessor database is at http://mcassessor.maricopa.gov/. Also, perform tax appeal lookups at SBOE site at www.sboe.state.az.us/cgi-bin/name_lookup.pl. Search treasurers tax data and parcels by number free at http://treasurer.maricopa.gov/.

Mohave County *Recorded Documents Records* https://www.mohavecounty.us/ContentPage.aspx?id=129 Access the Recorder's System free (to view documents, $58.00 monthly fee) at http://eagleweb.co.mohave.az.us/recorder/web/login.jsp. Records from 1/1/1970 to present. Registration-password required; sign-up with Recorder Dept at x4701.
Property, Taxation Records Property sales history back to 2000 free at www.mohavecounty.us/ContentPage.aspx?id=111&cid=869. Also, the treasurer's tax sale parcel search is at https://eagletreas.mohavecounty.us/treasurer/web/.

Navajo County *Recorded Documents Records* www.navajocountyaz.gov/Departments/Recorder Access to the recorder's database at www.thecountyrecorder.com/Disclaimer.aspx?jsEnabled=1. Index goes back to 1989; unofficial images to 1995.
Property, Taxation Records Access property assessor database free at www.navajocountyaz.gov/Departments/Assessor.

Pima County *Recorded Documents Records* https://www.recorder.pima.gov/ Access to records for free at https://www.recorder.pima.gov/PublicDocServices/Search. Records available from 1/14/1985 to present. Records prior to 1/14/1985 have not been digitally indexed.
Property, Taxation Records Records on the Pima County Tax Assessor database are free at www.asr.co.pima.az.us/links/frm_AdvancedSearch_v2.aspx?search=Parcel. A name/parcel/property tax appeals may be performed free on the SBOE site at www.sboe.state.az.us/cgi-bin/name_lookup.pl.

Pinal County *Recorded Documents Records* http://pinalcountyaz.gov/Recorder/Pages/Recorder.aspx Access to the recorder's index is free at http://pinalcountyaz.gov/recorder/Pages/DocumentSearch.aspx.
Property, Taxation Records Search the assessor's property tax database free at http://pinalcountyaz.gov/ASSESSOR/Pages/ParcelSearch.aspx. Also, access to the county treasurer's database free at https://treasurer.pinalcountyaz.gov/ParcelInquiry/.

Santa Cruz County *Recorded Documents Records* www.co.santa-cruz.az.us/287/Recorder Access to the recorder's database of indices is free at www.thecountyrecorder.com/Disclaimer.aspx?jsEnabled=1. Index back to 1986.
Property, Taxation Records Access County Assessor data free at http://gis.santacruzcountyaz.gov/asr/index.html.

Yavapai County *Recorded Documents Records* www.yavapai.us/recorder/ Access to the recording office Eagle Web database is free at http://eweb.co.yavapai.az.us/recorder/web/. Records from 1976 to present; images from 1976 to present.
Property, Taxation Records Assessor and land records on County GIS database are free at http://gis.yavapai.us/v4/.

Yuma County *Recorded Documents Records* www.yumacountyaz.gov/government/recorder Access to records for free at http://recorder.yumacountyaz.gov/recorder/web/. Records go back to 9/1/1993.
Property, Taxation Records Access county assessment sales data free at http://treasurer.yumacountyaz.gov/treasurer/web/login.jsp.

Arkansas

Capital: Little Rock
             Pulaski County
Time Zone: CST
Population: 2,978,204
# of Counties: 75

Useful State Links

Website: **http://portal.arkansas.gov/**
Governor: **http://governor.arkansas.gov**
Attorney General: **www.ag.state.ar.us**
State Archives: **www.ark-ives.com**
State Statutes and Codes: **www.lexisnexis.com/hottopics/arcode/Default.asp**
Legislative Bill Search: **http://leginfo.legislature.ca.gov/faces/codes.xhtml**
Unclaimed Funds: **https://www.ark.org/auditor/unclprop/index.php/search/searchCrit**

State Public Record Agencies

Criminal Records

Arkansas State Police, Identification Bureau, https://www.ark.org/criminal/index.php   Online access available to only employers or their agents (with written consent on file), and professional licensing boards. A subscriber account with the Information Network of Arkansas (INA) is required, a $95 annual fee is imposed. The search fee is $22.00. Searches are conducted by name. Search results includes registered sex offenders. Accounts must maintain the signed release documents in-house for three years. Visit https://www.ark.org/subscribe/index.php for an excellent overview of all record types available. Or call 501-324-8900. Results show felony and misdemeanor conviction record, any pending Arkansas felony arrests within the last three years, and whether the person is a registered sex offender or is required to be registered.

Sexual Offender Registry

Arkansas Crime Information Center, Sexual Offender Registry, http://acic.org/citizens/Pages/sexOffenderInfo.aspx   Searching is available at https://www.ark.org/offender-search/index.php. Search by name or location (county). Includes Level 3 and Level 4 offenders. One may request email and phone notifications of updates of offender addresses. You can subscribe for notifications on as many addresses as you like and agency will notify you if an offender moves into the specified radius of the address submitted.   *Other Options:* Download the SOR data at https://www.ark.org/Registration/so_bulk.php. Fee is $.10 per record. For questions call 877-727-3468.

Incarceration Records

Arkansas Department of Correction, Records Supervisor, http://adc.arkansas.gov/   The online access at http://adc.arkansas.gov/inmate_info/index.php has many search criteria capabilities. This file is updated weekly.

Corporation, Fictitious Name, LLC, Partnerships (LP, LLP LLLP, Foreign)

Secretary of State, Business & Commercial Service Division, www.sos.arkansas.gov/BCS/Pages/default.aspx   The Internet site permits free searching of many types of business entity records at www.sos.arkansas.gov/BCS/Pages/default.aspx#bcsonlineservices. More extensive record searching is available in a fee-based format from Arkansas.gov. There is annual subscription is $95.00; other record services are available. The site also provides Franchise Tax filings, with both batch and single request services. Also, search securities companies registered with the state at www.securities.arkansas.gov/star/portal/arasd/portal.aspx. *Other Options:* Subscribers can download lists for $.10 per record with a $10.00 minimum, or obtain bulk downloads for $2000 per month. Visit www.arkansas.gov/services/list/category/ina-account-services; other record services are available.

Trademarks/Servicemarks

Secretary of State, Trademarks Section, www.sos.arkansas.gov/BCS/Pages/trademarkServiceMark.aspx Searching is available at no fee at www.sos.arkansas.gov/corps/trademk/index.php. Search by name, owner, city, or filing number. Search via email at corprequest@sos.arkansas.gov *Other Options:* Records can be provided in bulk for $.50 per page. Call 501-682-3409 or visit website for details.

Uniform Commercial Code, Federal Tax Liens

UCC Division - Commercial Svcs, Secretary of State, www.sos.arkansas.gov/BCS/Pages/uniformCommercialCodeServices.aspx Subscribers of Arkansas.gov can search by file number or debtor name; subscription fees and search fees involved. See www.sos.arkansas.gov/aboutOffice/Pages/SoSOnlineServices.aspx for subscription details. *Other Options:* A download of UCC data is available via Arkansas.gov to subscribers. Fee is $2,000.00 per month for weekly, bi-weekly or monthly downloads.

Vital Records

Arkansas Department of Health, Division of Vital Records, www.healthy.arkansas.gov/programsServices/certificatesVitalRecords/Pages/default.aspx Orders can be placed via a state designated vendor. Go to www.vitalchek.com. Extra fees are involved. *Other Options:* Research projects require the approval of the director.

Workers' Compensation Records

Workers Compensation Commission, Operations/Compliance, www.awcc.state.ar.us To perform an online claim search, one must be a subscriber to Arkansas.gov. Records are from May 1, 1997 forward. There is an annual $95 subscriber fee. Each record request is $3.50; if more than 20 are ordered in one month, the fee is $2.50 each request over 20. For more information, visit www.awcc.state.ar.us/electron.html OR https://www.ark.org/subscribe/index.php. *Other Options:* Subscribers to t Arkansas.gov can obtain a bulk download s for a one-time $5000 fee then $100 per month. Visit www.arkansas.gov/sub_services.php. Annual subscription is $95.00; other record services are available.

Driver Records

Department of Driver Services, Driving Records Division, www.dfa.arkansas.gov/offices/driverServices/Pages/default.aspx Access is available through Arkansas.gov. The system offers both batch and interactive service. The system is only available to INA subscribers who have statutory rights to the data. The record fee is $10.00 for Insurance record or $13.00 for Commercial record. Visit www.arkansas.gov/services/list/category/ina-account-services. The annual subscription fee is $95.00, other record services are available. AR drivers may purchase their own record, to view and print, online at https://www.ark.org/personal_tvr/index.php. The same fees apply. The date the DL was issued is required with name, DOB, DL#, and partial SSN. Medical Cert Information on CDL drivers is provided on both the manually processed and electronic version of the Commercial driving record, but not the Insurance Record. *Other Options:* Driver Watch is a available to subscribers who have statutory rights to the data The program allows firms to monitor the driving record status of their employees and have the system notify them of a change in driving status.

Vehicle Ownership & Registration

Office of Motor Vehicles, MV Title Records, www.dfa.arkansas.gov/offices/motorVehicle/Pages/default.aspx Approved, DPPA compliant accounts may access records online by VIN, plate, or title number. The fee is $1.50. Name searches and certificated documents may be ordered. For further info, go to www.arkansas.gov/services/list/category/ina-account-services. There is a $95 annual subscription fee, other records are also available. *Other Options:* The bulk purchase of records, except for recall or statistical purposes, is prohibited.

Voter Registration, Campaign Finance, PAC, Lobbyists

Secretary of State, Voter Services, www.sos.arkansas.gov/elections/Pages/default.aspx Search one's voter registration information at https://www.voterview.ar-nova.org/VoterView/RegistrantSearch.do. Name and DOB required. A financial disclosure search for all election related entities, including lobbyists, PACs and candidates, is found at www.sos.arkansas.gov/elections/Pages/financialDisclosure.aspx. *Other Options:* The voter registration CD as described above is available for $2.50. If bulk data is requested on other formats, including paper, the cost is considerably higher.

Occupational Licensing Boards

These licenses are all searchable at
www.healthy.arkansas.gov/programsServices/hsLicensingRegulation/HealthFacilityServices/Pages/ProviderLists.aspx

Abortion Clinics	Health Facility	Laboratory
Alcohol/Drug Abuse Program	HMO	Medicare Certified Facility
Birthing Center	Home Health Agency	Permanent Cosmetic/Tattoo Artist
Clinics, Health	Hospice Facility	Radiologic Technician
Gas Fitter/Trainee	Hospital Maintenance Plumber	Rehabilitation Facilities

The Rest:

Accountant-CPA	https://www.ark.org/asbpa_olr/app/search.html
Acupuncturist	www.asbart.org/licensees.htm
Asbestos Inspector/Planner	https://www.adeq.state.ar.us/home/databases.aspx

Asbestos Training Provider/Removal Provider... https://www.adeq.state.ar.us/home/databases.aspx
Athletic Trainer (Sports)...................................... www.aratb.org/search.php
Athletic Trainer/Agent (Health) .... www.aratb.org/search.php
Attorney .... https://attorneyinfo.aoc.arkansas.gov/info/attorney_search/info/attorney/attorneysearch.aspx
Auctioneer.. https://www.ark.org/aalb/licensing/index.php/roster
Audiologist .... www.arkansas.gov/abespa_licv/app/enter.html
Bank.. www.sos.arkansas.gov/corps/search_all.php
Barber College/Instructor.................................... www.arbarber.com/barber_college_list.html
Catastrophe Adjuster .... https://a5w.insurance.arkansas.gov/CatastropheAdjusters/View_Registration.a5w
Cemetery, Perpetual Care................................... www.securities.arkansas.gov/contact/default.asp?DeptID=27
Check Casher .... www.asbca.org/collect_search/
Check Seller/Money Services.............................. www.securities.arkansas.gov/page/339/money-services
Chemical, List 1, Wholesale Distr .... www.ark.org/asbp/roster/index.php
Child Care Provider .... https://dhs.arkansas.gov/dccece/cclas/FacilitySearch.aspx
Collection Agency/ Collector/Mgr .... www.asbca.org/collect_search/
Contractor http://aclb2.arkansas.gov/clbsearch.php
Counselor, Professional....................................... www.accessarkansas.org/abec/search.php
Court Interpreters... https://courts.arkansas.gov/directories/court-interpreters-registry
Court Mediator .... https://courts.arkansas.gov/administration/adr/certified-mediators
Dental Assistant... https://www.ark.org/asbde_darenewal/app/roster.html
Dental Hygienist... www.dentalboard.arkansas.gov/rdhroster/search.php
Dentist.. www.dentalboard.arkansas.gov/ddsroster/search.php
Drugs, Legend, Wholesale Distr .... www.ark.org/asbp/roster/index.php
Electrician Journeyman/ Master/Contractor .... https://www.ark.org/labor/electrician/search.php
Embalmer/Embalmer Apprentice......................... www.arkansas.gov/fdemb/index.html
Emergency Medical Tech/Paramedic.................. https://aremslicense.adh.arkansas.gov/lookup/
Employee Leasing Firm .... https://sbs-ar.naic.org/Lion-Web/jsp/sbsreports/AgentLookup.jsp
Engineer/Engineer in Training .... www.arkansas.gov/pels/search/search.php
Farm Mutual Aid Assoc.. https://sbs-ar.naic.org/Lion-Web/jsp/sbsreports/AgentLookup.jsp
Fire Equipment Inspector/Repairer..................... www.arfireprotection.org/roster/index.html
Fire Extinguisher Sprinkler Inspector................. www.arfireprotection.org/roster/index.html
Forester .... https://www.ark.org/foresters_rsearch/app/enter.html
Funeral Director/Apprentice................................ www.arkansas.gov/fdemb/index.html
Funeral Home/Crematory .... www.arkansas.gov/fdemb/index.html
Funeral Transport .... www.arkansas.gov/fdemb/index.html
Geologist.. www.pgboard.ar.gov/directory.html
Ginseng Dealers .... http://plantboard.arkansas.gov/PlantIndustry/Pages/LicenseHolders.aspx
Hearing Disciplinary Action/Enforcement .... www.arec.arkansas.gov/enforcement/Pages/DisciplinaryAction.aspx
HMO Medicare.. https://sbs-ar.naic.org/Lion-Web/jsp/sbsreports/AgentLookup.jsp
Home Inspector .... www.ahib.org/
Homebuilders.. http://aclb2.arkansas.gov/clbsearch.php
Hospital Medical Service .... https://sbs-ar.naic.org/Lion-Web/jsp/sbsreports/AgentLookup.jsp
Insurance Agency... www.sos.arkansas.gov/corps/search_all.php
Insurance Company.. https://sbs-ar.naic.org/Lion-Web/jsp/sbsreports/AgentLookup.jsp
Insurance Sales Agent... https://a5w.insurance.arkansas.gov/AIDSearches/agent.a5w
Investment Advisor www.securities.arkansas.gov/page/337/securities
Landscape Contractors... http://plantboard.arkansas.gov/PlantIndustry/Pages/LicenseHolders.aspx
Lay Midwive/Apprintice.. www.healthy.arkansas.gov/programsServices/familyHealth/WomensHealth/Pages/LayMidwifery.aspx
Licensed Mold Investigator .... http://plantboard.arkansas.gov/PlantIndustry/Pages/LicenseHolders.aspx
Life Care .... https://sbs-ar.naic.org/Lion-Web/jsp/sbsreports/AgentLookup.jsp
Lobbyist .... www.sos.arkansas.gov/filing_search/index.php/filing/search/new
Marriage & Family Therapist .... www.accessarkansas.org/abec/search.php
Massage Therapy Tech/Masseur/M'use .... www.arkansasmassagetherapy.com/Roster.htm
Medicaid Provider .... https://www.medicaid.state.ar.us/provider/logon.aspx
Medical Corporation... www.armedicalboard.org/public/verify/default.aspx

Midwife	https://www.ark.org/arsbn/statuswatch/index.php/nurse/search/new
Mortgage Loan Broker/Company	www.securities.arkansas.gov/page/355/finra-broker-check
Motor Club	https://sbs-ar.naic.org/Lion-Web/jsp/sbsreports/AgentLookup.jsp
Motor Vehicle Dealer/Distributor	http://amvc.arkansas.gov/licensee.html
Motor Vehicle Mfg/Rep, New	http://amvc.arkansas.gov/licensee.html
Moxibustion Provider	www.asbart.org/licensees.htm
Multiple Employee Welfare Assoc	https://sbs-ar.naic.org/Lion-Web/jsp/sbsreports/AgentLookup.jsp
Notary Public	http://bcs.sos.arkansas.gov/NotarySearch
Nurse Anesthetist	https://www.ark.org/arsbn/statuswatch/index.php/nurse/search/new
Nurse-LPN	https://www.ark.org/arsbn/statuswatch/index.php/nurse/search/new
Nursery Dealers	http://plantboard.arkansas.gov/PlantIndustry/Pages/LicenseHolders.aspx
Nurseryman	http://plantboard.arkansas.gov/PlantIndustry/Pages/LicenseHolders.aspx
Nursing Home Facility	www.arhspa.org/agency_decisions.html
Occupational Therapist/Assistant	www.armedicalboard.org/public/verify/default.aspx
Optometrist	www.arbo.org/find_opt.php
Oriental Medicine	www.asbart.org/licensees.htm
Orthotist/Orthotist Assistant	www.healthy.arkansas.gov/opp/verification/index.php
Osteopathic Physician	www.armedicalboard.org/public/verify/default.aspx
P & C Company	http://insurance.arkansas.gov/pclh/pcweb.asp
Pedorthist	www.healthy.arkansas.gov/opp/verification/index.php
Pharmacist/Intern/Technician	www.ark.org/asbp/roster/index.php
Pharmacy, Hospital/Institution	www.ark.org/asbp/roster/index.php
Pharmacy, Specialty	www.ark.org/asbp/roster/index.php
Pharmacy-In-State or Out-of-State, Retail	www.ark.org/asbp/roster/index.php
Physical Therapist	www.arptb.org/ptroster/search.php
Physician/Medical Doctor/Surgeon/Assistant	www.armedicalboard.org/public/verify/default.aspx
Podiatrist	www.podiatricmedicine.arkansas.gov/licensing
Political Action Committee	www.sos.arkansas.gov/filing_search/index.php/filing/search/new
Pre-Need Seller	https://sbs-ar.naic.org/Lion-Web/jsp/sbsreports/AgentLookup.jsp
Prosthetist/Assistant	www.healthy.arkansas.gov/opp/verification/index.php
Psychologist/Examiner	https://www.ark.org/psych_lic_ver/index.php
Pump Installer	www.arkansas.gov/awwcc/
Real Estate Agent/Broker/Sales	https://www.ark.org/arec_renewals/index.php/search/agent
Real Estate Schools	www.arec.arkansas.gov/licensing/Pages/EducationProviders.aspx
Reins Intermediary	https://sbs-ar.naic.org/Lion-Web/jsp/sbsreports/AgentLookup.jsp
Reinsurer	https://sbs-ar.naic.org/Lion-Web/jsp/sbsreports/AgentLookup.jsp
Respiratory Care Practitioner	www.armedicalboard.org/public/verify/default.aspx
School Principal/Admin/Super	https://adeaels.arkansas.gov/AelsWeb/Search.aspx
Securities Agent/Broker/Dealer	www.securities.arkansas.gov/page/337/securities
Securities Exemption	www.securities.arkansas.gov/star/portal/arasd/portal.aspx
Septic Tank Cleaner	www.healthy.arkansas.gov/Pages/certsLicensesPermits.aspx
Service Contract Provider	https://sbs-ar.naic.org/Lion-Web/jsp/sbsreports/AgentLookup.jsp
Social Worker	www.accessarkansas.org/swlb/search/index.html
Social Worker Disciplinary Action	www.accessarkansas.org/swlb/pdfs/Disciplinary_Action_Descending_Order.pdf
Solid Waste Facility Operator	https://www.adeq.state.ar.us/home/databases.aspx
Speech Pathologist	www.arkansas.gov/abespa_licv/app/enter.html
Supplier of Legend Device/Med Gas	www.ark.org/asbp/roster/index.php
Supplier of Med Equipment	www.ark.org/asbp/roster/index.php
Surplus Lines Insurer	https://sbs-ar.naic.org/Lion-Web/jsp/sbsreports/AgentLookup.jsp
Surveyor, Land/Surveyor-in-Training	www.arkansas.gov/pels/search/search.php
Teacher	https://adeaels.arkansas.gov/AelsWeb/Search.aspx
Waste Water Plant Operator	https://www.adeq.state.ar.us/water/enforcement/wwl/
Water Supply Operator	www.healthy.arkansas.gov/Pages/certsLicensesPermits.aspx
Water Well Driller	www.arkansas.gov/awwcc/

State and Local Courts

About Arkansas Courts: Circuit Courts are the courts of general jurisdiction and are arranged in 28 circuits. Circuit Courts consist of five subject matter divisions: criminal, civil, probate, domestic relations, and juvenile. A Circuit Clerk handles the records and recordings, however some counties have a County Clerk that handles probate.

District Courts exercise countywide jurisdiction over misdemeanor cases, preliminary felony cases, and civil cases in matters of less than $5,000, including small claims.

There are **State District Courts** and **Local District Courts**, depending on which agency pays the judge (state or local). Local District courts hear civil cases with a limit of $5,000. State District Courts hear civil cases with a limit of $25,000. An additional group of counties will have their Local District Courts become State District Courts in 2017. The City Courts operate in smaller communities where District Courts do not exist and exercise citywide jurisdiction.

The web page for the Arkansas Judiciary is https://courts.arkansas.gov/

Appellate Courts: Search Supreme and Appellate Opinions and Disciplinary Decisions at https://courts.arkansas.gov/opinions-and-disciplinary-decisions.

About Court Online Access

The AOC has a growing number of Courts participating in a limited online docket look-up by name or case number called CourtConnect at https://caseinfo.aoc.arkansas.gov and you will be re-directed to a very lengthy URL

There are **two levels** of record searching; **one is thorough, one is very limited.** The Web mentioned above has lists of counties/courts with full and with limited data - but this is list not always up-to-date. One may use the Help tab for what appears to be updated information, but this list is also very iffy at times. The best suggestion is to perform sample searches.

Thorough Level System

The **Thorough level** has approx. 55 Circuit Courts, plus District Courts from 9 counties, and 2 Counties with Probate only participating. The data provided is fairly detailed information that goes back in time a good number of years. The system provides links to case images for some records. Cases available include civil, criminal, domestic relations, and probate. If you do not provide a DOB, there is no DOB provided. In the coming year more counties will be added to the system.

Lower Level System

The **Lower level** has approx. 19 Circuit Courts participating, but these courts provide very limited data online - all cases are not included. What is shown for these courts is only the data as provided on paper coversheets to the Administrative Office of the Courts and the participating Circuit Courts may not report all case types on paper. The searches are not onsite equivalent. If you do not provide a DOB, there is no DOB provided.

Circuit Courts (Counties) on Thorough Level System:

Baxter	Dallas	Lincoln	Ouachita	Sharp
Benton	Faulkner	Little River	Phillips	St. Francis
Boone	Franklin	Logan	Pike	Union
Calhoun	Garland	Lonoke	Poinsett	Van Buren
Carroll	Grant	Madison	Polk(Probate only)	Washington
Clark	Hempstead (Probate	Marion	Pope	White
Cleveland	only)	Miller	Prairie	Woodruff
Columbia	Hot Spring	Mississippi	Pulaski	Yell
Conway	Howard	Monroe	Saline	
Craighead	Jefferson	Montgomery	Scott	
Crawford	Johnson	Nevada	Searcy	
Cross	Lee	Newton	Sevier	

District Courts (Counties) on Thorough Level System:

Crawford	Hot Spring - Malvern Dept.	Pulaski County and Little Rock Dept.
Faulkner - Conway Dept.	Independence - Batesville Dept.	White - Searcy Dept.
Garland	Polk	
Grant	Pulaski	

Circuit Courts (Counties) on Lower Level System:

Ashley	Bradley	Chicot	Clay	Cleburne

Crittenden	Fulton	Izard	Lawrence	Sebastian
Desha	Greene	Jackson	Perry	Stone
Drew	Independence	Lafayette	Randolph	

County Sites Not Listed Above:

Arkansas County
Circuit Court - Northern District in Stuttgart   www.arcocircuitclerk.com/
Civil: Click on document search from the home page. Although this service leads to Title Searcher, the court has placed court records on this system. There is a monthly fee of $70.00 for unlimited searching and a $3.00 fee to view an image plus an $.25 per name searched. Images are available from 2005, the docket index goes back to 1996. Includes both Circuit Courts in this county. *Criminal:* same
Circuit Court - Southern District in DeWitt   www.arcocircuitclerk.com/
Civil: Click on document search from the home page. Although this service leads to Title Searcher, the court has placed court records on this system. There is a monthly fee of $70.00 for unlimited searching and a $3.00 fee to view an image. Images are available from 2005, the docket index goes back to 1996. *Criminal:* same

Ashley County
Circuit Court
Civil: A pay system is available for court records and images from 05/07/2003 to present at http://titlesearcher.com/. *Criminal:* same

Bradley County
Circuit Court
Civil: Two systems. A pay system is available for court records and images from 11/01/2010 to present at http://titlesearcher.com/. Fee is $70.00 per month.   *Criminal:* same

Cleburne County
Circuit Court
Civil: A pay system is available for court records and images from 01/01/2003 to present at http://titlesearcher.com/. Fee is $70.00 per month. *Criminal:* same

Craighead County
Western District Circuit Court - Jonesboro   www.craigheadcounty.org/circuit-court-clerk/
Civil: Judgments (not court records) may be viewed online for a fee. Cost of search is $5.95, each printed page is $.50. See https://tapestry.fidlar.com/Tapestry2/Search.aspx. *Criminal:* same
Eastern District Circuit Court - Lake City
Civil: Judgments (not court records) may be viewed online for a fee. Cost of search is $5.95, cost of each printed page is $.50. See https://tapestry.fidlar.com/Tapestry2/Search.aspx.
Western Division District Court - Jonesboro   www.craigheadcounty.org/craighead-county-district-court/
Civil: Judgments (not court records) may be viewed online for a fee. Cost of search is $5.95, cost of each printed page is $.50. See https://tapestry.fidlar.com/Tapestry2/Search.aspx.

Cross County
Circuit Court   www.crosscountyar.org/page.php?id=2
Civil: Judgments (not court records) may be viewed online for a fee. Cost of search is $5.95, cost of each printed page is $.50. See https://tapestry.fidlar.com/Tapestry2/Search.aspx.
Wynne District Court
Civil: Judgments (not court records) may be viewed online for a fee. Cost of search is $5.95, cost of each printed page is $.50. See https://tapestry.fidlar.com/Tapestry2/Search.aspx.

Desha County
Circuit Court   http://deshacounty.arkansas.gov/officials
Civil: A pay system is available for court records and images from 2008 to present at http://titlesearcher.com/. Fee is $70.00 per month. Judgments (not court records) may be viewed online for a fee. Cost of search is $5.95, cost of each printed page is $.50. See https://tapestry.fidlar.com/Tapestry2/Search.aspx.   *Criminal:* A pay system is available for court records and images from 2008 to present at http://titlesearcher.com/. Fee is $70.00 per month.
Dumas Local District Court
Civil: Judgments (not court records) may be viewed online for a fee. Cost of search is $5.95, cost of each printed page is $.50. See https://tapestry.fidlar.com/Tapestry2/Search.aspx.

Independence County
Circuit Court   www.independencecircuitclerk.com/
Civil: Online access to recorded judgments (not court records) available by subscription; see www.independencecircuitclerk.com/node/6 for details. *Civil & Criminal:* A pay system is available for court records from 2/2/1981 and images 11/1/2010 to present at http://titlesearcher.com/. Fee is $70.00 per month.

Little River County

Circuit Court   www.littlerivercounty.org/index.php/county-officials
Civil: Judgments (not court records) may be viewed online for a fee. Cost of search is $5.95, cost of each printed page is $.50. See https://tapestry.fidlar.com/Tapestry2/Search.aspx.
Local District Court
Civil: Judgments (not court records) may be viewed online for a fee. Cost of search is $5.95, cost of each printed page is $.50. See https://tapestry.fidlar.com/Tapestry2/Search.aspx.

Miller County
Circuit Court   http://millercountyar.org/county-circuit-clerk.html
Civil: Online access to circuit court dockets by subscription through RecordsUSA.com. Credit card, username and password is required; choose either monthly or per-use plan. Visit the website for sign-up or call Rob at 888-633-4748 x17 for information. Judgments (not court records) may be viewed online for a fee. Cost of search is $5.95, cost of each printed page is $.50. See https://tapestry.fidlar.com/Tapestry2/Search.aspx. *Criminal:* Online access to circuit court dockets by subscription through RecordsUSA.com. Credit card, username and password is required; choose either monthly or per-use plan. Visit the website for sign-up or call Rob at 888-633-4748 x17 for information.
Texarkana District Court - City Division   http://arkansas.txkusa.org/departments/district-court/
Civil: Judgments (not court records) may be viewed online for a fee. Cost of search is $5.95, cost of each printed page is $.50. See https://tapestry.fidlar.com/Tapestry2/Search.aspx. *Criminal:*

Montgomery County
Circuit Court
Civil: Judgments (not court records) may be viewed online for a fee. Cost of search is $5.95, cost of each printed page is $.50. See https://tapestry.fidlar.com/Tapestry2/Search.aspx.
Local District Court
Civil: Judgments (not court records) may be viewed online for a fee. Cost of search is $5.95, cost of each printed page is $.50. See https://tapestry.fidlar.com/Tapestry2/Search.aspx. *Criminal:*

Saline County
Circuit Court   www.salinecounty.org/
Civil: A court records index search is free at https://www.ark.org/grs/app/saline but fees are changed for record copies. Annual subscription account is $75.00 and the cost per record is $1.00. *Criminal:* same

Sebastian County
Circuit Court - Greenwood Division   www.sebastiancountyar.gov/Departments/Circuit-Clerk
Civil: Two systems are accessible from www.sebastiancountyar.gov/Departments/Circuit-Clerk/Resources/Circuit-Clerk-Inquiry. One system is up to June 2015, the other after June 2015. *Criminal:* same
Circuit Court - Fort Smith   www.sebastiancountyar.gov/Departments/Circuit-Clerk
Civil: Two systems are accessible from www.sebastiancountyar.gov/Departments/Circuit-Clerk/Resources/Circuit-Clerk-Inquiry. One system is up to June 2015, the other after June 2015. *Criminal:* same
Greenwood State District Court   www.sebastiancountyar.gov/Courts/Greenwood-District-Court
Civil: The index to civil records, including Small Claims from 1998 forward is at www.sebastiancountyar.gov/Courts/Greenwood-District-Accees is from www.sebastiancountyar.gov/Courts/Greenwood-District-Court/GWDC-Access.   *Criminal:* The index to criminal records from 1985 forward is at www.sebastiancountyar.gov/Courts/Greenwood-District-Court/GWDC-Access.

Fort Smith State District Court   www.districtcourtfortsmith.org
Civil: Access court records free at www.districtcourtfortsmith.org/Online%20Services.html. *Criminal:* same

Sevier County
Circuit & District Court   www.seviercountyar.com/index.php/county-officials/county-circuit-clerk.html
Civil: Judgments (not court records) may be viewed online for a fee. Cost of search is $5.95, cost of each printed page is $.50. See https://tapestry.fidlar.com/Tapestry2/Search.aspx.

Stone County
Circuit Court
Civi & Criminal: A pay system is available for court records and images from 01/17/2012 to present at http://titlesearcher.com/. Fee is $70.00 per month.

Union County
State District Court
Civil: Judgments (not court records) may be viewed online for a fee. Cost of search is $5.95, cost of each printed page is $.50. See https://tapestry.fidlar.com/Tapestry2/Search.aspx. *Criminal:*

Washington County
Circuit Court   www.co.washington.ar.us/index.aspx?page=59
Civil: Search pre-1973 court indices free at www.co.washington.ar.us/ArchiveSearch/CourtRecordSearch.asp.   *Criminal:* Pre-1933 criminal court indices free at www.co.washington.ar.us/ArchiveSearch/CourtRecordSearch.asp. Note that these cases are very old.

Recorders, Assessors, and Other Sites of Note

About Arkansas Recording Offices: 75 counties, 85 recording offices. The recording officer is the Clerk of Circuit Court who is Ex Officio Recorder. 10 counties have 2 recording offices - Arkansas, Carroll, Clay, Craighead, Franklin, Logan, Mississippi, Prairie, Sebastian, and Yell.

About Tax Liens: Federal tax liens on personal property of businesses are filed with the Secretary of State. Other federal and all state tax liens are filed with the Circuit Clerk.

Online Access

Recorded Documents

There is no statewide access to recorded documents, but data is accessible from at least 35 individual counties.

Assessor & Property Data

There is no statewide access to assessor or tax collector data; however, all counties (with the exception of Lincoln) cooperate with (sell data to) at least one commercial vendor. These vendors are listed below.

- Free and subscription data for at least 67 counties is at www.arcountydata.com. This site also offers a free public search of Assessor/Real Estate (40 counties) and Tax Collector/Tax Records (64 counties) records. This vendor also owns the site at www.countyservice.net.

- Both a subscription and a free limited service to access various property records are available at www.datascoutpro.com/ for all 75 counties. Five counties on this system also offer access to recorded documents. The same company has a second web page at https://www.actdatascout.com/

County Sites:

Arkansas County (Both Districts) *Recorded Documents* www.arcocircuitclerk.com/   Access to online document searches at www.arcocircuitclerk.com/node/3. Fees are $70.00 monthly for unlimited access or $3.00 per viewed image + $.25 per name searched. Can also call 866-604-3673 for more information. Deeds and indexes valid from 1995 to present. Images are viewable from 2005 to present.
Property, Taxation Records   A free search to Assessor and Tax Collector records is at www.arcountydata.com/. A more robust subscription service is also offered.

Ashley County *Recorded Documents*   Access to records for a fee at http://titlesearcher.com/. Deeds and indexes from 12/1/69 to present; images from 2009 to present.
Property, Taxation Records   A free search to Tax Collector records is at www.arcountydata.com/. A more robust subscription service is also offered. Search Assessor and tax collector records free at https://www.actdatascout.com/ or https://www.datascoutpro.com/ (same company).

Baxter County *Recorded Documents* www.baxtercounty.org/clerk.php   Access to indexes and images for a fee at www.titlesearcher.com/countyInfo.php?cnum=AR4. Deeds and indexes from 1/1/1981 to present; images are viewable from 1/1/2007 to present.
Property, Taxation Records   A free search to Assessor and Tax Collector records is at www.arcountydata.com/. A more robust subscription service is also offered. Search Assessor and tax collector records free at https://www.actdatascout.com/ or https://www.datascoutpro.com/ (same company).

Benton County *Recorded Documents*
http://bentoncountyar.gov/BCHome.aspx?info=Agency/info/CIRInfo.html&page=/Agency/CircuitClerk/default.aspx   Circuit court data for a fee at https://gov.propertyinfo.com/AR-Benton/#. Fee is $60.00 per month per account or can do a non subscribers payment of $.50 per page. Also, for a fee access land records at http://etitlesearch.com/. Can do a name search, fees vary depending on the usage.
Property, Taxation Records   A free search to Assessor and Tax Collector records is at www.arcountydata.com/. A more robust subscription service is also offered. Also, access to GIS/mapping for free at http://bentoncountyar.gov/BCHome.aspx.

Boone County *Recorded Documents* http://boonecountyar.com/circuit_clerk   Land records are at http://portal.propertyinfo.com/government. Name searches available; choose from $45.00 monthly subscription or per click account.
Property, Taxation Records   A free search to Assessor and Tax Collector records is at www.arcountydata.com/. A more robust subscription service is also offered.. Search Assessor and tax collector records free at https://www.actdatascout.com/ or https://www.datascoutpro.com/ (same company).

Bradley County *Recorded Documents*   Access to indexes and images for a fee at www.titlesearcher.com/countyInfo.php?cnum=S2. Deeds valid from 4/28/2009 to present, indexes and images valid from 1/1/2010 to present.
Property, Taxation Records   A free search to Assessor and Tax Collector records is at www.arcountydata.com/. A more robust subscription service is also offered.

Calhoun County *Property, Taxation Records*   A free search to Assessor and Tax Collector records is at www.arcountydata.com/. A more robust subscription service is also offered..

Carroll County (Both Districts) *Property, Taxation Records*   A free search to Tax Collector records is at www.arcountydata.com/. A more robust subscription service is also offered. Search Assessor and tax collector records free at https://www.actdatascout.com/ or https://www.datascoutpro.com/ (same company).

Chicot County *Property, Taxation Records*   A free search to Assessor and Tax Collector records is at www.arcountydata.com/. A more robust subscription service is also offered.

Clark County *Property, Taxation Records*   A free search to Tax Collector records is at www.arcountydata.com/. A more robust subscription service is also offered. Search Assessor and tax collector records free at https://www.actdatascout.com/ or https://www.datascoutpro.com/ (same company).

Clay County (Both Districts) *Property, Taxation Records*   A free search to Assessor and Tax Collector records is at www.arcountydata.com/. A more robust subscription service is also offered.

Cleburne County *Recorded Documents*   Access to indexes and images for a fee at www.titlesearcher.com/countyInfo.php?cnum=AR4. Indexes and images (liens) valid from 12/1/2012 to present.
Property, Taxation Records   A free search to Tax Collector records is at www.arcountydata.com/. A more robust subscription service is also offered. Search Assessor and tax collector records free at https://www.actdatascout.com/ or https://www.datascoutpro.com/ (same company).

Cleveland County *Property, Taxation Records*   A free search to Tax Collector records is at www.arcountydata.com/. A more robust subscription service is also offered.

Columbia County *Property, Taxation Records*   A free search to Assessor and Tax Collector records is at www.arcountydata.com/. A more robust subscription service is also offered.

Conway County *Property, Taxation Records*   Search Assessor and tax collector records free at https://www.actdatascout.com/ or https://www.datascoutpro.com/ (same company).

Craighead County *Recorded Documents*   www.craigheadcounty.org/circuit-court-clerk/   The county works with https://tapestry.fidlar.com/Tapestry2/Default.aspx for record access. Base fee is $5.95 per search and $.50 per print image. You can pay as you go using a credit or pre-pay using a subscription. Also, one may purchase a software program Laredo (www.fidlar.com/laredo.aspx) with extensive search features. Contact the county for details and pricing.
Property, Taxation Records   A free search to Assessor records is at www.arcountydata.com/. A more robust subscription service is also offered. Search Assessor and tax collector records free at https://www.actdatascout.com/ or https://www.datascoutpro.com/ (same company).

Crawford County *Recorded Documents*   www.crawford-county.org/circuit_clerk.aspx   Also, access to indexes and images for a fee at www.titlesearcher.com/countyInfo.php?cnum=AR4. Deeds and indexes valid from 1/1/1984 to present. Images are viewable from 1/1/2005 to present.
Property, Taxation Records   A free search to Tax Collector records is at www.arcountydata.com/. A more robust subscription service is also offered. Search Assessor and tax collector records free at https://www.actdatascout.com/ or https://www.datascoutpro.com/ (same company).

Crittenden County *Recorded Documents*   http://crittenden.ark.org/   The county works with https://tapestry.fidlar.com/Tapestry2/Default.aspx for record access. Base fee is $5.95 per search and $.50 per print image. You can pay as you go using a credit or pre-pay using a subscription. Also, one may purchase a software program Laredo (www.fidlar.com/laredo.aspx) with extensive search features. Contact the county for details and pricing.
Property, Taxation Records   A free search to Assessor and Tax Collector records is at www.arcountydata.com/. A more robust subscription service is also offered. Search Assessor and tax collector records free at https://www.actdatascout.com/ or https://www.datascoutpro.com/ (same company).

Cross County *Recorded Documents*   www.crosscountyar.org/page.php?id=2   The county works with https://tapestry.fidlar.com/Tapestry2/Default.aspx for record access. Base fee is $5.95 per search and $.50 per print image. You can pay as you go using a credit or pre-pay using a subscription. Also, one may purchase a software program Laredo (www.fidlar.com/laredo.aspx) with extensive search features. Contact the county for details and pricing.
Property, Taxation Records   A free search to Tax Collector records is at www.arcountydata.com/. A more robust subscription service is also offered. Search Assessor and tax collector records free at https://www.actdatascout.com/ or https://www.datascoutpro.com/ (same company).

Dallas County *Recorded Documents*   Also, access to indexes and images for a fee at www.titlesearcher.com/countyInfo.php?cnum=AR4. Deeds, indexes and images valid from 1/1/1998 to present.
Property, Taxation Records   A free search to Assessor and Tax Collector records is at www.arcountydata.com/. A more robust subscription service is also offered.

Desha County *Recorded Documents*   http://deshacounty.arkansas.gov/index   The county works with https://tapestry.fidlar.com/Tapestry2/Default.aspx for record access. Base fee is $5.95 per search and $.50 per print image. You can pay as you go using a credit or pre-pay using a subscription. Also, one may purchase a software program Laredo (www.fidlar.com/laredo.aspx) with extensive search features. Contact the county for details and pricing.

Property, Taxation Records A free search to Assessor and Tax Collector records is at www.arcountydata.com/. A more robust subscription service is also offered.

Drew County ***Property, Taxation Records*** Search Assessor and tax collector records free at https://www.actdatascout.com/ or https://www.datascoutpro.com/ (same company).

Faulkner County ***Property, Taxation Records*** A free search to Assessor and Tax Collector records is at www.arcountydata.com/. A more robust subscription service is also offered. This county participates two vendors - www.countyservice.net/ for property tax and ownership; https://www.ark.org/propertytax/faulkner/index.php for tax payments.

Franklin County (Both Districts) ***Property, Taxation Records*** A free search to Assessor and Tax Collector records is at www.arcountydata.com/. A more robust subscription service is also offered. Search Assessor and tax collector records free at https://www.actdatascout.com/ or https://www.datascoutpro.com/ (same company).

Fulton County ***Property, Taxation Records*** A free search to Assessor and Tax Collector records is at www.arcountydata.com/. A more robust subscription service is also offered.

Garland County ***Recorded Documents*** https://gov.propertyinfo.com/AR-Garland/ Access to document images and index information for a fee at https://gov.propertyinfo.com/AR-Garland/. Fee is $60.00 per month per account. Registration is free.
Property, Taxation Records Search Assessor and tax collector records free at https://www.actdatascout.com/ or https://www.datascoutpro.com/ (same company).

Grant County ***Property, Taxation Records*** A free search to Assessor and Tax Collector records is at www.arcountydata.com/. A more robust subscription service is also offered.

Greene County ***Property, Taxation Records*** A free search to Assessor and Tax Collector records is at www.arcountydata.com/. A more robust subscription service is also offered.

Hempstead County ***Recorded Records Records*** www.hempsteadcountyar.com/circuitclerk.html For a fee access land records at http://etitlesearch.com/. Name searches available. Fees vary depending on the usage.
Property, Taxation Records A free search to Assessor records is at www.arcountydata.com/. A more robust subscription service is also offered. Search Assessor and tax collector records free at https://www.actdatascout.com/ or https://www.datascoutpro.com/ (same company).

Hot Spring County ***Property, Taxation Records*** Search Assessor and tax collector records free at https://www.actdatascout.com/ or https://www.datascoutpro.com/ (same company).

Howard County ***Property, Taxation Records*** Access to tax payment records for free at http://howardcountytaxcollection.com/search/. Need name or parcel number. A free search to Assessor records is at www.arcountydata.com/. A more robust subscription service is also offered. Search Assessor and tax collector records free at https://www.actdatascout.com/ or https://www.datascoutpro.com/ (same company).

Independence County ***Recorded Documents*** www.titlesearcher.com Access to indexes and images for a fee at www.titlesearcher.com/countyInfo.php?cnum=AR4. Deeds and indexes valid from 1/3/1967 to present. Images are viewable from 11/1/2010 to present.
Property, Taxation Records A free search to Assessor records is at www.arcountydata.com/. A more robust subscription service is also offered. Search Assessor and tax collector records free at https://www.actdatascout.com/ or https://www.datascoutpro.com/ (same company).

Izard County ***Property, Taxation Records*** A free search to Assessor and Tax Collector records is at www.arcountydata.com/. A more robust subscription service is also offered. See www.countyservice.net/disabled?c=Izard for GIS and property tax and ownership. Search Assessor and tax collector records free at https://www.actdatascout.com/ or https://www.datascoutpro.com/ (same company).

Jackson County ***Property, Taxation Records*** A free search to Assessor records is at www.arcountydata.com/. A more robust subscription service is also offered. Search Assessor and tax collector records free at https://www.actdatascout.com/ or https://www.datascoutpro.com/ (same company).

Jefferson County ***Property, Taxation Records*** A free search to Assessor records is at www.arcountydata.com/. A more robust subscription service is also offered. Search Assessor and tax collector records free at https://www.actdatascout.com/ or https://www.datascoutpro.com/ (same company).

Johnson County ***Property, Taxation Records*** A free search to Assessor and Tax Collector records is at www.arcountydata.com/. A more robust subscription service is also offered.

Lafayette County ***Recorded Documents*** www.lafayettecounty.arkansas.gov/index.php The county works with https://tapestry.fidlar.com/Tapestry2/Default.aspx for record access. Base fee is $5.95 per search and $.50 per print image. You can pay as you go using a credit or pre-pay using a subscription. Also, one may purchase a software program Laredo (www.fidlar.com/laredo.aspx) with extensive search features. Contact the county for details and pricing.
Property, Taxation Records Search Assessor and tax collector records free at https://www.actdatascout.com/ or https://www.datascoutpro.com/ (same company).

Lawrence County *Property, Taxation Records*   A free search to Tax Collector records is at www.arcountydata.com/. A more robust subscription service is also offered Search Assessor and tax collector records free at https://www.actdatascout.com/ or https://www.datascoutpro.com/ (same company).

Lee County *Property, Taxation Records*   A free search to Assessor and Tax Collector records is at www.arcountydata.com/. A more robust subscription service is also offered.

Lincoln County *Property, Taxation Records*   Search Assessor and tax collector records free at https://www.actdatascout.com/ or https://www.datascoutpro.com/ (same company).

Little River County *Recorded Documents* www.littlerivercounty.org/index.php/county-officials   The county works with https://tapestry.fidlar.com/Tapestry2/Default.aspx for record access. Base fee is $5.95 per search and $.50 per print image. You can pay as you go using a credit or pre-pay using a subscription. Also, one may purchase a software program Laredo (www.fidlar.com/laredo.aspx) with extensive search features. Contact the county for details and pricing.
Property, Taxation Records   A free search to Tax Collector records is at www.arcountydata.com/. A more robust subscription service is also offered. Search Assessor and tax collector records free at https://www.actdatascout.com/ or https://www.datascoutpro.com/ (same company).

Logan County (Both Districts) *Property, Taxation Records*   A free search to Assessor and Tax Collector records is at www.arcountydata.com/. A more robust subscription service is also offered.

Lonoke County *Recorded Documents* www.lonokecircuitclerk.com/   Access to court record indexes for free at https://caseinfo.aoc.arkansas.gov/cconnect/PROD/public/ck_public_qry_main.cp_main_idx.
Property, Taxation Records   A free search to Assessor and Tax Collector records is at www.arcountydata.com/. A more robust subscription service is also offered.

Madison County *Recorded Documents* www.madisoncircuitclerk.com   Access to indexes and images for a fee at www.titlesearcher.com/countyInfo.php?cnum=AR4. Deeds valid from 1/1/1977 to present. Indexes and images are viewable from 1//1/1995 to present. Fee is $70.00 per month unlimted access or pay as you go for $.25 per search and $3.00 per viewed image.
Property, Taxation Records   A free search to Tax Collector records is at www.arcountydata.com/. A more robust subscription service is also offered. Search Assessor and tax collector records free at https://www.actdatascout.com/ or https://www.datascoutpro.com/ (same company).

Marion County *Property, Taxation Records*   A free search to Assessor and Tax Collector records is at www.arcountydata.com/. A more robust subscription service is also offered. Search Assessor and tax collector records free at https://www.actdatascout.com/ or https://www.datascoutpro.com/ (same company).

Miller County *Recorded Documents* www.millercountyar.org/county-circuit-clerk.html   The county works with https://tapestry.fidlar.com/Tapestry2/Default.aspx for record access. Base fee is $5.95 per search and $.50 per print image. You can pay as you go using a credit or pre-pay using a subscription. Also, one may purchase a software program Laredo (www.fidlar.com/laredo.aspx) with extensive search features. Contact the county for details and pricing.
Property, Taxation Records   A free search to Tax Collector records is at www.arcountydata.com/. A more robust subscription service is also offered. Search Assessor and tax collector records free at https://www.actdatascout.com/ or https://www.datascoutpro.com/ (same company).

Monroe County *Property, Taxation Records*   A free search to Assessor and Tax Collector records is at www.arcountydata.com/. A more robust subscription service is also offered.

Montgomery County *Recorded Documents*   The county works with https://tapestry.fidlar.com/Tapestry2/Default.aspx for record access. Base fee is $5.95 per search and $.50 per print image. You can pay as you go using a credit or pre-pay using a subscription. Also, one may purchase a software program Laredo (www.fidlar.com/laredo.aspx) with extensive search features. Contact the county for details and pricing.
Property, Taxation Records   A free search to Tax Collector records is at www.arcountydata.com/. A more robust subscription service is also offered. Search Assessor and tax collector records free at https://www.actdatascout.com/ or https://www.datascoutpro.com/ (same company).

Nevada County *Property, Taxation Records*   A free search to Tax Collector records is at www.arcountydata.com/. A more robust subscription service is also offered. Search Assessor and tax collector records free at https://www.actdatascout.com/ or https://www.datascoutpro.com/ (same company).

Newton County *Property, Taxation Records*   A free search to Assessor and Tax Collector records is at www.arcountydata.com/. A more robust subscription service is also offered.

Ouachita County *Property, Taxation Records*   A free search to Tax Collector records is at www.arcountydata.com/. A more robust subscription service is also offered. Search Assessor and tax collector records free at https://www.actdatascout.com/ or https://www.datascoutpro.com/ (same company).

Perry County *Property, Taxation Records*   A free search to Tax Collector records is at www.arcountydata.com/. A more robust subscription service is also offered. Search Assessor and tax collector records free at https://www.actdatascout.com/ or https://www.datascoutpro.com/ (same company).

Phillips County *Property, Taxation Records* This county participates with one or more of the vendors listed in the Summary Section. Search Assessor and tax collector records free at https://www.actdatascout.com/ or https://www.datascoutpro.com/ (same company).

Pike County *Property, Taxation Records* A free search to Assessor and Tax Collector records is at www.arcountydata.com/. A more robust subscription service is also offered. Search Assessor and tax collector records free at https://www.actdatascout.com/ or https://www.datascoutpro.com/ (same company).

Poinsett County *Recorded Documents* www.poinsettcounty.us/county-officials.htm The county works with https://tapestry.fidlar.com/Tapestry2/Default.aspx for record access. Base fee is $5.95 per search and $.50 per print image. You can pay as you go using a credit or pre-pay using a subscription. Also, one may purchase a software program Laredo (www.fidlar.com/laredo.aspx) with extensive search features. Contact the county for details and pricing.
Property, Taxation Records A free search to Assessor and Tax Collector records is at www.arcountydata.com/. A more robust subscription service is also offered.

Polk County *Recorded Documents* Online access to land records is by subscription through RecordsUSA.com. Images are available. Visit the website for sign-up or call Rob at 888-633-4748 x17 for info.
Property, Taxation Records Access property tax for free at www.deltacomputersystems.com/MS/MS01/INDEX.HTML.A free search to Tax Collector records is at www.arcountydata.com/. A more robust subscription service is also offered. Search Assessor and tax collector records free at https://www.actdatascout.com/ or https://www.datascoutpro.com/ (same company).

Pope County *Property, Taxation Records* A free search to Assessor and Tax Collector records is at www.arcountydata.com/. A more robust subscription service is also offered.

Prairie County (Both Districts) *Property, Taxation Records* A free search to Tax Collector records is at www.arcountydata.com/. A more robust subscription service is also offered. Search Assessor and tax collector records free at https://www.actdatascout.com/ or https://www.datascoutpro.com/ (same company).

Pulaski County *Recorded Documents, Voter Registration, Marriage Records* www.pulaskiclerk.com/ Free access is at http://69.152.184.8/search/.
Property, Taxation Records A free search to Assessor records is at www.arcountydata.com/. A more robust subscription service is also offered.

Randolph County *Property, Taxation Records* A free search to Tax Collector records is at www.arcountydata.com/. A more robust subscription service is also offered.

Saline County *Recorded Documents* www.salinecounty.org/circuit_clerk The county works with https://tapestry.fidlar.com/Tapestry2/Default.aspx for record access. Base fee is $5.95 per search and $.50 per print image. You can pay as you go using a credit or pre-pay using a subscription. Also, one may purchase a software program Laredo (www.fidlar.com/laredo.aspx) with extensive search features. Contact the county for details and pricing.
Property, Taxation Records Search tax collector records free at https://www.ark.org/propertytax/saline/index.php. A free search to Assessor and Tax Collector records is at www.arcountydata.com/. A more robust subscription service is also offered.

Scott County *Property, Taxation Records* TA free search to Assessor and Tax Collector records is at www.arcountydata.com/. A more robust subscription service is also offered.

Searcy County *Recorded Documents* Access to indexes and images for a fee at www.titlesearcher.com/countyInfo.php?cnum=AR4. Deeds valid from 1/3/2001 to present. Indexes and images are viewable from 11/7/2011 to present.
Property, Taxation Records Access to GIS/mapping for free at http://tascgis.maps.arcgis.com/apps/webappviewer/index.html?id=d6f94d03ab3346e08111fb919af16cea.

Sebastian County (Both Districts) *Recorded Documents* www.sebastiancountyar.gov/Departments/County-Clerk The county works with https://tapestry.fidlar.com/Tapestry2/Default.aspx for record access. Base fee is $5.95 per search and $.50 per print image. You can pay as you go using a credit or pre-pay using a subscription. Also, one may purchase a software program Laredo (www.fidlar.com/laredo.aspx) with extensive search features. Contact the county for details and pricing.
Property, Taxation Records Access to GIS/mapping for free at http://tascgis.maps.arcgis.com/apps/webappviewer/index.html. A free search to Assessor and Tax Collector records is at www.arcountydata.com/. A more robust subscription service is also offered.

Sevier County *Recorded Documents* www.seviercountyar.com/ The county works with https://tapestry.fidlar.com/Tapestry2/Default.aspx for record access. Base fee is $5.95 per search and $.50 per print image. You can pay as you go using a credit or pre-pay using a subscription. Also, one may purchase a software program Laredo (www.fidlar.com/laredo.aspx) with extensive search features. Contact the county for details and pricing.
Property, Taxation Records A free search to Tax Collector records is at www.arcountydata.com/. A more robust subscription service is also offered. Search Assessor and tax collector records free at https://www.actdatascout.com/ or https://www.datascoutpro.com/ (same company).

Sharp County *Property, Taxation Records* A free search to Assessor and Tax Collector records is at www.arcountydata.com/. A more robust subscription service is also offered.

St. Francis County *Property, Taxation Records*   A free search to Assessor and Tax Collector records is at www.arcountydata.com/. A more robust subscription service is also offered.

Stone County *Recorded Documents*   Access to indexes and images for a fee at www.titlesearcher.com/countyInfo.php?cnum=AR4. Deeds valid from 5/1/1972 to present. Indexes and images are viewable from 1/17/2012 to present.
Property, Taxation Records   A free search to Assessor and Tax Collector records is at www.arcountydata.com/. A more robust subscription service is also offered.

Union County *Recorded Documents*   www.unioncountyar.com/circuit-clerk.html   The county works with https://tapestry.fidlar.com/Tapestry2/Default.aspx for record access. Base fee is $5.95 per search and $.50 per print image. You can pay as you go using a credit or pre-pay using a subscription. Also, one may purchase a software program Laredo (www.fidlar.com/laredo.aspx) with extensive search features. Contact the county for details and pricing.
Property, Taxation Records   Search Assessor and tax collector records free at https://www.actdatascout.com/ or https://www.datascoutpro.com/ (same company).

Van Buren County *Recorded Documents*   www.vanburencountycircuitclerk.com/   Access to indexes and images for a fee at www.titlesearcher.com/countyInfo.php?cnum=AR4. Deeds valid from 1878 to present. Indexes are viewable from 11/15/1971 to present. Images vewable-Deeds, 1878, Misc-1946 and Mortgages-1972.
Property, Taxation Records   A free search to Assessor and Tax Collector records is at www.arcountydata.com/. A more robust subscription service is also offered.

Washington County *Recorded Documents, Vital Records Records*   www.co.washington.ar.us/index.aspx?page=59   Search Clerk's indexed records at http://esearch.co.washington.ar.us/external/User/Login.aspx?ReturnUrl=%2fexternal. Also, search court record archives at www.co.washington.ar.us/ArchiveSearch/CourtRecordSearch.asp.
Property, Taxation Records   Search property records for free at www.co.washington.ar.us/PropertySearch/MapSearch.asp. Also, search assessor real estate and property tax records free at www.countyservice.net. A free search to Tax Collector records is at www.arcountydata.com/. A more robust subscription service is also offered. Search Assessor and tax collector records free at https://www.actdatascout.com/ or https://www.datascoutpro.com/ (same company).

White County *Property, Taxation Records*   A free search to Assessor and Tax Collector records is at www.arcountydata.com/. A more robust subscription service is also offered. Search Assessor and tax collector records free at https://www.actdatascout.com/ or https://www.datascoutpro.com/ (same company).

Woodruff County *Property, Taxation Records*   A free search to Tax Collector records is at www.arcountydata.com/. A more robust subscription service is also offered.

Yell County (Both Districts) *Property, Taxation Records*   A free search to Assessor and Tax Collector records is at www.arcountydata.com/. A more robust subscription service is also offered.

California

Capital: Sacramento
             Sacramento County
Time Zone: PST
Population: 39,144,818
# of Counties: 58

Useful State Links

Website: **www.ca.gov/**
Governor: **https://www.gov.ca.gov/home.php**
Attorney General: **http://oag.ca.gov**
State Archives: **www.sos.ca.gov/archives/archives/**
State Statutes and Codes: **http://leginfo.legislature.ca.gov/faces/codes.xhtml**
Legislative Bill Search: **www.leginfo.ca.gov/bilinfo.html**
Unclaimed Funds: **www.sco.ca.gov/upd_msg.html**

State Public Record Agencies

Sexual Offender Registry

Department of Justice, Sexual Offender Program,   www.meganslaw.ca.gov/   The web page offers online searching by a sex offender's specific name or by geographic location including ZIP Code, county or within a predetermined radius of a selected address, park, or school. The site provides access to information on nearly 53,000 persons required to register in California as sex offenders. Specific home addresses are displayed on more than 41,000 offenders. This online search CANNOT be used for pre-employment purposes unless the applicant is applying for a job that deals specifically with vulnerable people.

Incarceration Records

Dept of Corrections, Corrections & Rehabilitation ID Unit,   www.cdcr.ca.gov/   Identification Unit / Inmate Locator is free at http://inmatelocator.cdcr.ca.gov/. Either the name or Inmate Number must be provided. A name search provides the Inmate Number and the name of the facility.

Corporation, LLC, LP, LLP

Secretary of State, Information Retrieval/Certification Unit,   www.sos.ca.gov/business/   The website at http://kepler.sos.ca.gov/ offers access to business entity information including corporation, LLC, and LP. Information available includes status, file number, date of registration, jurisdiction and agent for service of process. The file is updated weekly. Also one may search securities companies registered with the state at www.dbo.ca.gov/CalEASI/CalEASI.asp. (This is a different agency).   *Other Options:* Information regarding bulk lists and other forms of records access is available by contacting the Sec. of State's Information Technology Division at 916-653-8905.

Trademarks/Servicemarks

Secretary of State, Trademark Unit,   www.sos.ca.gov/business-programs/ts/   One may request a search via email to tm@sos.ca.gov.   *Other Options:* Microfilm is sold on monthly basis with year contract.

Uniform Commercial Code, Federal & State Tax Liens

Business Programs Division, UCC Section - Sec. of State,   www.sos.ca.gov/business-programs/ucc/   UCC Connect provides an online service at https://uccconnect.sos.ca.gov/acct/acct-login.asp to conduct a variety of inquiries and place orders for copies and debtor search certificates on records and submit UCC filings. Ongoing requesters can become subscribers. Fees are based on name inquires ($5.00 per name) and images viewed ($1.00).

Sales Tax Registrations

Board of Equalization, Sales and Use Tax Department,   www.boe.ca.gov   The Internet site provides a permit verification service at https://efile.boe.ca.gov/boewebservices/verification.jsp?action=SALES. Permit number is needed. System is open 5AM to midnight.   *Other Options:*

Lists, available for a fee, are sorted in a number of ways including CA Industry Code. For further information and fees, call the Technical Services Division at 916-445-5848

Death Records

State Department of Health Svcs, Office of Vital Records - MS 5103, www.cdph.ca.gov/certlic/birthdeathmar/Pages/default.aspx   Access death records 1940 thru 1997 at http://vitals.rootsweb.ancestry.com/ca/death/search.cgi.

Workers' Compensation Records

Division of Workers' Compensation, Headquarters, www.dir.ca.gov/dwc/dwc_home_page.htm   Members of the public may search the Division of Workers' Compensation's database for information related to active cases in the Adjudication Unit (ADJ). . This is an informational only. There is no name searching, and it is not in real time, but updated nightly.   Go to www.dir.ca.gov/dwc/eams/EAMS_PublicInformationSearch.htm.

Driver Records

Department of Motor Vehicles, Information Services Branch,   www.dmv.ca.gov   The Department offers online batch and interactive batch record requests through the Internet using Secure File Transfer (SFT). The fee is $2.00 per record. The system is available 24 hours, 7 days a week. For more information call 916-657-5582. A $10,000 one-time setup fee is required. Authorized Requester End-Users can obtain access to DMV records through an authorized Service Provider/Reseller. Service Provider Resellers or End Users who access direct must meet all DMV's programming, security, and technical requirements.   *Other Options:* Employers may monitor their drivers using the Pull Notice Program. The DMV informs the organization when there is activity on enrolled drivers. For more information visit the website at www.dmv.ca.gov/vehindustry/epn/epnformlist.htm.

Vehicle, Vessel Ownership & Registration

Department of Motor Vehicle, Office Information Services Branch,   www.dmv.ca.gov   24 hour online access is limited to certain Authorized Vendors. Requesters may not use data for direct marketing, solicitation, nor resell for those purposes. A bond of $50,000 is required and a $10,000 one-time permit fee is mandatory. Records are $2.00 ea. Both batch and interactive processing is offered via SFT. For additional information, contact Electronic Access Administration Section at 916-657-5582. There is a free online check at https://vfr.dmv.ca.gov/CISA/index.html. Must have plate number and either the PIN or last 5 digits of the VIN. See www.smogcheck.ca.gov/pubwebquery/Vehicle/PubTstQry.aspx for a Smog Test History. *Other Options:* California offers electronic delivery of registration information within special parameters. Release of information is denied for commercial marketing purposes.

Voter Registration, Campaign Finance, PACs, Lobbyists

Secretary of State, Elections Division,   www.sos.ca.gov/elections/   Cal-Access provides financial information supplied by state candidates, donors, lobbyists, and others. Records of campaign finance can be viewed at http://cal-access.sos.ca.gov/campaign/. Find data on PACs and major donors at http://cal-access.ss.ca.gov/Campaign/Committees/. To find persons spending $5,000 or more to influence legislation or administration see http://cal-access.ss.ca.gov/Lobbying/Payments/. Data on lobbyists is found at http://cal-access.ss.ca.gov/Lobbying/. *Other Options:* The state will sell CDs with all or portions of the statewide voter registration database for political or pre-approved purposes. Call for details.

HSET-GED Certificates

ETS - GED Records Center, 1430 N Street,   www.cde.ca.gov/ta/tg/gd/   Third parties are routed to set up an account at: http://exchange.parchment.com/ged-receiver-registration-page. Parchment verifies that they are who they say they are so that they can place orders on behalf of students. Parchment contacts the third party and provides training on the site for ordering. During this training any orders they have are placed. After this the third party can order on behalf of students.   They still must upload a consent form for each student during the process. See https://www.diplomasender.com/ for TASC.

Occupational Licensing Boards

These Contractor Licenses are all searchable at
https://www2.cslb.ca.gov/OnlineServices/CheckLicenseII/CheckLicense.aspx

Air Conditioning Contractor	Flooring/Floor Covering Contractor	Refrigeration Contractor
Building Contr, General-Class B	Glazier	Roofing Contractor
Cabinet/Millwork Contractor	Heating & Warm-Air Vent Contr	Sanitation System Contractor
Concrete Contractor/Company	Insulation/Acoustical Contractor	Sheet Metal Contractor
Contractor, Business/Individual	Landscaping Contractor	Solar Energy Contractor
Drywall Contractor	Masonry Contractor	Specialty Contractor-Class C
Earthwork/Paving Contractor	Ornamental Metal Contractor	Steel Contractor
Electrical Contr & Electric Sign Contr	Painting/Decorating Contractor	Swimming Pool Contractor
Elevator Installation Contractor	Parking/Highway Improvement Contr	Tile Contractor, Ceramic/Mosaic
Fencing Contractor	Plastering Contractor	Water Well Driller
Fire Protection	Plumber	

These licenses are all searchable at https://www.breeze.ca.gov/datamart/selSearchTypeCADCA.do

Barber Instructor/School	Esthetician	Physical Therapist/Assistant
Barber/Barber Shop/Apprentice	Manicurist	Podiatrist
Continuing Education Provider	Marriage & Family Therapist	Psychologist, Educational
Cosmetician/Cosmetologist	Nurse-RN	Psychologist/Assistant
Cosmetology School	Nursing Continued Edu Provider	Respiratory Care Practitioner
Cosmetology/Electrology Firm/Instr	Optometric Corporation	Social Worker, Clinical
Electrologist	Optometrist	Veterinarian/Technician/Veterinary Hospitals
Electrology School	Optometry Practice/Branch Office	

The Rest:

Accountant-CPA/Firm	www.dca.ca.gov/cba/consumers/lookup.shtml
Acupuncturist	www2.dca.ca.gov/pls/wllpub/wllqryna$lcev2.startup?p_qte_code=AC&p_qte_pgm_code=6500
Acupuncturist Board Actions	www.acupuncture.ca.gov/consumers/board_actions.shtml
Adoption Agency	http://ccld.ca.gov/PG3581.htm
Agricultural Engineer	www.bpelsg.ca.gov/consumers/lic_lookup.shtml
Alarm Firm/Employee/Mngr	www.bsis.ca.gov/forms_pubs/online_services/verify_license.shtml
Appraiser, Real Estate	www.orea.ca.gov/html/SearchAppraisers.asp
Apprentice Program, Skilled Labor	www.dir.ca.gov/databases/das/aigstart.asp
Architect	www.cab.ca.gov/consumers/license_verification.shtml
Asbestos Consultant/Surveillance	www.dir.ca.gov/databases/doshcaccsst/caccsst_query_1.html
Asbestos Contractor	www.dir.ca.gov/databases/doshacru/acrusearch.html
Asbestos Trainer	www.dir.ca.gov/databasedown.asp
Asbestos Worker/Trainee	www.dir.ca.gov/DOSH/ACRU/TP_AsbestosTrainingCertificates.html
Attorney	www.calbar.ca.gov/
Audiologist	www2.dca.ca.gov/pls/wllpub/wllqryna$lcev2.startup?p_qte_code=LIC&p_qte_pgm_code=7700
Automobile Dealer/Repair	www.bar.ca.gov/Consumer/Verify_License.html
Bank Agencies/Facility/Branches, Foreign	www.dbo.ca.gov/Licensees/search_directory.asp
Bank, State Chartered	www.dbo.ca.gov/Licensees/search_directory.asp
Bank, State Chartered, Industr'l	www.dbo.ca.gov/Licensees/search_directory.asp
Baton Training Facility/Instruct	www.bsis.ca.gov/forms_pubs/online_services/verify_license.shtml
Bedding Mfg/Renovator/Ret/Whlse	www.bearhfti.ca.gov/enforcement/lookup.shtml
Brake & Lamp Adjuster/Station	www.bar.ca.gov/Consumer/Verify_License.html
Business/Industrial Developm't Firm	www.dbo.ca.gov/Licensees/search_directory.asp
Car Washing/Polishing	https://www.dir.ca.gov/databases/dlselr/carwash.html
Care Facility for Chronically Ill	http://ccld.ca.gov/PG3581.htm
Care Facility, Children, Transitional	http://ccld.ca.gov/PG3581.htm
Cemetery, Cemetery Broker/Seller	www.cfb.ca.gov/consumer/lookup.shtml
Child Care Center	http://ccld.ca.gov/PG3581.htm
Chiropractic Corporation/Satellite/Referal Svc	www.chiro.ca.gov/consumers/lic_lookup.shtml
Chiropractor	www.chiro.ca.gov/consumers/lic_lookup.shtml
Clinic Pharmaceutical Permit	www.pharmacy.ca.gov/about/verify_lic.shtml
Colleges of Mortuary Science	www.cfb.ca.gov/consumer/funeral.shtml#info
Community Treatment Facility	http://ccld.ca.gov/PG3581.htm
Conscious Sedation Permit	www.dbc.ca.gov/verification/license_verification.shtml
Construction Permit, Excava'n/Shoring	www.dir.ca.gov/dosh/PermitHolder/PermitHolder.asp
Court Reporter/Shorthand Reporter	www2.dca.ca.gov/pls/wllpub/wllqryna$lcev2.startup?p_qte_code=CSR&p_qte_pgm_code=8100
Crane Operator	www.dir.ca.gov/databases/crane/cranesearch.html
Credit Union	www.dbo.ca.gov/Licensees/search_directory.asp
Cremated Remains Disposer	www.cfb.ca.gov/consumer/lookup.shtml
Crematory	www.cfb.ca.gov/consumer/lookup.shtml
Day Care, Adult/Child	http://ccld.ca.gov/PG3581.htm
Dental Anesthesia Permit	www.dbc.ca.gov/verification/license_verification.shtml
Dental Assistant/Hygienist	www.dbc.ca.gov/verification/license_verification.shtml

Dental Registered Provider .... www.dbc.ca.gov/verification/license_verification.shtml
Dentist.. www.dbc.ca.gov/verification/license_verification.shtml
Dentist Fictitious Name...................................... www.dbc.ca.gov/verification/license_verification.shtml
Diagnostic Radiologic Technology School .... www.cdph.ca.gov/certlic/radquip/Documents/X-raySchoolPassRates.pdf
Driving School/Instructor................................... http://dmv.ca.gov/portal/dmv/detail/portal/olinq2/welcome
Drug Wholesaler/Drug Room .... www.pharmacy.ca.gov/about/verify_lic.shtml
Electronic & Appliance Repair .... www.bearhfti.ca.gov/enforcement/lookup.shtml
Embalmer/Embalmer Apprentice....................... www.cfb.ca.gov/consumer/lookup.shtml
Engineer (various disciplines)............................ www.bpelsg.ca.gov/consumers/lic_lookup.shtml
Family Child Care Home.................................... http://ccld.ca.gov/PG3581.htm
Farm Labor Contractor .... https://permits.dir.ca.gov/FLC_External/CreateVerificationSearchForm.do
Firearm Permit.. www.bsis.ca.gov/forms_pubs/online_services/verify_license.shtml
Firearm Training Facility/Instr .... www.bsis.ca.gov/forms_pubs/online_services/verify_license.shtml
Foster Family Agency.. http://ccld.ca.gov/PG3581.htm
Funeral Director/Establishment .... www.cfb.ca.gov/consumer/lookup.shtml
Funerary Training Establ/Apprentice .... www.cfb.ca.gov/consumer/lookup.shtml
Furniture and Bedding Retailer.......................... www.bearhfti.ca.gov/enforcement/lookup.shtml
Furniture Mfg/Retailer/Whlse .... www.bearhfti.ca.gov/enforcement/lookup.shtml
Garment Manufacturer....................................... www.dir.ca.gov/databases/dlselr/Garmreg.html
Geologist/Geophysicist, Engineering................. www.bpelsg.ca.gov/consumers/lic_lookup.shtml
Group Home http://ccld.ca.gov/PG3581.htm
Guide Dog for the Blind Instructors .... www.guidedogboard.ca.gov/consumers/instructors_list.shtml
Guide Dog for the Blind Schools .... www.guidedogboard.ca.gov/consumers/school_list.shtml
Hearing Aid Dispenser...................................... www2.dca.ca.gov/pls/wllpub/wllqryna$lcev2.startup?p_qte_code=LIC&p_qte_pgm_code=7700
Hemodialysis Tech, Certified............................. http://cvl.cdph.ca.gov/SearchPage.aspx
Home Care Aide .... https://secure.dss.ca.gov/ccld/hcsregistry/About.aspx
Home Furnishings.. www.bearhfti.ca.gov/enforcement/lookup.shtml
Home Health Aide... http://cvl.cdph.ca.gov/SearchPage.aspx
Horse Racing (license type) .... www.chrb.ca.gov/licensing.html
Hospital Pharmaceutical Exemptee.................... www.pharmacy.ca.gov/about/verify_lic.shtml
Hydrogeologist.. www.bpelsg.ca.gov/consumers/lic_lookup.shtml
Hypodermic Needle & Syringe Dist .... www.pharmacy.ca.gov/about/verify_lic.shtml
Industrial Loan Company, Premium .... www.dbo.ca.gov/Licensees/search_directory.asp
Infant Center http://ccld.ca.gov/PG3581.htm
Insurance Adjuster.. www.insurance.ca.gov/license-status/index.cfm
Insurance Agent/Broker/Producer .... www.insurance.ca.gov/license-status/index.cfm
Insurance Company... www.insurance.ca.gov/license-status/index.cfm
Investment Advisor .... www.dbo.ca.gov/Licensees/licensee_search.asp
Land Surveyor-in-Training .... www.bpelsg.ca.gov/consumers/lic_lookup.shtml
Landscape Architect .... www.latc.ca.gov/consumers/search.shtml
Lawyer Referral Service .... www.calbar.ca.gov/Public/LawyerReferralServicesLRS.aspx
Legal Specialization Provider .... http://lawhelpca.org/
Lobbyist/Lobbying Firm/Employer .... http://cal-access.ss.ca.gov/Lobbying/
Locksmith/Locksmith Company.......................... www.bsis.ca.gov/forms_pubs/online_services/verify_license.shtml
Medical Evaluator .... www.dir.ca.gov/databases/dwc/qmestartnew.asp
Midwife... www.mbc.ca.gov/Breeze/License_Verification.aspx
Money Order Issuer .... www.dbo.ca.gov/Licensees/search_directory.asp
Notary Education Vendor .... http://notaryeducation.sos.ca.gov/
Notary Public .... www.sos.ca.gov/notary/notary-public-listing/
Nurse Assistant, Certified .... http://cvl.cdph.ca.gov/SearchPage.aspx
Nursing Home Administrator .... http://cvl.cdph.ca.gov/SearchPage.aspx
Occupational Therapist/Assistant....................... www2.dca.ca.gov/pls/wllpub/wllqryna$lcev2.startup?p_qte_code=OT&p_qte_pgm_code=1475
Optician, Dispensing... www.mbc.ca.gov/Breeze/License_Verification.aspx
Osteopath .... www.opsc.org/search/custom.asp?id=2062
Patrol Operator, Private..................................... www.bsis.ca.gov/forms_pubs/online_services/verify_license.shtml

Pesticide Applicator/Operator/Field Rep .... www.pestboard.ca.gov/license.shtml
Pharmaceutical Dist, Out-of-State .... www.pharmacy.ca.gov/about/verify_lic.shtml
Pharmaceutical Wholesale/Exemptee .... www.pharmacy.ca.gov/about/verify_lic.shtml
Pharmacist/Pharmacist Intern .... www.pharmacy.ca.gov/about/verify_lic.shtml
Pharmacy/Pharmacy Technician .... www.pharmacy.ca.gov/about/verify_lic.shtml
Photogrammetrist .... www.bpelsg.ca.gov/consumers/lic_lookup.shtml
Physician Assistant .... www.pac.ca.gov/forms_pubs/online_services/license_lookup.shtml
Physician/Medical Doctor/Surgeon .... www.mbc.ca.gov/Breeze/License_Verification.aspx
Premium Finance Company .... www.dbo.ca.gov/Licensees/search_directory.asp
Private Investigator .... www.bsis.ca.gov/forms_pubs/online_services/verify_license.shtml
Psychiatric Technician .... www.bvnpt.ca.gov/consumers/license_verification.shtml
Psychoanalyst, Research .... www.mbc.ca.gov/Breeze/License_Verification.aspx
Public Works Trainer .... www.dir.ca.gov/databases/das/pwaddrstart.asp
Real Estate Agent/Seller/Broker/Corp www2.dre.ca.gov/PublicASP/pplinfo.asp
Repossessor Agency/Mgr/Employee .... www.bsis.ca.gov/forms_pubs/online_services/verify_license.shtml
Representative (Banking) Foreign .... www.dbo.ca.gov/Licensees/search_directory.asp
Residential Care/Facility for Adult/Elderly http://ccld.ca.gov/PG3581.htm
Ringside Physicians .... www.dca.ca.gov/csac/forms_pubs/publications/ringside_physicians.shtml
Sanitizer of Home Furnishings .... www.bearhfti.ca.gov/enforcement/lookup.shtml
Savings & Loan Association .... www.dbo.ca.gov/Licensees/search_directory.asp
School Teacher, Elementary, Secondary .... https://educator.ctc.ca.gov/esales_enu/start.swe
Securities Broker/Dealer .... www.dbo.ca.gov/Licensees/licensee_search.asp
Security Guard .... www.bsis.ca.gov/forms_pubs/online_services/verify_license.shtml
Service Contract Seller, Appliance .... www.bearhfti.ca.gov/enforcement/lookup.shtml
Shelter, Temporary http://ccld.ca.gov/PG3581.htm
Smog Check Station/Technician .... www.bar.ca.gov/Consumer/Verify_License.html
Social Rehabilitation Facility http://ccld.ca.gov/PG3581.htm
Speech Pathologist Assistant/Audiologist Aide .. www2.dca.ca.gov/pls/wllpub/wllqryna$lcev2.startup?p_qte_code=LIC&p_qte_pgm_code=7700
Speech-Language Pathologist .... www2.dca.ca.gov/pls/wllpub/wllqryna$lcev2.startup?p_qte_code=LIC&p_qte_pgm_code=7700
Studio Teacher .... https://www.dir.ca.gov/databases/dlselr/studtch.html
Support Center, Adult http://ccld.ca.gov/PG3581.htm
Surgical Clinic Pharm, Nonprofit .... www.pharmacy.ca.gov/about/verify_lic.shtml
Surveyor, Land .... www.bpelsg.ca.gov/consumers/lic_lookup.shtml
Talent Agency .... https://www.dir.ca.gov/databases/dlselr/talag.html
Tax Education Provider .... https://www.ctec.org/Preparer/ApprovedProvider
Thermal Insulation Manufacturer .... www.bearhfti.ca.gov/enforcement/lookup.shtml
Thrift & Loan Company .... www.dbo.ca.gov/Licensees/search_directory.asp
Traffic Violator School https://www.dmv.ca.gov/portal/dmv/detail/portal/oling2/welcome
Trainer, Public Works .... www.dir.ca.gov/databases/das/pwaddrstart.asp
Travelers Checks Issuer .... www.dbo.ca.gov/Licensees/search_directory.asp
Trust Company .... www.dbo.ca.gov/Licensees/search_directory.asp
Upholsterer, Custom .... www.bearhfti.ca.gov/enforcement/lookup.shtml
Veterinary Food/Animal Drug Retailer .... www.pharmacy.ca.gov/about/verify_lic.shtml
Viatical Settlement Insurer .... www.insurance.ca.gov/license-status/index.cfm
Vocational Nurse .... www.bvnpt.ca.gov/consumers/license_verification.shtml

State and Local Courts

About California Courts: **Superior Courts** have jurisdiction over all felonies, misdemeanors, traffic matters, and all civil cases including family law, probate, juvenile, and general civil matters.

Between 1998 and 2000 individual counties unified the Superior Courts and Municipal Courts within their respective counties. Some courts that were formerly Municipal Courts became **Limited Jurisdiction Superior Courts**. They generally hear civil cases under $25,000. Appeals in limited civil cases (where $25,000 or less is at issue) and misdemeanors are heard by the appellate division of the Superior Court. When a small claims case is appealed, a Superior Court judge decides the case.

If there is more than one court of a type within a county, then where the case is tried and where the record is held depends on how a citation is written, or where the infraction occurred, or where the filer chose to file the case. It is important to note that Limited Courts may try minor felonies.

In the last few years the state judiciary has closed a number of courts. For example, the BRB database has 59 closed courts linked to a new location.

The web page for the Judicial Branch is www.courts.ca.gov.

Appellate Courts: The Courts of Appeal are organized into six districts. The website above provides access to all opinions from the Supreme Court and Appeals Courts from 1850 to present. Click on *Case Information*.

About Court Online Access

There is no statewide online access available for the trial court record index. However, many counties have their own online access system and some provide web access at no fee. Of note, the Los Angeles County has an extensive free and fee-based online system at www.lacourt.org/onlineservices/ON0001.aspx. The fee based service has separate charges for a name search or for downloading a case file. The free portion is only available if you know the case number.

County Sites:
Alameda County
All Superior Court Locations www.alameda.courts.ca.gov/
Civil: Civil: A fee-based name search is offered at https://publicrecords.alameda.courts.ca.gov/PRS/Home/Disclaimer for Civil and Small Claims from 1997 and Probate/Family Law from 2001. Fee is $1.00 per search. A search by case number is also for free at https://publicrecords.alameda.courts.ca.gov/PRS/Case/SearchByCaseNumber. Online access to calendars and Register of Actions is free from the home page. *Criminal:* Online access is available at https://criminalrecords.alameda.courts.ca.gov:453/CRRWeb/, However, a simple name search is not available. One must have name and either DOB and date of arrest, or have DOB and date of conviction. Records are not available on an interactive basis, they are transmitted. Copies may be requested. Fees are involved..

Amador County
Superior Court www.amadorcourt.org
Civil: A free docket search index is offered at https://www.amadorcourt.org/pa/paprod.urd/pamw6500.display. Records go back to 2002. Court calendars are by date up to 7 days ahead at www.amadorcourt.org/courtcal/courtcal.html. Personal identifiers are name and case number. *Criminal:* same

Butte County
All Superior Court Locations www.buttecourt.ca.gov
Civil: Limited case index searching by name is free at https://cabutteodyprod.tylerhost.net/Portal. There is also a calendar lookup at www.buttecourt.ca.gov/calendarlookup/cmscalendarlookup.cfm. *Criminal:* same

Colusa County
All Superior Court Locations www.colusa.courts.ca.gov
Civil: The web search site is http://cms.colusa.courts.ca.gov/ for a civil or family case index search. Can search by name or case number. *Criminal:* same

Contra Costa County
All Superior Court Locations www.cc-courts.org
Civi only: With registration, use Open Access to view Civil, Probate, Family and Small Claims information is free at http://icms.cc-courts.org/iotw/. Also, lookup your court case info free at http://icms.cc-courts.org/tellme/. Online civil search results include month/year of birth.

El Dorado County
All Superior Court Locations www.eldoradocourt.org/
Civil & Criminal: Access alpha Case Index lists back to year 2000 free at www.eldoradocourt.org/caseindex/case_index.aspx. Search monthly calendars free at http://eldocourtweb.eldoradocourt.org/calendar.aspx..

Fresno County
All Superior Court Locations - Civil www.fresnosuperiorcourt.org
Civil: Access to civil general and limited, probate, family law, and small claims cases is free at www.fresnosuperiorcourt.org/case_info/ or https://publicportal.fresno.courts.ca.gov/FRESNOPORTAL/. Unlawful Detainer cases are not available for sixty days after the complaint is filed with the court. In cases filed in the Civil Department, the three initials of the judge assigned to the case are being listed at the end of the case number on documents and notices *Criminal:* Access to criminal and traffic index data is free at www.fresnosuperiorcourt.org/case_info/ or https://publicportal.fresno.courts.ca.gov/FRESNOPORTAL/. Unlawful Detainer cases are not available for sixty days after the complaint is filed with the court.

Glenn County

Superior Court   www.glenncourt.ca.gov
Civil: Search case index at www.glenncourt.ca.gov/online_index/. All non-confidential, non-sealed, case types are available (Civil, Criminal, Family Law, Probate, Small Claims, Traffic, etc.).   *Criminal:* same Criminal case information prior to 11/2002 will need to be searched in person.

Kern County

All Superior Court Locations   www.kern.courts.ca.gov
Civil & crimina: Search civil records free at https://odyprodportal.kern.courts.ca.gov/portalprod.   *Criminal:* Search criminal record database at https://www.kern.courts.ca.gov/online_services/criminal_case_search_disclaimer.   Access   defendant   hearings   schedule   at www.co.kern.ca.us/courts/crimcal/crim_hearing_srch.asp.

Kings County

All Superior Court Locations   www.kings.courts.ca.gov
Civil & criminal: A free online docket look-up is available at https://cakingsodyprod.tylerhost.net/CAKINGSPROD/. Search by name or attorney name or case number. Financial case information for cases filed prior to October 24, 2014, will not be accessible through this web-portal.

Lassen County

All Superior Court Locations   www.lassencourt.ca.gov
Civil: The court provides a free index search at www.lassencourt.ca.gov/online_services/casesearch.shtml. The search includes civil and family law. Search by name or case number.   *Criminal:* The court provides a free index search at www.lassencourt.ca.gov/online_services/casesearch.shtml. The search includes criminal and traffic. Search by name or case number.

Los Angeles County

All Los Angeles Superior Court Locations - Civil   www.lasuperiorcourt.org
A number of searches are offered at www.lacourt.org/onlineservices/ON0001.aspx for civil, small claims, probate and family law. The fee for a name search depends on the number of searches done per month: 1 to 10 is $1.00, 11-99 is $4.75; 100 -999 is $4.50; 1,000 to 10,000 is $4.25 and if over 10,000 then $4.00 each. Purchase online documents for $1.00 per page first 5 pages, then $.40 per page.
All Los Angeles Superior Court Location - Criminal   www.lasuperiorcourt.org
A number of searches are offered at www.lacourt.org/onlineservices/ON0001.aspx for felony and misdemeanor records. The fee for a name search depends on the number of searches done per month: 1 to 10 is $1.00, 11-99 is $4.75; 100 -999 is $4.50; 1,000 to 10,000 is $4.25 and if over 10,000 then $4.00 each. Includes felony cases records from 1980 to the present and misdemeanor case records from 1988 to present. Also, purchase online documents for $1.00 per page first 5 pages, then $.40 per page. If available, counts, current charges, disposition and disposition dates are shown.

Marin County

Superior Court   www.marincourt.org/
Civil: Access to the court index back to the 1970s is free at www.marincourt.org/PublicIndex/Default.aspx. The Register of Actions (for probate, civil and small claims) is free at http://apps.marincounty.org/BeaconRoa/BeaconROAStart.aspx.   *Criminal:* Access to the court index back to the 1970s is free at www.marincourt.org/PublicIndex/Default.aspx. Access Traffic Court matters by case #, citation #, or DL # at https://www.marincourt.org/MarinTrafficWeb/TrafficMain.aspx.

Mendocino County

All Superior Court Locations   www.mendocino.courts.ca.gov
Civil: Search index at www.mendocino.courts.ca.gov/caseindex.html. Online index may be up to 2 months behind. For cases prior to 2000, there are various indices to search at this page, depending on the case date and location.   *Criminal:* same

Merced County

All Superior Court Locations   www.merced.courts.ca.gov/
Civil: The docket index is searchable at https://jpportal.mercedcourt.org/mercedprod. There are several searches available. One requires the DOB, one does not. There is also a feature to search current hearings. The site does not indicate the thoughput.   *Criminal:* same

Monterey County

All Superior Court Locations   www.monterey.courts.ca.gov
Civil: Access   court   data   free   at   https://www.justicepartners.monterey.courts.ca.gov/Public/JPPublicIndex.aspx.   Search   calendars   at https://www.justicepartners.monterey.courts.ca.gov/Public/JPPublicCalendarSearch.aspx, When searching court record index online there could be missing identifiers, and computer systems are not always up-to-date, and do not have as wide a date range as when searching onsite.   *Criminal:* same.

Napa County

All Superior Court Locations   www.napa.courts.ca.gov
Criminal: Online access to criminal and traffic index is at https://secure.napa.courts.ca.gov/redlight_CS.html. Search by name or case number. Researchers state that a 2-part last name cannot be searched on the system, use caution. There is also an online search request for criminal and traffic data at http://secure.napa.courts.ca.gov/GetWeb/RecordSearch.html. Search by name or case number. The fees are the same as charged for mail or walk-in requesters.

Nevada County

All Superior Court Locations www.nevadacountycourts.com/
Civil: Access to case docket information is free at http://eaccess.nevadacountycourts.com/eservices/home.page.2. Search civil, family, probate, and also Truckee cases. Online does not show any part of the DOB. *Criminal:* same

Orange County

All Superior Court - Civil Locations www.occourts.org
Civil: Access civil case index and calendars free at www.occourts.org/online-services/case-access/. A name search is available Family court calendars also shown. Civil, small claims, probate cases index for the county can be purchased on CD; index goes back to 12/31/01 or can be purchased on monthly basis. *Criminal:* Search by case number free for criminal, traffic and calendars free at www.occourts.org/online-services/case-access. One must sign-up and be approved for the name search feature available. Only attorneys and justice personnel have online access to case file images. Search results include dispositions, dismissals, sentences, and participants, but no DOB. Also shows names, aliases, and Court True name. Index rarely goes back beyond 2002.

Placer County

All Superior Court - Civil Locations www.placer.courts.ca.gov/
Civil: An online index search is available at www.placer.courts.ca.gov/case-search.html for cases back to 1999. The online Court Index search does not include Juvenile Delinquency, Juvenile Dependency, Unlawful Detainer, Mental Health, Traffic Cases or confidential case files. *Criminal:* An online index search is available at www.placer.courts.ca.gov/case-search.html for cases back to 1999. Data is updated once a week.

Riverside County

All Superior Court - Civil Locations www.riverside.courts.ca.gov/
Civil: Searches offered at http://public-access.riverside.courts.ca.gov/OpenAccess. If a civil case number is provided, the register of actions for that case may be viewed free of charge. For a name search, the fee is $1 for 1 search, $3.50 for 5 searches, or $5 for 10 searches, or $25 for 75 searches. A flat fee of $250 per 30 days provides an unlimited number of online searches. If a civil case number is provided, the register of actions for that case may be viewed free of charge. Also, there is an online copy request at www.riverside.courts.ca.gov/onlinecopyorder.shtml. *Criminal:* Search by either name or case number at http://public-access.riverside.courts.ca.gov/OpenAccess. For either search is $1 for 1 search, $3.50 for 5 searches, or $5 for 10 searches, or $25 for 75 searches. A flat fee of $250 per 30 days provides an unlimited number of online searches. Riverside Superior Court uses two (2) databases. The Riverside (Banning and all locations west) database and the Indio (Indio, Palm Springs & Blythe) database. To accomplish a countywide search you must search both databases. Each search requires using a search credit, so two search credits will be required to do a countywide search.

Sacramento County

Superior Court www.saccourt.ca.gov/
Civil: Access court records back to 1993 at https://services.saccourt.ca.gov/publiccaseaccess/home/index/. Fees charged: $1.00 for 1 name, $2.50 for 5 names, $25.00 for 75 names; or $250 for 30 days, unlimited for $2,500 per year. Separate fees for downloading documents are $1.00 per page for first 5 pages, then $.40 per page ea add'l with a $40.00 maximum. The system provides criminal, probate, small claims (2001 forward), unlawful detainer, family as well as civil. *Criminal:* Access case info from 1989 to present at https://services.saccourt.ca.gov/PublicCaseAccess/Criminal. Fees charged: $1.00 for 1 name, $2.50 for 5 names, $25.00 for 75 names; or $250 for 30 days, unlimited for $2,500 per year. Separate fees for downloading documents are $1.00 per page for first 5 [ages, then $.40 per page ea add'l with a $40.00 maximum. The system provides civil, probate, small claims (2001 forward), unlawful detainer, family as well as criminal.

San Bernardino County

All Superior Court Locations www.sb-court.org/
Civil: Online access to civil cases is free atwww.sb-court.org/Divisions/Civil/CaseInformationOnline.aspx. Court Case information is available at no charge. There is also an enhanced service providing remote access to document images from case filings in civil matters. The fee for access to the documents is $0.50 per page, up to a maximum charge of $50.00 per document. *Criminal:* Access to criminal cases and traffic is free at www.sb-court.org/Divisions/Civil/CaseInformationOnline.aspx. Includes calendars. Note that this Internet service is provided 'as is' with no warranties, express or implied, including the implied warranty of fitness for a particular purpose, the court does not guarantee or warrant the completeness. Caution.

San Diego County

All Superior Court Locations - Civil www.sdcourt.ca.gov
Civil: Online search for case information for civil and probate cases initiated after 01/01/2008 is free at www.sdcourt.ca.gov/portal/page?_pageid=55,1056871&_dad=portal&_schema=PORTAL. Also lists calendars and new filings. *Criminal:* Online search for case information, calendars, and new filings is free at http://courtindex.sdcourt.ca.gov/CISPublic/enter.

San Francisco County

Superior Court - Civil www.sfsuperiorcourt.org/
The San Francisco Superior Court offers online queries by case number or name search. Documents included for cases in the following departments: Civil, Family Law, Probate, and Small Claims. Visit www.sfsuperiorcourt.org/online-services.

San Joaquin County

All Superior Court Locations www.stocktoncourt.org/courts/

Civil: A search of civil, small claims and probate cases is at https://www.sjcourts.org/online-services/. Records to family law, juvenile court, guardianship and conservatorship, mental health, criminal, civil harassment, workplace violence prevention are not available online. One may also fill out an online request form - see https://www.sjcourts.org/online-services/records-request/. Must have case file number. *Criminal:* Traffic and misdemeanor record search is at https://www.sjcourts.org/online-services/. Both the case number and name are needed. The date range may be limited - at one time the historical index was removed 04/01/2011. One may also fill out an online request form - see https://www.sjcourts.org/online-services/records-request/. Must have case file number.

San Mateo County

All Superior Court Locations www.sanmateocourt.org

Civil: Online access to the docket index is free at from the home page, click on the Online Services tab. *Criminal:* same

Santa Barbara County

All Superior Court Locations - Civil www.sbcourts.org/index.asp

Civil: Search general civil index 1975 to present or limited civil back to 1977 free at www.sbcourts.org/pubindex/. Daily calendars free at www.sbcourts.org/pubcal/.Also, a CD-Rom of monthly court indices from all divisions is for $40.00.

Santa Clara County

All Superior Court Locations - www.sccsuperiorcourt.org

Civil: Civil, Family, Probate, and Small Claims case records and court calendars are free online at www.sccaseinfo.org/. CD-ROM is also available, fee-$150.00. *Criminal:* Access to the criminal case index back to 2004 is at www.scscourt.org/court_divisions/criminal/index_search.asp. Traffic and Local Ordinance case information is at www.sccaseinfo.org.

Santa Cruz County

All Superior Court locations - Civil www.santacruzcourt.org

Civil: Access civil records free at http://ww.santacruzcourt.org/node/65. Includes civil, small claims, family law, probate. There is a disclaimer - data provided as is.

Shasta County

All Superior Court Locations www.shastacourts.com

Civil: Access to civil division index free back to 1993 at http://caselookup.shastacourts.com:8080/cgi-bin/webcase01r. Search by case, name, or date. Also, the county offers access to the Integrated Justice System (IJS), this is meant for attorneys and requires a password. And registration. *Criminal:* Access to the criminal docket index is free back to 1993 at http://caselookup.shastacourts.com:8080/cgi-bin/webcase01r. Search by case, name, or date.

Siskiyou County

All Superior Court Locations www.siskiyou.courts.ca.gov

Civil: Access to county superior court records is free at www.siskiyou.courts.ca.gov/WebInquiry/default.aspx. Includes traffic but not juvenile or confidential cases. *Criminal:* Online access to criminal and traffic records is same as civil

Solano County

All Superior Court Locations www.solano.courts.ca.gov/

Civil: Online access to countywide civil record index is free online. Click on Court Connect from the home page. Also, civil tentative rulings and probate notes are available at www.solanocourts.com/TentativeRulings.html. Online search provides a case number and limited docket entry information, no personal identifiers except name. Online search request does not allow for add'l identifiers. Missing records can be avoided with an in person search. *Criminal:* Online access to countywide court record index (back to year 2000 generally) is free at http://courtconnect.solanocourts.com/courtconnect/ck_public_qry_main.cp_main_idx. Online search provides a case number and limited docket entry information, no personal identifiers except name. Online search request does not allow for add'l identifiers. Missing records, often older felonies, can be avoided with an in person search.

Sonoma County

Superior Court www.sonomasuperiorcourt.com/index.php

Civil: Limited free search is at http://sonoma.courts.ca.gov/online-services/calendars for court calendars, cases recently filed, tentative rulings. *Criminal:* Search free calendars directly at http://sonoma.courts.ca.gov/online-services/calendars/daily-criminal. Online index does not provide register of actions, just case number and parties. Goes back 3 months.

Stanislaus County

Superior Court www.stanct.org/

Civil: The case look-up is found at www.stanct.org/case-index-lookup. Superior Court Case Index is available alphabetically on a CD Case Index is updated quarterly and includes cases filed 1900-1999, and 2000-present day. Cost is $15.00 each CD set, which includes S&H. *Criminal:* same.

Tulare County

Superior Court www.tularesuperiorcourt.ca.gov

Civil: Daily calendar and civil tentative rulings and probate recommendations at www.tularesuperiorcourt.ca.gov/. *Criminal:* Daily calendar at www.tularesuperiorcourt.ca.gov/.

Ventura County
All Superior Court Locations www.ventura.courts.ca.gov
Civil: Access to Civil, Small Claims, and Probate case dockets and calendars is free at www.ventura.courts.ca.gov/CivilCaseSearch/. Search Family Law at www.ventura.courts.ca.gov/FamilyCaseSearch/. For all searches, search by name or case number or date range.   *Criminal:* Access to case idocket back to 1995 and current calendars and dockets is free at https://secured.countyofventura.org/courtservices/CourtServiceHome.aspx.

Yolo County
Superior Court www.yolo.courts.ca.gov/
Civil: Calendars are online free at www.yolo.courts.ca.gov/online-services/court-calendar. Search Probate Notes at www.yolo.courts.ca.gov/online-services/probate-notes. Calendars are online free at www.yolo.courts.ca.gov/online-services/court-calendar.

Recorders, Assessors, and Other Sites of Note

About California Recording Offices: 58 counties, 58 recording offices. The recording officer is the County Recorder. Recordings are usually located in a Grantor/Grantee or General Index.

About Tax Liens: Federal and state tax liens on personal property of businesses are filed with the Secretary of State. Other federal and state tax liens are filed with the County Recorder, and state tax liens on individuals can be found at both the Secretary of State and the county level.

Online Access

Recorded Documents:
At least 47 California counties offer individual online access to recorded documents.

Assessor Records:
Also, at least 49 California counties provide online access to assessor and/or GIS data. A private vendor has parcel databases for all 58 California counties. Go to www.parcelquest.com/ for information on how to subscribe.

County Sites:

Alameda County   *Recorded Documents, Voter Registration Records*   www.acgov.org/auditor/clerk/   Access the clerk-recorder's official public records and fictitious name databases for free at http://rechart1.acgov.org/. Also, check voter registration status at https://www.acgov.org/alco_ssl_app/rov/voter_info/voter_profile.jsp?formLanguage=E.
Property, Taxation Records   Access to the Property Assessment database is free at www.acgov.org/MS/prop/index.aspx but no name searching. Also, GIS/mapping for free at www.acgov.org/assessor/resources/parcel_viewer.htm. Also, property tax data is found at www.acgov.org/propertytax/online.htm.

Alpine County   *Recorded Documents*   www.alpinecountyca.gov/Index.aspx?NID=141   Official records are searchable from 1986 forward at http://alpinepublic.countyrecords.com/. There is no fee, there are no images on this system.

Amador County   *Recorded Documents*   www.co.amador.ca.us/government/recorder-clerk   Access to the county's recorded documents is free at http://criis.com/index.html. Documents from 1991 to present.
Property, Taxation Records   Access parcel maps for free at www.co.amador.ca.us/government/assessor/assessor-parcel-maps.

Butte County   *Recorded Documents*   http://clerk-recorder.buttecounty.net/   Access to the recorder's database of official documents is free at http://clerk-recorder.buttecounty.net/Riimsweb/Asp/ORInquiry.asp. Records go back to 1980. Marriages, births and deaths are no longer available. There is also a search of Fictitious Business Names at http://clerk-recorder.buttecounty.net/RiimsWeb/ASP/FBNInquiry.asp.
Property, Taxation Records   View property tax data free at www.buttecounty.net/assessor/PropertyAssessment/AssessedValue.aspx.

Calaveras County   *Property, Taxation Records*   Access property tax data and GIS/mapping for free at http://calaverasgov.us/QuickLinks/PropertyInfo.aspx. No name searching.

Colusa County   *Property, Taxation Records*   Access to GIS/mapping free at www.countyofcolusa.com/index.aspx?nid=139.

Contra Costa County   *Recorded Documents*   www.contracostacore.us/   Access to the county's recorded documents is free at http://criis.com/index.html. Records from 1986 to present. There is a fee to order vital records.
Property, Taxation Records   Access to GIS/mapping records for free at www.ccmap.us/interactive_maps.aspx.

Del Norte County   *Recorded Documents*   http://elections.co.del-norte.ca.us/   Access to indexes of real estate records for free at http://recorder.co.del-norte.ca.us/. Images must be purchased. Contact the Recorder's office at 707-464-7216 for prices and procedures for purchasing.
Property, Taxation Records   Access to parcels, assessor maps, etc indexes for free at https://assr.parcelquest.com/Home. ParcelQeust is a third party system that gets data directly from the county assessor's office.

El Dorado County *Fictitious Name Index Records* www.edcgov.us/CountyClerk/   Access to the county's fictitious business documents is free at www.criis.com/cgi-bin/fbn_search.cgi?COUNTY=eldorado&YEARSEGMENT=current&TAB=1.
Property, Taxation Records   Parcel, tax, and personal property information available free at http://main.edcgov.us/CGI/WWB012/WWM400/A.

Fresno County *Recorded Documents* www.co.fresno.ca.us/Departments.aspx?id=186   Access to the county's recorded documents is free at http://criis.com/index.html. Records are from current back to 2000; 1999 back to 1992 and 1991 back to 1981.
Property, Taxation Records   Download the Assessment Roll at www.co.fresno.ca.us/DepartmentPage.aspx?id=12324.

Humboldt County *Property, Taxation Records*   Download GIS data from www.humboldtgov.org/201/Maps-GIS-Data. A property assessment search is at http://humboldtgov.org/231/Online-Search.

Imperial County *Recorded Documents* www.co.imperial.ca.us/Recorder/index.asp   Access the Recorder's Official records index free at http://implookup.co.imperial.ca.us/RecorderWorks/. Index goes back to 1986, but no images available. Fictitious business names are at http://implookup.co.imperial.ca.us/clerkdocsinternet/eFBN/fbnmain.asp.
Property, Taxation Records   A GIS-mapping site can assist in finding parcel data free at https://www.geoviewer8.com/?username=icpublic&password=icpublic. No name searching.

Inyo County *Recorded Documents* http://clerkrecorder.inyocounty.us/   Access to the county's recorded documents and fictitious business documents are free at http://criis.com/index.html. Documents from 1982 to present.
Property, Taxation Records   Access to parcels/maps for free at www.parcelquest.com/.

Kern County *Recorded Documents, Fictitious Business Name Records* http://recorder.co.kern.ca.us/index.php   Search county clerk's fictitious business name database free at www.kerncountyclerk.com/en/dba/FBN-Search.aspx#.V6iueBJNrkd. Also, search historical sales price data at www.kerndata.com/.
Property, Taxation Records   Assessor database records available free at http://assessor.co.kern.ca.us/propertysearch/index.php. Search tax collector data at www.kcttc.co.kern.ca.us/payment/mainsearch.aspx.

Kings County *Recorded Documents* www.countyofkings.com/departments/assessor/clerk-recorder   Access to records for free at http://publicrecords.countyofkings.com/.
Property, Taxation Records   A subscription-based access system is available, contact the office for more info. There is a $60 one-time set-up fee. There are no monthly fees. A Flat usage fee of $.15 per page that is accessed beginning with the Main Menu. Data available includes ownership including history, taxes, assessor maps, and boat and airplane information.

Lake County *Recorded Documents* www.co.lake.ca.us/Government/Directory/Assessor-Recorder.htm   Limited index display of official records can be accessed at www.co.lake.ca.us/Government/Directory/Assessor-Recorder/SearchIndex.htm.
Property, Taxation Records   Parcel records on the GIS Mapping site available by clicking on Lake County Base Maps free at http://gis.co.lake.ca.us/. No name searching.

Lassen County *Property, Taxation Records*   Access to real estate for a fee at https://assr.parcelquest.com/Home/Disclaimer. Also, access to tax sales lists is free through a private company at www.bid4assets.com/.

Los Angeles County *Recorded Documents, Fictitious Business Names Records* www.lavote.net/   Access to records for a fee from a vendor (Lexis - https://paymentsolutions.lexisnexis.com/pc/ca/co/rrccrecords). The county does not make these records availablel online. Search the Fictitious Business names database for free at http://rrcc.lacounty.gov/clerk/FBN_Search.cfm.
Property, Taxation Records   Property database subscription access at http://assessor.lacounty.gov/online-property-database-access. $100 monthly for maintaining the account, plus $1.00 per inquiry/screen, and $168.00 signup fee. Also search property/assessor data free at http://maps.assessor.lacounty.gov/GVH_2_2/Index.html?configBase=http://maps.assessor.lacounty.gov/Geocortex/Essentials/REST/sites/PAIS/viewers/PAIS_hv/virtualdirectory/Resources/Config/Default.

Marin County *Recorded Documents* www.marincounty.org/depts/ar   Search the county Grantor/Grantee index, sales, etc- free at www.marincounty.org/depts/ar. Search fictitious business names for free at http://apps.marincounty.org/fbn/search/fbnsearch.aspx.
Property, Taxation Records   Access to property records for free at www.marincounty.org/depts/ar/property.

Mendocino County *Property, Taxation Records*   A free property tax search is at www.co.mendocino.ca.us/tax/cgi-bin/pTax.pl. Must search by street address or parcel number - name search not available.

Merced County *Recorded Documents* www.co.merced.ca.us/index.aspx?NID=239   Access to the recorder official records index PARIS system is free at www.recorder.merced.ca.us/. Also, access Grantee/Grantor records for free at http://web2.co.merced.ca.us/RecorderWorksInternet/
Property, Taxation Records   Search parcel maps at www.co.merced.ca.us/index.aspx?NID=196. Search by fee parcel number or assessment number at www.co.merced.ca.us/index.aspx?NID=193 but no name searching.

Modoc County *Recorded Documents* www.co.modoc.ca.us/departments/recorder   Access to the county's recorded documents and fictitious business documents are free at http://criis.com/index.html. Documents from 1984 to present.

Mono County *Property, Taxation Records* Access property data free at www.monocounty.ca.gov/assessor/page/assessor-data-inquiry, but no name searching. GIS searching provided at https://gis.mono.ca.gov/site/.

Monterey County *Recorded Documents* www.co.monterey.ca.us/government/departments-a-h/assessor/assessor-county-clerk-recorder
Access the county PARIS system including official records and fictitious business names free at http://192.92.176.8/. Official records go back to 1978. When searching recorded documents online there could be missing identifiers, and computers are not always up-to-date, and do not have as wide a date range as when searching onsite.
Property, Taxation Records Access to parcel data for free at https://assr.parcelquest.com/Home/Disclaimer. The county tax defaulted property list is at www.co.monterey.ca.us/taxcollector/Auction_Internet.html.

Napa County *Recorded Documents* www.countyofnapa.org/Recorder-Clerk/ Access Official Records by subscription; fee- $3600 per year. Index and images go back to 1848. Also, search Official Records Inquiry site for real estate and Grantor/Grantee index back to 1848 free at http://services.countyofnapa.org/OfficialRecordsPublic/.
Property, Taxation Records Search assessor's property tax payments free at www.countyofnapa.org/PropertyTaxPayments/, but no name searching. Also, search for property data for free at www.countyofnapa.org/assessorparceldata/. Also search for property data on the GIS-mapping site for a fee at www.countyofnapa.org/Assessor/. Must signup with Username and Password.

Nevada County *Recorded Documents, Index Recorded Maps Records* www.mynevadacounty.com/nc/recorder/Pages/Home.aspx
Access to the county clerk database of recordings and assumed names is free at http://recorder.nevcounty.net/oncoreweb/. Also, subscription access to the recorders full database is $200 per month fee. This is only the index, cannot view images online.
Property, Taxation Records Access to parcel data and maps free at www.mynevadacounty.com/nc/assessor/Pages/Home.aspx. Also, view and pay property tax records at www.mynevadacounty.com/nc/ttc/Pages/View-and-Pay-Your-Tax-Bill-.aspx.

Orange County *Recorded Documents* http://ocgov.com/gov/clerk/ Orange County Grantor/Grantee index is free online at https://cr.ocgov.com/recorderworks/. Records are from 1982 to present. Also, search fictitious business names at https://efbn.ocgov.com/eFBNweb/default.aspx.
Property, Taxation Records Search tax parcel data, aircraft, and vessels free at http://tax.ocgov.com/tcweb/search_page.asp but no name searching.

Placer County *Recorded Documents* www.placer.ca.gov/Departments/Recorder.aspx Recorder office index records are free at https://countyfusion4.propertyinfo.com/countyweb/login.do?countyname=Placer. For detailed information must register.
Property, Taxation Records Assessor's property assessment data free at www.placer.ca.gov/departments/assessor/assessment-inquiry. Also, search GIS data at http://maps.placer.ca.gov/lis/.

Riverside County *Recorded Documents* http://riverside.asrclkrec.com Access to records for free at www.asrclkrec.com/Assessor/AssessorServices/PropertyInformationCenter.aspx. Also, access to county fictitious name database is free at www.asrclkrec.com/Clerk/OnlineFBNSearch.aspx.
Property, Taxation Records Access property tax data free at http://pic.asrclkrec.com/Default.aspx but no name searching.

Sacramento County *Recorded Documents* www.ccr.saccounty.net/Pages/default.aspx Access Clerk-Recorder Grantee/Grantor index back to 1850 for free at https://erosi.saccounty.net/. Search fictitious names at https://actonline.saccounty.net/CitizenAccess/SACCO_FBNSearch.aspx.
Property, Taxation Records Search property tax & parcels at https://eproptax.saccounty.net/; no name searching. Also, find property data at http://assessorparcelviewer.saccounty.net/jsviewer/assessor.html; no name searching. Search fictitious names free at https://actonline.saccounty.net/CitizenAccess/SACCO_FBNSearch.aspx.

San Benito County *Recorded Documents* http://sbcvote.us/ Records from 01/01/1989 forward are searchable at http://sbcvote.us/county-recorder/official-records-database-inquiry/. Name searching available.
Property, Taxation Records A parcel search is offered at www.parcelquest.com/. Access to GIS/mapping free at www.lynxgis.com/sanbenitoco/.

San Bernardino County *Recorded Documents* www.sbcounty.gov/arc/ Access to records for free at www.sbcounty.gov/assessor/pims/(S(glrc1duczdwse3h25erou3nh))/PIMSINTERFACE.ASPX. Search fictitious business names at http://acrparis.sbcounty.gov/fbn/index.html.
Property, Taxation Records Records on the County Assessor database are free at www.mytaxcollector.com/trSearch.aspx. No name searching.

San Diego County *Recorded Documents, Fictitious Name Records* https://arcc.sdcounty.ca.gov/Pages/default.aspx Access to recorded documents for free at https://arcc-acclaim.sdcounty.ca.gov/. Search fictitious business names at https://arcc.sdcounty.ca.gov/Pages/fictitious.aspx.
Property, Taxation Records From the county home page above or at https://arcc.sdcounty.ca.gov/Pages/parcelmaps.aspx search for assessor data on the parcel mapping site. Search for property sales data at https://arcc.sdcounty.ca.gov/Pages/Property-Sales.aspx; no name searching. Assessor date also available in bulk, see https://arcc.co.san-diego.ca.gov/subscription/login.aspx or call 619-685-2455.

San Francisco County *Recorded Documents* www.sfassessor.org/ Access to the county's recorded documents and fictitious business documents are free at http://criis.com/index.html. Documents from 1990 to present. Limited vital statistic data is searchable at www.sfgenealogy.com/sf/, a privately operated site.

San Joaquin County *Recorded Documents* https://www.sjgov.org/assessor_recorder/ Access to grantor/grantee database free at https://www.sjgov.org/recorder/grantorgrantee.
Property, Taxation Records Access property value online at https://www.sjgov.org/assessor/roll. Access parcels and values at www.parcelquest.com/. Access GIS and parcel maps www.sjmap.org/.

San Luis Obispo County *Recorded Documents* www.slocounty.ca.gov/clerk Search the recorder database for free at http://clerk.slocounty.ca.gov/officialrecords/Search.aspx.
Property, Taxation Records Access property information search free at www.slocounty.ca.gov/Page81.aspx. Also, GIS/mapping for free at www.slocounty.ca.gov/Assessor/Mapping.htm.

San Mateo County *Recorded Documents, Fictitious Business Names Records* www.smcare.org/ Access the recorder's grantor/grantee index free at www.smcare.org/apps/LandDocs/grantee_index.asp. Also, search fictitious business names at www.smcare.org/clerk/fictitious/default.asp.
Property, Taxation Records Property Tax Assessment Rolls is free at www.smcare.org/assessor/homeownerresources/tax_rolls.asp, View secured or unsecured property tax status by parcel, address or account at www.sanmateocountytaxcollector.org/index.html.

Santa Barbara County *Real Estate, Grantor/Grantee, Deed, Lien Records* www.sbcrecorder.com/Home.aspx Search the recorder's grantor/grantee index at www.sbcrecorder.com/ClerkRecorder/GrantorGranteeIndex.aspx.
Property, Taxation Records Access to assessor online property info system (OPIS) in free at www.sbcassessor.com/Assessor/AssessorRealEstateServices.aspx but no name searching. Records go back to 1989. Also, search parcels and maps for free at at www.sbcassessor.com/Assessor/AssessorParcelMap.aspx

Santa Clara County *Recorded Documents* https://www.sccgov.org/sites/rec/Pages/Office-of-the-Clerk-Recorder.aspx Access to the County Clerk-Recorder database is free at www.clerkrecordersearch.org/. Search births 1905-1995 free at www.mariposaresearch.net/php/. Also, search fictitious business names for free at www.clerkrecordersearch.org/cgi-bin/FBNSearch.html/input.
Property, Taxation Records Search the assessment roll free a https://www.sccassessor.org/index.php/online-services/property-search/real-property. Also, access to GIS/mapping for free at www.sccgov.org/arcgis/giswelcome/. Also, search the tax collector database at https://payments.sccgov.org/propertytax. No name searching.

Santa Cruz County *Recorded Documents* www.co.santa-cruz.ca.us/rcd/index.htm Access to the recorder's official records is free at http://clerkrecorder.co.santa-cruz.ca.us/. Online indexes go back to 1978. Images from 4/1/97.
Property, Taxation Records Access the assessor's parcel data free at http://sccounty01.co.santa-cruz.ca.us/ASR/. No name searching. Also, search for property data using the GIS map at www.co.santa-cruz.ca.us/default.aspx?tabid=93.

Shasta County *Recorded Documents* www.co.shasta.ca.us/index/recorder_index.aspx See http://apps.co.shasta.ca.us/riimspublic/Asp/ORPublicInquiry.asp for free access to index. Search by name, document type or document ID. Records available for viewing from 1/2/1924 to present.
Property, Taxation Records Search assessor documents for free at www.co.shasta.ca.us/index/assessor_index/assessment_inquiry.aspx#. Records on the City of Redding Parcel Search By Parcel Number Server are free at http://cor400.ci.redding.ca.us/nd/gow3lkap.ndm/input. CA state law has removed owner names.

Sierra County *Property, Taxation Records* Access to tax sales lists is free through a private company at www.bid4assets.com/.

Siskiyou County *Recorded Docume[...].co.siskiyou.ca.us/page/recorder-division Access to the county's recorded documents and fictitious business documents are free at http://cr[...]dex.html. Documents from 1974 to present.

Solano County *Recorded Documents* www.solanocounty.com/depts/ar/home.asp Access the recorder's indexes free at http://recorderonline.solanocounty.com. Access to online property information for free at www.solanocounty.com/depts/ar/viewpropertyinfo.asp.
Property, Taxation Records Access to Treasurer/tax collector property taxes and tax sales for free at www.solanocounty.com/depts/ttcc/default.asp.

Sonoma County *Recorded Documents* www.sonoma-county.org/recorder/aboutus.asp Access recorder index records for a fee at https://crarecords.sonomacounty.ca.gov/recorder/web/login.jsp. Must register. Also, with address, ZIP, and DOB search voter registration records free at https://secure.sonoma-county.org/vote/voter_registration_status.aspx?sid=1070. www.sonoma-county.org/deeds
Property, Taxation Records Access assessor information free at http://sonoma-county.org/assessor/.

Stanislaus County *Recorded Documents* www.stancounty.com/clerkrecorder/ Access to the county's recorded documents and fictitious business documents are free at http://criis.com/index.html. Documents from 1980 to present.
Property, Taxation Records Access to GIS/mapping for free at http://sbtapp1.co.stanislaus.ca.us/AssessorWeb/public/MapBooks.

Sutter County *Recorded Documents* www.suttercounty.org/doc/government/depts/cr/crhome Access the recorder database free at www.suttercounty.org/apps/recordsquery/clerk/. Records go back to 12/29/1994.
Property, Taxation Records Access assessment and property tax records free at www.suttercounty.org/doc/apps/recordsquery/recordsquery but no name searching.

Tehama County *Recorded Documents* www.co.tehama.ca.us/dep-clerk-and-recorder   Search recorder's official public record indexes free at http://tehamapublic.countyrecords.com/. Deed index only back to 1975. Images are not currently available for purchase online. The cost to purchase images is $1.50 per page.

Property, Taxation Records   Search property tax data on the county unsecured tax information lookup at www.co.tehama.ca.us/assessor-info-and-maps.

Trinity County *Fictitious Business Name Records* www.trinitycounty.org/index.aspx?page=57   Access to the Recorder's fictitious business names database is free at http://halfile.trinitycounty.org. For user name, enter fbn; leave password field empty.

Tulare County *Recorded Documents* www.tularecounty.ca.gov/clerkrecorder/   Search the recorders database including births, marriages, deaths free at http://riimsweb.co.tulare.ca.us/riimsweb/Asp/ORInquiry.asp. Subscription fee for all images and recorder's services is $780/00 per month.

Property, Taxation Records   Access the Assessor's maps for free at http://maps.tularecounty.ca.gov/InteractiveMaps/maphome.html.

Tuolumne County *Recorded Documents* www.co.tuolumne.ca.us/index.aspx?NID=214   Access the recorder grantor/grantee index at https://www.records.co.tuolumne.ca.us/default.htm. Logon using 'web' for free access; turn off pop-up blocker.

Property, Taxation Records   Access to parcel search information for a fee at https://assr.parcelquest.com/. No name searches.

Ventura County *Recorded Documents, Fictitious Name Records* http://recorder.countyofventura.org/county-recorder/   Access the county clerk & recorder database free at http://recorder.countyofventura.org/county-recorder/official-records/. Also, access to Grantor/Grantee records for free at http://apps.countyofventura.org/ailis5/.

Property, Taxation Records   Search property tax data for free at http://prop-tax.countyofventura.org/ but no name searching. Also, access to parcel maps free at http://assessor.countyofventura.org/research/mappage.asp.

Yolo County *Recorded Documents* www.yolorecorder.org   Access to recordings on the county clerk database are free at www.yolorecorder.org/recsearch. County Fictitious Business Name at www.yolorecorder.org/recording/fictitious/lookup. Search City of Davis business licenses free at http://cityofdavis.org/ed/business/.

Property, Taxation Records   Search for parcels free at www.yolocounty.org/general-government/general-government-departments/assessor/parcel-quest.

Yuba County *Recorded Documents* www.co.yuba.ca.us/departments/clerk/   Access recorded document index free at https://recorder.co.yuba.ca.us/recorder/web/.

Property, Taxation Records   Access to property records is free at www.co.yuba.ca.us/services/Parcel%20Search/, but no name searching.

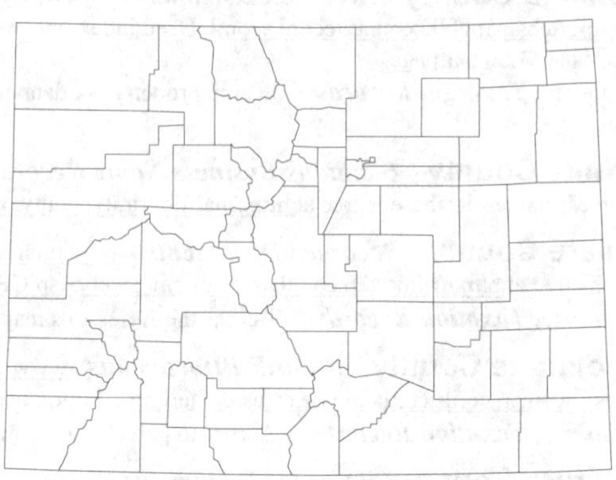

Colorado

Capital: Denver
             Denver County
Time Zone: MST
Population: 5,456,574
# of Counties: 64

Useful State Links

Website: **https://www.colorado.gov/**
Governor: **https://www.colorado.gov/governor/**
Attorney General: **www.coloradoattorneygeneral.gov/**
State Archives: **www.archives.state.al.us**
State Statutes and Codes: **www.lexisnexis.com/hottopics/Colorado/**
Legislative Bill Search: **www.leg.state.co.us/clics/cslFrontPages.nsf/HomeSplash?OpenForm**
Unclaimed Funds: **www.colorado.gov/treasury/gcp/**

State Public Record Agencies

Criminal Records

CO Bureau of Investigation, State Repository, Identification Unit,   https://www.colorado.gov/cbi   There is Internet access at https://www.cbirecordscheck.com/. The system is operated by a vendor - KTI. Requesters must use a credit card, an account does not need to be established. However, account holders may set up a batch system with KTI. The fee is $6.85 per record. Account holders must place a minimum of $200 in the account. Arrests which are not supported by fingerprints are not included in this database. Note warrant information, sealed records, and juvenile records are not available to the public.

Sexual Offender Registry

Colorado Bureau of Investigation, SOR Unit,   https://www.colorado.gov/apps/cdps/sor/?SOR=home.caveat   The website gives access to only certain high-risk registered sex offenders in the following categories: Sexually Violent Predator (SVP), Multiple Offenses, Failed to Register, and adult felony conviction.

Incarceration Records

Colorado Department of Corrections, Offender Records,   https://www.colorado.gov/cdoc/   Search the Inmate Locater at www.doc.state.co.us/oss/. This is not a historical search; only active offenders and parolees are listed. Offender's name on record is their arresting/prosecuted name and may not be their legal name. Plus, one may submit a record request pursuant to CORA or CCJRA from this web page: www.doc.state.co.us/contact/contact-open-records-request.

Corporation, LLC, LP, LLP, LLLP, Trademarks/Servicemarks, Fictitious/Assumed Name, Trade Name

Secretary of State, Business & Licensing,   www.sos.state.co.us/pubs/business/businessHome.html?menuheaders=2   There are a variety of searches available from www.sos.state.co.us/biz/BusinessEntityCriteriaExt.do including a business name, trademark or trade name. Other searches from the SOS home page include lobbyists and charities & fundraisers. Several other sites, not from this agency, are worthy of mention herein. Search securities dept. enforcement action at https://www.colorado.gov/pacific/dora/enforcement-actions. Search for charitable nonprofit members of CANPO at https://www.coloradononprofits.org/membership/nonprofit-member-directory.   Search   Registered   Charities   and   Fundraisers   at https://www.sos.state.co.us/ccsa/pages/search/basic.xhtml.   *Other Options:* Various information is available as a one time order or via subscription. Transmittal can be through CDs, tapes or FTP.

Uniform Commercial Code, Federal Tax Liens

Secretary of State, UCC Division,   https://www.sos.state.co.us/pubs/UCC/uccHome.html   There are a number of search options at https://www.sos.state.co.us/ucc/pages/home.xhtml. There a standard search, advanced search, a master list of Farm Product related filings, and one can also validate or certify a search. More extensive data is also available via subscription for ongoing business requesters.   *Other Options:* Various information is available as a one time order or via subscription. Transmittal can be through CDs, tapes or FTP. The program may be delayed due to the redaction of SSNs.

Sales Tax Registrations

CO Dept of Revenue, Taxpayer Service Division,   https://www.colorado.gov/tax   You can verify a sales tax license or exemption number at https://www.colorado.gov/revenueonline/_/#2.

Birth Certificates

Department of Public Health & Environment, Vital Records Section HSVR-A1,   https://www.colorado.gov/pacific/cdphe/birth-certificates   Records can be ordered online from state designated vendor. Go to https://www.vitalchek.com/default.aspx. Must have a major credit card. Historical records from the Archives are searchable at https://www.colorado.gov/pacific/archives/archives-search.

Death Records

Department of Public Health & Environment, Vital Records Section HSVR-A1,   https://www.colorado.gov/pacific/cdphe/deathrecords   Records can be ordered online from state designated vendors. Go to https://www.vitalchek.com/. Historical records from the Archives are searchable at https://www.colorado.gov/pacific/archives/archives-search.

Marriage Certificates, Divorce Records

Department of Public Health & Environment, Vital Records Section HSVR-A1,   https://www.colorado.gov/pacific/cdphe/verification-marriage-civil-union-dissolution-divorce   Records can be ordered online from state designated vendors. Go to https://www.vitalchek.com/.

Workers' Compensation Records

Division of Workers' Compensation, Customer Service,   https://www.colorado.gov/cdle/dwc   One may verify if an employer ahs coverage - see https://www.ewccv.com/cvs/.   *Other Options:* Lists and/or labels of carriers, adjusting companies, and attorneys are available upon request. Fees range from $3.00 to $7.00 (for list, not per name) plus postage.

Driver Records

Division of Motor Vehicles, Driver Control/Traffic Record Room 150,   https://www.colorado.gov/dmv   Colorado Interactive is the entity designated by the state to provide online access to driving records to registered users. Both interactive and batch processing is offered. Requesters must be approved per state compliance requirements with DPPA. There is an annual $75.00 registration fee, records are $2.00 each. Submit DL and either last name or DOB. For more information visit www.colorado.gov/registration or contact Amy Sawyer at 303-534-3468 extension 102.   *Other Options:* A driver monitoring program is offered by Colorado Interactive.

Voter Registration, Campaign and Finance Disclosures, Lobbyists

Department of State, Elections Department,   www.sos.state.co.us/pubs/elections/main.html?menuheaders=5   Verify voter registration status at https://www.sos.state.co.us/voter-classic/secuRegVoterIntro.do.   An   overall   search   site   with   many   options   is   at http://tracer.sos.colorado.gov/PublicSite/homepage.aspx.   View   campaign   finance   documents   at www.sos.state.co.us/ImageView/MainSearch.do?division=5. Search registered lobbyists at www.sos.state.co.us/lobby/Home.do.   *Other Options:* The entire database of voter registration is available on CD-ROM. The cost is $500. No customization is available.

GED Certificates

GED Testing Program,   www.cde.state.co.us/postsecondary/hse   Records may be requested from https://www.diplomasender.com. A credit card is needed. Request must be ordered by the test taker. Employers and third parties must receive an email and/or Authentication Code from the test taker to then access the authorized documents. Turnaround time is 1-3 days.

Occupational Licensing Boards

These licenses are all searchable at
https://www.colorado.gov/dora/licensing/Lookup/LicenseLookup.aspx

Accountant-CPA	Dentist/Dental Hygienist	Midwife
Acupuncturist	Drug Company (DRU) Mfg/Dist/Whlse	Nurse-RN/LPN/Aide
Addiction Counselor	Electrical Contractor/Master/Apprentice	Nursing Home Administrator
Architect	Electrician Journeyman/Master	Optometrist
Athletic Trainer	Engineer/Engineer Intern	Outfitter-River
Audiologist	Hearing Aid Dealer	Pharmacist/Pharmacist Intern
Barber	Land Surveyor/Land Surveyor Intern	Pharmacy Limited License
Chiropractor	Licensee Discipline Lookup	Pharmacy/Out-of-State/In-State/PDO
Cosmetologist/Manicurist	Marriage & Family Therapist	Physical Therapist/Assistants
Counselor, Professional	Mental Health Psychotherap't	Physician/Physician Assistant/Osteopathy

Plumber/Master/Apprentice/Residential	Ski Lift	Veterinarian
Podiatrist	Social Work	Wireman, Residential
Private Investigator	Tramway	

The Rest:

Alcohol Wholesalers	https://www.colorado.gov/pacific/enforcement/liquor-licenses
Attorney	www.coloradosupremecourt.com/Search/AttSearch.asp
Bus, Charter/Scenic/Children's	www.dora.state.co.us/pls/real/puc_permit.search_form
CDL Third-Party Tester/School	https://www.colorado.gov/pacific/sites/default/files/CDLschools.pdf
Charitable Organization	https://www.sos.state.co.us/ccsa/Login.do
Child Care Facility	www.colorado.gov/apps/jboss/cdhs/childcare/lookup/index.jsf
Collection Agency/Debt Collector	www.coloradoattorneygeneral.gov/car/licensing
Common Carrier/Contract Carrier	www.dora.state.co.us/pls/real/puc_permit.search_form
Credit Union	https://www.colorado.gov/dora/node/100231
Fundraising Consultant	www.sos.state.co.us/ccsa/PfcInquiryCriteria.do
HazMat Carrier	www.dora.state.co.us/pls/real/puc_permit.search_form
Household Goods/Property Carrier	www.dora.state.co.us/pls/real/puc_permit.search_form
Insurance Agency/Agent	https://www.sircon.com/ComplianceExpress/Inquiry/consumerInquiry.do
Limousine	www.dora.state.co.us/pls/real/puc_permit.search_form
Lobbyist/Volunteer	www.sos.state.co.us/lobby/Home.do
Motor Vehicle Dealer, Franchiser	https://www.colorado.gov/myverification/
Notary Public	https://www.sos.state.co.us/notary/pages/public/verifyNotary.xhtml
Off-Road Charter	www.dora.state.co.us/pls/real/puc_permit.search_form
Real Estate Agent	https://apps.colorado.gov/dre/licensing/Lookup/LicenseLookup.aspx
Savings & Loan	https://www.colorado.gov/dora/node/100231
School Administrator/Principal	https://apps.colorado.gov/cde/licensing/Lookup/LicenseLookup.aspx
School Special Service Associate	https://apps.colorado.gov/cde/licensing/Lookup/LicenseLookup.aspx
Solicitor, Paid	www.sos.state.co.us/pubs/charities/FAQ/consumers.html
Solicitor/Telemarketer	www.coloradoattorneygeneral.gov/licensing/telemarketing
Supervised Lenders/Disciplinary History	www.coloradoattorneygeneral.gov/uccc/licensing
Teacher/Substitute/Vocational	https://apps.colorado.gov/cde/licensing/Lookup/LicenseLookup.aspx
Towing Carrier	www.dora.state.co.us/pls/real/puc_permit.search_form
Vehicle Dealer	http://dmv.ca.gov/portal/dmv/detail/portal/oling2/welcome

State and Local Courts

State Court Structure: **District Courts** hear civil cases in any amount (District and County Courts have overlapping jurisdiction over civil cases involving less than $15,000), as well as domestic relations, criminal, juvenile, probate, and mental health cases. **County Courts** handle civil cases under $15,000, misdemeanors, traffic infractions, felony complaints (which may be sent to District Court), protection orders, and small claims. County court decisions may be appealed to the District Court.

About Combined Courts. Nearly every county has combined their offices and personnel of the District and County courts into one operation and formally now use the name XXX County Combined Court. Courts and judges are still separate, but record keeping is centralized which mean a record search will encompass a search of the combined courts' record databases.

Water Courts have exclusive jurisdiction over cases relating to the determination of water rights, use and administration of water, and all other water matters. There are seven Water Courts - one per major river basins - located in Weld, Pueblo, Alamosa, Montrose, Garfield, Routt, and La Plata counties.

The **Denver Court System** differs from those in the rest of the state, in part because Denver is both a city and a county. The Denver County Court functions as a municipal and a county court and is paid for entirely by Denver taxes, rather than by state taxes. The Denver County Court is not part of the state court system; the District Court is.

Municipal Courts deal with violations of city laws committed within the city limits. Generally these laws involve traffic, shoplifting, and minor offenses such as disturbances and dog leash violations. Denver is the only county where the **Probate Court** and **Juvenile Court** is separate from the District Court.
The web page for the Judicial Branch is https://www.courts.state.co.us/

Appellate Courts: The page at www.courts.state.co.us gives access to Appellate opinions and summaries.

About Court Online Access

Online access to the trial court dockets is not available directly through the Colorado Judicial Branch website, but from several state-designated vendors. The vendors provide a statewide search. A Register of Actions available on commercial sites includes civil, civil water, small claims, domestic, felony, misdemeanor, and traffic cases. Fees vary. To search records form either vendor go to www.courts.state.co.us/Administration/Program.cfm/Program/11.   See https://www.courts.state.co.us/dockets for a free search of current dockets by county.

The limited jurisdiction Denver County Court is not in the statewide system, but has its own separate online access system, see below.

Document image copies are not available from any of the websites; file copies may only be obtained from the local court of record.

County Sites (not including the statewide site mentioned above):

Delta County
Combined Courts   http://7thjudicialdistrictco.org/trial-courts/delta/
Civi & Criminal: Civil case look-up at http://7thjudicialdistrictco.org/docket-search/. One week of data only available.

Denver County
County Court - Civil Division   https://www.denvercountycourt.org/
Online search of Denver County Civil Division court cases is at https://www.denvercountycourt.org/search/. There is no fee to do a look-up by docket number, but there is a $2.00 fee to do a name search. DOBs do not always appear on Denver online results.
County Court - Criminal Division   https://www.denvercountycourt.org/
Name search of the criminal case index is $2.00 per name at www.denvergov.org/apps/newcourt/court_select.aspx. Denver case histories go back at least 10 years; results include case, party and action information. A series of free, limited searches is provided at https://www.denvercountycourt.org/search/

El Paso County
El Paso Combined Court   http://gofourth.org/clerkoffelp.htm
Civi & Criminal: Email requests to 04researchrequest@judicial.state.co.us..

Recorders, Assessors, and Other Sites of Note

About Colorado Recording Office: 63 counties, 63 recording offices. The recording officer is the County Clerk and Recorder.

About Tax Liens: Federal tax liens are filed with the Secretary of State. State Tax liens, handled by the Department of Revenue, are filed with the County Clerk and Recorder.

Online Access

There is no statewide access to recorded documents or assessment data. All but two counties (Jackson and Prowers) offer online access. There is a general mix between counties who have their own system and those who use the services of a vendor.

Recorded Documents: These vendors are prevalent:
- www.thecountyrecorder.com/
- http://icounty.org/

Both a free and subscription level searches are usually offered.

Property tax and assessor data: This vendor is prevalent:
- www.qpublic.net/co/ (aka www.coassessors.com).

County Sites:

Adams County   *Recorded Documents, Marriage, Death Records*   www.co.adams.co.us/index.aspx?nid=140   Search recorded documents free at http://apps.adcogov.org/oncoreweb/default.aspx.
Property, Taxation Records   Records from the Adams County Assessor database are free at http://gisapp.adcogov.org/quicksearch/.

Alamosa County   *Recorded Documents, Marriage Records*   www.alamosacounty.org/departments/clerk-a-recorder   Access to recording data back to 1985 is by subscription to I County; fee is $20.00 per day or $250.00 per month; for info and sign up, contact the Recording Office.
Property, Taxation Records   Access parcel maps free at http://slvgis.maps.arcgis.com/apps/Solutions/s2.html?appid=219e0404a52e4f89964bba864f992b93. Assessor records free at www.alamosacounty.org/index.php?option=com_content&view=article&id=8&Itemid=21.

Arapahoe County   *Recorded Documents*   www.co.arapahoe.co.us/index.aspx?nid=287   Access to the recorders database is free at www.co.arapahoe.co.us/oncoreweb/default.aspx. Unofficial images are now available online from 2/1/1996 and forward. No fee for unofficial images, non-certified-$.25 per page, certified copies-$.25 per page plus $1.00 per document. A convenience fee of $2.00 is added to all orders. Certified copies must be mailed out.
Property, Taxation Records   Centrally assessed tax data is available free at www.co.arapahoe.co.us/index.aspx?NID=1106 but no name searching. Search business personal property free at www.co.arapahoe.co.us/index.aspx?NID=1085. Search county foreclosures free at http://foreclosuresearch.arapahoegov.com/foreclosure/.

Archuleta County   *Recorded Documents*   www.archuletacounty.org/index.aspx?nid=84   Access record data by subscription at http://icounty.org/, fee is $300 monthly. Call Recording office for further info and sign-up. 24 hr search $52.00 plus credit card service fee (Visa, M/C fee is 3.5%, Discover and AMEX fee is 3.7%). Copies are $.25 per image printed. Data from 1985 to present, images from 1997 to present.
Property, Taxation Records   Search index data free at http://64.234.218.210/cgi-bin/colorado_links.cgi. Also search assessor data by name or address via the free mapping site at http://assessorrecords.archuletacounty.org/.

Baca County   *Recorded Documents*   www.springfieldcolorado.com/bacacountygov.html   Search recorded documents at www.thecountyrecorder.com/Disclaimer.aspx?jsEnabled=1. Index goes back to 1997.

Bent County   *Recorded Documents, Vital Records Records*   Access to recorded data is available by subscription. Fee is $200 per month. To print documents, an add'l fee of $.25 per page applies. To sign-up, contact Patti Nickell; a sign up form will be faxed to requester or go to http://icounty.org/ for daily use or 1 month use.

Boulder County   *Recorded Documents*   www.bouldercounty.org/dept/clerkrecorder/pages/default.aspx   Recorder data for free at https://recorder.bouldercounty.org/countyweb/login.do?countyname=Boulder. Can use Guest login.
Property, Taxation Records   Search property tax records at https://treasurer.bouldercounty.org/treasurer/web/. Also, access to property searches for free at http://maps.boco.solutions/propertysearch/. Also, access to GIS/mapping for free at www.bouldercounty.org/property/gis/pages/default.aspx.

Broomfield County   *Recorded Documents (index only) Records*   www.broomfield.org/index.aspx?NID=191   Search recorded documents free at https://egov.broomfield.org/recorder/web/.
Property, Taxation Records   Access to GIS/mapping for free at www.broomfield.org/index.aspx?NID=1356.

Chaffee County   *Recorded Documents*   www.chaffeecountyclerk.org/   Access to records for a fee at http://icounty.org/.
Property, Taxation Records   Search assessor database free at http://assessorsearch.chaffeecounty.org/RWDataMartPropertyInquiry/Inquiry.aspx. Access property record search at http://qpublic.net/co/chaffee/.

Cheyenne County   *Recorded Documents*   www.co.cheyenne.co.us/countydepartments/clerkandrecorder.htm   The agency sends online requesters of recorded documents to www.thecountyrecorder.com/Disclaimer.aspx?jsEnabled=1. Index goes back to 7/1/1995. All general books have been imaged and can be accessed by a Book-Page reference. These documents have not been indexed and are not searchable. General books from 10/29/1889-6/30/95; Deed Book A from 7/14/1888-10/10/1888 and mortgage book 2 from 6/26/1905-1/30/1925. Known Missing: Mortgage Book 1 from 5/8/1889-4/23/1909.
Property, Taxation Records   Search the county property sales lists (include town sales and Rural sales) free at www.co.cheyenne.co.us/countydepartments/assessor.htm. Lookups at bottom of webpage. Also, access to Map Viewer for free at http://209.139.208.16/mapguide/cheyenne/.

Clear Creek County   *Recorded Documents*   www.co.clear-creek.co.us/index.aspx?nid=104   Access to records free at https://erecording.co.clear-creek.co.us:8443/clearcreekrecorder/web/. Recorded documents from 8/30/83 to present. Images are not available at this time.
Property, Taxation Records   Access to property record search database free at http://assessor.co.clear-creek.co.us/Assessor/web/.

Conejos County   *Recorded Documents*   www.conejoscounty.org/departments/elected/clerk   Access to recorder office index back to 1978 is by subscription. Call recorder for signup and info. Fee is $200.00 per month plus $.25 per document.
Property, Taxation Records   Access to GIS/mapping for free at www.slvgis.info/conejos/parcelviewer.htm. A vendor provides data from the final tax roll free at http://qpublic.net/co/conejos/.

Costilla County   *Recorded Documents*   https://www.colorado.gov/costillacounty/costilla-county-clerk-recorder   Access to daily/monthly subscription at http://icounty.org/. All documents available from 1997 to present. Documents prior to 1997 coming soon.
Property, Taxation Records   Access to Assessor property search for free at www.co.pueblo.co.us/cgi-bin/webatrallbroker.wsc/ackatrcos.p. There is an older system (pre-2008) at Access assessor property data free at http://64.234.218.210/cgi-bin/colorado_links.cgi?county=costilla.

Crowley County   *Property, Taxation Records*   Access a parcel search, owner search, and location search at www.qpublic.net/co/crowley/index.html. Subscription required for full property data and sales. Also, access property assessment data by subscription at http://64.234.218.210/cgi-bin/colorado.pl.

Custer County   *Recorded Documents*   http://custercountygov.com/index.php?pg=clerk   Access to land record searching for a fee at http://icounty.org/. For a fee of $25.00 there is a 24 hour search. Indexing starts in 1986 and images start in 2004.
Property, Taxation Records   Access assessor final tax roll data free at http://qpublic.net/co/custer/. Subscription required for full property data and sales.

Delta County   *Recorded Documents*   www.deltacounty.com/4/Clerk-and-Recorder   Access recorder records free at https://acclaimweb.deltacounty.com/. Alpha indexing goes back to 1988. With reception number images back to 1883 can be found.
Property, Taxation Records   Access Assessor data on the GIS site for free at http://itax.deltacounty.com/assessor/web/.

Denver County   *Foreclosures Records*   https://www.denvergov.org/content/denvergov/en/denver-office-of-the-clerk-and-recorder.html   Search foreclosures at https://www.denvergov.org/ForeclosurePortal/Home.aspx/Search.
Property, Taxation Records   Assessor database at https://www.denvergov.org/property. Search business personal property at https://www.denvergov.org/apps/perspropertyapplication/persproperty.asp.

Dolores County   *Recorded Records Records*   Access to Recorder's office records free at www.thecountyrecorder.com/Disclaimer.aspx?jsEnabled=1. Index goes back to 1996.
Property, Taxation Records   Assessor information with subscription and log-on found at http://64.234.218.210/cgi-bin/colorado.pl.

Douglas County   *Recorded Documents, Marriage Records*   www.douglas.co.us/government/departments/clerk-and-recorder   Access to recorders index is free at https://apps.douglas.co.us/LandmarkWeb.
Property, Taxation Records   Records on the county assessor database are free at www.douglas.co.us/assessor/. May also download related list data from the site. Also, access to property sales search for free at http://apps.douglas.co.us/apps/assessor/comps/compsBySubdivision.do.

Eagle County   *Recorded Documents, Vital Records Records*   www.eaglecounty.us/Clerk/   Search clerk and recorder data free at https://acclaim.eaglecounty.us/. Access to images by prepaid escrow account or credit card. Charges to view documents or page is $1.00 per page. Contact recording@eaglecounty.us to set up account.
Property, Taxation Records   Search comps sales at www.eaglecounty.us/Assessor/Comparable_Sales_Data/. Access to GIS/mapping for free at www.eaglecounty.us/Assessor/Eagle_County_Parcel_Maps/.

El Paso County   *Recorded Documents*   http://car.elpasoco.com/Pages/default.aspx   Search the grantor/grantee index at http://recordingsearch.car.elpasoco.com/rsui/opr/Search.aspx.
Property, Taxation Records   Records on the county Assessor database are free at http://land.elpasoco.com/. Also, access to recent sales database for free at http://asr.elpasoco.com/Pages/Recent%20Sales%20Database.aspx.

Elbert County   *Recorded Documents*   www.elbertcounty-co.gov/clerk_and_recorder.php#.VigXbG5Nrkd   Access to records search at http://elbertco.tyler-esubmittal.com/recorder/web/. Free is access to recorded documents without images, User ID and Password required for view/print images, based on subscription type.
Property, Taxation Records   Search Assessor data free at http://elbertco.tyler-esubmittal.com/assessor/web/ but no name searching; free registration required. Find taxes owed from Treasurer's office at http://elbertco.tyler-esubmittal.com/treasurer/web/.

Fremont County   *Recorded Documents*   www.fremontco.com/clerkandrecorder/index.shtml   There is no subscription service, but agency offers a escrow account program to pay for document images. Call or email susan.justus@fremontco.com for more information. Copies are $.25 per page and $.50 per instrument.
Property, Taxation Records   Access the assessors property and sales database free at https://erecords.fremontco.com/assessor/web/login.jsp. Must register before using.

Garfield County   *Recorded Documents*   www.garfield-county.com/clerk-recorder/index.aspx   Access recording data free at https://act.garfield-county.com/recorder/web/. Images not available at this time.
Property, Taxation Records   Search the assessor and treasurer property and tax data free at https://act.garfield-county.com/assessor/web/. Also, may search assessor sales data by subscription at https://act.garfield-county.com/assessor/web/login.jsp?submit=Enter+EagleWeb. Also, access PDF parcel maps and property information free at http://garfieldco.mygisonline.com/. Also, access to mapping for free at www.mapquest.com/directions/to/us-co-glenwood+springs-109+8th+st-81601+3303/L1;39.546739,-107.326664.

Gilpin County   *Property, Taxation Records*   Assessor data is found at http://gilpin.infoenvoy.com/.

Grand County *Recorded Documents* http://co.grand.co.us/143/Clerk-Recorder   Access to Clerk-Recorder index is free at http://gcgovernmentapps.com/aptitude/oncoreweb/.
Property, Taxation Records   Access assessor data free at http://assessor.co.grand.co.us/assessor/web/.

Gunnison County *Recorded Documents* www.gunnisoncounty.org/143/Clerk-Recorders-Office   Access records for a fee at https://www.idocmarket.com/Sites.
Property, Taxation Records   Access to property records and sales list for free at http://qpublic6.qpublic.net/co_gunnison_search.php.

Hinsdale County *Recorded Documents* www.hinsdalecountycolorado.us/clerk.html   Access to records for a fee at http://icounty.org/ contact the Clerk's office for application.
Property, Taxation Records   Access to Tax rolls (latest shown as of 1/2/15), vacant land sales, commercial sales and residential sales for free at www.hinsdalecountycolorado.us/files/2013TAXROLL.pdf.

Huerfano County *Recorded Documents* www.huerfano.us/Clerk_s_Office.php   Access to Recorder database records free at www.thecountyrecorder.com/Disclaimer.aspx?jsEnabled=1. Index goes back to 1997.

Jefferson County *Recorded Documents* http://jeffco.us/clerk-and-recorder/   Search the recorder's records for free at https://landrecords.co.jefferson.co.us/. Index goes back to 1963; images to 1994.
Property, Taxation Records   Records on the county Assessor database are free at http://ats.jeffco.us/ats/splash.do. No name searching.

Kiowa County *Recorded Documents* www.kiowacounty-colorado.com/kiowa_county_clerk_&_recorder.htm   Access to recording index is free from a 3rd party company at www.thecountyrecorder.com/Disclaimer.aspx?jsEnabled=1. Index goes back only to July, 2001.

Kit Carson County *Property, Taxation Records*   Access to property record search and GIS for free at http://209.139.208.16/mapguide/kitcarson/.

La Plata County *Recorded Documents* www.co.laplata.co.us/government/elected_officials/clerk_and_recorder_s_office   Access to basic online index and images free at http://records.laplata.co.us/. Also, access to online records for a fee at https://www.idocmarket.com/.
Property, Taxation Records   Property information is available at http://eagleweb.laplata.co.us/assessor/web/. Must register to use.

Lake County *Recorded Documents* www.lakecountyco.com/clerkandrecorder/   Online subscription available-contact Carl at 719-486-4131.
Property, Taxation Records   Access county assessor property data free at http://64.234.218.210/cgi-bin/colorado_links.cgi or at http://qpublic.net/co/lake/index.html.

Larimer County *Recorded Documents, Voter Registration Records* www.larimer.org/clerk/   Search the county Public Record Databases (indexing only-no images) for free at http://records.larimer.org/LandmarkWeb/home/index. Search registered voter list free at https://www.sos.state.co.us/voter-classic/pages/pub/olvr/findVoterReg.xhtml.
Property, Taxation Records   Search assessor property data free at www.larimer.org/assessor/propertyExplorer/propertyexplorer.html or www.co.larimer.co.us/assessor/query/search.cfm. Search treasurer property taxes free at www.larimer.org/treasurer/query/search.cfm but no name searching.

Las Animas County *Recorded Documents* www.lasanimascounty.net/departments/clerk-a-recorder.html   Access to records for a fee at http://icounty.org/. Fees are $300.00 monthly or $20.00 for 24 hours.
Property, Taxation Records   Access data from the final tax roll free at http://qpublic.net/co/lasanimas/. There are also 3 levels of subscription service based on customers needs.

Lincoln County *Recorded Documents* http://lincolncountyco.us/clerk_recorder/clerk_recorder.html   Assess to documents free at www.thecountyrecorder.com/Disclaimer.aspx?jsEnabled=1. Index goes back to 1997.
Property, Taxation Records   Access data from the final tax roll free at http://qpublic.net/co/lincoln/. There are also 3 levels of subscription service based on customers needs. Also, access to property records for free at http://assessor.lincolncountyco.us/assessor/web/. For advanced search, must subscribe.

Logan County *Recorded Documents* https://www.colorado.gov/pacific/logan/county-clerk-and-recorder   Enter the recorder's database site at https://loganco.tyler-esubmittal.com/recorder/web/, registration and username/password required to view and print images. Sub fee is $300 per month.
Property, Taxation Records   Access to assessor property data is free at www.logancountycoaat.com/Search/Disclaimer.aspx?FromUrl=../search/commonsearch.aspx?mode=owner.

Mesa County *Recorded Documents* http://clerk.mesacounty.us/   Search the recorder's Grantor/Grantee index free at https://recording.mesacounty.us/landmarkweb. Can purchase a subscription, fees depend on amount documents accessed per month.
Property, Taxation Records   GIS/mapping and property data at http://gis.mesacounty.us/default.aspx.

Mineral County *Property, Taxation Records*   Access data from the final tax roll free at http://qpublic.net/co/mineral/. There are also 3 levels of subscription service based on customers needs.

Moffat County *Recorded Documents* https://www.colorado.gov/moffatcounty   Online records available online for $250.00 per month or $25.00 per day (24 hours) or $.25 per copy at http://icounty.org/. Contact Debbie Winder for more information.
Property, Taxation Records   Access to assessor property data free at http://moffat.infoenvoy.com/. Also, search the treasurer's tax database free at http://moffat.visualgov.com/SearchSelect.aspx.

Montezuma County *Recorded Documents, Marriage, Death Records* http://montezumacounty.org/web/departments/clerk-recorder/ Access recorded records data back to 6/3/1996 free at http://eagleweb.co.montezuma.co.us/recorder/web/. Index only. For more detail image view and print web subscription for $350.00 per month.
Property, Taxation Records   Access county property tax data free at http://montezumacounty.org/web/assessor-property-inquiry/. Also, access to GIS-mapping for free at http://montezumacounty.org/web/departments/gis-mapping/gis-viewer/.

Montrose County *Recorded Documents* www.montrosecounty.net/72/Clerk-Recorder   Access to records free at http://landmarkweb.montrosecounty.net/LandmarkWeb/.
Property, Taxation Records   Access to Property Information EagleWeb System is free at http://eagleweb.montrosecounty.net/eagleassessor/web/. Also, access to GIS/mapping for free at http://montrosecoparcel.mygisonline.com/.

Morgan County *Recorded Documents, Marriage Records* www.co.morgan.co.us/CountyClerk.html   Access the recorder's online index free as a public user or by subscription for images for $300 per year at www.co.morgan.co.us/recorder/web/splash.jsp.
Property, Taxation Records   Search the assessor database free at www.co.morgan.co.us/assessor/web/login.jsp. Must register before use.

Otero County *Recorded Documents* www.oterogov.com/elected-officials/clerk-and-recorder   Access to recorded data is by subscription only. Fee is $250 per month or $25.00 per day plus $.25 per page for copies printed. Contact the Clerk/Recorder office for more info and sign-up.
Property, Taxation Records   Access property data free at www.qpublic.net/co/otero/search.html.

Ouray County *Recorded Documents, Marriage Records* www.ouraycountyco.gov/325/Clerk-Recorder   Access the record data free at www.thecountyrecorder.com/Disclaimer.aspx?jsEnabled=1.
Property, Taxation Records   Access recorder data free at http://ouraycountyassessor.org/assessor/web/. With registration, can also create and print reports for properties free of charge.

Park County *Recorded Documents* www.parkco.us/72/Clerk-Recorder   Access to records for a fee at http://icounty.org/. Contact Lori at 719-836-4225 for county access.
Property, Taxation Records   Records on the county Assessor database are free at www.parkco.org/Search2.asp, including tax data, owner, address, building characteristics, legal and deed information.

Phillips County *Property, Taxation Records*   Access to property record search for free at http://phillipsco.tyler-esubmittal.com/assessor/web/.

Pitkin County *Recorded Documents* www.pitkinclerk.org/   Search recorded documents free at www.pitkinclerk.org/oncoreweb/. Also, probate records from 1881 to 1953 and divorce records from 1931 to 1964 are at https://www.colorado.gov/archives.
Property, Taxation Records   Records on the county Assessor database are free at www.pitkinassessor.org/Assessor/.

Pueblo County *Recorded Documents, Marriage Records* http://county.pueblo.org/government/county/department/clerk-and-recorder Access clerk & recorder index of recorded docs at https://erecording.co.pueblo.co.us/recorder/web/. Search documents recorded since 05/01/1991.
Property, Taxation Records   Access county assessor data free at www.co.pueblo.co.us/cgi-bin/webatrallbroker.wsc/ackatr.p.

Rio Blanco County *Recorded Documents* www.rbc.us/176/Clerk-Recorder   Access to records at https://www.idocmarket.com/Sites. Can do a basic search for free or for more detailed information must subscribe. Indexing and images available from 4/1983 to present.
Property, Taxation Records   Access assessor property data free at http://rioblanco.valuewest.net/.

Rio Grande County *Recorded Documents* www.riograndecounty.org/index.php?option=com_content&view=article&id=9&Itemid=7   Access to records for a fee at http://icounty.org/.
Property, Taxation Records   Access to GIS/mapping for free to go www.co.pueblo.co.us/cgi-bin/webatrallbroker.wsc/ackatrig.p.

Routt County *Recorded Documents, Property Sale Records* www.co.routt.co.us/index.aspx?nid=133   Search records for free at https://countyfusion2.propertyinfo.com/countyweb/login.do?countyname=RouttCO. For detailed information, must subscribe. Indexing is from 1/1983 to present.
Property, Taxation Records   Records on the county Assessor are free at http://agner.co.routt.co.us/assessor/web/. Treasurer records free at http://agner.co.routt.co.us:8080/treasurer/web/.

Saguache County *Recorded Documents* www.saguachecounty.net/index.php/departments/clerk-and-recorder   Access Recorder database free at www.thecountyrecorder.com/Disclaimer.aspx?jsEnabled=1. Index goes back to 1994; unofficial images back to 1996.
Property, Taxation Records   Search Assessor tax roll database free at www.qpublic.net/co/saguache/.

San Juan County *Recorded Documents* www.sanjuancountycolorado.us/clerk--recorder.html   Access to recording index is free from a 3rd party company at www.thecountyrecorder.com/Disclaimer.aspx?jsEnabled=1. Index goes back to 1997.

Property, Taxation Records   Access to county online property search for free at www.co.pueblo.co.us/cgi-bin/webatrallbroker.wsc/atrpropertysearchall.html.

San Miguel County   *Recorded Documents*   www.sanmiguelcounty.org/163/Clerk-Recorder   Access to recording index is free from a 3rd party company at www.sanmiguelcounty.org/155/County-Clerk-Recorders-Office-Disclaimer.

Property, Taxation Records   Assessor data is viewable online at https://onlinepayments.sanmiguelcountyco.gov/treasurer/web/. The treasurer data is at https://onlinepayments.sanmiguelcounty.org/treasurer/web/. A database of property foreclosures is at http://foreclosures.sanmiguelcounty.org/. All searches are free.

Sedgwick County   *Recorded Documents*   www.sedgwickcountygov.net/county-officials/clerk-recorder/   Access to recorded records free at www.thecountyrecorder.com/Disclaimer.aspx?jsEnabled=1. Index goes back to 1973.

Property, Taxation Records   Access data from the final tax roll free at http://qpublic.net/co/sedgwick/. There are also 3 levels of subscription service based on customers needs.

Summit County   *Property, Taxation Records*   Access to the GIS/mapping site property data is free at http://gis.co.summit.co.us/Map/. Also, access to foreclosure property search free at http://apps.summitcountyco.gov/ForeclosureSearch/index.aspx.

Teller County   *Recorded Documents*   www.co.teller.co.us/CR/default.aspx   Access the county clerk real estate database free at www.thecountyrecorder.com/Disclaimer.aspx?jsEnabled=1. Searchable documents exist starting in 1991. Images not available for Public access.

Property, Taxation Records   Search the assessor database free at www.co.teller.co.us/assessor/databasehome.aspx. Search by name or address.

Washington County   *Recorded Documents*   Access to recorded records for free to go www.thecountyrecorder.com/Disclaimer.aspx?jsEnabled=1. Index goes back to 1996.

Property, Taxation Records   Access data from the final tax roll free at http://qpublic.net/co/washington/.

Weld County   *Recorded Documents*   http://cr.weldgov.com/index.html   Access to records go to https://searchicris.co.weld.co.us/recorder/web/. Query is free. Documents available from 1/1/1865, maps from 1865.

Property, Taxation Records   Access assessor data, property sales, ownership listings, transfers, property cards free at www.co.weld.co.us/Departments/Assessor/index.html.

Yuma County   *Recorded Documents*   www.yumacounty.net/clerk_recorder.html   Access to online records for a fee at https://www.idocmarket.com/.

Property, Taxation Records   Access data from the final tax roll free at http://qpublic.net/co/yuma/. Also, access to GIS/mapping for free at http://yumaco.mygisonline.com/.

Connecticut

Capital: Hartford
                Hartford County
Time Zone: EST
Population: 3,590,886
# of Counties: 8

Useful State Links

Website: **http://portal.ct.gov/**

Governor: **http://portal.ct.gov/governor/**

Attorney General: **www.ct.gov/ag/site/default.asp**

State Archives: **http://ctstatelibrary.org/state-archives/**

State Statutes and Codes: **https://www.cga.ct.gov/current/pub/titles.htm**

Legislative Bill Search: **https://www.cga.ct.gov/asp/CGABillInfo/CGABillInfoRequest.asp**

Unclaimed Funds: **www.ctbiglist.com/**

State Public Record Agencies

Sexual Offender Registry

Division of State Police, Sex Offender Registry Unit,   www.communitynotification.com/cap_office_disclaimer.php?office=54567   The search site is www.communitynotification.com/cap_office_disclaimer.php?office=54567. There are many search options including by name.   *Other Options:* Record data can be purchased in bulk.

Incarceration Records

Connecticut Department of Corrections, Public Information Office,   www.ct.gov/doc/site/default.asp   Current inmates may be searched at www.ctinmateinfo.state.ct.us/. DOB is shown. The agency indicates that a person's current incarceration does not necessarily indicate they have been convicted of a crime, as Connecticut's correctional system also holds those who are awaiting trial.

Corporation, LP, LLC, LLP, Statutory Trust, Trademarks/Servicemarks

Secretary of the State, Commercial Recording Division,   www.sots.ct.gov/sots/site/default.asp   Click on the CONCORD option at the website for free access to corporation and UCC records. The system is open from 7AM to 11PM. You can search by business name, business ID or by filing number. The web also offers online filing. Go to   www.concord-sots.ct.gov/CONCORD/index.jsp.   Search securities division enforcement actions at www.ct.gov/dob/cwp/view.asp?a=2246&q=401762   *Other Options:* Bulk data is available on disk, there are many options. Please call for details.

Uniform Commercial Code, Federal & State Tax Liens

UCC Division, Secretary of State,   www.concord-sots.ct.gov/CONCORD/index.jsp   An free index search is offered at www.concord-sots.ct.gov/CONCORD/online?sn=PublicInquiry&eid=9755. The link is on the home page.   *Other Options:* Bulk lists and CDs are available for purchase. Call the Financial Area at 860-509-6165.

Birth, Death, Marriage Records

Department of Public Health,   www.ct.gov/dph/site/default.asp   Online ordering is provided by a designated vendor - www.vitalchek.com.

Driver Records

Department of Motor Vehicles, Copy Records Unit,   www.ct.gov/dmv/site/default.asp   Electronic access is provided to approved businesses that enter into written contract. The contract requires a $37,500 prepayment deposit for the first 2,500 records. The online system is operational for interactive and batch modes. The fee is $15.00 for per inquiry made, including no record found reports. The driver's license number, first name, last name, middle initial and DOB are required when ordering. Write to the Data Access unit at the same address listed above. Also, a free Non-CDL Status Check is at https://www.dmvselfservice.ct.gov/LicenseStatusService.aspx?dmvPNavCtr=|#56360. must enter DL#. The state's Judicial Branch offers a free look-up of motor vehicle convictions at www.jud2.ct.gov/crdockets/SearchByDefDisp.aspx. Search by name and court location.

Vehicle Ownership & Registration

Department of Motor Vehicles, Copy Record Unit, www.ct.gov/dmv/site/default.asp   There is no online access to full records, but one may check registration expiration dates by entering the plate number at www.dmvselfservice.ct.gov/RegistrationVerificationService.aspx.   *Other Options:* Vehicle record information is available on a volume basis to approved businesses that enter into a written agreement and approved use. The contract requires an annual fee and a surety bond. For more information, write to Data Access at the address above.

Crash Reports

Department of Public Safety, Reports and Records Unit,   www.ct.gov/despp/cwp/view.asp?a=4212&q=494530   Access online is available via a designated vendor; see www.docview.us.com. A $6.00 convenience fee is added. Please note, not all accidents will be available on Docview.

Campaign Finance & Committees

State Elections Enforcement Commission,   www.ct.gov/seec/site/default.asp   Search campaign finance and committee fundraising at the Campaign Reporting Information System at http://seec.ct.gov/eCris/DocumentSearch/DocumentSearchHome.aspx?seecNav=| Political committees are shown at www.ct.gov/seec/lib/seec/committeelists/ongoing_political_committees.pdf. State contractors prohibited from contributing to statewide office candidates are shown at www.ct.gov/seec/cwp/view.asp?a=3560&Q=421136   *Other Options:* An electronic file of all registered voters is available for $300.

Occupational Licensing Boards

These licenses are all searchable at https://www.elicense.ct.gov/Lookup/LicenseLookup.aspx

Accountant-CPA/Firm	Electrical Cont/Inspector	Liquor License
Acupuncturist	Electrical Journeyman/Apprentice	Liquor Mfg/Dist/Whlse
Alcohol/Drug Counselor	Electrical Sign Installer	Liquor Permittee
Antenna Svcs Dealer/Technician	Electrician	Liquor Store/Broker/Shipper
Apple Product Mfg	Electrologist/Hypertricologist	Marriage & Family Therapist
Architect/Architectural Firm	Electronics Service Dealer/Tech	Martial Arts Facility
Asbestos Consultant/Contractor	Elevator Inspector/Mechanic	Massage Therapist
Asbestos Worker/Supvr	Embalmer	Mausoleum
Assisted Living Service	Emergency Med Svc Professional	Medical Gas/Vacuum System
Association Manager	EMS First Responder	Medical Marijuana Related
Athletic Promoter	EMS Instructor	Medical Response Technician
Audiologist	Engineer/Engineer-in-Training	Mental Health Facility/Clinic
Automobile Glass Technician	Fire Protection Inspector/Contractor	Midwife
Bakery	Fire Sprinkler Technician	Mobile Home Park/Seller
Barber	Fund Raiser, Paid	Naturopathic Physician
Bedding Mfg/Renovation	Funeral Director/Home	New Home Construction Contr
Bedding Supply/Sterilizer	Gasoline Dealer, Retail	Nurse-Advance Registered Practice
Beverage/Water Bottler	Glazier	Nurse-LPN/Aide
Boxer/Boxing Professional	Hairdresser	Nursing Home
Building Contractor	Health Club	Nursing Home Administrator
Caterer/Concessioner, Liquor	Hearing Instrument Specialist	Occupational Therapist/Assistant
Charitable Solicitor	Heating/Piping/Cooling Cont/Journey'n	Optical Shop
Child Day Care, Substitute, Asst, Consultant	Home Health Aide Agency/Homemaker	Optician
Chiropractor	Home Heating Fuel Dealer	Optometrist
Closing Out Sale, Promoter	Home Improvement Contr/Seller	Osteopathic Physician
Construction Inspector	Home Inspector	Paramedic
Contractor, Mechanical/Major	Homemaker Companion	Perfusionist
Controlled Substance Lab/Practioner	Homeopathic Physician	Pharmacist/Pharmacist Intern
Convalescent Nursing Home	Hospice	Pharmacy/Technician
Cosmetologist	Hypnotist	Physical Therapist/Assistant
Counselor, Professional	Interior Designer	Physician/Doctor/Assistant
Crematorium	Interstate Land Sale	Pipefitter
Dental Anesthesia/Sedation Permittee	Juice Producer	Plumber
Dentist/Dental Hygienist	Kennel/Commercial	Podiatrist
Dietician/Nutritionist	Land Sale, Interstate	Poultry Facility
Drug/Cosmetic Whlse/Mfg	Landscape Architect/Land Surveyor/Surveyor	Psychologist
Druggist Liquor Permittee	Firm	Public Service Technician

Radiographer

Real Estate Agent/Broker/Sales/Appraiser

Real Estate Educ Provider

Respiratory Care Practitioner

Sanitarian

Sheet Metal Contr/Journeyman

Shorthand Court Reporter

Social Worker

Solar Energy Contr/Journeyman

Speech Pathologist

Sprinkler Layout Technician

Student Athlete Agent

Telecommunication Technician

Television/Radio License

Vending Machine Operator

Vendor, Itinerant

Veterinarian

Water Distribution System Operator

Water Treatment Plant Operator

Weigher

Weights/Measures Dealer/Repair/Regul'r

Well Driller

Winery Farm

Wrestler/Wrestling Manager

The Rest:

Airport/Heliport	http://ctairports.org/
Appraiser, MVPD/MVR	www.cidverifylicense.ct.gov/CLIC/VerifyLicense.aspx
Attorney/Attorney Firm	www.jud2.ct.gov/attorneyfirming/AttorneyFirmInquiry.aspx
Automobile Insurance Adjuster	www.cidverifylicense.ct.gov/CLIC/VerifyLicense.aspx
Automobile Parts Mfg'r	www.ct.gov/dmv/cwp/view.asp?a=799&q=401814&dmvPNavCtr=|#48712
Automobile Racing Permit	www.ct.gov/dmv/cwp/view.asp?a=799&q=401814&dmvPNavCtr=|#48712
Automobile Renter/Leaser	www.ct.gov/dmv/cwp/view.asp?a=799&q=401814&dmvPNavCtr=|#48712
Bail Bondsman	www.ct.gov/dps/lib/dps/special_licensing_and_firearms/licensed_bondsman.pdf
Bail Enforcement Agent	www.ct.gov/dps/lib/dps/special_licensing_and_firearms/licensed_bea.pdf
Bail Enforcement Instructor	www.ct.gov/dps/lib/dps/special_licensing_and_firearms/bea_instructors.pdf
Bank & Trust Company	www.ct.gov/dob/cwp/view.asp?a=2228&q=296954&dobNAV_GID=1660
Bank Branch/Banking Office, Non-depository	www.ct.gov/dob/cwp/view.asp?a=2228&q=296954&dobNAV_GID=1660
Bank CEO	www.ct.gov/dob/cwp/view.asp?a=2239&Q=298138&dobNAV_GID=1659&dobNav=|
Beekeeper	www.ct.gov/caes/cwp/view.asp?a=2818&q=376964
Business Opportunity Offering	www.ct.gov/dob/cwp/view.asp?a=2239&Q=298138&dobNAV_GID=1659&dobNav=|
Casualty Adjuster	www.cidverifylicense.ct.gov/CLIC/VerifyLicense.aspx
Check Cashing Service	www.ct.gov/dob/cwp/view.asp?a=2239&Q=298138&dobNAV_GID=1659&dobNav=|
Child Caring Agency/Facility	www.dir.ct.gov/dcf/Licensed_Facilities/listing_CCF.asp
Child Placing Agency	www.dir.ct.gov/dcf/Licensed_Facilities/listing_CPA.asp
Child Psychiatric Clinic/Outpatient	www.dir.ct.gov/dcf/Licensed_Facilities/listing_OPCC.asp
Collection Agency	www.ct.gov/dob/cwp/view.asp?a=2239&Q=298138&dobNAV_GID=1659&dobNav=|
College/University-State Supported	www.ctohe.org/HEWeb/CollegesList.asp
Credit Union	www.ct.gov/dob/cwp/view.asp?a=2237&q=298042&dobNAV_GID=1660
Day Treatment Facility, Extended	www.dir.ct.gov/dcf/Licensed_Facilities/listing_EDT.asp
Debt Adjuster	www.ct.gov/dob/cwp/view.asp?a=2239&Q=298138&dobNAV_GID=1659&dobNav=|
Decertified Police Officers	www.ct.gov/post/lib/post/certification/list_of_decertified_officers.pdf
Driver Education Instr/School	www.ct.gov/dmv/cwp/view.asp?a=799&q=401814&dmvPNavCtr=|#48712
Family Residence, Permanent	www.dir.ct.gov/dcf/Licensed_Facilities/listing_PFR.asp
Hazardous Waste Transporter	www.ct.gov/deep/cwp/view.asp?a=2718&q=455558&depNav_GID=1967&depNav
Health Care Center Insurer	www.cidverifylicense.ct.gov/CLIC/VerifyLicense.aspx
Honey Bee Registration	www.ct.gov/caes/cwp/view.asp?a=2818&q=376964
Insurance Adjuster/Appraiser	www.cidverifylicense.ct.gov/CLIC/VerifyLicense.aspx
Insurance Agent, Fraternal/Consultant	www.cidverifylicense.ct.gov/CLIC/VerifyLicense.aspx
Insurance Company/Producer	www.cidverifylicense.ct.gov/CLIC/VerifyLicense.aspx
Investment Advisor/Agent	www.ct.gov/dob/cwp/view.asp?a=2239&Q=298138&dobNAV_GID=1659&dobNav=|
Junkyard Operator	www.ct.gov/dmv/cwp/view.asp?a=799&q=401814&dmvPNavCtr=|#48712
Loan Company, Small	www.ct.gov/dob/cwp/view.asp?a=2239&Q=298138&dobNAV_GID=1659&dobNav=|
Lobbyist	https://www.oseapps.ct.gov/NewLobbyist/security/loginhome.aspx
Marshall, State	www.jud.ct.gov/faq/marshals.htm
Medication Admin for Ment'y Retarded	www.ct.gov/dds/cwp/view.asp?a=3620&q=424134
Money Forwarder	www.ct.gov/dob/cwp/view.asp?a=2239&Q=298138&dobNAV_GID=1659&dobNav=|
Money Order/Travelers Check Issuer	www.ct.gov/dob/cwp/view.asp?a=2233&q=297862&dobNAV_GID=1663
Mortgage Broker/Lender	www.ct.gov/dob/cwp/view.asp?a=2239&Q=298138&dobNAV_GID=1659&dobNav=|
Motor Vehicle Recycler	www.ct.gov/dmv/cwp/view.asp?a=799&q=401814&dmvPNavCtr=|#48712

Nursery Plant/Dealer .... www.ct.gov/caes/cwp/view.asp?a=2818&q=376964
Premium Finance Company .... www.cidverifylicense.ct.gov/CLIC/VerifyLicense.aspx
Private Investigator/Agency .... www.ct.gov/dps/lib/dps/special_licensing_and_firearms/licensed_pi_security_companies.pdf
Private Occupational & Hospital-Based Schools www.ctohe.org/HEWeb/CollegesList.asp
Reinsurance Intermediary .... www.cidverifylicense.ct.gov/CLIC/VerifyLicense.aspx
Rental Car Company .... www.cidverifylicense.ct.gov/CLIC/VerifyLicense.aspx
Risk Purchasing/Retention Group .... www.cidverifylicense.ct.gov/CLIC/VerifyLicense.aspx
Sales Finance Company .... www.ct.gov/dob/cwp/view.asp?a=2239&Q=298138&dobNAV_GID=1659&dobNav=|
Savings Bank/Savings & Loan Association .... www.ct.gov/dob/cwp/view.asp?a=2239&Q=298138&dobNAV_GID=1659&dobNav=|
School Principal/Superintendent .... www.csde.state.ct.us/public/csde/reports/SuperintendentContacts.asp
Security Company/ Firearms Instr .... www.ct.gov/dps/lib/dps/special_licensing_and_firearms/certified_security_officers_firearms_instructors-
blue_cards.pdf
Security Officer Instructor .... www.ct.gov/dps/lib/dps/special_licensing_and_firearms/approved_cj_security_instructor_(public).pdf
Security Service .... www.ct.gov/dps/lib/dps/special_licensing_and_firearms/licensed_pi_security_companies.pdf
Solid Waste Facility Operator .... www.ct.gov/deep/cwp/view.asp?a=2718&q=455558&depNav_GID=1967&depNav
Surplus Lines Broker .... www.cidverifylicense.ct.gov/CLIC/VerifyLicense.aspx
Teacher .... http://sdeportal.ct.gov/CECSFOI/FOILookup.aspx
Towing Operator .... www.ct.gov/dmv/cwp/view.asp?a=799&q=401814&dmvPNavCtr=|#48712
Utilization Review Company .... www.cidverifylicense.ct.gov/CLIC/VerifyLicense.aspx
Vehicle Dealer/Repairer .... www.ct.gov/dmv/cwp/view.asp?a=799&q=401814&dmvPNavCtr=|#48712
Viatical Settlement Broker/Provider .... www.cidverifylicense.ct.gov/CLIC/VerifyLicense.aspx
Wildlife Control Operator/ Rehabilitator .... www.ct.gov/deep/cwp/view.asp?a=2709&Q=518202&deepNav_GID=1643

State and Local Courts

About Connecticut Courts: The **Superior Court** is the sole court of original jurisdiction for all causes of action, except for matters over which the **Probate Courts** have jurisdiction as provided by statute. The state is divided into 13 Judicial Districts, 20 Geographic Area Courts, and 13 Juvenile Districts. The Superior Court - comprised primarily of the **Judicial District Courts** and the **Geographical Area Courts** - has 5 divisions: Criminal, Civil, Family, Juvenile, and Administrative Appeals. When not combined, the Judicial District Courts handle felony and civil cases while the Geographic Area Courts handle misdemeanors, and most handle small claims. Divorce records are maintained by the Chief Clerk of the Judicial District Courts. Probate is handled by city Probate Courts and those courts not part of the state court system. In May, 2006 the state centralized all small claims cases to the Centralized Small Claims Office. This location holds all records since that date.

The web page for the Judicial Branch is www.jud.ct.gov/.

Appellate Courts: The Courts of Appeal hears appeals from the Superior Courts. The website above provides access to all opinions; click on *Case Look-up*.

About Court Online Access

There is a statewide system for each of serveral types of records.

The Judicial Branch offers web look-up to case docket information at www.jud.ct.gov/jud2.htm. Case look-ups are segregated into five types; civil/family, criminal/motor vehicle, housing, juvenile, and small claims. Search statewide or by location for civil; only by location for criminal. The year of birth shows for criminal, but not for civil. The criminal and the motor vehicle case docket data is available on cases up to ten years after a disposition or bond forfeiture occurred. The system is strict about the ten year rule, no matter how serious the criminal case. The web page states civil cases are available from no less than one year and no more than ten years after the disposition date depending on location, but the number is usually closer to ten. There may be missing or unviewable data on the online system if the civil case was e-filed.

Criminal searches are generally considered to be onsite equivalent - civil searches are not.

Note the Housing case record search at www.jud.ct.gov/housing.htm is available only for Hartford, New Haven, New Britain, Bridgeport, Norwalk and Waterbury districts. However, Case records for summary process matters in Tolland and Meriden Judicial Districts can be found using the Civil/Family look-up.

There are no individual Connecticut courts offering online access beyond the statewide sites mentioned above.

Recorders, Assessors, and Other Sites of Note

About Connecticut Recording Offices: 8 counties and 169 towns/cities. **There is no county recording in Connecticut, all recording is at the town/city level**. The recording officer is the Town/City Clerk. Be careful not to confuse searching in the following towns/cities as equivalent to a countywide search (since they have the same names): Fairfield, Hartford, Litchfield, New Haven, New London, Tolland, and Windham.

About Tax Liens: All federal and state tax liens on personal property are filed with the Secretary of State. Federal and state tax liens on real property are filed with the Town/City Clerk. In generalm, towns will not perform tax lien searches.

Online Access

Recorded Documents

There is access to approximately 72 Town Clerks' record indexes and images for a fee at https://connecticut-townclerks-records.com/User/Login.aspx. Images are shown to subscribers. Throughput dates are shown. Subscriptions range from one day to one year. Images are $1.00 per page. There is a 5% service fee if paying with PayPal.

A vendor provides free access to an index of recorded documents for approximately 17 Town Clerks at www.searchiqs.com/. One can also sign-up for user account to print images. Print fees are $1.50 per image.

Another vendor provides a free search of recorded real estate records for at least 37 Town Clerks at https://www.uslandrecords.com/ctlr/. To view images, pay-per access service is available.

Assessor Information

A number of towns offer free access to Assessor information. Several vendors provide access for various Connecticut jurisdictions.

A vendor providing Assessor property records, usually free, is at www.vgsi.com/vision/Applications/ParcelData/Home.aspx. There are at least 84 participating jurisdictions. However data is not necessarily current. The web page shows when last updated.

The Northeastern Connecticut Council of Governments (NECCOG) provides a free GIS Map Viewer for 8 cities at http://54.174.182.81/html5viewer/?viewer=neccoggis2.

Local Online Sites

Note: All recording and property assessment is at the town level. Therefore this section is provided in town /city order. The county is indicated.

Andover Town in Tolland County *Property, Taxation Records* Search town assessor database at https://www.mytaxbill.org/inet/bill/home.do?town=andover. This is for viewing or paying taxes.

Ansonia City in New Haven County *Recorded Documents* www.cityofansonia.com/content/2524/2614/default.aspx Access to record indexes and images for a fee at https://connecticut-townclerks-records.com/User/Login.aspx?ReturnUrl=%2f. Subscription range from one day to one year. Images are $1.00 per page. There is a 5% service fee if paying with PayPal.
Property, Taxation Records Access to GIS/mapping free at http://ansonia.mapxpress.net/.

Ashford Town in Windham County *Recorded Documents* www.ashfordtownhall.org/government/admin-and-finance/town-clerk/ Access to record indexes and images for a fee at https://connecticut-townclerks-records.com/User/Login.aspx?ReturnUrl=%2f. Subscription range from one day to one year. Images are $1.00 per page. There is a 5% service fee if paying with PayPal.
Property, Taxation Records Access to property assessment free at http://gis.vgsi.com/ashfordct/. Also, access to GIS/mapping for free at http://gis.neccog.org/Municipal/Ashford/AssessorMaps/. Another GIS/mapping site for free at http://54.174.182.81/html5viewer/?viewer=neccoggis2.

Avon Town in Hartford County *Recorded Documents* www.avonct.gov/town-clerk Access to record indexes and images for a fee at https://connecticut-townclerks-records.com/User/Login.aspx?ReturnUrl=%2f. Subscription range from one day to one year. Images are $1.00 per page. There is a 5% service fee if paying with PayPal.
Property, Taxation Records Access to property data is free at www.avonassessor.com/index.shtml.

Barkhamsted Town in Litchfield County *Recorded Documents*
http://barkhamsted.us/Departments/TownClerk/tabid/96/Default.aspx   Access to land records for free at https://www.uslandrecords.com/ctlr/. Indexes are free, pay-per access service available to view images. Records from 1/1/.1957 to present.
Property, Taxation Records   Access to GIS/mapping free at https://barkhamstedct.mapgeo.io/.

Berlin Town in Hartford County *Recorded Documents* www.town.berlin.ct.us/department/?structureid=26   Access to record indexes and images for a fee at https://connecticut-townclerks-records.com/User/Login.aspx?ReturnUrl=%2f. Subscription range from one day to one year. Images are $1.00 per page. There is a 5% service fee if paying with PayPal.
Property, Taxation Records   Search the Town of Berlin Geographic and Property Network for property maps and abutting property at www.berlingis.com/.

Bethany Town in New Haven County *Property, Taxation Records*   For property assessments for free at
http://host.appgeo.com/sccog/. Also, access to GIS/mapping for free at http://bethany.mapxpress.net/. Also, access to online property field cards at www.equalitycama.com/#Towns. Click on Bethany.

Bethel Town in Fairfield County *Recorded Documents* www.bethel-ct.gov/content/117/452/default.aspx   Access to record indexes and images for a fee at https://connecticut-townclerks-records.com/User/Login.aspx?ReturnUrl=%2f. Subscription range from one day to one year. Images are $1.00 per page. There is a 5% service fee if paying with PayPal.
Property, Taxation Records   Access to the Assessor's field cards and GIS mapping for free at www.bethel-ct.gov/content/117/125/129.aspx.

Bethlehem Town in Litchfield County *Recorded Documents* www.ci.bethlehem.ct.us   Access to land records for free at https://www.uslandrecords.com/ctlr/. Indexes are free, pay-per access service available to view images.
Property, Taxation Records   Search town assessor database at www.qpublic.net/ct/bethlehem/search.html.

Bloomfield Town in Hartford County *Recorded Documents* http://bloomfieldct.org/Plugs/town-clerk.aspx   Access to index/indices for free at https://www.uslandrecords.com/ctlr/. Indexes are free, pay-per ($2.00) access service available to view images.
Property, Taxation Records   Access to Assessor's online database free at www.qpublic.net/ct/bloomfield/search.html.

Bolton Town in Tolland County *Recorded Documents* www.bolton.govoffice.com/index.asp   Access to record indexes and images for a fee at https://connecticut-townclerks-records.com/User/Login.aspx?ReturnUrl=%2f. Subscription range from one day to one year. Images are $1.00 per page. There is a 5% service fee if paying with PayPal.
Property, Taxation Records   Access to GIS/mapping for free at http://mapgeo.com/crcogct/. Also, search the town assessor database at http://gis.vgsi.com/BoltonCT/.

Bozrah Town in New London County *Recorded Documents* http://townofbozrah.org/departments/town-clerk   Access to record indexes and images for a fee at https://connecticut-townclerks-records.com/User/Login.aspx?ReturnUrl=%2f. Subscription range from one day to one year. Images are $1.00 per page. There is a 5% service fee if paying with PayPal.

Branford Town in New Haven County *Recorded Documents* www.branford-ct.gov/TownClerk   Access to town clerk's recording records for a fee at https://connecticut-townclerks-records.com/User/Login.aspx?ReturnUrl=%2f. Land records go back to 1/1993; trade names indexes and images back to 2005. Maps go back to 191/1/1962.
Property, Taxation Records   Search the town assessor database at http://gis.vgsi.com/branfordct/.

Bridgeport Town in Fairfield County *Recorded Documents* www.bridgeportct.gov/content/89019/89914/default.aspx   Access to land records for free at https://www.uslandrecords.com/ctlr/. Indexes are free, pay-per access service available to view images. Images are available from 1988 to present.
Property, Taxation Records   Search town assessor database free at http://gis.vgsi.com/bridgeportct/. Also, access to GIS/mapping free at www.bridgeportct.gov/content/89019/89751/91181.aspx.

Bridgewater Town in Litchfield County *Recorded Documents*
www.bridgewatertownhall.org/Pages/BridgewaterCT_TownClerk/index   Access to record indexes and images for a fee at https://connecticut-townclerks-records.com/User/Login.aspx?ReturnUrl=%2f. Subscription range from one day to one year. Images are $1.00 per page. There is a 5% service fee if paying with PayPal.
Property, Taxation Records   Access to the Assessor's maps for free at
www.bridgewatertownhall.org/pages/BridgewaterCT_Assessor/maps/S01E5F3B6. Also, access to Tax Assessor's database for free at http://gis.vgsi.com/bridgewaterct/.

Bristol City in Hartford County *Recorded Documents* www.bristolct.gov/index.aspx?nid=281   Access to land record indexes from 1/1/1899 to present for free (as a guest) at
http://cottweb.ci.bristol.ct.us/External/User/Login.aspx?ReturnUrl=%2fExternal%2fLandRecords%2fprotected%2fSrchQuickName.aspx. For detailed information must subscribe. For a small annual convenience fee of $250, can access the land record images from 1/1/1958 to present and the trade name images.
Property, Taxation Records   Search town assessor database free at http://gis.vgsi.com/bristolct/.

Brookfield Town in Fairfield County   *Property, Taxation Records*   Search town assessor database at http://gis.vgsi.com/brookfieldct/. Also, access to GIS/mapping for free at http://brookfield.mapxpress.net/.

Brooklyn Town in Windham County   *Recorded Documents*   www.brooklynct.org/town-clerk   Access to land records for free at https://www.uslandrecords.com/ctlr/. Indexes are free, pay-per access service available to view images. Images are available from 1985 to present.
Property, Taxation Records   Access to vacant land summary for free at www.brooklynct.org/sites/brooklynct/files/file/file/vacant_land_sales_0.pdf. Search the assessor database free at http://gis.vgsi.com/brooklynct/.

Burlington Town in Hartford County   *Recorded Documents*   www.burlingtonct.us/town-clerk   Access to record indexes and images for a fee at https://connecticut-townclerks-records.com/User/Login.aspx?ReturnUrl=%2f. Subscription range from one day to one year. Images are $1.00 per page. There is a 5% service fee if paying with PayPal.
Property, Taxation Records   Access to GIS/mapping for free at http://burlington.mapxpress.net/.

Canaan Town in Litchfield County   *Recorded Documents*   www.canaanfallsvillage.org/   Access to record indexes and images for a fee at https://connecticut-townclerks-records.com/User/Login.aspx?ReturnUrl=%2f. Subscription range from one day to one year. Images are $1.00 per page. There is a 5% service fee if paying with PayPal.
Property, Taxation Records   Search town assessor database at http://gis.vgsi.com/CanaanCT/.

Canterbury Town in Windham County   *Property, Taxation Records*   Access assessor property data free at http://gis.vgsi.com/canterburyct/. Also, access to GIS/mapping for free at http://54.174.182.81/html5viewer/?viewer=neccoggis2.

Canton Town in Hartford County   *Recorded Documents*   www.townofcantonct.org/content/19178/19248/default.aspx   Access to record indexes and images for a fee at https://connecticut-townclerks-records.com/User/Login.aspx?ReturnUrl=%2f. Subscription range from one day to one year. Images are $1.00 per page. There is a 5% service fee if paying with PayPal.
Property, Taxation Records   Search of property address, search by owner name, or search sales at www.propertyrecordcards.com/SearchMaster.aspx?towncode=023.

Chaplin Town in Windham County   *Recorded Documents*   www.chaplinct.org/department.htm?id=qx09gkbt   Access to record indexes and images for a fee at https://connecticut-townclerks-records.com/User/Login.aspx?ReturnUrl=%2f. Subscription range from one day to one year. Images are $1.00 per page. There is a 5% service fee if paying with PayPal.
Property, Taxation Records   Access to GIS/mapping for free at http://54.174.182.81/html5viewer/?viewer=neccoggis2.

Cheshire Town in New Haven County   *Recorded Documents*   www.cheshirect.org/town-clerk   Access to land records at https://www.uslandrecords.com/ctlr/. Indexes are free, pay-per access service available to view images. Images available from 4/10/2001.
Property, Taxation Records   Access to online property field cards at www.propertyrecordcards.com/searchmaster.aspx?towncode=025.

Chester Town in Middlesex County   *Recorded Documents*   www.chesterct.org/departments/townclerk.htm   Access to record indexes and images for a fee at https://connecticut-townclerks-records.com/User/Login.aspx?ReturnUrl=%2f. Subscription range from one day to one year. Images are $1.00 per page. There is a 5% service fee if paying with PayPal.
Property, Taxation Records   Access to online property field cards at www.propertyrecordcards.com/searchmaster.aspx?towncode=026.

Clinton Town in Middlesex County   *Recorded Documents*   http://clintonct.org/181/Town-Clerk   Access to record indexes and images for a fee at https://connecticut-townclerks-records.com/User/Login.aspx?ReturnUrl=%2f. Subscription range from one day to one year. Images are $1.00 per page. There is a 5% service fee if paying with PayPal.
Property, Taxation Records   Access assessor property data free at http://gis.vgsi.com/clintonct/.

Colchester Town in New London County   *Recorded Documents*   www.colchesterct.gov/Pages/ColchesterCT_Dept/CTC/index   Access to record indexes and images for a fee at https://connecticut-townclerks-records.com/User/Login.aspx?ReturnUrl=%2f. Subscription range from one day to one year. Images are $1.00 per page. There is a 5% service fee if paying with PayPal.
Property, Taxation Records   Access to parcel information for free at http://colchester.mapxpress.net/.

Columbia Town in Tolland County   *Recorded Documents*   www.columbiact.org/index.asp?Type=B_BASIC&SEC={3B271787-786D-4DD1-8927-02A8BF0B3258}   Access to record indexes and images for a fee at https://connecticut-townclerks-records.com/User/Login.aspx?ReturnUrl=%2f. Subscription range from one day to one year. Images are $1.00 per page. There is a 5% service fee if paying with PayPal.
Property, Taxation Records   Access to GIS/mapping free at http://beta.mapgeo.com/crcogct/#.

Coventry Town in Tolland County   *Recorded Documents*   www.coventryct.org/index.aspx?nid=134   Access to land records for free at www.searchiqs.com/. Index data (only) from 7/1983 to 10/15/2003, index data and images from 10/16/2003 to present. Can sign-up for free user account, print fees are $1.50 per image.

Cromwell Town in Middlesex County   *Recorded Documents*   www.cromwellct.com/dept-townclerk.htm   Access to land records for free at https://www.uslandrecords.com/ctlr/. Indexes are free, pay-per access service available to view images. Images are available from 1851 to present.
Property, Taxation Records   Access to GIS/mapping and record cards for free at https://cromwellct.mapgeo.io/.

Danbury City in Fairfield County *Recorded Document Index Records* www.ci.danbury.ct.us/ Access to records free at http://tc.danbury-ct.gov/external/LandRecords/protected/SrchQuickName.aspx.
Property, Taxation Records Access assessor property data free at http://gis.vgsi.com/danburyct/.

Darien Town in Fairfield County *Property, Taxation Records* Access to Assessor's database free at http://assessment.darienct.gov/Main/Home.aspx.

Deep River Town in Middlesex County *Recorded Documents* www.deepriverct.us/Pages/DeepRiverCT_Clerk/index Access to record indexes and images for a fee at https://connecticut-townclerks-records.com/User/Login.aspx?ReturnUrl=%2f. Subscription range from one day to one year. Images are $1.00 per page. There is a 5% service fee if paying with PayPal.
Property, Taxation Records Access to property records for free at http://gis.vgsi.com/deepriverct/.

Derby City in New Haven County *Property, Taxation Records* Access to GIS/mapping for free at http://derby.mapxpress.net/.

Durham Town in Middlesex County *Recorded Documents* www.townofdurhamct.org/content/28562/27556/27777/default.aspx Access to record indexes and images for a fee at https://connecticut-townclerks-records.com/User/Login.aspx?ReturnUrl=%2f. Subscription range from one day to one year. Images are $1.00 per page. There is a 5% service fee if paying with PayPal.
Property, Taxation Records Access the assessor's database at http://durham.univers-clt.com/.

East Granby Town in Hartford County *Recorded Documents* http://eastgranbyct.org/town-clerk.html Access to record indexes and images for a fee at https://connecticut-townclerks-records.com/User/Login.aspx?ReturnUrl=%2f. Subscription range from one day to one year. Images are $1.00 per page. There is a 5% service fee if paying with PayPal.
Property, Taxation Records Access to property tax for free at http://gis.vgsi.com/EastGranbyCT/. Also, access to GIS/mapping free at http://eastgranbyct.org/assessor-maps.html.

East Haddam Town in Middlesex County *Recorded Documents*
www.easthaddam.org/index.cfm?fuseaction=trees.treePage&treeID=97 Access to land records for free at https://www.uslandrecords.com/ctlr/. Indexes are free, pay-per access service available to view images. Images from 5/1992 to present.
Property, Taxation Records Search the town assessor database at http://gis.vgsi.com/easthaddamct/.

East Hartford Town in Hartford County *Recorded Documents* www.easthartfordct.gov/town-clerk Access to land records for free at https://www.uslandrecords.com/ctlr/. Indexes are free, pay-per access service available to view images. Images are available from 7/8/1971 to present.
Property, Taxation Records Access to GIS/mapping free at www.easthartfordct.gov/assesor/pages/property-information-gis.

East Haven Town in New Haven County *Recorded Documents* www.townofeasthavenct.org/town-clerk Access to land records for free at https://www.uslandrecords.com/ctlr/. Indexes are free, pay-per access service available to view images.
Property, Taxation Records Access property data free at http://host.appgeo.com/sccog/. Also, access to GIS/mapping for free at http://easthaven.mapxpress.net/. Also, access to online property field cards at www.propertyrecordcards.com/searchmaster.aspx?towncode=044.

East Lyme Town in New London County *Recorded Documents* http://eltownhall.com/government/departments/town-clerk-2/ Access to land records for free at https://www.uslandrecords.com/ctlr/. Indexes are free, pay-per access service available to view images.
Property, Taxation Records Access assessor property data free at http://gis.vgsi.com/eastlymect/.

East Windsor Town in Hartford County *Property, Taxation Records* Access property data free at http://host.appgeo.com/sccog/. Also, access to online property field cards at www.propertyrecordcards.com/searchmaster.aspx?towncode=047.

Eastford Town in Windham County *Recorded Documents* Access to record indexes and images for a fee at https://connecticut-townclerks-records.com/User/Login.aspx?ReturnUrl=%2f. Subscription range from one day to one year. Images are $1.00 per page. There is a 5% service fee if paying with PayPal.
Property, Taxation Records Access to town mapping for free at http://54.174.182.81/html5viewer/?viewer=neccoggis2. Access to property records for free at http://gis.vgsi.com/EastfordCT/.

Easton Town in Fairfield County *Recorded Documents* www.eastonct.gov/town-clerk Access to land records for a fee at http://24.89.162.123/Subscription/Default.aspx.
Property, Taxation Records Access property data free at http://host.appgeo.com/sccog/. Also, access to online property field cards at www.propertyrecordcards.com/searchmaster.aspx?towncode=046.

Ellington Town in Tolland County *Recorded Documents* http://ellington-ct.gov/233/Town-Clerks-Office Access to record indexes and images for a fee at https://connecticut-townclerks-records.com/User/Login.aspx?ReturnUrl=%2f. Subscription range from one day to one year. Images are $1.00 per page. There is a 5% service fee if paying with PayPal.
Property, Taxation Records Access assessor property data free at http://gis.vgsi.com/EllingtonCT/. Also, access to GIS/mapping for free at https://ellingtonct.mapgeo.io/.

Enfield Town in Hartford County   *Property, Taxation Records*   Search for parcel data free on the GIS-mapping site at http://host.cdmsmithgis.com/EnfieldCT/. Also, access to property lookup for free at http://gis.vgsi.com/EnfieldCT/.

Essex Town in Middlesex County   *Recorded Documents*   www.essexct.gov/town-clerk   Access to record indexes and images for a fee at https://connecticut-townclerks-records.com/User/Login.aspx?ReturnUrl=%2f. Subscription range from one day to one year. Images are $1.00 per page. There is a 5% service fee if paying with PayPal.
Property, Taxation Records   Access to on-line property viewer, GIS/mapping free at https://essexct.mapgeo.io/?latlng=41.3533%2C-72.4211&zoom=13. Also, access to records for free at http://gis.vgsi.com/essexct/.

Fairfield Town in Fairfield County   *Recorded Documents*   www.fairfieldct.org/townclerk   Access to land records for free at www.searchiqs.com/. Index data from 4/1977 to 12/30/1998, index data and images from 12/31/1998 to present. Can sign-up for free user account, print fees are $1.50 per image.
Property, Taxation Records   Access assessor property data free at http://gis.vgsi.com/fairfieldct/.

Farmington Town in Hartford County   *Recorded Documents*   www.farmington-ct.org/departments/town-clerk   Access to record indexes and images for a fee at https://connecticut-townclerks-records.com/User/Login.aspx?ReturnUrl=%2f. Subscription range from one day to one year. Images are $1.00 per page. There is a 5% service fee if paying with PayPal.

Glastonbury Town in Hartford County   *Recorded Records Records*   www.glastonbury-ct.gov/departments/department-directory-l-z/town-clerk   Access town clerks recorded document index free at http://tcweb.glastonbury-ct.gov/wb_or1/disclaim.asp. Online land record indexes go back to 1693. One and two year subscriptions available to view images for $1.00 per page plus small convenience fee to print copies.
Property, Taxation Records   Access assessor property data free at http://gis.vgsi.com/glastonburyct/.

Goshen Town in Litchfield County   *Property, Taxation Records*   Access GIS/property data free at http://goshen.mapxpress.net/.

Granby Town in Hartford County   *Recorded Documents*   www.granby-ct.gov/Public_Documents/GranbyCT_Clerk/index   Access to record indexes and images for a fee at https://connecticut-townclerks-records.com/User/Login.aspx?ReturnUrl=%2f. Subscription range from one day to one year. Images are $1.00 per page. There is a 5% service fee if paying with PayPal.
Property, Taxation Records   Access assessor property data free at www.qpublic.net/ct/granby/search.html.

Greenwich Town in Fairfield County   *Recorded Documents*   www.greenwichct.org/government/departments/town_clerk/   Access to land records for free at https://www.uslandrecords.com/ctlr/. Indexes are free, pay-per access service available to view images. Images are available from 1988 to present.
Property, Taxation Records   Search current tax records free at www.greenwichct.org/government/departments/assessor/. Click on view and pay taxes. Can also search real estate, personal property, and motor vehicles.

Griswold Town in New London County   *Recorded Documents*   www.griswold-ct.org/townclerk.html   Access to record indexes and images for a fee at https://connecticut-townclerks-records.com/User/Login.aspx?ReturnUrl=%2f. Subscription range from one day to one year. Images are $1.00 per page. There is a 5% service fee if paying with PayPal.
Property, Taxation Records   Access to records for free at www.qpublic.net/ct/griswold/.

Groton Town in New London County   *Recorded Documents*   www.groton-ct.gov/depts/twnclk/   Access to record indexes and images for a fee at https://connecticut-townclerks-records.com/User/Login.aspx?ReturnUrl=%2f. Subscription range from one day to one year. Images are $1.00 per page. There is a 5% service fee if paying with PayPal.
Property, Taxation Records   Access property data free at http://gis.groton-ct.gov/Disclaimer.asp. Records back to 1990. Search taxes/payments for free at https://www.mytaxbill.org/inet/bill/home.do?town=groton.

Guilford Town in New Haven County   *Recorded Documents*   www.ci.guilford.ct.us/town-clerk.htm   Access to record indexes and images for a fee at https://connecticut-townclerks-records.com/User/Login.aspx?ReturnUrl=%2f. Subscription range from one day to one year. Images are $1.00 per page. There is a 5% service fee if paying with PayPal.
Property, Taxation Records   Access property data by address for free at http://host.appgeo.com/sccog/.

Haddam Town in Middlesex County   *Property, Taxation Records*   Access to the Assessor's maps for free at www.haddam.org/assessor.html. Scroll down to the bottom of page for the maps. Also, access to the Town Assessor database at http://gis.vgsi.com/haddamct/.

Hamden Town in New Haven County   *Property, Taxation Records*   Search the town assessor's database free at http://gis.vgsi.com/hamdenct/.

Hampton Town in Windham County   *Recorded Documents*   www.hamptonct.org/department.htm?id=5rkujjim   Access to record indexes and images for a fee at https://connecticut-townclerks-records.com/User/Login.aspx?ReturnUrl=%2f. Subscription range from one day to one year. Images are $1.00 per page. There is a 5% service fee if paying with PayPal. Records back to 1/1/1994. Also, access to land records for free at https://www.uslandrecords.com/ctlr/. Indexes are free, pay-per access service available to view images.
Property, Taxation Records   Look-up tax bills for free at https://www.mytaxbill.org/inet/bill/home.do?town=hampton. Also, access to assessment database for free at http://gis.vgsi.com/EastHamptonCT/.

Hartford City in Hartford County *Recorded Documents* www.hartford.gov/townclerk   Access to land records for free at https://www.uslandrecords.com/ctlr/. Indexes are free, pay-per access service available to view images.Images are available from 2002 to present.
Property, Taxation Records   Search city assessor data free at http://assessor1.hartford.gov/Default.asp.

Hartland Town in Hartford County *Recorded Documents* www.hartlandct.org/   Access to record indexes and images for a fee at https://connecticut-townclerks-records.com/User/Login.aspx?ReturnUrl=%2f. Subscription range from one day to one year. Images are $1.00 per page. There is a 5% service fee if paying with PayPal.

Harwinton Town in Litchfield County *Recorded Documents* www.harwinton.us/town-clerk   Access to record indexes for a fee at https://connecticut-townclerks-records.com/User/Login.aspx?ReturnUrl=%2f. Subscription range from one day to one year. Images are $1.00 per page. There is a 5% service fee if paying with PayPal.
Property, Taxation Records   Access to assessment tax roll information for free at www.harwinton.us/assessor/pages/search-records.

Hebron Town in Tolland County *Recorded Documents* http://hebronct.com/town-departments/town-clerk/   Access to land records for free at https://www.uslandrecords.com/ctlr/. Indexes are free, pay-per access service available to view images. Document images are available from 1978 to present.
Property, Taxation Records   Access property data free at http://host.appgeo.com/sccog/. Also, Access to GIS/mapping free at www.mainstreetmaps.com/CT/Hebron/public.asp. Also, access to the Assessor's database for free at http://nereval.com/SearchInfo.aspx?town=Hebron.

Kent Town in Litchfield County *Recorded Documents* www.townofkentct.org/town-clerk   Access to land records for free at www.searchiqs.com/. Can sign-up for free user account, print fees are $1.50 per image.
Property, Taxation Records   Access to tax maps for 2013 (latest shown as of 1/2/15) found at www.townofkentct.org/dokument.php?id=2701 for free. Also, access to assessor's record site for free at www.qpublic.net/ct/kent/search.html. Search the town assessor database at http://gis.vgsi.com/KentCT/.

Killingly Town in Windham County *Recorded Documents* www.killingly.org/town-clerk   Access to land records for free at www.searchiqs.com/. Index data (only) from 1/4/1939-1/20/2004, index data and images from 1/21/2004 to present. Can sign-up for free user account, print fees are $1.50 per image.
Property, Taxation Records   Access assessor records of real estate sales for free at www.killingly.org/assessor/pages/real-estate-sales.

Killingworth Town in Middlesex County *Recorded Documents* www.townofkillingworth.com/offices/town_clerk.html   Access to record indexes and images for a fee at https://connecticut-townclerks-records.com/User/Login.aspx?ReturnUrl=%2f. Subscription range from one day to one year. Images are $1.00 per page. There is a 5% service fee if paying with PayPal.
Property, Taxation Records   Access property data free at http://host.appgeo.com/sccog/. Also, access to online property field cards at www.propertyrecordcards.com/searchmaster.aspx?towncode=070.

Lebanon Town in New London County *Recorded Documents* www.lebanontownhall.org/department.htm?id=ht1u4fda   Access to record indexes and images for a fee at https://connecticut-townclerks-records.com/User/Login.aspx?ReturnUrl=%2f. Subscription range from one day to one year. Images are $1.00 per page. There is a 5% service fee if paying with PayPal.
Property, Taxation Records   Access to GIS/mapping free at www.mainstreetmaps.com/CT/Lebanon/.

Ledyard Town in New London County *Property, Taxation Records*   Access to GIS/mapping for free at https://www.mapsonline.net/ledyardct/index.html.

Lisbon Town in New London County *Recorded Documents* www.lisbonct.com/town_clerk.php   Access to land records for free at https://www.uslandrecords.com/ctlr/. Indexes are free, pay-per access service available to view images. Images from 7/31/1992 to present.

Litchfield Town in Litchfield County *Recorded Documents* www.townoflitchfield.org/Pages/LitchfieldCT_Clerk/index   Access to land records for free at https://www.uslandrecords.com/ctlr/. Indexes are free, pay-per access service available to view images.
Property, Taxation Records   Search town assessor property data free at http://gis.vgsi.com/LitchfieldCT/.

Madison Town in New Haven County *Recorded Documents* www.madisonct.org/153/Town-Clerk   Access to land records for free at https://www.uslandrecords.com/ctlr/. Indexes are free, pay-per access service available to view images.
Property, Taxation Records   Search the town assessor database at http://gis.vgsi.com/madisonct/.

Manchester Town in Hartford County *Recorded Documents* http://townclerk.townofmanchester.org/   Access to the town records for free to go http://tcweb.townofmanchester.org/External/LandRecords/protected/SrchQuickName.aspx. Also, access to record indexes and images for a fee at https://connecticut-townclerks-records.com/User/Login.aspx?ReturnUrl=%2f. Subscription range from one day to one year. Images are $1.00 per page. There is a 5% service fee if paying with PayPal.
Property, Taxation Records   Search the town assessor database at http://gis.vgsi.com/manchesterct/. Free registration required. Also, Access to GIS/mapping free at www.manchestergis.com/ but no name searching.

Mansfield Town in Tolland County *Recorded Documents* www.mansfieldct.gov/content/1914/1916/default.aspx   Access to record indexes and images for a fee at https://connecticut-townclerks-records.com/User/Login.aspx?ReturnUrl=%2f. Subscription range from one day to one year. Images are $1.00 per page. There is a 5% service fee if paying with PayPal.
Property, Taxation Records   Access property and GIS/mapping free at www.mainstreetmaps2.com/ct/mansfield/public.asp.

Marlborough Town in Hartford County *Recorded Documents* www.marlboroughct.net/index.php/town-clerk   Access to record indexes and images for a fee at https://connecticut-townclerks-records.com/User/Login.aspx?ReturnUrl=%2f. Subscription range from one day to one year. Images are $1.00 per page. There is a 5% service fee if paying with PayPal.
Property, Taxation Records   Access to GIS/mapping free at https://marlboroughct.mapgeo.io/.

Meriden City in New Haven County *Recorded Documents* www.cityofmeriden.org/Content/City_Clerk/   Access to land records for free at https://www.uslandrecords.com/ctlr/. Indexes are free, pay-per access service available to view images.
Property, Taxation Records   Search by parcel ID or address for property assessor data at http://gis.meridenct.gov/meriden/default.aspx. Also, access to tax sales for free at www.cttaxsales.com/. Also, access to the Assessor's database for free at www.nereval.com/Home.html?aspxerrorpath=/OnlineDatabases.aspx.

Middlebury Town in New Haven County *Recorded Documents* www.middlebury-ct.org/government/town-clerk/   Access to land records for free at https://www.uslandrecords.com/ctlr/. Indexes are free, pay-per access service available to view images.
Property, Taxation Records   Access assessor and property data free at http://gis.vgsi.com/middleburyct/.

Middlefield Town in Middlesex County *Property, Taxation Records*   Access to property records for free at http://gis.vgsi.com/MiddlefieldCT/.

Middletown City in Middlesex County *Recorded Documents* www.middletownct.gov/content/117/123/181/default.aspx   Access to record indexes and images for a fee at https://connecticut-townclerks-records.com/User/Login.aspx?ReturnUrl=%2f. Subscription range from one day to one year. Images are $1.00 per page. There is a 5% service fee if paying with PayPal.
Property, Taxation Records   Access GIS/mapping for free at http://gis.vgsi.com/MiddletownCT/.

Milford City in New Haven County *Recorded Documents* www.ci.milford.ct.us/city-clerk   Access to record indexes and images for a fee at https://connecticut-townclerks-records.com/User/Login.aspx?ReturnUrl=%2f. Subscription range from one day to one year. Images are $1.00 per page. There is a 5% service fee if paying with PayPal.
Property, Taxation Records   Search the town assessor's database at http://gis.vgsi.com/milfordct/.

Monroe Town in Fairfield County *Recorded Documents* www.monroect.org/Town-Clerk   Access to land records for free at https://www.uslandrecords.com/ctlr/. Indexes are free, pay-per access service available to view images.
Property, Taxation Records   Access to Tax search information, that includes maps, field cards, etc. for free at www.monroect.org/Assessor. Search the town assessor database at http://gis.vgsi.com/monroect/.

Montville Town in New London County *Recorded Documents, Land Records Records* www.townofmontville.org/Content/Town_Clerk/   Access to record indexes and images for a fee at https://connecticut-townclerks-records.com/User/Login.aspx?ReturnUrl=%2f. Subscription range from one day to one year. Images are $1.00 per page. There is a 5% service fee if paying with PayPal.

Morris Town in Litchfield County *Recorded Documents* www.townofmorrisct.com/nm/templates/pages-government.aspx?articleid=43&zoneid=2   Access to record indexes and images for a fee at https://connecticut-townclerks-records.com/User/Login.aspx?ReturnUrl=%2f. Subscription range from one day to one year. Images are $1.00 per page. There is a 5% service fee if paying with PayPal.
Property, Taxation Records   Access to Assessor's records for free at www.qpublic.net/ct/morris/index.html.

Naugatuck Town in New Haven County *Recorded Documents* www.naugatuck-ct.gov/content/113/123/125/429/default.aspx   Access to land records for free at https://www.uslandrecords.com/ctlr/. Indexes are free, pay-per access service available to view images.
Property, Taxation Records   Access to GIS/mapping for free at http://naugatuck.mapxpress.net/.

New Britain City in Hartford County *Recorded Documents* www.newbritainct.gov/index.php/city-services/town-clerk.html   Access to land record indexes only, free at http://cotthosting.com/CTNewBritainExternal/LandRecords/protected/SrchQuickName.aspx. Also, access to record indexes and images for a fee at https://connecticut-townclerks-records.com/User/Login.aspx?ReturnUrl=%2f. Subscription range from one day to one year. Images are $1.00 per page. There is a 5% service fee if paying with PayPal.
Property, Taxation Records   Search the city assessor database at http://gis.vgsi.com/newbritainct/.

New Canaan Town in Fairfield County *Recorded Documents* www.newcanaan.info/content/9490/293/329/default.aspx   Access to record indexes and images for a fee at https://connecticut-townclerks-records.com/User/Login.aspx?ReturnUrl=%2f. Subscription range from one day to one year. Images are $1.00 per page. There is a 5% service fee if paying with PayPal.
Property, Taxation Records   Access to land records free at www.newcanaan.info/content/9490/293/325/6553/default.aspx.

New Fairfield Town in Fairfield County *Property, Taxation Records* Access the assessor database free at http://gis.vgsi.com/newfairfieldct/.

New Hartford Town in Litchfield County *Recorded Documents* www.town.new-hartford.ct.us/town-clerk Access to record indexes and images for a fee at https://connecticut-townclerks-records.com/User/Login.aspx?ReturnUrl=%2f. Subscription range from one day to one year. Images are $1.00 per page. There is a 5% service fee if paying with PayPal.
Property, Taxation Records Access to GIS/mapping free at www.newhartfordgis.com/.

New Haven City in New Haven County *Recorded Documents* www.cityofnewhaven.com/TownClerk/index.asp Access to land records for free at www.searchiqs.com/. Index data and images from 6/30/1955 to present.
Property, Taxation Records Search the city assessor database free at http://gis.vgsi.com/newhavenct/. Also, access to GIS/mapping for free at https://northhavenct.mapgeo.io/.

New London City in New London County *Recorded Documents* http://ci.new-london.ct.us/content/7429/7431/7443/default.aspx Access to land records for free at https://www.uslandrecords.com/ctlr/. Indexes are free, pay-per access service available to view images.
Property, Taxation Records Access to GIS/mapping free at http://host.appgeo.com/sccog/. Select New London Town. Also, search the town assessor's database at http://gis.vgsi.com/monroect/.

New Milford Town in Litchfield County *Recorded Documents* www.newmilford.org/TownClerk Access to record indexes and images for a fee at https://connecticut-townclerks-records.com/User/Login.aspx?ReturnUrl=%2f. Subscription range from one day to one year. Images are $1.00 per page. There is a 5% service fee if paying with PayPal.
Property, Taxation Records Search the town assessor database at http://gis.vgsi.com/newmilfordct/.

Newington Town in Hartford County *Recorded Documents* www.newingtonct.gov/content/78/118/148/2078.aspx Access to record indexes and images for a fee at https://connecticut-townclerks-records.com/User/Login.aspx?ReturnUrl=%2f. Subscription range from one day to one year. Images are $1.00 per page. There is a 5% service fee if paying with PayPal.
Property, Taxation Records Access to assessor property records is free at www.newingtonct.gov/content/78/118/120/7768.aspx.

Newtown Town in Fairfield County *Recorded Documents* www.newtown-ct.gov/Public_Documents/NewtownCT_Clerk/index Access to record indexes and images for a fee at https://connecticut-townclerks-records.com/User/Login.aspx?ReturnUrl=%2f. Subscription range from one day to one year. Images are $1.00 per page. There is a 5% service fee if paying with PayPal.
Property, Taxation Records Access property data free at http://host.appgeo.com/sccog/. Search the town assessor's database free at http://gis.vgsi.com/newtownct/.

Norfolk Town in Litchfield County *Recorded Documents* http://norfolkct.org/town-government/town-offices/town-clerk-registrar-of-vital-statistics Access to land records for free at www.searchiqs.com/. Can sign-up for free user account, print fees are $1.50 per image.
Property, Taxation Records Access the Assessor's online database for free at http://qpublic.net/ct/norfolk/.

North Branford Town in New Haven County *Recorded Documents* www.townofnorthbranfordct.com/newweb/government/departments/town-clerk.aspx Access to record indexes and images for a fee at https://connecticut-townclerks-records.com/User/Login.aspx?ReturnUrl=%2f. Subscription range from one day to one year. Images are $1.00 per page. There is a 5% service fee if paying with PayPal.
Property, Taxation Records Search assessor records at http://gis.vgsi.com/northbranfordct/. Also, access to GIS/mapping free at http://107.20.209.214/NorthBranfordCT_Public/index.html.

North Haven Town in New Haven County *Recorded Documents* www.northhaven-ct.gov/government/town_departments/departments_%28s_-_z%29/town_clerk/index.php Access to limited land records and trade names free at http://cotthosting.com/CTNHAVENExternal/User/Login.aspx. For detailed records must subscribe. Land record indes from 1/4/1965-present; Tradenames index from 1/5/2010 to present.
Property, Taxation Records Access property data free at http://gis.vgsi.com/northhavenct/. Also, access GIS/mapping free at www.mapgeo.com/northhavenct/.

North Stonington Town in New London County *Recorded Documents* www.northstoningtonct.gov/Pages/NStoningtonCT_Dept/TC/index Access to land records for free at https://www.uslandrecords.com/ctlr/. Indexes are free, pay-per access service available to view images. Indexes are from 3/8/74 to present. Images from 11/2000.
Property, Taxation Records Access to GIS/mapping free at www.northstoningtongis.com/.

Norwalk City in Fairfield County *Recorded Documents* www.norwalkct.org/index.aspx?nid=155 Access to the town clerk's Official Records is free at http://my.norwalkct.org/Searchweb/default.aspx.
Property, Taxation Records Access to Norwalk property record cards is free at http://gis.vgsi.com/NorwalkCT/.

Norwich City in New London County *Recorded Documents* www.norwichct.org/index.aspx?NID=179 Access to the clerk's town land records is online by subscription. Index goes back to 1929 and images to 1/1/1978. Fee is $400.00 per year; sign-up online at www.norwichct.org/index.aspx?NID=184 or call 860-823-3732.

Property, Taxation Records   Access to records for free at http://gis.vgsi.com/NorwichCT/.

Old Lyme Town in New London County   *Recorded Documents*   www.oldlyme-ct.gov/Pages/OldlymeCT_Clerk/index   Access to
record indexes and images for a fee at https://connecticut-townclerks-records.com/User/Login.aspx?ReturnUrl=%2f. Subscription range from one day to
one year. Images are $1.00 per page. There is a 5% service fee if paying with PayPal.
Property, Taxation Records   Search the town Assessor's database at http://gis.vgsi.com/oldlymect/. Also, access to GIS/mapping free at
https://oldlymect.mapgeo.io/.

Old Saybrook Town in Middlesex County   *Recorded Documents*   www.oldsaybrookct.org/Pages/OldSaybrookCT_clerk/index
Access to record indexes and images for a fee at https://connecticut-townclerks-records.com/User/Login.aspx?ReturnUrl=%2f. Subscription range from
one day to one year. Images are $1.00 per page. There is a 5% service fee if paying with PayPal.
Property, Taxation Records   Access to records for free at http://gis.vgsi.com/oldsaybrookct/.

Orange Town in New Haven County   *Recorded Documents*   www.orange-ct.gov/govser/townclerk.htm   Access to record indexes
and images for a fee at https://connecticut-townclerks-records.com/User/Login.aspx?ReturnUrl=%2f. Subscription range from one day to one year. Images
are $1.00 per page. There is a 5% service fee if paying with PayPal.
Property, Taxation Records   Access to property assessment free at http://gis.vgsi.com/orangect/.

Oxford Town in New Haven County   *Recorded Documents*   www.oxford-ct.gov/town-clerk   Access to record indexes and images
for a fee at https://connecticut-townclerks-records.com/User/Login.aspx?ReturnUrl=%2f. Subscription range from one day to one year. Images are $1.00
per page. There is a 5% service fee if paying with PayPal.
Property, Taxation Records   Access property data free at http://host.appgeo.com/sccog/. Also, access to the assessor's database at
http://gis.vgsi.com/oxfordct/.

Plainfield Town in Windham County   *Recorded Documents*   www.plainfieldct.org/townclerk.asp   Access to records for free
(indexes only) at https://www.searchiqs.com/ctpla/Login.aspx. For further details must subscribe for a fee. indexes back to 1937, images to 2004.
Property, Taxation Records   Search the assessor's database at http://gis.vgsi.com/PlainfieldCT/.

Plainville Town in Hartford County   *Recorded Documents*   www.plainvillect.com/town-clerk   Access to record indexes and images
for a fee at https://connecticut-townclerks-records.com/User/Login.aspx?ReturnUrl=%2f. Subscription range from one day to one year. Images are $1.00
per page. There is a 5% service fee if paying with PayPal.
Property, Taxation Records   Access town assessor property data free at http://plainville.univers-clt.com/. Also, access to GIS/mapping for free at
http://plainville.mapxpress.net/.

Plymouth Town in Litchfield County   *Property, Taxation Records*   Access to the Assessor's database free at
http://plymouth.univers-clt.com/. Also, access to GIS/mapping for free at http://plymouth.mapxpress.net/.

Pomfret Town in Windham County   *Recorded Documents*   www.pomfretct.gov/town-clerk   Access to land records for free at
https://www.uslandrecords.com/ctlr/. Indexes are free, pay-per access service available to view images. Land/real estate indexes back to 1852. document
images back to 12/8/1966.
Property, Taxation Records   Search town assessor database free at http://gis.vgsi.com/pomfretct/.

Portland Town in Middlesex County   *Recorded Documents*   www.portlandct.org/Departments/TownClerk.aspx   Access to land
records for free at https://www.uslandrecords.com/ctlr/. Indexes are free, pay-per access service available to view images.
Property, Taxation Records   Access to Assessors data for free at http://portland.univers-clt.com/.

Preston Town in New London County   *Property, Taxation Records*   Access assessor data free at http://gis.vgsi.com/prestonct/.

Prospect Town in New Haven County   *Property, Taxation Records*   Access property data free at http://host.appgeo.com/sccog/.

Putnam Town in Windham County   *Recorded Documents*   www.putnamct.us/town-clerk   Access to land records for free at
https://www.uslandrecords.com/ctlr/. Indexes are free, pay-per access service available to view images.
Property, Taxation Records   Access assessor property data free after registration at www.putnamct.us/assessor/pages/assessors-maps-and-property-
record-cards. Also, access to GIS/mapping for free at http://54.174.182.81/html5viewer/?viewer=neccoggis2.

Redding Town in Fairfield County   *Recorded Documents*   http://townofreddingct.org/government/town-administration/town-clerk/
Access to record indexes and images for a fee at https://connecticut-townclerks-records.com/User/Login.aspx?ReturnUrl=%2f. Subscription range from
one day to one year. Images are $1.00 per page. There is a 5% service fee if paying with PayPal.
Property, Taxation Records   Access to GIS/mapping free at http://townofreddingct.org/government/land-records/gis/. Search the city assessor
database at http://gis.vgsi.com/reddingct/.

Ridgefield Town in Fairfield County   *Land Records Index Only Records*   www.ridgefieldct.org/content/46/108/default.aspx
Access to land records for free at https://cott.ridgefieldct.org/External/LandRecords/protected/SrchQuickName.aspx.

Property, Taxation Records   Access to property searches for free at www.equalitycama.com/tvweb/mainsearch.aspx?city=Ridgefield. Also, to access GIS/mapping for free at http://host.appgeo.com/sccog/. Also, access to Assessor's field cards for free at www.propertyrecordcards.com/SearchMaster.aspx?towncode=118.

Rocky Hill Town in Hartford County   *Recorded Documents, Marriage, Death, Trade Name, Map Records*
www.rockyhillct.gov/departments/town_clerk/index.php   Access to the Town Clerk's Index Search is free at www.rockyhillct.gov/resolution/. Land records go back to 1973; Marriages/Deaths to 1990; trade names to 1987; maps to 1982. Also, access to record indexes and images for a fee at https://connecticut-townclerks-records.com/User/Login.aspx?ReturnUrl=%2f. Subscription range from one day to one year. Images are $1.00 per page. There is a 5% service fee if paying with PayPal.
Property, Taxation Records   Access to property data/GIS/mapping for free at https://www.mapsonline.net/rockyhillct/web_assessor/search.php. Also, access to GIS/mapping free at https://www.mapsonline.net/rockyhillct/index.html.

Roxbury Town in Litchfield County   *Recorded Documents*   www.roxburyct.com/Pages/RoxburyCT_TownClerk/index   Access to land records for free at https://www.uslandrecords.com/ctlr/. Indexes are free, pay-per access service available to view images.
Property, Taxation Records   Access to property records for free at http://qpublic.net/ct/roxbury/search.html.

Salem Town in New London County   *Recorded Documents*   www.salemct.gov/Pages/SalemCT_Clerk/index   Access to land records for a fee at www.salemct.gov/Pages/SalemCT_Clerk/Public%20Search. Free index searches, but must subscribe for detailed information.
Property, Taxation Records   Access to the Assessor's database free at http://gis.vgsi.com/salemct/. Also, access to mapping (interactive, download, advanced search and gallery) at http://salem.mapxpress.net/. Also, access to GIS/mapping free at http://host.appgeo.com/sccog/.

Salisbury Town in Litchfield County   *Recorded Documents*   www.salisburyct.us/offices/townclerk   Access to land records for free at https://www.searchiqs.com/ctsal/Login.aspx. Can sign-up for free user account, print fees are $1.50 per image.
Property, Taxation Records   Purchase Assessor's field cards for $1.00, ($.50 per page for vacant land), email assessor@salisburyct.us

Scotland Town in Windham County   *Property, Taxation Records*   Access to GIS/mapping for free at http://54.174.182.81/html5viewer/?viewer=neccoggis2.

Seymour Town in New Haven County   *Recorded Documents*   www.seymourct.org/Town-Clerk/   Access to land records for free at https://www.uslandrecords.com/ctlr/. Indexes are free, pay-per access service available to view images. Indices from 8/1/1975 to present. Images from 6/21/1982 to present.
Property, Taxation Records   Access to GIS/mapping free at www.seymourgis.com/.

Sharon Town in Litchfield County   *Recorded Documents*   www.sharonct.org   Access to Town Clerk records for free at https://www.searchiqs.com/ctsha/Login.aspx. Can log-in as guest for limited records.
Property, Taxation Records   Access to records for free at http://gis.vgsi.com/SharonCT/.

Simsbury Town in Hartford County   *Recorded Documents*   www.simsbury-ct.gov/town-clerk   Access to record indexes and images for a fee at https://connecticut-townclerks-records.com/User/Login.aspx?ReturnUrl=%2f. Subscription range from one day to one year. Images are $1.00 per page. There is a 5% service fee if paying with PayPal.
Property, Taxation Records   For property assessments for free at http://host.appgeo.com/sccog/. Also, access to online property field cards at www.propertyrecordcards.com/searchmaster.aspx?towncode=128.

Somers Town in Tolland County   *Recorded Documents*   www.somersct.gov/townclerk.cfm   Access to record indexes and images for a fee at https://connecticut-townclerks-records.com/User/Login.aspx?ReturnUrl=%2f. Subscription range from one day to one year. Images are $1.00 per page. There is a 5% service fee if paying with PayPal.
Property, Taxation Records   Search the town assessor's database free at http://gis.vgsi.com/somersct/.

South Windsor Town in Hartford County   *Recorded Documents*   www.southwindsor.org/town-clerk   Access to record indexes and images for a fee at https://connecticut-townclerks-records.com/User/Login.aspx?. Subscription range from one day to one year. Images are $1.00 per page. There is a 5% service fee if paying with PayPal.
Property, Taxation Records   Search the town Assessor's database at http://gis.vgsi.com/southwindsorct/. Also, access to the Grand List for free at www.southwindsor.org/pages/swindsorct_assessor/index#glist.

Southbury Town in New Haven County   *Recorded Documents*   http://southbury-ct.org/   Access to land records for free at https://www.uslandrecords.com/ctlr/. Indexes are free, pay-per access service available to view images.
Property, Taxation Records   Search the town Assessor's database free at http://gis.vgsi.com/southburyct/..

Southington Town in Hartford County   *Recorded Documents, Voter Registration Records*
www.southington.org/content/17216/17534/default.aspx   Access to record indexes and images for a fee at https://connecticut-townclerks-records.com/User/Login.aspx?ReturnUrl=%2f. Subscription range from one day to one year. Images are $1.00 per page. There is a 5% service fee if paying with PayPal. Access the voter registration lookup free at www.southington.org/content/17216/17323/default.aspx.
Property, Taxation Records   Access to GIS/mapping free at http://gis.southington.org/. The Grand Lists are found at www.southington.org/content/17216/17235/default.aspx. Also, search the assessor's database at http://gis.vgsi.com/southingtonct/.

Stafford Town in Tolland County   *Recorded Documents (index only) Records*   www.staffordct.org/clerk.php   Access town clerk land records back to 1/03/1977 free at http://records.staffordct.org/Resolution/search_menu.asp but free registration is required. Also, access to record indexes and images for a fee at https://connecticut-townclerks-records.com/User/Login.aspx?ReturnUrl=%2f. Subscription range from one day to one year. Images are $1.00 per page. There is a 5% service fee if paying with PayPal.
Property, Taxation Records   Search the town assessor's database free at http://gis.vgsi.com/staffordct/.

Stamford City in Fairfield County   *Recorded Documents*   www.stamfordct.gov/town-clerk   Search the city registry of trade names for free at www.stamfordct.gov/town-clerk/pages/trade-name-information. Also, land records search for a fee at https://landrecords.cityofstamford.org/landrecordssearch/. Fee is $750.00 for 2 years.
Property, Taxation Records   Search the assessor's database at http://gis.vgsi.com/stamfordct/.

Sterling Town in Windham County   *Property, Taxation Records*   Access to Assessor's database free at http://sterling.ias-clt.com/parcel.list.php. Also, access to GIS/mapping free at http://107.20.209.214/sterlingct_public/default.html.

Stonington Town in New London County   *Recorded Documents*   www.stonington-ct.gov/town-clerk   Access to record indexes and images for a fee at https://connecticut-townclerks-records.com/User/Login.aspx?ReturnUrl=%2f. Subscription range from one day to one year. Images are $1.00 per page. There is a 5% service fee if paying with PayPal.
Property, Taxation Records   Access to GIS/mapping data free at http://gis.stonington-ct.gov/ags_map/.

Stratford Town in Fairfield County   *Recorded Documents*   www.townofstratford.com/content/39832/39846/39945/default.aspx   Access to record indexes and images for a fee at https://connecticut-townclerks-records.com/User/Login.aspx?ReturnUrl=%2f. Subscription range from one day to one year. Images are $1.00 per page. There is a service fee if paying with PayPal.
Property, Taxation Records   Access to records for free at www.townofstratford.com/content/39832/39846/64651/default.aspx.

Suffield Town in Hartford County   *Recorded Documents*   www.suffieldtownhall.com/townclerk   Access to record indexes and images for a fee at https://connecticut-townclerks-records.com/User/Login.aspx?ReturnUrl=%2f. Subscription range from one day to one year. Images are $1.00 per page. There is a 5% service fee if paying with PayPal.
Property, Taxation Records   Search the town assessor database at http://gis.vgsi.com/SuffieldCT/.

Thomaston Town in Litchfield County   *Recorded Documents*   www.thomastonct.org/Content/Town_Clerk_.asp   Access to record indexes and images for a fee at https://connecticut-townclerks-records.com/User/Login.aspx?ReturnUrl=%2f. Subscription range from one day to one year. Images are $1.00 per page. There is a 5% service fee if paying with PayPal.
Property, Taxation Records   Search property data free at http://host.appgeo.com/sccog/. Also, access to GIS/Mapping for free at http://thomaston.mapxpress.net/.

Thompson Town in Windham County   *Recorded Documents*   www.thompsonct.org/index.php/departments-157/town-clerk.html   Access to land records for free at https://www.uslandrecords.com/ctlr/. Indexes are free, pay-per access service available to view images. Images are available from 6/2004 to present.
Property, Taxation Records   Search the town assessor database free at http://gis.vgsi.com/thompsonct/.

Tolland Town in Tolland County   *Recorded Documents*   www.tolland.org/town-clerk   Access to land records for free at https://www.uslandrecords.com/ctlr/. Indexes are free, pay-per access service available to view images.
Property, Taxation Records   Search town assessor database free at http://gis.vgsi.com/Tollandct/. Also, access to GIS/mapping for free at https://tollandct.mapgeo.io/.

Torrington City in Litchfield County   *Recorded Documents*   www.torringtonct.org/Public_Documents/TorringtonCT_Clerk/index   Access to records for free at www.torringtonct.org/Public_Documents/TorringtonCT_Clerk/Land%20Records%20&%20eRecording. Also, access to land records for free at www.searchiqs.com/. Index data (only) from 1/3/1955-4/15/1997, index data and images from 12/30/1988 to present (starts @ Vol. 450). Can sign-up for free user account, print fees are $1.50 per image.
Property, Taxation Records   Access to online property field cards at www.propertyrecordcards.com/SearchMaster.aspx?towncode=143.

Trumbull Town in Fairfield County   *Recorded Documents*   www.trumbull-ct.gov/content/10623/10655/11079/default.aspx   Free access to land records indexes available at http://71.11.0.182/External/LandRecords/protected/SrchQuickName.aspx. Land record index from 1/1/50 to present, trade names from 3/24/30 to present. Images are not available.
Property, Taxation Records   Search the assessor database free at http://gis.vgsi.com/trumbullct/.

Union Town in Tolland County   *Recorded Documents*   www.unionconnecticut.org/clerk.html   Access to record indexes and images for a fee at https://connecticut-townclerks-records.com/User/Login.aspx?ReturnUrl=%2f. Subscription range from one day to one year. Images are $1.00 per page. There is a 5% service fee if paying with PayPal.
Property, Taxation Records   Search the assessor database at http://gis.vgsi.com/UnionCT/. Also, access to GIS/mapping for free at http://54.174.182.81/html5viewer/?viewer=neccoggis2.

Vernon Town in Tolland County   *Property, Taxation Records*   Access to GIS/mapping free at www.vernon-ct.gov/gis-info. Also, access to property record cards for free at www.vernon-ct.gov/propertycard.

Voluntown Town in New London County *Property, Taxation Records* Access to records free at http://gis.vgsi.com/voluntownct/. Also, access to GIS/mapping for free at http://54.174.182.81/html5viewer/?viewer=neccoggis2.

Warren Town in Litchfield County *Recorded Documents* www.warrenct.org/town-clerk Access to land records for free at www.searchiqs.com/. Index data and images from 6/13/2984 to present. Can sign-up for free user account, print fees are $1.50 per image. Also, access land records for a fee at http://landrecordsearch.webtownhall.com/.
Property, Taxation Records Access to records for free at www.qpublic.net/ct/warren/search.html.

Washington Town in Litchfield County *Recorded Documents* www.washingtonct.org/town-clerk Access to land records for free at https://www.uslandrecords.com/ctlr/. Indexes are free, pay-per access service available to view images.
Property, Taxation Records Access to the Grand Lists for Real Estate, Motor Vehicles and Personal Property for free at www.washingtonct.org/assessor/pages/grand-lists.

Waterbury City in New Haven County *Recorded Documents* www.waterburyct.org/content/9569/9605/9640/default.aspx Real Estate records and lien lists can be accessed at free www.waterburyct.org/content/9569/9605/9640/10285.aspx. Access to land records for free at www.searchiqs.com/. Index data and images from 1983 to present. Can sign-up for free user account, print fees are $1.50 per image.
Property, Taxation Records Access to property records for free at www.propertyrecordcards.com/searchmaster.aspx?towncode=151. Also, access to GIS/mapping free at http://gis.waterburyct.org/GIS/Maps_Assessor.asp.

Waterford Town in New London County *Recorded Documents* www.waterfordct.org/town-clerk Access to land records for free at https://www.uslandrecords.com/ctlr/. Indexes are free, pay-per access service available to view images.
Property, Taxation Records Access property data free at http://host.appgeo.com/sccog/, but no name searching. Also, access to property records for free at http://gis.vgsi.com/waterfordct/.

Watertown Town in Litchfield County *Recorded Documents* www.watertownct.org/content/10298/4189/default.aspx Access to land records for free at https://www.uslandrecords.com/ctlr/. Indexes are free, pay-per access service available to view images.

West Hartford Town in Hartford County *Recorded Documents* https://www.westhartfordct.gov/gov/departments/townclerk/default.asp Access to the records index for free at http://cotthosting.com/ctwesthartford/User/Login.aspx. Choose option to Sign in as a guest.
Property, Taxation Records Access to the assessor property records on the GIS-mapping site is free at http://host.appgeo.com/westhartfordct/. Also, search the assessor database with the property tax data lookup free at http://gis.vgsi.com/westhartfordct/.

West Haven City in New Haven County *Recorded Documents* www.cityofwesthaven.com/156/City-Clerks-Office Access to public records for free at www.searchiqs.com/westhaven.html. Can log-in as guest, for detailed information must register. Land index from 7/1968 to present; images from 5/14/2002 to present. Maps from 1/1/12-present. Tradenames index from 1990's, images from 2011.
Property, Taxation Records Search GIS/mapping for free at www.westhavengis.com. Also, access to property lookup for free at http://gis.vgsi.com/westhavenct/.

Westbrook Town in Middlesex County *Recorded Documents* www.westbrookct.us/townclerk.php Access to record indexes and images for a fee at https://connecticut-townclerks-records.com/User/Login.aspx?ReturnUrl=%2f. Subscription range from one day to one year. Images are $1.00 per page. There is a 5% service fee if paying with PayPal. Access to land records for free at www.searchiqs.com/. Index data and images from 1983 to present. Can sign-up for free user account, print fees are $1.50 per image.
Property, Taxation Records Access to property records for free at http://gis.vgsi.com/westbrookct/.

Weston Town in Fairfield County *Recorded Documents* www.westonct.gov/townhall/27652/27718/28002 Access to record indexes only for free at https://connecticut-townclerks-records.com/User/Login.aspx?ReturnUrl=%2f.
Property, Taxation Records Access to property data and values on parcels for free at www.qpublic.net/ct/weston/.

Westport Town in Fairfield County *Recorded Documents* www.westportct.gov/index.aspx?page=134 Access to record indexes and images for a fee at https://connecticut-townclerks-records.com/User/Login.aspx?ReturnUrl=%2f. Subscription range from one day to one year. Images are $1.00 per page. There is a 5% service fee if paying with PayPal.
Property, Taxation Records Search assessor data free at http://gis.vgsi.com/westportct/. Also, search the GIS-mapping site at https://geopower.jws.com/westport/.

Wethersfield Town in Hartford County *Recorded Documents* http://wethersfieldct.com/content/398/434/default.aspx Access to land records for free at https://www.uslandrecords.com/ctlr/. Indexes are free, pay-per access service available to view images.
Property, Taxation Records Access to Assessor's database for free at https://wethersfieldct.mapgeo.io/.

Willington Town in Tolland County *Recorded Documents* http://willingtonct.virtualtownhall.net/Public_Documents/WillingtonCT_TownClerk/townclerk2 Access to record indexes and images for a fee at https://connecticut-townclerks-records.com/User/Login.aspx?ReturnUrl=%2f. Subscription range from one day to one year. Images are $1.00 per page. There is a 5% service fee if paying with PayPal.

Property, Taxation Records Access to GIS/mapping free at www.mapgeo.com/crcogct/. Also, search the assessor database at http://gis.vgsi.com/WillingtonCT/.

Wilton Town in Fairfield County
Recorded Documents www.wiltonct.org/departments/clerk/clerk.html   Access to land records for free at https://www.uslandrecords.com/ctlr/. Indexes are free, pay-per access service available to view images. Indices from 1942 to present.
Property, Taxation Records Search the town assessor database free at http://gis.vgsi.com/wiltonct/.

Winchester Town in Litchfield County
Recorded Documents www.townofwinchester.org/town-clerk   Access to record indexes and images for a fee at https://connecticut-townclerks-records.com/User/Login.aspx?ReturnUrl=%2f. Subscription range from one day to one year. Images are $1.00 per page. There is a 5% service fee if paying with PayPal.
Property, Taxation Records Access to assessment database for free at http://gis.vgsi.com/winchesterct/. Also, access to tax maps for free at www.townofwinchester.org/tax-assessor/pages/tax-assessor-maps.

Windham Town in Windham County
Recorded Documents www.windhamct.com/department.htm?id=i9g86evd&m=boards   Access to land records for free at www.searchiqs.com/. Land index (only) data from 1/3/1966-7/26/2004, index data and images from 7/27/2014-present. Can sign-up for user account.
Property, Taxation Records Access assessor valuation data free at http://windham.univers-clt.com/. Also, access to GIS/mapping free at http://107.20.209.214/sterlingct_public/default.html.

Windsor Locks Town in Hartford County
Recorded Documents www.windsorlocksct.org/   Access to record indexes and images for a fee at https://connecticut-townclerks-records.com/User/Login.aspx?ReturnUrl=%2f. Subscription range from one day to one year. Images are $1.00 per page. There is a 5% service fee if paying with PayPal.
Property, Taxation Records Access the Assessor's office records for free at http://gis.vgsi.com/windsorlocksct/. Also, access to GIS/mapping for free at http://host.cdmsmithgis.com/WindsorLocksCT/.

Windsor Town in Hartford County
Recorded Documents http://townofwindsorct.com/townclerk/   Search the town clerk's land records index back to 1970 free at http://townofwindsorct.com/townclerk/index.php?page=68. Images available for $1.00 per page (add'l $.50 per page fee also applies). Town services search page at www.townofwindsorct.com/. Also, access to land records for free at www.searchiqs.com/. Index data (only) from 1/1/1970-6/25/1971, index data and images from 1/1/1970 to present. Can sign-up for free user account, print fees are $1.50 per image.
Property, Taxation Records Search the town GIS database at http://info.townofwindsorct.com/gis/. Also, access to property card information for free at www.townofwindsorct.com/assessor/property-card.php.

Wolcott Town in New Haven County
Recorded Documents www.wolcottct.org/pages/page_content/secondary_town-departments_town-clerk_town-clerks-office.aspx   Access to record indexes and images for a fee at https://connecticut-townclerks-records.com/User/Login.aspx?ReturnUrl=%2f. Subscription range from one day to one year. Images are $1.00 per page.
Property, Taxation Records Search the town assessor database at http://gis.vgsi.com/wolcottct/. Also, access to GIS/mapping for free at http://wolcott.mapxpress.net/.

Woodbridge Town in New Haven County
Recorded Documents www.woodbridgect.org/content/6585/6647/default.aspx   Access to land records for free at https://www.uslandrecords.com/ctlr/. Indexes are free, pay-per access service available to view images. Images from 7/26/58 to present.
Property, Taxation Records Search the assessor database at http://gis.vgsi.com/WoodbridgeCT/. Also, access to tax maps for free at http://woodbridge.mapxpress.net/.

Woodbury Town in Litchfield County
Recorded Documents http://woodburyct.org/index.asp?SEC=DA5A52A5-C42E-44AD-867C-214A87BF4F4E&Type=B_BASIC   Access to record indexes and images for a fee at https://connecticut-townclerks-records.com/User/Login.aspx?ReturnUrl=%2f. Subscription range from one day to one year. Images are $1.00 per page.
Property, Taxation Records Access to online property field cards at www.propertyrecordcards.com/SearchMaster.aspx?towncode=168. Also, access to GIS/mapping for free at http://woodbury.mapxpress.net/.

Woodstock Town in Windham County
Recorded Documents www.woodstockct.gov/town-departments/town-clerk.html   Access to land records for free at www.searchiqs.com/. Index data (only) from 1/1954 to 12/1983, index data and images from 12/1983 to present. Can sign-up for free user account, print fees are $1.50 per image.
Property, Taxation Records Search the assessor database at http://gis.vgsi.com/woodstockct/.

# Chapter 5

Delaware

Capital: Dover
        Kent County
Time Zone: EST
Population: 945,934
# of Counties: 3

Useful State Links

Website: **http://delaware.gov**
Governor: **http://governor.delaware.gov/index.shtml**
Attorney General: **http://attorneygeneral.delaware.gov/**
State Archives: **http://archives.delaware.gov/**
State Statutes and Codes: **http://delcode.delaware.gov/**
Legislative Bill Search: **http://legis.delaware.gov/**
Unclaimed Funds: **http://revenue.delaware.gov/unclaimedproperty.shtml**

State Public Record Agencies

Sexual Offender Registry

Delaware State Police, Sex Offender Central Registry, https://sexoffender.dsp.delaware.gov/ Statewide registry can be searched at https://sexoffender.dsp.delaware.gov. Be patient as sometimes it takes a while for the page to open. There are a variety of searches available. The site gives the ability to search by last name, Development, and city or Zip Code. Any combination of these fields may be used; however, a search cannot be performed if both a city and Zip Code are entered.

Incarceration Records

Delaware Department of Corrections, Director of Central Offender Records, http://doc.delaware.gov/ The state's web page links to a vendor - VINELink found at https://www.vinelink.com/vinelink/siteInfoAction.do?siteId=8000. *Other Options:* Escapees and death penalty lists are available online at http://doc.delaware.gov/escapees/escapees.shtml.

Corporation, LLC, LP, LLP, General Partnerships, Trademarks/Servicemarks

Secretary of State, Corporation Records, www.corp.delaware.gov/ Check an entity name for corporate status, file number, incorporation/formation date, registered agent name, address, phone number and residency from https://icis.corp.delaware.gov/Ecorp/EntitySearch/NameSearch.aspx. A search of Trade, Business, or Fictitious names is found at www.courts.delaware.gov/tradenames/. Note this is from the courts, not from the Sec. of State. Also, the DE Department of Finance provides a free search of business licenses at https://dorweb.revenue.delaware.gov/scripts/bussrch/bussrch.dll.

Sales Tax Registrations

Finance Department - Div. Rev., Gross Receipt Tax Registration, http://revenue.delaware.gov/ Search for a business license at https://dorweb.revenue.delaware.gov/scripts/bussrch/bussrch.dll. There is also a "door-to-door salesperson search."

Birth, Death, Marriage Records

Department of Health, Office of Vital Statistics, www.dhss.delaware.gov/dhss/dph/ss/vitalstats.html Access available at https://www.vitalchek.com/vital-records/delaware/delaware-vital-records-georgetown, a state designated vendor. Additional fees incurred.

Workers' Compensation Records

Labor Department, Industrial Accident Board, https://dia.delawareworks.com/workers-comp/ To check on an employer's insurance history visit http://dia.delawareworks.com/workers-comp/workers-comp-search.php.

Driver Records

Division of Motor Vehicles, Driver Services Department, www.dmv.de.gov/ The Direct Access Program is provided 24 hours via the web. The fee is $15.00 per record (will increase to $25.00 effective Oct. 1, 2015). Searches are done by submitting the driver's license number. Requesters must be pre-approved, a signed contract application is required. Online searching is by single inquiry only; no batch request mode is offered. For more information about establishing an account, call 302-744-2723.

Vehicle Ownership & Registration

DMV - Administration, Vehicle Records, www.dmv.de.gov/ The Direct Access Program is provided 24 hours via the web. The fee is $15.00 per name. Requesters must be pre-approved; a signed contract application is required. Online searching is by single inquiry only; no batch request mode is offered. For more information about establishing an account, call 302-744-2723. This program is strictly monitored and not available to those with a non-permissible use.

Voter Registration, Campaign Finance

Commissioner of Elections, Voter Registration Records, http://elections.delaware.gov/index.shtml The site to view information on contributions is https://cfrs.elections.delaware.gov/Public/ViewReceiptsMain/. A list of PACs is found at http://elections.delaware.gov/information/campaignfinance/pdfs/PAC%20List.pdf. Find data on lobbyists, courtesy of the Public Integrity Commission at https://egov.delaware.gov/lobs/Home/. *Other Options:* As stated, the entire state voter registration database is available on CD for $10. The file is provided in Access. Candidates who filed to run for office may request the Statewide CD at no cost.

Occupational Licensing Boards

Search these licenses at https://dpronline.delaware.gov/mylicense%20weblookup/Search.aspx

Accountant-CPA	Dietician/Nutritionist	Occupational Therapist/Assistant
Adult Entertainment	Electrical Inspector	Osteopathic Physician
Aesthetician	Electrician	Pharmacist
Amateur Boxing-related	Electrologist	Pharmacy/Pharmacy-related Business
Architect	Emergency Medical Tech/Paramedic	Physical Therapist/Assistant
Athletic Agent	Funeral Director	Physician Assistant
Athletic Trainer	Gaming Control	Physician/Medical Doctor/Surgeon
Audiologist	Geologist	Pilot, River
Barber	Hearing Aid Dealer/Fitter	Plumber
Bodyworker	Landscape Architect	Podiatrist
Boxer/Boxing Professional	Massage	Psychological Assistant
Charitable Gaming Permittee	Medical Practice	Psychologist
Chiropractor	Mental Health Counselor	Real Estate Agent/Broker
Cosmetologist	Midwife	Real Estate Appraiser
Counselor, Professional	Nail Technician	Respiratory Care Practitioner
Deadly Weapons Dealer	Nurse	Social Worker
Dental Hygienist	Nursing Home Administrator	Speech Pathologist/Audiologist
Dentist	Nutritionist	Surveyor, Land

The Rest:

Counselor, Elem/Secondary School .... https://deeds.doe.k12.de.us/public/deeds_pc_findeducator.aspx
Engineer/Firm .... https://www.dape.org/users/login
Fire School... www.statefireschool.delaware.gov/
Insurance Adjuster/Advisor...................... https://sbs.naic.org/solar-web/pages/public/stateServices.jsf?dswid=-2444&state=DE
Insurance Agent/Consultant .... https://sbs.naic.org/solar-web/pages/public/stateServices.jsf?dswid=-2444&state=DE
Insurance Broker/Dealer/Company .... https://sbs.naic.org/solar-web/pages/public/stateServices.jsf?dswid=-2444&state=DE
Investment Adviser/Firm .... www.adviserinfo.sec.gov/
Library/Media Specialist .... https://deeds.doe.k12.de.us/public/deeds_pc_findeducator.aspx
Liquid Waste Hauler www.dnrec.delaware.gov/wr/Information/GWDInfo/Documents/Class%20F%20list.pdf
Lobbyist.. https://egov.delaware.gov/lobs/Explore/ExploreLobbyists
Optometrist... www.arbo.org/index.php?action=findanoptometrist
Pesticide Applicator .... www.kellysolutions.com/de/Applicators/index.htm
Pesticide Business.................................... www.kellysolutions.com/de/Business/index.htm
Pesticide Dealer....................................... www.kellysolutions.com/de/Dealers/index.htm

Pesticide, Registered.............................	www.kellysolutions.com/de/pesticideindex.htm
Public Officer	https://egov.delaware.gov/lobs/
Radiation Technician	http://dhss.delaware.gov/dhss/dph/hsp/files/orcradtechreg.pdf
Radiologic Technologist	http://dhss.delaware.gov/dhss/dph/hsp/files/orcradtechreg.pdf
Redoatopm Service Providers, Registered	http://dhss.delaware.gov/dhss/dph/hsp/files/orcradtechreg.pdf
School Admin Supervisor/Asst	https://deeds.doe.k12.de.us/public/deeds_pc_findeducator.aspx
School Counselor	https://deeds.doe.k12.de.us/public/deeds_pc_findeducator.aspx
School Principal/Superintendent	https://deeds.doe.k12.de.us/public/deeds_pc_findeducator.aspx
Surplus Lines Broker	https://sbs.naic.org/solar-web/pages/public/stateServices.jsf?dswid=-2444&state=DE
Teacher...	https://deeds.doe.k12.de.us/public/deeds_pc_findeducator.aspx
Veterinarian	https://dpronline.delaware.gov/mylicense%20weblookup/Search.aspx
Wholesalers/Importers	http://date.delaware.gov/OABCC/wholesalers.shtml

State and Local Courts

About Delaware Courts: The **Superior Court** has original jurisdiction over criminal and civil cases except equity cases. The Superior Court has exclusive jurisdiction over felonies and drug offenses, except drug offenses involving minors, and offenses involving possession of marijuana.

The **Court of Common Pleas** has jurisdiction in civil cases where the amount in controversy, exclusive of interest, does not exceed $50,000. In criminal cases, the Court of Common Pleas handles all misdemeanors occurring in the state except certain drug-related offenses and traffic offenses. Appeals may be taken to the Superior Court.

Court of Chancery cases consist largely of corporate matters, trusts, estates, and other fiduciary matters, disputes involving the purchase and sale of land, questions of title to real estate, and commercial and contractual matters in general.

The **Family Court** has jurisdiction over juvenile, child neglect, custody, guardianship, adoptions, divorces and annulments, property divisions, and separation agreements.

The **Justice of the Peace Court** jurisdiction will vary by court – not all courts have the same jurisdiction. Depending of the court, it may handle civil cases in which the disputed amount is less than $15,000, landlord/tenant proceedings, certain misdemeanors including DUIs and Truancy, and most motor vehicle cases (excluding felonies). The Court may act as Committing Magistrates for all crimes.

Alderman's Courts usually have jurisdiction over misdemeanors, municipal ordinances, and traffic offenses that occur within their town limits.

The web page for the Unified Judicial System is http://judicial.alabama.gov/

Appellate Courts: The **Supreme Court** has appellate jurisdiction in criminal cases in which the sentence exceeds certain minimums, in civil cases as to final judgments and for certain other orders of the Court of Chancery, the Superior Court, and the Family Court. Chancery, Superior, Common Pleas, and Supreme Courts opinions and orders are available free online at http://courts.delaware.gov/opinions/?ag=all courts.

About Court Online Access: There are a number of statewide sites.

- A free site to search trial court **civil** case information and **judgments**, **eviction** case data from Superior, Court of Common Pleas and Justice of the Peace Courts is at http://courts.delaware.gov/docket.aspx. Click on **CourtConnect**. Note the site states *Any commercial use of data obtained through the use of this site is strictly prohibited.* Results basically give parties, case number, and status. There are no identifiers shown.

- Supreme, Superior. Common Pleas Courts **calendars** are available free at http://courts.delaware.gov/calendars.

- **Archived Probate** records are found at http://archives.delaware.gov/collections/probate.shtml.

- In the Superior Court in each county there is a Prothonotary which is where the registration of **Business, Trade and Fictitious Names** must be filed. There is a free online access page to this data, go to http://courts.delaware.gov/Superior/trade_names.stm.

No individual DE courts offer online access beyond the statewide sites mentioned above.

Recorders, Assessors, and Other Sites of Note

About Delaware Recording Offices: Delaware has 3 counties and 3 recording offices. The recording officer is the County Recorder.

About Tax Liens: Federal tax liens on personal property of businesses are filed with the Secretary of State. Other federal and all state tax liens on personal property are filed with the County Recorder.

Online Access

There is no statewide online system for county recorded documents. However each county has an affiliated site. Searching is free, but each site requires registration and a monthly fee to access document images.

County Sites:

Kent County *Recorded Documents* www.co.kent.de.us/recorder-of-deeds-office.aspx   Search the Land/Deed Record Data at https://de.uslandrecords.com/delr/DelrApp/index.jsp. Registration is required with a $50 monthly fee.
Property, Taxation Records   Locate parcels on the GIS-mapping site free at www.co.kent.de.us/Apps/KentCountyMapping/.

New Castle County *Recorded Documents, Marriage Records* www.nccde.org/136/Recorder-of-Deeds   Free text searches to the Recorder of Deeds database found at www.nccde.org/144/Document-Search. Must sign up with a credit card to view images. Fee is $1.00 per page or $100.00 per month per user, unlimited use.
Property, Taxation Records   County property data is found at www3.nccde.org/parcel/search/. No name searching. Also, access to tax maps for free at www.nccde.org/576/Tax-Assessment-Maps.

Sussex County *Recorded Documents, Real Property Records* www.sussexcountyde.gov/recorder-deeds   Search the Land/Deed Record Data for a fee at https://de.uslandrecords.com/delr/DelrApp/index.jsp. There is a $1.00 fee per page to print. A subscription account is also available at $50.00 per month and $.25 per page.
Property, Taxation Records   Search parcels on GIS-mapping site free at http://map.sussexcountyde.gov/. Search current sheriff sale list free at www.sussexcountyde.gov/sheriff-sales. Search county tax data free at www.sussexcountyde.gov/zoning-and-sales-information.

District of Columbia

Time Zone: EST
Population: 672,228
# of Divisions/Counties: 1

Useful State Links

Website: **http://dc.gov/**
Mayor: **http://mayor.dc.gov/**
Attorney General: **http://oag.dc.gov/**
District Archives: **http://os.dc.gov/service/district-columbia-archives**
District Statutes and Codes: **http://www.dcregs.dc.gov/**
Unclaimed Funds: **http://cfo.dc.gov/service/unclaimed-property**

State Public Record Agencies

Sexual Offender Registry

Metropolitan Police Department, Sex Offender Registry Unit, http://mpdc.dc.gov/service/sex-offender-registry   A list of Class A & B registered sex offenders is provided at http://mpdc.dc.gov/service/search-sex-offender-registry.

Incarceration Records

District of Columbia Department of Corrections, 2000 14th Street NW, 7th Fl, http://doc.dc.gov/   The agency directs online searching to a third party at https://www.vinelink.com/vinelink/siteInfoAction.do?siteId=9900.

Corporation, LP, LLC, Trade Name, Fictitious Name

Corporations Division, Department of Consumer & Regulatory Affairs, http://dcra.dc.gov   An online search by name or file number or registered agent's name of all registered entities with expanded entity information to include report and trade name history is free after registration. See https://corp.dcra.dc.gov/Account.aspx/LogOn?ReturnUrl=%2fHome.aspx.   Also, one may verify a Business License at http://pivs.dcra.dc.gov/BBLV/Default.aspx.   *Other Options:* For information concerning lists and bulk file purchases, contact the Office of Information Services.

Uniform Commercial Code, Federal & State Tax Liens, Recorded Documents

UCC Recorder, District of Columbia Recorder of Deeds, http://otr.cfo.dc.gov/service/recorder-deeds-document-images   Search the index by name or document number at https://gov.propertyinfo.com/DC-Washington/. This is a vendor site promoted by this agency. Data is provided from 1921 forward. Both a non-subscriber system (which requires registration) and a subscriber account are offered. Subscribers receive unlimited view of index data and pay $2.00 per document, plus a $175 fee per month. A registered "non-subscriber" pays no fee to view documents and $4.00 per document mage downloaded. Registration is required. Use of a credit card is required. Note that this system provided access to all recorded documents - not just UCC filings.

Birth Certificates

Department of Health, Vital Records Division, http://doh.dc.gov/service/birth-certificates   Orders may be placed online via a state designated vendor at www.vitalchek.com.

Death Records

Department of Health, Vital Records Division, http://doh.dc.gov/service/death-certificates   Orders may be placed online via a state designated vendor at www.vitalchek.com. Also, a Nationwide Gravesite Locator is located at http://gravelocator.cem.va.gov/. Includes VA, national, state, military, veteran, DOI, and where grave is marked with a government grave marker.

Driver Records

Department of Motor Vehicles, Driver Records Division, http://dmv.dc.gov   Online requests are taken throughout the day and are available in batch the next morning after 8:15 am. There is no minimum order requirement. Fee is $13.00 per record; only the ten-year record is sold. This system is restricted to high volume, ongoing users. Each requester must be approved, sign a contract and pay a $3,500 annual fee. Billing is a "bank" system which draws from pre-paid account. For more information, call 202-727-5692.   There is driver license number verification site at https://public.dmv.washingtondc.gov/BusinessPages/DL/DriverLicenseVerification.aspx. Also, DC drivers may obtain their driving record at http://dmv.dc.gov/service/request-driver-record.

Vehicle Ownership & Registration

Department of Motor Vehicles, Vehicle Records, http://dmv.dc.gov DC provides a Vehicle Registration Verification at https://public.dmv.washingtondc.gov/BusinessPages/VR/VehicleRegistrationVerification.aspx and an Out-of-State Title Status at https://public.dmv.washingtondc.gov/scripts/VS/OutOfStateTitleStatus.aspx. *Other Options:* Bulk requests can be obtained for commercial purposes upon approval by the Director, Department of Motor Vehicles if it is determined that the requested use "is for the public interest." Commercial purposes are not permitted.

Voter Registration

DC Board of Elections, Voter Registration Records, https://www.dcboee.org/home.asp One may check voter registration status at https://www.dcboee.org/voter_info/reg_status/index.asp. Name, DOB and ZIP are required. *Other Options:* Records can be purchased on CD. A variety of data is available from party registration to voter history. Minimum fee $2 for CD. Call 202-727-2525 for details. Form at www.dcboee.org/pdf_files/Data_Request_Form.pdf.

Campaign Finance, Lobbyists

Office of Campaign Finance, Frank D. Reeves Municipal Building, http://ocf.dc.gov/ Financial Reports Images Searches available at http://ocf.dc.gov/node/566202. Contributions and expenditures records are searchable at https://efiling.ocf.dc.gov/ContributionExpenditure. Search lobbyists activities at http://ocf.dc.gov/service/archived-lobbyist-activity.

GED Certificates

GED Testing Center, One Judiciary Square, http://osse.dc.gov/ged Third parties are routed to set up an account at: http://exchange.parchment.com/ged-receiver-registration-page. Parchment verifies that they are who they say they are so that they can place orders on behalf of students. Parchment contacts the third party and provides training on the site for ordering. During this training any orders they have are placed. After this the third party can order on behalf of students. They still must upload a consent form for each student during the process.

Occupational Licensing Boards

The following licenses are all searchable at http://pivs.dcra.dc.gov//bblv/default.aspx

Air Conditioning/Refrigeration	Electrician	Plumber
Alarm Technician	Engineer	Real Estate Agent/Broker/Seller
Amusement Park, Mechanical Machine, Related	Firearms Instructor	Restaurant, Caterers, Candy Manufacturer, Related
Asbestos Contractor/Worker	Firearms Permit	School, Degree/Non-Degree Granting
Auctioneer, Auction Sales	Funeral Director/Establishment	Secondhand Dealer, Related
Automobile, Rental, Repossessor, Wash	Health Spa	Securities Agent
Barber, Shop, Related	Interior Designer	Securities Broker/Dealer
Bed & Breakfast, Billiard Parlor, Bowling Alley	Motor Vehicle Dealer/Salesperson	Security Agency/Guard, Related
Contractor, Mechanical/Resident'l	Parking Lot Attendant, Related	Security Alarm Dealer/Agent, Related
Cosmetologist, Shop, Related	Pesticide Applicator	Solicitor
Driving School	Pesticide Dealer	Solid Waste, Related
	Pesticide Employee/Operator	

The following licenses are all searchable at https://app.hpla.doh.dc.gov/Weblookup/

Counselor, Professional	Nurse-Clinical	Physical Therapist
Dance Therapist	Nurse-LPN/RN	Physician Assistant
Dentist/Dental Hygienist	Nursing Home Administrator	Physician/Medical Doctor
Dietitian/Nutritionist	Occupational Therapist	Podiatrist
Massage Therapist/Establishment	Optometrist	Psychologist
Midwife	Osteopath	Recreational Therapist
Nurse Anesthetist	Pharmacist/Pharmacy	Respiratory Care

The Rest:

Bank	http://disb.dc.gov/service/verify-financial-institution-or-representative-licensed-disb
Check Casher	http://disb.dc.gov/service/verify-financial-institution-or-representative-licensed-disb
Chiropractor	https://app.hpla.doh.dc.gov/Weblookup/
Cigarette Retail/Wholesale	http://pivs.dcra.dc.gov/BBLV/Default.aspx

Emergency Medical Technician...............	https://octo.quickbase.com/db/bjjq68583
EMS Education Institutions......................	http://doh.dc.gov/service/ems-training-and-certification
Hearing Aid Dispenser............................	https://app.hpla.doh.dc.gov/Weblookup/
Insurance Broker/Agent, Company..........	https://sbs-dc.naic.org/Lion-Web/jsp/sbsreports/AgentLookup.jsp
Investment Advisor..................................	http://www.adviserinfo.sec.gov/
Investment Advisor Rep..........................	http://www.adviserinfo.sec.gov/
Limousine Company................................	https://octo.quickbase.com/db/bkzdccmbr
Money Lender, Transmitter......................	http://disb.dc.gov/service/verify-financial-institution-or-representative-licensed-disb
Mortgage Broker/Lender..........................	http://disb.dc.gov/service/verify-financial-institution-or-representative-licensed-disb
Naturopath..	https://app.hpla.doh.dc.gov/Weblookup/
Notary Public..	http://geospatial.dcgis.dc.gov/agencyapps/notary.aspx
Sales Finance Company..........................	http://disb.dc.gov/service/verify-financial-institution-or-representative-licensed-disb
Social Worker..	https://app.hpla.doh.dc.gov/Weblookup/
Taxicab/Limousine Operator....................	https://octo.quickbase.com/db/bkzdccmbr

Courts

About the DC Courts: The **Superior Court** handles all local trial matters and consists of five divisions: Civil, Criminal, Family, Probate, and Domestic Violence.

The **Civil Division** is divided into four branches: the Civil Actions Branch, the Quality Review Branch, the Landlord and Tenant Branch and the Small Claims Branch. The **Criminal Division** hears all local criminal matters including felony, misdemeanor, and serious traffic cases. The **Family Court** Operations Division receives and processes the following types of cases: child abuse and neglect, juvenile delinquency, adoption, divorce, custody, guardianship, visitation, paternity, child support, termination of parental rights, as well as mental health and habilitation. The **Probate Division** has jurisdiction over estates guardianships of minors and of incapacitated adults.

Appellate Online Access: The Court of Appeals opinions are at www.dccourts.gov/internet/welcome.jsf.
The DC Courts & Online Access:
Superior Court - Criminal   www.dccourts.gov/internet/superior/org_criminal/main.jsf
Access criminal case information free at www.dccourts.gov/internet/CCO.jsf. Although the system provides case summary data, it does not provide images, address, SSNs, DOB, and phone numbers. Some sentencing and dockets are incorrect compared to onsite court records. The public information on the Remote Access to Case Dockets (RACD) System reflects the docket entries in civil, criminal, domestic violence and tax cases, probate, disclaimers of interest, major litigation, wills and foreign estate proceedings.
Superior Court - Civil   www.dccourts.gov/internet/superior/org_civil/smallclaimsbranch.jsf
Access civil records free at www.dccourts.gov/internet/CCO.jsf. Although the system provides case summary data it does not provide images, address, SSNs, DOB, and phone numbers. The public information on the Remote Access to Case Dockets (RACD) System reflects the docket entries in civil, criminal, domestic violence and tax cases, probate, disclaimers of interest, major litigation, wills and foreign estate proceedings.
Superior Court - Landlord and Tenant Branch   www.dccourts.gov/internet/public/aud_civil/lease.jsf
Access information using the civil record index at www.dccourts.gov/internet/CCO.jsf. There is no fee. Although the system provides case summary data it does not provide images, address, SSNs, DOB, or phone numbers.

Recorder, Assessor

Recording Office: *Recorded Documents* http://otr.cfo.dc.gov/service/otr-recorder-deeds   Search the index by name or document number at https://countyfusion4.propertyinfo.com/countyweb/login.do?countyname=WashingtonDC. Data is provided from 1921 forward. Both a subscriber and non-subscriber system are offered. Subscribers receive unlimited view of index data and pay $2.00 per document, plus a $175 fee per month. A registered non-subscriber pays no fee to view documents and $4.00 per document image to download. Use of a credit card is required for subscribers. Also, a real property assessment database and real estate sales database are serachable from http://otr.cfo.dc.gov/node/388872.
Property, Taxation Records   Search the real property tax database as well as property sales at http://otr.cfo.dc.gov/page/real-property-tax-database-search.

Florida

Capital: Tallahassee
             Leon County

Time Zone: EST

> Florida's ten western-most counties are CST:
> They are: Bay, Calhoun, Escambia, Gulf, Holmes,
> Jackson, Okaloosa, Santa Rosa, Walton, Washington.

Population: 20,271,272

# of Counties: 67

Useful State Links

Website: **www.myflorida.com**

Governor: **www.flgov.com/**

Attorney General: **http://myfloridalegal.com**

State Archives: **http://dos.myflorida.com/library-archives/**

State Statutes and Codes: **www.flsenate.gov/Laws/Statutes**

Legislative Bill Search: **www.leg.state.fl.us**

Unclaimed Funds: **https://www.fltreasurehunt.org/**

State Public Record Agencies

Criminal Records

Florida Department of Law Enforcement, User Services Bureau/Criminal History Srvs,   www.fdle.state.fl.us/cms/home.aspx   Criminal history information may be ordered over the Department Program Internet site at https://web.fdle.state.fl.us/search/app/default?0. The $24.00 fee applies. These records are not certified. Credit card ordering will return records to your screen or via email. Search multiple types of state's wanted list at http://pas.fdle.state.fl.us/pas/pashome.a. Included are most wanted or missing persons, and stolen items such as vehicles, boats, plates, etc.

Sexual Offender Registry

Florida Department of Law Enforcement, Florida Offender Registration and Tracking Svcs,   http://offender.fdle.state.fl.us/offender/homepage.do Search the registry from the web page. Searching can be done by name or by geographic area.

Incarceration Records

Florida Department of Corrections, Central Records Office,   www.dc.state.fl.us   Extensive search capabilities are offered at www.dc.state.fl.us/inmateinfo/inmateinfomenu.asp. Click on Inmate Population Information Search. *Other Options:* Bulk data may be purchased on a CD.

Corporation, LP, LLC, Trademarks/Servicemarks, Fictitious Names, Federal Tax Liens

Division of Corporations, Department of State,   www.sunbiz.org   The state's excellent Internet site gives detailed information on all corporate, trademark, limited liability company and limited partnerships; fictitious names; and lien records. Images of filed documents are available from 1996/7 to present. See www.sunbiz.org/search.html, there are lots of choices.   *Other Options:* The agency offers downloadable record information from the web page. Data is released quarterly. See www.sunbiz.org/corp_pur.html.

Uniform Commercial Code

UCC Filings, Image API, Inc,   https://www.floridaucc.com/uccweb/   The Internet site https://www.floridaucc.com/uccweb/SearchDisclaimer.aspx? allows access for no charge. Search by name or document number, for records 1997 to present. Debtor names are stored in two separate data fields in the debtor database record. One field contains the debtor name as keyed into the database, and the other field contains the compacted debtor name that is indexed for searching. TIFF images of Florida UCC filings can be downloaded from the Internet for all filings from 1997 to present. Tax Liens are not included with UCC filing information. *Other Options:* Microfilm reels and CD's of images are available for bulk purchase requesters. Call for more information.

Vital Records

Department of Health, State Office of Vital Statistics, www.floridahealth.gov/certificates/certificates/birth/index.html - www.vitalchek.com. There are additional fees for use of a credit card.

Workers' Compensation Records

Workers Compensation Division, Data Quality Section, www.myfloridacfo.com/division/wc/ There is no statewide access to trial court data, but quite a few counties offer access to court record data view their own web page. MyFlorida.com, a vendor site operated by a group of county officials the Court Clerks, offers access to civil judgment data for all but 5 counties (Broward, Miami-Dade, Monroe, Orange, and Seminole). See https://www.myfloridacounty.com. A search of the index is free, but registration and fees are charged for images or further data. Subscription fee is $120.00 per year plus additional transaction fees for copies. Search Supreme Court dockets at http://jweb.flcourts.org/pls/docket/ds_docket_search. Docket Appeals at http://199.242.69.70/pls/ds/ds_docket_search.

Driver Records

Division of Motorist Services, Bureau of Records, https://www.flhsmv.gov/ Record access online has been privatized through Network Providers. Requesters with 5,000 or more records per month are considered Network Providers. Requesters with less than 5,000 requests per month (called Individual Users) are directed to a Provider. Call 850-617-2014 to become a Provider. A list of providers is found at http://flhsmv.gov/data/internet.html. The state fee is as stated above; Providers add a service fee, which varies by vendor. Online requests are processed on an interactive basis. Check the status of any Florida driver license free at https://services.flhsmv.gov/DLCheck/?Aspx&AspxAutoDetectCookieSupport=1. Simply enter the driver license number. *Other Options:* This agency will process batch data via FTP for approved users. Contact DataProcessingUnit@flhsmv.gov or call 850-617-2634.

Vehicle Ownership & Registration

Division of Motorist Services, Record Information & Research Unit -MS91, www.flhsmv.gov/html/titlinf.html For a free vehicle status check enter the title # or VIN to check vehicle status at https://services.flhsmv.gov/MVCheckWeb/. A personalized license plate inquiry at https://services.flhsmv.gov/MVCheckPersonalPlate/ lets user know availability. Florida has contracted to release detailed vehicle information through approved Network Providers. Accounts must first be approved by the state. The SSN is not released. The access is transactional oriented. The cost will vary usually between $.52 and $1.25 per record fee plus a transactional fee based on the type of connection and software. The link to the list of vendors on the Dept web site is at http://flhsmv.gov/data/internet2.html. *Other Options:* There are bulk record services available with DPPA procedures enforced. Customized search parameters are offered. Typical fees are $.01 per record, $1.00 for the CD and $4.50 for shipping. Call 850-617-2805.

Crash Reports

DHSMV-, Crash Records-MS-28, https://www.flhsmv.gov/florida-highway-patrol/traffic-crash-reports/ Crash reports can be purchased online at www.buycrash.com, a state designated vendor. The fee is $16.00, use of a credit card or PayPal is required. *Other Options:* List or bulk purchase is available by special request.

Voter Registration, Campaign Finance & Contributions, PACs

Dept of State - Division of Elections, 500 South Bronough St, http://dos.myflorida.com/elections/ A number of searches are provided at http://dos.myflorida.com/elections/candidates-committees/campaign-finance/ including filed campaign documents, contribution and expenditure records, and PACs Check a person's voter status at http://registration.elections.myflorida.com/CheckVoterStatus. *Other Options:* The only format for bulk release of voter reg. records is via DVD for $5.00. The content includes name, address, party, gender, voting history, and the telephone if provided on registration or if not marked confidential.

GED Certificates

FL GED Testing Office, GED Transcripts/Certificates, www.fldoe.org/academics/career-adult-edu/hse Third parties are routed to set up an account at: http://exchange.parchment.com/ged-receiver-registration-page. Parchment verifies that they are who they say they are so that they can place orders on behalf of students

Occupational Licensing Boards

These licenses are all searchable at www.myfloridalicense.com/wl11.asp

Accountant-CPA	Building Inspector	Food Services Establishment
Air Conditioning Contractor/Svc	Community Assoc Manager	Gas Line Specialty Contractor
Alcoholic Beverage Permit	Construction Qualified Business	Geologist/Geology Firm
Architect/Architectural Firm	Contractor, General	Hair Braider
Athletic Agent	Contractor, Residential	Home Inspector
Auctioneer/Auction Firm	Cosmetologist, Nails/Salon	Hotel/Restaurant
Barber/Barber Assist/Shop	Drywall/Gypsum Specialty Contr	Interior Design Business/Individual
Boxer	Electrical Contractor	Internal Pollutant Storage Tank Lining
Building Code Administrator	Elevator Certificates of Operation	Kickboxer
Building Contractor	Employee Leasing Company	Labor Org Business Agent

Labor Organization
Land Sale, Condominiums
Landscape Architecture Firm/Individ'l
Liquor Store
Lodging Establishment
Mechanical Contractor
Mobile Home
Motel/Restaurant
Nail Specialist
Pari-Mutuel Wagering

Pilot, State/Deputy
Plumbing Contractor
Pollutant Storage System Contr
Precision Tank Tester
Racing, Dog/Horse
Real Estate Agent/Broker/Sales
Real Estate Appraiser
Roofing Contractor
Sheet Metal Contractor
Solar Contractor

Specialty Structure Contractor
Surveyor, Mapping
Swimming Pool/Spa Contr/Svc
Talent Agency
Tobacco Wholesale
Underground Utility Contractor
Veterinarian/Veterinary Establishment
Yacht & Ship Broker/Salesman

These licenses are all searchable at https://appsmqa.doh.state.fl.us/MQASearchServices/Home

Acupuncturist
Athletic Trainer
Audiologist
Chiropractic-related Occupation
Chiropractor
Clinical Lab Personnel
Dentist/Dental Assistant
Dietician/Nutritionist
Electrologist/Electrologist Facility
Hearing Aid Specialist
Marriage & Family Therapist
Massage Therapist/School/Facility
Medical Doctor, Limited
Medical Faculty Member
Mental Health Counselor

Midwife
Naturopath
Naturopathic Physician
Nuclear Radiology Physicist
Nurse/Practical/Aide
Nursing Home Administrator
Nutrition Counselor
Occupational Therapist
Optician/Optician Apprentice
Optometrist
Orthotist/Prosthetist
Osteopathic Physician
Pedorthist
Pharmacist, Consulting
Pharmacist/Pharmacist Intern

Physical Therapist/Assistant
Physician/Medical Doctor/Assistant
Physicist-Medical
Psychologist/Ltd License Psycholog't
Radiologic Physician
Radiologist
Respiratory Care Therapist/Provider
School Psychologist
Social Worker, Clinical/Master
Speech-Language Pathologist
Therapeutic Radiologic Physician
Visiting Mental Health Faculty
X-Ray Podiatric Assistant (certified)

The Rest:

Attorney	www.floridabar.org/divpgm/lronline.nsf/wreferral6?OpenForm
Bank	https://real.flofr.com/ConsumerServices/FinancialInstitutions/InstSrch.aspx
Broker, Burial Rights	www.myfloridacfo.com/data/Pnslicensesearch/index.htm
Cemetery	www.myfloridacfo.com/data/Pnslicensesearch/index.htm
Cemetery Lot Salesperson	www.myfloridacfo.com/data/Pnslicensesearch/index.htm
Child Care Center	http://dcfsanswrite.state.fl.us/Childcare/provider/
Company in Liquidation/Rehabilitation/Colsed	www.myfloridacfo.com/division/receiver/Companies/default.htm#.U3FCOqIVDVo
Concealed Weapon	https://licensing.freshfromflorida.com/CWStatusCheck/CWStatusChk.aspx
Credit Union	https://real.flofr.com/ConsumerServices/FinancialInstitutions/InstSrch.aspx
Crematory	www.myfloridacfo.com/data/Pnslicensesearch/index.htm
Day Care/Child Care Ctr/Nursery Sch'l	http://dcfsanswrite.state.fl.us/Childcare/provider/
Embalmer/Apprentice	www.myfloridacfo.com/data/Pnslicensesearch/index.htm
Engineer	https://www.fbpe.org/index.php/licensure/licensee-search
Engineering Firm	https://www.fbpe.org/index.php/licensure/licensee-search
Finance Company, Consumer	www.flofr.com/StaticPages/VerifyALicense.htm
Firearm Instructor/School/Agency	www.freshfromflorida.com/Divisions-Offices/Licensing/Private-Investigation/Search-for-a-Licensee
Firearm License, Statewide	https://licensing.freshfromflorida.com/access/individual.aspx
Funeral Director	www.myfloridacfo.com/data/Pnslicensesearch/index.htm
Funeral Home	www.myfloridacfo.com/data/Pnslicensesearch/index.htm
Health Facility	www.floridahealthfinder.gov/facilitylocator/facloc.aspx
Home Improvement Financer	www.flofr.com/StaticPages/VerifyALicense.htm
In Home Family Day Care Center	http://dcfsanswrite.state.fl.us/Childcare/provider/
Installment Seller, Retail	www.flofr.com/StaticPages/VerifyALicense.htm
Insurance Adjuster/Agent/Title Agent	www.myfloridacfo.com/data/aar_alis1/
Insurance-related Company	www.floir.com/companysearch/

International Bank Office	https://real.flofr.com/ConsumerServices/FinancialInstitutions/InstSrch.aspx
Investment Advisor	www.flofr.com/StaticPages/VerifyALicense.htm
Licensed Dealer Training School	www.flhsmv.gov/dmv/L_Dealer_Trng_Sch.pdf
Lobbying Firms	https://floridalobbyist.gov/
Lobbyist/Lobby Principal	https://floridalobbyist.gov/LobbyistInformation/LobbyistSearch
Money Transmitter	www.flofr.com/StaticPages/VerifyALicense.htm
Monument Dealer	www.myfloridacfo.com/data/Pnslicensesearch/index.htm
Mortgage Broker/Firm	www.flofr.com/StaticPages/VerifyALicense.htm
Mortgage Business School	www.flofr.com/StaticPages/VerifyALicense.htm
Notary Public	http://notaries.dos.state.fl.us/not001.html
Pest Control, Structural/Operator	http://ceupublicsearch.freshfromflorida.com/
Pesticide Applicator/Dealers/Companies	http://ceupublicsearch.freshfromflorida.com/
Polygraph Assn Member	www.floridapolygraph.org/
Polygraph PCSOT Examiner	www.floridapolygraph.org/
Polygraphist, Certified	www.floridapolygraph.org/
Preneed Seller, Funeral	www.myfloridacfo.com/data/Pnslicensesearch/index.htm
Private Investigator/Agency/School	www.freshfromflorida.com/Divisions-Offices/Licensing/Private-Investigation/Search-for-a-Licensee
Recovering Agent/School/Instruct/Mgr	www.freshfromflorida.com/Divisions-Offices/Licensing/Private-Investigation/Search-for-a-Licensee
Sales Finance Company	www.flofr.com/StaticPages/VerifyALicense.htm
Savings & Loan Association, Charter	https://real.flofr.com/ConsumerServices/FinancialInstitutions/InstSrch.aspx
Securities Agent	www.flofr.com/StaticPages/VerifyALicense.htm
Securities Broker Dealer/Branch Office	www.flofr.com/StaticPages/VerifyALicense.htm
Securities Broker/Seller/Associate	www.flofr.com/StaticPages/VerifyALicense.htm
Security Officer/Instructor/School	www.freshfromflorida.com/Divisions-Offices/Licensing/Private-Investigation/Search-for-a-Licensee
Solid Waste Facility Operator	https://fldeploc.dep.state.fl.us/www_rcra/reports/handler_sel.asp
Teacher	http://app4.fldoe.org/edcert/Certification_Status.aspx
Trust Company	https://real.flofr.com/ConsumerServices/FinancialInstitutions/InstSrch.aspx

State and Local Courts

About Florida Courts: The trial jurisdiction of **Circuit Courts** includes, among other matters, original jurisdiction over felonies, civil disputes involving more than $15,000, estates, minors and persons adjudicated as incapacitated, juveniles tax disputes; title and boundaries of real property; suits for declaratory judgments. Circuit Courts also have general trial jurisdiction over matters not assigned by statute to the county courts and also hear appeals from county court cases. There can be as many as 7 counties and few as 1 county assigned to the 20 Circuits. Note Miami-Dade has five full-service District Court locations, two limited-service offices.

The trial jurisdiction of **County Courts** includes civil disputes involving $15,000 or less, misdemeanors, traffic and small claims. The majority of non-jury trials in Florida take place before the County Court. The County Courts are sometimes referred to as *the People's Courts.*

The web page for the Judicial System is www.flcourts.org.

Appellate Courts: The Supreme Court is the court of last resort. The web page provides opinions and dockets from www.floridasupremecourt.org. However, most appeals are heard by the five District Courts of Appeal. See www.flcourts.org/florida-courts/district-court-appeal.stml.   Search   Supreme   Court   dockets   at http://jweb.flcourts.org/pls/docket/ds_docket_search. and Docket Appeals at http://199.242.69.70/pls/ds/ds_docket_search.

About Court Online Access

While a number of counties offer online access, there is one primary free search system with quite a few participants using the same core site with a different numeric ending. For example, Baker County is https://www.civitekflorida.com/ocrs/county/02 and Bradford County is https://www.civitekflorida.com/ocrs/county/04/

There is also a vendor - MyFlorida.com operated by the Florida Association of Court Clerks Services Group - offering access to certified court judgments and other county information such as recorded land documents for many participating courts and county recorder's offices. A search of the index is free, but registration and fees are charged for images or further data. Subscription fee is

$120.00 per year. Records may be ordered. Non-subscribers pay between $3.50 and $13.00 for every official record ordered. Subscribers pay a fixed, discounted fee of $2.00 per record. See https://www.myfloridacounty.com/.

The Clerk of the Circuit Court cannot place an image or copy of the following documents on a publicly available website for general public display: military discharges; death certificates; court files, records or papers relating to Family Law, Juvenile Law, or Probate Law cases.

County Sites:
Alachua County
Circuit & County Courts - Criminal   www.alachuacounty.us/Depts/Clerk/Pages/Clerk.aspx/
Search limited criminal and traffic citations at https://www.alachuaclerk.org/court_records/.
Circuit & County Courts - Civil   www.alachuacounty.us/Depts/Clerk/Pages/Clerk.aspx
Search civil record index free at https://www.alachuaclerk.org/court_records/. Also, access to an index of judgments & recorded documents at www.myfloridacounty.com. Fees involved to order copies. Also, search the probate index (no images) and other ancient records free at www.alachuaclerk.org/Archive/default.cfm. Court accepts record requests by email osr@alachuacounty.org. Also, search the probate index (no images) and other ancient records free at www.alachuaclerk.org/Archive/default.cfm. Court accepts record requests by email osr@alachuacounty.org

Baker County
Circuit & County Courts - Civil http://208.75.175.18/clerk/
There is a free docket search at https://www.civitekflorida.com/ocrs/county/02/. Includes Circuit civil cases back to 11/4/92, County to 01/22/88, Small Claims to 9/27/91, Probate/Guardianship to 4/18/95. An initial free search of court judgments is at https://www2.myfloridacounty.com/ori/index.do. Records may be ordered. Non-subscribers pay between $3.50 and $13.00 for every official record ordered. Subscribers pay a fixed, discounted fee of $2.00 per record. Access to liens and recorded documents also offered.
Circuit & County Courts - Criminal   http://208.75.175.18/clerk/
There is a free docket search at https://www2.myfloridacounty.com/ori/index.do. Includes Felony cases back to 7/13/70, misdemeanor to 5/6/81, traffic to 6/20/97, and Muni Infractions to 11/13/2012. A 2nd search site is available at https://www.civitekflorida.com/ocrs/county/02/disclaimer.xhtml, The site does not indicate the throughput..

Bay County
Circuit & County Courts - Civil www.baycoclerk.com
Search the court cases, including traffic and probate, for free a thttps://court.baycoclerk.com/BenchmarkWeb2/Home.aspx/Search. Florida Attorneys may request secure access subscription and access information by emailing CIS@baycoclerk.com. Also, access an index of judgments, liens, recorded documents at www.myfloridacounty.com. Fees involved to order copies; save $1.50 per record by becoming a subscriber.
Circuit & County Courts - Criminal www.baycoclerk.com
Search the courts case database free at https://court.baycoclerk.com/BenchmarkWeb2/Home.aspx/Search. For a free search and additional searches available for subscribers see https://www.myfloridacounty.com/official_records/index.html.

Bradford County
Circuit & County Courts - Civil   www.bradfordcountyfl.gov/clerkIndex.html
A free search is offered at https://www.civitekflorida.com/ocrs/county/04. This is county wide. An initial free search of court judgments is at https://www2.myfloridacounty.com/ori/index.do. Records may be ordered. Non-subscribers pay between $3.50 and $13.00 for every official record ordered. Subscribers pay a fixed, discounted fee of $2.00 per record. Access to liens and recorded documents also offered.
Circuit & County Courts - Criminal   www.bradfordcountyfl.gov/clerkIndex.html
A free search is offered at https://www.civitekflorida.com/ocrs/county/04. This is county wide. Search by name or SSN. A second site is at https://www2.myfloridacounty.com/ori/index.do.

Brevard County
Circuit & County Courts - Civil http://brevardclerk.us/
Access public information of the records index free at https://vweb1.brevardclerk.us/facts/facts_search.cfm. Attorneys of record have access to images per a separate account. A subscription account is also available, see http://brevardclerk.us/official-records-view. One may request copies and pay for research at https://vweb1.brevardclerk.us/webapps_ssl/rcrc/default.cfm. Overall, online civil records can be searched by name or case number from 1987 to present.
Circuit & County Courts - Criminal http://brevardclerk.us/
Access public information of the records index free at https://vweb1.brevardclerk.us/facts/facts_search.cfm. Attorneys of record have access to images per a separate account. A subscription account is also available, see http://brevardclerk.us/official-records-view. One may request copies and pay for research at https://vweb1.brevardclerk.us/webapps_ssl/rcrc/default.cfm.

Broward County
Circuit & County Courts - www.clerk-17th-flcourts.org/ClerkWebsite/welcome2.aspx
Civil: Basic information is free at https://www.browardclerk.org/Web2/. Search by name, case number or case type. There is also a premium case subscription service available to registered users and free to one-time users. Direct email record requests to eclerk@browardclerk.org. *Criminal:* Basic information free at https://www.browardclerk.org/Web2/. Search by name, case number or case type. Also, there is a 'Premium Access' for detailed case information; requires a fee, registration and password. Call 954-831-5654..

Criminal: Basic information free at https://www.browardclerk.org/Web2/. Search by name, case number or case type. Includes search of traffic tickets. Also, there is a 'Premium Access' for detailed case information; requires a fee, registration and password. Call 954-831-5654.

Calhoun County
Circuit & County Court   www.calhounclerk.com/
Civil: Access civil, probate, guardianship, and small claims records at https://www.civitekflorida.com/ocrs/county/07. *Criminal:* Access index of felony, misdemeanor, and traffic records at https://www.civitekflorida.com/ocrs/county/07.

Charlotte County
Circuit & County Courts - Civil Division   http://co.charlotte.fl.us/Default.aspx
Civil: Access civil court records free at https://courtsweb.co.charlotte.fl.us/BenchmarkWeb/Home.aspx/Search. Also, access an index of judgments, liens, recorded documents at www.myfloridacounty.com fees for copies.
Circuit & County Courts - Criminal Division   http://co.charlotte.fl.us/Default.aspx
Criminal: Access index free at https://courtsweb.co.charlotte.fl.us/BenchmarkWeb/Home.aspx/Search. Name only required to search. One may search traffic and domestic violence cases as well.

Citrus County
Circuit Court   www.clerk.citrus.fl.us/nws/home.jsp?section=1&item=1
Civil: View court record index (no images) free at http://search.clerk.citrus.fl.us/courts/login.asp; Subscription system giving full identifiers also available. Also there is an index of judgments, liens, recorded documents at www.myfloridacounty.com. Fees involved to order copies; save $1.50 per record by becoming a subscriber.   *Criminal:* View court record index (no images) free at www.clerk.citrus.fl.us/courts/search. Also, see www.clerk.citrus.fl.us/nws/home.jsp?section=1&item=17 for a subscription system giving full address and DOB identifiers also available.
County Court   www.clerk.citrus.fl.us/nws/home.jsp?section=1&item=1
Civil: View court record index (no images) free at https://scorss.clerk.citrus.fl.us/; Subscription system with identifiers also available. Free index search does not give DOB or full address, subscription system does. Anonymous users are required to complete the Captcha requirements for each search request. Access an index of judgments, liens, recorded documents at www.myfloridacounty.com/services/officialrecords_intro.shtml; Fees involved to order copies; save $1.50 per record by becoming a subscriber.   *Criminal:* View court record index (no images) free at https://scorss.clerk.citrus.fl.us/. Subscription system with identifiers also available. Anonymous users are required to complete the Captcha requirements for each search request. Free index search does not give DOB or full address, subscription system does.

Clay County
Circuit Court   www.clayclerk.com/
Civil: Clerk of the circuit court provides free access to record index of civil actions and judgments at www.clayclerk.com/recording-department/how-to-search-official-records/. Also, from an approved vendor, access an index of judgments, liens, recorded documents at www.myfloridacounty.com. Fees involved to order copies; save $1.50 per record by becoming a subscriber.   *Criminal:* Access to criminal record index is free at www.clayclerk.com/recording-department/how-to-search-official-records/.

County Court   www.clayclerk.com/court-services/criminal-court/#county-criminal-court
Civil: Access civil, family, and probate docket info to 1992 free at http://pa.clayclerk.com/PublicAccess/default.aspx. Also, access an index of judgments, liens, recorded documents at www.myfloridacounty.com. Fees involved to order copies; save $1.50 per record by becoming a subscriber.   *Criminal:* Access criminal records free at http://pa.clayclerk.com/PublicAccess/default.aspx.

Collier County
Circuit & County Court   www.collierclerk.com/
Civil: Online access is free at https://www.collierclerk.com/records-search/public-inquiry. *Criminal:* same.

Columbia County
Circuit & County Courts   www.columbiaclerk.com/
Civil: Access to County Clerk of Circuit Court records is at https://www.civitekflorida.com/ocrs/county/12 Attorneys and regular users may register and have access to images, fees involved.   *Criminal:* Access to County Clerk of Circuit Court felony, misdemeanor, and traffic records is at https://www.civitekflorida.com/ocrs/county/12. The newer site is https://www.civitekflorida.com/ocrs/county/12/. At the newer site attorneys and regular users may register and have access to images, fees involved.

De Soto County
Circuit & County Courts   www.desotoclerk.com
Civil: Free access to civil information, marriage/divorce, small claims, traffic/parking, Muni ordinances, domestic relations, name changes, foreclosures from 1980 to present at www.desotoclerk.com. An initial free search of court judgments is at https://www2.myfloridacounty.com/ori/index.do. Records may be ordered. Non-subscribers pay between $3.50 and $13.00 for every official record ordered. Subscribers pay a fixed, discounted fee of $2.00 per record. Access to liens and recorded documents also offered. *Criminal:* Traffic Criminal cases are free at www.desotoclerk.com/dpa/cvweb.asp. Access index of felony, misdemeanor, and traffic records at https://www.civitekflorida.com/ocrs/county/14.

Dixie County
Circuit & County Courts   http://dixieclerk.com/
Civil: Access to County Clerk of Circuit Court records is at https://www.civitekflorida.com/ocrs/county/15   *Criminal:* Access to index of felony, misdemeanor and traffic records is at https://www.civitekflorida.com/ocrs/county/15.

Duval County

Circuit & County Courts   www.duvalclerk.com/ccWebsite/

Civil: Access court records back to 1986 from all courts in the county free at https://core.duvalclerk.com/. One may also apply for a log-in to view enhanced records, as explained at the site. Also, access an index of judgments, liens, recorded documents at https://www.myfloridacounty.com/. Fees involved to order copies; save $1.50 per record by becoming a subscriber. *Criminal:* Access court records back to 1986 from all courts in the county free at https://core.duvalclerk.com/. One may also apply for a log-in to view enhanced records, as explained at the site.

Escambia County

Circuit & County Courts   www.escambiaclerk.com/clerk/index.aspx

Civil: end email requests to publicrecords@escambiaclerk.com. Online access to county clerk records is free at http://public.escambiaclerk.com/xml/xml_web_1a.asp. Search by name, citation, or case number. Small claims, traffic, and marriage data also available. Access an index of judgments, liens, recorded documents at www.myfloridacounty.com. Fees involved to order copies; save $1.50 per record by becoming a subscriber. *Criminal:* Online access to felony, criminal traffic and municipal ordinance records is free and active at http://public.escambiaclerk.com/xml/xml_web_1a.asp. Search by name, citation, or case number. Send email requests to publicrecords@escambiaclerk.com.

Flagler County

Circuit & County Courts   www.flaglerclerk.com/

Civil: Access clerk's civil records free at hhttps://apps.flaglerclerk.com/Benchmark/Home.aspx/Search. Also, access an index of judgments, liens, recorded documents at www.myfloridacounty.com. Fees involved to order copies. Additional documents may be viewed online by completing and submitting a Registration Agreement. Also, you may email record requests to records@flaglerclerk.com. *Criminal:* Access clerk's criminal records free at https://apps.flaglerclerk.com/Benchmark/Home.aspx/Search. Additional documents may be viewed online by completing and submitting a Registration Agreement.

Franklin County

Circuit & County Courts   www.franklinclerk.com

Civil: Access index and records free at https://www.civitekflorida.com/ocrs/county/19. Circuit goes back to 3/1997; County to 10/1998; Probate back to 2/1982. Also, access an index of judgments with other recorded documents at https://www3.myfloridacounty.com/official_records/index.html. Fees involved to order copies; save $1.50 per record by becoming a subscriber. *Criminal:* Access index and records free at https://www.civitekflorida.com/ocrs/county/19. Felony goes back to 3/4/1984; Misdemeanors back to 1989. Also, access criminal records by subscription at https://www.myfloridacounty.com/subscription/. Fees are involved.

Gadsden County

Circuit & County Courts   www.gadsdenclerk.com/

Civil: The index of civil court judgments is free to view at http://gadsdenclerk.com/courtscribepublicinquiry/. Also, subscription access an index of judgments, liens, recorded documents at www.myfloridacounty.com. Fees involved to order copies; save $1.50 per record by becoming a subscriber. *Criminal:* The index of criminal and traffic case files is free to view at http://gadsdenclerk.com/courtscribepublicinquiry/.

Gilchrist County

Circuit & County Courts   www.gilchristclerk.com/

Civil: Access to County Clerk of Circuit Court records is at https://www.civitekflorida.com/ocrs/county/21 Search judgments (and liens) online at https://www.myfloridacounty.com/ori/index.do   Criminal: same

Glades County

Circuit & County Courts   www.gladesclerk.com/

Civil: Access civil, probate, guardianship, and small claims records at https://www.civitekflorida.com/ocrs/county/22. *Criminal:* Access index of felony, misdemeanor, and traffic records at https://www.civitekflorida.com/ocrs/county/22.

Gulf County

Circuit & County Courts   http://gulfclerk.com/

Civil: Access an index of civil judgments and small claims at https://www.civitekflorida.com/ocrs/county/23. Fees involved to order copies; save $1.50 per record by becoming a subscriber. Circuit civil goes back to 7/31/1984, County civil to 3/31/1986. *Criminal:* Access an index of felony and misdemeanor cases at https://www.civitekflorida.com/ocrs/county/23. Fees involved to order copies; save $1.50 per record by becoming a subscriber. Records go back to 2/22/1979 for felony, 4/6/1973 for misdemeanor and 01/04 /82 for traffic.

Hamilton County

Circuit & County Courts   www.hamiltoncountyflorida.com/cd_clerk.aspx

Civil: Access the docket index, including small claims, probate/guardianship, and domestic relations at https://www.civitekflorida.com/ocrs/county/24. Few identifiers are shown. Purchase office copies of certified judgments at https://www.myfloridacounty.com/official_records/index.html. Save $1.50 a record by becoming a subscriber. *Criminal:* Access the docket index for felony, misdemeanor and traffic at https://www.civitekflorida.com/ocrs/county/24

Hardee County

Circuit & County Courts   www.hardeeclerk.com/

Civil: Access to civil, domestic relations, small claims, guardianship, and probate is available at https://www.civitekflorida.com/ocrs/county/25. Records go back at least 25 years. *Criminal:* Access to felony, misdemeanor, traffic is available at https://www.civitekflorida.com/ocrs/county/25. Felony records go back to 9/17/1973.

Hendry County
Circuit & County Courts   www.hendryclerk.org/
Civil: Access civil and guardianship case dockets free back to 05/1992 at https://www.civitekflorida.com/ocrs/county/26. Fees involved to order copies; save $1.50 per record by becoming a subscriber. *Criminal:* Access felony to 6/18/1985, misdemeanor to 5/19/1986, and traffic to 08/21/1988 free at https://www.civitekflorida.com/ocrs/county/26

Hernando County
Circuit & County Courts   http://hernandoclerk.com/
Civil: An initial free search of court judgments is at https://www2.myfloridacounty.com/ori/index.do. Records may be ordered. Non-subscribers pay between $3.50 and $13.00 for every official record ordered. Subscribers pay a fixed, discounted fee of $2.00 per record. Access to liens and recorded documents also offered. *Criminal:* same

Highlands County
Circuit & County Courts   www.hcclerk.org/Home.aspx
Civil: Access to county clerk civil and probate records is free at www.hcclerk.org/Home/Search-Court-Records.aspx back to 1991. Also includes small claims, probate, and tax deeds. An initial free search of court judgments is at https://www2.myfloridacounty.com/ori/index.do. Records may be ordered. Non-subscribers pay between $3.50 and $13.00 for every official record ordered. Subscribers pay a fixed, discounted fee of $2.00 per record. Access to liens and recorded documents also offered. *Criminal:* Subscribe for access to court records at http://courts.hcclerk.org/iquery/. Access free index of felony, misdemeanor, and traffic records at https://www.civitekflorida.com/ocrs/county/28.

Hillsborough County
Circuit & County Courts   www.hillsclerk.com/publicweb/home.aspx
Civil: The newer search site is at https://hover.hillsclerk.com/. The search is free and regsitered use can view case images. Also online access is at http://pubrec10.hillsclerk.com/Unsecured/default.aspx. . Using the site map, one can order case files online at www.hillsclerk.com/publicweb/SiteMap.aspx. A vendor search site is at http://pubrec10.hillsclerk.com/Unsecured/default.aspx. Access index of judgments, liens, recorded documents at www.myfloridacounty.com. Fees involved to order copies; save $1.50 per record by becoming a subscriber. *Criminal:* The newer search site is at https://hover.hillsclerk.com/. The search is free and registered use can view case images. Using the site map, one can order case files online at www.hillsclerk.com/publicweb/SiteMap.aspx. A vendor search site is at http://pubrec10.hillsclerk.com/Unsecured/default.aspx.

Holmes County
Circuit & County Courts   https://www.myfloridacounty.com/ori/index.do
Civil: Access to County Clerk of Circuit Court records is from a link on the home page or go to https://www.civitekflorida.com/ocrs/county/30. Note that there is a disclaimer that states this search should not be used as an authoritative public record. *Criminal:* Access to County Clerk of Circuit Court records is from a link on the home page or go tohttps://www.civitekflorida.com/ocrs/county/30.

Indian River County
Circuit & County Courts   www.clerk.indian-river.org/en/
Free access to the index for civil, family, and probate is at https://court.indian-river.org/BenchmarkWeb/home.aspx/search/. Full access to court records for attorneys only is via the clerk's subscription service. Fee is $25.00 per month. For information about the fee access, call Gary at 772-567-8000 x1216. *Criminal:* Free access to the index for criminal and traffic is at https://court.indian-river.org/BenchmarkWeb/home.aspx/search/. All access to court records for attorneys only is via the clerk's subscription service. Fee is $25.00 per month.

Jackson County
Civil: Access civil, probate, guardianship, and small claims at https://www.civitekflorida.com/ocrs/county/32. Access an index of judgments (not dockets) is at www.myfloridacounty.com. Fees involved to order copies; save $1.50 per record by becoming a subscriber. *Criminal:* Access index of felony, misdemeanor, and traffic at https://www.civitekflorida.com/ocrs/county/32.

Jefferson County
Circuit & County Courts   www.jeffersonclerk.com/
Civil: Access to County Clerk of Circuit Court records is at https://www.civitekflorida.com/ocrs/county/33/disclaimer.xhtml   *Criminal:* same

Lafayette County
Circuit & County Courts   http://lafayetteclerk.com/
Civil: Access civil, probate, guardianship, and small claims records at https://www.civitekflorida.com/ocrs/county/34. Fees involved to order copies; save $1.50 per record by becoming a subscriber. *Criminal:* Access criminal, traffic and ordinance records at https://www.civitekflorida.com/ocrs/county/34.

Lake County
Circuit & County Courts   www.lakecountyclerk.org/
Civil: Online access to Court records free at www.lakecountyclerk.org/record_searches/court_records_agreement.aspx. Civil records back to 1985; Circuit records back to 9/84. *Criminal:* same

Lee County

Circuit & County Courts   www.leeclerk.org

Civil: Access records free at www.leeclerk.org, click on Courts then Search Court Cases. Online records go back to 1988. Includes small claims and probate. Access an index of judgments, liens, recorded documents at www.leeclerk.org or www.myfloridacounty.com. Search free but fees involved to order certified copies; save the per-record copy fee by becoming a subscriber; sub fee is $25.00 per month.   *Criminal:* Access records free at www.leeclerk.org, click on Courts then Search Court Cases. Online records go back to 1988. Includes traffic, felony, misdemeanor. Subscription service is available for attorneys.

Leon County

Circuit & County Courts   https://cvweb.clerk.leon.fl.us/public/login.asp

Civil: Search all types of civil and probate cases free at https://cvweb.clerk.leon.fl.us/public/login.asp. Access an index of judgments, liens, recorded documents at www.myfloridacounty.com. Fees involved to order copies; save $1.50 per record by becoming a subscriber. *Criminal:* Criminal case records are not online, but search traffic infraction cases free at https://cvweb.clerk.leon.fl.us/public/login.asp. Also access an inmate search at www.leoncountyso.com/leon-county-jail/jail-inmate-search.

Levy County

Circuit & County Courts   www.levyclerk.com

Civil: A search of the civil docket index is free at www.levyclerk.com/electronic-court-records-access/. Search civil for Circuit and County separate or together. Can also search probate, guardianship, small claims, and domestic relations. Recorded judgments available on the Clerk of the Circuit Court Official Records Index free at http://oncore.levyclerk.com/oncoreweb/.   *Criminal:* A search of the criminal docket index is free at www.levyclerk.com/electronic-court-records-access/. Search felony, misdemeanor, traffic, Muni infractions, and criminal traffic. Felony and misdemeanor go back to 1989.

Liberty County

Circuit & County Courts   www.libertyclerk.com/

Civil: Three entry points are available at https://www.civitekflorida.com/ocrs/county/39. One for the public, one for attorneys, and one for registered users. The latter 2 require a user ID and password and images may be purchased.. An initial free search of court judgments is at https://www2.myfloridacounty.com/ori/index.do. Records may be ordered. Non-subscribers pay between $3.50 and $13.00 for every official record ordered. Subscribers pay a fixed, discounted fee of $2.00 per record. Access to liens and recorded documents also offered. *Criminal:* The docket index is available at https://www2.myfloridacounty.com/ccm/disclaimer.jsp?county=39.

Madison County

Circuit & County Courts   www.madisonclerk.com/

Civil: Access civil, probate, guardianship, and small claims records at https://www.civitekflorida.com/ocrs/county/40.   *Criminal:* Access index of felony, misdemeanor, and traffic records at https://www.civitekflorida.com/ocrs/county/40.

Manatee County

Circuit & County Courts   www.manateeclerk.com

Civil: Access public court record index and images at clerk's office free at www.manateeclerk.org. Both a public access and a subscription service is offered. Civil record available from July 18, 2001. Also, you may direct email record requests to lori.tolksdorf@manateeclerk.com. *Criminal:* Access public court record index and images at clerk's office at www.manateeclerk.org. Both a public access and a subscription service are offered. This is a new Pilot program for FL that went live. Felony records available from June 5, 2002; misdemeanor from Jan. 2003.

Marion County

Circuit & County Courts   www.marioncountyclerk.org

Civil: Online access to civil and probate records from 1983 forward is free at www.marioncountyclerk.org/index.cfm?Pg=OfficialRecords1. Click on 'Search Records Now.' Also, access an index of judgments, liens, recorded documents at www.myfloridacounty.com. Fees involved to order copies; save $1.50 per record by becoming a subscriber.   *Criminal:* Online access to county clerk records is free at www.marioncountyclerk.org/index.cfm?Pg=OfficialRecords1. Click on 'Search Records Now. Felony, misdemeanor and traffic case information available since 1991.

Martin County

Circuit & County Courts   www.martinclerk.com/

Civil: Access civil, probate, guardianship, and small claims records at https://www.civitekflorida.com/ocrs/county/43 Also includes small claims, recordings, other document types. Search online by name. There is a disclaimer - the information provided is not official record. *Criminal:* Access index of felony, misdemeanor, and traffic records at https://www.civitekflorida.com/ocrs/county/43. Online results include partial address, sex, race, alias.

Miami-Dade County

Circuit & County Courts - Civil   www.miami-dadeclerk.com/courts_civil.asp

Free and commercial fee-based online services are available. Search most all case types free at https://www2.miami-dadeclerk.com/CJIS/CaseSearch.aspx. Commercial consumers have access to either bulk data in FTP format or to API (Application Programming Interfaces) for retrieval of case information. For details and fees see https://www2.miami-dadeclerk.com/Developers.

Circuit & County Courts - Criminal   www.miami-dadeclerk.com/

Free and commercial fee-based online services are available. Search felony, misdemeanor, civil and county ordinance violations free at https://www2.miami-dadeclerk.com/CJIS/CaseSearch.aspx. Commercial consumers have access to either bulk data in FTP format or to API (Application Programming Interfaces) for retrieval of case information. For details and fees see https://www2.miami-dadeclerk.com/Developers.

Monroe County
Circuit & County Courts   https://gov.propertyinfo.com/fl-monroe/
Civil: Online access to civil cases is free at https://gov.propertyinfo.com/fl-monroe/searchCivilCases.asp. Also, search probate cases free at https://gov.propertyinfo.com/fl-monroe/searchProbateCases.asp. *Criminal:* Online access to criminal records is free at https://gov.propertyinfo.com/fl-monroe/searchTrafficCriminalCases.asp. Includes traffic cases online.

Nassau County
Circuit & County Courts   www.nassauclerk.com
Civil: A search of the docket index is provided for free at https://www.civitekflorida.com/ocrs/county/. Access an index of judgments, sentences, county commitments, uniform state commitments, disposition notices and nolle prosecution only at www.myfloridacounty.com. Fees involved to order copies; save $1.50 per record by becoming a subscriber. *Criminal:* same

Okaloosa County
Circuit & County Courts   www.okaloosaclerk.com
Civil: Civil record index search is free at www.okaloosaclerk.com/index.php/records-disclaimers/78-court-records-disclaimer. Records go back to 1/83. Search civil index by defendant or plaintiff, date, or file type. Also, access an index of judgments, liens, recorded documents back to 11/1986 at www.myfloridacounty.com. Fees involved to order copies; save $1.50 per record by becoming a subscriber. *Criminal:* Search online includes felony and misdemeanor and civil/criminal traffic record docket at www.okaloosaclerk.com/index.php/records-disclaimers/78-court-records-disclaimer.

Okeechobee County
Circuit & County Courts   www.clerk.co.okeechobee.fl.us
Civil: There is a free docket search at https://www.civitekflorida.com/ocrs/county/47. Wireless access to the public system is provided in the courthouse. *Criminal:* Index of criminal judgments (and recorded documents) can be searched free at https://www.civitekflorida.com/ocrs/county/47.

Orange County
Circuit & County Courts   https://myorangeclerk.com/
Civil: The free Myclerk Case Inquiry System is at https://myeclerk.myorangeclerk.com/. Civil and Probate records available.   *Criminal:* Access criminal records free on the Myclerk Case Inquiry System at https://myeclerk.myorangeclerk.com/.

Osceola County
Circuit & County Courts   www.osceolaclerk.com/
Civil: nline access to court records on the Clerk of Circuit Court database is free at https://courts.osceolaclerk.org/BenchmarkWeb/Home.aspx/Search. Also, access an index of judgments, liens, recorded documents at www.myfloridacounty.com. Fees involved to order copies; save $1.50 per record by becoming a subscriber.   *Criminal:* Online access to court records on the Clerk of Circuit Court database is free at https://courts.osceolaclerk.org/benchmarkweb/Home.aspx/Search. Submit email requests to research@osceolaclerk.org.

Palm Beach County
Circuit & County Courts   www.mypalmbeachclerk.com/
Civil: Access to the countywide online remote system is free. Civil index goes back to '88. Records also include probate, traffic and domestic. See www.mypalmbeachclerk.com/cctrecordsearch.aspx. Bulk case data can be purchases as well. See https://applications.mypalmbeachclerk.com/clerkcart/ *Criminal:* Same

Pasco County
Circuit & County Courts   www.pascoclerk.com/
Civil: Access court records free at https://www.civitekflorida.com/ocrs/county/51/. Search by case file number at www.pascoclerk.com/public-online-services-disclaimer-search.asp. An initial free search of court judgments is at https://www2.myfloridacounty.com/ori/index.do. Records may be ordered. Non-subscribers pay between $3.50 and $13.00 for every official record ordered. Subscribers pay a fixed, discounted fee of $2.00 per record. Access to liens and recorded documents also offered.   *Criminal:* Access court records free at https://www.civitekflorida.com/ocrs/county/51/. Search by case file number at www.pascoclerk.com/public-online-services-disclaimer-search.asp.

Pinellas County
Circuit & County Courts - www.pinellasclerk.org
Civil: Access court dockets free at https://ccmspa.pinellascounty.org/PublicAccess/default.aspx. Also, access index of judgments and recorded docs at www.myfloridacounty.com. Fees to order copies; subscribers save $1.50 per record.   *Criminal:* Access court dockets free at https://ccmspa.pinellascounty.org/PublicAccess/default.aspx.

Polk County
Circuit & County Courts - www.polkcountyclerk.net/home/
Civil: Free online access to dockets at https://ori2.polk-county.net/ct_web1/search.asp. Searchable online record index does not provide addresses; in-person search at court will only provide most recent address. Also, access to County Clerk of Circuit Court records is at https://www2.myfloridacounty.com/ccm/?county=53.$$$ *Criminal:* Free online access to dockets at https://pro.polkcountyclerk.net/PRO. Includes all

case types countywide. There is also an enhanced version for attorneys or parties involved in a case - registration required. Sheriff warrants and most wanted are at www.polksheriff.org/FugitivesOffenders/Pages/FugitivesPredators.aspx.

Putnam County

Circuit & County Courts - Civil Division   www.putnam-fl.com/coc/

Civil: Access to the countywide remote online system requires $400 setup fee and $40. monthly charge plus $.05 per minute over 20 hours. Civil records go back to 1984. System includes criminal and real property records. Contact Putnam County IT Dept at 386-329-0390 to register. Also, access a free index of dockets at https://www.putnam-fl.com/peas/public_menu.php. Access civil, probate, guardianship, and small claims records at https://www2.myfloridacounty.com/ccm/?county=54.

Criminal: Access to the countywide criminal online system by subscription at https://www.putnam-fl.com/subscribe/login.php. Fees are not displayed, but thought to be requires $400 setup fee and $40. monthly charge plus $.05 per minute over 20 hours. Criminal records go back to 1972. System includes ability to download criminal and traffic records. Call 386-329-0390. Access a free index of dockets at https://www.putnam-fl.com/peas/public_menu.php. Access index of felony, misdemeanor, and traffic records at https://www2.myfloridacounty.com/ccm/disclaimer.jsp?county=54.

Santa Rosa County

Circuit & County Courts - Civil Division   www.santarosaclerk.com

Free search of civil index is at https://www.civitekflorida.com/ocrs/county/57/. An initial free search of court judgments is at https://www2.myfloridacounty.com/ori/index.do. Records may be ordered. Non-subscribers pay between $3.50 and $13.00 for every official record ordered. Subscribers pay a fixed, discounted fee of $2.00 per record. Access to liens and recorded documents also offered.

Circuit & County Courts - Criminal Division   www.santarosaclerk.com

Access to the record index is offered at https://www.civitekflorida.com/ocrs/county/57/. Felony records go back to 3/19/1976. Misdemeanor records to 10/26/1979.

Sarasota County

Circuit & County Courts - Civil   www.sarasotaclerk.com

Civil: The site at www.sarasotaclerk.com/default1308.html?Page=170 offers access to civil and probate records. Registration is required. Judgments and liens may be accessed as well. Also, access an index of judgments, liens, recorded documents at https://www.myfloridacounty.com/ori/index.do. Fees involved to order copies; save $1.50 per record by becoming a subscriber.

Circuit & County Courts - Criminal   www.sarasotaclerk.com

Criminal: A search site at www.sarasotaclerk.com/default1308.html?Page=170 offers access to criminal and traffic case information. Registration is required. Judgments and liens may be accessed as well. Images are often available on or after 09/09/2002.

Seminole County

Circuit & County Courts   www.seminoleclerk.org

Civil: Access to judgment records is free at http://officialrecords.seminoleclerk.org/. Images related to Probate cases are not available on the Clerk's website. The court does not provide a DOB on name search results either online or on the public terminal. *Criminal:* Access criminal dockets free at www.seminoleclerk.org, click on Criminal Dockets Search. Partial DOB shown.

St. Johns County

Circuit & County Courts - Civil Division   www.clk.co.st-johns.fl.us/

Civil: A free search is offered at http://doris.clk.co.st-johns.fl.us/benchmarkweb/. Search by name or case number. Access an index of judgments, liens, recorded documents at www.myfloridacounty.com. Fees involved to order copies; save $1.50 per record by becoming a subscriber at $25.00 per month.

Circuit & County Courts - Criminal Division   www.clk.co.st-johns.fl.us/

Criminal: A free search is offered at http://doris.clk.co.st-johns.fl.us/benchmarkweb/. Search by name or case number. Can search traffic records also.

St. Lucie County

Circuit & County Courts - Civil Division   http://stlucieclerk.com

Civil: View case information for civil cases at https://courtcasesearch.stlucieclerk.com/BenchmarkWebExternal/Home.aspx/Search. A list of current dockets is also shown from this site. To receive access to select court case documents and reports, you must complete, notarize, and return an original agreement form.

Circuit & County Courts - Criminal Division   http://stlucieclerk.com

View case information for misdemeanor, felony, and traffic cases at https://courtcasesearch.stlucieclerk.com/BenchmarkWebExternal/Home.aspx/Search. A list of current dockets is also shown from this site. To receive access to select court case documents and reports, you must complete, notarize, and return an original agreement form.

Sumter County

Circuit & County Courts - Civil Division   www.sumterclerk.com/index.cfm/civil

Civil: An initial free search of court judgments is at https://www2.myfloridacounty.com/ori/index.do. Records may be ordered. Non-subscribers pay between $3.50 and $13.00 for every official record ordered. Subscribers pay a fixed, discounted fee of $2.00 per record. Access to liens and recorded documents also offered.

Circuit & County Courts - Criminal Division   www.sumterclerk.com/index.cfm/

Criminal: Access an index of felony, criminal traffic and misdemeanor records at https://www.civitekflorida.com/ocrs/county/60. Felony records available from 2/10/1958, misdemeanor from 02/06/1985, traffic from 05/13/1991. Race, sex, city and ZIP Shown.

Suwannee County
Circuit & County Courts www.suwgov.org/
Civil: Access to civil judgment records is available by subscription at https://www.myfloridacounty.com/official_records/index.html.

Taylor County
Circuit & County Courts www.taylorclerk.com/
Civil: Access an index of judgments (not docket) is at www.myfloridacounty.com. Fees involved to order copies; save $1.50 per record by becoming a subscriber.

Union County
Circuit & County Courts http://circuit8.org
Access an index of judgments (not dockets) is at www.myfloridacounty.com. Fees involved to order copies; save $1.50 per record by becoming a subscriber. An initial free search of court judgments is at https://www2.myfloridacounty.com/ori/index.do. Records may be ordered. Non-subscribers pay between $3.50 and $13.00 for every official record ordered. Subscribers pay a fixed, discounted fee of $2.00 per record. Access to liens and recorded documents also offered. *Criminal:* Access the circuit-wide criminal quick lookup at http://circuit8.org. Account and password is required; restricted usage. Also, limited free search of felony, misdemeanor, and traffic records is at https://www.civitekflorida.com/ocrs/county/63.

Volusia County
Circuit & County Courts - Civil Division www.clerk.org
Civil: There is both a free and pay site. Access to the countywide Clerk of Circuit Court record index for 1982 to present is free at http://app02.clerk.org/ccms/. Also, access an index of judgments, liens, recorded documents at www.myfloridacounty.com with fees for copies.
Criminal: There is both a free and pay site. Access to the countywide Clerk of Circuit Court record index for 1982 to present is free at http://app02.clerk.org/ccms/. Access to restricted data is $100 setup fee. Access to the database of Citation Violations and 24-hour Arrest Reports for 1990 forward is free at www.clerk.org/index.html.

Wakulla County
Circuit & County Courts www.wakullaclerk.com
Civil: Access to County Clerk of Circuit Court records is at https://www.civitekflorida.com/ocrs/county/65   *Criminal:* same

Walton County
Circuit & County Courts http://clerkofcourts.co.walton.fl.us
Civil: Access final judgments or orders on closed cases at http://orsearch.clerkofcourts.co.walton.fl.us/ORSearch/. An initial free search of court judgments is at https://www2.myfloridacounty.com/ori/index.do. Records may be ordered. Non-subscribers pay between $3.50 and $13.00 for every official record ordered. Subscribers pay a fixed, discounted fee of $2.00 per record. Access to liens and recorded documents also offered.   *Criminal:* Access to County Clerk of Circuit Court records is at https://www.civitekflorida.com/ocrs/county/66.

Washington County
Circuit & County Courts www.washingtonclerk.com
Civil: Access an index of civil dockets at https://www.civitekflorida.com/ocrs/county/67.   Circuit Civil back to 1/6/1986, County Civil back to 11/25/1986, Small Claims to 01/03/1986, Probate to 04/01/1961.   *Criminal:* Access an index of dockets at https://www.civitekflorida.com/ocrs/county/67. Felony back to 4/16/1976, Misdemeanor 50 6/5/1969, Municipal Ordinance to 2/2/1989, criminal traffic to 6/4/1984

Recorders, Assessors, and Other Sites of Note

About Florida Recording Offices: 67 counties, 67 recording offices. The recording officer is the Clerk of the Circuit Court. All transactions are recorded in the Official Record which is the grantor/grantee index. Some counties will search by type of transaction while others will return everything on the index.

About Tax Liens: Federal tax liens on personal property of businesses are filed with the Secretary of State. All other federal and state tax liens on personal property are filed with the county Clerk of Circuit Court. Usually tax liens on personal property are filed locally in the same index with UCC financing statements and real estate transactions.

Online Access

Recorded Documents

There are numerous county agencies that provide online access to records, but the system MyFlorida.com predominates. MyFloridaCounty.com is maintained and operated by the Florida Association of Court Clerks Services Group.

MyFlorida offers access to all but 7 counties (Brevard, Broward, Flagler, Indian River, Miami-Dade, Monroe, Seminole). Data includes Circuit Clerks of Court recorded indexes, including real estate records, liens, judgments, marriages, deaths at https://www.myfloridacounty.com/ori/index.do. A search of the index is free, but registration and fees are charged for images or further data. Record copies may be ordered. Non-subscribers pay between $3.50 and $13.00 for every official record ordered. Subscribers pay a fixed, discounted fee of $2.00 per record. plus their a is an annual subscription fee of $120.00.

Note that MyFloridaCounty has a program available to users who need high-volume access. Contact David Porter (porter@flclerks.com or 850.921.0808) for details.

Assessor and/or Tax Collector Records

All counties provide invidualized online access to property tax records.

County Sites:

Since all but 7 counties offer online access via https://www.myfloridacounty.com/ori/index.do, redunancy text is omitted below for each county. Please refer to the details provided above.

Alachua County   *Recorded Documents, Marriage Records*   www.alachuacounty.us/Depts/Clerk/Pages/Clerk.aspx   Access Clerk's recording database free at www.alachuacounty.us/Depts/Clerk/PublicRecords/Pages/PublicRecords.aspx. Index goes back to 1971; images to 1990. Search ancient records (pre-1940 plats, pre-1970 marriages, deeds, transcriptions, more- free at www.alachuaclerk.org/archive/default.cfm.
Property, Taxation Records   Search Appraiser's Property pages free at www.acpafl.org/. Various other searches also here.

Baker County   *Recorded Documents*   http://208.75.175.18/clerk/   Access to public records free at http://208.75.175.18/landmarkweb.
Property, Taxation Records   Search appraiser data free at www.bakerpa.com/index_disclaimer.asp. Also, search the Tax Collector database free at http://bakercountyfl.org/taxcollector/.

Bay County   *Recorded Documents, Death, Marriage Records*   http://baycoclerk.com/   Access to the Clerk's recorded database is free at http://baycoclerk.com/public-records/official-record-search/. *Property, Taxation Records*   Search property appraiser data free at www.baypa.net/search.html. Also, Search the tax collector data at http://tc.co.bay.fl.us//

Bradford County   *Property, Taxation Records*   Search the property appraiser database plus GIS/mapping at www.bradfordappraiser.com/.

Brevard County   *Recorded Documents, Marriage Records*   http://brevardclerk.us/   Free index access at http://web1.brevardclerk.us/oncoreweb/search.aspx. Also, an electronic fully automated case tracking system at https://vweb1.brevardclerk.us/FACTS/facts_search.cfm. Also, access tax lien & indexed records (1981-present), land records (1981-present), registration/password required for full data. Access marriage indices from 1938-1982; 1986-1994, 1981-1995;1995-1998 & 1995 to current free at http://brevardclerk.us/marriage-licenses-search. A fee of $25.00 annual grants access to images, including recorded Probate and Guardianship documents.

Broward County   *Recorded Documents*   www.broward.org/RecordsTaxesTreasury/Records/Pages/Default.aspx   Access to online records for a fee at www.broward.org/RecordsTaxesTreasury/Records/Pages/PublicRecordsSearch.aspx.
Property, Taxation Records   Search property tax data for free at www.bcpa.net/RecMenu.asp.

Calhoun County   *Recorded Documents, Historical Indexes Records*   www.calhounclerk.com/   Access to Historical Indexes free at www.calhounclerk.com/historical.html. Also, access to Historical books are at www.calhounclerk.com/historical-books.html.
Property, Taxation Records   Search assessor's data free at http://calhounpa.net and click on 'Search Records.'

Charlotte County   *Recorded Documents, Marriage Records*   www.co.charlotte.fl.us/Default.aspx   Search recorded data and marriages free at www.co.charlotte.fl.us/Default.aspx.
Property, Taxation Records   Sales records are on the tax collector database free at https://www.bidcharlottecounty.com/.

Citrus County   *Recorded Documents*   www.clerk.citrus.fl.us/nws/home.jsp?section=1&item=1   Access to the Clerk of Circuit Court recorded records is free at https://search.clerk.citrus.fl.us/LandmarkWeb. Also, download land sales data free at www.clerk.citrus.fl.us/nws/home.jsp?section=8&item=88.
Property, Taxation Records   Search property appraiser and personal property records free at www.citruspa.org/_dnn/Search. Also, download land sales data by year free. Search property and other related-tax records free at https://www.citrus.county-taxes.com/tcb/app/main/home.

Clay County   *Property, Taxation Records*   Access property appraiser records free at http://qpublic6.qpublic.net/fl_search_dw.php?county=fl_clay. Search treasurer RE and tangibles personal property at http://fl-clay-taxcollector.governmax.com/collectmax/collect30.asp.

Collier County   *Recorded Documents*   https://www.collierclerk.com/   Access court, lien, real property and vital records free at https://www.collierclerk.com/records-search.
Property, Taxation Records   Access Property Appraiser data (includes GIS/mapping) free at www.collierappraiser.com/. Search property tax roll at www.colliertax.com/search/.

Columbia County   *Recorded Documents, Marriage, Death Records*   www.columbiaclerk.com/   Access Clerk's recorded database index free at www.columbiaclerk.com/search/. Generally, documents go back to 1987.

Property, Taxation Records Search property appraiser records free at http://g2.columbia.floridapa.com/GIS/Search_F.asp?. Also, search the tax rolls and occupational licenses for free at http://fl-columbia-taxcollector.governmax.com/collectmax/collect30.asp.

De Soto County ***Recorded Documents*** www.desotoclerk.com Access to court records free at www.desotoclerk.com/Disclaimer.htm.
Property, Taxation Records Access the property appraiser data free at http://qpublic.net/desoto/search.html. Also, assess to record searches and GIS/mapping system for free at www.desotopa.com/GIS/Search_F.asp?GIS.

Dixie County ***Property, Taxation Records*** Access assessor's property data free at www.qpublic.net/dixie/search.html.

Duval County ***Recorded Documents*** www2.duvalclerk.com/ Access Clerk of Circuit Court and City of Jacksonville Official Records index free at www2.duvalclerk.com/records/. This site also includes OnCore (official records).
Property, Taxation Records Search Property Appraiser records free at http://apps.coj.net/pao_propertySearch/Basic/Search.aspx. Search parcel data free at http://maps.coj.net/jaxgis/ click on Duval Maps. Search tax collector real estate, personal property data free at http://fl-duval-taxcollector.publicaccessnow.com/.

Escambia County ***Recorded Documents, Vital Records Records*** www.escambiaclerk.com/clerk/coc_official_records.aspx Access to the Clerk of Court Public Records database is free at www.escambiaclerk.com/clerk/coc_online_public_records.aspx. This includes grantor/grantee index and marriage, traffic, court records, tax sales.
Property, Taxation Records Search the real estate record search for free at www.escpa.org/cama/Search.aspx. Also, Access to GIS/mapping free at www.escpa.org/MapMain.aspx. Property sale list for free at www.escpa.org/cama/SaleSearch.aspx. Also, access the tax collector's Property Tax database free at http://escambiataxcollector.governmaxa.com/collectmax/collect30.asp.

Flagler County ***Recorded Documents*** https://flaglerclerk.com/ Search recording records free at https://apps.flaglerclerk.com/landmark/?redirected=OnCore&old=/Search.aspx.
Property, Taxation Records Search appraiser property data free at http://flaglerpa.com/. Check property sales at www.qpublic.net/flagler/flaglersearch.html. Also, name search the tax collector tax records site free at http://fl-flagler-taxcollector.governmax.com/collectmax/collect30.asp.

Franklin County ***Property, Taxation Records*** Property record search form appraiser is free at http://qpublic.net/franklin/.

Gadsden County ***Recorded Documents*** www.gadsdenclerk.com/ Access to official records index is free at www.gadsdenclerk.com/PublicInquiry/Search.aspx?Type=Name. Records go back to 1985.
Property, Taxation Records Access to the property appraiser database including property sales is free at www.qpublic.net/gadsden/search.html. Also, search tax collector records at http://fl-gadsden-taxcollector.governmax.com/collectmax/collect30.asp.

Gilchrist County ***Property, Taxation Records*** Access the property appraiser database free at http://qpublic6.qpublic.net/fl_search_dw.php?county=fl_gilchrist.

Glades County ***Property, Taxation Records*** Sales searches are at www.gladesflpa.com/.

Gulf County ***Property, Taxation Records*** Access the property appraiser database free at www.gulfpa.com/. Click on 'Search Records'.

Hamilton County ***Property, Taxation Records*** Access the property appraiser database free at www.hamiltoncountytaxcollector.com/Property/SearchSelect.

Hardee County ***Property, Taxation Records*** Access to the property appraiser data is free at www.qpublic.net/hardee/search.html.

Hendry County ***Property, Taxation Records*** Access the property appraiser database at www.hendryprop.com/GIS/Search_F.asp.

Hernando County ***Recorded Documents, Marriage, Tax Deeds Records*** http://hernandoclerk.com/ Access to the clerk's Official Records database at http://hernandoclerk.com/. Click on Official Records. Browser must be JavaScript enabled. Images that are available can be printed for free. Includes recordings, marriages, and court records, but domestic relations judgments/court papers not viewable.
Property, Taxation Records Access to property record search for free at https://www.hernandocountygis-fl.us/PropertySearch/. Also, access to GIS/mapping for free at https://www.hernandopa-fl.us/PAWebSite/%28S%28tntmk20t42g2n3cjpfjssxj1%29%29/Default.aspx?xml=GISMaps.

Highlands County ***Recorded Documents*** www.hcclerk.org/Home.aspx Access records from the county recording database is free at http://records.hcclerk.org/OnCoreWeb/default.aspx.
Property, Taxation Records Property appraiser records are free at www.hcpao.org/; tangible personal property records available. Also, Access to GIS/mapping free at www.hcpao.org/gis/. Also, county tax collector database free at https://www.highlands.county-taxes.com/tcb/app/re/accounts.

Hillsborough County ***Recorded Documents*** www.hillsclerk.com/publicweb/home.aspx Access records for free at http://pubrec3.hillsclerk.com/oncore/Search.aspx. Images are from 1965 to present. Also, search for similar tax data free on the tax collector site at https://hillsborough.county-taxes.com/public.
Property, Taxation Records A basic property search is free at http://gis.hcpafl.org/propertysearch/#/nav/Basic Search. A business search with property values is at http://gis.hcpafl.org/tppsearch/. Also, search for similar tax data free on the tax collector site at https://hillsborough.county-taxes.com/public. Search on GIS site at http://gis.hcpafl.org/gissearch/.

Holmes County   *Property, Taxation Records*   Access property appraiser data free including property, sales and sales lists free at http://qpublic.net/holmes/.

Indian River County   *Recorded Documents*   www.clerk.indian-river.org/en/   Access to Clerk's recording indices are free at http://ori.indian-river.org/. Records go back to 1983. Full court records from the Clerk of the Circuit Court is at their fee site; subscriptions start at $25.00 per month. For info about free and fee access, call 772-226-1204. Fees involved to order copies; save $1.50 per record by becoming a subscriber. *Property, Taxation Records*   Appraiser records free at www.ircpa.org/.

Jackson County   *Property, Taxation Records*   Access to property records free at www.qpublic.net/jackson/search.html.

Jefferson County   *Property, Taxation Records*   Access Property Appraiser data free at www.jeffersonpa.net/GIS/Search_F.asp?GIS. Includes GIS/mapping and parcel details. Search the tax collector database free at http://jeffersoncountytaxcollector.com/.

Lafayette County   *Property, Taxation Records*   Search appraiser's property data free at http://g2.lafayettepa.com/GIS/Search_F.asp. Also, search property sales free at http://g2.lafayettepa.com/GIS/Search_F.asp?SalesReport.

Lake County   *Recorded Documents, Marriage Records*   www.lakecountyclerk.org   Access the county clerk official records database free at http://officialrecords.lakecountyclerk.org/. Records go as far back as 1887. *Property, Taxation Records*   Search the County Property Assessor parcel and tax data also property sales free at www.lakecopropappr.com/. Also, search property on the tax collector site free at https://www.lake.county-taxes.com/public.

Lee County   *Property, Taxation Records*   Search property tax rolls for either real estate or personal property at www.leetc.com/search-records. A tax certificate search is at https://www.leetc.com/ncp/search_criteria.asp?searchtype=TC. Search property GIS/mapping free at http://gissvr.leepa.org/GeoView2/.

Leon County   *Recorded Documents*   https://cvweb.clerk.leon.fl.us/public/login.asp   Real Estate, lien, and foreclosure records are free at https://cvweb.clerk.leon.fl.us/public/clerk_services/official_records/index.asp. *Property, Taxation Records*   Search Property Appraiser database records free at www.leonpa.org/pt/Search/Disclaimer.aspx?FromUrl=../search/commonsearch.aspx?mode=realprop. Access to GIS/mapping for free at www.leonpa.org/_dnn/Search/Map-Search.

Levy County   *Recorded Documents*   www.levyclerk.com   Access the Clerk of Circuit Court recording database free at http://online.levyclerk.com/landmarkweb. Search by name, book/page, file number or document type. *Property, Taxation Records*   Access to the property appraiser data is free at www.qpublic.net/levy/, also has sales searches and GIS/mapping.

Liberty County   *Property, Taxation Records*   Access assessor property records free at www.qpublic.net/liberty/.

Madison County   *Property, Taxation Records*   Access property assessor and sale data free at www.madisonpa.com/GIS/Search_F.asp.

Manatee County   *Recorded Documents, Death, Marriage, Condominium Records*   www.manateeclerk.com   Access to search and view real estate and recordings records free from the Clerk of Circuit Court and Comptroller's database at https://records.manateeclerk.com/OfficialRecords/Search. Also, access to service that includes recordings and probate available at www.manateeclerk.org/Home/tabid/57/Default.aspx. *Property, Taxation Records*   Property Appraiser records for a fee at www.manateepao.com/ManateeFL/Search/Disclaimer.aspx?FromUrl=../search/commonsearch.aspx?mode=owner.

Marion County   *Recorded Documents, Death, Marriage Records*   www.marioncountyclerk.org/index.cfm?Pg=ClerkOfCourt   Search recorder records free at http://216.255.240.38/SearchNG_Application/. *Property, Taxation Records*   Access the Appraiser property search from the home page. Search county tax rolls free at https://www.mariontax.com/itm.asp. Also, access property data free at www.pa.marion.fl.us/.

Martin County   *Recorded Documents*   www.martinclerk.com/   Access to the clerk's recordings database is free at http://or.martinclerk.com/, there is also an enhanced (fee) search from this page. *Property, Taxation Records*   A number of searches are offered from https://www.pa.martin.fl.us/tools/property-map-searches, including real property search, tangible property search, and interactive maps.

Miami-Dade County   *Recorded Documents, Marriage, Voter Registration Records*   www.miami-dadeclerk.com/   Access records and index free at http://miamidade.gov/wps/portal. Recorded docs at https://www2.miami-dadeclerk.com/public-records/. Access voter registration check site free at www.miamidade.gov/elections/. *Property, Taxation Records*   Access assessor property search for free at www.miamidade.gov/pa/property_search.asp. Also, lookup property tax free at https://www.miamidade.county-taxes.com/public.

Monroe County   *Recorded Documents*   https://gov.propertyinfo.com/FL-Monroe/   Access to the clerk of circuit courts database is free at https://gov.propertyinfo.com/FL-Monroe/. *Property, Taxation Records*   Access to property appraiser data is free on the GIS-mapping site at www.mcpafl.org/GISMaps.aspx. Also, search property tax and tax deed sales free at www.monroetaxcollector.com/.

Nassau County   *Recorded Documents, Marriage Records*   www.nassauclerk.com/   Access recorders database free at www.nassauclerk.com/publicrecords/oncoreweb/.
Property, Taxation Records   Access property data free at www.nassauflpa.com/. Also, access to tax deed sales for free at www.nassauclerk.com/default.cfm?pid=taxdeedsales.

Okaloosa County   *Recorded Documents, Marriage Records*   www.okaloosaclerk.com/   Access clerk's land and official records for free at https://clerkapps.okaloosaclerk.com/Landmarkweb; includes marriage, civil, traffic records.
Property, Taxation Records   Access property appraiser records and sales lists free at www.okaloosapa.com/. Access tax collector data at https://www.okaloosa.county-taxes.com/tcb/app/pt/main. Access property data on the GIS-mapping site free at ftp://sdrftp03.dor.state.fl.us/Map%20Data/.

Okeechobee County   *Recorded Documents*   www.clerk.co.okeechobee.fl.us   Search the Clerk of Courts Tax Deed data, foreclosure sale, court records and official records free at www.clerk.co.okeechobee.fl.us/.
Property, Taxation Records   Search assessor data on the GIS site free at www.okeechobeepa.com/GIS/Search_F.asp.

Orange County   *Recorded Documents*   www.occompt.com   Real Estate, Lien, and Marriage records on the county Comptroller database are free at http://or.occompt.com/recorder/web/login.jsp.
Property, Taxation Records   Access appraiser records free at www.ocpafl.org/Searches/ParcelSearch.aspx#%23. Search appraiser site free www.ocpafl.org/default.aspx includes tax sales. Search Property on the GIS site at http://maps.ocpafl.org/webmap/.

Osceola County   Access recording/land records at https://courts.osceolaclerk.org/benchmarkweb/Home.aspx/Search.
Property, Taxation Records   Subscription required for property appraiser records at https://osceola.county-taxes.com/public.

Palm Beach County   *Recorded Documents, Vital Records Records*   www.mypalmbeachclerk.com/   Access clerk's recording database free at www.mypalmbeachclerk.com/officialrecords/search.aspx. Records go back to 1968; images back to 1968; includes marriage records 1979 to present.
Property, Taxation Records   Access property appraiser records at http://pbcgov.com/papa/Asps/GeneralAdvSrch/SearchPage.aspx. Search real estate, property tax, personal property data at https://www.pbctax.com/.

Pasco County   *Recorded Documents, Vital Records Records*   www.pascoclerk.com   Free access to indexes and copies at www.pascoclerk.com/. Click on 'public records.
Property, Taxation Records   Access property appraiser data and sales data and maps free at http://appraiser.pascogov.com. Also, access to tax records search for free at www.pascotaxes.com/records-search/.

Pinellas County   *Recorded Documents*   www.pinellasclerk.org/aspInclude2/ASPInclude.asp?pageName=index.htm   Access records free at https://public.co.pinellas.fl.us/login/clerkloginx.jsp. Guest access is limited to 100 transactions per day. For full range access must subscribe.
Property, Taxation Records   Assessor property records are free at www.pcpao.org/. Also, search tax collector data free at https://www.pinellas.county-taxes.com/tcb/app/pt/main/. Tax deed sales lists are at www.pinellasclerk.org/tributeweb/searchcases.aspx.

Polk County   *Recorded Documents*   www.polkcountyclerk.net/home/   Search the county clerk database for free at http://ori2.polk-county.net/SearchNG_Application/.
Property, Taxation Records   Access appraiser property tax, personal property, and sales data free at www.polkpa.org/CamaDisplay.aspx. Search tax deeds at www.polkcountyclerk.net/Tax-Deeds-Search/.

Putnam County   *Recorded Documents*   www.putnam-fl.com/coc/   Access to official records free at https://www.putnam-fl.com/peas/public_disclaimer.php.   *Property, Taxation Records*   Access to GIS/mapping and sales for free at http://pa.putnam-fl.com/index.php/gis-mapping-sales. Also, search the online tax rolls at http://pa.putnam-fl.com/index.php/property-search.

Santa Rosa County   *Recorded Documents*   www.santarosaclerk.com/   Access the Clerk's index of recorded documents at http://oncoreweb.srccol.com/oncoreweb/.   *Property, Taxation Records*   Access the appraiser property records free at www.srcpa.org/search.html.

Sarasota County   *Recorded Documents, Vital Records, Marriage Records*   www.sarasotaclerk.com/   Access Clerk of Circuit Court recordings database free at www.sarasotaclerk.com/default1308.html?Page=170. Other public records included in this URL.
Property, Taxation Records   Access property appraiser data free at www.sc-pa.com/propertysearch/; includes subdivision/condominium sales. Also, search tax collector and occ licenses at http://sarasotataxcollector.governmax.com/collectmax/collect30.asp.

Seminole County   *Recorded Documents*   www.seminoleclerk.org   Access the clerk of circuit court's recordings database free at http://seminoleclerk.org/. Click on Official Records Search.
Property, Taxation Records   Property appraisal tax records free at www.scpafl.org/. Access property and real estate tax data free at http://seminoletax.org/Tax/TaxSearch.shtml. Search tax deed sales for free at www.seminoleclerk.org/TaxDeedSales/default.jsp.

St. Johns County   *Recorded Documents, Probate Records*   www.sjccoc.us/   Access to the county Clerk of Circuit Court recording database is free at www.sjccoc.us/Misc/onlinesearch.html. Includes civil and probate records, UCCs, and other public records.
Property, Taxation Records   Access county property appraiser database free at www.sjccoc.us/Misc/onlinesearch.html.

St. Lucie County   *Recorded Documents, Marriage, Fictitious Name Records*   www.stlucieclerk.com/   Access public records including recorded documents at http://stlucieclerk.com/index.php/public-search-gen.
Property, Taxation Records   Access property appraiser records free at www.paslc.org/main/index.html#/. Click on Property Search. Also, access to tax records for free at https://www.stlucie.county-taxes.com/tcb/app/re/accounts.

Sumter County   *Property, Taxation Records*   Access to property record searches, GIS/mapping and sales report searches for free at www.sumterpa.com/.

Suwannee County   *Recorded Documents, Marriage, Death Records*   www.suwgov.org/   Access of the county clerk of circuit database index is free at www.suwgov.org/. This directs to the statewide database; search index free; subscription required for documents.
Property, Taxation Records   Search property assessor data free at http://g2.suwanneepa.com/GIS/Search_F.asp. Official records search also at http://records.suwgov.org/LandmarkWeb/Home/index. Also, search the tax collector database free at http://fl-suwannee-taxcollector.manatron.com/ also register to view tax deed sale records.

Taylor County   *Recorded Documents*   www.taylorclerk.com/   Access voter registration for names free at https://www.electionsfl.org/taylor/index.php?mais=Y.
Property, Taxation Records   Access to tax collector tax roll data free at http://fl-taylor-taxcollector.governmax.com/collectmax/collect30.asp. Also, access to public records search free at www.taylorcountypa.com/.

Union County   *Property, Taxation Records*   Access assessor's records free at www.unioncountytc.com/Property/SearchSelect?ClearData=True. Search property sales free at http://g2.union.floridapa.com/GIS/Search_F.asp?SalesReport. Also, search the GIS-mapping site for assessor property data free at http://g2.union.floridapa.com/GIS/Search_F.asp?GIS.

Volusia County   *Recorded Documents*   www.clerk.org/   Recording data is free at http://app02.clerk.org/menu/default.aspx. Recorder indices go back to 1990. Arrest ledger, tax deed sales and citations also at this website. County also offers full real estate, lien, court and vital records on a commercial site; set up is $100 with $25 monthly. For info, contact clerk.
Property, Taxation Records   Access property search free at http://vcpa.vcgov.org/searches.html#moved.

Wakulla County   *Recorded Documents, Death, Marriage, Probate, Divorce, Judgment Records*   www.wakullaclerk.com/   Access an index of a wide array of recorded and public records/documents at www.wakullaclerk.com/landmarkweb. Also, the Clerk's office has plat images online free at www.wakullaclerk.com/plats.asp.
Property, Taxation Records   Access assessor property data free at www.qpublic.net/wakulla/search1.html. Access clerk of court's foreclosure monthly lists and Tax Deed Sales Free at www.wakullaclerk.com/index.asp. Click on Link in Quick Links Section. Search tax collector data free at www.wakullacountytaxcollector.com/Property/SearchSelect?ClearData=True.

Walton County   *Recorded Documents, Vital Records Records*   http://clerkofcourts.co.walton.fl.us/   Free record search back to 1/1976 at www.clerkofcourts.co.walton.fl.us/public_records/official_records_new.html. Incudes recorded judgments.
Property, Taxation Records   Property appraiser records are free at http://qpublic6.qpublic.net/fl_search_dw.php?county=fl_walton.

Washington County
Property, Taxation Records   Search the property appraiser sales and property records for free at www.washcofl.com/pa/.

Georgia

Capital: Atlanta
Fulton County
Time Zone: EST
Population: 10,214,860
# of Counties: 159

Useful State Links

Website: **http://georgia.gov/**
Governor: **http://gov.georgia.gov/**
Attorney General: **http://law.ga.gov/**
State Archives: **http://sos.georgia.gov/archives/**
State Statutes and Codes: **www.lexisnexis.com/hottopics/gacode/default.asp**
Legislative Bill Search: **www.legis.ga.gov/en-US/default.aspx**
Unclaimed Funds: **https://dor.georgia.gov/unclaimed-property-program**

State Public Record Agencies

Criminal Records

Georgia Bureau of Investigation, Attn: GCIC, http://gbi.georgia.gov/obtaining-criminal-history-record-information The Georgia Technology Authority (GTA) provides an online system called Georgia Felon Search. The search returns the top five closest matches based on the criteria entered. See http://gta.georgia.gov/georgia-felon-search. The search will verify whether individuals have committed and been convicted for felony offenses in the State of Georgia. The fee is $15.00, and ongoing requesters may set up an account. SSNs are supressed. If questions, call 404-463-2300 (note this is a different phone number than listed above).

Sexual Offender Registry

Georgia Bureau of Investigations, GCIC - Sexual Offender Registry, http://gbi.georgia.gov/georgia-sex-offender-registry Records may be searched at http://state.sor.gbi.ga.us/Sort_Public/. Earliest records go back to 07/01/96. Close to 80% of registered offenders have photographs on the web site. Searches may be conducted for sex offenders, absconders, and predators. *Other Options:* One may download an Excel file of offenders. The file is updated quarterly and has over 19,500 names.

Incarceration Records

Georgia Department of Corrections, Inmate Records Office - 6th Fl, East Tower, www.dcor.state.ga.us/ The website has an extensive array of search capabilities. You can search by the GDC ID, case number, or by name with a variety of personal identifiers. One may search current inmates of those not currently incarcerated. See www.dcor.state.ga.us/GDC/Offender/Query.

Corporation, LP, LLP, LLC, Not-for-Profits

Sec of State - Corporation Division, Record Searches, https://ecorp.sos.ga.gov/ The onlien search is at https://ecorp.sos.ga.gov/BusinessSearch. A numbrer of searching options are offered including a search by an offcier's name, the registered agent, the control numenr or the business. Plus one can use partial words or names as awell as an exact match. There is an onlien system to obtin copies or certified documenst for a fee. One must be registered. See https://ecorp.sos.ga.gov/Account. Also, search licensed charities at http://verify.sos.ga.gov/Verification/.

Trademarks/Servicemarks

Secretary of State, Trademark Division, http://sos.ga.gov/index.php/corporations/trademarks__service_marks2 A record database is searchable from http://sos.ga.gov/index.php/corporations/search_the_trademarks_and_service_mark_database. The DB is updated daily. Pending applications are not listed. Search by registration #, mark name, description, connection, owner, or classification.

Uniform Commercial Code

GA Superior Court Clerks' Cooperative Authority, https://www.gsccca.org/learn/projects-programs/ucc-system Free name searching is available at https://www.gsccca.org/search. Also search by secured party, tax payer ID, date, or file number. In order to view images, ongoing requesters can open a

Premium subscription account. There is a monthly charge of $24.95 for unlimited access to images. Billing is monthly. Requests for certified searches are offered for $10.00 per name. The system is open 24 hours daily. The website also includes searches of the real estate index w/images, lien index, and notary index. Visit https://www.gsccca.org/search.   *Other Options:* The entire UCC Central Index System can be purchased on a daily, weekly, biweekly basis. For more information, contact Mike Smith.

Birth, Death Records Certificates

Department of Human Resources, Vital Records Unit,   http://dph.georgia.gov/birth-records   Can order certificate at http://gta.georgia.gov/rover for a fee.   *Other Options:* The death index is available for the years 1919-1998 on microfiche for $50.00 or more.

Workers' Compensation Records

State Board of Workers Compensation,   http://sbwc.georgia.gov/   Form a link at the home page verify if an employer has WC coverage at http://sbwc.georgia.gov/online-employers-workers-compensation-coverage-verification.

Driver Records

Department of Driver Services, MVR Unit,   www.dds.ga.gov   Electronic record access is available for insurance, employment, credit, rental car agency and for a Limited Rating Information (LRI) only available to the insurance industry. For each purpose and use, a requester will be assigned a separate user-ID and password. Both the $6.00 three-year history and $8.00 seven-year history are available online. A LRI is $1.70. Requesters must complete several applications and user agreement forms. See https://onlinemvr.dds.ga.gov/mvr/gettingcert.aspx or call 404-463-2300 and ask for Bulk Sales. Also, one may conduct an immediate, free driver's license status check at https://online.dds.ga.gov/DLStatus/default.aspx.

Vehicle Ownership & Registration

DOR - Motor Vehicle Division, Research Unit,   http://dor.georgia.gov/motor-vehicles   Online subscription record access is available to Georgia dealers only; registration is required. The MVD provides a free public Vehicle Insurance Status Check at http://onlinemvd.dor.ga.gov/vinstatuscheck/vinstatus.aspx.   *Other Options:* A lien or security interest on non-title vehicles is recorded with Clerk of the Superior Court's office in the county where the vehicle owner resides under the provisions of the Uniform Commercial Code. See https://www.gsccca.org/file/ucc-forms.

Crash Reports

Department of Transportation, GDOT Crash Reporting Unit,   www.dot.ga.gov/DS/Data   The agency has outsourced the online purchase of accident reports through a private vendor. See www.buycrash.com. Users can search for their crash reports utilizing a number of search options including their name, date of crash, road of occurrence and VIN. This agency also accepts mail requests, a form is at the web page. The fee for reports will vary between $5.00 and $12.00 depending on the investigating agency that is supplying the report to the DOT. The online site will not tell you the fee until you nearly complete the request transaction.

Vessel Ownership & Registration

Georgia Dept of Natural Resources, License and Boat Registration Unit,   www.georgiawildlife.com/boating   A download of the boat registration information by county or statewide is available on the web. The exact URL is at https://hfwa.centraltechnology.net/gdnr_vrs/downloads/boatData.do. You must have MS Access or Excel. Online files are available for subscribers at https://jc.activeoutdoorsolutions.com/.

Voter Registration, Campaign Finance, PACs

Secretary of State - Elections Division, 1104 West Tower,   http://sos.ga.gov/index.php/Elections/register_to_vote   Name and DOB needed to search unofficial registration information at http://mvp.sos.state.ga.us/. The results will provide address and district-precinct information; no SSNs released. Campaign contribution and disclosure reports are searchable at http://sos.ga.gov/elections/disclosure/disclosure.htm. This includes PACs. Verify voter registration status ans poll locator at https://www.mvp.sos.ga.gov/MVP/mvp.do.   *Other Options:* Voter Registration CDs, Internet files, disks, and paper lists are available for purchase for non-commercial purposes. For fees go to http://sos.georgia.gov/elections/voter_registration/voter_reg_lists.htm

Occupational Licensing Boards

These licenses are all searchable at http://verify.sos.ga.gov/Verification/

Animal Technician, Veterinary	Cosmetologist/Cosmetology Shop	Geologist
Architect	Counselor	Hearing Aid Dealer/Dispenser
Athletic Agent	Dietitian	Interior Designer
Athletic Trainer	Electrical Contractor	Landscape Architect
Auctioneer/Auction Dealer	Embalmer	Manicurist
Audiologist	Engineer	Marriage Counselor
Barber/Barber Shop	Esthetician	Nail Care
Boxing Related	Family Therapist	Nurse-RN/LPN
Cemeteries	Forester	Nurse-RN/LPN
Charity	Funeral Director/Apprentice	Nursing Home Administrator
Chiropractor	Funeral Establishment	Occupational Therapist/Assistant

Optician, Dispensing
Optometrist
Physical Therapist/Therapist Asst
Plumber Journeyman/Contractor
Podiatrist
Private Investigator
Psychologist
Rebuilder of Motor Vehicles
Salvage Pool Operator
Salvage Yard Dealer

School Librarian
Securities Salesperson/Dealer
Security Guard/Agency
Social Worker
Speech-Language Pathologist
Surveyor, Land
Ticket Broker
Used Car Dealer
Used Car Parts Dist
Utility Contractor

Veterinarian/Veterinary Technician
Veterinary Faculty
Waste Water Lab Analyst
Waste Water System Operator
Wastewater Collection System Operator
Wastewater Industrial
Water Distribution System Operator
Water Laboratory Operator
Water Operator Class 1-4
Wrestling

The Rest:

Accountant-CPA	https://www.cpaverify.org/
Acupuncturist	https://services.georgia.gov/dch/mebs/jsp/index.jsp
Appraiser School	www.grec.state.ga.us/info/wcls_school_list?p_auth_group=AP-ED
Attorney	https://www.gabar.org/membership/membersearch.cfm
Boiler & Pressure Vessel	https://www.oci.ga.gov/AdministrativeProcedures/OpenRecords.aspx
Court Reporter-Inactive/Suspension Lists	http://bcr.georgiacourts.gov/content/license-verification?menu=main
Court Reporting Firm-Active/Inactive	http://bcr.georgiacourts.gov/content/license-verification?menu=main
Dental Hygienist	https://gadch.mylicense.com/verification/Search.aspx
Dentist	https://gadch.mylicense.com/verification/Search.aspx
Detox Specialist	https://services.georgia.gov/dch/mebs/jsp/index.jsp
Drug Whlse/Retail/Mfg (Hospital)	https://gadch.mylicense.com/verification/Search.aspx
Elevator, Escalator	https://www.oci.ga.gov/AdministrativeProcedures/OpenRecords.aspx
Emergency Medical Technician	https://sendss.state.ga.us/sendss/!ems_lic_query
Financial Statement (Ethics Dept)	http://media.ethics.ga.gov/Search/Lobbyist/Lobbyist_ByName.aspx
Home Inspector	http://gahi.com/directory
Insurance Adjuster	https://www.oci.ga.gov/Agents/AgentStatus.aspx
Insurance Agent/Counselor/ Education Providers	https://www.oci.ga.gov/Agents/AgentStatus.aspx
Insurance Company	https://www.oci.ga.gov/Insurers/CompanySearch.aspx
Liquor Licensing	https://gtc.dor.ga.gov/_/#4
Lobbyist	http://media.ethics.ga.gov/Search/Lobbyist/Lobbyist_ByName.aspx
Notary Public	http://search.gsccca.org/notary/search.asp
Nuclear Pharmacist	https://gadch.mylicense.com/verification/Search.aspx
Osteopathic Physician	https://services.georgia.gov/dch/mebs/jsp/index.jsp
Perfusionist	https://services.georgia.gov/dch/mebs/jsp/index.jsp
Pesticide Applicator	http://agr.georgia.gov/pesticide-contractors.aspx
Pesticide Contractor/Employee	http://agr.georgia.gov/pesticide-contractors.aspx
Pharmacist	https://gadch.mylicense.com/verification/Search.aspx
Pharmacy School, Clinic Researcher	https://gadch.mylicense.com/verification/Search.aspx
Physician Assistant	https://services.georgia.gov/dch/mebs/jsp/index.jsp
Physician Teacher	https://services.georgia.gov/dch/mebs/jsp/index.jsp
Physician/Medical Doctor	https://services.georgia.gov/dch/mebs/jsp/index.jsp
Poison Pharmacist	https://gadch.mylicense.com/verification/Search.aspx
Prosthetist	https://services.georgia.gov/dch/mebs/jsp/index.jsp
Public Adjuster	https://www.oci.ga.gov/Agents/AgentStatus.aspx
Real Estate Agent/Seller/Broker	www.grec.state.ga.us/clsweb/realestate.aspx
Real Estate Appraiser	www.grec.state.ga.us/clsweb/appraiser.aspx
Real Estate Community Assn Mgr	www.grec.state.ga.us
Real Estate Firm	www.grec.state.ga.us/clsweb/company.aspx
Real Estate Instructor	www.grec.state.ga.us/clsweb/instructors.aspx
Real Estate School	www.grec.state.ga.us/info/wcls_school_list?p_auth_group=RE-ED
Real Estate/Appraiser Disciplinary Sanctions	www.grec.state.ga.us/
Respiratory Care Practitioner	https://services.georgia.gov/dch/mebs/jsp/index.jsp

School Administrator/Supervisor .... www.gapsc.com/Certification/Lookup.aspx
Surplus Line Broker .... https://www.oci.ga.gov/Agents/AgentStatus.aspx
Teacher... www.gapsc.com/Certification/Lookup.aspx
Tobacco Licensing... https://gtc.dor.ga.gov/_/#4

State and Local Courts

About Georgia Courts: The Georgia court system has five classes of trial-level courts: the Magistrate, Probate, Juvenile, State, and Superior courts. In addition, there are approximately 370 municipal courts operating locally. The **Superior Court**, is the court of general jurisdiction. It has exclusive, constitutional authority over felony cases, divorce, equity and cases regarding title to land. By law, **State Courts** may exercise jurisdiction over all misdemeanor violations, including traffic cases, and all civil actions, regardless of the amount claimed, unless the Superior Court has exclusive jurisdiction. However counties may sue local rules to vary case assignments. Most State Courts will hear traffic violations, misdemeanors, issue search and arrest warrants, hold preliminary hearings in criminal cases, and try civil matters not reserved exclusively for the Superior Courts. In counties where there is not a State Court, traffic violations can be held in a variety of courts, including Magistrate, Probate, or Superior, depending on the county. **Magistrate Court** jurisdiction includes civil claims of $15,000 or less; certain minor criminal offenses; distress warrants and dispossessory writs; county ordinance violations; deposit account fraud (bad checks); preliminary hearings; and summonses, arrest and search warrants. An informative site provided by the Council of Magistrate Court Clerks is found at http://cmcss.georgiacourts.gov.

Municipal Courts try municipal ordinance violations, issue criminal warrants, conduct preliminary hearings, and may have concurrent jurisdiction over shoplifting cases and cases involving possession of one ounce or less of marijuana.

The jurisdiction of **Juvenile Courts** extends to delinquent children under the age of 17 and deprived or unruly children under the age of 18. Juvenile courts have concurrent jurisdiction with Superior Courts in cases involving capital felonies, custody and child support cases, and in proceedings to terminate parental rights. Note the Superior Courts have original jurisdiction over those juveniles who commit certain serious felonies.

Probate Courts can, in certain jurisdictions, issue search and arrest warrants, and hear miscellaneous misdemeanors, or local ordinance violations.

The web page for the Judicial System is www.georgiacourts.gov.

Appellate Courts: Opinions and summaries are available from the web page at www.gasupreme.us.

Online Court Access

There is no statewide online access available. A limited number of counties offer online access.

County Sites:
Atkinson County
Superior Court   www.cscj.org/courts/atkinson
Civil: Civil and domestic relations document images are available at www.peachcourt.com. No fee to register, $.50 per page to download. Records from 2014 forward available instantly. Prior records to approx 2005 can be ordered and received by email. Search by name, attorney name, case number, or judge. No personal identifiers are displayed.

Bartow County
Superior Court   www.bartowga.org/departments/courts/clerk_of_superior_court.php
Civil: Civil and domestic relations document images are available at www.peachcourt.com. No fee to register, $.50 per page to download. Records from 2014 forward available instantly. Prior records to approx 2005 can be ordered and received by email. Search by name, attorney name, case number, or judge. No personal identifiers are displayed.

Ben Hill County
Superior Court   www.eighthdistrict.org/c_benhill.htm
Civil: Civil and domestic relations document images are available at www.peachcourt.com. No fee to register, $.50 per page to download. Records from 2014 forward available instantly. Prior records to approx 2005 can be ordered and received by email. Search by name, attorney name, case number, or judge. No personal identifiers are displayed.

Berrien County
Superior Court   www.cscj.org/courts/berrien

Civil: Civil and domestic relations document images are available at www.peachcourt.com. No fee to register, $.50 per page to download. Records from 2014 forward available instantly. Prior records to approx 2005 can be ordered and received by email. Search by name, attorney name, case number, or judge. No personal identifiers are displayed.

Bibb County

Superior Court www.maconbibb.us/superior-court/

Civil: A subscription service is offered at https://bibbclerkindexsearch.com/external/User/Login.aspx?ReturnUrl=%2fexternal%2findex.aspx. Fee is $299.40 for a year, $24.95 for one month, or $7.95 per day. Includes civil and criminal. In general, images are available from 1985 to present. Court calendars online at www.co.bibb.ga.us/CalendarDirectory/CalendarDirectory.asp. *Criminal:* same Search the District Attorney's criminal case index at www.co.bibb.ga.us/da/criminalcases/. The Superior court calendars are at www.co.bibb.ga.us/CalendarDirectory/CalendarDirectory.asp.

State Court www.maconbibb.us/state-court/

Civil: Search civil dockets at www.co.bibb.ga.us/CONStateCourtCivilDockets/Search.aspx   *Criminal:* Search criminal dockets at www.co.bibb.ga.us/CONStateCourtCriminalDockets/Search.aspx.

Magistrate Court - Civil Division www.maconbibb.us/civil-court/

Civil: Access the index at www.maconbibb.us/civil-court/. Search by name or case number back to 1980.

Burke County

Superior Court www.burkecounty-ga.gov/departments/courts/clerk-of-superior-court

Civil: Civil and domestic relations document images are available at www.peachcourt.com. No fee to register, $.50 per page to download. Records from 2014 forward available instantly. Prior records to approx 2005 can be ordered and received by email. Search by name, attorney name, case number, or judge. No personal identifiers are displayed.

State Court

Civil: Civil and domestic relations document images are available at www.peachcourt.com. No fee to register, $.50 per page to download. Records from 2014 forward available instantly. Prior records to approx 2005 can be ordered and received by email. Search by name, attorney name, case number, or judge. No personal identifiers are displayed.

Butts County

Superior Court https://www.gsccca.org/

Civil: Civil and domestic relations document images are available at www.peachcourt.com. No fee to register, $.50 per page to download. Records from 2014 forward available instantly. Prior records to approx 2005 can be ordered and received by email. Search by name, attorney name, case number, or judge. No personal identifiers are displayed.

Calhoun County

Superior Court www.calhouncourtclerk.com/

Civil: Civil and domestic relations document images are available at www.peachcourt.com. No fee to register, $.50 per page to download. Records from 2014 forward available instantly. Prior records to approx 2005 can be ordered and received by email. Search by name, attorney name, case number, or judge. No personal identifiers are displayed. Court civil calendars by month available at the website.

Camden County

Superior Court http://camdensuperiorclerk.com/

Civil: Online access is available at http://camdensuperiorclerk.com/superiorcourt_012.htm. Records are available from 1989 forward.   *Criminal:* Online access is available at http://camdensuperiorclerk.com/superiorcourt_012.htm. Records are available form 1989 forward.

Carroll County

Superior Court www.carrollcountyclerk.com/

Civil: Civil and domestic relations document images are available at www.peachcourt.com. No fee to register, $.50 per page to download. Records from 2014 forward available instantly. Prior records to approx 2005 can be ordered and received by email. Search by name, attorney name, case number, or judge. No personal identifiers are displayed.

Catoosa County

Superior Court www.catoosa.com/Judicial/Clerk%20Of%20Court.htm

Civil: Civil and domestic relations document images are available at www.peachcourt.com. No fee to register, $.50 per page to download. Records from 2014 forward available instantly. Prior records to approx 2005 can be ordered and received by email. Search by name, attorney name, case number, or judge. No personal identifiers are displayed.

Chatham County

Superior Court www.chathamcourts.org/Superior-Court

Civil: Search county civil dockets free at www.chathamcourts.org. Search by name or case number.   *Criminal:* Search county criminal dockets free at www.chathamcourts.org. Search by name or case number.

State Court www.chathamcourts.org/State-Court

Civil: Search county civil dockets free at www.chathamcourts.org. Search by name or case number.   *Criminal:* Search county criminal dockets free at www.chathamcourts.org. Search by name or case number.

Chattahoochee County

Superior Court www.cscj.org/courts/chattahoochee

Civil: Civil and domestic relations document images are available at www.peachcourt.com. No fee to register, $.50 per page to download. Records from 2014 forward available instantly. Prior records to approx 2005 can be ordered and received by email. Search by name, attorney name, case number, or judge. No personal identifiers are displayed.

Cherokee County
Superior Court   www.cherokeeclerkofcourt.com/webFormFrame.aspx?page=main
Civil: Search the docket index free at www.cherokeeclerkofcourt.com/webFormFrame.aspx?page=main. Search both the Superior and State Court data separate or together.   *Criminal:* same

State Court   www.cherokeeclerkofcourt.com/webFormFrame.aspx?page=main
Civil: Search the docket index free at www.cherokeeclerkofcourt.com/webFormFrame.aspx?page=main. Search both the Superior and State Court data separate or together.   *Criminal:* same

Clarke County
Superior Court   www.athensclarkecounty.com/324/Clerk-of-Superior-State-Courts
Civil: Public access available to the docket from the home page. Civil and domestic relations document images are available at www.peachcourt.com. No fee to register, $.50 per page to download. Records from 2014 forward available instantly. Prior records to approx 2005 can be ordered and received by email. Search by name, attorney name, case number, or judge. No personal identifiers are displayed.   *Criminal:* same

State Court   www.athensclarkecounty.com/324/Clerk-of-Superior-State-Courts
Civil: Public access available to the docket from the home page. Civil and domestic relations document images are available at www.peachcourt.com. No fee to register, $.50 per page to download. Records from 2014 forward available instantly. Prior records to approx 2005 can be ordered and received by email. Search by name, attorney name, case number, or judge. No personal identifiers are displayed.   *Criminal:* same

Clayton County
Superior Court   www.claytoncountyga.gov/courts/clerk-of-superior-court.aspx
Civil: Online access is the same as criminal, see below.   *Criminal:* Search records free at www.claytoncountyga.gov/courts/court-case-inquiry.aspx. Court calendars at www.claytoncountyga.gov/courts/court-calendars.aspx. Searches and records also available on the statewide system.

State Court   www.claytoncountyga.gov/courts/clerk-of-state-court.aspx
Criminal: Search criminal database from 1990 by name or case at http://weba.co.clayton.ga.us/casinqsvr/htdocs/index.shtml. Results shows year of birth.

Clinch County
Superior Court   www.gaclerks.org/Association/Clerks/default.aspx
Civil: Civil and domestic relations document images are available at www.peachcourt.com. No fee to register, $.50 per page to download. Records from 2014 forward available instantly. Prior records to approx 2005 can be ordered and received by email. No personal identifiers are displayed.

Cobb County
Superior Court   https://www.cobbsuperiorcourtclerk.com/
Civil: Civil indexes and images from Clerk of Superior Court are free at https://ctsearch.cobbsuperiorcourtclerk.com/. Search by name, type or case number. Data updated Fridays. Images go back thru 2004.   *Criminal:* Criminal indexes and images from Clerk of Superior Court are free at https://ctsearch.cobbsuperiorcourtclerk.com/. Search by name, type or case number. Data updated Fridays but indexing can be nearly a month behind.

Columbia County
Superior Court   www.columbiaclerkofcourt.com
Civil: Online search to docket from web page. Search by case number or name. Use last name, first name.   *Criminal:* same

Cook County
Superior Court   https://www.gsccca.org/clerks/clerk-results?cid=37
Civil: Civil and domestic relations document images are available at www.peachcourt.com. No fee to register, $.50 per page to download. Records from 2014 forward available instantly. Prior records to approx 2005 can be ordered and received by email. Search by name, attorney name, case number, or judge. No personal identifiers are displayed.

Coweta County
Superior Court   www.coweta.ga.us/Index.aspx?page=199
Civil: Access court records free online at http://sccweb.coweta.ga.us/cmwebsearchppp/. There is also a search with images, but a subscription is required with a pre-paid account. Call 770-254-2690. *Criminal:* same
State Court   www.coweta.ga.us/Index.aspx?page=197
Civil: Online access to index provided at www.coweta.ga.us/Index.aspx?page=1301. View case dockets by entering the case number, party's name, and/or CSE number.   *Criminal:* same

Crawford County
Superior Court   https://www.gsccca.org/
Civil: Civil and domestic relations document images are available at www.peachcourt.com. No fee to register, $.50 per page to download. Records from 2014 forward available instantly. Prior records to approx 2005 can be ordered and received by email. Search by name, attorney name, case number, or

judge. No personal identifiers are displayed. *Criminal:* There is a subscription service available to view and print case information. Please call the court, as this is an unadvertised service.

Dade County
Superior Court   www.dadegaclerkofcourt.com/
Civil: A search of the docket index for Civil, Domestic, and Child Support is found at www.dadesuperiorcourt.com/webFormFrame.aspx?page=main. There is an additioanal search for attroneys, a log-in is required.   *Criminal:* A search of the docket index is found at www.dadesuperiorcourt.com/webFormFrame.aspx?page=main. There is an additioanal search for attroneys, a log-in is required.

Dawson County
Superior Court   www.dawsonclerkofcourt.net/
Civil: Search the index for free at www.dawsonclerkofcourt.net/WebCaseManagement/webFormFrame.aspx?page=main. There is an advanced search for attroneys.   *Criminal:* same

De Kalb County
Superior Court   http://web.co.dekalb.ga.us/superior/index.html
Civil: Online access to the dicket index is free at https://ody.dekalbcountyga.gov/portal/. The system does not indicate how far back records go. Registered users may purchase images. This is an Odyssey system.   *Criminal:* same Search jail records at http://ojs.dekalbcountyga.gov/.

State Court   http://dekalbstatecourt.net/
Civil: Online access to the dicket index is free at https://ody.dekalbcountyga.gov/portal/. The system does not indicate how far back records go. Registered users may purchase images. This is an Odyssey system.   *Criminal:* Same, also wsearch jail records at http://ojs.dekalbcountyga.gov/.

Dodge County
Superior Court   www.dodgeclerkofcourt.com/
Civil: Civil and domestic relations document images are available at www.peachcourt.com. No fee to register, $.50 per page to download. Records from 2014 forward available instantly. Prior records to approx 2005 can be ordered and received by email. Search by name, attorney name, case number, or judge. No personal identifiers are displayed. *Criminal:* There is a subscription service offered for online access, however this is only made available to attorneys. The fee is 3140 per year. Please call the Clerk's office for details.

Dooly County
Superior Court   https://www.gsccca.org/
Civil: Civil and domestic relations document images are available at www.peachcourt.com. No fee to register, $.50 per page to download. Records from 2014 forward available instantly. Prior records to approx 2005 can be ordered and received by email. Search by name, attorney name, case number, or judge. No personal identifiers are displayed.

Douglas County
Superior & State Courts   www.celebratedouglascounty.com
Civil: All requests for access to the online system must be submitted to the Clerk of Superior Court who will issue a User ID and Password. Public access is limited to attorneys. System shows docket data.   *Criminal:* same

Effingham County
Superior Court   www.effinghamcounty.org/
Civil: Civil and domestic relations document images are available at www.peachcourt.com. No fee to register, $.50 per page to download. Records from 2014 forward available instantly. Prior records to approx 2005 can be ordered and received by email. Search by name, attorney name, case number, or judge. No personal identifiers are displayed.
State Court   www.effinghamcounty.org/
Civil: Civil and domestic relations document images are available at www.peachcourt.com. No fee to register, $.50 per page to download. Records from 2014 forward available instantly. Prior records to approx 2005 can be ordered and received by email. Search by name, attorney name, case number, or judge. No personal identifiers are displayed.

Fayette County
Superior Court   www.fayetteclerk.com/
Civil: Search dockets free at www.fayetteclerkofcourt.com/webFormFrame.aspx?page=main. Civil and domestic relations document images are available at www.peachcourt.com. No fee to register, $.50 per page to download. Records from 2014 forward available instantly. Prior records to approx 2005 can be ordered and received by email. Search by name, attorney name, case number, or judge. No personal identifiers are displayed. *Criminal:* same
State Court   www.fayetteclerk.com/
Civil: Search dockets free at www.fayetteclerkofcourt.com/webFormFrame.aspx?page=main. Civil and domestic relations document images are available at www.peachcourt.com. No fee to register, $.50 per page to download. Records from 2014 forward available instantly. Prior records to approx 2005 can be ordered and received by email. Search by name, attorney name, case number, or judge. No personal identifiers are displayed. *Criminal:* same

Forsyth County
Superior Court   www.forsythclerk.com/
Civil: Free online access to the docket index is available at http://cases.forsythco.com/default.aspx. The site includes a search of Family case records.
Criminal: Free online access to the docket index is available at http://cases.forsythco.com/default.aspx.

State Court www.forsythclerk.com/
Civil: Free online access to the docket index is available at http://cases.forsythco.com/default.aspx. The site includes a search of Family case records.
Criminal: Free online access to the docket index is available at http://cases.forsythco.com/default.aspx.

Franklin County

Superior Court https://www.gsccca.org/
Civil: There is online access to the docket index at www.franklinclerkofcourt.com/. The site does not indicate how far back records go, but a test indicates records back to at least 2003. Chrome works best. *Criminal:* same

Fulton County

Superior Court - Civil www.fcclk.org
Civil: Access Clerk of Superior Court Judicial civil records free at http://justice.fultoncountyga.gov/PASupCrtCM/default.aspx. Search by either party name, case number, and date range. There is a separate search for Family Court. Current dockets are at www.fultoncountydocket.com/.
State Court http://fultonstate.org/
Civil: Access the docket index online at https://publicrecordsaccess.fultoncountyga.gov/Portal. *Criminal:* same

Gwinnett County

Superior & State Courts www.gwinnettcourts.com/
Civil & Criminal: Online access to court case party index is free at www.gwinnettcourts.com/home.asp#partycasesearch/. Search by name or case number.

Hancock County

Superior Court https://www.gsccca.org/
Civil: Civil and domestic relations document images are available at www.peachcourt.com. No fee to register, $.50 per page to download. Records from 2014 forward available instantly. Prior records to approx 2005 can be ordered and received by email. Search by name, attorney name, case number, or judge. No personal identifiers are displayed.

Harris County

Superior Court www.harrisclerkofcourt.com/
Civil: Access court records by subscription; for information and signup contact Lisa Culpeper at 706-628-4944. Site is www.harrisclerkofcourt.com/WebCaseSearch/ but log-in required. *Criminal:* same

Hart County

Superior Court http://hartcountyga.gov/clerkcourt.html
Civil: Civil and domestic relations document images are available at www.peachcourt.com. No fee to register, $.50 per page to download. Records from 2014 forward available instantly. Prior records to approx 2005 can be ordered and received by email. Search by name, attorney name, case number, or judge. No personal identifiers are displayed.

Heard County

Superior Court https://www.gsccca.org/
Civil: Civil and domestic relations document images are available at www.peachcourt.com. No fee to register, $.50 per page to download. Records from 2014 forward available instantly. Prior records to approx 2005 can be ordered and received by email. Search by name, attorney name, case number, or judge. No personal identifiers are displayed.

Henry County

Superior Court www.co.henry.ga.us/SuperiorCourt/index.shtml
Civil: The court provides a free docket search at https://hcwebb.boca.co.henry.ga.us/SuperiorCMWebSearch/. Search by name or case number, or associated party. The DOB is not shown, it is hard to identify common names if used for a specific name search. Civil and domestic relations document images are available at www.peachcourt.com. No fee to register, $.50 per page to download. Records from 2014 forward available instantly. Prior records to approx 2005 can be ordered and received by email. Search by name, attorney name, case number, or judge. No personal identifiers are displayed.
Criminal: The court provides a free docket search at https://hcwebb.boca.co.henry.ga.us/SuperiorCMWebSearch/. Search by name or case number.
State Court www.co.henry.ga.us/StateCourt/
Civil: Search the docket index at https://hcwebb.boca.co.henry.ga.us/state_cmwebsearchpfp/Login.aspx. One must be registered first. There is no fee. One may order print images. *Criminal:* same

Houston County

State Court www.houstoncountyga.org/
Civil: The docket index is searchable free at www.houstoncountyga.org:8011/mrcjava/servlet/MRCPUBLIC.I00160s. Search by name with a date range.
Criminal: Search the index of misdemeanor and traffic records free at www.houstoncountyga.org:8011/mrcjava/servlet/MRCPUBLIC.I00170s. The year of birth is shown, along with address.

Irwin County

Superior Court https://www.gsccca.org/

Civil: Civil and domestic relations document images are available at www.peachcourt.com. No fee to register, $.50 per page to download. Records from 2014 forward available instantly. Prior records to approx 2005 can be ordered and received by email. Search by name, attorney name, case number, or judge. No personal identifiers are displayed.

Jasper County
Superior Court   www.gaclerks.org/Association/Clerks/default.aspx
Civil: Civil and domestic relations document images are available at www.peachcourt.com. No fee to register, $.50 per page to download. Records from 2014 forward available instantly. Prior records to approx 2005 can be ordered and received by email. Search by name, attorney name, case number, or judge. No personal identifiers are displayed.

Jones County
Superior Court   www.jonescountyclerkofcourt.org/
Civil: Civil and domestic relations document images are available at www.peachcourt.com. No fee to register, $.50 per page to download. Records from 2014 forward available instantly. Prior records to approx 2005 can be ordered and received by email. Search by name, attorney name, case number, or judge. No personal identifiers are displayed.

Lamar County
Superior Court   https://www.gsccca.org/
Civil: Civil and domestic relations document images are available at www.peachcourt.com. No fee to register, $.50 per page to download. Records from 2014 forward available instantly. Prior records to approx 2005 can be ordered and received by email. Search by name, attorney name, case number, or judge. No personal identifiers are displayed.

Lanier County
Superior Court   https://www.gsccca.org/
Civil: Civil and domestic relations document images are available at www.peachcourt.com. No fee to register, $.50 per page to download. Records from 2014 forward available instantly. Prior records to approx 2005 can be ordered and received by email. Search by name, attorney name, case number, or judge. No personal identifiers are displayed.

Liberty County
Superior Court   www.libertyco.com
Civil: The docket index is available for no charge at https://ww2.libertycountyga.com/publiccmwebsearch/. Record data available from 1986 forward. Search by case number or party name. Case file documents are not shown. Civil and domestic relations document images are available at www.peachcourt.com. No fee to register, $.50 per page to download. Records from 2014 forward available instantly. Prior records to approx 2005 can be ordered and received by email. Search by name, attorney name, case number, or judge. No personal identifiers are displayed.   *Criminal:* same

State Court   www.libertyco.com
Civil: The docket index is available for no charge at https://ww2.libertycountyga.com/publiccmwebsearch/. Record data available from 1986 forward. Search by case number or party name. Case file documents are not shown. Civil and domestic relations document images are available at www.peachcourt.com. No fee to register, $.50 per page to download. Records from 2014 forward available instantly. Prior records to approx 2005 can be ordered and received by email. Search by name, attorney name, case number, or judge. No personal identifiers are displayed.   *Criminal:* same

Madison County
Superior Court   www.madisonclerkofcourt.com/
Civil: Search the docket index at www.madisonsuperiorcourt.com/webFormFrame.aspx?page=main, records go to 1998. A more enhanced system is available for attorneys and frequent users, contact the office to set up an account.   *Criminal:* Search the criminal docket index at www.madisonsuperiorcourt.com/webFormFrame.aspx?page=main, records go to 1998. A more enhanced system is available for attorneys and frequent users, contact the office to set up an account.

Marion County
Superior Court   https://www.gsccca.org/
Civil: Civil and domestic relations document images are available at www.peachcourt.com. No fee to register, $.50 per page to download. Records from 2014 forward available instantly. Prior records to approx 2005 can be ordered and received by email. Search by name, attorney name, case number, or judge. No personal identifiers are displayed.

Meriwether County
Superior Court   www.meriwetherclerkofcourt.com/
Civil: Search the docket index online at www.meriwetherclerkofcourt.com/WebCaseManagement/webFormFrame.aspx?page=main. May search by name or case number. Records go back to 1990. No images shown. Civil and domestic relations document images are available at www.peachcourt.com. No fee to register, $.50 per page to download. Records from 2014 forward available instantly. Prior records to approx 2005 can be ordered and received by email. Search by name, attorney name, case number, or judge. No personal identifiers are displayed.   *Criminal:* Search the docket index online at www.meriwetherclerkofcourt.com/WebCaseManagement/webFormFrame.aspx?page=main. May search by name or case number. Records go back to 1990. No images shown.

Mitchell County
Superior Court   www.mitchellcountyga.net/superiorcourtclerk.html

Civil: Civil and domestic relations document images are available at www.peachcourt.com. No fee to register, $.50 per page to download. Records from 2014 forward available instantly. Prior records to approx 2005 can be ordered and received by email. Search by name, attorney name, case number, or judge. No personal identifiers are displayed.

State Court   www.mitchellcountyga.net/superiorcourtclerk.html

Civil: Civil and domestic relations document images are available at www.peachcourt.com. No fee to register, $.50 per page to download. Records from 2014 forward available instantly. Prior records to approx 2005 can be ordered and received by email. Search by name, attorney name, case number, or judge. No personal identifiers are displayed.

Monroe County

Superior Court   https://www.gsccca.org/

Civil: Civil and domestic relations document images are available at www.peachcourt.com. No fee to register, $.50 per page to download. Records from 2014 forward available instantly. Prior records to approx 2005 can be ordered and received by email. Search by name, attorney name, case number, or judge. No personal identifiers are displayed.

Montgomery County

Superior Court   https://www.gsccca.org/

Civil: Civil and domestic relations document images are available at www.peachcourt.com. No fee to register, $.50 per page to download. Records from 2014 forward available instantly. Prior records to approx 2005 can be ordered and received by email. Search by name, attorney name, case number, or judge. No personal identifiers are displayed.

Morgan County

Superior Court   www.morganga.org/

Civil: Search the docket index by name or case number at www.morgansuperiorcourt.org/. Records go back to 1987.   *Criminal:* same

Murray County

Superior Court   http://murraycountyga.org/index.aspx?nid=107

Civil: Civil and domestic relations document images are available at www.peachcourt.com. No fee to register, $.50 per page to download. Records from 2014 forward available instantly. Prior records to approx 2005 can be ordered and received by email. Search by name, attorney name, case number, or judge. No personal identifiers are displayed. Calendar look-up free at home page. *Criminal:* Calendar free at the website.

Muscogee County

Superior Court   www.muscogeecourts.com

Civil: Current dockets in pdf format are free at www.muscogeecourts.com. There is no historical data available online.   *Criminal:* same

State Court   www.muscogeecourts.com

Civil: Current dockets in pdf format are free at www.muscogeecourts.com. There is no historical data available online.   *Criminal:* same

Oconee County

Superior Court   www.oconeecounty.com/departments/clerk-of-courts-superior-magistrate-a-juvenile

Civil: Civil and domestic relations document images are available at www.peachcourt.com. No fee to register, $.50 per page to download. Records from 2014 forward available instantly. Prior records to approx 2005 can be ordered and received by email. Search by name, attorney name, case number, or judge. No personal identifiers are displayed.

Oglethorpe County

Superior Court   https://www.gsccca.org/clerks/clerk-results?cid=109

Civil: A free search of the civil docket is at http://oglethorpeclerkofcourt.com/WebCaseManagement/webFormFrame.aspx?page=main. Search includes Superior and State Court. The site includes access to Child Support, Domestic and Habeas Corpus. There is also an enhanced version for attorneys - a log-in is required. Call for information.   *Criminal:* A free search of the criminal docket is at http://oglethorpeclerkofcourt.com/WebCaseManagement/webFormFrame.aspx?page=main. There is also an enhanced version for attorneys - a log-in is required. Call for information.

Paulding County

Superior Court   www.paulding.gov/index.aspx?NID=92

Civil: Civil and domestic relations document images are available at www.peachcourt.com. No fee to register, $.50 per page to download. Records from 2014 forward available instantly. Prior records to approx 2005 can be ordered and received by email. Search by name, attorney name, case number, or judge. No personal identifiers are displayed.

Pike County

Superior Court   https://www.gsccca.org/

Civil: Civil and domestic relations document images are available at www.peachcourt.com. No fee to register, $.50 per page to download. Records from 2014 forward available instantly. Prior records to approx 2005 can be ordered and received by email. Search by name, attorney name, case number, or judge. No personal identifiers are displayed.

Putnam County

Superior & State Court   http://putnamcourtclerk.org/

Civil: Civil and domestic relations document images are available at www.peachcourt.com. No fee to register, $.50 per page to download. Records from 2014 forward available instantly. Prior records to approx 2005 can be ordered and received by email. Search by name, attorney name, case number, or judge. No personal identifiers are displayed.

Richmond County

Superior Court   www.augustaga.gov/804/Superior-Court

Civil: Access court index free at www.augustaga.gov/421/Case-Management-Search for records 2001 forward. Civil and domestic relations document images are available at www.peachcourt.com. No fee to register, $.50 per page to download. Records from 2014 forward available instantly. Prior records to approx 2005 can be ordered and received by email. Search by name, attorney name, case number, or judge. No personal identifiers are displayed. *Criminal:* Access court index free at www.augustaga.gov/421/Case-Management-Search.

State Court   www.augustaga.gov/1475/State-Court-of-Richmond-County

Civil: Name search civil dockets free at www.augustaga.gov/421/Case-Management-Search. Civil and domestic relations document images are available at www.peachcourt.com. No fee to register, $.50 per page to download. Records from 2014 forward available instantly. Prior records to approx 2005 can be ordered and received by email. Search by name, attorney name, case number, or judge. No personal identifiers are displayed. *Criminal:* Name search of misdemeanor cases is free at www.augustaga.gov/421/Case-Management-Search.

Civil Court   www.augustaga.gov/67/Civil-Magistrate-Court

Civil: Civil and domestic relations document images are available at www.peachcourt.com. No fee to register, $.50 per page to download. Records from 2014 forward available instantly. Prior records to approx 2005 can be ordered and received by email. Search by name, attorney name, case number, or judge. No personal identifiers are displayed.

Rockdale County

Superior Court   www.rockdaleclerk.com/

Civil: Online is only open to attorneys of record with cases before the court. Records associated with cases and court calendars in the county's Superior, State, Magistrate and Probate courts are available. Online access is not open to the public.   *Criminal:* same

State Court   www.rockdaleclerk.com/

Civil: Online is only open to attorneys of record with cases before the court. Records associated with cases and court calendars in the county's Superior, State, Magistrate and Probate courts are available. Online access is not open to the public.   *Criminal:* same

Schley County

Superior Court   https://www.gsccca.org/

Civil: Civil and domestic relations document images are available at www.peachcourt.com. No fee to register, $.50 per page to download. Records from 2014 forward available instantly. Prior records to approx 2005 can be ordered and received by email. Search by name, attorney name, case number, or judge. No personal identifiers are displayed.

Screven County

Superior & State Courts   www.gaclerks.org/Association/Clerks/default.aspx

Civil: Civil and domestic relations document images are available at www.peachcourt.com. No fee to register, $.50 per page to download. Records from 2014 forward available instantly. Prior records to approx 2005 can be ordered and received by email. Search by name, attorney name, case number, or judge. No personal identifiers are displayed.

Telfair County

Superior Court   www.telfairclerkofcourt.com/

Civil: Online access to the civil docket is at www.telfairclerkofcourt.com/search/webFormFrame.aspx?page=main. Separate searches for Child Support, Domestic and Habeas Corpus offered on the screen. The screen also offers access to State court records, but this county does not have a State Court. There is no indication of the date range available, but per the Clerk's office records are available since mid 2001. Civil and domestic relations document images are available at www.peachcourt.com. No fee to register, $.50 per page to download. Records from 2014 forward available instantly. Prior records to approx 2005 can be ordered and received by email. Search by name, attorney name, case number, or judge. No personal identifiers are displayed. *Criminal:* Online access to the criminal docket is at www.telfairclerkofcourt.com/search/webFormFrame.aspx?page=main. There is no indication of the date range available, but per the Clerk's office records are available since mid 2001.

Toombs County

Superior Court   https://www.gsccca.org/clerks/clerk-results?cid=138

Civil: Civil and domestic relations document images are available at www.peachcourt.com. No fee to register, $.50 per page to download. Records from 2014 forward available instantly. Prior records to approx 2005 can be ordered and received by email. Search by name, attorney name, case number, or judge. No personal identifiers are displayed.

State Court   https://www.gsccca.org/clerks/clerk-results?cid=138

Civil: Civil and domestic relations document images are available at www.peachcourt.com. No fee to register, $.50 per page to download. Records from 2014 forward available instantly. Prior records to approx 2005 can be ordered and received by email. Search by name, attorney name, case number, or judge. No personal identifiers are displayed.

Upson County

Superior Court   www.upsoncountyga.org/departments/clerk_court.htm

Civil: Search the docket index for free at www.upsonclerkofcourt.com/webFormFrame.aspx?page=main. Civil and domestic relations document images are available at www.peachcourt.com. No fee to register, $.50 per page to download. Records from 2014 forward available instantly. Prior records to approx 2005 can be ordered and received by email. Search by name, attorney name, case number, or judge. No personal identifiers are displayed. *Criminal:* same

Walker County

Superior Court   www.lmjc.net/walkerpage1.htm
Civil: Access to civil records for free go to http://walker.gaclerkofcourt.net/webFormFrame.aspx?page=main.   *Criminal:* Access to criminal records for free to go http://walker.gaclerkofcourt.net/webFormFrame.aspx?page=main.

State Court   www.lmjc.net/walkerpage1.htm
Civil: Access to civil records for free go to http://walker.gaclerkofcourt.net/webFormFrame.aspx?page=main.   *Criminal:* Access to criminal records for free to go http://walker.gaclerkofcourt.net/webFormFrame.aspx?page=main.

Webster County

Superior Court   https://www.gsccca.org/
Civil: Civil and domestic relations document images are available at www.peachcourt.com. No fee to register, $.50 per page to download. Records from 2014 forward available instantly. Prior records to approx 2005 can be ordered and received by email. Search by name, attorney name, case number, or judge. No personal identifiers are displayed.

Wheeler County

Superior Court   https://www.gsccca.org/
Civil: Civil and domestic relations document images are available at www.peachcourt.com. No fee to register, $.50 per page to download. Records from 2014 forward available instantly. Prior records to approx 2005 can be ordered and received by email. Search by name, attorney name, case number, or judge. No personal identifiers are displayed. :

Whitfield County

Superior Court   www.whitfieldcountyga.com/sc/scmain.htm
Civil: Civil and domestic relations document images are available at www.peachcourt.com. No fee to register, $.50 per page to download. Records from 2014 forward available instantly. Prior records to approx 2005 can be ordered and received by email. Search by name, attorney name, case number, or judge. No personal identifiers are displayed.

Wilcox County

Superior Court   www.wilcoxcountygeorgia.com/departments/clerk.html
Civil: Civil and domestic relations document images are available at www.peachcourt.com. No fee to register, $.50 per page to download. Records from 2014 forward available instantly. Prior records to approx 2005 can be ordered and received by email. Search by name, attorney name, case number, or judge. No personal identifiers are displayed.

Wilkinson County

Superior Court   www.wilkinsonclerkofcourt.com/
Civil: There is a public access system to basic info. There is also access to expanded docket information but it is limited to attorneys and to court officials. See www.wilkinsonclerkofcourt.com/webcasemanagement/webFormFrame.aspx?page=main. Search by name or case number for a specified date range in the public access system. Civil and domestic relations document images are available at www.peachcourt.com. No fee to register, $.50 per page to download. Records from 2014 forward available instantly. Prior records to approx 2005 can be ordered and received by email. Search by name, attorney name, case number, or judge. No personal identifiers are displayed. *Criminal:* There is a public access system to basic info. Eexpanded docket information limited to attorneys and to court officials is at www.wilkinsonclerkofcourt.com/webcasemanagement/webFormFrame.aspx?page=main. Search by name or case number for a specified date range.

Recorders, Assessors, and Other Sites of Note

About Georgia Recording Offices: 159 counties, 159 recording offices. The recording officer is the Clerk of Superior Court. All transactions are recorded in a "General Execution Docket." All tax liens on personal property filed with the county Clerk of Superior Court in a "General Execution Docket" (grantor/grantee) or "Lien Index."

About Tax Liens: All state and federal tax liens are filed with the District Recorder..

Online Access

Recorded Documents (Statewide)

The **Georgia Superior Court Clerk's Cooperative Authority (GSCCCA)** at https://www.gsccca.org/search offers free access to certain Recorded Documents for all Georgia counties. The Real Estate Index contains property transactions from all counties since January 1, 1997. There are both free and Premium (pay) services offered. The Lien Index includes liens filed on real and personal property. The UCC Index contains financing statement data from all counties and can be searched by name, taxpayer ID, file date and file number. Additionally, the actual image of the corresponding UCC statement can be downloaded for a fee. Visit the GSCCCA website for details.

Tax Assessor Data

Nearly every county is associated with **http://qpublic.net/ga** for a free limited data look-up online for that county's parcel data, tax digest data, and GIS maps. In addition, at least 25 counties participate in an enhanced data subscription service. Each county is linked from the home page.

There is a general links list to all Georgia County Tax Assessor web pages at www.gaassessors.com.

County Sites - Other Than the Two Sites Mentioned Above

Since all counties offer online access via https://www.gsccca.org/search and nearly all contires use the vendor http://qpublic.net/ga, these sites are omitted below.

Bibb County   *Recorded Documents Records*   www.maconbibb.us/office-of-the-superior-court-clerk/   Access land records (1/1/98-current), liens (pre-standard- 8/1/89, standard- 1/1/04) and hospital liens (7/8/02) for a fee at https://bibbclerkindexsearch.com/external/. Daily fee: $7.95; Monthly access: $24.95; Yearly access: $299.40 for Civil/Criminal cases or Real Estate ($39.95 monthly access for both). All access includes free printing from outside terminals. We charge $.50 per copy when copied in this office.
Property, Taxation Records   Free property records search at www.co.bibb.ga.us/TaxAssessors/index1.html. Also, search for property ownership for free at www.co.bibb.ga.us/engineering/property/search.htm. Also, Ad Valorem tax statements at www.co.bibb.ga.us/TaxBills/Searchpage.asp.

Carroll County   *Recorded Documents Records*   www.carrollcountyclerk.com/   Access to land records online for a fee at www.mainstreet-tech.com/Search/Default.aspx.

Chatham County   *Property, Taxation Records*   Search the assessor database for property sales for free at http://boa.chathamcounty.org/Home/Property-Sales. Free property records search at http://boa.chathamcounty.org/Home/Search-Property-Record-Cards.

Chattahoochee County   *Property, Taxation Records*   Access GIS site free at http://webmap.jws.com/chattahoochee/.

Cherokee County   *Recorded Documents Records*   www.cherokeega.com/Clerk-of-Courts/superior-court-clerk%27s-office/   Access recording records free at http://deeds.cherokeega.com/Search.aspx.
Property, Taxation Records   Free property records search from the Tax Assessor's Database at http://taxassessor.cherokeega.com/taxnet/.

Clayton County   *Property, Taxation Records*   Search property card index free at http://weba.co.clayton.ga.us/cluserver/htdocs/index.shtml. Access to real property and personal property records free at www.claytoncountyga.gov/departments/tax-assessor/property-search-information.aspx.

Cobb County   *Property, Taxation Records*   Property tax records search for free at www.cobbtax.org/taxes. Also, search for parcel data on the GIS-mapping site free at www.cobbgis.org:81/Html5Viewer/?viewer=cobbpublic. Also, property appraisal search and tax maps free at www.cobbassessor.org/cobbga/filesearch/filesearch.aspx.

Columbia County   *Property, Taxation Records*   Access to GIS/mapping for free at http://mapsonline.columbiacountyga.gov/columbiajs/.

Dade County   *Recorded Documents Records*   www.dadegaclerkofcourt.com/   Access to clerk records is available at www.mainstreet-tech.com/Search/Default.aspx. Must sign-up to use. To be able to view and print images, a subscription and print credits will be needed. Subscription will only allow image viewing. Print Credits will need to be purchased to print the image. Court calendars are available at www.dadegaclerkofcourt.com/.

DeKalb County   *Property, Taxation Records*   Search real estate data for free at http://taxcommissioner.dekalbcountyga.gov/PropertyAppraisal/realSearch.asp.

Dougherty County   *Recorded Documents Records*   www.albany.ga.us/content/1800/2887/2985/default.aspx   Access to the clerk of courts Dept. of Deeds public menu is at www.albany.ga.us/content/1800/2889/3011/3506/default.aspx. Click on Real Estate.

Douglas County   *Recorded Documents Records*
www.celebratedouglascounty.com/view/departments/view_dept/&cdept=33&department=Clerk%20of%20Superior%20Court   Access to land records free at http://deeds.co.douglas.ga.us/External/LandRecords/protected/v4/SrchName.aspx.
Property, Taxation Records   Access property data and GIS/mapping free at http://gis.co.douglas.ga.us/start.aspx.

Effingham County   *Property, Taxation Records*   Access to GIS/mapping free at www.effinghamcounty.org/Departments/GIS/CountyMaps/tabid/1573/Default.aspx.

Fayette County   *Recorded Documents Records*   www.fayetteclerk.com/   Access to records free at http://fccottweb.fayettecountyga.gov/external/LandRecords/protected/SrchQuickName.aspx.
Property, Taxation Records   Records are free on the GIS-mapping site at http://maps.fayettecountyga.gov/.

Forsyth County   *Recorded Documents Records*   www.forsythclerk.com/   Search land records, liens, plats, and trade names free at www.forsythclerk.com/index.php?option=com_content&view=article&id=5&Itemid=7.

Glynn County   *Property, Taxation Records*   Access the county assessor property tax records free on the GIS mapping site at www.glynncounty.org/656/GIS-Mapping

Gordon County *Property, Taxation Records*   Search property tax payment database free at https://gordon.paytaxes.net//customer/enhanced_property_tax_search.php. Access to GIS/mapping for free at www.gordoncountygis.org/.

Gwinnett County *Property, Taxation Records*   Access to GIS/mapping free at www.gwinnettassessor.manatron.com/IWantTo/PropertyGISSearch.aspx.

Hall County *Property, Taxation Records*   Access property data free on the GIS site at www.hallcounty.org/235/GIS.

Houston County *Recorded Documents Records*   www.houstoncountyga.com/government/houston-county-superior-court.aspx   The clerks recording indices of plats, land records, liens is free at http://cotthosting.com/GAHoustonExternal/LandRecords/protected/SrchQuickName.aspx.

Madison County *Property, Taxation Records*   Search tax bill data free at https://madison.paytaxes.net/customer/enhanced_property_tax_search.php.

Morgan County *Recorded Documents Records*   www.morganga.org/Index.aspx?NID=226   The county site is http://24.107.172.108/rewebsearch/default.htm. For the log-in use pub for username and password. To print images one is required to have an account. To create an account or if questions, call the Clerk's office at 706-342-3605.

Muscogee County *Property, Taxation Records*   Access to GIS/mapping for free at www.columbusga.org/engineering2/GIS.htm#TA.

Paulding County *Property, Taxation Records*   Access to Tax Assessor's records for free (limited data) or through a subscription service (all available features) go to http://gaassessors.com/loadpage.php?refurl=www.qpublic.net/ga/paulding.

Peach County *Property, Taxation Records*   Subscribe to the GIS-mapping site for property data at www.peachcounty.net/gis-county-mapping.cfm. For registration and password, contact the Tax Office at 478-825-5924.

Pickens County *Property, Taxation Records*   Access records on the mapping site free at www.tscmaps.com/cnty/pickens-ga/.

Richmond County *Property, Taxation Records*   Access GIS Maps at http://gismap.augustaga.gov/AugustaJS/.

Sumter County *Property, Taxation Records*   Access to address and parcel finder for free at http://maps.kcsgis.com/ga.americus_sumter_public/.

Union County *Property, Taxation Records*   Access to GIS/mapping for free at www.georgiagis.com/union/Frameset.cfm.

Walton County *Property, Taxation Records*   Search property tax data at www.waltoncountytax.com/taxSearch.

Warren County *Property, Taxation Records*   Access assessor parcel data free on the Central Savannah River Area GIS site at www.csrardc.org/. Click on Search then County then choose Warren.

Whitfield County *Recorded Documents Records*   www.whitfieldcountyga.com/coc/clerk.htm   Access to deeds, plats, etc free at https://www.uslandrecords.com/galr/.
Property, Taxation Records   Access to property tax data is available free at www.whitfieldcountyga.com/Indexgis.htm. A subscription service is also available for professions requiring full property data.

Hawaii

Capital: Honolulu
        Honolulu County
Time Zone: HT
Population: 1,431,603
# of Counties: 4

Useful State Links

Website: **http://portal.ehawaii.gov**
Governor: **http://governor.hawaii.gov**
Attorney General: **http://ag.hawaii.gov**
State Archives: **http://ags.hawaii.gov/archives**
State Statutes and Codes: **www.capitol.hawaii.gov/**
Legislative Bill Search: **www.capitol.hawaii.gov**
Unclaimed Funds: **https://www.ehawaii.gov/lilo/app**

State Public Record Agencies

Criminal Records

Hawaii Criminal Justice Data Center, CHRC Unit,   http://ag.hawaii.gov/hcjdc/   Online access is available at eCrim at https://ecrim.ehawaii.gov/ahewa/. There is a $5.00 search fee for each unique search. The cost of an official record is an additional $10.00. Unlimited eCrim searches are available for a monthly fee. Registration is required. Questions are directed to 808-587-4220   *Other Options:* A Bulk Criminal Data Download is available for $24,000/year. There is a minimum one year subscription. See http://portal.ehawaii.gov/subscriber-services.html.

Sexual Offender Registry

Hawaii Criminal Justice Data Center, Sexual Offender Registry,   http://sexoffenders.ehawaii.gov/sexoffender/welcome.html   Search at http://sexoffenders.ehawaii.gov/sexoffender/search.html. Search by name, street or ZIP Code.   *Other Options:* Download all sex offender data for the state of Hawai'i. Cost for the Sex Offender and Other Covered Offender Registry Data is $100 per download. For more information on purchasing Bulk COR Data, please call (808) 695-4622.

Incarceration Records

Hawaii Department of Public Safety, Inmate Classification,   http://dps.hawaii.gov/about/divisions/corrections/   The inmate locator is outsourced to a vendor service - see https://www.vinelink.com/vinelink/siteInfoAction.do?siteId=50000.

Corporation, LP, LLC, LLP, Trade Name, Assumed Name, Trademarks/Servicemarks

Dept of Commerce and Consumer Affairs, Business Registration Division,   http://cca.hawaii.gov/breg/   Note: For assistance during business hours, call 808-586-2727. Online access to business names is available at https://hbe.ehawaii.gov/documents/search.html?mobile=N&site_preference=normal. There are no fees. There are multiple online services provided. One can also purchase/search to see if business qualifies for a Good Standing report. Tax license searching is free at https://dotax.ehawaii.gov/tls/app. Search by name, ID number of DBA name. PDF copies may be purchased for $3.00. Thru the web page at business.ehawaii.gov, the agency provides a Mobile App to search a business name, find information or purchase filed documents. Use your device and the website will display a Mobile App version. *Other Options:* Bulk data can be purchased online through the List Builder program at https://hbe.ehawaii.gov/listbuilder/. One may build a customized list of registered businesses. Visit the website or call 808-695-4624for more information.

Uniform Commercial Code, Federal & State Tax Liens, Real Estate Recordings

UCC Division, Bureau of Conveyances,   http://dlnr.hawaii.gov/boc/   All of the available searches and images from this agency are available at http://dlnr.hawaii.gov/boc/online-services/. Search the all the indices from 1976 forward by grantor, grantee, business name. Includes real estate recordings. Uncertified copies of documents recorded as of January 1992 can be downloaded immediately after purchase at https://boc.ehawaii.gov/docsearch/nameSearch.html. For technical questions call 808-695-4620. *Other Options:* Commercial customers may subscribe to a monthly service for bulk download of record documents.

Birth Certificates

State Department of Health, Vital Records Section,   http://health.hawaii.gov/vitalrecords/   The Department provides an online ordering system at https://vitrec.ehawaii.gov/vitalrecords. The certified copies being ordered will be mail, and will not be issued online as a part of the transaction. Turnaround time is usually at least one month. The fee is the same as mentioned above PLUS $2.50 for processing. This system does exact matches only. Please enter data carefully as typographical errors will result in a failure to match.

Marriage, Civil Union Certificates

State Department of Health, Vital Records Section,   http://health.hawaii.gov/vitalrecords/   The Department provides an online ordering system at https://www.ehawaii.gov/doh/vitrec/exe/vitrec.cgi, The certified copies being ordered will be mail, and will not be issued online as a part of the transaction. Turnaround time is usually at least one month. The fee is the same as mentioned above PLUS $2.50 for processing. A tracking system is also in place. This system does exact matches only. Please enter data carefully as typographical errors will result in a failure to match.

Driver Records

Traffic Violations Bureau, Driving Records,   www.courts.state.hi.us/   Online ordering by DPPA complaint requesters is available from the state-designated entity - Hawaii Information Consortium (HIC). The record fee is $23.00 per record plus a $75.00 annual subscription fee is required. Record requests are accepted via FTP. Results, if clear, are returned via FTP. Results with hits on convictions on the record are returned on paper. Visit their website at https://portal.ehawaii.gov/page/subscriber-services/ or call HIC at 808-695-4620 for more information. Name checks of traffic court records may be ordered from the court.   *Other Options:* HIC offers a driver monitoring program. The fee is $.15 per driver per month. Call 808-695-4620 or 4624 for further details.

Vessel Ownership & Registration

Land & Natural Resources, Division of Boating & Recreation,   http://dlnr.hawaii.gov/dobor/   Go to http://hawaii.gov/dlnr/dbor/, click on Online Services, then on Vessel Registration, then click on Public Search tab to view registration data. Search by vessel name, hull number or vessel number. A name search is not offered.

Campaign Finance

Campaign Spending Commission, 235 S. Beretania Street, Room 300,   http://ags.hawaii.gov/campaign/   Campaign spending reports for all candidate committees and PACS are viewable using links on the right edge at http://ags.hawaii.gov/campaign/. This includes enforcement reports and court rulings. Also see the State Ethics Commission page at http://hawaii.gov/ethics for financial disclosures for legislators, state officials, and candidates.

Financial Disclosures, Lobbyists

State Ethics Commission, 1001 Bishop Street, Suite 970,   http://ethics.hawaii.gov/   A series of searches is available from the home page at http://ethics.hawaii.gov. Click on the Disclosures tab and the Lobbying tab.

GED Certificates

Community Education, HI State Dept of Education,   www.hawaiipublicschools.org/TeachingAndLearning/AdultEducation/Pages/Home.aspx   Third parties are routed to set up an account at: http://exchange.parchment.com/ged-receiver-registration-page. Parchment verifies that they are who they say they are so that they can place orders on behalf of students. Parchment contacts the third party and provides training on the site for ordering. During this training any orders they have are placed. After this the third party can order on behalf of students. They still must upload a consent form for each student during the process.

Occupational Licensing Boards

These licenses are all searchable at https://pvl.ehawaii.gov/pvlsearch/

Accountant-CPA/PA	Electrologist	Nursing Home Administrator
Acupuncturist	Emergency Medical Personnel, B & P	Occupational Therapist
Architect/Landscape Architect	Employment Agency	Optician, Dispensing
Auction	Engineer	Optometrist
Barber Shop	Guard/Agency	Osteopathic Physician
Barber/Barber Apprentice	Hearing Aid Dealer/Fitter	Pest Control Field Rep/Operator
Boxer	Investment Advisor/Representative	Pharmacist/Pharmacy
Cemetery/Pre-Need Funeral Authority	Marriage & Family Therapist	Physical Therapist
Chiropractor	Massage Therapist/Establishment	Physician/Medical Doctor/Assistant
Collection Agency	Mechanic	Pilot, Port
Contractor	Mortgage Broker/Solicitor	Plumber
Cosmetologist/School/Shop/Instructor	Motor Vehicle Dealer/Broker/SellerRepair	Podiatrist
Dental Hygienist	Dealer	Private Investigator/Agency
Dentist	Naturopathic Physician	Psychologist
Electrician	Nurse/RN/LPN/Aide	Real Estate Appraiser

Securities Salesperson	Speech Pathologist/Audiologist	Travel Agency
Social Worker	Timeshare	Veterinarian

The Rest:

Bank/Bank Agency/Office	http://cca.hawaii.gov/dfi/list-of-companies/#money_transmitters
Condominium Hotel Operator	https://insurance.ehawaii.gov/hils/
Condominium Managing Agent	http://insurance.ehawaii.gov/hils/
Credit Union	http://cca.hawaii.gov/dfi/list-of-companies/#money_transmitters
Elected Officials Financial Disclosure	http://ethics.hawaii.gov/2014-legislator-financial/
Escrow Company	http://cca.hawaii.gov/dfi/list-of-companies/#money_transmitters
Financial Services Loan Company	http://cca.hawaii.gov/dfi/list-of-companies/#money_transmitters
Insurance Adjuster/Agent/Producer/Solicitor	https://insurance.ehawaii.gov/hils/
Money Transmitter Companies	http://cca.hawaii.gov/dfi/list-of-companies/#money_transmitters
Notary Public	https://notary.ehawaii.gov/notary/public/publicsearch.html
Pesticide Dealer/Product	http://hdoa.hawaii.gov/pi/pest/restricted-use-pesticide-dealers/
Real Estate Agent/Broker/Sales	https://insurance.ehawaii.gov/hils/
Restricted Use Pesticides Distributor/Seller	http://hdoa.hawaii.gov/pi/pest/
Savings & Loan Association	http://cca.hawaii.gov/dfi/list-of-companies/#money_transmitters
Savings Bank	http://cca.hawaii.gov/dfi/list-of-companies/#money_transmitters
Special Local Needs Registered Pesticides	http://hdoa.hawaii.gov/pi/pest/
Tattoo Artist/Tattoo Shop	http://health.hawaii.gov/san/tattoo-lists/
Trust Company	http://cca.hawaii.gov/dfi/list-of-companies/#money_transmitters
Unlicensed Businesses/Applicators	http://hdoa.hawaii.gov/pi/pest/

State and Local Courts

About Hawaii Courts: Hawaii's trial level is comprised of **Circuit Courts** (includes Family Courts) and **District Courts**. These trial courts function in four judicial circuits: First (Oahu), Second (Maui-Molokai-Lanai), Third (Hawaii County), and Fifth (Kauai-Niihau). The Fourth Circuit was merged with the Third in 1943.

Circuit Courts are general jurisdiction and handle all jury trials, felony cases, and civil cases over $40,000, also probate and guardianship. However, there is **concurrent jurisdiction** with District Courts in **civil** non-jury cases of specific performance that specify amounts between **$5,000-$20,000**. Other cases heard by the Circuit Courts include mechanics' liens and misdemeanor violations transferred from the District Courts for jury trials. The District Court handles criminal cases punishable by a fine and/or less than one year imprisonment, landlord/tenant, traffic, DUI cases, civil cases, and small claims ($5,000 limit). The Family Court rules in all legal matters involving children, such as delinquency, waiver, status offenses, abuse and neglect, termination of parental rights, adoption, guardianships and detention. Also hears traditional domestic-relations cases, including divorce, nonsupport, paternity, uniform child custody jurisdiction cases and miscellaneous custody matters.

The web page for the Judiciary is www.courts.state.hi.us.

Appellate Courts: The Supreme Court hears appeals from the Intermediate Court of Appeals and reserved questions of law from the Circuit Courts, the Land Court, and the Tax Appeal court. The Intermediate Court of Appeals (ICA) is the court that hears nearly all appeals from trial courts and some state agencies in the State of Hawaii. There is also a Tax Appeal Court that hears appeals regarding real estate taxation and this is a court of record. Opinions and decisions from the Supreme and Appeals courts are on the home page above.

Online Court Access

There are **two free statewide online access systems** available.

1) See www.courts.state.hi.us/legal_references/records/hoohiki_disclaimer for the system known as Ho'ohiki. This provides civil and criminal case information from the Circuit and Family Courts and certain civil information in the District Courts. Search by name or case number. Most courts offer access back to mid 1980s. Case information provided by the Judiciary through this website is made available "as is," as a public service with no warranties, express or implied, including any implied warranties of merchantability, accuracy, non-infringement or fitness for a particular purpose.

2) For traffic cases, district court criminal and appellate cases on eCourt Kokua system, visit www.courts.state.hi.us/legal_references/records/jims_system_availability or access from the home page. This system also provides access to case information from the Hawaii Intermediate Court of Appeals, and the Hawaii Supreme Court. Note that juvenile traffic records are not available online.

There are no additional county sites for court records other than mentioned above.

Recorder and Assessor

About Hawaii Recording Offices: All UCC financing statements, tax liens, and real estate documents are filed centrally with the Bureau of Conveyances at http://hawaii.gov/dlnr/boc located in Honolulu. Details of searching below.

About Tax Liens: Federal and state tax liens are filed with the Bureau of Conveyances.

Online Access

Recorded Documents
Searches by name or document number as well as the ability to order certified copies are available at http://dlnr.hawaii.gov/boc/online-services/. Data is from 1976 forward. Uncertified copies of documents recorded as of January 1992 can be downloaded immediately after purchase from a link on this page. One can also subscribe to more detailed information, plus subscibers have the ability to obtain a bulk image monthly download of the DB.

Tax Assessor Data
Access to tax assessment is available from each individual county, see below.

County Sites (not mentioned above):
Hawaii County *Property, Taxation* Access to property tax data is free at http://qpublic9.qpublic.net/hi_honolulu_search.php. A name search is not offered. Access to TMK and Subdivision Maps is free at www.hawaiicounty.gov/rpt-tmk-sub.

Honolulu County *Property, Taxation* Access to real property assessment and tax billing info free at http://qpublic9.qpublic.net/hi_honolulu_search.php. There is no name search feature.

Kauai County *Property, Taxation* A free property search by location or parcel number is at http://qpublic9.qpublic.net/ga_search_dw.php?county=hi_kauai. A name search is only offered to registered users.

Maui County *Property, Taxation* View real property tax assessments free at http://qpublic9.qpublic.net/hi_maui_search.php. Search by location address, name, parcel number and map. A separate search of sales, and lists of sales by year, is also provided. Also, access to tax map images free at www.mauicounty.gov/757/Tax-Map-Information. Download parcel data extracts at www.co.maui.hi.us/DocumentCenter/Index/231

Idaho

Capital: Boise
             Ada County

Time Zone: MST

Idaho's ten northwestern-most counties are PST:
They are: Benewah, Bonner, Boundary, Clearwater,
Idaho, Kootenai, Latah, Lewis, Nez Perce, Shoshone.

Population: 1,654,930

# of Counties: 44

Useful State Links

Website: **www.idaho.gov/**

Governor: **https://gov.idaho.gov/**

Attorney General: **www.ag.idaho.gov/index.html**

State Archives: **https://history.idaho.gov/idaho-state-archives**

State Statutes and Codes: **https://legislature.idaho.gov/idstat/idstat.htm**

Legislative Bill Search: **www.legislature.idaho.gov**

Unclaimed Funds: **https://www.yourmoney.idaho.gov/**

State Public Record Agencies

Sexual Offender Registry

State Repository, Central Sexual Offender Registry,   https://isp.idaho.gov/sor_id/   Search records at https://www.isp.idaho.gov/sor_id/search.html. Inquires can be made by name, address, or by city or county or ZIP Code. Mapping is also available. Lists of violent and non-compliant offenders are viewable. Also, at the web page one may subscribe for notification on an address or offender.

Incarceration Records

Idaho Department of Correction, Records Bureau,   https://www.idoc.idaho.gov/   The database search at https://www.idoc.idaho.gov/content/prisons/offender_search provides in-depth information about offenders currently under Idaho Department of Correction jurisdiction meaning only those incarcerated, on probation, or on parole. Names of individuals who have served time and satisfied their sentence will appear - their convictions will not. If you need additional basic offender record information, contact inquire@idoc.idaho.gov. To make a formal request of public records, email publicrecord@idoc.idaho.gov.

Corporation, LP, LLP, LLC, Trademarks/Servicemarks, Assumed Name

Secretary of State, Corporation Division,   www.sos.idaho.gov/corp/index.html   Business Entity Searches at www.accessidaho.org/public/sos/corp/search.html?SearchFormstep=crit. This is a free Internet service open 24 hours daily. Includes not-for-profit entities. Be sure to check out the Search Tips link. Trademarks may be searched at www.accessidaho.org/public/sos/trademark/search.html.   *Other Options:* There are a variety of formats and media available for bulk purchase requesters. Requesters can subscriber to a monthly CD update.

Uniform Commercial Code, Federal & State Tax Liens

UCC Division, Secretary of State,   www.sos.idaho.gov/ucc/index.html   There is a free limited search at https://www.accessidaho.org/secure/sos/liens/search.html. We recommend professional searchers to subscribe to the extensive commercial service at this site. The fee is $3.00 per name searched with a $95.00 annual subscription fee. Note there is a 1-2 day delay before new filings are available online. See https://www.accessidaho.org/ai/subscription.html.   *Other Options:* A full extract of the data file is available for download,

Business and Sales/Use Tax Registrations

Revenue Operations Division, IO/Records Management,   http://tax.idaho.gov/i-1049.cfm   Verify a seller's permit at https://www.accessidaho.org/secure/istc/permit/validate.html. Email requests are accepted at leola.rees@tax.id.gov,

Vital Records

Vital Records, www.healthandwelfare.idaho.gov/Health/VitalRecordsandHealthStatistics/tabid/1504/Default.aspx   Requests can be made online via a vendor - vitalchek.com. Additional fees involved.   Alos, the agency has made the death index of records from 1911 - 1956 available at http://abish.byui.edu/specialCollections/fhc/Death/searchForm.cfm. There is no fee.

Driver Records

Idaho Transportation Department, Driver's Services,   www.itd.idaho.gov/dmv/   Note: Access Idaho refers to driving records as 'Driver License Records' or DLRs and refers to records related to vehicle title or registration as MVRs. Idaho offers online access (CICS) to the driver license files through its portal provider, Access Idaho. Fee is $9.00 per record. There is an annual $95.00 subscription fee. See www.accessidaho.org/ai/subscription.html. Idaho drivers can also order their own record from thttps://www.accessidaho.org/secure/itd/dlr/interactive/search.html, fee is $9.56, subscription nor required. There is a free DL status check at https://www.accessidaho.org/secure/itd/reinstatement/signin.html.   *Other Options:* Idaho offers bulk retrieval of basic drivers license information with a signed contract. For information, call 208-334-8602.

Vehicle Ownership & Registration, Vessel Ownership

Idaho Transportation Department, Vehicle Services,   http://itd.idaho.gov/dmv/vehicleservices/vs.htm   Idaho offers online and batch access to registration and title files through its portal provider Access Idaho. Records are $8.50 per record. For more information, call 208-332-0102 or visit https://www.accessidaho.org/online_services. There is a $95 annual subscription fee. A free HAZMAT status check is at https://www.accessidaho.org/secure/itd/motorcarrier/unitsearch/hazmat/tportal/search.html. Must have Carrier Acct #.   *Other Options:* Idaho offers bulk retrieval of registration, ownership, and vehicle information with a signed contract. For more information, call 208-334-8601.

Crash Reports

Idaho Transportation Department, Traffic and Highway Safety-Accident Records,   http://itd.idaho.gov/ohs/records.htm   One may view and print reports at https://www.accessidaho.org/secure/itd/ohs/crashreports/search.html. The total fee is $9.00. It may take several weeks before new records are available on this system.   *Other Options:* Computer files may be purchased with prepaid deposit plus computer charges. However, the file will not contain addresses, citation information, or drivers' license numbers and other personal information. Annual databases may be purchased.

Voter Registration, Campaign Finance Disclosure, Lobbyists

State Elections Office, Sec of State,   www.sos.idaho.gov/elect/index.html   A list of lobbyists and expenditures is found at www.sos.idaho.gov/elect/lobbyist/lobinfo.htm.   Election campaign and finance disclosure, including PACs, is searchable at www.sos.idaho.gov/elect/finance/index.html.   Some files are downloadable.   To check to see if registered go to www.idahovotes.gov/YPP_NEW/AmIRegistered.aspx. Must have full last name, partial first name is allowed and must have date of birth, also must know in what county registered.

GED Certificates

Division of Professional-Technical Education, GED Testing,   www.pte.idaho.gov/GED/Transcripts.html   Records may be requested from https://www.diplomasender.com. A credit card is needed. Request must be ordered by the test taker. Employers and third parties must receive an email and/or Authentication Code from the test taker to then access the authorized documents. Turnaround time is 1-3 days.

Occupational Licensing Boards

These licenses are all searchable at https://secure.ibol.idaho.gov/eIBOLPublic/LPRBrowser.aspx

Acupuncturist	Crematory	Nail Technician/Instructor
Appraiser, Real Estate/Gen/Residential/Trainee	Denturist	Naturopath
Architect/Architectural Examiners	Denturist Intern/Establishment	Nursing Care (Skilled) Facility
Athlete Agent	Drinking Water Professionals	Nursing Home Administrator
Athletic Commission/Boxing/Martial Arts	Driving Business	Occupational Therapists
Audiologist	Electrolysis, Electrolysis Instructor	Optometrist
Backflow Assembly Tester	Esthetician, Esthetician Instructor	Physical Therapist/Assistant
Barber/Barber Shop/Instructor/School	Funeral Director/Dir Trainee	Podiatrist
Boxer	Funeral Establishment	Psychologist
Boxing/Wrestling Event/Professional	Geologist	Psychology Service Extender
Chiropractor	Glamour Photography Studio	Real Estate Appraiser
Contracting Business	Hearing Aid Fitter/Dealer	Residential Care Administrator
Contractor, Registered	Landscape Architect	Residential Care Facility
Cosmetics Dealer, Retail	LPG Dealer/Facility	Shorthand Reporter
Cosmetologist/Cosmetology Salon	Marriage & Family Counselor	Social Worker
Cosmetology School/Instructor	Midwife	Speech/Language Pathologist
Counselor, Clinical	Mortician Temporary Permit	Waste Water Professionals
Counselor, Professional	Mortician/Mortician Resi Trainee	Waste Water Treatment Operator

Water Collection Operator	Water Treatment Operator
Water Distribution Operator	Wrestler

The Rest:

Accountant-CPA/LPA	https://isba.idaho.gov/htm/accountantsearch.htm
Applicator, Pesticide, Private/Commercial	www.agri.state.id.us/LicenseSearch/PesticideLicenses
Assignee (Lender)	www.finance.idaho.gov/LicenseeSearch.aspx
Athletic Trainer	https://isecure.bom.idaho.gov/BOMPublic/LPRBrowser.aspx
Attorney	https://isb.idaho.gov/licensing/attorney_roster.cfm
Bank	www.finance.idaho.gov/LicenseeSearch.aspx
Beer/Wine License, Whlse/Retail	https://isp.idaho.gov/abc/licenseSearch/
Brewery	https://isp.idaho.gov/abc/licenseSearch/
Building Inspector	https://web.dbs.idaho.gov/etrakit3/
Collection Agency/Collector	www.finance.idaho.gov/LicenseeSearch.aspx
Commodity Dealer	www.agri.state.id.us/AGRI/Categories/Warehouse/indexWarehouse.php
Construction Mgr, Public Works	https://web.dbs.idaho.gov/etrakit3/
Consumer Loan Co & Credit Seller	www.finance.idaho.gov/LicenseeSearch.aspx
Contractor, Public Works	https://web.dbs.idaho.gov/etrakit3/
Counselor, Debt/Credit	www.finance.idaho.gov/Escrow/EscrowLicense.aspx
Credit Seller	www.finance.idaho.gov/LicenseeSearch.aspx
Credit Union	www.finance.idaho.gov/LicenseeSearch.aspx
Dietitian	https://isecure.bom.idaho.gov/BOMPublic/LPRBrowser.aspx
Driller, Rotary	http://maps.idwr.idaho.gov/map/locator
Elections & Campaign Disclosure	www.sos.idaho.gov/eid/eos/CandSearch.aspx
Electrical Apprentice/Journeyman	https://web.dbs.idaho.gov/etrakit3/
Elevator Installation/Repairmen	https://web.dbs.idaho.gov/etrakit3/
Engineer	https://ipels.idaho.gov/rostersearch.cfm
Escrow Licensee	www.finance.idaho.gov/Escrow/EscrowLicense.aspx
Euthanasia Agency	https://bovm.idaho.gov/license_search/
Euthanasia Technician	https://bovm.idaho.gov/license_search/
Finance Company	www.finance.idaho.gov/LicenseeSearch.aspx
Fireworks License	www.doi.idaho.gov/SFM/Licensing/FireworksVendorList.aspx
Florist/Nurseryman	www.agri.state.id.us/LicenseSearch/NurseryLicenses
Guide	https://fishandgame.idaho.gov/ifwis/ioglb/
HVAC Contractor/Journeyman	https://web.dbs.idaho.gov/etrakit3/
Insurance Producer	www.doi.idaho.gov/insurance/search.aspx
Insurance Surplus Lines Broker	www.doi.idaho.gov/insurance/search.aspx
Insurer, Domestic/Mutual/Foreign	www.doi.idaho.gov/insurance/search.aspx
Investment Advisor	www.finance.idaho.gov/Securities/SecuritiesLicense.aspx
Liquor License, Retail	https://isp.idaho.gov/abc/licenseSearch/
Lobbyist	www.sos.idaho.gov/elect/lobbyist/index.html
Logging	https://web.dbs.idaho.gov/etrakit3/
Mail Order Pharmacy List	https://idbop.glsuite.us/GLSuiteWeb/Clients/IDBOP/Public/Verification/Search.aspx
Medical Resident	https://isecure.bom.idaho.gov/BOMPublic/LPRBrowser.aspx
Medical, Temporary	https://isecure.bom.idaho.gov/BOMPublic/LPRBrowser.aspx
Money Transmitter	www.finance.idaho.gov/LicenseeSearch.aspx
Mortgage Broker/Banker	www.finance.idaho.gov/LicenseeSearch.aspx
Mortgage Company	www.finance.idaho.gov/LicenseeSearch.aspx
Mortgage Loan Originator	www.finance.idaho.gov/LicenseeSearch.aspx
Notary Public	www.sos.idaho.gov/NotarySearch/
Osteopathic Physician	https://isecure.bom.idaho.gov/BOMPublic/LPRBrowser.aspx
Outfitter	https://fishandgame.idaho.gov/ifwis/ioglb/
Payday Lender	www.finance.idaho.gov/LicenseeSearch.aspx
Pesticide Applicat'r/Oper'r/Dealer/Mfg	https://ofmpub.epa.gov/apex/aps/f?p=GPWI:HOME::::::

Pharmacist/Pharmac't Intern/Preceptor............	https://idbop.glsuite.us/GLSuiteWeb/Clients/IDBOP/Public/Verification/Search.aspx
Physician Assistant..	https://isecure.bom.idaho.gov/BOMPublic/LPRBrowser.aspx
Physician/Medical Doctor	https://isecure.bom.idaho.gov/BOMPublic/LPRBrowser.aspx
Plumbing Apprentice/Journeyman....................	https://web.dbs.idaho.gov/etrakit3/
Plumbing Inspector/Contractor........................	https://web.dbs.idaho.gov/etrakit3/
Polysomnography Technician/Trainee	https://isecure.bom.idaho.gov/BOMPublic/LPRBrowser.aspx
Real Estate Agent/Broker/Company.................	https://apps.irec.idaho.gov/PublicSearch
Real Estate Instructor/School	https://apps.irec.idaho.gov/PublicSearch
Respiratory Therapist	https://isecure.bom.idaho.gov/BOMPublic/LPRBrowser.aspx
Securities Broker/Seller/Issuer/Dealer.............	www.finance.idaho.gov/LicenseeSearch.aspx
Seed Buyers/Company/Dealer	www.agri.state.id.us/AGRI/Categories/Warehouse/indexWarehouse.php
Surveyor, Land	https://ipels.idaho.gov/rostersearch.cfm
Temporary Medical...	https://isecure.bom.idaho.gov/BOMPublic/LPRBrowser.aspx
Title Loan Lender...	www.finance.idaho.gov/LicenseeSearch.aspx
Trust Company	www.finance.idaho.gov/LicenseeSearch.aspx
Veterinarian/Veterinary Technician	https://bovm.idaho.gov/license_search/
Warehouse, Bonded...	www.agri.state.id.us/AGRI/Categories/Warehouse/indexWarehouse.php
Water Rights Examiner.....................................	www.idwr.idaho.gov/WaterManagement/WaterRights/Examiners/examiners.htm
Water Well Driller..	www.idwr.idaho.gov/apps/well/licensedwelldrillers/
Winery..	https://isp.idaho.gov/abc/licenseSearch/

State and Local Courts

About Idaho Courts: **District Courts** have original jurisdiction over felony criminal cases and civil actions if the amount involved is more than $10,000, and hear appeals of decisions of the Magistrate Division. District judges may also hear domestic relation cases, such as divorces and child custody matters, but in most counties, such cases are handled by Magistrate judges.

The **Magistrate Courts** hears probate matters, divorce proceedings, juvenile proceedings, initial felony proceedings through the preliminary hearing, criminal misdemeanors, infractions, civil cases when the amount in dispute does not exceed $10,000. Magistrates also hear Small Claims cases, established for disputes of $5,000 or less.

The web page for the Unified Judicial System is https://isc.idaho.gov/

Appellate Courts: The Court of Appeals has limited jurisdiction to appeals from the District Courts which are assigned by the Supreme Court. Appellate and Supreme Court opinions are available at www.isc.idaho.gov/appeals-court/opinions.

Online Court Access

The state judiciary is in transition to a new case management system which includes an upgrade to public access online to trial court records. The new System is called the Portal. The existing system is called the Data Repository. At this time Ada and Twin Falls counties are on the new system at http://icourt.idaho.gov/. The remaining counties should be on the new system by the end of 2017.

Therefore, for all counties except Ada and Twin Falls, free access to trial court record index is provided on the Data Repository system at https://www.idcourts.us/repository/start.do. Records are searchable by name statewide or by individual county, and by case number. Results date back to 1995 or further depending on the county. Online results include identifiers year of birth and middle initial. The following personal information is not released: DL, address, first 6 characters of the SSN, and the month and day of birth.   In general, records go back to 1995.   Court calendars are also shown on this site. Send questions to repositoryaccess@idcourts.net.

The terminals at the court house go back further, show the class of record, and can have more dispositions reported when compared to the older online system. Thus, this online service is not thought to be equivalent to an onsite search at the courthouse.

It is not yet known if the new system will be online/onsite equivalent.

Note: No individual Idaho courts offer online access, other than as described above.

Recorders and Assessors

About Idaho Recording Offices: 44 counties, 44 recording offices. The recording officer is the County Recorder. Many counties utilize a grantor/grantee index containing all transactions recorded by them.

About Tax Liens: Federal tax liens on personal property of businesses are filed with the Secretary of State. Other federal tax liens are filed with the county recorder. All state tax liens are filed with the Secretaru of state.

Online Access

Recorded Documents

A few counties offer web access to recorded documents, but not many.

See www.canaanllc.com/index.php/canaanonline/availablecounties for a vendor who provides a links list to entities that service property title information for 29 participating counties. Pricing schedule is shown at this URL.

Assessor and GIS Data

Approximately 1/2 of the counties offer online access to property tax or mapping data.

Counties:

Ada County   *Recorded Documents*   https://adacounty.id.gov/clerk   Access to recorder's index is free at https://adacounty.id.gov/recsearch/. Images are not shown. Search by name or Instrument Number. To order document, must fill out order form (download, fill out and mail to Ada County Recorder along with fee of $1.00 per page).
Property, Taxation Records   Search the property assessor database for property data for free at www.adacountyassessor.org/propsys/. No name searching.

Bannock County   *Recorded Documents*   www.bannockcounty.us/clerk/   Access to records for a fee at www.canaanllc.com/index.php/canaanonline/availablecounties. Email contact Chris Bowman at cbowman@titlefc.com for posting procedures. Pricing fees at this URL.
Property, Taxation Records   Access to GIS/mapping and Planning and Zoning maps for free at www.co.bannock.id.us/assessor/.

Benewah County   *Recorded Documents*   www.idaho.gov/aboutidaho/county/benewah   Access to records for a fee at www.canaanllc.com/index.php/canaanonline/availablecounties. Email contact Chris Bowman at cbowman@titlefc.com for posting procedures. Pricing fees at this URL.

Bingham County   *Recorded Documents*   www.co.bingham.id.us/clerk/clerk.html   Access to records for a fee at www.canaanllc.com/index.php/canaanonline/availablecounties. Email contact Chris Bowman at cbowman@titlefc.com for posting procedures. Pricing fees at this URL.

Blaine County   *Recorded Documents*   www.co.blaine.id.us/index.asp?Type=B_BASIC&SEC={9CB9F97C-7CC7-4A0C-9ECF-7D73EEE74E69}   Access to records for a fee at www.canaanllc.com/index.php/canaanonline/availablecounties. Email contact Chris Bowman at cbowman@titlefc.com for posting procedures. Pricing fees at this URL.
Property, Taxation Records   Access to GIS/mapping free at http://maps.co.blaine.id.us/.

Boise County   *Recorded Documents*   www.boisecounty.us/Clerk_Auditor_Recorder.aspx   Access to records for a fee at www.canaanllc.com/index.php/canaanonline/availablecounties. Email contact Chris Bowman at cbowman@titlefc.com for posting procedures. Pricing fees at this URL.
Property, Taxation Records   Access to property data for free at http://property.boisecounty.us/default.aspx?p=home. Must have an account to login, otherwise you may use the username and password of public1 (for both) to sign-in.

Bonner County   *Recorded Documents*   http://bonnercounty.us/recording-office/   Access to records for a fee at www.canaanllc.com/index.php/canaanonline/availablecounties. Email contact Chris Bowman at cbowman@titlefc.com for posting procedures. Pricing fees at this URL.
Property, Taxation Records   Assessor's data extract and subdivision lists are available free at http://bonnercounty.us/assessor/data-files/.

Bonneville County   *Recorded Documents*   www.co.bonneville.id.us/index.php/clerks-recorders-office   Access to records for a fee at www.canaanllc.com/index.php/canaanonline/availablecounties. Email contact Chris Bowman at cbowman@titlefc.com for posting procedures. Pricing fees at this URL.
Property, Taxation Records   Access to GIS/mapping free at www.co.bonneville.id.us/index.php/gis. Also, access to the parcel viewer for free at http://bonneville.maps.arcgis.com/apps/Solutions/s2.html.

Boundary County   *Recorded Documents*   www.boundarycountyid.org/site-page/purchasing-real-estate   Access to records for a fee at www.canaanllc.com/index.php/canaanonline/availablecounties.   Email contact Chris Bowman at cbowman@titlefc.com for posting procedures. Pricing fees at this URL.

Butte County   *Recorded Documents*   www.idaho.gov/aboutidaho/county/butte   Access to records for a fee at www.canaanllc.com/index.php/canaanonline/availablecounties.   Email contact Chris Bowman at cbowman@titlefc.com for posting procedures. Pricing fees at this URL.
Property, Taxation Records   Access to GIS/mapping for free at http://data.idahoparcels.us/www/rib/butte.html.

Camas County   *Recorded Documents*   http://camascounty.id.gov/county-clerk/recorders-office/   Access to records for a fee at www.canaanllc.com/index.php/canaanonline/availablecounties.   Email contact Chris Bowman at cbowman@titlefc.com for posting procedures. Pricing fees at this URL.

Canyon County   *Recorded Documents*   www.canyonco.org/Elected-Officials/Clerk/Recorder.aspx   Access to Recorder's database search free at http://rec-search.canyonco.org/Recording/search.asp.
Property, Taxation Records   Access to property searches for free at http://id-canyon-assessor.governmaxa.com/propertymax/rover30.asp. Also, access to GIS/mapping for free at http://gis.canyonco.org/flexviewers/Test/.

Caribou County   *Property, Taxation Records*   Access to records for a fee at www.canaanllc.com/index.php/canaanonline/availablecounties. Email contact Chris Bowman at cbowman@titlefc.com for posting procedures. Pricing fees at this URL.
Property, Taxation Records   Access to GIS/mapping parcel info system for free at http://data.idahoparcels.us/www/rib/caribou.html.

Cassia County   *Recorded Documents*   www.cassiacounty.org/clerk-auditor-recorder/index.htm   Access to records for a fee at www.canaanllc.com/index.php/canaanonline/availablecounties.   Email contact Chris Bowman at cbowman@titlefc.com for posting procedures. Pricing fees at this URL.
Property, Taxation Records   Access to parcel/map information for free at http://cassia.idahoparcels.us/. A request form for public records is found at www.cassiacounty.org/county-code/misc-publications/forms/Public-Records-Request.pdf.

Clark County   *Recorded Documents*   www.clark-co.id.gov/officials.aspx   Access to records for a fee at www.canaanllc.com/index.php/canaanonline/availablecounties.   Email contact Chris Bowman at cbowman@titlefc.com for posting procedures. Pricing fees at this URL.

Custer County   *Recorded Documents*   www.co.custer.id.us/departments/executive/clerk/   Access to records for a fee at www.canaanllc.com/index.php/canaanonline/availablecounties.   Email contact Chris Bowman at cbowman@titlefc.com for posting procedures. Pricing fees at this URL.
Property, Taxation Records   Access to GIS/mapping free at www.greenwoodmap.com/custer/.

Elmore County   *Property, Taxation Records*   Access to a parcel information map for free at http://data.idahoparcels.us/www/rib/elmore.html.

Franklin County   *Recorded Documents*   www.franklincountyidaho.org/clerk   Access to records for a fee at www.canaanllc.com/index.php/canaanonline/availablecounties.   Email contact Chris Bowman at cbowman@titlefc.com for posting procedures. Pricing fees at this URL..
Property, Taxation Records   Access to GIS/mapping free at http://data.idahoparcels.us/www/rib/franklin.html.

Fremont County   *Recorded Documents*   www.co.fremont.id.us/departments/clerk/index.htm   Access to records for a fee at www.canaanllc.com/index.php/canaanonline/availablecounties.   Email contact Chris Bowman at cbowman@titlefc.com for posting procedures. Pricing fees at this URL.
Property, Taxation Records   Access to maps and tax assessor data free at http://maps.greenwoodmap.com/fremontid/.

Gem County   *Property, Taxation Records*   Access to property search and new parcel number search for free at www.co.gem.id.us/assessor/default.htm.

Gooding County   *Recorded Documents*   www.goodingcounty.org/151/Clerk-Auditor-Recorder   Access to records for a fee at www.canaanllc.com/index.php/canaanonline/availablecounties.   Email contact Chris Bowman at cbowman@titlefc.com for posting procedures. Pricing fees at this URL.
Property, Taxation Records   Access to GIS/mapping free at http://gooding.idahoparcels.us/.

Idaho County   *Property, Taxation Records*   Access to the county parcels for free at http://idaho.idahoparcels.us/.

Jefferson County   *Recorded Documents*   www.co.jefferson.id.us/clerk.php   Access to records for a fee at www.canaanllc.com/index.php/canaanonline/availablecounties.   Email contact Chris Bowman at cbowman@titlefc.com for posting procedures. Pricing fees at this URL.
Property, Taxation Records   Access to GIS/mapping free at www.co.jefferson.id.us/gis_mapping.php.

Jerome County *Recorded Documents* www.jeromecountyid.us/index.asp?Type=B_BASIC&SEC={10D4A0A1-0FDB-41DC-BE28-77AF1096A206} Access to records for a fee at www.canaanllc.com/index.php/canaanonline/availablecounties. Email contact Chris Bowman at cbowman@titlefc.com for posting procedures. Pricing fees at this URL.
Property, Taxation Records Access to GIS/mapping for free at http://jerome.idahoparcels.us/.

Kootenai County *Recorded Documents* www.co.kootenai.id.us/departments/recorder/ Access to records for a fee at www.canaanllc.com/index.php/canaanonline/availablecounties. Email contact Chris Bowman at cbowman@titlefc.com for posting procedures. Pricing fees at this URL.
Property, Taxation Records Access assessor data free on the mapping site at www.kcgov.us/departments/mapping/mapSearch/. Login as Guest to search without registration.

Latah County *Property, Taxation Records* Access to plat maps of (incorporated cities, rural section and rural subdivisions is free at https://www.latah.id.us/assessor/Assessor_Plat_Map/disclaimer_form.php.

Lemhi County *Recorded Documents* www.lemhicountyidaho.org/clerkauditors.htm Subscription service available, Contact Terri or Brenda at above listed number.
Property, Taxation Records Access to GIS/mapping free at http://data.idahoparcels.us/www/rib/lemhi.html.

Lewis County *Property, Taxation Records* Access property data for free at http://data.idahoparcels.us/www/rib/lewis.html.

Lincoln County *Recorded Documents* www.lincolncountyid.us/page3.php Access to records for a fee at www.canaanllc.com/index.php/canaanonline/availablecounties. Email contact Chris Bowman at cbowman@titlefc.com for posting procedures. Pricing fees at this URL.

Madison County *Recorded Documents* www.co.madison.id.us/index.php/depts/clerk Access to records for a fee at www.canaanllc.com/index.php/canaanonline/availablecounties. Email contact Chris Bowman at cbowman@titlefc.com for posting procedures. Pricing fees at this URL.
Property, Taxation Records Access to GIS/mapping for free at http://rexburg.org/pages/GIS.

Minidoka County *Recorded Documents* www.minidoka.id.us/clerk-auditor-recorder/default.htm Access to records for a fee at www.canaanllc.com/index.php/canaanonline/availablecounties. Email contact Chris Bowman at cbowman@titlefc.com for posting procedures. Pricing fees at this URL.

Nez Perce County *Recorded Documents* www.co.nezperce.id.us/ElectedOfficials/ClerkAuditor/Recorder.aspx Access to records for a fee at www.canaanllc.com/index.php/canaanonline/availablecounties. Email contact Chris Bowman at cbowman@titlefc.com for posting procedures. Pricing fees at this URL. *Property, Taxation Records* Maps may be used at ftp://ftp.co.nezperce.id.us/Assessor/.

Owyhee County *Property, Taxation Records* Access to parcel maps for free at http://data.idahoparcels.us/www/rib/owyhee.html.

Payette County *Recorded Documents* www.payettecounty.org/index.php/clerk Access to recorded documents is free at www.payettecounty.org/index.php/clerk/recorded-documents.
Property, Taxation Records Access to property tax information for free to go www.payettecounty.org/index.php/treasurer/property-tax-information. User ID is: guest_id-payette-assessor and Password is: manatron. Also, access to GIS/Mapping for free at http://data.idahoparcels.us/www/rib/payette.html.

Power County *Recorded Documents* Access to records for a fee at www.canaanllc.com/index.php/canaanonline/availablecounties. Email contact Chris Bowman at cbowman@titlefc.com for posting procedures. Pricing fees at this URL.

Shoshone County *Recorded Documents* www.shoshonecounty.org/index.php Access to records for a fee at www.canaanllc.com/index.php/canaanonline/availablecounties. Email contact Chris Bowman at cbowman@titlefc.com for posting procedures. Pricing fees at this URL.
Property, Taxation Records Access to GIS/mapping free at https://6e88028fbb0e8bcadb45296ce0a4b9de45f305ce.googledrive.com/host/0B0J_A50xWBAqNHZqVlUxSkNUbWs/Shoshone.html.

Teton County *Recorded Documents* www.tetoncountyidaho.gov/department.php?deptID=5&menuID=1 Access to records for a fee at www.canaanllc.com/index.php/canaanonline/availablecounties. Email contact Chris Bowman at cbowman@titlefc.com for posting procedures. Pricing fees at this URL.

Twin Falls County *Recorded Documents* www.twinfallscounty.org/clerk/ Access to records for a fee at www.canaanllc.com/index.php/canaanonline/availablecounties. Email contact Chris Bowman at cbowman@titlefc.com for posting procedures. Pricing fees at this URL.

Valley County *Recorded Documents* www.co.valley.id.us/departments/clerk/ Access to records for a fee at www.canaanllc.com/index.php/canaanonline/availablecounties. Email contact Chris Bowman at cbowman@titlefc.com for posting procedures. Pricing fees at this URL.

Illinois

Capital: Springfield
          Sangamon County
Time Zone: CST
Population: 12,859,995
# of Counties: 102

Useful State Links
Website: **www.illinois.gov**
Governor: **www.illinois.gov/gov/Pages/default.aspx**
Attorney General: **www.ag.state.il.us**
State Archives: **www.cyberdriveillinois.com/departments/archives/databases/home.html**
State Statutes and Codes: **www.ilga.gov/legislation/ilcs/ilcs.asp**
Legislative Bill Search: **www.ilga.gov/legislation/default.asp**
Unclaimed Funds: **https://icash.illinoistreasurer.gov/**

State Public Record Agencies

Criminal Records
IL State Police Bureau of Identification, Bureau of Identification,   www.isp.state.il.us/crimhistory/chri.cfm   Name based inquiries are available through the Criminal History Information Response Process (CHIRP), The fee is $10.00 for a name check It takes about one month to set up an account. Upon signing an interagency agreement with ISP and establishing an escrow account, users can submit inquiries by email. Responses are sent back in 24 to 48 hours by either email or fax. Users must be able to receive electronic encrypted responses. Visit https://chirp.isp.state.il.us/TruePassSample/AuthenticateUserRoamingEPF.html for enrollment info. If questions, then call 815-740-5160. There is a free search for entities that have participated in methamphetamine manufacturing - go to www.isp.state.il.us/meth/.

Sexual Offender Registry
Illinois State Police, SOR Unit,   www.isp.state.il.us/sor/   The home page (www.isp.state.il.us/sor/) provides an online listing of sex offenders required to register in the State of Illinois. The database is updated daily and allows searching by name, city, county, or ZIP Code.

Incarceration Records
Illinois Department of Corrections,   www.illinois.gov/health-safety/Pages/PoliceAndPrisons.aspx   An inmate search is offered at www.illinois.gov/IDOC/OFFENDER/Pages/InmateSearch.aspx.   *Other Options:* A CD of data since 1982 may be purchased for $45. Send request to FOIA Officer at address above.

Corporation, LLC, LP, LLP, LLLP, RLLP, Trade Names, Assumed Name
Department of Business Services, Corporate Department,   www.ilsos.net/departments/business_services/home.html   The website gives free access to corporate and LLC status at www.ilsos.gov/corporatellc/. A commercial access program is also available. Fees vary. Potential users must submit in writing the purpose of the request. Submit your request to become involved in this program to the Director's Office. Search the database for registrations of LP, LLP, LLLP, and RLLP at www.ilsos.gov/lprpsearch/.   *Other Options:* List or bulk file purchases are available. Contact the Director's office for details.

Uniform Commercial Code, Federal Tax Liens
Secretary of State, UCC Division,   www.cyberdriveillinois.com/departments/business_services/uniform_commercial_code/ucc_instructions.html   An index search is offered at www.ilsos.gov/UCC/. No images are available.   *Other Options:* The entire database can be purchased and for $2500 with weekly updates at $200 per week. A CD update service for images is available for $250 per month.

Sales Tax Registrations
Revenue Department, Sales & Use Tax Services,   www.tax.illinois.gov/   One may verify a registered business at https://www.revenue.state.il.us/app/bgii/. Either an IL tax number or license number for FUIN is needed.

Birth Certificates

IL Department of Public Health, Division of Vital Records,   www.idph.state.il.us/vitalrecords/default.htm   Records may requested from www.vitalchek.com, a state-endorsed vendor. Also, detailed instructions are at the website. Requests are processed within 3-5 days.

Death Records

IL Department of Public Health, Division of Vital Records,   www.idph.state.il.us/vitalrecords/deaths/Pages/default.htm   Records may be requested from www.vitalchek.com, a state-endorsed vendor. Detailed instructions are at the website. Also, the state archives database of Illinois Death Certificates 1916-1950 is available free at www.cyberdriveillinois.com/departments/archives/databases/idphdeathindex.html.

Marriage Certificates, Divorce Records

Department of Public Health, Division of Vital Records,   www.idph.state.il.us/vitalrecords/default.htm   Find record for a fee at https://www.vitalchek.com/vital-records/illinois/illinois-dept-of-public-health?click_id=567735461817679874&ppc=0. There is a free online search of a statewide   Marriage   Index   for   1763-1900   found   at   the   Illinois   State   Archives   website   at www.cyberdriveillinois.com/departments/archives/databases/marriage.html.

Workers' Compensation Records

IL Workers' Compensation Commission,   www.iwcc.il.gov   Case information for any case is available at www.iwcc.il.gov/caseinfo.htm. You can obtain information online for all open and closed cases, starting with cases that were open when the mainframe computer system started in 1983. You can search by employee name, employer name, or case number.

Driver Records

Abstract Information Unit, Drivers Services Department,   www.cyberdriveillinois.com/   Find record for a fee at https://www.vitalchek.com/vital-records/illinois/illinois-dept-of-public-health?click_id=567735461817679874&ppc=0. A program for high volume, approved users is available. Records are $12.00 each. Call 217-785-3094 for further information. Also, there is a special, free page that parents or guardians may use to view the driving record of their children under 18. Go to https://www.ilsos.gov/parentalaccess/.   Other Options: Overnight cartridge batch processing may be available to high volume users (there is a 200 request minimum per day). Call 217-785-3094 for more information.

Vehicle Ownership & Registration

Vehicle Services Department, Vehicle Record Inquiry,   www.cyberdriveillinois.com/departments/vehicles/home.html   Online access to records is not available, but Illinois provides a free Title and Registration Status Inquiry at www.ilsos.gov/regstatus. Must enter the VIN.   Other Options: This agency will sell customized, bulk requests upon approval of purpose and with a signed contract. Contact the Data Processing Division in Room 400.

Crash Reports

Illinois State Police, Patrol Records Section,   www.isp.state.il.us   One may request and pay for a copy of a crash report online using a credit card. Go to www.isp.state.il.us/traffic/crashreports.cfm. There is an additional $1.00 fee plus the $5.00 per record fee for this service. Credit cards are accepted for payment online. Using E-PAY, one may also request, pay for and receive the traffic crash report by email.

Voter Registration, Campaign Finance & Disclosure, PACs

IL State Board of Elections, Voter Registration Services,   www.elections.state.il.us   At www.elections.state.il.us/, click on the search option to find many   searchable   data   sets   dealing   campaign   finance   and   contributions.   Search   committees   and   PACs   at www.elections.state.il.us/CampaignDisclosure/CommitteeSearch.aspx.   A   general   contributions   search   is   at www.elections.state.il.us/campaigndisclosure/ContributionsSearchByAllContributions.aspx   One   may   verify   registration   at www.elections.il.gov/votinginformation/registrationlookup.aspx.

Occupational Licensing Boards

These licenses are all searchable at **https://ilesonline.idfpr.illinois.gov/DPR/Lookup/LicenseLookup.aspx**

Accountant-CPA (Public)	Environmental Health Practitioner	Occupational Aide
Acupuncturist	Funeral Director/Embalmer	Occupational Therapist
Architect	Geologist	Optometrist
Athletic Trainer/Agent	Interior Designer	Orthotist
Collection Agency	Landscape Architect	Osteopathic Physician
Counselor/Clinical Prof Counselor	Marriage & Family Therapist	Pedorthist
Dentist/Dental Hygienist	Massage Therapist	Perfusionist
Design Firm	Medical Corporation	Pharmacist/Pharmacy
Dietitian/Nutrition Counselor	Naprapath	Physical Aide
Engineer/Engineer Intern	Nurse-LPN/RN/APN	Physical Therapist/Assistant
Engineer/Structural	Nursing Home	Physician/Medical Doctor

Podiatrist
Polygraph/Deception Detect Examiner
Private Investigator
Private Security Contractor
Psychologist
Psychology Business

Rehabilitation Aide
Respiratory Care Practitioner
Roofer
Roofing Contractor
Shorthand Reporter
Social Worker

Speech-Language Pathologist
Surgical Technician
Surveyor/Land
Timeshare
Veterinarian

The Rest:

Alcohol Abuse Counselor ....www.iaodapca.org/?page_id=1075
Ambulatory Surgical Treatment Center ....www.idph.state.il.us/healthcarefacilities/astc.htm
Aquaculturist..www.dnr.illinois.gov/LPR/Pages/CommercialLicensesFees.aspx
Attorney ....https://www.iardc.org/lawyersearch.asp
Auctioneer...https://www.idfpr.com/LicenseLookUp/LicenseLookup.asp
Bank..www.obrelookupclear.state.il.us/default.asp
Bilingual Teacher, Transitional ....www.isbe.net/ELIS/default.htm
Bingo Operation...https://mytax.illinois.gov/_/
Boiler Repair Firms ....www.sfm.illinois.gov/Commercial/boilers/licensedrepair
Business Broker...www.ilsos.gov/brokersearch/
Business Opportunity Offering......................www.ilsos.gov/brokersearch/
Charitable Game..https://mytax.illinois.gov/_/
Check Seller/Distributor...............................https://www.idfpr.com/LicenseLookUp/LicenseLookup.asp
Driver Training School..................www.cyberdriveillinois.com/departments/drivers/driver_education/commercial_driver_training/cdlcertschools.pdf
Early Childhood Teacher ....www.isbe.net/ELIS/default.htm
Elevator Contractor/Inspector/Company ....www.sfm.illinois.gov/Commercial/Elevators/Elevator-Contractors-Inspectors-and-Inspection-Companies
Fire Equipment Distributor www.sfm.illinois.gov/Portals/0/docs/FirePreventionDocs/FireEquipmentDistributors.pdf
Fish Dealer ....www.dnr.illinois.gov/LPR/Pages/CommercialLicensesFees.aspx
Fisherman, Commercial................................www.dnr.illinois.gov/LPR/Pages/CommercialLicensesFees.aspx
Gambling Addiction Counselor ....www.iaodapca.org/?page_id=1075
Gaming/Gambling Supplier...........................www.igb.illinois.gov/RiverboatSuppliers.aspx
Home Health Aide (CNAs-ASHHA) ....www.idph.state.il.us/nar/home.htm
Home Health Care Agency ....www.idph.state.il.us/healthcarefacilities/homehealth_list.htm#hha
Home Inspector ....https://www.idfpr.com/LicenseLookUp/LicenseLookup.asp
Hospital...www.idph.state.il.us/healthcarefacilities/hospital_list.htm
Hunting Area Operator..................................www.dnr.illinois.gov/LPR/Pages/CommercialLicensesFees.aspx
Insurance Producer ....https://sbs-il.naic.org/Lion-Web/jsp/sbsreports/AgentLookup.jsp
Lead Contractor...http://dph.illinois.gov/licensing-certification?page=2
Lead Risk Assessor/Insp/Supr ....http://dph.illinois.gov/licensing-certification?page=2
Lead Training Provider ....http://dph.illinois.gov/licensing-certification?page=2
Liquor License, Retail/Dist/Mfg.....................www.illinois.gov/ilcc/SitePages/LicenseLookup.aspx
Loan Broker ....www.ilsos.gov/brokersearch/
Lobbyist ....www.cyberdriveillinois.com/departments/index/lobbyist/home.html
Long Term Care Insurance Firm ....https://sbs-il.naic.org/Lion-Web/jsp/sbsreports/AgentLookup.jsp
Mental Health Counselor ....www.iaodapca.org/?page_id=1075
Mortgage Banker/Broker...............................www.obrelookupclear.state.il.us/default.asp
Not Current Authorized Attorney ....https://www.iardc.org/home/rra_search.aspx
Notary Public ....www.ilsos.gov/notary/
Nurses Aide ....www.idph.state.il.us/nar/home.htm
Nursing Home Administrator ....https://www.idfpr.com/licenselookup/licenselookup.asp
Pawnbroker..https://www.idfpr.com/LicenseLookUp/LicenseLookup.asp
Police Trainer/Training Facility ....www.ptb.state.il.us/resources/ptb-id-lookup/
Pull Tab Operator ....https://mytax.illinois.gov/_/
Real Estate Agent/Broker/Seller...................https://www.idfpr.com/LicenseLookUp/LicenseLookup.asp
Real Estate Appraiser..................................https://www.idfpr.com/LicenseLookUp/LicenseLookup.asp
Red Tag Tank ....http://webapps.sfm.illinois.gov/ustsearch/Redtagtanks.aspx

Savings & Loan Association	https://www.idfpr.com/LicenseLookUp/LicenseLookup.asp
Savings Bank	https://www.idfpr.com/LicenseLookUp/LicenseLookup.asp
Special Teacher	www.isbe.net/ELIS/default.htm
Substance Abuse Counselor	www.iaodapca.org/?page_id=1075
Substitute Teacher	www.isbe.net/ELIS/default.htm
Taxidermist	www.dnr.illinois.gov/LPR/Pages/CommercialLicensesFees.aspx
Teacher	www.isbe.net/ELIS/default.htm
Timeshare/Land Sales	https://www.idfpr.com/LicenseLookUp/LicenseLookup.asp
Trust Company	www.obrelookupclear.state.il.us/default.asp
Underground Storage Tank	http://webapps.sfm.illinois.gov/ustsearch/Search.aspx
Video Gaming	www.igb.illinois.gov/VideoLists.aspx

State and Local Courts

About Illinois Courts: The **Circuit Court** is the Unified Trail Court in Illinois and has jurisdiction for all matters properly brought before it and shares jurisdiction with the Supreme Court to hear cases relating to revenue, mandamus, prohibition, and habeas corpus. Illinois is divided into twenty-four circuits. Six are single county circuits (Cook, Will, DuPage, Lake, McHenry, and Will) and the remaining eighteen circuits comprise as few as two and as many as twelve counties each. There are two types of judges in the Circuit Court: circuit judges and associate judges. Circuit judges, elected for six years, can hear any kind of case. An associate judge can hear any case, except criminal cases punishable by a prison term of one year or more (felonies).

Probate is handled by the Circuit Court in all counties.

The web page for the Judicial System is www.illinoiscourts.gov.

Appellate Courts: There are five Appellate Court Districts. Opinions and dockets for the Supreme and Appellate Courts are available from the home page shown above.

Online Court Access

There is no statewide public online system available to trial courts. However, at least 76 counties participate in some manner with a vendor - Judici.com.

About Judici.com

The site at www.judici.com provides a free index search and there is also a premium subscription service with more detailed information. The Multicourt program (subscription) allows a user to search for all participating courts on a single search. One may view case documents for approx. 30% of the participating courts. Available data includes: litigant information; criminal charges, dispositions, and sentences; civil judgments, and case minutes. Visit the site to find the participating counties; they are shown by map and with a drop-down box. There are plans to add more counties. There is also a separate subscription to obtain information about Wills.

Counties Participating on Judici.com:

Adams	Crawford	Iroquois	Marshall	Randolph
Alexander	Cumberland	Jackson	Mason	Richland
Bond	DeWitt	Jasper	Massac	Rock Island
Boone	Douglas	Jefferson	Mercer	Saline
Brown	Edgar	Jersey	Montgomery	Schuyler
Bureau	Edwards	Jo Daviess	Morgan	Scott
Calhoun	Effingham	Johnson	Moultrie	Shelby
Carroll	Fayette	Lawrence	Ogle	Stark
Cass	Ford	Lee	Perry	Stephenson
Christian	Franklin	Livingston	Piatt	Tazewell
Clark	Greene	Logan	Pike	Union
Clay	Grundy	Macon	Pope	Vermilion
Clinton	Hamilton	Macoupin	Pulaski	Wabash
Coles	Henry	Marion	Putnam	Warren

Washington   White   Williamson
Wayne   Whiteside   Woodford

Other County Online Sites:

Adams County
Circuit Court   www.co.adams.il.us/Circuit_Clerk/index.htm
Civil & Criminal: Direct email search requests to lgeschwander@co.adams.il.us. The county inmate list and warrant list is at the home page.

Cook County
Circuit Court - Civil Division   www.cookcountyclerkofcourt.org/?section=DDPage&DDPage=3700
Search full case dockets free at www.cookcountyclerkofcourt.org and click on Online Case Info. Among the choices are dockets, case snapshots, probate and traffic. Search by name, number, or date. Data includes attorneys, case type, filing date, the amount of damages sought, division/district, and most current court date. There is a Mobile App connection at www.cookcountyclerkofcourt.org/?section=MobileApp.
Circuit Court - Law Division   www.cookcountyclerkofcourt.org/?section=DDPage&DDPage=3300
Civil: Search full case dockets free at www.cookcountyclerkofcourt.org and click on Online Case Info. Be sure to choose Law in the Division name box. Search by name, number, or date. Data includes attorneys, case type, filing date, the amount of damages sought, division/district, and most current court date. There is a Mobile App connection at www.cookcountyclerkofcourt.org/?section=MobileApp.
Skokie District 2   www.cookcountyclerkofcourt.org/?section=DDPage&DDPage=2800
Civil: Online case information is available at www.cookcountyclerkofcourt.org. Click on Online Case Info. There are a number of searching options. There is a Mobile App connection at www.cookcountyclerkofcourt.org/?section=MobileApp.
Rolling Meadows District 3   www.cookcountyclerkofcourt.org/?section=DDPage&DDPage=2900
Civil: Online case information is available at www.cookcountyclerkofcourt.org. Click on Online Case Info. There are a number of searching options. Search by case number or name. There is a Mobile App connection at www.cookcountyclerkofcourt.org/?section=MobileApp.
Maywood District 4   www.cookcountyclerkofcourt.org/?section=DDPage&DDPage=3000
Civil: Online case information is available at www.cookcountyclerkofcourt.org. Click on Online Case Info. There are a number of searching options. There is a Mobile App connection at www.cookcountyclerkofcourt.org/?section=MobileApp.
Bridgeview District 5   www.cookcountyclerkofcourt.org/?section=DDPage&DDPage=3100
Civil: Online case information is available at www.cookcountyclerkofcourt.org. Click on Online Case Info. There are a number of searching options. There is a Mobile App connection at www.cookcountyclerkofcourt.org/?section=MobileApp.
Markham District 6   www.cookcountyclerkofcourt.org/?section=DDPage&DDPage=3200
Civil: Online case information is available at www.cookcountyclerkofcourt.org. Click on Online Case Info. There are a number of searching options. There is a Mobile App connection at www.cookcountyclerkofcourt.org/?section=MobileApp.

De Kalb County
Circuit Court   www.circuitclerk.org/
Civil: A free search of the index of records 2004 to present is athttp://gis.dekalbcounty.org/circuitclerkcourtdata/CircuitClerkCivilSearch.asp. The vendor subscription product is also offered (see description in Criminal Records section).   *Criminal:* A free search of the index is at http://gis.dekalbcounty.org/circuitclerkcourtdata/CircuitClerkSearch.asp. his website contains DeKalb County traffic and criminal cases filed in 2013 to present. Visit www.clericusmagnus.com or www.janojustice.com or call 800-250-9884 for details ands signup. Online access via subscription requires a setup fee plus annual subscription of $240 for this county, or $300/yr for all participating IL counties - Champaign, DeKalb, Kendall, LaSalle, Madison, Sangamon, Will.

Du Page County
Circuit Court   www.co.dupage.il.us/courtclerk/
Civil: The online site at https://www.dupagecase.com/Clerk/ is meant to find basic information. The disclaimer states '*ATTENTION - This site is not for research. It is to only be used by defendants for case payments or finding their next court date. All attorneys, researchers and other non-defendants should leave this site immediately and are advised to contact the Circuit Clerk's office. Failure to do so may cause the service to be suspended from you. *Criminal:* The online site at https://www.dupagecase.com/Clerk/ is meant to find basic information. The disclaimer states *ATTENTION - This site is not for research. It is to only be used by defendants for case payments or finding their next court date.

Jersey County
Circuit Court   www.jerseycounty-il.us
Civil: Current court records may be accessed free at http://66.117.103.46/jersey/caseinfo.htm. Also, online access is free at www.judici.com/. A premium fee service is also available with multi-county search capabilities and other features. Case files are available from 1990. *Criminal:* same

Kane County
Circuit Court   www.cic.co.kane.il.us
Civil: Online access at http://kocis.countyofkane.org/KOCIS/KOCIS.html#.   *Criminal:* Online access at http://kocis.countyofkane.org/KOCIS/KOCIS.html#. Electronic results may include DL u number.

Kankakee County

Circuit Court   www.co.kankakee.il.us/circuitclerk.html

Civil: Online access to the civil dockets is free at http://173.165.39.26/eservices/home.page. Note the data entry requirements if searching by case number. There are search options for range of DOB and File Date.   *Criminal:* Online access to the criminal dockets is free at http://173.165.39.26/eservices/home.page. Note the data entry requirements if searching by case number. Includes Traffic. There are search options for range of DOB and File Date.

Kendall County

Circuit Court   www.co.kendall.il.us/circuit-clerk/

Civil: A free record search is at www.co.kendall.il.us/circuit-clerk/online-court-records/. Also access to civil court records on a subscription basis is the same as criminal, see below.   *Criminal:* A free record search is at www.co.kendall.il.us/circuit-clerk/online-court-records/, includes traffic. Also, a subscription service is at www.clericusmagnus.com or www.janojustice.com or call 800-250-9884 for details ands signup. This requires a setup fee plus annual subscription of $240 for this county, or $300/yr for all participating IL counties - Champaign, DeKalb, Kendall, LaSalle, Madison, Sangamon, Will.

Knox County

Circuit Court   www.9thjudicial.org/Knox/knox-circuit-clerk.html

Civil: Access to case searches at www.9thjudicial.org/search.html. Can search by name or case number.   *Criminal:* same

La Salle County

Circuit Court - Civil Division   http://lasallecounty.com/

Civil: A vendor provides online access via subscription is a $59 setup fee plus annual subscription of $240 for this county, or $300/yr for all counties - Champaign, Dekalb, Kendall, Madison, Sangamon, Will and Winnebago. Visit www.clericusmagnus.com/. A less powerful, free site is available at http://lasallecounty.com/online-court-records-2/. Search by case number, name of DL number.

Circuit Court - Criminal Division   http://lasallecounty.com/

Criminal: Online access via subscription requires a setup fee plus annual subscription of $240 for this county, or $300/yr for all participating IL counties - Champaign, DeKalb, Kendall, LaSalle, Madison, Sangamon, Will. Visit www.clericusmagnus.com or www.janojustice.com or call 800-250-9884 for details and signup. A less powerful, free site is available at http://lasallecounty.com/online-court-records-2/. Search by case number, name of DL number.

Lake County

Circuit Court   www.lakecountycircuitclerk.org/

Civil: Online access is at https://circuitclerk.lakecountyil.gov/publicAccess/html/common/index.xhtml. Includes certain traffic records. There is a strong disclaimer including a statement that that data cannot be used for commercial resale. Use caution depending on level of due diligence needed. There is alos an enhanced subscription product at www.lakecountycircuitclerk.org/enhanced-access. Fees are based on number of users starting at $240 for one user. Uses PayPal.   *Criminal:* same There is also an enhanced subscription product at www.lakecountycircuitclerk.org/enhanced-access. Fees are based on number of users starting at $240 for one user. Uses PayPal.

Macon County

Circuit Court   www.cclerk.co.macon.il.us/

Civil: Access to court records is free at http://search.co.macon.il.us/templates/searchcaseinfo.htm. Search docket information back to 04/96. Includes traffic, probate, family, small claims. Online access is free at www.judici.com/. A premium fee service is also available with multi-county search capabilities and other features.   *Criminal:* Access to court records is free online at http://search.co.macon.il.us/templates/searchcaseinfo.htm. Search docket information back to 04/96.

Madison County

Circuit Court - Civil/Misdemeanor Division   www.co.madison.il.us/departments/circuit_court/index.php

Civil: A free docket search is offered at http://madisoncountycircuitclerkil.org/index.php/court-records-search. Search by name, case number or DL#. A vendor provides online access via subscription is a $59 setup fee plus annual subscription of $240 for this county, or $300/yr for all 7 counties - Champaign, Dekalb, Kendall, Madison, Sangamon, Will and Winnebago. Visit www.clericusmagnus.com/.   *Criminal:* Online access to misdemeanor records is free at http://madisoncountycircuitclerkil.org/index.php/court-records-search. Search by name, case number or DL#. Note - Felony records are also included.

Circuit Court - Felony Division   www.co.madison.il.us/departments/circuit_court/criminal_court.php

Criminal: A   free   docket   search   is   offered   at   www.co.madison.il.us/CircuitClerk/eMagnusLite.shtml   or http://madisoncountycircuitclerkil.org/index.php/court-records-search. Search by name, case number or DL#. Online access via subscription requires a setup fee plus annual subscription of $240 for this county, or $300/yr for participating IL counties - Champaign, DeKalb, Kendall, LaSalle, Madison, Sangamon, Will. Visit www.clericusmagnus.com.

McHenry County

Circuit Court   https://www.co.mchenry.il.us/county-government/courts

Civil: Free docket search to civil, traffic and domestic at http://68.21.116.46/wow65/runApp?id=0. Search by name or case number. One may order copies online from the home page, same copy and search fees apply. Use caution. The User is expressly prohibited from reproducing, publishing on-line, selling, reselling or otherwise disseminating data or information accessed pursuant to this Agreement. The information accessed is not intended or permitted to be used for commercial resale.   *Criminal:* Free docket search is at http://68.21.116.46/wow65/runApp?id=0. Use caution. The User is expressly prohibited from reproducing, publishing on-line, selling, reselling or otherwise disseminating data or information accessed pursuant to this Agreement. The information accessed is not intended or permitted to be used for commercial resale. For complete case file information, access to records on the subscription system requires $750 license fee and $92.50 set-up fee, plus $50 per month. Records date back to 1990 with civil, criminal, probate, traffic, and domestic records. For more info, call 815-334-4302.

McLean County
Circuit Court   www.mcleancountyil.gov
Civil: See http://webapp.mcleancountyil.gov/%28X%281%29S%2840clyje35gtjwjyyuoio533t%29%29/webapps/PublicAccess/PubAC_SearchCivil.aspx. Search by name, business name, or case number. However the thruput is limited. Closed cases are only included for the past year, but all open cases are shown some even going back to 2008. Should a name and case number appear with a no information available message, a written inquiry including the name and case number should be submitted to the Circuit Clerk.   *Criminal:* Free public access at hhttp://webapp.mcleancountyil.gov/webapps/PublicAccess/PubAC_SearchCriminal.aspx. The system has traffic as well as criminal index. Dockets from the Circuit Clerk are available from 1991-present.

Peoria County
Circuit Court   www.peoriacounty.org/circuitclerk/
Civil: Access to docket index free at http://justice.peoriacounty.org/default.aspx. Search by name, case number or attorney for Civil, Family or probate records. Few if any identifiers are shown.   *Criminal:* Access to docket index free at http://justice.peoriacounty.org/default.aspx. Search by name, case number or attorney for criminal or traffic records. One may search jail records from this site also. Few if any identifiers are shown.

Perry County
Circuit Court   www.illinoiscourts.gov/circuitcourt/circuitmap/20th.asp#Perry
Civil: Online access is free at www.judici.com/. A premium fee service is also available with multi-county search capabilities and other features. *Criminal:* same

Rock Island County
Circuit Court   www.rockislandcounty.org/CircuitClerk/CivilDiv/Home/
Civil: Full access to court records on the remote online system requires contract and fees. Civil, criminal, probate, traffic, and domestic records can be accessed by name or case number. Online access is free at www.judici.com/. A premium fee service is also available with multi-county search capabilities and other features. Case files are available from 1989. *Criminal:* same

Sangamon County
Circuit Court   www.sangamoncountycircuitclerk.org
Civil: Online access via subscription requires a setup fee plus annual subscription of $240 for this county, or $300/yr for all participating IL counties - Champaign, DeKalb, Kendall, LaSalle, Madison, Sangamon, Will. Visit www.clericusmagnus.com or www.janojustice.com or call 800-250-9884 for details and signup. A free search is also offered at http://67.128.239.91/sccc/Home.sc, but this is a limited search and not official unless certified, but does include images for some records. A daily court docket is found at www.infax.com/docket/sangamoncountydocket/. *Criminal:* same

St. Clair County
Circuit Court   www.circuitclerk.co.st-clair.il.us/Pages/default.aspx
Civil: Search the court index online at www.circuitclerk.co.st-clair.il.us/courts/Pages/icj.aspx.   *Criminal:* same

Warren County
Circuit Court   www.9thjudicial.org/Warren/warren-circuit-clerk.html
Civil: Access to case searches at www.9thjudicial.org/search.html. Can search by name or case number. Online access is free at www.judici.com/. A premium fee service is also available with multi-county search capabilities and other features.   *Criminal:* same

Will County
Circuit Court   www.circuitclerkofwillcounty.com/
Civil: Online access to civil court records is at https://ipublic.il12th.org/SearchPrompt.php. *Criminal:* same

Winnebago County
Circuit Court   www.cc.co.winnebago.il.us
Civil: Online access to civil court records is at http://fce.wincoil.us/fullcourtweb/start.do.   One may also request documents online at https://www.cc.co.winnebago.il.us/document-requests/.   Same fees apply as onsite.   *Criminal:* Online access is at http://fce.wincoil.us/fullcourtweb/start.do.   Search by party name or case number.   One may also request documents online at https://www.cc.co.winnebago.il.us/document-requests/. Same fees apply as onsite.

Recorders, Assessors, and Other Sites of Note

About Illinois Recording Offices: 102 counties, 102 recording offices. The recording officer is the County Recorder, but some counties prefer the name Recorder of Deeds. In some counties the two positions are combined as the County Clerk and Recorder. Cook County had separate offices for real estate recording and UCC filing until they combined offices June 30, 2001. Since that date only UCC extension, amendments or terminations can be filed on exisiting UCCs, with exception of UCCs on real estate related collateral whch are still filed here.

About Tax Liens: Federal tax liens on personal property of businesses are filed with the Secretary of State. Other federal and all state tax liens on personal property are filed with the County Recorder.

Online Access

Recorded Documents

A number of counties offer online access. There is no statewide system, but there is an agency-supported vendor for the 43 counties shown below. The county works with https://tapestry.fidlar.com/Tapestry2/Default.aspx for record access. The base fee is $5.95 per search and $.50 per print image, but the county may set their own pricing. You can pay as you go using a credit or pre-pay using a subscription. Also, per the same vendor one may purchase a software program called Laredo (www.fidlar.com/laredo.aspx) with extensive search features. Contact the county for details and pricing.

Counties participating on the Laredo or Tapestry System.

Adams	De Witt	La Salle	Randolph
Boone	Du Page	Lee	Rock Island
Bureau	Edgar	Livingston	Sangamon
Carroll	Fulton	Logan	Shelby
Cass	Henry	Madison	St. Clair
Champaign	Iroquois	McHenry	Vermilion
Christian	Jackson	Monroe	Warren
Clinton	Jefferson	Montgomery	Whiteside
Coles	Jo Daviess	Moultrie	Will
Cook	Kankakee	Ogle	Winnebago
Crawford	Knox	Perry	

Assessor Records

Many counties offer online access to tax assessor records and/or GIS data. There is no statewide system.

County Sites (Profiles do not include counties participating on the Tapestry & Laredo System, shown above.)

Adams County *Property, Taxation Records*   Access to property tax inquiry for free at http://illinoisassessors.com/. Also, access to the property tax online inquiry for free at http://taxrecords.co.adams.il.us/.

Boone County *Property, Taxation Records*   Access to property data is free at http://booneil.devnetwedge.com/. Also, Access to GIS/mapping free at www.boonecountyil.org/department/gis. Access land data on commercial site - PropertyMax - at http://booneilpropertymax.governmaxa.com/propertymax/rover30.asp. Subscription packages from $20.00 per month.

Brown County *Property, Taxation Records*   Access to parcels and GIS/mapping for free at http://gis.browncountyengineer.org/MAPS-2015/MAP-GENERAL.aspx.

Bureau County *Property, Taxation Records*   Access to property tax, parcel info and property sales for free at www.fikeandfike.com/propertytax/home/Disclaimer.aspx?c=6.

Carroll County *Property, Taxation Records*   Access to Assessor parcel data for free at http://carroll.illinoisassessors.com/search.php.

Cass County *Property, Taxation Records*   Search assessor property data for a fee on the GIS system at https://beacon.schneidercorp.com/.

Champaign County *Property, Taxation Records*   Search property tax records free at www.co.champaign.il.us/ccao/Assessors.htm. Also, search the treasurer's real estate property tax database free at www.co.champaign.il.us/taxlookup, but no name searching. Also, access to GIS/mapping for free at www.maps.ccgisc.org.

Christian County *Property, Taxation Records*   Access to property tax data for free at www.fikeandfike.com/propertytax/Home/Disclaimer.aspx?c=11. Also, access to a parcel search for free at http://christian.il.bhamaps.com/.

Clark County *Recorded Documents* www.clarkcountyil.org/clerk.htm   Access to records for a fee at https://cotthosting.com/ILPortal/User/Login.aspx. Index records from 1/1/2005 to present; Images from 1/3/2005 to present.
Property, Taxation Records   Access to GIS/mapping free at http://clark.il.bhamaps.com/.

Clay County *Recorded Documents* http://claycountyillinois.org/clerkrecorder/   Access to records for free (limited) at https://esearch.cichosting.com/. For detailed information, must subscribe.
Property, Taxation Records   Access to GIS/mapping for free at http://clayil.mygisonline.com/.

Clinton County   *Property, Taxation Records*   Access to property search for free at http://il-clinton-assessor.governmax.com/svc/default.asp

Coles County   *Property, Taxation Records*   Access property tax data free at http://colesil.devnetwedge.com/. Also, access to GIS/mapping for free at www.co.coles.il.us/flexviewers/TaxMapViewer/.

Cook County   *Property, Taxation Records*   Access to property tax inquiry for free at http://illinoisassessors.com/. Also, search assessor data at www.cookcountyassessor.com/ but no name searching.

Crawford County   *Property, Taxation Records*   Access to property sales reports for free at www.crawfordcountycentral.com/webedit/index.php?p=assessor_sales&t=table. Also, access to GIS/mapping for free at http://crawfordil.mygisonline.com/?_h=true.

Cumberland County   *Property, Taxation Records*   Access to GIS/mapping for free at http://cumberland.il.bhamaps.com/.

De Kalb County   *Recorded Documents*   http://dekalbcounty.org/CoClerk/index.html   Access to records for free at http://lrs.dekalbrecorder.com/. Must create an account and sign-in.
Property, Taxation Records   Search property assessor data free at http://dekalbcounty.org/GIS/TASDisclaimer.html. Also, access to property tax inquiry for free at http://illinoisassessors.com/. Also, access to GIS/mapping free at http://dekalbcounty.org/GIS/GISWebDisclaimer.html.

De Witt County   *Property, Taxation Records*   Access property tax data free at www.fikeandfike.com/propertytax/home/Disclaimer.aspx?c=20. Also, access to GIS/mapping for free at https://dewittil.mygisonline.com/#.

Douglas County   *Property, Taxation Records*   Access to record searches for free at http://douglas.illinoisassessors.com/. Subscription available for advanced searches and advanced parcel searches for a fee. Must be registered, there is a log-in.

Du Page County   *Property, Taxation Records*   Search Wheatland Township records at http://wheatlandassessor.com/SD/wlt/content/default.aspx?ID=6. Search Wayne Township records at www.waynetownshipassessor.com/. Search Bloomingdale Township property records at www.bloomingdaletownshipassessor.com/SD/BT/content/default.aspx. Search Addison Township records at http://addisontownship.com/SD/addison/content/Detail.aspx?ID=2&CID=893fc6c7-629a-4b82-bf31-955cedae7efc. No name searches in any of these sites.

Edgar County   *Property, Taxation Records*   Access to the property search site for free at http://il-edgar-county.publicaccessnow.com/PropertySearch.aspx.

Effingham County   *Property, Taxation Records*   Access to property taxes for free at http://propertyinquiry.co.effingham.il.us/.

Fayette County   *Recorded Documents*   www.fayettecountyillinois.org/2160/County-Clerk-Recorder   Access to records for free (limited) at https://esearch.cichosting.com/. For detailed information, must subscribe.
Property, Taxation Records   Access to GIS/mapping for free at https://fayetteil.mygisonline.com/.

Ford County   *Property, Taxation Records*   Search property data free ot two locations: old serach at http://il-ford-assessor.governmax.com/svc/; new search at https://il985.cichosting.com/atasportal/. Also, access to GIS/mapping for free at http://fordil.mygisonline.com/.

Gallatin County   *Recorded Documents*   Access to records for a fee at https://cotthosting.com/ILPortal/User/Login.aspx. Index from 3/1/1991 to present, images from 4/3/2006 to present.

Grundy County   *Recorded Documents*   www.grundyco.org/county-clerkrecorder/   Access to records for free (limited) at https://esearch.cichosting.com/. For detailed records, must subscribe.
Property, Taxation Records   The county assessor's official search site is www.grundycntysa.org/. A vendor has a site at www.fikeandfike.com/propertytax/Grundy/Inquiry.aspx?c=32.

Hamilton County   *Recorded Documents*   Access to recorded documents for a fee at https://cotthosting.com/ilhamiltonexternal/User/Login.aspx. Must contact the Recorder's office for contract.

Hancock County   *Property, Taxation Records*   Search by name, address, or parcel number at http://hancockil.devnetwedge.com/. Also, access to property tax inquiry for free at http://illinoisassessors.com/.

Henderson County   *Property, Taxation Records*   Access to Assessor's database information free at http://henderson.illinoisassessors.com/search.php.

Henry County   *Property, Taxation Records*   Access to the assessor property inquiry database is free at www.henrycty.com/Departments/Assessments/Online-Mapping-and-Property-Inquiry. Access the treasurer's tax payment data free at www.henrycty.com/Departments/Treasurer-Property-Taxes. Search county foreclosure list free at https://www.foreclosure.com/search.html?rsp=6252&st=IL&cno=073.

Jackson County *Property, Taxation Records* Access to property tax for free at http://jacksonil.devnetwedge.com/. Also, access to GIS/mapping for free at http://jackson.il.bhamaps.com/.

Jasper County *Property, Taxation Records* Also, access to property tax inquiry for free at http://illinoisassessors.com/.

Jersey County *Property, Taxation Records* Access to records for free at http://jersey.il.bhamaps.com/.

Johnson County *Recorded Documents* Access to records for a fee at https://esearch.cichosting.com/. Must subscribe.

Kane County *Recorded Documents* www.kanecountyrecorder.net/ Access recorders real estate records free at http://lrs.kanecountyrecorder.net/. Documents printed at the website are unofficial and the Recorder's Office cannot guarantee they will be considered legal in a court of law. Official documents may be acquired at the Recorder's Office.
Property, Taxation Records Search the Tax Assessment database at http://kaneapplications.countyofkane.org/taxassessor//. Search by parcel number or address only; no name searching. Access to GIS/mapping for free at http://gistech.countyofkane.org/kanegis/kanegis.html#.

Kankakee County *Property, Taxation Records* The Treasurer offers a free property inquiry at http://treasurer.k3county.net/. Also, limited access to GIS/mapping for free at www.k3gis.com/. Subscription allows more functionality and information than the free site.

Kendall County *Recorded Documents* www.kendallcountyrecorder.net/ Access to land records free at www.kendallcountyrecorder.net/lrs/Source/Home.aspx.
Property, Taxation Records Search property data/GIS Viewer for free at http://gis.co.kendall.il.us/GISViewer_Gallery.aspx?/#CAMA.

Knox County *Property, Taxation Records* Access to records for free at http://taxinq.knoxtreasurer.org/.

La Salle County *Property, Taxation Records* Property tax data available at www.fikeandfike.com/propertytax/LaSalle/Inquiry.aspx?c=50.

Lake County *Recorded Documents* www.lakecountyil.gov/258/Recorder-of-Deeds Access to county recorded documents is by subscription; Index back to 1980; images back to 1800's. See website for information.
Property, Taxation Records Search property by address or legal description for free on the GIS-mapping site at http://maps.lakecountyil.gov/mapsonline/. Also, access to property tax inquiry for free at http://illinoisassessors.com/.

Lawrence County *Property, Taxation Records* Also, access to property tax inquiry for free at http://illinoisassessors.com/.

Lee County *Property, Taxation Records* Access to GIS/mapping for free at www.leecountyil.com/index.php?option=com_content&view=article&id=141.

Livingston County *Property, Taxation Records* Free parcel search at http://livingston.illinoisassessors.com/search.php. For more detailed information, must subscribe for a fee. Contact the assessor's office for subscription information.

Logan County *Property, Taxation Records* Search the tax assessor database at http://loganil.devnetwedge.com/. Access to GIS/mapping free at www.centralilmaps.com/LoganGIS/.

Macon County *Recorded Documents* www.co.macon.il.us/recorder.php Searching recorded data free at www.recorder.co.macon.il.us/Rap/Search.aspx. A subscription service is also available, see www.recorder.co.macon.il.us/Rap/registerlogin.aspx.
Property, Taxation Records Access the county GIS mapping site by address at http://maconcounty.maps.arcgis.com/apps/Solutions/s2.html?appid=e34e6e8d49e446ebb3d4922e5f4feb9a. A vendor proviodes access to property tax records at www.fikeandfike.com/propertytax/Macon/Inquiry.aspx?c=55.

Macoupin County *Recorded Documents* www.macoupincountyil.gov/county_clerk.htm Recorded land documents, including images, will be available from 1/1/2001 to present. The account will have a username and password. Fees are 30 day Sub=$25.00, 180 day Sub=$125.00 and 1 year Sub=$200.00. Call the Recorder's office at X708 to set up account. The search site is at www.macoupincountyil.gov/county_clerk_remote.htm.
Property, Taxation Records Access to parcel search for free at http://macoupin.il.bhamaps.com/.

Madison County *Property, Taxation Records* Access tax data and Mapping for free at www.co.madison.il.us/departments/chief_county_assesment_office/index.php. Also, access to property tax inquiry for free at http://illinoisassessors.com/.

Marion County *Recorded Documents* www.assessorsoffice.net/countyappraisal.asp?state=Illinois&county=Marion Access to records for free (limited) at https://esearch.cichosting.com/. For detailed records, must subscribe.
Property, Taxation Records Access to GIS/mapping free at http://marionil.mygisonline.com/. Also, access to property tax inquiry for free at http://illinoisassessors.com/.

Marshall County *Property, Taxation Records* Access to property tax inquiry for free at http://illinoisassessors.com/. Also, access to property tax data free at www.fikeandfike.com/propertytax/Marshall/MainMenu.aspx?c=59.

Mason County *Property, Taxation Records* Access to parcel data and Parcel File free at www.masoncountyil.org/assessment.htm.

Massac County *Recorded Documents*   Access to records for a fee at
https://cotthosting.com/ILPortal/User/Login.aspx?ReturnUrl=%2filportal%2fIndex.aspx. Index from 1/2/1991 to present, images from 2/29/1992 to present.
Property, Taxation Records   Also, access to property tax inquiry for free at http://illinoisassessors.com/.

McHenry County *Recorded Documents*   Access to land record search free at http://68.21.116.60/freewebsearch/default.aspx.
Property, Taxation Records   Records on the County Treasurer Inquiry site are free at https://www.co.mchenry.il.us/county-government/departments-j-z/treasurer. Sheriff's foreclosure list is free at www.mchenrysheriff.org/side-nav-pages/side-nav-item-5.aspx.

McLean County *Recorded Documents*   www.mcleancountyil.gov/index.aspx?nid=791   Access recorder official records free at http://recorder.mcleancountyil.gov/External/User/Login.aspx?ReturnUrl=%2fexternal%2fIndex.aspx. A registered user account required. Also, at access http://webapp.mcleancountyil.gov/webapps/(X(1)S(q2ps32as0vcpxa45wumlwh55))/Tax/MobileHomeSearch.aspx access county parcel and mobile home lots free. Also, search unclaimed property list at www.mcleancountyil.gov/index.aspx?nid=560.
Property, Taxation Records   Access to parcel information for free at
http://webapp.mcleancountyil.gov/webapps/%28X%281%29S%28qsmw0wq4byg5el552yikfv55%29%29/Tax/TaxParcelInfo.aspx.

Menard County *Property, Taxation Records*   Access to GIS/mapping free at http://gis.menard.il.bhamaps.com/.

Mercer County *Property, Taxation Records*   Access to property tax/search for free at http://merceril.devnetwedge.com/.

Monroe County *Property, Taxation Records*   Access property tax data free at
www.fikeandfike.com/propertytax/Monroe/Inquiry.aspx?c=67. Also, access to GIS/mapping free at http://monroeil.mygisonline.com/.

Montgomery County *Property, Taxation Records*   Access to GIS/mapping for free at https://beacon.schneidercorp.com/.

Moultrie County *Property, Taxation Records*   Access assessor records at www.fikeandfike.com/propertytax/Moultrie/Inquiry.aspx?c=70.

Ogle County *Property, Taxation Records*   Search assessor property data for a fee on the GIS system at https://beacon.schneidercorp.com/ but registration and username required for a name search. Also, access to property tax inquiry for free at http://illinoisassessors.com/. Also, access to property owners, parcel number and assessed values free at http://oglecounty.org/departments/supervisor-of-assessments/property-owners/ by numerical or alphabetical.

Peoria County *Recorded Documents*   www.peoriacounty.org/deedsrecorder/   Access to limited public search data for free at https://recorder.peoriacounty.org/recorder/web/. For full detail searches must subscribe.
Property, Taxation Records   Access to property tax database free at http://66.99.203.101/assessor/realasp1.asp.

Piatt County *Property, Taxation Records*   Access to tax search for free at http://piattil.devnetwedge.com/. Also, access to GIS/mapping for free at http://maps.piattcounty.org/.

Pulaski County *Property, Taxation Records*   Access to property tax data for free at
www.fikeandfike.com/propertytax/Home/Home.aspx?c=77. Also, access to property tax inquiry for free at http://illinoisassessors.com/.

Putnam County *Property, Taxation Records*   Access to GIS/mapping free at http://putnam.il.wthgis.com/. Also, access to real estate sales for free at www.co.putnam.il.us/county-offices/supervisor-of-assessments/real-estate-sales.

Richland County *Property, Taxation Records*   Access to property tax inquiry for free at http://illinoisassessors.com/.

Rock Island County *Property, Taxation Records*   Access to property tax searches at www.rockislandcounty.org/TaxSearch/. Moline Town assessor records are free at www.molinetownship.com/OnlineSearch/Search.asp. No name searching. Also, access to property tax inquiry for free at http://illinoisassessors.com/.

Saline County *Property, Taxation Records*   Access to property tax inquiry for free at http://illinoisassessors.com/.

Sangamon County *Property, Taxation Records*   View the status of property tax payments or property assessments at http://tax.co.sangamon.il.us/SangamonCountyWeb/app/homeAction.action. Also, access to GIS/mapping for free at http://gismaps.co.sangamon.il.us/gallery/.

Shelby County *Property, Taxation Records*   Access to a parcel search for free at http://shelby.il.bhamaps.com/. Search proprty tax data at www.fikeandfike.com/propertytax/Shelby/Inquiry.aspx?c=86.

St. Clair County *Property, Taxation Records*   Access parcel data free at www.co.st-clair.il.us/departments/assessor/Pages/parcel.aspx.

Stark County *Property, Taxation Records*   Access to property tax records for free at
www.fikeandfike.com/propertytax/Stark/Inquiry.aspx?c=88.

Stephenson County *Recorded Documents*   www.co.stephenson.il.us/clerk/   Access to property search for free at http://stephensonil.devnetwedge.com/.
Property, Taxation Records   Access to property search for free at http://stephensonil.devnetwedge.com/.

Tazewell County   *Recorded Documents*   www.tazewell.com/CountyClerk/CountyClerk&Recorder.html   Access to records for free (limited) at https://esearch.cichosting.com/. For detailed records, must subscribe.

Property, Taxation Records   Access to property search information for free at http://il-tazewell-assessor.governmax.com/propertymax/rover30.asp. Also, access to GIS/mapping for free at http://gis.tazewell.com/public/.

Vermilion County   *Property, Taxation Records*   Find information on subscribing to the county's property tax database at www.vercounty.org/TechServ/taxinquiry.pdf.

Wabash County   *Recorded Dcouments Records*   Access to recorded documents for free (limited time) at https://esearch.cichosting.com/. Must subscribe after time is over.

Wayne County   *Recorded Documents*   www.fairfield-il.com/county.html   Access to index records and images for a fee at https://cotthosting.com/ILPortal/User/Login.aspx. Index from 6/1/1988 to present; images from 12/2/1996; online index books 1/1/1890.

White County   *Property, Taxation Records*   Access to GIS/mapping free at http://whiteil.mygisonline.com/.

Whiteside County   *Property, Taxation Records*   Search assessor property data for a fee on the GIS system at https://beacon.schneidercorp.com/. Also, access to property tax inquiry for free at http://whitesideil.devnetwedge.com/.

Will County   *Property, Taxation Records*   Access to property/parcel number for free at www.willcountysoa.com/disclaimer.aspx.

Williamson County   *Recorded Documents*   www.williamsoncountyil.gov/county-clerk-and-recorder/   Access to records for a fee at https://cotthosting.com/ILPortal/User/Login.aspx. Index and images from 1992 to present.

Winnebago County   *Property, Taxation Records*   Access county parcel and assessment data free at http://assessor.wincoil.us/assessment/search/. Also, search parcel data free on the treasurer search site free at http://treasurer.wincoil.us/. Also, access property data via the GIS-mapping site free at http://ims.wingis.org/. Also, search Rockford Township assessment data free at www.rockfordtownshipassessor.net/propertysearch.asp.

Woodford County   *Property, Taxation Records*   A list of Township Assessors with address and phone numbers is at www.woodford-county.org/index.php?section=191,

Indiana

Capital: Indianapolis
                Marion County
Time Zone: EST

   11 western Indiana counties are CST and observe DST. They are: Gibson, Jasper, Laporte,
   Lake, Newton, Porter, Posey, Spencer, Starke, Vanderburgh, Warrick. The remainder are
    EST and do not observe DST except for Clark, Dearborn, Floyd, Harrison, Ohio.

Population: 6,619,930
# of Counties: 92

Useful State Links

Website: **www.in.gov**
Governor: **www.in.gov/gov**
Attorney General: **www.in.gov/attorneygeneral**
State Archives: **www.in.gov/iara/**
State Statutes and Codes: **http://iga.in.gov/legislative/laws/2016/ic/**
Legislative Bill Search: **https://iga.in.gov/**
Bill Monitoring: **www.in.gov/apps/lsa/session/billwatch/**
Unclaimed Funds: **https://indianaunclaimed.gov/**

State Public Record Agencies

Criminal Records

Indiana State Police, Criminal History Records, www.in.gov/isp/   The agency offers a Limited Criminal History that contains only felonies and Class A misdemeanor arrests, based upon county participation. See available at www.in.gov/ai/appfiles/isp-lch/. Using a credit card, the search fee is $16.32. Subscribers to accessIndiana can obtain records for $15.00 per search or for no charge if statutorily exempt, or $7.00 with a government exemption. Response of No Records Found is an official search result. Records go back to the mid 1930's.

Sexual Offender Registry

Sex and Violent Offender Directory Registry, 302 W. Washington St., www.in.gov/idoc/3285.htm   The website has a searching capabilities by name and city or county at www.icrimewatch.net/indiana.php. Each county must be searched separately. This is no statewide search feature. As mentioned, local sheriffs maintain and update sex offender registration information including the information found on this site.

Incarceration Records

Indiana Department of Correction, IGCS, Records Section, Room E-334, www.in.gov/idoc/   At the website, click on Offender Locator or visit www.in.gov/apps/indcorrection/ofs/ofs. To search provide either first and last name or the inmate number.

Corporation, LP, LLC, LLP, Fictitious/Assumed Name, Notary, Service of Process

Business Services Division, Secretary of State, https://secure.in.gov/sos/business/index.htm   Requests may be emailed to mmercado@sos.in.gov. Requests will be emailed back in PDF form within 3-5 business days with an invoice attached. Individuals can conduct Business Entity searches free at https://bsd.sos.in.gov/publicbusinesssearch. The basic seacrch enables one to search by business name, registered agent, filing number. A more robust advanced search is alos availabel form this page.   Also while not part of this agency, search securities companies registered with the state at www.in.gov/apps/sos/securities/sos_securities.   *Other Options:* Monthly lists of all new registered businesses, bulk data and specialized searches are available at http://in.gov/sos/business/2441.htm. There is $25 minimum fee, if request is over 1,000 then add $.25 per ea add'l name. Subscription is available.

Trademarks/Servicemarks

Secretary of State, Trademark Division, https://secure.in.gov/sos/business/2379.htm Visit www.in.gov/sos/business/2374.htm. Search by name of trademark, description of trademark, or owner of trademark. Results allow one to view application, certificate or the mark. To access the certificate, you must have Adobe Reader. *Other Options:* One may download the database and purchase monthly or weekly updates. See www.in.gov/ai/appfiles/sos-trademark-bulk/ for prices and details.

Uniform Commercial Code

UCC Division, Secretary of State, www.in.gov/sos/business/2380.htm A variety are searches are found at https://secure.in.gov/sos/bus_service/online_ucc/welcome.asp. You may browse lien records at https://secure.in.gov/sos/bus_service/online_ucc/browse/default.asp. There is no charge. An official search may be performed for $4.59 use of credit card required. Ongoing requesters should subscribe to IN.Gov at www.ai.org/accounts/, then fee to obtain record is $3.50. Subscribers can also purchase customized data for as little as $25.00 per 1,000 records; example is all liens on a secured party in a date range. Filing services are also available to subscribers. *Other Options:* The master data table with images is available for $3,000; if updated weekly then $25,000 annually; if updated monthly then $15,000 annually. Call 800-236-5446.

Sales Tax Registrations

IN Dept of Revenue, Sales Tax Registrations, www.in.gov/dor/ A look-up to tax delinquent business is found at www.in.gov/apps/dor/rrmc/Default.aspx.

Birth, Death Certificates

State Department of Health, Vital Records Office, www.in.gov/isdh/20243.htm Records may be ordered online via the website above or go to https://vitalrecords.egov.com/CDC.VitalRecordsMVC.Web/Wizard/IN/Municipality/SelectMunicipality. Also, records may requested from www.vitalchek.com, a state-endorsed vendor.

Workers' Compensation Records

Workers Compensation Board, Indiana Government Center, www.in.gov/wcb/ Two searches are offered. Search Disputed Claims at https://wcbnec03.wcb.state.in.us/search.asp. Multiple ways to search are available. Search for the First Report of Injury at https://wcbnec03.wcb.state.in.us/jcn.asp. A SSN and date of injury are needed.

Driver Records

BMV-Driving Records, 100 N Senate Ave, Room N412, www.in.gov/bmv/ IN.gov is the state owned interactive information and communication system which provides batch and interactive access to driving records. Subscribers must be approved and enter into an agreement on usage. There is an annual $95.00 fee. Fee is $7.50 per record. Call 317-233-2010 or visit www.in.gov/accounts. Subscribers may also validate one's IN driver's license for $1.00 per transaction. Non-subscribers can obtain a driving record, use of credit card equired. Same fees apply. All records returned through this service will contain only the personal information that the requesting party submit with their request. See www.in.gov/accounts/2333.htm. A person of record may obtain his/her own record at www.in.gov/bmv/2331.htm by creating an account and sufficiently establishing identity. The record can be viewed free of charge, same fees apply if mailed or printed..

Vehicle, Vessel Ownership & Registration

Bureau of Motor Vehicles, Records, www.in.gov/bmv/ Subscribers may search the Indiana Bureau of Motor Vehicles database for title and lien information by VIN and SSN or by title # and SSN. Requesters must be approved and sign an agreement on usage. Visit www.in.gov and click on Account Center. The fee is $5.00 per record for a title and lien search, and $15.00 for a vehicle registration search. One must be a subscriber paying the annual fee of $95.00. If not a subscriber, one may purchase either of these two records using a credit card for $16.32 per record.

Crash Reports

Crash Records Section, c/o Appriss, https://www.buycrash.com/ Crash reports can be purchased online at www.buycrash.com, a state designated vendor. The fee is $12.00, use of a credit card or PayPal is required. *Other Options:* For information about bulk file purchasing, contact the Data Section at 317-233-5133.

Voter Registration, Campaign Finance, PACs

Election Division, www.in.gov/sos/elections/ A number of campaign search sites are indexed at http://campaignfinance.in.gov/PublicSite/Search.aspx including contributions, expenditures and committees. Campaign finance reports are viewable at www.in.gov/sos/elections/2394.htm. This includes PACs.

GED Certificates

Dept of Workforce Development, 10 N Senate Ave #10, www.in.gov/dwd/adulted.htm Records may be requested from https://www.diplomasender.com. A credit card is needed. Request must be ordered by the test taker. Employers and third parties must receive an email and/or Authentication Code from the test taker to then access the authorized documents. Turnaround time is 1-3 days.

Occupational Licensing Boards

These licenses are all searchable at https://mylicense.in.gov/eGov/

Accountant-CPA	Esthetician	Physical Therapist/Therapist Asst
Acupuncturist	Funeral/Cemetery Director	Physician Assistant
Appraiser, Real Estate/Gen/Residential	Hazardous Waste Facility/Handler	Physician/Medical Doctor
Appraiser, Trainee/Temp	Health Services Administrator	Plumber/Plumbing Contractor
Architect & Landscape Architects	Hearing Aid Dealer	Podiatrist
Asbestos Contractor	Hypnotist	Private Investigator
Asbestos Disposal Mgr/Worker	Investigation Firm/Employee	Psychologist
Asbestos Mgmt Planner	Lead Inspector/Contractor	Radiologic Technologist
Asbestos Training Provider	Lead Project Designer/Supervisor	Radon Testers/Mitigators
Athletic Trainer	Lead Risk Assessor/Lead Worker	Real Estate Agent/Broker/Seller
Auctioneer	Lead Training Course Provider	Real Estate Appraiser
Audiologist	Manicurist	Respiratory Care Practitioner
Barber/Barber Instructor/Cosmetology	Marriage & Family Therapist	Shampoo Operator
Boxer	Medical Residency Permit	Social Worker
Boxing Occupation	Mental Health Counselor	Social Worker, Clinical
Chiropractor	Midwife	Solid Waste Facility
Clinical Nurse Specialist	Nurse-RN/LPN	Speech Pathologist
Dental Anesthetist/Hygienist	Nursing Home Administrator	Surveyor, Land
Dentist	Occupational Therapist/Assistant	Veterinarian
Dietitian	Optometrist	Veterinary Tech
Electrologist	Optometrist Drug Certification	Waste Tire Processor/Transporter
Embalmer	Osteopathic Physician	Waste Water Treatm't Plant Operator
Engineer/Engineering Intern	Pharmacist/Pharmacist Intern	Yard Waste Composting Facility
Environmental Health Specialist	Pharmacy Technician	

The Rest:

Alcoholic Bev. Dealer/Mfg/Dist/Retail/employee	www.in.gov/ai/appfiles/atc-license-lookup/
Asbestos Inspector/Supvr/Designer	www.in.gov/idem/airquality/2585.htm
Attorney	www.in.gov/judiciary/ble/2361.htm
Bank & Trust Company	http://extranet.dfi.in.gov/Depository/DepositoryListing
Check Casher	http://extranet.dfi.in.gov/Depository/DepositoryListing
Child Care Center	https://secure.in.gov/apps/fssa/carefinder/index.html
Child Care Home/Provider	https://secure.in.gov/apps/fssa/carefinder/index.html
Collection Agency	www.in.gov/apps/sos/securities/sos_securities
Consumer Credit Grantor	http://extranet.dfi.in.gov/ConsumerCredit
Credit Union	http://extranet.dfi.in.gov/Depository/DepositoryListing
Feed, Fertilizer & Seed Inspectors	www.oisc.purdue.edu/inspection_program.html
Grain Bank/Warehouse	www.in.gov/isda/2399.htm
Grain Buyer	www.in.gov/isda/2399.htm
Home Inspector	www.in.gov/pla/hi.htm
Insurance Agent/Consultant	https://www.sircon.com/ComplianceExpress/Inquiry/consumerInquiry.do
Investment Advisor	www.in.gov/apps/sos/securities/sos_securities
Lender, Small	http://extranet.dfi.in.gov/Depository/DepositoryListing
Loan Broker/Firms	www.in.gov/apps/sos/securities/sos_securities
Lobbyist, Executive Branch	https://secure.in.gov/apps/ilrc/registration/browse
Lobbyist, Legislative	https://secure.in.gov/apps/ilrc/registration/browse
Money Transmitter	http://extranet.dfi.in.gov/Depository/DepositoryListing
Mortgage Lenders	http://extranet.dfi.in.gov/Depository/DepositoryListing
Notary Public	https://myweb.in.gov/SOS/notaryapp/Common/NotarySearch.aspx?isReapplying=0
Pawnbroker	http://extranet.dfi.in.gov/Depository/DepositoryListing

Pesticide Applicator	https://oisc.purdue.edu/oiscweb/#!/publicrecords/licensing/searchlicensing
Pesticide Investigators (OISC)	www.oisc.purdue.edu/pesticide/pdf/investigator_territories.pdf
Pesticide Registered Products	http://npirspublic.ceris.purdue.edu/state/state_menu.aspx?state=IN
Pesticide Technician/Consultant	https://oisc.purdue.edu/oiscweb/#!/publicrecords/licensing/searchlicensing
Placement Officer, School	https://licenselookup.doe.in.gov/teacherinquiry.aspx
Polygraph Examiner	www.indianapolygraphassociation.com/members.asp
Rental Purchase Lender	http://extranet.dfi.in.gov/Depository/DepositoryListing
Savings & Loan	http://extranet.dfi.in.gov/Depository/DepositoryListing
School Administr'r/Principal/Director	https://licenselookup.doe.in.gov/teacherinquiry.aspx
School Counselor	https://licenselookup.doe.in.gov/teacherinquiry.aspx
School Nurse	https://licenselookup.doe.in.gov/teacherinquiry.aspx
Securities Broker/Dealer	www.in.gov/apps/sos/securities/sos_securities
Teacher	https://licenselookup.doe.in.gov/teacherinquiry.aspx
Trust Company	http://extranet.dfi.in.gov/Depository/DepositoryListing
Warehouse, Agricultural, etc	www.in.gov/isda/2399.htm

State and Local Courts

State Court Structure: Indiana has 92 counties, and 90 of these counties comprise their own circuit, with their own **Circuit Court**. The remaining two small counties (Ohio and Dearborn counties) have combined to form one circuit. **Circuit Courts** traditionally hear all types of civil and criminal cases and have unlimited trial jurisdiction, except when exclusive or concurrent (shared) jurisdiction is conferred to a Superior Court. Circuit Courts also have appellate jurisdiction over appeals from City and Town Courts. In general, **Superior Courts often** hear lower level felonies (Level 5 or 6), misdemeanors, lower level civil matters including small claims, evictions, probate, and certain traffic cases. However, there are a number of counties where the civil and criminal cases are assigned on a pure random or a workload basis. The Felony Classification System is shown below.

The terms County Clerk and Clerk of the Court" (or Clerk of the Circuit Court) are often used interchangeably. The key fact to know is that all record searching is performed by the Office of the Clerk, and not by the Court.

In counties without Superior Courts, the Circuit Courts handle small claims cases for civil disputes involving less than $6,000, and minor offenses, such as misdemeanors, ordinance violations, and Level 6 felonies.

The web page for the Unified Judicial System is www.in.gov/judiciary

Appellate Courts: The Court of Appeals of Indiana is an intermediate appellate court and Indiana's second-highest court. Decisions and case records from the Supreme and Appellate Courts are viewable online from the home page mentioned above.

Online Court Access

There are two primary online systems in the state providing docket information from the Circuit and Superior courts, plus some of the City courts. Neither system provides all counties in the state.

1. Doxpop.com

The system with the most participating counties (89) counties with a search of the case index is https://www.doxpop.com/prod/. A list of case numbers with name (and DOB for some records) is displayed for free. 20 limited searches are free per month. To see full case details, then fees are involved. Their fees range from $30.00 to $1,020.00 per month depending on number of searches. In general, the service does not provide case files or images, as the IN courts are cautious about providing this material. Therefore an onsite search may be necessary to pull case file information, especially if a case involves a civil judgment. Although not statewide, this is nonetheless an expanding service that is also adding recording office data. This system also includes a number of City Courts.

Counties on Doxpop:

89 Counties: ALL COUNTIES except Lake, Pulaski, and Crawford. Note Boone County is included, but is not complete.

2. Mycase.in.gov

The second system - Odyssey (https://mycase.in.gov/default.aspx or https://public.courts.in.gov/mycase/#/vw/Search - has courts in over 50 counties participating - but that does not necessarily mean all courts from a county are reporting. This is a free search of the docket. More counties are scheduled to be added over time On Odyssey one may search for 1) Criminal and Citation case records;

or 2) Civil, Family and Probate case records. Note all counties on Odyssey are on also on Doxpop. But neither system offers a true statewide search.

Per feedback from local PIs and record searchers, there are several cautionary additional facts to keep in mind about the Odyssey System:

1. Certain counties do not provide sentencing details, especially regarding plea bargains, on criminal records. The system merely shows there is a disposition date. Therefore one must pull the case file in person.
2. For criminal cases, Odyssey does not display identifiers other than name and address (at time of charging and filed updates), thus no DOBs. Note that Doxpop will display DOBs on criminal records. Neither system displays DOBs on civil records.
3. Odyssey shows the date the county started on the system, but NOT thru date. This means users must individually contact each county on Odyssey in order to determine the extent to which data has been converted onto the system.

Counties on Mycase.in.gov:

Allen	Floyd	Jackson	Owen	Steuben
Benton	Fountain	Jasper	Parke	Tippecanoe
Blackford	Franklin	Jennings	Perry	Tipton
Carroll	Grant	Johnson	Porter	Union
Cass	Greene	Knox	Posey	Vanderburgh
Clark	Hamilton	LaPorte	Randolph	Vigo
Clinton	Hancock	Madison	Rush	Warren
DeKalb	Harrison	Marion	Saint Joseph	Washington
Delaware	Hendricks	Miami	Scott	
Elkhart	Henry	Monroe	Shelby	
Fayette	Huntington	Orange	Starke	

Note Bartholomew and Crawford will be added in early 2017.

Other County Online Sites:
Porter County
Circuit Court & Superior Courts www.porterco.org
Civil: Subscription access to court records is available via Enhanced Access for $50 per month, $25 each add'l user. Info not shown on web page, call 219-465-3547.47. Online subscription service at https://www.doxpop.com. Fees involved. Records date from 01/2000. A limited free search of open cases is available. Judgments are shown at https://in-portercounty.civicplus.com/DocumentCenter/Index/175. One must view separate PDF docs.

Recorders, Assessors, and Other Sites of Note

About Indiana Recording Offices: 92 counties, 92 recording offices. The recording officer is the County Recorder.
About Tax Liens: All federal tax liens on personal property are filed with the County Recorder. State tax liens on personal property are filed with the Circuit Clerk in a different office than the Recorder. Refer to the County Court section for information on Indiana Circuit Courts.

Online Access

Recorded Documents
There is no statewide access but many counties offer online services, usually via a vendor.

An agency-supported vendor at https://tapestry.fidlar.com/Tapestry2/Default.aspx covers for the 44 counties shown below for record access. The base fee is $5.95 per search and $.50 per print image, but the county may set their own pricing. You can pay as you go using a credit or pre-pay using a subscription. Also, per the same vendor one may purchase a software program called Laredo (www.fidlar.com/lardao.aspx) with extensive search features. Contact the county for details and pricing.

Counties On Tapestry and Laredo
Allen	Elkhart	Howard	Lagrange	Miami
Cass	Floyd	Huntington	LaPorte	Noble
Crawford	Fulton	Jackson	Madison	Owen
Dekalb	Greene	Johnson	Marion	Perry
Delaware	Harrison	Know	Marshall	Porter

Posey	Starke	Wabash	White
Spencer	Tippecanoe	Warrick	Whitley
St. Joseph	Vanderburgh	Washington	

Also there is a free name-only without identifiers search of Recorded Documents at www.doxpop.com/prod/recorder. A subscription is necessary to obtain detailed information including images. There are 39 counties available on this site.

Tax Assessor Data:

There are three statewide government sites that provide a wealth of information regarding with property assessment, taxes and ownership. Each site gives the ability to search by name or property on a county basis.

1. Property Assessed Value: www.in.gov/dlgf/4931.htm

2. Property Sales Disclosures: http://gatewaysdf.ifionline.org/Search.aspx

3. Property Tax Bill - Past Dues: www.in.gov/dlgf/4929.htm

County Sites (To Avoid Redundancy, the tapestry Counties listed above and the three statewdie Government Sites are omitted on all profiles.)

Adams County   *Recorded Documents*   www.adams-county.com/185/Recorders-Office   A free name-only without identifiers search of recorded document index from 1/1990 forward at https://www.doxpop.com/prod/. A subscription is necessary to obtain detailed information, images available from 1/1990.
Property, Taxation Records   Access to GIS/mapping site free at www.adams-county.com/180/Geographical-Information-Systems-GIS.

Allen County   *Recorded Documents*   www.allencountyrecorder.us/Home.aspx   Access to recorders portal for a fee go to https://indiana-countyrecorders-records.com/User/Login.aspx. Fees are charged for acces, see the web page.
Property, Taxation Records   Access property database card data free at www.allencounty.us/custom/property_record_cards/search.php. No name searches.

Bartholomew County   *Recorded Documents*   www.bartholomew.in.gov/recorder.html   Access to index free at www.bartholomew.in.gov/recorder.html#records-search. Indexes available from 8/1985 to present. Images are available online for a fee. A free name-only without identifiers search of recorded document index from 1/1983 forward at www.doxpop.com/prod/common/ViewCountyDetails?countyId=18005. A subscription is necessary to obtain detailed information, images available from 1/1983.
Property, Taxation Records   Access to GIS/mapping free at http://bartholomewin.egis.39dn.com/#. Must register for detailed information.

Benton County   *Recorded Documents*   www.bentoncounty.in.gov/recorder   A free name-only without identifiers search of recorded document index from 5/5/1970 forward at https://www.doxpop.com/prod/. A subscription is necessary to obtain detailed information.
Property, Taxation Records   Access to GIS/mapping free at http://benton.in.wthgis.com/.

Blackford County   *Recorded Documents*   http://gov.blackfordcounty.org/pages.asp?Page=Recorder&PageIndex=367   A free name-only without identifiers search of recorded document index from 1/1992 forward at https://www.doxpop.com/prod/. A subscription is necessary to obtain detailed information, images available from 9/2000.
Property, Taxation Records   Access property data at https://beacon.schneidercorp.com/.

Boone County   *Recorded Documents*   www.boonecounty.in.gov/Default.aspx?tabid=151   Access to records free at https://www.uslandrecords.com/inlr/. Land records index from 1/93 to present.
Property, Taxation Records   Search for property data free on the GIS-mapping site at http://50.73.115.85/boone/map.phtml.

Brown County   *Recorded Documents*   http://browncounty-in.gov/Departments/Recorder.aspx   A free name-only without identifiers search of recorded document index from 7/1988 forward at https://www.doxpop.com/prod/. A subscription is necessary to obtain detailed information, images available from 7/1988.

Carroll County   *Recorded Documents*   www.carrollcountygovernment.org/recorders-office.html   A free name-only without identifiers search of recorded document index from 1/1994 forward at https://www.doxpop.com/prod/. A subscription is necessary to obtain detailed information, images available from 1/1994.
Property, Taxation Records   Access to GIS/mapping information for free at https://beacon.schneidercorp.com/.

Clark County   *Recorded Documents*   www.co.clark.in.us/index.php/clark-county-indiana-government/clark-county-indiana-recorder-s-office   A free name-only without identifiers search of recorded document index from 11/1999 forward at https://www.doxpop.com/prod/. A subscription is necessary to obtain detailed information, images available from 11/1999.
Property, Taxation Records   Online access to property records is available at http://counties.azurewebsites.net/clark/parcelsearch.aspx.

Clay County *Property, Taxation Records* A GIS search is available at http://clay.in.wthgis.com. Registration is necessary of enhanced system. Three state search sites provide a wealth of information: Property Assessed Value at www.in.gov/dlgf/4931.htm; Property Tax Bill - Past Dues at www.in.gov/dlgf/4929.htm; and Property Sales Disclosures at http://gatewaysdf.ifionline.org/Search.aspx

Clinton County *Property, Taxation Records* Search assessor property data for a fee on the GIS system at https://beacon.schneidercorp.com/. Registration and username required.

Crawford County *Property, Taxation Records* Access to property sales dislosures for free at http://gatewaysdf.ifionline.org/Search.aspx.

Daviess County *Recorded Documents* www.daviess.org/department/index.php?structureid=24 A free name-only without identifiers search of recorded document index from 1/1997 forward at https://www.doxpop.com/prod/. A subscription is necessary to obtain detailed information, images available from 1/1997.
Property, Taxation Records Online access to property records is available at http://counties.azurewebsites.net/daviess/parcelsearch.aspx.

Dearborn County *Recorded Documents* www.dearborncounty.org/department/index.php?structureid=28 A free name-only without identifiers search of recorded document index from 1/2000 forward at https://www.doxpop.com/prod/. A subscription is necessary to obtain detailed information. *Property, Taxation Records* Access to free property search go to https://beacon.schneidercorp.com/.

Decatur County *Recorded Documents* www.decaturcounty.in.gov/recorder/recorder.htm A free name-only without identifiers search of recorded document index from 1/1994 forward at https://www.doxpop.com/prod/. A subscription is necessary to obtain detailed information, images available from 1/1994.
Property, Taxation Records Access county property data for free at https://beacon.schneidercorp.com/.

DeKalb County *Property, Taxation Records* Access to Assessor database information for free at http://counties.azurewebsites.net/dekalb/.

Delaware County *Property, Taxation Records* Access to property searches for free at http://munsan.spinweb.net/parcel/.

Dubois County *Recorded Documents* www.duboiscountyin.org/offices/recorder.html A free name-only without identifiers search of recorded document index from 04/1994 forward at https://www.doxpop.com/prod/. A subscription is necessary to obtain detailed information, images available from 12/1999.
Property, Taxation Records Access property search information free at www.duboiscountyassessor.com/propertymax/rover30.asp

Elkhart County *Recorded Documents* www.elkhartcountyindiana.com/Departments/Recorder/index.htm Access to simple guest browse/print at http://in2laredo.fidlar.com/INElkhart/DirectSearch/Default.aspx. Access to records for a fee at https://tapestry.fidlar.com/Tapestry2/Default.aspx. Contact 309-794-3283 or kylec@fidlar.com for subscription information. Search fee is $5.95 each, printed images $.75 each unless otherwise noted.
Property, Taxation Records Search parcel data for free at www.macoggis.com/ and includes Michiana area which is St Joseph and Elkhart Counties. Also, access to GIS/mapping for a fee at https://elkhartin.elevatemaps.io/.

Fayette County *Property, Taxation Records* Access assessor property record cards and tax records free at http://fayette.in.wthgis.com/.

Fountain County *Recorded Documents* www.fountaincounty.net/index.html A free name-only without identifiers search of recorded document index from 6/1992 forward at https://www.doxpop.com/prod/. A subscription is necessary to obtain detailed information, images available from 1/2003. *Property, Taxation Records* Access the assessor property tax and property sales data free at http://in-fountain-assessor.governmax.com/propertymax/rover30.asp.

Franklin County *Recorded Documents* www.franklincounty.in.gov/countyoffices/recorder/ A free name-only without identifiers search of recorded document index from 1/2002 forward at https://www.doxpop.com/prod/. A subscription is necessary to obtain detailed information, images available from 1/2002, (deeds-1974 to present; mortgage-1990 to present).
Property, Taxation Records Access the GIS web map free at http://franklin.in.wthgis.com/.

Fulton County *Property, Taxation Records* Access to GIS/mapping for free at http://fulton.in.wthgis.com/.

Gibson County *Property, Taxation Records* Access property assessor parcel data free at https://beacon.schneidercorp.com/.

Grant County *Recorded Documents* http://recorder.grantcounty27.us/ Access to recorders portal for a fee go to https://indiana-countyrecorders-records.com/User/Login.aspx. Fees are charged for acces, see the web page.
Property, Taxation Records Access to GIS data is found at https://grantin.elevatemaps.io/.

Hamilton County *Recorded Documents* www.hamiltoncounty.in.gov/520/Recorders-Office A free name-only without identifiers search of recorded document index from 01/1987 forward at https://www.doxpop.com/prod/. A subscription is necessary to obtain detailed information, images available from 2/1996. *Property, Taxation Records* Access parcel and tax info for free at www3.hamiltoncounty.in.gov/propertyreports/.

Hancock County *Recorded Documents* http://hancockcoingov.org/hancock-county-government-departments/hancock-county-indiana-recorder A free name-only without identifiers search of recorded document index from 01/1990 forward at https://www.doxpop.com/prod/. A subscription is necessary to obtain detailed information, images available from 1/2001.

Property, Taxation Records Access to the assessor property data is free on the GIS/mapping site at https://beacon.schneidercorp.com/. Also, sales disclosure data is free at http://hancockcoingov.org/hancock-county-assessor-sales-disclosure.

Harrison County ***Property, Taxation Records*** Access property and assessor data free on the GIS-mapping search site at http://harrisonin.egis.39dn.com/#.

Hendricks County ***Recorded Documents*** www.co.hendricks.in.us/department/index.php?structureid=20 Access to records for a fee athttps://www.doxpop.com/prod/. Doxpop provides a range of subscription levels, from no-cost access for individual citizens to full-featured plans designed to help legal professionals and researchers excel at their work.
Property, Taxation Records Search the GIS mapping for Town of Plainfield data free at https://beacon.schneidercorp.com/.

Henry County ***Recorded Documents*** www.henryco.net/RecordersOffice.aspx A free name-only without identifiers search of recorded document index from 01/1990 forward at https://www.doxpop.com/prod/. A subscription is necessary to obtain detailed information, images available from 1/1991. ***Property, Taxation Records*** Access property assessment free at https://beacon.schneidercorp.com/.

Howard County ***Property, Taxation Records*** Search assessor property data free on the GIS system at https://beacon.schneidercorp.com/ with registration and username required.

Huntington County ***Property, Taxation Records*** Access to GIS/mapping and property record cards for free at https://beacon.schneidercorp.com/. Three state search sites provide a wealth of information: Property Assessed Value at www.in.gov/dlgf/4929.htm; Property Tax Bill - Past Dues at www.in.gov/dlgf/4929.htm; and Property Sales Disclosures at http://gatewaysdf.ifionline.org/Search.aspx.

Jackson County ***Property, Taxation Records*** Access to property tax, GIS/mapping and assessments for free at http://thinkopengis.jackson.in.wthtechnology.com/.

Jasper County ***Property, Taxation Records*** Access to GIS/mapping free at www.jaspercountyin.gov/eGov/apps/services/index.egov?view=detail;id=7.

Jay County ***Recorded Documents*** www.jaycounty.net/plugins/content/content.php?content.34 A free name-only without identifiers search of recorded document index from 01/1997 forward at https://www.doxpop.com/prod/. A subscription is necessary to obtain detailed information, images available from 1/1997.

Jefferson County ***Property, Taxation Records*** Access to GIS/mapping free at http://jefferson.in.wthgis.com/.

Jennings County ***Recorded Documents*** www.jenningscounty-in.gov/recorder/index.php A free name-only without identifiers search of recorded document index from 11/91 forward at https://www.doxpop.com/prod/. A subscription is necessary to obtain detailed information, images available from 11/91.
Property, Taxation Records Access to the assessor property data is free on the GIS/mapping at http://jennings.in.wthgis.com/.

Johnson County ***Recorded Documents*** http://co.johnson.in.us/government/taxpropertyfinance/recorders-office/ Access to records for a fee at https://indiana-countyrecorders-records.com/User/Login.aspx?ReturnUrl=%2fIndex.aspx.
Property, Taxation Records Access to the assessor GIS database of property and sales data is free at https://beacon.schneidercorp.com/.

Kosciusko County ***Recorded Documents*** www.kcgov.com/department/index.php?fDD=20-0 A free name-only without identifiers search of recorded document index from 01/1991 forward at https://www.doxpop.com/prod/. A subscription is necessary to obtain detailed information, images available from 2/1992.
Property, Taxation Records Access to property records on the searchable GIS mapping site at https://beacon.schneidercorp.com/.

La Porte County ***Property, Taxation Records*** Access to GIS/mapping free at https://beacon.schneidercorp.com/.

Lake County ***Property, Taxation Records*** Access property tax data online at http://in-lake-assessor.governmaxa.com/propertymax/rover30.asp. Search free as Guest, but no name searching. Subscription service allows name searching; sub fee is $19.95 per month.

Madison County ***Property, Taxation Records*** Access to parcel searches isfree at http://counties.azurewebsites.net/madison/parcelsearch.aspx.

Marion County ***Property, Taxation Records*** Access to property cards for free at http://maps.indy.gov/AssessorPropertyCards/.

Marshall County ***Property, Taxation Records*** Search property data free at https://beacon.schneidercorp.com/.

Martin County ***Recorded Documents*** A free name-only without identifiers search of recorded document index from 1/2003 forward at https://www.doxpop.com/prod/. A subscription is necessary to obtain detailed information, images available from 1/2003.

Miami County ***Property, Taxation Records*** View GIS, tax and property information at www.miamicountyin.gov/GIS39dn.htm.

Monroe County ***Recorded Documents*** www.co.monroe.in.us/tsd/Government/TaxProperty/Recorder.aspx Access to records at https://www.doxpop.com/prod/. Residents get 6 free searches per month, and businesses pay a subscription fee based upon usage.

Property, Taxation Records   Access to GIS/Maps information for free at www.co.monroe.in.us/tsd/GIS.aspx.

Montgomery County *Recorded Documents* www.montgomeryco.net/department/?fDD=12-0   A free name-only without identifiers search of recorded document index from 01/1995 forward at https://www.doxpop.com/prod/. A subscription is necessary to obtain detailed information, images available from 1/1995.
Property, Taxation Records   Access to property tax and property assessment data for free at https://beacon.schneidercorp.com/. Also, access to GIS/mapping free at www.montgomeryco.net/department/?fDD=20-0.

Morgan County *Recorded Documents* http://morgancountyrecorder.com/   A free name-only without identifiers search of recorded document index from 05/1994 forward at https://www.doxpop.com/prod/. A subscription is necessary to obtain detailed information, images available from 1/1/94 to present. *Property, Taxation Records*   Access to GIS/mapping (basic) for a fee at https://beacon.schneidercorp.com/.

Newton County *Property, Taxation Records*   Access assessor's property database free at https://beacon.schneidercorp.com/.

Noble County *Recorded Documents* www.noblecountyrecorder.com/   Access the township land ownership roster (2010 only) for free at www.noblecountyrecorder.com/downloads/Land_Ownership_Roster.pdf.

Ohio County *Recorded Documents*   A free name-only without identifiers search of recorded document index from 11/1997 forward at https://www.doxpop.com/prod/. A subscription is necessary to obtain detailed information, images available from 11/1999.

Owen County *Recorded Documents* www.owencounty.in.gov/index.php?q=content/recorder   Access to records for a fee at https://tapestry.fidlar.com/Tapestry2/Default.aspx. Contact the Recorder's Office for subscription information. Search fee is $6.95 each, printed images $1.00 each unless otherwise noted.

Parke County *Recorded Documents* www.parkecounty-in.gov/recorder   A free name-only without identifiers search of recorded document index from 1/1996 forward at https://www.doxpop.com/prod/. A subscription is necessary to obtain detailed information, images available from 1/1996.

Perry County *Property, Taxation Records*   Access to GIS/mapping free at http://perry.in.wthgis.com/.

Pike County *Recorded Documents*   Access land records for a fee at https://www.uslandrecords.com/inlr/. Indexed from 1/4/1064 to present.

Porter County *Property, Taxation Records*   Access to property assessment data and sales is free at http://search.portercountyassessor.com/. Also, access to GIS/mapping for free at http://porterin.mygisonline.com/.

Posey County *Recorded Documents* www.poseycountyin.gov/about-us/recorders-office/   Access to records for a fee at https://tapestry.fidlar.com/Tapestry2/Default.aspx. Contact 309-794-3283 or kylec@fidlar.com for subscription information. Search fee is $6.95 each, printed images $1.00 each unless otherwise noted. Unlimited Laredo for $250.00 or access 250 minutes for $50.00. Print images are $1.00. Deeds indexed back to 1956.
Property, Taxation Records   Access to property search information for free at http://in-posey-assessor.governmax.com/svc/default.asp.

Pulaski County *Recorded Documents* http://gov.pulaskionline.org/recorder/   A free name-only without identifiers search of recorded document index from 1/1994 forward at https://www.doxpop.com/prod/. A subscription is necessary to obtain detailed information.

Putnam County *Recorded Documents* www.co.putnam.in.us/Recorder/   A free name-only without identifiers search of recorded document index from 01/1992 forward at https://www.doxpop.com/prod/.

Randolph County *Recorded Documents* http://randolphcounty.us/departments/recorder   A free name-only without identifiers search of recorded document index from 01/1993 forward at https://www.doxpop.com/prod/. A subscription is necessary to obtain detailed information, images available from 5/2003. *Property, Taxation Records*   Access to property/GIS information for free at http://randolph.in.wthgis.com/.

Ripley County *Recorded Documents* www.ripleycounty.com/recorder/   A free name-only without identifiers search of recorded document index from 7/1975 forward at www.doxpop.com/prod/common/ViewCountyDetails?countyId=18137. A subscription is necessary to obtain detailed information, images available from 7/1975.

Rush County *Recorded Documents* www.rushcounty.in.gov/Public/CountyOffices/Recorder/index.cfm   A free name-only without identifiers search of recorded document index from 08/97 forward at https://www.doxpop.com/prod/. A subscription is necessary to obtain detailed information, images available from 12/98.
Property, Taxation Records   Access to parcel searches for free at https://beacon.schneidercorp.com/.

Scott County *Recorded Documents*   A range of subscription levels for records at https://www.doxpop.com/prod/ from no-cost access for individuals to full-featured plans designed for legal professionals and researchers.

Shelby County *Recorded Documents* www.co.shelby.in.us/Default.aspx?alias=www.co.shelby.in.us/recorder   A free name-only without identifiers search of recorded document index from 5/1998 forward at https://www.doxpop.com/prod/. A subscription is necessary to obtain detailed information, images available from 5/1998. *Property, Taxation Records*   Access to GIS/mapping free at http://shelby.in.wthgis.com/.

St. Joseph County *Property, Taxation Records*   Search parcel data for free at www.macoggis.com, includes Michiana area which is St Joseph and Elkhart Counties. Also, access to property searches free at http://in-stjoseph-assessor.governmax.com/propertymax/rover30.asp.

Starke County   *Property, Taxation Records*   Access to property record cards for free at http://thinkopengis.starke.in.wthtechnology.com/.

Steuben County   *Recorded Documents*   www.co.steuben.in.us/departments/recorder/index.php   A free name-only without identifiers search of recorded document index from 1/1992 forward at https://www.doxpop.com/prod/. A subscription is necessary to obtain detailed information, images available from 1/1994.
Property, Taxation Records   Access property data free on the GIS mapping site at https://beacon.schneidercorp.com/.

Sullivan County   *Recorded Documents*   A free name-only without identifiers search of recorded document index from 8/2/2004 forward at https://www.doxpop.com/prod/. A subscription is necessary to obtain detailed information, images available from 8/2/2004.

Tippecanoe County   *Property, Taxation Records*   Access to tax and assessment databases free at www.tippecanoe.in.gov/151/Access-Property-Tax-Assessment-Records. Also, access to GIS-mapping site free for county and city of Lafayette at http://gis2.tippecanoe.in.gov/PublicSL/Viewer.html?Viewer=Public.

Tipton County   *Property, Taxation Records*   Search assessor property data free on the GIS system at the Tipton county site or https://beacon.schneidercorp.com/.

Union County   *Recorded Documents*   www.unioncountyin.gov/recorder.html   A free name-only without identifiers search of recorded document index from 1/2000 forward at https://www.doxpop.com/prod/. A subscription is necessary to obtain detailed information, images available from 1/2000. *Property, Taxation Records*   Access to GIS/mapping for free to http://union.in.wthgis.com/.

Vanderburgh County   *Property, Taxation Records*   Access assessor property database free at www.vanderburghassessor.org/NewDisclaimer.aspx. Three state search sites provide a wealth of information: Property Assessed Value at www.in.gov/dlgf/4931.htm; Property Tax Bill - Past Dues at www.in.gov/dlgf/4929.htm; and Property Sales Disclosures at http://gatewaysdf.ifionline.org/Search.aspx

Vermillion County   *Recorded Documents*   www.vermilliongov.us/recorder.html   A free name-only without identifiers search of recorded document index from 8/1994 forward at https://www.doxpop.com/prod/. A subscription is necessary to obtain detailed information, images available from 12/1997. *Property, Taxation Records*   Access to GIS/mapping free at http://thinkopengis.vermillion.in.wthtechnology.com/.

Vigo County   *Recorded Documents*   www.vigocounty.in.gov/department/index.php?structureid=10   A free name-only without identifiers search of recorded document index from 11/96 forward at https://www.doxpop.com/prod/. A subscription is necessary to obtain detailed information, images available from 12/2001.
Property, Taxation Records   Search Vigo County property data by parcel, name or address at https://beacon.schneidercorp.com/, includes City of Terra Haute.

Wabash County   *Property, Taxation Records*   Access property data free from the Property List at http://assessor.wabash.in.datapitstop.us/. Click on Property Tax Information.

Warrick County   *Property, Taxation Records*   Access property data free at http://in-warrick-assessor.publicaccessnow.com/. Also, GIS Map information available at http://thinkopengis.warrick.in.wthengineering.com

Washington County   *Property, Taxation Records*   Access to GIS/mapping free at http://washington.in.wthgis.com/.

Wayne County   *Recorded Documents, Marriage Records*   http://co.wayne.in.us/recorder/   A free name-only without identifiers (12 are free) search of recorded document index from 1/1994 forward at https://www.doxpop.com/prod/. A subscription (after 12) is necessary to obtain detailed information, images available from 4/2000. Recorded deeds are being added irregularly. Plat information from 1/2/1815 to present. Also, marriage records from the County Clerk's office being added irregularly to the website at www.co.wayne.in.us/marriage/retrieve.cgi. Records are from 1811 forward.
Property, Taxation Records   Access county property records free at http://prc.co.wayne.in.us. Must register. Also, search current property tax records free at the GIS/mapping site at www.gis.co.wayne.in.us/. Free registration required.

Wells County   *Property, Taxation Records*   Access assessor records free on the GIS-mapping site at https://beacon.schneidercorp.com/.

White County   *Property, Taxation Records*   Property and tax data is available at http://in-white-treasurer.governmax.com/collectmax/collect30.asp?sid=4D9AE443CCE84C4FA4A1037D62330980.

Whitley County   *Recorded Documents*   www.whitleygov.com/department/index.php?structureid=8   Access to records for a fee at https://tapestry.fidlar.com/Tapestry2/Default.aspx. Contact 800-747-4600 or support@fidlar.com for subscription information. Search fee is $6.95 each, printed images $1.00 per page.
Property, Taxation Records   Search assessor property data free on the GIS system at https://beacon.schneidercorp.com/.

Iowa

Capital: Des Moines
         Polk County
Time Zone: CST
Population: 3,123,899
# of Counties: 99

Useful State Links

Website: **https://www.iowa.gov/**
Governor: **https://governor.iowa.gov/**
Attorney General: **https://www.iowaattorneygeneral.gov**
State Archives: **https://iowaculture.gov/history/**
State Statutes and Codes: **https://www.legis.iowa.gov/law/statutory**
Legislative Bill Search: **https://www.legis.iowa.gov/legislation/billTracking**
Unclaimed Funds: **https://www.greatiowatreasurehunt.gov/owners/search/**

State Public Record Agencies

Criminal Records

Division of Criminal Investigation, Support Operation Bureau, www.dps.state.ia.us/DCI/index.shtml   The Iowa Department of Public Safety, Division of Criminal Investigation's (DCI) Criminal History Record Check website at https://iowacriminalhistory.iowa.gov/default.aspx provides a criminal record check. Fee is $15.00 This website will not provide criminal history data on any arrest information that is older than 18 months without a final disposition or any completed deferred judgment information. Thus this record is not the complete history.

Sexual Offender Registry

Division of Criminal Investigations, SOR Unit,   www.iowasexoffender.com/   The website at www.iowasexoffender.com/search permits name searching, enables a requester to be notified on the movement of an offender, and provides a map of registrants. One may even search by vehicle plate number. RSS feed and API also available. There are approx. 5,700 registrants listed on this website.

Incarceration Records

Iowa Department of Corrections, 510 E 12th Street,   www.doc.state.ia.us   A free search of inmates is at www.doc.state.ia.us/OffenderInformation. There is also a vendor site at https://vinelink.com/#/home/site/16000.   *Other Options:* Bulk records are not available. This was a mis-use of the deferred judgment records by vendors, and database purchases are no longer offered.

Corporation, LLC, LP, Fictitious Name, Trademarks/Servicemarks

Secretary of State - Business Services Div, 321 E 12th Street,   https://sos.iowa.gov   From home page, click on the Search Databases tab to find Business Entities. Search by name on this free search. Information is also maintained on trademarks registered with the office. All this information can be accessed from this web site.   *Other Options:* This agency will sell the records in database format. Call the number listed above and ask for Karen Ubaldo for more information.

Uniform Commercial Code, Federal Tax Liens

UCC Division - Sec of State, 321 E 12th Street,   https://sos.iowa.gov/business/UCCInfo.html   Visit https://sos.iowa.gov/search/ucc/search.aspx?ucc. This search uses the filing office standard search logic for UCC or federal tax liens. It allows one to print a certified lien search report. By default the search reveals all liens that have not reached their lapse date. UCC searches have the option to include liens that have lapsed within the past year. An additional, alternative search is at https://sos.iowa.gov/search/uccAlternative/search.aspx. This is helpful in finding names that are similar too but not exactly the same as the name searched.   *Other Options:* This agency will sell the database of records. Call the number listed above and ask for Karen Ubaldo.

Birth Certificates

Iowa Department of Public Health, Bureau of Vital Records,   http://idph.iowa.gov/health-statistics/vital-records   The agency promotes a vendor - www.vitalchek.com - as the online means to order records. Additional fees ($13.00) involved and use of credit card required.

Driver Records

Department of Transportation, Driver Service Records Section,   www.iowadot.gov/mvd/index.htm   The state requires that all ongoing requesters/users access records via IowaAccess. The fee is $8.50 per record, the service is interactive or batch. Requesters must be approved and open an account. The records contain personal information, so requesters must comply with DPPA. For more information, contact IowaAccess at 515-323-3468 or 866-492-3468. Iowa drivers may view their own record online for free at https://mymvd.iowadot.gov/Account/Login. The fee to order a certified record is $7.00, use of a credit card or debit card is required.

Vehicle Ownership & Registration

Department of Transportation, Office of Vehicle & Motor Carrier Services,   www.iowadot.gov/mvd/   Online access is available to those who qualify per DPPA including dealers, Iowa licensed investigators and security companies. There is no fee. All accounts must register and be pre-approved per DPPA. Write to the Office of Motor Vehicle, explaining purpose/use of records.   *Other Options:* Iowa makes the entire vehicle file or selected data available for purchase. Weekly updates are also available for those purchasers. Requesters subject to DPPA requirements. For more information, call 515-237-3110.

Campaign Finance, PACs

Iowa Ethics & Campaign Disclusre Board, 510 E 12th St, Ste 1A,   www.iowa.gov/ethics/   Search campaign disclosure reports at https://webapp.iecdb.iowa.gov/publicview/ContributionSearch.aspx. Search by individual, candidate, party or PAC. Almost all records from 2003 forward are online.

HSED (GED) GED Certificates

Attn: HSED Records, ID Dept of Edu, Adult Education and Literacy,   https://www.educateiowa.gov/   All access is available via the vendor at https://www.diplomasender.com/. For information about their Third Party Program, visit https://www.diplomasender.com/AgencyProgram.aspx. One may also agencysupport@diplomasender.com to ask questions.

Occupational Licensing Boards

These licenses are all searchable at
https://ibplicense.iowa.gov/PublicPortal/Iowa/IBPL/publicsearch/publicsearch.jsp

Athletic Trainer	Funeral Director/Home	Optometrist
Audiologist	Hearing Aid Dispenser/Dealer	Physical Therapist/Assistant
Barber	Manicurist	Physician Assistant
Chiropractor	Marriage & Family Therapist	Podiatrist
Cosmetologist	Massage Therapist	Psychologist
Cosmetol'y Salon/School/Instruct	Mental Health Counselor	Respiratory Therapist
Crematory	Mortuary Science	Social Worker
Dietitian	Nail Technologist	Speech Pathologist/Audiologist
Electrologist	Nursing Home Administrator	Tattoo Artist
Esthetician	Occupational Therapist/Assistant	

The Rest:

Accountant-CPA	https://eservices.iowa.gov/licensediniowa/index.php
Acupuncturist	www.medicalboard.iowa.gov/find_physician/index.html
Adoption Firms	www.dhs.iowa.gov/docs/LicFacs.xls
Alcoholic Beverage Retail/Whlse/Mfg	https://elicensing.iowaabd.com/LicenseSearch.aspx
Ambulance/Air Ambulance/Transport	http://idph.iowa.gov/bets/ems/services
Anesthesiologist	www.medicalboard.iowa.gov/find_physician/index.html
Appraiser	https://eservices.iowa.gov/licensediniowa/index.php
Architect	https://eservices.iowa.gov/licensediniowa/index.php
Asbestos Contractor/Worker	www2.iwd.state.ia.us/LaborServices/LabrAsbs.nsf
Asbestos Project Designer/Planner	www2.iwd.state.ia.us/LaborServices/LabrAsbs.nsf
Attorney	https://www.iacourtcommissions.org/icc/SearchLawyer.do
Attorney Disability/Disciplinary Orders	https://www.iacourtcommissions.org/icc/SearchDiscipline.do
Bank	www.idob.state.ia.us/public/license/Financesrch/licenseVerify.aspx

Controlled Substance Registrant	https://pharmacy.iowa.gov/miscellaneous/verifications
Day Care	https://ccmis.dhs.state.ia.us/ClientPortal/ProviderSearch.aspx
Debt Management Company	www.idob.state.ia.us/public/license/Financesrch/licenseVerify.aspx
Delayed Deposit Service Business	www.idob.state.ia.us/public/license/Financesrch/licenseVerify.aspx
Dental Assistant	https://eservices.iowa.gov/PublicPortal/Iowa/IDB/licenseQuery/LicenseQuery.jsp
Dental Hygienist	https://eservices.iowa.gov/PublicPortal/Iowa/IDB/licenseQuery/LicenseQuery.jsp
Dentist	https://eservices.iowa.gov/PublicPortal/Iowa/IDB/licenseQuery/LicenseQuery.jsp
Drug Distributor/Whlse/Mfg	https://pharmacy.iowa.gov/miscellaneous/verifications
Emergency Med Tech-Paramedic	http://idph.iowa.gov/bets/ems/provider-list
EMS Disciplinary Actions	http://idph.iowa.gov/BETS/EMS/Discipline
EMS Provider/Service/Bureau Staff	http://idph.iowa.gov/bets/ems/provider-list
Engineer	https://eservices.iowa.gov/licensediniowa/index.php
Finance Company	www.idob.state.ia.us/public/license/Financesrch/licenseVerify.aspx
First Response Paramedic	http://idph.iowa.gov/bets/ems/provider-list
Gambling Device Manufacturer/Distributor	https://irgc.iowa.gov/document/current-licensees
Insurance Agency/Company	https://sbs-ia.naic.org/Lion-Web/jsp/sbsreports/AgentLookup.jsp
Insurance Producer	https://sbs-ia.naic.org/Lion-Web/jsp/sbsreports/AgentLookup.jsp
Landscape Architect	https://eservices.iowa.gov/licensediniowa/index.php
Lobbyist	http://coolice.legis.iowa.gov/Cool-ICE/default.asp?Category=Matt&Service=Lobby
Money Transmitter	www.idob.state.ia.us/public/license/Financesrch/licenseVerify.aspx
Mortgage Banker/Broker	www.idob.state.ia.us/public/license/Financesrch/licenseVerify.aspx
Mortgage Loan Service	www.idob.state.ia.us/public/license/Financesrch/licenseVerify.aspx
Notary Public	https://sos.iowa.gov/search/notary/search.aspx
Nurse-Advance Registered Practice	https://eservices.iowa.gov/PublicPortal/Iowa/IBON/public/license_verification.jsp
Nurse-LPN	https://eservices.iowa.gov/PublicPortal/Iowa/IBON/public/license_verification.jsp
Orthopedic Doctor	www.medicalboard.iowa.gov/find_physician/index.html
Osteopathic Physician	www.medicalboard.iowa.gov/find_physician/index.html
Pediatrician	www.medicalboard.iowa.gov/find_physician/index.html
Pesticide Commercial Applicator	www.kellysolutions.com/ia/Business/index.asp
Pesticide Commercial Certification	www.kellysolutions.com/ia/Applicators/index.asp
Pesticide Dealer	www.kellysolutions.com/ia/Dealers/index.asp
Pesticide Private Applicator	www.kellysolutions.com/ia/Applicators/index.asp
Pharmacist/Pharmacist Tech/Intern	https://pharmacy.iowa.gov/miscellaneous/verifications
Pharmacy	https://pharmacy.iowa.gov/miscellaneous/verifications
Physician/Medical Doctor	www.medicalboard.iowa.gov/find_physician/index.html
Psychiatrist	www.medicalboard.iowa.gov/find_physician/index.html
Real Estate Agent/Broker/Sales	https://eservices.iowa.gov/licensediniowa/index.php
Real Estate Appraiser	https://eservices.iowa.gov/licensediniowa/index.php
Real Estate Appraiser Disciplinary Index	https://plb.iowa.gov/real-estate-appraisers/disciplinary-index
School Coach	https://www.iowaonline.state.ia.us/boee/
School Counselor	https://www.iowaonline.state.ia.us/boee/
School Principal/Superintendent	https://www.iowaonline.state.ia.us/boee/
Shorthand Reporter	https://www.iacourtcommissions.org/icc/SearchCsr.do
Surveyor, Land	https://eservices.iowa.gov/licensediniowa/index.php
Teacher	https://www.iowaonline.state.ia.us/boee/
Waste Water Lagoon/Treatm't Oper'tor	https://programs.iowadnr.gov/wwisard/home.aspx
Water Distribution Operator	https://programs.iowadnr.gov/wwisard/home.aspx
Water Treatment Operator	https://programs.iowadnr.gov/wwisard/home.aspx
Well Driller	https://programs.iowadnr.gov/wwisard/home.aspx

State and Local Courts

About Iowa Courts: The **District Court** is the court of general jurisdiction and handles all civil, criminal, juvenile, and probate matters in the state. There are three levels of judges within District court: district judges have general jurisdiction over all types of cases; associate judges (district associate, associate juvenile, associate probate) and magistrates have limited jurisdiction.

The web page for the Unified Judicial System is www.iowacourts.gov.

Appellate Courts: The Iowa Court of Appeals is an intermediate appellate court. It reviews appeals from trial court decisions that have been transferred to the Court of Appeals by the Supreme Court. From the home page above one may access Supreme Court and Appellate Court opinions.

Online Court Access

All courts participate in the systems described below.

The Iowa Courts Online Search System (ICIS) provides several options for options for obtaining case docket information from Trial Courts and Appellate Court, including options for free searching and a more robust Advanced Case Search.

The Advanced Case Search for the Trial Courts is a pay service for registered users. The services are found at https://www.iowacourts.state.ia.us/ESAWebApp/SelectFrame. Information on juveniles and other confidential cases is not available.

About the Trial Court Free System

Basic Information available for all 99 District Courts includes criminal, civil, divorce cases with financials/custody data, probate, and traffic. Name searches can be performed on either a statewide or specific county basis. Search results include cases entered into the ICIS System through the end of the last business day. Search by name or case number. Once a case is selected from the search results, the case data displayed is up-to-the-minute as entered by the Clerk of Court.

About the Advanced (Pay) Trial Court System

A subscription system (Advanced Case Search) provides more detailed information; fee is $25.00 per month paid in advance. Plus both the search results and case information are current. The drawback to this system is that only one county can be searched at a time. While this is an excellent site with much information and are updated daily, note that the historical records are provided from different starting dates per county. Images are not shown. The DOB is not entered when searching, but is often shown on search results. Registered users are limited to 1,000 searches per calendar day.

Online/Onsite Equivalency

The pay system provides more details than the free system and is considered equivalent to an onsite search. The free search is NOT considered to be onsite-online equivalent.

No individual Iowa courts offer online access, other than as described above.

Recorders and Assessors

About Iowa Recording Offices: All 99 counties, 100 recording offices. Lee County has two recording offices. The recording officer is the County Recorder.

About Tax Liens: Federal tax liens on personal property of businesses are filed with the Secretary of State. Other federal and all state tax liens on personal property are filed with the County Recorder.

Online Access

Recorded Documents:

Provided by the Iowa County Recorders Association, the Iowa Land Records system at https://iowalandrecords.org/portal offers statewide searching and pdf images of deeds, liens, even UCCs and judgments. There are also features for monitoring new documents and saving documents. Registration is currently free, however certification and copy fees are charged.

Since this system appears in every county and to avoid redundancy, details are ommited in the County profiles to follow.

Assessor Data:

A links list for county assessor web pages and sites with accesible records for most Iowa counties plus cities of Ames, Cedar Rapids, Clinton, Davenport, Dubuque, Iowa City, Mason City and Souix City is at www.iowaassessors.com/.

Search basic assessor property data free on the GIS system for over 50% of the counties at https://beacon.schneidercorp.com/. Registration and username required, fees may apply. Search basic assessor property data free on the GIS system at http://beacon.schneidercorp.com/. Registration and username required, fees may apply.

County Sites:

(To Avoid Redundancy, info on the Iowa County Recorders Association site is Omitted on All Profiles.)

Adair County *Property, Taxation Records*   Access to the assessor database of property and sales data is free at http://adair.iowaassessors.com/.

Adams County *Property, Taxation Records*   Access to the assessor database of property and sales data is free at http://adams.iowaassessors.com/.

Allamakee County *Property, Taxation Records*   Search assessor property data and/or GIS sites for free at https://beacon.schneidercorp.com/. For detailed information, must subscribe for a fee.

Appanoose County *Property, Taxation Records*   Access to the Assessor's database for free at http://appanoose.iowaassessors.com/.

Audubon County *Property, Taxation Records*   Search assessor property data and/or GIS sites for free at https://beacon.schneidercorp.com/. For detailed information, must subscribe for a fee.

Benton County *Property, Taxation Records*   Search assessor property data and/or GIS sites for free at https://beacon.schneidercorp.com/. For detailed information, must subscribe for a fee.

Black Hawk County *Property, Taxation Records*   Access to tax mapping and owenership data for free at www.co.black-hawk.ia.us/377/Real-Estate-Mapping. Also, search the tax delinquencies list free, manually at www.co.black-hawk.ia.us/334/Delinquencies.

Boone County *Property, Taxation Records*   Search assessor property data and/or GIS sites for free at https://beacon.schneidercorp.com/. For detailed information, must subscribe for a fee.

Bremer County *Property, Taxation Records*   Search assessor property data and/or GIS sites for free at https://beacon.schneidercorp.com/. For detailed information, must subscribe for a fee.

Buchanan County *Property, Taxation Records*   Access county property data free at http://buchanan.iowaassessors.com/ but no name searching. Includes property sales.

Buena Vista County *Property, Taxation Records*   Search the property assessor and Ag sales databases for free at www.bvcountyiowa.com/index.php/assessors. Also, access county property data free at http://buchanan.iowaassessors.com/ but no name searching. Includes property sales.

Butler County *Property, Taxation Records*   Also, access county property data free at http://butler.iowaassessors.com/ but no name searching. Includes property sales.

Calhoun County *Property, Taxation Records*   Access to the assessor database of property and sales data is free at http://calhoun.iowaassessors.com/.

Carroll County *Property, Taxation Records*   Access to GIS/mapping for free at http://carrollia.mygisonline.com/. Also, access county property data free at http://carroll.iowaassessors.com/ but no name searching. Includes property sales.

Cass County *Property, Taxation Records*   Search assessor property data and/or GIS sites for free at https://beacon.schneidercorp.com/. For detailed information, must subscribe for a fee. Also, access to property record cards, GIS/mapping, sales, building, etc for free at http://cass.iowaassessors.com/.

Cedar County *Property, Taxation Records*   Search county property and sales data free at http://cedar.iowaassessors.com/.

Cerro Gordo County *Property, Taxation Records*   Access to the County and Mason City property records is free at http://old.co.cerro-gordo.ia.us/property_search/property_search.cfm. Also, search assessor property data and/or GIS sites for free at https://beacon.schneidercorp.com/. For detailed information, must subscribe for a fee.

Cherokee County *Recorded Documents* http://cherokeecountyiowa.com/offices/recorder/index.htm   An inquiry of Recorded Documents for free is at http://lti.gmdsolutions.com/cherokee/rindex.html. At https://iowalandrecords.org/portal/, an index of recorded land records is available from 1/2000, images available from 03/2002.

Property, Taxation Records   Access to real estate and tax information for free at http://cherokee.iowaassessors.com/search.php. Search county property and sales data free at http://cherokee.iowaassessors.com/.

Chickasaw County   *Property, Taxation Records*   Search assessor property data and/or GIS sites for free at https://beacon.schneidercorp.com/?site=ChickasawCountyIA. For detailed information, must subscribe for a fee.

Clarke County   *Property, Taxation Records*   Search parcels free on the GIS-mapping site at www.clarkecoiagis.com/.

Clay County   *Recorded Documents*   www.co.clay.ia.us/offices/recorder/index.htm   Access recorded doc index free at http://lti.gmdsolutions.com/clay/rindex.html.
Property, Taxation Records   Search assessments, parcels, and sales free at http://clay.iowaassessors.com/. Also, search tax sale certificates free at http://lti.gmdsolutions.com/clay/tindex.html. Also, search land and tax database free at http://lti.gmdsolutions.com/clay/index.html.

Clayton County   *Property, Taxation Records*   Search county property records free at http://clayton.iowaassessors.com/. Search assessor property data and/or GIS sites for free at https://beacon.schneidercorp.com/. For detailed information, must subscribe for a fee.

Clinton County   *Recorded Documents*   www.clintoncounty-ia.gov/Page/Recorder.aspx?nt=497   Access to electronic plats for free at www.clintoncounty-ia.gov/page/Recorders_Plat_Index.aspx?nt=497.
Property, Taxation Records   Access to the assessor database of property and sales data is free at www.qpublic.net/clinton/search1.html. Also, GIS/mappiing for free at www.clintoncounty-ia.gov/Clinton_County_GIS. Search assessor property data and/or GIS sites for free at http://beacon.schneidercorp.com. For detailed information, must subscribe for a fee.

Crawford County   *Property, Taxation Records*   Search county property records free at http://crawford.iowaassessors.com/ but no name searching or sales info unless subscription is made.

Dallas County   *Recorded Documents* Access to indexing inquiry for free at http://lti.gmdsolutions.com/dallas/rindex.html.
Property, Taxation Records   Access to the assessor database of property and sales data is free at www.assessorweb.co.dallas.ia.us/Searchv3.aspx.

Davis County   *Property, Taxation Records*   Search assessor property data and/or GIS sites for free at https://beacon.schneidercorp.com/. For detailed information, must subscribe for a fee.

Delaware County   *Property, Taxation Records*   Search assessor property data and/or GIS sites for free at https://beacon.schneidercorp.com/. For detailed information, must subscribe for a fee. Also, access to assessor data free at http://delaware.iowaassessors.com/.

Des Moines County   *Property, Taxation Records*   Access to GIS/mapping free at www.dmcgis.com/. Also, access to property cards for free at http://desmoines.iowaassessors.com/.

Dickinson County   *Property, Taxation Records*   Search assessor property data and/or GIS sites for free at https://beacon.schneidercorp.com/. For detailed information, must subscribe for a fee. Also, access to assessor's database for free at http://dickinson.iowaassessors.com/.

Dubuque County   *Recorded Documents* http://dubuquecounty.org/recorder/   Access recorder general, tax lien, and corporations indexes free at http://cotthosting.com/iadubuque/LandRecords/protected/SrchQuickName.aspx. Only the Indexes from 1972 through 1996 are available online. The records for this time period can only be viewed in the recorder's office. Also, at http://iowalandrecords.org/portal/clris/SwitchToCountiesTab, view index and images of recorded land records from 1/1987.
Property, Taxation Records   Search assessor property data and/or GIS sites for free at https://beacon.schneidercorp.com/. For detailed information, must subscribe for a fee.

Emmet County   *Property, Taxation Records*   Search assessor property data and/or GIS sites for free at https://beacon.schneidercorp.com/. For detailed information, must subscribe for a fee.

Fayette County   *Property, Taxation Records*   Search assessor property data and/or GIS sites for free at https://beacon.schneidercorp.com/. For detailed information, must subscribe for a fee.

Floyd County   *Property, Taxation Records*   Search assessor property data and/or GIS sites for free at https://beacon.schneidercorp.com/. For detailed information, must subscribe for a fee. Also, access property and sales data is free at www.floydcoia.org/309/GIS.

Franklin County   *Property, Taxation Records*   Search assessor property data and/or GIS sites for free at https://beacon.schneidercorp.com/. For detailed information, must subscribe for a fee.

Greene County   *Property, Taxation Records*   Access to the assessor database of property and sales data is free at http://greene.iowaassessors.com. Also, access to GIS/mapping free at http://greeneia.mygisonline.com/.

Grundy County   *Property, Taxation Records*   Search assessor property data and/or GIS sites for free at https://beacon.schneidercorp.com/. For detailed information, must subscribe for a fee.

Guthrie County *Property, Taxation Records*   Access to the assessor database of property and sales data is free at http://guthrie.iowaassessors.com/search.php?mode=search&showdis=true. Also, search assessor property data and/or GIS sites for free at https://beacon.schneidercorp.com/. For detailed information, must subscribe for a fee.

Hamilton County *Property, Taxation Records*   Search assessor property records and residential and commercial sales free at http://hamilton.iowaassessors.com/.

Hancock County *Property, Taxation Records*   Access to a variety of free searches at http://hancock.iowaassessors.com/. Includes building, sales, and real estate.

Hardin County *Property, Taxation Records*   Search assessor property data and/or GIS sites for free at https://beacon.schneidercorp.com/. For detailed information, must subscribe for a fee.

Harrison County *Property, Taxation Records*   Search assessor property data and/or GIS sites for free at https://beacon.schneidercorp.com/. For detailed information, must subscribe for a fee.

Henry County *Property, Taxation Records*   Search assessor property data and/or GIS sites for free at https://beacon.schneidercorp.com/. For detailed information, must subscribe for a fee.

Howard County *Property, Taxation Records*   Access to assessor records for free at http://howard.iowaassessors.com/.

Humboldt County *Property, Taxation Records*   Assessor property records and sales free at http://humboldt.iowaassessors.com/.

Iowa County *Property, Taxation Records*   Access to the assessor database of property and sales data is free at http://iowa.iowaassessors.com/. Also search free at http://lti.gmdsolutions.com/iowa/index.html.

Jackson County *Property, Taxation Records*   Search assessor property data and/or GIS sites for free at https://beacon.schneidercorp.com/. For detailed information, must subscribe for a fee.

Jasper County *Recorded Documents* www.co.jasper.ia.us/index.aspx?page=101   Access to real estate records for free at http://cotthosting.com/IAJasperRodExternal/LandRecords/protected/SrchQuickName.aspx.
Property, Taxation Records   Access to the assessor database of property and sales data is free at http://jasper.iowaassessors.com/. Also, access to parcel searches for free at https://www.iowatreasurers.org/index.php. Search assessor property data and/or GIS sites for free at https://beacon.schneidercorp.com/. For detailed information, must subscribe for a fee.

Jefferson County *Property, Taxation Records*   Access to the assessor database of property and sales data is free at http://jefferson.iowaassessors.com/.

Johnson County *Recorded Documents Records* www.johnson-county.com/dept_recorder.aspx?id=1155   Access the recorders data free at http://recorder.johnson-county.com/External/LandRecords/protected/SrchQuickName.aspx. Images and indexes go back to 11/1983, Book 670 and are updated daily.
Property, Taxation Records   Search assessor property data and/or GIS sites for free at https://beacon.schneidercorp.com/. For detailed information, must subscribe for a fee. Also, access to Iowa City assessor and property data is free at http://iowacity.iowaassessors.com.

Jones County *Property, Taxation Records*   Search assessor property data and/or GIS sites for free at https://beacon.schneidercorp.com/. For detailed information, must subscribe for a fee.

Keokuk County *Property, Taxation Records*   Search assessor property data and/or GIS sites for free at https://beacon.schneidercorp.com/. For detailed information, must subscribe for a fee.

Kossuth County *Property, Taxation Records*   Access to the assessor database of property and sales data is free at http://kossuth.iowaassessors.com/showResBldgSearch.php.

Lee County *Property, Taxation Records*   Search assessor property data and/or GIS sites for free at https://beacon.schneidercorp.com/. For detailed information, must subscribe for a fee.

Linn County *Recorded Documents* www.linncountyrecorder.com/   Access to recorder database free at http://cotthosting.com/ialinn/LandRecords/protected/SrchQuickName.aspx.
Property, Taxation Records   Access to the assessor database of property data is free at http://linn.iowaassessors.com/. Also, access to City of Cedar Rapids property data is free at http://cedarrapids.iowaassessors.com/. No name searching.

Louisa County *Property, Taxation Records*   Search assessor property data and/or GIS sites for free at https://beacon.schneidercorp.com/. For detailed information, must subscribe for a fee.

Lucas County *Property, Taxation Records*   Access to assessor's database free at http://lucas.iowaassessors.com/.

Lyon County *Property, Taxation Records*   Search assessor property data and/or GIS sites for free at https://beacon.schneidercorp.com/. For detailed information, must subscribe for a fee.

Madison County   *Recorded Documents* www.madisoncoia.us/offices/recorder/index.htm   Search the indexing inquiry page for free at http://lti.gmdsolutions.com/madison/rindex.html.

Property, Taxation Records   Access the assessor database of property data (includes tax sales certificates) free at http://lti2.gmdsolutions.com/drupal/BasicShell?ctid=61&BSI=Search_Realestate&tabid=127337. Also search free at http://madison.iowaassessors.com/. Also, search assessor property data and/or GIS sites for free at https://beacon.schneidercorp.com/. For detailed information, must subscribe for a fee.

Mahaska County   *Property, Taxation Records*   Search assessor property data and/or GIS sites for free at https://beacon.schneidercorp.com/. For detailed information, must subscribe for a fee.

Marion County   *Property, Taxation Records*   Search assessor property data and/or GIS sites for free at https://beacon.schneidercorp.com/. For detailed information, must subscribe for a fee.

Marshall County   *Property, Taxation Records*   Access to the assessor property record card system and sales data is free at www.co.marshall.ia.us/assessor/cgi/frameset.cgi.

Mills County   *Property, Taxation Records*   Search assessor property data and/or GIS sites for free at https://beacon.schneidercorp.com/. For detailed information, must subscribe for a fee.

Mitchell County   *Property, Taxation Records*   Access to assessor's database free at http://mitchell.iowaassessors.com/.

Monona County   *Property, Taxation Records*   Access to records for a fee at http://monona.iowaassessors.com/.

Monroe County   *Recorded Documents Records* www.monroecoia.us/offices/recorder/index.htm   A specific county site is offered at http://lti2.gmdsolutions.com/drupal/BasicShell?ctid=68&BSI=SelectRecordedDoc&tabid=122717, search by name or by book and page.

Property, Taxation Records   Access to assessor's database free at http://monroe.iowaassessors.com/.

Montgomery County   *Property, Taxation Records*   Search assessor property data and/or GIS sites for free at https://beacon.schneidercorp.com/. For detailed information, must subscribe for a fee.

Muscatine County   *Property, Taxation Records*   Search assessor property data and/or GIS sites for free at https://beacon.schneidercorp.com/. For detailed information, must subscribe for a fee.

Osceola County   *Property, Taxation Records*   Search assessor property data and/or GIS sites for free at https://beacon.schneidercorp.com/. For detailed information, must subscribe for a fee.

Page County   *Property, Taxation Records*   Search assessor property data and/or GIS sites for free at https://beacon.schneidercorp.com/. For detailed information, must subscribe for a fee.

Palo Alto County   *Property, Taxation Records*   Access to assessor's database for free to go http://paloalto.iowaassessors.com/.

Plymouth County   *Property, Taxation Records*   Access the assessor database of property and sales data free at http://plymouth.iowaassessors.com/. Access to Agricultural Land Sale Searches free at www.co.plymouth.ia.us/Services/forms.htm from 2008 to 2015.

Pocahontas County   *Property, Taxation Records*   Search assessor property data and/or GIS sites for free at https://beacon.schneidercorp.com/. For detailed information, must subscribe for a fee.

Polk County   *Recorded Documents* www.polkcountyiowa.gov/recorder   Access to deeds, liens, etc. free at http://landrecords.polkcountyiowa.gov/LandRecords/protected/SrchQuickName.aspx. Index records from 1992 to present; view/print documents from 7/1/2002 to present; No vital record or Military information is available online. Also, download residential, commercial, or agricultural data free at www.assess.co.polk.ia.us/web/basic/exports.html.

Property, Taxation Records   Access to the Polk County assessor database is free at www.assess.co.polk.ia.us/web/basic/search.html. Search by property or by sales. Also, download residential, commercial, or agricultural data free at www.assess.co.polk.ia.us/web/basic/exports.html. Also, access to property search data for free at http://web.assess.co.polk.ia.us/cgi-bin/web/tt/infoqry.cgi?tt=home/index.

Pottawattamie County   *Recorded Documents Records* www.pottcounty.com/departments/recorder/overview/   Access to real estate parcel information free at http://rec.pottcounty.com/avaweb/#/.   The county works with https://tapestry.fidlar.com/Tapestry2/Default.aspx for record access. Base fee is $5.95 per search and $.50 per print image. You can pay as you go using a credit or pre-pay using a subscription. Also, one may purchase a software program Laredo (www.fidlar.com/laredo.aspx) with extensive search features. Contact the county for details and pricing.

Property, Taxation Records   Records on the County Courthouse/Council Bluffs property database and sales are free at www.pottco.org/. Search by owner name, address, or parcel number. Records since 7/1/89, images since 10/20/2002.

Poweshiek County   *Property, Taxation Records*   Search assessor property data and/or GIS sites for free at https://beacon.schneidercorp.com/. For detailed information, must subscribe for a fee.

Ringgold County   *Property, Taxation Records*   Search assessor property data and/or GIS sites for free at https://beacon.schneidercorp.com/. For detailed information, must subscribe for a fee.

Sac County *Property, Taxation Records* Search assessor property data and/or GIS sites for free at https://beacon.schneidercorp.com/. For detailed information, must subscribe for a fee.

Scott County *Recorded Documents* See http://cotthosting.com/iascott/LandRecords/protected/SrchQuickName.aspx; includes land, lien, plats, incorporations, trade names, and UCCs back to 1/1989.

Property, Taxation Records Access to assessor property parcel search for free at www.scottcountyiowa.com/parcels. Also, sheriff sales lists free at www.scottcountyiowa.net/sheriff/temp-sales.php. Also, access to GIS/mapping for free at http://maps.scottcountyiowa.com/.

Shelby County *Property, Taxation Records* Search assessor property data and/or GIS sites for free at https://beacon.schneidercorp.com/. For detailed information, must subscribe for a fee.

Sioux County *Property, Taxation Records* Access property data information free at http://assessor.siouxcounty.org/assessmenthome.asp. Also, search the treasurer's property tax records at http://treasurer.siouxcounty.org/ for free.

Story County *Property, Taxation Records* Search assessor property data and/or GIS sites for free at https://beacon.schneidercorp.com/. For detailed information, must subscribe for a fee.

Tama County *Property, Taxation Records* Access to the assessor database of property and sales data is free at http://tama.iowaassessors.com/.

Taylor County *Property, Taxation Records* Access to GIS/mapping for free at https://taylor.integritygis.com/.

Union County *Property, Taxation Records* Search assessor property data and/or GIS sites for free at https://beacon.schneidercorp.com/. For detailed information, must subscribe for a fee.

Van Buren County *Property, Taxation Records* Search parcel data information free at http://vanburen.iowaassessors.com/.

Wapello County *Property, Taxation Records* Search assessor property and sales data free at http://wapello.iowaassessors.com/.

Warren County *Property, Taxation Records* Search assessor property data and/or GIS sites for free at https://beacon.schneidercorp.com/. For detailed information, must subscribe for a fee.

Washington County *Property, Taxation Records* Access to the assessor database of property and sales data is free at http://washington.iowaassessors.com. Also, access to GIS/mapping for free at http://washingtonia.mygisonline.com/.

Wayne County *Property, Taxation Records* Access to parcel searches and property sales for free at www.wayne.iowaassessors.com/.

Webster County *Property, Taxation Records* Access to the assessor database of property and sales data is free at www.webstercountyia.org/. Also, property data is free at www.webstercountyia.org/web-plugin/. Also, access to Assessor property searches for free at http://webster.iowaassessors.com/.

Winnebago County *Property, Taxation Records* Search assessor property data and/or GIS sites for free at https://beacon.schneidercorp.com/. For detailed information, must subscribe for a fee. Also, access to records free at https://iowalandrecords.org/portal/clris/SwitchToSearchSimpleTab#firstLevelTabs.

Winneshiek County *Property, Taxation Records* Search assessor property data and/or GIS sites for free at https://beacon.schneidercorp.com/. For detailed information, must subscribe for a fee.

Woodbury County *Property, Taxation Records* Search assessor property data and/or GIS sites for free at https://beacon.schneidercorp.com/. For detailed information, must subscribe for a fee.

Worth County *Property, Taxation Records* Access to assessor's database free at http://worth.iowaassessors.com/.

Wright County *Property, Taxation Records* Search assessor property data and/or GIS sites for free at https://beacon.schneidercorp.com/. For detailed information, must subscribe for a fee. Also, access to land search data for free at http://wright.iowaassessors.com/.

Reminder:

Recorded documents for all counties are available on the state system.

Provided by the Iowa county Recorders Association, the Iowa Land Records system at http://iowalandrecords.org/portal offers statewide searching and pdf images of deeds, liens, even UCCs and judgments. While free now, the site states this service may begin charging at any time. There are also features for monitoring new documents and saving documents.

Kansas

Capital: Topeka
           Shawnee County

Time Zone: CST

    Kansas' five western-most counties are MST:
    They are: Greeley, Hamilton, Kearny, Sherman, Wallace.

Population: 2,911,641
# of Counties: 105

Useful State Links

Website: **www.kansas.gov**
Governor: **http://governor.ks.gov**
Attorney General: **http://ag.ks.gov/home**
State Archives: **www.kshs.org**
State Statutes and Codes: **http://kslegislature.org/li/**
Legislative Bill Search: **http://kslegislature.org/li/**
Unclaimed Funds: **https://www.kansascash.com/prodweb/up/unclaimed-property.php**

State Public Record Agencies

Criminal Records

Kansas Bureau of Investigation, Criminal Records Division, www.kansas.gov/kbi/criminalhistory/ Anyone may obtain non-certified criminal records online at https://www.kansas.gov/criminalhistory/. The fee is $20.00 per record; credit cards accepted online. The system is also available for premium subscribers of accessKansas. Note the system is unavailable between the hours of midnight and 4 AM daily.

Sexual Offender Registry

Kansas Bureau of Investigation, Offender Registration, www.kbi.ks.gov/registeredoffender/ Searching is available at the website, there are several searches including by name, a geographical search, by phone number and by email or Facebook page.. All open registrants are searchable. The information contained in a registration entry was provided by the registrant. Neither the Kansas Bureau of Investigation (KBI) nor the sheriff's office can guarantee the accuracy of this information. The online Offender Registry is for notification and public information only, and does not contain all offender required to register by law, nor does it contain all information about any offender's criminal history.

Incarceration Records

Kansas Department of Corrections, Records Division, www.dc.state.ks.us/ Web access to the database known as KASPER gives information on offenders who are: currently incarcerated; under post-incarceration supervision; and, who have been discharged from a sentence. The database does not have information available about inmates sent to Kansas under the provisions of the interstate compact agreement. Go to https://kdocrepository.doc.ks.gov/kasper/. Also, view the Parole Absconders Escapees list at the same site. *Other Options:* Bulk lists are available on CD for $.01 per record.

Corporation, LP, LLC

Sec. of State - Business Srvs, Memorial Hall, 1st Floor, www.sos.ks.gov/business/business_entity.html Free entity searching from a link at https://www.kansas.gov/bess/flow/main?execution=e3s1. Search by company name of business entity ID numbers. Also search chartable organizatoins, trademark/service-mark and name availability at this site. *Other Options:* Bulk purchase is offered. Call Anne at 785-296-2908.

Trademarks/Servicemarks

Sec of State - Business Srvs, Trademarks/Servicemarks Division, www.kssos.org/business/trademark/trademark_search.aspx Free searching at www.kssos.org/business/trademark/trademark_search.aspxbusiness/trademark/trademark_search.aspx by a variety of ways (keyword, owner, trademark, etc.). *Other Options:* For bulk file purchase call Anne at 785-296-2908.

Uniform Commercial Code, Federal & State Tax Liens

Secretary of State - UCC Searches, Memorial Hall, 1st Fl,   www.sos.ks.gov/business/business.html   One must be a subscriber. UCC records are $10.00 per record plus $1.00 per copy. Go to www.sos.ks.gov/other/ucc_debtor_search_requests.html or for more information call at 800-4-KANSAS. The system is open 24 hours daily. The subscription requires a modest annual fee. This is the same online system used for obtaining business entity records and driving records.   *Other Options:* Records in a bulk or database format is available from the subscription mentioned above.

Vital Records

Kansas Department of Health & Environment, Office of Vital Statistics,   www.kdheks.gov/vital/   Records may be ordered online via a state designated vendor VitalChek at www.vitalchek.com. Add $11.00 for expedited service.

Driver Records

Department of Revenue, Driver Control Bureau,   www.ksrevenue.org/vehicle.html   There is a free DL status check at https://www.kdor.org/DLStatus/login.aspx?ReturnUrl=%2fdlstatus%2fsecure%2fdefault.aspx. Kansas has contracted with the Kansas.gov (800-452-6727) to service all electronic media requests of driver license histories at www.kansas.gov/subscribers/. The fee per record is $6.00 for batch requests or $6.60 for immediate inquiry. There is an annual subscription fee of $95. Billing is monthly. If not paid via EFT, a 3% surcharge is added. The system is open 24 hours a day, 7 days a week. Batch requests are available at 7:30 am (if ordered by 10 pm the previous day).   *Other Options:* Kansas offers a monitoring system or notification program for insurance companies to monitor any changes that occur during the month for records with a traffic conviction and/or administrative action added to the record.

Crash Reports

Kansas Highway Patrol, GHQ - Records Section,   www.kansashighwaypatrol.org/   With a Kansas.Gov account, one may request an accident report online, but only if the accident occurred since May 2013. See https://www.kansas.gov/accident-reports/. Same fees apply. The Kansas Highway Patrol Crash Log online application at https://www.accesskansas.org/ssrv-khp-crashlogs/index.do allows one to retrieve any crash log posted, but only for the last 30 days. Search the crash logs by date, county, and type of crash.

Vehicle Ownership & Registration

Division of Vehicles, Title and Registration Bureau,   www.ksrevenue.org/vehicle.html   The fee is $6.50 to search by title number or by plate number or by VIN. No name searching is permitted. Visit www.kansas.gov/subscribers for a complete description of obtaining records from Kansas.gov (800-452-6727), the state authorized vendor. Email questions to helpcenter@ink.org. There is an annual $95 fee to access records from Kansas, note many other records are available, including driving records.

Voter Registration, Campaign Finance. PACs, Lobbyists

Secretary of State - Elections Division, Memorial Hall, 1st Floor,   www.sos.ks.gov/elections/elections_registration.html   Check campaign finance including spending and contribution, individual candidates, and PACs at www.sos.ks.gov/elections/cfr_viewer/cfr_examiner_entry.aspx. Lobbyists data is shown at   www.kssos.org/elections/elections_lobbyists.html.   Search polling place location by voter information at https://myvoteinfo.voteks.org/VoterView/PollingPlaceSearch.do.   View registration information at https://myvoteinfo.voteks.org/VoterView/RegistrantSearch.do.   *Other Options:* This agency will sell the voter registration database for political purposes by CD or email. The entire DB is $200.00 or purchase by subdivision. The form is at www.kssos.org/forms/elections/CVR.pdf. Email bryan.caskey@sos.ks.gov if questions.

GED Certificates

Kansas Board of Regents, GED Records,   www.kansasregents.org/students/kansas_ged_information   Records may be requested from https://www.diplomasender.com. A credit card is needed. Request must be ordered by the test taker. Employers and third parties must receive an email and/or Authentication Code from the test taker to then access the authorized documents. Turnaround time is 1-3 days.

Occupational Licensing Boards

Accountant Firm	http://oitsapps.ks.gov/boa/searchforfirms.aspx
Accountant-CPA	http://oitsapps.ks.gov/boa/searchforindividual.aspx
Alcohol License	https://www.kdor.org/abc/licensee/default.aspx
Alcohol/Drug Counselor	https://www.kansas.gov/bsrb-verification/index.do
Alcoholic Brand Lookup	https://ks.productregistrationonline.com/activebrands
Ambulance Attendant	https://www.accesskansas.org/ssrv-aivel/ac/search.html
Ambulance Service	www.ksbems.org/ems/?page_id=18
Athletic Trainer	https://www.accesskansas.org/ssrv-ksbhada/search.html
Attorney	http://tpka-oas-01.kscourts.org:8888/pls/ar/attorney_registration_pkg.request_attorney
Behavioral Sciences Disciplinary Actions	http://ksbsrb.ks.gov/complaints/disciplinary-actions
Charity Organization	www.kscharitycheck.org/
Chiropractor	https://www.accesskansas.org/ssrv-ksbhada/search.html

Clinical Psychotherapist	https://www.kansas.gov/bsrb-verification/index.do
Coroners/District and Deputy	http://ksbma.ks.gov/resources/license-listings
Cosmetology Disciplinary Action Reports	www.kansas.gov/kboc/DisciplinaryActionReports.htm
Cosmetology-related School	www.kansas.gov/kboc/Docs/School_Directory.pdf
Counselor, Professional	https://www.kansas.gov/bsrb-verification/index.do
Crematory	http://ksbma.ks.gov/resources/license-listings
Dental Hygienist	www.kansas.gov/dental-verification/index.do
Dentist	www.kansas.gov/dental-verification/index.do
Disciplinary Cases from 10/25/96 to present	www.kscourts.org/rules-procedures-forms/attorney-discipline/cases.asp
Discontinued/Restricted Use Pesticide Products	http://agriculture.ks.gov/divisions-programs/pesticide-fertilizer/pesticide-applicator
Embalmer	http://ksbma.ks.gov/resources/license-listings
EMS Disciplinary Action	https://www.accesskansas.org/ssrv-aivel/dl/search.html
Funeral Director/Assis't Financial Dir.	http://ksbma.ks.gov/resources/license-listings
Funeral Establishment	http://ksbma.ks.gov/resources/license-listings
Instructor/Teacher	https://www.accesskansas.org/ssrv-aivel/tc/search.html
Insurance Agent, Company	http://towerii.ksinsurance.org/agent/index.jsp
Investment Advisor	www.adviserinfo.sec.gov/
Lobbyist	www.kssos.org/elections/lobbyist_online.aspx
Marriage & Family Therapist	https://www.kansas.gov/bsrb-verification/index.do
Medical School	https://www.accesskansas.org/ssrv-ksbhada/search.html
Nurse	www.kansas.gov/ksbn-verifications/
Nurses Aide	https://ksdhe.glsuite.us/glsuiteweb/Clients/KSDHE/public/main.html
Occupational Therapist/Assistant	https://www.accesskansas.org/ssrv-ksbhada/search.html
Optometrist	https://www.accesskansas.org/ssrv-optometry/index.html
Osteopathic Physician	https://www.accesskansas.org/ssrv-ksbhada/search.html
Pesticide Applicator	http://agriculture.ks.gov/divisions-programs/pesticide-fertilizer/pesticide-applicator
Pesticide Dealer	http://agriculture.ks.gov/divisions-programs/pesticide-fertilizer/pesticide-dealer
Pharmacist	https://ksbop.elicensesoftware.com/portal.aspx
Physical Therapist/Assistant	https://www.accesskansas.org/ssrv-ksbhada/search.html
Physician/Medical Doctor/Assistant	https://www.accesskansas.org/ssrv-ksbhada/search.html
Podiatrist	https://www.accesskansas.org/ssrv-ksbhada/search.html
Provider/Sponsor	https://www.accesskansas.org/ssrv-aivel/ps/search.html
Psychologist	https://www.kansas.gov/bsrb-verification/index.do
Psychologist, Masters Level	https://www.kansas.gov/bsrb-verification/index.do
Radiologic Technologist	https://www.accesskansas.org/ssrv-ksbhada/search.html
Real Estate Agent/Seller/Broker	https://www.kansas.gov/krec-verification/index.do
Real Estate Appraiser	www.kansas.gov/appraiser-directory/index.do
Respiratory Therapist/Student	https://www.accesskansas.org/ssrv-ksbhada/search.html
School Administrator	https://online.ksde.org/TLL/SearchLicense.aspx
School Counselor	https://online.ksde.org/TLL/SearchLicense.aspx
School Nurse	https://online.ksde.org/TLL/SearchLicense.aspx
Securities Broker/Dealer	http://brokercheck.finra.org/
Social Worker	https://www.kansas.gov/bsrb-verification/index.do
Teacher	https://online.ksde.org/TLL/SearchLicense.aspx
Tobacco Registration/License	https://www.kdor.org/abc/licensee/default.aspx
Veterinarian	http://agriculture.ks.gov/divisions-programs/division-of-animal-health/kansas-board-of-veterinary-examiners/licensee-information

State and Local Courts

About Kansas Courts: The **District Court** is the court of general jurisdiction. with general original jurisdiction over all civil and criminal cases, including divorce and domestic relations, damage suits, probate and administration of estates, guardianships, conservatorships, care of the mentally ill, juvenile matters, and small claims. There is a District Court in each county and an Office of the Clerk of the Court where cases may be filed.

A **Municipal Court** can hear only cases involving alleged violations of municipal ordinances legally enacted by the governing body of the city. A Municipal Court in Kansas has no civil jurisdiction. The Municipal Court has jurisdiction to hear a case involving any traffic ordinance violation when the accused person is at least 14 years of age. If an individual in Municipal Court wants a jury trial, the request must be filed de novo in a District Court. Marriage and divorce records are found with the Clerk of the District Court where the action occurred as well as at the state vital records agency.

The web page for the Unified Judicial System is http://judicial.alabama.gov/

Appellate Courts: Published opinions and case information from the Appellate Courts and Supreme Court are available at www.kscourts.org.

Online Court Access

All courts participate in the system described below.

Commercial online access for civil, criminal, and traffic records is available for District Court records from the state's judicial system managed by Kansas.gov. Note that Sedgwick County cases prior to 2003 and Wyandotte County Cases prior to July 2004 are not available on the system and there are certain limitations with Johnson County (see below).   See https://www.kansas.gov/countyCourts/courtDates.gsp for a list of start dates when new filings where entered for each county.

Record searching is offered to the general public at https://www.kansas.gov/countyCourts/. The site works with smartphones or tablets. A subscription account is also available, see http://www.kansas.gov/subscribers/. For either system the fee is $1.00 per search, per county, PLUS $1.00 per case retrieved for view. Users may perform a name search of multiple counties. A credit card is required for payment, unless the requester has a subscription. Subscribers pay an annual $95 subscription fee and receive monthly billing. Interestingly and although the web page does not state this, **Johnson County records are available only to subscribers**—if a requester uses the public site (and pays with a credit card) Johnson County records are NOT available.

Other County Sites (not mentioned above):

Johnson County

District Court   http://www.jococourts.org/
Civil: Search Johnson County District Court records available free at www.jococourts.org with index back to 1980. Access is web-based at https://www.accesskansas.org/countyCourts/. Fee is $1.00 per search and $1.00 per case retrieved for view. A credit card is required. Or pay a $95.00 annual subscription which will provide monthly billing and access to other Kansas public records. *Criminal:* same

Shawnee County

District Court   http://www.shawneecourt.org
Civil: Go to https://public.shawneecourt.org/PublicAccess/publicAccess/?service=PublicAccess to view the county's online access to dockets. Daily dockets lists are free at http://public.shawneecourt.org/docket/. Access is web-based at https://www.accesskansas.org/countyCourts/. Fee is $1.00 per search and $1.00 per case retrieved for view. A credit card is required. Or pay a $95.00 annual subscription which will provide monthly billing and access to other Kansas public records.
Criminal: Access is web-based at https://www.accesskansas.org/countyCourts/. Fee is $1.00 per search and $1.00 per case retrieved for view. A credit card is required. Or pay a $95.00 annual subscription which will provide monthly billing and access to other Kansas public records. Search is by county, not statewide. No identifiers shown. Go to https://public.shawneecourt.org/PublicAccess/publicAccess/?service=PublicAccess to view the county's online access to dockets. Daily dockets lists are free at http://public.shawneecourt.org/docket/.

Recorders and Assessors

About Kansas Recording Offices: 105 counties, 105 recording offices. The recording officer is the Register of Deeds. Many counties utilize a "Miscellaneous Index" for tax and other liens, separate from real estate records.

About Tax Liens: Per KS Statute 79-2614, federal tax liens on personal property of businesses are filed with the Secretary of State. Other federal tax liens and all state tax liens on personal property are filed with the county Register of Deeds.

Online Access

There is no statewide system to either recorded documents or tax assessor records.

At least 26 counties individually provide online access to recorded documents and 74 counties provide online access to property tax records or GIS records.

County Sites:

Allen County   *Recorded Documents* www.allencounty.org/regdeeds.html   The county works with https://tapestry.fidlar.com/Tapestry2/Default.aspx for record access. Base fee is $5.95 per search and $.50 per print image. You can pay as you go using a credit or pre-pay using a subscription. Also, one may purchase a software program Laredo (www.fidlar.com/laredo.aspx) with extensive search features. Contact the county for details and pricing.

Property, Taxation Records   Access to property tax information for free at http://ks388.cichosting.com/security/default.aspx?Module=TAX. Also, access to property information and GIS/mapping for free at http://jade.kgs.ku.edu/orka2/CoSelect.aspx.

Anderson County   *Property, Taxation Records*   Access to property information and GIS/mapping for free at http://jade.kgs.ku.edu/orka2/CoSelect.aspx.

Atchison County   *Property, Taxation Records*   Search the property and tax database free at www.atchisoncountyks.org/Appraisal.aspx. Not regularly updated. Also, access to property information and GIS/mapping for free at http://jade.kgs.ku.edu/orka2/CoSelect.aspx.

Barber County   *Property, Taxation Records*   Access to property information and GIS/mapping for free at http://orka.kansasgis.org/IntroPage.aspx.

Barton County   *Property, Taxation Records*   Access to property information and GIS/mapping for free at http://jade.kgs.ku.edu/orka2/CoSelect.aspx.

Bourbon County   *Recorded Documents* www.bourboncountyks.org/index.php/government/register-of-deeds   This office has an online subscripton site. Contact office for details.
Property, Taxation Records   Access to property data index for a fee at www.bourboncountyks.org/index.php/how-to-find/parcel-search. Contact Appraiser's office at 620-223-3800 x36 for subscription information. They do have a limited public search. Also, search property tax information free at http://ks1055.cichosting.com/ttp/tax/Search/search_tax.aspx. Also, access to property information and GIS/mapping for free at http://jade.kgs.ku.edu/orka2/CoSelect.aspx.

Brown County   *Recorded Documents* http://ks-brown.manatron.com/RegisterofDeeds/tabid/5348/Default.aspx   Access to recorded docs and tax records and ORION online is currently under development; see http://ks-brown.manatron.com/RegisterofDeeds/DMSOnline/tabid/5617/Default.aspx. Contact Register's Office at 785-742-7602 for more information. Registration fee is $250.00 per year.
Property, Taxation Records   Search assessment data free or by subscription at www.brown.kansasgov.com/parcel/. Basic searches free, more detailed searches are subscription.

Butler County   *Recorded Documents* www.bucoks.com/Directory.aspx?did=17   An index of recorded real estate records from 1950 forward is available at http://maps.bucoks.com/rmis/search.aspx.

Chase County   *Recorded Documents* www.wycokck.org/Internetdept.aspx?id=2600&menu_id=1024&banner=15284   The county works with https://tapestry.fidlar.com/Tapestry2/Default.aspx for record access. Base fee is $5.95 per search and $.50 per print image. You can pay as you go using a credit or pre-pay using a subscription. Also, one may purchase a software program Laredo (www.fidlar.com/laredo.aspx) with extensive search features. Contact the county for details and pricing.

Chautauqua County   *Property, Taxation Records*   Access to property information and GIS/mapping for free at http://orka.kansasgis.org/IntroPage.aspx.

Cherokee County   *Property, Taxation Records*   Assess to county parcel data for free at www.cherokee.kansasgov.com/parcel/. Can search as Public and contact Appraiser's Office to register. Also, access to property information and GIS/mapping for free at http://jade.kgs.ku.edu/orka2/CoSelect.aspx.

Cheyenne County   *Property, Taxation Records*   Access to property information and GIS/mapping for free at http://jade.kgs.ku.edu/orka2/CoSelect.aspx.

Clark County   *Property, Taxation Records*   Access to Appraisal's parcel search is free at www.clark.kansasgov.com/parcel/. Click on parcel search public for free information. A tax roll search is free at www.ecountyworks.com/clark/. Also, access to property information and GIS/mapping for free at http://jade.kgs.ku.edu/orka2/CoSelect.aspx.

Clay County   *Property, Taxation Records*   Access to property lookup for free at www.claycountykansas.org/property_lookup. Also, access to property information and GIS/mapping for free at http://jade.kgs.ku.edu/orka2/CoSelect.aspx.

Cloud County *Property, Taxation Records*   Access to parcel data for free at https://ks1120.cichosting.com/webportal/Login.aspx. Also, access to property information and GIS/mapping for free at http://jade.kgs.ku.edu/orka2/CoSelect.aspx. Also, access to tax search data free at https://ks1120.cichosting.com/tax/Search/search_tax.aspx.

Coffey County *Property, Taxation Records*   Access to tax and property searches for free at www.coffeycountyks.org/county_appraiser.php?Overview-1.

Cowley County *Property, Taxation Records*   Search property data free at https://ks275.cichosting.com/webportal/Login.aspx. Must register.

Crawford County *Recorded Documents* www.crawfordcountykansas.org/county-register-of-deeds.html   The county works with https://tapestry.fidlar.com/Tapestry2/Default.aspx for record access. Base fee is $5.95 per search and $.50 per print image. You can pay as you go using a credit or pre-pay using a subscription. Also, one may purchase a software program Laredo (www.fidlar.com/laredo.aspx) with extensive search features. Contact the county for details and pricing. Index and images go back to 1989.
Property, Taxation Records   Access to parcel search for free at www.crawford.kansasgov.com/parcel/. Must register to enter. Also, access to property information and GIS/mapping for free at http://orka.kansasgis.org/IntroPage.aspx.

Dickinson County *Property, Taxation Records*   Access to GIS/mapping free at www.dkcoksgis.org/ParcelSearch/. Also, access to property information and GIS/mapping for free at http://jade.kgs.ku.edu/orka2/CoSelect.aspx.

Doniphan County *Property, Taxation Records*   Access to GIS/mapping free at https://doniphan.integritygis.com/. Also, access to property information and GIS/mapping for free at http://jade.kgs.ku.edu/orka2/CoSelect.aspx.

Douglas County *Recorded Documents* www.douglascountyks.org/depts/register-of-deeds   Register of Deeds data by subscription; for info and signup call IL Dept at 785-832-5183/5299.
Property, Taxation Records   Access property records and GIS/mapping for free at www.douglascountyks.org/depts/appraiser

Elk County *Property, Taxation Records*   Access to property information and GIS/mapping for free at http://jade.kgs.ku.edu/orka2/CoSelect.aspx.

Ellis County *Property, Taxation Records*   Access to real estate record searches for free at https://ks292.cichosting.com/webportal/Login.aspx. Must register.

Ellsworth County *Property, Taxation Records*   Access to property information and GIS/mapping for free at http://jade.kgs.ku.edu/orka2/CoSelect.aspx.

Finney County *Recorded Documents* www.finneycounty.org/index.aspx?nid=147   Access to records for a fee at http://ks-finneycounty.civicplus.com/index.aspx?NID=379; $120.00 for 3 months or $360.00 per year; contact office at 620-272-3628. Imaged documents starting in January, 1990 to present. Access to records prior to above-$150.00 for 3 months.
Property, Taxation Records   Access to land tax records for free at www.finney.kansasgov.com/parcel/DisclaimerReg.asp.

Ford County *Recorded Documents* www.fordcounty.net/rod/index.html   The county works with https://tapestry.fidlar.com/Tapestry2/Default.aspx for record access. Base fee is $5.95 per search and $.50 per print image. You can pay as you go using a credit or pre-pay using a subscription. Also, one may purchase a software program Laredo (www.fidlar.com/laredo.aspx) with extensive search features. Contact the county for details and pricing.
Property, Taxation Records   Property information including parcels and taxes for free are available at www.fordcounty.net/appraisal/index.html.

Franklin County *Recorded Documents* www.franklincoks.org/index.aspx?NID=136   Contact Appraisers office about subscription fees for online info (785-229-3420).
Property, Taxation Records   Access to GIS/mapping free at www.franklin.kansasgis.com/. For detailed information must register and pay fees.

Geary County *Property, Taxation Records*   Access to Tax search for free at http://geary.kansasgov.com/tax/.

Gove County *Recorded Documents* www.govecountyks.com/latest-news/register-of-deeds   Access to document records search for a fee at https://esearch.cichosting.com/. Must subscribe. Covers 13 counties.

Grant County *Recorded Documents* www.grantcoks.org/index.aspx?nid=126   Access to property tax search free at www.ecountyworks.com/grant/.

Gray County *Recorded Documents* www.grayco.org/Government/RegisterofDeeds/tabid/3921/Default.aspx   Access to record searches free at www.grayco.org/.
Property, Taxation Records   Access to tax and parcel searches free at www.grayco.org/.

Greeley County *Cemetery Directory Records* www.greeleycounty.org/?page_id=1557   Access to the County Cemetery Directory for free at www.greeleycounty.org/?page_id=1358.

Greenwood County *Property, Taxation Records* Access to property information and GIS/mapping for free at http://jade.kgs.ku.edu/orka2/CoSelect.aspx.

Harper County *Property, Taxation Records* Access to GIS/mapping free at www.harpercountyks.gov/index.aspx?NID=375.

Harvey County *Property, Taxation Records* Access property tax records from the appraiser and treasurer free at www.harvey.kansasgis.com/. For detailed information must register for a fee.

Hodgeman County *Property, Taxation Records* Access to property information and GIS/mapping for free at http://jade.kgs.ku.edu/orka2/CoSelect.aspx.

Jackson County *Property, Taxation Records* Access to GIS/mapping, parcel search and tax search for free at www.jackson.kansasgis.com/.

Jefferson County *Recorded Documents* www.jfcountyks.com/index.aspx?nid=352 The county works with https://tapestry.fidlar.com/Tapestry2/Default.aspx for record access. Base fee is $5.95 per search and $.50 per print image. You can pay as you go using a credit or pre-pay using a subscription. Also, one may purchase a software program Laredo (www.fidlar.com/laredo.aspx) with extensive search features. Contact the county for details and pricing.
Property, Taxation Records Access parcel, tax and GIS/mapping data free at www.jfcountyks.com/index.aspx?NID=101. For more detailed information must subscribe. Also, access to property information and GIS/mapping for free at http://jade.kgs.ku.edu/orka2/CoSelect.aspx.

Jewell County *Property, Taxation Records* Access to property information and GIS/mapping for free at http://jade.kgs.ku.edu/orka2/CoSelect.aspx.

Johnson County *Property, Taxation Records* Search records on the Land Records database free at http://land.jocogov.org/default.aspx. No name searching.

Kingman County *Property, Taxation Records* Access to property information and GIS/mapping for free at http://jade.kgs.ku.edu/orka2/CoSelect.aspx.

Labette County *Property, Taxation Records* Access to assessment maps for free at www.labettecounty.com/eGov/apps/document/center.egov?view=item;id=16.

Leavenworth County *Recorded Dcouments Records* www.leavenworthcounty.org/rod/default.asp The county works with https://tapestry.fidlar.com/Tapestry2/Default.aspx for record access. Base fee is $5.95 per search and $.50 per print image. You can pay as you go using a credit or pre-pay using a subscription. Also, one may purchase a software program Laredo (www.fidlar.com/laredo.aspx) with extensive search features. Contact the county for details and pricing.
Property, Taxation Records Free search of county parcel data at www.leavenworth.kansasgov.com/parcel/. Also, access to property information and GIS/mapping for free at http://jade.kgs.ku.edu/orka2/CoSelect.aspx.

Lincoln County *Property, Taxation Records* Access to property information and GIS/mapping for free at http://jade.kgs.ku.edu/orka2/CoSelect.aspx.

Linn County *Property, Taxation Records* Access to parcel searches for free at www.linn.kansasgov.com/parcel/. Also, access to property information and GIS/mapping for free at http://jade.kgs.ku.edu/orka2/CoSelect.aspx.

Lyon County *Recorded Documents* www.lyoncounty.org/Register_of_Deeds.html T The county works with https://tapestry.fidlar.com/Tapestry2/Default.aspx for record access. Base fee is $5.95 per search and $.50 per print image. You can pay as you go using a credit or pre-pay using a subscription. Also, one may purchase a software program Laredo (www.fidlar.com/laredo.aspx) with extensive search features. Contact the county for details and pricing.
Property, Taxation Records Access parcel data free at https://beacon.schneidercorp.com/. Also, access to property information and GIS/mapping for free at http://jade.kgs.ku.edu/orka2/CoSelect.aspx.

Marion County *Property, Taxation Records* Access property tax records free at www.marion.kansasgov.com/Tax/TaxSearch.asp. Also, access to property information and GIS/mapping for free at http://jade.kgs.ku.edu/orka2/CoSelect.aspx.

Marshall County *Property, Taxation Records* Access property values free at www.marshall.kansasgov.com/Parcel/. Also, tax information for free at www.marshall.kansasgov.com/tax/.

McPherson County *Property, Taxation Records* Access to property map data for free at www.dkcoksgis.org/MPOrka/Default.aspx. Also, access to property information and GIS/mapping for free at http://jade.kgs.ku.edu/orka2/CoSelect.aspx.

Meade County *Property, Taxation Records* Access to county tax search and parcel search for free, go to www.meade.kansasgis.com/.

Miami County *Recorded Documents* www.miamicountyks.org/229/Register-of-Deeds The county works with https://tapestry.fidlar.com/Tapestry2/Default.aspx for record access. Base fee is $5.95 per search and $.50 per print image. You can pay as you go using a credit or pre-pay using a subscription. Also, one may purchase a software program Laredo (www.fidlar.com/laredo.aspx) with extensive search features. Contact the county for details and pricing.

Property, Taxation Records   Access property data and cemetery data free at http://beacon.schneidercorp.com/?site=MiamiCountyKS. Registration, username and password required.

Mitchell County   *Property, Taxation Records*   Access to county tax search for free at www.mitchell.kansasgov.com/Tax/. Also, access to parcel searches free at www.mitchell.kansasgov.com/parcel/.

Montgomery County   *Property, Taxation Records*   Access to parcel search for free at www.montgomery.kansasgov.com/parcel/. Must register for access. Also, access to property information and GIS/mapping for free at http://jade.kgs.ku.edu/orka2/CoSelect.aspx.

Morton County   *Recorded Documents*   www.mtcoks.com/register/register.html   Access to records for a fee at https://esearch.cichosting.com/. Must subscribe.

Nemaha County   *Recorded Documents*   http://ks-nemaha.manatron.com/ElectedOfficials/RegisterofDeeds/tabid/6342/Default.aspx   Access to the Real Estate Portal for a fee at http://ks284.cichosting.com/WebPortal/appraiser/Default.aspx. There is a public access button that can be clicked on for basic information. Must subscribe for full information.
Property, Taxation Records   Access to property information and GIS/mapping for free at http://jade.kgs.ku.edu/orka2/CoSelect.aspx.

Neosho County   *Property, Taxation Records*   Access to parcel search for free at www.neosho.kansasgov.com/parcel/. Also, access to property information and GIS/mapping for free at http://jade.kgs.ku.edu/orka2/CoSelect.aspx.

Ness County   *Recorded Documents*   http://nesscountyks.com/register-of-deeds.html   Online subscription is availabe, contact the Register of Deeds office for details.

Osage County   *Property, Taxation Records*   Online access to the registered user application is at www.osageco.org/Services/Documents/tabid/3637/Default.aspx. Fee is $150.00 annually. Also, access to county records free at www.osage.kansasgis.com/crs/DisclaimerReg.asp.

Ottawa County   *Property, Taxation Records*   Search property data for free at www.ottawa.kansasgov.com/parcel/. Also, search county tax records free at www.ottawa.kansasgov.com/tax/.

Pawnee County   *Property, Taxation Records*   Access the parcel search site for free at www.pawnee.kansasgis.com/.

Pottawatomie County   *Property, Taxation Records*   Access county parcel search free at www.pottawatomie.kansasgov.com/parcel/. For fuller data, obtain username and password from Appraiser's Office. Also search GIS maps free at www.pottcounty.org/Flex/PottCo/.

Reno County   *Property, Taxation Records*   Parcel Information, Election Results, Tax Information, Tax Sale information free at http://renogis3.renogov.org/rn_vb/MainPage.aspx. Also, access to GIS/mapping for free at www.renogov.org/465/GIS-Map. Also, access to property information and GIS/mapping for free at http://jade.kgs.ku.edu/orka2/CoSelect.aspx.

Republic County   *Recorded Documents*   The county works with https://tapestry.fidlar.com/Tapestry2/Default.aspx for record access. Base fee is $5.95 per search and $.50 per print image. You can pay as you go using a credit or pre-pay using a subscription. Also, one may purchase a software program Laredo (www.fidlar.com/laredo.aspx) with extensive search features. Contact the county for details and pricing.
Property, Taxation Records   Access to parcel/property records for free at www.republiccounty.org/parcel/. There is both a public search and a registered user search with more data available. Also, a vendor offers access to property tax data free at www.ecountyworks.com/republic/index.php. Also, access to property information and GIS/mapping for free at http://jade.kgs.ku.edu/orka2/CoSelect.aspx.

Rice County   *Recorded Documents*   http://ricecounty.us/departments/register-of-deeds/   Access to property search data for free at http://ks486.cichosting.com/orion/Login.aspx. Must register with userID and password.
Property, Taxation Records   Access to property tax information for free at http://ks486.cichosting.com/tax/.

Riley County   *Recorded Documents*   www.rileycountyks.gov/418/Register-of-Deeds   Access to recorder office land data is by subscription at http://idoc.rileycountyks.gov. Records go back to 1/3/1995.
Property, Taxation Records   Access to online appraisal data for free at www.riley.kansasgov.com/parcel/.

Rooks County   *Property, Taxation Records*   Access to property information and GIS/mapping for free at http://jade.kgs.ku.edu/orka2/CoSelect.aspx.

Russell County   *Property, Taxation Records*   Also, access to property information and GIS/mapping for free at http://jade.kgs.ku.edu/orka2/CoSelect.aspx.

Saline County   *Recorded Documents*   www.saline.org/RegisterofDeeds.aspx   Access to record indexing for a fee at https://www.idocmarket.com/Subscription/Subscribe?county=SalineKS. Records from 1/1/1995 to present.
Property, Taxation Records   Access property data free at www.saline.org/Appraiser/ParcelHome.aspx. Also, access to GIS/mapping for free at www.saline.org/GISMapping.aspx. Includes property ownership (tax purposes only), parcel search, votiing districts, etc. Also, access to property information and GIS/mapping for free at http://jade.kgs.ku.edu/orka2/CoSelect.aspx.

Sedgwick County *Recorded Documents* www.sedgwickcounty.org/deeds/ Access recorder deeds free at www.sedgwickcounty.org/deeds/document_search.asp. Must register before use.

Property, Taxation Records Search property appraisal/tax data at https://ssc.sedgwickcounty.org/propertytax/disclaimer.aspx. Also, access to property information and GIS/mapping for free at http://jade.kgs.ku.edu/orka2/CoSelect.aspx.

Seward County *Property, Taxation Records* Access to records free at www.seward.kansasgov.com/parcel/. There is both a public search and an enhanced search that one must register for. Also, access to property information and GIS/mapping for free at http://jade.kgs.ku.edu/orka2/CoSelect.aspx.

Shawnee County *Recorded Documents* www.snco.us/rd/ A The county works with https://tapestry.fidlar.com/Tapestry2/Default.aspx for record access. Base fee is $5.95 per search and $.50 per print image. You can pay as you go using a credit or pre-pay using a subscription. Also, one may purchase a software program Laredo (www.fidlar.com/laredo.aspx) with extensive search features. Contact the county for details and pricing.

Property, Taxation Records Access the residential property list free at www.co.shawnee.ks.us/AP/R_prop/Disclaimer.shtm. Also search the county mapping site for parcel owner and map data at http://gis.snco.us/publicgis/.

Smith County *Property, Taxation Records* Search parcel data or tax data for free at www.smithcoks.com/RegisterofDeeds/tabid/4252/Default.aspx.

Stafford County *Property, Taxation Records* Access to property information and GIS/mapping for free at http://jade.kgs.ku.edu/orka2/CoSelect.aspx.

Stevens County *Property, Taxation Records* Access to property information and GIS/mapping for free at http://jade.kgs.ku.edu/orka2/CoSelect.aspx.

Sumner County *Property, Taxation Records* Access to parcel search for free at www.sumner.kansasgis.com/. For detailed information must register.

Thomas County *Property, Taxation Records* Parcel search is for paid subscribers only. Contact the County Appraiser for more information.

Wabaunsee County *Property, Taxation Records* Access to the assessor parcel search data for free is at http://ks-wabaunsee.manatron.com/CountyOffices/Appraiser/ParcelSearch/tabid/10768/Default.aspx. Also, access the treasurer's property tax data free at http://ks-wabaunsee.manatron.com/ElectedOfficials/Treasurer/TaxSearch/tabid/10757/Default.aspx. Also, access to property information and GIS/mapping for free at http://jade.kgs.ku.edu/orka2/CoSelect.aspx.

Washington County *Property, Taxation Records* Access to limited parcel data for free at www.washington.kansasgov.com/parcel/DisclaimerReg.asp. For detailed information must subscribe.

Wilson County *Property, Taxation Records* Access to property information and GIS/mapping for free at http://jade.kgs.ku.edu/orka2/CoSelect.aspx.

Woodson County *Property, Taxation Records* Access property data free or by registering for full subscription access at www.woodson.kansasgov.com/parcel/. Click on 'Parcel Search Public' for free access and name search. Subscription service for full data is $200 per year.

Wyandotte County *Recorded Documents* www.wycokck.org/Internetdept.aspx?id=2600&menu_id=1024&banner=15284 The county works with https://tapestry.fidlar.com/Tapestry2/Default.aspx for record access. Base fee is $5.95 per search and $.50 per print image. You can pay as you go using a credit or pre-pay using a subscription. Also, one may purchase a software program Laredo (www.fidlar.com/laredo.aspx) with extensive search features. Contact the county for details and pricing.

Property, Taxation Records The property dial-up services requires a $20 set up fee, $5 monthly minimum and $.05 each transaction. Lending agency info also available. Contact Louise Sachen 913-573-2885 for signup. There is a real estate search and a parcel search at http://appr.wycokck.org/appraisal/publicaccess/.

Kentucky

Capital: Frankfort
                Franklin County

Time Zone: EST

Kentucky's forty western-most counties are CST.

CST counties are– Adair, Allen, Ballard, Barren, Breckinridge, Butler, Caldwell, Calloway, Carlisle, Christian, Clinton, Crittenden, Cumberland, Daviess, Edmonson, Fulton, Graves, Grayson, Hancock, Hart, Henderson, Hickman, Hopkins, Livingstone, Logan, Marshall, McCracken, McLean, Metcalfe, Monroe, Muhlenberg, Ohio, Russell, Simpson, Todd, Trigg, Union, Warren, Wayne, and Webster.

Population: 4,425,092
# of Counties: 120

Useful State Links

Website: **http://kentucky.gov**
Governor: **http://governor.ky.gov**
Attorney General: **http://ag.ky.gov**
State Archives: **http://kdla.ky.gov/Pages/default.aspx**
State Statutes and Codes: **http://www.lrc.ky.gov/statutes/**
Legislative Bill Search: **www.lrc.ky.gov/legislation.htm**
Unclaimed Funds: **https://secure.kentucky.gov/treasury/unclaimedProperty/Default.aspx**

State Public Record Agencies

Sexual Offender Registry

Kentucky State Police, Sex Offender Registry:, www.kentuckystatepolice.org/sor.htm   Access is available at http://kspsor.state.ky.us/. All registrants are listed. Online searches must provide one of the following fields: Last Name, City, ZIP, or County.   *Other Options:* None

Incarceration Records

Kentucky Department of Corrections, Offender Information Services,

Corporation, LP, LLP, LLC, Assumed Name Records

Secretary of State, Corporate Records - Records,   www.sos.ky.gov/bus/businessrecords/Pages/default.aspx   A number of distinct searches are available at https://app.sos.ky.gov/ftsearch/. Search business filings and records and also business organizations. Also search by registered agent, founding or current officer name. Another good search site for business filings is http://sos.ky.gov/business/filings/online/. Also, search securities companies registered with the state at http://kfi.ky.gov/search/Pages/default.aspx.   *Other Options:* Bulk data and monthly lists of new corporations are available. See www.sos.ky.gov/bus/Pages/File-Descriptions.aspx for all options and prices. Business records are $2,000 per month.

Trademarks/Servicemarks

Secretary of State, Trademarks Service Marks Section,   www.sos.ky.gov/bus/tmandsm/Pages/default.aspx   The direct site to the free searchable database is http://apps.sos.ky.gov/business/trademarks/.   *Other Options:* Bulk data available by request. Call for info and fees.

Uniform Commercial Code

UCC Branch, Secretary of State,   www.sos.ky.gov/bus/UCC/Pages/default.aspx   UCC record searching is offered free of charge at www.sos.ky.gov/bus/UCC/Pages/Online-Services.aspx. Search by debtor name or file number. SSNs are withheld from the online system. Although you can perform a partial name search online, only full name search results can be certified.   *Other Options:* Monthly, weekly or daily lists of new UCC filing are available, see http://sos.ky.gov/bus/Pages/Bulk-Data-Service.aspx for all options and prices. A subscription agreement must be completed. UCC filins are $1,500 per month, images $300 per month.

Birth Certificates

Department for Public Health, Vital Statistics,   http://chfs.ky.gov/dph/vital/   Records may be ordered online via a state designated vendor at www.vitalchek.com.

Death Records

Department for Public Health, Vital Statistics,   http://chfs.ky.gov/dph/vital/   In cooperation with the University of Kentucky, there is a searchable death index at http://ukcc.uky.edu/vitalrec/. This is for non-commercial use only. Records are from 1911 through 1992. Also, there is a free genealogy site at http://vitals.rootsweb.ancestry.com/ky/death/search.cgi. Death Indexes from 1911-2000 are available. Search by surname, given name, place of death, residence, or year. Records may be ordered online via a state designated vendor at www.vitalchek.com.

Marriage, Divorce Certificates

Department for Public Health, Vital Statistics,   http://chfs.ky.gov/dph/vital/   In cooperation with the University of Kentucky, a searchable index is available on the Internet at http://ukcc.uky.edu/vitalrec/. The index runs from 1973 through 1993. This is for non-commercial use only. Records may be ordered online via a state designated vendor at www.vitalchek.com.   *Other Options:* Contact Libraries and Archives.

Driver Records

Division of Driver Licensing, Attention: MVRs,   http://transportation.ky.gov/Driver-Licensing/Pages/default.aspx   There are 2 systems, both accessible from Kentucky.gov. Requesters who are permitted to obtain personal information can order by batch. Fee is $5.00 per record, billing is monthly. Accounts must be approved by the Commissioner's office. For more details, call Kentucky.gov at 502-875-3733 or email support@kentucky.gov. Information about this service is not available on the web. Three-year records without personal information can be obtained on an interactive basis at https://secure.kentucky.gov/dhronline. A $5.50 fee applies and use of a credit card is required.

Vehicle, Vessel Ownership & Registration

KY Transportation Cabinet, Division of Motor Vehicle Licensing,   https://mvl.ky.gov/MVLWeb/   Electronic access is available to approved, ongoing requesters with a permissible use. The system, known as OVIS, is run by Kentucky.gov. OVIS is open 24/7 and provides immediate results after requests are sent. Data available includes vehicle info, registration, data, plate data, and liens. The fee is $0.44 per record. Requesters must first be approved by the Commissioner's office as well as have an account with Kentucky.gov. There is a $75.00 annual subscription fee. For more information, call Kentucky.gov at 502-875-3733 or visit http://kentucky.gov/register/Pages/subscribe.aspx.   *Other Options:* Kentucky has the ability to supply customized bulk delivery of vehicle registration information. The request must be in writing with the intended use outlined. For more information, call 502-564-5301.

Crash Reports

Kentucky State Police, Criminal ID/Records Branch,   http://kentuckystatepolice.org/   Online reports are outsourced to a vendor at https://www.buycrash.com/Public/Home.aspx. The DL # or the badge number of the investigating Officer is required to search. The fee is $10.00. Use of a credit card or PayPal is required.   *Other Options:* Specific accident statistics may be obtained by phoning the statistics coordinator.

Voter Registration

State Board of Elections,   http://elect.ky.gov/Pages/default.aspx   The agency offers a voter information status search at https://vr.sos.ky.gov/vic/. First name, last name and DOB are required. For questions, contact sheila.walker@ky.gov.   *Other Options:* Bulk lists data is available on CD-Rom, labels or lists for eligible persons, pursuant to state statutes. See http://elect.ky.gov/requestforvoterreg/Pages/default.aspx.

Campaign Finance & Disclosure, PACs and Contributors

KY Registry of Election Finance,   http://kref.ky.gov/Pages/default.aspx   The agency offers a searchable database of all records for 1998 to present at www.kref.state.ky.us/krefsearch/. When candidates submit financial records by using electronic filing software, the disbursement figures are available to download. Lobbyist data at the Ethics Commission at http://klec.ky.gov/Reports/Pages/Employers-and-Legislative-Agents.aspx.

Occupational Licensing Boards

Accountant-CPA	https://secure.kentucky.gov/FormServices/CPA/LicenseRenewal/Search
Accountant-CPA Company	https://secure.kentucky.gov/formservices/CPA/FirmRenewal/search
Addiction Psychiatrist MD	http://web1.ky.gov/gensearch/LicenseSearch.aspx?AGY=5
Alcohol/Drug Counselor	https://kyonp.force.com/public/LicenseVerification
Anesthesiologist	http://web1.ky.gov/gensearch/LicenseSearch.aspx?AGY=5
Architect	https://secure.kentucky.gov/cidRosterSearch/
Art Therapist	https://kyonp.force.com/public/LicenseVerification
Athlete Agent	https://kyonp.force.com/public/LicenseVerification
Athletic Trainer, Medical	http://web1.ky.gov/gensearch/LicenseSearch.aspx?AGY=21
Attorney	www.kybar.org/search/custom.asp?id=2947
Auctioneer, Livestock, Ltd	http://web1.ky.gov/GenSearch/LicenseSearch.aspx?AGY=3
Auctioneer, Tobacco, Ltd	http://web1.ky.gov/GenSearch/LicenseSearch.aspx?AGY=3

Auctioneer/Auctioneer Apprentice .... http://web1.ky.gov/GenSearch/LicenseSearch.aspx?AGY=3
Audiologist .... https://kyonp.force.com/public/LicenseVerification
Bank... www.kfi.ky.gov/search/Pages/default.aspx
Barber Colleges .... http://barbering.ky.gov/schools/Pages/colleges.aspx
Boiler Contractor/Insp/Installer .... https://ky.joportal.com/License/Search/license_lookup.asp
Building Inspector .... https://ky.joportal.com/License/Search/license_lookup.asp
Check Casher/Seller... www.kfi.ky.gov/search/Pages/default.aspx
Child Care Facility http://chfs.ky.gov/NR/rdonlyres/14A77B8F-F406-4055-B765-
                                                                                                            43C7674599D3/0/LicensedChildCareCenterDirectory5102010.xls
Chiropractor .... http://web1.ky.gov/gensearch/LicenseSearch.aspx?AGY=22
Clean-Up Contractor of Meth Lab................................. http://waste.ky.gov/SFB/MethLabCleanup/Documents/ListofContractors.pdf
Cosmetologist .... https://www.hnslicense.net/index.cfm?
Cosmetologist Disciplinary Actions.............................. http://kbhc.ky.gov/Pages/Disciplinary-Actions.aspx
Cosmetology School.. http://kbhc.ky.gov/Pages/Cosmetology-Schools.aspx
Counselor, Pastoral/Professional .... https://kyonp.force.com/public/LicenseVerification
Credit Union.. www.kfi.ky.gov/search/Pages/default.aspx
Dental Hygienist.. https://secure.kentucky.gov/renewalservices/kybd/search.aspx
Dental Laboratory .... http://web1.ky.gov/gensearch/LicenseSearch.aspx?AGY=13
Dentist.. https://secure.kentucky.gov/renewalservices/kybd/search.aspx
Dentistry Disciplinary Actions .... http://dentistry.ky.gov/About-Us/Pages/Disciplinary-Actions.aspx
Dialysis Technician .... https://secure.kentucky.gov/kbn/bulkvalidation/basic.aspx
Dietitian/Nutritionist.. https://kyonp.force.com/public/LicenseVerification
Director of Pupil Transportation .... http://applications.education.ky.gov/sdci/other.aspx
Electrical Contractor/Inspector .... https://ky.joportal.com/License/Search/license_lookup.asp
Elevator Inspector... https://ky.joportal.com/License/Search/license_lookup.asp
Embalmer .... http://kbefd.ky.gov/Pages/License-Directory.aspx
EMT-First Response/Basic... https://kemsis.kbems.kctcs.edu/licensure/public/kentucky/portal/lookup/
Engineer/Land Surveyor Firm....................................... http://elsweb.kyboels.ky.gov/kboels-web/Searchable-Roster.aspx
Engineer/Land Surveyor/Firm Disciplinary Action .... http://elsweb.kyboels.ky.gov/kboels-web/DisciplinaryAction.aspx
Esthetician .... https://www.hnslicense.net/index.cfm?
Exterminator .... www.kyagr.com/consumer/pesticide-ceu-search.aspx
Fire Alarm System Inspector .... https://ky.joportal.com/License/Search/license_lookup.asp
Fire Protection Sprinkler Installer .... https://ky.joportal.com/License/Search/license_lookup.asp
Fire Suppression System Inspector.............................. https://ky.joportal.com/License/Search/license_lookup.asp
Funeral Director/Apprentice.. http://kbefd.ky.gov/Pages/License-Directory.aspx
Funeral Establishment .... http://kbefd.ky.gov/Pages/License-Directory.aspx
Geologist.. https://kyonp.force.com/public/LicenseVerification
Health Care Facility .... http://chfs.ky.gov/os/oig/ltckarkrs.htm
Hearing Instrument Specialist....................................... https://kyonp.force.com/public/LicenseVerification
Holding Co/HUD.. www.kfi.ky.gov/search/Pages/default.aspx
Home Health Aid.. https://secure.kentucky.gov/kbn/bulkvalidation/basic.aspx
Home Inspector .... https://ky.joportal.com/License/Search/license_lookup.asp
HVAC Contractor/Journeyman/Master/Mechanic........ https://ky.joportal.com/License/Search/license_lookup.asp
Industrial Loan/Consumer Loan .... www.kfi.ky.gov/search/Pages/default.aspx
Insurance Adjuster.. http://insurance.ky.gov/Company/Default.aspx?MenuID=47&Div_id=2
Insurance Agent.. http://insurance.ky.gov/Company/Default.aspx?MenuID=47&Div_id=2
Insurance CE Provider... http://insurance.ky.gov/Company/Default.aspx?MenuID=47&Div_id=2
Insurance Company/Insurer .... http://insurance.ky.gov/Company/Default.aspx?MenuID=47&Div_id=2
Insurance Consultant/Solicitor...................................... http://insurance.ky.gov/Company/Default.aspx?MenuID=47&Div_id=2
Interpreters for the Deaf.. https://kyonp.force.com/public/LicenseVerification
Legislative Employer of Lobbyists .... http://apps.klec.ky.gov/searchregister.asp
Liquor License .... https://dppweb.ky.gov/ABCStar/portal/abconline/page/License_Lookup/portal.aspx
Loan Company, Comm/Industrial .... www.kfi.ky.gov/search/Pages/default.aspx
Loan Officer/Processor.. www.kfi.ky.gov/search/Pages/default.aspx
Lobbyist .... http://apps.klec.ky.gov/searchregister.asp

Malt Beverage Distributor/Storage	https://dppweb.ky.gov/ABCStar/portal/abconline/page/License_Lookup/portal.aspx
Marriage & Family Therapist	https://kyonp.force.com/public/LicenseVerification
Midwife	https://secure.kentucky.gov/kbn/bulkvalidation/basic.aspx
Milk Inspector	www.rs.uky.edu/regulatory/inspectors/
Mines, Licensed	http://minesafety.ky.gov/Pages/MinesLicensedinKentucky.aspx
Money Transmitter	www.kfi.ky.gov/search/Pages/default.aspx
Mortgage Broker/Loan Company	www.nmlsconsumeraccess.org/
Nail Technician	https://www.hnslicense.net/index.cfm?
Nurse Anesthetist/Clinical Specialist	https://secure.kentucky.gov/kbn/bulkvalidation/basic.aspx
Nurse Work Permit	https://secure.kentucky.gov/kbn/bulkvalidation/basic.aspx
Nurse-RN/LPN/Aide	https://secure.kentucky.gov/kbn/bulkvalidation/basic.aspx
Nursing Home Administrator	https://kyonp.force.com/public/LicenseVerification
Occupational Therapist/Assistant	https://kyonp.force.com/public/LicenseVerification
Ophthalmic Dispenser	http://oop.ky.gov/lic_search.aspx
Optician/Apprentice	https://kyonp.force.com/public/LicenseVerification
Optometrist	http://web1.ky.gov/gensearch/LicenseSearch.aspx?AGY=8
Paramedic	https://kemsis.kbems.kctcs.edu/licensure/public/kentucky/portal/lookup/
Pesticide Applicator/Dealer	www.kyagr.com/consumer/pesticide-ceu-search.aspx
Pesticide Product Registration	http://npirspublic.ceris.purdue.edu/state/state_menu.aspx?state=KY
Pharmacist/Pharmacy	https://secure.kentucky.gov/pharmacy/licenselookup/
Physical Therapist/Assistant	http://pt.ky.gov/LicenseSearch/Pages/default.aspx
Physician Assistant	http://web1.ky.gov/gensearch/LicenseSearch.aspx?AGY=20
Physician/Surgeon	http://web1.ky.gov/gensearch/LicenseSearch.aspx?AGY=5
Plans & Specifications Inspector	https://ky.joportal.com/License/Search/license_lookup.asp
Plumber	https://ky.joportal.com/License/Search/license_lookup.asp
Podiatrist	http://web1.ky.gov/gensearch/LicenseSearch.aspx?AGY=24
Private Investigator	https://kyonp.force.com/public/LicenseVerification
Proprietary Education School	https://kyonp.force.com/public/LicenseVerification
Psychiatrist MD	http://web1.ky.gov/gensearch/LicenseSearch.aspx?AGY=5
Psychologist	https://kyonp.force.com/public/LicenseVerification
Real Estate Agent/Broker/Firm	https://secure.kentucky.gov/KREC/databasesearch
Real Estate Appraiser	http://kreab.ky.gov/Pages/KLAMC.aspx
Retired LPN	https://secure.kentucky.gov/kbn/bulkvalidation/basic.aspx
Sanitarian	https://prd.chfs.ky.gov/regsan/
School Administrator	https://wd.kyepsb.net/EPSB.WebApps/KECI/
School Bus Driver Trainer	http://education.ky.gov/districts/trans/Documents/2014%20DriverTrainerDirectory.pdf
School Guidance Counselor	https://wd.kyepsb.net/EPSB.WebApps/KECI/
School Media Librarian	https://wd.kyepsb.net/EPSB.WebApps/KECI/
School Nurse	https://wd.kyepsb.net/EPSB.WebApps/KECI/
School Social Worker/Psychologist	https://wd.kyepsb.net/EPSB.WebApps/KECI/
Sexual Assault Nurse Examiner	https://secure.kentucky.gov/kbn/bulkvalidation/basic.aspx
Social Worker	https://secure.kentucky.gov/formservices/kbsw/socialworkrenewal/
Speech-Language Pathologist	https://kyonp.force.com/public/LicenseVerification
Surgical Assistant	http://web1.ky.gov/gensearch/LicenseSearch.aspx?AGY=23
Teacher	https://wd.kyepsb.net/EPSB.WebApps/KECI/
Veterinarian	https://kyonp.force.com/public/LicenseVerification
Waste Water System Operator	https://dep.gateway.ky.gov/eSearch/Search_License.aspx

State and Local Courts

About Kentucky Courts: The **Circuit Court** is the court of general jurisdiction and hears civil matters involving more than
    $5,000, capital offenses and felonies, land dispute title cases and contested probate cases. The **Family Court** is a division of the

Circuit Court and has concurrent jurisdiction with certain domestic abuse matters. However, the Family Court division retains primary jurisdiction in cases involving dissolution of marriage; child custody; visitation; maintenance and support; equitable distribution of property in dissolution cases; adoption; and, termination of parental rights.

District Court is the court of limited jurisdiction and handles juvenile matters, city and county ordinances, misdemeanors, violations, traffic offenses, probate of wills, arraignments, felony probable cause hearings, small claims ($2,500 or less), civil cases involving $5,000 or less, voluntary and involuntary mental commitments and cases relating to domestic violence and abuse.

Ninety percent of all Kentuckians involved in court proceedings appear in District Court.

The web page for the Unified Judicial System is http://courts.ky.gov.

Appellate Courts: The Court of Appeals hears all appeals from the lower courts. Divorces may not be appealed; however, child custody and property rights decisions may be appealed. Search opinions and case information from the Supreme Court and Court of Appeals at http://apps.courts.ky.gov/Appeals/COA_Dockets.shtm.

Online Court Access

All courts participate in the system described below.

There are three systems offered.

1. The KY Admin. Office of Courts provides a criminal record online ordering system at http://kcoj.kycourts.net/PublicMenu/Default.aspx?header=AOC+FastCheck. Called AOC Fast Check, the program charges $20.00 per record. This is not an interactive system; requesters receive an e-mail notification when the results are available. A vender, designated by the state, handles the credit card transactions and charges a reported 5% surcharge. The following case types are not available - juvenile, mental health, and civil/domestic violence.

    Two Cautionary Notes:

    a. The AOC is NOT the state mandated official site for criminal records. State law dictates that the Kentucky State Police Records Branch is responsible for holding records with confirmed dispositions, not the AOC.

    b. The subject of the search is notified of the request, sent a copy of the record, and is given the name of the requester.

2. A limited free search (few historical records are provided) for both civil and criminal record dockets is offered at https://kcoj.kycourts.net/kyecourts/login/guestlogin. Search by county or statewide and by party name, case number, or by citation number. Most of the cases lists are pending. Results essential shown are only the name and case number and if an arraignment is scheduled. Note there is a separate, enhanced system offered to members of the Kentucky Bar Association See https://kcoj.kycourts.net/kyecourts/Login. A log-in is required.

3. A free search site for daily court calendars by county is found at http://kcoj.kycourts.net/dockets/.

Note: No individual Kentucky courts offer online access, other as described above.

Recorders, Assessors, and Other Sites of Note

About Kentucky Recording Offices: 120 counties, 121 recording offices. The recording officer is the County Clerk. Kenton County has two recording offices.

About Tax Liens: All federal and state tax liens on personal property on either individuals or businesses are filed with the County Clerk, often in an Encumbrance Book.

Online Access

Recorded Documents

Access to index/images with limited records for a fee for 40 counties at https://www.ecclix.com. Must subscribe. See vendor web page for fees.

Access to recorded documents (and tax records) is provided for 14 Kentucky counties by a vendor at www.kylandrecords.com/. Fees are involved, must chose "per land or tax." Image files provided.

Assessor Records

A number of counties offer free access to assessor or property records. Several counties provide a more robust search using a vendor systems.

County Sites:

Adair County *Recorded Land Documents Records* http://adairwp.clerkinfo.net/ Access to recorded land records for a fee from a vendor at www.kycountyrecords.com/. Images included. Fees are $62.00 per month, per county (this is a recurring monthly charge) or $22.00 per county, per record type. To subscribe contact via email at administrator@kylandrecords.com or call 888-486-6258 or 270-443-1610.
Property, Taxation Records Access to tax records for a fee at www.kylandrecords.com/. Images included.

Allen County *Recorded Documents* http://allencountyclerk.com/ Access index/images with limited records for a fee at https://www.ecclix.com/. Must subscribe. See vendor web page for fees.
Property, Taxation Records Access property search data for free at www.qpublic.net/ky/allen/index.html.

Anderson County *Recorded Documents* http://andersoncountyclerk.ky.gov/Pages/default.aspx Access index/images with limited records for a fee at https://www.ecclix.com/. Must subscribe. See vendor web page for fees.
Property, Taxation Records Access to basic property record searches for free at http://qpublic.net/ky/anderson/search.html. For detailed information must subscribe.

Barren County *Recorded Documents* http://barrencountyclerk.com/ Access index/images with limited records for a fee at https://www.ecclix.com/. Must subscribe. See vendor web page for fees.
Property, Taxation Records Access to property records for free (limited data) go to http://qpublic5.qpublic.net/ky_barren_taxroll.php. For all available features must subscribe to service for a fee.

Bath County *Recorded Land Documents Records* http://bathcounty.ky.gov/Pages/default.aspx Access to recorded land records for a fee from a vendor at www.kycountyrecords.com/. Images included. Fees are $62.00 per month, per county (this is a recurring monthly charge) or $22.00 per county, per record type. To subscribe contact via email at administrator@kylandrecords.com or call 888-486-6258 or 270-443-1610.
Property, Taxation Records Access to tax records for a fee at www.kycountyrecords.com/?AspxAutoDetectCookieSupport=1

Boone County *Property, Taxation Records* Assessor property data is available at http://boonepva.ky.gov/.

Bourbon County *Recorded Land Documents Records* www.bourbon.clerkinfo.net/ Access to recorded land records for a fee from a vendor at www.kycountyrecords.com/. Images included. Fees are $62.00 per month, per county (this is a recurring monthly charge) or $22.00 per county, per record type. To subscribe contact via email at administrator@kylandrecords.com or call 888-486-6258 or 270-443-1610.
Property, Taxation Records Access to tax records for a fee at www.kylandrecords.com/. Images included.

Boyd County *Recorded Documents* http://boydcountyky.gov/ Access index/images with limited records for a fee at https://www.ecclix.com/. Must subscribe. See vendor web page for fees.
Property, Taxation Records Access to tax rolls for free at http://qpublic5.qpublic.net/ky_boyd_taxroll.php.

Boyle County *Property, Taxation Records* Access to tax rolls for free at http://qpublic5.qpublic.net/ky_boyle_taxroll.php. For more product, can pay for subscription for 120 records-$100, 300 records-$200, 600 records-$400, 1200 records-$750.

Bracken County *Property, Taxation Records* Access to records for free (limited data) at www.qpublic.net/ky/. For more detailed information must subscribe for a fee.

Breathitt County *Recorded Documents* http://breathittcountyclerk.com/ Access index/images with limited records for a fee at https://www.ecclix.com/. Must subscribe. See vendor web page for fees.

Breckinridge County *Recorded Documents* www.breckinridgecountyky.com/index.asp?cookiesEnabled=false Access to land index back to 1996 and images to by subscription at www.titlesearcher.com/countyInfo.php?cnum=S99.
Property, Taxation Records Access to property search data for free at www.qpublic.net/ky/breckinridge/search.html. For deeper information, subscription is available for a fee.

Bullitt County *Recorded Documents* www.bullittcountyclerk.com/ Access index/images with limited records for a fee at https://www.ecclix.com/. Must subscribe. See vendor web page for fees.

Butler County *Recorded Documents* http://butlercounty.ky.gov/County-Government/Pages/County-Clerk.aspx Access to land records for a fee at www.mainstreet-tech.com/Search/Default.aspx.
Property, Taxation Records Access to tax roll/parcel data for free (limited data) or for all available features on subscription (pay) go to http://qpublic5.qpublic.net/ky_butler_taxroll.php.

Caldwell County *Recorded Documents* Register to receive free username and password to search recording indexes free at http://216.135.47.158/recordsearch/.
Property, Taxation Records Access to records for free at www.qpublic.net/ky/caldwell/.

Calloway County *Recorded Land Documents Records* http://calloway.clerkinfo.net/   Access to recorded land records for a fee from a vendor at www.kycountyrecords.com/. Images included. Fees are $62.00 per month, per county (this is a recurring monthly charge) or $22.00 per county, per record type. To subscribe contact via email at administrator@kylandrecords.com or call 888-486-6258 or 270-443-1610.
Property, Taxation Records   Access to property data is free at http://qpublic.net/ky/calloway/. Access to tax records for a fee at www.kylandrecords.com/. Images included.

Campbell County *Recorded Documents* http://campbellcountyclerkky.com/   Access index/images with limited records for a fee at https://www.ecclix.com/. Must subscribe. See vendor web page for fees.
Property, Taxation Records   Access the Property Valuation Administrator assessment search at www.campbellcountykypva.org/. Search by any or all: owner name, parcel ID, street name, street number, property type, district, sale date, sale price, deed book, deed page.

Carlisle County *Recorded Documents* http://carlislecounty.ky.gov/Pages/default.aspx   Access index/images with limited records for a fee at https://www.ecclix.com/. Must subscribe. See vendor web page for fees.

Carter County *Recorded Land Documents Records* http://cartercounty.ky.gov/Pages/default.aspx   Access to recorded land records for a fee from a vendor at www.kycountyrecords.com/. Images included. Fees are $62.00 per month, per county (this is a recurring monthly charge) or $22.00 per county, per record type. To subscribe contact via email at administrator@kylandrecords.com or call 888-486-6258 or 270-443-1610.
Property, Taxation Records   Access to the tax roll for free at www.qpublic.net/ky/carter/. For detailed information, must subscribe.

Christian County *Recorded Documents* www.christiancountyky.gov/qcms/index.asp?Page=county%20clerk   Access recorded docs by subscription at https://cotthosting.com/kychristian/User/Login.aspx. Marriage index back to 1973, wills back to 8/2002, mortgage index from 1940-1984, mortgage and land recording index and images back to 1987.
Property, Taxation Records   Access property tax data by subscription at http://qpublic5.qpublic.net/ky_christian_taxroll.php.

Clark County *Property, Taxation Records*   Access to the Tax Roll for a fee at www.qpublic.net/ky/clark/taxroll.html.

Clay County *Recorded Land Documents Records* http://claycounty.ky.gov/Pages/default.aspx   Access to recorded land records for a fee from a vendor at www.kycountyrecords.com/. Images included. Fees are $62.00 per month, per county (this is a recurring monthly charge) or $22.00 per county, per record type. To subscribe contact via email at administrator@kylandrecords.com or call 888-486-6258 or 270-443-1610.

Clinton County *Recorded Land Documents Records* www.clinton.clerkinfo.net/   Access to recorded land records for a fee from a vendor at www.kycountyrecords.com/. Images included. Fees are $62.00 per month, per county (this is a recurring monthly charge) or $22.00 per county, per record type. To subscribe contact via email at administrator@kylandrecords.com or call 888-486-6258 or 270-443-1610.
Property, Taxation Records   Access to tax records for a fee at www.kycountyrecords.com/. Images included.

Crittenden County *Property, Taxation Records*   Access to tax rolls for a fee at http://qpublic5.qpublic.net/ky_crittenden_taxroll.php.

Elliott County *Property, Taxation Records*   Access to records for a fee at http://qpublic5.qpublic.net/ky_asearch.php?county=ky_elliott.

Estill County *Recorded Documents* www.estillky.com/county-clerk.html   Access index/images with limited records for a fee at https://www.ecclix.com/. Must subscribe. See vendor web page for fees.
Property, Taxation Records   Access to tax list for free at www.estillky.com/tax-information.html.

Fayette County *Property, Taxation Records*   Search property index free at http://qpublic9.qpublic.net/ky_fayette_gtos.php. Name searches with subscription only.

Fleming County *Recorded Documents* http://flemingcountyclerk.com/   Access index/images with limited records for a fee at https://www.ecclix.com/. Must subscribe. See vendor web page for fees.

Floyd County *Recorded Records Records*   Access to land records online for a fee at www.mainstreet-tech.com/Search/Default.aspx.
Property, Taxation Records   Access to property record search for a fee at www.qpublic.net/ky/floyd/search.html.

Franklin County *Recorded Documents* www.franklincountyclerkky.com/   Access index/images with limited records for a fee at https://www.ecclix.com/. Must subscribe. See vendor web page for fees.
Property, Taxation Records   Access to property index is free at www.franklincountypva.com/PublicSearch/tabid/673/Default.aspx. A subscription is required for full data; $150 per 6 months or $250 per year.

Fulton County *Property, Taxation Records*   Access to the delinquent taxes list for free at www.fulton.clerkinfo.net/index.php?option=com_wrapper&view=wrapper&Itemid=62.

Garrard County *Recorded Documents* http://garrardcountyclerk.com/   Access to records for a fee at www.landrecordskentucky.com/. Access index/images with limited records for a fee at https://www.ecclix.com/. Must subscribe. See vendor web page for fees.
Property, Taxation Records   Access to property records and GIS/mapping for a fee are found at www.garrardpva.com/PublicSearch.aspx.

Grant County *Recorded Documents* http://grantcounty.ky.gov/   Access index/images with limited records for a fee at https://www.ecclix.com/. Must subscribe. See vendor web page for fees.

Property, Taxation Records   Access property index free at http://qpublic5.qpublic.net/ky_grant_taxroll.php. Subscription required for GIS map and full data.

Graves County *Property, Taxation Records*   Access to property tax roll for free at www.qpublic.net/ky/graves/.

Grayson County *Recorded Documents* http://graysoncountyclerk.ky.gov/Pages/default.aspx   Access to land records for a fee at www.mainstreet-tech.com/Search/Default.aspx. Records from 1986 to present.
Property, Taxation Records   A list of delinquent debtors for free at http://revenue.ky.gov/Property/Pages/Delinquent-Property-Tax.aspx.

Green County *Recorded Documents* www.greencountyky.us/countyclerk.html   Access index/images with limited records for a fee at https://www.ecclix.com/. Must subscribe. See vendor web page for fees.

Greenup County *Recorded Documents* www.greenupcountyclerk.com   Access index/images with limited records for a fee at https://www.ecclix.com/. Must subscribe. See vendor web page for fees.

Hancock County *Recorded Documents* http://hancockcountyclerk.com/   Access index/images with limited records for a fee at https://www.ecclix.com/. Must subscribe. See vendor web page for fees.
Property, Taxation Records   Access to the tax roll for free at http://qpublic5.qpublic.net/ky_hancock_taxroll.php. More detailed information is available via subscription service (for more information about the subscription go to http://qpublic5.qpublic.net/ky_hancock_login.php?subscribe=1. Also, delinquent taxes list for free at www.hancockky.us/Government/DelTaxBill.htm.

Hardin County *Recorded Documents* www.hccoky.org   Access the Clerk's permanent and temporary records search page free at www.hccoky.org/eSearch/User/Login.aspx. Deeds go back to 1970; mortgages to 1971.
Property, Taxation Records   Access to property records for a fee at www.qpublic.net/ky/hardin/search.html

Harrison County *Property, Taxation Records*   Access to public records for free at www.harrisoncountypva.com/PublicSearch.aspx.

Hart County *Property, Taxation Records*   Access to property tax/assessment records for free at http://qpublic.net/ky/hart/search.html. Must register and pay a fee for detailed records.

Henderson County *Recorded Records Records* www.hendersonky.us/clerk.php   Access to records for a fee at www.titlesearcher.com/countyInfo.php?cnum=K4.
Property, Taxation Records   Access county property assessment index free at http://qpublic.net/ky/henderson/search.html. For full data, a subscription is required.

Henry County *Recorded Documents* www.henrycountyclerk.ky.gov/   Access index/images with limited records for a fee at https://www.ecclix.com/. Must subscribe. See vendor web page for fees.
Property, Taxation Records   Access to property valuation data for free at www.henrypva.com/PublicSearch/tabid/674/Default.aspx.

Hopkins County *Property, Taxation Records*   Access property assessment index free at http://qpublic.net/ky/hopkins/search.html. Subscription available for more detailed information at http://qpublic5.qpublic.net/ky_hopkins_login.php?subscribe=1.

Jefferson County *Recorded Documents* www.jeffersoncountyclerk.org/   Access county land records free at http://search.jeffersondeeds.com/.
Property, Taxation Records   Access to the county property valuation administrator's assessment roll is free at https://jeffersonpva.ky.gov/property-search/. No name searching. There is also a subscription service for a fee, click on choose a plan at same site.

Jessamine County *Recorded Documents* http://jessaminecountyclerk.com/   Access index/images with limited records for a fee at https://www.ecclix.com/. Must subscribe. See vendor web page for fees.
Property, Taxation Records   Access to property and sales searches free at www.jessaminepva.com/?page_id=90.

Johnson County *Recorded Documents* http://johnsoncountyclerkky.com/   Access index/images with limited records for a fee at https://www.ecclix.com/. Must subscribe. See vendor web page for fees.
Property, Taxation Records   Access to records (limited) free at http://qpublic5.qpublic.net/ky_johnson_taxroll.php. Subscription service (all available features) available for a fee. Access to the delinquent tax list for free at http://kydtax.smllc.us/DTaxPDFs/JohnsonDTAX.pdf.

Kenton County (1st District) *Recorded Documents* http://kentoncountykyclerk.com/main/   Access to public records for free at http://kcor.org/. Records back to 5/1991. More detailed information require an account fee.
Property, Taxation Records   Access to GIS/mapping for a fee at http://kcky.maps.arcgis.com/apps/webappviewer/index.html?id=914171b6f0804aa9a0b949c2774ef9be.

Kenton County (2nd District) *Property, Taxation Records*   Access the county Property Valuation database at http://kcor.org/. Search for free by using 'Guest Access.' For full, professional property data can subscribe; fee for username and password is varied depending on Clerk's, PVA or both records required

Knott County *Property, Taxation Records*   Access to Delelinquent tax bills lists for free at http://cts.ky.gov/Property+Tax/.

Knox County *Property, Taxation Records*   Access to property records for free (limited data) at www.qpublic.net/ky/knox/search.html. For detailed information, must subscribe.

Larue County *Recorded Documents* http://laruecountyclerk.com/   Access to records for free at http://laruecountyclerk.com/index.cfm.

Laurel County *Property, Taxation Records*   Access the property records free at www.qpublic.net/ky/laurel/search.html.

Leslie County *Property, Taxation Records*   Access to property records for free at www.qpublic.net/ky/leslie/.

Lewis County *Recorded Land Documents* http://lewiscountyclerk.ky.gov/Pages/default.aspx   Access to recorded land records for a fee from a vendor at www.kycountyrecords.com/. Images included. Fees are $62.00 per month, per county (this is a recurring monthly charge) or $22.00 per county, per record type. To subscribe contact via email at administrator@kylandrecords.com or call 888-486-6258 or 270-443-1610.
Property, Taxation Records   Access to tax records for a fee at www.kylandrecords.com/. Images included. Also, access to delinquent taxes for free at www.kylandrecords.com/taxads/lewis.php.

Lincoln County *Property, Taxation Records*   Access to public records for free at http://qpublic.net/ky/lincoln/about.html.

Livingston County *Recorded Documents* www.livingstoncountyky.com/countyclerk/   Access index/images with limited records for a fee at https://www.ecclix.com/. Must subscribe. See vendor web page for fees.

Logan County *Property, Taxation Records*   Access to property tax and property sale information for a fee at http://qpublic5.qpublic.net/ky_logan_taxroll.php.

Lyon County *Recorded Documents* www.lyoncounty.ky.gov/   Access to records for free at http://68.222.251.95/recordsearch/. From this site one may do a delinquent tax search.
Property, Taxation Records   Access to tax roll information for free at http://qpublic5.qpublic.net/ky_lyon_taxroll.php.

Madison County *Recorded Documents* http://madisoncountyclerk.us/   Access index/images with limited records for a fee at https://www.ecclix.com/. Must subscribe. See vendor web page for fees.
Property, Taxation Records   Access to property records for a fee at http://qpublic.net/ky/madison/search.html.

Magoffin County *Property, Taxation Records*   Access to delinquent taxes for free at http://magoffincountyclerk.ky.gov/Pages/dt.aspx.

Marion County *Recorded Documents* www.marioncounty.ky.gov/elected/coclerk.htm   Access records lookup free at www.marioncountykyclerk.com/. Click on DocSearch.

Marshall County *Property, Taxation Records*   Access to PVA property data requires registration, username and password at http://marshallpva.ky.gov/PVA/. Subscription fees apply. Access to tax records for a fee at www.kylandrecords.com/. Images included.

Martin County *Recorded Documents*   Access index/images with limited records for a fee at https://www.ecclix.com/. Must subscribe. See vendor web page for fees.

Mason County *Recorded Documents* http://masoncountyclerkky.com/   Access index/images with limited records for a fee at https://www.ecclix.com/. Must subscribe. See vendor web page for fees.
Property, Taxation Records   Access to records for free at http://qpublic.net/ky/mason/search.html.

McCracken County *Recorded Documents* http://mccrackencountyclerk.net/   Access to land records, marriage, etc records for free at www.mccrackenrecords.com/. Includes delinquent taxes.
Property, Taxation Records   Access to GIS/mapping free at http://map-gis.org/disclaimer.

McCreary County *Recorded Documents* www.mccrearycountyclerk.com/   Access index/images with limited records for a fee at https://www.ecclix.com/. Must subscribe. See vendor web page for fees.

McLean County *Recorded Documents* http://mcleancounty.ky.gov/Pages/default.aspx   Access index/images with limited records for a fee at https://www.ecclix.com/. Must subscribe. See vendor web page for fees.

Meade County *Recorded Documents* http://meadecountyclerk.com/   Access index/images with limited records for a fee at https://www.ecclix.com/. Must subscribe. See vendor web page for fees.

Menifee County *Recorded Documents*   Access index/images with limited records for a fee at https://www.ecclix.com/. Must subscribe. See vendor web page for fees.

Mercer County *Recorded Documents* http://mercercounty.ky.gov/Pages/default.aspx   Access index/images with limited records for a fee at https://www.ecclix.com/. Must subscribe. See vendor web page for fees.
Property, Taxation Records   Access to online subscription for tax roll access for a fee at www.mercercountypva.com/ContactUs/SubscriberApplication/tabid/763/Default.aspx. Fees are $250.00-1 year; each add'l sub $125.00-1 year each; short term $50.00-1 month each. Also, access to property valuation data for free at www.mercercountypva.com/PublicSearch.aspx.

Metcalfe County   *Recorded Documents*   www.metcalfecountyclerk.com/   Access to county records for a fee at www.mainstreet-tech.com/Search/UserAnon/ChooseCounty.aspx?CCodeRedir=1. Unlimited printing is available with a purchased subscription.

Monroe County   *Recorded Documents*   www.monroecountyclerkky.com/   Access index/images with limited records for a fee at https://www.ecclix.com/. Must subscribe. See vendor web page for fees.

Montgomery County   *Recorded Documents*   http://montgomerycountyclerk.com/   Access index/images with limited records for a fee at https://www.ecclix.com/. Must subscribe. See vendor web page for fees.
Property, Taxation Records   Access to PVA property data for a fee requires registration, username and password at http://qpublic5.qpublic.net/ky_montgomery_taxroll.php.

Morgan County   *Property, Taxation Records*   Access to delinquent taxes for free at www.morgan.clerkinfo.net/index.php?option=com_wrapper&view=wrapper&Itemid=62.

Muhlenberg County   *Recorded Documents*   www.muhlenbergcountyclerk.com/Home.aspx   Access index/images with limited records for a fee at https://www.ecclix.com/. Must subscribe. See vendor web page for fees.
Property, Taxation Records   Access to property record searches for free at http://qpublic.net/ky/muhlenberg/search.html.

Nelson County   *Recorded Documents*   www.nelsoncountyclerk.com   Access to records for a fee at www.nelsoncountyclerk.com/. Unlimited monthly access for up to 5 simultaneous users for $40.00 per month.
Property, Taxation Records   Access to property records and GIS/mapping for a fee are found at www.qpublic.net/ky/nelson/search.html (limited information is provided to guests for free, but to access entire database, must subscribe to website).

Nicholas County   *Property, Taxation Records*   Access to records for a fee at http://qpublic5.qpublic.net/ky_nicholas_taxroll.php.

Ohio County   *Recorded Documents*   http://ohiocountyclerk.ky.gov/Pages/default.aspx   Access index/images with limited records for a fee at https://www.ecclix.com/. Must subscribe. See vendor web page for fees.
Property, Taxation Records   Access to the property search for free at www.pvdnetwork.com/PVDNet.asp?SiteID=103.

Oldham County   *Recorded Documents*   http://oldhamcountyclerkky.com/   Access index/images with limited records for a fee at https://www.ecclix.com/. Must subscribe. See vendor web page for fees.
Property, Taxation Records   Access to property tax records free at http://qpublic5.qpublic.net/ky_oldham_taxroll.php. For detailed information, must subscribe.

Owen County   *Recorded Documents*   www.owencountyky.us/county-agencies/owen-county-clerk.html   Access to index back to 1986 and images back to 1986 by subscription at www.titlesearcher.com/countyInfo.php?cnum=T66.
Property, Taxation Records   Access to property records for free at http://qpublic.net/ky/owen/search.html. For detailed information must subscribe.

Owsley County   *Property, Taxation Records*   Access to property records for a fee at www.qpublic.net/ky/owsley/search.html.

Pendleton County   *Recorded Land Documents Records*   http://pendletonwp.clerkinfo.net/   Access to recorded land records for a fee from a vendor at www.kycountyrecords.com/. Images included. Fees are $62.00 per month, per county (this is a recurring monthly charge) or $22.00 per county, per record type. To subscribe contact via email at administrator@kylandrecords.com or call 888-486-6258 or 270-443-1610.

Perry County   *Property, Taxation Records*   Access to property records for free at www.qpublic.net/ky/perry/.

Pike County   *Recorded Land Documents Records*   http://pike.clerkinfo.net/   Access to recorded land records for a fee from a vendor at www.kycountyrecords.com/. Images included. Fees are $62.00 per month, per county (this is a recurring monthly charge) or $22.00 per county, per record type. To subscribe contact via email at administrator@kylandrecords.com or call 888-486-6258 or 270-443-1610.
Property, Taxation Records   Access to tax records for a fee at www.kylandrecords.com/. Images included.

Powell County   *Recorded Land Documents*   www.powellcounty.ky.gov/elected/coclerk.htm   Access to recorded land records for a fee from a vendor at www.kycountyrecords.com/. Images included. Fees are $62.00 per month, per county (this is a recurring monthly charge) or $22.00 per county, per record type. To subscribe contact via email at administrator@kylandrecords.com or call 888-486-6258 or 270-443-1610.
Property, Taxation Records   Access to tax records for a fee at www.kylandrecords.com/. Images included.

Pulaski County   *Property, Taxation Records*   Access to property index is free at www.qpublic.net/ky/pulaski/search.html. Also, access to the delinquent tax list for free at www.pulaskicountycourtclerk.com/Delinquent_Taxes.html.

Rowan County   *Recorded Documents*   http://rowancountyclerk.com/   Access index/images with limited records for a fee at https://www.ecclix.com/. Must subscribe. See vendor web page for fees.
Property, Taxation Records   Access to county tax rolls requires registration and password; fees apply, see http://qpublic5.qpublic.net/ky_rowan_login.php. 120 records over 12 months is $100, up to 1200 records for $750. Email questions to carmen.swim@ky.gov.

Russell County   *Recorded Land Documents Records*   www.russell.clerkinfo.net/   Access to recorded land records for a fee from a vendor at www.kycountyrecords.com/. Images included. Fees are $62.00 per month, per county (this is a recurring monthly charge) or $22.00 per county, per record type. To subscribe contact via email at administrator@kylandrecords.com or call 888-486-6258 or 270-443-1610.
Property, Taxation Records   Access to tax roll data for free (limited) go to http://qpublic5.qpublic.net/ky_russell_taxroll.php. For detailed information (all available features) must subscribe for a fee. Access to tax records for a fee at www.kylandrecords.com/. Images included.

Scott County   *Recorded Documents*   http://scottcountyclerk.com/   Access index/images with limited records for a fee at https://www.ecclix.com/. Must subscribe. See vendor web page for fees.
Property, Taxation Records   Access property tax roll data and recent sales for free at http://qpublic.net/ky/scott/.

Shelby County   *Recorded Documents*   www.shelbycountyclerk.com   Access index/images with limited records for a fee at https://www.ecclix.com/. Must subscribe. See vendor web page for fees.
Property, Taxation Records   Access to property index is free at www.qpublic.net/ky/shelby/. A subscription is required for full data.

Simpson County   *Property, Taxation Records*   Access to the delinquent tax list for free at http://simpsoncountyclerk.ky.gov/Documents/Simpson%20County%202014%20Delinquent%20Tax.pdf

Spencer County   *Recorded Documents*   www.spencercountyclerk.com/new/   Access index/images with limited records for a fee at https://www.ecclix.com/. Must subscribe. See vendor web page for fees.

Taylor County   *Recorded Documents*   www.tcclerk.com/   Access to entire index and selected images free at www.tcclerk.com/index.cfm. Images include deeds and mortgages from 1982 to present; Marriages from 1977 and all documents imaged from 2000.

Trigg County   *Recorded Documents*   http://triggcountyclerk.ky.gov/Pages/default.aspx   Access index/images with limited records for a fee at https://www.ecclix.com/. Must subscribe. See vendor web page for fees.
Property, Taxation Records   Access to tax records for a fee at www.kylandrecords.com/. Images included.

Trimble County   *Recorded Documents*   www.trimblecounty.ky.gov/gov/cclerk.htm   Access index/images with limited records for a fee at https://www.ecclix.com/. Must subscribe. See vendor web page for fees.

Union County   *Recorded Documents*   www.unioncounty.ky.gov/index.php/countygovernment/countyclerk   Access to records for a fee at https://cotthosting.com/kyunionexternal/User/Login.aspx. Must have user ID and password.

Warren County   *Recorded Documents*   www.warrencountyky.gov/county-clerk   Access index/images with limited records for a fee at https://www.ecclix.com/. Must subscribe. See vendor web page for fees.
Property, Taxation Records   Access to property data for free at www.qpublic.net/ky/warren/.

Wayne County   *Recorded Documents*   http://waynecounty.ky.gov/eo/Pages/coclerk.aspx   Access to records free at www.waynecountyky.com/. Must register before use. Must also install Alternatiff image view in order to view images. Can get this program at this site.
Property, Taxation Records   Access to property tax records for free at http://taxbills.g-uts.com/%28S%28e1sqz455mkuxf255cgi22v55%29%29/default.aspx?siteid=20&taxbill=1. Access to property records and GIS/mapping for a fee are found at www.pvdnetwork.com/PVDNet.asp?SiteID=100.

Webster County   *Recorded Land Documents*   http://webstercountyclerk.ky.gov/Pages/default.aspx   Access to recorded land records for a fee from a vendor at www.kycountyrecords.com/. Images included. Fees are $62.00 per month, per county (this is a recurring monthly charge) or $22.00 per county, per record type. To subscribe contact via email at administrator@kylandrecords.com or call 888-486-6258 or 270-443-1610.
Property, Taxation Records   Access GIS-mapping and property data for a fee at www.webstercountypva.com/maps.htm. Contact by email (jeffd.kelley@ky.gov) for registration information.

Wolfe County   *Recorded Land Documents*   Access to recorded land records for a fee from a vendor at www.kycountyrecords.com/. Images included. Fees are $62.00 per month, per county (this is a recurring monthly charge) or $22.00 per county, per record type. To subscribe contact via email at administrator@kylandrecords.com or call 888-486-6258 or 270-443-1610.
Property, Taxation Records   Access to tax records for a fee at www.kylandrecords.com/. Images included.

Woodford County   *Property, Taxation Records*   Access to property records and GIS/mapping for a fee are found at http://qpublic5.qpublic.net/ky_gsearch.php?county=ky_woodford.

Louisiana

Capital: Baton Rouge
         East Baton Rouge Parish
Time Zone: CST
Population: 4,670,724
# of Parishes: 64

Useful State Links

Website: http://louisiana.gov/
Governor: http://gov.louisiana.gov/
Attorney General: www.ag.state.la.us
State Archives: www.sos.la.gov/HistoricalResources/LearnAboutTheArchives/Pages/default.aspx
State Statutes and Codes: www.legis.la.gov/legis/LawSearch.aspx
Legislative Bill Search: www.legis.la.gov/legis/home.aspx
Unclaimed Funds: https://www.treasury.state.la.us/ucpm/UP/index.asp

Primary State Agencies

Criminal Records

State Police, Bureau of Criminal Identification,   www.lsp.org/index.html   Authorized agencies can utilize LAAPPS and submit their information and receive a response instantaneously provided
if there is no criminal history information. The site is https://ibc.dps.louisiana.gov/program.aspx. Use of Microsfot Silverlightis required, Also, one may print an official receipt from the site with a unique audit number so that the user may reference a submission at any time. The fee is $26.00.

Sexual Offender Registry

State Police, Sex Offender and Child Predator Registry,   www.lsp.org/socpr/default.html   Search by name, ZIP Code, city or parish or view the entire list at the website. Also search by city, school area or parish. Also, email requests are accepted, use SOCPR@dps.state.la.us.

Incarceration Records

Department of Public Safety and Corrections, PO Box 94304,   www.corrections.state.la.us/   Currently, the Department does not have inmate locator capabilities. However, the web page refers searchers to https://www.vinelink.com/.

Corporation, LP, LLP, LLC, Trademarks/Servicemarks

Commercial Division, Corporation Department,   www.sos.la.gov/BusinessServices/Pages/default.aspx   Search by individual's name or charter's name or document number at www.sos.la.gov/BusinessServices/SearchForLouisianaBusinessFilings/Pages/default.aspx. Instructions are given for ordering documents or retrieving an order..   *Other Options:* Bulk sale of corporation, LLC, partnership, and trademark information is available for approved entities. For more info, call 225-925-4704.

Uniform Commercial Code, Federal Tax Liens

Secretary of State, UCC Division,   www.sos.la.gov/BusinessServices/UniformCommercialCode/Pages/default.aspx   An annual $400 fee gives unlimited access to UCC filing information at Direct Access 24/7. However, the agreements states that the purchaser can only use the data for internal purposes, and data is not transferable. Although federal tax liens are filed at the parish level, they do appear on the index of this service. State tax liens do not appear on this database search. For further information, call the number above or 225-922-1193. The application form on the web may not be connected.   *Other Options:* If one needs a paper copy of a federal or state tax lien, it must be obtained at the local parish.

Birth, Death Records

Vital Records Registry, Office of Public Health,   http://dhh.louisiana.gov/index.cfm/page/634/n/235   Orders can be placed online at www.vitalchek.com, a state-approved vendor; see expedited services.

Driver Records

Dept of Public Safety and Corrections, Office of Motor Vehicles,   www.expresslane.org/Pages/default.aspx   There are two methods. The commercial requester, interactive mode is available from 7 AM to 9:30 PM daily. There is a minimum order requirement of 2,000 requests per month. A bond or large deposit is required. Fee is $16.00 per record. Users must post a bond or submit a deposit; thereafter, the state bills monthly. Users also must pass background checks and vetting. For more information, call 225-925-6032 Also, individuals may view and print their own record at https://expresslane.dps.louisiana.gov/ODRPublic/ODR1.aspx. The fee is $17.00 and requires a credit card. There is a Driver Reinstatement Status check at https://expresslane.dps.louisiana.gov/ReinstatementInquiry/ReinstatementInquiry.aspx. The Dl and last four digits of the DSSN are needed. The search is per DPPA requirements and not open to the public..

Crash Reports

Louisiana State Police, Traffic Records Unit - A27,   www.lsp.org/technical.html#traffic   One may purchase a crash report from the request link at www.lsp.org/technical.html#traffic. The request requires first and last name, date of crash, and parish location of crash. A login/ID must be created to finalize the transaction. The fee is $8.50. After payment, the requester may print a PDF version of the report. Records go back five years. Use of a credit card is required.

Voter Registration

Louisiana Secretary of State, Voter Registration Div,   www.sos.la.gov/ElectionsAndVoting/Pages/default.aspx   One may find voter information at https://voterportal.sos.la.gov/. There is an Inactive Voter Search at www.sos.la.gov/ElectionsAndVoting/Pages/InactiveVoters.aspx. Also request data via email at voterlistrequest@sos.la.gov.   *Other Options:* The agency will sell the database statewide or by parish per request. Media formats include email, labels, CD, and paper lists. There are no restrictions regarding purchasing for marketing purposes. Email questions to cate.mcritchie@sos.louisiana.gov.

Campaign Finance

Louisiana Board of Ethics, PO Box 4368,   http://ethics.la.gov/   Campaign Finance Reports, Opinions, PAC lists, and outstanding fines, lobbyist data and more are available using the Tabs at http://ethics.la.gov.

Occupational Licensing Boards

Accountant-CPA	https://elicense.cpaboard.la.gov/Lookup/LicenseLookup.aspx
Acupuncturist	https://services.lsbme.org/verifications/
Addiction Counselor	www.la-adra.org/index.php/2012-05-25-02-39-47
Adult Residential Care	https://webapps.dcfs.la.gov/carefacility/facility
Agricultural Consultant	www.ldaf.state.la.us/ldaf-programs/pesticide-environmental-programs/
Alcoholic Beverage Vendor	http://204.196.140.121:81/Lookup/LicenseLookup.aspx
Arborist/Utility Arborist	www.ldaf.state.la.us/consumers/horticulture-programs/louisiana-horticulture-commission/
Architect/Architectural Firm	www.lastbdarchs.com/roster.htm
Athletic Trainer	https://services.lsbme.org/verifications/
Attorney	https://www.lsba.org/Public/MembershipDirectory.aspx
Auctioneer Schools	www.lalb.org/approved_schools.php
Auto Buyer/Salesman/Dealer, New & Used	https://license.lumvc.louisiana.gov/Lookup/LicenseLookup.aspx
Automobile Parts Dealer, Used	https://license.lumvc.louisiana.gov/Lookup/LicenseLookup.aspx
Automotive Dismantler & Parts Recycler	https://license.lumvc.louisiana.gov/Lookup/LicenseLookup.aspx
Bank	www.ofi.state.la.us
Bond For Deed Agency	www.ofi.state.la.us
Burglar Alarm Contractor	http://sfm.dps.louisiana.gov/lic_contractors.htm#3
Cemetery	www.lcb.state.la.us/search.html
Check Casher	www.ofi.state.la.us
Chemical Engineer	https://renewals.lapels.com/Lookup/LicenseLookup.aspx
Child Residential Care/Child Placing Agency	https://webapps.dcfs.la.gov/carefacility/facility
Chiropractor/X-Ray Tech	www.lachiropracticboard.com/licensees.htm
Clinical Lab Personnel	https://services.lsbme.org/verifications/
Collection Agency	www.ofi.state.la.us
Construction Project, +$50000	www.lslbc.louisiana.gov/contractor-search/
Consumer Credit Grantor	www.ofi.state.la.us
Contractor	www.lslbc.louisiana.gov/contractor-search/
Contractor, General/Subcontractor	www.lslbc.louisiana.gov/contractor-search/
Cosmetologist/Cosmetology Instructor	www.lsbc.louisiana.gov/Public/Default.aspx
Counselor (Drug/Addiction) Disciplinary Actions	www.la-adra.org/index.php/complaints

Counselor, Professional (LPC)	www.lpcboard.org/LPC_new.php
Credit Repair Agency	www.ofi.state.la.us
Credit Union	www.ofi.state.la.us
Crematory	www.lsbefd.state.la.us/wp-content/uploads/2017.Crematories.pdf
Day Care Facility	https://webapps.dcfs.la.gov/carefacility/facility
Dentist/Dental Hygienist	www.lsbd.org/licenseverification.htm
Dietitian	https://www.lbedn.org/index.cfm/licensee-search
Electrical Engineer	https://renewals.lapels.com/Lookup/LicenseLookup.aspx
Electrolysis Schools	http://lsbee.org/Page_4.html
Embalmer	www.lsbefd.state.la.us/wp-content/uploads/2016.embalmer.web_.list_.b.pdf
Engineer/Engineer Intern/Firm	https://renewals.lapels.com/Lookup/LicenseLookup.aspx
Environmental Engineer	https://renewals.lapels.com/Lookup/LicenseLookup.aspx
Esthetician	www.lsbc.louisiana.gov/Public/Default.aspx
Exercise Physiologist, Clinical	https://services.lsbme.org/verifications/
Fire Alarm Contractor	http://sfm.dps.louisiana.gov/lic_contractors.htm#3
Fire Extinguisher Contractor	http://sfm.dps.louisiana.gov/lic_contractors.htm#3
Fire Protection Sprinkler Contractor	http://sfm.dps.louisiana.gov/lic_contractors.htm#3
Florist, Retail/Wholesale	www.ldaf.state.la.us/consumers/horticulture-programs/louisiana-horticulture-commissioh/
Foster Care/Adoption Care	https://webapps.dcfs.la.gov/carefacility/facility
Funeral Director	www.lsbefd.state.la.us/wp-content/uploads/2016.funeral.director.web_.list_.b.pdf
Funeral Establishment	www.lsbefd.state.la.us/wp-content/uploads/2016.Funeral.Homes_.web_.list_.b.pdf
Home Improvem't Cont'r +$75,000	www.lslbc.louisiana.gov/contractor-search/
Horticulturist	www.ldaf.state.la.us/consumers/horticulture-programs/louisiana-horticulture-commission/
Insurance Agent/Broker/Producer/LHA/PC	https://www.ldi.la.gov/onlineservices/ActiveCompanySearch/
Interior Designer	http://lsbid.org/licensees.asp
Juvenile Detention	https://webapps.dcfs.la.gov/carefacility/facility
Land Surveyor/Surveyor Intern/Firm	https://renewals.lapels.com/Lookup/LicenseLookup.aspx
Landscape Architect/Contractor	www.ldaf.state.la.us/consumers/horticulture-programs/louisiana-horticulture-commission/
Lender	www.ofi.state.la.us
Lobbyist	http://ethics.la.gov/LobbyistLists.aspx
Manicurist	www.lsbc.louisiana.gov/Public/Default.aspx
Marriage and Family Therapist	www.lpcboard.org/LMFT_new.php
Massage Therapist/Establlshment	https://www.labmt.org/find_a_therapist
Maternity Home	https://webapps.dcfs.la.gov/carefacility/facility
Medical Disciplinary Actions	http://apps.lsbme.la.gov/disciplinary/actionsDetail.aspx
Medical Gas Piping Installer	www.spbla.com/rosters-find-a-license-plumber/
Midwife	https://services.lsbme.org/verifications/
Mold Remediation	www.lslbc.louisiana.gov/contractor-search/
Motor Auction	https://license.lumvc.louisiana.gov/Lookup/LicenseLookup.aspx
Motor Vehicle Agent/Sellerman	www.lmvc.la.gov/
Motor Vehicle Crusher/Shredder	https://license.lumvc.louisiana.gov/Lookup/LicenseLookup.aspx
Motor Vehicle Dealer; New/Used	www.lmvc.la.gov/
Motor Vehicle Leasing/Rental Firm	www.lmvc.la.gov/
Motor Vehicle Mfg/Distributor	https://license.lumvc.louisiana.gov/Lookup/LicenseLookup.aspx
Motor Vehicle Sales Finance Firm	www.lmvc.la.gov/
Motored Products, New	https://license.lumvc.louisiana.gov/Lookup/LicenseLookup.aspx
Notary Public	www.sos.la.gov/NotaryAndCertifications/SearchForLouisianaNotaries/Pages/default.aspx
Notification Filer	www.ofi.state.la.us/Notification%20Licensees.htm
Nuclear Engineer	https://renewals.lapels.com/Lookup/LicenseLookup.aspx
Nuclear Medicine Technologist	www.lsrtbe.org/search.cfm
Nurse-LPN	www.lsbpne.com/license_verification.phtml
Nurse-RN	https://services.lsbn.state.la.us/services/service.asp?s=1&sid=8
Nurses Aide	https://tlc.dhh.la.gov/
Nutritionist	https://www.lbedn.org/index.cfm/licensee-search
Occupational Therapist/Technologist	https://services.lsbme.org/verifications/

Optometrist	http://weoassociation.com/default.aspx?PID=4
Osteopathic Physician	https://services.lsbme.org/verifications/
Payday Lender	www.ofi.state.la.us/
Pesticide Applicator	www.ldaf.state.la.us/ldaf-programs/pesticide-environmental-programs/
Pesticide Dealer/Operator	www.ldaf.state.la.us/ldaf-programs/pesticide-environmental-programs/
Pharmacist/Pharmacy	https://secure.pharmacy.la.gov/Lookup/LicenseLookup.aspx
Pharmacy Intern (College)	https://secure.pharmacy.la.gov/Lookup/LicenseLookup.aspx
Pharmacy Tech/Candidate	https://secure.pharmacy.la.gov/Lookup/LicenseLookup.aspx
Pharmacy/Hospital	https://secure.pharmacy.la.gov/Lookup/LicenseLookup.aspx
Physical Therapist/Therapist Asst	https://www.laptboard.org/index.cfm/pt-search
Physician/Medical Doctor/Assistant	https://services.lsbme.org/verifications/
Plumber Journeyman/Master	www.spbla.com/rosters-find-a-license-plumber/
Podiatrist	https://services.lsbme.org/verifications/
Prevention Specialist (Social Work)	www.la-adra.org/index.php/2012-05-25-02-39-47
Psychologist	https://www.lsbepportal.com/LicenseVerification.aspx
Radiation Therapy Technologist	www.lsrtbe.org/search.cfm
Radiographer/Radiologic Technologist	www.lsrtbe.org/search.cfm
Radiologic Technologist, Private	https://services.lsbme.org/verifications/
Real Estate Agent/Broker/Firm	https://www.lrec.state.la.us/licensee-search/
Real Estate Appraiser/Trainee	www.reab.state.la.us/dbfiles/appraiserinfo_new.htm
Real Estate School/Instruct/Educator	www.lrec.state.la.us/pre-license-education/
Residential Construction +$50,000	www.lslbc.louisiana.gov/contractor-search/
Respiratory Therapist/Therapy Tech	https://services.lsbme.org/verifications/
Retort Operator	www.lsbefd.state.la.us/wp-content/uploads/2017.Retort-Operators.pdf
Social Worker/Clinic Supervisor	https://www.labswe.org/page/licensee-info
Solicitor	https://www.ldi.la.gov/onlineservices/ActiveCompanySearch/
Speech Pathologist/Audiologist	https://www.lbespa.org/index.cfm/licensee-search
Substance Abuse Counselor	www.la-adra.org/index.php/2012-05-25-02-39-47
Vocational Rehabilitation Counselor	http://lrcboard.org/licensee_database.asp
Water Supply Piping	www.spbla.com/rosters-find-a-license-plumber/

State and Local Courts

About Louisiana Courts: The trial court of general jurisdiction in Louisiana is the **District Court**. A District Court Clerk in each Parish holds all the records for that Parish. Each Parish has its own clerk and courthouse.

City Courts are courts of record and handle misdemeanors, limited civil, juvenile, traffic and evection. The amount of civil is concurrent with the District Court based where the amount in controversy does not exceed $15,000 to $50,000 depending on the court. (See CCP 4843 - http://legis.la.gov/Legis/law.aspx?d=112087).

In criminal matters, City Courts generally have jurisdiction over ordinance violations and misdemeanor violations of state law. City judges also handle a large number of traffic cases.

Parish Courts exercise jurisdiction in civil cases worth up to $10,000 to 25,000 and criminal cases punishable by fines of $1,000 or less, or imprisonment of six months or less. Cases are appealable from the Parish Courts directly to the courts of appeal.

A **Mayor's Court** handles certain traffic cases and minor infractions for towns and municipalities.

The **Justice of the Peace Courts** are organized by Ward within a Parish. They have jurisdiction in civil matters when the amount in dispute does not exceed $5,000 and can perform marriage ceremonies. They do not have jurisdiction when a title to real estate is involved, when the state or any political subdivision is a defendant, or in successions or probate matters.

The web page for the Judicial System is www.lasc.org/judicial_admin/default.asp/

Appellate Courts: There are five Courts of Appeals that are the intermediate courts of appeal between the District Courts and the Supreme Court. Search opinions at www.lasc.org/opinion_search.asp. Supreme Court Dockets going back approx. 2 years are shown at www.lasc.org/docket/default.asp.

Online Court Access

There is no statewide system open to the public for trial court dockets, but a number of parishes offer online access.

Ascension Parish

23rd District Court - Donaldsonville   www.ascensionclerk.com/default.aspx

Civil: Access to civil judgments, etc, available by subscription; $100 set-up charge single user; $250 multiple user up to 5, plus $50.00 monthly and $.50 per image printed; includes recorded document index; see www.ascensionclerk.com/onlineservices.aspx. *Criminal:* Access to criminal case data available by subscription; $100 set-up charge single user; $250 multiple user up to 5, plus $50.00 monthly and $.50 per image printed; includes civil and recorded document index; see www.ascensionclerk.com/onlineservices.aspx.

Assumption Parish

23rd District Court - Napoleonville   http://assumptionclerk.com/

Civil: The site is at http://assumptionclerk.com/record-search/. Registration is required. Registration is $50 per month or $500 a year with $1.00 per page to print images. Please note that there may be records that have been assigned Official numbers but not yet completely indexed or available on this search. *Criminal:* The site is at http://assumptionclerk.com/record-search/. Registration is $50 per month or $500 a year with $1.00 per page to print images.

Avoyelles Parish

12th District Court - Marksville

Civil: An online subscription service to record images is available at http://cotthosting.com/laavoyelles. Monthly rate is $75.00, other fees are $.50 for each printed page plus a service fee to use PayPal. *Criminal:* same

Beauregard Parish

36th District Court - DeRidder   www.beauregardclerk.org/

Civil: Search the index at www.beauregardclerk.org/search-our-records. Records go back to 6/1/2009. Fee is $100 a month or $15.00 a day. *Criminal:* Search the index at www.beauregardclerk.org/search-our-records. Records go back to 3/12/2009. Fee is $100 a month or $15.00 a day.

Bienville Parish

2nd District Court - Arcadia   http://clerk.bienvilleparish.org/

Civil: An online subscription service is available for $50.00 a month. Contact the Clerk of Court for details and pricing.

Bossier Parish

26th District Court - Benton   www.bossierclerk.com

Civil: Access to the Parish Clerk of Court online records requires $85 setup fee and a $35 monthly flat fee, see the home page. Civil, criminal, probate, traffic and domestic index information is by name or case number. Call 318-965-2336 for more information. The system occasionally lacks identifiers that would otherwise be found in person. *Criminal:* same

Caddo Parish

1st District Court- Shreveport   www.caddoclerk.com

Civil: Online access to civil records back to 1994 and name index back to 1984 is through county Internet service. Fee is $360 per year. Marriage and recording information is also available. Online images $.30 each to print. For information and sign-up, call 318-226-6523. The online system for the District Court may occasionally have court records missing or lack identifiers that would otherwise be found in person. *Criminal:* Online access to criminal record index back to 1994 and name index back to 1984 is through county Internet service. Fee is $360 per year. Recorded documents also available.

Shreveport City Court   www.shreveportcitycourt.org/

Civil: Using the home page there are separate searches (in the Civil tab) to search by name, or by docket number. A calendar search is also provided. *Criminal:* Search by citation number at http://apps.shreveportla.gov/citycourt/criminalbycitationtest.aspx. Search by name at http://apps.shreveportla.gov/citycourt/criminaltest.aspx.

Calcasieu Parish

14th District Court Lake Charles   www.calclerkofcourt.com

Civil: Online access to civil records is the same as criminal, see below.   *Criminal:* Online access to court record indices is free at http://207.191.42.34/resolution/. Registration and password required. Full documents requires $100.00 per month subscription.

Cameron Parish

38th District Court-Cameron

Civil: Online access is offered, but by contract only and fees involved. Call Susan Racca at 337-775-5316 for details. *Criminal:* same

De Soto Parish

42nd District Court-Mansfield   www.desotoparishclerk.org/

Civil: Access index via a web-based subscription service. Search index, view, & print image fee is $100.00 per month, plus a one-time setup fee of $150.00. Call 318-872-3110 to set-up an account of visit www.desotoparishclerk.org/online.html. *Criminal:* same

East Baton Rouge Parish

19th District Court-Baton Rouge   www.ebrclerkofcourt.org

Civil: Online access to the clerk's database is by subscription. Civil record indexes go back to '88; case tracking of civil and probate back to 1988. Setup fee is $100.00 plus $50.00 per month for 1st password, $25.00 for each add'l passwords. Call MIS Dept at 225-389-5295 for info or visit the website. *Criminal:* Online access to the clerk's database is by subscription. Setup fee is $100.00 plus $50.00 per month for 1st password, $25.00 for each add'l passwords.

Baton Rouge City Court-Baton Rouge   www.brgov.com/dept/citycourt/

Civil: Access city court's database including attorneys and warrants free at from the web page.   *Criminal:* Access city court's criminal dockets database and warrants free at http://brgov.com/dept.citycourt.

East Feliciana Parish

20th District Court-Clinton   www.eastfelicianaclerk.org/court.html

Civil: Online subscription service is available. $400.00 per quarter permits access to viewable documents; $250 per quarter permits access in indices. This database also includes recordings, conveyances, mortgages, and marriage records. *Criminal:* Criminal online also requires a subscription for full access, must be approved. Call for details.

Evangeline Parish

13th District Court-Ville Platte   www.evangelineparishclerkofcourt.com/

Civil: View index of civil suits back 40 01/01/1989 and marriages back to 01.01.1911 at https://cotthosting.com/LaEvangeline/User/Login.aspx

Iberia Parish

16th District Court-New Iberia   www.iberiaclerk.com

Civil: Search the civil index back to 01/01/09 and probate to 01/01/2000 at www.iberiaclerk.com/resolution/default.asp. A user ID and password are required, it may be necessary to call for help on obtaining.   *Criminal:* search criminal record index from 01/01/2000 to the last day of the previous month. A user ID and password are required, it may be necessary to call for help on obtaining.

Iberville Parish

18th District Court-Plaquemine   www.ibervilleclerk.com/

Civil: There is no free online access to court records - but if a civil judgment has been recorded, a subscription service to images of recorded documents is available at www.ibervilleclerk.com/html_pages/online.html.

Jefferson Parish

24th District Court-Gretna   www.jpclerkofcourt.us

Civil: Access to court records on JeffNet is $100, plus $50.00 monthly, $.75 per printed page. Includes recordings, marriage index, and assessor rolls. The service also offers a day rate - $20.00 for a 24 hour period. Civil case activity is available from 01/01/1986. For further information and sign-up, visit the website and click on Jeffnet or call 504-364-2976. One may also email to jeffnet@jpclerkofcourt.us. *Criminal:* Access to court records on JeffNet is $100, plus $50.00 monthly, $.75 per printed page, from 04/28/1994. The service also offers a day rate - $20.00 for a 24 hour period. For further information and sign-up, visit the website and click on Jeffnet or call 504-364-2976. One may also email to jeffnet@jpclerkofcourt.us.

Lafayette Parish

15th District Court-Lafayette   www.lafayetteparishclerk.com

Civil: Access to the remote online system requires $100 setup fee plus $65 subscription fee per month. Civil index goes back to 10/1964. For more information, call 337-291-6435 or visit www.lafayetteparishclerk.com/onlineIndex.cfm. The. system includes scanned images and pleadings back to 10/1994. *Criminal:* Access to criminal and traffic index back to 1986 on the remote online system requires $100 setup fee plus $65 subscription fee per month. There is a $10.00 fee per printed minute entry, and a $1.00 charge for printing other documents. For more information, call 337-291-6329 or visit www.lafayetteparishclerk.com/onlinerecords.cfm.

Livingston Parish

District Court-Livingston   www.livclerk.org

Civil: Civil indexing is available to online subscribers. Civil images are available to online subscribers with a Louisiana Bar Number. Call 225-686-2216 for more information. *Criminal:* Online access is available to local attorneys only, with registration, call 225-686-2216 x1107. $50.00 per year fee for online access.

Natchitoches Parish

10th District Court-Natchitoches   www.npclerkofcourt.org/

Civil: With username and password to WebView you can search and access civil records, judgments. $50 setup fee, then $50.00 monthly, plus $.50 per image. Includes conveyance and marriage records. Direct subscription inquires to Linda Cockrell at 318-352-8152. *Criminal:*

Orleans Parish

Civil District Court-New Orleans   www.orleanscdc.com/

Civil: CDC Remote provides access to civil case index from 1985 and First City Court cases as well as parish mortgage and conveyance indexes. Case files are not provided. The annual fee is $500 or monthly is $100. Credit cards are accepted. Call 504-592-9264 for more information.

New Orleans City Court   www.orleanscdc.com/

Civil: CDC Remote provides access to First City Court cases from 1988 as well as civil cases, parish mortgage and conveyance indexes. The fee is $250 or $300 per year. Call 504-407-0380 for more information.

Ouachita Parish

4th District Court-Monroe   www.opclerkofcourt.com

Civil: Civil records are available online. Civil records included are from Oct 1, 2000 forward. See https://cotthosting.com/laouachita/User/Login.aspx?ReturnUrl=%2flaouachita%2f.   *Criminal:* A subscription service to the record index is at https://cotthosting.com/laouachita/User/Login.aspx?ReturnUrl=%2flaouachita%2f. There is a one day ($12.50) or one month ($100) or one year ($1080) unlimited access fee to the index and images. There is an additional $1.00 per page fee to print. Establish an account with a credit card. Access to criminal records are July 9, 2002.

Plaquemines Parish
25th District Court-Belle Chasse   www.plaqueminesparishclerkofcourt.com/
Civil: Search the docket index online from the home page.   *Criminal:* same

Red River Parish
39th District Court-Coushatta   http://redriverclerk.com/
Civil: A subscription service is offered at https://cotthosting.com/LARedRiverExternal/User/Login.aspx. Fee is $50.00 per month or $20 per a 24-hour period. Add $1.00 for every page printed. Civil records available from 07/01/2000 to present.   *Criminal:* A subscription service is offered at https://cotthosting.com/LARedRiverExternal/User/Login.aspx. Fee is $50.00 per month or $20 per a 24-hour period. Add $1.00 for every page printed. Criminal records available form 03/01/2014 to present.

Sabine Parish
11th District Court-Many   www.sabineparishclerk.com/
Civil: Access civil and succession-probate court records by subscription at www.sabineparishclerk.com/pages/online-access. The $100 per month fee includes access to conveyance, mortgage, marriage records. Civil suits go back to 1/1985; Probate to 1920.   *Criminal:* Access to criminal records for subscribers available at http://cotthosting.com/lasabineqgov/main/login.aspx. There is a $100.00 per month fee. The docket index goes back to 07/01/1990.

St. Bernard Parish
34th District Court-Chalmette   http://stbclerk.com
Civil: Search civil case records back to 1/1989 is by subscription at http://records.stbclerk.com/User/Login.aspx. A variety of plans are available. Images may be printed for an additional $1.00 per page.   *Criminal:* Search criminal case records back to 1/1989 is by subscription at http://records.stbclerk.com/User/Login.aspx. A variety of plans are available.

St. Charles Parish
29th District Court-Hahnville   www.stcharlesgov.net/
Civil: This is the same subscription system described under criminal records. However, civil records are much more current, generally within 1 week old.   *Criminal:* Note the online system has old data - criminal record data up to and not beyond 13/31//2006. The log-in page is at https://records.stcharlesparish-la.gov/User/Login.aspx?ReturnUrl=%2findex.aspx. Images to 1999, index to 1988. Fee is $50 per month plus $1.00 per page for copies. All fees paid by credit card.

St. Landry Parish
27th District Court-Opelousas   www.stlandry.org
Civil: Online subscription access program to civil cases is available. The fee ranges from $50.00 to $300 per month. Includes civil court records back to 1997, also includes land indexes and images. Contact the court or visit the web page for details. *Criminal:*

St. Martin Parish
16th District Court-St. Martinville   www.stmartinparishclerkofcourt.com
Civil: The online system is by subscription only. Fee is $750 annual, or $400 for 6 months or $125 one month or $20 one day. Add $1.00 per page for copies. Data available images back to 1989/1990. Judgments are found with Recorder's Office data indices available at www.stmartinparishclerkofcourt.com.   *Criminal:* The online system is by subscription only. Fee is $750 annual, or $400 for 6 months or $125 one month or $20 one day. Add $1.00 per page for copies. Data available images back to 1989/1990. Those interested in subscribing to this service should please call Tricia at 337-394-2210.

St. Mary Parish
16th Judicial District Court-Franklin   www.stmaryparishclerkofcourt.com/
Civil: Access the civil index (among others) from 07/01/1980 or probate from 02/01/1983 forward. Fees: 1year is $750; 6 months is $400; 30 days is $125; one day is $20.00. If a credit card is used, there is a 3% surcharge. The access and sign-up link is at the home page.   *Criminal:* Access the criminal index from 02/01/1983 forward. Fees: 1year is $750; 6 months is $400; 30 days is $125; one day is $20.00. If a credit card is used, there is a 3% surcharge. The link an more information is at the home page. Indexes that are available for search are Conveyances, Mortgages, Civil Suits, Criminal, Probate, Marriages, Bonds, Chattel Mortgage, Incorporation, Military Discharge, Miscellaneous, Notarial Adoptions, Oaths and Partnerships.

St. Tammany Parish
22nd District Court-Covington   www.sttammanyclerk.org/
Civil: Internet access to civil records is from the Clerk of Court. There are two plans - basic and premium. Basic is $5.00 per day or $30 per month. Premium is $50 set up and $50 a month. Premium includes document images. For information, call Kristie Howell at 985-809-8787. Civil index goes back to 1992; images 1994 to present. *Criminal:* Internet access to criminal records is from the Clerk of Court. There are two plans - basic and premium. Basic is $5.00 per day or $30 per month. Premium is $50 set up and $50 a month. Premium includes document images. Includes records 1998 to present.

Tangipahoa Parish
21st District Court-Amite   www.tangiclerk.org

Civil: Online access to index of civil records is at www.tangiclerk.org/. You can Sign in as a Guest to view indexes at no cost; images are only available with a paid subscription). Index back to 1974. When civil data is shown is dependent on the type of subscription, be sure to read this information on the site.

Terrebonne Parish

32nd District Court-Houma   www.terrebonneclerk.org/

Civil: An online subscription is offered (see home page) to civil and criminal dockets. No images are provided. The rate is $50 per month. Subscribers can also obtain land records with or without images, for additional fees. One may print for $1.00 per page. *Criminal:* same Note that there is no option to subscribe to only civil or only criminal.

Union Parish

3rd District Court-Farmerville   http://upclerk.com/

Civil: From the home page click on Court Records Search. This is a subscription service based on a one day ($20), one month ($100), or one year ($1080) basis. Civil and probate available from 06/09/2001 forward. *Criminal:* From the home page click on Court Records Search. This is a subscription service based on a one day ($20), one month ($100), or one year ($1080) basis.

Washington Parish

22nd District Court-Franklinton   www.22ndjdc.org/default.aspx

Civil: The records, including file images are searchable online. The fee is $75 per month (or $20 for 24-hours) to view plus $1.00 for each printed page. Sign-up is at https://cotthosting.com/LAWashington/User/Login.aspx?ReturnUrl=%2fLAWashington%2f. *Criminal:* The records index only are searchable online. The fee is $75 per month (or $20 for 24-hours) to view plus $1.00 for each printed page. The sign-up is at https://cotthosting.com/LAWashington/User/Login.aspx?ReturnUrl=%2fLAWashington%2f.

Webster Parish

26th District Court-Minden   www.websterclerk.org/

Civil: Access court records by subscription; fee is $50.00 per month for index searches and images. Civil index goes back to 01/1986; images back to 2005. Sub includes criminal, probate, civil, traffic, also marriages and conveyances. Login, signup or find more information at www.websterclerk.org/records.html. *Criminal:* Access to criminal index and images is included in the general subscription service described in the civil section, above. The criminal subscription index goes back to 11/28/1992; images go back to early 2007.

West Baton Rouge Parish

18th District Court-Port Allen   www.wbrclerk.org/

Civil: Online access is available from home page. Click on Public Records under services and follow the menu, as there is a disclaimer and acceptance required. The index is free to view. There is a cost of $50 a month or $20 a day to subscribe view images. Subscribers can also print documents for $1.00 per page. *Criminal:* same

West Feliciana Parish

20th District Court-St Francisville   www.westfelicianaclerkofcourt.org/

Civil: Access to civil and probate index and images for a fee at https://cotthosting.com/lawestfeliciana/User/Login.aspx. Fee is $20 for 24 hours, or $100 for 30 days or $1080 for 365 days. Must have user ID and password.

Recorders, Assessors, and Other Sites of Note

About Louisiana Recording Offices: 64 parishes, 64 recording offices. One parish – St. Martin – has two non-contiguous segments. In Orleans Parish, deeds are recorded in a different office from mortgages.

About Tax Liens: All federal and state tax liens are filed at the parish level. However note that federal tax liens are placed in the state UCC database and state tax liens are not.

Online Access

Recorded Documents

A number of parishes offer online access to recorded documents. Most are commercial fee systems but newer systems are allowing for free index searching, then a fee for images, usually $1.00 each.

There is a statewide online access system for UCC information. Although federal tax liens are filed at the parish level, they do appear on this search. State tax liens do not appear on this database search. For more information, visit www.sos.la.gov/BusinessServices/HTMLPages/AbouttheDirectAccessService.htm.

- The Louisiana Clerks Remote Access Authority ("LCRAA") provides a free search web page at www.laclerksportal.org for viewing recorded mortgages and conveyances. One must register before use but viewing is free. There are at least 38 participating counties with more planned.

Parish's active on this site:

Allen	Concordia	Plaquemines	Terrebonne
Ascension	East Baton Rouge	Red River	Union
Assumption	East Carroll	Sabine	Vernon
Beauregard	East Feliciana	St. Bernard	Washington
Bienville	Grant	St. Charles	Webster
Bossier	Lafourche	St. James	West Baton Rouge
Caddo	La Salle	St. Martin	West Feliciana
Caldwell	Livingston	St. Mary	Winn
Calcasieu	Madison	St. Tammany	
Catahoula	Natchitoches	Tangipahoa	

Property Tax Records - Statewide Site

- See www.latax.state.la.us/Menu_ParishTaxRolls/TaxRolls.aspx for free access to each parish's assessor tax roll data. Note all parishes do not necessarily update their records to the current year.

Parish Sites Other Than the Two Bulleted Systems Mentioned Above:

Acadia Parish *Recorded Documents* www.acadiaparishclerk.com/   Access to conveyance and mortgage indexing and image records by subscription at www.acadiaparishclerk.com/online-services. Must fill out online contract, pay fee and be approved before use. The index records for conveyance and mortgage are from 1970 to present. Images are from 1977 to present. Also the court's civil indexing are from 1983 to current with images going back to around 2000.
Property, Taxation Records   Access to property data free at www.acadiaassessor.org/SearchForm.aspx.

Allen Parish *Recorded Documents* www.laclerksofcourt.org/Parishs/allenparish.htm   Access to the land mortgage and conveyance index is free at www.laclerksportal.org/. Must register before first use. Document images not available at this time.

Ascension Parish *Recorded Documents, Judgment Records* www.ascensionclerk.com/   Access available by subscription; $100 set-up charge single user; $250 multiple user up to 5, plus $50.00 monthly and $1.00 per image printed; see www.ascensionclerk.com/onlineservices.aspx. Also have $25.00 online day use. Access to the land mortgage and conveyance index is free at www.laclerksportal.org/. Must register before first use. Document images not available at this time.
Property, Taxation Records   Access to the property search site for free at www.ascensionassessor.com/Search.

Assumption Parish *Recorded Documents, Probate, Marriage Records* http://assumptionclerk.com/   Online access by subscription at https://cotthosting.com/LAAssumption/User/Login.aspx. User ID and password required. Access to the land mortgage and conveyance index is free at www.laclerksportal.org/. Must register before first use. Document images not available at this time.

Avoyelles Parish *Recorded Documents* http://avoyellesparishclerkofcourt.com/   Access to land record at https://cotthosting.com/laavoyelles/User/Login.aspx. A monthly service fee of $75.00 is charged or $25.00 for daily fee.

Beauregard Parish *Recorded Documents* www.laclerksofcourt.org/Parishs/Beauregardparish.htm   Access to Recorded Documents www.beauregardclerk.org/search-our-records. Records go back to 3/17/2008. Fee is $100 a month or $15.00 a day. Access to the land mortgage and conveyance index is free at www.laclerksportal.org/. Must register before first use. Document images not available at this time.

Bienville Parish *Recorded Documents* http://clerk.bienvilleparish.org/index.php   Access to records for a fee at http://clerk.bienvilleparish.org/ucc.php, or contact Eddie Holmes at 318-263-2123 X10 for more subscription information. Conveyance records from 2/13/13 to present; mortgage records from 1/1/86 to present; civil records from 7/1/89 to present. The dates for all records will broaden as they continue to integrate older records into the digital system. Access to the land mortgage and conveyance index is free atwww.laclerksportal.org/. Must register before first use. Document images not available at this time.

Bossier Parish *Recorded Documents* www.bossierclerk.com   Access to the clerk's WebView System is by subscription; one-time signup fee is $50 plus $35 per month, plus small fee per image printed. Monthly billing. Mortgages go back to 1984, marriages to 1843, courts back to 1980s; see http://209.209.204.34/WebInquiry/login.aspx?ReturnUrl=%2fWebInquiry%2fDefault.aspx. This online system may occasionally have records missing or lack identifiers that would otherwise be found in person. This office now issues Birth Certificates for $24.00 each and Death Certificates for $17.00 each. Also, access to the land mortgage and conveyance index is free at www.laclerksportal.org/. Must register before first use. Document images not available at this time.
Property, Taxation Records   Free public address search available at www.bossierparishassessor.org/cgi-bin/pro_search.pl. Access to full data requires username and login ID, signup online; fee amounts to less than $1.00 per day. For more information, call 318-221-8718.

Caddo Parish *Recorded Documents* www.caddoclerk.com   Access to the Parish online records requires a $380.00 per year free, plus $.30 per page for imaging printing. Mortgages and indirect conveyances index dates back to 1983; direct conveyances date back to 1914. Lending agency data is available. Mortgage images back to 1981. Also, access marriage licenses free back to 1838; use username 'muser' and password 'caddo.' Signup and info at www.caddoclerk.com/remote.htm or call 318-226-6523. Online system may occasionally have records missing or lack identifiers that would otherwise be found in person. Also, access to the land mortgage and conveyance index is free at www.laclerksportal.org/. Must register before first use. Document images not available at this time.

Calcasieu Parish *Recorded Documents, Marriage Records* www.calclerkofcourt.com   Online access to court record indices is free at www.calclerkofcourt.com/depts-servcs/IT-Services/Search-Main-Page. Registration and password required. Image and print are fee based. Also, access to the land mortgage and conveyance index is free at www.laclerksportal.org/. Must register before first use. Document images not available at this time.
Property, Taxation Records   Access to property search for free at www.calcasieuassessor.org/Search. Also, access to GIS/mapping free at www.cppj.net/index.aspx?page=120.

Caldwell Parish *Recorded Documents* www.caldwellparishclerkofcourt.com/recording_fees.aspx   Access to the land mortgage and conveyance index is free at www.laclerksportal.org/. Must register before first use. Document images not available at this time.

Cameron Parish *Recorded Documents* www.laclerksofcourt.org/Parishs/cameronparish.htm   Access to mortgage and conveyance info for a fee at www.deltacomputersystems.com/search.html. For subscription service contact Susan Racca.

Catahoula Parish *Recorded Documents* www.laclerksofcourt.org/clerksofcourt.htm   Access to the land mortgage and conveyance index is free at www.laclerksportal.org/. Must register before first use. Document images not available at this time.

Concordia Parish *Recorded Documents* www.concordiaclerk.org   Access to the land mortgage and conveyance index is free at www.laclerksportal.org/. Must register before first use. Document images not available at this time.

De Soto Parish *Recorded Documents* www.desotoparishclerk.org/   Access Clerk of Court records index by subscription at www.desotoparishclerk.org/; One-time set-up fee is $250.00 plus $100 per month for index, doc viewing, and images. Conveyance images and index back to 1843. Other public records included in this URL. Contact Jayme Maxie, Tabitha Sant, or Katie Procell at (318) 872-3110 to set up account.

East Baton Rouge Parish *Recorded Documents* www.ebrclerkofcourt.org/   Access to online records requires a $100 set up fee with a $50-$75 monthly fee. Lending agency data is available. For info, contact Robin White at 225-389-7851. Access to the land mortgage and conveyance index is free at www.laclerksportal.org/. Must register before first use. Document images not available at this time.

East Carroll Parish *Recorded Documents* www.laclerksofcourt.org/Parishs/eastcarrolparish.htm   Access to the land mortgage and conveyance index is free at www.laclerksportal.org/. Must register before first use. Document images not available at this time.

East Feliciana Parish *Recorded Documents* www.eastfelicianaclerk.org/   Access to online records requires a subscription, $20.00 for 24 hrs, $100.00 per month, $1000.00 per year plus copy cost for indices plus images. Conveyances go back to 1825, mortgages to 1981; viewable back to 6/18/1982. Marriages go back to 1987, viewable to 1995, and miscellaneous index goes back to 1984. For info, contact clerk's office at 225-683-5145 or visit www.eastfelicianaclerk.org/. Access to the land mortgage and conveyance index is free at www.laclerksportal.org/. Must register before first use. Document images not available at this time.

Evangeline Parish *Recorded Documents, Marriage Records* www.evangelineparishclerkofcourt.com/   Access to records for a fee at https://cotthosting.com/LaEvangeline/User/Login.aspx. Subscription fees are: Daily (24 hour access) $20.00; Monthly (30 days) $75.00; 6 Month (180 days) $400.00; 1 Year (365 days) $750.00. Also printing fee is $1.00 per page. Marriage records also available back to 1911.
Property, Taxation Records   Search tax roll data on statewide website, www.latax.state.la.us/Menu_ParishTaxRolls/TaxRolls.aspx.

Grant Parish *Recorded Documents* www.laclerksofcourt.org/parishs/grantparish.htm   Access to the land mortgage and conveyance index is free at www.laclerksportal.org/. Must register before first use. Document images not available at this time.

Iberia Parish *Recorded Documents* www.iberiaclerk.com   Access to the Parish online records requires a usage fee, 1 yr=$750/$1.00 per page, 6 months-$400/$1.00 per page, 30 days-$125/$1.00 per page, 1 day-$20/$1.00 per page. Lending agency data is available. For info, contact Mike Thibodeaux at 337-365-7282. Registration is also required for the Clerk's index search at https://cotthosting.com/laiberia/User/Login.aspx?ReturnUrl=%2flaiberia%2findex.aspx which includes conveyances and mortages back to 1959.

Iberville Parish *Recorded Documents* www.ibervilleclerk.com/   Access to records for a fee at https://ibervilleparishrecordsearch.com/External/User/Login.aspx?ReturnUrl=%2fExternal%2fIndex.aspx. Subscriptions are from 24 hours to 1 year.

Jackson Parish *Recorded Documents* www.jacksonparishclerk.org/   Access to the clerk's WebView Online Records system is available by subscription; $50 installation and account setup fee plus $50.00 per month usage fee; Contact Tanya at 318-259-2424 or email at clerk@jacksonparishclerk.org or go the subscription form at http://64.239.220.231/Webinquiry_Jackson/%28S%2802zgt255y5ekda3cs4xkod45%29%29/login.aspx.
Property, Taxation Records   Access to property search for free at www.jacksonassessor.org/Search.

Jefferson Davis Parish *Recorded Documents* www.jeffdavisclerk.org/pages?id=12   access to mortgage & conveyance information for a fee at http://sites.deltacomputersystems.com/home/la27/. Fee is $100.00 per month, $25.00 per day or $1200.00 per year. Conveyance index from 1976 to present, mortgage index from 1978 to present.
Property, Taxation Records   Access to property search for free at www.jeffdavisassessor.org/Search.

Jefferson Parish   *Recorded Documents*   www.jpclerkofcourt.us   Access to the clerk's JeffNet database is by subscription; set-up fee is $100.00 plus $50.00 monthly and $.50 per image printed. Mortgage and conveyance images go back to 1971 and changing; index to 1967. Marriage and property records go back to 1992. For info, visit https://ssl.jpclerkofcourt.us/JeffnetSetup/default.asp.
Property, Taxation Records   Search the assessor property records free at www.jpassessor.com/search.php.

La Salle Parish   *Recorded Documents*   www.laclerksofcourt.org/Parishs/lasalleparish.htm   Access to the land mortgage and conveyance index is free at www.laclerksportal.org/. Must register before first use. Document images not available at this time.

Lafayette Parish   *Recorded Documents*   www.lpclerk.com/   Access to Parish online records requires a $100 set up fee plus $65 per month. Conveyances date back to 1936; mortgages to 1948; other records to 1986. Lending agency data is available.
Property, Taxation Records   Assessor property data is free at http://lafayetteassessor.com/PropertySearch.cfm, but no name searching.

Lafourche Parish   *Recorded Documents*   http://lafourcheclerk.com/   Access to public records for a fee at http://lafourcheclerk.com/recordsSearch.html. This is a subscription fee to be paid by credit card online. Contact person is Annette M Fontana. Access to the land mortgage and conveyance index is free at www.laclerksportal.org/. Must register before first use. Document images not available at this time.
Property, Taxation Records   Property tax searches for free at www.lpao.net/Search.

Lincoln Parish   *Property, Taxation Records*   Access property assessor data at https://www.actdatascout.com/State/LA/Lincoln. Also, search by owner name for parcel and property data free on the GIS-mapping site at www.lincolnparish.org/gis/pages/online_maps.php/.

Livingston Parish   *Recorded Documents*   www.livclerk.org/   Access the clerk's search pages for a fee at https://cotthosting.com/LALPCOCExternal/User/Login.aspx. User name and password require to search; $50.00 yearly fee for an account plus $1.00 per page fee for printing of images. They also offer a one day (24 hr) subscription for $20.00 (land records only) plus printing fees. For assistance, call Vanessa Barnett at 225-686-2216 x4007 or 225-505-8200 (cell) or email to questions@livclerk.org. Access to the land mortgage and conveyance index is free at www.laclerksportal.org/. Must register before first use. Document images not available at this time.
Property, Taxation Records   Access to GIS/mapping for free at http://atlas.geoportalmaps.com/livingston. Also, access to county online tax rolls for free at http://livingstonassessor.com/Jobs/Benefits.asp.

Madison Parish   *Recorded Documents*   www.laclerksofcourt.org/Parishs/madisonparish.htm   Access to the land mortgage and conveyance index is free at www.laclerksportal.org/. Must register before first use. Document images not available at this time.

Natchitoches Parish   *Recorded Documents*   www.npclerkofcourt.org/   With username and password to WebView, access to marriage and property records back to 1976. $50 setup fee, then $50.00 monthly, plus $.50 per image. Direct subscription inquires to http://12.197.249.67/WebInquiry_Natchitoches/%2815uiy35543h142fjh25zo3nv%29/login.aspx. Access to the land mortgage and conveyance index is free at www.laclerksportal.org/. Must register before first use. Document images not available at this time.
Property, Taxation Records   Access assessor property data free at www.natchitochesassessor.org/SearchProperty.aspx.

Orleans Parish   *Recorded Documents*   www.orleanscivilclerk.com/   Access the Parish online records requires a $700 yearly subscription fee. Records date back to 1989. Access includes real estate, liens and civil. For info/signup, email civil clerk land records at orleanscdc.com. Conveyances back to 1989, mortgages to 9/21/97.
Property, Taxation Records   Access to property records for free at http://qpublic.net/la/orleans/search.html

Ouachita Parish   *Recorded Documents, Marriage Records*   www.opclerkofcourt.com/   Access to online access for a fee at https://cotthosting.com/laouachita/User/Login.aspx. Public records included in this URL (mortgage, deeds, criminal, civil and plats). Conveyance books from 1/2/1980 to present; marriage books from 1/8/1996 to present (NOTE: marriage license ONLY viewable, not printable), criminal records from 7/9/2002 to present and civil records from 10/1/2000 to present.
Property, Taxation Records   Access to assessor property data is free at https://www.actdatascout.com/State/LA/Ouachita.

Plaquemines Parish   *Recorded Documents*   http://clerk25th.com/   Access to record searches free at https://cotthosting.com/laplaquemines/User/Login.aspx. For more detailed information must sign up and pay fees. Access to the land mortgage and conveyance index is free at www.laclerksportal.org/. Must register before first use. Document images not available at this time.

Pointe Coupee Parish   *Property, Taxation Records*   Access to GIS/mapping free at www.ptcoupeeassessor.com/PageDisplay.asp?p1=1988. Also, access to the assessments free at www.ptcoupeeassessor.com/assessments. Can search by name, address, parcel number, subdivision or section, township and range.

Rapides Parish   *Recorded Documents*   www.rapidesclerk.org   Access to subscription service contact Ken Parks at 318-619-5816.
Property, Taxation Records   Access to property records for free at https://www.actdatascout.com/State/LA/Rapides.

Red River Parish   *Recorded Documents*   www.redriverclerk.com/   Access to records for a fee at https://cotthosting.com/LARedRiverExternal/User/Login.aspx. Access to the land mortgage and conveyance index is free at www.laclerksportal.org/. Must register before first use. Document images not available at this time.
Property, Taxation Records   Access to GIS/mapping for free at http://atlas.geoportalmaps.com/redriver.

Richland Parish   *Recorded Documents*   http://laclerksofcourt.org/Parishs/richlandparish.htm   Access to record images for a fee at https://www.uslandrecords.com/lalr/. Images available from 6/1/1980 to present, $2.00 per page for view of any document available.

Property, Taxation Records   Access to current assessment listing for free at www.rpao.org/SearchForm.aspx. Also, access to GIS/mapping for free at http://76.73.192.244:8008/mapguide/SpatialNet/Richland/.

Sabine Parish   ***Recorded Documents***   www.sabineparishclerk.com/   Access deeds, civil court and succession-probate court records by subscription along with conveyance, mortgage records at https://cotthosting.com/lasabine/User/Login.aspx. Conveyance index and images are from 1843 to present, mortgage index and images from 1843 to present. Civil suits index from 1/1/85 to present and images from 1998 to present. Criminal index and images from 7/1/90 to present. Probate index from 1/1/1920 to present and images from 1998 to present. Marriage records from 1/1/1930 to present. Also, access to the land mortgage and conveyance index is free at www.laclerksportal.org/. Must register before first use. Document images not available at this time.

St. Bernard Parish   ***Recorded Documents***   http://stbclerk.com/?s=Clerk+of+court   Search clerk's court and recording records indexes free at http://records.stbclerk.com/User/Login.aspx?ReturnUrl=%2fLandRecords%2fprotected%2fSrchQuickName.aspx. Mortgages back to 1849, marriages back to 4/1877, conveyances back to 1/1849 and partnerships back to 1/1967, courts and chattel back to 1/1989, Misc. and bonds and partnerships back to1/1967. Access to the land mortgage and conveyance index is free at www.laclerksportal.org/. Must register before first use. Document images not available at this time.

St. Charles Parish   ***Recorded Documents***   www.scpclerkofcourt.com/   Access to subscription for records go to https://records.stcharlesparish-la.gov/User/Login.aspx?ReturnUrl=%2fIndex.aspx. Fee is $50.00 per month plus $1.00 per page to print. Conveyance indices & images from 1960-present; mortgage indices 1958-present; mortgage images 1973-present; marriage license indices 1954-present. Access to the land mortgage and conveyance index is free at www.laclerksportal.org/. Must register before first use. Document images not available at this time.
Property, Taxation Records   Access to property searches for free at http://stcharlesassessor.azurewebsites.net/Search.

St. James Parish   ***Recorded Land Documents Records***   www.laclerksofcourt.org/parishs/stjamesparish.htm   Access to the land mortgage and conveyance index is free at www.laclerksportal.org/. Must register before first use. Document images not available at this time.
Property, Taxation Records   Access to GIS/mapping for free at http://stjamesassessor.com/gis-data Also, access to county tax roll search for free at www.stjamesassessor.com/PageDisplay.asp?p1=3555.

St. John the Baptist Parish   ***Property, Taxation Records***   Access property data free at www.stjohnassessor.org/Search.

St. Landry Parish   ***Recorded Documents***   http://stlandry.org/   Access to recorder office land records is by subscription; fee is $35-50 per month. Data includes mortgages and conveyances, also perhaps court records. For registration and password contact Ms Lisa Doyla at Clerk of Court office, extension 103.
Property, Taxation Records   Access to property search for free at www.stlandryassessor.org/Search. No name searches. Also, access to GIS/mapping for free at http://stlandrymapping.azurewebsites.net/.

St. Martin Parish   ***Recorded Documents***   www.stmartinparishclerkofcourt.com/   Access to the land mortgage and conveyance index is free at www.laclerksportal.org/. Must register before first use. Document images not available at this time.
Property, Taxation Records   Access to GIS/mapping records free at http://atlas.geoportalmaps.com/stmartin. Also, access to assessment list free at www.stmartinassessor.org/propsrch_disclaim.html.

St. Mary Parish   ***Recorded Documents***   www.stmaryparishclerkofcourt.com/   Acces to the online data for a fee at ttps://cotthosting.com/LAstMaryExternal/User/Login.aspx. Fees are: 1 year-$750; 6 months-$400; 30 days-$125; one day-$20. If credit card used, 3% surcharge fee. Indexes available for search: Conveyances, Mortgages, Civil Suits, Criminal, Probate, Marriages, Bonds, Chattel Mortgage, Incorporation, Militiary Discharge, Miscellaneous, Notarial Adoptions, Oaths and Partnerships. Access to the land mortgage and conveyance index is free at www.laclerksportal.org/. Must register before first use. Document images not available at this time.
Property, Taxation Records   A property search by name or parcel or address is free at www.smpassessor.net/Search.

St. Tammany Parish   ***Recorded Documents***   www.sttammanyclerk.org/   There are two plans - basic and premium. Basic is $5.00 per day or $30 per month. Premium is $50 set up and $50 a month. Records date back to 1961; viewable images on conveyances back to 1976. For info, go to www.sttammanyclerk.org/Online-Services/Public-Records-Search. Access to the land mortgage and conveyance index is free at www.laclerksportal.org/. Must register before first use. Document images not available at this time.
Property, Taxation Records   Search assessor and property value database free at www.stassessor.org/property-search.

Tangipahoa Parish   ***Recorded Documents***   www.tangiclerk.org/   Access to Parish online records found at https://cotthosting.com/LATangipahoa/User/Login.aspx. Indexes available at no cost, Images are only available with a paid subscription. Access to the land mortgage and conveyance index is free at www.laclerksportal.org/. Must register before first use. Document images not available at this time.
Property, Taxation Records   The county offers a subscription service which includes a mapping service with assessor property information. Also, access to assessor records for free at www.tangiassessor.com/tangi-assessment-search.html.

Terrebonne Parish   ***Recorded Documents***   www.terrebonneclerk.org/   Access to records for a fee at https://search.terrebonneclerk.org/External/User/Login.aspx?ReturnUrl=%2fexternal%2findex.aspx. Access to the land mortgage and conveyance index is free at www.laclerksportal.org/. Must register before first use. Document images not available at this time.
Property, Taxation Records   Search property, maps and tax estimator for free at www.tpassessor.org/Search.

Union Parish   *Recorded Documents*   http://upclerk.com/   Access to the online subscription for a fee at http://cotthosting.com/LAUnion/User/Login.aspx and follow directions to sign-up. Credit cards accepted. Access to the land mortgage and conveyance index is free at www.laclerksportal.org/. Must register before first use. Document images not available at this time.
Property, Taxation Records   Access property index free at https://www.unionparishassessor.com/publicsearch/Search.aspx but for full data registration and fees based on usage are required.

Vermilion Parish   *Recorded Documents*   www.vermilionparishclerkofcourt.com/   Access to mortgage and conveyance info for a fee at http://sites.deltacomputersystems.com/home/la57/.

Vernon Parish   *Recorded Documents*   www.vernonclerk.com/   For Information to a subscription for Recorded Documents, contact Jeff Skidmore. Access to the land mortgage and conveyance index is free at www.laclerksportal.org/. Must register before first use. Document images not available at this time.

Washington Parish   *Recorded Documents*   www.wpclerk.org/   Access to subscription to records for a fee at https://cotthosting.com/LAWashington/User/Login.aspx. Access to the land mortgage and conveyance index is free at www.laclerksportal.org/. Must register before first use. Document images not available at this time.
Property, Taxation Records   Search tax roll data on statewide website, www.latax.state.la.us/Menu_ParishTaxRolls/TaxRolls.aspx. Also, an assessment search for free at www.washingtonparishassessor.org/SiteDisclaimer.aspx.

Webster Parish   *Recorded Documents*   www.websterclerk.org/   Access to the land mortgage and conveyance index is free at www.laclerksportal.org/. Must register before first use. Document images not available at this time.

West Baton Rouge Parish   *Recorded Records Records*   www.wbrclerk.org/   Access to records free at www.wbrclerk.org/CatSubCat/CatSubCatDisplay.asp?p1=139&p2=Y&p7=0&p8=1010&p9=CSC1. Sign in as a Guest. For more detailed records a subscription for a fee is available. Access to the land mortgage and conveyance index is free at www.laclerksportal.org/. Must register before first use. Document images not available at this time.
Property, Taxation Records   Access assessments, digital maps and qualified sales for free at www.wbrassessor.org/.

West Feliciana Parish   *Recorded Documents, oil and Gas leases, marriages, autopsy reports Records*
www.westfelicianaclerkofcourt.org/   Access to index and images for a fee at https://cotthosting.com/lawestfeliciana/User/Login.aspx. Fee is $20 for 24 hours, or $100 for 30 days or $1080 for 365 days. Must have user ID and password. Access to the land mortgage and conveyance index is free at www.laclerksportal.org/. Must register before first use. Document images not available at this time.
Property, Taxation Records   Local property tax for free at www.wfassessor.com/tools/search-tax/2014-07-09-22-55-08. Also, access to GIS/mapping free at http://atlas.geoportalmaps.com/westfeliciana.

Winn Parish   *Recorded Land Documents Records*   www.laclerksofcourt.org/Parishs/winnparish.htm   Access to the land mortgage and conveyance index is free at www.laclerksportal.org/. Must register before first use. Document images not available at this time.

Reminder:

- The Louisiana Clerks Remote Access Authority ("LCRAA") provides a free search web page at www.laclerksportal.org for 38 counties to view recorded mortgages and conveyances. One must register before use but viewing is free.

- See www.latax.state.la.us/Menu_ParishTaxRolls/TaxRolls.aspx for free access to each parish's assessor tax roll data. Note all parishes do not necessarily update their records to the current year.

Maine

Capital: Augusta
   Kennebec County
Time Zone: EST
Population: 1,329,828
# of Counties: 16

Useful State Links

Website: **www.maine.gov/**
Governor: **www.mass.gov/governor**
Attorney General: **www.maine.gov/ag/**
State Archives: **www.maine.gov/sos/arc/**
State Statutes and Codes: **www.mainelegislature.org/legis/statutes/**
Legislative Bill Search: **www.mainelegislature.org/LawMakerWeb/search.asp**
Unclaimed Funds: **www.maine.gov/treasurer/unclaimed_property/**

State Public Record Agencies

Criminal Records

State Bureau of Identification, State House Station #42,   https://www5.informe.org/online/pcr/   One may request a record search from the web. Results are usually returned via e-mail in 2 hours. Fee is $31.00 and use of credit card required. There is a discount fee of $21.00 only if the subscriber lives in state. There is a $95.00 annual fee to be a subscriber.

Sexual Offender Registry

State Bureau of Identification, Sex Offender Registry,   http://sor.informe.org/cgi-bin/sor/index.pl   Search at http://sor.informe.org/cgi-bin/sor/index.pl. Information is only provided for those individuals that are required to register pursuant to Title 34-A MRSA, Chapter 15. Records date to 01/01/82 and forward. The date of the last address verification is indicated next to the registrant's address.

Incarceration Records

Maine Department of Corrections, Inmate Records,   www.maine.gov/corrections/   There is a free search of current adult prisoners and probationers on the web page - see https://www1.maine.gov/online/mdoc/search-and-deposit/index.htm. One may also do a search by sending an email to Corrections.Webdesk@maine.gov. Include your full name, address, and reasons for the search. Public information is provided.

Corporation, LP, LLP, LLC, Trademarks/Servicemarks, Assumed Name

Secretary of State, Reports & Information Division,   www.maine.gov/sos/cec/corp/   A free search of basic information about the entity including address, corporate ID, agent, and status is found at https://icrs.informe.org/nei-sos-icrs/ICRS. A commercial subscriber account also gives extensive information and ability to download files. Also, search securities Division Enforcement Actions and Consent Agreements free at www.maine.gov/pfr/securities/enforcement.shtml.   *Other Options:* Bulk data purchase is available, a list of available databases for sale if found at the web. Monthly lists of new entities filed with this office are also available. Call 207-624-7752 or view www.maine.gov/sos/cec/corp/miscellaneous.html.

Uniform Commercial Code, Federal & State Tax Liens

Secretary of State, UCC Records Section,   www.maine.gov/sos/cec/ucc/index.html   For search and purchase of official UCC documents and fees visit www.maine.gov/sos/cec/ucconline/index.htm. Several different searches are offered including an unofficial debtor search for no fee. Find name variations using this unofficial search of debtor name variations of active or lapsed filings (within 1 year past lapsed date). Some fee-based services may require the use of a credit card or subscription with InforME.   *Other Options:* UCC Bulk Database: $1,200 for all; $1,500 for–images; $600 monthly download; $300 weekly download; $500 weekly images. Available to subscribers.

Sales Tax Registrations

Maine Revenue Services, Sales, Fuel & Special Tax Division,   www.maine.gov/revenue/   Maine Revenue Service provides an online Sales and Service Provider Tax Lookup Program. This program can be used to determine whether a customer's Resale Certificate or Sales Tax Exemption Certificate is currently valid. See https://portal.maine.gov/certlookup/.

Birth Certificates

Department of Health and Human Services, Office of Vital Records,   www.maine.gov/dhhs/mecdc/public-health-systems/data-research/vital-records/index.shtml   Records may be ordered online via www.vitalchek.com, a designated vendor.   *Other Options:* Physical birth lists are available for purchase, excluding restricted information.

Death Records

Department of Health and Human Services, Office of Vital Records,   www.maine.gov/dhhs/mecdc/public-health-systems/data-research/vital-records/index.shtml   Search a free genealogy site at http://vitals.rootsweb.ancestry.com/me/death/search.cgi has Death Indexes from 1960-1997. Search by surname, given name, place or year.   *Other Options:* Bulk file purchases are available, with the exclusion of restricted data.

Workers' Compensation Records

Workers Compensation Board,   www.maine.gov/wcb/   Not online - but requests are accepted by email - sandra.wade@maine.gov. Records may be returned by email upon request.   *Other Options:* Computer data is available, but requests are screened for purpose.

Driver Records

BMV - Driver License Services, 101 Hospital Street,   www.maine.gov/sos/bmv/   Access is through the Driver Record Check program. There are two access systems. The fee for either system is $7.00 per request for a 3-year record and $12.00 for a 10-year record. Casual requesters can obtain records that have personal information cloaked. See the Driver Record Check at www.maine.gov/bmv/drc/ There is a subscription service for approved requesters, records contain personal information as records are released per DPPA. There is a $95.00 annual fee for the subscription service. A myriad of other state government records are available. Visit www.maine.gov/informe/subscribers/services.html or call 207-621-2600.   *Other Options:* InforME offers "Driver Cross Check" - a program for employers, to provide notification when activity occurs on a specific record. See Visit www.maine.gov/informe/subscribers/services.html.

Vehicle Ownership & Registration

Department of Motor Vehicles, Registration Section,   www.maine.gov/sos/bmv/   Maine offers online access to title and registration records via InforME. The fee is $5.50 per title and $5.00 per registration record plus there is an additional $2.00 portal fee. Search title records by VIN or title number. Search registration records by name and DOB, or by plate number. Records are available as interactive online or FTP with a subscription account. There are many other services available with the subscription. A service provided to financial institutions is notification of abandoned vehicles with liens. There is a $95.00 annual fee. For more information email customerservice@informe.org. or visit www.maine.gov/informe/subscribers/services.html.

Crash Reports

Maine State Police, Traffic Division,   https://www1.maine.gov/online/mcrs/   Records from 01/2003 forward may be ordered from www.informe.org/mcrs/ for $10.00 per record. If you do not have a subscription to InforME, then a credit card must be used. Resulting reports is either returned by mail, or emailed in a PDF format. Search by name, date of birth, crash location, crash date, or investigating agency (police department). These reports may include officer narratives. Records prior to 2003 must be ordered as a manual search.   *Other Options:* Subscribers may purchase monthly database updates or use the "Crash Tracker" notification program for no charge.

Campaign Finance, PACs, Lobbyists

Commission on Ethics & Election Practices,   www.state.me.us/ethics/   The home page allows the public to view the campaign finance data for the State of Maine. There are several options for searching, viewing and printing campaign finance report information. Data available includes information on PACs and lobbyists. All searches and downloads are available from http://mainecampaignfinance.com/PublicSite/Homepage.aspx.

GED (HiSET) Certificates

Dept of Education, GED (HiSET) Office,   www.maine.gov/doe/adulted/   A number of searches are provided at http://dos.myflorida.com/elections/candidates-committees/campaign-finance/ including filed campaign documents, contribution and expenditure records, and PACs Records may be requested from https://www.diplomasender.com. A credit card is needed. Request must be ordered by the test taker. Employers and third parties must receive an email and/or Authentication Code from the test taker to then access authorized documents. Turnaround time is 1-3 days.

Occupational Licensing Boards

Search these licenses at https://www.pfr.maine.gov/ALMSOnline/ALMSQuery/SearchIndividual.aspx

Accountant-CPA	Barber	Counselor
Alcohol/Drug Abuse Counselor	Boiler	Dietitian
Architect	Charitable Solicitation	Electrician
Athletic Trainer	Chiropractor	Elevator/Tramway
Auctioneer	Cosmetologist	Forester

Funeral Service
Geologist/Soil Scientist
Insurance Advisor/Consultant
Insurance Agent/Agency/Company
Interpreter
Landscape Architect
Manufactured Housing
Massage Therapist
Nurse/Practical
Occupational Therapist/Assistants

Osteopathic Physician Extender
Osteopathic Physician/Physician Asst
Osteopathic Resident/Intern
Pharmacist
Physical Therapist
Physician/Medical Doctor/Assistant
Plumber
Podiatrist
Psychologist
Radiologic Technician

Real Estate Appraiser
Real Estate Broker
Respiratory Care Therapist
RN/Advanced Practice/Professional
Social Worker
Speech Pathologist/Audiologist
Surveyor, Land
Veterinarian/Veterinary Technician

The Rest:

Accountant-CPA	https://www.pfr.maine.gov/ALMSOnline/ALMSQuery/SearchIndividual.aspx
Active Agency Store Liquor Resellers	https://www1.maine.gov/dafs/bablo/licensing/search_large.php
Alcohol/Drug Abuse Counselor	https://www.pfr.maine.gov/ALMSOnline/ALMSQuery/SearchIndividual.aspx
Alcoholic Beverage Distributor	https://www1.maine.gov/dafs/bablo/licensing/search_large.php
Ambulatory Surgical Ctr	https://gateway.maine.gov/dhhs-apps/aspen/
Architect	https://www.pfr.maine.gov/ALMSOnline/ALMSQuery/SearchIndividual.aspx
Assisted Living Facility	https://gateway.maine.gov/dhhs-apps/aspen/
Athletic Trainer	https://www.pfr.maine.gov/ALMSOnline/ALMSQuery/SearchIndividual.aspx
Attorney	https://www1.maine.gov/cgi-bin/online/maine_bar/attorney_directory.pl
Auctioneer	https://www.pfr.maine.gov/ALMSOnline/ALMSQuery/SearchIndividual.aspx
Bottle Club, Alcohol	https://www1.maine.gov/dafs/bablo/licensing/search_large.php
Brewery/Winery	https://www1.maine.gov/dafs/bablo/licensing/search_large.php
Catering, Liquor, Special	https://www1.maine.gov/dafs/bablo/licensing/search_large.php
Child Care Resource/Day Care	www.childcarechoices.me/SearchForChildcare.aspx
Dental Hygienist/Radiographer	https://www.pfr.maine.gov/almsonline/almsquery/welcome.aspx
DentistDenturist	https://www.pfr.maine.gov/almsonline/almsquery/welcome.aspx
Disciplinary Actions	https://www.pfr.maine.gov/almsonline/almsquery/SearchCase.aspx
Emergency Medical Technician	www.maine.gov/ems/public/ProviderLookup.html
Employee Leasing Company	https://www.pfr.maine.gov/almsonline/almsquery/welcome.aspx
EMS Authorized Training Centers	www.maine.gov/ems/providers/training/centers.html
Engineer/Intern	https://www1.maine.gov/professionalengineers/roster.html
HMO	https://www.pfr.maine.gov/almsonline/almsquery/welcome.aspx
Home Health Care Svc Agency	https://gateway.maine.gov/dhhs-apps/aspen/
Hospice	https://gateway.maine.gov/dhhs-apps/aspen/
Hospital	https://gateway.maine.gov/dhhs-apps/aspen/
Insurance Adjuster	https://www.pfr.maine.gov/almsonline/almsquery/welcome.aspx
Insurance Producer	https://www.pfr.maine.gov/almsonline/almsquery/welcome.aspx
Intermediate Care Facility (Retarded)	https://gateway.maine.gov/dhhs-apps/aspen/
Liquor License, On & Off Premise	www.maine.gov/dafs/bablo/active_liquor/Active_Licenses.htm
Liquor Salesperson	https://www1.maine.gov/dafs/bablo/licensing/search_large.php
Liquor Store/Wholesaler	www.maine.gov/dafs/bablo/active_liquor/Active_Agency_Liquor_Stores.htm
Lobbyist	http://mainecampaignfinance.com/PublicSite/SearchPages/LobbyingInfoSearch.aspx
Lottery Retailer	www.mainelottery.com/players_info/where_to_buy.html
Notary Public	www5.informe.org/online/notary/search/
Nurse/Practical Adverse Actions	www.maine.gov/boardofnursing/Discipline/AdverseActions.htm
Nursing Home	https://gateway.maine.gov/dhhs-apps/aspen/
Optometrist	https://www.pfr.maine.gov/almsonline/almsquery/
Portable X-Ray Providers	https://gateway.maine.gov/dhhs-apps/aspen/
Preferred Provider Organization	https://www.pfr.maine.gov/almsonline/almsquery/welcome.aspx
Registered Pesticide Products	http://npirspublic.ceris.purdue.edu/state/state_menu.aspx?state=ME
Residential Care	https://gateway.maine.gov/dhhs-apps/aspen/
Surplus Lines Company	https://www.pfr.maine.gov/almsonline/almsquery/welcome.aspx

Swarm Collectors..www.maine.gov/dacf/php/apiary/index.shtml
Temporary Nursing Agency........................https://gateway.maine.gov/dhhs-apps/aspen/

State and Local Courts

About Maine Courts: A **Superior Court** – the court of general jurisdiction – is located in each of Maine's sixteen counties, except for Aroostook County which has two Superior Courts. A Superior Court may hear almost any kind of civil or criminal case that may be brought to trial. Criminal offenses are divided by the Maine Criminal Code into classes according to the seriousness of the offense and the penalty. Classes A, B and C are the more serious offenses; Classes D and E, the least. The Superior Court hears Class D and E cases if there is a jury; otherwise the case is heard by the **District Court**. Thus both the Superior and District Courts handle misdemeanor and felony cases, with jury trials being held in Superior Court only.

The Legislature created a special class of civil actions that includes offenses not regarded as serious enough to be dealt with as crimes. These less serious offenses are called **civil violations**. They include minor traffic infractions, possession of a small amount of marijuana, and violations of town and city called ordinances. One may be fined, but not imprisoned, for a civil violation.

As stated, the **District Court** hears both civil and criminal and always sits without a jury. Within the District Court is the **Family Division**, which hears all divorce and family matters including those involving children, child support and paternity cases. The District Court also hears child protection cases, and serves as the Juvenile Court. Actions for protection from abuse or harassment, mental health, small claims cases ($6,000 limit), and money judgments are filed in the District Court. All traffic violation hearings take place in the District Court in the Division in which the infraction is alleged to have been committed. The traffic violations are then processed the centralized Violations Bureau, part of the District Court system. The District Court has jurisdiction over all **civil actions** where no equitable relief has been demanded and the damages claimed do not exceed $30,000.00. If a civil case is less than $30,000 and there is a demand for a jury trial, the case is heard in the Superior Court.

The **Business and Consumer Court**, also known as the BCD, is a statewide docket comprised of selected actions involving business and /or consumer disputes,

Probate Courts are part of the county's court system, not the state system. Although the Probate Court may be housed with other state courts, the court is generally on a different phone system and calls may not be transferred.

The web page for the Judicial Branch is www.courts.maine.gov.

Appellate Courts: The Supreme Court is the court of last resort. An Appellate Division of the Court hears appeals from criminal sentences when the penalty is one year or more of incarceration. The website offers access to Maine Supreme Court opinions and administrative orders, but not all documents are available online.

Online Court Access

No individual Maine courts offer online access, other than to probate records as described below.

Search probate records at www.maineprobate.net/search.html. An account is $10.00 per month: $2.00 fee for images, $1.00 if account holder. Also have guardianship, conservatorship, name changes and adoption records at this court.

Recorders, Assessors, and Other Sites of Note

About Maine Recording Offices: The recording officer is the County Register of Deeds.1 There are 16 counties and 18 recording offices (registry districts). Aroostock and Oxford Counties each have 2 recording offices.

About Tax Liens: All tax liens on real estate are filed with the Register of Deeds, otherwise tax liens are filed with the Secretary of State.

Online Access

Recorded Documents

A number of counties offer online access, many outsource to vendors There is no statewide access.

Tax Assessor Records

The Tax assessor is at the city or town level - not at the county level. A private vendor provides access to assessor records and GIS data, http://www.vgsi.com/vision/Applications/ParcelData/ME/Home.aspx for at least 37 participating jurisdictions. A list is shown on this site along with the date of the last update.

The tax Assess sites displayed below are associated with the county seats.

County Sites:

Androscoggin County   *Recorded Documents*   www.androscoggincountymaine.gov/Deeds/Deeds.htm   Search for free at www.androscoggindeeds.com/. To print from the web, registration is required. Online indexes and images go back to 1854. For info and sign-up information regarding a subscription service, contact Registry of Deeds at 207-753-2500. Online indexes and images go back to 1854.
Property, Taxation Records   City of Auburn tax assessor data is free at www.auburnmaine.gov/pages/government/city-of-auburn-webgis. Also, property assessment data free at http://auburnme.patriotproperties.com/default.asp.

Aroostook County (Both Districts)   *Recorded Documents*   http://www.aroostook.me.us/departments/deeds.html   Remote access via a commercial online system has been replaced by a subscription internet-based system. Data on the internet system includes deeds, mortgages, liens, judgment, and land recording generally. Records go back to 1960. Subscription fee is $100 for South and North Districts. For more info and signup, see http://www.aroostook.me.us/departments/deeds.html
Property, Taxation Records   Access to GIS/mapping for the Town of Holton free at http://www.axisgis.com/HoultonME/.

Cumberland County   *Recorded Documents*   www.cumberlandcounty.org/477/Registry-of-Deeds   Searching and viewing for free at https://i2a.uslandrecords.com/ME/. Effective October 9, 2013, for each calendar year the first 500 pages per person* are free, then $.50 per page thereafter. *Person is defined as a person, corporation, partnership or any other entity.
Property, Taxation Records   Access to Cumberland online database free at http://gis.vgsi.com/cumberlandme/Search.aspx. Also, free access to property tax and personal property info for the Town of Falmouth, ME at https://falmouthme.munisselfservice.com/citizens/default.aspx. For Cape Elizabeth go to www.capeelizabeth.com/services/land_use/maps/assessors_maps/home.shtml.

Franklin County   *Recorded Documents*   www.franklincountydeedsme.com/   Access to recorders data index is free at www.franklincountydeedsme.com/. Land index goes back to 1984; images go back to part of 1985 (in process). For full access and to print documents, registration and fees are required.

Hancock County   *Recorded Documents*   www.hancockcountydeeds.com/   Access to the county registry of deeds database at www.hancockcountydeeds.com/. Fee is $.50 per page, is required for printable pages.
Property, Taxation Records   Access to Mount Desert assessor's database free at http://gis.vgsi.com/mountdesertme/. Also, download land records (spreadsheet) from http://ellsworthmaine.gov/files/reweb.txt.

Kennebec County   *Recorded Documents*   https://gov.propertyinfo.com/ME-kennebec/   Register free and search recorder index free at https://gov.propertyinfo.com/ME-kennebec/. The first 500 images per calendar year are free. Fees charged after that 500.
Property, Taxation Records   Search City of Augusta assessor database at http://gis.vgsi.com/augustame/.

Knox County   *Recorded Documents*   www.knoxcountymaine.gov/index.asp?Type=B_BASIC&SEC={F52A773D-3C3C-4657-AB9C-D49F67E6D3F9}   Search property records at www.searchiqs.com/. Indexes and images available from 1/1/1950 to present. NOTE: Land data search may not reflect everything from 1950-1965. Check Infodex indexes for complete listings. Each calendar yeare the first 500 pages per person* are free, then $.50 per page thereafter. (*person is defined as a person, corporation, partnership, or any other entity)

Lincoln County   *Recorded Documents*   www.lincolncountymaine.me/pg_deeds.htm   Search Register of Deeds indices and images back to 1954 for free at https://www.searchiqs.com/meLin/Login.aspx. Must register to use. With the passage of LD 559 beginning on October 9, 2013 the first 500 images acquired from the Lincoln County website is free, printing fee is $.50 per image. If Registry staff is involved in preparing copies the regular rate will be charged.

Oxford County (Both Districts)   *Recorded Documents*   www.oxfordcounty.org/deeds-east.php   Search records of the Eastern portion of county for free at https://www.searchiqs.com/meoxe/Login.aspx. For detailed records can register with them.

Penobscot County   *Recorded Documents*   https://penobscotdeeds.com/   Search the Register of Deeds index back to 1967 and images back to 1967 for free at https://penobscotdeeds.com/. A fee is charged for copies.
Property, Taxation Records   Access to tax maps for free at www.bangormaine.gov/taxmaps. Also, search the City of Old Town real estate database for free at www.mygovnow.com/oldtci/Invision/assessing/index.htm.

Piscataquis County   *Recorded Documents*   https://i2a.uslandrecords.com/ME/   Access Register of Deeds site for free at https://i2a.uslandrecords.com/ME/Piscataquis/D/Default.aspx. Each calendar year the first 500 pages per person* are free, then $.50 per page thereafter. * Person is defined as a person, corporation, partnership or any other entity.

Property, Taxation Records   Access to tax maps and property cards for free at http://dover-foxcroft.org/index.asp?SEC=096EF06A-4FF2-447C-8C23-2DEA7A7641AD&Type=B_BASIC.

Sagadahoc County   ***Recorded Documents***   http://sagcounty.com/departments/deeds/   Register of Deeds records are online at Laredo/Tapestry. Go to http://sagcounty.com/departments/registry-of-deeds/ for detailed information. For the land records search site go to http://mesagadahoc.fidlar.com/DirectSearch/Default.aspx.

Property, Taxation Records   Search records on the City of Bath Assessor database free at http://assessdb.cityofbath.com/parcel.list.php.

Somerset County   ***Recorded Documents***   www.somersetcounty-me.org/141/Registry-of-Deeds   Access real estate records free at https://i2a.uslandrecords.com/ME/Somerset/D/Default.aspx. Each calendar year the first 500 pages per person* are free, then $.50 per page thereafter. * Person is defined as a person, corporation, partnership or any other entity.

Waldo County   ***Recorded Documents***   www.waldocountyme.gov/rod/index.html   Access real estate records by subscription at https://i2a.uslandrecords.com/ME/Waldo/D/Default.aspx. Index and images back to 1980. Plan index and images back to 1800's. Each calendar year the first 500 pages per person* are free, then $.50 per page thereafter. * Person is defined as a person, corporation, partnership or any other entity.

Washington County   ***Recorded Documents***   www.washingtoncountymaine.com/index.php/county-government/registry-of-deeds   Access to land deed's records go to https://i2a.uslandrecords.com/ME/Washington/D/Default.aspx. Searching and document viewing is free, printing and/or downloading will incur charges. Document index and images from 1945 thru 1971 under Virtual Books and from 1972 to present under Recorded Land; survey plan index and images from 1784 to present.

York County   ***Recorded Documents***   https://gov.propertyinfo.com/ME-York/Default.asp   Search Register of Deeds records at https://gov.propertyinfo.com/ME-York/. Must register first, then search basic index free; purchase copies of documents for $.50 per page (that are printed out on personal printers). Credit card purchases only. Search parameters are the same online as they are in the registry office. Online research only goes back to January, 1966 thru the present.

Property, Taxation Records   Access to the Assessors database free at http://gis.vgsi.com/yorkme/.

Maryland

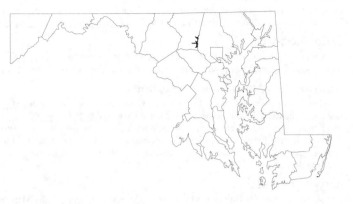

Capital: Annapolis
             Anne Arundel County
Time Zone: EST
Population: 6,006,401
# of Counties: 23

Useful State Links

Website: **www.maryland.gov**
Governor: **http://msa.maryland.gov/**
Attorney General: **https://www.oag.state.md.us/**
State Archives: **http://msa.maryland.gov/**
State Statutes and Codes: **http://mgaleg.maryland.gov/webmga/frmStatutes.aspx**
Legislative Bill Search: **http://mgaleg.maryland.gov/webmga/frmLegislation.aspx**
Unclaimed Funds: **https://interactive.marylandtaxes.com/Individuals/Unclaim/default.aspx**

State Public Record Agencies

Sexual Offender Registry

Criminal Justice Information System, Sex Offender Registry Unit, www.socem.info   Online access is free at www.socem.info/. Search by name or ZIP Code. An interactive map is also available.   *Other Options:* A printout is available of partial or complete SOR. Request must be in writing,

Incarceration Records

DPS and Correctional Services, Central Headquarters, www.dpscs.state.md.us   Search inmates online at https://vinelink.com/#/home/site/20000. *Other Options:* Public Records Requests form is found at www.mass.gov/eopss/agencies/doc/public-records-requests.html. Only questions pertaining to the PRR process or status should be sent to this site.

Corporation, LP, LLP, LLC, Fictitious Name, Trade Name

Department of Assessments and Taxation, Charter Corporate Division, http://dat.maryland.gov/Pages/default.aspx   At the main website, search by company name or file number for records of domestic corporations, limited liability companies, limited partnerships and of foreign corporations, and limited partnerships qualified to transact business in the state. Search for corporate name and trade name records for http://sdat.dat.maryland.gov/ucc-charter/Pages/CharterSearch/default.aspx. A Certificate of Good Standing is available online at https://certificate.dat.maryland.gov/Pages/default.aspx for a $40.00 fee. Certificates of Status are not available for trade names, name reservations, and sole proprietorships. The Secretary of State also offers a search of Charities at http://sos.maryland.gov/Charity/Pages/SearchCharity.aspx.   *Other Options:* This agency will release information in a bulk output format through a contactor. Obtain prices, formats, production schedules, etc. from Specprint, Inc. Contact Mr. Joe Jenkins of Specprint, Inc. at 410- 561-9600.

Trademarks/Servicemarks

Secretary of State, Trademarks Division, http://sos.maryland.gov/Pages/Trademarks/Trademarks.aspx   Online searching is available at http://sos.maryland.gov/Pages/Trademarks/TMSearch.aspx. Search can be by keyword in the description field, the service or product, the owner, the classification, or the mark name or keyword in the mark name. The site also offers application forms to register, renew, or assign trade and service marks, and general info about registration.   *Other Options:* A computer printout of all marks registered, renewed or assigned within a 3 month period is available for $.05 per trademark.

Uniform Commercial Code

UCC Division-Taxpayer's Services, Department of Assessments & Taxation, https://egov.maryland.gov/sdat/uccfiling/uccmainpage.aspx   The site at https://egov.maryland.gov/SDAT/UCCFiling/MainMenu.aspx provides a chocie of either a name search or search by filing number.   *Other Options:* The agency has available for sale copies of public release master data files including corporation, real estate, and UCC. In addition, they can produce customized files on paper or disk. Visit the website for more information.

Sales Tax Registrations

Taxpayer Services, Revenue Administration Division,   www.marylandtaxes.com/taxes.asp   Using the web, one can determine if a MD sales tax account number is valid. See https://interactive.marylandtaxes.com/Business/VerifyExempt/User/Home.aspx.

Vital Records

Department of Health, Division of Vital Records,   http://dhmh.maryland.gov/vsa/Pages/birth.aspx   Records may be ordered from a designated vendor at www.vitalchek.com. Use of credit card is required and additional $9.75 fee required.

Workers' Compensation Records

Workers' Compensation Commission, Claim Information,   www.wcc.state.md.us   Free access is provided and there is a more in-depth service available for a fee. The free Public Information is found at www.wcc.state.md.us/WFMS/public_inquiry.html. There is no search fee, but programming fees must be paid in advance. The system is open 24 hours a day to only in-state accounts. Write to the Commission at address above, care of Information Technology Division, or at 410-864-5170. Information on insolvent insurance companies is found at www.wcc.state.md.us/Gen_Info/Insolvent.html.   *Other Options:* This agency will sell its entire database depending on the use of the purchaser. Intended use must be validated and approved. Contact the commission for further information.

Driver Records

MVA, Driver Records Unit, Rm 145,   www.mva.maryland.gov   The Maryland Motor Vehicle Administration partners with NICUSA regarding the access of driver and vehicle records previously accessed through MVA's subscription services (DARS, LMS, etc.). The fee is $12.00 per record for either interactive or batch access. There is a $95.00 subscription fee (which was waived for existing subscribers to DARS). For more information go to https://www.egov.maryland.gov/register/ or call 888-963-3468. Drivers may view their own record online at https://securetransactions.mva.maryland.gov. *Other Options:* A License Monitoring System (LMS) is available to employers. For more information go to https://www.egov.maryland.gov/register or call 888-963-3468.

Vehicle Ownership & Registration

Motor Vehicle Administration, Data Management,   www.mva.maryland.gov   The Maryland Motor Vehicle Administration partners with NICUSA regarding the access of vehicle records previously accessed through MVA's subscription services (DARS, LMS, etc.). The fee is $12.00 per record for either interactive or batch access. There is a $95.00 subscription fee (which was waived for existing subscribers to DARS). For more information go to https://www.egov.maryland.gov/register/ or call 888-963-3468.

Voter Registration, Campaign Finance, PACs

State Board of Elections,   www.elections.state.md.us   Campaign finance reports are at www.sos.ms.gov/elections3.aspx. A lobbyist and client search is at www.sos.ms.gov/elec/portal/msel/page/search/portal.aspx. Search the campaign finance database and disclosure of expenditures and contributions at www.elections.state.md.us/campaign_finance/index.html. Search PAC data at https://campaignfinancemd.us/Public/ViewCommittees. Note that lobbyists are managed by a different agency - see http://ethics.gov.state.md.us/listing.htm.

Occupational Licensing Boards

Accountant-CPA	www.dllr.state.md.us/pq/
Acupuncturist	https://mdbnc.dhmh.md.gov/ACUPTVerification/default.aspx
Architect	https://www.dllr.state.md.us/cgi-bin/ElectronicLicensing/OP_search/OP_search.cgi?calling_app=AR::AR_qselect
Architectural Partnership/Corp	www.dllr.state.md.us/pq/
Attorney	www.courts.state.md.us/cpf/attylist.html
Audiologist	https://mdbnc.dhmh.md.gov/AUDVerification/Default.aspx
Bail Bondsman	https://sbs-md.naic.org/Lion-Web/jsp/sbsreports/AgentLookup.jsp
Barber	https://www.dllr.state.md.us/cgi-bin/ElectronicLicensing/OP_search/OP_search.cgi?calling_app=BAR::BAR_qselect
Business, Any Licensed	www.kellysolutions.com/md/Business/index.htm
Carrier Vehicle	http://webapp.psc.state.md.us/intranet/transport/GetCarrier_new.cfm
Charity	www.sos.state.md.us/Charity/Pages/SearchCharity.aspx
Chiropractor/Chiropractic Assist	https://mdbnc.dhmh.md.gov/chiroverification/default.aspx
Contractor, Subcontractor	https://www.dllr.state.md.us/cgi-bin/ElectronicLicensing/OP_search/OP_search.cgi?calling_app=HIC::HIC_qselect
Cosmetologist	https://www.dllr.state.md.us/cgi-bin/ElectronicLicensing/OP_search/OP_search.cgi?calling_app=COS::COS_qselect
Day Care Provider	www.checkccmd.org/
Dental Assistant/Hygienist/Teacher	https://maryland.mylicense.com/mdbodverif/Search.aspx
Dentist	https://maryland.mylicense.com/mdbodverif/Search.aspx

Dietitian/Nutritionist	https://mdbnc.dhmh.md.gov/dietVerification/Default.aspx
Driver For Hire	http://webapp.psc.state.md.us/Intranet/Transport/ForHireDriver_new.cfm
Election	www.elections.state.md.us/
Electrician, Master	www.dllr.state.md.us/pq/
Electrologist	http://167.102.241.39/verification/Search.aspx
Engineer, Examining	www.dllr.state.md.us/pq/
Engineer, Professional	www.dllr.state.md.us/pq/
Esthetician	https://www.dllr.state.md.us/cgi-bin/ElectronicLicensing/OP_search/OP_search.cgi?calling_app=COS::COS_qselect
For Hire Carrier Suspended	http://webapp.psc.state.md.us/Intranet/Transport/ForHireSuspendedCarriers_new.cfm
Forester	www.dllr.state.md.us/pq/
Fund Raising Counsel	www.sos.state.md.us/Charity/Pages/SearchCharity.aspx
Gem Dealer	www.dllr.state.md.us/pq/
Hearing Aid Dispenser	https://mdbnc.dhmh.md.gov/AUDVerification/Default.aspx
Home Improvement Contractor	www.dllr.state.md.us/pq/
Home Improvement Salesperson	https://www.dllr.state.md.us/cgi-bin/ElectronicLicensing/OP_search/OP_search.cgi?calling_app=HIC::HIC_qselect
Home Inspector	www.dllr.state.md.us/pq/
HVACR Contractor	www.dllr.state.md.us/pq/
Insurance Broker/Advisor/Agent	https://sbs-md.naic.org/Lion-Web/jsp/sbsreports/AgentLookup.jsp
Interior Designer	www.dllr.state.md.us/pq/
Landscape Architect/Land Surveyor	www.dllr.state.md.us/pq/
Lobbyist/Employer	http://ethics.maryland.gov/lobbyists/listing/
Manicurist/Nail Technician	https://www.dllr.state.md.us/cgi-bin/ElectronicLicensing/OP_search/OP_search.cgi?calling_app=COS::COS_qselect
Massage Therapist	https://mdbnc.dhmh.md.gov/chiroverification/default.aspx
Notary Public	www.sos.state.md.us/Notary/Pages/NotarySearch.aspx
Nurse-RN/LPN/Aide	http://mbon.maryland.gov/Pages/lic-lookup.aspx
Nursery, Plant	http://mda.maryland.gov/plants-pests/Pages/nurseries_plant_dealers.aspx
Nursing Home Administrator	https://mdbnc.dhmh.md.gov/NHAVerification/Default.aspx
Nursing Occupation	http://mbon.maryland.gov/Pages/lic-lookup.aspx
Occupational Therapist/Assistant	https://maryland.mylicense.com/mdbotverif/
Optometrist	https://mdbnc.dhmh.md.gov/optverification/default.aspx
Pawnbroker	www.dllr.state.md.us/pq/
Pesticide Applicator/Operator/Consultant	www.kellysolutions.com/md/
Pesticide Business/Dealer	www.kellysolutions.com/md/
Physical Therapist/Assistant	https://mdbnc.dhmh.md.gov/bptverification/default.aspx
Physician/Medical Doctor	https://www.mbp.state.md.us/bpqapp/
Plant Broker/Dealer	www.mda.state.md.us/plants-pests/Pages/nurseries_plant_dealers.aspx
Plumber	www.dllr.state.md.us/pq/
Polygraph Examiner/School/Sales	www.mdpolygraph.org/info.htm
Precious Metal & Gem Dealer	www.dllr.state.md.us/pq/
Real Estate Agent/Broker	https://www.dllr.state.md.us/cgi-bin/ElectronicLicensing/RE/certification/RECertification1.cgi
Real Estate Appraiser	www.dllr.state.md.us/pq/
Security Agency/Guar.	http://mdsp.maryland.gov/Organization/Pages/CriminalInvestigationBureau/LicensingDivision/ProfessionalLicenses/SecurityGuard.aspx
Speech & Language Pathologists	https://mdbnc.dhmh.md.gov/AUDVerification/Default.aspx
Subcontractor	https://www.dllr.state.md.us/cgi-bin/ElectronicLicensing/OP_search/OP_search.cgi?calling_app=HIC::HIC_qselect
Taxicab	http://webapp.psc.state.md.us/Intranet/Transport/TaxicabDriver_new.cfm
Transportation Permit Holder	http://webapp.psc.state.md.us/Intranet/Transport/GetPermitList_new.cfm
Veterinarian	https://www.mdavet.org/Login.aspx

State and Local Courts

About Maryland Courts: Circuit Courts generally handle the State's major civil cases and more serious criminal matters, along with juvenile cases, family matters such as divorce, and most appeals from the District Court, orphans' courts and administrative agencies. The Circuit Courts also can hear cases from the District Court (civil or criminal) in which one of the parties has requested a jury trial, under certain circumstances.

The **District Court** hears both civil and criminal cases involving claims up to $30,000, and has exclusive jurisdiction over peace order cases and landlord/tenant, replevin (recovery of goods claimed to be wrongfully taken or detained), other civil cases involving amounts at or less than $5,000, certain juvenile case, and traffic cases.. The District Court also handles motor vehicle/boating violations and other misdemeanors and limited felonies, although the circuit courts share jurisdiction if the penalties authorized are three years or more in prison, a fine of $2,500 or more, or both. Both trial courts can hear domestic violence cases. A case in the District Court is argued before a judge only: there are no jury trials in District Court.

Orphans' Courts handle wills, estates, and other probate matters. In addition, they have jurisdiction—along with the circuit courts—to appoint guardians of the person, and to protect the estates of un-emancipated minors (minors who remain under parental authority).

The Circuit Court handles **probate** in only Montgomery and Harford counties. In other counties, probate is handled by the **Orphan's Court**. The clerk is called the **Register of Wills** and is a county, not a court, function.

Note there is both a **Baltimore County** and the **City of Baltimore**; each has its own courts.

Municipalities are towns or cites that are self governing and these entities handle local infractions. See a list at http://msa.maryland.gov/msa/mdmanual/01glance/html/mun.html.

The web page for the Judicial System is www.mdcourts.gov.

Appellate Courts: The Maryland Court of Appeals is the highest court in the state (commonly called the Supreme Court in other states). The Court of Special Appeals is Maryland's intermediate appellate court and generally considers any reviewable judgment, decree, order, or other action of the circuit and orphans' courts. The web page www.mdcourts.gov gives access to opinions.

Online Court Access

All courts participate in the systems described below.

See http://casesearch.courts.state.md.us/casesearch//inquiry-index.jsp for a free search of dockets of the trial courts, including **civil, traffic and criminal**.

Below are some key aspects of this site:

- Minor traffic infractions generally only appear for 36 months. A search of civil or criminal includes all District and Circuit courts in the state - but a search of liens and judgments do not include District Courts and Circuit Court for Prince George's County.

- Note the DOB is shown on some but not all dockets. The web page does state that *Effective July 9, 2013 Case Search to Display Date of Birth.* Records are updated daily, but case information from Montgomery and Prince George's counties usually lag one additional day. All case information may be searched by party name or case number. The amount of historical information may vary by county based on when an automated case management system was deployed in that county and how the system has evolved. There is a disclaimer: "This site reflects the electronic record of the cases presented and may not always reflect the information maintained within the official case file. The data may not be reliable in the sense that further action may occur in the case that would affect the record."

- Federal and state tax liens are recorded in the Circuit Courts, however, the data may not be available in Case Search, depending on the process used by the court to record the liens. To determine whether a court is recording Federal and state tax lien data for Case Search, you must contact the court directly.

One may search by Decedent, Guardian, Interested Party, Minor, personal Representative, or estate number. Records from the Register of Wills of all counties go back to at least 1998. A free Estate Search of the Register of Wills records is offered at two sites. See:

1. http://jportal.mdcourts.gov/willsandtrusts/index.jsf
2. http://registers.maryland.gov/main/search.html.

Counties with Sites Not Mentioned Above:

Montgomery County

Circuit Court   www.montgomerycountymd.gov/ciatmpl.asp?url=/content/circuitcourt/index.asp
The daily calendar is free at www.montgomerycountymd.gov/mc/judicial/circuit/docket.html.

Recorders, Assessors, and Other Sites of Note

About Maryland Recording Offices: 23 counties and one independent city; 24 recording offices. The recording officer is the Clerk of the Circuit Court. Baltimore City has a recording office separate from the County of Baltimore.

About Tax Liens: All tax liens are filed with the county Clerk of Circuit Court.

Online Access

Recorded Documents - Statewide Site

The Maryland Judiciary, the 24 elected Maryland Court Clerks, and Maryland State Archives all joined in partnership to provide this up-to-date access to all verified land record instruments in Maryland. This service is currently being provided free to individuals who apply for a user name and password. See https://mdlandrec.net/main/

Assessor/Property Tax Records

Statewide - From the Government:

- The State Dept. of Planning offers MDProperty View with property maps/parcels and assessments via the web or CD-rom. Visit http://planning.maryland.gov/OurProducts/PropertyMapProducts/FinderOnlineProduct.shtml. Registration required, there is no name searching.

- The State Archives provides a web service site for viewing land surveys, condominium, and survey plats at: http://msa.maryland.gov/megafile/msa/stagser/s1500/s1529/html/0000.html

- A free search for property tax record data is at http://sdat.dat.maryland.gov/RealProperty/Pages/default.aspx. No name searching, search by street address, parcel number, or property account identifier..

Statewide - But Not Updated Since 01/15/2010

- A   free   search   for   property   tax   record   data,   for   counties   ia   provided   at http://sdat.dat.maryland.gov/RealProperty/Pages/default.aspx. No name searching, search by street address, parcel number, or property account identifier.

Counties with Sites Not Mentioned Above:

Baltimore City   *Property, Taxation Records*   Search property tax and ownership at http://cityservices.baltimorecity.gov/realproperty/default.aspx.

Caroline County   *Property, Taxation Records*   Access to property tax search free at www.carolinemd.org/509/Pay-Property-Taxes. No name searching.

Charles County   *Property, Taxation Records*   Access to property tax data is free at www.charlescounty.org/treas/taxes/acctinquiry/selection.jsp. Registration required, there is no name searching.

Montgomery County   *Property, Taxation Records*   Access to the assessor's property tax account database is free at https://www2.montgomerycountymd.gov/realPropertyTax/Default.aspx.

Prince George's County   *Property, Taxation Records*   Search the Treasurer's property tax inquiry system at http://taxinquiry.princegeorgescountymd.gov.

Washington County   *Property, Taxation Records*   Access to real estate property tax inquiry/payment for free at https://payments.washco-md.net/MSS/default.aspx.

Worcester County   *Property, Taxation Records*   Search by county for property tax data free at http://sdat.resiusa.org/RealProperty/Pages/default.aspx. No name searching.

Massachusetts

Capital: Boston
                Suffolk County
Time Zone: EST
Population: 6,794,422
# of Counties: 14

Useful State Links

Website: **www.mass.gov/portal**
Governor: **www.mass.gov/governor**
Attorney General: **www.mass.gov/ago**
State Archives: **www.sec.state.ma.us/arc/**
State Statutes and Codes: **https://malegislature.gov/Laws/GeneralLaws**
Legislative Bill Search: **www.malegislature.gov**
Unclaimed Funds: **www.mass.gov/treasury/unclaimed-prop/**

State Public Record Agencies

Criminal Records

MA Dept of Criminal Justice, Information Services,   www.mass.gov/eopss/agencies/dcjis/   The online system known as iCORI provides access to criminal offender record information. All accounts must be approved and registered. The data provided is entered and maintained by the Office of the Commissioner of Probation and is not supported by any type of biometric identifier, including fingerprints. This system requires use of a credit card. Note the agency recently stopped taking business checks. The Open Access record is $50.00, Personal is $25.00; Standard Request is $25.00.

Sexual Offender Registry

Sex Offender Registry Board,   www.mass.gov/eopss/agencies/sorb/   There is a free search at http://sorb.chs.state.ma.us/. A variety of searches are offered, including by town.This includes Level 3 sex offenders, plus Level 2 offenders who were classified by the board after July 12, 2013.

Incarceration Records

Executive Office of Public Safety & Security, Department of Correction,   www.mass.gov/eopss/agencies/doc/   No online search for inmates is offered by this agency; however the agency promotes a private company with free web access to DOC offenders at https://www.vinelink.com/vinelink/siteInfoAction.do?siteId=20000. DOC most wanted is at www.mass.gov/eopss/law-enforce-and-cj/prisons/doc-most-wanted/

Corporation, LLP, LP, LLC, Trademarks/Servicemarks,

Secretary of the Commonwealth, Corporation Division,   www.sec.state.ma.us/cor/coridx.htm   There are a number of free searches from the home page including: trademark, corporate database, corporate rejected filings, UCCs, and liens.   *Other Options:* Bulk sale on CD is available.

Uniform Commercial Code

UCC Division, Secretary of the Commonwealth,   www.sec.state.ma.us/cor/corpweb/corucc/uccmain.htm   There is free access to record index from http://corp.sec.state.ma.us/corpweb/uccsearch/uccSearch.aspx. Search by name, organization or file number. There is a separate search for financing statements with at least one year after the lapse date has passed. Also, there is a search for Child Support Liens and Tax Liens at http://corp.sec.state.ma.us/CorpWeb/liens/lienssearch.aspx.   *Other Options:* CDs may be purchased.

Sales Tax Registrations

Revenue Department - Taxpayer Resources, Sales Tax Registrations,   www.mass.gov/dor/individuals/taxpayer-help-and-resources/   Verification of Sales Tax Certificate is free at https://mtc.dor.state.ma.us/mtc/_/#2 View the complete list of tax delinquents owing more than $25,000 in outstanding tax liabilities to the Commonwealth at https://wfb.dor.state.ma.us/dorcommon/PublicDisclosure/disclosure.aspx.

Birth Certificates
Registry of Vital Records and Statistics,   www.mass.gov/eohhs/gov/departments/dph/programs/admin/dmoa/vitals/   Orders can be placed via a state designated vendor. Go to www.vitalchek.com. Extra fees are involved. he cost for the first certified copy is $50.00, and each additional copy of the same record is $42.00. Expedited service is available for an additional fee.

Death Records
Registry of Vital Records and Statistics,   www.mass.gov/eohhs/gov/departments/dph/programs/admin/dmoa/vitals/   Orders can be placed via a state designated vendor. Go to www.vitalchek.com. Extra fees are involved. he cost for the first certified copy is $50.00, and each additional copy of the same record is $42.00. Expedited service is available for an additional fee.

Marriage Certificates
Registry of Vital Records and Statistics,   www.mass.gov/eohhs/gov/departments/dph/programs/admin/dmoa/vitals/   Orders can be placed via a state designated vendor. Go to www.vitalchek.com. Extra fees are involved. he cost for the first certified copy is $50.00, and each additional copy of the same record is $42.00. Expedited service is available for an additional fee.

Workers' Compensation Records
Keeper of Records, Department of Industrial Accidents,   www.mass.gov/lwd/workers-compensation/   Outside parties legally entitled to access may view database. There is an online insurance inquiry as well for account holders. The links are very lengthy, use the home page above.

Driver Records-Registry
Registry of Motor Vehicles, Court Records Department,   www.massrmv.com/   High volume accounts, approved accounts may purchase record for $8.00 per record.The driver license number is needed for input. Records are generally available in batch mode (afternoon requests ready early the next morning) or within minutes interactive. Call the above number for further details. Also the public may order an unattested record in PDF format for $8.00, or order an attested (certified) record to be mailed for $20.00. The record is only mailed to the address shown on the license-holder's DL. Use of a credit card is required. One may view or order a record on another as long as complete information is disclosed about the requesters. See https://secure.rmv.state.ma.us/DrvRecords/intro.aspx A free License/Permit and ID Inquiry is at https://secure.rmv.state.ma.us/LicInquiry/intro.aspx. No personal information is displayed. *Other Options:* The RMV offers a Driver Verification System (DVS). DVS is a web based application that allows companies, cities, towns, state agencies and authorities to track the license statuses of their employees. Email dvs@state.ma.us or call 617-351-9521.

Driver Records-Insurance
Merit Rating Board, Attn: Detailed Driving History Records,   www.massrmv.com/MeritRatingBoard.aspx   An online service is available to authorized insurance companies and agents to view driving records maintained by the MRB. This service is available through the RMV Uninsured Motorist System (www.mass.gov/rmv/ums). The information is used to adjust automobile insurance rates. Per statute, this method is not available to the general public.

Vehicle Ownership & Registration
Registry of Motor Vehicles, Document Control,   www.massrmv.com/   The Title/Lien Inquiry Transaction is for vehicle owners and lienholders to track a title, to verify lienholder accuracy, or to ensure a title has been sent to the appropriate party. Visit https://secure.rmv.state.ma.us/TitleLookup/intro.aspx. The Registration Inquiry Transaction works in a similar manner. Requesters must have the vehicle's registration plate type and registration number as printed on the vehicle registration card. Visit https://secure.rmv.state.ma.us/RegInquiry/intro.aspx. Both systems display no personal information. *Other Options:* Bulk retrieval media is available for permitted commercial vendors, exclusive of bulk marketing and solicitation purposes which is not permitted.

Crash Reports
Accident/Crash Records, Registry of Motor Vehicles,   www.massrmv.com/rmv/forms/accident.htm   Online ordering is provided at https://secure.rmv.state.ma.us/CrRequest/Public/Intro.aspx to request a standard or certified copy of a motor vehicle police crash report that has been filed and processed with the MA Registry of Motor Vehicles (RMV). The fee is $20.00 per record request, non-refundable. Currently, only crash reports filed by state or local MA police agencies are available through this on-line request method. *Other Options:* Quarterly or yearly tapes are available for $2,500.

Voter Registration, Lobbyists
Sec. of the Commonwealth - Elections Division, One Ashburton Place, Rm 1705.,   www.sec.state.ma.us/ele/eleidx.htm   Voter registration status is offered at   www.sec.state.ma.us/VoterRegistrationSearch/MyVoterRegStatus.aspx.   A   public   search   of   lobbyists   is   offered   at www.sec.state.ma.us/LobbyistPublicSearch/. Records prior to registration year 2005 are not available online.

Campaign Finance, Donations, Expenditures, PACs
Office of Campaign & Political Finance, One Ashburton Place,   www.ocpf.us/Home/   At the main website, click on Offender Lookup. The information reflects the records on file of offenders sentenced to a term of probation or incarceration within the Oklahoma Department of Corrections Search for and find reports for campaign finance, donations, expenditures, and PACs from links at www.sec.state.ma.us/ele/eleidx.htm.

HSE (GED) Certificates
Mass Dept of Elem. & Sec. Education, GED Records,   www.doe.mass.edu/hse/   A voter registration status link is found at https://www.votercheck.necvr.ne.gov/. Registered lobbyists are found at http://nebraskalegislature.gov/reports/lobby.php. Records may be requested from https://www.diplomasender.com. A credit card is needed. Request must be ordered by the test taker. Employers and third parties must receive an email and/or Authentication Code from the test taker to then access the authorized documents. Turnaround time is 1-3 days.

Occupational Licensing Boards

These licenses are all searchable at http://license.reg.state.ma.us/pubLic/licque.asp

Accountant-CPA/Firm	Funeral Director	Plumber/Shop
Aesthetician/School/Shop	Gas Fitter/Firm	Podiatrist
Alarm Installer/Burglar/Fire	Health Profession, Allied/Health Offices	Psychologist, Educational
Architect	Home Inspector	Radio & TV Repair Technician
Athletic Trainer	Land Surveyor/Landscape	Real Estate Agent/Broker/Firm, Related
Audiologist	Landscape Architect	Real Estate Appraiser
Barber/School/Shop	Marriage & Family Therapist	Rehabilitation Therapist
Chiropractor/Facility	Mental Health Counselor	Sanitarian
Cosmetologist/Shop/School, Related	Mental Health/Human Svcs Pro, Allied	Social Worker
Electrician/Shop	Occupational Therapist/Assistant	Speech-Language Pathologist
Electrologist/School	Optician/Dispensing	Veterinarian
Embalmer	Optometrist	Water Supply Facility Operator
Engineer/Professional	Physical Therapist/Assistant/Shop	

The Rest:

Adoption Center	http://www.eec.state.ma.us/ChildCareSearch/AdoptFoster.aspx
Alcoh'l Bev/Wine Seller/Broker/Whlse	www.mass.gov/abcc/statelicenselistspage.htm
Alcoh'l Bev/Wine Transport Permit	www.mass.gov/abcc/statelicenselistspage.htm
Ambulance Service	www.mass.gov/eohhs/gov/departments/dph/programs/hcq/oems/ambulance-services/
Ambulatory Surgical Ctr	www.mass.gov/eohhs/gov/departments/dph/programs/hcq/dhpl/
Amusement Device Inspector	http://elicense.chs.state.ma.us/Verification/Search.aspx
Attorney	http://massbbo.org/bbolookup.php
Automobile Repair Shop	www.aib.org/ContentPages/Public/RepairGlass.aspx
Bank & Savings Institution	https://services.oca.state.ma.us/LicenseeLookup/licenseelist.asp
Bank, Cooperative	https://services.oca.state.ma.us/LicenseeLookup/in-choose.asp
Birthing Center	www.mass.gov/eohhs/gov/departments/dph/programs/hcq/dhpl/
Blood Bank	www.mass.gov/eohhs/gov/departments/dph/programs/hcq/dhpl/
Boxer/ Boxing Professional	http://elicense.chs.state.ma.us/Verification/Search.aspx
Boxing Physician	http://elicense.chs.state.ma.us/Verification/Search.aspx
Brewery/Pub/Sacramen'l Wine	www.mass.gov/abcc/statelicenselistspage.htm
Brewery/Winery Storer/Farmer	www.mass.gov/abcc/statelicenselistspage.htm
Check Casher	www.nmlsconsumeraccess.org/
Check Casher/Seller	www.mass.gov/ocabr/government/oca-agencies/dob-lp/download-a-list-of-approved-licensees.html
Cigar Distributor	www.mass.gov/dor/businesses/help-and-resources/cigarette-and-tobacco-tax/licensed-massachusetts-cigar-distributors.html
Cigarette Seller	www.mass.gov/dor/businesses/help-and-resources/cigarette-and-tobacco-tax/licensed-massachusetts-cigarette-retailers-.html
Clinic	www.mass.gov/eohhs/gov/departments/dph/programs/hcq/dhpl/
Collection Agency	https://services.oca.state.ma.us/LicenseeLookup/licenseelist.asp
Concrete Testing Laboratory	www.mass.gov/eopss/docs/dps/buildingcode/inf4/concrete-testing.doc
Consumer Credit Grantor	https://services.oca.state.ma.us/LicenseeLookup/licenseelist.asp
Credit Union	https://services.oca.state.ma.us/LicenseeLookup/in-choose.asp
Debt Collector	www.nmlsconsumeraccess.org/
Dentist/Dental Hygienist	https://checkalicense.hhs.state.ma.us/MyLicenseVerification/
Dietitian/Nutritionist	https://checkalicense.hhs.state.ma.us/MyLicenseVerification/
Electrologist	https://checkalicense.hhs.state.ma.us/MyLicenseVerification/
Elevator Operator/Construction/Maintenance	http://elicense.chs.state.ma.us/Verification/Search.aspx
Elevator School	www.mass.gov/eopss/consumer-prot-and-bus-lic/license-type/elevators/approved-elevator-schools.html
Emergency Medical Technician	https://checkalicense.hhs.state.ma.us/MyLicenseVerification/

Employment Agency, Placing/Temp	www.mass.gov/lwd/docs/dos/ea/ea-licensed.pdf
EMS Training Institution	www.mass.gov/eohhs/gov/departments/dph/programs/hcq/oems/emt-training-inst/public-health-oems-training-institutions.html
Engineers/Fireman School	www.mass.gov/eopss/agencies/dps/schools-approved-by-the-department.html
Family Child Care Provider	www.eec.state.ma.us/ChildCareSearch/CCRR.aspx
Fire Sprinkler Contractor/Fitter	http://elicense.chs.state.ma.us/Verification/Search.aspx
Fireman, 1st/2nd Class/Engineer	http://elicense.chs.state.ma.us/Verification/Search.aspx
Foreign Transmittal Agency	www.mass.gov/ocabr/government/oca-agencies/dob-lp/download-a-list-of-approved-licensees.html
Foster Care Provider	www.eec.state.ma.us/ChildCareSearch/AdoptFoster.aspx
Funeral Services/Embalming	https://checkalicense.hhs.state.ma.us/MyLicenseVerification/
Hearing Instrument Specialist	https://checkalicense.hhs.state.ma.us/MyLicenseVerification/
Hoisting Machinery Operator	http://elicense.chs.state.ma.us/Verification/Search.aspx
Home Health Care Provider	www.mass.gov/lwd/docs/dos/ea/ea-licensed.pdf
Hospital / Hospice	www.mass.gov/eohhs/gov/departments/dph/programs/hcq/dhpl/
Insurance Premium Financer	www.mass.gov/ocabr/government/oca-agencies/dob-lp/download-a-list-of-approved-licensees.html
Laboratory, Medical-related	www.mass.gov/eohhs/gov/departments/dph/programs/hcq/dhpl/
Loan Company, Small/Servicer	www.nmlsconsumeraccess.org/
Lobbyist/Lobbyist Employer	www.sec.state.ma.us/LobbyistPublicSearch/
Lumber Producer, Native	www.mass.gov/eopss/consumer-prot-and-bus-lic/license-type/lumber-producers/native-lumber-producers.html
Manufactured Building Producer	www.mass.gov/eopss/consumer-prot-and-bus-lic/license-type/csl/manufactured-buildings.html
Mortgage Broker/Lender	www.nmlsconsumeraccess.org/
Motor Vehicle Sales Financer	www.mass.gov/ocabr/government/oca-agencies/dob-lp/download-a-list-of-approved-licensees.html
Nuclear Plant Engineer/Oper'tor	http://elicense.chs.state.ma.us/Verification/Search.aspx
Nurse-LPN/RN	https://checkalicense.hhs.state.ma.us/MyLicenseVerification/
Nurses Aide in Long-term-care Facility	www.mass.gov/eohhs/gov/departments/dph/programs/hcq/dhpl/
Nursing Home	http://webapps.ehs.state.ma.us/nursehome/
Nursing Home Administrator/ Health Officer	https://checkalicense.hhs.state.ma.us/MyLicenseVerification/
Oil Burner Technician/Contr	http://elicense.chs.state.ma.us/Verification/Search.aspx
Out-Patient Rehabilitation Facility	www.mass.gov/eohhs/docs/dph/quality/healthcare/healthcare-facilities.xls
Perfusionist	https://checkalicense.hhs.state.ma.us/MyLicenseVerification/
Pesticide Enforcement Inspectors	www.mass.gov/eea/agencies/agr/pesticides/contact-an-enforcement-inspector.html
Pharmacist	https://checkalicense.hhs.state.ma.us/MyLicenseVerification/
Physician Assistant	https://checkalicense.hhs.state.ma.us/MyLicenseVerification/
Physician Assistant Disciplinary Actions	www.mass.gov/eohhs/gov/departments/dph/programs/hcq/dhpl/physician-assistants/disciplinary-and-other-board-actions.html
Physician/Medical Doctor	http://profiles.ehs.state.ma.us/Profiles/Pages/FindAPhysician.aspx
Pipefitter/School	www.mass.gov/eopss/agencies/dps/schools-approved-by-the-department.html
Private Detective	www.mass.gov/eopss/agencies/msp/prof-stds/cert-unit/
Private Investigator	www.mass.gov/eopss/agencies/msp/prof-stds/cert-unit/
Promoter/Referee/Judge	http://elicense.chs.state.ma.us/Verification/Search.aspx
Radiologic Technologist	http://webapps.ehs.state.ma.us/radtechs/default.aspx
Refrigeration Technician School/Contractor	http://elicense.chs.state.ma.us/Verification/Search.aspx
Renal Dialysis, End Stage	www.mass.gov/eohhs/gov/departments/dph/programs/hcq/dhpl/
Residential Care, Youth	www.eec.state.ma.us/ChildCareSearch/RPMap.aspx
Respiratory Care Therapist	https://checkalicense.hhs.state.ma.us/MyLicenseVerification/
Retail Installment Financer	https://services.oca.state.ma.us/LicenseeLookup/licenseelist.asp
Ringside Physician	http://elicense.chs.state.ma.us/Verification/Search.aspx
Sprinkler Fitting School	http://elicense.chs.state.ma.us/Verification/Search.aspx
Theatrical Booking Agent	http://elicense.chs.state.ma.us/Verification/Search.aspx
Ticket Reseller	http://elicense.chs.state.ma.us/Verification/Search.aspx
Timekeepers/Trainers/Managers/Professional Combatants	http://elicense.chs.state.ma.us/Verification/Search.aspx
Trauma Center	https://www.facs.org/search/trauma-centers
Trust Company	https://services.oca.state.ma.us/LicenseeLookup/licenseelist.asp

State and Local Courts

About Massachusetts Courts: The Massachusetts Trial Court is organized by Departments and within each Department there are "Divisions." The **Superior Court** has original jurisdiction in civil actions over $25,000 and in matters where equitable relief is sought, in labor disputes where injunctive relief is sought, has exclusive authority to convene medical malpractice tribunals, has appellate jurisdiction over certain administrative proceedings, and may hold sittings for naturalization in any city or town. The court has exclusive original jurisdiction of first degree murder cases and original jurisdiction of all other crimes.

The **Superior Court** has concurrent civil jurisdiction with the **District** and **Boston Municipal Court** departments; however, most plaintiffs seeking damages of $25,000 or less file in the District Court, the Boston Municipal Court, or the **Housing Court**. District, Boston Municipal, and Housing Court departments resolve small claims matters which are $7,000 or less.

District Court criminal jurisdiction extends to all felonies punishable by a sentence up to five years, and other specific felonies with greater potential penalties; all misdemeanors; and all violations of city and town ordinances and by-laws.

In **civil** matters, District Court judges conduct both jury and jury-waived trials, and determine with finality any matter in which the likelihood of recovery does not exceed $25,000, plus Small Claims to $7,000 as stated above.

Eviction cases may be filed at a county District Court or at the regional "**Housing Court**." A case may be moved from a District Court to a Housing Court, but never the reverse. Housing Courts also hear misdemeanor *Code Violation* cases and prelims. There is one **Probate and Family Court** per county, but several counties have additional full sessions and satellite office locations – including Essex, Bristol Middlesex, and Plymouth.

The majority of Boston's **Municipal Courts** cases involve traffic and ordinance matters.

Probate filing is a function of the Circuit Court; however, each county has a **Register in Probate** who maintains and manages the probate records, guardianship, and mental health records.

The web page for the Judicial System is www.mass.gov/courts/

Appellate Courts: Search the Appeals Court docket and calendar at www.ma-appellatecourts.org/index.php. Appellate Courts and Supreme Court opinions are available at www.mass.gov/courts/court-info/sjc/about/reporter-of-decisions/.

Online Court Access

Online access to trial courts is available to the public on **civil actions, contact/business cases, equitable remedies, torts**, and actions involving the state or municipalities. See www.masscourts.org/eservices/home.page. Criminal record data is not included. ; The system became statewide with the addition of Suffolk County on November 12, 2015.

No individual Massachusetts courts offer online access, other than as described above.

Recorders, Assessors, and Other Sites of Note

About Massachusetts Recording Offices: Masschusetts is unique. In Massachusetts, Registries of Deeds deal only with title to real property. Other aspects of property ownership, such as building type/size, property taxes, zoning, etc. fall under the jurisdiction of the municipality where the property is located.

County Level

Documents affecting real estate, such as deeds and mortgages, and tax liens on real estate are filed and recorded at the Register of Deeds. There are 14 counties with 21 Registry Districts (recording offices). Berkshire and Bristol counties each have three Registry Districts. Essex, Middlesex, and Worcester counties each have two Registry Districts. The recorded real estate documents are indexed by grantor, grantee, document type, and address.

City/Town Level

All other liens, judgments, State Tax liens on personal property are filed with the Town/City Clerk or the Tax Collector. Federal tax liens may be filed either locally or with the Clerk of U.S. District Court. There are at least 352 cities and towns that record documents. An excellent cross-reference list of city/town to county is found at http://www.sec.state.ma.us/rod/rodgde/gdeidx.htm.

About Tax Liens: As mentioned above, State tax liens on personal property are filed with the Town/City Clerk or the Tax Collector. All tax liens against real estate are filed with county Register of Deeds. Federal tax liens on personal property may be are filed with the U.S. District Court in Boston as well as with the towns/cities.

Online Access - County Level

Recorded Documents

All 21 county level Registry Districts provide access to information on recorded documents at www.masslandrecords.com. This site is sponsored by the state of Massachusetts.

A statewide system to search court records related to the Land Court Division in each county is free at http://www.masscourts.org/eservices/home.page.2. This gateway does not give details on the throughput and can be somewhat slow at times.

Tax Liens

A list of Tax Lien cases going back 3 months is shown at www.mass.gov/courts/docs/pdf-new/casesfiledbydatetaxlien.pdf.

Also, search Child Support Liens and Tax Liens from the Secretary of State at http://corp.sec.state.ma.us/CorpWeb/liens/lienssearch.aspx. However, there is no information explaining what type of tax liens this search provides.

County Sites Online - Followed by Town/City Sites

County Sites

Barnstable County   *Recorded Documents*   www.barnstabledeeds.org/   Access to County records is free at https://search.barnstabledeeds.org/. Search for free, but to print requires a $50 annual fee. Land record indexes and images date back to 1704. Also, access to Registry of Deeds data is free at www.masslandrecords.com/.

Berkshire County (Middle District)   *Recorded Documents*   www.berkshiremiddledeeds.com/   Access to Registry of Deeds data is free at www.masslandrecords.com/.

Berkshire County (Northern District)   *Real Estate Recorded Documents*   www.sec.state.ma.us/rod/rodbrknth/brknthidx.htm Access to Registry of Deeds data is free at www.masslandrecords.com/.

Berkshire County (Southern District)   *Recorded Documents*   www.berkshiresouthdeeds.com/   Access to Registry of Deeds data is free at www.masslandrecords.com/.

Bristol County (Fall River District)   *Recorded Documents*   A free search of recorded land documents is at https://www.fallriverdeeds.com/D/Default.aspx. Also, access to Registry of Deeds data is free at www.masslandrecords.com/.

Bristol County (Northern District)   *Recorded Documents*   www.tauntondeeds.com   Access recorded real property searches at www.tauntondeeds.com/Default.aspx. There is an advanced image search as well. Also, access to Registry of Deeds data is free at www.masslandrecords.com/.

Bristol County (Southern District)   *Recorded Document*   www.newbedforddeeds.com/   Access to recorded documents for free at www.newbedforddeeds.com/. Common records indices available from 1/2/78 to present. Land Court indices available from 1/1/90 to present. Most recent images available for Recorded Land.   Also, access to Registry of Deeds data is free at www.masslandrecords.com/.

Dukes County   *Recorded Document Records*   http://dukescounty.org/Pages/DukesCountyMA_Deeds/index   Access to Registry of Deeds data is free at www.masslandrecords.com/.

Essex County (Northern District)   *Recorded Documents*   http://74.8.243.156/essexnorth/   Search the recorder database for free at http://50.241.73.83/ALIS/WW400R.HTM?WSIQTP=SY00. Also, access to Registry of Deeds data is free at www.masslandrecords.com/.

Essex County (Southern District)   *Recorded Documents*   http://salemdeeds.com/salemdeeds/Default2.aspx   Records on the Essex County South Registry of Deeds database are free at http://salemdeeds.com/salemdeeds/Default2.aspx. Advanced deeds search from 1640 to present. Classic deeds search from 1951-present.   Also, access to Registry of Deeds data is free at www.masslandrecords.com/.

Franklin County   *Recorded Documents*   www.masslandrecords.com/franklin/(X(1)S(djepk5vd30nwykydp51s1lq3))/Default.aspx   Access to Registry of Deeds data is free at www.masslandrecords.com/.

Hampden County   *Recorded Documents*   www.registryofdeeds.co.hampden.ma.us/   Access to the county index of land records is free at http://50.203.30.58/html/search.html. Copies can be printed at no charge. Records go back to 1956. Also, access to Registry of Deeds data is free at www.masslandrecords.com/.

Hampshire County   *Recorded Document*   https://www.sec.state.ma.us/rod/rodhamp/hampidx.htm   Access to records for free at www.masslandrecords.com/Hampshire/; index back to 1948, images back to 1786.

Middlesex County (Northern District)   *Recorded Documents*   www.lowelldeeds.com/   Access to Registry of Deeds data is free at www.masslandrecords.com/, but the agency does have separate searches at www.lowelldeeds.com.

Middlesex County (Southern District) *Recorded Document* www.masslandrecords.com/MiddlesexSouth   Access to Registry of Deeds data is free at www.masslandrecords.com/.

Nantucket County *Recorded Documents* www.nantucket-ma.gov/234/Registry-of-Deeds   Access to Registry of Deeds data is free at www.masslandrecords.com/.

Norfolk County *Recorded Document Records* www.norfolkdeeds.org/   Access to county online records is on two levels, both accessible via http://research.norfolkdeeds.org/ALIS/WW400R.HTM?WSIQTP=SY00. Search images and indices free, however, to print requires a subscription; $100 per year plus $1.00 per page. Land records go back to 1900; images to 1793. Land court records go back to 9/1984, with images back to 1901. Also, access to Registry of Deeds data is free at www.masslandrecords.com/.

Plymouth County *Real Estate Recorded Documents* www.plymouthdeeds.org/   Access to Registry of Deeds data is free at www.masslandrecords.com/. Also, access to record search with county for free at http://titleview.org/plymouthdeeds/.

Suffolk County *Real Estate, Deed, Lien, Judgment Records* www.suffolkdeeds.com/   Records on the County Registry of Deeds database are free at www.masslandrecords.com/Suffolk/.

Worcester County (Northern) *Recorded Documents* www.sec.state.ma.us/rod/rodnw/nwidx.htm   Access to Registry of Deeds is free at http://74.8.243.133/ALIS/WW400R.HTM?WSIQTP=SY00. Small fee to copy or certify documents. Land index back to 1956; images to 1868. Also, access to Registry of Deeds data is free at www.masslandrecords.com/.

Worcester County (Southern) *Recorded Document Records* www.worcesterdeeds.com/   Access to Registry of Deeds data is free at www.masslandrecords.com/.

Town and City Sites Online

About Property Tax Records - At Town or City Level

Many towns provide their own online search sites for Assessor data. But many towns also work with a vendor or have sold data to a vendor. As a courtesy, three vendors with widest coverage are listed below.

1. **DataVision: www.vgsi.com/vision/applications/parceldata/MA/Home.aspx. There are over 70 participating jurisdictions.**

Abington	Foxborough	Lakeville	Norwood	Sutton
Amesbury	Georgetown	Lawrence	Palmer	Taunton
Avon	Gloucester	Lexington	Paxton	Tewksbury
Blackstone	Gosnold	Longmeadow	Plympton	Walpole
Boxford	Groton	Marlborough	Quincy	Wareham
Chelmsford	Hamilton	Marion	Randolph	Wayland
Chelsea	Hampden	Medford	Rochester	Westfield
Concord	Hanover	Middleboro	Rowley	Westwood
Dartmouth	Harvard	Millbury	Sharon	Wilbraham
Dedham	Hingham	Nantucket	Shrewsbury	Wilmington
Dracut	Holden	Newburyport	Somerville	Winthrop
Dudley	Holland	Norfolk	Southbridge	Woburn
Duxbury	Hubbardston	North Attleboro	Southampton	Worcester
Easton	Hudson	Northbridge	Southwick	Yarmouth
Edgartown	Kingston	Norwell	Sturbridge	

2. **Patriot Properties: www.patriotproperties.com/. There are at least 83 participating jurisdictions.**

Arlington	Cohasset	Gill	Littleton	Melrose
Bedford	Dalton	Groveland	Lynn	Merrimacx
Belchertown	Danvers	Hatfield	Lynnfield	Methuen
Bellingham	Essex	Haverhill	Malden	Middleton
Beverly	Everett	Holbrook	Manchester-by-the-	Milford
Billerica	Fairhavenl	Holyoke	Sea	Millville
Blandford	Fall Riverl	Hopedale	Marblehead	Milton
Braintree	Falmouth	Hopkinton	Marshfield	Montague
Brimfield	Fitchburg	Hull	Maynard	Montgomery
Burlington	Framingham	Ipswich	Medfield	Nahant
Charltonr	Franklin	Leicester	Medway	Newbury

North Adams	Raynham	Shirley	Wakefieldx	Westford
Northborough	Reading	Stoneham	Waltham	Whitman
Orange	Revere	Stoughton	Watertown	Winchester
Pembroke	Salem	Swampscott	West Bridgewater	Worthington
Pepperell	Salisbury	Topsfield	West Newbury	
Plymouth	Sherborn	Tyngsborough	Westborough	

3. **EPAS: http://epas.csc-ma.us/PublicAccess/Pages/AllCommunitySearchParcel.aspx?town=AllCommunities has 55 participating jurisdictions.**

Adams	Chester	Lancaster	Princeton	Warwick
Alford	Clarksburg	Lee	Richmond	Washington
Ashby	Cummington	Lunenburg	Royalston	Wendell
Ashland	Dighton	Middlefield	Saugus	West Brookfield
Ayer	East Brookfield	Monroe	Seekonk	West Stockbridge
Becket	Egremont	New Braintree	Sheffield	Westhampton
Berkley	Grafton	North Andover	Shelburne	Williamsburg
Bernardston	Great Barrington	North Brookfield	Somerset	Williamstown
Bolton	Hardwick	Northborough	Southborough	Windsor
Brookfield	Hinsdale	Peru	Tolland	
Charlemont	Holliston	Plainfield	Uxbridge	

Town and City Sites: - Sites from DataVision, Patriot Properties, and EPAS Omitted - See Lists Above

Acton Town in Middlesex County   *Property, Taxation Records*   Access to GIS/mapping free at http://host.appgeo.com/ActonMA/.

Adams Town in Berkshire County   *Property, Taxation Records*   Access to parcel searches free at http://adamsma.virtualtownhall.net/Public_Documents/AdamsMA_Assessor/index.

Amherst Town in Hampshire County   *Property, Taxation Records*   Access to property search for free at www.amherstma.gov/1844/Amherst-Property-Search.

Andover Town in Essex County   *Property, Taxation Records*   Property tax records on the Assessor's database are free at http://andoverma.gov/assessors/values.php. Access to GIS/Mapping for free at http://andoverma.gov/gis/. Also, access to tax maps for free at http://andoverma.gov/gis/taxmaps/.

Aquinnah Town in Dukes County   *Property, Taxation Records*   Access to GIS/mapping for free at www.axisgis.com/AquinnahMA/.

Ashburnham Town in Worcester County   *Property, Taxation Records*   Access to GIS/mapping for free at www.axisgis.com/AshburnhamMA/.

Ashby Town in Middlesex County   *Property, Taxation Records*   Access to parcel maps for free at www.ci.ashby.ma.us/assessors/maplink.html.

Ashfield Town in Franklin County   *Property, Taxation Records*   Access to Assessor's maps for free at http://ashfield.org/assessors-maps.html.

Ashland Town in Middlesex County   *Property, Taxation Records*   Access to GIS/mapping for free at www.ashlandmass.com/157/Geographic-Information-System-GIS-Maps.

Athol Town in Worcester County   *Property, Taxation Records*   Access to GIS/mapping free at www.axisgis.com/AtholMA/.

Attleboro City in Bristol County   *Property, Taxation Records*   Access to the Assessor's database free at www.nereval.com/Home.html?aspxerrorpath=/OnlineDatabases.aspx.

Auburn Town in Worcester County   *Property, Taxation Records*   Access to Real Estate tax lookup free at https://www.mapsonline.net/auburnma/tax_collector/search.php. Also, access to GIS/mapping for free at https://www.mapsonline.net/auburnma/index.html.

Avon Town in Norfolk County *Property, Taxation Records*   Access to Assessor maps for free at www.avon-ma.gov/assessors/pages/assessor-maps.

Ayer Town in Middlesex County *Property, Taxation Records*   Access to GIS/mapping free at www.ayer.ma.us/assessor/pages/assessors-maps.

Barnstable Town in Barnstable County *Property, Taxation Records*   Access to town assessor records for free at http://www.townofbarnstable.us/Assessing/propertydisplay16.asp.

Becket Town in Berkshire County *Property, Taxation Records*   Access to Assessor maps free at www.townofbecket.org/Public_Documents/BecketMA_Maps/.

Belmont Town in Middlesex County *Property, Taxation Records*   Access to the property database free at http://jfryan.com/belmont/.

Beverly City in Essex County *Property, Taxation Records*   Access to GIS/mapping free at https://beverlyma.mapgeo.io/?latlng=42.565159%2C-70.857627&zoom=13.

Billerica Town in Middlesex County *Property, Taxation Records*   Access to GIS/mapping free at https://www.mapsonline.net/billericama/public.html.

Blackstone Town in Worcester County *Property, Taxation Records*   Access to GIS/mapping free at https://blackstonema.mapgeo.io/.

Blandford Town in Hampden County *Property, Taxation Records*   Access to property assessment maps for free at www.townofblandford.com/assessors/AssessorsMaps.pdf.

Bolton Town in Worcester County *Property, Taxation Records*   Access to Assessor maps free at www.townofbolton.com/pages/BoltonMA_Assessors/Assessor%20MAPS.

Boston City in Suffolk County *Property, Taxation Records*   Records on the City of Boston Assessor database are free at www.cityofboston.gov/assessing/search/. Also, property tax bill and payment is searchable by parcel number for free at https://www.invoicecloud.com/portal/(S(i3ytvepjezo2fjlkqrpyvph3))/Site.aspx?G=13377843-58b1-429b-be78-ab0ebba80835

Bourne Town in Barnstable County *Property, Taxation Records*   Access to property taxes free go to www.assessedvalues2.com/index.aspx?jurcode=36.

Boxborough Town in Middlesex County *Property, Taxation Records*   Access to Assessor's maps free at www.boxborough-ma.gov/home/pages/maps.

Boxford Town in Essex County *Property, Taxation Records*   Access to property parcel maps for free at www.town.boxford.ma.us/Pages/BoxfordMA_Assessors/maps/index.

Boylston Town in Worcester County *Property, Taxation Records*   Access to GIS/mapping for free at www.axisgis.com/West_BoylstonMA/. Also, access to Assessor maps for free at www.boylston-ma.gov/assessors-office/pages/maps.

Brewster Town in Barnstable County *Property, Taxation Records*   Access to assessors' property data at www.assessedvalues2.com/index.aspx?jurcode=41.

Bridgewater Town in Plymouth County *Property, Taxation Records*   Access property data free on the GIS-mapping site at www.bridgewaterma.org/Government/Depts/Assessors/ParcelMaps.cfm. No name searching. Also, access to Assessor's online database for free at www.assessedvalues2.com/index.aspx?jurcode=42.

Brockton City in Plymouth County *Property, Taxation Records*   Access to the Assessors database free at www.brockton.ma.us/Online/AssessorsDB.aspx. Also, access to the Assessor's maps for free at www.brockton.ma.us/Online/AssessorsMaps.aspx.

Brookfield Town in Worcester County *Property, Taxation Records*   Access to Assessor's maps for free at www.brookfieldma.us/.

Brookline Town in Norfolk County *Property, Taxation Records*   Records on the Town of Brookline Assessors database are free at http://apps.brooklinema.gov/assessors/propertylookup.asp. Also, access assessor's maps for free at www.brooklinema.gov/716/Land-Records.

Cambridge City in Middlesex County *Property, Taxation Records*   Search city assessor database at www.cambridgema.gov/PropertyDatabase.

Canton Town in Norfolk County *Property, Taxation Records*   Access assessed value data at www.assessedvalues2.com/index.aspx?jurcode=50.

Carver Town in Plymouth County *Property, Taxation Records*   Access to Assessor's online database free at www.assessedvalues2.com/index.aspx?jurcode=52. Also, access to GIS/mapping for free at www.carverma.gov/assessors-maps.

Charlton Town in Worcester County   *Property, Taxation Records*   Access to MuniMapper for free at http://maps.massgis.state.ma.us/map_ol/charlton.php. Also, access to GIS/mapping free at www.townofcharlton.net/assessors.htm#AssessorsMaps.

Chatham Town in Barnstable County   *Property, Taxation Records*   Free access to assessor database at https://www.mapsonline.net/chathamma/web_assessor/search.php. Also, access to GIS/mapping for free at https://www.mapsonline.net/chathamma/index.html.

Chester Town in Hampden County   *Property, Taxation Records*   Access to GIS/mapping for free at http://pvpc.maps.arcgis.com/apps/Solutions/s2.html?appid=90d2cd46a3074629b527386311a74999.

Chesterfield Town in Hampshire County   *Property, Taxation Records*   Access to Assessor's online database free at www.assessedvalues2.com/index.aspx?jurcode=60. Also, access to GIS/mapping for free at www.townofchesterfieldma.com/Files/parcels/parcels.html. Also, another GIS/mapping site at http://maps.massgis.state.ma.us/map_ol/chesterfield.php.

Chicopee City in Hampden County   *Property, Taxation Records*   Access to the Assessor's database free at http://chicopee.univers-clt.com/.

Clinton Town in Worcester County   *Property, Taxation Records*   Access to field cards and parcel sheets for free at www.clintonma.gov/departments/Assessors/fieldcards/default.aspx. Also. Access to GIS/mapping for free at https://mrmapper.mrpc.org/webapps/clinton-public/.

Colrain Town in Franklin County   *Property, Taxation Records*   Access to mapping for free at http://colrain-ma.gov/assessor-maps.html.

Cummington Town in Hampshire County   *Property, Taxation Records*   Access to GIS/mapping free at www.mainstreetmaps.com/MA/Cummington/.

Dalton Town in Berkshire County   *Property, Taxation Records*   Access to property maps for free at https://dalton.govoffice2.com/admin/index.asp.

Danvers Town in Essex County   *Property, Taxation Records*   Access to GIS/mapping free at www.danversma.gov/index.asp?Type=B_BASIC&SEC={02FAF51E-E3E9-4D86-90E6-05D068FE7A83}.

Dedham Town in Norfolk County   *Property, Taxation Records*   Ssearch the GIS mapping site for owner and property data free at www.dedham-ma.gov/index.cfm?pid=12650.

Deerfield Town in Franklin County   *Property, Taxation Records*   Access to GIS/mapping free at www.axisgis.com/DeerfieldMA/.

Dennis Town in Barnstable County   *Property, Taxation Records*   Access to assessor property records is free at www.assessedvalues2.com/index.aspx?jurcode=75. Also, access to GIS/mapping for free at https://www.mapsonline.net/dennisma/index.html.

Dighton Town in Bristol County   *Property, Taxation Records*   Access to GIS/mapping for free at https://dightonma.mapgeo.io/.

Douglas Town in Worcester County   *Property, Taxation Records*   Access to GIS/mapping free at www.axisgis.com/DouglasMA/.

Dover Town in Norfolk County   *Property, Taxation Records*   Access to the assessor property values data is free at www.doverma.org/town-government/town-offices/assessor/.

Dracut Town in Middlesex County   *Property, Taxation Records*   Access to maps for free at www.dracut-ma.us/sites/dracutma/files/file/file/index_map_2_0.pdf.

Dudley Town in Worcester County   *Property, Taxation Records*   Access to tax maps and zoning maps for free at www.dudleyma.gov/taxmaps/.

Dunstable Town in Middlesex County   *Property, Taxation Records*   Access to Assessor's maps for free at www.dunstable-ma.gov/Pages/DunstableMA_Bcomm/BOA/index.

East Bridgewater Town in Plymouth County   *Property, Taxation Records*   Access to Assessor's online database free at www.assessedvalues2.com/index.aspx?jurcode=83. Also, access to GIS/mapping for free at https://www.mapsonline.net/eastbridgewaterma/index.html.

East Longmeadow Town in Hampden County   *Property, Taxation Records*   Access to street GIS/mapping for free at http://maps.eastlongmeadowma.gov/search/.

Eastham Town in Barnstable County   *Property, Taxation Records*   Assessor's online database free at https://www.mapsonline.net/easthamma/web_assessor/search.php.

Easthampton City in Hampshire County   *Property, Taxation Records*   Access to GIS/mapping for free at www.axisgis.com/EasthamptonMA/.

Easton Town in Bristol County   *Vital Records Records*   Acess to Family Vital Records from 1725-1843 for free at www.easton.ma.us/departments/town_clerk1/birth_death_marriage_records.php.

Edgartown Town in Dukes County *Property, Taxation Records* Access to GIS/mapping for free at www.axisgis.com/EdgartownMA/.

Egremont Town in Berkshire County *Property, Taxation Records* Access to GIS/mapping for free at http://www.axisgis.com/EgremontMA/Default.aspx

Erving Town in Franklin County *Property, Taxation Records* Access to the property maps for free at www.erving-ma.org/publications/assessors-maps/170-assessors-maps.

Fairhaven Town in Bristol County *Property, Taxation Records* Access to GIS/mapping for free at www.fairhaven-ma.gov/Pages/FairhavenMA_Assessors/Maps/.

Fall River City in Bristol County *Recorded Documents* Access to land records for free at https://www.fallriverdeeds.com/D/Default.aspx. Also, access to Registry of Deeds data is free at www.masslandrecords.com/.

Fitchburg City in Worcester County *Property, Taxation Records* Access Assessor's maps for free at http://fitchburgma.gov/DocumentCenter/Index/35.

Franklin Town in Norfolk County *Property, Taxation Records* Access to GIS/mapping for free at www.axisgis.com/FranklinMA/.

Freetown Town in Bristol County *Property, Taxation Records* Access property data free at http://assessedvalues2.com/index.aspx?jurcode=102. Also, access to GIS/mapping for free at www.axisgis.com/FreetownMA/.

Gardner City in Worcester County *Property, Taxation Records* Search the city assessor data at www.gardner-ma.gov/162/City-Assessor

Goshen Town in Hampshire County *Property, Taxation Records* Access to town maps (latest shown as of 1/2/15) for free at www.egoshen.net/media/23749/goshen_assessors_maps_2010.pdf.

Grafton Town in Worcester County *Property, Taxation Records* Access to GIS/mapping free at https://graftonma.mapgeo.io/.

Granville Town in Hampden County *Property, Taxation Records* Access to the Assessors database free at www.assessedvalues2.com/index.aspx?jurcode=112. Also, access to GIS/mapping for free at www.axisgis.com/GranvilleMA/.

Greenfield Town in Franklin County *Property, Taxation Records* Access to online property information and GIS/mapping website free at www.mainstreetmaps.com/MA/Greenfield/.

Groveland Town in Essex County *Property, Taxation Records* Access to tax maps for free at www.grovelandma.com/Pages/GrovelandMA_Assessors/MAP/.

Hadley Town in Hampshire County *Property, Taxation Records* Access to GIS/mapping free at www.axisgis.com/HadleyMA/.

Halifax Town in Plymouth County *Property, Taxation Records* Access to the Assessor's online database free at www.assessedvalues2.com/index.aspx?jurcode=118. Also, access to the Assessor's maps for free at http://town.halifax.ma.us/Pages/HalifaxMA_Bcomm/Assessor/maps.pdf/.

Hamilton Town in Essex County *Property, Taxation Records* Access to the Assessor's maps for free at www.hamiltonma.gov/Pages/HamiltonMA_Assessors/MAPS/.

Hardwick Town in Worcester County *Property, Taxation Records* Access to GIS/mapping free at www.townofhardwick.com/assessorsmaps1.html.

Harvard Town in Worcester County *Property, Taxation Records* Access to the GIS/mapping records for free at www.axisgis.com/HarvardMA/.

Harwich Town in Barnstable County *Property, Taxation Records* Access to mapping for free at www.harwich-ma.gov/assessing/pages/assessors-maps.

Hatfield Town in Hampshire County *Property, Taxation Records* Access to Assessor data for free at www.mainstreetmaps.com/ma/hatfield/public.asp.

Heath Town in Franklin County *Property, Taxation Records* Access to the town map index for free at www.townofheath.org/?attachment_id=5221.

Hingham Town in Plymouth County *Property, Taxation Records* Access to GIS/mapping for free at https://www.mapsonline.net/hinghamma/index.html.

Holbrook Town in Norfolk County *Property, Taxation Records* Access to Assessor's maps for free at http://holbrookma.gov/Pages/HolbrookMA_Assessors/Maps.

Holden Town in Worcester County   *Property, Taxation Records*   Access to GIS/mapping for free at www.mapsonline.net/holdenma/index.html.

Holland Town in Hampden County   *Property, Taxation Records*   Access to GIS/mapping for free at www.axisgis.com/HollandMA/.

Hopkinton Town in Middlesex County   *Property, Taxation Records*   Access Board of Assessors maps free at www.hopkinton.org/assessor/listing.htm; no name searching.

Hudson Town in Middlesex County   *Property, Taxation Records*   Access GIS/mapping for free at www.townofhudson.org/public_documents/HudsonMA_GIS/Requests.

Hull Town in Plymouth County   *Property, Taxation Records*   Access to Assessor's maps for free at www.town.hull.ma.us/Public_Documents/HullMA_Assessors/assessor%20maps/.

Huntington Town in Hampshire County   *Property, Taxation Records*   Access to property maps for free at http://huntingtonma.us/propMaps.html. Also, access to GIS/Mapping for free at http://humboldtgov.org/231/Online-Search.

Ipswich Town in Essex County   *Property, Taxation Records*   Access to GIS/mapping free at http://maps.massgis.state.ma.us/map_ol/oliver.php.

Lancaster Town in Worcester County   *Property, Taxation Records*   Access to GIS/mapping free at www.axisgis.com/LancasterMA/.

Lanesborough Town in Berkshire County   *Property, Taxation Records*   Access to GIS/mapping free at www.axisgis.com/LanesboroughMA/.

Lee Town in Berkshire County   *Property, Taxation Records*   Access to tax maps for free at www.lee.ma.us/assessor/pages/tax-maps.

Lenox Town in Berkshire County   *Property, Taxation Records*   Access and search assessor's data free at www.assessedvalues2.com/index.aspx?jurcode=152. Also, access to the Property Maps for free at www.townoflenox.com/Public_Documents/LenoxMA_Assessor/index. Click on Property Maps.

Leominster City in Worcester County   *Property, Taxation Records*   Search the assessor's older maps for free to go www.leominster-ma.gov/depts/management/assessor/old_maps.asp.

Leverett Town in Franklin County   *Property, Taxation Records*   Access to Assessor property maps for free at http://leverett.ma.us/content/assessor-property-maps.

Lincoln Town in Middlesex County   *Property, Taxation Records*   Access to property cards, maps and assessment list for free at www.lincolntown.org/index.aspx?nid=241.

Littleton Town in Middlesex County   *Property, Taxation Records*   Access to Assessor's Maps for free at www.littletonma.org/content/19455/53/1044/97/5904/default.aspx.

Lowell City in Middlesex County   *Property, Taxation Records*   Access property assessment data and GIS/mapping data for free at www.lowellma.gov/mis/Pages/General/GIS.aspx.

Ludlow Town in Hampden County   *Property, Taxation Records*   Access to GIS/mapping free at http://107.20.209.214/ludlowma_public/.

Lunenburg Town in Worcester County   *Property, Taxation Records*   Access to GIS/mapping for free at www.axisgis.com/LunenburgMA/.

Malden City in Middlesex County   *Property, Taxation Records*   Access to GIS/mapping for free at https://maldenma.mapgeo.io/.

Mansfield Town in Bristol County   *Property, Taxation Records*   Access to GIS/mapping free at http://gis.mansfieldma.com/parcels/disclaimer.htm.

Marion Town in Plymouth County   *Property, Taxation Records*   Access to property values for free at https://marionma.mapgeo.io. Also, access to Assessor's maps for free at www.marionma.gov/Pages/MarionMA_Assessors/maps/.

Mashpee Town in Barnstable County   *Property, Taxation Records*   Search Town of Mashpee Assessor database free at www.assessedvalues2.com/index.aspx?jurcode=172. Access to tax maps for free at www.mashpeema.gov/gis-e911/pages/interactive-town-map.

Mattapoisett Town in Plymouth County   *Property, Taxation Records*   Access to GIS/mapping for free at https://www.mapsonline.net/mattapoisettma/index.html.

Medford City in Middlesex County   *Property, Taxation Records*   Search the city assessor database/maps at https://www.scribd.com/collections/4394098/Assessors-Maps.

Medway Town in Norfolk County   *Property, Taxation Records*   Parcel Maps available free via the link on the Assessor webpage.

Melrose City in Middlesex County   *Property, Taxation Records*   Access to the Assessor's maps for free at https://www.mapsonline.net/melrosema/index.html.

Mendon Town in Worcester County   *Property, Taxation Records*   Access to GIS/mapping free at http://maps.massgis.state.ma.us/map_ol/mendon.php.

Merrimac Town in Essex County   *Property, Taxation Records*   Access to Assessor's maps free at http://mimap.mvpc.org/merrimacPropertySelector/default.aspx?town=merrimac.

Middleton Town in Essex County   *Property, Taxation Records*   Access to the Assessor's Maps for free at www.townofmiddleton.org/Pages/MiddletonMA_Assessor/Assessors%20Maps/.

Millbury Town in Worcester County   *Property, Taxation Records*   Access to GIS/mapping for free at http://107.20.209.214/millburyma_public/default.html.

Millis Town in Norfolk County   *Property, Taxation Records*   Access to GIS/mapping free at www.axisgis.com/MillisMA/Default.aspx?Splash=True.

Millville Town in Worcester County   *Property, Taxation Records*   Town maps for free at www.millvillema.org/maps/.

Monson Town in Hampden County   *Property, Taxation Records*   Access to GIS/mapping free at http://107.20.209.214/MonsonMA_public/Default.html.

Montague Town in Franklin County   *Property, Taxation Records*   Access to GIS/mapping for free at www.mainstreetmaps.com/MA/Montague/public.asp.

Monterey Town in Berkshire County   *Property, Taxation Records*   Access to GIS/mapping free at www.axisgis.com/MontereyMA/.

Nantucket Town in Nantucket County   *Property, Taxation Records*   Access to GIS/mapping for free at www.nantucket-ma.gov/151/GIS-Maps.

Natick Town in Middlesex County   *Property, Taxation Records*   Search town assessments free at www.natickma.org/assess/assessinfo.asp. Includes name searches.

Needham Town in Norfolk County   *Property, Taxation Records*   Access to parcels searches and sales searches for free at www.needhamma.gov/index.aspx?NID=57.

New Bedford City in Bristol County   *Property, Taxation Records*   Access to the assessor property database is free at www.newbedford-ma.gov/assessors/parcel-lookup/.

Newbury Town in Essex County   *Property, Taxation Records*   Access to the Assessor's maps for free at www.townofnewbury.org/Pages/NewburyMA_Assessors/Maps2013/index.

Newburyport City in Essex County   *Property, Taxation Records*   Access to the city maps for free at http://mimap.mvpc.org/newburyportpropertyselectorpublic/default.aspx?town=Newburyport.

Newton City in Middlesex County   *Property, Taxation Records*   Records on the City of Newton Fiscal 2003 assessment database are free at http://assessing.newtonma.gov/NewtonMAWebApp/. Data represents market value as of January of current year.

Norfolk Town in Norfolk County   *Property, Taxation Records*   Access tax maps for free at www.virtualnorfolk.org/public_documents/norfolkma_assess/Norfolk_TaxMaps/.

North Adams City in Berkshire County   *Property, Taxation Records*   Access to GIS/mapping for free at www.axisgis.com/North_AdamsMA/.

North Andover Town in Essex County   *Property, Taxation Records*   Access to 2014 street listings for free at www.townofnorthandover.com/Pages/NAndoverMA_Assessor/st14.pdf.

North Reading Town in Middlesex County   *Property, Taxation Records*   Access assessor rolls and property sales free at http://csc-ma.us/PROPAPP/Opening.do?subAction=NewSearch&town=NreadingPubAcc. No name searches.

Northampton City in Hampshire County   *Property, Taxation Records*   Access to property evaluation information for free at www.northamptonassessor.us/.

Northborough Town in Worcester County   *Property, Taxation Records*   Access to maps for free at www.town.northborough.ma.us/Pages/NorthboroughMA_MIS/maplibrary.

Northbridge Town in Worcester County   *Property, Taxation Records*   Access to alphabetical street listing for free at www.northbridgemass.org/sites/northbridgema/files/file/file/northbridgevalues4.pdf.

Norton Town in Bristol County   *Property, Taxation Records*   Access to Assessor's database free at www.assessedvalues2.com/index.aspx?jurcode=218. Also, access to GIS/mapping for free at https://nortonma.mapgeo.io/.

Oak Bluffs Town in Dukes County   *Property, Taxation Records*   Access to property record cards and GIS/mapping free at www.assessedvalues2.com/index.aspx?jurcode=221.

Orange Town in Franklin County   *Property, Taxation Records*   Access to GIS/mapping for free at www.axisgis.com/OrangeMA/.

Orleans Town in Barnstable County   *Property, Taxation Records*   Search the Assessor's online database free at www.assessedvalues2.com/index.aspx?jurcode=224.

Otis Town in Berkshire County   *Property, Taxation Records*   Access to property data for free at https://www.mapsonline.net/otisma/web_assessor/search.php.

Oxford Town in Worcester County   *Property, Taxation Records*   Search the property assessments by name or address at https://security.town.oxford.ma.us/WebUserInterface/(S(yzur0vk4k3bcmeqov4mqtb4r))/WebPortal/WEB_PT_MAIN.aspx?command=. There is a $.25 per transaction fee. Also, access to GIS/mapping for free at https://www.mapsonline.net/oxfordma/index.html. Assessor's maps found at www.town.oxford.ma.us/Pages/OxfordMA_Assessor/maps/index.

Palmer Town in Hampden County   *Property, Taxation Records*   Access to GIS/mapping for free at www.townofpalmer.com/assessor.

Paxton Town in Worcester County   *Property, Taxation Records*   Access to tax maps for free at www.townofpaxton.net/index.asp?SEC=FFF0D9D6-0C7C-4C8E-B6DA-4C0CA4E06378&Type=B_BASIC

Peabody City in Essex County   *Property, Taxation Records*   Access property data free at http://host.appgeo.com/PeabodyMA/.

Phillipston Town in Worcester County   *Property, Taxation Records*   Access to Assessors property data free at www.axisgis.com/PhillipstonMA/.

Plainville Town in Norfolk County   *Property, Taxation Records*   Access to the Assessor's database free at www.nereval.com/Home.html?aspxerrorpath=/OnlineDatabases.aspx.

Plympton Town in Plymouth County   *Property, Taxation Records*   Access to the Assessor's maps for free at www.town.plympton.ma.us/assessors/pages/online-maps.

Princeton Town in Worcester County   *Property, Taxation Records*   GIS/mapping available for free at http://town.princeton.ma.us/Pages/PrincetonMA_Assessors/Maps/.

Provincetown Town in Barnstable County   *Property, Taxation Records*   Access to property record cards for free at https://www.mapsonline.net/provincetownma/web_assessor/search.php. Access to GIS/mapping free at www.provincetown-ma.gov/index.aspx?NID=161.

Randolph Town in Norfolk County   *Property, Taxation Records*   Access to GIS/mapping free at https://randolphma.mapgeo.io/?disclaimer=true&latlng=42.1711%2C-71.0608&zoom=13.

Raynham Town in Bristol County   *Property, Taxation Records*   Access the Online Property Viewer free at https://raynhamma.mapgeo.io/.

Reading Town in Middlesex County   *Property, Taxation Records*   Access to property tax maps for free at www.readingma.gov/PropertyMaps.

Rehoboth Town in Bristol County   *Property, Taxation Records*   Access to GIS/mapping and property cards for free at https://rehobothma.mapgeo.io/.

Rochester Town in Plymouth County   *Property, Taxation Records*   Access to Assessor's Maps for free at www.townofrochestermass.com/bdassessors.htm.

Rockland Town in Plymouth County   *Property, Taxation Records*   Access to assessment listings for 2014-2015 for free at http://rockland-ma.gov/town-departments/town-assessor/.

Rockport Town in Essex County   *Property, Taxation Records*   Access GIS/mapping for free at www.rockportma.gov/assessors/pages/assessors-maps-gis. Access to parcel and ownership records free at https://www.mapsonline.net/rockportma/web_assessor/search.php.

Russell Town in Hampden County   *Property, Taxation Records*   Access to GIS/mapping for free at www.townofrussell.us/assessors.html.

Rutland Town in Worcester County *Property, Taxation Records* Access to GIS/mapping free at www.axisgis.com/RutlandMA/Default.aspx?Splash=True.

Salem City in Essex County *Property, Taxation Records* Access to GIS/mapping free at www.salem.com/gis-and-maps.

Salisbury Town in Essex County *Property, Taxation Records* Access to tax maps for free at www.salisburyma.gov/assessor/pages/salisbury-tax-maps.

Sandwich Town in Barnstable County *Property, Taxation Records* Access to GIS/mapping free at https://sandwichma.mapgeo.io/.

Saugus Town in Essex County *Property, Taxation Records* Access to GIS/mapping free at www.saugus-ma.gov/assessors-office/pages/assessors-plate-maps.

Scituate Town in Plymouth County *Property, Taxation Records* Search the Assessor property data for free at www.assessedvalues2.com/index.aspx?jurcode=264.

Sharon Town in Norfolk County *Property, Taxation Records* Access to GIS/mapping free at www.mainstreetmaps.com/MA/Sharon/.

Shelburne Town in Franklin County *Property, Taxation Records* Assessor's tax maps for free at http://townofshelburne.com/assessors-maps.html.

Sherborn Town in Middlesex County *Property, Taxation Records* Access to town maps free at www.sherbornma.org/Pages/SherbornMA_Assessor/2010mapstable.

Shirley Town in Middlesex County *Property, Taxation Records* Access to GIS/mapping for free at https://mrmapper.mrpc.org/shirleyassessors_public/index.html.

Shrewsbury Town in Worcester County *Property, Taxation Records* Access to GIS/mapping free at https://www.mapsonline.net/shrewsburyma/index.html.

Shutesbury Town in Franklin County *Property, Taxation Records* Online maps and property information is at www.mainstreetmaps.com/MA/Shutesbury/.

Somerville City in Middlesex County *Property, Taxation Records* Access to the town maps for free at www.somervillema.gov/departments/finance/assessing/maps.

South Hadley Town in Hampshire County *Property, Taxation Records* Access to Assessor maps free at www.southhadley.org/225/Find-a-Map-and-Parcel. Also, GIS/mapping for free at www.axisgis.com/South_HadleyMA/.

Southampton Town in Hampshire County *Property, Taxation Records* Access assessor property data in spreadsheet format for free at www.townofsouthampton.org/Assessor/FY2015VALUES.pdf. Also, access to tax maps, property cards and muni-mapper for free at http://townofsouthampton.org/administration/finance/assessors/.

Southbridge Town in Worcester County *Property, Taxation Records* Access to GIS/mapping for free at https://southbridgema.mapgeo.io/.

Spencer Town in Worcester County *Property, Taxation Records* Access to GIS/mapping free at https://spencerma.mapgeo.io/.

Springfield City in Hampden County *Recorded Documents* Search city properties/owners with tax liens free at www.springfield-ma.gov/finance/taxtitle/.
Property, Taxation Records Access to city assessor property valuations is free at www.springfield-ma.gov/finance/assessors/. Also, search the city GIS-mapping site for property data at https://maps.springfield-ma.gov/gis/.

Sterling Town in Worcester County *Property, Taxation Records* Access GIS/mapping for free at www.axisgis.com/SterlingMA/.

Stockbridge Town in Berkshire County *Property, Taxation Records* Access to GIS/mapping free at www.axisgis.com/StockbridgeMA/. Also, access to the property maps for free at http://townofstockbridge.com/wp/town-government/assessors/.

Stow Town in Middlesex County *Property, Taxation Records* Free access to the Assessor's database at http://stow.univers-clt.com/. No name searches. Free access to 2012 (only) property maps at www.stow-ma.gov/Pages/StowMA_Assessor/Stow%20Property%20Maps%202012/.

Sturbridge Town in Worcester County *Property, Taxation Records* Access to tax maps free at www.town.sturbridge.ma.us/public_documents/sturbridgema_assessor/Tax_Maps/.

Sudbury Town in Middlesex County *Property, Taxation Records* Access to the property valuations list for current year is free at https://sudbury.ma.us/assessors/2013-sudbury-property-valuation/. No name searching on this address index list.

Swampscott Town in Essex County   *Property, Taxation Records*   Access to GIS/mapping free at
http://host.cdmsmithgis.com/swampscottma/.

Swansea Town in Bristol County   *Property, Taxation Records*   Access GIS/mapping free at www.town.swansea.ma.us/board-of-
assessors/pages/assessors-maps. Also, access to the Assessor's database for free at www.nereval.com/Home.html?aspxerrorpath=/OnlineDatabases.aspx.

Taunton City in Bristol County   *Property, Taxation Records*   Also, access to GIS/mapping for free at
www.mapgeo.com/TauntonMa/.

Templeton Town in Worcester County   *Property, Taxation Records*   Access to property cards and maps free at
www.axisgis.com/TempletonMA/.

Tewksbury Town in Middlesex County   *Property, Taxation Records*   Search lists of yearly tax assessments free at
www.tewksbury-ma.gov/assessors-office/pages/assessment-values. Also, access tax maps for free at
www.tewksbury.net/Pages/TewksburyMA_Assessor/TaxMaps.

Tisbury Town in Dukes County   *Property, Taxation Records*   Access to GIS/mapping free at www.axisgis.com/TisburyMA/. Also,
access to the assessor's maps for free at www.tisburyma.gov/Pages/tisburyma_assessorsmaps/mapsindex.

Tolland Town in Hampden County   *Property, Taxation Records*   Access parcel listing by owner name free at www.tolland-
ma.gov/Public_Documents/TollandMA_Assessor/Tolland_Parcel_Listing_by_Owner_Name_2013.pdf.

Townsend Town in Middlesex County   *Property, Taxation Records*   Access to Assessor's database free at
http://realprop.townsend.ma.us/realform.htm.

Truro Town in Barnstable County   *Property, Taxation Records*   Access to Assessor's database free at
www.assessedvalues2.com/index.aspx?jurcode=300. Also, access to GIS/mapping for free at www.axisgis.com/TruroMA/.

Tyringham Town in Berkshire County   *Property, Taxation Records*   Access to Assessor's maps for free at
www.assessedvalues2.com/index.aspx?jurcode=302.

Upton Town in Worcester County   *Property, Taxation Records*   Access to tax maps free at www.uptonma.gov/assessor/pages/tax-
maps. Also, access to the Assessor's database for free at www.nereval.com/Home.html?aspxerrorpath=/OnlineDatabases.aspx.

Uxbridge Town in Worcester County   *Property, Taxation Records*   Access to GIS/mapping for free at
www.axisgis.com/UxbridgeMA/.

Wareham Town in Plymouth County   *Property, Taxation Records*   Access to Assessor maps for free at
www.wareham.ma.us/assessing-department/pages/assessors-maps.

Warren Town in Worcester County   *Property, Taxation Records*   Assessor maps and data are available at
www.axisgis.com/WarrenMA/Default.aspx?Splash=True.

Wayland Town in Middlesex County   *Property, Taxation Records*   Access to GIS/mapping for free at
www.wayland.ma.us/Pages/WaylandMA_GIS/atlas.

Webster Town in Worcester County   *Property, Taxation Records*   Access to GIS/mapping free at
http://107.20.209.214/WebsterMA_Public/Default.html.

Wellesley Town in Norfolk County   *Property, Taxation Records*   Property tax records on the Assessor's database are free at
http://wellesleyma.virtualtownhall.net/Pages/WellesleyMA_Assessor/index. Click on Assessment Information at left of page.

Wellfleet Town in Barnstable County   *Property, Taxation Records*   Access to property assessment records for free at
www.assessedvalues2.com/index.aspx?jurcode=318. Also, access to GIS/mapping for free at www.wellfleet-ma.gov/assessor/pages/assessors-map-online.

Wenham Town in Essex County   *Property, Taxation Records*   Access to GIS/mapping free at www.axisgis.com/WenhamMA/.

West Boylston Town in Worcester County   *Property, Taxation Records*   Access to GIS/mapping free at www.westboylston-
ma.gov/Pages/WBoylstonMA_WebDocs/gis.

West Newbury Town in Essex County   *Property, Taxation Records*   Access to the property finder for free at
http://mimap.mvpc.org/westnewburypropertyselector/default.aspx?town=West+Newbury. Also, access to town maps for free at
www.wnewbury.org/pages/WestNewburyMA_Assessor/maps/index.

West Springfield Town in Hampden County   *Property, Taxation Records*   Search the town assessor database at
www.townofwestspringfield.org/public_documents/wspringfieldma_assr/index#!assessor/c6z5.

West Stockbridge Town in Berkshire County   *Property, Taxation Records*   Assessors' maps and property cards for free at
www.weststockbridge-ma.gov/Pages/WestStockbridgeMA_Assessor/Assessor_Maps.

West Tisbury Town in Dukes County *Property, Taxation Records* Access to GIS/mapping free at www.axisgis.com/West_TisburyMA/.

Westborough Town in Worcester County *Property, Taxation Records* Access to GIS/mapping for free at https://westboroughma.mapgeo.io/?latlng=42.2658%2C-71.6103&zoom=13.

Westford Town in Middlesex County *Property, Taxation Records* Access the town online offerings - property, GIS-mapping for free at www.westfordma.gov/pages/onlineservices/gis. Also, access to parcel look-up free at www.westfordma.gov/Pages/Government/TownDepartments/WestfordMA_MapsGIS/.

Westminster Town in Worcester County *Property, Taxation Records* Access to Assessor maps for free at www.westminster-ma.gov/assessors

Weston Town in Middlesex County *Property, Taxation Records* Access to GIS/mapping free at https://www.mapsonline.net/westonma/index.html.

Westport Town in Bristol County *Property, Taxation Records* Access to GIS/mapping free at https://westportma.mapgeo.io/.

Westwood Town in Norfolk County *Property, Taxation Records* Access to GIS/mapping for free at www.townhall.westwood.ma.us/index.cfm/page/GIS-Maps-and-Data/pid/25580.

Weymouth Town in Norfolk County *Property, Taxation Records* Access to property data is free at www.weymouth.ma.us/geographic-information-system-gis/pages/property-viewer-31.

Whately Town in Franklin County *Property, Taxation Records* Access to GIS/mapping for free at www.axisgis.com/WhatelyMA/.

Whitman Town in Plymouth County *Recorded Documents* Access to deeds searches for free at http://titleview.org/plymouthdeeds/%28X%281%29S%28f2dz2nqkqve2vv45sygfklad%29%29/Default.aspx?AspxAutoDetectCookieSupport=1. Fees for printing and must have subscription, $30.00 per month and $1.00 per page.
Property, Taxation Records Access to GIS/mapping for free at http://maps.massgis.state.ma.us/map_ol/whitman.php.

Williamstown Town in Berkshire County *Property, Taxation Records* Access to GIS/mapping for free at www.axisgis.com/WilliamstownMA/.

Winchendon Town in Worcester County *Property, Taxation Records* Access to assessor's property maps and cards for free at www.axisgis.com/WinchendonMA/.

Worcester City in Worcester County *Property, Taxation Records* Online access to the City Real Estate Tax/CML database is free at www.worcesterma.gov/e-services/search-public-records/real-estate-tax-cml.

Wrentham Town in Norfolk County *Property, Taxation Records* Access to the Assessor's database free at www.assessedvalues2.com/index.aspx?jurcode=350.

Yarmouth Town in Barnstable County *Property, Taxation Records* Access to mapping for free at http://yarmouth.ma.us/DocumentCenter/Index/52.

Michigan

Capital: Lansing
             Ingham County
Time Zone: EST

    Four NW Michigan counties are in the CST:

    They are: Dickinson, Gogebic, Iron, Menominee.

Population: 9,922,576
# of Counties: 83

Useful State Links

Website: **www.michigan.gov**
Governor: **www.michigan.gov/snyder**
Attorney General: **www.michigan.gov/ag**
State Archives: **www.michigan.gov/mhc/0,4726,7-282-61083---,00.html** |
State Statutes and Codes: **www.legislature.mi.gov**
Legislative Bill Search: **www.legislature.mi.gov**
Unclaimed Funds: **www.michigan.gov/treasury/0,1607,7-121-44435---,00.html**

State Public Record Agencies

Criminal Records

Michigan State Police, Criminal History Section, Criminal Justice Information Center, www.michigan.gov/cjic Online access is available. All felonies and serious misdemeanors that are punishable by over 93 days are required to be reported to ICHAT by the state repository by law enforcement agencies, prosecutors, and courts in all 83 Michigan counties. Register at http://apps.michigan.gov/ICHAT/Home.aspx. Fee is $10.00 per name. Call 517-241-0606. Also, you are allowed up to three variations on one name search. Suppressed records and warrant information are not available through ICHAT. Use of a MasterCard, Discover or VISA is required. This is the only method available for a non-fingerprint search.

Sexual Offender Registry

Michigan State Police, SOR Section, www.communitynotification.com/cap_main.php?office=55242/ One may search the registry at www.icrimewatch.net/index.php?AgencyID=55242, there is no charge. Other search options include published lists to download. Data includes an offender's registerable offense, his/her photo (if available), physical description, offender's last reported address, if offender is attending and/or employed at a post secondary school and any aliases Email questions to PSORS@Michigan.gov.

Incarceration Records

Michigan Department of Corrections, Central Records Office, www.michigan.gov/corrections The online access found from a link at http://mdocweb.state.mi.us/OTIS2/otis2.aspx has many search offender status capabilities. The site does not include information about offenders who have been off supervision for more than three years. *Other Options:* Bulk sales of database information is available.

Corporation, LLC, LP, LLP, Assumed Name

Department of Licensing and Reg. Affairs, Corp., Sec., & Commercial Licensng - Corps Div., www.michigan.gov/lara/0,4601,7-154-61343---,00.html At the main website, search by company name or file number for records of domestic corporations, limited liability companies, limited partnerships and of foreign corporations, and limited partnerships qualified to transact business in the state. Click on Business Entity Search or go to www.dleg.state.mi.us/bcs_corp/sr_corp.asp. Per the web page, the Business Entity Search is no longer compatible with the Google Chrome web browser. *Other Options:* The database is for sale by contract.

Trademarks/Servicemarks

Dept of labor & Economic Growth, Commercial Svcs - Trademarks & Service Marks, www.michigan.gov/lara/0,4601,7-154-61343_35413_35431---,00.html Download files of Registered Marks at www.michigan.gov/lara/0,4601,7-154-61343_35413_35431-390048--,00.html.

Uniform Commercial Code, Federal & State Tax Liens

MI Department of State, UCC Section,   http://services.sos.state.mi.us/UCC/Home.aspx   A free search by individual name or organization ("Debtor Name Quick Search") is at http://services.sos.state.mi.us/UCC/QuickSearch.aspx. Also, an official search with documents may be ordered for a fee. Registration is required. A credit card is necessary unless the requester has an established billing account. Click on Information Request on left panel. *Other Options:* A monthly subscription service is available for the bulk purchase of UCC filings on CDs. The fee is $50 or actual cost, whichever is greater. Call 517-322-1144 for additional information.

Vital Records

Department of Health, Vital Records Requests,   www.michigan.gov/mdhhs/0,5885,7-339-71551_4645---,00.html   Records can be ordered from the web site, credit card is required. Processing time is 2 weeks.

Workers' Compensation Records

Department of Labor & Economic Dev., Workers' Compensation Agency,   www.michigan.gov/wca   Go to the website and follow the links to see if an employer has coverage. The site does not allow searching by employee name.

Driver Records

Department of State, Record Lookup Unit,   www.michigan.gov/sos   Online ordering is available on an interactive or batch basis. There is a 100 minimum for batch requests. Ordering is by DL or name and DOB. An account must be established and billing is monthly. Fee is $8.00 per record. A $25,000 surety bond is required. Also, the agency offers an activity notification service for employers who register their drivers. Account holders may also access vehicle and watercraft records. For more information on either program, call 517-322-6281 or email CommercialServices@michigan.gov for further information.   *Other Options:* The state offers the license file for bulk purchase to approved requesters. Customized runs are $64 per thousand records; complete database can be purchased for $16 per thousand. A $25,000 surety bond is required. Call 517-322-1042.

Vehicle, Vessel Ownership & Registration

Department of State, Record Lookup Unit,   www.michigan.gov/sos   Online searching via the Internet is single inquiry and requires a VIN or plate number (no name searches). An account is required with a $25,000 surety bond. Fee is $8.00 per record. For more information, call 517-322-6281. The program is called Direct Access and details are found on the web. A unique service offered is the Repeat Offender Inquiry. This web search function allows dealers and others to learn if a vehicle purchaser is ineligible for license plates and subject to registration denial under Michigan's Repeat Offender Law. Search results state if the purchaser is eligible, not eligible, or if not on file. The web site is https://services.sos.state.mi.us/RepeatOffender/Inquiry.aspx.   *Other Options:* Michigan offers bulk retrieval from the VIN and plate database. A written request letter, stating purpose, must be submitted and approved. A $25,000 surety bond is required upon approval. Please call 517-322-1042.

Crash Reports

Department of State Police, Criminal Justice Information Center,   www.michigan.gov/msp/0,4643,7-123-1878_15889---,00.html   Records may be viewed and printed from the Traffic Crash Purchasing System at http://mdotjboss.state.mi.us/TCPS/login/welcome.jsp. The fee is $10.00, a credit card must be used unless billing arrangements are made. Reports are not mailed.. Records are available going back 10 years. For specific questions email CrashPurchaseTCPS@michigan.gov.

Voter Registration, Campaign Finance, Lobbyists, PACs

Secretary of State, Bureau of Elections,   www.michigan.gov/sos/1,1607,7-127-1633---,00.html   Single name voter registration searches are to https://webapps.sos.state.mi.us/mivote/votersearch.aspx. Must have first and last name, birth month and year and residential zip code. Campaign finance disclosures and lobbyist disclosures are available from links at www.michigan.gov/sos/1,1607,7-127-1633---,00.html. Search lobbyists from a different Division at http://miboecfr.nicusa.com/cgi-bin/cfr/lobby_srch.cgi.   *Other Options:* The agency will sell district, statewide or customized subsets of the voter registration database on CD. Fees are usually $23.00, depending on data requested.

Occupational Licensing Boards

These licenses are all searchable at https://w2.lara.state.mi.us/VAL/License/Search

Acupuncture	Marriage & Family Therapist	Physician/Medical Doctor/Assistant
Ambulance Attendant	Massage Therapist	Podiatric Medicine & Surgery
Athletic Trainer	Medical First Responder	Podiatrist
Audiology	Medicine	Psychologist
Chiropractor	Nurse/Aide	Respiratory Care
Counselor	Nursing Home Administrator	Sanitarian
Dentist	Occupational Therapist	Social Worker
Dentist/Dental Assistant/Hygienist	Optometrist	Speech-Language Pathologist
Emergency Medical Personnel	Osteopathic Physician	Veterinarian/Veterinary Technician
EMT Advanced/Specialist/Instructor	Paramedic	Veterinary Medicine
Health Facility/Laboratory	Pharmacist, Pharmacy	
Mammography Facility	Physical/Occupational Therapist	

These licenses are all searchable at https://www.lara.michigan.gov/colaLicVerify/lName.jsp

Accountant-CPA
Alarm System Service
Amusement Ride
Appraiser, Real Estate/Gen/Residential
Architect
Barber
Barber Shop/School
Boxing/Wrestling Occupation
Builder, Residential
Carnival
Cemetery
Collection Manager
Community Planner

Community Planner (Mfg Home)
Contractor, Residential
Cosmetologist
Cosmetology Shop/School
Employment Agency, fee only
Engineer
Forester
Funeral Home/Salesperson
Funeral, Prepaid Contract Regis
Hearing Aid Dealer
Landscape Architect
Manufactured Home Installer/Svcs/Retail
Manufactured Home Community

Mortuary Science
Ocularist
Personnel Agency
Polygraph Examiner
Private Investigator/Detective
Private Security/Secur'y arrest author'y
Real Estate Agent/Broker/Seller
Security Agency
Security Alarm Installer
Security Guard, Private
Surveyor, Professional

The Rest:

Adoption/Child Placing Agency	www.dleg.state.mi.us/brs_cwl/sr_cwl.asp
Adult Foster Care/Homes for Aged	www.dleg.state.mi.us/brs_afc/sr_afc.asp
Aircraft Dealer	www.michigan.gov/statelicensesearch/0,4671,7-180-24786-76010--,00.html
Animal Shelter	www.michigan.gov/documents/mda/Licensed_Animal_Shelter_List_By_County_Report_222946_7.pdf
Aquaculture Operation	www.michigan.gov/documents/mda/mda_aquaculture_192478_7.pdf
Asbestos Accreditation, Individ'l	www.dleg.state.mi.us/asbestos_program/sr_individual.asp
Asbestos Contractor	www.dleg.state.mi.us/asbestos_program/sr_contractor.asp
Asbestos Training Provider	www.dleg.state.mi.us/asbestos_program/sr_tcp.asp
Attorney, State Bar	www.michbar.org/memberdirectory/home
Auto Dealer/Mech'/Repair Facility	www.michigan.gov/sos/0,4670,7-127-49534_50301-51047--,00.html
Bank & Trust Company	http://difs.state.mi.us/fis/ind_srch/cht_bank/
Boilermaker/Boiler Installer/Repairer	https://aca3.accela.com/lara/
Camp, Child/Adult Foster Care	www.dleg.state.mi.us/brs_afc/sr_afc.asp
Check Seller	http://difs.state.mi.us/fis/ind_srch/ConsumerFinance/
Child Care Family/Group/Center	www.dleg.state.mi.us/brs_cdc/sr_lfl.asp
Child Care Institution/Facility, Court Operated	www.dleg.state.mi.us/brs_cdc/sr_lfl.asp
Construction Disciplinary Action Report	www.michigan.gov/lara/0,4601,7-154-10575_17394_56071---,00.html
Consumer Financial Service	http://difs.state.mi.us/fis/ind_srch/ConsumerFinance/
Credit Card Issuer	http://difs.state.mi.us/fis/ind_srch/ConsumerFinance/
Credit Union	http://difs.state.mi.us/fis/ind_srch/CreditUnion/
Debt Management	http://difs.state.mi.us/fis/ind_srch/ConsumerFinance/
Electrician (various types)	https://aca3.accela.com/lara/
Elevator Contractor/Service	https://aca3.accela.com/lara/
Flight School	www.michigan.gov/documents/aero/Licensed_Flight_Schools_529990_7.pdf
Grain Dealer/Trucker	www.michigan.gov/documents/mda/5_16_11_MI_Licensed_Grain_Dealers_352969_7.pdf
HMO	www.michigan.gov/difs/0,5269,7-303-13251_13262---,00.html
Insurance Adjuster	www.michigan.gov/difs/0,5269,7-303-13251_13262---,00.html
Insurance Agent/Counsel/Solicit/Admin	www.michigan.gov/difs/0,5269,7-303-13251_13262---,00.html
Insurance Counselor/Solicitor	https://difs.state.mi.us/fis/ind_srch/ins_agnt/
Insurance-related Entity	www.michigan.gov/difs/0,5269,7-303-13251_13262---,00.html
Investment Adviser/Firm	www.adviserinfo.sec.gov/
Liquor Dist/Whlse/Mfg	www.michigan.gov/lara/0,4601,7-154-10570_12905---,00.html
Liquor Finance Division	https://www.lara.michigan.gov/llist/
Liquor Hearings & Appeals	https://www.lara.michigan.gov/llist/
Liquor License/Licensing Director	https://www.lara.michigan.gov/llist/
Livestock Dealer	www.michigan.gov/documents/mda/LIVESTOCK_MARKET_LIST_BY_COUNTY_215927_7.pdf
Living Care Facility	www.michigan.gov/documents/cis_ofis_lclist_25541_7.pdf
Loan Originator	http://difs.state.mi.us/fis/ind_srch/ConsumerFinance/

Long Term Care Company	www.michigan.gov/difs/0,5269,7-303-13251_13262---,00.html
Mechanical Construction	https://aca3.accela.com/lara/
Mortgage Licensee	http://difs.state.mi.us/fis/ind_srch/ConsumerFinance/
Motor Vehicle Loan Seller/Financer	http://difs.state.mi.us/fis/ind_srch/ConsumerFinance/
Nursery Dealer/Grower	www.michigan.gov/mdard/0,4610,7-125-1569_2459-13069--,00.html
Pesticide Application Business	www.michigan.gov/mdard/0,4610,7-125-1569_2459-11993--,00.html
Plumber	https://aca3.accela.com/lara/
Potato Dealer	www.michigan.gov/documents/mdard/MILicensedWholesalePotatoDealersList_5-12_385840_7.pdf
Premium Finance Company	http://difs.state.mi.us/fis/ind_srch/ConsumerFinance/
Pump Installer	www.michigan.gov/documents/deq/deq-dwrpd-gws-wcu-Reg-Contractors-By-County_215316_7.pdf
Savings Bank	http://difs.state.mi.us/fis/ind_srch/cht_bank/
Surety Company	www.michigan.gov/difs/0,5269,7-303-13251_13262---,00.html
Surplus Line Broker	www.michigan.gov/difs/0,5269,7-303-13251_13262---,00.html
Teacher	https://mdoe.state.mi.us/MOECS/PublicCredentialSearch.aspx
Third-Party Administrator	www.michigan.gov/difs/0,5269,7-303-13251_13262---,00.html
Weights & Measures Person/Agency	www.michigan.gov/mdard/0,4610,7-125-1569_2459-66367--,00.html
Well Contractor	www.michigan.gov/documents/deq/deq-dwrpd-gws-wcu-Reg-Contractors-By-County_215316_7.pdf

State and Local Courts

About Michigan Courts: The **Circuit Court** is the court of general jurisdiction. In general, the Circuit Court handles all civil cases with claims of more than $25,000 and all felony criminal cases (cases where the accused, if found guilty, could be sent to prison). The **Family Division** of Circuit Court handles all cases regarding divorce, paternity, adoptions, personal protection actions, emancipation of minors, treatment and testing of infectious disease, safe delivery of newborns, name changes, juvenile offenses, and child abuse and neglect. In addition, the Circuit Court hears cases appealed from the other trial courts or from administrative agencies.

The **District Court** handles most traffic violations, civil cases with claims up to $25,000, landlord-tenant matters, most traffic tickets, and all misdemeanor criminal cases (generally, cases where the guilty, cannot be sentenced to more than one year in jail). Small claims cases are heard by a division of the District Court.

Four municipalities have chosen to retain a **Municipal Court** rather than create a District Court. These Municipal Courts have limitations (Civil limit is $3,000). The **Probate Court** handles wills, administers estates and trusts, appoints guardians and conservators, and orders treatment for mentally ill and developmentally disabled persons. There is a **Court of Claims** in Lansing that is a function of the Michigan Court of Appeals with jurisdiction over claims against the state of Michigan.

The web page for the Judicial System is http://courts.mi.gov/Pages/default.aspx/

Appellate Courts: Court of Appeals opinions are free online to view at http://courts.mi.gov/opinions_orders/Pages/default.aspx. Subscribe to free email updates of appellate opinions at http://courts.mi.gov/opinions_orders/subscribe-to-opinions-and-orders/pages/default.aspx.

Online Court Access

There is no statewide program offered for online access. However there are at least 50 local courts with online access. Several counties (Barry, Berrien, Iron, Isabella, Lake, and Washtenaw) plus courts in the 46th Judicial Circuit are participating in a *Demonstration Pilot* project designed to streamline court services and consolidate case management. Note that these courts may refer to themselves as County Trial Courts.

County Sites:
Alpena County
26th Circuit Court   www.alpenacounty.org/circuit%20court.html
Civil: There is online access to public case information at https://records.alpenacounty.org/. Cases may be searched and cross-referenced by case number, party name, judge, prosecutor and/or attorney of record.   *Criminal:* same

Antrim County
13th Circuit Court   www.13thcircuitcourt.org/149/13th-Circuit-Court
Civil: Access to a record index is at http://online.co.grand-traverse.mi.us/iprod/clerk/cccivil.html.   *Criminal:* Access to criminal record index is found at http://online.co.grand-traverse.mi.us/iprod/clerk/cccriminal.html.

86th District Court   www.co.grand-traverse.mi.us/304/86th-District-Court
Civil: Access to a list of cases is found at http://districtcourt.co.grand-traverse.mi.us/c86_cases/.   *Criminal:* same

Barry County
5th Circuit Court   www.barrycounty.org/depts/courts/circuit/
Civil: A free search of the civil and family docket is at https://webinquiry.courts.michigan.gov/WISearch/Search?Name=C05.   *Criminal:* same

Bay County
18th Circuit Court   www.baycountycourts.com/
Access the county courts' open case records for free at home page or at http://12.221.137.17/c74/c74_cases.php. Calendar of scheduled cases at http://12.221.137.17/c74/c74_calendar.php.   *Criminal:* same

74th District Court   www.baycountycourts.com/
Civil: Access the county courts' open case records for free at home page or at http://12.221.137.17/c74/c74_cases.php. Calendar of scheduled cases at http://12.221.137.17/c74/c74_calendar.php.   *Criminal:* Same

Berrien County
County Trial Court - 2nd Circuit Level   www.berriencounty.org
Civil: A free search of the civil and family docket is at https://webinquiry.courts.michigan.gov/WIGroups/Agree?Name=BERRIEN.

Calhoun County
10th District Court   https://www.calhouncountymi.gov/government/district_court/
Civil: A Register of Actions look-up is at www.calhouncountymi.gov/government/district_court/register_of_actions_lookup/. The DOB may show on the detail pages. A daily docket schedule is found at www.calhouncountymi.gov/government/district_court/daily_docket_schedule/.   *Criminal:* same

Cheboygan County
89th District Court   www.cheboygancounty.net/89th-district-court-78/
Civil: Court dispositions are searchable at http://24.236.154.154:81/c89_cases/. Calendars are at the home page.   *Criminal:* Court dispositions are searchable at http://216.109.207.51:81/c89_cases/. Calendars are at the home page. Traffic is included.

Clinton County
29th Circuit Court   https://www.clinton-county.org/304/Circuit-Court
Civil: Free search of the docket is at http://webinquiry.courts.michigan.gov/WIGroups/Agree?Name=C29. Search by name or case number.   *Criminal:* same

65th District Court   https://www.clinton-county.org/149/65A-District-Court
Civil: Free search of the Register of Actions (docket) is at https://www.clinton-county.org/496/Court-Case-Inquiry. A court schedule inuiry is also available from this site.   *Criminal:* Free search of the Register of Actions (docket) is at https://www.clinton-county.org/496/Court-Case-Inquiryx.

Crawford County
46th Circuit Court   www.Circuit46.org
Civil: Online access to court case records is limited (closed cases for 90 days only) and free at www.circuit46.org/Crawford/c46c_cases.php.   *Criminal:* same. Case information is not applicable for background checks.

87C District Court   www.Circuit46.org
Civil: Online access to a limited index of records at www.circuit46.org/Crawford/c46c_cases.php. Search results show case number.   *Criminal:* same. Case information is not applicable for background checks.

Eaton County
56th Circuit Court   www.eatoncounty.org/departments/circuit-court-clerk
Civil: A free searchof the civil docket is at https://webinquiry.courts.michigan.gov/WISearch/Search?Name=C56. Divorce judgments are also searchable. *Criminal:* A free search of the criminal docket is at https://webinquiry.courts.michigan.gov/WISearch/Search?Name=C56.

Genesee County
7th Circuit Court   www.gc4me.com/departments/circuit_court_7th/index.php
Civil: Online access to court records is free at www.gc4me.com/departments/circuit_court_7th/online_records.php.   *Criminal:* same

67th District Court - Central Court - Flint   www.gc4me.com/departments/district_court/index/index.php
Civil: Online access to court records is free, but two sites must be searched. For records prior to 8-1-2014 see www.co.genesee.mi.us/cgi-bin/gweb.exe?mode=7800&sessionname=genpool. For records 8-1-2014 and forward see www.co.genesee.mi.us/roawebinq/default.aspx.   *Criminal:* same

Grand Traverse County

13th Circuit Court   www.co.grand-traverse.mi.us/149/13th-Circuit-Court
Civil: Search civil records free at http://online.co.grand-traverse.mi.us/iprod/clerk/cccivil.html. 1964 through 1985 contain only index information. 1986 to present include case information and register of actions. Database updated nightly.   *Criminal:* Access to a record index is found at http://online.co.grand-traverse.mi.us/iprod/clerk/cccriminal.html.

86th District Court   www.co.grand-traverse.mi.us/304/86th-District-Court
Civil: Access to a list of cases is found at http://districtcourt.co.grand-traverse.mi.us/c86_cases/. A second site is at http://online.co.grand-traverse.mi.us/iprod/clerk/cccivil.html   *Criminal:* same

Gratiot County

29th Circuit Court   www.gratiotmi.com/Law-Justice/29th-Circuit-Court
Civil: A free search of the civil and family docket is at https://webinquiry.courts.michigan.gov/WIGroups/Agree?Name=C29_G . *Criminal:* same. Case information is not applicable for background checks.

Ingham County

30th Circuit Court - Lansing   http://cc.ingham.org/
Civil: Access court docket records and schedules at https://courts.ingham.org/. Records go back to 1986 for both civil and probate. Search by name and case number. At one time a fee was charged, but the fee has been waived.   *Criminal:* Access court docket records and schedules at https://courts.ingham.org/. However, the full DOB must be presented in the search for either criminal or traffic cases. Records date back to 1986. At one time a fee was charged, but the fee has been waived.

54 A District Court - Lansing   www.lansingmi.gov/District_Court
Civil: The court has a link to online records at https://secure.courts.michigan.gov/jis/, Records go back to 2009.   *Criminal:* same

54 B District Court - East Lansing   www.cityofeastlansing.com/676/54B-District-Court
Civil: The docket index is searchable at www.cityofeastlansing.com/681/Court-Case-Lookup. General Civil, Small Claims, and Landlord/tenant can be searched by name.   *Criminal:* Same. Includes landlord/tenant actions.

55th District Court - Mason   http://dc.ingham.org/
Civil: Search by name or case number free at https://secure.courts.michigan.gov/jis/?court=MASON. Records back to 2009 at https://secure.courts.michigan.gov/jis/?court=MASON.   *Criminal:* same

Jackson County

4th Circuit Court   www.co.jackson.mi.us/county_courts/CNP.asp
Civil: Access court records free at http://173.241.216.100/c12/c12_cases.php.   *Criminal:* same

12th District Court   www.d12.com/county_courts/d12/index.asp
Civil: Access court records free at www.d12.com/county_courts/d12/court_records.asp.   *Criminal:* same

Kalkaska County

46th Circuit Court   www.circuit46.org/Kalkaska/c46k_home.html
Civil: Online access to court case records (open or closed cases for 90 days only) is free at www.circuit46.org/Kalkaska/c46k_cases.php.   *Criminal:* same

87-B District Court   www.Circuit46.org
Civil: Online access to limited index of court records is free at www.circuit46.org/Kalkaska/c46k_cases.php.   *Criminal:* same

Kent County

17th Circuit Court - Grand Rapids   https://www.accesskent.com/Courts/17thcc/default.htm
Civil: Search for $6.00 per name at https://www.accesskent.com/CourtNameSearch/. DOB not required but credit card is for record found. Also, search hearings schedule free at https://www.accesskent.com/CCHearing/   *Criminal:* Search for $6.00 per name at https://www.accesskent.com/CourtNameSearch/. DOB and credit card required for results. Also, search for accident reports at $3.00 per name at https://www.accesskent.com/AccidentReports/

61st District Court - Grand Rapids   https://www.grcourt.org/
Civil: Axccess the docket index at https://records.grcourt.org/fullcourtweb/start.do.   *Criminal:* Search at https://records.grcourt.org/fullcourtweb/start.do. The information for case dates that begin in 1996 and end in 1999 is limited to a judgment of sentence or register of actions for criminal and traffic codes only.

Leelanau County

13th Circuit Court - Suttons Bay   www.leelanau.cc/courts.asp
Civil: Access to a record index is at http://online.co.grand-traverse.mi.us/iprod/clerk/cccivil.html . Family court records also included. Search by name or case number.   *Criminal:* Access to a record index is found at http://online.co.grand-traverse.mi.us/iprod/clerk/cccriminal.html. Search by name or case number to 1981.

86th District Court - Leland   www.co.grand-traverse.mi.us/304/86th-District-Court

Civil: Access to a list of cases is found at http://districtcourt.co.grand-traverse.mi.us/c86_cases/. DOB is shown. A second site is at http://online.co.grand-traverse.mi.us/iprod/clerk/cccivil.html   *Criminal:* same

Livingston County
44th Circuit Court - Howell   https://www.livgov.com/courts/circuit/clerk/Pages/default.aspx
Civil: Access civil name index and abbreviated case summary online free or by more detailed data subscription at https://www.livingstonlive.org/CourtRecordValidation/. The subscription fee is $6.00 for the verification and $2.50 for an abbreviated summary. Search cases for the 53rd District, 44th Circuit Court, Juvenile & Family Courts. *Criminal:* Access criminal name index and abbreviated case summary back to 1997 free or more detailed by subscription at https://www.livingstonlive.org/CourtRecordValidation/; a DOB is required to search. The subscription fee is $6.00 for the verification and $2.50 for an abbreviated summary.
53 District Court - Howell   https://www.livgov.com/courts/district/Pages/default.aspx
Civil: Access civil records after registration or by subscription at https://www.livingstonlive.org/CourtRecordValidation/. $6.00 fee for each name and court searched; $2.50 for each summary or case history. Search cases for the 53rd District, 44th Circuit Court, Juvenile & Family Courts. *Criminal:* Access criminal records back to 1997 after registration or by subscription at https://www.livingstonlive.org/CourtRecordValidation/ but a DOB is required to search on the free access. $6.00 fee for each name and court searched; $2.50 for each summary or case history.
53 B District Court - Brighton   https://www.livgov.com/courts/district/Pages/default.aspx
Civil: Access civil records after registration using a credit card or by subscription at https://www.livingstonlive.org/CourtRecordValidation/. Search cases for the 53rd District, 44th Circuit Court, Juvenile & Family Courts.   *Criminal:* Access criminal records back to 1997 after registration using a credit card or by subscription at https://www.livingstonlive.org/CourtRecordValidation/ but a DOB is required to search on the free access.

Macomb County
16th Circuit Court - Mt Clemens   http://circuitcourt.macombgov.org/
Civil: Access Circuit Court index for free at http://courtpa.macombgov.org/eservices/home.page.2. From this site one may order document copies. Document images, addresses, SSNs, and phone numbers are not available. Probate records are also available.   *Criminal:* same

Marquette County
25th Circuit Court - Marquette   www.co.marquette.mi.us/departments/courts/circuit_court/index.php#
Civil: The county partners with a vendor to provide docket entries, name searches, divorce judgments for a fee at http://orders.paymentsolutions.lexisnexis.com/mi/marquetteco/. *Criminal:* The county partners with a vendor to provide docket entries and name searches for a fee at http://orders.paymentsolutions.lexisnexis.com/mi/marquetteco/.

Midland County
42nd Circuit Court   https://co.midland.mi.us/Courts/42ndCircuitCourt.aspx
Civil: Public case information is available at https://mcc.co.midland.mi.us/. Search by party name, attorney, or case code. Court calendars are shown at https://co.midland.mi.us/Courts/CourtCalendar.aspx.   *Criminal:* Public case information is available at https://mcc.co.midland.mi.us/. Search by party name, attorney, or case code. Court calendars are shown at https://co.midland.mi.us/Courts/CourtCalendar.aspx.

Muskegon County
14th Circuit Court   www.co.muskegon.mi.us/circuitcourt/
Civil: There is a subscription based online record search at https://www.muskegongov.org/MCCircuitSearch/. The fee for each name searched is $6.00 and $2.50 for each Register of Action viewed. *Criminal:* same

Oakland County
6th Circuit Court   https://www.oakgov.com/courts/circuit/Pages/default.aspx
Civil: Register of Actions free at https://www.oakgov.com/clerkrod/pages/courtexplorer.aspx. Order document copies online, note there is an additional enhanced access fee starting at $2.50, and can be higher with more volume. *Criminal: Criminal:* same
52nd District Court - All Divisions -   https://www.oakgov.com/courts/dc52div1/Pages/default.aspx
Civil: This court recently converted to a new Case Management System with online access. Civil records prior to 2011 may not be available online. See https://secure.courts.michigan.gov/jis/.   *Criminal:* same

Otsego County
46th Circuit Trial Court - District Court   www.circuit46.org/Otsego/c46g_home.html
Civil: Online access to limited index (generally only open cases) is free at www.circuit46.org/Otsego/c46g_cases.php.   *Criminal:* Access to online limited index (generally only open cases) is free at www.circuit46.org/Otsego/c46g_cases.php There are limitations, this system is not meant to be used for background checks, it is supplemental only.

Ottawa County
20th Circuit Court - Grand Haven   www.miottawa.org/Courts/20thcircuit/
Civil: A fee-service is offered at https://www.miottawa.org/CourtRecordLookup/. One may set-up an account. Search by name or case numbers. The search includes the 20th Circuit Court and 58th District Court. There is a $12.00 cost for each name searched and a $2.50 cost for each case history or summary viewed. *Criminal:* A fee-service is offered at https://www.miottawa.org/CourtRecordLookup/. One may set-up an account. Search by name or case numbers. Includes traffic. The search includes the 20th Circuit Court and 58th District Court.

58th District Court - Hudsonville   www.miottawa.org/Courts/58thDistrict/
Civil: A fee-service is offered at https://www.miottawa.org/CourtRecordLookup/. One may set-up an account. Search by name or case numbers. There is a $12 cost for each name searched and a $2.50 cost for each case history or summary viewed.   *Criminal:* A fee-service is offered at https://www.miottawa.org/CourtRecordLookup/. One may set-up an account. Search by name or case numbers. Includes traffic.

58th District Court - Holland   www.miottawa.org/Courts/58thDistrict/
Civil: A fee-service is offered at https://www.miottawa.org/CourtRecordLookup/. One may set-up an account. Search by name or case numbers. The search includes the 20th Circuit Court and 58th District Court. There is a $12.00 cost for each name searched and a $2.50 cost for each case history or summary viewed. One may download 4 months of case information for $.04 a record, see https://www.miottawa.org/DistrictCaseExtract/.   *Criminal:* A fee-service is offered at https://www.miottawa.org/CourtRecordLookup/. One may set-up an account. Search by name or case numbers. Includes traffic. The search includes the 20th Circuit Court and 58th District Court. There is a $12.00 cost for each name searched and a $2.50 cost for each case history or summary viewed.

58th District Court - Grand Haven   www.miottawa.org/Courts/58thDistrict/
Civil: A fee-service is offered at https://www.miottawa.org/CourtRecordLookup/. One may set-up an account. Search by name or case numbers. There is a $12.00 cost for each name searched and a $2.50 cost for each case history or summary viewed.   *Criminal:* A fee-service is offered at https://www.miottawa.org/CourtRecordLookup/. One may set-up an account. Search by name or case numbers. Includes traffic.

Saginaw County

10th Circuit Court   www.saginawcounty.com/CircuitCourt.aspx?AspxAutoDetectCookieSupport=1
Civil: Search civil records from 2000 forward online free at www.saginawcounty.com/Apps/ClerkSearches/CircuitCivilSearch.aspx.   *Criminal:* Search criminal records online free at www.saginawcounty.com/Apps/ClerkSearches/CircuitCriminalSearch.aspx. Records shown are from 2000 to present.

St. Clair County

31st Circuit Court   www.stclaircounty.org/Offices/courts/
Civil: A index of records can be viewed at www.stclaircounty.org/Offices/courts/circuit/Default.aspx.   *Criminal:* Records index can be viewed at www.stclaircounty.org/Offices/courts/circuit/Default.aspx.

72nd District Court - Port Huron & Marine City   www.stclaircounty.org/Offices/courts/
Civil: Access court case index free at www.stclaircounty.org/DCS/search.aspx.   *Criminal:* same

Van Buren County

36th Circuit Court - Paw Paw   www.vbco.org/vbcfoc.asp
Civil: A free search of the civil and family docket is at https://webinquiry.courts.michigan.gov/WIGroups/Agree?Name=C36.

Washtenaw County

22nd Circuit Court - Ann Arbor   www.washtenawtrialcourt.org
Civil: Access to civil case indexes for free at https://tcweb.ewashtenaw.org/PublicAccess/default.aspx.   *Criminal:* Access to criminal case indexes for free at https://tcweb.ewashtenaw.org/PublicAccess/default.aspx.

15th District Court - Criminal Division - Ann Arbor   www.a2gov.org/departments/15D/Pages/default.aspx
Criminal: Access court records free at www.a2gov.org/departments/15D/online-services/Pages/Case-Search.aspx. Includes cases files on or after 08/05/2006. Older cases are found at https://secure.a2gov.org/15darchive/login.asp. A search of current dockets is at www.a2gov.org/departments/15D/online-services/Pages/Docket-Search.aspx.

15th District Court - Civil Division - Ann Arbor   www.a2gov.org/departments/15D/Pages/default.aspx
Civil: Access court records free at www.a2gov.org/departments/15D/online-services/Pages/Case-Search.aspx. Includes cases filed on or after 08/05/2006. Older cases available at https://secure.a2gov.org/15darchive/login.asp.

14A - District Court - Ann Arbor   http://14adistrictcourt.org/locations/
Civil: Online access to the docket index is at https://secure.courts.michigan.gov/jis/?court=WashtenawAnnArbor. Dockets and calendars are searchable at www.14adistrictcourt.org/cases.   *Criminal:* same

14A-2 District Court - Ypsilanti   http://14adistrictcourt.org/locations/14a-2
Civil: Current dockets and calendars only are searchable online at www.14adistrictcourt.org/cases.   *Criminal:* same

14A-3 District Court - Chelsea   http://14adistrictcourt.org/locations/14a-3
Civil: Dockets and calendars are searchable at www.14adistrictcourt.org/cases.   *Criminal:* same

14A-4 District Court - Saline   http://14adistrictcourt.org
Civil: Dockets and calendars are searchable at www.14adistrictcourt.org/cases.   *Criminal:* same

Wayne County

3rd Circuit Court -Detroit   https://www.3rdcc.org/
Civil: Free access to the docket index at https://www.3rdcc.org/OPA.aspx. *Criminal:* same
23rd District Court-Taylor   www.cityoftaylor.com/court
Civil: Name searching of the docket is free at https://secure.courts.michigan.gov/jis/?court=TAYLOR.   *Criminal:* same

29th District Court-Wayne   www.ci.wayne.mi.us/index.php/29th-district-court

Civil: Name searches available at https://secure.courts.michigan.gov/jis/?court=wayne. This site is just for the 29th District. *Criminal:* Name searches available at https://secure.courts.michigan.gov/jis/?court=wayne. This site is just for the 29th District.

33rd District Court-Woodhaven www.d33.courts.mi.gov/
Civil: Docket information is offered at www.d33.courts.mi.gov/jisdocket/Default.aspx, searchable by name. attorney, judge or case number. Also, search the Register of Action by name or case number at www.d33.courts.mi.gov/JISROA/Default.aspx. *Criminal:* same

Recorders, Assessors, and Other Sites of Note

About Michigan Recording Offices: 83 counties, 83 recording offices. The recording officer is the County Register of Deeds.

About Tax Liens: Federal and state tax liens on personal property of businesses are filed with the Secretary of State. Other federal and state tax liens are filed with the Register of Deeds. Note that a Notice of State Tax Lien is a legal instrument sent to the debtor by the state. After a period of 35 days if the debt is unpaid, then the lien is filed at the county level.

Online Access

Recorded Documents

There is no statewide online access to recorded documents, but a number of counties offer free access.

Property Ownership and Tax Assessor Data

There are a number of sites that offer access to property information.

The site at www.dleg.state.mi.us/platmaps/sr_subs.asp maintained by the Dept. of Licensing and Regulatroy Affairs provides free access to digital images - with print capability - of the plats and related documents of land subdivisions in the State of Michigan's construction plat files. Search by location or subdivision. Covers all 83 counties.

Access local property record data from over 794 Michigan jurisdictions (towns, townships, cities, etc.) at a vendor site: https://is.bsasoftware.com/bsa.is/SelectUnit.aspx. See the vendor site for the complete list of jurisdiction and when last updated. The index search is free for most locations. Tax information searches may also be available. Some units charge a small convenience fee to view records. A business account allows the user to perform lookups without paying up-front; monthly billing is available.

County Sites:

Alcona County *Recorded Land Documents* http://alconacountymi.com/?page_id=390 To access land records for a fee at https://mi.uslandrecords.com/milr/MilrApp/index.jsp. Land records from 1980 to present.
Property, Taxation Records Access to property tax search for free at http://alcona.mi.govern.com/.

Allegan County *Property, Taxation Records* Search index by name or address at https://is.bsasoftware.com/bsa.is/SelectUnit.aspx, includes 10 local cities or townships, 2 are fee based.

Alpena County *Property, Taxation Records* Access to delinquent tax records for free at https://www.accessmygov.com/Home/Index?uid=1940. Search index by name or address at https://is.bsasoftware.com/bsa.is/SelectUnit.aspx, includes 4 local cities or townships, 3 are fee based.

Antrim County *Recorded Documents* www.antrimcounty.org/registerofdeeds.asp Access to land records for a fee at https://mi.uslandrecords.com/milr/MilrApp/index.jsp. Records from 1/1/93 to present. The county works with https://tapestry.fidlar.com/Tapestry2/Default.aspx for record access. Base fee is $5.95 per search and $.50 per print image. You can pay as you go using a credit or pre-pay using a subscription. Also, one may purchase a software program Laredo (www.fidlar.com/lardao.aspx) with extensive search features. Contact the county for details and pricing.
Property, Taxation Records Search parcel data information free at www.antrimcounty.org/parcel_search.asp. Also, search index by name or address at https://is.bsasoftware.com/bsa.is/SelectUnit.aspx, includes 10 local cities or townships, 7 are fee based.

Arenac County *Recorded Documents* www.arenaccountygov.com/register_of_deeds/ Access to public records available at https://rodweb.arenaccountygov.com/LandShark/login.jsp? User name and password are both PUBLIC, please remember this is case sensitive.
Property, Taxation Records Access to property searches and county maps for free at www.arenaccountygov.com/arenac_county_maps/. Also, search index by name or address at https://is.bsasoftware.com/bsa.is/SelectUnit.aspx, includes 2 local townships, 1 is fee based.

Baraga County *Property, Taxation Records* Search index by name or address at https://is.bsasoftware.com/bsa.is/SelectUnit.aspx for a fee.

Barry County *Recorded Documents* www.barrycounty.org/depts/register/ Access recorded Indexes back to 1987 free at https://internal.barrycounty.org:8443/recorder/web/. Images from 8/1/87 to present (and being added). Also, search Vital Records data free at http://internal.barrycounty.org:8081/clerk/web/. Also The Register of Deeds has images available from 1973 (or book 364) on the computer system. These documents are not indexed yet, so can only be retrieved by the book and page number. Documents are currently indexed back to February 1988.
Property, Taxation Records Access to county parcel data is free at http://barryco.readyhosting.com/xsea.asp. County property Index is from 12/95 to 12/2005; assessment rolls should not be used for a title search or legal description. Also, search index by name or address at https://is.bsasoftware.com/bsa.is/SelectUnit.aspx, includes 13 local townships, all are fee based.

Bay County *Recorded Documents* www.baycounty-mi.gov/ROD/ Access the register's land records data after registration, login with username and password at www.baycounty-mi.gov/ROD/. Index goes back to 1976; images now available with copy cost and $5.00 login fee.
Property, Taxation Records Search index by name or address at https://is.bsasoftware.com/bsa.is/SelectUnit.aspx, includes 15 local cities or townships, 12 are fee based.

Benzie County *Recorded Documents* www.benzieco.net/government/county_register_of_deeds/index.php T The county works with https://tapestry.fidlar.com/Tapestry2/Default.aspx for record access. Base fee is $5.95 per search and $.50 per print image. You can pay as you go using a credit or pre-pay using a subscription. Also, one may purchase a software program Laredo (www.fidlar.com/lardao.aspx) with extensive search features. Contact the county for details and pricing. Also, access to land records search for free at http://deeds-srv1.benzieco.net/DirectSearch/Default.aspx.
Property, Taxation Records Access to parcel search and mapping for free at http://rs1.liaa.org/benzieco/. Also, search index by name or address at https://is.bsasoftware.com/bsa.is/SelectUnit.aspx, includes 4 local cities or townships. All are fee based.

Berrien County *Recorded Documents* http://berriencounty.org/RegisterofDeeds Access to records from register of deeds at https://regofdeeds.berriencounty.org/countyweb/login.do?countyname=BerrienDeeds. Indices are available for free, printing any image is $1.00 per page and a $5.00 credit card/IT handling fee. Images for Deeds and Miscellaneous records are from 1950 forward, images for all records exist from 1967 forward. After accessing the site, click on 'Login as Guest' and then 'Search Public Records.' Images will initially appear with a black block across the image, but the image will print cleanly when payment verification is received.
Property, Taxation Records Access to information on real estate properties, see http://berriencounty.org/inside.php?action=property_listing_search&dept=8. GIS data is at https://beacon.schneidercorp.com/. Search index by name or address at https://is.bsasoftware.com/bsa.is/SelectUnit.aspx, includes 44 local cities or townships, 5 are fee based.

Branch County *Real Estate, Deed, Liens* www.countyofbranch.com/departments/26 The county works with https://tapestry.fidlar.com/Tapestry2/Default.aspx for record access. Base fee is $5.95 per search and $.50 per print image. You can pay as you go using a credit or pre-pay using a subscription. Also, one may purchase a software program Laredo (www.fidlar.com/lardao.aspx) with extensive search features. Contact the county for details and pricing.
Property, Taxation Records Search index by name or address at https://is.bsasoftware.com/bsa.is/SelectUnit.aspx, includes 4 local cities or townships, 1 is fee based.

Calhoun County *Real Estate, Grantor/Grantee, Deed, Liens* www.co.calhoun.mi.us/ Access the recorder's Land Records Index free back to 1/3/1966 at https://rod.co.calhoun.mi.us/indexsearch.html. Guests: May search the index free of charge and purchase PDF copies of documents via credit card at a cost of $1.00 per page. There is an add'l online transaction fee of $5.00 per order.
Property, Taxation Records Search index by name or address at https://is.bsasoftware.com/bsa.is/SelectUnit.aspx, includes 22 local cities or townships, 11 are fee based.

Cass County *Property, Taxation Records* Access county property tax records free at www.cass.mi.govern.com/parcelquery.php. Also, search index by name or address at https://is.bsasoftware.com/bsa.is/SelectUnit.aspx, includes 4 local cities or townships, all are fee based.

Charlevoix County *Recorded Documents* www.charlevoixcounty.org/register_of_deeds/index.php Access to online records for a fee at http://198.108.193.197/recorder/web/. Images are purchased on a document by document basis. Copy fees are $1.05 per page plus a $.30 per CART transaction fee..
Property, Taxation Records Access the assessor's basic property data or property tax payment free at http://charlevoixcountymi.documents-on-demand.com/. Also, search index by name or address at https://is.bsasoftware.com/bsa.is/SelectUnit.aspx, includes 9 local cities or townships, 6 are fee based.

Cheboygan County *Recorded Documents* www.cheboygancounty.net/county-clerkregister-of-deeds-11/ Access to land record index for free at https://clerk.cheboygancounty.net:4430/landweb.dll/$/. Fee to print documents $10.00 per page plus $5.00 access fee (payable by credit card). Indexes available from 1/2/1935 to present.
Property, Taxation Records Search index by name or address at https://is.bsasoftware.com/bsa.is/SelectUnit.aspx, includes 2 local townships, both are fee based. Also, Access to GIS/mapping free at www.cheboygancounty.net/equalization-97/#sect-972.

Chippewa County *Recorded Documents* www.chippewacountymi.gov/rod.html Access to limited records index free at www.chippewacountymi.gov/rod_online_searching.html. Indexes available from 1/1/1950 to present. No online viewing of documents available.
Property, Taxation Records Access to parcel records for free at http://mi-chippewa-equalization.governmax.com/collectmax/collect30.asp. Also, search index by name or address at https://is.bsasoftware.com/bsa.is/SelectUnit.aspx, includes 1 local city that is fee based.

Clare County   *Property, Taxation Records*   Search index by name or address at https://is.bsasoftware.com/bsa.is/SelectUnit.aspx, includes 9 local cities or townships, 8 are fee based.

Clinton County   *Recorded Documents*   https://www.clinton-county.org/218/Register-of-Deeds   Register to search free on the recorders database at https://www.clinton-county.org/278/Deeds-Index-Search. Username & password is required. Copies of documents online can be purchased with a credit card. Rate depends on the number of pages purchased.
Property, Taxation Records   Search index by name or address at https://is.bsasoftware.com/bsa.is/SelectUnit.aspx, includes 16 local cities or townships, 9 are fee based.

Crawford County   *Recorded Documents*   www.crawfordco.org/deeds/deeds.htm   Access to the online services for free at http://recording.crawfordco.org/recorder/web/. Must register to search records, view images and purchase copies.
Property, Taxation Records   Search index by name or address at https://is.bsasoftware.com/bsa.is/SelectUnit.aspx, includes 5 local cities or townships, all are fee based.

Delta County   *Property, Taxation Records*   Search index by name or address at https://is.bsasoftware.com/bsa.is/SelectUnit.aspx, includes 3 local cities or townships, 2 are fee based. Also, access to mapping for free at http://deltacounty.geoquickserver.com/.

Dickinson County   *Property, Taxation Records*   Search index by name or address at https://is.bsasoftware.com/bsa.is/SelectUnit.aspx, includes 3 local cities or townships, all are fee based.

Eaton County   *Recorded Documents*   www.eatoncounty.org/index.php/departments/register-of-deeds   Access to records free at https://countyfusion3.propertyinfo.com/countyweb/login.do?countyname=Eaton. No fee to access index (under login as guest), however to view images and print images must open account and pay. Copy fees are $1.00 per page; there is also an add'l fee of $1.00 per transaction (not per document) to use this option.
Property, Taxation Records   Search index by name or address at https://is.bsasoftware.com/bsa.is/SelectUnit.aspx, includes 13 local cities or townships, 8 are fee based.

Emmet County   *Recorded Documents*   www.emmetcounty.org/officials-departments/register-of-deeds/free-online-records-search/   Access recorder land records for free, log-in as Public User at http://apps1.emmetcounty.org:8080/Recorder/web/. Must register for log-in and password before use. Also, full online access to view and print images is available for $1.03 per page, payable via credit card/PayPal.
Property, Taxation Records   Search index by name or address at https://is.bsasoftware.com/bsa.is/SelectUnit.aspx, includes 3 local cities or townships, all are non-fee based.

Genesee County   *Recorded Documents*   www.gc4me.com/departments/register_of_deeds/index/index.php   Access to records for free at https://www.co.genesee.mi.us/pax/. Must purchase copies and can do that through PayPal. Record index data through 3/28/13. Also, online access to the county clerk's marriage (back to 1963) and death (back to 1930) indexes are free at www.co.genesee.mi.us/vitalrec/.
Property, Taxation Records   Search property index at www.co.genesee.mi.us/tax/tax.html. Also, search index by name or address at https://is.bsasoftware.com/bsa.is/SelectUnit.aspx, includes 24 local cities or townships. 12 are fee based.

Gladwin County   *Recorded Documents*   www.gladwinco.com/Departments/RegisterofDeeds.aspx   Access to index of records for a fee at https://www.idocmarket.com/Subscription/Subscribe?county=GladwinMI. Indexes back to 12/11/1875; images from 1/1/1952 to present.
Property, Taxation Records   Search index by name or address at https://is.bsasoftware.com/bsa.is/SelectUnit.aspx, includes 3 local cities or townships, 2 are fee based. Also, access to land records portal for free at https://www.fetchgis.com/gladwinlrp/appauth/GladwinLRP.html.

Gogebic County   *Property, Taxation Records*   Search index by name or address at https://is.bsasoftware.com/bsa.is/SelectUnit.aspx, includes 2 local cities or townships, both are fee based. Also, access to GIS/mapping for free at www.gogebic.org/colman.html.

Grand Traverse County   *Recorded Documents*   www.co.grand-traverse.mi.us/587/Register-of-Deeds-Office   Recorder's document index search back to 1986 is free at http://deeds.co.grand-traverse.mi.us/DirectSearch/default.aspx. Images require fee; pay by credit card. Deaths go back to 1867; marriages to 1853. The county works with https://tapestry.fidlar.com/Tapestry2/Default.aspx for record access. Base fee is $5.95 per search and $.50 per print image. You can pay as you go using a credit or pre-pay using a subscription. Also, one may purchase a software program Laredo (www.fidlar.com/lardao.aspx) with extensive search features. Contact the county for details and pricing.
Property, Taxation Records   Search index by name or address at https://is.bsasoftware.com/bsa.is/SelectUnit.aspx, includes 12 local cities or townships, 8 are fee based. Also, access to parcel information and GIS/mapping for free at www.co.grand-traverse.mi.us/551/Parcel-Information.

Gratiot County   *Recorded Documents*   www.gratiotmi.com/Departments/Register-of-Deeds   Access to land record indexes for free at http://216.111.203.221/landweb.dll/$/. Indexes are available from 1/185 to present. Copies are charged a fee of $1.00 per page. There is an add'l transaction fee of $5.00 per order.
Property, Taxation Records   Free access to GIS/mapping is found at www.fetchgis.com/gratiotweb/rma/GratiotMapViewer.html#. Also, search index by name or address at https://is.bsasoftware.com/bsa.is/SelectUnit.aspx, includes 7 local cities or townships. 5 are fee based.

Hillsdale County   *Recorded Documents*   http://co.hillsdale.mi.us/index.php/deeds   Access to the recorder's index is free. Records go back to 9/1968 and more being added. Subscription fee is $300.00 for recorder, or $50.00 for just the assessor's equalization records. Copies included. Call recorder for signup. The office does allow credit card purchases online in addition to sub. Also, access to recorders index is free via a private firm at https://countyfusion1.propertyinfo.com/countyweb/login.do?countyname=Hillsdale. Search free as Guest. Fees to print images.

Property, Taxation Records   Search parcels free at www.hillsdalecounty.info/parcelsearch.asp, no name searching. Also, search index by name or address at https://is.bsasoftware.com/bsa.is/SelectUnit.aspx, includes 5 local cities or townships. 4 are fee based. Map searching is available at www.hillsdalecounty.info/mapspage0002.asp. See County Register of Deeds section for subscription info for county assessment data.

Houghton County   *Recorded Documents*   www.houghtoncounty.net/directory-register-of-deeds.php   The county works with https://tapestry.fidlar.com/Tapestry2/Default.aspx for record access. Base fee is $5.95 per search and $.50 per print image. You can pay as you go using a credit or pre-pay using a subscription. Also, one may purchase a software program Laredo (www.fidlar.com/lardao.aspx) with extensive search features. Contact the county for details and pricing.

Property, Taxation Records   Search index by name or address at https://is.bsasoftware.com/bsa.is/SelectUnit.aspx, includes 4 local cities or townships. 3 are fee based.

Huron County   *Recorded Documents*   www.co.huron.mi.us/departments_rdeeds.asp   Access to land records for free at http://208.99.238.3/landweb.dll/$/. Indexes from 1/2/1981 to present.

Property, Taxation Records   Also, search index by name or address at https://is.bsasoftware.com/bsa.is/SelectUnit.aspx, includes 4 local cities or townships. All are fee based. Also, access to online assessing and tax search for free at https://www.accessmygov.com/?uid=737.

Ingham County   *Real Estate, Grantor/Grantee, Deed, Marriage, Fictitious Name Records*   http://rd.ingham.org/   Access the Register of Deeds online database for a fee, there are 3 ways to access-1. AVA - https://ava.fidlar.com/michigan/ingham/ava (this information is delayed for 30 days), This is a free search, images are available for $1.10 per page; 2. Tapestry - https://tapestry.fidlar.com/Tapestry2/Default.aspx, Fee is $5.95 per search, copies of images are $1.00 per page; and 3. Laredo - www.fidlar.com/, subscription plan rates plus images are $1.00 per page.

Property, Taxation Records   Also, search index by name or address at https://is.bsasoftware.com/bsa.is/SelectUnit.aspx, includes 21 local cities or townships. 10 are fee based. Also, access to GIS/mapping free at http://ingham-equalization.rsgis.msu.edu/.

Ionia County   *Recorded Documents*   www.ioniacounty.org/register-of-deeds/   Access recorder records free at www.ioniacounty.org/online-services/.

Property, Taxation Records   Access county property data and GIS/mapping free at www.ioniacounty.org/online-services/. Also, search index by name or address at https://is.bsasoftware.com/bsa.is/SelectUnit.aspx, includes 5 local cities or townships, 3 are fee based.

Iosco County   *Recorded Documents*   www.iosco.net/departments/register-of-deeds/   Access to records for a fee at http://rod.ioscocounty.org/landweb.dll/$/. Indexes from 1/2/1979 to present.

Property, Taxation Records   Also, search index by name or address at https://is.bsasoftware.com/bsa.is/SelectUnit.aspx, includes8 local cities or townships, 5 are fee based.

Iron County   *Recorded Documents*   http://ironmi.org/departments/register-of-deeds/   Access to land records for free at www.ironcountyrecords.com/landweb.dll/$/. Indexes are available 1/3/55 to present. Copy fees are $1.00 per page. There is an additional online transaction fee of $5.00 per order.

Property, Taxation Records   Search index by name or address at https://is.bsasoftware.com/bsa.is/SelectUnit.aspx, includes 4 local townships, 3 are fee based.

Isabella County   *Recorded Documents*   www.isabellacounty.org/dept/deeds   Access recorder land data back to 1940 on ACS at https://www.uslandrecords.com/milr/options_073.htm. Fees involved. New free search that gives images. Also, access to deeds 'Super Search' for a fee at www.isabelladeeds.com/.

Property, Taxation Records   Also, search index by name or address at https://is.bsasoftware.com/bsa.is/SelectUnit.aspx, includes 5 local cities or townships, 3 are fee based. Also, access to GIS/mapping for free at www.fetchgis.com/isabellaweb/rma/IsabellaMapViewer.html#.

Jackson County   *Recorded Documents*   www.co.jackson.mi.us/rod/   Search recorded documents for free as a Login as Guest at https://countyfusion3.propertyinfo.com/countyweb/login.do?countyname=Jackson. Must subscribe with a fee for add'l services.

Property, Taxation Records   Search index by name or address at https://is.bsasoftware.com/bsa.is/SelectUnit.aspx, includes 18 local cities or townships, 12 are fee based. Also, search GIS-mapping site for property free at www.co.jackson.mi.us/CountyGIS/index.htm. Search tax sale data free at www.jacksoncountytaxsale.com/index.asp.

Kalamazoo County   *Recorded Deeds, Vital Records Records*   www.kalcounty.com/clerk/index.htm   Access to public records go to https://clerkregister.kalcounty.com:8443/eaglerecorder/web/. The public search allows users to search the index only; images are not available. Once registered, can purchase single documents by credit card for $1.00 per page. Also, a free vital records search available at https://clerkregister.kalcounty.com:8444/eagleclerk/web/login.jsp.

Property, Taxation Records   Access property assessor data free at www.kalcounty.com/equalization/parcel_search.php. Also, search index by name or address at https://is.bsasoftware.com/bsa.is/SelectUnit.aspx, includes 22 local cities or townships, 9 are fee based. Also, access to GIS/mapping at www.kalcounty.com/planning/gis.htm.

Kalkaska County   *Recorded Documents*   www.kalkaskacounty.net/regdeeds.asp   The county works with https://tapestry.fidlar.com/Tapestry2/Default.aspx for record access. Base fee is $5.95 per search and $.50 per print image. You can pay as you go using a credit or pre-pay using a subscription. Also, one may purchase a software program Laredo (www.fidlar.com/lardao.aspx) with extensive search features. Contact the county for details and pricing. Frequent users contact JoAnn DeGraaf for details and monthly subscriptions.

Property, Taxation Records   Access to property search for free at www.kalkaskacounty.net/propertysearch.asp. Also, access to GIS/mapping for free to go www.kalkaskacounty.net/mapindex.asp.

Kent County   *Recorded Documents*   https://www.accesskent.com/Departments/RegisterofDeeds/   Access Kent deeds index for a fee at https://www.accesskent.com/deeds/. Fee for document $2.00 per page plus a $.50 convenience fee. Search and purchase accident reports $13.00 at https://www.accesskent.com/Sheriff/accident.htm.
Property, Taxation Records   Access to property search for free at https://www.accesskent.com/Property/. Also, search index by name or address at https://is.bsasoftware.com/bsa.is/SelectUnit.aspx, includes 31 local cities or townships, 10 are fee based.

Lake County   *Recorded Documents*   www.lakecounty-michigan.com/Courthouse/RegisterofDeeds.aspx   Access to indexes for free at http://lrs.lakecounty-michigan.com/landweb.dll/$/. Indexes available from 1/3/1989 to present. PDF copy fees are $1.00 per page. There is an add'l online transaction fee of $5.00 per order.
Property, Taxation Records   Also, search index by name or address at https://is.bsasoftware.com/bsa.is/SelectUnit.aspx, includes 12 local cities or townships, 2 are fee based.

Lapeer County   *Recorded Documents*   www.lapeercountyweb.org/   Access recorder index free by name by clicking on Guest Login at http://207.72.70.14/. Registration and fees required for full search. Pop-up blocker must be off. No images online. Indexes available from 1/1/1801 thru present.
Property, Taxation Records   Access index by name or address at https://is.bsasoftware.com/bsa.is/SelectUnit.aspx, includes 15 local cities or townships, 11 are fee based.

Leelanau County   *Recorded Documents*   www.leelanau.cc/registerofdeeds.asp   Access the recorders database of indexes free at www.leelanau.cc/rodsearch.asp. Records go back 1/1/1972 but may be subject to errors and omissions. Subscription service for full data and images; $1.25 per page.
Property, Taxation Records   Access assessor property data free at www.leelanau.cc/PropertySearch.asp. Also, search index by name or address at https://is.bsasoftware.com/bsa.is/SelectUnit.aspx, includes 6 local cities or townships. All are fee based.

Lenawee County   *Recorded Documents*   www.lenawee.mi.us/259/Register-of-Deeds   Access recorder records free at https://countyfusion2.propertyinfo.com/countyweb/login.do?countyname=Lenawee. Login as guest for free name search. More detailed must register with fees.
Property, Taxation Records   Also, search index by name or address at https://is.bsasoftware.com/bsa.is/SelectUnit.aspx, includes 7 local cities or townships, 6 are fee based.

Livingston County   *Recorded Documents*   https://www.livgov.com/rod/Pages/default.aspx   Web access to county records occasional users for free; convenience fee schedule is at https://www.livingstonlive.org/html/LCFeeSchedule.html. See https://www.livingstonlive.org/Deeds/. Also, search the county death indices from 1867 to 1948 for free at www.memoriallibrary.com/MI/Livingston/Death/. The county works with https://tapestry.fidlar.com/Tapestry2/Default.aspx for record access. Base fee is $5.95 per search and $.50 per print image. You can pay as you go using a credit or pre-pay using a subscription. Also, one may purchase a software program Laredo (www.fidlar.com/lardao.aspx) with extensive search features. Contact the county for details and pricing.
Property, Taxation Records   Also, search index by name or address at https://is.bsasoftware.com/bsa.is/SelectUnit.aspx, includes 19 local cities or townships, 9 are fee based. Also, access property data for a fee at https://www.livingstonlive.org/Property/.

Luce County   *Property, Taxation Records*   Search index by name or address at https://is.bsasoftware.com/bsa.is/SelectUnit.aspx, includes 2 local cities or townships, 1 is fee based.

Mackinac County   *Property, Taxation Records*   Search index by name or address at https://is.bsasoftware.com/bsa.is/SelectUnit.aspx, includes 1 local city. City of St Ignace is fee based. Also, access to assessing, delinquent tax and tax records for free at https://accessmygov.com/?uid=708.

Macomb County   *Recorded Documents*   http://clerk.macombgov.org/?q=Clerk-ROD   Access recorder land data at https://www.uslandrecords.com/milr/options_073.htm. Fees involved. New search that gives images. Also, county recorder index and images (back to 1818) from a private source at www.courthousedirect.com/. Fees/registration required.
Property, Taxation Records   Search index by name or address at https://is.bsasoftware.com/bsa.is/SelectUnit.aspx, includes 26 local cities or townships, 6 are fee based.

Manistee County   *Recorded Documents*   www.manisteecountymi.gov/index.php?option=com_content&view=article&id=53&Itemid=92   The county works with https://tapestry.fidlar.com/Tapestry2/Default.aspx for record access. Base fee is $5.95 per search and $.50 per print image. You can pay as you go using a credit or pre-pay using a subscription. Also, one may purchase a software program Laredo (www.fidlar.com/lardao.aspx) with extensive search features. Contact the county for details and pricing.. Also, access to land records for free at http://register.manisteecountymi.gov/directsearch/default.aspx.
Property, Taxation Records   Access property records free at www.liaa.org/manisteeparcels/propertysearch.asp. Also, search index by name or address at https://is.bsasoftware.com/bsa.is/SelectUnit.aspx, includes 3 local cities or townships. All are fee based.

Marquette County   *Recorded Documents*   www.co.marquette.mi.us/departments/register_of_deeds/index.php#.U3O2nHYVDVo   The county works with https://tapestry.fidlar.com/Tapestry2/Default.aspx for record access. Base fee is $5.95 per search and $.50 per print image. You can pay

as you go using a credit or pre-pay using a subscription. Also, one may purchase a software program Laredo (www.fidlar.com/lardao.aspx) with extensive search features. Contact the county for details and pricing.

Property, Taxation Records   Access building records free with registration at www.co.marquette.mi.us/departments/building_codes/index.php#.Uw5Ja85tbVo. Also, Access to GIS/mapping free at www.co.marquette.mi.us/departments/equalization_tax_roll/gis_mapping.php#.Uw5I9s5tbVo. Also, search index by name or address at https://is.bsasoftware.com/bsa.is/SelectUnit.aspx, includes 12 local cities or townships. 11 are fee based.

Mason County   *Recorded Documents*   www.masoncounty.net/departments/register-of-deeds/   Search county Register database at http://97.86.80.147/WebSense/Default.aspx. Search this Websense index free; other two require registration and fees. The county works with https://tapestry.fidlar.com/Tapestry2/Default.aspx for record access. Base fee is $5.95 per search and $.50 per print image. You can pay as you go using a credit or pre-pay using a subscription. Also, one may purchase a software program Laredo (www.fidlar.com/lardao.aspx) with extensive search features. Contact the county for details and pricing.

Property, Taxation Records   Access county property data at www.liaa.org/masonparcels/propertysearch.asp. Also, access property tax data and GIS-maps for a fee at www.dnr.state.mi.us/spatialdatalibrary/pdf_maps/topomaps/county_files/mason/mason_topo.htm. Also, search index by name or address at https://is.bsasoftware.com/bsa.is/SelectUnit.aspx, includes 3 local cities or townships. All are non-fee based.

Mecosta County   *Recorded Documents*   www.co.mecosta.mi.us/RegDeeds.html   Access to land records for a fee at https://mi.uslandrecords.com/milr/MilrApp/index.jsp. Records are available from 1968 to present. Also, access to record search for free at www.mecostadeeds.com/.

Property, Taxation Records   Search index by name or address at https://is.bsasoftware.com/bsa.is/SelectUnit.aspx, includes 6 local cities or townships, 4 are fee based.

Menominee County   *Recorded Land Documents Records*   www.menomineecounty.com/departments

Property, Taxation Records   Search index by name or address at https://is.bsasoftware.com/bsa.is/SelectUnit.aspx, includes 5 local cities or townships, 3 are fee based.

Midland County   *Recorded Documents*   https://www.co.midland.mi.us/RegisterofDeeds.aspx   Access to records free at https://webapps.co.midland.mi.us/countyweb/login.do?countyname=Midland. No fee to access index (under login as guest), however to view image thumbnails and print images must open account and pay.

Property, Taxation Records   Search index by name or address free at https://is.bsasoftware.com/bsa.is/SelectUnit.aspx, includes 1 local city. County access via www.co.midland.mi.us/ also includes delinquent tax and animal license data.

Missaukee County   *Property, Taxation Records*   Search index by name or address for free at https://is.bsasoftware.com/bsa.is/SelectUnit.aspx, includes 9 local cities/townships, 8 are fee based.

Monroe County   *Recorded Documents*   www.co.monroe.mi.us/officials_and_departments/officials/register_of_deeds/index.php   The county works with https://tapestry.fidlar.com/Tapestry2/Default.aspx for record access. Base fee is $5.95 per search and $.50 per print image. You can pay as you go using a credit or pre-pay using a subscription. Also, one may purchase a software program Laredo (www.fidlar.com/lardao.aspx) with extensive search features. Contact the county for details and pricing.

Property, Taxation Records   Search index by name or address at https://is.bsasoftware.com/bsa.is/SelectUnit.aspx, includes 22 local cities or townships, 18 are fee based.

Montcalm County   *Recorded Documents*   The county works with https://tapestry.fidlar.com/Tapestry2/Default.aspx for record access. Base fee is $5.95 per search and $.50 per print image. You can pay as you go using a credit or pre-pay using a subscription. Also, one may purchase a software program Laredo (www.fidlar.com/lardao.aspx) with extensive search features. Contact the county for details and pricing.

Property, Taxation Records   Search index by name or address at https://is.bsasoftware.com/bsa.is/SelectUnit.aspx, includes 10 local cities or townships, 9 are fee based.

Montmorency County   *Property, Taxation Records*   To view land records free at https://www.fetchgis.com/montlrp/appauth/MontLRP.html#. To get further information on property must register and pay fees. Also, search index by name of address at https://is.bsasoftware.com/bsa.is/SelectUnit.aspx, includes 2 local townships, both are fee based.

Muskegon County   *Recorded Documents*   www.co.muskegon.mi.us/deeds/   Login as Great, password Muskegon, to search recorder land records free at www.co.muskegon.mi.us/deeds/record_search.htm. Must register, indexes free, to view and print documents for a fee (single documents by credit card-$1.00 per page plus a convenience fee). Also can purchase a monthly subscription.

Property, Taxation Records   Access to the GIS/mapping for free at www.muskegoncountygis.com/. Also, search index by name or address at https://is.bsasoftware.com/bsa.is/SelectUnit.aspx, includes 11 local cities or townships, 9 are fee based. Access the county genealogical death index system for free at www.co.muskegon.mi.us/clerk/websearch.cfm. Records 1867-1965.

Newaygo County   *Recorded Documents*   www.countyofnewaygo.com/RegisterOfDeeds.aspx   Access the county land records search system free at www.countyofnewaygo.com/RODWeb.aspx. Login as Guest. Subscription required for full access, $500 monthly plus $1 per page. Indexes available from 11/27/1854 to present.

Property, Taxation Records   Search property data free on the GIS-mapping site at http://countyofnewaygo.com/GIS.aspx. Also, search index by name or address at https://is.bsasoftware.com/bsa.is/SelectUnit.aspx, includes 15 local cities or townships, 14 are fee based.

Oakland County   *Recorded Documents, Business/Assumed Name Records*   https://www.oakgov.com/clerkrod/Pages/default.aspx
Search fictitious/assumed names for free at https://www.oakgov.com/clerkrod/vital_records/Pages/dba.aspx. Also, access to real property records for a fee at https://www.oakgov.com/clerkrod/rod/Pages/landaccess.aspx. Fees-$6.00 for 1st doc, $1.00 each add'l doc per transaction. Also, access to land records for a fee at https://mi.uslandrecords.com/milr/MilrApp/index.jsp.
Property, Taxation Records   Access to Oakland property data is by subscription, available monthly or per use. For info or sign-up, visit https://www.oakgov.com/accessok/Pages/default.aspx or call Information Services at 248-858-0861. Search Rochester Hills tax assessor data at www.rochesterhills.org/index.aspx?NID=134. Also, search index by name or address at https://is.bsasoftware.com/bsa.is/SelectUnit.aspx, includes 34 local cities or townships, 16 are fee based.

Oceana County   *Recorded Documents*   http://oceana.mi.us/register-of-deeds/   Access the record index for a fee at https://mi.uslandrecords.com/milr/MilrApp/index.jsp. Land records are certified from 1/1/2002 through present. Uncertified from 1/1/1995 through 1/1/2002. If the document number or Liber/Page is known, images are available back to 1/1/1970 by changing the Recorded Date range From date.
Property, Taxation Records   Search index by name or address at https://is.bsasoftware.com/bsa.is/SelectUnit.aspx, includes 10 local cities or townships, 6 are fee based. Also, access property tax data and GIS-maps for a fee at www.liaa.org/oceanaparcels/.

Ogemaw County   *Property, Taxation Records*   Access assessor equalization data free at http://ogemaw.mi.govern.com/parcelquery.php. Also, access property data free at http://ogemawgis.com/parcelquery/website/.

Osceola County   *Property, Taxation Records*   Search index by name or address at https://is.bsasoftware.com/bsa.is/SelectUnit.aspx, includes 6 local cities or townships, all are fee based.

Oscoda County   *Recorded Documents*   www.oscodacountymi.com/register-of-deeds/   *Recorded Documents* www.co.monroe.mi.us/officials_and_departments/officials/register_of_deeds/index.php   The county works with https://tapestry.fidlar.com/Tapestry2/Default.aspx for record access. Base fee is $5.95 per search and $.50 per print image. You can pay as you go using a credit or pre-pay using a subscription. Also, one may purchase a software program Laredo (www.fidlar.com/lardao.aspx) with extensive search features. Contact the county for details and pricing.
Property, Taxation Records   Access to Equalization records for free at http://mi-oscoda-equalization.governmax.com/svc/default.asp.

Otsego County   *Recorded Documents*   www.otsegocountymi.gov/county-government-2/register-of-deeds/   Access to records free at http://rod.otsegocountymi.gov/Landweb.dll/$/. Indexes available from 3/5/1864 to present.
Property, Taxation Records   Search property and assessment data on the Equalization Dept search site at www.otsegocountymi.gov/county-government-2/equalization/property-search/. Also, search index by name or address at https://is.bsasoftware.com/bsa.is/SelectUnit.aspx, includes 4 local cities or townships, 3 are fee based.

Ottawa County   *Recorded Documents, Vital Records Records*   www.miottawa.org/Departments/CountyClerk/ROD/   *Recorded Documents*   www.co.monroe.mi.us/officials_and_departments/officials/register_of_deeds/index.php   The county works with https://tapestry.fidlar.com/Tapestry2/Default.aspx for record access. Base fee is $5.95 per search and $.50 per print image. You can pay as you go using a credit or pre-pay using a subscription. Also, one may purchase a software program Laredo (www.fidlar.com/lardao.aspx) with extensive search features. Contact the county for details and pricing.. Access to vital records for a fee at www.miottawa.org/Departments/CountyClerk/VitalRecord/.
Property, Taxation Records   Access Treasurer and Equalization tax records at https://www.miottawa.org/Property/noLogin.do. Also, search index by name or address at https://is.bsasoftware.com/bsa.is/SelectUnit.aspx, includes access to 20 local cities or townships, 8 are fee based.

Presque Isle County   *Property, Taxation Records*   Search property tax data free at www.presqueisle.mi.govern.com/parcelquery.php. Also, search index by name or address at https://is.bsasoftware.com/bsa.is/SelectUnit.aspx, includes 7 local cities or townships, all are fee based.

Roscommon County   *Recorded Documents*   www.roscommoncounty.net/196/Register-of-Deeds   Access land recorded index for a fee at https://mi.uslandrecords.com/milr/MilrApp/index.jsp. Select Roscommon.
Property, Taxation Records   Also, search index by name or address at https://is.bsasoftware.com/bsa.is/SelectUnit.aspx, includes 10 local cities or townships, 9 are fee based.

Saginaw County   *Recorded Documents*   www.saginawcounty.com/Rod/Default.aspx   Search the Register of Deeds index for free at www.saginawcounty.com/Rod/Default.aspx. Click on ROD Simple or Advanced Search at right of page. Access county clerks assumed names, marriages, death free at www.saginawcounty.com/Clerk/Search.aspx. Vital statistic records go back to 1995.
Property, Taxation Records   Search equalization board tax records at www.saginawcounty.com/Apps/Equal/PropertySearch.aspx. Also, a general property and sales search on the GIS site is free at www.saginawcounty.com/OnlineServices.aspx. Also, search index by name or address at https://is.bsasoftware.com/bsa.is/SelectUnit.aspx, includes 8 local cities or townships, 6 are fee based.

Sanilac County   *Recorded Documents (Index Only) Records*   www.sanilaccounty.net/PublicPages/Entity.aspx?ID=220   Access to records free at www.sanilaccounty.net/PublicPages/Entity.aspx?ID=220. Indexes available from 1/1969 to present. Images available with approved escrow account.
Property, Taxation Records   Access to parcel information for free at www.fetchgis.com/Sanilaclrp/app/SanilacLRP.html#. Also, search index by name or address at https://is.bsasoftware.com/bsa.is/SelectUnit.aspx, includes 12 local cities or townships, 11 are fee based.

Schoolcraft County   *Property, Taxation Records*   Also, search index by name or address at https://is.bsasoftware.com/bsa.is/SelectUnit.aspx, includes 2 local cities or townships, both are fee based.

Shiawassee County   *Recorded Documents*   https://countyfusion2.propertyinfo.com/ShiawasseeMI/website/index.htm   Access to public records go to https://countyfusion2.propertyinfo.com/countyweb/login.do?countyname=Shiawassee. Can login as guest, for more detailed information can sign in for a fee for subscription.
Property, Taxation Records   Also, search index by name or address at https://is.bsasoftware.com/bsa.is/SelectUnit.aspx, includes 18 local cities or townships, 14 are fee based.

St. Clair County   *Real Estate, Deed, Lien, Death Records*   www.stclaircounty.org/Offices/register_of_deeds/   Access register of deeds database is free at http://publicdeeds.stclaircounty.org/. Land records are available to view online from 1984 to present. A more extensive subscription is available for $150.00 per year. Subscribers may view and print images for $1.00 per page.
Property, Taxation Records   Search parcel data free by name or address at www.stclaircounty.org/offices/equalization/search.aspx. Also, a tax search request is at www.stclaircounty.org/Offices/treasurer/TaxRequest.aspx. Also, search index by name or address at https://is.bsasoftware.com/bsa.is/SelectUnit.aspx, includes 28 local cities or townships, 19 are fee based.

St. Joseph County   *Recorded Documents*   www.stjosephcountymi.org/deeds/   Access to land indexes for free at www.stjosephcountymi.org/deeds/land_records_search.htm. Printing any image is $1.00 per page and a $1.00 credit card transaction fee. Indexes for deeds and misc records from 1987 to present.
Property, Taxation Records   Search parcel records for free at www.stjosephcountymi.org/taxsearch/default.asp. Also offered is a subscription service with additional features. Also, search index by name or address at https://is.bsasoftware.com/bsa.is/SelectUnit.aspx, includes 21 local cities or townships, 18 are fee based.

Tuscola County   *Recorded Documents*   www.tuscolacounty.org/rod/   Access to the recorder's index for free at https://mi.uslandrecords.com/milr/MilrApp/index.jsp. Index searches are free, images are $1.00 each.
Property, Taxation Records   Acess to GIS/mapping for free at https://www.fetchgis.com/tuscolaweb/rmaauth/TuscolaMapViewer.html#. Also, search index by name or address at https://is.bsasoftware.com/bsa.is/SelectUnit.aspx, includes 7 local cities or townships, 6 are fee based.

Van Buren County   *Property, Taxation Records*   Also, search index by name or address at https://is.bsasoftware.com/bsa.is/SelectUnit.aspx, includes 7 local cities or townships, 2 are fee based. Also, access to property tax searches free at https://accessmygov.com/?uid=2070.

Washtenaw County   *Recorded Documents*   www.ewashtenaw.org/government/clerk_register/cr_clkdeeds.html   Access a menu of searchable databases at https://rod.ewashtenaw.org/recorder/web/. Document index data and images from 1/12/1959 to 12/31/1968.
Property, Taxation Records   Search index by name or address at https://is.bsasoftware.com/bsa.is/SelectUnit.aspx, includes 28 local cities or townships, 13 are fee based. Also, access to GIS/mapping for free at www.ewashtenaw.org/government/departments/gis/MapWashtenaw_Main.htm. Also, for Property/Parcel Lookup free at https://secure.ewashtenaw.org/ecommerce/property/pStart.do.

Wayne County   *Recorded Documents*   www.waynecounty.com/deeds/index.htm   Search county recorder land records database for a fee at https://www.waynecountylandrecords.com/recorder/web/, call 313-967-6857 for info/sign-up or see above website. Access to unclaimed property free at www.michigan.gov/treasury/0,1607,7-121-44435-7924--,00.html.
Property, Taxation Records   Dearborn property Assessment data free at http://addlapps.cityofdearborn.org/dbnassessor/. No name searching. Search index by name or address at https://is.bsasoftware.com/bsa.is/SelectUnit.aspx, includes 42 local cities or townships, 15 are fee based.

Wexford County   *Recorded Documents*   www.wexfordcounty.org/Services/RegisterofDeeds.aspx   Access to recorded documents for a fee at https://mi.uslandrecords.com/milr/. Records available from 1/1976 to present.
Property, Taxation Records   Access the land parcel and Assessment roll site free at http://ws6.liaa.org/wexford/propertysearch.asp. Search index by name or address at https://is.bsasoftware.com/bsa.is/SelectUnit.aspx, includes 4 local cities or townships, is fee based.

Minnesota

Capital: St. Paul
             Ramsey County
Time Zone: CST
Population: 5,489,594
# of Counties: 87

Useful State Links

Website: **www.mn.gov/portal/**
Governor: **http://mn.gov/governor/**
Attorney General: **www.ag.state.mn.us**
State Archives: **www.mnhs.org**
State Statutes and Codes: **https://www.revisor.mn.gov/pubs/**
Legislative Bill Search: **www.leg.state.mn.us/leg/legis.aspx**
Unclaimed Funds: **https://mn.gov/commerce/consumers/your-money/**

State Public Record Agencies

Criminal Records

Bureau of Criminal Apprehension, MNJIS - Criminal History Access Unit,   https://dps.mn.gov/divisions/bca/pages/background-checks.aspx   Access to the Public CCH (15 years, no consent) is available free at https://cch.state.mn.us/ or https://cch.state.mn.us/pcchOffenderSearch.aspx. Search for Methamphetamine offenders at https://mor.state.mn.us/.   *Other Options:* A public database is available on CD-ROM. Monthly updates can be purchased. Data is in ASCII format and is raw data. Fee is $40.00

Sexual Offender Registry

Bureau of Criminal Apprehension, Minnesota Predatory Offender Program,   https://por.state.mn.us/   Offenders and non-compliant offender if 16 or older may be searched at https://por.state.mn.us/OffenderSearch.aspx. Risk level 3 search available at DOC site https://coms.doc.state.mn.us/Level3/. Data is updated within 48 of being reported.

Incarceration Records

Minnesota Department of Corrections, Records Management Unit,   www.doc.state.mn.us/PAGES/   A series of searches are available at www.doc.state.mn.us/PAGES/index.php/search-offenders-fugitives/. The Offender Search provides public information about adult offenders who have been committed to the Commissioner of Corrections, and who are still under our jurisdiction (i.e. in prison, or released from prison and still under supervision). There is also a search for Active DOC Fugitives as well as non-compliant predatory offenders.

Corporation, LLC, LP, Assumed Name, Trademarks/Servicemarks

Business Services, Secretary of State,   www.sos.state.mn.us/   Go to https://mblsportal.sos.state.mn.us/Business/Search for free look-ups of business names and corporation files. Information includes Registered Office Address and Agent/CEO and PPPB address when applicable and Name Availability Searches Online orders or copies and Good Standing certificates are available for add'l fee of $10.00 fee. Good Standing Certs purchased online are downloaded immediately and copy orders are emailed out.   *Other Options:* Information can be purchased in bulk format. Call for more information.

Uniform Commercial Code, Federal & State Tax Liens

UCC/CNS & Notary Services, Secretary of State,   https://mblsportal.sos.state.mn.us/Secured/SearchUCC   A free search by filing number is at https://mblsportal.sos.state.mn.us/Secured/SearchUCC. One may set-up an account to search and order copies. The fee is $250 for 25 searches, a Standard Searrch option is also available for $20 per name . Use of a credit card is required.   Searches are non-certifed. One may allso order UCC, Tax llien data tables on a weekly basis and CNS Farm data on a monthly list. See https://mblsportal.sos.state.mn.us/Secured/Subscriptions

Birth, Death Records

Minnesota Department of Health, Central Cashiering - Vital Records, www.health.state.mn.us/divs/chs/osr/birth.html Search the archived Birth Certificates Index and archived Death Certificates Index free at http://search.mnhs.org/?brand=people. Email requests to health.issuance@state.mn.us. .

Workers' Compensation Records

Labor & Industry Department, Workers Compensation Division - File Review, www.doli.state.mn.us/workcomp.asp Copies of decision decided by the Minnesota Workers' Compensation Court of Appeals (WCCA) can be found at http://mn.gov/workcomp/. An insurance verification on an employer is found at www.inslookup.doli.state.mn.us/. One may also report an emiployer operating without worker's comp insurance.

Driver Records

Driver & Vehicle Services, Records Section, https://dps.mn.gov/divisions/dvs/Pages/default.aspx Online access to records is offered to entities with an approved Business Partner Records Access Agreement. The online access fee is $5.00 per record. Online inquiries can be processed either as interactive or as batch files (overnight) 24 hours a day, 7 days a week. Requesters operate from a "bank." Records are accessed by either DL number or full name and DOB. The DVS has plans to upgrade this system later in 2014; there will be changes to the display. Call Data Services at 651-297-5352 for more information. A free view of a DL status report is available at https://dutchelm.dps.state.mn.us/dvsinfo/dv02/dv02frame.asp.. The DL# is needed, no personal information is released. *Other Options:* Minnesota will sell its entire database of driving record information with monthly updates per DPPA guidelines. Customized request sorts are available. Fees vary by type with programming and computer time and are quite reasonable.

Vehicle Ownership & Registration

Driver & Vehicle Services, Vehicle Record Requests, https://dps.mn.gov/divisions/dvs/Pages/default.aspx Approved accounts have the ability to request and receive title and registration records. DVS establishes a unique account for each customer. The customer must maintain funds in the account sufficient to cover customer use. The fee for each inquiry is $5.00. The account balance is displayed at time of log on. For more information call 651-297-5352. Also, to obtain a renewal status report on a plate go to https://dutchelm.dps.state.mn.us/dvsinfo/info/DLTitleStatus/DLTitle_main.asp. Need the plate number or the VIN. Only public information is released.

Voter Registration

Secretary of State-Election Division, Voter Registration Lists, www.sos.state.mn.us/elections-voting/ Check voter registration status at https://mnvotes.sos.state.mn.us/VoterStatus.aspx.

Campaign Finance, Disclosures, PACs, Lobbyists

Campaign Finance & Public Disclosure, 190 Centennial Office Building, www.cfboard.state.mn.us/ A myriad of searchable database are available from links at www.cfboard.state.mn.us/. Search contributions and expenditures for candidates and PACs. Also search lobbyists and the associations that hire them by either lobbyist or association name.

Occupational Licensing Boards

These licenses are all searchable at www.commerce.state.mn.us/LicenseLookupMain.html

Abstractor/Abstractor Company	Contractor/Remodeler, Resid'l	Managing General Agent
Adjuster	Credit Union	Manicurist
Appraiser/Appraisal Mgmt Co	Currency Exchange	Motor Vehicle Financer
Bondsman (Insurance)	Debt Collector	Notary Public
Broker/Closing Agent/Company	Debt Prorate Company	Real Estate Agent/Broker/Dealer
Building Contractor, Residen'l	Esthetician	Re-Insurance Intermediary
Campground Membership Agent	Insurance Agent/Seller/Agency	Securities Salesperson/Inves't Advisor
Collection Agency	Lender, Small	Thrift/Industrial Loan Company
Consumer Credit/Payday Lender	Loan Company	

The Rest:

Accountant Firm	www.boa.state.mn.us/Licensing/findFirm.html
Accountant-CPA	www.boa.state.mn.us/Licensing/findCPA.html
Acupuncturist	http://mn.gov/boards/medical-practice/public/find-practitioner/
Alcohol/Drug Counselor	https://bht.hlb.state.mn.us/DesktopModules/ServiceForm.aspx?svid=37&mid=178
Ambulance Service/Personnel	https://mn.gov/elicense/gateway/selSearchType.do
Architect	http://mn.gov/aelslagid/roster.html
Asbestos Contractor/Worker/Supervisor	www.health.state.mn.us/divs/eh/asbestos/find_person/index.cfm
Athletic Trainer	http://mn.gov/boards/medical-practice/public/find-practitioner/
Attorney	http://mars.courts.state.mn.us/
Barber	https://mn.gov/boards/barber-examiners/registrations/registrationverification.jsp

Behovoroal Health & Therapy Disciplinary Actions .https://mn.gov/boards/assets/Public%20disc%20actions-BBHT_tcm21-27315.pdf
Bingo Operation...http://mn.gov/gcb/linked-bingo-game-providers.html
Boats for Hire..http://workplace.doli.state.mn.us/ccld/BLBoat.pdf
Boiler Inspector...https://secure.doli.state.mn.us/lookup/licensing.aspx
Building Code Jurisdiction Directory.......................http://workplace.doli.state.mn.us/jurisdiction/
Camp Doctor..http://mn.gov/boards/medical-practice/public/find-practitioner/
Chemical & Mental Health ....http://licensinglookup.dhs.state.mn.us/
Child Care Facility..http://licensinglookup.dhs.state.mn.us/
Children's Service...http://licensinglookup.dhs.state.mn.us/
Chiropractor/Firm...https://chi.hlb.state.mn.us/app/index.html#/LicenseVerification
Cosmetologist/Cosmetology Instr'r/School.............https://bcegl.hlb.state.mn.us/glsuiteweb/Clients/MNBoC/Public/Verification/Search.aspx
Crematory ....www.health.state.mn.us/divs/hpsc/mortsci/mortsciselect.cfm
Dental Lab ....http://mn.gov/boards/dentistry/licensure/dentallab/dentallabverificationpage.jsp
Dietitian ....https://dnp.hlb.state.mn.us/app/index.html#/LicenseVerification
Drug Mfg/Whlse/Dist...https://bopgl.hlb.state.mn.us/glsuiteweb/clients/mnbopharm/public/licenseesearch.aspx
Electrical Contractor ....https://secure.doli.state.mn.us/lookup/licensing.aspx
Electrical Inspector ....www.dli.mn.gov/CCLD/ElectricalInspect.asp
Electrical Technology System Contractor................https://secure.doli.state.mn.us/lookup/licensing.aspx
Electrician ....https://secure.doli.state.mn.us/lookup/licensing.aspx
Electronic Gaming ....http://mn.gov/gcb/assets/electronic-game-sites.pdf
Elevator Contractor...https://secure.doli.state.mn.us/lookup/licensing.aspx
Emergency Medical Technician....................................https://mn.gov/elicense/gateway/selSearchType.do
EMS Disciplinary Actions..http://mn.gov/boards/emsrb/disciplinary/disciplinary-actions.jsp
EMS Examiner..https://mn.gov/elicense/gateway/searchForExaminer.do
Engineer ....http://mn.gov/aelslagid/roster.html
Foster Care Program ....http://licensinglookup.dhs.state.mn.us/
Funeral Director/Establishment ....www.health.state.mn.us/divs/hpsc/mortsci/mortsciselect.cfm
Gambling Equipment Distributor.................................http://mn.gov/gcb/manufacturers.html
Gambling Equipment Manufacturer............................http://mn.gov/gcb/manufacturers.html
Gambling Organizations ....http://mn.gov/gcb/index.html
Gambling, Lawful Organization ....http://mn.gov/gcb/index.html
Geologist..http://mn.gov/aelslagid/roster.html
Grain Licensing..www2.mda.state.mn.us/webapp/lis/default.jsp
Hearing Aid Dispenser...https://pqc.health.state.mn.us/hopVerify/loginAction.do
Interior Designer ....http://mn.gov/aelslagid/roster.html
Landscape Architect...http://mn.gov/aelslagid/roster.html
Liquor Store, On-sale Retail/Municipal ....https://app.dps.mn.gov/age/
Livestock Dealer/Market/Weigher..............................www2.mda.state.mn.us/webapp/lis/default.jsp
Lobbyist ....www.cfboard.state.mn.us/lob_lists.html
Lottery Retailer ....https://www.mnlottery.com/buy_tickets/find_a_retailer/
Manufactured Home Installer ....https://secure.doli.state.mn.us/lookup/licensing.aspx
Manufactured Home Mfg/Dealer ....https://secure.doli.state.mn.us/lookup/licensing.aspx
Manufactured Structures Section ....https://secure.doli.state.mn.us/lookup/licensing.aspx
Marriage & Family Therapist/Associate...................https://mft.hlb.state.mn.us/app/index.html#/LicenseVerification
Medical Gas Mfg/Whlse/Dist ....https://bopgl.hlb.state.mn.us/glsuiteweb/clients/mnbopharm/public/licenseesearch.aspx
Medical Professional Firm...http://mn.gov/boards/medical-practice/public/find-practitioner/
Mental Health, Chem'l Depend'cy Prof....................http://licensinglookup.dhs.state.mn.us/
Midwife...http://mn.gov/boards/medical-practice/public/find-practitioner/
Mortician ....www.health.state.mn.us/divs/hpsc/mortsci/mortsciselect.cfm
Naturopathic Doctor..http://mn.gov/boards/medical-practice/public/find-practitioner/
Nurse-APRN...http://mn.gov/boards/nursing/public/aprn-license-verification/
Nurse-LPN/RN...https://www.hlb.state.mn.us/mbn/Portal/DesktopDefault.aspx
Nursing Home Administrator ....http://mn.gov/boards/nursing-home/licensees/verify-a-license.jsp
Nursing Home Facility...http://mn.gov/boards/nursing-home/licensees/verify-a-license.jsp
Nutritionist...https://dnp.hlb.state.mn.us/app/index.html#/LicenseVerification

Occupational Therapist/Assistant .... https://pqc.health.state.mn.us/hopVerify/loginAction.do
Optometrist/Firm .... https://opt.hlb.state.mn.us/app/index.html#/LicenseVerification
Pesticide Applicator Company .... www.mda.state.mn.us/licensing/license-lookup.aspx
Pesticide Applicator, Private https://www2.mda.state.mn.us/webapp/PrivApp/default.jsp
Pharmaceutical Technician .... https://bopgl.hlb.state.mn.us/glsuiteweb/clients/mnbopharm/public/licenseesearch.aspx
Pharmacist/Pharmacy .... https://bopgl.hlb.state.mn.us/glsuiteweb/clients/mnbopharm/public/licenseesearch.aspx
Physician/Medical Doctor/Assistant .... http://mn.gov/boards/medical-practice/public/find-practitioner/
Podiatrist .... https://pod.hlb.state.mn.us/app/index.html#/Login
Political Action Committee .... www.cfboard.state.mn.us/campfin/pcfatoz.html
Political Candidate .... www.cfboard.state.mn.us/cand_lists.html
Private Investigator .... https://dps.mn.gov/entity/pdb/Pages/license-holders.aspx
Psychologist .... https://mnit.force.com/license
Psychologist Disciplinary Actions .... http://mn.gov/boards/psychology/public/discipline/
Radiology Schools .... www.health.state.mn.us/divs/eh/radiation/xray/radschools.pdf
Respiratory Care Practitioner .... http://mn.gov/boards/medical-practice/public/find-practitioner/
Sanitarian .... www.health.state.mn.us/divs/eh/san/sani_query.cfm
Security Agent/Protective Agent .... https://dps.mn.gov/entity/pdb/Pages/license-holders.aspx
Social Worker .... https://lsoc.hlb.state.mn.us/DesktopDefault.aspx
Soil Scientist .... http://mn.gov/aelslagid/roster.html
Speech-Language Audiologist/Pathologist .... https://pqc.health.state.mn.us/hopVerify/loginAction.do
Surgeon .... http://mn.gov/boards/medical-practice/public/find-practitioner/
Surveyor, Land .... http://mn.gov/aelslagid/roster.html
Teacher http://w20.education.state.mn.us/LicenseLookup/lookup
Telemedicine .... http://mn.gov/boards/medical-practice/public/find-practitioner/
Undergr'nd Storage Tank Contr/Supvr .... www.pca.state.mn.us/index.php/view-document.html?gid=15373
Veterinarian .... https://vet.hlb.state.mn.us/app/index.html#/LicenseVerification
X-Ray Physicist .... www.health.state.mn.us/divs/eh/radiation/xray/servproviders/physicists.pdf
X-Ray Service Provider .... www.health.state.mn.us/divs/eh/radiation/xray/servproviders/spvendorcy.pdf

State and Local Courts

About Minnesota Courts: **District Courts** hear everything from traffic tickets, to civil and family conflicts, to first degree murder trials. Some District Courts may have separate divisions, such as criminal, civil, probate, family, and juvenile courts. Gnerlay each county has one or more Traafic Courts that are housed where criminal cases are heard.

The **Conciliation Court** is a division of Civil Court and handles small claims. The limit for small claims is $10,000 unless the case involves a consumer credit transaction, then the limit is $4000 or $15,000.00 if the claim involves money or personal property subject to forfeiture under section 84.7741, 169A.63, 609.5311, 609.5312, 609.531 4, or 609.5318. This is the limit set by law. You cannot file a claim involving title to real estate, libel, slander, class actions or medical malpractice in a conciliation Court.

There are eleven **Tribal Courts** that have jurisdiction on tribal land.
The web page for the Unified Judicial System is www.mncourts.gov.

Appellate Courts: The Court of Appeals reviews all final decisions of the trial courts, state agencies and local governments, except from the Minnesota Tax Court, the Minnesota Workers' Compensation Court of Appeals, first-degree murder cases and statewide election contests. Supreme and Appellate opinions are found at the home page mentioned above.

Online Court Access
All courts participate in the system described below.

Minnesota offers the Trial Court Public Access (MPA) of searching statewide or by county. Records available include criminal, civil, family, and probate. Searches can be performed using a case number or by name. See www.mncourts.gov/Access-Case-Records.aspx.

There are a number of caveats, especially for criminal record searches. **Certain publicly-accessible case records or data fields found at the courthouse cannot be viewed online.** For example, comment fields for all case types are not available online but are available at the courthouse. Party street address and name searches on criminal, traffic, and petty misdemeanor pre-conviction case records are not accessible online, but are at the courthouse. Further, a criminal/traffic/petty search **excludes** all Hennepin County and Ramsey County payable citations except: 1) those that result in a court appearance; and 2) Ramsey DNR payable citations. The excluded payable citations are processed through a separate system called VIBES.

Of course the federal Violence Against Women Act (VAWA) prevents all states from displaying harassment and domestic abuse case records online, but these convictions are available at the courthouse. Online users are not notified when such public data is restricted from online viewing.

No individual Minnesota courts offer online access, other than as described above.

Recorders, Assessors, and Other Sites of Note

About Minnesota Recording Offices: 87 counties, 87 recording offices. The recording officer is the County Recorder.

About Tax Liens: Federal and state tax liens on personal property of businesses and on individuals can be filed either with the Secretary of State or with the County Recorder. Both locations must be searched..

Online Access

Recorded Documents

There is no statewide system. However, a number of counties offer web access to recorded data. There are two several vendors of note below.

- Access to recorded documents is offered by https://idocmarket.com/. A subscription is required for searching, viewingand printing. There are 17 participating counties.
- Access recorded land data by subscription on the Tapestry System for 17 participating counties. One can either use a credit card and pay $5.95 per image or take advantage of a subcription with a flat rate. See https://tapestry.fidlar.com/Tapestry2/Search.aspx for details. Payment is made to the County Recorder.

Property Assessor and GIS

Search assessor GIS property data from 25 jurisdictions for a fee on the GIS system at https://beacon.schneidercorp.com/ with registration and username required.

County Sites:

Aitkin County   *Property, Taxation Records*   Access property data free at http://gisweb.co.aitkin.mn.us/link/jsfe/index.aspx. To access more detailed building information, including dimensions and sales report generating capability, a subscription to WebFusion is required. Call 218-927-7327 for more information.

Anoka County   *Property, Taxation Records*   Access property data at https://prtinfo.co.anoka.mn.us/(b4uc2leotcvloc55xkuzoh55)/search.aspx.

Becker County   *Recorded Documents*   www.co.becker.mn.us/dept/recorder/default.aspx   Access for iDoc database for online real estate for a fee at https://idocmarket.com/Sites#. Fee is $50.00 per month, (limited); $150.00 per month, unlimited access & copies. Must sign-up & pay before use. Records available index & image: 1970 to present.
Property, Taxation Records   Access to parcel informatin for free at http://gis-server.co.becker.mn.us/www/parcel_search.aspx. Also, search plat images free at www.co.becker.mn.us/dept/recorder/plats_online.aspx. Also, access to GIS/mapping for free at http://gis-server.co.becker.mn.us/link/jsfe/index.aspx. Also, access to property sales for free at http://gis-server.co.becker.mn.us/www/sales_search.aspx.

Beltrami County   *Recorded Documents*   www.co.beltrami.mn.us/Departments/Recorder/Recorder.html   The county works with https://tapestry.fidlar.com/Tapestry2/Default.aspx for record access. Base fee is $5.95 per search and $.50 per print image. You can pay as you go using a credit or pre-pay using a subscription. Also, one may purchase a software program Laredo (www.fidlar.com/laredo.aspx) with extensive search features. Contact the county for set-up and pricing.
Property, Taxation Records   Access to GIS/mapping free at http://beltramicounty.maps.arcgis.com/apps/PublicGallery/index.html?appid=efda5687eaef418cb787d8c62cbc6dc1.

Benton County   *Recorded Documents*   www.co.benton.mn.us/County_Recorder/index.php   Landshark is now available. Contact the Recorder's office at 320-968-5037 for more information.

Property, Taxation Records Free search of Auditor property tax data at https://beacon.schneidercorp.com/. Also, at this site-search property records and GIS/mapping for free.

Big Stone County
Recorded Documents www.bigstonecounty.org/recorder/recorder.vbhtml Access to land records for a fee at https://tapestry.fidlar.com/Tapestry2/. Fee for search is $5.95, each printed page is add'l $.50 per page.
Property, Taxation Records Access to sales listing for free at www.bigstonecounty.org/assessor/sales.vbhtml.

Blue Earth County
Recorded Documents www.blueearthcountymn.gov/index.aspx?nid=332 A The county works with https://tapestry.fidlar.com/Tapestry2/Default.aspx for record access. Base fee is $5.95 per search and $.50 per print image. You can pay as you go using a credit or pre-pay using a subscription. Also, one may purchase a software program Laredo (www.fidlar.com/laredo.aspx) with extensive search features. Contact the county for set-up and pricing.
Property, Taxation Records Access to the property data search database is free at http://mn-blueearth.manatron.com/. No name searching but subscription is available at this site. Also, access to various maps for free at www.blueearthcountymn.gov/index.aspx?nid=158. Also, free search of Auditor property tax data at https://beacon.schneidercorp.com/. Also, at this site-search property records and GIS/mapping for free.

Brown County
Recorded Records Records www.co.brown.mn.us/departmentslink/recorders-office Access to records in subscription for $50.00 per month, $1.00 per doc viewed, contact Betti Kamolz, Recorder at 507-233-6653.
Property, Taxation Records Access to GIS/mapping free at www.co.brown.mn.us/gis-a-property-info.

Carlton County
Documents Recorded Records www.co.carlton.mn.us/index.asp?SEC=C8B001FA-6CA3-4422-938B-B62B53268995&Type=B_BASIC Access for iDoc database for online real estate for a fee at https://idocmarket.com/Sites#. Fee is $50.00 per month, (limited); $150.00 per month, unlimited access & copies. Must sign-up & pay before use. Data and images from 1/3/1989, prior images available if document number is known (back to 6/1/1960).
Property, Taxation Records Access to parcel information for free at www.parcelinfo.com/index.php.

Carver County
Recorded Document Records www.co.carver.mn.us/departments/property-financial-services/property-records Access to recorder land records available by subscription at http://landshark.co.carver.mn.us/LandShark/login.jsp. No fee to search, fee for images. Fee schedule is online under fees.
Property, Taxation Records Access property and tax roll data free at http://mn-carver.manatron.com/Tabs/TaxSearch.aspx but no name searching. Also search the GIS-mapping site free at www.co.carver.mn.us/departments/public-services/information-services/gis. Also, access to property data for free at https://gis.co.carver.mn.us/publicparcel/.

Cass County
Recorded Documents Access for iDoc database for online real estate for a fee at https://idocmarket.com/Sites#. Fee varies depending on plan desired. Must sign-up & pay before use. Data and images available for abstract documents back to 3/4/1965.
Property, Taxation Records Access to GIS/mapping data for free at www.co.cass.mn.us/services/land/maps/index.php.

Chippewa County
Recorded Documents www.co.chippewa.mn.us/recorder.htm Access for iDoc database for online real estate for a fee at https://idocmarket.com/Sites#. Fee varies depending on plan desired. Must sign-up & pay before use. Indexing back to 1991, images back to 8/1997.
Property, Taxation Records Access property tax records free at www.co.chippewa.mn.us/taxdisclaim.htm but no name searching.

Chisago County
Property, Taxation Records Access parcel data at the GIS-mapping site at https://gis.chisagocounty.us/Link/jsfe/index.aspx.

Clay County
Recorded Documents http://claycountymn.gov/245/Recorder The county works with https://tapestry.fidlar.com/Tapestry2/Default.aspx for record access. Base fee is $5.95 per search and $.50 per print image. You can pay as you go using a credit or pre-pay using a subscription. Also, one may purchase a software program Laredo (www.fidlar.com/laredo.aspx) with extensive search features. Contact the county for set-up and pricing.
Property, Taxation Records Search property data for City of Moorhead and Clay County free at http://claycountymn.gov/296/Property-Map-Search. Also, access to GIS/mapping free at http://claycountymn.gov/661/Maps-Online.

Clearwater County
Property, Taxation Records Access to GIS mapping/E911 Rural Addressing System for free at www.co.clearwater.mn.us/index.asp?Type=B_LIST&SEC={A45A7FBB-7EB4-4C1C-95DD-12490F634AC6}.

Cook County
Recorded Documents www.co.cook.mn.us/2016site/index.php/home/2016-06-09-18-42-22/2016-01-15-01-30-35 Access for iDoc database for online real estate for a fee at https://idocmarket.com/Sites#. Fee varies depending on plan desired. Must sign-up & pay before use. Data and images back to 1/1/1960. Images of certificates of Title back to 1/1/1931 (certificates have also been indexed).
Property, Taxation Records Access to GIS/mapping for free at http://cookcountymn.maps.arcgis.com/home/index.html.

Cottonwood County
Recorded Documents www.co.cottonwood.mn.us/county-departments/recorder/ The county works with https://tapestry.fidlar.com/Tapestry2/Default.aspx for record access. Base fee is $5.95 per search and $.50 per print image. You can pay as you go using a credit or pre-pay using a subscription. Also, one may purchase a software program Laredo (www.fidlar.com/laredo.aspx) with extensive search features. Contact the county for set-up and pricing.
Property, Taxation Records Free search of Auditor property tax data at https://beacon.schneidercorp.com/. Also, at this site-search property records and GIS/mapping for free. For specific information, must subscribe.

Crow Wing County   *Recorded Documents*   http://crowwing.us/197/Customer-Services   Access to recorder data is available by subscription, $50.00 per month and $.25 per image. Email the County Recorder at kathy.ludenia@crowwing.us for info and signup, or login at http://erecord.co.crow-wing.mn.us/LandShark/login.jsp.
Property, Taxation Records   Access to GIS/mapping free at http://crowwing.us/1238/County-Maps.

Dakota County   *Recorded Documents*   https://www.co.dakota.mn.us/HomeProperty/Recording/Pages/default.aspx   Access to recorded documents requires a subscription and an escrow account set up with Property Taxation & Records. Fee varies per plan. To obtain a Login ID and Password, contact 651-438-4355.
Property, Taxation Records   Search foreclosure data free by address at https://www.co.dakota.mn.us/HomeProperty/Foreclosed/Pages/ForeclosureSearch.aspx.

Dodge County   *Recorded Documents*   www.co.dodge.mn.us/departments/land_records/recorder_s_office.php   Online subscription available with a set-up escrow account.A monthly subscription fee and search fees charged.
Property, Taxation Records   Access to property information, GIS/mapping for free at www.co.dodge.mn.us/departments/land_records/gis.php.

Douglas County   *Recorded Documents*   www.co.douglas.mn.us/dc/recorder.aspx   Access to database for a fee at www.landshark.co.douglas.mn.us/LandShark/login.jsp?url=http%3A%2F%2F.
Property, Taxation Records   Look-up assessor property tax data free at www.co.douglas.mn.us/dc/parcel-info-lookup.aspx. Also, access GIS/mapping for free at www.co.cass.mn.us/services/land/maps/index.php.

Faribault County   *Recorded Documents*   http://faribaultcountyrecorder.com/   Access to records for a fee at https://tapestry.fidlar.com/Tapestry2/Default.aspx. Contact 507-526-6252 or sherry.asmus@co.faribault.mn.us. Search fee is $5.95 each, printed images $.50 each unless otherwise noted. Quarterly subscriptions to Laredo also available at $50.00 per month.
Property, Taxation Records   Free search of Auditor property tax data at https://beacon.schneidercorp.com/. Also, at this site-search property records and GIS/mapping for free. For specific information, must subscribe.

Fillmore County   *Recorded Documents*   www.co.fillmore.mn.us/recorder   Access for iDoc database for online real estate for a fee at https://idocmarket.com/Sites#. Fee varies depending on plan desired. Must sign-up & pay before use. Documents back to 1/1/1964.
Property, Taxation Records   Access to public viewing on GIS/mapping free at www.co.fillmore.mn.us/gis, a fee subscription available for more detailed information, at same site.

Freeborn County   *Property, Taxation Records*   Free search of Auditor property tax data at https://beacon.schneidercorp.com/. Also, at this site-search property records and GIS/mapping for free. For specific information, must subscribe.

Goodhue County   *Property, Taxation Records*   Search GIS/mapping for free at www.co.goodhue.mn.us/524/Maps. Also, access to sale informatin for free at http://goodhue.minnesotaassessors.com/showResSaleSearch.php. Also, access to property data for free at http://goodhue.minnesotaassessors.com/search.php.

Grant County   *Recorded Documents*   www.co.grant.mn.us/177/Recorder   The county works with https://tapestry.fidlar.com/Tapestry2/Default.aspx for record access. Base fee is $5.95 per search and $.50 per print image. You can pay as you go using a credit or pre-pay using a subscription. Also, one may purchase a software program Laredo (www.fidlar.com/laredo.aspx) with extensive search features. Contact the county for set-up and pricing. The Grant County Recorder provides a free online subscription to Property Fraud Alert service which notifies the subscriber/property owner when a document is recorded in the Grant County Recorder's Office with their name on it. See www.propertyfraudalert.com/GrantMN/Disclaimer.aspx.
Property, Taxation Records   Look-up assessor property tax data free at www.co.grant.mn.us/350/Tax-Parcel-Search.

Hennepin County   *Recorded Documents*   www.hennepin.us/residents/property/real-estate-recording-information   Access to Hennepin County online records requires a $35 annual fee with a charge of $5 per hour from 7AM-7PM, or $4.15 per hour at other times. Records date back to 1988. Only lending agency data is available. An Automated phone system is also available; 612-348-3011.
Property, Taxation Records   Search parcel property tax records on county Property Information Search database free at www16.co.hennepin.mn.us/pins/. Also, access to GIS/mapping for free at www.hennepin.us/your-government/open-government/gis-open-data.

Houston County   *Recorded Documents*   www.co.houston.mn.us/Recorder.aspx   Online access by subscription to records starting in 1991 forward. Contact the Recorder's Office. Land records in this office data back to 1855.
Property, Taxation Records   Free search of Auditor property tax data at https://beacon.schneidercorp.com/. Also, at this site-search property records and GIS/mapping for free. For specific information, must subscribe.

Hubbard County   *Recorded Documents*   www.co.hubbard.mn.us/Recorder.htm   Access for iDoc database for online real estate for a fee at https://idocmarket.com/Sites#. Fee varies depending on plan desired. Must sign-up & pay before use.
Property, Taxation Records   Access to GIS/mapping free at www.co.hubbard.mn.us/maps.htm. For more detailed information must subscribe.

Isanti County   *Recorded Documents*   www.co.isanti.mn.us/isanti/departments/recorder   Access to Online records for a fee at https://landshark.co.isanti.mn.us/LandShark/login. Fee is $50.00 per month, unlimited access and $.25 per page for copies. Must sign-up and pay before use. See website for more information.

Property, Taxation Records Access monthly sales sheets by Town of electronic certificate of real estate value for free at www.revenue.state.mn.us/CRV/Pages/eCRV.aspx. Free search of Auditor property tax data at https://beacon.schneidercorp.com/. Also, at this site-search property records and GIS/mapping for free. For specific information, must subscribe.

Itasca County *Recorded Documents* www.co.itasca.mn.us/Home/Departments/Recorders/Pages/default.aspx Access for iDoc database for online real estate for a fee at https://idocmarket.com/Sites#. Fee varies depending on plan desired. Must sign-up & pay before use. Index and images back to 4/1/1987.
Property, Taxation Records Access property and parcel data free from a private company at www.parcelinfo.com/index.php. Also, access to GIS/mapping for free at http://207.171.101.128/website/AssessorInternet/viewer.htm.

Jackson County *Property, Taxation Records* Free search of Auditor property tax data at https://beacon.schneidercorp.com/. Also, at this site-search property records for free. For specific information, must subscribe.

Kanabec County *Recorded Documents* www.kanabeccounty.org/index.asp Access to LandShark is available for a fee. Contact Rhonda or Lisa at 320-679-6466. *Property, Taxation Records* Free search of Auditor property tax data at https://beacon.schneidercorp.com/. Also, at this site-search property records and GIS/mapping for free. For specific information, must subscribe.

Kandiyohi County *Recorded Documents* www.co.kandiyohi.mn.us/departments/recorder/index.php Access to records for a fee at https://tapestry.fidlar.com/Tapestry2. Search fee is $5.95 each, printed images $.50 each unless otherwise noted. Additional information on Laredo Software at www.co.kandiyohi.mn.us/departments/recorder/access_agreement.php.
Property, Taxation Records Look-up assessor property tax data free athttp://cpuimei.com/tax/disclaimer_value.asp?cid=34. Also, access to GIS/mapping free at http://gis.co.kandiyohi.mn.us/.

Kittson County *Property, Taxation Records* Access to property tax look-up and payment at http://mn-kittsoncounty.civicplus.com/2161/Property-Tax-Look-Up-Payment.

Koochiching County *Recorded Documents* Access for iDoc database for online real estate for a fee at https://idocmarket.com/Sites#. Fee varies depending on plan desired. Must sign-up & pay before use. Indexing of abstract documents back to 10/2/1979.
Property, Taxation Records Access to property and parcel data is free from a private company at www.parcelinfo.com/.

Lac qui Parle County *Recorded Documents* www.lqpco.com/recorder.php Access to online access for index and images of recorded documents for a fee contact Josh Amland at 320-598-3724. fee is $50.00 per month of unlimited access at this time.
Property, Taxation Records Access to parcel data and the Lake Finder for free at www.parcelinfo.com/index.php.

Lake County *Recorded Documents* www.co.lake.mn.us/departments/recorder_and_vitals/index.php Access for iDoc database for online real estate for a fee at https://idocmarket.com/Sites#. Fee varies depending on plan desired. Must sign-up & pay before use. Indexed data and images back to 1/1/1978.

Lake of the Woods County *Recorded Documents* www.co.lake-of-the-woods.mn.us/Recorder.aspx Access for iDoc database for online real estate for a fee at https://idocmarket.com/Sites#. Fee varies depending on plan desired. Must sign-up & pay before use. Index and images back to 7/1/1991. *Property, Taxation Records* Access to GIS/mapping free at http://oak.co.lake-of-the-woods.mn.us/link/jsfe/index.aspx.

Le Sueur County *Recorded Documents* www.co.le-sueur.mn.us/departments/recorder/index.php Access to recorder's land records back to 5/1/1991 is by subscription through LandShark at https://landshark.co.le-sueur.mn.us/LandShark/login.jsp. Fees of $50.00 installation, $2.00 per doc viewed, $50.00 per month, username and password required.
Property, Taxation Records Free search of Auditor property tax data at https://beacon.schneidercorp.com/. Also, at this site-search property records and GIS/mapping for free. For specific information, must subscribe.

Lincoln County *Recorded Documents* www.lincolncounty-mn.us/Departments/Recorder.htm The county works with https://tapestry.fidlar.com/Tapestry2/Default.aspx for record access. Base fee is $5.95 per search and $.50 per print image. You can pay as you go using a credit or pre-pay using a subscription. Also, one may purchase a software program Laredo (www.fidlar.com/laredo.aspx) with extensive search features. Contact the county for set-up and pricing. *Property, Taxation Records* Access to GIS/mapping free at www.lincolncounty-mn.us/Departments/gis_maps.htm.

Lyon County *Recorded Documents* www.lyonco.org/recorder The county works with https://tapestry.fidlar.com/Tapestry2/Default.aspx for record access. Base fee is $5.95 per search and $.50 per print image. You can pay as you go using a credit or pre-pay using a subscription. Also, one may purchase a software program Laredo (www.fidlar.com/laredo.aspx) with extensive search features. Contact the county for set-up and pricing.
Property, Taxation Records Look-up assessor property tax data free at http://geomoose.lyonco.org/.

Martin County *Recorded Documents* www.co.martin.mn.us/index.php/government/recorder Access to records for a fee at https://tapestry.fidlar.com/Tapestry2/Default.aspx. Search fee is $5.95 each, printed images $.50 each unless otherwise noted. For subscription, contact the Recorder's Office. *Property, Taxation Records* Free search of Auditor property tax data at https://beacon.schneidercorp.com/. Also, at this site-search property records and GIS/mapping for free. For specific information, must subscribe.

McLeod County   *Recorded Documents*   www.co.mcleod.mn.us/mcleodco.cfm?pageID=25&sub=yes   Access recorder data by subscription at http://landshark.co.mcleod.mn.us/LandShark/login.jsp. Set-up $50 plus $50.00 per month, plus $2.00 per image.
Property, Taxation Records   Access to GIS/mapping free at www.co.mcleod.mn.us/mcleodco.cfm?pageID=591&sub=yes2. Check property taxes and delinquent taxes online at http://mcleod.visualgov.com/. Info goes back to 1993.

Meeker County   *Recorded Documents*   www.co.meeker.mn.us/209/Recorder   Access to records for a fee at https://tapestry.fidlar.com/Tapestry2/Default.aspx. Search fee is $5.95 each, printed images $.50 each unless otherwise noted. For subscription, contact the Recorder's Office.

Mille Lacs County   *Recorded Documents*   www.co.mille-lacs.mn.us/   Access to LandShark for a fee at http://136.234.73.242/LandShark/login.jsp?url=http%3A%2F%2F136.234.73.242%2FLandShark%2Fsearchname.jsp.
Property, Taxation Records   Look-up assessor property tax data free at http://cpuimei.com/tax/disclaimer_value.asp?cid=48.

Morrison County   *Recorded Documents*   www.co.morrison.mn.us   Access is via Landshark subscription 1-user service; $50 setup fee; several monthly service plans; first doc image free then $.25 per downloaded page. Info and signup at directly with Eileen at 320-632-0145 or 0146. Visit http://landshark.co.morrison.mn.us/LandShark/login.jsp - tract index by legal disc. back to 1897, images start at 245403 6/1/72.
Property, Taxation Records   Free search of Auditor property tax data at https://beacon.schneidercorp.com/. Also, at this site-search property records and GIS/mapping for free. For specific information, must subscribe.

Mower County   *Recorded Documents*   www.co.mower.mn.us/recorder.html   Access to real estate records for a fee at https://landrecords.co.mower.mn.us/web/login.aspx?ReturnUrl=%2fweb%2f. Grantor/Greantee indexes back to 1/3/1983, images of abstract real estate documents back to 1/2/1980. Contact Recorder's Office for copies
Property, Taxation Records   Search property assessor data free at http://mower.minnesotaassessors.com/. No name searching for free, but a sub service is available which does.

Murray County   *Property, Taxation Records*   Access to real estate tax inquiry for free at http://cpuimei.com/tax/disclaimer.asp?cid=51.

Nicollet County   *Recorded Documents*   www.co.nicollet.mn.us/292/Recorders-Office   Access to LandShark for a fee at https://landshark.co.nicollet.mn.us/LandShark/login.jsp?url=https%3A%2F%2Flandshark.co.nicollet.mn.us%2FLandShark%2Fsearchname.jsp. Also, access to a subscripton site at www.co.nicollet.mn.us/581/RecordEASE-Web.   *Property, Taxation Records*   Access to property information for free at http://nicollet.minnesotaassessors.com/. Also, free search of Auditor property tax data at https://beacon.schneidercorp.com/. Also, at this site-search property records and GIS/mapping for free. For specific information, must subscribe.

Nobles County   *Property, Taxation Records*   Look-up assessor property tax data free at http://206.145.187.205/tax/disclaimer_value.asp?cid=53. Also, free search of Auditor property tax data at https://beacon.schneidercorp.com/. Also, at this site-search property records and GIS/mapping for free. For specific information, must subscribe.

Norman County   *Property, Taxation Records*   Access to GIS/mapping for free at http://gismap.co.norman.mn.us/link/jsfe/index.aspx.

Olmsted County   *Recorded Documents*   https://www.co.olmsted.mn.us/prl/Pages/default.aspx   Recording office land records information by subscription via Landshark at http://landshark.co.olmsted.mn.us/LandShark/login.jsp. Yearly or monthly signup required, plus escrow account for usage. Occasional user option now available. See website or contact Wendy at 507-328-7634.
Property, Taxation Records   Property records and GIS-map data is available free at https://webapp.co.olmsted.mn.us/propertytax/Site/Default.aspx.

Otter Tail County   *Recorded Documents*   www.co.otter-tail.mn.us/445/Recorders-Office   Access recorder office real estate data by Tapestry at www.co.otter-tail.mn.us/1093/Tapestry. Fee based. This is a pay as you go site. For a subscription based site go to www.co.otter-tail.mn.us/1094/Laredo.   *Property, Taxation Records*   Search property tax data at www.co.otter-tail.mn.us/589/Property-Tax-Resources. Includes delinquent property taxes list and tax payment lookup.

Pennington County   *Recorded Documents*   http://co.pennington.mn.us/departments/recorder.asp   Access for iDoc database for online real estate for a fee at https://idocmarket.com/Sites#. Fee varies depending on plan desired. Must sign-up & pay before use. Indexing back to 1/1/1989, images back to 1989.

Pine County   *Recorded Documents*   www.co.pine.mn.us/index.asp   Access to land records for a fee at https://landshark.co.pine.mn.us/LandShark/login. Must register and subscribe.
Property, Taxation Records   Free search of Auditor property tax data at https://beacon.schneidercorp.com/. Also, at this site-search property records and GIS/mapping for free. For specific information, must subscribe.

Pipestone County   *Recorded Documents*   www.pipestone-county.com/board/recorder.php   Access for iDoc database for online real estate for a fee at https://idocmarket.com/Sites#. Fee varies depending on plan desired. Must sign-up & pay before use.
Property, Taxation Records   Access to GIS/mapping free at http://co.pipestone.mn.us:8080/pipestonemoose26/index.html.

Polk County   *Recorded Documents*   www.co.polk.mn.us/index.asp   Access for iDoc database for online real estate for a fee at https://idocmarket.com/Sites#. Must sign-up & pay before use. Images back to 1890. All indexed by the document number. Grantors/Grantees are indexed back to 1991.   *Property, Taxation Records*   Access to real estate records and sale searches for free at http://polk.minnesotaassessors.com/.

Pope County *Recorded Documents* www.co.pope.mn.us/recorder.php   Access to records for a fee at https://tapestry.fidlar.com/Tapestry2/Default.aspx. Search fee is $5.95 each, printed images $.50 each unless otherwise noted. For subscription, contact the Recorder's Office.
Property, Taxation Records   Look-up assessor property tax data free at http://cpuimei.com/tax/disclaimer_value.asp?cid=61.

Ramsey County *Recorded Documents (indexes only) Records* https://www.ramseycounty.us/residents/property/recorders-office   This agency's extensive search product including recorded documents is available by subscription; see http://rrinfo.co.ramsey.mn.us/public/document/index.asp. *Property, Taxation Records*   Search the property assessment rolls free at http://rrinfo.co.ramsey.mn.us/public/characteristic/index.aspx but no name searching.

Redwood County *Property, Taxation Records*   Access to free search of Auditor property tax data at https://beacon.schneidercorp.com/. Also, at this site-search property records and GIS/mapping for free.

Renville County *Recorded Documents* www.renvillecountymn.com/departments/tax_and_property_records/recorder/index.php   Access to records for a fee. Subscriptions offered on 4 separate levels of access. Go the this website for more information.
Property, Taxation Records   Look-up assessor property tax data free at http://cpuimei.com/tax/disclaimer.asp?cid=65. Also, access to property taxes for free at http://cpui.us/tax/disclaimer.asp?cid=65.

Rice County *Recorder Records Records* www.co.rice.mn.us/departments/recorder   Access to LandShark database for a fee at http://landshark.co.rice.mn.us/LandShark/login. Must register with user name and password.
Property, Taxation Records   Free search of Auditor property tax data at https://beacon.schneidercorp.com/. Also, at this site-search property records and GIS/mapping for free. For specific information, must subscribe. Also, access to county maps for free at www.co.rice.mn.us/departments/maps.

Rock County *Recorded Documents* www.co.rock.mn.us   A Access to records for a fee at https://tapestry.fidlar.com/Tapestry2/Default.aspx. Search fee is $5.95 each, printed images $.50 each unless otherwise noted. For subscription, contact the Recorder's Office.
Property, Taxation Records   Access to GIS/mapping free at http://rock.houstoneng.com/. Free search of property tax data fir the City of Luvern at https://beacon.schneidercorp.com/. Also, at this site-search property records and GIS/mapping for free. For specific information, must subscribe.

Roseau County *Property, Taxation Records*   Access to GIS/mapping free at http://gis.co.roseau.mn.us/link/jsfe/index.aspx. Also, access to the Sales List for free at www.co.roseau.mn.us/assessor.html.

Scott County *Recorded Documents* www.co.scott.mn.us/Pages/DepartmentDetail.aspx?LID=14   Access to the images, or print copies, of multiple recorded documents or certificates of title for a monthly fee go to www.co.scott.mn.us/PropertyGISLand/LandRecords/Pages/Land%20Records.aspx.
Property, Taxation Records   Search assessor and a variety of other property data for a fee at www.co.scott.mn.us/PropertyGISLand/propertyassessment/Pages/PropertyAssessment.aspx. Must subscribe. Also, access to GIS/mapping for a fee at www.co.scott.mn.us/PROPERTYGISLAND/GEOGRAPHICINFORMATIONSYSTEMS/Pages/GeographicInformationSystems.aspx.

Sherburne County *Recorded Records Records* www.co.sherburne.mn.us/recorder/index.php   Call Samantha for information on their online access.
Property, Taxation Records   Free search of Auditor property tax data at https://beacon.schneidercorp.com/. Also, at this site-search property records and GIS/mapping for free. For specific information, must subscribe.

Sibley County *Recorded Documents* www.co.sibley.mn.us/recorder/index.php   Access to Sibley County Land Records from Aug. 1994 to present, by Landshark. Access fees for LandShark are $50 installation, $50 per month and $2 per document viewed.
Property, Taxation Records   Access to tax records for free at www.co.sibley.mn.us/treasurer/property_tax_information.php.

St. Louis County *Recorded Documents* www.stlouiscountymn.gov/LANDPROPERTY/RealEstateRecording.aspx   Access the recorder database by subscription. Fee is $140 monthly and includes assessment records. Contact the Auditor or Recorder office for sign up, or visit the Recorder office website and click on Online Contract.
Property, Taxation Records   Access to parcel tax look-up information for free at http://apps.stlouiscountymn.gov/auditor/parcelInfo2005Iframe/. No name look-ups.

Stearns County *Recorded Documents* www.co.stearns.mn.us/Government/CountyDepartments/RecordersOffice   Access to land records for a fee at https://erecording.co.stearns.mn.us/LandShark/about.jsp?aboutKey=LandShark.
Property, Taxation Records   Free search of Auditor property tax data at https://beacon.schneidercorp.com/. Also, at this site-search property records and GIS/mapping for free. For specific information, must subscribe.

Steele County *Recorded Documents* www.co.steele.mn.us/   A Access to records for a fee at https://tapestry.fidlar.com/Tapestry2/Default.aspx. Search fee is $5.95 each, printed images $.50 each unless otherwise noted. For subscription, contact the Recorder's Office.
Property, Taxation Records   Search parcel data, sales, and GIS-mapping site free at http://steele.minnesotaassessors.com/search.php.

Stevens County *Property, Taxation Records*   Access to GIS/mapping for free at http://gis.co.stevens.mn.us/gis/geomoose.html

Swift County Land Records *Property, Taxation Records*   Access parcel data by address, ID, or book/page for free at http://206.145.187.205/tax/disclaimer.asp?cid=76.

Todd County *Recorder Documents Records* www.co.todd.mn.us/departments/recorder/recorder_frontpage_panel   Access to recorder's records for a fee at Landshark. Contact Cheryl Perish at 320-732-4459 or cheryl.perish@co.todd.mn.us.
Property, Taxation Records   Access property data on the GIS-mapping site free at http://gis.mytoddcounty.com/gisviewer/. Also, look-up assessor property/parcel tax data and free at http://cpuimei.com/tax/disclaimer.asp?cid=77.

Traverse County *Recorded Documents* www.co.traverse.mn.us/departments/departments/county-recorder/   Access for iDoc database for online real estate for a fee at https://idocmarket.com/Sites#. Fee varies depending on plan desired. Must sign-up & pay before use. Computer indexing and imaging back to 1/1/2004.
Property, Taxation Records   Access to assessor records for free at http://cpuimei.com/tax/disclaimer_value.asp?cid=78.

Wabasha County *Property, Taxation Records*   Free search of Auditor property tax data at https://beacon.schneidercorp.com/. Also, at this site-search property records and GIS/mapping for free. For specific information, must subscribe.

Wadena County *Property, Taxation Records*   Access to parcel database free at http://206.145.187.205/tax/disclaimer.asp?cid=80. Also, access to GIS/mapping for free at http://gis.co.wadena.mn.us/link/jsfe/index.aspx.

Waseca County *Recorded Documents* www.co.waseca.mn.us/index.aspx?nid=131   With registration, username and password can access recording data on LandShark system at http://landshark.co.waseca.mn.us/LandShark/login.jsp. Fee is $50.00 per month, plus copy fee for images.
Property, Taxation Records   Access to GIS/mapping free at http://gis.co.waseca.mn.us/jsfe/index.aspx. Also, access to the sales data for free at www.co.waseca.mn.us/index.aspx?NID=239.

Washington County *Recorded Documents* https://www.co.washington.mn.us/index.aspx?nid=721   Access to county tract records requires a $50.00 set up fee and $50.00 monthly fee; abstract images go back to 1/1984; Torrens images to 1/1984; tracts to 1984. UCC and Torrens cert, data is not on this system. Go to https://www.co.washington.mn.us/index.aspx?NID=1131 for more information.
Property, Taxation Records   Access to property records/GIS/mapping for free at http://maps.co.washington.mn.us/PropertyViewer/. Also, access to real estate sales for free at http://washington.minnesotaassessors.com/showResSaleSearch.php. Also, access to real estate search for free at http://washington.minnesotaassessors.com/search.php.

Watonwan County *Recorded Land Documents Records* www.co.watonwan.mn.us/index.aspx?nid=195   Access to records for a fee at https://tapestry.fidlar.com/Tapestry2/Default.aspx. Search fee is $5.95 each, printed images $.50 each unless otherwise noted. For subscription, contact the Recorder's Office.
Property, Taxation Records   Free search of Auditor property tax data at https://beacon.schneidercorp.com/. Also, at this site-search property records for free. For specific information, must subscribe.

Winona County *Recorded Documents* www.co.winona.mn.us/page/2464   Access to (informational only-no tract index) recorded sales, rural land sales and foreclosures free at www.co.winona.mn.us/page/2464. Also, access to land records for a fee at http://ls.winonaco.com/LandShark/login.
Property, Taxation Records   Access to property records for free at www.qpublic.net/mn/winona/. Also, free search of Auditor property tax data at https://beacon.schneidercorp.com/. Also, at this site-search property records and GIS/mapping for free. For specific information, must subscribe.

Wright County *Recorded Documents* www.co.wright.mn.us/195/Recorder   Access to Land Title database (data only) free at https://landshark.co.wright.mn.us/LandShark/login.jsp?url=https%3A%2F%2Flandshark.co.wright.mn.us%2FLandShark%2Fsearchname.jsp. No images. Data & images available with LandShark remote access, fee based.
Property, Taxation Records   Search the property tax database free at https://intranet2.co.wright.mn.us/proptax2/. Also, free search of Auditor property tax data at https://beacon.schneidercorp.com/, includes City of Buffalo. Also, at this site-search property records and GIS/mapping for free. For specific information, must subscribe.

Yellow Medicine County *Recorded Documents* www.co.ym.mn.gov/index.asp   Access for iDoc database for online real estate for a fee at https://idocmarket.com/Sites#. Fee varies depending on plan desired. Must sign-up & pay before use. Abstract documents indexed/imaged back to 1/1/2003.
Property, Taxation Records   Access to 2012-2016 tillable land estimated market values for free at www.co.ym.mn.us/index.asp?Type=B_BASIC&SEC={5B1C3107-AC4A-4783-A571-4B2A56B301D3}.

Mississippi

Capital: Jackson
              Hinds County
Time Zone: CST
Population: 2,992,333
# of Counties: 82

Useful State Links

Website: **www.ms.gov**
Governor: **www.governorbryant.com/**
Attorney General: **www.ago.state.ms.us**
State Archives: **www.mdah.ms.gov/new/**
State Statutes and Codes: **www.legislature.ms.gov/Pages/default.aspx**
Legislative Bill Search: **www.legislature.ms.gov/Pages/default.aspx**
Unclaimed Funds: **www.treasurerlynnfitch.com/unclaimedproperty/Pages/default.aspx**

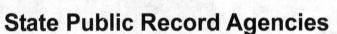

State Public Record Agencies

Sexual Offender Registry

DPS- MS Bureau of Investigation, Sex Offender Registration,   http://state.sor.dps.ms.gov/   The state Sex Offender Registry can be accessed at the website http://state.sor.dps.ms.gov. Search by last name, city, county, or ZIP Code. One may also sign-up for Community Notifications for offenders within one, two or three miles of a designated address.

Incarceration Records

Mississippi Department of Corrections, Records Department,   www.mdoc.ms.gov/Pages/default.aspx   There is an inmate search by name or ID number at https://www.ms.gov/mdoc/inmate. Also, search the Parole Board records at https://www.ms.gov/mdoc/parolee.

Corporation, LP, LLP, LLC, Trademarks/Servicemarks

Secretary of State, Business Services,   www.sos.ms.gov/BusinessServices/Pages/default.aspx   An online search service is available at https://corp.sos.ms.gov/corp/portal/c/page/corpBusinessIdSearch/portal.aspx?#clear=1.   Also, search securities companies registered with the state at www.sos.ms.gov/Applications/Pages/Securities-Filings-Search.aspx.   *Other Options:* The Data Division offers bulk release of information on an annual subscription basis ($1500). Monthly subscription to list of new corporations and new qualifications is $25.00.

Uniform Commercial Code, Federal & State Tax Liens

Secretary of State, Business Services - UCC,   www.sos.ms.gov/BusinessServices/Pages/UCC.aspx   Free searching for UCC debtors is at www.sos.ms.gov/BusinessServices/Pages/UCC-Search.aspx for basic search. For more detailed information must sign-up for the subscription.   *Other Options:* A monthly list of farm liens is available for purchase.

Sales Tax Registrations

Department of Revenue, Sales and Use Tax Bureau,   www.dor.ms.gov/Business/Pages/Sales-Use-Tax-landing.aspx   Verify a Perment Number at https://tap.dor.ms.gov/_/#1

Vital Records

State Department of Health, Vital Statistics & Records,   www.msdh.ms.gov/phs/   Orders can be placed via a state designated vendor. Go to www.vitalchek.com. Extra fees are involved.

Workers' Compensation Records

Workers Compensation Commission,   www.mwcc.state.ms.us/#/home   The First Report of Injury, proof of coverage by an employer, and other documents are available via the web. There is no fee, but users might need to register for some services.

Driver Records

Department of Public Safety, Driver Services, www.dps.state.ms.us/driver-services/ In 2012, the processing of electronic driving record requests was taken over by Mississippi Interactive (MSI), an affiliate of NIC. This is in concert with the new state portal for Mississippi. The fee is $14.00 per record. All requesters are required to be initially approved by the DPS and must sign a subscription agreement with MS.gov. There is an annual $95 subscription fee for new accounts. Billing is monthly. At present there are no details about this service on the web page. Interested new subscribers should contact the MSI at 877-290-9487.

Vehicle Ownership & Registration

Department of Revenue, Motor Vehicle Licensing Bureau, www.dor.ms.gov/TagsTitles/Pages/default.aspx Electronic access to vehicle records is available to approved, DPPA compliant entities. Accounts must pay an annual $100 registration fee, record search fees are the same as listed above. Access is via the web. *Other Options:* Mississippi offers some standardized files as well as some customization for bulk requesters of VIN and registration information. For more information, contact MLVB at the address listed above.

Crash Reports

Safety Responsibility, Accident Records, www.dps.state.ms.us/online-collision-reports/ Persons legally eligible to obtain a copy of the report can do so online by visiting http://reportbeam.com. Select "Purchase a Report" under the "Public Access" tab. The fee is $20.00. Reports are available from local law enforcement and from the Highway Patrol.

Vessel Ownership & Registration

Wildlife, Fisheries, & Parks Dept, Boating Registration, www.mdwfp.com/license/boating-registration.aspx One may do a search at the registration renewal site https://www.ms.gov/gf/boating/index.jsp. There is no name searching; both the MI Number and Serial (HIN) must be input. *Other Options:* This agency makes records available electronically and on printed lists. Fees vary.

Voter Registration, Campaign Finance, Lobbyists

Secretary of State, Elections Division, www.sos.ms.gov/elections.aspx Campaign finance reports are at www.sos.ms.gov/elections3.aspx. A lobbyist and client search is at www.sos.ms.gov/elec/portal/msel/page/search/portal.aspx. A PAC list is at www.sos.ms.gov/links/elections/home/tab1/PACReport_100610.pdf. *Other Options:* Voter registration lists are available for purchase. Call for details.

GED Certificates

Mississippi Community College Board, GED Office, www.sbcjc.cc.ms.us/adulted/addefault.aspx Third parties are routed to set up an account at: http://exchange.parchment.com/ged-receiver-registration-page. Parchment verifies that they are who they say they are so that they can place orders on behalf of students. Parchment contacts the third party and provides training on the site for ordering. During this training any orders they have are placed. After this the third party can order on behalf of students. They still must upload a consent form for each student during the process.

Occupational Licensing Boards

Alcoholic Beverage Retailer	www.dor.ms.gov/ABC/Pages/Authorized-Wholesale.aspx
Architect/Landscape Architect/Interior Designer	https://www.msboa.ms.gov/secure/licensesearch.asp
Asbestos Contractor/Insp/Supv/Worker	http://opc.deq.state.ms.us/report_asbestos_el.aspx
Asbestos Project Designer/Planner	http://opc.deq.state.ms.us/report_asbestos_el.aspx
Athletic Trainer	https://apps.msdh.ms.gov/licreviews/index.aspx
Attorney/Attorney Firm	http://msbar.org/lawyer-directory.aspx
Audiologist	https://apps.msdh.ms.gov/licreviews/index.aspx
Bank	www.dbcf.state.ms.us/documents/banking/mslist.pdf
Beauty School	www.msbc.ms.gov/Pages/School-List.aspx
Body Piercing/Tattoo Operator	https://apps.msdh.ms.gov/licreviews/index.aspx
Charity/Fund Raiser	https://charities.sos.ms.gov/online/portal/ch/page/charities-search/Portal.aspx
Child Care Facility	www.msdh.state.ms.us/msdhsite/_static/30,332,183,438.html
Chiropractor	www.msbce.ms.gov/msbce/msbce.nsf/Search?OpenForm
Contractor, Commercial/Residential	www.msboc.us/OnlineServices/CheckLicenseRequest.html
Counselor, Professional	https://www.lpc.ms.gov/secure/licensesearch.asp
Dental Hygienist/Radiologist	www.dentalboard.ms.gov/msbde/msbdesearch.nsf/WebStart
Dentist	www.dentalboard.ms.gov/msbde/msbdesearch.nsf/WebStart
Dietician	https://apps.msdh.ms.gov/licreviews/index.aspx
Dietitian	https://apps.msdh.ms.gov/licreviews/index.aspx
Emergency Medical Technician	https://mississippi.emsbridge.com/licensure/public/mississippi/lookup/
Engineer	www.pepls.state.ms.us/pepls/web.nsf/webpages/LN_LV_PAGE_LV?OpenDocument
Eye Enucleator	https://apps.msdh.ms.gov/licreviews/index.aspx

Funeral Director/Service Practitioner	https://www.msbfs.ms.gov/secure/licenseverification.asp
Funeral Home/Establishment	https://www.msbfs.ms.gov/secure/licenseverification.asp
Geologist	www.msbrpg.ms.gov/MSBRPG%20Documents/git.htm
Health Facility	http://msdh.ms.gov/msdhsite/_static/resources/4662.pdf
Hearing Aid Dealer (Specialist)	https://apps.msdh.ms.gov/licreviews/index.aspx
HMO	https://www.mid.ms.gov/licensing-search/licensing-search.aspx
Home Inspector	http://appserver.mrec.ms.gov/findlicensee.asp
Insurance Agent/Solicitor/Advisor	https://www.mid.ms.gov/licensing-search/licensing-search.aspx
Insurance/Domestic Insurance Company	https://www.mid.ms.gov/licensing-search/licensing-search.aspx
Lobbyist	www.sos.state.ms.us/elections/Lobbying/Lobbyist_Dir.asp
Long Term Care Insurance Firm	https://www.mid.ms.gov/licensing-search/licensing-search.aspx
Marriage & Family Therapist	www.swmft.ms.gov/swmft/Roster.nsf/webpage/Therapist_1?editdocument
Medical Radiation Technician	https://apps.msdh.ms.gov/licreviews/index.aspx
Notary Public	www.sos.ms.gov/Applications/Pages/Notary-Search.aspx
Nurse-LPN/RN	https://gateway.licensure.msbn.ms.gov/Verification/search.aspx
Nursing Home Administrator	https://www.msnha.ms.gov/secure/licenseverification.asp
Occupational Therapist/Assistant	https://apps.msdh.ms.gov/licreviews/index.aspx
Optometrist	www.msbo.ms.gov/SitePages/License%20Verification.aspx
Osteopathic Physician	https://www.ms.gov/medical_licensure/renewal/verificationSearch.jsp
Pawn Shop/Pawnbroker	www.dbcf.state.ms.us/documents/lists/pawnbroker.pdf
Pharmacist/Pharmacy/Intern/Technician	https://elicense.mbp.state.ms.us/portal.aspx
Physical Therapist/Assistant	https://apps.msdh.ms.gov/licreviews/index.aspx
Physician/Medical Doctor	https://www.ms.gov/medical_licensure/renewal/verificationSearch.jsp
Podiatrist	https://www.ms.gov/medical_licensure/renewal/verificationSearch.jsp
Polygraph Examiner	www.mississippipolygraph.com/member-directory.php
Psychologist	http://dsitspe01.its.ms.gov/msbp/roster.nsf/webpage/psych_1?editdocument
Real Estate Agent/Seller/Broker	http://appserver.mrec.ms.gov/findlicensee.asp
Real Estate Appraiser	http://appserver.mrec.ms.gov/findappraiser.asp
Respiratory Care Therapist	https://apps.msdh.ms.gov/licreviews/index.aspx
Social Worker	www.swmft.ms.gov/swmft/Roster.nsf/webpage/Therapist_1?editdocument
Speech-Language Pathologist	https://apps.msdh.ms.gov/licreviews/index.aspx
Surplus Lines Insurer	https://www.mid.ms.gov/licensing-search/licensing-search.aspx
Surveyor, Land	www.pepls.state.ms.us/pepls/web.nsf/webpages/LN_LV_PAGE_LV?OpenDocument

State and Local Courts

About Mississippi Courts: **Circuit Courts** hear felony criminal prosecutions and civil lawsuits. **Chancery Courts** have jurisdiction over matters involving equity; domestic matters including adoptions, custody disputes and divorces; guardianships; sanity hearings; probate, wills; and challenges to constitutionality of state laws. Land records are filed in Chancery Court. Chancery Courts have jurisdiction over juvenile matters in counties which have no County Court.

County Courts have exclusive jurisdiction over eminent domain proceedings and juvenile matters, among other things. In counties which have a County Court, a County Court judge also serves as the Youth Court judge. County Courts share jurisdiction with Circuit and Chancery Courts in some civil matters. The jurisdictional limit of County Courts is up to $200,000. County Courts may handle non-capital felony cases transferred from Circuit Court. **County Courts have concurrent jurisdiction with Justice Courts in all matters, civil and criminal.** The operations of Circuit and County Courts are usually combined in a county, except in Harrison County.

Justice Courts have jurisdiction over small claims civil cases involving amounts of $3,500 or less, eviction cases, misdemeanor criminal cases and any traffic offense that occurs outside a municipality.

Municipal Courts have jurisdiction over misdemeanor crimes, municipal ordinances and city traffic violations.

Drug Courts are special courts which address crimes committed by persons addicted to drugs or alcohol. **Youth Courts** generally deal with matters in involving abuse and neglect of juveniles, as well as offenses committed by juveniles.

The web page for the Judiciary is http://courts.ms.gov//

Appellate Courts: The Court of Appeals hears cases assigned by the Supreme Court and is also an error correction court. Decisions of the Chancery, Circuit and County Courts and of the Court of Appeals may be appealed to the Supreme Court. The home page above offers searching of the MS Supreme Court and Court of Appeals decisions and dockets.

Online Court Access

Mississippi is implementing the **Mississippi Electronic Courts System (MEC)**. The MEC System is a comprehensive case management system which allows courts to offer electronic case filing and to maintain electronic case files using the Web. The system closely resembles the Federal Courts' CM/ECF case management system. **37+ counties have courts** participating at this time. Most of the participating courts are Chancery Courts. There are a handful of Circuit and County Courts that participate as well, but these court general limit access to Civil records only. More courts planning to participate in the near future.

How MEC Works:

MEC provides access to case documents filed electronically. There is a $10.00 annual registration fee and a charge of $.20 per page to view documents. Criminal, civil, probate, and eviction cases are among those cases available. Divorce, adoption, mental committement and debt collection cases are not available. Records may be searched by case number, file date, nature of the case or suit, attorney name, and by party name. However there are no identifiers used as part of a name search and limited identifiers are shown on results. Also this time there is no indication on the web page of the through put of records for the participating courts, but in general throughput is 5 years or less. Some courts are adding their historical electronic case files and some courts do not have historical electronic cases to place on the system. Attorneys registered with MEC may file and view documents from any court participating on the system.

In summary, at this time the MEC is not an online/onsite equivalent system, use caution. For details visit http://courts.ms.gov/mec/mec.html.

A number of counties particpate with a vendor to provide access to document images on a subscription basis. These counties are indicated in the profiles.

Adams County
Circuit & County Courts   https://www.adamscountyms.net/circuit-court
Civil: The Circuit Court Case and Judgment Roll Information is $30/monthly or $330/yearly. A user account must be created and subscription purchased to use this service at http://www.deltacomputersystems.com/MS/MS01/ *Criminal:* same

Benton County
Circuit Court   http://bentoncountyms.gov/circuit.html
Civil: Commercial access ($30 monthly or $330 annual sub.) to civil index is via a vendor at http://www.deltacomputersystems.com/ms/bccc/index.html.
Criminal: Commercial access ($30 monthly or $330 annual sub.) to criminal index is via a vendor at http://www.deltacomputersystems.com/ms/bccc/index.html.

Clay County
Circuit Court   http://www.claycountyms.com/index.php/court_systems/circuit_court
Civil: Online access is provided to subscribers at http://courts.ms.gov/mec/mec.html. This is an electronic case filing system, so not all historical cases are included. There is a $10.00 annual fee and a $.20 per page view. Search by case number, type of case, attorney name or party name. No identifiers are provided. Includes eviction. *Criminal:* same Search by case number, type of case, attorney name or party name. No identifiers are provided.

De Soto County
Circuit & County Courts   http://www.desotocountyms.gov/index.aspx?nid=116
Civil: Search docket information, records and judgments at http://www.deltacomputersystems.com/ms/ms17/index.html. Fee is $30 monthly or $330 annually. Online access is provided to subscribers at http://courts.ms.gov/mec/mec.html. This is an electronic case filing system, so not all historical cases are included. There is a $10.00 annual fee and a $.20 per page view. No identifiers are provided. *Criminal:* same

Hancock County
Circuit Court   http://www.hancockcounty.ms.gov/Pages/Circuit.aspx
Civil: Commercial access ($30 monthly or $330 annual sub.) to civil index is via a vendor at http://www.deltacomputersystems.com/ms/ms23/index.html.
Criminal: Commercial access ($30 monthly or $330 annual sub.) to criminal index is via a vendor at http://www.deltacomputersystems.com/ms/ms23/index.html.

Harrison County
Circuit Court - 1st District - Gulfport   http://co.harrison.ms.us/elected/circuitclerk/
Civil: Access to Judicial District judgments are free at http://co.harrison.ms.us/elected/circuitclerk/jroll/. Search current court dockets free by date at http://co.harrison.ms.us/dockets/. Online access is provided to subscribers at http://courts.ms.gov/mec/mec.html. This is an electronic case filing system, so not all historical cases are included. There is a $10.00 annual fee and a $.20 per page view. Search by case number, type of case, attorney name or party name. No identifiers are provided. Includes eviction.
Circuit Court - 2nd District - Biloxi   http://co.harrison.ms.us/elected/circuitclerk/
Civil: Access to Judicial District judgments are free at http://co.harrison.ms.us/elected/circuitclerk/jroll/. Search current court dockets free by date at http://co.harrison.ms.us/dockets/. Online access is provided to subscribers at http://courts.ms.gov/mec/mec.html. This is an electronic case filing system,

so not all historical cases are included. There is a $10.00 annual fee and a $.20 per page view. Search by case number, type of case, attorney name or party name. No identifiers are provided. Includes eviction. *Criminal:* Search current court dockets by date free at http://co.harrison.ms.us/dockets/.

County Court - Both Districts - Gulfport   http://co.harrison.ms.us/elected/circuitclerk/

Civil: Access to Judicial District judgments are free at http://co.harrison.ms.us/elected/circuitclerk/jroll/. Search current court dockets free by date at http://co.harrison.ms.us/dockets/. Online access is provided to subscribers at http://courts.ms.gov/mec/mec.html. This is an electronic case filing system, so not all historical cases are included. There is a $10.00 annual fee and a $.20 per page view. Search by case number, type of case, attorney name or party name. No identifiers are provided. Includes eviction.   *Criminal:*   Search current court dockets by date free at http://co.harrison.ms.us/dockets/

All Chancery Courts - http://co.harrison.ms.us/elected/chanceryclerk/chancourt.asp
Search Chancery Court dockets for free at http://co.harrison.ms.us/dockets/.

Hinds County

Circuit Court - 2nd District - Raymond   http://www.hindscountyms.com/elected-offices/circuit-clerk

Civil: Access the clerk's judgment rolls free at www.co.hinds.ms.us/pgs/apps/jridx_query.asp. Online access is provided to subscribers at http://courts.ms.gov/mec/mec.html. This is an electronic case filing system, so not all historical cases are included. There is a $10.00 annual fee and a $.20 per page view. Search by case number, type of case, attorney name or party name. No identifiers are provided. Includes eviction.

Circuit Court - 1st District - Jackson   http://www.hindscountyms.com/elected-offices/circuit-clerk

Civil: Search civil and county case info at http://www.co.hinds.ms.us/pgs/apps/gindex.asp. Judgment information is also available. Online access is provided to subscribers at http://courts.ms.gov/mec/mec.html. This is an electronic case filing system, so not all historical cases are included. There is a $10.00 annual fee and a $.20 per page view. Search by case number, type of case, attorney name or party name. No identifiers are provided. Includes eviction.

County Court - 1st District - Jackson   http://www.hindscountyms.com/elected-offices/circuit-clerk

Civil: Search civil and county case info at http://www.co.hinds.ms.us/pgs/apps/gindex.asp. Judgment information is also available. Online access is provided to subscribers at http://courts.ms.gov/mec/mec.html. This is an electronic case filing system, so not all historical cases are included. There is a $10.00 annual fee and a $.20 per page view. Search by case number, type of case, attorney name or party name. No identifiers are provided. Includes eviction.

County Court - 2nd District - Raymond   http://www.hindscountyms.com/elected-offices/circuit-clerk

Civil: Access the clerk's judgment rolls free at www.co.hinds.ms.us/pgs/apps/jridx_query.asp. Online access is provided to subscribers at http://courts.ms.gov/mec/mec.html. This is an electronic case filing system, so not all historical cases are included. There is a $10.00 annual fee and a $.20 per page view. Search by case number, type of case, attorney name or party name. No identifiers are provided. Includes eviction.

Jackson County

Circuit Court   http://www.co.jackson.ms.us/courts/circuit-court/

Civil: Access to only Circuit Court monthly dockets is free at www.co.jackson.ms.us/courts/circuit-court/docket.php.   *Criminal:* Online access to criminal dockets is the same as civil. Search back to 2010.

Jefferson Davis County

Circuit Court

Civil: Online access is provided to subscribers at http://courts.ms.gov/mec/mec.html. This is an electronic case filing system, so not all historical cases are included. There is a $10.00 annual fee and a $.20 per page view. No identifiers are provided. *Criminal:* same

Jones County

All Circuit Courts   http://www.jonescountyms.com/index.php/courts/
Civil: Access the circuit court judgment roll free at http://www.deltacomputersystems.com/MS/MS34/INDEX.HTML.
All County Courts - 1st District - Ellisville   http://www.jonescountyms.com/index.php/courts/
Civil: Access the circuit court judgment roll free at www.deltacomputersystems.com/MS/MS34/INDEX.HTML.

Lafayette County

Circuit Court   http://lafayettems.com/us/elected-officials/circuit-clerk/
Civil: Search the docket index free at http://www.deltacomputersystems.com/MS/MS36/INDEX.HTML.

Lawrence County

Circuit Court

Civil: Online access is provided to subscribers at http://courts.ms.gov/mec/mec.html. This is an electronic case filing system, so not all historical cases are included. There is a $10.00 annual fee and a $.20 per page view. No identifiers are provided. *Criminal:* same

Leflore County

Circuit Court

Civil: A private company permits online access to civil records; go to www.recordsusa.com - subscription required.
County Court   http://leflorecountycourt.com/index.html
Civil: A private company permits online access to civil records; go to www.recordsusa.com - subscription required. :

Lincoln County

Circuit Court   http://www.deltacomputersystems.com/ms/lccc/

Civil: Free access to the dockets plus judgment roll and marriage records at http://www.deltacomputersystems.com/ms/lccc/. One may also purchase document copies for $1.00 per document. Users can subscribe for either $25 per month or $300 per year for unlimited access to scanned documents. *Criminal:* A free search of the dockets is at http://www.deltacomputersystems.com/ms/lccc/. One may also purchase document copies for $1.00 per document.

Lowndes County

Circuit & County Courts   http://lowndescountyms.com/elected-officials/circuit-clerk/

Civil: Online access is via a designated vendor at www.deltacomputersystems.com/search.html, the fee is $30 monthly fee or an $330 annual fee. Circuit Court civil cases and the Judgment Roll are available from 1993 to present are included - images from 2008. Marriage licenses are available for 1991. *Criminal:* Same, criminal cases from 1993 to present are included - images from September 2008.

Madison County

Circuit Court   http://www.madison-co.com/court-systems/circuit-court/

Civil: Online access is provided to subscribers at http://courts.ms.gov/mec/mec.html. This is an electronic case filing system, so not all historical cases are included. There is a $10.00 annual fee and a $.20 per page view. Search by case number, type of case, attorney name or party name. No identifiers are provided. Includes eviction. Records go back to 2010.

County Court   http://www.madison-co.com/court-systems/county-court/

Civil: Online access is provided to subscribers at http://courts.ms.gov/mec/mec.html. This is an electronic case filing system, so not all historical cases are included. There is a $10.00 annual fee and a $.20 per page view. Search by case number, type of case, attorney name or party name. No identifiers are provided. Includes eviction.

Marshall County

Circuit Court

Civil: Commercial access ($30 monthly or $330 annual sub.) to civil index is via a vendor at www.deltacomputersystems.com/ms/mccc/. *Criminal:* Commercial access ($30 monthly or $330 annual sub.) to criminal index is via a vendor at www.deltacomputersystems.com/ms/mccc/.

Oktibbeha County

Circuit Court   http://www.oktibbehacountyms.org/?q=node/78

Civil: Access the county civil circuit records and judgment roll per subscription account at http://www.deltacomputersystems.com/MS/MS53/INDEX.HTML. Fee is $30 monthly or $330 annual. *Criminal:* Access the county criminal circuit records back to 1997 at http://www.deltacomputersystems.com/MS/MS53/INDEX.HTML. Fee is $30 monthly or $330 annual.

Pike County

Circuit & County Courts   http://co.pike.ms.us/departments/circuit_clerk

Civil: Search the judgment roll free at http://co.pike.ms.us/index.php/research_records/judgement_roll. The civil index is available by subscription at http://co.pike.ms.us/court_case_information. Fee is either $30 monthly or $330 annually. *Criminal:* same

Rankin County

Circuit Court   https://www.rankincounty.org/department/index.php?structureid=3

Civil: Online access is provided to subscribers at http://courts.ms.gov/mec/mec.html. This is an electronic case filing system, so not all historical cases are included. There is a $10.00 annual fee and a $.20 per page view. No identifiers are provided.

County Court   https://www.rankincounty.org/department/index.php?structureid=3

Civil: Online access is provided to subscribers at http://courts.ms.gov/mec/mec.html. This is an electronic case filing system, so not all historical cases are included. There is a $10.00 annual fee and a $.20 per page view. No identifiers are provided.

Tate County

Circuit Court

Civil: Online access is provided to subscribers at http://courts.ms.gov/mec/mec.html. This is an electronic case filing system, so not all historical cases are included. There is a $10.00 annual fee and a $.20 per page view. No identifiers are provided. *Criminal:* same

Tippah County

Circuit Court

Civil: Commercial access ($30 monthly or $330 annual sub.) to civil index is via a vendor at http://www.deltacomputersystems.com/ms/ms70/index.html *Criminal:* Commercial access ($30 monthly or $330 annual sub.) to criminal index is via a vendor at http://www.deltacomputersystems.com/ms/ms70/index.html.

Warren County

Circuit & County Court   http://co.warren.ms.us/circuit-clerk/

Civil: Online access is provided to subscribers at http://courts.ms.gov/mec/mec.html. This is an electronic case filing system, so not all historical cases are included. There is a $10.00 annual fee and a $.20 per page view. Search by case number, type of case, attorney name or party name. No identifiers are provided. Includes eviction.

Recorders, Assessors, and Other Sites of Note

About Mississippi Recording Offices: 82 counties, 92 recording offices. The recording officers are Chancery Clerk, and the Clerk of Circuit Court for state tax liens. Ten counties have two separate recording offices - Bolivar, Carroll, Chickasaw, Harrison, Hinds, Jasper, Jones, Panola, Tallahatchie, Yalobusha.

About Tax Liens: Federal tax liens on personal property of businesses are filed with the Secretary of State. Federal tax liens on personal property of individuals are filed with the county Chancery Clerk.

Online Access

Recorded Documents

A limited number of counties offer online access to records. There is no statewide system

Property Tax Data

A vendor - Delta's PropertyLink System - provides access to variety of county data including property tax data. The service varies by individual county. Some counties require a subscription, some provide free information. Approximately 43 counties plus 2 cities participate. See www.deltacomputersystems.com/search.html

Partcipating Counties on Delta:

Adams	Greene	Leake	Pike
Alcorn	Grenada	Lee	Rankin
Benton	Hancock	Lincoln	Scott
Chickasaw	Harrison	Lowndes	Smith
Claiborne	Itawamba	Marion	Stone
Clarke	Jackson	Marshall	Tippah
Covington	Jasper	Neshoba	Union
Desoto	Jones	Newton	Walthall
Forrest	Lafayette	Oktibbeha	Warren
Franklin	Lamar	Pearl River	Washington
George	Lauderdale	Perry	Wayne

County Sites (Delta Online Property Tax Data Sites Omitted Below):

Adams County   *Recorded Documents*   https://www.adamscountyms.net/chancery-clerk   Access judgment rolls and marriage records for a fee at www.deltacomputersystems.com/MS/MS01/INDEX.HTML. Subscription fees are $30/monthly or $330/yearly.

Benton County   *Recorded Documents*   http://bentoncountyms.gov/   Access to deeds and records free at www.deltacomputersystems.com/MS/MS05/index_chancery.html. Unofficial copies of scanned records are $1.50 per page. From 1994-present.

Clarke County   *Mapping*   Find mapping at http://tscmaps.com/cnty/clarke-ms/,

Clay County   *Property, Taxation Records*   Access to property data for free at http://cs.datasysmgt.com/tax?state=MS&county=13.

Copiah County   *Property, Taxation Records*   Access to real property tax and map databases for free at http://tscmaps.com/.

De Soto County   *Recorded Documents*   www.desotocountyms.gov/index.aspx?nid=111   Access to Chancery Clerk grantor/grantee index is available at www.desotoms.info/; click on Chancery Clerk. For voter registration data, click on Circuit Clerk and then Voter Registration tab. Also available, county board and planning commission minutes. For courts and marriages, click on Circuit Clerk.
Property, Taxation Records   Access to GIS/mapping free at www.desotoms.info/. Click on Tax Assessor or Tax Collector..

Forrest County   *Recorded Documents*   http://forrestcountyms.us/?page_id=136   Access to the case information index for free at www.deltacomputersystems.com/MS/MS18/mclinkquerych.html.

George County   *Recorded Documents*   www.georgecountyms.com/chancery_clerk.html   A private company permits online access by subscription; go to www.recordsusa.com/ or call Rob at 888-633-4748 x17 for info and demo.

Grenada County   *Property, Taxation Records*   Search assessor real property and tax sale free at http://tscmaps.com/cnty/grenada-ms/ but no name searching.

Hancock County   *Property, Taxation Records*   Access property data free through the GIS-mapping site owner search page free at http://atlas.geoportalmaps.com/hancock. Search parcel data generally on the mapping site free www.dor.ms.gov/.

Harrison County (Both Districts)   *Recorded Documents, Marriage Records*   http://co.harrison.ms.us/elected/chanceryclerk/
Access general instruments, recorded land records, and marriage records at http://co.harrison.ms.us/services.
Property, Taxation Records   Access property tax data free at http://co.harrison.ms.us/elected/taxassessor/landroll.

Hinds County (Both Districts)   *Recorded Documents*   www.hindscountyms.com/elected-offices/chancery-clerk   Access a list of free
County search databases at www.co.hinds.ms.us/pgs/newindex.asp.
Property, Taxation Records   Search the assessor land roll query for free at www.co.hinds.ms.us/pgs/apps/landroll_query.asp. Also, a property
billing roll query can be searched at www.co.hinds.ms.us/pgs/apps/bppmf/personal_property_billing_roll_query.asp.

Jackson County   *Recorded Documents*   www.co.jackson.ms.us/officials/chancery-clerk/   Access to Chancery Court cases for free at
www.deltacomputersystems.com/search.html. Also, access to the land record index for free at http://landrecords.co.jackson.ms.us/. Click on Chancery
Clerk, then land records. Index and images from 7/29/2002 to present.

Jones County (Both Districts)   *Judgment Records*   www.jonescountyms.com/index.php/gov_admin/chancery_clerk/   Access county
judgment roll a fee at www.deltacomputersystems.com/search.html. Fees are-$30 monthly; $330 annually.
Property, Taxation Records   County appraisal and tax records are available by subscription at www.deltacomputersystems.com/search.html. Fees
are- $30 monthly; $330 annually.

Lawrence County   *Property, Taxation Records*   Search appraisal, Real Property Tax, and tax sales lists free at
www.tscmaps.com/mg/ms/lawrence/index.asp.

Leflore County   *Recorded Judgments, Marriage Records*   www.leflorecounty.org/chancery-clerk   Access judgment rolls and marriage
records from a vendor. Fees involved. See www.recordsusa.com/

Madison County   *Recorded Documents*   www.madison-co.com/elected-offices/chancery-clerk/   Access the Chancery clerks recorded deed
records free at www.madison-co.com/elected-offices/chancery-clerk/court-house-search/deed-record-lookup.php. Also, search at www.madison-
co.com/online_services/index.php for Federal Lien, Chancery Ct, Plat, Covenant, and more.
Property, Taxation Records   Access Land Roll data free at http://tscmaps.com/. Also, search personal property tax data free at www.madison-
co.com/elected-offices/tax-assessor/personal-property-tax-roll.php. Also, access to GIS/mapping for free at http://gis.cmpdd.org/madison/.

Monroe County   *Property, Taxation Records*   Access property records free on the mapping site at http://tscmaps.com/pg/state-of-
mississippi/.

Oktibbeha County   *Recorded Documents*   www.oktibbehachanceryclerk.com/index.php   Search county information at
www.oktibbehachanceryclerk.com/online-search/index.php. Must have username and password. Contact Larry Bellipani at 601-583-7373 to create an
account.
Property, Taxation Records   Online access to property records, appraisals, tax sale lists free at http://tscmaps.com/pg/state-of-mississippi/.

Panola County (Both Districts)   *Property, Taxation Records*   Access to GIS/mapping for free at
http://panolams.geopowered.com/propertysearch/.

Pike County   *Property, Taxation Records*   Search property assessor and tax records free at http://co.pike.ms.us/departments/assessor.

Pontotoc County   *Property, Taxation Records*   Access to property tax information for free at www.geoportalmaps.com/atlas/pontotoc/.

Rankin County   *Recorded Documents*   https://www.rankincounty.org/department/index.php?structureid=16   Access to records for a fee at
https://mscountyrecording.com/.
Property, Taxation Records   Access to GIS/mapping for free at http://gis.cmpdd.org/rankinnew/.

Scott County   *Recorded Documents*   Access to online records, contact Paul at Syscon (205) 758-2000 x8107 or
paul.sellers@syscononline.com.

Tunica County   *Property, Taxation Records*   Access to parcel/mapping for free at http://tunicamaps.com/cnty/tunica-ms/.

Winston County   *Property, Taxation Records*   Access to real property information for free at
http://cs.datasysmgt.com/dsmh/WWREALH1. Also, access to mapping for free at http://winston.tscmaps.com/ms/winston/.

Missouri

Capital: Jefferson City
              Cole County
Time Zone: CST
Population: 6,083,672
# of Counties: 114

Useful State Links

Website: **www.mo.gov**
Governor: **http://governor.mo.gov**
Attorney General: **www.ago.mo.gov**
State Archives: **http://s1.sos.mo.gov/archives/default**
State Statutes and Codes: **www.moga.mo.gov/htmlpages2/Statuteconstitutionsearch.aspx**
Legislative Bill Search: **www.house.mo.gov/billcentral.aspx**
Unclaimed Funds: **www.treasurer.mo.gov/UnclaimedProperty/Main.aspx**

State Public Record Agencies

Criminal Records

Missouri State Highway Patrol, Criminal Justice Information Srvs Division, www.mshp.dps.missouri.gov/MSHPWeb/PatrolDivisions/CRID/crimRecChk.html Online access and retrieval is available at https://www.machs.mshp.dps.mo.gov/MACHSFP/home.html. An account must be first created and use of a credit card is required. The same $12.00 fee applies plus a 'convenience fee' for each transaction. This fee is $1.25 for 1 to 4 records, when more than 4 records are ordered, a sliding scale is used which will vary from $1.75 to $2.15. Once an account is created, users may submit the name, date of birth, and/or SSN of a person. Requesters receive all Missouri open record criminal history information related to the individual - meaning convictions, arrests within 30 days, pending charges and suspended imposition of sentences during probation. All completed records are emailed in a PDF format to the user's account, usually within seconds unless further research is need to determine a disposition. Data includes felonies, misdemeanors, and selected municipal ordinance violations.

Sexual Offender Registry

Missouri State Highway Patrol, Sexual Offender Registry,   www.mshp.dps.mo.gov/CJ38/search.jsp   The name index can be searched at the website, by name, county or ZIP Code. The web page also gives links lists to the county sheriffs who have online access. The Division offers a community notification program, to enroll visit https://www.mshp.dps.missouri.gov/CJ38Comm/logon.jsp. There is a tab to download a complete record file as well. *Other Options:* There is a spreadsheet (Excel) that can be downloaded from the search page - see the tab Download File.

Incarceration Records

Missouri Department of Corrections, Offender Inquiry,   http://doc.mo.gov/   Inmate searching is offered at https://web.mo.gov/doc/offSearchWeb/. Includes probationers and parolees. But the search does not provide information on discharged offenders.

Corporation, LLC, LP, Fictitious/Assumed Name, Trademarks/Servicemarks

Secretary of State, Corporation Services,   www.sos.mo.gov/business/corporations/   Search free online by name, Charter Number or Registered Agent at https://bsd.sos.mo.gov/loginwelcome.aspx?lobID=1. Also, with an established account one may order copies and certified documents online. Use of a credit card is required.   *Other Options:* Bulk listings are available for a fee, call for details.

Uniform Commercial Code

UCC Division,   http://s1.sos.mo.gov/ucc   The web address is https://bsd.sos.mo.gov/loginwelcome.aspx?lobID=0. All users must have an account, and can then both file a UCC lien and conduct any UCC searches. The same search fee applies. Use of a credit card incures a convenience fee (approx. 2.15%), Echeck payemnst incure a $.50 per transaction fee.   *Other Options:* The agency will release information for bulk purchase, call for procedures and pricing.

Vital Records

Department of Health & Senior Svcs, Bureau of Vital Records, http://health.mo.gov/data/vitalrecords/index.php   Orders may be placed online at www.vitalchek.com. Records prior to 1910 are available by county at www.sos.mo.gov/archives/resources/birthdeath/.

Workers' Compensation Records

Labor & Industrial Relations Department, Workers Compensation Division, http://labor.mo.gov/dwc   Online access is available to claimants using a pre-assigned PIN. Appeal decisions are shown to public at www.labor.mo.gov/LIRC/Forms/WC_Decisions/. To check if an employer has coverage, visit http://labor.mo.gov/areyoucovered.

Driver Records

Department of Revenue, Motor Vehicle and Driver Licensing, http://dor.mo.gov/drivers/   Electronic access is different in MO compared to other states. Two methods are offered. Fees are not based on a per record basis, but instead on a batch or file purchase basis. The fee is $52.00 per batch, regardless of the number of requests included. There are set-up fees involved for state programmer's time. If requests are sent by 2AM, results can be picked up at 6AM same day. Also, approved users or vendors may purchase the entire file for drivers and histories (for $2035) and then purchase daily or monthly updates. For further information, call 573-526-3669 or e-mail dlrecords@dor.mo.gov. Requests for driver records may be e-mailed to dlrecords@dor.mo.gov. Customer's request must include all credit card information (type, number, expiration date, etc.) in order for the request to be processed.   *Other Options:* The Bulk Purchase Program described above enables entities to construct their own monitoring programs for themselves or clients. For more information, call 573-526-3669, option 6.

Vehicle, Vessel Ownership & Registration

Department of Revenue, Motor Vehicle and Driver Licensing Div, http://dor.mo.gov/motorv/   Vehicle lienholder data and registration and ownership information is available to registered requesters. There is an approval process since records are only released per permissible use. Two forms are required. The applicant must qualify to have a security access code (DPPA number) issued by the Department. For more information, call 573-526-3669, option 2 The fee is $.0382 per record and is automatically withdrawn through the requestor's ACH account. Access is via the Internet. Visit the web page for more information.   *Other Options:* Missouri has an extensive range of records and information available on electronic format or labels or paper. Besides offering license, vehicle, title, dealer, and marine records, specific public report data is also available. Call 573-526-3669 x6.

Crash Reports

Missouri State Highway Patrol, Traffic Records Division, www.mshp.dps.missouri.gov/MSHPWeb/PatrolDivisions/PRD/index.html   Preliminary information on accidents investigated by the Highway Patrol is found at https://www.mshp.dps.missouri.gov/HP68/search.jsp. Date is posted here for just one year. The site also porvides a list of recent crashes displayed.   *Other Options:* Some crash reconstruction reports may be available via CD, depending on date of crash. CD includes photos and other attachments.

Campaign Finance, Disclosure, Lobbyists, PACs

Missouri Ethics Commission, Division of Elections, www.mec.mo.gov/   A number of searches are available at www.mec.mo.gov/. View campaign finance reports, search and view lobbyist reports, search contribution and expenditures for candidates. Email questions to helpdesk@mec.mo.gov

GED (HSE) Certificates

GED (HSE) Office, http://dese.mo.gov/adult-learning-rehabilitation-services/high-school-equivalency   Individuals, colleges, universities, verifying services and employers can instantly view transcripts for free at https://apps.dese.mo.gov/GEDManagement/Transcript_Search.aspx. To get access to transcript information, 3 pieces of unique information must be entered.: last 4 digits of the SSN, the DOB, and the last name.

Occupational Licensing Boards

These licenses are all searchable at https://renew.pr.mo.gov/licensee-search.asp

Accountant-CPA/Firm	Cosmetologist	Geologist/Registrant in Training
Acupuncturist	Cosmetologist/School/Instructor/Shop	Hearing Instrument Specialist
Anesthesia Permit, Dental	Counselor, Professional/Trainee	Insurance Consultant, Chiropractic
Announcer, Athletic Event/Ring	Dental Hygienist/Specialist	Interior Designer
Architect	Dentist	Interpreter for the Deaf
Athletic Event/Physician/Timekeeper	Drug Distributor	Landscape Architect
Athletic Trainer	DSGA Permit/Site Certificate	Marital & Family Therapist
Audiologist	ECS Permit/Site Certificate	Martial Artist/Martial Art Occupation
Audiologist, Clinical	Embalmer	Massage Therapist/Business
Barber/Barber Shop/Instructor/School	Engineer	Midwife
Body Piercer/Brander/Branding Estab	Esthetician/Manicurist	Nurse-RN/LPN/PA
Boxer/Boxing Professional	Funeral Director/Establishment	Nursing School
Cemetery	Funeral Pre-Need Provider/Seller	Occupation'l Therapist/Therapist Ass't
Chiropractor	General Anesthesia Permit	Optometrist

Parenteral Conscious Sedation
PCS Permit/Site Certificate
Perfusionist
Pharmacist/Pharmacy/Intern/Technician
Physical Therapist
Physical Therapist Assistant
Physician Assistant
Physician/Medical Doctor

Podiatrist/Ankle Specialist
Psychologist
Real Estate Agent/Seller/Broker/Partner
Real Estate Appraiser
Real Estate Instructor/School
Real Estate Officer/Corp/Association
Respiratory Care Practitioner
School Nurse

Social Worker, Baccalaureate/Clinical
Speech-Language Pathologist
Surveyor, Land
Tattoo Artist/Establishment
Veterinarian/Veterinary Tech/Facility
Wrestler/Wrestling Professional

The Rest:

Attorney .... www.mobar.org/LawyerSearch.aspx
Bail Bond Agents/Surety Recovery Agents ...... http://insurance.mo.gov/agents/documents/Licensed_033.pdf
Child Care Facility https://webapp01.dhss.mo.gov/childcaresearch/searchengine.aspx
Insurance Enforcement Action .... http://insurance.mo.gov/CompanyAgentSearch/search/SearchEnforcementActions.php
Investment Advisor .... www.sos.mo.gov/securities/mipc/brokercheck.asp
Lobbyist Report .... http://mec.mo.gov/MEC/Lobbying/Lob_SearchLob.aspx
Lobbyist/Active .... http://mec.mo.gov/MEC/Lobbying/Lob_SearchLob.aspx
Notary Public .... www.sos.mo.gov/Notary/NotarySearch/NotarySearch.aspx
Nursing Home Administrator .... http://health.mo.gov/information/boards/bnha/pdf/administrators.pdf
Pesticide Applicator/Technician .... https://apps.mda.mo.gov/moplants/PesticideApplicator/ApplicationExternalSearch.aspx
Pesticide Brand .... https://apps.mda.mo.gov/moplants/ProductRegFSA/BrandSearch.aspx
Pesticide Dealer/Registered/Business .... https://apps.mda.mo.gov/moplants/PesticideApplicator/ApplicationExternalSearch.aspx
Private Investigator/Agency/Branch/Trainer ..... https://renew.pr.mo.gov/pi-licensee-search.asp
Private Investigator/Fire Investigator .... https://renew.pr.mo.gov/pi-licensee-search.asp
Securities Agent/Broker/Dealer .... www.sos.mo.gov/securities/mipc/brokercheck.asp
Teacher .... https://apps.dese.mo.gov/HQT/CredentialListerChecker.aspx

State and Local Courts

About Missouri Courts: Missouri Circuit Courts are courts of original civil and criminal jurisdiction. Within the Circuit Court, there are various divisions, such as Criminal, Associate Circuit (**lower level civil cases usually under $25,000**), Small Claims, Municipal, Family, Probate, and Juvenile. The type of case determines the division to which a particular case is assigned.

At one time, every county had a separate **Associate Circuit Court** which heard a variety of case types. Since 01/01/2010, all Associate Courts have been absorbed into the Circuit Court as Divisions. The judges in this Division generally hear civil cases under $25,000 and misdemeanors.

The **Municipal Court** has original jurisdiction on municipal ordinance violations. A List of Municipal Courts is found at www.courts.mo.gov/page.jsp?id=7418.

The web page for the Unified Judicial System is www.courts.mo.gov.

Appellate Courts: The Missouri Court of Appeals is the intermediate appellate court and handles appeals from the Circuit Courts and all other appeals except those in the Supreme Court's exclusive jurisdiction. Appellate and Supreme Court opinions are available at the web page.

Online Court Access

All courts participate in the system described below.

Available at https://www.courts.mo.gov/casenet/base/welcome.do is **Missouri CaseNet**, an online system for access to civil, paternity, adult & child protection, and criminal docket data. The system includes all Circuit Courts, City of St. Louis, the Eastern, Western, and Southern Appellate Courts, the Supreme Court, and Fine Collection Center. Cases can be searched case number, filing date, or litigant name. A number of Municipal Courts also participate.

CaseNet search results show full name and address, and only the year of birth if available (click on Parties and Attorneys at case result page).

CaseNet system is what the counties' courthouse public access terminals show on their screens, an online search of CaseNet is considered to be equivalent to an initial search of the public access terminal at the courthouse. The advantage of being at the courthouse is one can look at case files to try and determine the true identity of a search subject if there is a possibility of a false positive.

Not all courts have electronic documents available, only those using the Document Management System (DMS) within the Judicial Information System (JIS). If a document is available for viewing and printing it shows as a blue hyperlink on the screen.

Note that some individual courts offer access to probate records outside of CaseNet. Since June 29, 2012, final judgment documents on domestic relations cases are longer available on Casenet.

An additional service added in 2016 is that Case.net users may register to receive email notifications when docket entries are made or updated on selected cases.

County Sites Other Than the Statewide Casenet System Mentioned Above:

Jackson County
Circuit Court - Probate - Kansas City   https://www.16thcircuit.org/
Online access to probate records is free at www.16thcircuit.org/publicaccess.asp.

Recorders, Assessors, and Other Sites of Note

About Missouri Recording Offices: 114 counties and one independent city; 115 recording offices. The recording officer is the Recorder of Deeds. The City of St. Louis has its own recording office.

About Tax Liens: All federal and state tax liens are filed with the county Recorder of Deeds.

Online Access

Recorded Documents
A number of counties offer online access to records; there is no statewide system except the Secretary of State's UCC access. Twenty-one counties work with https://tapestry.fidlar.com/Tapestry2/Default.aspx for record access. The base fee is $5.95 per search and $.50 per print image, but the county may set their own pricing. You can pay as you go using a credit or pre-pay using a subscription. Also, per the same vendor one may purchase a software program called Laredo (www.fidlar.com/laredo.aspx) with extensive search features. Contact the county for details and pricing.

Tax Assessor and GIS Data
Search assessor GIS property data from 10 jurisdictions for a fee on the GIS system at https://beacon.schneidercorp.com/ with registration and username required. Participating Counties: Audrain. Cass, Callaway, Greene, Jasper, Pettis, Pike, Platte, and St. Louis City, Taney.

A fee based service to property title information for 7 participating counties is managed by a vendor at www.canaanllc.com/index.php/canaanonline/availablecounties, Participating Counties: Boone, Butler, Mississippi, New Midrid, Pemiscot, Scott, Stoddard.

County Sites:

Adair County   *Property, Taxation Records*   Access to parcel search for free at http://adair.missouriassessors.com/. Note this is a vendor site.

Atchison County   *Recorded Documents* www.atchisoncountyrecorder.com/   Access to index and images of deeds or marriage licenses (no images) for a fee at www.atchisoncountyrecorder.com/OnLineRecords.aspx. Contact the Recorder at 660-744-2707 for an application and fees. Real Estate records from 1993 to present.

Audrain County   *Recorded Documents* http://audraincounty.org/county-offices/157-2/   Access to records for a fee at https://tapestry.fidlar.com/Tapestry2/Default.aspx. Search fee is $5.95 each, printed images $.50 each unless otherwise noted. For subscription, contact the Recorder's Office.
Property, Taxation Records   Search assessor property data for a fee on the GIS system at https://beacon.schneidercorp.com/. Registration and username required. At the default website, choose Missouri then Audrain County, then register. Access to parcel search for free at http://audrain.missouriassessors.com/.

Barry County   *Recorded Documents*   Access to records for free at https://cotthosting.com/moportal/User/Login.aspx. For detailed records must subscribe. Index and images available from 1/1/1990 to present.

Bates County   *Recorded Documents*   http://batescounty.net/recorder.php   Access to records for free at http://mo830.cichosting.com/Search.aspx. A note to genealogical researchers: The Butler Public Library has a copy of the land records from 1840 through 1902 and marriage records from 1860 through 1940 are available on microfilm. Also, access to records for a fee at https://esearch.cichosting.com/.
Property, Taxation Records   Access to GIS/mapping free at http://bates.integritygis.com/. Must be authorized to use with user ID and password.

Benton County   *Property, Taxation Records*   Access to GIS/mapping free at http://bentoncogis.com/.

Bollinger County   *Property, Taxation Records*   Access to property data for free at http://bollingermo.devnetwedge.com/.

Boone County   *Recorded Documents*   www.showmeboone.com/RECORDER/   Access to the recorder database is free at www.showmeboone.com/recorder/. Also, access to records for a fee at www.canaanllc.com/. Contact Jon Gilmore at 573-471-6005 for posting procedures. Pricing schedule is at this URL.
Property, Taxation Records   Assessor data of real and personal property is free at www.showmeboone.com/assessor/. Free registration and password required.

Buchanan County   *Recorded Documents*   www.co.buchanan.mo.us/167/Recorder-of-Deeds-Office   Access the recorder database for a fee at http://newvisions.co.buchanan.mo.us/searchng_application/. Fee for database is $250.00 per month by contract agreement. Now also have for occasional user agreement $.25 per minute.
Property, Taxation Records   Search the GIS-mapping site for property data free at www.buchanancomogis.com/ but no name searching.

Butler County   *Recorded Documents*   http://butler.countyportal.net/departments.php?id=recorder   Access to records for a fee at www.canaanllc.com/. Contact Jon Gilmore at 573-471-6005 for posting procedures. Pricing schedule is at this URL. Records from 1989 to present, with images available from 2000. Also, access to records for free (limited) at https://esearch.cichosting.com/. For detailed information, must subscribe.
Property, Taxation Records   Access to GIS/mapping free at http://butlergis.countyportal.net/.

Callaway County   *Recorded Documents*   http://callawaycounty.org/recorder/   Access to records for a fee at http://callawaymo.icounty.com/iRecordWeb2.0/Login.aspx.
Property, Taxation Records   Search assessor property data for free on the GIS system at https://beacon.schneidercorp.com/. Registration and username required. At the default website, choose Missouri then Callaway County, then register.

Camden County   *Property, Taxation Records*   Access to the GIS/mapping free at http://camdencogis.com/.

Cape Girardeau County   *Recorded Documents*   www.capecounty.us/Recorder/Recorders%20Office.aspx   Access to records for a fee at https://tapestry.fidlar.com/Tapestry2/Default.aspx. Search fee is $5.95 each, printed images $.50 each unless otherwise noted. For subscription, contact the Recorder's Office.

Cass County   *Recorded Documents*   www.casscounty.com/2164/Recorder-of-Deeds   Access to index searches are free, to view and copy images, contact Marilyn Morris at 816-380-8168 to set-up account. Fees are $150.00 per month or $.10 per minute. Go to http://209.153.83.8/searchng_application/ for information regarding accessing records and to set up an account.
Property, Taxation Records   Search assessor property data for a fee on the GIS system at https://beacon.schneidercorp.com/. Registration and username required. At the default website, choose Missouri then Cass County, then register. Access to property information for free at http://cass.missouriassessors.com.

Cedar County   *Recorded Documents*   http://cedarcountymo.gov/recorder   Access to records for free at http://cedarmo.icounty.com/iRecordWeb2.0/Login.aspx. The GUEST user provides access to the data, but does not allow viewing document images. Images are from a paid subscription. Contact 417-276-6700 x6 for subscription information.

Christian County   *Recorded Documents*   www.christiancountymo.gov/recorder.htm   Access the recording office records free at http://christianmo.icounty.com/iRecordWeb2.0/Login.aspx/. Real estate records go back to 12/30/1993; marriage records go back to 1865; tax liens back to 1/3/2000. Username and password is Guest.
Property, Taxation Records   Access to parcel information for free at https://www.missouricountygov.com/christian_assess/mort/index.php. Use public for the username and password to have limited access to basic information. For detailed information must subscribe. Also, access to GIS/mapping for free at http://essentiallydata.maps.arcgis.com/apps/webappviewer/index.html?id=8a7b09fde8e0484fbf9e1324dea1b8d5.

Clay County   *Recorded Documents*   https://www.claycountymo.gov/recorder   Access to the recorder's database is free at http://recorder.claycountymo.gov/iRecordClient/. Must register to use.
Property, Taxation Records   Access assessor property records free at http://gisweb.claycogov.com/realEstate/realEstate.jsp but no name searching. Also, access real estate records from Collector's Office free at https://collector.claycountymo.gov/ascend/(cowatc55rk03xq55fpwy0iz0)/search.aspx.

Cole County   *Property, Taxation Records*   Access property and other mapping data for a fee at www.midmogis.com/colesl/.

Cooper County   *Recorded Documents*   Access to records for a fee at https://tapestry.fidlar.com/Tapestry2/Default.aspx. Search fee is $5.95 each, printed images $.50 each unless otherwise noted. For subscription, contact the Recorder's Office.

Property, Taxation Records   Access to GIS/mapping for free at https://cooper.integritygis.com/.

Dade County   *Property, Taxation Records*   Access to property records for free at http://qpublic7.qpublic.net/ga_search.php?county=ga_dade.

Dallas County   *Recorded Documents*   www.buffalococ.com/dallasgov.htm   Access to land/tax lien records for a fee at http://dallasmo.icounty.com/iRecordWeb2.0/Login.aspx. Must sign up for access to data.
Property, Taxation Records   Access to GIS/mapping for free at www.dallascogis.com/.

Dent County   *Property, Taxation Records*   Access to mapping for free at http://dentgis.countyportal.net/.

Franklin County   *Recorded Documents*   www.franklinmo.org/Recorder/Recorder.htm   Access to records for a fee at https://tapestry.fidlar.com/Tapestry2/Default.aspx. Search fee is $5.95 each, printed images $.50 each unless otherwise noted. For subscription, contact the Recorder's Office. Also, access to document search for free at www.franklinmo.net/fcrd/search.asp. Also, access to records for free at https://cotthosting.com/moportal/User/Login.aspx. For detailed records must subscribe.
Property, Taxation Records   Access to Assessor records for free at www.franklinmo.net/assr/Assessor.aspx.

Gasconade County   *Recorded Documents*   Access to records for a fee at https://tapestry.fidlar.com/Tapestry2/Default.aspx. Search fee is $5.95 each, printed images $.50 each unless otherwise noted. For subscription, contact the Recorder's Office.

Greene County   *Recorded Documents*   www.greenecountymo.org/recorder/   Search the recorder database for free at www.greenecountymo.org/recorder/real_estate_search/index.php. Search tax liens at www.greenecountymo.org/recorder/tax_lien_search/index.php.
Property, Taxation Records   Search assessor property data for a fee on the GIS system at https://beacon.schneidercorp.com/.

Henry County   *Property, Taxation Records*   Access to GIS/mappiing for free at http://maps.hornershifrin.com/henrycountymo/.

Hickory County   *Recorded Documents*   Access to records for a fee at https://tapestry.fidlar.com/Tapestry2/Default.aspx. Search fee is $5.95 each, printed images $.50 each unless otherwise noted. For subscription, contact the Recorder's Office.

Jackson County   *Recorded Documents, Marriage, UCC Records*   www.jacksongov.org/267/Recorder-of-Deeds   Search the recorder records database for free at http://records.jacksongov.org/.
Property, Taxation Records   Search real estate sales, tax payments, parcel info at https://ascendweb.jacksongov.org/ascend/%28pjb5zy550fc0u3mfswy30srl%29/search.aspx.

Jasper County   *Recorded Documents*   www.jaspercounty.org/recorder.html   Access to indexes (except for images and soldier's discharges) for free at http://recorder.jaspercounty.org/. Click on Recorder's Office. For images must subscribe for a fee.
Property, Taxation Records   Search assessor property data for free on the GIS system at https://beacon.schneidercorp.com/. Registration and username required.

Jefferson County   *Recorded Documents*   www.jeffcomo.org/Recorder.aspx?nodeID=Recorder   Access to records for a fee at https://tapestry.fidlar.com/Tapestry2/Default.aspx. Search fee is $5.95 each, printed images $.50 each unless otherwise noted. For subscription, contact the Recorder's Office. Also, access to records for free at https://cotthosting.com/moportal/User/Login.aspx. For detailed records must subscribe.
Property, Taxation Records   Search assessor property data for free at www.jeffcomo.org/Assessor.aspx?nodeID=Assessor.

Johnson County   *Recorded Documents*   www.jocorecorder.com/   Access to recorder records for a fee at www.jocorecorder.com/#!public-searching/kahok. Must sign a contract for subscription.
Property, Taxation Records   Access to tax records/payments for a fee at https://epay.4gov.com/jqePayTax/start?county=Johnson.

Laclede County   *Recorded Documents (index only), Marriage Records*   http://lacledecountymissouri.org/index.php?page=recorder   Access to recorders documents indexes is free at http://lacledecountymissouri.org/index.php?page=free-on-line-search. Images of land records are available with a charge card.
Property, Taxation Records   Access to real estate/property look-up for a fee at www.lacledecollector.com/. Must fill out user form and be issued user-name and password.

Lafayette County   *Recorded Documents*   www.lafayettecountymo.com/P-63/Recorder-of-Deeds.aspx   Access to records for a fee at https://tapestry.fidlar.com/Tapestry2/Default.aspx. Search fee is $5.95 each, printed images $.50 each unless otherwise noted. For subscription, contact the Recorder's Office.
Property, Taxation Records   Access to personal property records for free at www.lafayettecountyassessor.com/onlinepers/index.php. Must have PIN number for search.

Lawrence County   *Recorded Documents*   Access to records for free at https://cotthosting.com/moportal/User/Login.aspx. For detailed records must subscribe. Index and images available from 1/4/1988 to present.
Property, Taxation Records   Access to GIS/mapping free at https://lawrence.integritygis.com/SL/viewer.html?Viewer=Lawrence_Public.

Lincoln County   *Recorded Documents*   http://lincolncountyrecorder.com/   Access to records for free at https://cotthosting.com/moportal/User/Login.aspx. For detailed records must subscribe. Index and images of deeds from 1819-1987, Right of Ways from

1927-1947. Can sign-in as a guest but info is limited. Also, access to records for free at http://lincolncountyrecorder.com/. Includes comtemporary dates from 1988 to present, historical dates from 1819 to 1987 and marriage licenses from 8/1825 to present.
Property, Taxation Records   For free parcel searches go to https://lincoln.integritygis.com/. Also, access to Assessor's database free at http://lincoln.missouriassessors.com/.

Linn County   *Recorded Documents*   Access to records for a fee at https://tapestry.fidlar.com/Tapestry2/Default.aspx. Search fee is $5.95 each, printed images $.50 each unless otherwise noted. For subscription, contact the Recorder's Office.
Property, Taxation Records   Also, access to Assessor's database free at http://linn.missouriassessors.com/. Must subscribe.

Livingston County   *Recorded Documents*   www.livingstoncountymo.com/recorder.htm   Access to records for a fee at https://www.idocmarket.com/. Subscription based.
Property, Taxation Records   Also, access to Assessor's database free at http://livingston.missouriassessors.com/.

Macon County   *Recorded Documents*   www.maconcountymo.com/recorder-of-deeds.html   Access to records for a fee at https://tapestry.fidlar.com/Tapestry2/Default.aspx. Search fee is $5.95 each, printed images $.50 each unless otherwise noted. For subscription, contact the Recorder's Office.

Maries County   *Recorded Documents*   For subscription service call Mark Bushmann for more information.

Marion County   *Recorded Documents*   http://marioncountymo.com/departments/recorder-of-deeds/   Access to records for a fee at https://tapestry.fidlar.com/Tapestry2/Default.aspx. Search fee is $5.95 each, printed images $.50 each unless otherwise noted. For subscription, contact the Recorder's Office.
Property, Taxation Records   Also, access to Assessor's database free at http://marion.missouriassessors.com/.

McDonald County   *Recorded Documents*   www.mcdonaldcountygov.com/depts/recorder.php   Access to records for free at https://cotthosting.com/moportal/User/Login.aspx. For detailed records must subscribe. Index and images of deeds from 1/1/1978 to present, Mortgages from 1/1/1998 to present, Surveys from 1880 to present. images). Tax lien and survey images are available. Guest index search only for free.
Property, Taxation Records   Access to GIS/mapping free at http://mcdonaldgis.countyportal.net/.

Miller County   *Property, Taxation Records*   Access to GIS/mapping free at www.millercomogis.com/.

Mississippi County   *Recorded Documents*   www.misscomo.net/countyofficeindex/recorderofdeeds.html   Access to records for a fee at www.canaanllc.com/. Contact Jon Gilmore at 573-471-6005 for posting procedures. Pricing schedule at this URL. Records from 1950 to present.

Moniteau County   *Recorded Dcouments Records*   Online access available. Call 816-295-1540.

Monroe County   *Recorded Documents*   Access to records for a fee at https://tapestry.fidlar.com/Tapestry2/. Search fee is $5.95 each, printed images $.50 each unless otherwise noted. Records back to 1996, anything prior to 1996 has to be searched in office.

Morgan County   *Property, Taxation Records*   Access to GIS/mapping for free at www.morgancomogis.com/.

New Madrid County   *Recorded Documents*   www.new-madrid.mo.us/index.aspx?NID=38   Access to records for a fee at www.canaanllc.com/. Contact Jon Gilmore at 573-471-6005 for posting procedures. Pricing schedule is at this URL. Records from 1989 to present.

Newton County   *Recorded Documents, Vital Records Records*   www.ncrecorder.org   Search the index free at www.ncrecorder.org/search.htm. Use guest for userID and password. Request and pay for copy on website, then emailed or faced. Fee is $1.00 per page with PayPal or credit card. ***Property, Taxation Records***   Access to property records free at http://newtoncountyassessor.com/onlinepers/perspin.php. Must have OL number (located on the left side of address label).

Nodaway County   *Recorded Documents*   www.nodawaycountymo.us/county-offices/elected-officials/recorder-deeds/   Access to Recorder documents for free at http://search.nodawaycountyrecorder.com/iRecordWeb2.0/Login.aspx. Guest access for searching online indexes is offered. For images must register.

Pemiscot County   *Recorded Documents*   www.pemiscotcounty.org/recorder-2/   Access to records for a fee at www.canaanllc.com/. Contact Jon Gilmore at 573-471-6005 for posting procedures. Pricing schedule is at this URL. Records from 1980 to present.

Perry County   *Recorded Documents*   www.perrycountymo.us/index.aspx?nid=76   Access to records for a fee at https://tapestry.fidlar.com/Tapestry2/Default.aspx. Search fee is $5.95 each, printed images $.50 each unless otherwise noted. For subscription, contact the Recorder's Office. ***Property, Taxation Records***   Access to property search information go to http://perry.missouriassessors.com/. Basic search free, more detailed search for a yearly fee. Contact office for more information.

Pettis County   *Recorded Documents*   www.pettiscomo.com/rec.html   A Access to records for a fee at https://tapestry.fidlar.com/Tapestry2/Default.aspx. Search fee is $5.95 each, printed images $.50 each unless otherwise noted. For subscription, contact the Recorder's Office.
Property, Taxation Records   Search assessor property data for a fee on the GIS system at https://beacon.schneidercorp.com/. Registration and username required. At the default website, choose Missouri then Pettis County, then register.

Phelps County *Recorded Documents* www.phelpscounty.org/recorder/recorder.htm   Access to records for a fee at https://tapestry.fidlar.com/Tapestry2/Default.aspx. Search fee is $5.95 each, printed images $.50 each unless otherwise noted. For subscription, contact the Recorder's Office.
Property, Taxation Records   Access to GIS/mapping for a fee at http://phelpscomogis.com/. Also, access to direct parcel access for free at http://phelps.missouriassessors.com/direct.php. Must have password (parcel password is printed on real estate property tax statement or in change in assessment notice).

Pike County *Property, Taxation Records*   Search assessor property data for a fee on the GIS system at https://beacon.schneidercorp.com/. Registration and username required. At the default website, choose Missouri then Pike County, then register.

Platte County *Recorded Documents* https://platte-county-u18x.squarespace.com/recorder   To access recorder's indexes online, complete the online deed form at http://co.platte.mo.us/docs/recorder/online_search_agree.pdf and a password will be issued. Fees vary depending on amount of documents per month (fees are shown on the form).
Property, Taxation Records   Assessor data available free at http://maps.co.platte.mo.us/. Also, access the Collector's tax payments data free at www.plattecountycollector.com/wrapper.php?page=1 but parcel ID or account number required. Search assessor property data for free on the GIS system at https://beacon.schneidercorp.com/. Registration and username required. At the default website, choose Missouri then Platte County, then register.

Polk County *Recorded Documents*   Access to database for free at http://polkmo.icounty.com/iRecordWeb2.0/Login.aspx. Must register before use. For more detailed information must register for subscription. Contact staff at 417-326-4924 for more information.

Pulaski County *Recorded Documents* www.showmepulaski.org/#!recorder-of-deeds   Access to land records for a fee at http://pulaskimo.icounty.com/iRecordWeb2.0/Login.aspx.
Property, Taxation Records   Access to GIS/mapping free at www.pulaskicogis.com/.

Putnam County *Property, Taxation Records*   Free parcel search at http://putnam.missouriassessors.com/search.php.

Ralls County *Property, Taxation Records*   Access to GIS/mapping free at http://rallscogis.com/.

Randolph County *Recorded Documents* www.randolphcounty-mo.com/recorder-of-deeds/   Access to records for free at http://randolphmo.icounty.com/iRecordWeb2.0/Login.aspx. Must register for use. Images are for a fee. Contact them at 660-277-4718 for more information.
Property, Taxation Records   Access to property search free at www.rcao.com/namesearch.php. Also, access to GIS/mapping and tax maps for free at www.randolphcounty-mo.com/assessor/.

Ray County *Property, Taxation Records*   Free assessor parcel search at http://ray.missouriassessors.com/search.php.

Reynolds County *Recorded Documents* http://reynoldscountyrecorder.com/   Access to deeds and marriage records for a fee at http://reynoldscountyrecorder.com/OnLineRecords.aspx.

Saline County *Recorded Documents* https://www.deeds.com/recorder/missouri/saline/   Access to records for a fee at https://tapestry.fidlar.com/Tapestry2/Default.aspx. Search fee is $5.95 each, printed images $.50 each unless otherwise noted. For subscription, contact the Recorder's Office.

Scott County *Recorded Documents* www.scottcountymo.com/recorder.php   Access to records for a fee at www.canaanllc.com/. Contact Jon Gilmore at 573-471-6005 for posting procedures. Pricing schedule is at this URL. Records from 1997 to present.
Property, Taxation Records   Access to GIS/mapping free at www.semogis.com/flexviewers/Scott/.

Shelby County *Recorded Documents* http://shelbyrecorder.com/   Access to land records at http://shelbyrecorder.com/. Guest login. Index from 1992 to present. Also access to land records/marriage records index from 1835-2001 at http://shelby.mogenweb.org.

St. Charles County *Property, Taxation Records*   Search property assessment data free at https://lookups.sccmo.org/assessor. No name searching.

St. Francois County *Recorded Documents* www.sfcgov.org/Recorder.html   Access to records for a fee at https://tapestry.fidlar.com/Tapestry2/Default.aspx. Search fee is $5.95 each, printed images $.50 each unless otherwise noted. For subscription, contact the Recorder's Office.
Property, Taxation Records   Access property assessor data free at www.sfcassessor.org/parcel_search.html.

St. Louis City *Recorded Documents* https://www.stlouis-mo.gov/government/departments/recorder/   Access to records for a fee at https://tapestry.fidlar.com/Tapestry2/Default.aspx. Search fee is $5.95 each, printed images $.50 each unless otherwise noted. For subscription, contact the Recorder's Office.
Property, Taxation Records   Access the mapping site free at http://maps.stlouisco.com/propertyview/. Also, access address and property search data for free at http://stlouis-mo.gov/data/address-search/index.cfm. Search personal property by account number, address, or name at http://revenue.stlouisco.com/Collection/ppInfo/. Assessor property data for a fee on the GIS system at http://beacon.schneidercorp.com. Registration and username required. At the default website, choose City of Wildwood, then register.

St. Louis County *Recorded Documents* www.stlouisco.com/YourGovernment/CountyDepartments/Revenue/RecorderofDeedsDivision Access to records for a fee at https://tapestry.fidlar.com/Tapestry2/Default.aspx. Search fee is $5.95 each, printed images $.50 each unless otherwise noted. For subscription, contact the Recorder's Office.
Property, Taxation Records Access county property data free at http://revenue.stlouisco.com/ias/. Search personal property tax data free at http://revenue.stlouisco.com/Collection/ppInfo/.

Ste. Genevieve County *Recorded Documents* www.stegencounty.org/recorder_of_deeds Access to records for a fee at https://www.idocmarket.com/. Data indexed 1896 to present. Images and data from 6/1990 to present.

Stoddard County *Recorded Documents* Access to the record index is free at http://stoddardmo.icounty.com/iRecordWeb2.0/Login.aspx. Image fees are as follows-$25.00 for 25 doc, $50.00 for 50 docs, $75.00 for 75 doc, etc. Records from 1991 to present. Also, access to records for a fee at www.canaanllc.com/. Contact Jon Gilmore at 573-471-6005 for posting procedures. Pricing schedule is at this URL.

Stone County *Recorded Documents* www.stoneco-mo.us/Recorder.htm Access to recorder data is free through land access.com at https://www.uslandrecords.com/molr/. Indexes and images back to 1/1/1993. For detailed information (any document that has been recorded at the county office) must subscribe.
Property, Taxation Records Access property data from the GIS interactive map at https://stone.integritygis.com/.

Taney County *Recorded Documents* www.taneycounty.org/index.php?section=departments&department=18 Access to records for a fee at https://tapestry.fidlar.com/Tapestry2/Default.aspx. Search fee is $5.95 each, printed images $.50 each unless otherwise noted. For subscription, contact the Recorder's Office. Also, office has DOCUWARE system for plats and surveys for free. Must call into the office and request access and provide office with username and password.
Property, Taxation Records Search assessor property data for free on the GIS system at https://beacon.schneidercorp.com/. Registration and username required. At the default website, choose Missouri then Tanney County, then register.

Vernon County *Property, Taxation Records* Access to personal property search for free at http://vernon.missouriassessors.com/ppSearch.php.

Warren County *Recorded Documents* www.warrencountymo.org/ Access to records for a fee at https://tapestry.fidlar.com/Tapestry2/Default.aspx. Search fee is $5.95 each, printed images $.50 each unless otherwise noted. For subscription, contact the Recorder's Office.

Wayne County *Recorded Documents* http://waynecountyrecorder.com/ To sign-up for the online paid subscription go to http://waynecountyrecorder.com/OnLineRecords.aspx for information.

Webster County *Recorded Documents* www.webstercountymo.gov/recorders-office/ Access to recorded data is by subscription; $200.00 per month. Get info and register through the recorder's office.
Property, Taxation Records Access to GIS/mapping at www.webstercountymo.gov/service-center/assessors-office/. Click on free version or Subscribers for more detailed mapping. To subscribe contact the Assessors Office at above number.

Montana

Capital: Helena
             Lewis and Clark County

Time Zone: MST

Population: 1,032,949

# of Counties: 56

Useful State Links

Website: **http://mt.gov/**

Governor: **http://governor.mt.gov/**

Attorney General: **https://doj.mt.gov/agooffice**

State Archives: **http://mhs.mt.gov**

State Statutes and Codes: **http://leg.mt.gov/bills/mca_toc/index.htm**

Legislative Bill Search: **http://leg.mt.gov/css/bills/default.asp**

Unclaimed Funds: **http://revenue.mt.gov/home/businesses/unclaimed_property**

State Public Record Agencies

Criminal Records

Department of Justice, Montana Criminal Records,   https://dojmt.gov/enforcement/crime-information-bureau/   Access is available for "public users" or "registered users" at https://app.mt.gov/choprs/. Fee is $13.000 per record. Registered users receive monthly bills and have access to other data. There is a $100 annual fee. Search using the name and DOB. The SSN is helpful but not required. Results include up to 4 aliases, dispositions, detentions, sentences, and correctional status.

Sexual Offender Registry

Sexual or Violent Offender Registration Unit, Division of Criminal Investigation,   https://app.doj.mt.gov/apps/svow/   The state's sexual offender search is at https://app.doj.mt.gov/apps/svow/search.aspx. Both an Offender Basic Search and a Neighborhood Search are offered. You may search by offender name; by city, county or zip code; or by offender type (sexual or violent or both). The percent sign (%) may be used as a wildcard character in the Last Name field to represent one or more other characters.

Incarceration Records

Montana Department of Corrections, Directors Office,   http://cor.mt.gov/   Search current or former inmates on the ConWeb system at https://app.mt.gov/conweb/. Search by ID# or by name. A list of parole violators at large is found at https://app.mt.gov/cgi-bin/boppviolator/boppviolator.cgi.   *Other Options:* Entire offender database is available for purchase; call Discovering Montana, 406-449-3468. Academic or social researchers can acquire the same database for no charge. See https://app.mt.gov/conweb/Help/RequestDatabase.

Corporation, LLC, LP, Fictitious/Assumed Name, Trademarks/Servicemarks

Business Services Division, Secretary of State,   http://sos.mt.gov/Business/index.asp   Visit https://app.mt.gov/bes/ for free searches of MT business entities. Certified copies may be ordered online at https://app.mt.gov/ccop/ for $10.00 using a credit card. Certified copies may be ordered online at https://app.mt.gov/ccop/ for $10.00 using a credit card. Add $5.00 to have documents faxed. One-hour and 24-hour service not available online. There is a commercial service for finding registered principles as well, but one must have an account. Visit https://app.mt.gov/rps/.   *Other Options:* One may purchase a download a customized list of new business entities. Various ways to customize a list and fees are found at https://app.mt.gov/corprecords/.

Uniform Commercial Code, Federal Tax Liens

Business Services Division, Secretary of State, Rm 260,   http://sos.mt.gov/business/index.asp   A web-based subscription service provides information about all active liens filed with the office. To use the service you need to establish an account with Discovering Montana for a fee of $25 per month. See https://www.montanasos.com/. Accounts may view active lien information and also perform and print unlimited certified search certificates. Bulk downloads are available for $1,000 per month. Contact Discovering Montana at 101 N Rodney #3, Helena MT 59601, or call 866-449-3468, or visit the website above. *Other Options:* Registered users may receive farm bill filings lists on a monthly basis for $5.00 per category on paper or via online. Data on CDs is no longer offered.

Birth Certificates

Montana Department of Health & Human Services, Vital Records, https://dphhs.mt.gov/vitalrecords.aspx Orders can be placed at https://vitalrecords.egov.com/CDC.VitalRecordsMVC.Web/Wizard/MT/Municipality/SelectMunicipality add $3.00 per record. Or via a state designated vendor at www.vitalchek.com. Extra fees are involved. Also, one may order a record from the state designated vendor at www.vitalchek.com. Extra fees are involved.

Death Records

Montana Department of Health & Human Services, Vital Records, https://dphhs.mt.gov/vitalrecords.aspx Orders can be placed at https://vitalrecords.egov.com/CDC.VitalRecordsMVC.Web/Wizard/MT/Municipality/SelectMunicipality add $3.00 per record. Or via a state designated vendor at www.vitalchek.com. Extra fees are involved. Also, one may order a record from the state designated vendor at www.vitalchek.com. Extra fees are involved.

Driver Records

Motor Vehicle Division, Driver's Services, https://dojmt.gov/driving/ There are two methods offered, one for Public User requests and a subscription service. The fee is $7.25. The Public Access results do not offer address information. For registered subscribers, an agreement must be signed and there is an annual $100.00 registration fee. Services online also include a License Status Conviction Activity batch or monitoring search, at a reduced price. For more about online services visit https://app.mt.gov/dojdrs/ or call 406-449-3468. *Other Options:* Under the License Status Conviction Activity (LSCA) program, approved requesters may submit a monthly list of names, at $.15 per name. If there is conviction activity within the past 30 days, the requester is sent a driving record for the $7.25 fee.

Vehicle, Vessel Ownership & Registration

Department of Justice, Title and Registration Bureau, https://dojmt.gov/driving/vehicle-title-and-registration/ Both "Public User" and Registered User" interfaces are offered . See https://app.mt.gov/dojvs/public for the Public Users., which is for MT citizens or users with an occasional need to know the ownership history of a pre-owned car. Sensitive information, such as the SSN or home address is not released. A $5.00 fee applies and a credit card must be used. The Registered User system is for ongoing registered accounts approved by the Motor Vehicle Division. The Registered User system is for ongoing registered accounts approved by the Motor Vehicle Division. The fee is $2.25 per search. There is an annual $100.00 registration fee for 10 users. See https://app.mt.gov/registered. Depending on the level of authority granted, the following is available: Vehicle Information, License Plate Information, Vehicle Owner Information, Lien History, Title History and Registration Information. *Other Options:* Bulk or batch ordering of registration information is available on tape, disk, or paper. The user must fill out a specific form, which gives the user the capability of customization. For further information, contact the Registrar at address above.

Voter Registration

Secretary of State, Elections and Government Srvs, http://sos.mt.gov/Elections/ Access voter registration records at https://app.mt.gov/voterfile/select_criteria.html. Records can be purchased for non-commercial use only. *Other Options:* This agency database or customized portions can be purchased on disk or CD-ROM for $200 or less. Fee to purchase entire database is $1,000 or $5,000 for subscription with updates. For more information, call 406-449-2468 ext 228.

Campaign Finance, Lobbyist

Commissioner of Politcial Practices, http://politicalpractices.mt.gov/default.mcpx At www.scstatehouse.gov/, search by bill number, subject, or sponsor. The site has a myriad of data including state codes, laws and regulations. Laws can be searched at www.scstatehouse.gov/code/statmast.php Search for a lobbyist and principal at https://app.mt.gov/cgi-bin/camptrack/lobbysearch/lobbySearch.cgi. Search and download campaign data at https://camptrackext.mt.gov/CampaignTracker/dashboard. This includes contributions and expenditures. Search committee reports at https://campaignreport.mt.gov/forms/committeesearch.jsp. A number of searches on complaints and opinions are available from the home page.

Occupational Licensing Boards

These licenses are all searchable at https://ebiz.mt.gov/pol/

Accountant-CPA/LPA	Chiropractor	Engineer
Acupuncturist	Clinical Social Worker	Euthanasia Agency/ Technician
Addiction Counselor	Cosmetologist/Cosmetol'y Instr/Sch'l	Firearms Instructor
Alarm Response Runner	Crematory/Crematory Oper/Tech	Funeral Director
Architect	Dangerous Drug Researcher	Hearing Aid Dispenser
Athletic Event/Event Timekeeper	Dentist/Dental Assistant/Hygienist	Land Surveyor
Audiologist	Denturist	Landscape Architect
Barber/Barber Shop/Instruct'r	Electrician	Landscape Architects
Boxer/Boxing Prof/Mgr/Promoter/Judge	Electrologist/Esthetician/Manicurist	Midwife, Apprentice
Cemetery, Privately Owned	Emergency Medical Technician	Mortuary/Mortician

Naturopathic Physician
Nurse Anesthetist/Clinical Specialist
Nurse-RN/LPN/PA
Nutritionist
Occupational Therapist
Optometrist
Osteopathic Physician
Outfitter/Guide, Hunting/Fishing
Pharmacist
Physical Therapist/Assistant
Physician//Medical Doctor/Assistant

Plumber
Podiatrist
Private Investigator/Trainee
Private Security Guard
Process Server
Property Manager
Psychologist
Radiologic Technologist
Real Estate Agent/Broker/Sales
Real Estate Appraiser/Trainee
Referee

Resident Manager
Respiratory Care Practitioner
Security Alarm Installer/Company
Security Org, Proprietary
Social Worker, LSW
Speech Pathologist
Timeshare Broker/Salesperson
Veterinarian
Wholesale Drug Distributor
Wrestler
X-Ray Technician

The Rest:

Adoption Agency	http://dphhs.mt.gov/CFSD/Adoption/PrivateAdoptionAgencies
Adult Day Care Center	https://dphhs.mt.gov/qad/Licensure/lbcontact.aspx
Attorney	http://montanabar.site-ym.com/search/custom.asp?id=2249
Child Care Provider	http://ccubs-sanswrite.hhs.mt.gov/MontanaPublic/ProviderSearch.aspx
Construction Blaster	https://buildingpermits.mt.gov/Licenses/licenses.aspx
Contractor, Revoked License	http://erdepc.dli.mt.gov:8080/birt2.5/frameset?__report=RevlCListreport.rptdesign
Discount Card Companies	https://sbs-mt.naic.org/Lion-Web/jsp/sbsreports/AgentLookup.jsp
Group Home, Youth	http://dphhs.mt.gov/qad/Licensure/HealthCareFacilityLicensure/LBFacilityApplications/YouthCareFacility.aspx
Group Home/Shelter Care/Therapeutic	http://dphhs.mt.gov/qad/Facility
Health Care Facilities, Various	http://dphhs.mt.gov/qad/Facility
Insurance Adjuster/Producer	https://sbs-mt.naic.org/Lion-Web/jsp/sbsreports/AgentLookup.jsp
Lobbyist/Lobbying Principal	https://app.mt.gov/cgi-bin/camptrack/lobbysearch/lobbySearch.cgi
Maternity Goup Home	http://dphhs.mt.gov/qad/Facility
Pesticide Applicator/Dealer	http://services.agr.mt.gov/Pesticide_Applicators/
School Guidance Couns'r/Psycholog'st	https://apps3.opi.mt.gov/SSO/Login/Login.aspx
School Principal	https://apps3.opi.mt.gov/SSO/Login/Login.aspx
School Superintendent	https://apps3.opi.mt.gov/SSO/Login/Login.aspx
Teacher	https://apps3.opi.mt.gov/SSO/Login/Login.aspx
Underground Tank Inspector/Intal/Remover	http://deq.mt.gov/Land/ust/OperatingPermitStatus

State and Local Courts

State Court Structure: The **District Courts,** the courts of general jurisdiction, handle all felony cases and probate cases, most civil cases at law and in equity, and other special actions and proceedings.

The courts of limited jurisdiction are **Justice Courts**, **City Courts** and **Municipal Courts**. Although the jurisdiction of these courts differs slightly, collectively they address cases involving misdemeanor offenses, civil cases for amounts up to $12,000, small claims valued up to $7,000, landlord/tenant disputes, local ordinances, forcible entry and detainer, protection orders, certain issues involving juveniles, and other matters. Some Justice Courts and City Courts have consolidated.

Also, Montana has a Water Court and a Workers' Compensation Court.

The web page for the Unified Judicial System is http://courts.mt.gov/.

Appellate Courts: Montana does not have an intermediate appellate court. Consequently, the Supreme Court hears direct appeals from all of the District Courts across Montana, as well as from the Workers' Compensation Court and the Water Court. Supreme Court opinions, orders, and recently filed briefs may be found http://searchcourts.mt.gov.

Online Court Access

There is no statewide access to docket information from the trial courts. Several courts respond to email requests, but none offer online access to records.

The state does have an exsiting centralized case management system and is working towards implmenting an e-filing system sometime in the future.

Recorders, Assessors, and Other Sites of Note

About Montana Recording Offices: 57 counties, 56 recording offices. Yellowstone National Park is considered a county but is not included as a filing location. The recording officer is the County Clerk and Recorder, and Clerk of District Court can be used for state tax liens.

About Tax Liens: Federal and state tax liens on personal property of businesses and on individuals can be filed either with the Secretary of State or with the County Clerk and Recorder. State tax liens on individuals can also be filed with the Clerk of District Court.

Online Access

Recorded Documents

There is no statewide search for recorded documents at the county level, but an increasing number of counties offer data online free or via a vendor for a fee.

Assessor and Mapping

All counties participate in a **free search for a Montana property owner** by name and county on the Montana Cadastral Mapping Project GIS mapping database at http://svc.mt.gov/msl/mtcadastral/.

A fee based service to property title information for 23 participating counties listed below is managed by a vendor at www.canaanllc.com/index.php/canaanonline/availablecounties

Beaverhead	Gallatin	Lincoln	Petroleum
Cascade	Glacier	Madison	Pondera
Dawson	Granite	McCone	Ravalli
Deer Lodge	Judith Basin	Meagher	Sanders
Fergus	Lake	Mineral	Toole
Flathead	Liberty	Missoula	

Counties: (Data on the above two sites omitted on the profiles below)

Beaverhead County *Recorded Documents* www.beaverheadcounty.org/html/clerk_and_recorder.html   Access to records for a fee at www.canaanllc.com/. Email contact Neal Morris at Neal.Morris@CanaanLLC.com or call 870-330-7007 for posting procedures.

Broadwater County *Recorded Documents* http://townsendmt.com/chd_sec4pg3.asp   Data available by paid subscription. Contact the office for more information.

Butte-Silver Bow County *Recorded Documents* www.co.silverbow.mt.us/155/Clerk-Recorder   Access to recorded documents for a fee at https://www.idocmarket.com/sites. Must subscribe before use. Fees vary depending on plan picked. Computer indexing back to 10/1990, imaging back to 2/2009.

Carbon County *Property, Taxation Records* Access to county tax search free at http://mtcounty.com/bmsrdl/tax_search.php?customer_id=454.

Cascade County *Recorded Documents* www.cascadecountymt.gov/departments/clerk-and-recorder   Recording office land data available at http://clerkrecorder.co.cascade.mt.us/Recorder/web/; registration and fees required.
Property, Taxation Records Access to GIS/mapping for a nominal charge at www.cascadecountymt.gov/departments/geographic-information-system.

Fergus County *Property, Taxation Records* Access to iTax for a fee at https://itax.tylertech.com/FergusMT/.

Flathead County *Recorded Documents* http://flathead.mt.gov/clerk_recorder/   Access to recorded documents for a fee at https://www.idocmarket.com/sites. Must subscribe before use. Fees vary depending on plan picked. Computer indexing back to 1/1/1984, imaging back to 1984.

Gallatin County *Recorded Documents* http://gallatincomt.virtualtownhall.net/Public_Documents/gallatincomt_clerk/clerk   Access to records free at https://eagleweb.gallatin.mt.gov/recorder/web/. Searches are free but individual images must be purchased. Also can subscribe to full image access for $200.00 a year.
Property, Taxation Records Search property tax for free at http://itax.gallatin.mt.gov/. Also, access to GIS/mapping for free at http://webapps.gallatin.mt.gov/mappers/.

Glacier County   *Property, Taxation Records*   Free search of complete property information including ownership, taxes, dwelling info and more at http://svc.mt.gov/msl/mtcadastral. Also, access to Property tax payment search for free at www.glaciercountygov.com/tax-payments/. Glacier County has a Clerk & Recorders' Office only, no Assessing Office.

Golden Valley County   *Property, Taxation Records*   Free search of complete property information including ownership, taxes, dwelling info and more at http://svc.mt.gov/msl/mtcadastral.

Jefferson County   *Recorded Documents*   www.jeffersoncounty-mt.gov/clerk_recorder.html   Access to recorded documents for a fee at https://www.idocmarket.com/sites. Must subscribe before use. Fees vary depending on plan picked. Computer indexing back to 4/2/1990.

Lake County   *Property, Taxation Records*   Access to the GIS/mapping for free at www.lakemt.gov/gis/index.html. Also, search treasurer's tax payment list after registration at www.mtcounty.com/bmsrdl/tax_pay_search.php?customer_id=321.

Lewis and Clark County   *Recorded Documents*   www.lccountymt.gov/car.html   Search Grantor/Grantee index and recorder records free at https://eagle-web.lccountymt.gov/recorder/web/. Public users can search recorded documents without images, must subscribe for images. This new automation includes document imaging via subscription online service. Search Certificate of Survey and Corner Records recorded since January 1, 1865.
Property, Taxation Records   Search property tax data free at https://itax.tylertech.com/LewisAndClarkMT/.

Lincoln County   *Recorded Documents*   www.lincolncountymt.us/clerkandrecorder/index.html   Access to online documents for a fee at www.lincolncountymt.us/clerkandrecorder/onlinesearch.html.
Property, Taxation Records   Access to tax search free at www.mtcounty.com/bmsrdl/tax_search.php?customer_id=188.

Mineral County   *Recorded Documents*   http://co.mineral.mt.us/departments/clerkrecorder/   Recording office land data to be available at a later date at www.etitlesearch.com/; registration and fees required.

Missoula County   *Recorded Documents*   www.missoulacounty.us/government/administration/clerk-treasurer   Recording office land data to be available at a later date at www.etitlesearch.com; registration and fees required.
Property, Taxation Records   Access the county property data system free at www.co.missoula.mt.us/owner/. Property search by Address, Tax ID, Geocode, Map. Records search by Tax ID, Geocode, Book/Page. No name searching.

Musselshell County   *Recorded Documents*   http://musselshellcounty.org/Government/index.cfm?gid=Clerk%20and%20Recorder   Access to parcel searches free at http://svc.mt.gov/msl/mtcadastral/.

Park County   *Recorded Documents*   www.parkcounty.org/Government-Departments/Clerk-Recorder/   Access to recorded documents for a fee at https://www.idocmarket.com/sites. Must subscribe before use. Fees vary depending on plan picked. Computer document indexing back to 3/13/1972. Imaging can be access by entering roll and page number, if known.
Property, Taxation Records   Access to tax records free at http://tax.parkcounty.org/.

Ravalli County   *Recorded Documents*   http://ravalli.us/129/Clerk-Recorder   Access to recorded documents for a fee at https://www.idocmarket.com/sites. Must subscribe before use. Fees vary depending on plan picked. Indexing back to 1988, imaging back to 1999.

Sanders County   *Recorded Documents*   http://co.sanders.mt.us/departments/clerk-recorder/   Access to tax, document indexing and plat maps free at www.mtcounty.com/bmsrdl/doc_search.php?customer_id=220.

Sweet Grass County   *Recorded Documents*   http://sweetgrasscountygov.com/government-departments/county-govt/clerk-recorder/   Access to recorded documents for a fee at https://www.idocmarket.com/sites. Must subscribe before use. Fees vary depending on plan picked. Computer indexing back to 9/1/2000, imaging back to 9/1/2000.

Valley County   *Property, Taxation Records*   Access county tax data free at www.mtcounty.com/bmsrdl/tax_search.php?customer_id=113.

Yellowstone County   *Recorded Documents*   www.co.yellowstone.mt.gov/clerk/   Access county clerk & recorder indexes free at https://crdocs.co.yellowstone.mt.gov/recorder/eagleweb/. Can purchase individual document images or subscribe to view and print unlimited images. Must register to subscribe.
Property, Taxation Records   Access tax assessor maps free at www.co.yellowstone.mt.gov/assessor/index.asp.

Nebraska

Capital: Lincoln
               Lancaster County

Time Zone: CST

Nebraska's nineteen western-most counties are MST. They are: Arthur,
Banner, Box Butte, Chase, Cherry, Cheyenne, Dawes, Deuel, Dundy, Garden,
Grant, Hooker, Keith, Kimball, Morrill, Perkins, Scotts Bluff, Sheridan, Sioux.

Population: 1,895,190

# of Counties: 93

Useful State Links

Website: **www.nebraska.gov**

Governor: **www.governor.nebraska.gov**

Attorney General: **www.ago.ne.gov**

State Archives: **www.nebraskahistory.org/lib-arch/index.shtml**

State Statutes and Codes: **http://uniweb.legislature.ne.gov/**

Legislative Bill Search: **http://uniweb.legislature.ne.gov/**

Unclaimed Funds: **https://treasurer.nebraska.gov/up/**

State Public Record Agencies

Criminal Records

Nebraska State Patrol, Criminal Identifcation Division,   https://statepatrol.nebraska.gov/vnews/display.v/ART/56c76a2fd44fb   One may submit a request online at https://www.nebraska.gov/apps-nsp-limited-criminal. The fee is $18.00. All major credit cards are accpeted. You will receive either a "No Record" response or "Request is being researched" response. If you receive a "No Record" response you will be able to download and/or print the dissemination report immediately. If you receive a "Request is being researched" response, the information entered is not unique and must be reviewed by a Criminal Records Technician. The results will be returned within 3 business days.

Sexual Offender Registry

Nebraska State Patrol, Sexual Offender Registry,   https://sor.nebraska.gov/   Three different types of searches are available at https://sor.nebraska.gov/. The records may be searched by either ZIP Code, last name, first name, city, or county. Search or review the entire list of names. Email questions to nsp.sor@nebraska.gov.

Incarceration Records

Nebraska Department of Correctional Services, Central Records Office,   www.corrections.nebraska.gov   Click on the Inmate Locator tab at the website for a search of incarcerated nmates.

Corporation, LLC, LP, Trade Names, Trademarks/Servicemarks

Secretary of State, Corporation Division,   www.sos.ne.gov/business/corp_serv/   There are several services. The free lookup at https://www.nebraska.gov/sos/corp/corpsearch.cgi?nav=search provides general information to obtain information on the status of corporations and other business entities registered in this state. The state has designated Nebraska.gov (800-747-8177) to facilitate online retrieval of records in a batch mode from https://www.nebraska.gov/SpecialRequestSearches/index.cgi. Cost for batch requests of Secretary of State business entity requests is $15 per 1000 records (Nebraska Revised Statutes 33-101) Also, search securities companies registered with the state at www.ndbf.ne.gov/searches/securities.shtml. *Other Options:* Nebraska.gov has the capability of offering database purchases.

Uniform Commercial Code, Federal & State Tax Liens

UCC Division, Secretary of State, Rm 1301,   www.sos.ne.gov/business/ucc/   Access is outsourced to Nebraska.gov To set an account, go to www.nebraska.gov/subscriber/index.html. The system is available 24 hours daily. There is an annual $50.00 fee in addition to charges to view records.

Call 800-747-8177 for more information. *Other Options:* Check with Nebrask.gov for bulk purchase via UCC/EFS, there is a per record rate of $2.00 for the first 1,000 records then a flat rate afterward. Also, by debt location the rate is $15 per 1000 records.

Sales Tax Registrations

Revenue Department, Taxpayer Assistance, www.revenue.nebraska.gov/salestax.html Summaries of court cases are displayed at www.revenue.nebraska.gov/legal/court_cases/court.html. *Other Options:* Bulk data on registered businesses and new businesses is available for purchase.

Vital Records

Health & Human Services System, Vital Statistics Section, http://dhhs.ne.gov/publichealth/Pages/vital_records.aspx Records may be ordered online via the web page. For Internet requests, fax to 402-471-8230 the indicating name(s) on the record(s) requested and the Internet confirmation number.

Workers' Compensation Records

Workers' Compensation Court, Administrative Offices, www.wcc.ne.gov A search of court decisions and orders is at http://dtsearch.wcc.ne.gov/. One may reuquest records online at https://www.wcc.ne.gov/apps/IPUBA0003Afrm.aspx. *Other Options:* Request for bulk access are considered. Send request to Su Perk Davis at address listed.

Driver Records

Department of Motor Vehicles, Driver & Vehicle Records Division, www.dmv.nebraska.gov/ Nebraska outsources all electronic record requests, incluing a Driver License Monitoring system to Nebraska.gov at www.nebraska.gov/subscriber/index.html# or call 402- 471-7810. The system allows one to become an electronic subscriber or an electronic non-subscriber (also known as the One-Time Search). Search methods require DL# or SSN and name and date of birth - there is no name only search for non-subscribers. The system is interactive and open 24 hours a day, 7 days a week. Fee is $3.00 per record. Subscribers pay annual fee of $50.00 and are billed for record searches. An online status check is offered at https://www.nebraska.gov/dmv/reinstatements/client.cgi. Enter the full name, dob and either the DL or SSN. There is no fee. *Other Options:* Bulk requesters must be authorized by state officials. Purpose of the request and subsequent usage are reviewed. For information, call 402-471-3885.

Vehicle & Vessel Title & Registration, Vessel Title

Department of Motor Vehicles, Driver & Vehicle Records Division, www.dmv.nebraska.gov/ Electronic access is through Nebraska.gov at www.nebraska.gov/subscriber/index.html#. There is an annual $50.00 up fee addition to the $1.00 per record fee. The system is open 24 hours a day, 7 days a week. Call 800-747-8177 for more information. Title Status, lien notation confirmation and brand information may be obtained at no fee using the Vehicle identification number (VIN), go to www.clickdmv.ne.gov and select Title Inquiry. *Other Options:* Bulk requesters must be authorized by state officials. Purpose of the request and subsequent usage are reviewed. For more information, call 402-471-3885

Crash Reports

Department of Roads, Accident Records Bureau, www.transportation.nebraska.gov/highway-safety/ Investigator's reports are available online at www2.dor.state.ne.us/storefront. Must be purchased using a credit card or Pay Pal. The agency offers electronic access to daily reports involving injury (intended for attorneys, etc.) for $750 plus tax. *Other Options:* Records can be purchased in bulk from the computer database (1988 to present).

Campaign Finance, Lobbyists, Conflicts of Interest

NE Accountability and Disclosure Commission, PO Box 95086, www.nadc.nebraska.gov/ View campaign filings at www.nadc.nebraska.gov/ccdb/search.cgi. A list of registered PACs is at www.nadc.nebraska.gov/cf/active_pacs.html. View lobbyists reports at http://nebraskalegislature.gov/reports/lobby.php. To obtain actual copies of documents which were not filed in electronic format, please email lobby@leg.ne.gov. View enforcement actions at www.nadc.nebraska.gov/en/EnforcementActionsOfTheCommission.html. *Other Options:* Current law dictates the database can only be sold for political purposes and not for commercial purposes. A statewide CD can be purchased for $500.

Voter Registration

Secretary of State, Elections Division-Records, www.sos.ne.gov/dyindex.html A voter registration status link is found at https://www.votercheck.necvr.ne.gov/. Registered lobbyists are found at http://nebraskalegislature.gov/reports/lobby.php. *Other Options:* Current law dictates the database can only be sold for political purposes and not for commercial purposes. A statewide CD can be purchased for $500.

Occupational Licensing Boards

These licenses are all searchable at https://www.nebraska.gov/LISSearch/search.cgi

Adult Day Care	Child Care Center/Child Caring/Placing Agency	Electrician, Heating & Cooling
Alarm, Fire/Installer	Chiropractor	Electrician/Apprentice
Alcohol/Drug Tester	Cosmetologist/Nail Care/Salon/School	Electrologist/Electrology Facility
Animal Technician	Dental Hygienist/Anesthesia Permit	Embalmer
Asbestos Worker/Supvr	Dentist	Emergency Medical Care Facility
Asbestos-Related Occupation	Developmentally Disabled/Mentally Retarded Care	Environmental Health Specialist
Assisted Living Facility	Service	Esthetician/Esthetician Establishment
Athletic Trainer	Drug Distributor, Wholesale	Funeral Director/Establishment
Audiologist	Drug Wholesale Facility	Health Clinic

Hearing Aid Dispenser/Fitter
Home Health Agency
Hospice
Hospital
Intermediate Care Facility (Retarded)
Labor/Delivery Service/Clinic
Laboratory
Lead Abatement Worker, etc
Local Anesthesia Certification
Long Term Care Center
Marriage & Family Therapist
Massage Establishment/Massage Therapy School
Mental Health Center
Nurse-RN/LPN

Nursing Home/Administrator
Nutrition Therapy, Medical
Occupational Therapist
Optometrist
Osteopathic Physician
Pharmacist/Pharmacy/Pharmacy, Mail Order
Physical Therapist
Physician/Medical Doctor/Assistant
Podiatrist
Preschool
Psychologist
Radiographer
Radon Mitigation Specialist/Technician
Rehabilitation Agency

Respiratory Care Practitioner
Respite Care Service
Social Worker
Speech-Language Pathologist
Substance Abuse Treatment Center
Swimming Pool Operator
Veterinarian/Veterinary Technician
Water Operator
Water Treatment Plant Operator
Well Driller/Pump Installer
X-Ray Equipment (Portable)

The Rest:

Abstractor/Abstractor Company .... www.nebraska.gov/abstracters/license-search/license_search.phtml
Accountant-CPA .... www.nbpa.ne.gov/search/
Athletic Event, Contestant/Judge/Manager .... www.athcomm.nebraska.gov/certificationcourses.html
Athletic Event, Physician, Timekeeper .... www.athcomm.nebraska.gov/certificationcourses.html
Attorney .... www.nebar.com/search/
Bank.. www.ndbf.ne.gov/searches/fisearch.shtml
Boxer .... www.athcomm.nebraska.gov/certificationcourses.html
Check Seller .... www.ndbf.ne.gov/searches/fisearch.shtml
Club, Amateur.. www.athcomm.nebraska.gov/certificationcourses.html
Collection Agency .... www.sos.ne.gov/licensing/collection/index.html
Credit Union.. www.ndbf.ne.gov/searches/fisearch.shtml
Debt Management Agency .... www.sos.ne.gov/licensing/debt.html
Delayed Deposit Service .... www.ndbf.ne.gov/searches/fisearch.shtml
Fund Transmission .... www.ndbf.ne.gov/searches/fisearch.shtml
Geologist.. www.nebog.nebraska.gov/pdf/roster.pdf
Insurance Agency/Agent/Broker/Prod .... www.doi.nebraska.gov/entity-search.html
Insurance Agent/Agency Closed Actions .... www.doi.nebraska.gov/legal/agaction/agaction.html
Insurance Company/Consultant .... www.doi.nebraska.gov/entity-search.html
Investment Advisor/Advisor Rep .... www.ndbf.ne.gov/searches/fisearch.shtml
Landscape Architect .... www.nsbla.nebraska.gov/registrants.pdf
Liquor Retailers/ Whlse/Shipper .... https://www.nebraska.gov/nlcc/license_search/licsearch.cgi
Lobbyist .... www.nebraskalegislature.gov/feature/lobbyists.php
Matchmaker .... www.athcomm.nebraska.gov/certificationcourses.html
Pesticide Applicator/Dealer .... www.kellysolutions.com/ne/
Polygraph Examiner, Private/Public .... www.sos.ne.gov/licensing/poly_menu.html
Private Investigator/Agency.. www.sos.ne.gov/licensing/private_eye/index.html
Real Estate Agent/Seller/Broker.. www.nrec.ne.gov/licinfodb/index.cgi
Real Estate Appraiser.. www.appraiser.ne.gov/appraiser_listing.html
Referee .... www.athcomm.nebraska.gov/certificationcourses.html
Sales Finance Company .... www.ndbf.ne.gov/searches/fisearch.shtml
Saving & Loan .... www.ndbf.ne.gov/searches/fisearch.shtml
Seconds, Athletic Event.. www.athcomm.nebraska.gov/certificationcourses.html
Securities Agent/Broker/Dealer .... www.ndbf.ne.gov/searches/fisearch.shtml
Surveyor, Land .... www.nbels.nebraska.gov/lsalpha.html
Teacher.. https://dc2.education.ne.gov/nclblookup/main.aspx
Trust Company .... www.ndbf.ne.gov/searches/fisearch.shtml
Voice Stress Examiner/Analyzer .... www.sos.ne.gov/licensing/poly_menu.html
Wrestler/Wrestling/Boxing Matches.......................... www.athcomm.nebraska.gov/certificationcourses.html

State and Local Courts

About Nebraska Courts: District Courts have original jurisdiction in all felony cases, equity cases, domestic relations cases, and civil cases where the amount in controversy involves more than $52,000. However many District Judges will accept cases over $15,000. District Courts also have appellate jurisdiction in certain matters arising out of County Courts.

County Courts have original jurisdiction in probate matters, violations of city or village ordinances, juvenile court matters without a separate juvenile court, adoptions, preliminary hearings in felony cases, and eminent domain proceedings. The County Courts have concurrent jurisdiction in civil matters when the amount in controversy is $52,000 or less, criminal matters classified as misdemeanors or infractions, some domestic relations matters, and paternity actions. Nearly all misdemeanor cases are tried in the County Courts. As a rule of thumb, only District Courts can enter a sentence which incarcerates a defendant for more than one year.

Traffic cases are part of the County Courts, with the exception of Enhanced DUIs, which are part of the District Court records since they are felonies. County Courts have juvenile jurisdiction in all but 3 counties. Douglas, Lancaster, and Sarpy counties have separate Juvenile Courts. Also, there is a separate Workers' Compensation Court – see www.wcc.ne.gov.

The web page for the Judicial Branch is https://supremecourt.nebraska.gov/.

Appellate Courts: The Court of Appeals is generally the first court to hear appeals of judgments and orders in criminal, juvenile, civil, domestic relations and probate matters. In addition, the Court of Appeals has appellate jurisdiction over decisions originating in a number of state administrative boards and agencies. Opinions are available from the home page above.

Online Court Access

All courts participate in the system described below.

An online access subscription service is available for all Nebraska County Courts and all District Courts. Douglas County An online access service is available for all Nebraska County Courts and all District Courts. The data can be access by individual on a pay-as-you-go basis at https://www.nebraska.gov/justicecc/ccname.cgi. Entities that are frequent requesters may set-up a subscription (see below). The fee for a onetime search using a credit card is $15.00.

Douglas County District Court was the last county added in April 2011. Case details, all party listings, payments, and actions taken for criminal, civil, probate, juvenile, and traffic are available. District Courts and County Courts must be searched separately. The system starts with a name search and resulting list gives full DOB. Both convictions and pending cases are available in the criminal search.

About the Subscription Service

Subscribers who register with Nebraska.gov pay an annual fee for $50.00 and then a fee of $1.00 per case file viewed record. Those entities who view at least 500 cases a month may have access for a flat rate of $500.00 per month. Go to www.nebraska.gov/faqs/justice or call 402-471-7810 for more information.

The system essentially displays the same docket information as shown on the public terminals available at the county court house, when available.

There are no other online court sites.

Recorders, Assessors, and Other Sites of Note

About Nebraska Recording Offices: 93 counties and offices. The recording officer is the Register of Deed; however, in many counties this is a combined position with the County Clerk.

About Tax Liens: Since July 1, 1999, all federal and state tax liens are initially filed at the UCC Division at the state. The UCC Division then forwards the filing to the County Register of Deeds.

Online Access

Recorded Documents

Below are the 37 counties affiliated with a vendor for access to Register of Deeds data - see http://nebraskadeedsonline.us/. Data fields available include the instrument, date, type, grantor, grantee, and legal descriptions.

Antelope	Frontier	Nemaha	Sioux
Banner	Gage	Nuckolls	Stanton
Boyd	Garden	Pawnee	Thayer
Brown	Garfield	Phelps	Washington
Burt	Hamilton	Pierce	Wayne
Clay	Keith	Platte	Webster
Colfax	Knox	Red Willow	York
Cuming	Madison	Saline	
Dawes	Merrick	Scotts Bluff	
Fillmore	Nance	Seward	

Property Tax and Ownership

Access real estate or personal property tax data free for the following 64 counties at www.nebraskataxesonline.us.

Adams	Dixon	Jefferson	Phelps
Antelope	Dodge	Johnson	Platte
Banner	Douglas	Keith	Red Willow
Boone	Dundy	Kimball	Richardson
Box Butte	Fillmore	Knox	Saline
Buffalo	Franklin	Lincoln	Saunders
Burt	Frontier	Logan	Scotts Bluff
Cass	Furnas	Madison	Seward
Cedar	Gage	Merrick	Stanton
Chase	Garden	Morrill	Thayer
Clay	Gosper	Nance	Thomas
Colfax	Greeley	Nemaha	Thurston
Cuming	Hamilton	Nuckolls	Wayne
Dawes	Hayes	Otoe	Webster
Dawson	Hitchcock	Pawnee	Wheeler
Deuel	Holt	Perkins	York

County Sites (Not Listed Above):

Adams County   *Recorded Documents* www.adamscounty.org/register-of-deeds   Access to records free at http://deeds.adamscounty.org/DeedSifter/Disclaimer.aspx?ReturnUrl=%2fdeedsifter%2fdefault.aspx.
Property, Taxation Records   Click on Adams County. Also, access to property tax for free at http://assessor.adamscounty.org/Appraisal/PublicAccess/. Also, access to GIS/mapping free at http://gis.adamscounty.org/map/.

Antelope County   *Recorded Documents* https://antelopecounty.nebraska.gov/register-deeds   Access to deeds online go to www.nebraskadeedsonline.us/, then select a county. Index is free to view.
Property, Taxation Records   Access to property search for free at www.antelope.assessor.gisworkshop.com/.

Box Butte County   *Property, Taxation Records*   Access to property search info free at http://boxbutte.gisworkshop.com/.

Brown County   *Property, Taxation Records*   Access to GIS/mapping free at http://brown.gisworkshop.com/.

Buffalo County   *Recorded Documents* www.buffalocounty.ne.gov/REGISTER-OF-DEEDS   Access to deeds for a fee Laredo or Tapestry. Go to www.buffalocounty.ne.gov/DEEDS-RECORDS-ONLINE and click on Deeds Records Online for more information.
Property, Taxation Records   Click on Buffalo County. Also, access to GIS/mapping free at http://buffalo.gisworkshop.com/.

Burt County
Property, Taxation Records   Access to GIS/mapping for free at http://burt.gisworkshop.com/.

Butler County   *Property, Taxation Records*   Search assessor property data on the GIS site free at http://butler.gisworkshop.com/.

Cass County   *Property, Taxation Records*   Access GIS and Assessor data free at http://cass.gisworkshop.com/#.

Cedar County   *Property, Taxation Records*   Click on Cedar County. Also, access to GIS/mapping for free at http://cedar.gisworkshop.com/#.

Cherry County   *Property, Taxation Records*   Access to GIS/mapping free at www.cherry.gisworkshop.com/.

Cheyenne County   *Property, Taxation Records*   Access to GIS/mapping free at http://cheyenne.assessor.gisworkshop.com/.

Clay County   *Property, Taxation Records*   Access to GIS/mapping free at http://clay.assessor.gisworkshop.com/.

Cuming County   *Property, Taxation Records*   Access to GIS/mapping for free at www.cuming.assessor.gisworkshop.com/#.

Custer County   *Property, Taxation Records*   Access to TaxSifter Parcel search for free at http://custerne.taxsifter.com/taxsifter/disclaimer.asp. Also, access to GIS/mapping for free at www.custer.gisworkshop.com/.

Dakota County   *Property, Taxation Records*   Access to GIS/mapping free at http://dakota.gisworkshop.com/.

Dawes County   *Property, Taxation Records*   Access to GIS/mapping free at http://dawes.assessor.gisworkshop.com/#.

Dawson County   *Property, Taxation Records*   Access to GIS/mapping for free at http://dawson.gisworkshop.com/.

Dixon County   *Property, Taxation Records*   Access to GIS/mapping for free at http://dixon.gisworkshop.com/.

Dodge County   *Recorded Documents* www.registerofdeeds.com/   Access to land records for a fee at http://dodgene.landlinkportal.com:9081/LandShark/login.jsp?url=http%3A%2F%2Fdodgene.landlinkportal.com%3A9081%2FLandShark%2Fuseredit.jsp. Records from 1/1/1998 to present.
Property, Taxation Records   Access assessor records free at www.dodgerealproperty.nebraska.gov/Appraisal/PublicAccess/.

Douglas County   *Recorded Documents, Marriage Records* www.dcregisterofdeeds.org/home   Search the clerk/comptroller marriage database free at www.douglascountyclerk.org/marriage-licenses/marriagelicensesearch. A subscription service is available at www.dcregisterofdeeds.org/premium-services. Images of deeds and Misc document types are available from 1987-forward. All other document types are available from 1993-forward. There are 4 pricing tiers, based on the number of users. Basic 'On-Demand Users' are charged a $5.00 convenience fee per print order. The premium Plus with up to user unlimited access is $1,000 per month.
Property, Taxation Records   Access to GIS/mapping for free at http://douglascone.wgxtreme.com/. Also, access to the county assessor property valuation lookup is free at http://douglasne.mapping-online.com/DouglasCoNe/static/valuation.jsp.

Fillmore County   *Property, Taxation Records*   Access to GIS/mapping free at http://fillmore.assessor.gisworkshop.com/.

Frontier County   *Property, Taxation Records*   Access to basic property assessor data is available free at http://frontier.gisworkshop.com/. A subscription is required for full data including sales, photos, history, buildings for $200 per year.

Gage County   *Property, Taxation Records*   Access property data via the county Assessor GIS/mapping service free at https://gage.gisworkshop.com/.

Garden County   *Property, Taxation Records*   Access to GIS/mapping for free at http://garden.gisworkshop.com/.

Garfield County   *Property, Taxation Records*   Access parcel records and mapping for free at www.garfieldcounty.ne.gov/webpages/about/maps.html. Also, access to GIS/mapping for free at http://garfield.gisworkshop.com/.

Gosper County   *Property, Taxation Records*   Access to GIS/mapping for free at www.gosper.gisworkshop.com/.

Grant County   *Property, Taxation Records*   Access to GIS/mapping free at https://grant.gisworkshop.com/.

Greeley County   *Property, Taxation Records*   Access parcel records free at www.nebraskaassessorsonline.us/search.aspx?county=Greeley. Also, access to GIS/mapping for free at http://greeley.gisworkshop.com/.

Hall County   *Recorded Documents* www.hallcountyne.gov/content.lasso?page=6089   Access to the county Register of Deeds Document Search is free at http://deeds.hallcountyne.gov/.
Property, Taxation Records   Access GIS/mapping free at http://grandislandne.map.beehere.net/. Also, access to parcel search for free at http://taxsifter.hallcountyne.gov/taxsifter/disclaimer.asp.

Hamilton County   *Property, Taxation Records*   Access parcel records free at http://hamilton.gisworkshop.com/.

Harlan County *Property, Taxation Records* Access parcel records free at www.harlanrealproperty.nebraska.gov/Appraisal/PublicAccess/. Also, access to GIS/mapping for free at http://harlan.gisworkshop.com/.

Hayes County *Property, Taxation Records* Access to property search for free at www.hayes.assessor.gisworkshop.com/.

Hitchcock County *Property, Taxation Records* Access to GIS/mappiing for free at http://hitchcock.gisworkshop.com/.

Holt County *Property, Taxation Records* Access to GIS/mapping for free at http://holt.gisworkshop.com/.

Howard County *Property, Taxation Records* Access to GIS/mapping free at http://howard.gisworkshop.com/.

Johnson County *Property, Taxation Records* Access property data free at http://johnson.assessor.gisworkshop.com/.

Kearney County *Property, Taxation Records* Access property data and parcel records free at http://kearney.gisworkshop.com/.

Keith County *Property, Taxation Records* Also access GIS/mapping free at http://keith.gisworkshop.com/.

Keya Paha County *Property, Taxation Records* Access to GIS/mapping free at http://keyapaha.gisworkshop.com/#.

Kimball County *Property, Taxation Records* Access to GIS/mapping for free at http://kimball.gisworkshop.com/.

Property, Taxation Records Access to GIS/mapping free at http://knox.gisworkshop.com/.

Lancaster County *Recorded Documents* http://lancaster.ne.gov/assessor/index.htm Search register of deeds Grantor/Grantee index free at https://lancasterne-recorder.tylertech.com/lancasterrecorder/web/. Use Public Login or register for more detailed data (images).
Property, Taxation Records Access to GIS/mapping for free at http://lancaster.ne.gov/assessor/gis.htm. Also, access to property information and tax payment for free at http://lincoln.ne.gov/aspx/cnty/cto/default.aspx.

Lincoln County *Recorded Documents* www.co.lincoln.ne.us/deeds/ Access to records for free (limited) at https://esearch.cichosting.com/. For detailed records, must subscribe.
Property, Taxation Records Access to GIS/mapping free at http://lincoln.gisworkshop.com/.

Madison County *Property, Taxation Records* Also access assessor records free at http://madison.gisworkshop.com/.

Merrick County *Property, Taxation Records* Access to GIS/mapping for free at http://merrick.gisworkshop.com/.

Nance County *Property, Taxation Records* Access to GIS/mapping and property search for free at www.nance.gisworkshop.com/.

Nemaha County *Property, Taxation Records* Access to GIS/mapping free at www.nemaha.assessor.gisworkshop.com/.

Nuckolls County *Property, Taxation Records* Access to GIS/mapping for free at http://nuckolls.gisworkshop.com/.

Otoe County *Property, Taxation Records* Access property search and GIS/mapping for free at www.otoe.gisworkshop.com/.

Pawnee County *Property, Taxation Records* Access to GIS/mapping for free at www.pawnee.gisworkshop.com/.

Perkins County *Property, Taxation Records* Access to property searches for free at www.perkins.gisworkshop.com/.

Phelps County *Property, Taxation Records* Access to records for free at http://phelps.gisworkshop.com/.

Pierce County *Property, Taxation Records* Access to property records/GIS/mapping free at http://pierce.assessor.gisworkshop.com/.

Platte County *Property, Taxation Records* Access the GIS/mapping at http://platte.assessor.gisworkshop.com/.

Polk County *Property, Taxation Records* Search property and mapping free at http://polk.assessor.gisworkshop.com/#. Access the treasurer county tax record search free at http://polk.treasurer.gisworkshop.com/.

Red Willow County *Property, Taxation Records* Search auditor's county property data on the gis-mapping site free at http://redwillow.gisworkshop.com/.

Richardson County *Property, Taxation Records* Access to property search for free at www.richardson.assessor.gisworkshop.com/.

Rock County *Property, Taxation Records* Access to property search and mapping for free at http://rock.assessor.gisworkshop.com/

Saline County *Property, Taxation Records* Access property data free at http://saline.gisworkshop.com/.

Sarpy County *Recorded Documents* www.sarpy.com/deeds/ Search the historical grantor/grantee index 1857-1990 free at www.sarpy.com/rodggi/.
Property, Taxation Records A simple property search is available free at www.sarpy.com/sarpyproperty/ but no name searching. A premium subscription service based on needs is available starting at $240 per year and goes higher; see contract at www.sarpy.com/oldterra/SarpyContract.pdf. Also, register to accept tax sales lists at www.sarpy.com/taxsale/.

Saunders County *Property, Taxation Records* Access assessment data for free at www.saundersrealproperty.nebraska.gov/Appraisal/PublicAccess/. Also, access to property tax search for free at www.nebraskataxesonline.us/. Click on Saunders County. Also, access to GIS/mapping for free at http://saunders.gisworkshop.com/.

Scotts Bluff County *Recorded Land Documents Records* www.scottsbluffcounty.org/register-deeds/deeds.html Access recorded documents from www.scottsbluffcounty.org/register-deeds/deeds-disclaimer-do.html. There are several options and links available from this page. Also, access to deeds online go to www.nebraskadeedsonline.us/, then select a county. Index is free to view.
Property, Taxation Records Access to property tax search for free at www.nebraskataxesonline.us/. Click on Scotts Bluff County.

Seward County *Recorded Documents* www2.connectseward.org/cgov/clerk.htm Access to deeds online go to www.nebraskadeedsonline.us/, then select a county. Index is free to view.
Property, Taxation Records Free access to property tax searches at www.nebraskataxesonline.us/. Click on Seward County. Also, access GIS/mapping for free at http://seward.gisworkshop.com/.

Sheridan County *Property, Taxation Records* Access to GIS/mapping free at http://sheridan.gisworkshop.com/.

Sherman County *Property, Taxation Records* Access to parcel records free at http://sherman.assessor.gisworkshop.com/.

Sioux County *Property, Taxation Records* Access to GIS/mapping for free at http://sioux.gisworkshop.com/.

Stanton County *Property, Taxation Records* Access to GIS/mapping for free at www.stanton.gisworkshop.com/.

Thayer County *Property, Taxation Records* Access to GIS/mapping for free at http://thayer.assessor.gisworkshop.com/.

Thomas County *Property, Taxation Records* Access to GIS/mapping free at http://thomas.assessor.gisworkshop.com/.

Thurston County *Property, Taxation Records* Access to GIS/mapping for free at http://thurston.gisworkshop.com/.

Valley County *Property, Taxation Records* Access to GIS/mapping free at www.valley.gisworkshop.com/.

Washington County *Property, Taxation Records* Access to GIS/mapping for free at http://washington.gisworkshop.com/.

Webster County *Property, Taxation Records* Access to GIS/mapping for free at http://webster.gisworkshop.com/.

York County *Property, Taxation Records* Access to property search for free at http://york.assessor.gisworkshop.com/.

Nevada

Capital: Carson City
              Carson City County
Time Zone: PST
Population: 2,890,845
# of Counties: 17

Useful State Links

Website: **http://nv.gov/**
Governor: **http://gov.state.nv**
Attorney General: **http://ag.nv.gov/**
State Archives: **http://nsla.nv.gov/**
State Statutes and Codes: **www.leg.state.nv.us/NRS/**
Legislative Bill Search: **www.leg.state.nv.us**
Unclaimed Funds: **www.nevadatreasurer.gov/Unclaimed_Property/UP_Home/**

State Public Record Agencies

Criminal Records

Dept. of Public Services, General Services Division,   http://gsd.nv.gov/   A system called Civil Name Check provides criminal history record information to only authorized Repository users (direct employers and third party agencies who provide background services to employers). See http://gsd.nv.gov/Services/Civil_Name_Check/. Signed releases are required and everyone in the data chain (who sees report) must be fingerprinted & approved. All user accounts are audited. The fee is $20.00. Results are reported same day, but sometimes it can take days if there are excessive hits. A significant issue is the data can not be directly disseminated to the end user (employer). The data on the report MUST be verified at each court where this is a record. So an onsite court search is required for every hit.

Sexual Offender Registry

Records and Technology Division, Sex Offender Registry,   www.nvsexoffenders.gov/   Note: Per state law (NRS 179B.270), a search of this free public database at www.nvsexoffenders.gov/Search.aspx, CANNOT be used for employment screening purposes. Information available on the website is extensive, including aliases, photograph (where available), conviction information, and latest registered address. Search by name, ZIP Code, or license plate number. There is no fee. Information is provided for sex offenders with a risk assessment score of a TIER Level 3 or TIER Level 2.

Incarceration Records

Nevada Department of Corrections, Attn: Records,   http://doc.nv.gov/   Search inmates at http://167.154.2.76/inmatesearch/form.php.

Corporation, LP, LLC

Secretary of State, Records,   www.nvsos.gov   Search online at http://nvsos.gov/sosentitysearch/CorpSearch.aspx. Also includes Trademarks, Trade Names, Service Marks, Reserved Names & Business Licenses. Search by corporate name, resident agent, corporate officers, or by file number. To broaden the search, enter only the main name without entity suffixes (Inc, LLC, LP etc.) Also, good standing certificates can be ordered online - no add'l search fee. Email search requests are encouraged, copies@sos.nv.gov. Note that most orders may be emailed back if email is provided. There is also a search offered at the state's Business Portal at www.nvsilverflume.gov/home.   *Other Options:* Reports and data downloads available - Foreign Corporation lists, Non-Profits, for example - under the Online Services tab at the website; fees vary.

Trademarks/Servicemarks

Secretary of State, Corporate Expedite Office,   www.nvsos.gov/index.aspx?page=246   Search marks at http://nvsos.gov/sosentitysearch/. While this may look like a business entity search, it will bring up marks. Look on the document number; SM is servicemark; TM is trademark.

Uniform Commercial Code, Federal & State Tax Liens

UCC Division, Secretary of State,   http://nvsos.gov/index.aspx?page=155   After registration, searching is available at https://nvsos.gov/NVUCC/user/login.asp. To receive documents the fee is $30.00, an order form may be downloaded. A full commercial system is also available. *Other Options:* Bulk purchase services are available. Must have an account with email and password. Go to https://nvsos.gov/NVUCC/user/login.asp and sign in.

Birth, Death Records

Nevada Department of Health & Human Services, Office of Vital Statistics, http://dpbh.nv.gov/Programs/Office_of_Vital_Statistics/ Online ordering available from state designated vendor at www.vitalchek.com.

Workers' Compensation Records

Davison of Industrial Relations, Workers' Compensation Section, http://dir.nv.gov/WCS/home/ For the Employers' Workers' Compensation coverage verification link go to http://dirweb.state.nv.us/WCS/cvs.htm. Coverage Verification Service (CVS) users can verify workers' compensation coverage of employers who have policies with private carriers. A search resulting in NO RECORDS FOUND on CVS does not necessarily indicate that coverage does not exist.

Driver Records

Department of Motor Vehicles, Records Section, www.dmvnv.com/ The state has an FTP system available for high volume users. All files received by 5:30 PM are processed and returned at 6:30 PM. Fee is $8.00 per record. Call 775-684-4702 for details. Also, a batch processing system has recently be added for higher volume accounts. Only three-year histories are available electronically A person may order his or her own record at online at https://dmvapp.nv.gov/dmv/dl/OL_DH/Drvr_Usr_Info.aspx. The fee is $8.00.

Vehicle Ownership & Registration

Department of Motor Vehicles, Motor Vehicle Record Section, www.dmvnv.com A registration status inquiry is at https://dmvapp.nv.gov/dmv/vr/vr_dev/VR_reg/VR_Reg_Default.aspx. The license plate number and last four digits of the VIN are required to display the registration information. There is no fee. *Other Options:* Database is available for sale to permissible users under DPPA at costs varying from $500 to $2,500.

Voter Registration, Campaign Finance, PACs

Secretary of State, Elections Division, http://nvsos.gov/index.aspx?page=3 First, create an online web account. Then submit the Official Request for List of Registered Voters form. This submission must be made by made, fax or in person. Upon acceptance (which can take 7 days), the requester is notified by email. Then the approved requester may download online. View registered PACs at http://nvsos.gov/index.aspx?page=111. View campaign finance reports at www.nvsos.gov/SOSCandidateServices/AnonymousAccess/CEFDSearchUU/Search.aspx#individual_search *Other Options:* Bulk access of voter registration is available for purchase in electronic format. See the web page listed above for details.

GED (HSE) Transcripts

NV Department of Education, State HSE Office, www.nevadaadulteducation.org Records may be requested from https://www.diplomasender.com. A credit card is needed. Request must be ordered by the test taker. Employers and third parties must receive an email and/or Authentication Code from the test taker to then access the authorized documents. Turnaround time is 1-3 days.

Occupational Licensing Boards

These Contractor licenses are all searchable at www.nvcontractorsboard.com

Building Mover	Glazier Contractor	Roofer
Carpentry Contractor	Heating & Air Conditioning Mechanic	Sewerage Contractor
Concrete Contractor	Insulation Installer Contractor	Sheet Metal Fabricator
Contractor, General	Landscape Contractor	Siding Installer
Electrical Contractor	Mason	Sign Erector
Elevator/Conveyor	Painter/Paper Hanger	Solar Contractor
Engineering, General	Plasterer/Drywall Installer/Lather	Steel Contractor
Fencing	Playground Builder	Tank Installer, Pressure/Storage
Fire Protection Contractor	Plumber	Well Driller
Floor/Tile/Carpet Layer	Pump Installer	Wrecker/Demolisher
Gas Fitter	Refractory/Firebrick Contractor	

The Rest:

Accountant-CPA/Accountancy-Auditor .... www.nvaccountancy.com/search.fx
Aesthetician .... https://nvboc.glsuite.us/glsuiteweb/Clients/NVBOC/Public/Verification/Search.aspx
Ambulatory Surgery Ctr (Pharm) .... https://pharmacy.bop.nv.gov/datamart/mainMenu.do
Appraiser (MVD) .... http://doi.nv.gov/licensing-search/
Architect .... http://nsbaidrd.state.nv.us/?page=7
Attorney .... https://www.nvbar.org/find-a-lawyer/

Audiologist	https://nvaud.glsuite.us/GlsuiteWeb/Clients/NVAUD/Public/Verification/Search.aspx
Automobile/ Mfg'r/Transporter	https://dmvapp.nv.gov/DMV/OBL/Business_Reports/Pages/BusinessLicenses.aspx
Automobile/ Wrecker/Salvage Pool	https://dmvapp.nv.gov/DMV/OBL/Business_Reports/Pages/BusinessLicenses.aspx
Automobile/Garage, Registered/Rebuilder	https://dmvapp.nv.gov/DMV/OBL/Business_Reports/Pages/BusinessLicenses.aspx
Body Shop	https://dmvapp.nv.gov/DMV/OBL/Business_Reports/Pages/BusinessLicenses.aspx
Cemetery	http://funeral.nv.gov/Licensees/Licensees/
Chiropractor	https://nvbochiro.glsuite.us/GLSuiteWeb/Clients/NVBOChiro/Public/Licensee/LicenseeSearch.aspx
Claims Adjuster	http://doi.nv.gov/licensing-search/
Cosmetologist/Hair Stylist (Designer)	https://nvboc.glsuite.us/glsuiteweb/Clients/NVBOC/Public/Verification/Search.aspx
Cosmetology Instructor/School	https://nvboc.glsuite.us/glsuiteweb/Clients/NVBOC/Public/Verification/Search.aspx
Court Reporter, Certified	http://crptr.nv.gov/consumer/License_Verification/
Crematorium	http://funeral.nv.gov/Licensees/Licensees/
Denied/Unsuitable Gaming Individual	http://gaming.nv.gov/index.aspx?page=76
Dentist/Dental Hygienist	http://dental.nv.gov/Consumers/License_Verification/
Driving School/DUI School	https://dmvapp.nv.gov/DMV/OBL/Business_Reports/Pages/BusinessLicenses.aspx
Drug Wholesaler/Dist/Mfg	https://pharmacy.bop.nv.gov/datamart/mainMenu.do
Electrologist	https://nvboc.glsuite.us/glsuiteweb/Clients/NVBOC/Public/Verification/Search.aspx
Embalmer	http://funeral.nv.gov/Licensees/Licensees/
Emergency Medical Service Nurse	http://nevadanursingboard.org/licensure-and-certification/verify-licenses-and-certificates/
Engineer	www.nvboe.org/rosters/
Euthanasia Technician (Animal)	https://pharmacy.bop.nv.gov/datamart/mainMenu.do
Euthanasia/Animal Technician	https://www.nvvetboard.us/glsuiteweb/clients/nvbov/public/LicenseeList.aspx
Funeral Director	http://funeral.nv.gov/Licensees/Licensees/
GCB Most-Wanted & Banned List	http://gaming.nv.gov/index.aspx?page=76
Guard Dog Handler	https://nevadapilb.glsuite.us/
Hearing Aid Specialist/Apprentice	https://nvaud.glsuite.us/GlsuiteWeb/Clients/NVAUD/Public/Verification/Search.aspx
Home Inspector	www.inspectordatabase.com/state.php?statecode=NV
Homeopathic Physician/Assistant	http://nvbhme.org/licensees.html
Homeopathic Practitioner, Advanced	http://nvbhme.org/licensees.html
Hospital Pharmacy-Institutional	https://pharmacy.bop.nv.gov/datamart/mainMenu.do
Insurance Agent/Company/Agency	http://doi.nv.gov/licensing-search/
Interior Designer	http://nsbaidrd.state.nv.us/?page=7
Landscape Architect	http://nsbla.nv.gov/LA/LicensedArchitects/
Lobbyist	www.leg.state.nv.us/AppCF/lobbyist/
Long Term Care Disciplinary Action Report	http://beltca.nv.gov/Disciplinary_Actions/Disciplinary_Actions/
LPG Gas Distributor/Technician	https://nvlpgboard-46a24c8ecff038.sharepoint.com/LP-Gas%20Board%20Active%20Licensees/default.aspx
Manicurist	https://nvboc.glsuite.us/glsuiteweb/Clients/NVBOC/Public/Verification/Search.aspx
Medical Device-Equipment or Gas	https://pharmacy.bop.nv.gov/datamart/mainMenu.do
Medical Doctor, Disciplinary Action	http://medverification.nv.gov/verification/
Mobile Home Dealer/Ltd Dealer	http://mhd.nv.gov/Content/Inspections/Licensed_Companies/
Mobile Home Salesman	http://mhd.nv.gov/Content/Inspections/Licensed_Companies/
Mobile/Manufactured Home RME	http://mhd.nv.gov/Content/Inspections/Licensed_Companies/
Narcotic Treatment Center	https://pharmacy.bop.nv.gov/datamart/mainMenu.do
Notary Public Suspensions	http://nvsos.gov/SOSNotaryApp/AnonymousAccess/SuspendedNotaries.aspx
Nurse Anesthetist	http://nevadanursingboard.org/licensure-and-certification/verify-licenses-and-certificates/
Nurse/Adverse Action Report	www.nursingboard.state.nv.us/dactions/
Nurse/RN/LPN/Advanced Practice/Aide	http://nevadanursingboard.org/licensure-and-certification/verify-licenses-and-certificates/
Nurse-Adv'd Practitioner (Pharm)	https://pharmacy.bop.nv.gov/datamart/mainMenu.do
Nursing Home Administrator	http://beltca.nv.gov/Licensing/Licensing_Information/
Occupational Therapist/Assistant	https://nvbot.glsuite.us/GLSuiteWeb/Clients/NVBOT/Public/Verification/Search.aspx
Ophthalmic Dispenser/Apprentice	http://nvbdo.nv.gov/Consumers/LicenseVerification/
Optometrist	http://optometry.nv.gov/uploadedFiles/optometrynvgov/content/Licensure/LicenseeList.pdf
Osteopathic Physician/Assistant	https://license.k3systems.com/LicensingPublic/app?page=licenseeList&service=page
Patrol Company/Man, Private	https://nevadapilb.glsuite.us/

Pest Control Applicator/Company	http://agri.nv.gov/Plant/PEST/Licensed_Pest_Control_Companies/
Pharmacist/Pharmaceutical Tech	https://pharmacy.bop.nv.gov/datamart/mainMenu.do
Pharmacy/Pharmacy Practitioner	https://pharmacy.bop.nv.gov/datamart/mainMenu.do
Physical Therapist/Assistant	http://ptboard.nv.gov/License/Verification/
Physician Assistant (Pharm)	https://pharmacy.bop.nv.gov/datamart/mainMenu.do
Physician/Medical Doctor/Assistant	http://medverification.nv.gov/verification/
Podiatrist/Podiatric Hygienists	http://podiatry.nv.gov/Licensees/LicenseeLookup/
Polygraph Examiner	https://nevadapilb.glsuite.us/
Prison Pharmacy	https://pharmacy.bop.nv.gov/datamart/mainMenu.do
Private Investigator	https://nevadapilb.glsuite.us/
Process Server	https://nevadapilb.glsuite.us/
Psychologist	http://psyexam.nv.gov/Licensing/
Real Estate Agent/Seller	https://red.prod.secure.nv.gov/Lookup/LicenseLookup.aspx
Real Estate Broker	https://red.prod.secure.nv.gov/Lookup/LicenseLookup.aspx
Real Estate Pre-Licensing Schools	https://red.prod.secure.nv.gov/Lookup/LicenseLookup.aspx
Repossessor	https://nevadapilb.glsuite.us/
Residential Designer	http://nsbaidrd.state.nv.us/?page=7
Respiratory Care Practitioner	http://medverification.nv.gov/verification/
Ring Officials/Inspectors/Ringside Doctors	http://boxing.nv.gov/about/Ring_Officials_Inspectors/
Social Worker	http://socwork.nv.gov/Licensees/
Speech Pathologist	https://nvaud.glsuite.us/GlsuiteWeb/Clients/NVAUD/Public/Verification/Search.aspx
Surveyor, Land	www.nvboe.org/rosters/
Taxi Cab Company (Clark County)	http://taxi.nv.gov/Taxicab_Companies/Taxicab_Company_Information/
Taxi Wraps	http://taxi.nv.gov/About_Us/ALL/Taxi_Wraps/Taxi_Wraps/
Teacher	http://nvteachersearch.doe.nv.gov/
Traffic Safety School	https://dmvapp.nv.gov/DMV/OBL/Business_Reports/Pages/BusinessLicenses.aspx
Vehicle Broker/Dealer	https://dmvapp.nv.gov/DMV/OBL/Business_Reports/Pages/BusinessLicenses.aspx
Veterinarian/Facility	https://www.nvvetboard.us/glsuiteweb/clients/nvbov/public/LicenseeList.aspx
Water Well Driller	http://water.nv.gov/data/drillers/
Well Driller/Monitor	http://water.nv.gov/data/drillers/

State and Local Courts

About Nevada Courts: Note that Nevada does NOT have a unified court system.

The **District Courts** are the courts of general jurisdiction. The District Court Clerk maintains the official court record for felony or gross misdemeanor criminal, divorce, juvenile, probate, adoption, paternity, child support, and civil court cases in excess of $10,000.

The **Justice Courts** are generally named for the township of jurisdiction. Due to their small populations, some townships no longer have Justice Courts. The Justice Courts handle misdemeanor crime and traffic matters, small claims disputes, evictions, and other civil matters less than $10,000. The maximum amount for Small Claims increased from $5,000 to $7,500 in July 2011. The Justices of the Peace also preside over felony and gross misdemeanor arraignments and conduct preliminary hearings to determine if sufficient evidence exists to hold criminals for trial at District Court.

The **Municipal Courts** manage cases involving violations of traffic and misdemeanor ordinances that occur within the city limits of incorporated municipalities. Plus they can hear misdemeanor violations of state laws, so their jurisdiction goes beyond city infractions. Generally theses courts do not oversee civil matters. Generally they do not oversee civil matters.

The web page for the Judiciary is http://nvcourts.gov.

Appellate Courts: The primary constitutional function of the Supreme Court is to review appeals from decisions of the District Courts. Currently there is not an intermediate Court of Appeals in Nevada, but there is ongoing discussion of the formation of one. Opinions are accessible from http://nvcourts.gov/.

Online Court Access

Some Nevada courts have internal online computer systems, but only Clark and Washoe counties offer online access to the public for District Court records. The Clark County Justices courts and the Family Court are also online.

A state-sponsored court automation system is under discussion, but will be several years before it will be implemented.

There is an online site to search Appellate Case information from their Management System. See http://caseinfo.nvsupremecourt.us/public/publicActorSearch.do.

Clark County

8th Judicial District Court -Las Vegas   https://www.clarkcountycourts.us/ejdc/
Civil: Case records are searchable free at https://www.clarkcountycourts.us/Anonymous/default.aspx. Search by case number or party name or attorney. A wealth of data is available including calendars, but few personal identifiers.   *Criminal:* Case records are searchable free at https://www.clarkcountycourts.us/Anonymous/default.aspx. Search by case number or party name or attorney.

All Township Justice Courts   http://www.clarkcountynv.gov/justicecourt/boulder/Pages/default.aspx
Civil: Access the county's Justice Courts' case data at http://cvpublicaccess.co.clark.nv.us/eservices/home.page.2. Note the Las Vegas Justice Court has a separate site.   *Criminal:* Access the county's Justice Courts' case data at http://cvpublicaccess.co.clark.nv.us/eservices/home.page.2. Note the Las Vegas Justice Court has a separate site. Includes traffic citations, but it may take 2 to 3 weeks before citations are posted

Washoe County

2nd Judicial District Court https://www.washoecourts.com/
Civil: Three search options are available at from the case inquiry tab at the home page. On can search by case number, perosn's name, or company name. *Criminal:* same

Recorders, Assessors, and Other Sites of Note

About Nevada Recording Offices: 16 counties and one independent city; 17 recording offices. The recording officer is the County Recorder. Carson City has a separate filing office.

About Tax Liens: Federal tax liens on personal property of businesses are filed with the Secretary of State. Federal tax liens on personal property of individuals are filed with the County Recorder. Although not called state tax liens, employment withholding judgments have the same effect and are filed with the County Recorder.

Online Access

There is no statewide access, however all but one county (White Pine) provides a search of recorded documents and all counties provide a search to Property Assessor data.

Carson City   *Recorded Documents* www.carson.org/government/departments-a-f/clerk-recorder   Most all recordings are indexed online at www.carson.org/how-do-i/view/public-records. Images available.
Property, Taxation Records   Access assessor data of parcels and secured property free at www.ccapps.org/cgi-bin/aswmenu. Find Carson city parcel maps searchable by parcel number at www.carson.org/government/departments-a-f/assessor/assessor-parcel-maps.

Churchill County *Recorded Documents* www.churchillcounty.org/index.aspx?nid=168   Access recorder records at www.churchillcounty.org/index.aspx?NID=215. Documents 2000 and forward can be viewed, all maps (excluding mining plat maps) can be viewed.
Property, Taxation Records   Access assessor property records free at www.churchillcounty.org/index.aspx?nid=88.

Clark County *Recorded Documents, Marriage Records* www.clarkcountynv.gov/recorder/pages/default.aspx   Access to the Recorder's real estate records free at https://recorder.co.clark.nv.us/recorderecommerce/ but no images. Can purchase a document for a fee. Also, access to fictitious firm filing free at http://sandgate.co.clark.nv.us:8498/clarkcounty/clerk/clerkSearch.html. Business license- www.clarkcountynv.gov/business-license/Pages/BLSearch.aspx. Voter Reg- www.clarkcountynv.gov/election/Services/pages/VoterRegistration.aspx.
Property, Taxation Records   Property records, assessor maps, manufactured housing, road documents, and business personal property on the county Assessor database are free at www.clarkcountynv.gov/assessor/pages/recordsearch.aspx. Property-GIS at http://gisgate.co.clark.nv.us/openweb/. Must install Microsoft Silverlight to use this site.

Douglas County *Recorded Documents* www.douglascountynv.gov/66/Recorder   Access recorded documents index back thru 1983 free at https://recorder-search.douglasnv.us/Recording/search.asp. Indexed online from 1/1/83 to present. Also, access to parcel maps for free at www.douglascountynv.gov/615/Parcel-Maps.
Property, Taxation Records   Parcel records on the Assessor's database are free at www.douglascountynv.gov/45/Assessor. Also, access GIS/ maps at www.douglascountynv.gov/104/Geographic-Information-Systems. Also, the clerk/treasurer property tax database is free at https://cltr.douglasnv.us/treasurytaxes/.

Elko County   *Recorded Documents, Marriage Records*   www.elkocountynv.net/departments/recorder/index.php   Access to the recorder database free at www.elkocountynv.net/departments/recorder/recorder/public_records.php.   *Property, Taxation Records*   Access to the assessor database including personal property and sales records is free at www.elkocountynv.net/public_record/index.php.

Esmeralda County   *Recorded Documents*   http://accessesmeralda.com/county_offices/auditor_recorder/index.php   A free index search is offered at www.esmeraldacountynv.net:1401/cgi-bin/diw200. Search by name, document number, document type or recording date.   *Property, Taxation Records*   Access the Assessor's Sales Data Inquiry for free at www.esmeraldacountynv.net:1401/cgi-bin/asw300.

Eureka County   *Recorded Documents*   www.co.eureka.nv.us/audit/auditor01.htm   Access to document inquiry free at http://eurekacounty.net:1403/cgi-bin/diw200. There are over 50 types of document to choose from.   *Property, Taxation Records*   There are three searches available from the Assessor's DB at http://eurekacounty.net:1401/cgi-bin/aswmenu. Search the treasurer's secured property tax roll at http://eurekacounty.net:1401/cgi-bin/tcw100.

Humboldt County   *Recorded Documents*   www.hcnv.us/recorder/recorder.htm   Access to record indexes and images for free at www.hcnv.us/recorder/recorder.htm. Must call office for copies of documents.   *Property, Taxation Records*   Access assessor property records free at www.hcnv.us:1401/cgi-bin/aswmenu.

Lander County   *Recorded Documents*   http://landercountynv.org/lander-county-elected-officials/recorder-office   Access to documents index for free at http://landercountynv.org/recorder%E2%80%99s-document-index. Index goes back to 1963, documents back to 1/5/1996.   *Property, Taxation Records*   Access to plat maps free at www.landercounty.org:1401/maps/LANDER_INDEX_MAP.pdf. Also, access to GIS/mapping for free at http://landercountynv.org/gis-interactive-map.

Lincoln County   *Recorded Documents*   www.lincolncountynv.org/ra/index.htm   Access to document inquiry for free at http://ibm1.lincolnnv.com:1401/cgi-bin/diw200.   *Property, Taxation Records*   Access to the Assessor data for free at http://ibm1.lincolnnv.com:1401/cgi-bin/aswmenu. Also, access to GIS/mapping for free at http://maps.gnomon.com/website/WMR_Lincoln/, and access to the parcel maps for free at www.lincolncountynv.org/assessor/parcelbooks.html.

Lyon County   *Recorded Documents, Maps Records*   www.lyon-county.org/Directory.aspx?did=18   Access recorder records free at www.lyon-county.org/110/Browse-Records; images go back to 1/1997. This site includes UCC database and map database. There is a charge for all credit card payments (minimum fee is $2.00).   *Property, Taxation Records*   Search assessor data at www1.lyon-county.org:403/cgi-bin/aswmenu.

Mineral County   *Recorded Documents, Marriage Records*   www.mineralcountynv.us/government/recorder_auditor.php   Search recorded documents free by name, type, document number or recording date at http://records.mineralcountynv.us:1401/cgi-bin/diw200   *Property, Taxation Records*   Search Property Assessor records at http://records.mineralcountynv.us:1401/cgi-bin/aswmenu.

Nye County - Pahrump   *Recorded Documents*   www.nyecounty.net/index.aspx?nid=210   Also access to recorder database free at http://nye.nv.countygovernmentrecords.com/nyecounty/web/. Index available from 1/1/86 to present. Images are added on a daily basis. If an image is available an image link will appear. If the image is not available no image link will be present.   *Property, Taxation Records*   Search property assessor data free at http://asdb.co.nye.nv.us:1401/cgi-bin/asw100. Access secured tax data sheets free at www.nyecounty.net/.

Nye County - Tonopah   *Recorded Documents*   www.nyecounty.net/index.aspx?nid=210   Also access to recorder database free at http://nye.nv.countygovernmentrecords.com/nyecounty/web/. Index available from 1/1/86 to present. Images are added on a daily basis. If an image is available an image link will appear. If the image is not available no image link will be present.   *Property, Taxation Records*   Search property assessor data free at http://asdb.co.nye.nv.us:1401/cgi-bin/asw100. Access secured tax data sheets free at www.nyecounty.net/index.aspx?NID=88.

Pershing County   *Recorded Documents*   http://pershingcounty.net/index.php/Recorder/   Access to the document inquiry site for free at www.pershingcountynv.net:1401/cgi-bin/diw200.   *Property, Taxation Records*   Access to Assessor data for free at www.pershingcountynv.net:1401/cgi-bin/aswmenu.

Storey County   *Recorded Documents*   www.storeycounty.org/338/Recorder   Access to records free at www.storeycountynv.org:1401/cgi-bin/diw200.   *Property, Taxation Records*   Search assessor's assessment roll free at www.storeycounty.org/134/Assessment-Roll. Also, access to secured tax inquiry for free at www.storeycountynv.org:1401/cgi-bin/tcw100p.

Washoe County   *Recorded Documents*   https://www.washoecounty.us/recorder/   Access grantor/grantee index free at http://icris.washoecounty.us/recorder/web/. Data from 11/19/1991 to present, images from 8/16/1999 to present. Must register.   *Property, Taxation Records*   Access property tax data at www.washoecounty.us/assessor/cama/index.php. Download property sales 2002-2015 YTD data free at https://www.washoecounty.us/assessor/online_data/sales_reports.php. Also, search aircraft, business property, mobile home data free at https://www.washoecounty.us/assessor/index.php. Click in Search Our Data.

White Pine County   *Property, Taxation Records*   Access to the property records for free at www.whitepinecountytreasurer.org:1401/cgi-bin/aswmenu. Also, access to GIS/mapping for free at http://whitepinenv.mygisonline.com/. Also, access to tax rolls for free at https://nv-whitepinecounty.civicplus.com/index.aspx?NID=435.

New Hampshire

Capital: Concord
                 MerrimackCounty
Time Zone: EST
Population: 1,330,608
# of Counties: 10

Useful State Links

Website: **www.nh.gov/**
Governor: **http://governor.nh.gov/**
Attorney General: **http://doj.nh.gov**
State Archives: **http://sos.nh.gov/arch_rec_mgmt.aspx**
State Statutes and Codes: **http://gencourt.state.nh.us/rsa/html/indexes/default.html**
Legislative Bill Search: **http://gencourt.state.nh.us/index/**
Unclaimed Funds: **www.nh.gov/treasury/unclaimed-property/index.htm**

State Public Record Agencies

Sexual Offender Registry

Division of State Police, Special Investigations Unit-SOR,   http://business.nh.gov/NSOR/search.aspx   The web site at http://business.nh.gov/NSOR/search.aspx gives access to the NH Registration of Criminal Offenders. There are disclaimers as this information may not reflect all sexual offender acts. There is also a Warrants Non-compliant Criminal Offenders search at http://business.nh.gov/NSOR/Warrant.aspx.

Incarceration Records

New Hampshire Department of Corrections, Offender Records Office,   www.nh.gov/nhdoc/   An inmate locator is available on their web page or go to http://business.nh.gov/Inmate_locator/. The inmate locator displays the offender's current controlling sentence and does not show concurrent sentences also being served or consecutive sentences that have yet to be served.

Corporation, LP, LLP, LLC, Trademarks/Servicemarks, Trade Names

Secretary of State, Corporation Division,   http://sos.nh.gov/Corp_Div.aspx   A free business name lookup is available at the website. Results include a wealth of information including registered agent. Documents filed after 12/2004 and some older documents have been imaged and are also available in the entity's Filed Documents.   *Other Options:* Monthly lists of corporations, LLCs, or trade names are $50 per month or $500 for last 12 months. . A list of all non-profits on file is available for $250.00.

Uniform Commercial Code, Federal & State Tax Liens

UCC Division, Secretary of State,   http://sos.nh.gov/ucc.aspx   Visit https://corp.sos.nh.gov/ for commercial online access to records. Accounts may be established using either automated clearing house (ACH) debit account or credit card. The fee is $27.00 plus a $2.00 handling fee per debtor name on a pay as you go basis, or for a $5,000 subscription fee receive unlimited online searches for one full year. Users can apply for an ACH (Automated Clearing House) account to be used as a payment option for filings or search.

Vital Records

Department of State, Bureau of Vital Records,   http://sos.nh.gov/vital_records.aspx   Records may be ordered online from www.vitalchek.com (see expedited services). The Division's web page offers access to statistical data only at http://nhvrinweb.sos.nh.gov/. You can also produce data reports in a spreadsheet format.

Driver Records

Department of Motor Vehicles, Driving Records,   www.nh.gov/safety/divisions/dmv/   Electronic online access and FTP (file transfer protocol) are both offered for approved commercial accounts. Search by license number, or by name and DOB. Fee is $12.00 per record, will increase to $13.00 on 3/1/2016. The minimum daily order requirement is fifty requests. If more information is required, call 603-227-4050.

Voter Registration, Campaign Finance, PACs

Secretary of State, Election Division, http://sos.nh.gov/Elections.aspx View information of campaign finance and PACs at http://sos.nh.gov/CampFin.aspx. View what individuals have contributed.

Occupational Licensing Boards

Accountant-CPA/Firm	https://nhlicenses.nh.gov/Verification/
Action Schools	http://sos.nh.gov/auctioneers.aspx
Architect	https://nhlicenses2.nh.gov/cgi-bin/professional/nhprof/search.pl
Asbestos Worker	http://des.nh.gov/organization/divisions/air/cb/ceps/ams/documents/consultants.pdf
Attorney Discipline System	http://nhattyreg.org/search.php
Auctioneer	http://sos.nh.gov/auctioneers.aspx
Audiologist	www.nh.gov/hearing-care/
Barber/Cosmetologist Licensed Schools	www.nh.gov/cosmet/schools/index.htm
Boiler Inspector/Vessel	www.nh.gov/labor/inspection/boilers-pressure-vessels.htm
Cash Dispenser Machine, Non-bank	www.nh.gov/banking/consumer-credit/non-bank-cash-disp-machines.htm
Child Care Facility	https://nhlicenses.nh.gov/verification/?facility=Y
Chiropractor	www.nh.gov/chiropractic/
Court Reporter	https://nhlicenses.nh.gov/verification/
Dentist/Dental Hygienist	https://nhlicenses.nh.gov/Verification/
Drug Wholesaler/Manufacturer	www.nh.gov/pharmacy/licensing/verification.htm
Electrician, High/Medium Volt/Trainee	https://nhlicenses.nh.gov/Verification/
Electrician, Master/Journeyman/Apprentice	https://nhlicenses.nh.gov/Verification/
Embalmer	www.nh.gov/funeral/documents/embalmers-funeral-directors.pdf
Embalmer, Apprentice	www.nh.gov/funeral/documents/apprentice-embalmers.pdf
Engineer	https://nhlicenses2.nh.gov/cgi-bin/professional/nhprof/search.pl
Fireworks Competency License	www.nh.gov/safety/divisions/firesafety/special-operations/fireworks/index.html
Forester	https://nhlicenses2.nh.gov/cgi-bin/professional/nhprof/search.pl
Funeral Director	www.nh.gov/funeral/documents/embalmers-funeral-directors.pdf
Game Operators, Licensed	http://racing.nh.gov/game-operators/index.htm
Geologist	https://nhlicenses2.nh.gov/cgi-bin/professional/nhprof/search.pl
Hearing Aid Dispenser/Fitter/Dealer	www.nh.gov/hearing-care/
Insurance Agent/Broker/Producer	https://sbs-nh.naic.org/Lion-Web/jsp/sbsreports/AgentLookup.jsp
Liquor Keg Shipper, Direct	https://nhlicenses.nh.gov/MyLicense%20Verification/
Liquor Product/Store	www.nh.gov/liquor/enforcement/licensing/licensee-information-lookup.htm
Lobbyist	http://sos.nh.gov/lobby.aspx
Marital/Family Mediator	www.nh.gov/family-mediator/mediators/index.htm
Marriage & Family Therapist	https://nhlicenses.nh.gov/Verification/
Mental Health Counselor, Clinical	https://nhlicenses.nh.gov/Verification/
Midwife	http://nhmidwives.org/find-a-midwife-2.html
Nurse-LPN/Practical/Advanced/Assistant	https://nhlicenses.nh.gov/Verification/
Pastoral Psychotherapist	https://nhlicenses.nh.gov/Verification/
Pharmacist Pharmacy/Technician	www.nh.gov/pharmacy/licensing/verification.htm
Physician/Medical Doctor/Assistant	http://business.nh.gov/medicineboard/Disclaimer.aspx
Plumber	https://nhlicenses.nh.gov/Verification/
Psychologist	https://nhlicenses.nh.gov/Verification/
Public Health Clinic	www.nh.gov/pharmacy/licensing/verification.htm
Real Estate Agent/Seller/Broker/Firm	https://nhlicenses.nh.gov/Verification/
Real Estate Appraiser	https://nhlicenses.nh.gov/verification/
School Administrator	http://my.doe.nh.gov/profiles/educators/search.aspx
Scientist, Natural/Wetlands	https://nhlicenses2.nh.gov/cgi-bin/professional/nhprof/search.pl
Shorthand Reporter	https://nhlicenses.nh.gov/verification/
Social Worker, Clinical	https://nhlicenses.nh.gov/Verification/
Surveyor, Land	https://nhlicenses2.nh.gov/cgi-bin/professional/nhprof/search.pl

Teacher...http://my.doe.nh.gov/profiles/educators/search.aspx
Verbatim Court Reporter.................................https://nhlicenses.nh.gov/verification/
Veterinary Medicine ....https://nhlicenses.nh.gov/Verification/

State and Local Courts

About New Hampshire Courts: The **Superior Court** is the court of General Jurisdiction and has jurisdiction over a wide variety of cases, including criminal, domestic relations, and civil cases, and provides the only forum in this state for trial by jury. Felony cases include Class A misdemeanors. The Superior Court has exclusive jurisdiction over cases in which the damage claims exceed $25,000.

Effective July 1, 2011, a new **Circuit Court** system was established that consolidated the then existing 32 **District Courts**, 10 **Probate Courts**, and 25 **Family Courts**. Under the new rules, each county now has a Circuit Court with three Divisions: District, Family and Probate. All the current District Court locations remained open. In Cheshire County, the marital division continues to operate as part of the Cheshire County Superior Court. In all other counties, the Circuit Court Family Division operates at the same locations as before.

To view which town is associated with which court jurisdiction, use the toll found at www.courts.state.nh.us/courtlocations/index.htm.

The web page for the Judicial Branch is www.courts.state.nh.us.

Appellate Courts: The Supreme Court is the appellate court and has jurisdiction to review appeals from the State trial courts and from many State administrative agencies. It also has original jurisdiction to issue writs of certiorari, prohibition, habeas corpus and other writs. There is not an intermediate Court of Appeals. Opinions are accessible from the web page above.

Online Court Access

There is no statewide access available for historical trial court records.

No individual New Hampshire courts offer online access.

Recorders, Assessors, and Other Sites of Note

About New Hampshire Recording Offices: New Hampshire has 10 recording offices. The recording officer is the Register of Deeds.

Real estate transactions recorded at the county level; property taxes are handled at the town/city level, there are 233. Be careful to distinguish the following names that are identical for both a town/city and a county - Grafton, Hillsborough, Merrimack, Strafford, and Sullivan.

About Tax Liens: Federal and state tax liens on personal property of businesses are filed with the Secretary of State. Other federal and state tax liens on personal property are filed with the Town/City Clerk. Federal and state tax liens on real property are filed with the county Register of Deeds..

County Online Access - County Sites are followed by Town/City Sites

County Recorder Sites

Belknap County   *Recorded Documents* www.belknapcounty.org/pages/belknapcounty_deeds/index   Access to county register of deeds data is free at www.nhdeeds.com/belknap/BeDisclaimer.html. Online records go back to 1765. To establish an account for copies of documents from the internet, go to www.nhdeeds.com/belknap/BeCopyAcct.html. Fees are $2.00 per page from Internet.

Carroll County   *Recorded Documents* http://nhdeeds.com/carroll/CaHome.html There are two systems..The 1st site, which requires a subscription if images are needed, begins at the disclaimer at http://nhdeeds.com/carroll/CaDisclaimer.html. The 2nd site is a pay as you gos site via a vendor at http://nhdeeds.com/carroll/CaTapestry.html. Each name searched and each book and page input incurs a search charge of $5.95 and each page printed is charged $2.50/page.

Cheshire County   *Recorded Documents* www.co.cheshire.nh.us/Deeds/index.html   Access to county register of deeds data is free at www.nhdeeds.com/cheshire/ChDisclaimer.html. Indices and images are available from 1960.

Grafton County   *Recorded Documents*   www.nhdeeds.com/grafton/GrHome.html   Access to county register of deeds data for a fee at www.nhdeeds.com/grafton/GrTapestry.html. This is a -pay as you go- resource. A subscription is required to print images. Fee is $120.00 for set-up plus $1.00 per page. Access to county register of deeds data is free at www.nhdeeds.com/grafton/GrDisclaimer.html
Property, Taxation Records   Access assessor data by subscription at http://data.avitarassociates.com/logon.aspx. Fees range from $25 per month (1 town) to $500 per year (all towns).

Hillsborough County   *Recorded Documents*   www.nhdeeds.com/hillsborough/HiHome.html   Access to county register of deeds data is free at www.nhdeeds.com/hillsborough/HiDisclaimer.html. Online records go back to 1966.

Merrimack County   *Recorded Documents*   https://merrimackcountydeedsnh.com/   Access records on the county Registry of Deeds for a fee at https://merrimackcountydeedsnh.com/landmarkweb/. Must register. Index is available at no charge.

Rockingham County   *Recorded Documents*   www.nhdeeds.com/rockingham/RoHome.html   Access to the register of deeds database is free at www.nhdeeds.com/rockingham/RoDisclaimer.html. Index and image goes back to 1629; search by book, page numbers or grantor/grantee names.

Strafford County   *Recorded Documents*   http://co.strafford.nh.us/icons/registry-of-deeds   Access to county register of deeds data is free at http://nhdeeds.com/strafford/StDisclaimer.html. Online records go back to 1921.

Sullivan County   *Recorded Documents*   www.nhdeeds.com/sullivan/SuHome.html   Access to the county Register of Deeds database is free at www.nhdeeds.com/sullivan/SuDisclaimer.html. Index now in Real-Time, updated every 15 minutes. Access to record information is free, printing of images in not free (must have established account with Registry).

Town/City Online Access

About Property Tax Records - At Town or City Level

Online access is available for nearly all towns, often from a vendor. Two of the more widely used vendors are shown below followed by a list of the towns or cities they service.

- See www.vgsi.com/vision/Applications/ParcelData/NH/Home.aspx for 42 participating jurisdictions. Access varies; some allow free index searches, some require registration, and a few may charge for access. The web page gives the date when last updated.

Amherst Town	Durham Town	Hanover Town	Manchester City	Rindge Town
Bedford Town	Epping Town	Henniker Town	Meredith Town	Salem Town
Bow Town	Exeter Town	Hollis Town	Milford Town	Seabrook Town
Bridgewater Town	Fremont Town	Hooksett Town	Moultonborough Town	Strafford Town
Charlestown Town	Goffstown Town	Jaffrey Town	Newmarket Town	Swanzey Town
Chester Town	Grantham Town	Laconia City	North Hampton Town	Wilton Town
Claremont City	Greenland Town	Littleton Town	Pelham Town	
Concord City	Hampton Falls Town	Lyme Town	Portsmouth City	
Derry Town	Hampton Town	Lyndeborough Town	Raymond Town	

- See http://data.avitarassociates.com/logon.aspx for data on over 120 towns. Three fee structures offered, ranging from $25 for one town/one month to $500 for all towns for one year.

Albany Town	Brookfield Town	Dublin Town	Greenfield Town	Loudon Town
Alexandria Town	Brookline Town	Dummer Town	Greenville Town	Lyman Town
Allenstown Town	Canaan Town	East Kingston Town	Groton Town	Madbury Town
Alstead Town	Canterbury Town	Easton Town	Hampstead Town	Madison Town
Andover Town	Chatham Town	Effingham Town	Hancock Town	Mason Town
Atkinson Town	Chichester Town	Ellsworth Town	Harrisville Town	Merrimack Town
Auburn Town	Clarksville Town	Epsom Town	Hart's Location Town	Middleton Town
Barrington Town	Columbia Town	Farmington Town	Hebron Town	Milan Town
Barnstead Town	Cornish Town	Fitzwilliam Town	Hill Town	Milton Town
Bartlett Town	Croydon Town	Francestown Town	Lancaster Town	Monroe Town
Bennington Town	Dalton Town	Franconia Town	Landaff Town	Nelson Town
Berlin City	Danville Town	Gilmanton Town	Lee Town	New Boston Town
Boscawen Town	Deerfield Town	Gilsum Town	Lempster Town	New Castle Town
Bradford Town	Deering Town	Grafton County	Lisbon Town	New Ipswich Town
Bristol Town	Dorchester Town	Grafton Town	Litchfield Town	Newfields Town

Newport Town	Plainfield Town	South Hampton Town	Surry Town	Washington Town
Newton Town	Randolph Town	Springfield Town	Temple Town	Waterville Valley Town
Northfield Town	Richmond Town	Stark Town	Thornton Town	Weare Town
Nottingham Town	Rollinsford Town	Stewartstown Town	Tilton Town	Wentworth Town
Orange Town	Roxbury Town	Strafford Town	Tuftonboro Town	Westmoreland Town
Orford Town	Rumney Town	Stratford Town	Unity Town	Wilmot Town
Piermont Town	Sandwich Town	Stratham Town	Wakefield Town	Winchester Town
Pittsburg Town	Sharon Town	Sugar Hill Town	Walpole Town	Windsor Town
Pittsfield Town	Shelburne Town	Sullivan Town	Warren Town	Wolfeboro Town

Other Town and City Sites (To avoid redundancy, the two lists above are ommited.):

Allenstown Town in Merrimack County   *Property, Taxation Records*   Access to Town Assessments for free at www.axisgis.com/AllenstownNH/. Also, access to the tax Kiosh for free at https://nhtaxkiosk.com/?KIOSKID=ALLENSTOWN.

Andover Town in Merrimack County   *Property, Taxation Records*   Tax bill payment and invoices available at https://nhtaxkiosk.com/Default.aspx?KIOSKID=ANDOVER for free.

Antrim Town in Hillsborough County   *Property, Taxation Records*   Access to property cards, tax maps and zoning maps for free at www.antrimnh.org/Pages/index.

Atkinson Town in Rockingham County   *Property, Taxation Records*   Access to GIS/mapping free at www.town-atkinsonnh.com/assessor.html, at bottom of page.

Barnstead Town in Belknap County   *Property, Taxation Records*   Access to property tax information for free at https://nhtaxkiosk.com/Default.aspx?KIOSKID=BARNSTEAD.

Bedford Town in Hillsborough County   *Property, Taxation Records*   Access to GIS/mapping free at https://www.mapsonline.net/bedfordnh/index.html.

Belmont Town in Belknap County   *Property, Taxation Records*   Access to assessing cards and GIS/mapping for free at www.axisgis.com/BelmontNH/Default.aspx?Splash=True.

Berlin City in Coos County   *Property, Taxation Records*   Access assessor data by subscription at http://data.avitarassociates.com/logon.aspx?ReturnUrl=%2fDefault.aspx. Fees range from $25 per month (1 town) to $500 per year (all towns). Also, access to GIS/mapping for free at https://www.mapsonline.net/berlinnh/index.html.

Boscawen Town in Merrimack County   *Property, Taxation Records*   Access to the tax kiosk for free at www.boscawen.nhtaxkiosk.com/default.aspx.

Bridgewater Town in Grafton County   *Property, Taxation Records*   Access to GIS/mapping free at www.axisgis.com/BridgewaterNH/. Also, search the assessor database for free at http://gis.vgsi.com/bridgewaternh/Search.aspx.

Bristol Town in Grafton County   *Property, Taxation Records*   Access to tax kiosk for free at https://nhtaxkiosk.com/?KIOSKID=BRISTOL.

Brookfield Town in Carroll County   *Property, Taxation Records*   Access to tax maps for free at www.brookfieldnh.org/Pages/BrookfieldNH_Assessing/Tax%20Maps/.

Chichester Town in Merrimack County   *Property, Taxation Records*   Assessment card request at www.chichesternh.org/Public_Documents/ChichesterNH_WebDocs/AssessmentCardRequest. Also, access to the Tax Kiosk for free at www.nhtaxkiosk.com/default.aspx.

Claremont City in Sullivan County   *Property, Taxation Records*   Access to GIS/mapping for free at www.claremont.interactivegis.com/. Must register.

Colebrook Town in Coos County   *Property, Taxation Records*   Access to list of property owned by the Town of Colebrook at www.colebrook-nh.com/Public_Documents/ColebrookNH_Assessor/Town%20Property%20Inventory.

Conway Town in Carroll County   *Property, Taxation Records*   Access to tax maps for free at http://conwaynh.org/tax-maps/. Also, access to the property taxes review and pay for free at https://nhtaxkiosk.com/?KIOSKID=CONWAY.

Deerfield Town in Rockingham County   *Property, Taxation Records*   Access to GIS/mapping for free at www.axisgis.com/DeerfieldNH/Default.aspx?Splash=True.

Deering Town in Hillsborough County   *Property, Taxation Records*   Access tax maps for free at www.deering.nh.us/Public_Documents/docs//TaxMaps/2013_Tax_Maps (latest shown as of 1/2/15). Also, access to parcel list by owners name for free at www.deering.nh.us/Public_Documents/DeeringNH_Assessor/postings/owner%20index%20sorted%20by%20owner%20name.pdf.

Dover City in Strafford County   *Property, Taxation Records*   Access to property record cards and maps for free at https://dovernh.mapgeo.io/?disclaimer=true&latlng=43.187126%2C-70.890358&zoom=12.

Dummer Town in Coos County   *Property, Taxation Records*   Access to the tax kiosh for free at www.dummer.nhtaxkiosk.com/?KIOSKID=DUMMER.

Easton Town in Grafton County   *Property, Taxation Records*   Access to the tax kiosk of the county municipalities for free at www.nhtaxkiosk.com/.

Enfield Town in Grafton County   *Property, Taxation Records*   Access to tax maps for free at www.enfield.nh.us/Pages/EnfieldNH_Assessing/Maps/taxmaps .

Epping Town in Rockingham County   *Property, Taxation Records*   Access to property tax records for free at https://www.eb2gov.com/EB2gov.dll/Customer/TaxCenter?fn=Customer/PropertyTaxCenter.html&sid={103AD766-34DC-442D-9614-D0C32A6A93A3}&towncode=2820.

Franklin City in Merrimack County   *Property, Taxation Records*   Access to tax maps free at www.franklinnh.org/Pages/FranklinNH_PlanZoning/TaxMapsDoc. Also, access to the tax kiosk for free at https://nhtaxkiosk.com/?KIOSKID=FRANKLIN.

Fremont Town in Rockingham County   *Property, Taxation Records*   Search town assessor database at http://gis.vgsi.com/fremontnh/Search.aspx.

Gilford Town in Belknap County   *Property, Taxation Records*   Access to property tax cards for free at http://gilford.univers-clt.com/. Also, access assessor and other town online documents free at https://www.eb2gov.com/scripts/eb2gov.dll/townlaunch?towncode=110. Must register to use.

Gorham Town in Coos County   *Property, Taxation Records*   Access to property maps for free at www.gorhamnh.org/Pages/GorhamNH_Assessing/mapsfolder/maps.

Hampstead Town in Rockingham County   *Property, Taxation Records*   Access to expanded owner index sorted by parcel location for free at www.hampsteadnh.us/Pages/HampsteadNH_Assessing/address.pdf. Email questions to Townclerk@hampsteadnh.us.

Hampton Town in Rockingham County   *Property, Taxation Records*   Access to GIS/mapping for free at http://hamptonnh.gov/?page_id=52.

Hancock Town in Hillsborough County   *Property, Taxation Records*   The Tax Kiosk is found at https://nhtaxkiosk.com/?KIOSKID=HANCOCK for free. Also, access to GIS/mapping for free at www.axisgis.com/HillsboroughNH/Default.aspx?Splash=True.

Haverhill Town in Grafton County   *Property, Taxation Records*   Access to GIS/mapping free at www.axisgis.com/HaverhillNH/. Also, access assessor data by subscription at http://data.avitarassociates.com/logon.aspx. Fees range from $25 per month (1 town) to $500 per year (all towns).

Hebron Town in Grafton County   *Property, Taxation Records*   Access to property tax amounts for free at https://nhtaxkiosk.com/?KIOSKID=HEBRON.

Hill Town in Merrimack County   *Property, Taxation Records*   Access tax kiosk for free at https://nhtaxkiosk.com/?KIOSKID=HILL.

Hillsborough Town in Hillsborough County   *Property, Taxation Records*   Access to GIS/Mapping for free at www.axisgis.com/HillsboroughNH/Default.aspx?Splash=True.

Holderness Town in Grafton County   *Property, Taxation Records*   Access to tax maps for free at http://mapsonline.net/holdernessnh/index.html.

Hopkinton Town in Merrimack County   *Property, Taxation Records*   Access to property tax cards and GIS/mapping free at www.axisgis.com/HopkintonNH/.

Hudson Town in Hillsborough County   *Property, Taxation Records*   Access to property assessment data free at http://patriotproperties.com/.

Jackson Town in Carroll County   *Property, Taxation Records*   Access to property tax searches for free at www.jackson.nhtaxkiosk.com/default.aspx.

Keene City in Cheshire County   *Property, Taxation Records*   Online access to property values at http://keene.tylertech.com/Main/Home.aspx.

Kensington Town in Rockingham County   *Property, Taxation Records*   Access to parcel details for free at http://town.kensington.nh.us/assessor.htm. Click on "Parcel Detail". Also, access to tax maps for free at http://town.kensington.nh.us/assessor.htm. Scroll down to bottom of page.

Lancaster Town in Coos County   *Property, Taxation Records*   Access to property tax and maps for free at www.lancasternh.org/tax-collector.html.

Lebanon City in Grafton County   *Property, Taxation Records*   Access to property assessment data for free at http://qpublic.net/nh/lebanon/. Search interactive GIS maps free at http://ims.lebcity.com/LebCityAGS/.

Lee Town in Strafford County   *Property, Taxation Records*   Access to tax maps free at http://leenh.virtualtownhall.net/Pages/LeeNH_Assessor/maps.

Lempster Town in Sullivan County   *Property, Taxation Records*   Access to the Tax Kiosk for free at https://nhtaxkiosk.com/?KIOSKID=LEMPSTER.

Lincoln Town in Grafton County   *Property, Taxation Records*   Free access to GIS/mapping found at www.axisgis.com/LincolnNH/. Also, access to tax maps for free at www.lincolnnh.org/assessing-office/pages/tax-maps.

Littleton Town in Grafton County   *Property, Taxation Records*   Access to parcel maps and online maps for free at www.townoflittleton.org/taxmaps.php. Also, access to GIS/mapping for free atwww.axisgis.com/LittletonNH/Default.aspx?Splash=True.

Londonderry Town in Rockingham County   *Property, Taxation Records*   Access to property assessment data free at http://patriotproperties.com/. Also, access to GIS/mapping free at www.londonderrynh.org/Pages/LondonderryNH_Assessing/Maps/Index.

Lyme Town in Grafton County   *Property, Taxation Records*   Access to the assessing database free at http://gis.vgsi.com/lymeNH/. Also, access to tax maps for free at www.lymenh.gov/assessing-department/pages/tax-maps.

Madbury Town in Strafford County   *Property, Taxation Records*   Access assessor data by subscription at http://data.avitarassociates.com/logon.aspx. Fees range from $25 per month (1 town) to $500 per year (all towns). Also, access to property tax online review for free at https://nhtaxkiosk.com/?KIOSKID=MADBURY.

Madison Town in Carroll County   *Property, Taxation Records*   Access to GIS/mapping free at http://208.88.76.81/mapguide2011/mapviewernet/TISA.aspx?MID=Madison.

Manchester City in Hillsborough County   *Property, Taxation Records*   Search Property data on the GIS-mapping and Tax Collector account sites free at http://208.82.76.123/pubgis/ but no name searching.

Marlow Town in Cheshire County   *Property, Taxation Records*   Access to town property maps free at www.marlownewhampshire.org/town-property-maps.php.

Meredith Town in Belknap County   *Property, Taxation Records*   Access to tax maps free at www.meredithnh.org/Joomla/index.php/tax-maps-29. Also, access current assessment data free at http://gis.vgsi.com/meredithnh/Search.aspx.

Merrimack Town in Hillsborough County   *Property, Taxation Records*   Access to GIS/mapping for free at http://host.cdmsmithgis.com/merrimacknh/.

Milton Town in Strafford County   *Property, Taxation Records*   Access to tax kiosk for free at https://nhtaxkiosk.com/?KIOSKID=MILTON.

Moultonborough Town in Carroll County   *Property, Taxation Records*   Search town assessor database at www.axisgis.com/moultonboroughNH/.

Nashua City in Hillsborough County   *Property, Taxation Records*   Access to property assessment data for free at http://assessing.gonashua.com/default.asp. Also, access to property assessment data free at http://patriotproperties.com/. Also, access to GIS/mapping for free at http://citygisweb3.nashuanh.gov/NashuaNH/default.aspx.

Nelson Town in Cheshire County   *Property, Taxation Records*   Access to the Tax Kiosk for free at https://nhtaxkiosk.com/?KIOSKID=NELSON.

New Boston Town in Hillsborough County   *Property, Taxation Records*   Access to tax maps for free at www.newbostonnh.gov/Pages/NewBostonNH_Assessing/NBTaxMaps.

New Durham Town in Strafford County   *Property, Taxation Records*   Access tax maps for free at www.newdurhamnh.us/Pages/NewDurhamNH_Maps/Tax%20and%20Feature%20Maps%20of%20New%20Durham.

New Hampton Town in Belknap County   *Property, Taxation Records*   Access tax maps for free at www.new-hampton.nh.us/taxmaps.asp.

Newbury Town in Merrimack County   *Property, Taxation Records*   Access to assessing and mapping data for free at www.axisgis.com/Tri_TownNH/Default.aspx?Splash=True. This also includes the Town of Sunapee.

Newington Town in Rockingham County   *Property, Taxation Records*   Access to the Assessor's database free at http://newington-nh.univers-clt.com/. Also, access to the tax maps for free at www.newington.nh.us/sites/newingtonnh/files/file/file/tax_maps_2.pdf.

Ossipee Town in Carroll County   *Property, Taxation Records*   Access to GIS/mapping free at www.axisgis.com/OssipeeNH/. Also, access to the tax kiosk for free at https://nhtaxkiosk.com/?KIOSKID=OSSIPEE.

Peterborough Town in Hillsborough County   *Property, Taxation Records*   Access to GIS/mapping for free at https://webapps2.cgis-solutions.com/peterboroughnh/parcel/.

Pittsfield Town in Merrimack County   *Property, Taxation Records*   Access to property tax searches for free at https://nhtaxkiosk.com/?KIOSKID=PITTSFIELD.

Plaistow Town in Rockingham County   *Property, Taxation Records*   Property owner list free at www.axisgis.com/PlaistowNH/ Also, access to the tax maps for free at www.plaistow.com/assessor/pages/tax-maps.

Plymouth Town in Grafton County   *Property, Taxation Records*   Access to property cards and GIS/mapping for free at www.axisgis.com/PlymouthNH/.

Portsmouth City in Rockingham County   *Property, Taxation Records*   Access to tax maps for free at www.cityofportsmouth.com/maps/index.html. Also, access current assessment data free at http://gis.vgsi.com/PortsmouthNH/Search.aspx.

Raymond Town in Rockingham County   *Property, Taxation Records*   Access to Assessor's database, GIS/mapping and property maps for free at www.raymondnh.gov/assessing/assessing.php.

Rochester City in Strafford County   *Property, Taxation Records*   Access to property assessment data free at http://patriotproperties.com/. Also, access to GIS/mapping for free at www.axisgis.com/RochesterNH/Default.aspx?Splash=True.

Rollinsford Town in Strafford County   *Property, Taxation Records*   Access to property tax review for free at https://nhtaxkiosk.com/?KIOSKID=ROLLINSFORD.

Salisbury Town in Merrimack County   *Property, Taxation Records*   Access to town maps free at www.salisburynh.org/pages/planning_board/town_maps.html.

Sanbornton Town in Belknap County   *Property, Taxation Records*   Access to tax maps and property record maps free at www.sanborntonnh.org/Interactive%20maps/Property%20Record%20Master%20Pages/PR%20Home.htm.

Sandown Town in Rockingham County   *Property, Taxation Records*   Access to records for free at www.axisgis.com/SandownNH/.

Seabrook Town in Rockingham County   *Property, Taxation Records*   Access to town tax maps at http://seabrooknh.info/town-departments/assessing/seabrook-tax-maps/. Also, access current assessment data free at http://gis.vgsi.com/seabrooknh/Search.aspx.

Sharon Town in Hillsborough County   *Property, Taxation Records*   Access to the tax kiosk for free at https://nhtaxkiosk.com/?KIOSKID=SHARON.

Somersworth City in Strafford County   *Property, Taxation Records*   Access to property assessment data free at http://patriotproperties.com/. Also, access to tax maps for free at www.somersworth.com/departments-services/development/development-services/assessing/tax-maps/.

Stoddard Town in Cheshire County   *Property, Taxation Records*   Access to the official tax maps for free at www.stoddardnh.org/tax-collector/pages/official-tax-maps-of-the-town-of-stoddard.

Strafford Town in Strafford County   *Property, Taxation Records*   Access to the tax map index free at http://strafford.nh.gov/index.php?option=com_content&task=view&id=72&Itemid=1.

Stratham Town in Rockingham County   *Property, Taxation Records*   Access to the tax kiosk for free at https://nhtaxkiosk.com/?KIOSKID=STRATHAM.

Sullivan Town in Cheshire County   *Property, Taxation Records*   Access to tax billing information for free at https://nhtaxkiosk.com/?KIOSKID=SULLIVAN.

Sunapee Town in Sullivan County   *Property, Taxation Records*   Access to GIS/mapping for free at www.axisgis.com/Tri_TownNH/Default.aspx?Splash=True.

Warner Town in Merrimack County   *Property, Taxation Records*   Access to tax maps for free at http://warner.nh.us/index.php?page=taxmaps.

Warren Town in Grafton County   *Property, Taxation Records*   Access to the town Tax Kiosk for free at www.nhtaxkiosk.com/?KIOSKID=Warren.

Webster Town in Merrimack County   *Property, Taxation Records*   Access to property tax searches free at https://www.nhtaxkiosk.com/?KIOSKID=WEBSTER.

Wentworth Town in Grafton County   *Property, Taxation Records*   Access to the tax kiosk for free at https://nhtaxkiosk.com/?KIOSKID=WENTWORTH. Also, access to tax maps for free at www.wentworth-nh.org/htm/taxmaps.html.

Winchester Town in Cheshire County   *Property, Taxation Records*   Access to the tax kiosk for free at https://nhtaxkiosk.com/?KIOSKID=WINCHESTER.

Windham Town in Rockingham County   *Property, Taxation Records*   Access GIS/mapping for free at www.axisgis.com/WindhamNH/.

Windsor Town in Hillsborough County   *Property, Taxation Records*   Access to the tax kiosk for free at www.nhtaxkiosk.com/default.aspx.

Woodstock Town in Grafton County   *Property, Taxation Records*   Access to GIS/mapping free at www.axisgis.com/WoodstockNH/.

New Jersey

Capital: Trenton
             Mercer County
Time Zone: EST
Population: 8,958,013
# of Counties: 21

Useful State Links

Website: **www.state.nj.us**
Governor: **www.state.nj.us/governor**
Attorney General: **www.state.nj.us/lps**
State Archives: **www.state.nj.us/state/darm/index.html**
State Statutes and Codes: **www.njleg.state.nj.us**
Legislative Bill Search: **www.njleg.state.nj.us**
Unclaimed Funds: **http://www.unclaimedproperty.nj.gov/**

State Public Record Agencies

Sexual Offender Registry

Division of State Police, Sexual Offender Registry,   www.njsp.org/sex-offender-registry/index.shtml   Data can be searched online www.njsp.org/sex-offender-registry/index.shtml. There are a variety of searches available including geographic, individual, advanced, and fugitives, The law limits the information to be placed on the Internet to all high risk (Tier 3) offenders and some moderate risk (Tier 2) offenders. The law excludes all juvenile sex offenders (except for Tier 3 juvenile sex offenders. Most moderate risk offenders whose crimes were committed against members of their families or households, and most moderate sex offenders whose crimes were considered statutory because of age are also excluded.

Incarceration Records

New Jersey Department of Corrections, ATTN: Correspondence Unit,   http://njdoc.gov/pages/index.shtml   Extensive search capabilities are offered from the website; click on "Offender Search Engine" or visit https://www20.state.nj.us/DOC_Inmate/inmatefinder?i=I. An offender is removed from the Offender Search Web page one year after the completion of the custodial term or one year after expiration of the maximum sentence date or their mandatory parole supervision date (MPS), if applicable. Offenders sentenced to Community Supervision for Life (CSL) or Parole Supervision for Life (PSL) will not be removed from the Web site, as their custodial term does not have a completion date. Offenders on Work Release, Furlough, or in a Halfway House are not necessarily reflected as such in their profile. Also, search offenders and inmates on a private site free at https://www.vinelink.com/#/home/site/31000.

Corporation, LLC, LP, Fictitious Name

Division of Revenue, Corporate Records,   www.nj.gov/treasury/revenue/   A number of different searches are offered at www.nj.gov/treasury/revenue/. Available searches include trademarks and trade names. There is no fee to browse the site to locate a name; however fees are involved for copies or status reports. Reports are mailed. Also, search securities agency enforcement actions at www.njsecurities.gov/bosdisc.htm. (This is provided by a different agency.)

Trademarks/Servicemarks

Department of Treasury, Trademark Division,   www.nj.gov/treasury/revenue/   Search trademarks and trade names at www.nj.gov/treasury/revenue/. Search by Status Report of view Lists.

Uniform Commercial Code

NJ Dept of Revenue, UCC Unit,   https://www.njportal.com/Ucc/   The site at https://www.njportal.com/UCC/ gives several search options for UCC records, including certified and non-certified. There can be approx. a 3 week delay before new records are searchable. Same fees as above apply, but add

$5.00 for a portal for searches or $.20 per page for copies. *Other Options:* Bulk record downloads may also be purchased at https://www.njportal.com/UCC/.

Vital Records

Department of Health & Senior Svcs, Bureau of Vital Statistics, www.state.nj.us/health/vital/index.shtml Order online from www.state.nj.us/health/vital/expedited. Pay with credit card, there is additional processing fee of $5, online authentication fee of $5 (non-refundable) and $30 shipping fee via UPS carrier.

Workers' Compensation Records

Labor Department, Division of Workers Compensation, http://lwd.state.nj.us/labor/wc/wc_index.html COURTS on-line is a secure Internet website that provides authorized subscribers access to the Division's database for review of cases in which they are a party. Possible subscribers include: Insurance Carrier/Law Firms; Court Reporting Firms; and WC Forensic Experts (Physicians). See http://lwd.dol.state.nj.us/labor/wc/egov/col/courts2_index.html.

Driver Records

Motor Vehicle Commission, Driver History Abstract Unit, www.state.nj.us/mvc/ The commercial access system is called CAIR. Visit www.state.nj.us/mvcbiz/Records/CAIR.htm. The system is only available to those with a permissible use such as insurance companies, bus and truck companies, and highway/parking authorities. Both batch (SFT) and individual modes are offered. Records can only be accessed by using a driver license number, which will provide a five-year driver history abstract (there is no name only searching offered). Account holders may also obtain a License Status check for $2.00. NJ drivers may order their own record online at www.state.nj.us/mvc/Licenses/driver_history_page.htm. A user account must be opened first. The fee is $15.00 per record plus a $.75 service fee per record.

Vehicle, Vessel Ownership & Registration

Motor Vehicle Commission, Office of Communication, www.state.nj.us/mvc/ Online access is available for insurance companies, bus and truck companies, highway/parking authorities, and approved vendors. Vehicle record inquiries can only be made by submitting a VIN or plate number - not by name. The VIN number will produce the mileage, mileage status, owner/lien holder names and addresses and lessee information if the vehicle is leased. The license plate number will provide the owner's name, address, vehicle information, leased vehicle status. If using the Ownership History option (only available to insurance companies), the New Jersey VIN data will also be provided. The fee for a registration or title record including ownership history is $12.00 per record. For details visit www.state.nj.us/mvcbiz/Records/CAIR.htm.

Crash Reports

CriminlalJustice Records Bureau, Traffic/Crminal, www.njsp.org Online access to accident reports on Toll-Roads is available via a state designated vendor - www.buycrash.com. The same $10.00 fee the state charges plus a $3.00 vendor fee. Reports involving non-toll roads are available at https://www.njportal.com/njsp/crashreports/. Only Crash Reports for accidents that occurred on non-toll roads on or after Jan.1, 2013 can be ordered using this service. Each report costs $13.00, payable by Visa, MasterCard, Discover, or American Express credit or debit card. Allow at least 24 hours from the time of accident to use this search. Fulfillment of these searches may take anywhere from same day delivery to up to a week depending on their stage of processing. You will receive an email with instructions for how to download the report.

Voter Registration, Contributions. PACS, Lobbyists

Dept of State, Division of Elections, http://nj.gov/state/elections/index.html Search contributions to candidates and PACs at www.elec.state.nj.us/publicinformation/searchdatabase.htm, an advanced search is also offered at www.elec.state.nj.us/ELECReport/AdvancedSearch.aspx. *Other Options:* Bulk purchase is of voter registration records is available for political purposes.

GED Certificates

GED Testing Program, NJ Dept. of Education, www.state.nj.us/education/students/adulted/ Through the E-Transcripts process examinees can access their records at any time from the web as well as give permission to third parties and employers to verify a transcript - but only with an Access Code provided by the NJ DOE. GED graduates since April 1, 2007 can find their access code at the bottom center of their diplomas. Graduates prior to April 1, 2007 can obtain an access code by submitting a written request to the Department of Education's Office of GED Testing, along with proof of identity, or may request a code in person with proper ID. See the press release at www.state.nj.us/education/news/2007/0611ged.htm.

Occupational Licensing Boards

These licenses are all searchable at https://newjersey.mylicense.com/verification

Accountant-CPA/Firm/Municipal	Audiologist	Dental Assistant/Hygienist
Acupuncturist	Barber/Shop	Dental Clinic
Alcohol/Drug Counselor	Cemetery/Salesperson	Dentist
Appraiser/Apprentice, Real Estate	Chiropractor	Electrical Contractor
Architect	Cosmetologist/Hairstylist/Beautician/Shop	Embalmer
Architect Certificate of Authorization	Counselor, Professional	Employment Agency
Athletic Trainer	Court Reporter	Engineer/Survey Company

Funeral Practitioner/Home
Health Care Service Agency
Home Health Aide
Home Improvement/Home Elevation
Contractors
Home Inspector
Interior Design
Lab Director, Bio-Analytical
Landscape Architect
Manicurist/Manicurist Shop
Marriage/Family Counselor
Midwife
Modeling & Talent Agency

Mortician
Mover/Warehouseman
Nurse-Advance Practice
Nurse-LPN/RN
Nursing Registry Svc
Occupational Therapist/Assistant
Optician/Ophthalmic Technician/Dispenser
Optometrist
Orthopedist
Orthotist/Prosthetist
Pharmacist/Pharmacy
Physical Therapist/Assistant
Physician/Medical Doctor/Assistant

Planner, Professional
Plumber/Master Plumber/Journeyman
Podiatrist
Psychologist
Respiratory Therapist
Skin Care Specialist/Shop
Social Worker
Speech-Language Pathologist
Surveyor, Land
Temporary Help Agency
Veterinarian

The Rest:

Animal Facility	www.state.nj.us/health/animalwelfare/lic_facilities.shtml
Animal Control Officer Revocation	www.state.nj.us/health/cd/izdp/revoked.shtml
Attorney	https://njcourts.judiciary.state.nj.us/web15z/AttyPAWeb/pages/home.faces
Bank Mergers	www.state.nj.us/dobi/bankmerger_alpha.htm
Banks	www.state.nj.us/dobi/bankwebinfo.htm
Candidate Report	www.elec.state.nj.us/ELECReport/SearchContribCandidate.aspx
Consumer Lender	https://www20.state.nj.us/DOBI_LicSearch/bnkSearch.jsp
Contributor, Political	www.elec.state.nj.us/ELECReport/SearchContribCandidate.aspx
Debt Adjuster	https://www20.state.nj.us/DOBI_LicSearch/bnkSearch.jsp
Emergency Medical Technician	https://njems.rutgers.edu/jsp/verify_credential.jsp
Emergency Medical Training Sites	www.state.nj.us/health/ems/documents/education/ems_training_sites.pdf
Employment/Personnel Services	www.njconsumeraffairs.gov/epservices/Documents/New-Jersey-Licensed-and-Registered-Employment-and-Personnel-Services.pdf
Enforcement Activity	www.state.nj.us/dobi/division_banking/bankdivenforce.html
Foreign Money Transmitter	https://www20.state.nj.us/DOBI_LicSearch/bnkSearch.jsp
Health Clubs	www.njconsumeraffairs.gov/healthclubs/Documents/New-Jersey-Registered-Health-Spas.pdf
Hearing Aid Dispenser/Fitter	www.njconsumeraffairs.gov/had/Pages/verification.aspx
High Cost Home Loan Credit Counseling Svcs	https://www20.state.nj.us/DOBI_LicSearch/bnkSearch.jsp
Home Financing Agency	https://www20.state.nj.us/DOBI_LicSearch/bnkSearch.jsp
Home Repair Contractor/Seller	https://www20.state.nj.us/DOBI_LicSearch/bnkSearch.jsp
Insurance Agent/Public Adjuster	https://www20.state.nj.us/DOBI_LicSearch/insSearch.jsp
Insurance Carrier	www.state.nj.us/dobi/data/inscomp.htm
Insurance Premium Finiance	https://www20.state.nj.us/DOBI_LicSearch/bnkSearch.jsp
Landfill	www.nj.gov/dep/dshw/lrm/landfill.htm
Licensed Cashier of Checks	https://www20.state.nj.us/DOBI_LicSearch/bnkSearch.jsp
Lobbyist	www.elec.state.nj.us/PublicInformation/GAA_Annual.htm
Medical Waste Generator	www.nj.gov/dep/dshw/hwr/medwaste.htm
Money Transmitter	https://www20.state.nj.us/DOBI_LicSearch/bnkSearch.jsp
Mortgage (2nd) Lender	https://www20.state.nj.us/DOBI_LicSearch/bnkSearch.jsp
Motor Vehicle Installment Seller	https://www20.state.nj.us/DOBI_LicSearch/bnkSearch.jsp
New Banks Opened/Pending	www.state.nj.us/dobi/bnk_depositories/newbankwebinfo.htm
Notary Public	https://www.njportal.com/DOR/Notary
Nuclear Medicine Technologist	http://datamine2.state.nj.us/dep/DEP_OPRA/
Nursing Disciplinary Actions	www.njconsumeraffairs.gov/nur/Pages/actions.aspx
Nursing Home Administrator	http://nj.gov/health/healthfacilities/documents/list_active_lhna.pdf
Pawnbroker	https://www20.state.nj.us/DOBI_LicSearch/bnkSearch.jsp
Pest Management (IPM) School	www.nj.gov/dep/enforcement/pcp/ipm-contacts.htm
Pesticide Applicator/Operator	http://datamine2.state.nj.us/DEP_OPRA/OpraMain/categories?category=Pesticides

Pesticide Dealer	http://datamine2.state.nj.us/DEP_OPRA/OpraMain/categories?category=Pesticides
Plumber Disciplinary Actions	www.njconsumeraffairs.gov/plu/Pages/actions.aspx
Radiation Report	http://datamine2.state.nj.us/dep/DEP_OPRA/
Radiation Technologist/Therapist	http://datamine2.state.nj.us/dep/DEP_OPRA/
Radon Tester/Businesses	http://datamine2.state.nj.us/dep/DEP_OPRA/
Real Estate Agent/Broker/Seller/Schooll	https://www20.state.nj.us/DOBI_LicSearch/recSearch.jsp
Recycle Coordinator	www.nj.gov/dep/dshw/
Recycling Facility	www.nj.gov/dep/dshw/lrm/classbsch.htm
Sale Finance Company	https://www20.state.nj.us/DOBI_LicSearch/bnkSearch.jsp
Security Agencies, Licensed	www.njsp.org/info/pdf/pdet/010312_actagency.pdf
Viatical Settlement Broker	https://www20.state.nj.us/DOBI_LicSearch/insSearch.jsp
Waste Company	www.nj.gov/dep/dshw/

State and Local Courts

About New Jersey Courts: Each **Superior Court** has 3 divisions; Civil, Criminal, and Family. Search requests should be addressed separately to each division. Criminal cases are those in which a defendant stands accused of a serious crime, such as assault, theft, robbery, fraud, or murder. These indictable crimes consist of 4th, 3rd, 2nd and 1st Degree charges. Civil cases in which the amount in controversy exceeds $15,000 are heard in the Civil Division of Superior Court.

Cases in which the amounts in controversy are between $3,000 and $15,000 are heard in the Special Civil Part of the Civil Division. Those in which the amounts in controversy are less than $3,000 also are heard in the Special Civil Part and are known as Small Claims cases. Civil cases in which monetary damages are not being sought are heard in the General Equity Division of Superior Court. General Equity judges handle non-jury cases such as those involving trade secrets, labor matters, foreclosures and other disputes in which court relief, often in the form of restraining orders, is sought on an emergency basis.

Family related cases, such as those involving divorce, domestic violence, juvenile delinquency, child support, foster-care placements and termination of parental rights, are heard by the Family Division.

Probate can be handled by either the **Surrogates' Courts** or by the Chancery Division, Probate Part of the Superior Court.

More About Criminal Records: New Jersey is unique. NJ courts use the term "indictable offense" instead of felony. These offenses are called as such because the accused has the right to have his case presented to a grand jury. These matters are heard in the Superior Court and if a trial ensues, it is trial by jury. Less serious offenses are called "disorderly persons offenses." These offenses are similar to misdemeanors and encompass a wide array of lower level criminal offenses such as shoplifting (if under $200), disorderly conduct, simple assault, etc.

The web page for the Judicial Branch is www.judiciary.state.nj.us/.

Appellate Courts: The Appellate Division of the Superior Court is New Jersey's intermediate Appellate Court. Appellate Division judges hear appeals from decisions of the trial courts, the Tax Court and State administrative agencies. Opinions from the Supreme or Appellate Court are viewable from the home page above – click on *Opinions*.

Online Court Access

All courts participate in the systems described below.

There are four online search systems indvidually provided by the Judiciary for civil and criminal case information.

1. Criminal Dockets

A limited information system of criminal records - PROMIS/Gavel - has public access at https://ecourts.judiciary.state.nj.us/webe4/ExternalPGPA/. This is NOT the same system and content as displayed on the public access terminals at the court houses - although both are called PROMIS Gavel. The reason the online system is referred to as "filtered" is because the PGPA does not include soundex name searching. Also it does not show offenses or petty offenses recorded in the 530+ Municipal Courts, unless they are filed with indictables which are filed at the Superior Court. The more serious of these petty offenses include drug offenses, violence, theft, sexual assault, and pedophilia. An AOC press release about the PGPA states:

The court records obtained from PROMIS/Gavel do not constitute a criminal history records check, which must be obtained through law enforcement.

Therefore this online system is not equivalent to an onsite search and is considered to be only a supplemental search. In addition, **a** study performed by a NJ Private Investigator showed excessive data lacking from the online system.

2. Civil Dockets

A free statewide **access service (ACMS Public Access) to civil cases** is available at http://njcourts.judiciary.state.nj.us/web15z/ACMSPA/. One may search by name or docket number. If a name search is performed, it is name only - no personal identifiers are shown except an address on docket. There is a strong disclaimer that states

The Judiciary provides this information as a public service and makes no warranties, either expressed or implied, regarding accuracy, reliability, currency, completeness, or suitability for any particular purpose.

3. Civil Judgments and Liens

See https://njcourts.judiciary.state.nj.us/web15/JudgmentWeb/jsp/judgmentCaptcha.faces for an **of civil judgments and liens**. Also, the agency offers a much more robust program, called the **Electronic Access Program, to civil case docket and summary information** from four separate state information systems. Included are the Automated Case Management Systems (ACMS) (mentioned above), the Civil Judgment and Order Docket, the Family Automated Case Tracking System (FACTS), and the Automated Traffic System (ATS). The fee is $1.00 per minute. Subscribers receive only a screen view; the ability to perform downloads or data extraction (screen-scraping) is not offered. This information is in real-time. When a new case or document is entered by court personnel, the information is immediately available to the public for viewing. For more information and enrollment forms see the page at www.judiciary.state.nj.us/superior/eap_main.htm.

4. Judicial Calendar

Search the **Judiciary's civil motion calendar and schedule** at www.judiciary.state.nj.us/calendars.html. The database includes all Superior Court Motion calendars for the Civil Division (Law-Civil Part, Special Civil Part and Chancery-General Equity), and proceeding information for a six-week period (two weeks prior to the current date and four weeks following the current date).

No individual New Jersey courts offer online access, other than as described above.

Recorders, Assessors, and Other Sites of Note

About New Jersey Recording Offices: 21 counties, 21 recording offices. The recording officer title varies depending upon the county, either the Register of Deeds or the County Clerk.

About Tax Liens: All state and federal tax liens are filed with the District Recorder. The Clerk of Circuit Court records the equivalent of some state's tax liens.

Online Access

Recorded Documents

There is no statewide access to recorded documents from the government sites, however most (not all) counties offer online access. A links list to 8 county sites is at http://www1.njcountyrecording.com/NJCR/RecordSearch.aspx.

An online search at https://njcourts.judiciary.state.nj.us/web15/JudgmentWeb/jsp/judgmentCaptcha.faces. provides civil judgments and liens. Records considered confidential and not returned in search results include those involving child victims of sexual abuse, cases involving trade secrets, and records ordered impounded by a judge.

Property Tax Records

A vendor provides several online services from it's statewide database of property tax records. See www.taxrecords.com. The site is free to use to look up an individual property by address, lot, block or assessed value however a password is required. A very affordable paid subscription is required to download information for mail merges, mailing labels, search by name, or search by state.

Also, access property assessment data free for all counties free http://tax1.co.monmouth.nj.us/cgi-bin/prc6.cgi?menu=index&ms_user=glou&passwd=.

County Sites Other Than the Two Vendors Mentioned Above

Atlantic County   *Recorded Documents*   http://atlanticcountyclerk.org/   Search for free at http://24.246.110.8/or_web1/disclaim.asp. All documents recorded since 3/1/2000 are indexed and imaged. Index data for deed and mortgage documents go back to 3/8/1972. Note the online system is as accurate and current as indices at the courthouse and includes maps, tax sales, construction liens, and lis pendens.

Bergen County   *Recorded Documents*   www.bergencountyclerk.org/   A subscription and fees are required to search records at http://bergensearch.co.bergen.nj.us/countyweb/login.do?countyname=BergenRegistry.

Burlington County   *Recorded Documents*   www.co.burlington.nj.us/192/County-Clerk   Access to recorded property records for free at http://press.co.burlington.nj.us/press/index.aspx.

Cape May County   *Recorded Documents*   http://capemaycountynj.gov/189/County-Clerk   Property records for Cape May county are free to view online at http://50.195.106.200/ALIS/WW400R.PGM. To print, registration and login is required. Online documents go back to 1996, images to 2000. For assistance, telephone 609-465-1010.

Cumberland County   *Recorded Documents*   http://ccclerknj.com/   Access to unofficial copies of land records for free at http://cumberlandlookup.njtown.net/.

Gloucester County   *Recorded Documents*   www.gloucestercountynj.gov/depts/c/cclerk/default.asp   Access recording office land records free for individual verification at http://i2e.uslandrecords.com/NJ/Gloucester/D/Default.aspx.

Hudson County   *Property, Taxation Records*   Access to property searches for free at www.hudsoncountynj.org/property-search/. No name searching. Also, access to property tax records for free at www.taxrecords.com/. Must register. Subscription also available.

Mercer County   *Recorded Documents*   http://nj.gov/counties/mercer/officials/clerk/   Also, access to property searches free at http://records.mercercounty.org/RecordsNG_Search/. Non registered user gets view of full index, view of 1st 2 pages. Registered user get full index, view of all pages of doc, password required, no fee.

Middlesex County   *Recorded Documents*   www.middlesexcountynj.gov/Government/Departments/CS/Pages/County%20Clerk/County-Clerk.aspx   Access the county public access system index free at https://mcrecords.co.middlesex.nj.us/records/index.jsp. Printing clean copies of document images is a paid service.

Monmouth County   *Recorded Documents*   https://co.monmouth.nj.us/page.aspx?ID=125   Access county clerk deed and mortgage data free at http://oprs.co.monmouth.nj.us/oprs/clerk/ClerkHome.aspx?op=basic (informational only, not to be used for title searching). Deeds-1976 to present; Most other documents 1996 to present. Full access to Recorder of Deeds is by subscription at www.landex.com/remote/. Index goes back to 1930; images to 10/1996.

Morris County   *Recorded Documents*   www.morriscountyclerk.org/   Access the county clerk's records free at http://mcclerksng.co.morris.nj.us/or_wb1/default.asp.

Ocean County   *Recorded Documents*   www.oceancountyclerk.com   Land records on the County Clerk database are free at http://sng.co.ocean.nj.us/searchapplication/. Search by parties, document or instrument type. This online system includes maps, tax sales, construction liens and Lis Pendens.

Passaic County   *Recorded Documents*   www.passaiccountynj.org/Index.aspx?NID=131   The county recorded index is searchable from http://records.passaiccountynj.org/press/Clerk/ClerkHome.aspx?op=basic.

Salem County   *Recorded Documents*   http://salemcountyclerk.org   Search records at http://salemcountyclerk.org/public-records-search/. There is no fee. Site does not include Mortgage related documents such as: Cancellations, Discharges, Releases and Assignments

Somerset County   *Recorded Documents*   www.co.somerset.nj.us/government/elected-officials/county-clerk   Access to the County Clerk's recordings database for a fee at https://ccsearch.co.somerset.nj.us/ Also, see online notes in state summary at beginning of section.

Sussex County   *Recorded Documents*   http://sussexcountyclerk.org/   Records back to 1950 free at https://sussex.landrecordsonline.com/sussex/search.do. Also, see online notes in state summary at beginning of section.

Union County   *Recorded Documents*   http://ucnj.org/county-clerk/   Search recorded real estate related documents at https://clerk.ucnj.org/UCPA/DocIndex. Index goes from 6/1977 to present. Images from 12/1983 to present.

Warren County   *Recorded Documents*   www.co.warren.nj.us/countyclerk/   Access to land records for free at www.searchiqs.com/warren.html. Can sign-up for log-in for detailed records.

Reminder - Two vendors provide access to property and assessor records for all counties.

A vendor provides several online services from it's statewide database of property tax records. See www.taxrecords.com. The site is free to use to look up an individual property by address, lot, block or assessed value however a password is required. A very affordable paid subscription is required to download information for mail merges, mailing labels, search by name, or search by state.

Also, access property assessment data free for all counties free http://tax1.co.monmouth.nj.us/cgi-bin/prc6.cgi?menu=index&ms_user=glou&passwd=.

New Mexico

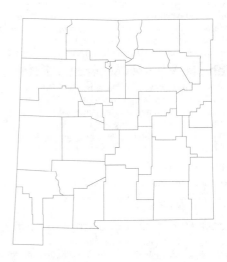

Capital: Santa Fe
              Santa Fe County
Time Zone: MST
Population: 2,085,013
# of Counties: 33

Useful State Links

Website: **www.newmexico.gov**
Governor: **www.governor.state.nm.us**
Attorney General: **www.nmag.gov/**
State Archives: **www.nmcpr.state.nm.us**
State Statutes and Codes: **www.nmonesource.com/nmnxtadmin/NMPublic.aspx**
Legislative Bill Search: **www.nmlegis.gov/Legislation/Bill_Finder**
Unclaimed Funds: **www.missingmoney.com** (state does not have its own site)

State Public Record Agencies

Sexual Offender Registry

Department of Public Safety, Records Bureau,   www.dps.state.nm.us/index.php/lerb/   The OffenderWatch program at http://sheriffalerts.com/counties.php?state=nm offers a variety of search methods including by name, county, city, and ZIP Code. The site also offers a complete state list and an absconder list.

Incarceration Records

New Mexico Corrections Department, Records Bureau,   http://cd.nm.gov/   The search site is http://search.cd.nm.gov/.   *Other Options:* A data subscription service is available. See details athttp://cd.nm.gov/offenders/NMCD_DATA_REQUESTS.pdf. Data may NOT be resold once purchased..

Corporation, LLC, LP, LLP Records,

Secretary of State, Corporations Bureau,   www.sos.state.nm.us/Business_Services/   There is no charge to view records at https://portal.sos.state.nm.us/BFS/online/Account. There are 12 searches available from this page including business serach, UCC search, verify cert.of existence or good standing, officers/diretcors/registered agents, and certificate of status.

Uniform Commercial Code

UCC   Division,   Secretary   of   State,   www.sos.state.nm.us/Business_Services/UCC_Overview.aspx   The   website https://portal.sos.state.nm.us/BFS/online/UCCSearch permits searching by name, organization, or file number. The site is not supported by some browsers, something to do with SSL certificates with 1024-bit RSA keys.   *Other Options:* Microfilm and images (from 7/99) on disk may be purchased.

Birth Certificates

Department of Health, Bureau of Vital Records,   https://nmhealth.org/about/erd/bvrhs/vrp/birth/   Online ordering is provided by a state designated vendor - www.vitalchek.com.

Death Records

Department of Health, Bureau of Vital Records,   https://nmhealth.org/about/erd/bvrhs/vrp/death/   Records can be ordered at www.vitalrecordsnm.org/vitalrecords.shtml via a state designated vendor. This is considered expedited service. This is also a look-up at www.usgwarchives.net/nm/deaths.htm for deaths 1899 to 1940.

Driver Records

Motor Vehicle Division, Driver Services Bureau,   www.mvd.newmexico.gov/   The New Mexico MVD contracts with New Mexico Interactive to provide all electronic media requests of driver license histories, title, registration and lien searches. Records are available to subscribers that meet federal and state standards. The annual subscription fee is $75 for up to 10 users. The fee for a driving record is $6.50, a non-hit result incurs a fee. Both single inquiry and batch modes are available for driving records. Monthly billing is provided. For more information call New Mexico Interactive at 877-660-3468 or visit www.mvd.newmexico.gov/online-services.aspx. NM drivers may order their own record online for $6.63 from the home page above. *Other Options:* New Mexico Interactive provides a driver monitoring program for approved subscribers. A monthly fee per driver is charged and if activity occurs, then a driving record is automatically ordered. Call 877-660-3468 for details.

Vehicle, Vessel Ownership & Registration
Motor Vehicle Division, Vehicle Services Bureau,   www.mvd.newmexico.gov/   The New Mexico MVD contracts with New Mexico Interactive to provide all electronic media requests of title, registration and lien searches, as well as driving records. Records are available to subscribers that meet federal and state standards. The annual subscription fee is $75 for up to 10 users. The fee is $4.95 per record. Records must be accessed by VIN or plate number - no name searching is provided. Monthly billing is provided. For more information call New Mexico Interactive at 505-982-8307 or visit the Online Services section at www.mvd.newmexico.gov/Online-Services/Pages/Subscriber-Services.aspx.   *Other Options:* Bulk requests for vehicle or ownership information must be approved by the Director's office. Once a sale is made, further resale is prohibited.

Crash Reports
Department of Public Safety, Attn: Records,   www.dps.nm.org/   One may also make a request online using a designated vendor. See https://ecrash.lexisnexis.com or call 866-215-2771. An account must be established. Records are available from 11 municipal police departments, 2 county sheriff offices and the New Mexico State Police. Fee is $10.00.

Voter Registration, Campaign Finance, PACs, Lobbyists
Secretary of State, Bureau of Elections,   www.sos.state.nm.us/Elections_Data/   A registrant verification is provided at https://voterview.state.nm.us/VoterView/RegistrantSearch.do. Results give zip code of registrant and polling place. View public information on PACS and campaigns from the home page at https://www.cfis.state.nm.us/media/.

GED Certificates
Department of Education - GED Testing, Higher Education Department,   http://ped.state.nm.us/ped/GED_index.html   Records may be requested from https://www.diplomasender.com. A credit card is needed. Request must be ordered by the test taker. Employers and third parties must receive an email and/or Authentication Code from the test taker to then access the authorized documents. Turnaround time is 1-3 days.

Occupational Licensing Boards
These licenses are all searchable at: www.rld.state.nm.us/LicenseeSearchIndex.aspx

Accountant-CPA	Direct Disposer/FSI (Funerary)	Optometrist
Acupuncturist	Dispens'g Physician Cont'd Substance	Oriental Medicine Doctor
Announcer, Athletic Event/Ring	Electrologist	Osteopathic Physician/Assistant
Armored Car Company	Electrophysician	Patrol Operator, Private
Art Therapist	Engineer	Pharmacist
Athletic Promoter/Matchmaker	Esthetician	Pharmacy, Non-Residential
Athletic Trainer	Funeral Director/Practitioner	Physical Therapist/Assistant
Audiologist	Funeral Home	Podiatrist
Bank	Funeral Service Intern	Polygraph Examiner
Barber	Hearing Aid Specialist	Private Investigator
Barber Shop/School	Interior Designer	Psychologist/Associate
Boiler Operator Journeyman	Landscape Architect	Real Estate Agent/Seller/Broker
Booking Agent	Loan Company, Small	Real Estate Appraiser
Boxer/Manager/Judge/Timekeeper	Manicurist	Referee
Cemetery, Endow'd/Perpet'l Care	Marriage & Family Therapist	Respiratory Care Therapist
Chiropractor	Martial Arts Contest	Savings & Loan
Collection Agency/Manager	Massage Therapist/Instr/Practitioner	Security Dog Company
Consumer Credit Grantor/Loaner	Massage Therapy School	Security Guard/Company
Cosmetologist	Medical Researcher/ Facility	Social Worker (LBSW, LI, LM)/Provisional
Cosmetology Shop/School	Medical Wholesale Company	Speech-Language Pathologist
Counseling/Therapy Practice	Mental Health Counselor	Substance Abuse Counselor/Intern
Credit Union	Money Order Agent/Firm/Exempts	Surveyor, Land
Crematory	Mortgage Firm/Loan Broker/Branch	Trust Company
Dental Assistant/Hygienist	Motor Vehicle Sales Financer	Wrestler
Dentist	Nursing Home Administrator/Facility	
Dietitian/Nutritionist	Occupational Therapist/Assistant	

The Rest:

Alcohol Server	http://verification.rld.state.nm.us/Search.aspx
Architect	www.bea.state.nm.us/Roster.aspx
Attorney Examination Results	http://nmexam.org/bar-exam/examination-results/
Clinical Nurse Specialist	https://www.bon.state.nm.us/lookup.html
Contractor	https://public.psiexams.com/index_login.jsp
Court Reporter	http://nmcra.wildapricot.org/page-1854932
Court Reporting Schools	http://nmcra.wildapricot.org/page-399048
Hemodialysis Technician	https://www.bon.state.nm.us/lookup.html
Insurance Agent/Producer/Company	http://164.64.160.41/?Submit=Agent,+Adjuster,+Company+and+Business+Entity+search
Journeyman Contractor	https://public.psiexams.com/index_login.jsp
Liquor Distributor	http://verification.rld.state.nm.us/Search.aspx
Lobbyist/Lobbying Organization	https://www.cfis.state.nm.us/media/
LP Gas License	https://public.psiexams.com/index_login.jsp
Manufactured Housing Dealer/Broker	http://verification.rld.state.nm.us/Search.aspx
Manufactured Housing Installer/Repair	http://verification.rld.state.nm.us/Search.aspx
Manufactured Housing Manufacturer	http://verification.rld.state.nm.us/Search.aspx
Manufactured Housing Salesperson	http://verification.rld.state.nm.us/Search.aspx
Medication Aide	https://www.bon.state.nm.us/lookup.html
Midwife	https://nmhealth.org/about/phd/fhb/mwp/
Nurse-LPN/RN/Anesthetist/Practitioner	https://www.bon.state.nm.us/lookup.html
Radiologic Technologist	https://www.env.nm.gov/nmrcb/documents/webreport.pdf
Teacher	www.ped.state.nm.us/Licensure/
Veterinarian/Veterinary Technician	http://directory.nmbvm.org/?option=com_sobi2&sobi2Task=search&Itemid=181

State and Local Courts

About New Mexico Courts: The **District Courts** hear felony, civil, tort, contract, real property rights, estate, exclusive domestic relations, mental health. The District Courts also handle appeals for administrative agencies and lower courts, miscellaneous civil jurisdiction; and misdemeanors.

The **Magistrate Court** handles tort, contract, landlord/tenant rights, civil, ($0-10,000); small claims, felony preliminary hearings; misdemeanor, DWI/DUI and other traffic violations.

Municipal Courts handle petty misdemeanors, DWI/DUI, traffic violations, and other municipal ordinance violations. The **Bernalillo Metropolitan Court** has jurisdiction in cases up to $10,000.

County Clerks hold the case files for "informal" or "uncontested" probate cases seen by the Probate Judge. The District Courts hold case files for "formal" or "contested" probate cases.
The web page for the Judicial Branch is www.nmcourts.com/.

Appellate Courts: The Supreme Court is the court of last resort and has superintending control over all lower courts and attorneys licensed in the state. The Court of Appeals has mandatory jurisdiction for civil, non-capital criminal, juvenile cases; discretionary jurisdiction in interlocutory decision cases and administrative agency appeals. Supreme Court opinions may be researched at www.nmcompcomm.us/nmcases/NMCases.aspx; Appellate Opinions at https://coa.nmcourts.gov/index.php.

Online Court Access

All District Courts participate in the system described below.

The page at https://caselookup.nmcourts.gov/caselookup/app offers free access to the District, Magistrate, and Municipal Court case information statewide with two exceptions listed below. In general, all other lower court records are available from June 1997 forward except:

- Municipal Court data is limited to criminal Domestic Violence and DWI historic convictions from September 1, 1991 forward.

- The site does not display Family Violence Protection Act Order of Protection cases on its Case Lookup Website (effective July 1, 2008). To access juvenile or order of protection information, please contact the court in which the case was filed.

Search by name & DL and/or DOB, and by county and type of case or by case number. Case lookup does not display the full date of birth, it displays only the year of birth. In addition, driver's license numbers are not displayed on records. A disclaimer reads: "Use of this site for any purpose other than viewing individual electronic court records, or attempts to download multiple records per transaction, are strictly prohibited." As mentioned, there is also a separate look-up for DWI Reports and DWI Offenders

Editor's Note: **Bernalillo County Metropolitan Court is available on this website. However, when this book was printed the text on the state system will send you to a different site for non-DWI data, but it is a loop that goes nowhere. The state has not updated the text in some time. Ignore the text about finding this court's data elsewhere and the bogus link.**

There are no other courts with online access, other than as described above.

Recorders, Assessors, and Other Sites of Note

About New Mexico Recording Offices: 33 counties, 33 recording offices. The recording officer is the County Clerk. Most New Mexico counties maintain both a grantor/grantee index and a miscellaneous index.

About Tax Liens: All federal and state tax liens are filed with the County Clerk.

Online Access

There is no statewide system. However, at least 11 counties offer indvidual online access to recorded documents and 21 counties provide online to property tax or GIS records.

Counties:

Bernalillo County *Recorded Documents* www.bernco.gov/clerk/ Search recorders data and Grantor/Grantee index free at http://eagleweb.bernco.gov:8080/recorder/web/. Free registration but small charge for copies. Records from 1978 to present. **$$$**
Property, Taxation Records Search assessor records at www.bernco.gov/property-tax-search-disclaimer/.

Chaves County *Property, Taxation Records* Access to property records for free at http://eagleweb.co.chaves.nm.us:8080/assessor/taxweb/.

Cibola County *Recorded Documents* www.co.cibola.nm.us/clerk.html Access to recorded documents go to http://cibola.tylerworksasp.com/cibola/web/login.jsp?submit=I+Acknowledge. Has public login for documents without images. Must register for a fee for more advanced records. **$$$**

Curry County *Recorded Documents* www.currycounty.org/elected-offices/clerks-office/ Access to records free at http://lookup.currycounty.org:8080/clerk.aspx?source=clerk.
Property, Taxation Records Access to property records for free at http://lookup.currycounty.org:8080/assessor.aspx?source=assessor.

Dona Ana County *Recorded Documents* www.donaanacounty.org/clerk/ Access to county database (search and view document recording information) free at http://records.donaanacounty.org/countyweb/login.do?countyname=DonaAna. Must login with user ID and password. Also access index of recorded documents at http://donaanacounty.org/clerk/docs/.
Property, Taxation Records Access assessor index free at www2.donaanacounty.org/search/realprop.php. Access property data free on the GIS-mapping site at http://gis.co.dona-ana.nm.us/advparcels/viewer.htm. No name searching. Use the black circle with the 'I' in it to show parcel data.**$$$**

Eddy County *Property, Taxation Records* Access to records and maps free at http://liveweb.co.eddy.nm.us/.

Lea County *Property, Taxation Records* Access to maps of county for a fee at www.emapsplus.com/. Must sign-up and purchase a subscription to a county.**$$$**

Lincoln County *Property, Taxation Records* Access to the assessor property records is free at www.lincolncountynm.net/new_county_offices/assessor/database_access.php. Registration, software, username and password is required. Follow prompts at website.

Los Alamos County *Recorded Documents* www.losalamosnm.us/clerk/Pages/default.aspx Access to recorded data at https://portal1.recordfusion.com/countyweb/login.do?countyname=LosAlamos username/password required or login free as Guest. **$$$**

Otero County *Recorded Documents* www.co.otero.nm.us/Clerk/clerk.htm   Access to the county documents go to http://occlerk.co.otero.nm.us/AppXtender/Login.aspx. Must register by contacting the clerk's office at above number. **$$$**
Property, Taxation Records   Search the treasurer's tax data inquiry site free at http://ocwebserver2.co.otero.nm.us:81/webtaxinq/default.asp?action=taxdatainq. Also, access to property data free at http://ocwebserver2.co.otero.nm.us:81/webproping/default.asp?action=stats. Also, access to GIS/mapping free at http://ocwebserver2.co.otero.nm.us/website/index.htm.

Sandoval County *Property, Taxation Records*   Access assessor property data free at http://etweb.sandovalcountynm.gov/Assessor/web/.

San Juan County *Recorded Documents, Marriage, Probate* www.sjcclerk.net./   Access to records for free to go https://portal2.recordfusion.com/countyweb/login.do?countyname=SanJuan. Recorded documents back to 9/16/1983, marriage records back to 1887, probate records back to 1887 and plats and surveys back to 1890. No fee to access index (under login as guest), however to veiw image thumbnails and print images put open account and pay. **$$$**
Property, Taxation Records   Access to county property tax data is free at www.sjcassessor.net/search.asp.

Santa Fe County *Recorded Documents* www.santafecountynm.gov/clerk   Access to recorder's grantor/grantee index available by subscription on the WEBXtender Document Imaging System. $36.00 setup fee and $25.00 monthly fee. There is a $7.00 per hour usage fee and $.50 per printer page. **$$$**
Property, Taxation Records   Access to county property data for free at www.santafecountynm.gov/assessor/appraisal_tax_information.**$$$**

Sierra County *Recorded Documents* www.sierracountynm.gov/department/138752-clerk   Access to recorded documents free at http://liveweb.sierracountynm.gov/clerk.aspx?source=clerk.
Property, Taxation Records   Access to records free at http://liveweb.sierracountynm.gov/assessor.aspx?source=assessor.

Taos County *Property, Taxation Records*   Access to records for free at http://lookup.taoscounty.org/assessor.aspx?source=assessor. Also, access to GIS/mapping free at http://lookup.taoscounty.org/assessor.aspx?source=assessor.

Valencia County *Recorded Documents , Probate Records* www.co.valencia.nm.us/departments/clerk/County_Clerk.html   Access to records free at http://publiclookup.co.valencia.nm.us/clerk.aspx?source=clerk.
Property, Taxation Records   Access to GIS/mapping for free at www.co.valencia.nm.us/departments/gis/GIS.html.

New York

Capital: Albany
           AlbanyCounty
Time Zone: EST
Population: 19,795,791
# of Counties: 62

Useful State Links

Website: **www.ny.gov**
Governor: **www.governor.ny.gov**
Attorney General: **www.oag.state.ny.us**
State Archives: **www.archives.nysed.gov/**
State Statutes & Codes: **http://public.leginfo.state.ny.us/lawssrch.cgi?NVLWO**:
Legislative Bill Search: **https://www.nysenate.gov/legislation**
Unclaimed Funds: **www.osc.state.ny.us/ouf/index.htm**

State Public Record Agencies

Sexual Offender Registry

Sex Offender Registry, Alfred E. Smith Building,   www.criminaljustice.ny.gov/SomsSUBDirectory/search_index.jsp   The sex offender registry of level 2 and 3 can be searched at www.criminaljustice.ny.gov/SomsSUBDirectory/search_index.jsp. Search by last name, or ZIP, or by county. If an offender is not be listed on this site, information about the offender is available through DCJS at 800-262-3257.

Incarceration Records

New York Department of Correctional Services, Building 2 - Central Files,   www.doccs.ny.gov/   Computerized inmate information is available from the Inmate Lookup at http://nysdoccslookup.doccs.ny.gov/kinqw00 or follow "inmate lookup" link at main site. Records go back to early 1970s. One may look up with exact last name and year of birth, or by partial/full last name. For the latter, a list of possibilities is presented. To acquire inmate DIN number, you may call 518-457-5000.

Corporation, LP, LLC, LLP

Division of Corporations, Dept. of State, One Commerce Plaza,   www.dos.ny.gov/corps/   A commercial account can be set up for direct access. Fee is $.75 per transaction through a draw down account. There is an extensive amount of information available including historical information. Also, the Division's corporate and business entity DB for not-for-profit corporations, LPs, LLCs, and LLPs   may be accessed without charge at www.dos.ny.gov/corps/bus_entity_search.html. Searches of assumed names used by corporations, LLCs or LPs must be made manually. Note general partnerships, sole proprietorships and limited liability partnerships file an assumed name certificate directly with the county clerk. Search the child support warrant notice system at www.dos.ny.gov/corps/child_support_search.html.   *Other Options:* One may submit an email search request to corporations@dos.state.ny.us.

Uniform Commercial Code, Federal & State Tax Liens

Department of State, UCC Unit - Records,   www.dos.ny.gov/corps/uccforms.html   Free access is available at https://appext20.dos.ny.gov/pls/ucc_public/web_search.main_frame. Search financing statements and federal tax lien notices by debtor name, or secured party name, or by filing number and date. Please note that UCC Images indicated as *N/A are unavailable on the website. The state's Tax Warrant Notice System can be searched at www.dos.ny.gov/corps/tax_warrant_search.html The State Child Support Enforcement Warrant Notice System is searchable from www.dos.ny.gov/corps/child_support_search.html.   *Other Options:* A UCC image subscription via the web is offered for $300 per month. Images are downloaded in TIFF format. Filings available 5 business days after filing and remain downloadable for 30 days. Call 518-486-5049.

Sales Tax Registrations

NY Dept of Taxation & Finance, Records Access - WA Harriman Campus,   https://www.tax.ny.gov/bus/   A registered sales tax look-up is offered at https://www7b.tax.ny.gov/TIVL/tivlStart.

Vital Records

Vital Records Section, Certification Unit,   www.health.ny.gov/vital_records/   Online ordering is available via an approved third party vendor, go to www.vitalchek.com.

Birth Certificate-New York City, Death Records-New York City

Department of Health, Bureau of Vital Records,   www.nyc.gov/html/doh/html/services/vr.shtml   Records may be requested via www.vitalchek.com. Use of credit card is required, additional fees charged.

Workers' Compensation Records

New York State Workers' Compensation Board, Records Access Officer,   www.wcb.ny.gov/index.jsp   FOIL request or PPPL request information at www.wcb.ny.gov/content/main/wclaws/FoilPPPL.jsp. Search www.wcb.ny.gov/content/ebiz/icempcovsearch/icempcovsearch_overview.jsp to determine if an employer has coverage.

Driver Records

Department of Motor Vehicles, MV-15 Processing,   https://dmv.ny.gov/   NY has implemented a "Dial-In Display" system which enables customers to obtain data online 24 hours a day. An application and pre-paid escrow account are required. The fee is $7.00 per record. For more information, visit https://dmv.ny.gov/records/dial-search-accounts or call 518-473-2137. Also, drivers may request their own DMV records at https://dmv.ny.gov/dmv-records/get-my-own-driving-record-abstract; however, records are returned by mail and the fee is $10.00. *Other Options:* This agency offers a program to employers so the employer is notified when a change posts to an employee's record. To find out about the "LENS" program, visit https://dmv.ny.gov/dmv-records/license-event-notification-service-lens-accounts.

Vehicle, Vessel Ownership & Registration

Department of Motor Vehicles, MV-15 Processing,   https://dmv.ny.gov/   New York offers plate, VIN and ownership data through the same network discussed in the Driving Records Section. The system is interactive and open 24 hours a day. The fee is $7.00 per record. All accounts must be approved, requesters must follow DPPA guidelines. Call 518-474-4293 or visit https://dmv.ny.gov/records/dial-search-accounts for more information. A free title/lien status check is at https://dmv.ny.gov/registration/check-title-or-lien-status. The VIN is needed; is not a name search. A free insurance status check (with control number) is at https://dmv.ny.gov/insurance/check-insurance-status. *Other Options:* DMV awards contracts for the sale of access to bulk of registration and ownership files to third party vendors, via a competitive bidding process. Stringent rules apply. For details, contact the DMV by email at DataServices@dmv.ny.gov.

Crash Reports

NYS - DMV, MV-198C processing,   https://dmv.ny.gov/get-accident-report   Online access is available to eligible requesters. There is a $7.00 search fee and a $15.00 report fee. There is no charge to simply view a list of accidents for a date and county. Available records go back 4 years. Reports can be viewed and printed. Visit the home page or go direct to https://transact.dmv.ny.gov/AccidentSales/.

Campaign Finance, Voter Registration

State Board of Elections, Public Information Officer,   www.elections.ny.gov/   View campaign finance reports at www.elections.ny.gov/CFViewReports.html. This database contains all financial disclosure reports filed with NYSBOE from July of 1999 to the present. Opinions from the Campaign Ethics Center is at www.nycourts.gov/ip/jcec/.

HSE (GED) Certificates

NY State Education Dept, HSE Testing Office,   www.acces.nysed.gov/hse/duplicate-diplomas-andor-transcripts   The agency offers an online status report for free at https://eservices.nysed.gov/ged/. To use this service, on must have the SSN or HSE ID number and the date of birth. Most records from 1982 and forward are available. These records are unofficial.

Occupational Licensing Boards

These licenses are all searchable at www.op.nysed.gov/opsearches.htm

Accountant-CPA	Audiologist	Interior Designer
Acupuncturist/Acupuncture Assis't	Chemical Dependence Operation	Landscape Architect
Addiction Counselor	Chiropractor	Massage Therapist
Addiction Treatment Center	Dental Hygienist/Dental Assistant	Midwife
Alcohol/Substance Abuse Counselor	Dentist	Nurse-LPN/RPN
Alcohol/Substance Abuse Provider	Dietitian	Nutritionist
Architect	Education/Training Providers	Occupational Therapist/Assistant
Athletic Trainer	Engineer	Ophthalmic Dispenser

Optometrist
Pharmacist
Physician/Medical Doctor/Assistant/Specialist
Podiatrist

Psychologist
Respiratory Therapist/Therapy Tech
Social Worker
Speech Pathologist/Audiologist

Surveyor-Land
Veterinarian/Veterinary Technician

These licenses are all searchable at 'https://appext20.dos.ny.gov/lcns_public/chk_load

Apartment Mgr/Vendor/Agent/Info Vendor
Apartment Sharing Manager
Appearance Enhancement Firm/Prof
Armored Car/Car Carrier/Guard
Athlete Agent
Bail Enforcement Agent
Barber Apprentice/Barber Shop

Bedding Manufacturing
Cosmetologist/Nail Technologist/Esthetics
Specialist
Dispatch Facility- Alarm/Sec/Fire
Guard/Patrol/Guard Dog Agency
Hearing Aid Dealer/Business
Home Inspector

Notary Public
Private Investigator
Real Estate Appraiser
Security Guard
Telemarketer Business
Upholster & Bedding Industry
Waxing Establishment/Operator/Tech

The Rest:

Adoption Agency .... http://ocfs.ny.gov/adopt/agcymenu.asp
Adult Care Medical Facility .... www.health.ny.gov/facilities/adult_care/
Adult Care Suspended List .... www.health.ny.gov/facilities/adult_care/memorandum.htm
Attorney .... http://iapps.courts.state.ny.us/attorney/AttorneySearch
Backflow Prev't'n Device Tester .... www.health.ny.gov/environmental/water/drinking/cross/backflow_testers/index.htm
Bail Bond Agent .... https://myportal.dfs.ny.gov/web/guest-applications/bail-bonds-search
Care Facility, Family Board-Sponsored http://ocfs.ny.gov/main/rehab/regionalListing1.asp
Charity, Registered .... https://www.charitiesnys.com/RegistrySearch/search_charities.jsp
Cigarette/Tobacco Tax Agent www8.tax.ny.gov/CGTX/cgtxHome
Cigarette/Tobacco Whlse/Retailer www8.tax.ny.gov/CGTX/cgtxHome
Day Care Center .... http://ocfs.ny.gov/main/childcare/looking.asp
Day Care, Farm Worker (ABCD) .... www.agriculture.ny.gov/programs/childdev.html
Family/Group Day Care .... http://ocfs.ny.gov/main/childcare/looking.asp
Farm Product Dealers .... www.agriculture.ny.gov/programs/apsf.html
Forest Ranger Roster www.dec.ny.gov/about/50303.html
Home Care Service .... https://profiles.health.ny.gov/
Hospice .... https://profiles.health.ny.gov/
Hospital .... https://profiles.health.ny.gov/
Insurance Adjuster/Appraiser .... https://myportal.dfs.ny.gov/web/guest-applications/prelicensing-providers
Insurance Company .... https://myportal.dfs.ny.gov/web/guest-applications/ins.-company-search
Juvenile Detention Facility http://ocfs.ny.gov/main/publications/Pub1160%20Facility%20Directory%20of%20Juvenile%20Detention%20Facilities.pdf
Kosher Food .... http://foodregistration.agriculture.ny.gov/kosher/search.aspx
Lobbyist/Client/Public Corporation .... http://prtl-drprd-web.nyc.gov/lobbyistsearch/
Mammography Facility .... www.accessdata.fda.gov/scripts/cdrh/cfdocs/cfMQSA/mqsa.cfm
Medicaid Long-Term Care Service .... www.health.ny.gov/health_care/managed_care/mltc/mltcplans.htm
Medical Disciplinary Action http://w3.health.state.ny.us/opmc/factions.nsf
Medical Examiner-Independent .... www.wcb.ny.gov/content/main/hcpp/ListofAuthIMENYC.jsp
Medical Personnel Profile .... www.nydoctorprofile.com/
Mental Health Facility .... www.omh.ny.gov/omhweb/aboutomh/omh_facility.html
Minority/Woman-owned Business .... https://ny.newnycontracts.com/FrontEnd/VendorSearchPublic.asp
Nursery/Plant Dealer/Greenhouse https://data.ny.gov/Economic-Development/Nursery-Growers-and-Greenhouse/qke7-n4w8
Nurses Aide .... https://registry.prometric.com/public
Nursing Home .... https://profiles.health.ny.gov/
Nursing Home Administrator .... www.health.ny.gov/professionals/nursing_home_administrator/licensed_nha/master_lnha.htm
Off-Track Betting .... https://license.gaming.ny.gov/
Pesticide Business/Agency .... www.dec.ny.gov/nyspad/?0
Pesticide Distributor .... www.dec.ny.gov/nyspad/?0
Pesticide/Commercial Applicator .... www.dec.ny.gov/nyspad/?0
Physician License Number Search .... www.health.ny.gov/professionals/doctors/conduct/license_lookup.htm

Racetrack...	https://license.gaming.ny.gov/
Racing Occupation	https://license.gaming.ny.gov/
Radiologic Technology School	www.health.ny.gov/professionals/doctors/radiological/schlist2.htm
Radon Testing Lab	www.wadsworth.org/regulatory/elap/certified-labs
Real Estate Agent/Broker/Office..............	https://appext20.dos.ny.gov/nydos/selSearchType.do
Real Estate Appraiser School..................	https://appext20.dos.ny.gov/nydos/selSearchType.do
Service Contract Providers, Registered	https://myportal.dfs.ny.gov/web/guest-applications/service-contract-providers
Teacher..	http://eservices.nysed.gov/teach/certhelp/CpPersonSearchExternal.jsp
Veteran - Skilled Nursing Home	www.nysvets.org/
Water Processing Facility, Bulk...............	www.health.ny.gov/environmental/water/drinking/bulk_bottle/bulkwter.htm
Water Treatment Plant Operator	www.health.ny.gov/environmental/water/drinking/operate/certified_operators/

State and Local Courts

About NY Courts: **Supreme and County Courts** are the highest trial courts in the state, equivalent to what may be called circuit or district in other states. New York's Supreme and County Courts may be administered together or separately. When separate, there is a clerk for each. Supreme and/or County Courts are not appeals courts. Supreme Courts handle civil cases – usually civil cases over $25,000 – but there are many exceptions. The County Courts handle felony cases and, in many counties, these County Courts also handle misdemeanors. The New York City Courts are structured differently.

For non-NYC courts (called Upstate Courts), **City Courts** handle misdemeanors and civil case claims up to $15,000, small claims, and eviction cases. Not all counties have City Courts, thus cases there fall to the Supreme and County Courts for civil and criminal respectively, or, in many counties, to the small **Town and Village Courts**, which can number in the dozens within a county.

Probate is handled by **Surrogate Courts**. Surrogate Courts may also hear Domestic Relations cases in some counties.

In **New York City**, the Supreme Court is the trial court with unlimited jurisdiction. The Civil Court of the City of New York has jurisdiction on civil matters up to $25,000. The Criminal Court of the City of New York has jurisdiction over misdemeanors and minor violations. The Family Court hears matters involving children and families. Probate is handled by the Surrogate's Court.

In the five boroughs of New York City the courts records are administered directly by the state **OCA – Office of Court Administration.**

The web page for the Judicial Branch is www.nycourts.gov.

Appellate Courts: The Court of Appeals is the state's highest court. The next step down is the four Appellate Divisions of the Supreme Court, one in each of the State's four Judicial Departments. These Courts resolve appeals from judgments or orders of the courts of original jurisdiction in civil and criminal cases, and review civil appeals taken from the Appellate Terms and the County Courts acting as appellate courts.

Appellate Terms of the Supreme Court in the First and Second Departments hear appeals from civil and criminal cases originating in the Civil and Criminal Courts of the City of New York. In the Second Department, Appellate Terms also have jurisdiction over appeals from civil and criminal cases originating in District, City, Town and Village Courts.

The County Courts in the Third and Fourth Departments (although primarily trial courts), hear appeals from cases originating in the City, Town and Village Courts.

Find decisions at www.nycourts.gov/decisions/index.shtml.

Statewide Court Online Access: There are a number of statewide systems - see below.
OCA Criminal Records

The OCA offers online access to criminal records. Requesters must apply for an account. There is a weekly minimum of searches required. This is not an interactive system - the search results are sent via email. Call the OCA at 212-428-2916 or visit www.nycourts.gov/apps/chrs/ for details on how to set up an account.

ECourts

A state search site at http://iapps.courts.state.ny.us/webcivil/ecourtsMain provides five resources, but know there limitations. The links accessible from this site works best as a **supplemental resource**. The site limitations are based on search logic issues. For example, when searching the civil index, the search index apparently only contains the name of the first defendant. Thus if there are multiple defendants, the site cannot be relied upon as being equivalent to an on-site search. The five resources are as follows:

1. **WebCriminal** provides pending criminal case data from 13 local and Supreme Courts - includes Mobil access.
2. **WebFamily** provides information on active Family Court cases in all 62 counties of New York State and Integrated Domestic Violence (IDV) Court cases in those counties with IDV Courts.
3. **WebCivil Supreme** contains information on both Active and Disposed Civil Supreme Court cases in all 62 counties of New York State. - includes Mobil access
4. The **WebCivil Local link** gives access to civil case data from City Courts and District Courts.
5. There is also a case tracking service called **eTrack**. This is case tracking service which automatically sends an email notification when activity occurs in cases shown on one's Case Notification list.

Note that **WebHousing was discontinued August 2015.** But information about Landlord-Tenant cases in the Housing Part of New York City Civil Court for Bronx, Kings (Brooklyn), New York (Manhattan), Queens Richmond (Staten Island) Counties is now found on the WebCivilLocal website.

Decisions

Search http://decisions.courts.state.ny.us/search/query3.asp for Supreme Court Civil and Criminal decisions, dating back to 2001. **Civil Cases** are from the following counties: Allegany, Bronx, Broome, Cattaraugus, Chautauqua, Cortland, Delaware, Erie, Kings, Livingston, Madison, Monroe, Nassau, New York, Niagara, Oneida, Onondaga, Ontario, Orange, Putnam, Queens, Richmond, Schuyler, Seneca, Steuben, Suffolk, Westchester and Wyoming Counties. **Criminal Cases** are from the following counties: Albany, Bronx, Broome, Cattaraugus, Cayuga, Chautauqua, Chemung, Delaware, Erie, Kings, Monroe, Nassau, New York, Oneida, Onondaga, Ontario, Orange, Oswego, Queens, Richmond, Seneca, Suffolk, and Wayne Counties.

Other County Sites Not Mentioned Above:

Bronx County

Supreme Court - Civil Division   www.courts.state.ny.us/courts/12jd/
Civi & Criminal: Access docket data free on the law case search at www.bronxcountyclerkinfo.com/law/UI/Admin/login.aspx. Sign in as a guest.

Broome County

County Clerk   http://gobroomecounty.com/clerk
Civil: Search clerk's court and judgment indexes free at https://www.searchiqs.com/nybro/Login.aspx. For civil records, the index goes back to 1986, images are available from 2007 forward.

Dutchess County

County Clerk   www.co.dutchess.ny.us/CountyGov/Departments/CountyClerk/CCIndex.htm
Civil: The county has its own online access at www.co.dutchess.ny.us/CountyGov/Departments/CountyClerk/12976.htm. Images can be viewed for free. Download uncertified documents for $.50 a page. *Criminal:* The county has its own online access at www.co.dutchess.ny.us/CountyGov/Departments/CountyClerk/12976.htm.

Erie County

County Clerk   www2.erie.gov/clerk/
Civil: Online access to the county clerk's database of civil judgments is free at http://ecclerk.erie.gov. Records go back to 01/93.

Madison County

County Clerk   https://www.madisoncounty.ny.gov/county-clerk/madison-county-clerk
Civil & Criminal: The fee for unlimited access to the Madison County Land/Court Records website includes an account activation fee of $50.00 and an additional $600 per quarter, payable in advance. See www.searchiqs.com/madison.html.

Orange County

County Clerk   www.co.orange.ny.us/content/124/861/default.aspx
Civi & Criminall: A county online system is offered at https://searchiqs.com/nyora/. Registration is required. There is a $150 fee of 90 days. Printing of documents is $.65 per page.

Rockland County

County Clerk   www.rocklandcountyclerk.com/index.php/en/
Civi & criminal: Online search to county clerk index is free at https://cotthosting.com/NYRocklandExternal/User/Login.aspx. Online includes civil judgments, real estate records, tax warrants. Once an account is established, registered users will be able to print documents at $.50 per page. The index goes back to 1/2/1947.

Schoharie County

County Clerk   www.schohariecounty-ny.gov/CountyWebSite/CountyClerk/countyclerkservice.html
Civil: The county has an online docket search at https://www2.schohariecounty-ny.gov/CountyClerkSearch/faces/Help.xhtml.

St. Lawrence County

County Clerk   www.co.st-lawrence.ny.us/departments/countyclerk/

Civil: Online access to index of a cases from 1/02/1990 to present is at www.searchiqs.com/stlaw.html.

Suffolk County
County Clerk www.suffolkcountyny.gov/departments/countyclerk.aspx
Civil & Criminal: Court minutes are online at www.suffolkcountyny.gov/Departments/CountyClerk/OnlineRecords.aspx.

Westchester County
County Clerk www.westchesterclerk.com
Civil & Criminal: Access cases on the county clerk database search site back to 2002 at https://wro.westchesterclerk.com/Login/Login.aspx?ReturnUrl=%2fdefault.aspx. Data includes liens, judgments, tax warrants, foreclosures, Divorces (no images).

Recorders, Assessors, and Other Sites of Note

About New York Recording Offices: 62 counties, 62 recording offices. Recording officer is the County Clerk except in the counties of Bronx, Kings, New York, and Queens where the recording officer is the New York City Register. Note that Staten Island/Richmond County also has a County Clerk.

About Tax Liens: Federal tax liens on personal property of businesses are filed with the Secretary of State and are usually indexed with UCC records. Other federal tax liens are filed with the County Clerk.

Online Access

Statewide or Multi-Jurisdiction Access: Many counties and towns offer free internet access to assessor records. Recording records are more likely to require registration and password; many also require a fee. Below are several notable sites.

- The New York City Register offers free access to all borough's real estate records (including Staten Island) on the ACRIS system at http://a836-acris.nyc.gov/Scripts/Coverpage.dll/index. Search by name, address, doc type, or legal description.

- New York Citty's Dept of Finance Property Assessment Rolls are free at http://nycprop.nyc.gov/nycproperty/nynav/jsp/selectbbl.jsp but no name searching.

- Use https://www.taxlookup.net to review localized property tax records free for limited communities in 40 or so counties.

County Sites:

Albany County *Recorded Documents* www.albanycounty.com/Government/Departments/CountyClerk.aspx View deeds and mortgages free at https://www.searchiqs.com/NYALB/Login.aspx. Fees required for subscription.
Property, Taxation Records Search Town of Guilderland property data free at https://www.taxlookup.net.

Allegany County *Recorded Documents* www.alleganyco.com/btn_county_clerk/templates/fw_layout.htm View deeds and mortgages free at https://www.searchiqs.com/NYALL/Login.aspx. Fees required for subscription.
Property, Taxation Records Access to land records, GIS/mapping and Tax maps for free at http://allegany.sdgnys.com/index.aspx.

Bronx County *Recorded Documents* www.nyc.gov/html/records/html/home/home.shtml Recording data from City Register is free at http://a836-acris.nyc.gov/CP/. Also, for deeper financial data back 10 years, subscribe to the NYC Dept of Finance dial-up system; fee-$250 monthly and $5.00 per item. Info/signup- call Richard Reskin 718-935-6523. NYC's Dept of Finance offers daily downloads for borough-wide transactions of UCCs, Fed lien, deeds, real estate at www1.nyc.gov/site/finance/index.page.
Property, Taxation Records Property tax and ownership is searchable at http://nycprop.nyc.gov/nycproperty/nynav/jsp/selectbbl.jsp. Another site state provides ability to find Bourough, block, and lot number, see http://webapps.nyc.gov:8084/cics/fin2/find001i?.

Broome County *Recorded Documents* www.gobroomecounty.com/clerk/ View deeds and mortgages free at https://www.searchiqs.com/NYBRO/Login.aspx. Fees required for subscription.
Property, Taxation Records Search City of Binghamton and Towns of Chenango, Conklin, Dickinson, Fenton, Kirkwood, Maine, Union, Vestal, and Windsor property tax data free at https://www.taxlookup.net/. City allows name searching; Town does not.

Cattaraugus County *Property, Taxation Records* Search for property info on the interactive map at http://maps.cattco.org/parcel_disclaimer.php.

Cayuga County *Recorded Documents* www.cayugacounty.us/Departments/County-Clerk Access to land records for a fee at https://www.nylandrecords.com/nylr/NylrApp/index.jsp. Indexing from 1972 to present, images are from 1984 to present.

Property, Taxation Records   Search tax data, rolls, final assessments free at www.cayugacounty.us/Departments/Real-Property/Assessment-Rolls. Also, access to property sales for free at www.cayugacounty.us/Departments/Real-Property/Current-Sales. Also, access to GIS/mapping for free at http://gis.cayugacounty.us/flexviewers/CCrpv/.

Chautauqua County   *Recorded Documents*   www.co.chautauqua.ny.us/168/County-Clerk   View deeds and mortgages free at www.searchiqs.com/chautauqua.html. Fees required for subscription.
Property, Taxation Records   Access to GIS/mapping free at www.co.chautauqua.ny.us/319/Geographic-Information-Systems. Also, access to real property tax lookup for free at http://app.co.chautauqua.ny.us/cctaxonline/#search.

Chemung County   *Recorded Documents*   www.chemungcounty.com/index.asp?pageId=115   Access to land records for a fee at www.landex.com/webstore/jsp/cart/DocumentSearch.jsp.
Property, Taxation Records   Search the treasurer's property tax data at http://chemung.sdgnys.com/index.aspx. Username and password is required for detailed data.

Chenango County   *Deeds, Mortgages, Judgments and other recorded documents. Records*   www.co.chenango.ny.us/clerk/   Access to records search for a fee at https://cotthosting.com/nychenango/User/Login.aspx. Must have a user ID and password.
Property, Taxation Records   Access to tax assessment rolls for 4 years free at www.co.chenango.ny.us/real-property-tax/rolls.php. Current town and village tax rolls also available. Another site for a fee is http://chemung.sdgnys.com/index.aspx.

Clinton County   *Recorded Documents*   www.clintoncountygov.com/Departments/CC/CountyClerkHome.html   Access to online records for a fee at https://secure.clintoncountygov.com/eSearch/User/Login.aspx?ReturnUrl=%2fesearch%2fIndex.aspx. Records from 1985 to present. Fees shown at website.
Property, Taxation Records   Access to the Public Access site is at http://clinton.sdgnys.com/index.aspx. Enhanced data for a fee, includes property taxes, tax maps and photos of parcels, call Tammy or Martine at 518-565-4763.

Columbia County   *Recorded Dcouments Records*   www.columbiacountyny.com/depts/ctyclerk/   View deeds and mortgages free at https://www.searchiqs.com/NYCOL/Login.aspx. Fees required for subscription.

Cortland County   *Recorded Documents*   www.cortland-co.org/cc/   View deeds and mortgages free at https://www.searchiqs.com/NYCOR/Login.aspx. Fees required for subscription. Deeds may be searched online from 1808 to 1985 on Infodex option.
Property, Taxation Records   Property data is available by $40 per month subscription. For information call 607-753-5040 or go to www.cortland-co.org/rpts/Imagemate.htm.

Dutchess County   *Recorded Documents*   www.co.dutchess.ny.us/CountyGov/Departments/CountyClerk/CCindex.htm   Access to records free at www.co.dutchess.ny.us/CountyGov/Departments/CountyClerk/12976.htm. To print or download documents there is a $.50 per page charge.
Property, Taxation Records   Search the county tax roll at http://geoaccess.co.dutchess.ny.us/parcelaccess/. Search the Town of East Fishkill property tax roll data free at https://www.taxlookup.net.

Erie County   *Recorded Documents*   www2.erie.gov/clerk/   Access to the county clerk's database index and images is at http://ecclerk.erie.gov/recordsng_web/. View index free. $5.00 fee to view full documents; a $250 initial escrow account required.
Property, Taxation Records   Parcel data is free at www2.erie.gov/ecrpts/index.php?q=real-property-parcel-search.

Essex County   *Recorded Documents*   https://www.co.essex.ny.us/wp/county-clerk/   View deeds and mortgages free at https://www.searchiqs.com/NYESS/Login.aspx. Fees required for subscription.
Property, Taxation Records   Parcel data, tax rolls are available for a fee at www.co.essex.ny.us/realproperty.asp. Also, a property tax search is at www.co.essex.ny.us/Treasurer/PropertyLookup.aspx?SearchReason=TaxSearch.

Franklin County   *Recorded Documents*   http://franklincony.org/content/Departments/View/59   View deeds and mortgages free at https://www.searchiqs.com/NYFRA/Login.aspx. Fees required for subscription.
Property, Taxation Records   Access to real property and GIS/mapping for free at http://franklin.sdgnys.com/index.aspx. For more detailed information, must sign-up and there is a fee.

Fulton County   *Property, Taxation Records*   Access tax assessor data at http://74.39.247.67/imo/index.aspx, assessment rolls at www.fultoncountyny.gov/index.php?word=departments/rolls.htm. Also, access to GIS/mapping for free at http://74.39.247.92/gis/.

Genesee County   *Property, Taxation Records*   Access to real property information for free at www.geneseecounty.oarsystem.com/. Also, GIS/mapping for free at www.co.genesee.ny.us/geneseecountymaps.html.

Greene County   *Property, Taxation Records*   Access to the Web Map for free at http://gis.greenegovernment.com/giswebmap/#. Also, access to assessment rolls for free at http://greene.sdgnys.com/index.aspx.

Hamilton County   *Property, Taxation Records*   Also, access to GIS/mapping free at www.hamcomaps.net/#.

Herkimer County   *Property, Taxation Records*   Access to tax searches free at http://herkimercounty.sdgnys.com/index.aspx. Also, search City of Little Falls property data free at https://www.taxlookup.net.

Jefferson County   *Recorded Documents*   www.co.jefferson.ny.us/index.aspx?page=51   View deeds and mortgages free at https://www.searchiqs.com/NYJEF/Login.aspx. Fees required for subscription.
Property, Taxation Records   Property assessment data offered online for free at http://jefferson.sdgnys.com/index.aspx. For more in depth records, must register. Also, access to GIS/mapping free at www.jeffcountymaps.com/.

Kings County   *Recorded Documents*   www.nyc.gov/html/kcpa/html/home/home.shtml   Recording data from City Register is free at http://a836-acris.nyc.gov/CP/. Also, for deeper financial data back 10 years, subscribe to the NYC Dept of Finance dial-up system; fee-$250 monthly and $5.00 per item. For info/signup, call Richard Reskin 718-935-6523.
Property, Taxation Records   Property tax and ownership is searchable at http://nycprop.nyc.gov/nycproperty/nynav/jsp/selectbbl.jsp. Another site state provides ability to find Bourough, block, and lot number, see http://webapps.nyc.gov:8084/cics/fin2/find001i?.

Lewis County   *Recorded Documents*   http://lewiscountyny.org/content/Departments/View/24?   Real property search free at http://lewiscountyny.org/content/RealProperty.
Property, Taxation Records   Access to real property data for free at http://lewiscountyny.org/content/RealProperty. Also, access to GIS/mapping for free at http://lewiscountyny.org/content/Generic/View/162.

Livingston County   *Recorded Documents*   www.co.livingston.state.ny.us/clerk.htm   Access to recorded data at https://countyfusion1.propertyinfo.com/countyweb/login.do?countyname=Livingston. Username/password required or logon free at Guest.
Property, Taxation Records   Access to real property tax services free at http://depot.livingstoncounty.us/rptx/rpsonlg2.pgm. Also, access to county real property tax maps for free at http://depot.livingstoncounty.us/rptx/RPSONLTXWN.pgm.

Madison County   *Recorded Documents*   https://www.madisoncounty.ny.gov/county-clerk/madison-county-clerk   View deeds and mortgages free at https://www.searchiqs.com/NYMAD/Login.aspx. Fees required for subscription.
Property, Taxation Records   A private company offers property assessment data online at www.madisoncounty.ny.gov/ImateWeb/index.aspx.

Monroe County   *Recorded Documents*   www2.monroecounty.gov/clerk-index.php   Access the county clerk database at https://gov.propertyinfo.com/NY-Monroe/. Index search is free but must register first. Fee for printing of images. Land records images from 1/1/75 to present; data from 1/1/73 to present. Also, access voter registration roll free at https://www.monroecounty.gov/etc/voter/.
Property, Taxation Records   Search the County Real Property Portal at www.monroecounty.gov/apps/propertyapp.php. Also search Town of Penfield property data free at https://www.taxlookup.net/.

Montgomery County   *Property, Taxation Records*   A private company offers property assessment data online at www.accuriz.com/index.aspx. Also, access property data via the GIS-mapping site free at http://ranger.co.montgomery.ny.us/IMO/index.aspx.

Nassau County   *Recorded Documents, Deeds, Land Records Records*   www.nassaucountyny.gov/458/County-Clerk   Access to land records for free at https://www.nylandrecords.com/nylr/NylrApp/index.jsp. Indexes are free, pay-per access service available to view images. Images are from 2/22/1994 to present.
Property, Taxation Records   Access to the county assessor tax data for free at http://lrv.nassaucountyny.gov/. No name searching, must search by address or lot and parcel number. Also, access to property reports is through a private company at www.courthousedirect.com/. Fee for data.

New York County   *Recorded Documents*   www.nyc.gov/html/records/html/home/home.shtml   Recording data from City Register is free at http://a836-acris.nyc.gov/CP/. Also, for deeper financial data back 10 years, subscribe to the NYC Dept of Finance dial-up system; fee-$250 monthly and $5.00 per item. For info/signup, call Rich Reskin 718-935-6523.
Property, Taxation Records   Property tax and ownership is searchable at http://nycprop.nyc.gov/nycproperty/nynav/jsp/selectbbl.jsp. Another site state provides ability to find Bourough, block, and lot number, see http://webapps.nyc.gov:8084/cics/fin2/find001i?.

Niagara County   *Recorded Documents*   www.niagaracounty.com/Departments/County-Clerk   View deeds and mortgages free at https://www.searchiqs.com/NYBRO/Login.aspx. Fees required for subscription.
Property, Taxation Records   Access to GIS/mapping free at http://gis2.erie.gov/HTML5/NiagaraCountyNY/PublicLaunchPage.aspx.

Oneida County   *Recorded Documents (Land Indexes Only) Records*   http://ocgov.net/countyclerk   View deeds and mortgages free at https://www.searchiqs.com/NYONE/Login.aspx. Fees required for subscription.
Property, Taxation Records   Access to tax rolls for free at http://ocgov.net/finance/2014TaxRolls.

Onondaga County   *Recorded Documents*   www.ongov.net/clerk/index.html   Access to records free at http://psi.ongov.net/PublicClerk/Search/Name.jsp. Images are not available at this time. For a copy of document, mail a self addressed stamped envelope and $.65 per page or $1.30 per document minimum.
Property, Taxation Records   Search for property data free on the GIS-mapping page at www.fsihost.com/onondaga/. Also, access to assessment rolls for free at www.ongov.net/rpts/assessmentrolls.html. Access county property data free at http://ocfintax.ongov.net/Imate/index.aspx, includes access to City of Syracuse property data. Also, search Town of Tully tax roll free at www.taxlookup.net/index.aspx.

Ontario County   *Recorded Documents*   www.co.ontario.ny.us/index.aspx?nid=102   Access to recorded data at https://countyfusion1.propertyinfo.com/countyweb/login.do?countyname=Ontario. Username/password required or login free at Guest.

Property, Taxation Records   City of Canandaigua property, assessment, and sales lists in pdf format available free at www.canandaiguanewyork.gov/index.asp?Type=B_BASIC&SEC={27669D54-CE6F-4445-9CED-0861BE56EFA0}. Also, assessment rolls for free at www.co.ontario.ny.us/DocumentCenter/Index/624.

Orange County   *Recorded Documents*   www.orangecountygov.com/content/124/861/default.aspx   View deeds and mortgages free at https://www.searchiqs.com/NYORA/Login.aspx. Fees required for subscription. ***Property, Taxation Records***   Real Property Tax Assessment Information is available free at http://propertydata.orangecountygov.com/imate/index.aspx. Registration and fees apply for fuller data. Also, search GIS-mapping site data at http://ocgis.orangecountygov.com/.

Orleans County   *Property, Taxation Records*   A private company offers property assessment data online at http://orleans.sdgnys.com/index.aspx. Also, access to assessment rolls for free at www.orleansny.com/Departments/TaxandFinance/RealProperty.aspx.

Oswego County   *Recorded Documents*   View deeds and mortgages free at www.searchiqs.com/oswego.html. Fees required for subscription. ***Property, Taxation Records***   Access tax roll data for Towns of Sandy Creek, Schroeppel, and Scriba free at www.taxlookup.net/#Oswego. Also, access GIS/mapping for free at http://rptsgisweb.oswegocounty.com/.

Otsego County   *Recorded Documents*   www.otsegocounty.com/depts/clk/   View deeds and mortgages free at https://www.searchiqs.com/NYOTS/Login.aspx. Fees required for subscription. ***Property, Taxation Records***   Search the county real property lookup free at http://imo.otsegocounty.com/index.aspx. Must subscribe for detailed info.

Putnam County   *Recorded Documents*   www.putnamcountyny.com/county-clerk/   Access to land records for a fee at https://www.nylandrecords.com/nylr/NylrApp/index.jsp. Images are from 2/22/1994 to present.

Queens County   *Recorded Documents*   Recording data from City Register is free at http://a836-acris.nyc.gov/CP/. Also, for deeper financial data back 10 years, subscribe to the NYC Dept of Finance dial-up system; fee-$250 monthly and $5.00 per item. For info/signup, call Richard Reskin 718-935-6523. ***Property, Taxation Records***   Property tax and ownership is at http://webapps.nyc.gov:8084/CICS/fin1/find001I and http://nycprop.nyc.gov/nycproperty/nynav/jsp/selectbbl.jsp.

Rensselaer County   *Recorded Documents*   www.rensco.com/departments_countyclerk.asp   Access to land records for a fee at https://www.nylandrecords.com/nylr/NylrApp/index.jsp.
Property, Taxation Records   Access to assessment rolls for free at www.rensco.com/departments_taxservices_assessmentrolls.asp.

Richmond County   *Recorded Documents*   www.richmondcountyclerk.com/   Recording data from City Register is free at http://a836-acris.nyc.gov/CP/. Also, for deeper financial data back 10 years, subscribe to the NYC Dept of Finance dial-up system; fee-$250 monthly and $5.00 per item. For info/signup, call Richard Reskin 718-935-6523. Also, access to land records for a fee at https://www.nylandrecords.com/nylr/NylrApp/index.jsp. Must register.
Property, Taxation Records   Property tax and ownership is at http://webapps.nyc.gov:8084/CICS/fin1/find001I and http://nycprop.nyc.gov/nycproperty/nynav/jsp/selectbbl.jsp.

Rockland County   *Recorded Documents*   www.rocklandcountyclerk.com/index.php/en/   Viewing of documents is free at https://cotthosting.com/NYRocklandExternal/User/Login.aspx. Documents can no longer be printed for free, must create an account, fee to print documents is $.50 per page.
Property, Taxation Records   Access to GIS/mapping free at https://geopower.jws.com/rockland/.

Saratoga County   *Property, Taxation Records*   A private company offers property assessment data online at http://saratoga.sdgnys.com/disclaimer.aspx.

Schenectady County   *Property, Taxation Records*   Access to property tax rolls with ownership information is at http://64.132.212.35/imate/index.aspx.

Schoharie County   *Recorded Documents*   www.schohariecounty-ny.gov/CountyWebSite/CountyClerk/countyclerkservice.html   Access to records free at https://www2.schohariecounty-ny.gov/CountyClerkSearch/.
Property, Taxation Records   Search property tax and ownership data free at http://imo.schohariecounty-ny.gov/index.aspx.

Schuyler County   *Property, Taxation Records*   Access to land records for free at http://schuyler.sdgnys.com/index.aspx. Guests may search free; registration and fees required for images, etc.

Seneca County   *Property, Taxation Records*   Access to tax assessment information and mapping for free at http://imo.co.seneca.ny.us/disclaimer.aspx.

St. Lawrence County   *Recorded Documents*   www.co.st-lawrence.ny.us/Departments/CountyClerk/   View deeds and mortgages free at https://www.searchiqs.com/NYSTL/Login.aspx. Fees required for subscription.
Property, Taxation Records   County assessor rolls available at www.co.st-lawrence.ny.us/Departments/RealProperty/#. Search property data and Treasurer's delinquent tax records for free at https://www.taxlookup.net.

Steuben County *Property, Taxation Records*   Search Steuben County assessment rolls free online at www.steubencony.org/Pages.asp?PGID=40. Search Town of Erwin Real Property Assessment Roll free online at www.erwinny.org/.

Suffolk County *Recorded Documents* www.suffolkcountyny.gov/departments/countyclerk.aspx   Access county land records, business names, and limited civil court records free at https://kiosk.suffolkcountyny.gov/KioskWeb/Notifications.aspx. Land records is index only.
Property, Taxation Records   The Areis Real Property subscription service is available, call Larry at 631-852-1550 or email Larry@suffolkcountyny.gov. View county accidents and details free at http://gis.co.suffolk.ny.us/website/accident/viewer.htm.

Sullivan County *Recorded Documents* http://co.sullivan.ny.us/Departments/CountyClerk/tabid/3373/Default.aspx   View deeds and mortgages free at https://www.searchiqs.com/NYSTL/Login.aspx. Fees required for subscription.
Property, Taxation Records   The agency has an agreement for property assessment data to be provided at http://webapps.co.sullivan.ny.us/IMO/index.aspx. Assessment Roll by town are provided at http://co.sullivan.ny.us/Departments/RealPropertyTaxServices/tabid/3319/Default.aspx. Private company offers property assessment data online at https://www.taxlookup.net.

Tioga County *Recorded Documents* www.tiogacountyny.com/departments/county-clerk/   Access to records for a fee at https://clerk.tiogacountyny.com/eSearch/User/Login.aspx?ReturnUrl=%2fesearch%2fIndex.aspx. Must register. Also, access to the basic property search database for free at http://imo.co.tioga.ny.us/index.aspx. For further details, must register.
Property, Taxation Records   Search Town of Owego property data free at https://www.taxlookup.net. Also, access to assessment rolls for free at www.tiogacountyny.com/departments/real-property-assessment-rolls/.

Tompkins County *Property, Taxation Records*   Access to property records on ImageMate system at http://tompkinscountyny.gov/assessment/online has 2 levels: basic free and a registration/password fee-based full system. Free version has no name searching. Fee service is $20 monthly or $200 per year. For info or registration for the latter, email assessment@tompkins-co.org.

Ulster County *Recorded Documents* http://ulstercountyny.gov/countyclerk/   Access to land records for a fee at https://www.nylandrecords.com/nylr/NylrApp/index.jsp. Land Records date back to 1984. Includes county court records back to 1987.
Property, Taxation Records   Access to county tax maps free at www.ulstercountyny.gov/real-property/tax-maps. Also, access to parcel records for free at http://ulstercountyny.gov/maps/parcel-viewer/.

Warren County *Recorded Documents* http://warrencountyny.gov/clerk/   View deeds and mortgages free at https://www.searchiqs.com/NYSTL/Login.aspx. Fees required for subscription.
Property, Taxation Records   Access to property information for free at http://warrencountyny.gov/rp/search.php.

Washington County *Recorded Documents* www.co.washington.ny.us/276/County-Clerks-Office   Access to land records for a fee at https://www.nylandrecords.com/nylr/NylrApp/index.jsp.
Property, Taxation Records   Access to GIS/mapping free at http://gis.co.washington.ny.us/webmap/index.htm.

Wayne County *Recorded Documents* http://web.co.wayne.ny.us/county-clerk/   Access to record indexes for free at http://web.co.wayne.ny.us/county-clerk/county-clerk-indexes/.
Property, Taxation Records   Access tax property data free at www.co.wayne.ny.us/RPT-TaxSearch/default.aspx. Also, access to the county tax maps for free at http://web.co.wayne.ny.us/wayne-county-real-property-tax-service/real-property-tax-maps/.

Westchester County *Recorded Documents* www.westchesterclerk.com/   Access to the clerk's recorded documents and liens is free at www.westchesterclerk.com/. There is also searches that feature images for a fee; registration is required. Data available also includes registrations of corporations, foreclosures, and divorces.
Property, Taxation Records   Access to the assessment rolls for free at http://orps1.tax.ny.gov/MuniPro/assessment_roll.cfm.

Wyoming County *Recorded Documents* www.wyomingco.net/cclerk/main.html   Access to land records for free at https://www.nylandrecords.com/nylr/NylrApp/index.jsp. Must register to use.
Property, Taxation Records   A private company offers property assessment data and GIS/mapping online at www.wyomingco.net/webgis/. Search by owner or address.

Yates County *Property, Taxation Records*   Access to property records for free at http://yates.sdgnys.com/disclaimer.aspx. Limited access is free; Subscription fee is $360.00 per year for full records access.

North Carolina

Capital: Raleigh
           Wake County
Time Zone: EST
Population: 10,042,802
# of Counties: 100

Useful State Links

Website: **www.nc.gov**
Governor: **www.governor.state.nc.us**
Attorney General: **www.ncdoj.gov/**
State Archives: **www.history.ncdcr.gov/**
State Statutes and Codes: **www.ncleg.net/gascripts/Statutes/Statutes.asp**
Legislative Bill Search: **www.ncleg.net**
Unclaimed Funds: **https://www.nctreasurer.com/Claim-Your-Cash/Claim-Your-NC_Cash/Pages/Search.aspx**

State Public Record Agencies

Sexual Offender Registry

State Bureau of Investigation, Criminal Information & Ident Sect - SOR Unit, http://sexoffender.ncsbi.gov/ Search Level 3 records at the website. Search by name or geographic region. Go to http://sexoffender.ncdoj.gov/disclaimer.aspx. One may also sign-up for email or telephone alerts. Portions of the registry information, and therefore its reliability, are based on information provided by the offender. For example, the offender reports his address, whether they are a student, etc. *Other Options:* Agency can provide data on CD-Rom.

Incarceration Records

North Carolina Department of Public Safety, Incarceration Records, https://www2.ncdps.gov/index2.cfm The web access allows searching by name or ID number for public information on inmates, escapes/captures, absoncers, and inmate releases robationers, or parolees since 1973. See http://webapps6.doc.state.nc.us/opi/offendersearch.do?method=view. Does not include county jail information. There is also a separate search for county jails, state prisons, sex offenders, and protective orders form a vendor - Vinelink - at https://www.vinelink.com/vinelink/siteInfoAction.do?siteId=34003.

Corporation, LP, LLC, Trademarks/Servicemarks

Secretary of State, Corporations Division, https://www.sosnc.gov/corporations/ The home page at https://www.sosnc.gov/corporations/ offers 5 different free searches: by corporate name, by new & dissolved entities, by new non-profits, by the registered agent., and by compnau official Document copies may be ordered online. Also, a free verification page is offered at https://www.sosnc.gov/verification/thepage.aspx where one can search by certificate or authority number. Search trademarks at https://www.sosnc.gov/trademrk/search.aspx. *Other Options:* This agency makes database information available for purchase via an FTP site. Contact Don Beckett at 919-807-2203 for details.

Uniform Commercial Code, Federal Tax Liens

UCC Division, Secretary of State, https://www.sosnc.gov/UCC/ A free search is offered at https://www.sosnc.gov/UCC/FilingSearch.aspx. Search by debtor name or filing number. A free serach of tax lines is at https://www.sosnc.gov/taxliens/filingsearch.aspx. *Other Options:* The UCC or tax lien database can be purchased on an annual basis via an FTP site. For more information, call 919-807-2219.

Sales Tax Registrations

Revenue Department, Sales & Use Tax Division, www.dornc.com/ Delinquent debtors are shown on the web at www.dor.state.nc.us/collect/delinquent.html. Three different tax registries can be viewed at www.dornc.com/taxes/sales/.

Vital Records

Department of Helath and Human Services, Vital Records Section, http://vitalrecords.nc.gov/ Online ordering is available using a credit card via a state-designated vendor at www.vitalchek.com. Additional fees are incurred for using a credit card and delivery.

Workers' Compensation Records

NC Industrial Commission, Worker's Comp Records,   www.ic.nc.gov/   The N.C. Industrial Commission provides public access to half a dozen full-text searchable public databases, including the Insurance Coverage Search System at www.ic.nc.gov/database.html. The search at the "Livelink Database" allows citizens to access Full Commission, Deputy Commissioner, and state appellate court decisions about workers' compensation and tort cases.

Driver Records

Division of Motor Vehicles, Driver License Records,   www.ncdot.gov/dmv/driver/   There are two systems. A commercial system is offered for approved, ongoing requesters. Records are $8.00 each. A minimum $500 security deposit is required. Call 919-861-3062 for details. NC drivers or requesters who attest to a valid reason for the request per DPPA may obtain records at www.ncdot.gov/dmv/online/records/. Requesters must first apply for a PIN which is sent by email. Non-certified records may be viewed and printed. fees are $8.00 uncertified or $14.00 if certified. Each request requires the first and last name, driver's license or ID card number, the SSN (or ITIN or U.S. VISA), and the DOB. Certified records, if ordered, are not viewable but are mailed within three days.

Voter Registration, Lobbyists, Campaign Finance

State Board of Elections,   www.ncsbe.gov/ncsbe/   A search of voter registration data is available free at https://enr.ncsbe.gov/voter_search_public/. A DOB is needed for best results. One may also have results emailed. Also, the agency has an FTP site available for requesters. See ftp://www.sboe.state.nc.us. Search campaign finance and lobbyists at http://ncsbe.azurewebsites.net/Campaign-Finance/report-search.   *Other Options:* Most records are sold in CD format, FTP or sent via email. The maximum fee is $25.00, subject to change if more than 2 CDs used.. Request forms are available at the webpage. This is the most prompt access to records, other than in person.

GED Certificates

NC Community College System, GED Office,   www.nccommunitycolleges.edu/college-and-career-readiness/high-school-equivalency/high-school-equivalency-records   Third party requesters looking for verifications or transcript records from 2002 forward must register and order online at http://exchange.parchment.com/ged-receiver-registration-page. Parchment verifies that they are who they say they are so that they can place orders on behalf of students. Parchment contacts the third party and provides training on the site for ordering.

Occupational Licensing Boards

Accountant-CPA/Firm	http://nccpaboard.gov/welcome/search-the-database/
Anesthesiologist Assistant	wwwapps.ncmedboard.org/Clients/NCBOM/Public/LicenseeInformationSearch.aspx
Anesthetist Nurse	https://apps.ncbon.com/LicenseVerification/Search.aspx
Architect	www.ncbarch.org/architect-search/
Architect/Architectural Firm	www.ncbarch.org/architect-search/
Armored Car	www.ncdps.gov/About-DPS/Boards-Commissions/Private-Protective-Services-Board/Licensees
Athletic Trainer/Disciplinary Action	www.ncbate.org/search-athletic-trainers.html
Attorney	https://www.ncbar.gov/for-the-public/finding-a-lawyer/member-directory/
Attorney Disciplinary Actions	https://www.ncbar.gov/
Auctioneer Disciplinary Action	www.ncalb.org/discActions.cfm
Auctioneer/Auctioneer Appren/Company	www.ncalb.org/search.cfm
Bail Bond Runner	https://sbs-nc.naic.org/Lion-Web/jsp/sbsreports/AgentLookup.jsp
Bank	https://www.nccob.org/Online/brts/BanksAndTrusts.aspx
Bank Branch	https://www.nccob.org/Online/brts/BankBranchSearch.aspx
Barber Inspector/Instructor	https://ncbob.glsuite.us/GLSuiteWeb/Clients/NCBOB/Public/Verification/Search.aspx
Barber School	https://ncbob.glsuite.us/GLSuiteWeb/Clients/NCBOB/Public/Verification/Search.aspx
Beauty Shop/Salon	https://www.nccosmeticarts.com/userman/UserAccounts/Login.aspx
Bodywork Therapist	www.theconjuredsolution.com/aspsearch/ncmassx_search.asp
Building Inspector	https://sbs-nc.naic.org/Lion-Web/jsp/sbsreports/AgentLookup.jsp
Cemetery	http://nccemetery.org/north-carolina-cemeteries/
Charitable/Sponsor Organization	https://www.sosnc.gov/search/index/csl
Check Casher	https://www.nccob.org/Online/CCS/CompanyListing.aspx
Chiropractor	www.cetrackerlive.com/ncboce/UserList-Active.php
Clinical Nurse Specialist	https://apps.ncbon.com/LicenseVerification/Search.aspx
Clinical Pharmacist Practitioner	wwwapps.ncmedboard.org/Clients/NCBOM/Public/LicenseeInformationSearch.aspx
Clinical Social Worker	www.ncswboard.org/page/license-lookup
Consumer Financer	https://www.nccob.org/online/CFS/CFSCompanyListing.aspx
Contractor, General	www.nclbgc.org/lic_fr.html
Cosmetologist Instruct/Appren/Practit'r	https://www.nccosmeticarts.com/userman/UserAccounts/Login.aspx

Cosmetology Disciplinary Action	https://www.nccosmeticarts.com/userman/UserAccounts/Login.aspx
Counselor, Professional	www.ncblpc.org/Verify.php
Courier Service	www.ncdps.gov/About-DPS/Boards-Commissions/Private-Protective-Services-Board/Licensees
Crematory	www.ncbfs.org/dir_crematoriesdb.html
Dentist/Dental Hygienist	www.ncdentalboard.org/license_verification.htm
DME-Rx Device	www.ncbop.org/ncbop_verification.htm
Electrical Contractor/Inspector	https://lookup.ncbeec.org/Lookup/LicenseLookup.aspx
Electronic Countermeasures Profession	www.ncdps.gov/About-DPS/Boards-Commissions/Private-Protective-Services-Board/Licensees
Elevator Inspection Data	https://www.labor.communications.its.state.nc.us/elevPublic/scripts/e_pa_1a.cfm
Engineer/Land Surveyor/Firm	https://www.membersbase.com/ncbels/search
Esthetician Instruc/Appren/Practition'r	https://www.nccosmeticarts.com/userman/UserAccounts/Login.aspx
Fire Sprinkler Contractor/Inspection Contr/Maintenance Tech	http://onlineweb.nclicensing.org/Lookup/LicenseLookup.aspx
Firearms Trainer	www.ncdps.gov/About-DPS/Boards-Commissions/Private-Protective-Services-Board/Licensees
Forester	www.ncbrf.org/list.htm
Fund Raiser Consultant/Solicitor	https://www.sosnc.gov/search/index/csl
Funeral Director/Service/Chapel	www.ncbfs.org/dir_licenseedb.html
Funeral Education Studied	www.ncbfs.org/list.html
Funeral Home	www.ncbfs.org/dir_funeralhomedb.html
Funeral Trainee	www.ncbfs.org/dir_traineesdb.html
Geologist/Firm	https://www.ncblg.org/licensees/
Guard Dog Service	www.ncdps.gov/About-DPS/Boards-Commissions/Private-Protective-Services-Board/Licensees
Hearing Aid Dispenser/Fitter	www.nchalb.org/Data/licensees.php
Heating Contractor	http://onlineweb.nclicensing.org/Lookup/LicenseLookup.aspx
HMO	http://infoportal.ncdoi.net/cmp_lookup.jsp
Home Inspector	https://apps.ncdoi.net/f?p=135:126
Hospital	https://www2.ncdhhs.gov/dhsr/reports.htm
Insurance Agent	https://sbs-nc.naic.org/Lion-Web/jsp/sbsreports/AgentLookup.jsp
Insurance Company	https://sbs-nc.naic.org/Lion-Web/jsp/sbsreports/CompanySearchLookup.jsp
Insurer, Life/Health	https://sbs-nc.naic.org/Lion-Web/jsp/sbsreports/AgentLookup.jsp
Insurer, Property/Casualty	https://sbs-nc.naic.org/Lion-Web/jsp/sbsreports/AgentLookup.jsp
Landscape Architect/Firms	www.ncbola.org/
Lobbyist	https://www.sosnc.gov/lobbyists/directory.aspx
Manicurist Instruct/Appren/Practitioner	https://www.nccosmeticarts.com/userman/UserAccounts/Login.aspx
Manuf'd Housing Retailer/Mfg/Contr/Seller/Qualifier	www.ncdoi.com/OSFM/Manufactured_Building.aspx
Massage Therapist	www.theconjuredsolution.com/aspsearch/ncmassx_search.asp
Midwife	https://apps.ncbon.com/LicenseVerification/Search.aspx
Money Transmitter	https://www.nccob.org/Online/MTS/MTSCompanyListing.aspx
Nurse-LPN/Practitioner/Aide	https://apps.ncbon.com/LicenseVerification/Search.aspx
Nursing Home	https://www2.ncdhhs.gov/dhsr/reports.htm
Nursing Home Administrator	www.ncbenha.org/licensees.html
Occupational Therapist/Therapy Assist	www.ncbot.org/OTpages/license_verification.html
Optometrist	http://web1.ncoptometry.org/verify.aspx
Osteopathic Physician	wwwapps.ncmedboard.org/Clients/NCBOM/Public/LicenseeInformationSearch.aspx
Paralegal	www.nccertifiedparalegal.gov/paralegal-search/
Pesticide Applicator/Dealer/Consultant	www.ncagr.gov/aspzine/str-pest/pesticides/data/advsearch.asp
Pharmacist	www.ncbop.org/ncbop_verification.htm
Pharmacy/Physician Pharmacy/Technician	www.ncbop.org/ncbop_verification.htm
Physical Therapist/Assistant	https://www.ncptboard.org/OnlineServices/Secure/VerifyTherapist/VerifyTherapist.php
Physician Assistant	wwwapps.ncmedboard.org/Clients/NCBOM/Public/LicenseeInformationSearch.aspx
Plumber	http://onlineweb.nclicensing.org/Lookup/LicenseLookup.aspx
Podiatrist	www.ncbpe.org/content/search-podiatrist
Polygraph Examiner	www.ncdps.gov/About-DPS/Boards-Commissions/Private-Protective-Services-Board/Licensees
Private Investigator	www.ncdps.gov/About-DPS/Boards-Commissions/Private-Protective-Services-Board/Licensees
Psychological Associate	www.ncpsychologyboard.org/license-verification/
Psychological Stress Evaluator	www.ncdps.gov/About-DPS/Boards-Commissions/Private-Protective-Services-Board/Licensees

Psychologist..www.ncpsychologyboard.org/license-verification/
RAL..https://www.nccob.org/online/RALS/RALSCompanyListing.aspx
Real Estate Agent/Broker/Dealer ....www.members-base.com/ncrec/oecgi3.exe/O4W_LIC_SEARCH_NEW
Real Estate Firm...www.members-base.com/ncrec/oecgi3.exe/O4W_FIRM_SEARCH_NEW
Sanitarian...www.ncrehs.com/rsboard-old/rsweb/directory/directory.htm
Security Guard & Patrol/ Armed/Unarmed .....www.ncdps.gov/About-DPS/Boards-Commissions/Private-Protective-Services-Board/Licensees
Social Worker/Manager ....www.ncswboard.org/page/license-lookup
Soil Scientist ....http://ncblss.org/lss-directory.pdf
Speech Pathologist/Audiologist ....www.ncboeslpa.org/search_members.asp
Therapist, Marriage & Family ....www.nclmft.org/public_resources/verify_a_licensee/
Trade Name Directory ....www.ncbar.gov/gxweb/wp_searchtradenames.aspx
Trust Company ....https://www.nccob.org/Online/BRTS/TrustLicensees.aspx

State and Local Courts

About North Carolina Courts: All felony criminal cases, civil cases involving more than $10,000 and misdemeanor and infraction appeals from District Court are tried in the **Superior Court**.

District Courts handle civil, misdemeanors and infractions, juvenile and magistrate. Civil cases include divorce, custody, child support and cases involving less than $10,000 or small claims ($5,000 or less). A **Magistrate** is a judicial officer of the District Court and the Magistrate presides over Small Claims Court and evictions. The principal relief sought in Small Claims Court is money, the recovery of specific personal property, or summary ejectment (eviction).

Uncontested Probate is handled by County Clerks.

The web page for the Judiciary is www.nccourts.org.

Appellate Courts: The Supreme Court is the court of last resort. The Court of Appeals is the state's only intermediate appellate court. Opinions are available from the home page.

Online Court Access

All courts participate in the systems described below.

- The state AOC provides ongoing, high volume requesters and vendors with portions of electronic criminal and civil records on an ongoing basis pursuant to a licensing agreement. For a list of the participating vendors visit the web at http://www.nccourts.org/Citizens/GoToCourt/Documents/cbccompanies.pdf.

- There are several other limited North Carolina online services that are free. Search current civil and criminal court calendars at www1.aoc.state.nc.us/www/calendars.html. Search the District and Superior Court Query system for current criminal defendants at hwww1.aoc.state.nc.us/www/calendars/CriminalQuery.html. At this site there are also queries for Impaired Driving, Citations, and Current Civil and Criminal Calendars.

- Also, note an eFiling Pilot Program is operational in Chowan, Davidson, and Wake counties.

Note: No individual North Carolina courts offer online access beyond the systems mentioned above.

Recorders, Assessors, and Other Sites of Note

About North Carolina Recording Offices: 100 counties, 100 recording offices. The recording officer is the Register of Deeds but for tax liens the officer is the Clerk of Superior Court.

About Tax Liens: Federal tax liens on personal property of businesses are filed with the Secretary of State. Other federal and all state tax liens are filed with the county Clerk of Superior Court. Oddly, even tax liens on real property are also filed with the Clerk of Superior Court, not with the Register of Deeds.

Online Access

Nearly every county offers free access to recorded documents and to assessor property records. Some county web search sites are provided by private vendors, but overall presence of a primary vendor-sponsored system among North Carolina counties is somewhat limited.

Counties:

Alamance County *Recorded Documents, Birth, Death, Marriage Records* www.alamance-nc.com/rod/ Access the recorded document database free at www.alamancerod.org/.

Alexander County *Recorded Documents* www.alexandercountync.gov/rod/ Access recorder land records free at http://cotthosting.com/ncalexander/LandRecords/protected/v4/SrchName.aspx.
Property, Taxation Records Access parcel data free on the GIS/mapping site a http://alexandercountync.gov/departments/gis/gis-real-estate-maps/. Search property tax records at http://alexander.ustaxdata.com/. There is an advanced search also available from this page.

Alleghany County *Recorded Documents* www.alleghanycounty-nc.gov/index.php?option=com_content&view=article&id=79&Itemid=92 Access to the Register of Deeds database is free at http://24.172.15.58/Opening.asp. All Deed images are online back thru 1859 to current. Real property indexes available 1859 to present week.
Property, Taxation Records Search for property data on a GIS mapping site at http://arcgis.webgis.net/nc/Alleghany/.

Anson County *Recorded Documents* www.co.anson.nc.us/CountyServices/RegisterofDeeds.aspx Access to land records free at www.ansonncrod.org/. Have access to both full system and imaging system only. Deeds from 1749 to present only.
Property, Taxation Records Search the county Online Tax Inquiry System free at www.co.anson.nc.us/pubcgi/taxinq/. Tax collections search at www.co.anson.nc.us/pubcgi/colinq/. Also, access to GIS/mapping for free at http://atlas.co.anson.nc.us/pubgis/.

Ashe County *Recorded Documents* www.ashecountygov.com/departments/register-of-deeds Access to the register of deeds real estate data is free at www.ashencrod.org/Opening.asp. Vital records not available on this website. Full system index goes back to 1/1995, scanned indexes and images go back to 1799.
Property, Taxation Records Access to tax records for free at https://qpublic.schneidercorp.com/.

Avery County *Recorded Documents* www.averydeeds.com/ Search the recorders database free at http://search.averydeeds.com/.
Property, Taxation Records Access to property data is free on the GIS mapping site at http://arcgis.webgis.net/nc/avery/. To name search click Quick Search. Also, access to tax bill search for free at http://webtax.averycountync.gov/.

Beaufort County *Recorded Documents* www.co.beaufort.nc.us/departments/register-of-deeds Access to real estate, marriage, death and birth records for free at www.beaufortcountyrod.com/.
Property, Taxation Records Access to GIS/mapping free at www.co.beaufort.nc.us/tax-admin-downloads.

Bertie County *Recorded Documents* www.co.bertie.nc.us/departments/rod/rod.html Access real property data back to 1/1/1983 free at http://bertie-live.inttek.net/ after registration.
Property, Taxation Records Access property records through GIS/mapping system free at www.co.bertie.nc.us/departments/tm/GISD.html.

Bladen County *Recorded Documents* www.bladenncrod.org/ Access to register of deeds site at www.bladenncrod.org/opening.asp; search comprehensive index or direct images. This System allows access to deed and plat book indexing information by searching on the following fields: grantor and/or grantee name, instrument number, or book and page.
Property, Taxation Records Search the GIS-mapping site for property info free at http://bladen2.connectgis.com/Map.aspx. Search property tax and ownership at http://bladen.ustaxdata.com/.

Brunswick County *Recorded Documents* http://rod.brunsco.net Access to the recorder database is free at http://rod.brunsco.net. Free registration, logon and password are required. Records are updated daily.
Property, Taxation Records Search the tax administration data for real property or vehicle for free at http://tax.brunsco.net/itsnet/.

Buncombe County *Recorded Documents* www.buncombecounty.org/governing/depts/RegisterDeeds/ Access to county Register of Deeds records is free at http://registerofdeeds.buncombecounty.org/External/LandRecords/protected/v4/SrchName.aspx. Includes marriages, deaths, deeds.
Property, Taxation Records County assessor tax records are free at www.buncombetax.org/Default.aspx. Also, GIS property search available at www.buncombecounty.org/Governing/Depts/GIS/Disclaimer.aspx. Also, search tax property sales free at www.buncombecounty.org/Governing/Depts/Tax/LegalDivision_Owned.aspx.

Burke County *Recorded Documents* www.burkenc.org/departments/register-of-deeds Access to public records free at https://rod.burkenc.org/.
Property, Taxation Records Access to property data is free on the GIS mapping site at http://gis.burkenc.org/. Also, access to a tax search/view/pay page for free at http://burkenctax.com/TaxSearch.

Cabarrus County   *Recorded Documents*   www.cabarrusncrod.org/Opening.asp   Access to the recorder records is free at www.cabarrusncrod.org/Opening.asp by two methods: full system or image-only system. Land records and images go back to 1792.
Property, Taxation Records   Search land records of all kinds including GIS free on the ClaRIS system at https://www.cabarruscounty.us/government/departments/information-technology/Pages/GIS.aspx.

Caldwell County   *Recorded Documents*   https://caldwellrod.org/   Access register of deeds recording data with images back to 19th Century free (as a guest user) at http://72.15.246.181/CaldwellNC/.
Property, Taxation Records   Access to GIS/mapping free at http://gis.caldwellcountync.org/maps/default.htm. Also, access to the real estate/tax bill and sales search database for free at http://tax.caldwellcountync.org/.

Camden County   *Recorded Dcouments Records*   www.camdencountync.gov/departments/register-of-deeds   Access to land conveyances for free at http://72.15.246.183/CamdenNC/.
Property, Taxation Records   Search property records on the GIS/mapping system free at http://maps2.roktech.net/CamdenCountyNC_GoMaps/index.html#.

Carteret County   *Recorded Documents*   http://nc-carteretcounty.civicplus.com/162/Register-of-Deeds   Access to Register of Deeds database is free at http://deeds.carteretcounty.com/.
Property, Taxation Records   Search tax parcel cards free at http://web3.mobile311.com/Carteretsearch/default.aspx. Also, free tax status search at http://carteretcountytax.com/taxes. Also, access to GIS/mapping for free at http://carteret2.connectgis.com/Disclaimer.aspx.

Caswell County   *Recorded Documents*   www.caswellcountync.gov/pView.aspx?id=8781&catid=600   Search recorded deeds at www.caswellrod.net/ and click Search Online. Images are shown.
Property, Taxation Records   Access to property data for a fee on the GIS mapping site at http://arcgis.webgis.net/nc/Caswell/.

Catawba County   *Recorded Documents*   www.catawbacountync.gov/depts/regdeed/default.asp   Also, search Register of Deeds records free at www.catawbarod.org/Opening.asp. Land index goes back to 1955; images to 9/30/1959.
Property, Taxation Records   Search property tax bill data free at www.catawbacountync.gov/Tax/billsearch.asp.

Chatham County   *Real Estate, Deed, Mortgage, UCC Records*   www.chathamnc.org/Index.aspx?page=905   Access land records free at www.chathamncrod.org/Opening.asp. Land Record Index Data back to 1771; UCC data goes back to 2008.
Property, Taxation Records   Access property data and tax records free at http://ustaxdata.com/nc/chatham/Search.cfm.

Cherokee County   *Real Estate, Deed, Lien Records*   www.cherokeecounty-nc.gov/index.aspx?page=137   Access to land records and imaging free at www.cherokeencrod.org/. Images go back to 07/1999, index back to 1993.
Property, Taxation Records   Access to Tax bill/sales records for free at www.cherokeecounty-nc.gov/ITSnet/.

Chowan County   *Recorded Documents*   www.chowancounty-nc.gov/index.asp   Access to real estate recording documents for free at http://72.15.246.183/ChowanNC/.
Property, Taxation Records   Access property tax records, sales and access to tax bill searches for free at http://208.27.112.94/itsnet/. Search property data on the GIS-mapping site free at http://chowancountygis.com/nc/chowan/.

Clay County   *Real Estate, Deed Records*   http://clayconc.com/county-offices/the-register-of-deeds/   Access to property and deeds indexes and images is via a private company at www.titlesearcher.com/. Fee/registration required. Deeds go back to 1/1995; indices back to 1/1/94; images to 8/22/1930. Also, access to deeds for free at http://search.claydeeds.com/.

Cleveland County   *Recorded Documents*   www.clevelandcounty.com/ccmain/   Access to selected indexes for free at https://www.countygovernmentrecords.com/. Grantor/Grantee indexes searches from 1/3/1995 to current. Document images for documents, plats and older large index book pages (prior to 1995) are available by entering the specific book and page number, if known.
Property, Taxation Records   Access property records free on the GIS-mapping site at http://quicksearch.webgis.net/search.php?site=nc_cleveland_co. Access to property data is free on the GIS mapping site at http://arcgis.webgis.net/nc/Cleveland/.

Columbus County   *Recorded Documents*   http://columbusdeeds.com/   Access to the Recorder's database is free at http://search.columbusdeeds.com/.   *Property, Taxation Records*   Access property tax data free at http://columbusco.org/GIS.aspx.

Craven County   *Recorded Documents*   www.cravencountync.gov/departments/reg.cfm   Search register of deeds free at www.cravencountync.gov/departments/reg/regwwwdisclaimer.cfm. Real estate 1995-present; Corporations 2002-3/2007; Births/Deaths 1914-2007; UCCs 1999-2001; older real estate 1984-1994; marriages 1964-present.
Property, Taxation Records   Access to assessor and property data is free at www.cravencountync.gov/departments/tax.cfm.

Cumberland County   *Recorded Documents*   www.ccrod.org   Search two systems free at www.ccrodinternet.org/Opening.asp. The land records index data dated from 1754 t0 1976 (scanned index books) and images from Book 1 (1754) to Book 2083 (2/68).
Property, Taxation Records   Assessor real estate search is free at http://mainfr.co.cumberland.nc.us/. Also, search property data free on the GIS mapping site at http://cumberlandgis.maps.arcgis.com/apps/OnePane/basicviewer/index.html?appid=c28216444cbb4a98aa10be7aee9e735d.

Currituck County *Recorded Documents* www.co.currituck.nc.us/Register-of-Deeds.cfm Access to land recorded documents is free at http://72.15.246.181/currituckNC/.
Property, Taxation Records Search property, sales, assessor data and more free at www.co.currituck.nc.us/Real-Estate-Searches.cfm. Also, name search for parcel ownership data free on the GIS-mapping site at www.co.currituck.nc.us/Interactive-Online-MappingDup2.cfm.

Dare County *Recorded Documents* www.darenc.com/deeds/ Recording office records are free at http://72.15.246.181/DareNC/.
Property, Taxation Records County assessor records free at www.darenc.com/tax/srchrcds.asp. Search property data on the GIS/mapping site free at www.darenc.com/gis/taxmaps/. Also, access to delinquent tax reports for free at www.darenc.com/tax/delinquentrpt.asp.

Davidson County *Recorded Documents* www.co.davidson.nc.us/ROD/ Access recorders database free at http://davidsoncorod.org/.
Property, Taxation Records Records on the county Tax Dept database are free at www.co.davidson.nc.us/taxnet/. Search for property info on the GIS mapping site for free at http://webgis.co.davidson.nc.us/.

Davie County *Recorded Documents* www.daviecountync.gov/index.aspx?nid=98 Access Register of Deeds site at www.daviecrod.org/. Land records go back to 1993. Accessed in three different ways - Full System, Imaging System Only, or Scanned Index Books.
Property, Taxation Records Access to real estate/tax searches for free at http://maps.daviecountync.gov/itsnet/basicsearch.aspx.

Duplin County *Recorded Documents* www.duplincountync.com/governmentOffices/registerOfDeeds.html Access to the Register's multiple databases is free at www.duplinrod.com/.
Property, Taxation Records Access assessment data on real estate and personal property free at http://duplintax.duplincounty.org/. Also, access to GIS/mapping for free at http://gis.duplincountync.com/.

Durham County *Recorded Documents* http://dconc.gov/government/departments-f-z/register-of-deeds Access the Register of Deeds database free at http://rodweb.co.durham.nc.us/.
Property, Taxation Records Search property records and tax bills free at www.ustaxdata.com/nc/durham/durhamtaxsearch.cfm. Search GIS mapping site free at http://gisweb.durhamnc.gov/sp/index.cfm.

Edgecombe County *Recorded Documents* www.edgecombecountync.gov/rod/rod.aspx Access the recorder's database free at http://cotthosting.com/ncedgecombeexternal/User/Login.aspx. Includes real property docs from 9/1/73 to present.

Forsyth County *Recorded Documents* www.co.forsyth.nc.us/ROD/ Access online record lookup for free at www.forsythdeeds.com/disclaimer.php. Also, access to property and deeds indexes and images is via a private company at www.titlesearcher.com/. Fee/registration required; monthly and per day access available. Deeds and indices go back to 1849.
Property, Taxation Records Access assessor records on Geo-Data free- www.co.forsyth.nc.us/Tax/geodata.aspx. Click 'Launch Geo-Data Explorer.' Search tax bills free at www.co.forsyth.nc.us/Tax/. Tax Admin tax bill svc free at www.co.forsyth.nc.us/Tax/taxbill.aspx Also, assessment data for City of Winston-Salem available free at https://www6.cityofws.org/assessmentliens/. Also, access to GIS/mapping for free at http://maps.co.forsyth.nc.us/forsythsales/.

Franklin County *Recorded Documents* www.franklincountync.us/services/register-of-deeds Access to recording records index free at http://deeds.co.franklin.nc.us/External/User/Login.aspx. For detailed records, must subscribe.
Property, Taxation Records Access to tax records free at www.franklincountytax.us/pt/forms/htmlframe.aspx?mode=content/home.htm. Also, access to GIS/mapping free at http://maps2.roktech.net/Franklin_GM4/.

Gaston County *Recorded Documents* www.gastongov.com/departments/register-of-deeds Access to recorded documents is free at https://deeds.co.gaston.nc.us/external/LandRecords/protected/v4/SrchName.aspx. Indexes prior to 1960 are now online.
Property, Taxation Records Access to GIS/mapping free at http://gis.gastongov.com/.

Gates County *Recorded Documents* www.gatesrod.net/ Access to county records for a fee at https://www.countygovernmentrecords.com/. Registration is free. Also, access to recorded documents free at www.gatesrod.net/.
Property, Taxation Records Access to GIS/mapping free at http://gatescountygis.com/nc/gates/.

Graham County *Recorded Documents* www.grahamcounty.org/grahamcounty_departments_registrar.html Access the consolidated real property database back to 1/1995 free at http://cotthosting.com/ncgraham/LandRecords/protected/v4/SrchName.aspx. Also search pre-1995 real estate 7/1/1978 to 12/31/1994. *Property, Taxation Records* Access to real estate search for free at http://taxsearch.grahamcounty.org/.

Granville County *Recorded Documents* www.granvillenc.govoffice2.com/index.asp Access recorders index free at www.granvillecountydeeds.org/External/LandRecords/protected/v4/SrchName.aspx.
Property, Taxation Records Access to GIS/mapping records free at www.granvillegis.org/.

Greene County *Property, Taxation Records* Access to GIS/mapping data for free at http://greenecountygis.com/nc/greene/.

Guilford County *Recorded Documents* www.myguilford.com/rod/ Access to register of deeds online records system for free at http://rdlxweb.co.guilford.nc.us/guilfordNameSearch.php.
Property, Taxation Records Access name search tax data free at http://taxweb.co.guilford.nc.us/CamaPublicAccess/.

Halifax County   *Recorded Documents*   www.halifaxnc.com/index.php?option=com_content&view=article&id=68&Itemid=66   Access to the Register's land records is at http://204.211.93.146/external/User/Login.aspx.
Property, Taxation Records   Search assessor property tax records free at http://qpublic.net/nc/halifax/. Also, access to GIS/mapping for free at www.halifaxnc.com/index.php?option=com_content&view=article&id=48&Itemid=48.

Harnett County   *Recorded Documents*   http://rod.harnett.org   County real estate and property tax data is free at http://rod.harnett.org. Search Births, Deaths, Marriages, UCCs and official public records. Also, access to real estate records for free at http://cama.harnett.org/BasicSearch.aspx.
Property, Taxation Records   Access property tax records free at http://tax.harnett.org/PublicWebAccess/.

Haywood County   *Recorded Documents*   www.haywoodnc.net/   Records on the Register of Deeds database are free at http://search.haywooddeeds.com/. Real estate grantor/grantee index from 01/01/86 to present. Grantor/Grantee index books from 1808-1985 available online. All deed books from 1808 forward are now available online.
Property, Taxation Records   Access property tax records and GIS mapping free at http://public.haywoodnc.net/. Also, search for property data on the GIS-mapping site for free at http://maps.haywoodnc.net/.

Henderson County   *Recorded Documents*   www.hendersoncountync.org/depts/deeds.html   Access to recorded documents free at http://72.15.246.181/HendersonNC/. Index records are from 1979 to present (images forthcoming).
Property, Taxation Records   Access the GIS mapping system free at http://henderson.roktech.net/ParcelMap/#. Also, access to tax bill/payment history data for free at http://taxdata.hendersoncountync.org/PublicWebAccess/.

Hertford County   *Recorded Documents*   www.hertfordrod.net/   Access recorded land data free at www.hertfordrod.net/.
Property, Taxation Records   Access to GIS data at http://maps2.roktech.net/hertfordags/#.

Hoke County   *Recorded Documents*   www.hokencrod.org   Access recorder data for free at www.hokencrod.org/Opening.asp. Land records index goes back to 7/1992; images back to 12/1994.
Property, Taxation Records   Access property data on GIS mapping site free at www.hokecounty.net/index.aspx?nid=211.

Hyde County   *Recorded Documents*   www.hyderod.net/   Access to grantor/grantee records for free at http://hyderod.net/.
Property, Taxation Records   Access to GIS/mapping free at http://hydecountygis.com/nc/hyde/.

Iredell County   *Recorded Documents*   https://www.co.iredell.nc.us/533/Register-of-Deeds   Access recorder property records for free at https://cotthosting.com/NCIredellExternal/User/Login.aspx. For detailed records, must subscribe.
Property, Taxation Records   Access to GIS/mapping resources for free at https://www.co.iredell.nc.us/554/GIS-Mapping-Department

Jackson County   *Recorded Dcouments Records*   www.jacksonnc.org/register-of-deeds.html   Access to indexed records for free at http://deeds.jacksonnc.org/External/LandRecords/protected/v4/SrchName.aspx.
Property, Taxation Records   Search assessor and property data free at http://maps.jacksonnc.org/gomapsags/#. Also, access to tax information for free at https://jacksonnctax.com/taxes.html#/.

Johnston County   *Recorded Documents*   www.johnstonnc.com/rod   Access to Register's indexes is free at http://erec.johnstonnc.com/recorder/web/. Land records go back to 1789; UCCs back to 7/2001.
Property, Taxation Records   Access property records free at https://www.bttaxpayerportal.com/itspublicjo.

Jones County   *Recorded Documents*   www.jonescountync.gov/index.asp?SEC=E1C244F1-2CC1-4306-9304-E7B2A3615402&Type=B_BASIC   Access to records free at http://cotthosting.com/ncjones/LandRecords/protected/v4/SrchName.aspx.
Property, Taxation Records   Access to GIS/mapping free at http://jonescountygis.com/nc/jones/.

Lee County   *Recorded Documents*   www.leecountync.gov/Departments/RegisterofDeeds.aspx   Access Register of Deeds index and images free at www.leencrod.org/Opening.asp. Land record index goes back to 1985; images to 1908-1984, and all plat images.
Property, Taxation Records   Access sales data and maps free at www.leecountync.gov/Departments/GISStrategicServices/tabid/124/Default.aspx.

Lenoir County   *Recorded Documents*   www.co.lenoir.nc.us/registerofdeeds.html   Access land records index and images back to 1976 at http://cottweb.co.lenoir.nc.us/external/User/Login.aspx.
Property, Taxation Records   Access property taxes free at www.lenoircountytaxes.com/.

Lincoln County   *Recorded Documents*   www.lincolncounty.org/index.aspx?nid=133   Access tax, property, and recording data for free at www.lincolncounty.org/index.aspx?NID=509. Grantor/Grantee indices go back to 1993. Images go back to Book 186. Search either of the 2 databases There is also a comparable properties search utility.
Property, Taxation Records   Access to the county GIS Land System is free at http://207.4.172.206/website/lcproperty2/viewer.htm.

Macon County   *Recorded Documents*   www.maconncdeeds.com/   Access deed images back to book 6 free and selected other recording types free at http://search.maconncdeeds.com/.
Property, Taxation Records   Access property tax records and land records for free at https://www.maconnctax.com/taxes.html#/. Also, access to GIS/mapping free at http://gis2.maconnc.org/lightmap/.

Madison County *Recorded Documents* http://madisonrod.net/ Access real property records free at http://madisonrod.net/.
Property, Taxation Records Access to property data for free at www.madcotax.com/.

Martin County *Recorded Documents* www.martincountyncgov.com/deeds Access to database free at www.martinrod.org/. Three ways to access-Full System, Imaging System Only & Scanned Index Books.
Property, Taxation Records Access to GIS/mapping free at www.martincountygis.com/. Also, access to the tax pay and search site for free at www.martincountyncgov.com/taxSearch.

McDowell County *Recorded Documents* www.mcdowelldeeds.com/ Access to basic property records for free at https://www.bttaxpayerportal.com/ITSPublicMD/.
Property, Taxation Records Access GIS property data free at http://mcweb1.co.morris.nj.us/MCTaxBoard/SearchTaxMaps.aspx. Also, access to property tax data for free at http://mcweb1.co.morris.nj.us/MCTaxBoard/SearchTaxRecords.aspx.

Mecklenburg County *Recorded Documents* http://charmeck.org/mecklenburg/county/ROD/Pages/default.aspx Access to records free at http://meckrod.manatron.com/. Also, access real estate from 1763 to 2/1990 for free at http://meckrodindex.com/oldindexsearch.php.
Property, Taxation Records Access to the assessors records for real estate, personal property, and tax bills are free at http://meckcama.co.mecklenburg.nc.us/relookup/. Search property ownership and data free on the GIS site at http://polaris3g.mecklenburgcountync.gov/.

Mitchell County *Recorded Documents* www.mitchellcounty.org/departments/registerofdeeds.html Access to county records free at http://search.mitchelldeeds.com/. Real estate books 62, 65 and 67-80 are not available online.
Property, Taxation Records Access to the tax roll for free at http://mitchell.webtaxpay.com/.

Montgomery County *Recorded Documents* www.montgomeryrod.net/ Access is free at www.montgomeryrod.net/.
Property, Taxation Records Search property records free on the GIS mapping site at https://www.webgis.net/nc/Montgomery/.

Moore County *Recorded Documents* https://www.moorecountync.gov/register-of-deeds Find a menu of search choices for recordings, land records at https://rod.moorecountync.gov/. No images are available online of birth & death records.
Property, Taxation Records Access property and tax data free at http://icare.moorecountync.gov/careprd/Search/Disclaimer.aspx?FromUrl=../search/commonsearch.aspx?mode=owner.

Nash County *Recorded Documents* www.co.nash.nc.us/index.aspx?nid=243 Search real estate and UCCs free back to 1970 free at www.deeds.co.nash.nc.us/eSearch/LandRecords/protected/v4/SrchName.aspx.
Property, Taxation Records Access to GIS/mapping free at http://gis.co.nash.nc.us/connectgis/nash/.

New Hanover County *Recorded Documents* http://registerofdeeds.nhcgov.com/ Access to the Register of Deeds database is free at http://registerofdeeds.nhcgov.com/services/records-search/.
Property, Taxation Records Access to tax records and tax bills free at http://tax.nhcgov.com/services/real-estate/. Also, access property data on the GIS-mappings site at http://maps.nhcgov.com/find-download-data/.

Northampton County *Property, Taxation Records* Access to GIS/mapping free at http://gis.northamptonnc.com/.

Onslow County *Recorded Documents, Birth, Death, Marriage Records* www.onslowcountync.gov/Register/ Access recorder office index data free at https://deeds.onslowcountync.gov/External/LandRecords/protected/v4/SrchName.aspx. Real estate records from 1734 to present; births 1/1930-8/2015; deaths through 12/2015, marriages from 1/93 to current (do not change the 'Good Through' date until the license has expired); will find other documents within these indexes in the system, but there is a gap, so they cannot list these dates.
Property, Taxation Records Access to property data is free at http://maps2.roktech.net/onslow/#. Also, access to property tax search, view and pay websiit at https://onslowco.munisselfservice.com/citizens/RealEstate/Default.aspx?mode=new.

Orange County *Recorded Documents* www.orangecountync.gov/departments/register_of_deeds/index.php Access to records database free at http://roam.orangecountync.gov/orangeweb/search.do.
Property, Taxation Records Access to property records on the GIS mapping site is free at http://server2.co.orange.nc.us/OrangeNCGIS/default.aspx.

Pamlico County *Recorded Documents* www.pamlicocounty.org/register-of-deeds.aspx Access to county records for a fee at https://www.countygovernmentrecords.com/. Must register. Also, access to register of deeds records free at http://cotthosting.com/ncpamlicoexternal/LandRecords/protected/v4/SrchName.aspx. Index books are from 1975 - 5/311988.
Property, Taxation Records Search the GIS-mapping site for property data free at www.pamlicocountygis.com/.

Pasquotank County *Recorded Documents* www.pasquotankrod.net/ Access to database free at www.pasquotankrod.net/.
Property, Taxation Records Search assessor database at www.co.pasquotank.nc.us/GIS/taxsearch.cfm. Search Sales histories free at www.co.pasquotank.nc.us/GIS/salessearch.cfm.

Pender County *Recorded Documents* www.pendercountync.gov/Government/Departments/RegisterofDeeds.aspx Access to online records for free at http://72.15.246.183/pendernc/.
Property, Taxation Records Property records are available for free at www.pendercountync.gov/OnlineServices/OnLineTaxInformation.aspx.

Perquimans County   *Recorded Documents* www.perquimansrod.us/   Access to county records for free at www.perquimansrod.us/.
Property, Taxation   Access assessor, tax, property card and GIS data free at www.co.perquimans.nc.us/property-cards-and-gistax-maps.html.

Person County   *Recorded Documents* www.personrod.net   Access to county real estate records is free at www.personrod.net/.

Pitt County   *Recorded Documents* www.pittcountync.gov/249/Register-of-Deeds   Access recorder land data for free at
http://regdeeds.pittcountync.gov/External/User/Login.aspx?ReturnUrl=%2fExternal%2fLandRecords%2fprotected%2fSrchQuickName.aspx.
Property, Taxation Records   Online access to property records is available at http://gis2.pittcountync.gov/opis/. Also, view overdue tax accounts at
www.pittcountync.gov/336/Tax-Foreclosures-for-Sale.

Polk County   *Recorded Documents* www.polknc.org/registrar_of_deeds.php#.UqHvoCdPDVp   Access to county records free at
http://cotthosting.com/ncpolkexternal/LandRecords/protected/v4/SrchName.aspx.
Property, Taxation Records   Access to GIS/mapping free at https://polknc.maps.arcgis.com/home/index.html.

Randolph County   *Recorded Documents* www.randrod.com/   Real Estate records and plats for free at
www.randrod.com/realestaterecords.html.
Property, Taxation Records   Access the county GIS database free at www.co.randolph.nc.us/gis.htm. Access property owners/property data, liens,
and foreclosure lists free at www.co.randolph.nc.us/tax/default.htm.

Richmond County   *Recorded Documents* www.richmondrod.net/   Access Register of Deeds land records free at www.richmondrod.net/.

Robeson County   *Recorded Documents* http://rod.co.robeson.nc.us   Access to recorder data is free at http://robeson.bislandrecords.com/.
Also, access to property and deeds indexes and images is via a private company at www.titlesearcher.com/. Fee/registration required. Deeds and images go
back to 1787; Indices back to 1787.
Property, Taxation Records   Access assessor property records free at www.ustaxdata.com/nc/robeson/robesonsearch.cfm.

Rockingham County   *Recorded Documents* www.registerofdeeds.info/   Access to Register of Deeds database is free at
http://72.15.246.181/RockinghamNC/. Land indexes 1996 to present.
Property, Taxation Records   Access to Tax Admin. property data (1996 forward) also tax bills are free at
www.ustaxdata.com/nc/rockingham/RockinghamSearch.cfm. Also, search property data free at the GIS/mapping site at
http://arcgis.webgis.net/nc/Rockingham/.

Rowan County   *Recorded Documents* www.rowancountync.gov/GOVERNMENT/Departments/RegisterOfDeeds.aspx   Access to the
Register of Deeds land records database after registration at http://rod.rowancountync.gov/external/User/Login.aspx.
Property, Taxation Records   Access to the county GIS mapping site is free at
www.rowancountync.gov/GOVERNMENT/Departments/PlanningDevelopment/GIS.aspx. Also, there is a tax inquiry quick search at
www.co.rowan.nc.us/taxinq/name/default.asp. More tax and property data available http://rowan.ustaxdata.com/.

Rutherford County   *Recorded Documents, Birth, Death, Marriage Records* http://rutherfordcountync.gov/registerofdeeds   Access
property data free at http://208.90.175.25/External/LandRecords/protected/v4/SrchName.aspx. RE goes back to 1974; births 1991 to 2006; Deaths and
marriages back to 1994/1995.
Property, Taxation Records   Access to GIS/mapping free at http://rutherfordcounty.connectgis.com/Disclaimer.aspx.

Sampson County   *Recorded Documents* www.sampsonnc.com/departments/register_of_deeds/index.php   Access to county Register of
Deeds land data is free at www.sampsonrod.org/Opening.asp. Index goes back to inception of county.

Scotland County   *Recorded Documents* www.scotlandcounty.org/register-of-deeds-1.aspx   Access ROD real estate records and also
financing statements from 1999 to 2/2004 free at http://rod.scotlandcounty.org/External/LandRecords/protected/v4/SrchName.aspx.
Property, Taxation Records   Access to online taxes for free to go www.scotlandcountytaxes.com/taxSearch.

Stanly County   *Recorded Documents* www.stanlyrod.net/   Access the Register of Deeds index back to 1841 at www.stanlyrod.net/.
Property, Taxation Records   Access property data on the GIS search free at www.stanlygis.net/.

Stokes County   *Recorded Documents* www.co.stokes.nc.us/deeds/   Access to the Register of Deeds Remote Access site is free at
www.stokescorod.org/Opening.asp. Land records go back to 1787, images to 1787; UCCs back to 1994.
Property, Taxation Records   Access to property info on the GIS mapping site is free at http://maps2.roktech.net/StokesGoMaps4/.

Surry County   *Recorded Documents* www.co.surry.nc.us/departments/(k_through_z)/register_of_deeds/index.php   Access recording index
free at http://rod.surryinfo.net/surryncnwpub/application.asp. Real property index goes back to 1/1980; financing statements 1989-6/30/2001; index to
plats are from 1889 to present. Must purchase a subscription to see images. Annual fee of $120.00 provides unlimited copying and viewing of Real Estate
index data and images.
Property, Taxation Records   A free tax status search on property and vehicles is found at https://www.surrytax.com/taxes.html#/. Also, Access to
GIS/mapping free at http://gis.surryinfo.net/maps/. Also, access to the foreclosure properties list for free at
www.co.surry.nc.us/departments/%28k_through_z%29/tax/foreclosure_properties_list.php.

Swain County   *Recorded Documents*   www.swaincorod.org/   Access to recorder land data is free at www.swaincorod.org/. There is a full system and an image only system. Land Record Indexing data goes back to 1/1995; images back to 8/1979.
Property, Taxation Records   Search "tax cards" at http://216.109.220.17/itspublicsw.

Transylvania County   *Recorded Documents*   www.transylvaniacounty.org/   Access real estate records for free at http://search.transylvaniadeeds.com/. Images are viewable back to 1/3/1973; deeds and indices back to 1/3/1973.
Property, Taxation Records   Access full or partial property data free on the GIS site at http://arcgis.webgis.net/nc/Transylvania/.

Tyrrell County   *Recorded Documents*   www.tyrrellrod.net/   Access to county records for free at www.tyrrellrod.net/.
Property, Taxation Records   Access to GIS/mapping for free at http://tyrrellcountygis.com/nc/tyrrell/.

Union County   *Recorded Documents*   www.co.union.nc.us/Government/RegisterofDeeds.aspx   Access to recorder land records is free at www.unionconrod.org/Opening.asp; index and images go back to 6/21/1993.
Property, Taxation Records   Access to records for free at www.co.union.nc.us/Government/ServiceAreas/TaxAdministration/RealPropertySearch.aspx.

Vance County   *Recorded Documents*   www.vancecounty.org/departments/register-of-deeds/   Access to Register records free at http://vancencrod.org/. *Property, Taxation Records*   Access to real estate property search for free at http://vance.ustaxdata.com/.

Wake County   *Recorded Documents*   www.wakegov.com/rod/Pages/default.aspx   Access Register of Deeds database free at http://services.wakegov.com/BOOKSweb/GenExtSearch.aspx. Records go back to 1785.
Property, Taxation Records   Free real estate property and tax bill search is at http://services.wakegov.com/realestate/search.asp. Also, access to property tax information for free at https://services.wakegov.com/ptax/main/billing/.

Warren County   *Recorded Documents*   www.warrenrod.org/   Access to remote access site free at www.warrenrod.org/opening.asp.
Property, Taxation Records   Access to GIS/mapping data is free at http://maps2.roktech.net/warren/#.

Washington County   *Recorded Documents*   www.washingtonrod.net/   Access to county records for free at www.washingtonrod.net/.
Property, Taxation Records   Search assessor property and building record cards free at http://taxweb.washconc.org/.

Watauga County   *Recorded Documents*   www.wataugacounty.org/App_Pages/Dept/Deeds/home.aspx   Access to register of deeds database is free at http://72.15.246.181/watauganc/.
Property, Taxation Records   Access to county tax search data is free at http://tax.watgov.org/WataugaNC/Search/Disclaimer.aspx.

Wayne County   *Recorded Documents, Marriage, Death Records*   www.waynegov.com/347/Register-of-Deeds   Access to the registers CRP, financing statement, and real estate databases is free at http://rod.waynegov.com/Resolution/LandRecords/protected/v4/SrchName.aspx. Real Estate includes records from 1969-1994. Beginning 1995 all real estate records are indexed under CRP. Birth and Death records online go back to 1995; marriages back to 1997. Plats are online beginning 1977.
Property, Taxation Records   Access property records free at from vendor at http://realestate.waynegov.com/ITSNet/. GIS mapping is at www.waynegov.com/232/Geographic-Information-Systems-GIS. Also, access to property tax information for free at http://152.34.232.218/publicwebaccess/.

Wilkes County   *Property, Taxation Records*   Free access to property data of the GIS-mapping site at http://maps2.roktech.net/wilkesgomaps4/. Also, free access to the real estate property taxes database found at https://tax.wilkescounty.net/MSS/citizens/RealEstate/Default.aspx?mode=new.

Wilson County   *Recorded Documents*   www.wilson-co.com/167/Register-of-Deeds   Access the Register of Deeds search site for free at http://rod.wilson-co.com/External/LandRecords/protected/v4/SrchName.aspx.
Property, Taxation Records   Access to the property tax database are free at www.wilson-co.com/229/Search-RecordsView-BillsPay-Taxes. Includes Real Property records and Tax Bills.

Yadkin County   *Recorded Documents*   www.yadkincountync.gov/index.aspx?nid=83   Access recorder's land records free at www.yadkincorod.org/. Two searches are offered. A Full System (index and image) or Image Only. For the Full Search, search by grantor and/or grantee name, instrument number, or book and page. Print all available images by clicking on the 'image' icon next to the indexing search results. The Image Only system is searchable by the appropriate book and page numbers - this is not a name search.
Property, Taxation Records   Search property tax date free at www.ustaxdata.com/nc/yadkin/.

Yancey County   *Recorded Documents, Real Estate, Grantor/Grantee, Deed, Lien Records*
http://yanceycountync.gov/departments/register-of-deeds   Access to index for free at www.yanceyrod.com/NorthCarolinaRecorder/web/. Users must first register.
Property, Taxation Records   Access to the Assessor's database free at http://yancey.univers-clt.com/.

North Dakota

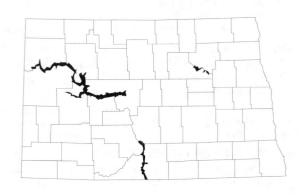

Capital: Bismarck
           Burleigh County

Time Zone: The southwestern area of North Dakota
  (west and south of the Missouri River) is in Mountain
  Time Zone. The remainder of the state is in
  the Central Time Zone.

Population: 756,927

# of Counties: 53

Useful State Links

Website: **www.nd.gov/**

Governor: **www.governor.state.nd.us**

Attorney General: **https://www.ag.nd.gov**

State Archives: **http://history.nd.gov/archives/**

State Statutes and Codes: **www.legis.nd.gov/general-information/north-dakota-century-code**

Legislative Bill Search: **www.legis.nd.gov/**

Unclaimed Funds: **https://land.nd.gov/UnclaimedProperty/**

State Public Record Agencies

Sexual Offender Registry

Bureau of Criminal Investigation, SOR Unit,   https://www.ag.nd.gov/BCI/BCI.htm   See www.sexoffender.nd.gov/ for list of all offenders. ND Native American offenders living on reservations are listed on Tribal websites. See http://mhanation.nsopw.gov for Mandan, Hidatsa, and Arikara Tribes. See http://swo.nsopw.gov for Sisseton, Wahpeton, and Oyate Tribes. See http://spiritlake.nsopw.gov for Spirit Lake Nation. See http://srst.nsopw.gov for Standing Rock Sioux, and see http://tmbci.nsopw.gov for Turtle Band of Chippewa.

Incarceration Records

Department of Corrections and Rehabilitation, Records Clerk,   www.nd.gov/docr/   A free lookup service of current inmates is at www.nd.gov/docr/search/. Search by last name, index screen shows full name and DOB. Results screen gives picture, estimated release date, and facility.

Corporation, LLC, LP, LLP, Trademarks/Servicemarks, Fictitious/Assumed Name

Secretary of State, Business Information/Registration,   http://sos.nd.gov/business/business-services   The Secretary of State's registered business database may be viewed at https://apps.nd.gov/sc/busnsrch/busnSearch.htm for no charge. Documents are not available online. Records include corporations, limited liability companies, limited partnerships, limited liability partnerships, limited liability limited partnerships, partnership fictitious names, trade names, trademarks, and real estate investment trusts. The database includes all active records and records inactivated within past twelve months. Access by the first few words of a business name, a significant word in a business name, or by the record ID number assigned. If questions, email sosbir@nd.gov. Also, search securities industry professionals database free at www.nd.gov/securities/industry-registration. *Other Options:* This agency provides a database purchase program. Cost is $35.00 per database and processing fees vary for type of media.

Uniform Commercial Code, Federal & State Tax Liens

UCC Division, Secretary of State,   http://sos.nd.gov/central-indexing-ucc   North Dakota provides, for a fee, direct access for three types of searches: Public, UCC-11 (without certificate), and Farm Products. There is an annual subscription $150 fee and a one-time $50.00 registration fee. The UCC-11 search fee (normally $7.00) applies, but documents will not be certified. Searches include UCC-11 information listing and farm product searches. *Other Options:* The agency offers bulk access via FTP or paper copy. Call for details.

Sales Tax Registrations

Office of State Tax Commissioner, Sales & Special Taxes Division, www.nd.gov/tax/user/businesses   A permit number may be verified online at www.nd.gov/tax/salesanduse/permitinquiry/. System indicates valid permit registered to company name.

Birth Certificates

ND Department of Health, Vital Records,   http://ndhealth.gov/vital/   Records may be ordered online from the Internet site or from vitalchek.com. Records are not returned online.

Death Records

ND Department of Health, Vital Records,   http://ndhealth.gov/vital/   Search the Public Death Index free at https://apps.nd.gov/doh/certificates/deathCertSearch.htm. Deaths within the past 12 months do not appear. Also, records may be ordered online from the Internet site or from vitalchek.com. Records are not returned online.

Workers' Compensation Records

Workforce Safety & Insurance, Workers' Compensation Records,   https://www.workforcesafety.com/   A claim look-up is available at https://www.workforcesafety.com/wsi/wsionlineservices/claimlookup.aspx. One must provide an injured worker's (SSN), Claim Number, or Name and DOB, and the injury date to retrieve claim verification information. An employer search is offered at https://www.workforcesafety.com/wsi/wsionlineservices/EmployerSearch.aspx.

Driver Records

Department of Transportation, Driver License Division,   www.dot.nd.gov   There are two systems. Ongoing, approved commercial accounts may request records with personal information via a commercial system. There is a minimum of 100 requests per month. For more information, call 701-328-4790. Also, from home page above one may view and print a limited record. The fee is $3.00 per record and a use of a credit card is required. The limited record does not include total points or convictions more than three years old, violations less than three points, or any crash information. No documents will be sent via mail. A free DL status check is found at https://apps.nd.gov/dot/dlts/dlos/requeststatus.htm; access by DL number.

Vessel Ownership & Registration

North Dakota Game & Fish Department, Boat Registration Records,   http://gf.nd.gov   There is a free public inquiry system at https://apps.nd.gov/gnf/onlineservices/lic/public/online/main.htm. Click on "Watercraft Registration and Renewals" to find registration number, or click on "Find Watercraft Safety Number" for that search. Requests may be submitted by email - ndgf@nd.gov. *Other Options:* Am electronic list is available of all registered vessels.

Voter Registration

Secretary of State, Elections Division,   https://vip.sos.nd.gov/PortalList.aspx   An offender locator is available at http://offender.doc.state.wi.us/lop/. Search campaign disclosure reports and filed statements at https://vip.sos.nd.gov/PortalListDetails.aspx?ptlhPKID=116&ptlPKID=2. Search lobbyists at http://sos.nd.gov/lobbyists/registered-lobbyists. Records can be ordered by email.

GED Certificates

Department of Public Instruction, GED Testing - CKEN-11,   https://www.nd.gov/dpi/students-parents/adulted/GED/   One may request records via email at JMarcellais@nd.gov. There is no fee, unless a transcript is ordered.

Occupational Licensing Boards

Accountant Firm	www.nd.gov/ndsba/stateboardsearch/sbasearch.asp
Accountant-CPA	www.nd.gov/ndsba/stateboardsearch/sbasearch.asp
Adoption Agency	www.nd.gov/dhs/services/childfamily/adoption/agencies.html
Alcoholic Beverage Control	https://www.ag.nd.gov/Licensing/LicenseHolders/LicenseHolders.htm
Amusement Device, Coin-Op	https://www.ag.nd.gov/Licensing/LicenseHolders/LicenseHolders.htm
Architect	www.ndsba.net/active-license-query/
Asbestos Contractor	www.ndhealth.gov/AQ/IAQ/ASB/Contractors.pdf
Attorney	www.ndcourts.gov/lawyers/
Bank, Commercial	www.nd.gov/dfi/regulate/reg/regulated.asp
Boxer/Boxing Professional	www.abcboxing.com/
Charitable Solicitation	https://apps.nd.gov/sc/busnsrch/busnSearch.htm
Chiropractor	http://ndsbce.org/doctor-search/
Collection Agency	www.nd.gov/dfi/regulate/reg/regulated.asp
Consumer Finance Company	www.nd.gov/dfi/regulate/reg/regulated.asp
Contractor/General Contractor	https://apps.nd.gov/sc/busnsrch/busnSearch.htm
Cosmetologist/Cosmetol'g't Instructor	www.ndcosmetology.com/license-lookup.aspx
Cosmetology School	www.ndcosmetology.com/schools.aspx

Counselor, Professional	www.ndbce.org/PDFs/counselor-list.pdf
Credit Union	www.nd.gov/dfi/regulate/reg/regulated.asp
Debt Collector	www.nd.gov/dfi/regulate/reg/regulated.asp
Deferred Presentment Provider	www.nd.gov/dfi/regulate/reg/regulated.asp
Dental Assistant/Hygienist	https://www.nddentalboard.org/verify/
Dentist	https://www.nddentalboard.org/verify/
Dietitian/Nutritionist	www.ndbodp.com/verify.html
Disapproved Medical School	https://www.ndbom.org/practitioners/physicians/newapp/disapprovedMedSchools.asp
Drug Mfg/Wholesaler	https://www.nodakpharmacy.com/verify.asp
Electrical Contractor	https://www.ndseb.com/search-1/find-a-licensed-contractor/
Electrician/Apprentice	https://www.ndseb.com/search-1/lookup-a-licensedregistered-electrician/
Engineer	http://ndpelsboard.org/search/
Esthetician	www.ndcosmetology.com/license-lookup.aspx
Fireworks, Wholesale/Distributor	https://www.ag.nd.gov/Licensing/LicenseHolders/LicenseHolders.htm
Funeral Home	www.ndfda.org/pg/ndk/directory.php
Gaming/Distributor/Manufacturer	https://www.ag.nd.gov/Licensing/LicenseHolders/LicenseHolders.htm
Insurance Agency/Agent/Broker	www.nd.gov/ndins/find/
Investment Advisor	www.nd.gov/securities/node/5498
Kickboxer/Mixed Fighting Style	www.abcboxing.com/
Laboratory Clinician	https://www.ndclinlab.com/verify/index.asp
Land Surveyor	http://ndpelsboard.org/search/
Lobbyist	http://sos.nd.gov/lobbyists
Manicurist	www.ndcosmetology.com/license-lookup.aspx
Medication Assistant	https://www.ndbon.org/verify_renew/verify_default.asp
Money Broker Firm	www.nd.gov/dfi/regulate/reg/regulated.asp
Nurse-LPN/RN/Assistant	https://www.ndbon.org/verify_renew/verify_default.asp
Nursing Home Administrator	www.ndnha.org/Admin%20List.pdf
Nutritionist	www.ndbodp.com/verify.html
Oil and Gas Active Driling Rig	https://www.dmr.nd.gov/oilgas/riglist.asp
Oil and Gas Broker	https://www.dmr.nd.gov/oilgas/findwellsvw.asp
Oil/Gas Well	https://www.dmr.nd.gov/oilgas/confidential.asp
Optometrist	www.ndsbopt.org/directory/
Osteopathic Physician	https://www.ndbom.org/public/find_verify/verify.asp
Pharmacist	https://www.nodakpharmacy.com/verify.asp
Pharmacy/Technician/Intern	https://www.nodakpharmacy.com/verify.asp
Physical Therapist/Assistant	https://www.ndbpt.org/verify.asp
Physician/Medical Doctor/Assistant	https://www.ndbom.org/public/find_verify/verify.asp
Physicians/Assistant Board Orders	https://www.ndbom.org/news/board_orders.asp#1217281
Private Investigator/Agency	www.nd.gov/pisb/holders.html
Real Estate Agent/Broker	www.realestatend.org/?id=42
Real Estate Schools	www.realestatend.org/education-providers/education-providers-2/
Respiratory Care Practitioner	https://www.ndsbrc.com/renewals/verify.asp
Sale of Check	www.nd.gov/dfi/regulate/reg/regulated.asp
Securities Agent/Dealer	www.nd.gov/securities/node/5498
Security Provider/Company	www.nd.gov/pisb/holders.html
Soil Classifier	https://www.ndsu.edu/pubweb/soils/BRPSCND/brpscnd_roster.html
Tobacco, Retail/Wholesale	https://www.ag.nd.gov/Licensing/LicenseHolders/LicenseHolders.htm
Transient Merchant	https://www.ag.nd.gov/Licensing/LicenseHolders/LicenseHolders.htm
Trust Company	www.nd.gov/dfi/regulate/reg/regulated.asp
Veterinarian/Veterinary Technician	www.ndbvme.org/

State and Local Courts

About North Dakota Courts: The **District Courts** have general jurisdiction over criminal, civil, and juvenile matters. At one time there were County Courts, but these courts merged with the District Courts statewide in 1995. These older County Court records are held by the 53 District Court Clerks in the 7 judicial districts.

Municipal Courts in North Dakota have jurisdiction for all violations of traffic and municipal ordinances, with some exceptions. **The web page for the Judicial Branch is www.ndcourts.gov.**

Appellate Courts: The Court of Appeals only hears cases assigned to it by the Supreme Court. Some years no cases are assigned. One may search North Dakota Supreme Court dockets and opinions at www.ndcourts.gov. Search by docket number, party name, or anything else that may appear in the text. Records are from 1982 forward. Email notification of new opinions is also available.

Online Court Access

All courts participate in the statewide system described below.

All District Courts and fifteen Muncipal Courts participate on an online access system for court record index data, including civil, criminal, probate, traffic, family case files as well as judgments. The web page is found at http://publicsearch.ndcourts.gov/default.aspx. There are a variety of searches, including by name, case number, attorney, and date filed. Results will provide year of birth for criminal (or entire DOB is entered as part of search), but not for civil, family or judgments.

Data throughput varies by each county; most counties go back at least 7 years. Some counties have data included from as early as 1991 and beyond; other counties that have been added in 2003 will have data for only the most recent cases. See www.ndcourts.gov/publicsearch/counties.aspx. for a list of counites and throughput starting dates. Data is current through the end of the previous business day.

The online site does not have access to case file images, but the public access terminals onsite at the court locations do. If the online system or the public access teminals give the full DOB for criminal record will depend on the county. Some search results may show a partial SSN.Note the site disclaimerstates the following:

> "The information provided on and obtained from this site does not constitute the official record of the Court. This information is provided as a service to the general public. Any user of this information is hereby advised that it is being provided "as is".

Further, the site warns name searches are not reliable. The information provided may be subject to errors or omissions. Visitors to this site agree that the Court is not liable for errors or omissions of any of the information provided." It is strongly urged to use this site only as a pre-screen. (See www.ndcourts.gov/publicsearch/counties.aspx).

Other Sites (not mentioned above):

Cass County

East Central Judicial District Court   http://www.ndcourts.gov
Probate: Search probate records from the 1870s to 1951 online at http://library.ndsu.edu/db/probate/. There is no fee.

Recorders, Assessors, and Other Sites of Note

About North Dakota Recording Offices: 53 counties, 53 recording offices. 53 counties, 53 recording offices. The recording officer is the County Recorder,

About Tax Liens: Effective March 1, 2016, all tax liens must be filed with the Secretary of State's office. Previously, federal tax liens on personal property of businesses are filed with the Secretary of State. Other federal and all state tax liens are filed with the County Recorder.

Online Access

Access to Recorded Documents is Statewide

The North Dakota Recorders Information Network (NDRIN) is an electronic central repository representing all North Dakota counties. The network offers Internet access to records for both indices and images. There is a $25 monthly usage fee, and a $1.00 charge per page printed. Register or request information via the website at www.ndrin.com.

Property Tax
Over half of the counties have a site. There is a links list to 18 county property tax sites at www.ndpropertytax.com

County Site (Omitted from profiles is the statewide access to recorded documents as described above):

Billings County *Property, Taxation Records*   Access to tax inquiry for free at www.billingscountynd.gov/taxinquire.txt. Also, access to GIS/mapping for free at http://mapservices.co.billings.nd.us/.

Bowman County *Property, Taxation Records*   Access to Mapservice for free at http://mapserver.co.bowman.nd.us/. Also, access to property record cards for free at http://bowman.northdakotaassessors.com/.

Burke County *Property, Taxation Records*   Access to GIS/mapping for free at http://burkend.mygisonline.com/.

Burleigh County *Property, Taxation Records*   Access to property tax information for free at http://www.co.burleigh.nd.us/property-information/default.asp?ID=383. No name searching. Also, parcel searches for free at http://burleigh.northdakotaassessors.com/search.php.

Cass County *Property, Taxation Records*   Access search data free at the Parcel Information site at http://fargoparcels.com/ but no name searching. Access record data at https://www.casscountynd.gov/county/depts/treasurer/proptax/app/Default.aspx#Search.

Cavalier County *Recorded Documents*   www.cavaliercounty.us/   Subscription access the recorder's land records via NDRIN's central repository at www.ndrin.com/. Registration and monthly fee applies. There is a $25 monthly usage fee, and a $1.00 charge per page printed. *Property, Taxation Records*   Access to GIS/mapping for free at http://cavaliernd.mygisonline.com/.

Divide County *Property, Taxation Records*   Access to real estate records for free at http://crosbycity.northdakotaassessors.com/index.php.

Dunn County *Property, Taxation Records*   Access to county tax information is free at http://ndpropertytax.org/tax/disclaimer.asp?cid=13.

Eddy County *Recorded Documents*   www.ndrin.org/recorders/county-profile.asp?CountyID=24   Subscription access the recorder's land records via NDRIN's central repository at www.ndrin.com/. Registration and monthly fee applies. There is a $25 monthly usage fee, and a $1.00 charge per page printed.

Emmons County *Property, Taxation Records*   Access to GIS/mapping free at http://emmonscounty.maps.arcgis.com/apps/Solutions/s2.html?appid=4ff10e43a379451287969b3fb5035720.

Golden Valley County *Property, Taxation Records*   Access to GIS/mapping free at http://goldenvalley.gisworkshop.com/#.

Grand Forks County *Recorded Documents*   http://gfcounty.nd.gov/?q=node/76   Access the recorder's Grantor/Grantee database free at http://gfcounty.nd.gov/?q=node/58. *Property, Taxation Records*   Access to GIS, property and document searches for free at http://gfcounty.nd.gov/?q=node/58.

Griggs County *Recorded Documents*   www.griggscountynd.gov/departments/recorder   Subscription access the recorder's land records via NDRIN's central repository at www.ndrin.com/. Registration and monthly fees ($25 monthly usage fee, and a $1.00 charge per page printed) apply. *Property, Taxation Records*   Access real estate tax statements (in PDF format) at https://www.griggscountynd.gov/resource/real-estate-tax-info.

Hettinger County *Property, Taxation Records*   Access to real estate tax records for free at http://hettinger.northdakotaassessors.com/.

La Moure County *Property, Taxation Records*   Access records at http://ndpropertytax.org/tax/disclaimer.asp?cid=23.

McKenzie County *Property, Taxation Records*   Access property tax information at http://ndpropertytax.org/tax/disclaimer.asp?cid=27.

McLean County *Property, Taxation Records*   Access records at http://mclean.northdakotaassessors.com/search.php.

Mercer County *Property, Taxation Records*   Access to property record searches for free at http://mercer.northdakotaassessors.com/.

Morton County *Property, Taxation Records*   Access property tax records at http://ndpropertytax.org/tax/disclaimer.asp?cid=30.

Mountrail County *Property, Taxation Records*   Access records at http://ndpropertytax.org/tax/disclaimer.asp?cid=31. Also, access to GIS/mapping for free at http://mountrailnd.mygisonline.com/.

Oliver County *Property, Taxation Records*   Access to real estate tax searches for free at http://oliver.northdakotaassessors.com/.

Pembina County *Property, Taxation Records*   Access records at http://ndpropertytax.org/tax/disclaimer.asp?cid=34.

Pierce County *Property, Taxation Records*   Access to real estate records for free at http://pierce.northdakotaassessors.com/.

Ramsey County *Property, Taxation Records*   Search property tax statements at www.co.ramsey.nd.us/Property-Tax-Statement-Search.

Ransom County *Property, Taxation Records*   Access records at http://ndpropertytax.org/tax/disclaimer.asp?cid=37.

Renville County   *Property, Taxation Records*   Access to real estate records for free at http://renville.northdakotaassessors.com/.

Richland County   *Property, Taxation Records*   Access to property tax information for free at www.co.richland.nd.us/index.php/tax. Also, access to GIS/mapping for free at www.co.richland.nd.us/rcims/.

Sargent County   *Property, Taxation Records*   Access records at http://ndpropertytax.org/tax/disclaimer.asp?cid=41.

Stark County   *Property, Taxation Records*   Access to real estate records for free at http://stark.northdakotaassessors.com/.

Stutsman County   *Property, Taxation Records*   Access to property tax information for free at https://portals.co.stutsman.nd.us/iTax/.

Traill County   *Property, Taxation Records*   Free access to GIS/mapping found at http://traillnd.mygisonline.com/. Also, access to property sales for free at www.co.traill.nd.us/departments/taxation/parcel-data.

Ward County   *Property, Taxation Records*   Access to property tax information for free at http://gis.wardnd.com/TaxParcelViewer/default.htm.

Williams County   *Property, Taxation Records*   Access to property tax information for free at http://www.williamsnd.com/Property/Search.

Reminder:

The North Dakota Recorders Information Network (NDRIN) is an electronic central repository representing all of the North Dakota counties. The network offers Internet access to records, indices, and images. There is a $25 monthly usage fee, and a $1.00 charge per page printed. Register or request information via the website at www.ndrin.com.

Ohio

Capital: Columbus
             Franklin County
Time Zone: EST
Population: 11,613,423
# of Counties: 88

Useful State Links

Website: **www.ohio.gov**
Governor: **http://governor.ohio.gov**
Attorney General: **www.ohioattorneygeneral.gov/**
State Archives: **www.ohiohistory.org/**
State Statues and Code: **www.legislature.ohio.gov/laws/ohio-codes**
Legislative Bill Search: **www.legislature.ohio.gov/legislation/search-legislation?1**
Unclaimed Funds: **www.com.ohio.gov/unfd/**

State Public Record Agencies

Criminal Records

Ohio Bureau of Investigation - BCI, Civilian Background Section,   www.ohioattorneygeneral.gov/Business/Services-for-Business/Webcheck   Civilian Background Checks (WebCheck) is a web-based system for all in-state record requests. Results are NOT returned via the Internet. The search fee is $22.00 per fingerprint record. Agencies can send fingerprint images and other data via the Internet using a single digit fingerprint scanner and a driver's license magnetic strip reader. Hardware costs are involved. Using WebCheck Letter Verifier, employers can check the validity of prospective or current employees' Ohio background check results showing no criminal history. This is a free service. The name and either DOB or last 4 digits of the SSN is required. See www.ohioattorneygeneral.gov/Business/Services-for-Business/WebCheck/WebCheck-letter-verifier.

Sexual Offender Registry

Sexual Offender Services, Dept. of Rehabilitation and Correction,   http://drc.ohio.gov/web/sexoffenderprogram.html   At the website, click on Offender Locator or visit www.in.gov/apps/indcorrection/ofs/ofs. To search provide either first and last name or the inmate number. Search www.icrimewatch.net/index.php?AgencyID=55149. Users can search by offender name, zip code, county and / or school district. Also, the page will list all offenders (over 17,500) in alpha order.

Incarceration Records

Ohio Department of Rehabilitation and Correction, Bureau of Records Management,   www.drc.ohio.gov/   From the website, in the Select a Destination box, select Offender Search or see www.drc.ohio.gov/OffenderSearch/Search.aspx. You can search by name, geographic location, or inmate number. The Offender Search includes all offenders currently incarcerated or under some type of Department supervision (parole, post-release control, or transitional control). Search Parole Violators at large at www.drc.ohio.gov/OffenderSearch/pvalListing.aspx.

Corporation, LLC, LP, Fictitious/Trade Name, Trademarks/Servicemarks

Secretary of State, Business Services,   www.sos.state.oh.us/SOS/Businesses.aspx   The agency provides free Internet searching for business and corporation records from the home page or form www5.sos.state.oh.us/ords/f?p=100:1. A Good Standing can be ordered. Validation is available for $5.00. A trademark search is available at www5.sos.state.oh.us/ords/f?p=100:3:0::NO. Also, not from this agency, but search securities exemption filings free at https://www.comapps.ohio.gov/secu/secu_apps/offering/offering.aspx,   and   securities   enforcement   orders   by   year   at https://www.comapps.ohio.gov/secu/secu_apps/FinalOrders/. *Other Options:* This agency makes the database available for purchase, call for details.

Uniform Commercial Code

UCC Records, Secretary of State, www.sos.state.oh.us/SOS/Businesses/UCC.aspx   The Internet site offers free online access to records. Search by debtor, secured party, or financing statement number at www5.sos.state.oh.us/ords/f?p=100:5:0::NO:::.   *Other Options:* The complete database is available on electronic media with weekly updates. Call for current pricing.

Birth Certificates

Ohio Department of Health, Office of Vital Statistics, www.odh.ohio.gov/vitalstatistics/vitalmisc/vitalstats.aspx   Records can be ordered from state's site at https://odhgateway.odh.ohio.gov/OrderBirthCertificates/. A credit card is needed.

Death Records

Ohio Department of Health, Office of Vital Statistics, www.odh.ohio.gov/vitalstatistics/vitalmisc/vitalstats.aspx   The Ohio Historical Society Death Certificate Index Searchable Database at http://apps.ohiohistory.org/death/index.php/ permits searching by name, county, index. Data is available from 1913 to 1944 only. Records can be ordered from state's site at https://odhgateway.odh.ohio.gov/OrderBirthCertificates/. A credit card is needed.

Workers' Compensation Records

Bureau of Workers Compensation, Customer Contact Center - Records Mgr, https://www.bwc.ohio.gov/Default.aspx   Injured workers, injured worker designees, representatives and managed care organizations (MCOs) can view a list of all claims associated with a given SSN, but are limited to viewing only the claims with which they are associated. Employers, their representatives or designees, and managed care organizations can view a list of all claims associated to their BWC policy number. Medical providers can view all claims associated with any given SSN. Access is through the website listed above. An account must be established. *Other Options:* Bulk data is released to approved accounts; however, the legal department must approve requesters. The agency has general information available on a website.

Driver Records

Bureau of Motor Vehicles, Record Requests, www.ohiobmv.com   A certified, three-year driver record abstract is available to anyone for purchase online at https://www.oplates.com. Also, using prepaid is suggested for requesters who order 100 or more motor vehicle reports per day in batch mode. The DL# or SSN and name are needed when ordering. Fee is $5.00 per record. For more information, call 614-752-7691. Also, Ohio drivers may view an unofficial copy of their record at www.ohiobmv.com/abstract.stm. There is no fee for a two year uncertified record. The BMV offers a free status check of an auto dealer. Go to https://ext.dps.state.oh.us/BMVOnlineServices.Public/DealerSearch.aspx. Find the issue date of a driver's license online at www.bmv.ohio.gov/registration_titling.stm.

Vehicle Ownership & Registration

Bureau of Motor Vehicles, Motor Vehicle Title Records, www.ohiobmv.com   Several different searches are offered for prepaid accounts - see http://bmv.ohio.gov/fiscal_prepaid_accounts.stm.   The   BMV   offers   a   limited,   free   search   at https://ext.dps.state.oh.us/BMVOnlineServices.Public/TitleSearch.aspx. This search includes watercraft and vehicles. Vehicle owners can check renewal status online at https://www.oplates.com/CheckRenewalStatus.aspx   *Other Options:* Bulk records are available for purchase, per DPPA guidelines. For more information contact the Records request Unit at 614-752-7548.

Crash Reports

OHIO State Highway Patrol, OPS Central Records,, http://statepatrol.ohio.gov/crash.stm   Reports of crashes may be ordered for the $4.00 fee online at www.statepatrol.ohio.gov/crash.stm; a record is returned via email within 24 hours. Crash photographs purchased online will be sent on a CD by mail. Use of   credit   card   is   required.   SSNs   are   not   released.   One   may   view   partial   non-official   crash   reports   at: https://ext.dps.state.oh.us/CrashRetrieval/OHCrashRetrieval.aspx. Viewing the partial report from this website will help you find out which agency handled the crash report.

Vessel Ownership & Registration

DNR-Division of Watercraft, Titles and Registration, http://watercraft.ohiodnr.gov/   A free inquiry of a watercraft title is available at https://ext.dps.state.oh.us/BMVOnlineServices.Public/TitleSearch.aspx. This is a search by title or ID number. This is not a DNR service, but is from the Ohio MBV. The title information available from this web page is obtained from Ohio county title offices. Records are from 1993 forward. This provides owner name only, no personal information.

Voter Registration, Campaign Finance, PACs

Secretary   of   State,   Elections   Division,   www.sos.state.oh.us   Search   campaign   finance   reports   at www.sos.state.oh.us/SOS/CampaignFinance/Search.aspx.   *Other Options:* Voter Reg. Records may obtained on disk in a text format. No customization is possible, only the entire database is released. For more information, contact Robin Fields.

GED Certificates

Ohio Dept of Education, GED Office, http://education.ohio.gov/Topics/Testing/Ohio-Options-for-Adult-Diploma/GED   Third parties will set up an account at: http://exchange.parchment.com/ged-receiver-registration-page. Parchment verifies that they are who they say they are so that they can place orders on behalf of students Parchment contacts the third party and provides training on the site for ordering. During this training any orders they have are placed. After this the third party can order on behalf of students. They still must upload a consent form for each student during the process. GED test takers can order duplicate copies of official Ohio GED transcripts and duplicate diplomas online at: www.gedtestingservice.com/testers/gedrequest-a-transcript

Occupational Licensing Boards

These licenses are all searchable at https://license.ohio.gov/lookup/default.asp

Accountant-CPA/PA/Firm
Acupuncturist
Anesthesiologist Assistant
Architect/Firm
Athletic Trainer
Barber/Instructor/Shop/School
Casino Gaming Operator/Employee
Chemical Dependency Counselor/Assistant
Chiropractor/Acupuncture Cert
Clinical Nurse Specialist
Cosmetic Therapist
Cosmetologist/Cosmetolog't,
Managing/Instructor
Counselor
Crematory
Dental Assistant Radiologist/Hygienist
Dentist
Dialysis Technician
Dietitian
DLR Dealer/Repair Shop
Drug Wholesaler/Distributor
Embalmer/Embalming Facility

Engineer
Engineering/Surveying Company
Esthetician/Managing Esthetician
Funeral Director
Funeral Home
Glass Repair Shop
Hearing Aid Dealer/Fitter
Landscape Architect
Manicuring/Esthetician Instructor
Manicurist/Managing Manicurist
Manufactured Homes Installer/Inspector
Manufactured Homes Related
Marriage and Family Therapist
Massage Therapist
Mechanotherapist
Midwife
Naprapath
Nurse-RN/LPN/Anesthetist/Practitioner
Occupational Therapist/Assistant
Ocularist/Ocularist Apprentice
Optical Dispenser
Optician/Optician Apprentice

Optometrist/ Diagnostic/Therapeutic
Oriental Medicine
Orthotics/ Prosthetics/Pedorthics
Osteopathic Physician
Pharmacist
Pharmacy/Pharmacy Dispensary
Physical Therapist/Assistant
Physician/Medical Doctor/Assistant
Podiatrist
Prescriptive Authority
Psychologist
Radiographer
Respiratory Home Medical Equipment Facility
Respiratory Therapist/Student/Facility
Sanitarian/In-Training/Training Agency
School Psychologist
Social Worker
Speech Pathologist/Audiologist/Aide
Surveyor, Land
Veterinarian/Veterinary Tech/Student
Veterinary Facility

The Rest:

Athlete Agent .... www.aco.ohio.gov/LinkClick.aspx?fileticket=Sfl849JRJJ8%3d&tabid=85
Attorney, Bar Assoc by Type .... https://www.zeekbeek.com/OSBA#region=OH
Attorney, State .... www.supremecourt.ohio.gov/AttySvcs/AttyReg/Public_AttorneyInformation.asp
Backflow Prev Assembly Insp .... https://www.comapps.ohio.gov/dic/dico_apps/bdcc/CertifiedBackFlowTesters/
Bank... https://elicense2-secure.com.ohio.gov/
Bedding/Furniture Dealer/Dist .... https://www.comapps.ohio.gov/dic/dico_apps/bedd/LicenseLookup/
Bedding/Furniture Mfg/Renovator .... https://www.comapps.ohio.gov/dic/dico_apps/bedd/LicenseLookup/
Boiler Contractor....................................... https://apps.com.ohio.gov/dico/BoilerContractors/
Boiler Inspector/Operator .... https://apps.com.ohio.gov/dico/BoilerContractors/
Boxer/Boxing Professional....................... www.aco.ohio.gov/LinkClick.aspx?fileticket=Ecq3TFsglyQ%3d&tabid=100
Boxing Promoter .... www.aco.ohio.gov/LinkClick.aspx?fileticket=xHWaVrfV7vo%3d&tabid=40
Check Cashing/Lending Service https://elicense2-secure.com.ohio.gov/
Child Care Type A or B House .... www.odjfs.state.oh.us/cdc/query.asp
Child Day Care Facility .... www.odjfs.state.oh.us/cdc/query.asp
Consumer Finance Company https://elicense2-secure.com.ohio.gov/
Contractor https://elicense4.com.ohio.gov/Lookup/LicenseLookup.aspx
Day Camp, Children's .... www.odjfs.state.oh.us/cdc/query.asp
Electrical Safety Inspector/Trainee........... https://www.comapps.ohio.gov/dic/dico_apps/bbst/ElectricalSafetyInspectors/
Electrician https://elicense4.com.ohio.gov/Lookup/LicenseLookup.aspx
Elevator Inspector.................................... https://apps.com.ohio.gov/dico/elevatorlookup/
EMS Training Facility............................... https://services.dps.ohio.gov/EMSSchools/TrainingFacility/
EMS/Fire Disciplinary Actions .... http://ems.ohio.gov/about-discipline.aspx
Fire Protection System Designer.............. https://www.comapps.ohio.gov/dic/dico_apps/bbst/FireProtectionSystemDesigners/
Gaming-Related Vendors http://casinocontrol.ohio.gov/Portals/0/Licensing/12-02-14%20Vendor%20Status%20for%20Website.pdf
Heating/Refrigeration (HVAC) https://elicense4.com.ohio.gov/Lookup/LicenseLookup.aspx
Horse Racing (license type) .... http://racing.ohio.gov/Licensing.html
Hydronic-related Occupation https://elicense4.com.ohio.gov/Lookup/LicenseLookup.aspx

Insurance Agent/Agency	https://gateway.insurance.ohio.gov/UI/ODI.Agent.Public.UI/AgentSearch.mvc/DisplaySearch
Legislative Agent/Agent Employer	www2.jlec-olig.state.oh.us/olac/
Liquor Store	https://www.comapps.ohio.gov/liqr/liqr_apps/PermitLookup/Agency.aspx
Liquor Temporary Permit/Event	https://www.comapps.ohio.gov/liqr/liqr_apps/PermitLookup/PermitTemporary.aspx
Lobbyist/Lobbyist Employer	www2.jlec-olig.state.oh.us/olac/
Lottery Retailer	https://www.ohiolottery.com/Find-A-Retailer.aspx
Milk Hauler	www.agri.ohio.gov/dairy/DairySearchIndex.aspx?type=mh
Milk Tanker, Active	www.agri.ohio.gov/dairy/DairySearchIndex.aspx?type=at
Milk Tester/Sampler	www.agri.ohio.gov/divs/dairy/DairySearchIndex.aspx?type=wst
Mixed Martial Arts Amateur	www.aco.ohio.gov/LinkClick.aspx?fileticket=NEhyr7hgVV0%3d&tabid=101
Mixed Martial Arts Professional	www.aco.ohio.gov/LinkClick.aspx?fileticket=nwRiRJYKcKU%3d&tabid=102
Mixed Martial Arts Promoter	www.aco.ohio.gov/LinkClick.aspx?fileticket=XlquIWJIjlo%3d&tabid=40
Mortgage Broker	https://elicense2-secure.com.ohio.gov/
Notary Public	www.sos.state.oh.us/SOS/recordsIndexes/Notary/Search.aspx
Pawnbroker	https://elicense2-secure.com.ohio.gov/
Pesticide Applicator Business	www.agri.ohio.gov/apps/odaprs/pestfert-PRS-index.aspx
Pesticide Applicator/Operator/Dealer	www.agri.ohio.gov/apps/odaprs/pestfert-PRS-index.aspx
Pesticide Limited Comm' l Applicator	www.agri.ohio.gov/apps/odaprs/pestfert-PRS-index.aspx
Plumber	https://elicense4.com.ohio.gov/Lookup/LicenseLookup.aspx
Plumbing Inspector	https://www.comapps.ohio.gov/dic/dico_apps/bdcc/PlumbingInspectorCertification/
Polygraph Examiner	www.ohiopolygraph.org/certified-examiners.asp
Precious Metals Dealer	https://elicense2-secure.com.ohio.gov/
Premium Finance Company	https://elicense2-secure.com.ohio.gov/
Private Investigator	https://ext.dps.state.oh.us/PISGS/Pages/Public/providersearch.aspx
Savings & Loan Association	https://elicense2-secure.com.ohio.gov/
Savings Bank	https://elicense2-secure.com.ohio.gov/
Securities Filing	https://www.comapps.ohio.gov/secu/secu_apps/offering/
Securities Salesperson/Dealer	https://www.comapps.ohio.gov/secu/secu_apps/recordrequest/
Security Guard	https://ext.dps.state.oh.us/PISGS/Pages/Public/providersearch.aspx
Spirituous Liquor Brand (greater than 42 proof)	https://www.comapps.ohio.gov/liqr/liqr_apps/PermitLookup/AgencyBrand.aspx
Steam Engineer	https://apps.com.ohio.gov/dico/BoilerContractors/
Teacher/Teacher's Aide	http://webapp1.ode.state.oh.us/emis/certification/courseSearch.asp
Wrestling Promoter	www.aco.ohio.gov/LinkClick.aspx?fileticket=qnR_c1H6eFQ%3d&tabid=40

State and Local Courts

About Ohio Courts: The **Court of Common Pleas** is the general jurisdiction court with separate divisions including General, Domestic Relations, Juvenile and Probate. Per the Supreme Court web page, the General Division has original jurisdiction in all criminal felony cases and in all civil cases in which the amount in controversy is more than $15,000. However, the Administrative Director's Office advises the Common Pleas can hear civil cases for $501 or more.

County and **Municipal Courts** handle virtually the same subject matter with some minor operational differences. Both have the authority to conduct preliminary hearings in felony cases, both have jurisdiction over traffic and non-traffic misdemeanors and, and have limited civil jurisdiction in which the amount of money in dispute does not exceed $15,000.

Mayor's Courts are not a part of the Judicial Banch and are not courts of record. A person convicted in a Mayor's Court may appeal the conviction to the Municipal or County court having jurisdiction within the municipal corporation. Ohio and Louisiana are the only two states that allow the mayors of municipal corporations to preside over a court.

The **Court of Claims** has original jurisdiction to hear and determine all civil actions filed against the state of Ohio and its agencies.

The web page for the Judicial System is www.supremecourt.ohio.gov.

Appellate Courts: The Supreme Court is the court of last resort. The primary function of the Court of Appeals is to hear appeals from the Common Pleas, Municipal and County courts. The Court of Appeals has twelve districts. The 10th District Court of Appeals in

Franklin County also hears appeals from the Ohio Court of Claims. Appellate and Supreme Court opinions may be researched from the website.

Online Court Access

Quite a few individual Common Pleas, County and Municipal courts offer online access. There is no statewide access. However the Supreme Court of Ohio is in the process of implementing the Ohio Court Network (OCN) for users from the court and justice systems. **There is no public access to OCN at this time**. This system will include court case docket information from all courts of record, including criminal, civil and traffic records.

County Sites:
Adams County
Common Pleas Court   https://adamscountyoh.gov/Clerk-of-Courts--Legal.asp
Civil & Criminal: Online access to the docket index is offered at http://courtrecords.adamscountyoh.gov/. Note there is a 24 hour or longer delay, this is not in real time. Includes search of County and Probated Courts.

County Court   https://adamscountyoh.gov/
Civil: Online access to the docket index is offered at http://courtrecords.adamscountyoh.gov. Note there is a 24 hour or longer delay, this is not in real time. Includes search of Court of Common Pleas.   *Criminal:* same

Allen County
Common Pleas Court   http://www.allencountyohio.com/commonpleas/ccom.php
Civil: Access civil records including judgment liens free at http://courtvweb.allencountyohio.com/eservices/home.page.2. No identifiers shown. Court records prior to 12/1/1988 are not available on Courtview. However they may appear as history.   *Criminal:* same

Lima Municipal Court   http://www.cityhall.lima.oh.us/index.aspx?NID=100
Civil: Search index information at http://connection.limamunicipalcourt.org/awc/Court/Default.aspx.   *Criminal:* same

Ashland County
Common Pleas Court   https://www.ashlandcounty.org/clerkofcourts/
Civil: Access docket index at http://www.ashlandcountycpcourt.org/eservices/home.page.2.   *Criminal:* same

Ashland Municipal Court   http://www.ashlandmunicourt.com/
Civil: Search the docket index for free at http://web1.civicacmi.com/Ashland/Court/. Search by either plaintiff or defendant.   *Criminal:* same

Ashtabula County
Common Pleas Court   http://courts.co.ashtabula.oh.us/
Civil: Access to index is free at http://courts.co.ashtabula.oh.us/eservices/home.page.2.   *Criminal:* same

County Court Eastern Division - Jefferson   http://courts.co.ashtabula.oh.us/eastern_county_court.htm
Civil: Access to records are free at http://courts.co.ashtabula.oh.us/pa.htm.   *Criminal:* same

County Court Western Division - Geneva   http://courts.co.ashtabula.oh.us/western_county_court.htm
Civil: Access records free at http://courts.co.ashtabula.oh.us/pa.htm.   *Criminal:* same

Ashtabula Municipal Court   http://www.ashtabulamunicipalcourt.com/
Civil: Online access to civil court cases are free at http://www.ashtabulamunicourt.com/searchcivildocket.asp?pageId=71.   *Criminal:* Online access to case information, including traffic, is free at http://www.ashtabulamunicourt.com/searchdocket.asp?pageId=32.

Athens County
Common Pleas Court   http://co.athensoh.org/departments/clerk_of_courts/index.php
Civil: Online access to CP court records are free at http://coc.athensoh.org/eservices/home.page.2.   *Criminal:* same

Athens Municipal Court   http://www.ci.athens.oh.us/index.aspx?nid=108
Civil: Online access to the court's civil records is free at http://docket.webxsol.com/athens/index.html. Records go back to 1992. Search by name or case number.   *Criminal:* same for criminal and traffic records

Auglaize County
Common Pleas Court   http://www2.auglaizecounty.org/courts/common-pleas
Civil: Access civil records back to 2/2000 free at www.auglaizecounty.org/pa/.   *Criminal:* same

Auglaize County Municipal Court - Wapakoneta   http://www2.auglaizecounty.org/courts/municipal
Civil: Access civil and small claims court records back to 4/1/1994 free at www.auglaizecounty.org/pa/.   *Criminal:* Access criminal and traffic records back to 10/1/1993 free at www.auglaizecounty.org/pa/. DOB shows sometimes.

Belmont County

Common Pleas Court - St Clairsville http://www.belmontcountyohio.org/common-pleas-court/
Civil: Access civil records for free at http://bceaccess.dyndns.org/. *Criminal:* Access criminal records for free at http://bceaccess.dyndns.org/.

County Court Western Division - St Clairsville http://www.belmontcountycourts.com/
Civil: View the docket index at http://eaccess.belmontcountycourts.com/eservices_e/home.page.2. There is no fee. *Criminal:* same

County Court Eastern Division - Bellaire http://www.belmontcountycourts.com/
Civil: View the docket index at http://eaccess.belmontcountycourts.com/eservices_e/home.page.2, there is no fee. *Criminal:* same

County Court Northern Division - Bellaire http://www.belmontcountycourts.com/
Civil: View the docket index at http://eaccess.belmontcountycourts.com/eservices_e/home.page.2. There is no fee. *Criminal:* same

Brown County

Common Pleas Court http://www.browncountyclerkofcourts.org/
Civil & Criminal: Search court records free at www.browncountyclerkofcourts.org/Search/. Document images available for cases file from 2013 forward.
County Municipal Court http://www.browncountycourt.org
Civl: Access to records are free at www.browncountycourt.org/search.html. *Criminal:* Access to records are free at www.browncountycourt.org/search.html. Includes a search of traffic. Online criminal search results include address and DOB.

Butler County

Common Pleas Court http://www.butlercountyclerk.org
Civil: Online access to the docket index for civil actions and liens is at http://pa.butlercountyclerk.org/eservices/home.page.2. Online access to Probate Court records is free at http://66.117.197.22/index.cfm?page=courtRecords. Search the Estate or Guardianship databases. *Criminal:* Online access to the docket index for criminal actions is at http://pa.butlercountyclerk.org/eservices/home.page.2.

All County Courts http://www.bcareacourts.org/
Civil: Online access to the docket index is free at http://docket.bcareacourts.org/. There will be at least a 24 hour delay before new information is posted. Search by name or case number. *Criminal:* Online access to the docket index is free at http://docket.bcareacourts.org/. There will be at least a 24 hour delay before new information is posted. Search by name or case number. Traffic cases included. Results show DOB if on the record.

Hamilton Municipal Court http://www.hamiltonmunicipalcourt.org
Civil & Criminal: Search record access free at http://www.hamiltonmunicipalcourt.org/AWC/Court/.
Fairfield Municipal Court http://www.fairfield-city.org/municipalcourt/index.cfm
Civil: Search records online back to 1988 free at www.fairfield-city.org/courtrecords/municipal-court-records.cfm. *Criminal:* same

Middletown Municipal Court http://www.cityofmiddletown.org/court/
Civil: Index to the civil docket is at https://court.cityofmiddletown.org/awc/Court/. *Criminal:* Search criminal and traffic records back to early 1990s and court schedules free at https://court.cityofmiddletown.org/awc/Court/.

Carroll County

County Municipal Court http://www.carrollcountycourt.org/
Civil: Search the online docket index at http://www.carrollcountycourt.org/recordSearch.php. There may be a 24-hour delay or more before new data is posted. There is no indication on the thruput dates. The search includes small claims. The address is shown on the details, but there is no DOB indicated. *Criminal:* Same - The search includes traffic and parking tickets.

Champaign County

Champaign County Municipal Court http://www.champaigncountymunicipalcourt.com
Civi & Criminall: Access court records back to 1992 free at http://web1.civicacmi.com/ChampaignCoMC/Court/Default.aspx includes traffic.

Clark County

Common Pleas Court http://www.clarkcountyohio.gov/index.aspx?nid=93
Civil: Online access to clerk's record index is free at http://66.192.124.85/pa/. *Criminal:* same

Clark County Municipal Court http://www.clerkofcourts.municipal.co.clark.oh.us/
Civil: Online access to case information is free at www.clerkofcourts.municipal.co.clark.oh.us/. Images available back to 4/15/06. Click on Cases. if you click on Dockets you only get current dockets. Online records go back to 3/90. *Criminal:* Same, Images available back to 4/15/06.

Clermont County

Common Pleas Court http://www.clermontclerk.org/Case_Access.htm
Civi &* Criminal: Online access to court records is free at www.clermontclerk.org/Case_Access.htm. Online records go back to 1/1987. Includes later Municipal Court records.
Clermont County Municipal Court http://www.clermontclerk.org
Civil & Criminal: Access to court records is free at www.clermontclerk.org/Case_Access.htm. Online records go back to 5/1/1996.

Clinton County

Common Pleas Court http://www.clintoncountycourts.org/index.php

Civil: Access the docket index at http://www.clintoncountycourts.org/recordSearch.php. This is not in real time, there can be a delay of at least 24 hours or more. Judgment liens may be searched, as well Appeals.   *Criminal:* same. Domestic Relation cases may be searched, as well as Appeals.

Clinton County Municipal Court   http://www.clintonmunicourt.org
Civil: Search court records online at www.clintonmunicourt.org/search.html.   *Criminal:* same

Columbiana County
Common Pleas Court   http://www.ccclerk.org
Civil: Access all county court index and docket records free at www.ccclerk.org/case_access.htm. Includes probate.   *Criminal:* Access all county court index and docket records free at www.ccclerk.org/case_access.htm.

Lisbon Municipal Court   http://www.ccclerk.org/the_courts.htm
Civil: Access all county court index and docket records free at http://www.ccclerk.org/case_access.htm.   *Criminal:* same

East Liverpool Municipal Court   http://www.elcourt.org/
Civi & Criminal: Access all county court index and docket records free at http://www.ccclerk.org/pa/paELIVER.urd/pamw6500.display.   Per the court, the online search is not equal to a clerk search onsite.

Coshocton County
Common Pleas Court   http://www.coshoctoncounty.net
Civil: Search civil and domestic relations cases back to 01/01/1999 at http://eaccess.coshoctoncounty.net/eservices/home.page. General identifiers given, but does not include DOB.   *Criminal:* same

Coshocton Municipal Court   http://www.coshoctonmunicipalcourt.com
Civil: Online access to civil records is at the website. Search by name, case number, attorney, date.   *Criminal:* same

Crawford County
Common Pleas Court   http://www.crawfordcocpcourt.org/Clerk%20of%20Court%20Page.htm
Civil: Online access to Common Pleas court record index is free at http://clerk.crawford-co.org/.   *Criminal:* same. Data is updated nightly.

Municipal Court East Div - Galion   http://www.crawfordcountymuni.org/
Civil: A free record search of the docket is at http://www.crawfordcountymuni.org/recordSearch.php. Online provides name, address, judgment, amount, and disposition of the case.   *Criminal:* same. Online provides name, address, violation and disposition only.

Municipal Court - Bucyrus   http://www.crawfordcountymuni.org/
Civil: A free record search of the docket is at http://www.crawfordcountymuni.org/recordSearch.php. Online provides name, address, judgment, amount, and disposition of the case.   *Criminal:* same. Online provides name, address, violation and disposition only.

Cuyahoga County
Common Pleas Court - General Division   http://cp.cuyahogacounty.us/internet/index.aspx
Civil: Online access to Common Please civil courts; click on Civil Case Dockets at http://cpdocket.cp.cuyahogacounty.us. Access Probate index at http://probate.cuyahogacounty.us/pa/.   *Criminal:* Online access to criminal records dockets is free at http://cpdocket.cp.cuyahogacounty.us. Alos, document images are available on Domestic Relations cases, but to registered attorneys. See http://coc.cuyahogacounty.us/en-US/efiling.aspx.

Cleveland Municipal Court - Criminal Division   http://clevelandmunicipalcourt.org/home.html
See https://clevelandmunicipalcourt.org/public-access for docket information. The site states data may not be current as rulings and or updates may not be posted. Use caution if relied upon for a full background search. There are limited personal identifiers to view as well. One can also use https://cmcoh.org.

Cleveland Municipal Court - Civil Division   http://clevelandmunicipalcourt.org/home.html
Civil: See https://clevelandmunicipalcourt.org/public-access for docket information. The site states data may not be current as rulings and or updates may not be posted. Use caution if relied upon for a full background search. There are limited personal identifiers to view as well.

Bedford Municipal Court   http://www.bedfordmuni.org/
Civil: Access index to court records at http://www.bedfordmuni.org/info.asp?pageId=5. Click on Case Information.   *Criminal:* same

East Cleveland Municipal Court   http://www.eccourt.com/
Civil: Limited court record data can be accessed for free at http://caseinfo.eccourt.com/search/searchcivildocket.asp. Daily dockets also available at the website.   *Criminal:* same

Euclid Municipal Court   http://www.cityofeuclid.com/community/court
Civil: Docket index and daily docket lists of civil cases available at http://www.cityofeuclid.com/community/court/HearingDocketsandCaseInformation.
Criminal: Same, includes Docket index and daily docket lists of misdemeanor and traffic cases.

Garfield Heights Municipal Court   https://www.ghmc.org/
Civil: Online access is limited to dockets; search by name, date or case number at https://docket.ghmc.org/recordSearch.php. There will be a delay between court filings and judicial action and the posting of such data. The delay could be at least twenty-four hours, and may be longer.   *Criminal:* same

Lakewood Municipal Court   http://www.lakewoodcourtoh.com
Civil: Search dockets at www.lakewoodcourtoh.com/casesearch.html.   *Criminal:* Same, includes traffic.

Lyndhurst Municipal Court   http://www.lyndhurstmunicipalcourt.org/
Civil & Criminal: Access current court dockets free at http://www.lyndhurstmunicipalcourt.org/info.asp?pageId=5.   There is a separate search for traffic.
Parma Municipal Court   http://www.parmamunicourt.org/
Civil: Access to the court dockets index is available free at http://www.parmamunicourt.org/info.asp?pageId=5. There will be a delay between court filings and judicial action and the posting of such data. The delay could be at least 24 hours and may be longer.   *Criminal:* same

Rocky River Municipal Court   http://www.rrcourt.net
Civil: Public access to record index at https://rrcourt.net/pa/pa.htm.   *Criminal:* same

Shaker Heights Municipal Court   http://www.shakerheightscourt.org/home/
Civil: Search case records and dockets at www.shakerheightscourt.org/home/.   *Criminal:* same

South Euclid Municipal Court   http://southeuclidcourt.com/
Civil: Access the docket index free athttp://apps.southeuclidcourt.com/record_search.php. There will be a delay (24 hours or more) between court filings and judicial action and the posting of such data by the clerk.   *Criminal:* same

Cleveland Heights Municipal Court   http://www.clevelandheightscourt.com
Civil: Search Muni civil (to $15,000) docket records from the home page or http://www.clevelandheightscourt.com/caseinformation.html. Search by name or case number.   *Criminal:* same

Berea Municipal Court   http://www.bereamunicipalcourt.org
Civil: Search docket information at http://www.bereamunicipalcourt.org/.   *Criminal:* same

Darke County
Common Pleas Court & County Municipal Court   http://www.darkecourts.com/
Civil: Free online access to the docket at http://www.darkecourts.com/. Includes judgments and divorce. *Criminal:* same

Defiance County
Common Pleas Court   http://www.defiance-county.com/commonpleas/index.php
Civil: Access the docket index at http://defianceclerkofcourts.com/eservices/home.page.2. The site does not disclose how far back records go, but cases seem to go back to at least 1995.   *Criminal:* same

Defiance Municipal Court   http://www.defiancemunicipalcourt.com
Civil: The Defiance Municipal Court computer record information is displayed at http://www.defiancemunicipalcourt.com/recordSearch.php. Search by name or case number.   *Criminal:* Same. Search by name or case number or ticket number (traffic).

Delaware County
Common Pleas Court   http://www.co.delaware.oh.us/index.php/clerk-of-courts
Civil: Access to court records is free at http://court.co.delaware.oh.us/eservices/home.page.2. Probate court index from 1852 to 1920 is free at www.midohio.net/dchsdcgs/probate.html.   *Criminal:* Access to court records is free at http://court.co.delaware.oh.us/eservices/home.page.2. Search the sheriff's county database of sex offenders, deadbeat parents, and most wanted list for free at www.delawarecountysheriff.com.

Delaware Municipal Court   http://www.municipalcourt.org/
Civil: Municipal courts records are at http://web1.civicacmi.com/DelawareMC/Court/.   *Criminal:* Same for misdemeanor and traffic case records.

Erie County
Common Pleas Court   http://www.eriecounty.oh.gov/departments-and-agencies/legal-resources/common-pleas-court/
Civil: Search record data free at http://clerkofcourts.eriecounty.oh.gov/eservices/home.page. Search by name. This is not the official record. Copied information from the years 2000 through 2009 may have increased inaccuracies since imaging was sporadically formulated within those years. Furthermore, there was no imaging from the years 2009 through February 2013.   *Criminal:* Same.

Erie County Municipal Court   http://muni.eriecounty.oh.gov/
Civil: A free search of the docket index is at http://muni.eriecounty.oh.gov/recordSearch.php. Search includes small claims.   *Criminal:* A free search of the docket index is at http://muni.eriecounty.oh.gov/recordSearch.php. Search inclldues traffic cases.

Sandusky Municipal Court   http://www.sanduskymunicipalcourt.org/
Civil: Access Muni court records free at http://www.sanduskymunicipalcourt.org/search.shtml.   *Criminal:* same

Vermilion Municipal Court   http://www.vermilionmunicipalcourt.org
Civil: Online access to Municipal court records at www.vermilionmunicipalcourt.org/search.shtml.   *Criminal:* same

Fairfield County
Common Pleas Court   http://www.fairfieldcountyclerk.com
Civil: Online access to County Clerk's court records database is free at http://courtview.co.fairfield.oh.us/eservices/home.page.2.   *Criminal:* same

Fairfield County Municipal Court   http://www.fcmcourt.org
Civil: Search civil case info online at http://12.49.195.19/cvsearch.shtml.   *Criminal:* Search criminal and traffic at http://12.49.195.19/trsearch.shtml.

Fayette County
Common Pleas Court   http://www.fayette-co-oh.com/clerk-of-courts.html
Civil: Search docket information free at https://courts.fayette-co-oh.com/ or at http://cp.onlinedockets.com/fayettecp/case_dockets/search.aspx. Search by name or case number. Includes access to divorces.   *Criminal:* Search docket info free at https://courts.fayette-co-oh.com/ or at http://cp.onlinedockets.com/fayettecp/case_dockets/search.aspx. Includes appeals from Muni court.

Wahington Court House Municipal Court   http://www.cityofwch.com
Civil: Search record index free at http://74.219.179.50/search.shtml.   *Criminal:* same

Franklin County
Common Pleas Court   http://clerk.franklincountyohio.gov/
Civil: Access records 3AM-11PM at http://fcdcfcjs.co.franklin.oh.us/CaseInformationOnline/ and includes domestic relations cases and appeals. The searchable online record index for court records often does not provide identifiers for civil and domestic case searches. One can also fill out an interactive request form at http://clerk.franklincountyohio.gov/PRRForm.cfm.   *Criminal:* Access records 3AM-11PM at http://fcdcfcjs.co.franklin.oh.us/CaseInformationOnline/. Most online index lists show the DOB, but not all. One can also fill out an interactive request form at http://clerk.franklincountyohio.gov/PRRForm.cfm.

Franklin County Municipal Court   http://www.fcmcclerk.com
Civil & Criminal: Search records from the Clerk of Court Courtview database free online at http://www.fcmcclerk.com/case/. Search by name, dates, ticket, address or case numbers.

Fulton County
Common Pleas Court   http://www.fultoncountyoh.com
Civil: Access an index of civil case records at http://pa.fultoncountyoh.com/pa/.   *Criminal:* same
County Court Western District - Wauseon   http://www.fultoncountyoh.com
Civil: Access court records back to 1995 free at www.fultoncountyoh.com/pa/.   *Criminal:* same

County Court Eastern District - Swanton   http://www.fultoncountyoh.com/
Civil: Access court records back to 1995 free at www.fultoncountyoh.com/pa/.   *Criminal:* same

Gallia County
Common Pleas Court   http://gallianet.net/index.php/justice-departments/common-pleas-court
Civil: Access the docket index at http://eaccess.gallianet.net/eservices/home.page.2. Includes judgments and divorce.   *Criminal:* Access the docket index at http://eaccess.gallianet.net/eservices/home.page.2. Includes criminal and domestic violence.

Gallipolis Municipal Court   http://www.cityofgallipolis.com/judicial_system/municipal_court.php
Civil: Search the record index at http://173.249.134.245/searchMC.shtml. Results show address.   *Criminal:* Same

Geauga County
Common Pleas Court   http://www.co.geauga.oh.us/commonpleas/
Civil: Search court record index free at http://web.geaugacourts.org/eservicesCP/home.page.2. Online records go back to 1990. Includes domestic cases. *Criminal:* Same. Includes traffic from the Muni court..

Chardon Municipal Court   http://www.co.geauga.oh.us/municourt/
Civil: Search court record index free at http://municourt.co.geauga.oh.us/eservices/home.page.2.   *Criminal:* same

Greene County
Common Pleas Court   http://www.co.greene.oh.us/index.aspx?nid=402
Civil: Online access to clerk of court records is free at https://courts.co.greene.oh.us/eservices/home.page.2. Search by name or case number. Also, search probate cases free at https://apps.co.greene.oh.us/probate/casesearch.aspx.   *Criminal:* same

Xenia Municipal Court   http://www.ci.xenia.oh.us/238/Municipal-Court
Civil: Online access to Municipal Court records free at http://www.ci.xenia.oh.us/251/Public-Access.   *Criminal:* same

Fairborn Municipal Court   http://www.fairbornmunicipalcourt.us/
Civil: Free online access to civil docket data is at http://www.fairbornmunicipalcourt.us/search.php. No images are shown.   *Criminal:* same. Search by ticket number, case number, or name.

Guernsey County
Common Pleas Court   http://www.guernseycounty.org/common-pleas-court/
Civil & Criminal: Access case index data free at http://clerkofcourts.guernseycounty.org/eservices/home.page.2. Judge calendars also available online.
Cambridge Municipal Court   http://www.cambridgeoh.org/court
Civil: Access Muni Court records free at http://webconnect03.civicacmi.com/cambridge/court/.   *Criminal:* same

Hamilton County
Common Pleas Court   http://www.courtclerk.org

Civil: Records and calendars from the court clerk are free at http://www.courtclerk.org/namesearch.asp. Online civil index goes back to 1991. Also, search probate records free at www.probatect.org/recordsearch/casesearch.asp. *Criminal:* Online access to criminal record docket is at http://www.courtclerk.org/queries.asp. Online criminal index goes back to 1986. Also, there is a subscription service for document access but this appears to be for attorneys only.

Hamilton County Municipal Court - Civil   http://www.hamilton-co.org/municipalcourt/
Civil: Information is available at http://www.courtclerk.org/. A login is needed. Very little information is provided regarding access or fees, you must call for an application if you are not an attorney.

Hancock County
Common Pleas Court   http://cp.co.hancock.oh.us/
Civil: Search records online back to 1985 at http://ea.co.hancock.oh.us/eservices/home.page.2/.   *Criminal:* same

Findlay Municipal Court   https://findlaymunicourt.com/municourt/
Civil: Search civil cases at https://findlaymunicourt.com/municourt/searchcivildocket.asp?pageId=71.   *Criminal:* Same, includes traffic.

Hardin County
Common Pleas Court   http://www.hardincourts.com/
Civil: Online access to the civil docket is available at http://www.hardincourts.com/CLSite/search.dis.shtml.   *Criminal:* same

Henry County
Common Pleas Court   http://www.henrycountyohio.com/clerk.htm
Civil: Online case search is offered at http://www.henrycountyohio.com/clerk.htm. Data is not in real time, can be 24 hours or more delay. Court schedule also online. Can search liens and judgments also.   *Criminal:* Same

Napoleon Municipal Court   http://www.napoleonmunicipalcourt.com/
Civil: A free record search is offered at http://www.napoleonmunicipalcourt.com/recordSearch.php. Note there is a delay of at least 24 hours before filings and actions are posted.   *Criminal:* same

Highland County
Common Pleas Court   http://www.hccpc.org/
Civil: Search the index online at http://eaccess.hccpc.org/eservices/home.page.2.   *Criminal:* same

Hillsboro Municipal Court   http://www.hillsboroohio.net/municipal%20court.html
Civil & Criminal: Online access is free at http://24.123.13.34/.

Hocking County
Common Pleas Court   http://www.hockingcountycommonpleascourt.com/
Civil: Access the court case index free at http://www.court.co.hocking.oh.us/cgi-bin/db2www.pgm/cpq.mbr/main.   *Criminal:* same

Hocking County Municipal Court   http://www.hockingcountymunicipalcourt.com
Civil & Criminal: Access civil records free at www.hockingcountymunicipalcourt.com/search.shtml. Shows case number, docket entry, charge, case type.

Holmes County
Common Pleas Court - General Div   http://www.co.holmes.oh.us/clerk-of-courts-overview
Civil: A free search of the court dockets is provided at http://courts.co.holmes.oh.us/eservices/home.page.2. Includes divorce, domestic relations, and civil judgment records.   *Criminal:* A free search of the court dockets is provided at http://courts.co.holmes.oh.us/eservices/home.page.2.

County Municipal Court   https://www.holmescountycourt.com/
Civil: Search by name or case number at https://www.holmescountycourt.com/recordSearch.php.   *Criminal:* Same, includes traffic.

Huron County
Common Pleas Court   http://www.huroncountyclerk.com
Civil: Search court dockets and public records free at the website http://www.huroncountyclerk.com/html/case_search.html Civil results on internet do not include DOB.   *Criminal:* Search court dockets and public records free at the website http://www.huroncountyclerk.com/html/case_search.html.

Norwalk Municipal Court   http://www.norwalkmunicourt.com
Civil: Access records free at www.norwalkmunicourt.com/search.php.   *Criminal:* same

Jackson County
Common Pleas Court   http://www.jcclerk.com/
Civil: Search the docket by name or case number at http://173.249.140.218/eservices/home.page.2.   *Criminal:* same

Jackson Municipal Court   http://www.jacksoncountymunicipalcourt.com/
Civil: Search record index free at www.jacksoncountymunicipalcourt.com/Search/.   *Criminal:* same

Jefferson County
Common Pleas Court - Steubenville   http://www.jeffersoncountyoh.com/
Civil: Access court index free at http://www.jeffersoncountyoh.com/CountyCourts/CommonPleas.aspx. No birthdates shown.   *Criminal:* same

All County Courts   http://www.jeffersoncountyoh.com/
Civil: Search court case index free at http://www.jeffersoncountyoh.com/CountyCourts/ClerkofCourts/tabid/156/Default.aspx.   *Criminal:* same

Steubenville Municipal Court   http://cityofsteubenville.us/municipal-court/
Civil: Online access to the docket index is at http://web1.civicacmi.com/Steubenville/court/.   *Criminal:* Online access to the criminal and traffic docket index is at http://web1.civicacmi.com/Steubenville/court/.

Knox County
Common Pleas Court   http://www.co.knox.oh.us/
Civil: Search court index, dockets, calendars free online at http://www.coc.co.knox.oh.us/eservices/home.page.3. Search by name or case number. *Criminal:* same

Mt Vernon Municipal Court   http://mountvernonmunicipalcourt.org
Civil: Access to the clerk's civil records are free at http://web1.civicacmi.com/MtVernonMC2/Court/Default.aspx.   *Criminal:* Same

Lake County
Common Pleas Court   http://www.lakecountyohio.com
Civil & Criminal: Online access to court records, dockets, and quick index, including probate records, is free at https://phoenix.lakecountyohio.gov/pa/.
Painesville Municipal Court   http://www.pmcourt.com
Civil: Free online access to index at www.pmcourt.com/search.shtml.   *Criminal:* same

Mentor Municipal Court   http://www.mentormunicipalcourt.org/
Civil: Record searches at http://www.mentormunicipalcourt.org/search.shtml. The initial docket list does not show identifiers, but click on the case number to find identifiers.   *Criminal:* Same.

Willoughby Municipal Court   http://www.willoughbycourt.com
Civil: Access the court's case lookup plus schedules free at http://www.willoughbycourt.com/WilloughbyMC/Court/Default.aspx.   *Criminal:* Same

Lawrence County
Common Pleas Court   http://www.lawrenceclerk.com/eservices/home.page.2
Civil: Online access to civil records is free at http://www.lawrenceclerk.com/eservices/home.page.2.   *Criminal:* same

Lawrence County Municipal Court   http://www.lawcomunicourt.com/
Civil: Click on Record Search at the web page for a search of the record index.   *Criminal:* Same. Note that SSNs are not available online.

Licking County
Common Pleas Court   http://www.lcounty.com/clerkofcourts/
Civil: County clerk's office offers free Internet access to current records at http://www.lcounty.com/TAGCPM.PA.PublicPortal/. Includes appeals for the Municipal Court and Probate Court.   *Criminal:* County clerk's office offers free Internet access to current records at http://www.lcounty.com/TAGCPM.PA.PublicPortal/. Includes appeals for the Municipal Court.

Licking County Municipal Court   http://www.lcmunicipalcourt.com
Civil: Online access to Municipal Court record docket is free at https://connection.lcmunicipalcourt.com/awc/Court/Default.aspx. Search by last name or business name of plaintiff or defendant.   *Criminal:* Online access to Municipal Court record docket is free at https://connection.lcmunicipalcourt.com/awc/Court/Default.aspx. Results include addresses.

Logan County
Common Pleas Court   http://co.logan.oh.us/192/Common-Pleas-Court
Civil: A supplemental free search is offered at http://caserecords.co.logan.oh.us/eservices/home.page.2.   *Criminal:* same

Bellefontaine Municipal Court   http://www.ci.bellefontaine.oh.us/municipal-court.html
Civil: Free access to the civil docket index is at https://web1.civicacmi.com/BellefontaineMC/Court/Default.aspx. Look up by name, including soundex, or case number. The site does not state the throughput, but records appear to go back at least 15 years.   *Criminal:* Same.

Lorain County
Common Pleas Court   http://www.loraincounty.com/clerk/
Civil: Free access to indices and dockets for common please court cases at http://cp.onlinedockets.com/loraincp/case_dockets/search.aspx. Access probate records at www.loraincounty.com/probate/search.shtml.   *Criminal:* same

Lorain Municipal Court   http://www.cityoflorain.org/municipal_court/
Civil: Access municipal court records free at http://www.cityoflorain.org/municipal_court/public_access. Search by name, date, case number or license number.   *Criminal:* same

Elyria Municipal Court   http://www.elyriamunicourt.org

Civil: Search at the docket at http://elyriamunicourt.org/index.php?id=records-schedules. Data is updated in real time. Also you can request information by email to civil@elyriamunicourt.org.   *Criminal:* Search misdemeanor and traffic docket back to 1992 at http://elyriamunicourt.org/index.php?id=records-schedules. Data is updated in real time.

Avon Lake Municipal Court   http://www.avonlakecourt.com/
Civil: Search docket index by name or case number at http://www.avonlakecourt.com/search.php.   *Criminal:* same

Oberlin Municipal Court   http://oberlinmunicipalcourt.org/
Civil: Access case information free online at http://oberlinmunicipalcourt.org/public-access/. Search by a variety of ways.   *Criminal:* same

Vermilion Municipal Court   http://www.vermilionmunicipalcourt.org
Civil: Online access to Municipal court records at www.vermilionmunicipalcourt.org/search.shtml.   *Criminal:* same

Lucas County

Common Pleas Court   http://www.co.lucas.oh.us/index.aspx?nid=83
Civil: Online access to clerk of courts dockets is free at http://www.co.lucas.oh.us/index.aspx?NID=99. Online docket goes back to 9/1997, online images back to 05/2005.. Search probate records at http://lucas-co-probate-ct.org:8080/web/guest/case-access.   *Criminal:* Online access to clerk of courts dockets is free at http://www.co.lucas.oh.us/index.aspx?NID=99. Online record go back to 9/1997. Search sex offenders at www.lucascountysheriff.org/sheriff/disclaimer.asp.

Toledo Municipal Court   http://www.tmc-clerk.com/
Civil: Dockets are online at http://www.tmc-clerk.com/caseinformation/civilcase/. Direct email requests to tmc-clerk@noris.org   *Criminal:* Same

Maumee Municipal Court   http://www.maumee.org/municipal_court/index.php
Civil & Criminal: Online access to web court system database is free at http://www.maumee.org/municipal_court/search_court_case_information.phpx. Online includes civil, criminal, traffic.

Oregon Municipal Court   http://www.oregonmunicipalcourt.us/view-court-records.html
Civil: Direct email civil search requests to court@oregonmunicipalcourt.com. Search court cases and schedules free at http://www.oregonmunicipalcourt.us/view-court-records.html.   *Criminal:* Same

Sylvania Municipal Court   http://www.sylvaniacourt.com
Civil: Online access free at http://courtsvr.sylvaniacourt.com/.   *Criminal:* same

Madison County

Common Pleas Court   http://co.madison.oh.us/commonpleas/
Civil: Search record index at http://co.madison.oh.us/clerkofcourts/Records_Search.html. Includes judgments and liens.   *Criminal:* same

Madison County Municipal Court   http://co.madison.oh.us/munict/
Civil: Access civil case record free at http://co.madison.oh.us/munict/Search.html. Shows case number, docket entry, charge, case type.   *Criminal:* Access criminal case record free at http://co.madison.oh.us/munict/Search.html. Shows case number, docket entry, charge, case type. Includes traffic.

Mahoning County

Common Pleas Court   http://www.mahoningcountyoh.gov/230/Common-Pleas-Court
Civil: For online access, see http://ecourts.mahoningcountyoh.gov/eservices/home.page.6. Some case data goes back to 1989.   *Criminal:* Access integrated justice system cases back to at least 1995 free at http://ecourts.mahoningcountyoh.gov/eservices/home.page.6. Some case data goes back to 1989.

All County Courts   http://www.mahoningcountyoh.gov/182/Clerk-of-Courts
Civil: For online access, see http://ecourts.mahoningcountyoh.gov/eservices/home.page.2. Some case data goes back to 1989.   *Criminal:* Access integrated justice system cases back to at least 1995 free at http://ecourts.mahoningcountyoh.gov/eservices/home.page.2. Some case data goes back to 1989.

Campbell Municipal Court   http://www.campbellohiomunicipalcourt.com/
Civil: Search the docket index free at http://records.campbellohiomunicipalcourt.com/. There is at least a 24 hour delay before a record is posted or modified. The search includes Small Claims. Search by name or case number.   *Criminal:* Same The search includes Traffic.

Struthers Municipal Court   http://www.cityofstruthers.com/court.aspx
Civil: Access court records at http://74.219.105.102. Records go back to 1996. Current records may not be on the system.   *Criminal:* same

Youngstown Municipal Court   http://www.youngstownmuniclerk.com/
Civil: Access cases record data back to 1998 free at http://www.youngstownmunicipalcourt.com/eservices/app/home.page.2. Search by name, case number, attorney or ticket number.   *Criminal:* same

Marion County

Common Pleas Court   http://www.co.marion.oh.us/clerk/
Civil: Court record access free at http://www.co.marion.oh.us/clerk/index.php/records-search. Records prior to August 31, 1991, may not be available on this web site.   *Criminal:* same

Marion Municipal Court   http://www.marionmunicipalcourt.org
Civil: Online record searching available at http://www.marionmunicipalcourt.org/search.php.   *Criminal:* same

Medina County
Common Pleas Court   http://www.clerk.medinaco.org/
Civi & Criminal: Search court documents, motion dockets, sexual predator judgments and court notices at the web page.
Medina Municipal Court   http://www.medinamunicipalcourt.org
Civil: Access the online Civil Case Lookup free from home page or go direct to http://24.144.216.42/MedinaMC/Court/. Records go back to 1989.
Criminal: Same

Wadsworth Municipal Court   http://www.wadsworthmunicipalcourt.com/
Civil: Access civil case lookups and case queries free at www.wadsworthmunicipalcourt.com/municipal-court/search-records.html.   *Criminal:* Same.

Meigs County
Common Pleas Court   http://www.meigscountyclerkofcourts.com/
Civil: The courts' docket information is searchable at http://www.meigscountyclerkofcourts.com/courtview_online_records.htm.   *Criminal:* same

County Court   http://www.meigscountycourt.org/
Civil: Access civil records free at http://docket.webxsol.com/meigs/index.html. Note that the heading on this web page reads Meigs County Municipal Court, but that is a typo. There is no Meigs County Municipal Court.   *Criminal:* Same

Mercer County
Common Pleas Court   http://www.mercercountyohio.org/clerk/
Civil: Online access for the public available from the home page.   *Criminal:* same

Miami County
Common Pleas Court   http://co.miami.oh.us/index.aspx?nid=132
Civil: Access the civil docket index for free at http://municipal.miamicountyohio.gov/eservicesMuni/home.page.2. When doing a search by Case number, it has to be Year, Case type, Case number; example: 15 CV 00000.   *Criminal:* Same

Municipal Court - Troy   http://www.co.miami.oh.us/index.aspx?nid=134
Civil: Online access to record index is free at http://municipal.miamicountyohio.gov/eservicesMuni/home.page.2. There is a separate search for attorneys. Note the disclaimer, as most recent updates or changes may not be posted.   *Criminal:* same

Monroe County
Common Pleas Court   http://www.monroecountyohio.net/government/common_pleas_court/index.php
Civil: Search records from November 2002 forward at http://173.249.129.210/. There is a delay of 24 hours or more of court filings and actions before they appear on the system.   *Criminal:* Same

County Court   http://www.monroecountyohio.com/government/county_court/index.php
Civil: Search records from November 2002 forward at http://173.249.129.210/. There is a delay of 24 hours or more of court filings and actions before they appear on the system.   *Criminal:* same

Montgomery County
Common Pleas Court   http://www.mcclerkofcourts.org/
Civil: Online access to the Courts countywide PRO system is free at http://www.mcclerkofcourts.org/internet-usage-disclaimer/. Access probate and guardianship record info free at http://www.mcohio.org/government/probate/prodcfm/casesearchg.cfm.   *Criminal:* same

Municipal Court - Western Division - New Lebanon   http://www.mccountycourts.org/
Civil: Search countywide records online at http://www.mcclerkofcourts.org/internet-usage-disclaimer/. The data is download each night, not quite real time.   *Criminal:* same

Municipal Court - Eastern Division - Huber Heights   http://www.mccountycourts.org/
Civil: Search countywide records online athttp://www.mcclerkofcourts.org/internet-usage-disclaimer/. The data is at least 24 hours old, it is not in real time.   *Criminal:* Same

Dayton Municipal Court -   https://daytonmunicipalcourt.org/
Civil: Online access to Dayton Municipal criminal and traffic court record search is free at http://www.wejis.com/pa/Search.cfm; includes traffic.
Criminal: Online access to civil Municipal court case summary is free at http://www.wejis.com/PA/CvSearch.cfm. Search by plaintiff, defendant, attorney name or filing date. There is a separate field if company is used. No personal identifiers shown.

Kettering Municipal Court   http://www.ketteringmunicipalcourt.com
Civil: Access case lookups free at http://caselookup.ketteringmunicipalcourt.com/awc/Court/Default.aspx. There is a disclaimer that the court does not warrant the accuracy of the data.   *Criminal:* same

Miamisburg Municipal Court   http://www.miamisburgcourts.com
Civil: Access case lookup options and case schedules for free at https://web1.civicacmi.com/MiamisburgMC/Court/Default.aspx.   *Criminal:* same

Vandalia Municipal Court   http://vandaliaohio.org/vandalia-municipal-court/
Civil: Search records, including traffic, at http://docket.vandaliacourt.com/.   *Criminal:* same

Morrow County

County Municipal Court   http://www.morrowcountymunict.org/
Criminal: Search upcoming or historical criminal and traffic case records at http://www.morrowcountymunict.org/.

Muskingum County

Common Pleas Court   http://clerkofcourts.muskingumcounty.org/
Civil: Online access to court records is available at http://clerkofcourts.muskingumcounty.org. Click on Online Search. Records indexed back to 1994.
Criminal: same

County Court   http://www.muskingumcountycourt.org
Civil: Access to county court records is free at http://www.muskingumcountycourt.org/recordSearch.php.   *Criminal:* same

Zanesville Municipal Court   http://www.coz.org/city-departments/municipal-court/
Civil: Online access free at http://74.219.84.227/searchMC.shtml   *Criminal:* Online access is free at http://74.219.84.227/searchMC.shtml and includes traffic and civil searching.

Ottawa County

Common Pleas Court   http://www.ottawacocpcourt.com
Civil: Record search and dockets free at http://www.ottawacocpcourt.com/records.htm.   *Criminal:* same

Ottawa County Municipal Court   http://www.ottawacountymunicipalcourt.com
Civil: Search record index is at http://www.ottawacountymunicipalcourt.com/search.php. Includes small claims.   *Criminal:* Same, includes traffic.

Paulding County

Common Pleas Court   http://www.pauldingcommonpleas.com
Civil: Online access to the docket index is free at http://www.pauldingcommonpleas.com/eservices/home.page.2 Includes search of certificate of judgments, divorce, and certain tax liens.   *Criminal:* same

County Court   http://www.pauldingcountycourt.com
Civil: Access to civil records is free at http://www.pauldingcountycourt.com/recordSearch.php.   *Criminal:* Access to criminal records is free at http://www.pauldingcountycourt.com/recordSearch.php.

Perry County

Common Pleas Court   http://pccommonpleas.com/
Civil: Access the civil docket and judgment liens index for free at http://pccommonpleas.com/recordSearch.php. Note that data may be posted with a delay of 24 hours or longer,   *Criminal:* Same

Perry County Court   http://www.perrycountycourt.com
Civil: Access court record index free at www.perrycountycourt.com/Search/.   *Criminal:* same

Pickaway County

Common Pleas Court   http://www.pickaway.org/
Civil: Search docket information at http://www.pickawaycountycpcourt.org/pa/.   *Criminal:* Same

Circleville Municipal Court   http://www.circlevillecourt.com
Civil: Search online at www.circlevillecourt.com/AccessCourtRecords.asp.   *Criminal:* Same.

Pike County

Pike County Court   http://www.pikecountycourt.org/
Civil: Search the index by name or case number or date at http://www.pikecountycourt.org/search.shtml. Results give full identifiers.   *Criminal:* Search the index by name or case number or date at http://www.pikecountycourt.org/search.shtml. Results give full identifiers. Includes traffic.

Portage County

Common Pleas Court   http://www.co.portage.oh.us/clerkofcourts.htm
Civil: For online records from 1977 forward, go to http://www.co.portage.oh.us/pa/pa.urd/pamw6500.display.   *Criminal:* For index from 1977 forward or images 06/2005 forward, http://www.co.portage.oh.us/pa/pa.urd/pamw6500.display. Direct questions about online access to Kathy Gray at 330-297-3648.

Portage Municipal Court - Ravenna Branch   http://www.co.portage.oh.us
Civil: Search records back to 1992 free at http://www.co.portage.oh.us/pa/pa.urd/pamw6500.display.   *Criminal:* Search records back to 1992 free at http://www.co.portage.oh.us/pa/pa.urd/pamw6500.display. Direct questions about online access to Cindy G. at 330-297-5654.

Portage Municipal Court - Kent Branch   http://www.co.portage.oh.us
Civil: Online records from 1992 forward at http://www.co.portage.oh.us/pa/pa.urd/pamw6500.display.   *Criminal:* Records from 1992 forward athttp://www.co.portage.oh.us/pa/pa.urd/pamw6500.display. Direct questions about online access to Robyn Godfrey at 330-296-2530.

Preble County
Common Pleas Court   http://www.preblecountyohio.net/
Civil: Access to court records and calendars free at www.preblecountyohio.net/.   *Criminal:* same

Eaton Municipal Court   http://www.eatonmunicipalcourt.com
Civil: Search by name or case number free at http://docket.webxsol.com/eaton/index.html. Records go back to 1989.   *Criminal:* Search by name or case number free at http://docket.webxsol.com/eaton/index.html. Computerized records begin in 1992 for online criminal and traffic cases.

Putnam County
Common Pleas Court   http://www.putnamcountyohio.gov/
Civil: Online access is free at http://common.putnamcountycourtsohio.com/eservices/home.page.2.   *Criminal:* Same

Putnam County Municipal Court   http://www.putnamcountyohio.gov/ElectedOfficials/Courts/MunicipalCourt.aspx
Civil: Online access is free at http://muni.putnamcountycourtsohio.com/eservices/home.page.2.   *Criminal:* same

Richland County
Common Pleas Court   http://richlandcourtsoh.us/
Civil: Access to civil records is at http://richlandcourtsoh.us/eservices/home.page.2. Most cases prior to 1990 are not available. This site also provides access to tax liens and certificates of judgments.   *Criminal:* Same. Most cases prior to 1990 are not available.

Mansfield Municipal Court   http://www.ci.mansfield.oh.us/departments-sp-783975672/municipal-court.html
Civil: Online access at http://ci.mansfield.oh.us/index.php?option=com_content&view=article&id=378 for records from 1992 forward.   *Criminal:* same

Ross County
Common Pleas Court   http://www.courts.co.ross.oh.us/
Civil: Search records back to 11/89 at http://eaccess.co.ross.oh.us/eservices/home.page.3.   *Criminal:* same

Chillicothe Municipal Court   http://www.chillicothemunicipalcourt.org
Civil: Search docket information at http://www.chillicothemunicipalcourt.org/Search/. Search by name or case number.   *Criminal:* Same, search traffic by ticket number.

Sandusky County
Common Pleas Court - Fremont   http://www.sandusky-county.com/index.php?page=common-pleas-court
Civil: Access the civil dockets at http://www.sandusky-county.org/Clerk/Disclaimer/All/default.asp. Search by name or case number.   *Criminal:* same.

All County Courts   http://www.sandusky-county.com/index.php?page=county-courts
Civil: Access civil docket online at http://www.sandusky-county.org/Clerk/Disclaimer/All/default.asp.   *Criminal:* Same for misdemeanor traffic and criminal data.

Scioto County
Common Pleas Court   http://www.sciotocountycpcourt.org/eservices/home.page.2
Civil: Online access to civil records back to 1/1986 is free at http://www.sciotocountycpcourt.org/eservices/home.page.2. Search by court calendar, quick index, general index or docket sheet.   *Criminal:* Online access to criminal record index back to 1/1986 is free at http://www.sciotocountycpcourt.org/eservices/home.page.2. Search by court calendar, quick index, general index or docket sheet.

Portsmouth Municipal Court   http://www.pmcourt.org
Civil: Access is free at www.pmcourt.org/disc.html.   *Criminal:* Access criminal records online free at www.pmcourt.org/disc.html.

Seneca County
Common Pleas Court   http://www.senecaco.org/clerk/index.php
Civil: Search dockets online at http://www.senecaco.org/cgi-bin/db2www.pgm/cpq.mbr/main.   *Criminal:* same

Tiffin Municipal Court   http://tiffinfostoriamunicipalcourt.org/
Civil: Access records free at http://tiffinfostoriamunicipalcourt.org/search.php.   *Criminal:* same
Fostoria Municipal Court   http://tiffinfostoriamunicipalcourt.org/
Civil: Search the index by name or case number at http://tiffinfostoriamunicipalcourt.org/search.php. The DOB is generally not shown for civil records.
Criminal: Same, can search for traffic. The DOB generally does show for criminal records and traffic tickets.

Shelby County
Common Pleas Court   http://co.shelby.oh.us/clerkofcourts/
Civil: Free online search of docket index is at http://co.shelby.oh.us/clerk-of-courts/public-records-search.   *Criminal:* same

Stark County
Common Pleas Court - Civil Division   http://starkcountyohio.gov/clerk/
Online access to the county online case docket database is free athttp://www.starkcjis.org/docket/main.html. Search by name or case number. There is an advanced search as well.

Common Pleas Court - Criminal Division   http://starkcountyohio.gov/clerk/
Online access to county case docket database is free at http://www.starkcjis.org/docket/main.htmll. Search by name, case number. Will accept requests by email at crim.clerk@co.stark.oh.us
Canton Municipal Court   http://www.cantoncourt.org/Forms/Default.aspx
Civil: Search docket information at http://www.cantoncourt.org/Forms/OnlineDocket.aspx or http://www.starkcjis.org/docket/main.html.   *Criminal:* Search docket info at http://www.starkcjis.org/docket/main.html. Includes search of traffic records.
Massillon Municipal Court   http://www.massilloncourt.org
Civil: Search the Online Case Docket of the Massillon Court at http://www.starkcjis.org/docket/main.html.   *Criminal:* Search the Online Case Docket of the Massillon Court at http://www.starkcjis.org/docket/main.html. Includes traffic and misdemeanor records.
Alliance Municipal Court   http://www.alliancecourt.org/
Civil: Search the Online Case Docket of the Alliance Court at http://www.starkcountycjis.org/cjis2/docket/main.html.   *Criminal:* Search the Online Case Docket of the Alliance Court at http://www.starkcountycjis.org/cjis2/docket/main.html includes traffic and misdemeanor records.

Summit County
Common Pleas Court   https://www.cpclerk.co.summit.oh.us/welcome.asp
Civil: Access to county clerk of courts record index is free at https://www.cpclerk.co.summit.oh.us/Disclaimer.asps. Search by name, case number, case type, or judge. Also, make a request at http://www.cpclerk.co.summit.oh.us/prr/prr.aspx. Access to probate records at http://search.summitohioprobate.com/eservices/home.page.2.   *Criminal:* Same

Akron Municipal Court   https://courts.ci.akron.oh.us/
Civil: Online access to court records and schedules is free at https://courts.ci.akron.oh.us/disclaimer.htm.   *Criminal:* same

Barberton Municipal Court   http://www.cityofbarberton.com/clerkofcourts/doc_home.html
Civil: Online records for Barberton, Green, Norton, New Franklin, Clinton, Copley and Coventry are free at http://www.cityofbarberton.com/clerkofcourts/. Includes civil and small claims.   *Criminal:* Same, includes traffic and criminal.

Stow Municipal Court   http://www.stowmunicourt.com/
Civil: Court docket information is free at www.stowmunicourt.com/docket.htm.   *Criminal:* Same

Trumbull County
Common Pleas Court   http://clerk.co.trumbull.oh.us/
Civil: Online access to court records is free at http://courts.co.trumbull.oh.us/eservices/home.page.2. Records go back to May, 1996. Includes divorce. Online access to probate court records is free at www.trumbullprobate.org/paccessfront.htm.   *Criminal:* Online access to criminal records is at http://courts.co.trumbull.oh.us/eservices/home.page.2.

Warren Municipal Court   http://warren.org/city_departments/municipal_court
Civil: Access to the docket is free at https://benchmark.warrenmuni.us/BenchmarkWeb/Home.aspx/Search. There is a 24 hour delay after filings and actions until the record is posted.   *Criminal:* Same. Includes traffic cases.

Girard Municipal Court   http://www.girardmunicipalcourt.com/
Civil: Access available at www.girardmunicipalcourt.com. Click on public access. Data is not in real time and is uploaded at night.   *Criminal:* Same

Niles Municipal Court   http://www.nilesmunicipalcourt.com/
Civil: Access the index free at http://www.nilesmunicipalcourt.com/recordSearch.php.   *Criminal:* Same Includes traffic.

Newton Falls Municipal Court   http://www.newtonfallscourt.com
Civil: Search record index free at www.newtonfallscourt.com/Search/.   *Criminal:* Same. Online results include violation, hearing info and disposition.

County Court Central - Cortland   http://www.centralcourt.co.trumbull.oh.us/
Civil: Access the docket index online at http://cdsearch.co.trumbull.oh.us/.   *Criminal:* same

County Court Eastern - Brookfield   http://www.easterncourt.co.trumbull.oh.us/
Civil: Access the docket index for this court at http://courts.co.trumbull.oh.us/eservices_east/home.page.2.   *Criminal:* same

Tuscarawas County
Common Pleas Court   http://www.co.tuscarawas.oh.us
Civil: Search dockets online at http://general.clerkweb.co.tuscarawas.oh.us/eservices/home.page.2.   *Criminal:* Search dockets online at http://general.clerkweb.co.tuscarawas.oh.us/eservices/home.page.2. Can view docket only, no images may be printed.

County Court   http://www.tusccourtsouthern.com/
Civil: Search records free at http://24.123.194.150. Link accessible from home page.   *Criminal:* Same. Warrants and Most Wanted are also available on the court website.

New Philadelphia Municipal Court   http://www.npmunicipalcourt.org
Civil: A record search of the index is available at http://www.npmunicipalcourt.org/search.php. Search by name or case number.   *Criminal:* Same

Union County
Common Pleas Court   http://www.co.union.oh.us/CommonPleasCourt/
Civil: Online access to the court clerk's public records and index is at http://www.co.union.oh.us/Public-Records-Search/. Records go back to 1/1990, older records added as accessed. Images go back to 1/2002.   *Criminal:* Same

Marysville Municipal Court   http://municourt.co.union.oh.us/
Civil: The record index may be searched for free at http://municourt.co.union.oh.us/recordSearch.php. Search by name, DOB, case number or ticket number. There will be a delay between court filings and judicial action and the posting of the data. The delay could be at least twenty-four hours, and may be longer.   *Criminal:* The record index may be searched for free at http://municourt.co.union.oh.us/recordSearch.php. Search by name, case number or ticket number.

Van Wert County
Common Pleas Court   http://www.vwcommonpleas.org
Civil: Court calendars available online. Access to civil records for free at http://eservices.vanwertcounty.org/eservices/home.page.3. Records back to 5/1998   *Criminal:* Same

Van Wert Municipal Court   http://www.vwmc.org/index.php
Civil: Access the docket index at http://www.vwmc.org/recordSearch.php. Includes Smaill Claiims. Overall throughput is not disclosed, but records appear to go back at least to mid 1990's   *Criminal:* Same.

Vinton County
Common Pleas Court
Civil: Civil records available at http://vintonco.com/clerk-of-courts/. Data is from 01/01/1998 to present and updated every 24 hours.   *Criminal:* Criminal records available at http://vintonco.com/clerk-of-courts/. Data is from 01/01/1998 to present and updated every 24 hours.

Warren County
Common Pleas Court   http://www.co.warren.oh.us/commonpleas/default.aspx
Civil: Access to civil and domestic relations case information is free at http://clerkofcourt.co.warren.oh.us/BenchmarkCP/Home.aspx/Search. Civil Stalking (CS) and Domestic Violence (DV) case file dockets are not available for viewing on the website. There is a special online access program for attorneys at http://www.co.warren.oh.us/AttorneyCourtSearch/login.aspx?ReturnUrl=%2fAttorneyCourtSearch%2fDefault.aspx   *Criminal:* Access to criminal case information is free at http://clerkofcourt.co.warren.oh.us/BenchmarkCP/Home.aspx/Search. Civil Stalking (CS) and Domestic Violence (DV) case file dockets are not available for viewing on the website.

Lebanon Municipal Court   http://court.lebanonohio.gov/
Civil: Search by name or case number at http://court.lebanonohio.gov/search.shtml. Results show address.   *Criminal:* Search by name or case number at http://court.lebanonohio.gov/search.shtml. Results show DOB and address.

County Court   http://www.co.warren.oh.us/countycourt/
Civil: Search court records on the CourtView system free at http://countycourt.co.warren.oh.us/BenchmarkCounty/Home.aspx/Search. Online records go back to 1990; no DOBs on civil results.   *Same*

Franklin Municipal Court   http://www.franklinmunicourt.com/
Civil: Free access to the docket index at http://eaccess.franklinohio.org/eservices/home.page.2. Includes small claims.   *Criminal:* Same, includes traffic.

Mason Municipal Court   http://www.masonmunicipalcourt.org
Civil: Online access to court records is free at http://courtconnect.masonmunicipalcourt.org/connection/court/.   *Criminal:* same

Washington County
Marietta Municipal Court   http://www.mariettacourt.com
Civil: Online access to from 1992 of court dockets is free at http://www.mariettacourt.com/search.shtml.   *Criminal:* same

Wayne County
Common Pleas Court   http://www.waynecourts.org
Civil: Online access to the docket is free at http://www.waynecourts.org/disclaimer. Case information is from 1995 to present. Search of Probate is included.   *Criminal:* Online access to the docket is free at http://www.waynecourts.org/disclaimer. Case information is from 1995 to present.

County Municipal Court   http://www.waynemunicipalcourt.org/
Civil: Online access to the docket is free at http://www.waynecourts.org/disclaimer. Case information is from 1995 to present. Search of Probate is included.   *Criminal:* Online access to the docket is free at http://www.waynecourts.org/disclaimer. Case information is from 1995 to present.

Williams County
Common Pleas Court   http://www.co.williams.oh.us/
Civil: Public search index available at http://www.co.williams.oh.us/. Choose Clerk of Courts tab, then public search. Searchers are to search on-line first, or they may do public search in the office as well. If website is down, you should fax over the search request. If data of birth of social needed to verify, fax or call. Records from 4/1988 to present.   *Criminal:* Same

Bryan Municipal Court   http://www.bryanmunicipalcourt.com

Civil: Muni Ct data available free at http://casesearch.bryanmunicipalcourt.com/. *Criminal:* same

Wood County
Common Pleas Court   http://clerkofcourt.co.wood.oh.us/
Civil: Access court index free at http://pub.clerkofcourt.co.wood.oh.us/eservices/home.page.2. *Criminal:* same

Perrysburg Municipal Court   http://www.perrysburgcourt.com
Civil: Online access to court record docket is free at https://www.perrysburgcourt.com/search.php. There is a 24 hour delay or more before record data is posted. Search traffic as well, by name or ticket number.   *Criminal:* Online access to court record docket is free at https://www.perrysburgcourt.com/search.php. The web page state there can be a 24 hour delay or more before record data is posted.

Bowling Green Municipal Court   http://www.bgcourt.org
Civil: Access is free to civil records at http://web1.civicacmi.com/BowlingGreenMC/Court/. *Criminal:* Same, includes traffic records.

Wyandot County
Common Pleas Court   http://www.co.wyandot.oh.us/clerk/index.php
Civil: Click on Common Pleas Inquiry from web page to view record index. *Criminal:* Same

Upper Sandusky Municipal Court   https://www.uppermunicourt.com/
Civil: A free search is provided at https://www.uppermunicourt.com/search.shtml. Generally the docket entry shows the address and DOB but the SSN is kept confidential. *Criminal:* same

Recorders, Assessors, and Other Sites of Note

About Ohio Recording Offices: 88 counties, 88 recording offices. The recording officer is the County Recorder.
About Tax Liens: All federal tax liens are filed with the County Recorder where the property is located. All state tax liens are filed with the Clerk of Common Pleas Court.

Online Access

Recorded Documents
Access to 40 Ohio county recorders' deeds, land, and UCC records is free at https://www.uslandrecords.com/ohlr3/. Participating counties are: Adams, Athens, Ashland, Auglaize, Belmont, Brown, Champaign, Clark, Clermont, Coshocton, Darke, Defiance, Fairfield, Fayette, Fulton, Geauga, Guernsey, Hancock, Hardin, Henry, Highland, Hocking, Logan, Madison, Mahoning, Monroe, Paulding, Perry, Pickaway, Pike, Richland, Ross, Sandusky, Seneca, Shelby, Van Wert, Washington, Wayne, and Williams.

Tax Assessor Data
Nearly all Ohio counties offer web access to Assessor and real estate ownership data. Usually the sites are free to use.

County Sites:

Adams County   *Property, Taxation Records*   Access the treasurer and auditor property tax data free at www.adamscountyauditor.org/.

Allen County   *Recorded Documents*   www.co.allen.oh.us/rec.php   Access recorder index and images free after registration, username and password at http://recorder.allencountyohio.com/ext/logon.asp. Contact the recorder for sign-up or get user agreement info at www.co.allen.oh.us/rec.php.
Property, Taxation Records   Access to the auditor property data is free at http://allencountyohpropertytax.com/. Also, access GIS/mapping for free at http://gis.allencountyohio.com/Freeance/Client/PublicAccess1/index.html?appconfig=AllenCountyGIS.

Ashland County   *Recorded Documents*   www.ashlandcounty.org/recorder   Access to county recorded land and UCC records is free at https://www.uslandrecords.com/ohlr3/.
Property, Taxation Records   Access property records and sales on the Auditor's database free at http://oh-ashland-auditor.publicaccessnow.com/.

Ashtabula County   *Recorded Documents*   http://ohiorecorders.com/ashtabul.html   Search real estate data back to 1/1984 at http://cotthosting.com/ohashtabula/LandRecords/protected/SrchQuickName.aspx.
Property, Taxation Records   Property records on the county Auditor's database are free at http://ashtabulaoh-auditor.ddti.net/Cookies.aspx. Also, access to GIS/mapping for free at http://gis2.ashtabulacounty.us/AshtabulaGIS/.

Athens County   *Recorded Documents*   www.ohiorecorders.com/athens.html   Access to county land and UCC records is free at https://www.uslandrecords.com/ohlr3/. Records go back to 1/1981.
Property, Taxation Records   Search the auditor's property data by name and the GIS/mapping from the home page at www.athenscountyauditor.org/.

Auglaize County   *Recorded Documents*   www2.auglaizecounty.org/elected-officials/recorder   Search recorder data free at https://www.uslandrecords.com/ohlr3/. Records from 1/1/1860 to present.
Property, Taxation Records   Look-up assessor property tax data free at www.auglaizeauditor.ddti.net/.

Belmont County   *Recorded Documents*   www.belmontcountyohio.org/recorder/   Access to recorder deed data is free at https://www.uslandrecords.com/ohlr3/. Records from 1/1/1992 to present.
Property, Taxation Records   Search auditor records at http://oh-belmont-auditor.publicaccessnow.com/home.aspx.

Brown County   *Recorded Documents*   www.ohiorecorders.com/brown.html   Access to record indexes free at https://www.uslandrecords.com/ohlr3/. Records from 1/3/1994 to present.
Property, Taxation Records   Access to GIS/mapping for free at www.browncountygis.com/PUBLIC-MAP/PUBLICMAP.HTM Also, access to property search data free at http://brownauditor.ddti.net/

Butler County   *Recorded Documents*   http://recorder.butlercountyohio.org/   Access recorded documents indexes and imaged free at http://esearch.butlercountyohio.org/External/User/Login.aspx. Can sign in as guest.
Property, Taxation Records   Search auditor property records free at www.butlercountyauditor.org/. Downloads also available from this site. Also, access to GIS/mapping for free at http://maps.butlercountyohio.org/.

Carroll County   *Recorded Documents*   www.carrollcountyohio.us/recorder.html   Access to the Recorder record database for free at http://50.42.31.139/Disclaimer.aspx.
Property, Taxation Records   Access to real estate taxes for free at http://carroll.mfcdsoftware.com/index.html.

Champaign County   *Recorded Document Index Records*   www.ohiorecorders.com/champaig.html   Access to land access free at https://www.uslandrecords.com/ohlr3/. Records from 9/19/1996 to present.
Property, Taxation Records   Online access to property records is free at http://champaignoh.ddti.net/. Also, access to GIS/mapping free at www.co.champaign.oh.us/engineer/Who_We_Are/GIS/gis.htm.

Clark County   *Recorded Documents*   www.ohiorecorders.com/clark.html   Access to county land and UCC records is free at https://www.uslandrecords.com/ohlr3/controller. Records go back to 1/1988.
Property, Taxation Records   Access to property records and GIS/mapping for free at http://gis.clarkcountyauditor.org/.

Clermont County   *Recorded Documents*   http://recorder.clermontcountyohio.gov/   Access to the recorder's property, deed, and UCC records back to 1/1/1800 at https://www.uslandrecords.com/ohlr3/.
Property, Taxation Records   Records from the auditor's county property database are free at www.clermontauditor.org/_dnn (scroll to bottom of page).

Clinton County   *Recorded Documents*   http://co.clinton.oh.us/government/recorder/   Access to recorder records free at http://cotthosting.com/ohclinton/LandRecords/protected/SrchQuickName.aspx.
Property, Taxation Records   Access the Auditor's property database including weekly sales for free at http://clintonoh.ddti.net/.

Columbiana County   *Recorded Documents*   www.columbianacountyrecorder.org/   Access the recorder index of official records back to 1993 and financing statements (index only) back to 3/1995 free at www.ccclerk.org/external/LandRecords/protected/SrchQuickName.aspx.
Property, Taxation Records   Access property records and tax sale land on the Auditor's database free at http://oh-columbiana-auditor.publicaccessnow.com/home.aspx. This site includes unclaimed funds, Sheriff's forfieted land sales and Dog Tags.

Coshocton County   *Recorded Documents*   www.coshoctoncounty.net/recorder/   Search the county 's system at http://eaccess.coshoctoncounty.net/eservices/home.page.2. Access to county land and UCC records is free at https://www.uslandrecords.com/ohlr3/. Records from 1/1980 to present.
Property, Taxation Records   Search property tax records for free at www.coshcoauditor.org/pt/forms/htmlframe.aspx?mode=content/home.htm. Also, access to GIS-mapping and deeds for free at http://gis.coshoctoncounty.net/index.aspx.

Crawford County   *Property, Taxation Records*   Access the auditor database of property search or sales search for free at www.crawfordauditor.info/. Access to GIS-mapping for free at http://gis.crawford-co.org/giswebsite/.

Cuyahoga County   *Recorded Documents*   http://fiscalofficer.cuyahogacounty.us/   Access the Recorders database free at http://recorder.cuyahogacounty.us/searchs/generalsearchs.aspx. Also, access to the Property Alert System for a fee go to http://recorder.cuyahogacounty.us/Members/Login.aspx?ReturnUrl=%2fmembers%2fnotific. This permits the subscriber to identify and monitor activity pertaining to parcels of land which have been identified as being of some interest to the user.
Property, Taxation Records   Search the auditor property tax database free at http://fiscalofficer.cuyahogacounty.us/en-US/REPI.aspx.

Darke County   *Recorded Dcouments Records*   http://mydarkecounty.com/offices/recorder/   Access to land records is free at https://www.uslandrecords.com/ohlr3/. Records go back to 5/1/1996.
Property, Taxation Records   Property and property tax records on the Darke County database are free at www.darkecountyrealestate.org/.

Defiance County *Recorded Documents* www.defiance-county.com/recorder/index.php   Free access to land record indexes found at https://www.uslandrecords.com/ohlr3/. Records from 6/1/1994 to present.
Property, Taxation Records   Free access to auditor real estate data found at http://defiance.ddti.net/.

Delaware County *Recorded Documents* www.co.delaware.oh.us/recorder/   Access to indexes for free at http://cotthosting.com/ohdelaware/User/Login.aspx. Must subscribe for images.
Property, Taxation Records   Access to auditor's property and sales data is free at http://delaware-auditor-ohio.manatron.com/.

Erie County *Recorded Documents* www.erie-county-ohio.net/recorder/   Free access to indexes at https://erieoh-web.tylertech.com/erieohweb/web/.
Property, Taxation Records   Free access to the auditor property database including weekly sales at http://erie.iviewauditor.com/.

Fairfield County *Recorded Documents* https://www.uslandrecords.com/ohlr3/controller   Access to land records is free at https://www.uslandrecords.com/ohlr3/controller. Records go back to 8/1/1996.
Property, Taxation Records   Access to the Auditor's property and sales database is free at http://realestate.co.fairfield.oh.us/.

Fayette County *Recorded Documents* www.fayette-co-oh.com/recorder.html   Access to land records is free at https://www.uslandrecords.com/ohlr3/. Indexes go back to 1/1/1976. Images are through official record Vol. #37.
Property, Taxation Records   Access the auditor's database for property data at http://fayettepropertymax.governmax.com/propertymax/rover30.asp. Access to property search for free at www.fayetteauditor.com/.

Franklin County *Recorded Documents* http://recorder.franklincountyohio.gov/   Access to the recorded data is free at https://countyfusion5.propertyinfo.com/countyweb/login.do?countyname=Franklin. Index coverage began 1/2/1914 for deeds and 1/2/1970 for mortgages.
Property, Taxation Records   Auditor's property data is at www.franklincountyauditor.com/your-property. Access auditor's GIS-data site with property lookup, history and more free at this same site.

Fulton County *Recorded Documents* www.fultoncountyoh.com/index.aspx?nid=274   Access to property, deed, and UCC records is to be free at https://www.uslandrecords.com/ohlr3/. Records from 8/1/1995 to present.
Property, Taxation Records   Search auditor property data and weekly sales free at http://fultonoh-auditor.ddti.net/. Search by name, address or parcel number.

Gallia County *Property, Taxation Records*   Property records on the county auditor real estate database are free at http://galliaauditor.ddti.net/. Also, property and GIS-mapping data free at http://galliacountygis.org/index.aspx.

Geauga County *Recorded Dcouments Records* www.ohiorecorders.com/geaugafaq.html#3   Access to land records is free at https://www.uslandrecords.com/ohlr3/. Records go back to 7/1/1984.
Property, Taxation Records   Search the Auditor's property database at http://geaugarealink.co.geauga.oh.us/ReaLink/.

Greene County *Recorded Documents, Marriage Records* www.co.greene.oh.us/index.aspx?nid=473   Access to the recorders index is free at https://apps.co.greene.oh.us/recorder/disclaimer.aspx. Indexed from 1984 to present and some internet images are available from 1997 to present. Also, Search marriages free at httsp://apps.co.greene.oh.us/probate/marriagesearch.aspx.
Property, Taxation Records   Access to GIS/mapping free at http://gis.co.greene.oh.us/onlinemaps/. Also, access to auditor data free at https://apps.co.greene.oh.us/auditor/ureca/default.aspx.

Guernsey County *Recorded Documents* www.guernseycounty.org/administrative-offices/recorder/   Access to court-related records free at http://clerkofcourts.guernseycounty.org/eservices/home.page.2. Also, access to records for free at https://www.uslandrecords.com/ohlr3/. Records from 1/1/1988 to present.
Property, Taxation Records   Access to property search for free at http://guernseycountyauditor.org/.

Hamilton County *Recorded Documents* http://recordersoffice.hamilton-co.org   Access to recorder land records is free at http://recordersoffice.hamilton-co.org/hcro-pdi/index.jsp. Can also search Military Discharges at this site.
Property, Taxation Records   Access to the auditor's tax records database is free at www.hamiltoncountyauditor.org/retax_menu_taxsummaries.asp. Assess to property search data free at www.hamiltoncountyauditor.org/realestateii/ROVER30.ASP.

Hancock County *Recorded Documents* http://co.hancock.oh.us/government-services/recorder   Access to recorder records is free at https://www.uslandrecords.com/ohlr3/. Records from 1/1/1986 to present.
Property, Taxation Records   Search the auditor's property database free at http://regis.co.hancock.oh.us/.

Hardin County *Recorded Documents* www.co.hardin.oh.us/recorder.php   Access to land record indexes for free at https://www.uslandrecords.com/ohlr3/. Records go back to 1/1/1990. Images not available.
Property, Taxation Records   Access property records from the auditor's database free at http://realestate.co.hardin.oh.us/cgi-bin/db2www.pgm/req.mbr/main?nuser=15:19:42&midf=&midn=. Also, search property data on the GIS-mapping site at www.hcgis.com/.

Harrison County *Recorded Documents* https://www.harrisoncountyohio.org/recorders-office   A free search is offered at https://www.harrisoncountyohio.org/property-search.

Henry County *Recorded Documents* www.henrycountyohio.com/recorder.htm   Access to land records for free at https://www.uslandrecords.com/ohlr3/. Records go back to 1/1/1990.
Property, Taxation Records   Access and search property data free at www.co.henry.oh.us/index.php. Also, search sheriff sales list for free at www.henrycountysheriff.com/SS/Sheriff%20Sales.html.

Highland County *Recorded Documents* www.co.highland.oh.us/Department%20Home%20Pages/Recorder.html   Access to recorders database is free at https://www.uslandrecords.com/ohlr3/. Records from 1/1/1987 to present.
Property, Taxation Records   Access and search property data free at www.highlandcountyauditor.org/.

Hocking County *Recorded Documents* www.co.hocking.oh.us/recorder/   Access to recorders database is free at https://www.uslandrecords.com/ohlr3/. Records from 1/1/1992 to present.
Property, Taxation Records   Access to county real estate assessor data for free at www.realestate.co.hocking.oh.us/cgi-bin/db2www.pgm/req.mbr/main?nuser=14:54:21&midf=&midn=.

Holmes County *Recorded Documents* http://co.holmes.oh.us/recorder-overview   For the advanced online records search go to www.fidlar.com/Laredo.aspx. Tax liens and certification of judgments are found for free at http://courts.co.holmes.oh.us/eservices/home.page.2.
Property, Taxation Records   Access the auditor's property data and sales free at www.holmescountyauditor.org/.

Huron County *Recorded Documents* http://recorder.huroncounty-oh.gov/   Search the recorder's land record indexes free at http://recorder.huroncounty-oh.gov/.
Property, Taxation Records   Access to the auditor data and property sales is free at www.huroncountyauditor.org/.

Jackson County *Property, Taxation Records*   Access property and sales data free at www.jacksoncountyauditor.org/ and click on Search.

Jefferson County *Recorded Documents* www.ohiorecorders.com/jefferso.html   Access to real estate records free at www.jeffersoncountyoh.com/OnLineServices/RealEstateSearch/tabid/199/Default.aspx. Also, search voter names free at www.voterfind.com/public/ohjefferson/pages/vtrlookup.asp. Access the sheriff, treasurer, and auditor foreclosure sales lists free at www.jeffersoncountysheriff.com/sales.html.
Property, Taxation Records   Access to the county auditor property data is free at http://public.jeffersoncountyoh.com/realtax/(X(1)S(h5zxfr45x2tage451v3wc43z))/MasterFrame.aspx?AspxAutoDetectCookieSupport=1. Also, download real estate data from the auditor's database free at http://public.jeffersoncountyoh.com/tax/realdown.htm. Also, access to GIS/mapping free at www.jeffersoncountyoh.com/OnLineServices/SubDivisionRealEstatePlats.aspx.

Knox County *Recorded Documents* www.co.knox.oh.us/offices/recorder/   Access index records free at www.recorder.co.knox.oh.us/external/LandRecords/protected/SrchQuickName.aspx.
Property, Taxation Records   Online access to property records is available at www.knoxcountyauditor.org/.

Lake County *Recorded Documents (indexes only) Records* www.lakecountyohio.gov/Default.aspx?alias=www.lakecountyohio.gov/recorder   Access the Recorder's Document Index free at www.lakecountyohio.gov/RS2009/Search.aspx/Search.aspx/Search.aspx. Records go back to 1986. UCCs are index only. Images of documents not available.
Property, Taxation Records   Access to the treasurer and auditor's real estate databases is free at www.lake.iviewauditor.com/. Also, access to GIS/mapping for free http://arcgis.lakecountyohio.gov/lakenavigator/index.html.

Lawrence County *Recorded Documents* www.lawrencecountyohiorecorder.org   Access to records free at www.lawrencecountyohiorecorder.org/record_search.htm. Deeds 1982 to present, mortgages 1988 to present, leases, liens and misc 1981 to present, financing statement 1989 to present.
Property, Taxation Records   Search the auditor's data free at www.lawrencecountyauditor.org/.

Licking County *Recorded Documents* www.lcounty.com/rec/   Access to the recorders database is free at www.lcounty.com/recordings/. NOTE: Documents recorded before 9/22/97 may not show all marginal notations on the imaged document.
Property, Taxation Records   Access the Assessor's county property database free at www.lcounty.com/OnTrac/. Also, access to GIS/mapping for free at www.lcounty.com/taxparcelviewer/default.htm.

Logan County *Recorded Documents* www.co.logan.oh.us/212/Recorder   Access to the recorders database is free at http://landrecords.co.logan.oh.us/. Treasurer's delinquent property tax lists free at www.co.logan.oh.us/218/Treasurer.
Property, Taxation Records   Records on the County Auditor's database are free at http://realestate.co.logan.oh.us/. Also, search the sheriff's sales lists at http://logansheriff.com/?option=com_content&view=article&id=154&Itemid=55.

Lorain County *Recorded Documents* www.loraincounty.com/recorder/   Access the recorder records free at http://162.39.12.36/External/User/Login.aspx. One may sign in as a guest. This site gives a list of avaibale records. Official records available since 1/1/1998.
Property, Taxation Records   Access property records and sales on the County Auditor's database free at www.loraincountyauditor.com/gis/. Both a free and advanced search are offered.

Lucas County *Recorded Documents* www.co.lucas.oh.us/index.aspx?nid=675 Access to recorder real estate records is free with registration at http://apps.co.lucas.oh.us/rec/logon.asp.
Property, Taxation Records Property records on the County Auditor's Real Estate Information System (AREIS) database are free at www.co.lucas.oh.us/index.aspx?nid=377.

Madison County *Recorded Documents* www.ohiorecorders.com/madison.html Access to land records is free at https://www.uslandrecords.com/ohlr3/. Records from 3/1/1920 to present for deeds, back to 1964 for mortgages, all others back to 5/1/1994.
Property, Taxation Records Access records on the County Auditor's database free at http://madisonoh.ddti.net/.

Mahoning County *Recorded Documents (Index Only) Records* http://gis.mahoningcountyoh.gov/215/Recorder Access to land records free at https://www.uslandrecords.com/ohlr3/. Records from 1/1/1985 to present.
Property, Taxation Records Property tax records on the Auditor's database are free at http://oh-mahoning-auditor.publicaccessnow.com/. Also, access property data free on the GIS site at http://gis.mahoningcountyoh.gov/161/GIS.

Marion County *Recorded Documents* www.co.marion.oh.us/recorder/ Access the recorders indexes only from 1983 to present at http://oh3laredo.fidlar.com/OHMarion/DirectSearch/Default.aspx.
Property, Taxation Records Access to the county auditor real estate database is free at http://propertysearch.co.marion.oh.us/. Also, access to GIS/mapping for free at http://mcogis.co.marion.oh.us/flex/viewer/. Also, access the sheriff sales list free at www.co.marion.oh.us/sheriff/index.php/sheriff-sales.

Medina County *Recorded Documents* www.recorder.co.medina.oh.us/ Access to indexes 1983 to present on the recorder database is free at www.recorder.co.medina.oh.us/documentsearch.html.
Property, Taxation Records Access property records, dog tags, and unclaimed funds on the Medina County Auditor database free at www.medinacountyauditor.org/allsearches.htm. Sheriff's county tax sale list is at www.medinacountyauditor.org/sheriffsales_php.php.

Meigs County *Property, Taxation Records* Access to Auditor database free from the home page www.meigscountyauditor.org/.

Mercer County *Recorded Documents* www.mercercountyrecorder.com/ Access recorder data free at www.mercercountyohio.org/LandmarkWebLive/.
Property, Taxation Records Access property records on County Auditor Real Estate database free at www2.mercercountyohio.org/auditor/ParcelSearch/.

Miami County *Property, Taxation Records* Access auditor data free at www.miamicountyauditor.org/.

Monroe County *Recorded Documents* www.ohiorecorders.com/monroe.html Access to recorders database is free at https://www.uslandrecords.com/ohlr3/. Records from 11/1/1993 to present.
Property, Taxation Records A commercial subscription program is available from the Auditor's office at http://monroecountyauditor.org. Call first to register, 740-472-0873; $15 fee per month fee applies.

Montgomery County *Recorded Documents* www.mcohio.org/government/elected_officials/recorder/index.php Access to the recorders indexes for free at http://public.mcrecorder.org/External/User/Login.aspx?ReturnUrl=%2fexternal%2findex.aspx. Must subscribe for detailed information.
Property, Taxation Records Search auditor's property data and GIS-data free at www.mcrealestate.org/Main/Home.aspx. Property tax records on the county treasurer tax information database are free at www.mctreas.org/. Also, search auditor's vendor license free at www.mcauditor.org/vendor_license_list.cfm?letter=D. Also, search sheriff sales at www.mcohio.org/sheriff/Real_Estate.cfm.

Morgan County *Property, Taxation Records* Access the auditor property data free at http://morgancountyauditor.org.

Morrow County *Property, Taxation Records* Access to the county auditor database is free at http://auditor.co.morrow.oh.us/.

Muskingum County *Recorded Documents* http://recorder.muskingumcounty.org/ Access the recorders database free at http://cotthosting.com/ohmuskingum/LandRecords/protected/SrchQuickName.aspx. Deeds back to 1977, Mortgages-1976, Liens & Misc-1975, Military Discharges back to 1865, Leases-1981, Plat-1800 and UCC's-1993. 4/1/11, if you want to search records before the above dates, Click on the 'Historical Indexes' tab. Also, the sheriff's site provides sale lists, sex offender data, inmate registry and most wanted date at www.ohiomuskingumsheriff.org/.
Property, Taxation Records Records on the county auditor database (includes parcel data dn GIS/mapping) are free at www.muskingumcountyauditor.org/.

Ottawa County *Property, Taxation Records* Access to the auditor's property database including sales is free at www.ottawacountyauditor.org/.

Paulding County *Recorded Documents* www.ohiorecorders.com/paulding.html Access recorder data free at https://www.uslandrecords.com/ohlr3/controller. Records from 1/1/1990 to present.
Property, Taxation Records Access to land searches for free at www.pauldingcountyauditor.com/.

Perry County *Recorded Documents* www.ohiorecorders.com/perry.html Access to record indexes free at https://www.uslandrecords.com/ohlr3/. Records from 1/1/1983 to present.

Property, Taxation Records   Access to property search records for free at www.perrycountyauditor.us/.

Pickaway County   *Recorded Documents*   www.pickaway.org/offices/recorder/index.html   Search recorder data free at https://www.uslandrecords.com/ohlr3/. Records from 1/1/1990 to present.

Property, Taxation Records   Access to the county auditor property data is www.pickaway.iviewauditor.com/.

Pike County   *Recorded Documents*   www.ohiorecorders.com/pike.html   Access to the recorder's database is free at https://www.uslandrecords.com/ohlr3/. Records from 8/1/1800 to present.

Property, Taxation Records   Access auditor databases free at www.realestate.pike-co.org/cgi-bin/db2www.pgm/req.mbr/main?nuser=14:06:38&midf=&midn=. Search sheriff sales lists at http://wp2.pikecosheriff.com/?page_id=924. Also, access to real estate records for free at www.realestate.pike-co.org/re/re-search.php.

Portage County   *Recorded Documents*   www.co.portage.oh.us/recorder.htm   Access to various records free at www.co.portage.oh.us/recorder.htm. Index is from 1995-present and documents from 2001 to present. Also has an index from 1979-1994 (deeds, POA and easements).

Property, Taxation Records   Access to the auditor's property records and sales is free at www.portagecountyauditor.org/. Access to the sheriff's property sales list is free at www.co.portage.oh.us/sheriffsales.htm. Also, access to GIS/mapping for free at www.co.portage.oh.us/gis.htm.

Preble County   *Property, Taxation Records*   Property records on the County Auditor's database are free at www.preblecountyauditor.org/.

Putnam County   *Recorded Documents*   www.putnamcountyrecorder.com/   Access to real estate indexes for free go to http://putnamcountyrecorder.com/Landmark/.

Property, Taxation Records   Access to real estate for free at http://co.putnam.oh.us/cgi-bin/db2www.pgm/req.mbr/main. Also, access to GIS/mapping free at www.putnamcountygis.com/.

Richland County   *Recorded Documents*   www.richlandcountyoh.us/Recorder/Recorder.html   Access county land records free at https://www.uslandrecords.com/ohlr3/. Records from 4/1/1989 to present. Also, access to tax liens and certificate of judgments at http://richlandcourtsoh.us/eservices/home.page.2.

Property, Taxation Records   Property records from the County Auditor database are free at www.richlandcountyauditor.org/pt/forms/htmlframe.aspx?mode=content/home.htm. Sales list also on this page.

Ross County   *Recorded Documents*   www.co.ross.oh.us/#!recorder/c13fs   Access to county land, recording and UCC records is free at https://www.uslandrecords.com/ohlr3/. Index from 1/1/1974 to present (not all images are in yet). Images can be printed out at $.10 per page.

Property, Taxation Records   Access to the auditor's property and sales data is free at http://auditor.co.ross.oh.us/.

Sandusky County   *Recorded Documents*   www.sandusky-county.com/index.php?page=recorder   Access to records for free at https://www.uslandrecords.com/ohlr3/. Records from 7/15/1996 to present.

Property, Taxation Records   Access to county auditor property data is free at www.sanduskycountyauditor.us/. Also, access to GIS/mapping for free at www.sanduskycountygis.org/sandgis/.

Scioto County   *Property, Taxation Records*   4 searches are offered at the home page http://sciotocountyauditor.org/: Address, owner, parcel number, and sales search.

Seneca County   *Recorded Documents*   www.ohiorecorders.com/seneca.html   Access to records for free at https://www.uslandrecords.com/ohlr3/. Records from 8/1/1987 to present.

Property, Taxation Records   Access to land records for free at www.senecacountyauditor.org/.

Shelby County   *Recorded Documents*   http://co.shelby.oh.us/recorders-office   Access to records for free at https://www.uslandrecords.com/ohlr3/. Records from 7/1/1989 to present.

Property, Taxation Records   Access to property search data for free at http://cama.shelbycountyauditors.com/cama/.

Stark County   *Recorded Documents*   http://starkcountyohio.gov/recorder/   Access the recorder's database free after registration at http://app.recorder.co.stark.oh.us/Recorder_Disclaimer.htm. Must register to retrieve public records.

Property, Taxation Records   Search auditor's property data free at http://ddti.starkcountyohio.gov/Disclaimer.aspx. Also, access to sheriff sales lists are at http://webapp.co.stark.oh.us/sheriff_sales/.

Summit County   *Property, Taxation Records*   Access tax map data from the county fiscal officer for free at http://summitgis.maps.arcgis.com/home/index.html. Also property appraisal, images and tax data are on this site. Also, search property tax bill and appraisal records free at https://fiscaloffice.summitoh.net/index.php/property-tax-search.

Trumbull County   *Recorded Documents*   http://recorder.co.trumbull.oh.us/   Access the recorder's database free at http://records.co.trumbull.oh.us/. Click on Find a Record?.

Property, Taxation Records   Search auditor property tax data free at http://property.co.trumbull.oh.us/. Also, search the Sheriff sales/land sales list free at http://sheriff.co.trumbull.oh.us/sheriffsale.htm.

Tuscarawas County *Recorded Documents* www.co.tuscarawas.oh.us/Recorder/index.htm Access to land records for free at http://auditor.co.tuscarawas.oh.us/.
Property, Taxation Records Access to online property searches for free at http://auditor.co.tuscarawas.oh.us/.

Union County *Recorded Documents* www.co.union.oh.us/Recorder/ Search recorded documents at www.co.union.oh.us/Recorder-Disclaimer/.
Property, Taxation Records Access to a variety of records for free at www.co.union.oh.us/index.cfm?fuseaction=trees.treepage&treeID=40393. Includes GIS/mapping, parcel, plats and payment of real estate taxes. Search the GIS mapping site at www4.co.union.oh.us/countymap/. Also, search the treasurer's list of delinquent taxpayers at www4.co.union.oh.us/treasurer/delinquent/Default.aspx/Default.aspx.

Van Wert County *Recorded Documents* http://vanwertcounty.org/recorders-office/ Access to county land and UCC records is free at https://www.uslandrecords.com/ohlr3/. Records from 1/1/1993 to present.
Property, Taxation Records Online access to property records free at www.co.vanwert.oh.us/re/re-search.php.

Vinton County *Property, Taxation Records* Search the data base at www.vintoncountyauditor.org/Cookies.aspx.

Warren County *Recorded Documents (index Only) Records* www.co.warren.oh.us/recorder/ Access Recorders indexes free back to 1979 at www.co.warren.oh.us/recorder/searchInfo.aspx.
Property, Taxation Records Access to the auditor Property Search database is free at www.co.warren.oh.us/property_Search/. Also, search sheriff sales records free at www.wcsooh.org/SheriffSales/default.aspx.

Washington County *Recorded Documents* www.washingtongov.org/index.aspx?NID=324 Access to records for free at https://www.uslandrecords.com/ohlr3/. Records from 12/1/1984 to present.
Property, Taxation Records Access to the county auditor's property search database is free at www.washingtoncountyauditor.us/Disclaimer.aspx. Search of manufactured homes is at www.washingtoncountyauditor.us/manufacturedhomes/.

Wayne County *Recorded Documents* www.ohiorecorders.com/wayne.html Access to land record indexes only for a fee at https://www.uslandrecords.com/ohlr3/controller. Indexes from 5/1/1988 to present.
Property, Taxation Records Access to the auditor's property and sales data is free at www.waynecountyauditor.org/. Click on Search. The late taxpayer list appears on the treasurer's website at http://waynecountytreasurer.org/LateTaxpayers.aspx.

Williams County *Recorded Documents* http://williamscountyrecorder.com/ Search recorder records free at https://www.uslandrecords.com/ohlr3/. Records from 1/1/1992 to present.
Property, Taxation Records Access to the auditor's property data and sales is free at http://williamsoh.ddti.net/.

Wood County *Recorded Documents (indexes only) Records* www.co.wood.oh.us/recorder/ Access to indexes free at http://woodrcd.co.wood.oh.us/Disclaimer.aspx.
Property, Taxation Records Access to the auditor's property data is free at http://auditor.co.wood.oh.us/. No name searching.

Wyandot County *Property, Taxation Records* A basic property search is at http://realestate.co.wyandot.oh.us/re/re-search.php. Search by name or address or parcel number.

Oklahoma

Capital: Oklahoma City
             Oklahoma County
Time Zone: CST
Population: 3,911,338
# of Counties: 77

Useful State Links

Website: **https://www.ok.gov/**
Governor: **www.ok.gov/governor/**
Attorney General: **www.oag.state.ok.us**
State Archives: **www.odl.state.ok.us/oar/index.htm**
State Statutes and Codes: **www.oklegislature.gov/osStatuesTitle.aspx**
Legislative Bill Search: **www.oklegislature.gov/**
Unclaimed Funds: **https://www.ok.gov/unclaimed/**

State Public Record Agencies

Criminal Records

OK State Bureau of Investigation, Criminal History Reporting,   https://www.ok.gov/osbi/Criminal_History/index.html   The agency provides the ACHS - Automated Criminal History System. $15.00 fee applies. Applications are only accepted for companies who currently conduct at least 50 record checks a month. See https://www.ok.gov/osbi/Criminal_History/Automated_Criminal_History_System/index.html. For questions on establishing an account, email carol.kinser@osbi.ok.gov. There is a User's manual found at https://www.ok.gov/osbi/documents/ACHS%20User%20Manual.pdf.

Sexual Offender Registry

Oklahoma Department of Corrections, Sex Offender Registry,   https://sors.doc.state.ok.us/   Two different online searches are offered from https://sors.doc.state.ok.us/. One search is for Sex Offenders Registry at https://sors.doc.state.ok.us/svor/f?p=119:1: The other for the Violent Offenders Registry - see https://vors.doc.state.ok.us/svor/f?p=101:1.   *Other Options:* Database and bulk purchases can be requested from the IT department. Call for pricing and media.

Incarceration Records

Oklahoma Department of Corrections, Offender Records,   https://www.ok.gov/doc/   Offender Lookup is at https://www.ok.gov/doc/Offenders/index.html. The information reflects the records on file of offenders sentenced to a term of probation or incarceration within the Oklahoma Department of Corrections There is a parole & pardon search at https://www.ok.gov/ppb/search/app/. A Most Wanted search is at http://204.62.19.160/fugitives/most_wanted.aspx.

Corporation, LLC, LP, LLP, Trade Name, Fictitious Name, Trademark

Secretary of State, Business Records Department,   https://www.sos.ok.gov/Default.aspx   Visit https://www.sos.ok.gov/corp/corpInquiryFind.aspx for free searches on business entities. Search trademarks at https://www.sos.ok.gov/trademarks/default.aspx. Customers may also order and receive status certificates as well as certified and plain copies. Fees vary, see the web page for details. There is a list of domestic LLCs. Also, search securities brokers/investment advisors/firms at www.securities.ok.gov/Firms-profs/DBSearch/DatabaseSearch.asp.   *Other Options:* A variety of database downloads are available. See the fees page for a list at https://www.sos.ok.gov/business/fees.aspx.

Uniform Commercial Code

UCC Central Filing Office, Oklahoma County Clerk,   http://countyclerk.oklahomacounty.org/registrar-of-deeds/ucc   Records of all UCC financing statements may be viewed free at http://countyclerk.oklahomacounty.org/registrar-of-deeds/rod-ucc-search. Search by debtor or secured party. The site gives a disclaimer stating there may be a significant delay between the filing of the record and availability to a requester on this site. Neither certified searches nor record requests are accepted at the web page.   *Other Options:* The entire database is available on microfilm or computer tapes. The initial history is $500 with $50 per update. Images are available for $.04 per image.

Sales Tax Registrations

Taxpayer Assistance - Sales Tax, Oklahome Tax Commission,   https://www.ok.gov/tax/   A free tax permit look-up service is provided at https://oktap.tax.ok.gov/OkTAP/Web/_/#1.   *Other Options:* Current sales tax permit holders are permitted to purchase the sales tax database on microfiche or disk. Monthly updates are available. Call for fees.

Birth, Death Records

State Department of Health, Vital Records Service,   https://www.ok.gov/health/Birth_and_Death_Certificates/index.html   Online ordering is available via a designated vendor - www.vitalchek. Their web page gives details - one may also order by phone. Additional fees are involved, use of a credit card is required.

Driver Records

MVR Desk, Records Management Division,   www.dps.state.ok.us/recm/   Electronic access is available for qualified, approved users through www.ok.gov. This is a batch mode process with plans for interactive service in the future. The $27.50 record fee includes a $2.50 service fee. There is an annual $75.00 subscription fee upon approval. Search by either the DL# or by the name, and DOB and gender. The full record fee applies for a no record found. For more information, call 800-955-3468 or visit https://www.ok.gov/idlr/index.php. Note OK drivers may order and view their own record at https://www.ok.gov/dps/mvr/app/index.php.   *Other Options:* The Driver Status Notification System (DSNS) is an online, notification service for employers (only) if CDL drivers. The annual fee is $50 plus $5 per driver enrolled and cost of an annual driving record. For more information, contact Records Management.

Vehicle, Vessel Ownership & Registration

Oklahoma Tax Commission, Motor Vehicle Division, Attn: Research,   https://www.ok.gov/tax/Individuals/Motor_Vehicle/index.html   Oklahoma offers an Insurance Verification online. The site allows one to verify compulsory liability insurance coverage on privately-owned vehicle insured by a personal policy of vehicle insurance It does not verify coverage for a vehicle covered by a commercial policy. The request must include the VIN and Policy Number. Visit https://www.dps.state.ok.us/insver/.   *Other Options:* Oklahoma does not offer bulk delivery of vehicle and ownership information except for purposes such as vehicle recall.

Voter Registration

State Election Board, Voter Records,   https://www.ok.gov/elections/   Confirm a registered voter at https://services.okelections.us/voterSearch.aspx. *Other Options:* Database CDs are provided for no charge. Contact the agency for more information.

Campaign Finance

Okalhoma Ethics Commission, 2300 N. Lincoln Blvd Rm. B-5,   https://www.ok.gov/ethics/   Search a myriad of financial information available to search at https://www.ok.gov/ethics/public/index.php. Also, opinions and investigations can be searched from the home page.

GED Records

ODCTE, Lifelong Learning,   http://sde.ok.gov/sde/general-educational-development-ged%C2%AE   Records may be requested from https://www.diplomasender.com. A credit card is needed. Request must be ordered by the test taker. Employers and third parties must receive an email and/or Authentication Code from the test taker to then access the authorized documents. Turnaround time is 1-3 days. You may choose to receive your document by email, fax, or mail.

Occupational Licensing Boards

Alarm Firm/Employee	https://www.ok.gov/odol/documents/Alarm_and_Locksmith_Licensed_Companies.pdf
Architect/Architectural Firm	https://apps.ok.gov/architects/app/licensee_search.php
Athletic Trainer/Apprentice	www.okmedicalboard.org/search
Attorney	www.oklahomafindalawyer.com/FindALawyer
Audiologist	https://www.ok.gov/obespa/LICENSE_INFORMATION/License_Verification/index.html
Bail Bondsman	https://sbs-ok.naic.org/Lion-Web/jsp/sbsreports/AgentLookup.jsp
Bank	https://www.ok.gov/banking/Bank_Listing.html
Beauty/Barber School	https://www.ok.gov/cosmo/Schools/index.html
Blacksmith	www.ohrc.org/dataaccess/OccupationalLicenseReceiptSearch.cfm
Burglar Alarm Svc/Instal/Seller	https://www.ok.gov/odol/documents/Alarm_and_Locksmith_Licensed_Companies.pdf
Counselor LPC/MLFT/LBP	https://www.ok.gov/health/counselor/app/index.php
Credit Services Organization	https://www.ok.gov/okdocc/Consumer_Resources/License_Rosters/
Credit Union	https://www.ok.gov/banking/Credit_Union_Listing.html
Dental Laboratory	https://www.ok.gov/dentistry/Licenses/index.html
Dentist/Dental Assistant/Hygienist	https://www.ok.gov/dentistry/Licenses/index.html

Dietitian/Provisional Dietitian	www.okmedicalboard.org/search
Disciplined Chiropractors	https://www.ok.gov/chiropracticboard/License_Information/Disciplined_Chiropractors/index.html
Electrologist	www.okmedicalboard.org/search
Embalmer/Funeral Director/Apprentice	https://ok.gov/funeral/License_Verification/index.html
Engineer	https://www.ok.gov/pels/search/search.php
Euthanasia Technician	https://pay.apps.ok.gov/okvetboard/renewal/search.php
Health Spa	https://www.ok.gov/okdocc/Consumer_Resources/License_Rosters/
Horse Racing (license type)	www.ohrc.org/dataaccess/OccupationalLicenseReceiptSearch.cfm
Insurance Adjuster	https://sbs-ok.naic.org/Lion-Web/jsp/sbsreports/AgentLookup.jsp
Insurance Agent/Representative	https://sbs-ok.naic.org/Lion-Web/jsp/sbsreports/AgentLookup.jsp
Insurance Company	https://sbs-ok.naic.org/Lion-Web/jsp/sbsreports/AgentLookup.jsp
Insurance Consultant	https://sbs-ok.naic.org/Lion-Web/jsp/sbsreports/AgentLookup.jsp
Jockey/Horse Trainer/Agent	www.ohrc.org/dataaccess/OccupationalLicenseReceiptSearch.cfm
Landscape Architect	https://apps.ok.gov/architects/app/licensee_search.php
Lobbyist	https://pay.apps.ok.gov/ethics/lobbyist/public_lobbyist_list.php?yr=2014
Locksmith/Company	https://www.ok.gov/odol/documents/Alarm_and_Locksmith_Licensed_Companies.pdf
LPG-Liquefied Petrol Dealer/Mfg/Mgr	www.oklpgas.org/search/index.php
Midwife	https://apps.ok.gov/nursing/verify/index.php
Money Order Agent/Company	https://www.ok.gov/banking/Money_Order_Licensee_Listing.html
Mortgage Broker	https://www.ok.gov/okdocc/Consumer_Resources/License_Rosters/
Notary Public	https://www.sos.ok.gov/notary/search.aspx
Nurse Anesthetist-Certified Registered	https://apps.ok.gov/nursing/verify/index.php
Nurse Practitioner-Adv'd Registered	https://apps.ok.gov/nursing/verify/index.php
Nurse-RN/LPN/Specialist-Clinical	https://apps.ok.gov/nursing/verify/index.php
Nursery, Plant	www.oda.state.ok.us/forms/cps/cps-nursdir.pdf
Occupational Therapist/Assistant	www.okmedicalboard.org/search
Optometrist	https://pay.apps.ok.gov/optometry/licensing/app/index.php
Optometrist Discipline List	http://optometry.ok.gov/
Orthotist/Prosthetist	www.okmedicalboard.org/search
Osteopathic Physician	http://docfinder.docboard.org/ok/df/oksearch.htm
Pawnbroker	https://www.ok.gov/okdocc/Consumer_Resources/License_Rosters/
Pedorthist	www.okmedicalboard.org/search
Perfusionist	www.okmedicalboard.org/search
Pesticide Applicator/Dealer	www.oda.state.ok.us/forms/cps/applist.pdf
Pesticide Certification/Registration	http://kellysolutions.com/ok/
Pharmacist/Pharmacy Intern/Technician	https://www.ok.gov/pharmacy/Board/Contact/index.html
Physical Therapist/Assistant	www.okmedicalboard.org/search
Physician/Medical Doctor/Assistant	www.okmedicalboard.org/search
Podiatrist	www.okpodiatrists.org/search
Precious Metals & Gem Dealer	https://www.ok.gov/okdocc/Consumer_Resources/License_Rosters/
Prosthetist	www.okmedicalboard.org/search
Psychologist	https://pay.apps.ok.gov/OSBEP/_app/search/index.php
Real Estate Appraiser	https://www.ok.gov/oid/documents/071416_Appraiser%20Roster.pdf
Real Estate Disciplinary Orders	https://www.ok.gov/oid/Regulated_Entities/Real_Estate_Appraiser_Board_(REAB)/Disciplinary_Orders.html
Registered Interior Designer	https://apps.ok.gov/architects/app/licensee_search.php
Rent to Own Dealer	https://www.ok.gov/okdocc/Consumer_Resources/License_Rosters/
Residential Child Care Facility	http://childcarefind.okdhs.org/childcarefind/
Respiratory Care Practitioner	www.okmedicalboard.org/search
Savings & Loan Association	https://www.ok.gov/banking/Savings_&_Loan_Listing.html
Social Worker	https://pay.apps.ok.gov/medlic/social/licensee_search.php
Speech Pathologist	https://www.ok.gov/obespa/LICENSE_INFORMATION/License_Verification/index.html
Surveyor, Land	https://www.ok.gov/pels/search/search.php
Trust Company	https://www.ok.gov/banking/Trust_Company_Listing.html
Veterinarian/Technician	https://pay.apps.ok.gov/okvetboard/renewal/search.php

State and Local Courts

About Oklahoma Courts: The **District Court** is the trial court and hears all cases except traffic and ordinance matters. There are 77 District Courts in 26 judicial districts. Creek County has three Divisions and Seminole County has two Divisions.

Cities with populations in excess of 200,000 (Oklahoma City and Tulsa) have a criminal **Municipal Courts of Record**. Cities with less than 200,000 do not have such courts.

There is also an Oklahoma Workers' Compensation Court.

The web page for the Judicial Branch is www.oscn.net.

Appellate Courts: Oklahoma is unique – it has two courts of last resort. The Supreme Court determines all issues of a civil nature; the Oklahoma Court of Criminal Appeals decides all criminal matters. There is also an intermediate appeals court – the Court of Civil Appeals. See /www.oscn.net/applications/oscn/NewDecisionsByCourt.asp for online access to opinions from the Supreme Court, the Court of Criminal appeals, the Court of Civil appeals, for OK Attorney General opinions, and OK session laws.

Online Court Access

Statewide Court Online Access: There are two systems.

All 77 Counties are on OSCN (Oklahoma State Courts Network)

Web access to docket information for civil and criminal docket information is free for all 77 counties including Cimarron (added June 2016). See www.oscn.net/dockets. Search by name or case number. One may also search traffic tickets. Be sure to check the Court Records Help link for searching help including the wild card characters. There is one caution: Researchers report there is a lack of identifiers which is an issue with common name searches. Another issue is that site does not indicate the throughput of records per county. One does not know how far back the records go. **Use caution** when using this site for strong due diligence needs.

At ODCR (On Demand Court Records) - A Vendor:

Online access is available for all county trial courts, except Cimarron, at www1.odcr.com.

An excellent service the ODCR site provides is a county status page. There is a *"records back to"* column plus the page shows in minutes when the last update was performed. See www1.odcr.com/status. Below is a description of the three service levels at ODCR.

1) **Free:** Search for docket info by partial name or case number of filed date range. The site also gives the throughput dates for each county. Most counties update within 24 hours or less.

2) **Advanced Subscription:** For $5.00 per month, enhanced searching procedures and results. Advanced search options include using the DOB, address, offense, and closed date range among others. There is also a case and party monitoring system.

3) **Image Access Subscription for Attorneys:** For $50.00 per month, attorneys have unlimited access to court images with the ability to download and print full case filings.

No individual Oklahoma courts offer online access, other than as described above.

Recorders, Assessors, and Other Sites of Note

About Oklahoma Recording Offices: 77 counties, 77 recording offices. The recording officer is the County Clerk, sometimes called the Clerk and Recorder.

About Tax Liens: Federal tax liens on personal property of businesses are filed with the County Clerk of Oklahoma County, which is the central filing office for the state. Other federal and all state tax liens are filed with the County Clerk.

Online Access

Recorded Documents

1. **Statewide:** Two versions of a statewide search for recorded documents and UCC filings from the centralized database are available at http://countyclerk.oklahomacounty.org/registrar-of-deeds/rod-ucc-search. This site is managed by the Oklahoma County Clerk's Office. Search by name, intruments type, boom and page, odocument type, or legal description.

2. **Nearly Statewide:** A private company provides a free search of for 64 counties of Oklahoma public land records including deeds, oil & gas leases, tax liens, judgments, at https://okcountyrecords.com. Fees are involved for viewing document images. (The counties not participating are Caddo, Canadian, Cleveland, Creek, Garfield, Grady, Hughes, Oklahoma, Payne, Pottawatomie, Tulsa, Wagoner, and Woods)

Treasurer, Assessor, and GIS Records

1. **Statewide:** See http://oklahoma.usassessor.com with Assessor and Appraisal data available from all Oklahoma counties. Both free and subscription services are offered.
2. **Statewide:** See www.countyassessor.info/freeaccess/free_login.aspx or their 2nd site at www.pvplus.com/freeaccess/free_login.aspx for access to Assessor and GIS data for all counties Both free and subscription services are offered.

County Sites:

(To avoid redundancy, the sites mentioned above are not included in the profiles.)

Atoka County *Property, Taxation Records*   Access treasurer's data free at http://okcountytreasurers.com/atoka/search.

Beaver County *Property, Taxation Records*   Access treasurer's data for a fee at http://okcountytreasurers.com/beaver.

Beckham County *Real Estate, Grantor/Grantee, Deed, Lien, Judgment, Fictitious Name, UCC Records*
http://beckham.okcounties.org/officials/officialpage.aspx?officerid=6   See the Summary of State's Recording Officers for information on vendors.
Property, Taxation Records   Access treasurer's data free at http://okcountytreasurers.com/beckham.

Blaine County *Property, Taxation Records*   Access treasurer's data free at www.tmconsulting.us.com/visitor/visitor_home.php?cnty=blaine.   Also,

Bryan County *Real Estate, Grantor/Grantee, Deed, Lien, Judgment, Fictitious Name, UCC Records*   See the Summary of State's Recording Officers for information on vendors.
Property, Taxation Records   Access treasurer's data free at http://okcountytreasurers.com/bryan.

Caddo County *Property, Taxation Records*   Access treasurer's data free at http://okcountytreasurers.com/caddo.

Canadian County *Real Estate, Grantor/Grantee, Deed, Lien, Judgment, Fictitious Name, UCC Records*
www.canadiancounty.org/index.aspx?nid=119   Access to recorders database is free http://search.cogov.net/okcana/. To download images, contact clerk's office for user name and password at 405-295-6122/6124/6123.
Property, Taxation Records   Access property search data for free at www.canadiancounty.org/index.aspx?NID=1104. Also, access treasurer's data free at www.tmconsulting.us.com/visitor/visitor_taxroll.php?cnty=Canadian.

Carter County *Property, Taxation Records*   Access to the Assessors property search for free at www.cartercountyassessor.org/search.asp. Also, access treasurer's data free at www.tmconsulting.us.com/visitor/visitor_taxroll.php?cnty=Carter.

Cleveland County *Real Estate, Grantor/Grantee, Deed, Lien, Judgment, Fictitious Name, UCC Records*
www.clevelandcountyok.com/130/County-Clerk   Also, access to index records for free at http://search.cogov.net/okclev/disclaimer.asp.
Property, Taxation Records   Access to property records is free at www.clevelandcountyassessor.us/. Access treasurer's data free at http://ok-cleveland-treasurer.governmax.com/collectmax/collect30.asp.

Coal County *Property, Taxation Records*   Access treasurer's data free at http://coal.okcountytreasurers.com/.

Comanche County *Property, Taxation Records*   Access treasurer property and tax data free at www.tmconsulting.us.com/visitor/visitor_taxroll.php?cnty=Comanche.

Craig County *Property, Taxation Records*   Access treasurer's data free at www.tmconsulting.us.com/visitor/visitor_home.php?cnty=Craig.

Creek County *Real Estate, Grantor/Grantee, Deed, Lien, Judgment, Fictitious Name, UCC Records*
www.creekcountyonline.com/county_clerk.htm   Data range and image range from 7/1997 to present. Also, access land records for free at http://24.173.220.139/creek/start.aspx.
Property, Taxation Records   Access treasurer's data free at www.tmconsulting.us.com/visitor/visitor_taxroll.php?cnty=Creek.

Custer County *Property, Taxation Records*   View Treasurer's data at www.tmconsulting.us.com/visitor/visitor_taxroll.php?cnty=Custer.

Delaware County *Property, Taxation Records*   View Treasurer's data at www.tmconsulting.us.com/visitor/visitor_taxroll.php?cnty=Delaware.

Garfield County *Property, Taxation Records*   Treasurer's data is free at www.tmconsulting.us.com/visitor/visitor_taxroll.php?cnty=Garfield.

Garvin County   *Real Estate, Grantor/Grantee, Deed, Lien, Judgment, Fictitious Name, UCC Records*   Also, access to recorded documents for a fee at https://okcountyrecords.com/search/garvin.
Property, Taxation Records   Access treasurer's data free at http://okcountytreasurers.com/garvin.

Grady County   *Property, Taxation Records*   Access assessor records free at http://grady.okcountyassessors.org/. Access treasurer data fee at www.tmconsulting.us.com/visitor/visitor_taxroll.php?cnty=Grady.

Grant County   *Property, Taxation Records*   Search treasurer data free at http://okcountytreasurers.com/grant/search.

Greer County   *Property, Taxation Records*   Access treasurer's data free at www.tmconsulting.us.com/visitor/visitor_taxroll.php?cnty=Greer.

Jackson County   *Real Estate, Grantor/Grantee, Deed, Lien, Judgment, Fictitious Name, UCC Records*
http://jackson.okcounties.org/officials/officialpage.aspx?officerid=6   Also, access to records for a fee at www.canaanllc.com/. Contact John Bailey at 580-477-0600 or email commodity1@cableone.net for posting procedures.
Property, Taxation Records   Access to treasurer's records free at http://okcountytreasurers.com/jackson.

Jefferson County   *Property, Taxation Records*   Access the treasurer records free at http://okcountytreasurers.com/jefferson.

Johnston County   *Property, Taxation Records*   Access treasurer's data free at http://okcountytreasurers.com/johnston.

Kay County   *Real Estate, Grantor/Grantee, Deed, Lien, Judgment, Fictitious Name, UCC Records*
www.courthouse.kay.ok.us/coclerk.html   Also, access to records for a fee at www.canaanllc.com/. Contact Kathy Leven at 580-362-2502 or email Kathy @securitytitleservice.com for posting procedures.
Property, Taxation Records   The assessor office has a subscription to property data; fee is $10.00 per month. A basic index search is to be available. Call 580-362-2565 for details. View Treasurer's data at www.tmconsulting.us.com/visitor/visitor_home.php?cnty=kay.

Kingfisher County   *Property, Taxation Records*   View treasurer's data free at www.tmconsulting.us.com/visitor/visitor_taxroll.php?cnty=Kingfisher.

Kiowa County   *Property, Taxation Records*   Treasurer's data free at www.tmconsulting.us.com/visitor/visitor_taxroll.php?cnty=Kiowa.

Latimer County   *Property, Taxation Records*   Access treasurer data free at http://latimer.okcountytreasurers.com/.

Le Flore County   *Property, Taxation Records*   Access treasurer data free at http://leflore.okcountytreasurers.com/.

Lincoln County   *Real Estate, Grantor/Grantee, Deed, Lien, Judgment, Fictitious Name, UCC Records*   Also access to records for a fee at www.canaanllc.com/. Contact Charles Holleman at 405-258-1244 x23 or email charlesh@abstractgty.com for posting procedures. Be sure to include Canaan On line-posting Question in the subject line of email.
Property, Taxation Records   Access treasurer's data free at www.tmconsulting.us.com/visitor/visitor_home.php?cnty=Lincoln.

Logan County   *Property, Taxation Records*   Access GIS/mapping for free at http://mapview-logan.com/. Also, access treasurer's data free at www.tmconsulting.us.com/visitor/visitor_home.php?cnty=Logan.

Love County   *Property, Taxation Records*   Access to Assessor records for free at http://okcountytreasurers.com/love/search.

Major County   *Recorded Documents*   https://okcountyrecords.com/search/major   Data range and image range from 7/1997 to present.

Marshall County   *Property, Taxation Records*   Access treasurer's data free at http://marshall.okcountytreasurers.com/.

Mayes County   *Real Estate, Grantor/Grantee, Deed, Lien, Judgment, Fictitious Name, UCC Records*
www.mayes.okcounties.org/officials/officialpage.aspx?officerid=6   See the Summary of State's Recording Officers for information on vendors.
Property, Taxation Records   Access treasurer's data free at www.tmconsulting.us.com/visitor/visitor_home.php?cnty=Mayes. Also, access to GIS/mapping for free at http://54.243.100.240/mayes/.

McClain County   *Property, Taxation Records*   Search the tax roll inquiry site free at www.tmconsulting.us.com/visitor/visitor_home.php?cnty=McClain.

McCurtain County   *Property, Taxation Records*   Access treasurer's data free at www.tmconsulting.us.com/visitor/visitor_home.php?cnty=mccurtain.

Murray County   *Property, Taxation Records*   Access treasurer's data free at www.tmconsulting.us.com/visitor/visitor_home.php?cnty=murray.

Muskogee County   *Property, Taxation Records*   Access treasurer's data free at www.tmconsulting.us.com/visitor/visitor_home.php?cnty=Muskogee.

Noble County   *Property, Taxation Records*   Look-up treasurer's data free at www.tmconsulting.us.com/visitor/visitor_home.php?cnty=Noble.

Nowata County   *Real Estate, Grantor/Grantee, Deed, Lien, Judgment, Fictitious Name, UCC Records*   See the Summary of State's Recording Officers for information on vendors.

Oklahoma County   *Property, Taxation Records*   Assessor and property data on county assessor database is free at www.oklahomacounty.org/assessor/disclaim.htm. Also, search the treasurer's property info at www.oklahomacounty.org/treasurer/.

Okmulgee County   *Property, Taxation Records*   Look-up treasurer's data free at www.tmconsulting.us.com/visitor/visitor_taxroll.php?cnty=Okmulgee.

Osage County   *Property, Taxation Records*   Look-up treasurer's data free at www.tmconsulting.us.com/visitor/visitor_taxroll.php?cnty=Osage.

Ottawa County   *Property, Taxation Records*   Search treasurer data free at http://okcountytreasurers.com/ottawa/search.

Pawnee County   *Property, Taxation Records*   Look-up treasurer's data free at www.tmconsulting.us.com/visitor/visitor_taxroll.php?cnty=Pawnee.

Payne County   *Real Estate, Grantor/Grantee, Deed, Lien, Judgment, Fictitious Name, UCC Records*   http://countyclerk.paynecounty.org/   Access to land records for free at http://24.173.220.139/payne/start.aspx.
Property, Taxation Records   Access treasurer's data free at www.tmconsulting.us.com/visitor/visitor_home.php?cnty=Payne. Also, access to land records free at www.qpublic.net/ok/payne/search.html.

Pittsburg County   *Property, Taxation Records*   Access treasurer's data free at http://pittsburg.okcountytreasurers.com/.

Pontotoc County   *Property, Taxation Records*   Access treasurer's data free at http://pontotoc.okcountytreasurers.com/.

Pottawatomie County   *Real Estate, Grantor/Grantee, Deed, Lien, Judgment, Fictitious Name, UCC Records*   Access to land records for free at https://www.uslandrecords.com/oklr/. Indexes back to 1/1/1985, image voluem back to 3/18/1993.
Property, Taxation Records   Look-up treasurer's data free at www.tmconsulting.us.com/visitor/visitor_taxroll.php?cnty=Pottawatomie.

Roger Mills County   *Real Estate, Grantor/Grantee, Deed, Lien, Judgment, Fictitious Name, UCC Records*   https://okcountyrecords.com/search/roger%20mills   Also, access to statewide records for a fee https://okcountyrecords.com/search/roger+mills.
Property, Taxation Records   Access to property records and GIS records free at www.oklahomacounty.org/assessor/disclaim.htm.

Rogers County   *Real Estate, Grantor/Grantee, Deed, Lien, Judgment, Fictitious Name, UCC Records*   www.rogerscounty.org/coclerk/index.htm   Also, access land records at http://etitlesearch.com; for registration and subscription, call 888-535-5776.
Property, Taxation Records   Access to the assessor database is free at www.rogerscounty.org/assessor/search_records.htm. Treasurer's data is free to view at www.tmconsulting.us.com/visitor/visitor_taxroll.php?cnty=RogerMills.

Seminole County   *Property, Taxation Records*   Search Treasurer's records at http://seminole.okcountytreasurers.com/.

Stephens County   *Property, Taxation Records*   Access treasurer property/taxes data free at http://okcountytreasurers.com/stephens.

Tillman County   *Real Estate, Grantor/Grantee, Deed, Lien, Judgment, Fictitious Name, UCC Records*   www.tillmancounty.org   See the Summary of State's Recording Officers for information on vendors
Property, Taxation Records   Access treasurer's data free at http://okcountytreasurers.com/tillman.

Tulsa County   *Real Estate, Grantor/Grantee, Deed, Lien, Judgment, Fictitious Name, UCC Records*   www.tulsacounty.org/TulsaCounty/dynamic.aspx?id=720   Access to Tulsa County's Land Records System, see www.tulsacounty.org/Tulsacounty/dynamic.aspx?id=2272. Monthly access fee is $30.00. Records go back to 1960.
Property, Taxation Records   Access to Tulsa County's Land Records System requires an agreement, username and password, and fees, see https://lrmis.tulsacounty.org/.

Wagoner County   *Real Estate, Grantor/Grantee, Deed, Lien, Judgment, Fictitious Name, UCC Records*   https://www.ok.gov/wagonercounty/Elected_Officials/County_Clerk/index.html   Also, access to land records free at http://24.173.220.138/wagoner/HomePage.aspx?ID=Wagoner%20County.
Property, Taxation Records   Access treasurer property tax data free at www.tmconsulting.us.com/visitor/visitor_taxroll.php?cnty=Wagoner. Also, access to plats free at www.wagonerassessor.com/. Also, access to Assessors data and records for

Washington County   *Property, Taxation Records*   Access treasurer property tax and parcel date free at www.tmconsulting.us.com/visitor/visitor_taxroll.php?cnty=Washington.

Woods County   *Property, Taxation Records*   Access treasurer's data free at http://woods.okcountytreasurers.com/.

Woodward County   *Property, Taxation Records*   View treasurer's data free at www.tmconsulting.us.com/visitor/visitor_taxroll.php?cnty=Woodward.

Oregon

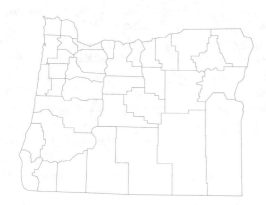

Capital: Salem
            Marion County
Time Zone: PST
Population: 4,028,977
# of Counties: 36

Useful State Links

Website: **www.oregon.gov**
Governor: **http://www.oregon.gov/gov/pages/index.aspx**
Attorney General: **www.attorneygeneral.gov/SplashPage.aspx**
State Archives: **http://arcweb.sos.state.or.us**
State Statutes and Codes: **www.oregonlegislature.gov/**
Legislative Bill Search: **https://www.oregonlegislature.gov/bills_laws**
Unclaimed Funds: **www.oregon.gov/DSL/UP/Pages/index.aspx**

State Public Record Agencies

Criminal Records

Oregon State Police, Unit 11, Criminal Justice Information System,   www.oregon.gov/OSP/ID/pages/index.aspx   A web based site is available for requesting and receiving criminal records is offered to registered users or to the public. Results are posted as "No Record" or "In Process" ("In Process" means a record will be mailed in 14 days). See www.oregon.gov/osp/ID/pages/public_records.aspx. Use the Open Records link to get into the proper site. Register with Open Records to obtain a business account. Fee is $10.00 per record.

Sexual Offender Registry

Oregon State Police, SOR Unit,   www.oregon.gov/OSP/SOR/Pages/index.aspx   Visit http://sexoffenders.oregon.gov/ for online searching of sex offenders who have been designated as Predatory. A mapping function is also offered. Be cautioned that the address and some of the information provided is information provided by the registrant and may not reflect the current residence, status, or other information regarding an offender. Two OR tribes have searchable sex offender registries. The Warm Springs Tribe is at http://warmsprings.nsopw.gov. The Confederated Tribes of the Umatilla Indian Reservation is at http://ctuir.nsopw.gov.   *Other Options:* Lists by city or ZIP can usually be requested for no fee, a statewide list be purchased for $85.00.

Incarceration Records

Oregon Department of Corrections, Offender Information & Sentence Computation,   www.oregon.gov/doc/Pages/index.aspx   An Offender Search is at http://docpub.state.or.us/OOS/intro.jsf. The site also lists contacts for each penitentiary or correction institution. The web page free web access at https://www.vinelink.com/vinelink/siteInfoAction.do?siteId=38000. A Corrections Most Wanted list in the pull down menu box. Use mary.a.jenkins@ doc.state.or.us to request by email. *Other Options:* Bulk sale of information is available. Contact ITS - Information Technology Services.

Corporation, LP, LLC, Trademarks/Servicemarks, Fictitious/Assumed Name

Corporation Division, Public Service Building,   http://sos.oregon.gov/business/Pages/default.aspx   There is free access at http://egov.sos.state.or.us/br/pkg_web_name_srch_inq.login for business registry information. Search by name or business registry number. Displays active and inactive records. There are several other related searches available at http://sos.oregon.gov/business/Pages/research-a-business.aspx such as s search for consumer complaints on OR businesses. Also, search a list of active trademarks at http://sos.oregon.gov/business/Pages/trademarks.aspx. *Other Options:* New business lists downloadable at http://sos.oregon.gov/business/Pages/oregon-business-data-stats.aspx.

Uniform Commercial Code, Federal & State Tax Liens

UCC Division, Attn: Records,   http://sos.oregon.gov/business/Pages/ucc.aspx   From the home page search for information on UCC secured transactions, as well as Farm Product notices, IRS Tax Liens, Agricultural searches Liens, Agricultural Produce Liens, Grain Producer's Liens, Revenue Warrants and Employment Warrants. See https://secure.sos.state.or.us/ucc/searchHome.action. There are three search tabs to choose from. The Farm

Products Registration and master List is available at http://sos.oregon.gov/business/Pages/farm-products-master-list.aspx. In general data is available one year after lapse of filing.   *Other Options:* Filing lists for last month are available online at http://sos.oregon.gov/business/Pages/ucc-data-lists.aspx.

Vital Records

Oregon Health Authority, Vital Records,   http://public.health.oregon.gov/BirthDeathCertificates/Pages/index.aspx   Order records online at www.vitalchek.com, the state's designated vendor. Phone orders are billed to credit cards and processed the same or next day. See a fee chart at http://public.health.oregon.gov/BirthDeathCertificates/GetVitalRecords/Documents/2016-fees-table.pdf. Fees range from $44.95 to $49.95.

Workers' Compensation Records

Department of Consumer & Business Svcs, Workers Compensation Division,   www.cbs.state.or.us/external/wcd/   Search by employer name at www4.cbs.state.or.us/ex/wcd/employer/.   Search   by   claims   number   or   by   employer's   claim   number   at www4.cbs.state.or.us/ex/imd/reports/rpt/index.cfm?ProgID=CE8039.

Driver Records

Driver and Motor Vehicle Services, Record Section,   www.oregon.gov/ODOT/DMV/   The fee for an electronic driving record is $9.63; the fee for a no record found is $9.13. For more information about obtaining an account contact the Records Policy Unit at 503-945-7950. TThe Agency also offers online ordering - with records retured by fax or mail. See www.oregon.gov/ODOT/DMV/pages/records/request_records.aspx. *Other Options:* The agency offers an automated "flag program" that informs customers of activity on a name list, for approved account holders only. Call the Automated Reporting Service at 503-945-5427 for more information.

Vehicle Ownership & Registration

Driver and Motor Vehicle Services, Record Section,   www.oregon.gov/ODOT/DMV/   Online ordering form option of records is available, but only for approved account holders. The fillable form may be downloaded from the web page. Records are returned by fax or mail, per requester's instructions. See https://dmv.odot.state.or.us/cf/vehiclerecrequest/index.cfm. Fees range from $1.50 to $22.50 depending on type of record needed. *Other Options:* Bulk lists available via FTP to qualified accounts. Call 503-945-8906 for more information.

Voter Registration, Campaign Finance, PACs

Secretary of State, Elections Division,   http://sos.oregon.gov/voting-elections/Pages/default.aspx   Access to campaign finance and PAC info is free at http://sos.oregon.gov/elections/Pages/orestar.aspx.   One   may   view   if   someone   is   regsotered   to   vote   at https://secure.sos.state.or.us/orestar/vr/showVoterSearch.do?lang=eng&source=SOS.

GED Certificates

Dept of Community Colleges/ Workforce Development, Oregon GED Program,   www.oregon.gov/CCWD/Pages/ged/index.aspx   Records may be requested from https://www.diplomasender.com. A credit card is needed. Request must be ordered by the test taker. Employers and third parties must receive an email and/or Authentication Code from the test taker to then access the authorized documents. Turnaround time is 1-3 days. You may choose to receive your document by email, fax, or mail.

Occupational Licensing Boards

These licenses are all searchable at https://elite.hlo.state.or.us/elitepublic/LPRBrowser.aspx

Athletic Trainer	Electrologist/Facial Technician/Technologist	Oral Pathology Endorsement
Barber	Electrology Instructor/School	Permanent Color Technician
Body Piercer	Environmental Health Specialist	Respiratory Care Practitioner
Cosmetologist/Hair Stylist/Hairdresser	Hair Salon	Respiratory Therapist
Denture Technologist	Hearing Aid Dealer/Dispenser	Sanitarian/Waste Water
Denturist	Hearing Aid Specialist	Tattoo Artist
Dietitian	Manicurist/Nail Technician	
Direct Entry Midwife	Nursing Home Administrator	

These licenses are all searchable at http://dfr.oregon.gov/gethelp/Pages/check-license.aspx

Bank/Registered Agent	Debt Consolidating Agency	Money Transmitter
Check/Money Order Seller	Digital Signature Authority	Mortgage Banker/Broker/Lender
Collection Agency	Endowment Care	Pawnbroker
Consumer Finance Company	Funeral Plan, Prearranged	Savings & Loan Association
Credit Service Organization	Investment Advisor	Special Qualifications Corporation
Credit Union	Manufactured Structures Dealer	

The Rest:

Accountant Disciplinary Action Report .... www.oregon.gov/BOA/Pages/index.aspx
Accountant-CPA/Firm .... http://fms13.oditech.com/fmi/iwp/cgi?-db=BoA_search&-loadframes
Acupuncturist .... www.oregon.gov/omb/licensing/Pages/License-Verification.aspx
Animal Euthanasia Technician/Facility .... https://hrlb.oregon.gov/ovmeb/licenseelookup/
Animal Feed (Livestock)/ Food Processor.............. www.oregon.gov/oda/licenses/Pages/default.aspx

Appraisal Management Companies	http://dfr.oregon.gov/gethelp/Pages/check-license.aspx
Architect/Architectural Firm	http://orbae.com/search-licensees/
Architect/Architectural Firm Disciplinary Actions	http://orbae.com/compliance-actions/
Attorney	www.osbar.org/members/membersearch_start.asp
Audiologist	https://hrlb.oregon.gov/bspa/licenseelookup/
Auditor-Municipal	www.oregon.gov/boa/BrdMemberPolicies/1.2015.pdf
Bakery	http://oda.state.or.us/dbs/licenses/search.lasso?&division=fsd
Boilermaker	www4.cbs.state.or.us/ex/all/mylicsearch/index.cfm?fuseaction=main.show_main&group_id=30
Brand (Livestock)/Brand Inspector	www.oregon.gov/oda/licenses/Pages/default.aspx
Cemetery	https://hrlb.oregon.gov/omcb/FacilityLookup/
Chiropractor/Chiropractic Assistant	http://obce.alcsoftware.com/liclookup.php
Christmas Tree Grower	http://oda.state.or.us/dbs/licenses/search.lasso?&division=nursery
Construction Contractor/Subcontr	www.ccb.state.or.us/search/
Counselor, Professional	https://hrlb.oregon.gov/oblpct/licenseelookup/index.asp
Crematorium	https://hrlb.oregon.gov/omcb/FacilityLookup/
Dairy Establishment	http://oda.state.or.us/dbs/licenses/search.lasso?&division=fsd
Dentist /Dental Hygienist/Specialist	http://obd.oregonlookups.com/
Diagnostic Radiologic Technologist	https://hrlb.oregon.gov/OBMI/LicenseeLookup/index.asp
Dog/Horse Racing Off Track Betting	www.portlandmeadows.com/offtrack-betting
Dog/Horse Racing Suspension List	www.oregon.gov/Racing/Pages/rul_index.aspx
Drug Manufacturer/Wholesaler/ Outlet	https://obop.oregon.gov/LicenseeLookup/
Egg Handler/Breaker	http://oda.state.or.us/dbs/licenses/search.lasso?&division=fsd
Electrician	www4.cbs.state.or.us/ex/all/mylicsearch/index.cfm?fuseaction=main.show_main&group_id=30
Elevator Journeyman, Limited	www4.cbs.state.or.us/ex/all/mylicsearch/index.cfm?fuseaction=main.show_main&group_id=30
Embalmer/Embalmer Apprentice	https://hrlb.oregon.gov/omcb/LicenseeLookup/
Emeritus Landscape Architect	http://oslab.orregistrants.org/search.php
Engineer	www.oregon.gov/Osbeels/Pages/Search_License.aspx
Escrow Agent/Agency	https://orea.elicense.irondata.com/Lookup/LicenseLookup.aspx
Farm/Forest Labor Contractor	https://apps.oregon.gov/SOS/LicenseDirectory/
Fertilizer/Mineral/Lime Registrant	http://oda.state.or.us/dbs/licenses/search.lasso?&division=pest
Florist	http://oda.state.or.us/dbs/licenses/search.lasso?&division=nursery
Food Establishment, Retail	http://oda.state.or.us/dbs/licenses/search.lasso?&division=fsd
Food Producer/Distributor/Storage Facility	http://oda.state.or.us/dbs/licenses/search.lasso?&division=fsd
Frozen Desert-Related Industry	http://oda.state.or.us/dbs/licenses/search.lasso?&division=fsd
Funeral Service Practitioner/Apprentice/Establishment	https://hrlb.oregon.gov/omcb/LicenseeLookup/
Geologist, Engineering	www.oregon.gov/OSBGE/Pages/registrants.aspx
Greenhouse Grower-Herbaceous Plant	http://oda.state.or.us/dbs/licenses/search.lasso?&division=nursery
Home Inspector	https://apps.oregon.gov/SOS/LicenseDirectory/
Immediate Disposition Company	https://hrlb.oregon.gov/omcb/FacilityLookup/
Insurance Adjuster/Agent/Consultant/Agency	https://sbs-or.naic.org/Lion-Web/jsp/sbsreports/AgentLookup.jsp
Interpreter, Legal	http://courts.oregon.gov/OJD/docs/osca/cpsd/interpreterservices/certifiedinterpreterroster.pdf
Landscape Architect Business	http://oslab.orregistrants.org/search.php
Landscape Business	www.oregonlcb.com/contractorsearch.aspx
Landscaper	http://oda.state.or.us/dbs/licenses/search.lasso?&division=nursery
Liquor Store	www.oregon.gov/OLCC/LIQUORSTORES/Pages/index.aspx
Livestock-Related Business	www.oregon.gov/oda/licenses/Pages/default.aspx
Lobbyist/Political Candidate Statement	www.oregon.gov/OGEC/Pages/public_records.aspx
Manufactured Housing Construction	www4.cbs.state.or.us/ex/all/mylicsearch/index.cfm?fuseaction=main.show_main&group_id=30
Marriage & Family Therapist	https://hrlb.oregon.gov/oblpct/licenseelookup/index.asp
Massage Therapist	https://hrlb.oregon.gov/obmt/licenseelookup/
Measuring Device	http://oda.state.or.us/dbs/search.lasso#msd
Milk Hauler/Milk Stabilizer/Handler	http://oda.state.or.us/dbs/licenses/search.lasso?&division=fsd
Mortuary/Cemetery Disciplinary Actions	www.oregon.gov/MortCem/Pages/discipline.aspx
Motor Fuel Quality	http://oda.state.or.us/dbs/search.lasso#msd
Naturopathic Physician	https://hrlb.oregon.gov/OBNM/licenseelookup/

Non-Alcoholic Beverage Plant	http://oda.state.or.us/dbs/licenses/search.lasso?&division=fsd
Nurse-LPN/Assistant	http://osbn.oregon.gov/OSBNVerification/Default.aspx
Nursery Stock/Native Plant Collector/Dealer	http://oda.state.or.us/dbs/licenses/search.lasso?&division=nursery
Occupational Therapist/Assistant	https://hrlb.oregon.gov/otlb/licenseelookup/
Optometrist	www.oregon.gov/obo/consumer/Pages/optometrist-search.aspx
Optometrist Disciplinary Actions	www.oregon.gov/obo/consumer/Pages/disciplinary-actions.aspx
Optometrist Medical Malpractice Reports	www.oregon.gov/obo/consumer/Pages/medical-malpractice-reports.aspx
Osteopathic Physician/Surgeon	www.oregon.gov/omb/licensing/Pages/License-Verification.aspx
Pesticide Applicator/Dealer/Consultant/Trainee	http://oda.state.or.us/dbs/licenses/search.lasso?&division=pest
Pesticide Product	http://oda.state.or.us/dbs/pest_productsL2K/search.lasso
Pharmacy/Pharmacist	https://obop.oregon.gov/LicenseeLookup/
Physical Therapist/Assistant	https://hrlb.oregon.gov/ptlb/licenseelookup/
Physician/Medical Doctor/Surgeon/Assistant	www.oregon.gov/omb/licensing/Pages/License-Verification.aspx
Plumber	www4.cbs.state.or.us/ex/all/mylicsearch/index.cfm?fuseaction=main.show_main&group_id=30
Podiatrist	www.oregon.gov/omb/licensing/Pages/License-Verification.aspx
Polygraph Examiner	www.oregon.gov/DPSST/Pages/sc/Polygraph.aspx
Private Investigator/Instructor/Business	www.oregon.gov/DPSST/PS/docs/PIContactInfo.pdf
Property Manager	https://orea.elicense.irondata.com/Lookup/LicenseLookup.aspx
Psychologist/Associate	http://obpe.alcsoftware.com/liclookup.php
Pump Installation Contr, Limited	www.cbs.state.or.us/bcd/licensing.html
Radiologic Technologist/ Therapy/ Ltd Permit	https://hrlb.oregon.gov/OBMI/LicenseeLookup/index.asp
Real Estate Agent/Seller/Broker	https://orea.elicense.irondata.com/Lookup/LicenseLookup.aspx
Real Estate Appraiser	http://oregonaclb.org/appraiser-database/
Real Estate Branch Office	https://orea.elicense.irondata.com/Lookup/LicenseLookup.aspx
Refrigerated Plant	http://oda.state.or.us/dbs/licenses/search.lasso?&division=fsd
Shellfish-related Industry	http://oda.state.or.us/dbs/licenses/search.lasso?&division=fsd
Sign Contractor, Limited	www.cbs.state.or.us/bcd/licensing.html
Slaughterhouse	http://oda.state.or.us/dbs/licenses/search.lasso?&division=fsd
Social Worker, Clinical, Licensed	https://hrlb.oregon.gov/BLSW/LicenseeLookup/index.asp
Speech Language Pathologist/Assistant	https://hrlb.oregon.gov/bspa/licenseelookup/
Surveyor, Land	www.oregon.gov/Osbeels/Pages/Search_License.aspx
Tax Consultant/Preparer/Business	https://apps.oregon.gov/Application/OBTPSearch
Teacher/Charter School Teacher	www.tspc.oregon.gov/lookup_application/lookup_query.asp
Therapeutic Radiologic Technologist	https://hrlb.oregon.gov/OBMI/LicenseeLookup/index.asp
Transaction Verification	http://oda.state.or.us/dbs/search.lasso#msd
Trust Company	www.cbs.state.or.us/external/dfcs/online.html
Veterinarian/Technician	https://hrlb.oregon.gov/ovmeb/licenseelookup/
Veterinary Clinic/Product, Livestock	http://oda.state.or.us/dbs/licenses/search.lasso?&division=vet_products
Waste Water System Operator	www.deq.state.or.us/wqpermitsearch/
Water Rights Examiner	www.oregon.gov/Osbeels/Pages/Search_License.aspx
Weighing Device	http://oda.state.or.us/dbs/search.lasso#msd

State and Local Courts

About Oregon Courts: Circuit Courts have original jurisdiction in all civil and criminal matters within the state, including probate, juvenile, and some traffic matters, as well as civil and criminal jury trials. The Small Claims limit is $5,000. The Clerk of Court is the record custodian.

The majority of **Municipal Court** cases involve traffic and ordinance matters.

Probate filing is a function of the Circuit Court; however, each county has a **Register in Probate** who maintains and manages the probate, guardianship, and mental health records.

The **Oregon Tax Court** has exclusive jurisdiction to hear tax appeals including personal income tax, property tax, corporate excise tax, timber tax, local budget law and property tax limitations. There are 2 divisions: Magistrate Division and Regular Division. **The web page for the Judicial Branch is www.courts.oregon.gov.**

Appellate Courts: The Supreme Court is the court of last resort. With the exception of a limited number of appeals that go directly to the Supreme Court (i.e. notably death penalty cases, ballot title cases, lawyer discipline matters, and tax court cases) the Court of Appeals receives appeals or judicial reviews from Oregon's trial courts and administrative agencies.

Supreme and Appellate court opinions are found at www.publications.ojd.state.or.us/.

Online Court Access

All courts participate in the system described below.

Online access is via the **OJCIN - Oregon Judicial Case Information Network**. Oregon recently modified their online system while upgrading to a new platform. OJCIN Online includes OECI (Oregon eCourt Case Information Network), and ACMS (Appellate Case Management System).

Regarding record or docket access, **OECI** is the **new system** (vendor is Odyssey) that replaced the OJIN **system** which had has been in place for many years, but was discontinued as of July 23, 2016. **OECI** is the **new system** (vendor is Odyssey) that all the Circuit Courts are using. This new system houses the records statewide since Circuit Courts were converted. The system is fee-based. Only one log-in is required.

See http://courts.oregon.gov/OJD/OnlineServices/OJIN/Pages/index.aspx.

Subscription Fees

For subscribers signing up after July 1, 2104, there is a $100.00 one time fee to establish the account and a fee of $35.00 per month per user, plus a monthly usage fee per user based on the type of search, if printed, and time of day, with a minimum monthly usage of $10.00. Prior to the date there was a one-time setup fee of $295.00 plus a monthly usage fee per user based on the type of search, if printed, and time of day, plus the minimum monthly usage is $10.00. For subscribers whose account was initiated before January 1, 2014, the monthly charge is the average monthly bill in 2013. For subscribers whose account was initiated after January 1, 2014 but before July 1, 2014, the monthly charge is the average monthly bill in 2014.

See http://courts.oregon.gov/OJD/OnlineServices/OJIN/Pages/accountingrates.aspx.

Feedback

As of press time, there has been some is pushback regarding the new system. Reportedly the new system is cumbersome; more time is needed to perform a search. The initial docket data displayed on OECI does not provide as many details as OJIN, so additional screens often must be viewed to see docket status or final disposition. Also there are inconsistent data elements displayed on OECI dockets. Researchers often have to pull case files to correctly ascertain case information. Reportedly there is a committee of attorneys working with Odyssey to overcome these problems. The ultimate purpose is to create a more modern, user-friendly environment for record access when compared to the older OJIN command line based system. But there may be still some issues to overcome.

No individual Oregon courts offer online access, other as described above.

Recorders, Assessors, and Other Sites of Note

About Oregon Recording Offices: 36 counties, 36 recording offices. The recording officer is the County Clerk.

About Tax Liens: All federal and state tax liens on personal property are filed with the Secretary of State. Other federal and state tax liens are filed with the County Clerk. Government agencies file 'warrants' that represent liens for unpaid taxes and other state fees. Certain warrants are filed with the Sec. of State such as those related to income tax and hazardous waste and are included in a UCC search. Other warrants are filed at the county level, such as those relating to employment taxes.

Online Access

Recorded Documents

Fourteen counties offer access to recorded documents. There is no statewide system.

Tax Assessor Records:

Nearly all counties offer Web access to assessor records. The ORMAP Tax Viewing System at http://www.ormap.net/ provides GIS maps free for all counties. Search by county, then by address. While there is no name searching and maps are pdfs arranged in folders (and you may zoom into a map location), this is a step toward owner identification.

Counties: (To avoid redundancy, information about the ORMAP tax site is omitted below,)

Baker County   *Recorded Documents*   www.bakercounty.org/clerks/clerks.html   Access to index searches free at www2.bakercounty.org/webclerks2/Index_Search.jsp.
Property, Taxation Records   Access to the assessor property database is free at www4.bakercounty.org:8080/webproperty/Assessor_Search.html.

Benton County   *Recorded Documents*   https://www.co.benton.or.us/records   Access to property related records for free at https://www.co.benton.or.us/records/page/property-records-index-search.
Property, Taxation Records   Assessor has a number of searches at https://www.co.benton.or.us/assessment/property_search. Also, see note at beginning of section. Also, access to GIS/mapping for free at https://www.co.benton.or.us/maps. A fee may apply to purchase of maps, etc.

Clackamas County   *Property, Taxation Records*   GIS/mapping at https://gis.oregonmetro.gov/metromap/ and at www.ormap.net. Tax roll statements are availabel as a lookup by account number or address at http://web3.clackamas.us/taxstatements/.

Clatsop County   *Property, Taxation Records*   Access to property data/maps for free at http://maps.co.clatsop.or.us/applications/login.asp.

Columbia County   *Property, Taxation Records*   Access assessment/tax data, property records/sales and GIS/mapping for free at www.co.columbia.or.us/departments/assessors-office/assessors-property-records-online.

Coos County   *Property, Taxation Records*   Access to GIS/mapping for free at http://coosmap.co.coos.or.us/CoosCountyMap/.

Crook County   *Property, Taxation Records*   Access property data free on the GIS-mapping site at http://gis.co.crook.or.us - but no name searching. Several search options, including by name, are offered using the map search at http://geo.maps.arcgis.com/apps/webappviewer/index.html

Curry County   *Recorded Documents*   www.co.curry.or.us/Departments/Recording   Access to subscription service contact Becky Ross at 541-247-3295.
Property, Taxation Records   Access to GIS/mapping free at http://gis.co.curry.or.us/imf/imf.jsp?site=external. Also, access to the Assessor's maps free at http://gis.co.curry.or.us/gis/AssessorMap/index.html.

Deschutes County   *Recorded Documents*   https://www.deschutes.org/clerk   Search real estate, deeds, mortgages, liens on the index for free at https://www.deschutes.org/clerk/page/records-research.   *Property, Taxation Records*   View records on the Assessor Inquiry System site at http://dial.deschutes.org/. There is also business property searching.

Douglas County   *Recorded Documents*   www.co.douglas.or.us/clerk/   Access to online subscription, contact Carol Engels at 541-440-4320. Index back to 1993, Images back to 1971.
Property, Taxation Records   Access to the assessor property data and sales is free at www.co.douglas.or.us/puboaa/puboaa_search.asp. Access to property sales is free at www.co.douglas.or.us/puboaa/ressales.asp. Also see note at beginning of section.

Gilliam County   *Property, Taxation Records*   Access maps via the statewide mapping site free at www.ormap.net/. Access to Gilliam county GIS/mapping for free at http://lcmaps.lanecounty.org/LaneCountyMaps/Gilliam.html?GroupName=Gilliam.

Harney County   *Recorded Documents*   www.co.harney.or.us/countyclerk.html   Access to records free at www.co.harney.or.us/records_research.html. Deed records are indexed back to 1950; Mortgage, Lien and Probate records are indexed back to 1984. All indexed records are current through today.
Property, Taxation Records   Access basic records for free at http://198.237.195.143/propertywebquery/MainQueryPage.aspx?QueryMode=&Query=. Fees due for the advanced search.

Hood River County   *Property, Taxation Records*   Access to WebMap online parcel viewer free at www.co.hood-river.or.us/index.asp?Type=B_BASIC&SEC={282D7000-DA1E-411C-9620-6B27BB917C50}.

Jackson County   *Recorded Documents*   http://jacksoncountyor.org/clerk   Access property deeds online for free at http://jacksoncountyor.org/clerk/Services/Property-Deeds.
Property, Taxation Records   Access to property data for free at http://web.jacksoncounty.org/pdo/index.cfm?btextonly=false.

Jefferson County   *Recorded Documents*   www.co.jefferson.or.us/CountyClerk/tabid/1382/language/en-US/Default.aspx   Access to subscription service for documents indexes and images for $25.00 per month. Contact the Clerk's Office.
Property, Taxation Records   Access assessor property and tax data free at http://199.48.41.18/AandTWebQuery/. A county GIS site is at http://maps.co.jefferson.or.us/.

Josephine County   *Recorded Documents*   www.co.josephine.or.us/SectionIndex.asp?SectionID=110   Access to recording office index and documents is by subscription; fee is $35 per month plus $45.00 set up fee, minimum 3 months. Contact Art at the recording office for signup, username and password.
Property, Taxation Records   Access property via the Map Book Viewer free at www.co.josephine.or.us/Page.asp?NavID=921 but no name searching. Also, search the tax map for free at www.ormap.net/flexviewer/index.html. Also see note at beginning of section.

Klamath County   *Property, Taxation Records*   Access to Assessor's Data for a fee at www.co.klamath.or.us:8008/.

Lane County *Recorded Documents* www.lanecounty.org/Departments/CAO/Operations/CountyClerk/pages/default.aspx Access recorded land data on the Reg. Land Information Database RLID by subscription. Visit www.rlid.org/ or call Eric at 541-682-4338 for info/signup. Initiation fee is $200; monthly access fee is $80.00.

Property, Taxation Records Access property and sales data on the Reg. Land Information Database RLID by subscription. Visit www.rlid.org/ or call Eric at 541-682-4338 for info/signup. Initiation fee is $200; monthly access fee is $80.00. Property records on the County Tax Map site are free at http://apps.lanecounty.org:80//TaxStatement/Search.aspx. No name searching.

Lincoln County *Recorded Documents* www.co.lincoln.or.us/clerk Access to real estate records for free at www.co.lincoln.or.us/clerk. Click on Recording Web Query.

Property, Taxation Records Access property info search tool and the GIS/mapping for free at www.co.lincoln.or.us/assessor.

Linn County *Property, Taxation Records* Tax assessor rolls and sales may be viewed at www.co.linn.or.us/assessorshomep/assessor.htm. Also, search property via the ELLA Maps site free at www.co.linn.or.us/assessorshomep/maps.htm. Also see note at beginning of section.

Malheur County *Recorded Documents* www.malheurco.org/countyclerk Access to indexes for free at http://info.malheurco.org/recording/Search.asp. Records go back to 1985. *Property, Taxation Records* Search assessment data free at http://assessor.malheurco.org/.

Marion County *Property, Taxation Records* Access assessor property data via the GIS-mapping pages at http://gis.co.marion.or.us/gisdownload/disclaimer.aspx. Also, property search for free at http://apps.co.marion.or.us/PropertyRecords/. Search free on the Mapper page at http://gis.co.marion.or.us/MYCIMA/ but no name searching.

Multnomah County *Recorded Documents* https://multco.us/recording Access to recorded documents for a fee at https://multco.us/services/recorded-documents-website. Fee is $150.00 for one-time setup in addition to $.24 per search. Must subscribe.

Property, Taxation Records Search assessor maps for free at https://multco.us/assessment-taxation/maps. Also, access to recorded documents for a fee at https://multco.us/recording/research-online. Fee is $150.00 for one-time setup in addition to $.24 per search. Must subscribe.

Polk County *Recorded Documents* www.co.polk.or.us/clerk Access to images are available on computer back to 1840. Only images back to 1983 are indexed. Contact office to sign up for the subscription. Fee is $20.00 per year.

Property, Taxation Records Access property data for a fee at http://pcwebquery.co.polk.or.us/. Offered by subscription only and costs $20.00 per year. Must sign-up and receive a username and password. Also, search for assessor maps for free at http://apps.co.polk.or.us/AandTMapSearch/mapsearch.htm but no name searching.

Tillamook County *Recorded Documents* www.co.tillamook.or.us/gov/clerk/default.htm Access to recorded document index free at www.co.tillamook.or.us/gov/clerk/Recording/recinq.htm; must register.

Property, Taxation Records Assessment and taxation records on the County Property database are free at www.co.tillamook.or.us/Documents/Search/query.asp. Search by property ID number or by name in the general query. Also, search for property info on the GIS-mapping service site at www.co.tillamook.or.us/gov/A&T/parcelmaps.htm. Also see note at beginning of section.

Umatilla County *Property, Taxation Records* Access to property taxes for free at www.co.umatilla.or.us/at/index.html.

Union County *Property, Taxation Records* Access property data free at http://union-county.org/assessor-tax-collector/record-search/.

Wallowa County *Property, Taxation Records* The Assessor/Collector has a property search site at http://assessor-search.co.wallowa.or.us. Search by name or address.

Washington County *Property, Taxation Records* Records on County GIS Intermap database are free at http://washims.co.washington.or.us/gis/ but no name searching. Also, GIS at https://gis.oregonmetro.gov/metromap/.

Yamhill County *Property, Taxation Records* Search assessor property data free at www.co.yamhill.or.us/content/yamhill-county-property-tax-search. No name searching.

Pennsylvania

Capital: Harrisburg
              Dauphin County
Time Zone: EST
Population: 12,802,503
# of Counties: 67

Useful State Links

Website: **www.pa.gov**
Governor: **www.governor.state.pa.us**
Attorney General: **https://www.attorneygeneral.gov**
State Archives: **www.phmc.state.pa.us**
State Statutes and Codes: **www.legis.state.pa.us/cfdocs/legis/LI/Public/cons_index.cfm**
Legislative Bill Search: **www.legis.state.pa.us/cfdocs/legis/home/session.cfm**
Unclaimed Funds: **www.patreasury.gov/claim/**

State Public Record Agencies

Criminal Records

State Police, Central Repository -164,   www.psp.pa.gov/Pages/Request-a-Criminal-History-Record.aspx#.V2s24BJi9Mg   Record check requests are available for approved agencies through the Internet on the Pennsylvania Access to Criminal History (PATCH). This is a commercial system with a $8.00 fee per name. Go to https://epatch.state.pa.us/Home.jsp. There are registered users. No new accounts are being added, but anyone can order on an individual basis using a credit card. Eighty-five percent of the time, "No Record" certificates are returned immediately. But note it can take three weeks for a response. This site refers users to the state court site for dispositions on some offenses.

Sexual Offender Registry

State Police Bureau of Records and Ident., Megan's Law Unit,   https://www.pameganslaw.state.pa.us/   Limited information on all registered sex offenders can be viewed online from the webpage. Complete address information is listed for all active offenders. Upon opening the offender's record, you are provided tabs to click on access details such as alias, address, offense, vehicle, and physical characteristics information.

Incarceration Records

Pennsylvania Department of Corrections, Population Mgmt and Central Office,   www.cor.pa.gov/Pages/default.aspx#.V2sFSBJNrkc   At the website, click on DOC Inmate Locator for information about each inmate currently under the jurisdiction of the Department of Corrections or visit http://inmatelocator.cor.pa.gov/#/. The site indicates where an inmate is housed, race, date of birth and other items. The Inmate Locator contains information only on inmates currently residing in a state correctional institution.

Corporation, LP, LLC, LLP, Trademarks/Servicemarks, Fictitious/Assumed Name

Bureau of Corporations & Charitable Organizations, Department of State,   www.dos.pa.gov/BusinessCharities/Business/Pages/default.aspx   There is free general searching by entity name or number from https://www.corporations.pa.gov/search/corpsearch. Searching by name provides a list of entities whose name starts with the search name entered. Users can click on any one entity in the list displayed to get more detailed information regarding that entity.   *Other Options:* The entire database of Image data is available for purchase. There is a $5,000 start fee and an annual fee of $12,000. Also, Business Lists may be purchased for $.25 per name. Contact Web Services.

Uniform Commercial Code

UCC Division, Department of State,   www.dos.pa.gov/BusinessCharities/Business/UCC/Pages/default.aspx#.V2msCxJNrkc   Search of UCC-1 financing statements filed with the Corporation Bureau by debtor name or financing statement no. at https://www.corporations.pa.gov/search/uccsearch. Note that this database is usually current within three days.   *Other Options:* UCC information is available in bulk via various formats. Call the number above for details.

Sales Tax Registrations

Revenue Department, Bureau of Business Trust Fund Taxes,   www.revenue.pa.gov/Pages/default.aspx   The agency has site where a financial institution can access a list of decedents by county to find specific decedents' financial accounts that the institution is required to report to the Department of Revenue.. See https://www.doreservices.state.pa.us/eServices/FinancialInstitutions/default.htm.

Birth Certificates

Department of Health, Division of Vital Records,   www.health.pa.gov/MyRecords/Certificates/Pages/11596.aspx#.V1S2NCFi9Mg   Records may be requested online at www.portal.state.pa.us/portal/server.pt/community/birth_certificates/14121/birth_records_-_by_internet/556818 The order is processed by a vendor - VitalChek. Add $10.00 to the fee. The processing can take 20 to 25 days. Public records are available for free by visiting the State Archives website at www.portal.state.pa.us/portal/server.pt/community/genealogy.

Death Records

Department of Health, Division of Vital Records, ATTN: Death Unit,   www.health.pa.gov/MyRecords/Certificates/Pages/11596.aspx#.V1S2NCFi9Mg Records may be requested online at www.vitalchek.com. The order is processed by a vendor - VitalChek. Add $10.00 to the fee. The processing can take 20 to 25 days. Public records are available for free by visiting the State Archives website at www.portal.state.pa.us/portal/server.pt/community/genealogy.

Driver Records

Department of Transportation, Driver Record Services,   www.dmv.state.pa.us   The online system is available to high volume requesters who must sign an agreement stating the individual authorizations are on file. The three-year driving record is released, unless the subject is a CDL holder, then the ten-year record is released. Fee is $9.00 per record. The driver's license number and first two letters of the last name are required. High volume vendors who represent end-users cannot transmit results via the web unless the process and the end-user are pre-approved. The resale of records by vendors to other vendors is generally forbidden. Call 717-705-1051 or go to www.dot33.state.pa.us/information/bus_acct_assistance.shtml for more information about establishing an account. Also, PA licensed drivers may order their own record at https://apps.pa.egov.com/idr using a credit card.

Voter Registration, Campaign Finance

Board of Commissions, Elections, & Leg., Voter Registration,   www.dos.pa.gov/VotingElections/Pages/default.aspx   Campaign finance reports can be searched at https://www.campaignfinanceonline.state.pa.us/pages/CFReportSearch.aspx. One may search data about lobbyists, but the requester must be registered.. See https://www.palobbyingservices.state.pa.us/ *Other Options:* A CD of the entire state or by county can be purchased for $20.00 per disk.

Occupational Licensing Boards

These licenses are all searchable at www.licensepa.state.pa.us/

Accountant-CPA/Firm
Acupuncturist
Amphetamine Program
Anesthesia Permit, Dental
Animal Health Technician
Appraiser, Real Estate/Gen/Residential
Appraiser/Broker
Architect/Architectural Firm
Athletic Trainer
Auctioneer Company/House
Auctioneer, Real Estate
Audiologist
Barber/School/Teacher/Shop/Manager
Builder/Owner, Real Estate
Campground Membership Seller
Cemetery Broker/Seller/Regis
Chiropractor
Cosmetologist/Cosmetician
Cosmetology Teacher/School
Counselor, Professional
Dental Assistant, Expanded Function/Hygienist

Dentist
Dietitian/Nutritionist LDN
Engineer
Evaluator, Appraisal
Funeral Director/Supervisor/Establishment
Geologist
Hearing Aid Fitter/Fitter Apprentice/Dealer
Hearing Examiner
Landscape Architect
Manicurist/Shop
Marriage & Family Therapist
Midwife
Nuclear Medicine Technologist
Nurse
Nursing Home Administrator
Occupational Therapist/Assistant
Optometrist
Osteopathic Acupuncturist
Osteopathic Physician/Surgeon/Assistant
Osteopathic Respiratory Care
Pharmacist/Pharmacy

Physical Therapist/Assistant
Physician/Medical Doctor/Assistant
Pilot, Navigational
Podiatrist
Psychologist
Radiation Therapy Technician
Radiologic Auxiliary, Chiropractic
Radiologic Technologist
Real Estate Agent/Broker/Sales/School
Real Estate Appraiser
Rental Listing Referral Agent
Respiratory Care Practitioner
Social Worker
Speech-Language Pathologist
Surveyor, Land
Therapist, Drugless
Timeshare Salesperson
Used Vehicle Lot
Vehicle Auction
Vehicle Dealer/Mfg'r/Dist/Salesperson
Veterinarian/Veterinary Techn'c'n

The Rest:

Athletic Agent..www.sac.state.pa.us/Pages/RegisteredAthleticAgents.aspx
Attorney ....www.padisciplinaryboard.org/look-up/pa-attorney-search.php
Attorney Disciplinary Reporter Search ....www.padisciplinaryboard.org/look-up/disciplinary-reporter-search.php

Bank	https://research.fdic.gov/bankfind/
Bondsman, Professional	http://apps02.ins.state.pa.us/producer/ilist1.asp
Campaign Finance Report	https://www.campaignfinanceonline.state.pa.us/pages/CFReportSearch.aspx
Child Day Care Facility	http://listserv.dpw.state.pa.us/ocd-pa-child-care-certification.html
Emergency Medical Technician	https://ems.health.state.pa.us/emsportal/
Insurance Agent/Company	http://apps02.ins.state.pa.us/producer/ilist1.asp
Liquor Distributor/Retailer/Whlse	https://plcbplus.pa.gov/pub/Login.aspx
Lobbyist/Lobbying Firm/Principal	https://www.palobbyingservices.state.pa.us/
Mortgage (1st) Banker/Broker/Limited Broker	www.nmlsconsumeraccess.org/
Mortgage (1st) Loan Correspondent	www.nmlsconsumeraccess.org/
Mortgage (2nd) Lender/ Broker/Agent	www.nmlsconsumeraccess.org/
Mortgage (accelerat'd) Paym't Provider	www.nmlsconsumeraccess.org/
Notary Public	https://www.notaries.state.pa.us/Pages/NotarySearch.aspx
Nursing Home	http://sais.health.pa.gov/commonpoc/nhLocatorie.asp
Political Contributor/Committee	https://www.campaignfinanceonline.state.pa.us/pages/CFReportSearch.aspx
Political Finance Statement	https://www.palobbyingservices.state.pa.us/
Public Adjuster/ Solicitor	http://apps02.ins.state.pa.us/producer/ilist1.asp
School Administrator/Superintendent	www.edna.ed.state.pa.us/Screens/wfSearchAdmin.aspx
Surplus Lines Broker	http://apps02.ins.state.pa.us/producer/ilist1.asp
Teacher	www.teachercertification.pa.gov/Screens/wfSearchEducators.aspx
Teacher Notification of Certification Actions	www.education.pa.gov/Teachers%20-%20Administrators/Certifications/Pages/Certificate-Actions.aspx#.Ve9Ag31Nrkc
Title Insurance	http://apps02.ins.state.pa.us/producer/ilist1.asp
Viatical Settlement Broker	http://apps02.ins.state.pa.us/producer/ilist1.asp

State and Local Courts

About Pennsylvania courts: The **Courts of Common Pleas** are the general trial courts, with jurisdiction over both civil and criminal matters and appellate jurisdiction over matters disposed of by the special courts. Note that the **civil records clerk** of the Court of Common Pleas is called the **Prothonotary**. The Prothonotary, who is elected by the county and is not a state employee, may also handle recorded documented (such as real estate). But Allegheny County (Pittsburgh) civil records are an exception - in 2008, a Dept. of Court Records Civil/Family Division was created and civil records were removed from the Prothonotary Office. The Superior Court is a Court of Appeals. Probate is handled by the Register of Wills.

The **Philadelphia Municipal Court** is a Court of Record and hears felony cases. Philadelphia also has its own Traffic Court. The **Pittsburgh Municipal Court** is not a court of record, but does have criminal, traffic, and non-traffic divisions.

The **Magisterial District Justice Courts**, which are designated as "special courts," also handle civil cases up to $12,000. These courts are in all counties except Philadelphia. Small claims cases are usually handled by the Magisterial District Justice Courts; however, all small claims are recorded with the other civil records through the Prothonotary Section of the Court of Common Pleas, which then holds the records. The same is true for misdemeanor records, they too go to the Court of Common Pleas. The only misdemeanor records "held" by the Magisterial District Courts are cases waived or dismissed. Thus it is not necessary to check with each Magisterial District Court, but rather to check with the county Common Pleas for criminal and Prothonotary for civil.

The web page for the Judicial Branch is www.pacourts.us.

Appellate Courts: The Appellate Court level has two courts - the **Commonwealth Court** and the **Superior Court**. The Commonwealth Court also acts as a court of original jurisdiction, or a trial court, when lawsuits are filed by or against the Commonwealth. View opinions and docket at www.pacourts.us/courts/supreme-court/court-opinions. View Appellate Decisions at https://ujsportal.pacourts.us/DocketSheets/Appellate.aspx.

Online Court Access

There are a number of multi-jurisdictional online resources.
Statewide access is available from the Judiciary

The web page at https://ujsportal.pacourts.us/ provides a variety of Judiciary's information. The Public Web Docket Sheets option provides free access to search, view and print the docket sheets for Appellate Courts, Criminal Courts of Common Pleas, Magisterial District Courts and the Philadelphia Municipal Court. In addition, a Court Summary Information report is available for Criminal Courts of Common Pleas and Philadelphia Municipal Court cases. There is also a tab with access to Court Calendars to the Common Pleas and Magisterial Districts courts schedules.

Also from this web page, there is an Attorney Services section that provides that provides attorneys and pro se litigants the option to file documents electronically on new and existing cases and view ongoing case data.

The Judiciary recently launched PAeDocket - a free app that provides a quick and simple search of court cases or dockets. To download the application, visit the app store and search for "PAeDocket".

Take caution using the free public accessible Docket Sheets system.

- Professional researchers indicate certain discrepancies: The UJS dockets may lack sentencing information, have incomplete gradings, lack mention of violation of probations, and alias' may not always listed. Also, per local researchers, there are instances when some records may have incomplete or missing terms of probation or amended charges on the UJS system. Plus the site states: *Recent entries made in the court filing offices may not be immediately reflected on these docket sheets.*

- The Disclaimer states: "Docket sheet information should not be used in place of a criminal history background check, which can only be provided by the Pennsylvania State Police. Employers who do not comply with the provisions of the Criminal History Record Information Act (18 Pa.C.S. Section 9101 et seq.) may be subject to civil liability as set forth in 18 Pa.C.S. Section 9183."

Several Vendors Provide Significant Resources

1) At least 30 PA counties participate with the Infocon County Access System to provide a commercial direct dial-up to primarily county real estate related public records. Some counties also include civil (**Prothonotary**) records. There is a $25.00 base set-up fee plus a minimum $25.00 per month with a $1.10 fee per minute. For information, call Infocon at 814-472-6066 or visit www.infoconcountyaccess.com.

2) A vendor at https://www.landex.com/land-records-access.asp provides access to the index and to some file images for Register of Will records from nineteen counties. Fees are involved. Participating counties include: Armstrong, Blair, Bradford, Cameron, Clearfield, Columbia, Crawford, Fayette, Franklin, Juniata, Luzerne, Monroe, Northumberland, Perry, Potter, Snyder, Sullivan, Susquehanna, and Tioga.

All courts participate in the Public Web Docket Sheets and Secure Web Docket Sheets, therefore this redundant description is omitted below.

However, the courts that participate with the InfoCon system are profiled below.

Allegheny County
Court of Common Pleas - Civil   https://www.alleghenycourts.us/Civil/Default.aspx
Civil: Search civil and family cases in the electronic filing system after registration at https://dcr.alleghenycounty.us/. Electronic access is blocked to current civil cases. Attorneys can register and file cases. Registration is for both Wills/Orphans court as well as Civil/Family. Note this search is CASE SENSITIVE. Search civil opinions at www.alleghenycourts.us/search/default.aspx?source=opinions_civil.

Armstrong County
Court of Common Pleas - Civil   www.co.armstrong.pa.us/departments/elected-officials/proth-coc
Civil: Online access is by subscription from private company-Infocon at www.infoconcountyaccess.com, 814-472-6066. See note in court summary section for fees. Images are not available; only the index.

Beaver County
Court of Common Pleas - Civil   www.beavercountypa.gov/prothonotary
Civil: Online access to civil records is by subscription from private company-Infocon at www.infoconcountyaccess.com, 814-472-6066. A link is at the court's home page. Also at the court's home page is a link to naturalization records.

Bedford County
Court of Common Pleas - Criminal/Civil   www.bedfordcountypa.org/Court_of_Common_Pleas.html

Civil: Online access is by subscription from private company-Infocon at www.infoconcountyaccess.com, 814-472-6066. See note in court summary section. Images are available. *Criminal:* Access is by subscription from private company-Infocon at www.infoconcountyaccess.com, 814-472-6066. See note at beginning of section.

Berks County
Court of Common Pleas - Civil   www.co.berks.pa.us/prothonotary/site/default.asp
Civil: The Prothonotary has a remote system to access dockets from 2002 forward. Subscription fee is $300 per year. For information, call 610-478-6970. A free genealogical search is offered at http://prothy.co.berks.pa.us/search_genealogical.

Blair County
Court of Common Pleas Civil   www.blairco.org/CourtAdministrator/Pages/BlairCountyCourtAdministrator.aspx
Civil: Online access is by subscription from private company-Infocon at www.infoconcountyaccess.com, 814-472-6066. See note in court summary section. Images are not available.

Bucks County
Court of Common Pleas - Civil   www.buckscounty.org/Courts/Civil
Civil: Access case searches for the Prothonotary Office and Family Court (excluding Support), please use the web link: http://propublic.co.bucks.pa.us/PSI/v/search/case. All documents purchased through the Bucks County Web Viewer will be charged $0.10 for each page, plus a Technology Fee of $1.00 per Cart. A convenience fee of either 2.39%, or $1.50 (minimum) will be charged by Value Payment Systems for the processing of all transactions.

Butler County
Court of Common Pleas - Criminal   www.co.butler.pa.us/
Search dockets online free at https://ujsportal.pacourts.us/DocketSheets/CP.aspx back to 1988 for complete index. Also, online access to the index and case files is by subscription from private company-Infocon at www.infoconcountyaccess.com, 814-472-6066. See note in court summary section for fees.
Court of Common Pleas - Civil   www.co.butler.pa.us/Prothonotary
Civil: Online access is by subscription from a private company - Infocon at www.infoconcountyaccess.com, 814-472-6066. See note in court summary section. Images are available.

Cambria County
Court of Common Pleas - Civil   www.cambriacountypa.gov/prothonotary.aspx
Civil: Access to civil index is available by subscription at Infocon.com; Signup online or get details at 814-472-6066. Images are now available.

Carbon County
Court of Common Pleas - Criminal   www.carboncourts.com
Online access to clerk of courts docket records is free at www.carboncourts.com/pubacc.htm. Registration required.
Court of Common Pleas - Civil   www.carboncourts.com
Civil: Online access to the clerk of courts docket records is by subscription at www.carboncourts.com/login-prothy.php. Registration required. There is a $300 annual fee.

Chester County
Court of Common Pleas - Criminal   www.chesco.org/202/Clerk-of-Courts
Search criminal dockets online free at https://ujsportal.pacourts.us/DocketSheets/CP.aspx back 20 to 25 years. There is a commercial online service at https://epin.chesco.org/EPIN/ which gives access to inmate records from this county. View the FAQ page for details on costs ($10 per month plus set up), but it also provides civil records.
Court of Common Pleas - Civil   www.chesco.org/1333/County-Court-of-Common-Pleas
Internet access to county records including court records requires a sign-up and credit card payment. Application fee: $50. There is a $10.00 per month minimum (no charge for no activity); and $.10 each transaction beyond 100. Sign-up and/or log-in at https://epin.chesco.org/EPIN/. Besides the civil data, this site also provides real estate data, recorded documents, information on wills, and some data held by the Sheriff.

Clarion County
Court of Common Pleas - Civil   www.co.clarion.pa.us/
Online access is by subscription from private company-Infocon at www.infoconcountyaccess.com, 814-472-6066. See note in court summary section. Images are not available.

Clinton County
Court of Common Pleas - Criminal/Civil   www.clintoncountypa.com/departments/court_services/county_courts/
Civil: Online access is by subscription from private company-Infocon at www.infoconcountyaccess.com, 814-472-6066. See note in court summary section for fees. Images are available. *Criminal:* Internet access to court records is by subscription from a private company-Infocon at www.ic-access.com, 814-472-6066. See note at beginning of section.

Crawford County
Court of Common Pleas - Civil   www.crawfordcountypa.net/portal/page?_pageid=393,824325&_dad=portal&_schema=PORTAL
Online access to Prothonotary records and Register of Wills is by subscription from private company-Infocon at www.infoconcountyaccess.com, 814-472-6066. See note in court summary section. Images not shown.

Cumberland County

Court of Common Pleas - Civil www.ccpa.net/121/Prothonotary

Civil: Online access available by subscription from private company-Infocon at www.infoconcountyaccess.com, 814-472-6066. See Summary of State Court System for more details. Images are available. Also, searchable civil records by docket # at https://www.ccpa.net/3805/Searchable-Civil-Recordss.

Dauphin County

Court of Common Pleas - Civil www.dauphincounty.org/government/Court-Departments/Pages/default.aspx

Civil: Access civil cases back to 11/2001, suits (1992-10/31/2001) and judgments back to 1983 free at www.dauphinc.org/onlineservices/public/header.asp.

Delaware County

Court of Common Pleas - Civil www.co.delaware.pa.us/courts/index.html

Online access to court civil records free (may begin charging in near future) at http://w01.co.delaware.pa.us/pa/publicaccess.asp. Search online by document type, document number, etc.

Erie County

Court of Common Pleas - Civil www.eriecountypa.gov/county-services/records/civil-records.aspx

Civil: Online access is by subscription from private company-Infocon at www.infoconcountyaccess.com, 814-472-6066. See note in court summary section. Images are available.

Fayette County

Court of Common Pleas - Civil www.co.fayette.pa.us/CourtAdmin/Pages/default.aspx

Internet access to court records is by subscription from a private company-Infocon at www.infoconcountyaccess.com/, 814-472-6066. See Summary of State Court System for more details. Images are available.

Forest County

Court of Common Pleas www.warrenforestcourt.org/

Civil: Online access available by subscription from private company-Infocon at www.infoconcountyaccess.com, 814-472-6066. See Summary of State Court System for more details. Images are available from 2006.

Franklin County

Court of Common Pleas - Civil www.franklincountypa.gov/index.php?section=judicial_prothonotary-office

Access index by subscription from private company-Infocon at www.infoconcountyaccess.com, 814-472-6066. See Summary of State Court System for more details. Images are not available.

Fulton County

Court of Common Pleas - Civil www.co.fulton.pa.us/court-common-pleas.php

Online access available by subscription from private company-Infocon at www.infoconcountyaccess.com, 814-472-6066. See Summary of State Court System for more details.

Huntingdon County

Court of Common Pleas - Civil http://huntingdoncountycourt.net/

Online access is by subscription from private company-Infocon at www.infoconcountyaccess.com, 814-472-6066. See note in court summary section. Images not shown.

Indiana County

Court of Common Pleas - Civil www.countyofindiana.org/Depts/Courts/Pages/default.aspx

Online access is by subscription. Details are only made available by calling this office at 724-465-3855.

Jefferson County

Court of Common Pleas - Civil www.pacourts.us/courts/courts-of-common-pleas/individual-county-courts/jefferson-county

Online access is by subscription from private company-Infocon at www.infoconcountyaccess.com, 814-472-6066. See note in court summary section. Images not shown. Data available from 1987 to present.

Lackawanna County

Court of Common Pleas - Civil www.lackawannacounty.org/index.php/judiciary

Civil: See www.lpa-homes.org/LPA_Applications.htm for access to the docket index from 2003 for the Civil and Family Court Divisions, including Register of Wills, Orphans' Court and Marriage Licenses.

Lawrence County

Court of Common Pleas - Criminal/Civil http://co.lawrence.pa.us/courts/court-of-common-pleas/

Civil: Online access is by subscription from private company-Infocon at www.infoconcountyaccess.com, 814-472-6066. See note in court summary section. Images shown. *Criminal:* Internet access to court records is by subscription from a private company-Infocon at www.ic-access.com, 814-472-6066. See note at beginning of section. Also, search dockets online free at https://ujsportal.pacourts.us/DocketSheets/CP.aspx back to 1968.

Lehigh County

Court of Common Pleas - Civil www.lccpa.org/civil/

Civil: Access to the county online system requires $300.00 annual usage fee. Search by name or case number. Call Lehigh Cty Fiscal Office at 610-782-3112 for more information.

Luzerne County
Court of Common Pleas - Civil   www.luzernecounty.org/county/row_offices/prothonotary
Civil: Civil record index may be viewed free online at https://www.searchiqs.com/paluz/Login.aspx.   View all documents filed in the Prothonotary's Office since 2005 (and some earlier cases). Copies of judgments are also viewable for this site.

McKean County
Court of Common Pleas - Civil
Civil: Online access is by subscription from private company-Infocon at www.infoconcountyaccess.com, 814-472-6066. Monthly usage fee and per minute fees apply.

Mercer County
Court of Common Pleas - Civil   https://www.mcc.co.mercer.pa.us/
Civil: Online access is by subscription from private company-Infocon at www.infoconcountyaccess.com, 814-472-6066. See note in court summary section. Images not shown.

Mifflin County
Court of Common Pleas - Civil   www.co.mifflin.pa.us/dept/Courts/Pages/default.aspx
Online access is by subscription from private company-Infocon at www.infoconcountyaccess.com, 814-472-6066. See note in court summary section. Images not shown. Court calendar available at main website.

Monroe County
Court of Common Pleas - Civil
Online access is by subscription from private company-Infocon at www.infoconcountyaccess.com, 814-472-6066. See note in court summary section. Images not shown.

Montgomery County
Court of Common Pleas - Civil   www.montcopa.org/97/Prothonotary
Search court and other record indices free from Prothonotary at https://courtsapp.montcopa.org/psi/v/search/case. This includes active and purged civil cases, also active probate cases, also calendars. Landlord/tenant actions are found at the local District Court level. A list of judges is found at www.montcopa.org/index.aspx?nid=186.

Montour County
Court of Common Pleas - Criminal/Civil   www.montourco.org/Pages/Prothonotary.aspx
Civil: Online access is by subscription from private company-Infocon at www.infoconcountyaccess.com, 814-472-6066. See note in court summary section. Images not shown. *Criminal:* Online access is by subscription from private company-Infocon at www.infoconcountyaccess.com, 814-472-6066. See note in court summary section. Images not shown. Record date back to 8/25/2005, no images. Search dockets online free at https://ujsportal.pacourts.us/DocketSheets/CP.aspx back to 1992.

Perry County
Court of Common Pleas - Civil   www.perryco.org/Dept/Courts/Prothonotary_ClerkOfCourts/Pages/ProthonotaryAndClerkOfCourts.aspx
Civil: Recorded judgments are on the County Recorder web page.

Philadelphia County
Court of Common Pleas - Civil   www.courts.phila.gov/common-pleas/
Access to 1st Judicial District Civil Trial records is free at https://fjdclaims.phila.gov/phmuni/login.do. Search by name, judgment and docket info.
Court of Common Pleas - Criminal Division   www.courts.phila.gov/common-pleas/trial/criminal/
Access docket info free at https://ujsportal.pacourts.us/DocketSheets/MC.aspx. Search new criminal filings by name or date at www.courts.phila.gov/apps/mcf/. Search the hearing list at www.courts.phila.gov/apps/criminal/. Search new criminal findings at www.courts.phila.gov/apps/mcf/.
Municipal Court - Civil Division   www.courts.phila.gov/municipal/civil/
Civil: Access to Muni court dockets on the court electronic filing system is free at http://fjdclaims.phila.gov/phmuni/login.do#, you may also register for a username and password.

Pike County
Court of Common Pleas   http://court.pikepa.org/
Civil: Online access is by subscription from private company-Infocon at www.infoconcountyaccess.com, 814-472-6066. See note in court summary section. Images shown. *Criminal:* Internet access to court records is by subscription from a private company-Infocon at www.infoconcountyaccess.com, 814-472-6066. See note at beginning of section. Images shown. Also, search dockets online free at https://ujsportal.pacourts.us/DocketSheets/CP.aspx back to 1993.

Potter County
Court of Common Pleas   www.pottercountypa.net/prothonotary_court.php
Civil: Online access is by subscription from private company-Infocon at www.infoconcountyaccess.com, 814-472-6066. See note in court summary section. Images shown.

Schuylkill County
Court of Common Pleas - Civil   www.co.schuylkill.pa.us

Civil: Access civil court records and judgments free at www.co.schuylkill.pa.us/info/Civil/Inquiry/Search.csp. Civil cases back 10 1989, judgment to 1999.

Somerset County

Court of Common Pleas - Civil   www.co.somerset.pa.us

Civil: Court calendars (no names) and daily schedules free at www.co.somerset.pa.us. Also, judgments may appear on the Landex system at www.landex.com/remote/ - registration and password required. Court calendars free at www.co.somerset.pa.us/courtcalendar/ but no name searching. Recorded judgments are filed by the Prothonotary, and are online for a fee at www.infoconcountyaccess.com.

Susquehanna County

Court of Common Pleas - Civil   http://susqco.com/court-offices/clerk-of-courts/

Civil: Online access is by subscription from private company-Infocon at www.infoconcountyaccess.com, 814-472-6066. See note in court summary section. Images not shown.

Venango County

Court of Common Pleas - Civil   www.co.venango.pa.us

Online access is by subscription from private company-Infocon at www.infoconcountyaccess.com, 814-472-6066. See note in court summary section for fees. Images are available.

Warren County

Court of Common Pleas - Civil   www.warrenforestcourt.org/

Online access is by subscription from private company-Infocon at www.infoconcountyaccess.com, 814-472-6066. See note in court summary section for fees. Images are not available; only the index.

Washington County

Court of Common Pleas - Criminal   www.washingtoncourts.us/pages/roClerkOfCourts.aspx

Search dockets online free at https://ujsportal.pacourts.us/DocketSheets/CP.aspx back to 1987. Access to the docket is by subscription; enroll at http://ers.co.washington.pa.us/ers/. Two subs are offered: Basic for $100 annual of 20 hours, and Professional for $150, same 20 hours plus hard copies are available. One may also register as a guest and view or print for a flat rate of $2.00 per page.

Court of Common Pleas - Civil   www.washingtoncourts.us/pages/home.aspx

Civil: Access to Prothonotary civil records including also orphans court is by subscription; enroll at http://ers.co.washington.pa.us/ers/. Two subs are offered: Basic for $100 annual of 20 hours, and Professional for $150, same 20 hours plus hard copies are available.. One may also register as a guest and view or print for a flat rate of $2.00 per page.

Westmoreland County

Court of Common Pleas - Civil   www.co.westmoreland.pa.us/index.aspx?nid=528

Civil: Access civil court dockets back to 1985 free at http://westmorelandweb400.us:8088/EGSPublicAccess.htm. Also, search Register of Wills and marriages free back to 1986. Access to full remote online system has $100 setup (no set-up if accessed via Internet) plus $20 monthly minimum. System includes civil, criminal, Prothonotary indexes and recorder data. For info, call 724-830-3874, or click on e-services at website.

York County

Court of Common Pleas - Civil   https://yorkcountypa.gov/courts-criminal-justice/court-courtrelated-offices/prothonotary.html

Civil: A civil case search is offered online, but the exact site depends on the users software. See https://yorkcountypa.gov/courts-criminal-justice/court-courtrelated-offices/prothonotary/civil-case-search.html. Documents filed on May 8, 2008 and thereafter are available as scanned images.

Recorders, Assessors, and Other Sites of Note

About Pennsylvania Recording Offices: 67 counties, 67 recording offices. All documents relating to real estate, uniform commercial code filings and notary public bonds and commissions, are filed in the **Recorder of Deeds Office**. .

About Tax Liens: All federal and state tax liens on personal property and on real property are filed with the Prothonotary. Usually, tax liens on personal property are filed in the judgment index of the Prothonotary.

Online Access

Recorded Documents

The Infocon County Access System is a cooperative fee-based subscriber service that provides web access to certain public records contained in participating County databases. Infocon has recorded record information (and often add'l data) for approximately 30 Pennsylvania counties. Visit www.infoconcountyaccess.com.

Access the recorded documents index for 29 counties via a private vendor free at www.landex.com/webstore/jsp/cart/DocumentSearch.jsp. This same vendor offers a commercial service with more capabilities from a page at https://www.landex.com/land-records-access.asp.

Assessor Records

At least 46 counties provide web access to assessor data. Many counties depend on online services provided by either Infocon or Landex as mentioned above.

County Sites:

Adams County   *Recorded Documents* www.adamscounty.us/Dept/RecOfDeeds/Pages/default.aspx   Access to public records for a fee at https://landrecordspa.adamscounty.us/external/User/Login.aspx?ReturnUrl=%2fexternal%2fIndex.aspx.
Property, Taxation Records   Access to GIS/mapping free at www.adamscounty.us/Dept/Planning/Pages/Interactive-Mapping.aspx.

Allegheny County   *Recorded Documents* www.county.allegheny.pa.us/real-estate/index.aspx   Search Recorder's Index for free at https://pa_allegheny.uslandrecords.com/palr/. Will be charged for each document image that is downloadedviewed online. Casual users fee is $1.00 per page for 1st 10 pages of doc, no fee for remaining pages. Commercial users fee is $.50 per page for 1st 10 pages of a doc, no fee for remaining pages. Also, access to records for a fee at www.county.allegheny.pa.us/real-estate/obtaining-records-online.aspx. Must subscribe, fees are $100 one-time fee (for registration) and $50.00 per month plus hourly usage fee (peak hrs-{8:30AM-4:30PM M-F}-$6.00per hour; non-peak hrs-$1.00 per hour).
Property, Taxation Records   Access to Allegheny County real estate database is free at www2.county.allegheny.pa.us/realestate/Default.aspx.

Armstrong County   *Recorded Documents* http://co.armstrong.pa.us/departments/elected-officials/reg-rec   Access to land records for a fee at www.landex.com/webstore/jsp/cart/DocumentSearch.jsp. Online and images for Recorder of Deeds from 1805 to present. Also, access to Recorder records/images for a fee at www.infoconcountyaccess.com/. Contact them at 814-472-6066 or icas@ic-access.com for subscription information.

Beaver County   *Recorded Documents* www.beavercountypa.gov/recorder-deeds   Access to the Recorder's database is free at www.beavercountypa.gov/recorder-deeds/recorder-deeds-online-search. Images from 1957 to present. Also, access land records for free at www.searchiqs.com/. Index data and inages from 1/1957 to present. For detailed records, can sign-up. Also, access to Recorder records/images for a fee at www.infoconcountyaccess.com/. Contact them at 814-472-6066 or icas@ic-access.com for subscription information.
Property, Taxation Records   Access property search for free at www.beavercountypa.gov/property-search.

Bedford County   *Recorded Documents* http://registerrecorder.webs.com/   Access to Recorder records/images for a fee at www.infoconcountyaccess.com/. Contact them at 814-472-6066 or icas@ic-access.com for subscription information.

Berks County   *Recorded Documents* www.co.berks.pa.us/recorder   Access recorder's records index and images at https://countyfusion4.propertyinfo.com/countyweb/login.do?countyname=Berks. Must register before using. Indexes for deeds recorded prior to 1959 and satisfied mortgages recorded prior to 1969, use the electronic Russell Index books. All indexes since 1752 via traditional search or computerized index books for all deeds, mortgages and misc documents including images.
Property, Taxation Records   Access parcel records free at http://gis.co.berks.pa.us/parcelsearch/.

Blair County   *Recorded Documents* www.blaircountyrecorder.com   Access to land records for a fee at www.landex.com/webstore/jsp/cart/DocumentSearch.jsp. Online for Recorder of Deeds from 1846 to present, images from 1963 to present. Also, access to Recorder records/images for a fee at www.infoconcountyaccess.com/. Contact them at 814-472-6066 or icas@ic-access.com for subscription information.

Bradford County *Recorded Documents* www.bradfordcountypa.org   Access to land records for a fee at www.landex.com/webstore/jsp/cart/DocumentSearch.jsp. Online and images for Recorder of Deeds from 1945-1950 & 1970 to present.
Property, Taxation Records   Access to property records and GIS/mapping free at www.bradfordappraiser.com/GIS/Search_F.asp.

Bucks County *Recorded Documents* www.buckscounty.org/government/RowOfficers/RecorderofDeeds   Access to land records for a fee at www.landex.com/webstore/jsp/cart/DocumentSearch.jsp. Online and images for Recorder of Deeds from 1980 to present.
Property, Taxation Records   Access Prothonotary records free at http://propublic.co.bucks.pa.us/PSI/Viewer/Search.aspx.

Butler County *Recorded Documents* www.co.butler.pa.us/recorder-of-deeds   Access deeds records free at www.co.butler.pa.us/recorder-of-deeds-access-deeds. Also access probate court estate and guardianship records free at http://66.117.197.22/index.cfm?page=home. At bottom of webpage, click on the type of lookup desired. Also, access to Recorder records/images for a fee at www.infoconcountyaccess.com/. Contact them at 814-472-6066 or icas@ic-access.com for subscription information.

Cambria County *Recorded Documents* www.cambriacountypa.gov/recorder-of-deeds-office.aspx   Access to Recorder records/images for a fee at www.infoconcountyaccess.com/. Contact them at 814-472-6066 or icas@ic-access.com for subscription information.
Property, Taxation Records   Access to GIS/mapping free at http://gis.co.cambria.pa.us/publicgis1/.

Cameron County *Recorded Documents*   Access to land records for a fee at www.landex.com/webstore/jsp/cart/DocumentSearch.jsp. Online for Recorder of Deeds from 1990 to present, images from 9/2005 to present.

Carbon County *Recorded Documents* www.carboncounty.com/index.php/2-uncategorised/40-recorder-of-deeds   Access to land records for a fee at www.landex.com/webstore/jsp/cart/DocumentSearch.jsp. Online for Recorder of Deeds from 1988 to present, images from 1994 to present. Also, access to Recorder records/images for a fee at www.infoconcountyaccess.com/. Contact them at 814-472-6066 or icas@ic-access.com for subscription information.
Property, Taxation Records   Access assessor property data free at www.carboncounty.com/index.php/public-records.

Centre County *Recorded Documents* http://centrecountypa.gov/index.aspx?NID=418   Access recorded data on the WEB IA subscription system from 1800 forward; fee is $10.00 set-up plus $.06 per click or other per click plan. This replaces the old dial-up system. See http://webia.co.centre.pa.us/login.asp.
Property, Taxation Records   Assessment data on the WEB IA subscription system; registration and per page fees apply; see http://webia.co.centre.pa.us/login.asp.

Chester County *Recorded Documents* www.chesco.org/169/Recorder-of-Deeds   Search unofficial Recorder of Deeds records free at http://chesterpa.countygovernmentrecords.com/ChesterRecorder/web/login.jsp. Must register to use. Also, full countywide search requiring registration and credit card payment is available at: http://chesterpa.countygovernmentrecords.com/ChesterRecorder/web/splash.jsp.

Clarion County *Recorded Documents* www.co.clarion.pa.us/government/register-and-recorders-office.html   Access to Recorder records/images for a fee at www.infoconcountyaccess.com/. Contact them at 814-472-6066 or icas@ic-access.com for subscription information.

Clearfield County *Recorded Documents* www.clearfieldco.org   Access to land records for a fee at www.landex.com/webstore/jsp/cart/DocumentSearch.jsp. Online for Recorder of Deeds from 1974 to present, images from 1974 to present.

Clinton County *Recorded Documents* www.clintoncountypa.com/departments/county_departments/register_recorder/   Access to Recorder records/images for a fee at www.infoconcountyaccess.com/. Contact them at 814-472-6066 or icas@ic-access.com for subscription information.
Property, Taxation Records   Access to GIS/mapping property and assessment data is free at www.clintoncountypa.com/departments/county_departments/gis/online_mapping.shtml.

Columbia County *Recorded Documents* www.columbiapa.org/registerrecorder/index.php   Access to land records for a fee at www.landex.com/webstore/jsp/cart/DocumentSearch.jsp. Online and images for Recorder of Deeds from 1974 to present
Property, Taxation Records   Access to GIS/mapping is free at http://gis.columbiapa.org/mapsonline/default.aspx. They now have general-purpose mapping service or paid subscription mapping service.

Crawford County *Property, Taxation Records*   Access to GIS/mapping free at www.crawfordcountypa.net/portal/page?_pageid=393,2539913&_dad=portal&_schema=PORTAL.

Cumberland County *Recorded Documents* https://www.ccpa.net/123/Recorder-of-Deeds   Access to land records for a fee at www.landex.com/webstore/jsp/cart/DocumentSearch.jsp. Online and images for Deeds from 1956 to present, mortgages from 1973 to present and misc from 1967 to present. Also, civil dockets (judgments, etc.) available free at http://records.ccpa.net/weblink_public/Browse.aspx?dbid=.
Property, Taxation Records   Access to the property assessment data is free at https://www.ccpa.net/2295/Web-Mapping. No name searching. Access property data on the GIS-mapping site free at http://gis.ccpa.net/PropertyMapper/. Search delinquent tax index at https://www.ccpa.net/2279/Delinquent-Real-Estate-Tax-Database, but no name searching. Tax Sale data at https://www.ccpa.net/2735/Upset-Real-Estate-Tax-Judicial-Sale.

Dauphin County   *Recorded Documents*   www.dauphincounty.org/government/Publicly-Elected-Officials/Recorder-of-Deeds/Pages/default.aspx   Access the register's land records database free at www.dauphincounty.org/government/Publicly-Elected-Officials/Recorder-of-Deeds/Pages/default.aspx. Indexes and images from 1979 to present.
Property, Taxation Records   Access to the GIS/mapping data is free at www.dauphincounty.org/government/About-the-County/County-Offices/Information-Technology/GIS/Pages/Interactive-Map.aspx. Access property and tax info free at www.dauphinpropertyinfo.org.

Delaware County   *Recorded Documents*   www.co.delaware.pa.us/depts/recorder.html   Access to the public access system is free at http://w01.co.delaware.pa.us/pa/publicaccess.asp. Other public records included in this URL.
Property, Taxation Records   Access to Real Estate and Assessment for free at http://w01.co.delaware.pa.us/pa/publicaccess.asp?real.x=71&real.y=50.

Elk County   *Recorded Documents*   www.co.elk.pa.us/regrecorder/   Access to records for free at https://countyfusion2.propertyinfo.com/countyweb/login.do?countyname=Elk. Must register with username and password.

Erie County   *Recorded Documents*   www.eriecountypa.gov/county-services/records/deeds-land-records.aspx   Access to Recorder records/images for a fee at www.infoconcountyaccess.com/. Contact them at 814-472-6066 or icas@ic-access.com for subscription information.
Property, Taxation Records   Access property records data free at www.eriecountygov.org/property-tax-records/property-records/property-tax-search.aspx, no name searching. Also, full data for real estate professionals is available by subscription, click on 'sign in' and follow the menu for details.

Fayette County   *Recorded Documents*   Access to real property records for a fee at https://pa.uslandrecords.com/palr2/controller. Also, access to Recorder records/images for a fee at www.infoconcountyaccess.com/. Contact them at 814-472-6066 or icas@ic-access.com for subscription information.

Forest County   *Recorded Documents*   www.co.forest.pa.us   Access to Recorder records/images for a fee at www.infoconcountyaccess.com/. Contact them at 814-472-6066 or icas@ic-access.com for subscription information.

Franklin County   *Recorded Documents*   www.franklincountypa.gov/index.php?section=government_register-record-office   Access to land records for a fee at www.landex.com/webstore/jsp/cart/DocumentSearch.jsp. Online for deeds from 1951 to present, mortgages from 1785; deed images from 1785 to present, mortgages from 1951 to present. Also, access to Recorder records/images for a fee at www.infoconcountyaccess.com/. Contact them at 814-472-6066 or icas@ic-access.com for subscription information.
Property, Taxation Records   Access to tax subscription service for a fee at http://webia.co.franklin.pa.us/login.asp. Also, access to the assessment database for free at http://gis.vgsi.com/franklincountypa/.

Fulton County   *Recorded Documents*   www.co.fulton.pa.us/prothonotary.php   Access to Recorder records/images for a fee at www.infoconcountyaccess.com/. Contact them at 814-472-6066 or icas@ic-access.com for subscription information.
Property, Taxation Records   Access to GIS/mapping free at http://gis.co.fulton.pa.us/. Must register. Also, can search assessment information for a fee.

Greene County   *Recorded Documents*   www.co.greene.pa.us/secured/gc2/depts/lo/rr/rr.htm   Access to the land record index for free at https://pa.uslandrecords.com/palr2/PalrApp/index.jsp. For detailed records, must subscribe. Subscription required for full access; view image for $.50 per page, max $5.00 per doc. Also, access to records for a fee at www.co.greene.pa.us/ImageSync/Login.aspx. Fees are $.30 per minute and $.50 per page to print from 1796-1940. Must subscribe.
Property, Taxation Records   Access to Assessor's database for free at http://gis.vgsi.com/GreenecountyPA/DEFAULT.aspx.

Huntingdon County   *Recorded Documents*   www.huntingdoncounty.net/Dept/CommonPleas/RegRec/Pages/default.aspx   Access to Recorder records/images for a fee at www.infoconcountyaccess.com/. Contact them at 814-472-6066 or icas@ic-access.com for subscription information.

Indiana County   *Recorded Documents*   www.countyofindiana.org/Depts/RegRec/Pages/default.aspx   Access is available by subscription at http://regrec.countyofindiana.org/countyweb/login.do?countyname=Indiana, but can login as Guest and search free.

Jefferson County   *Recorded Documents*   www.jeffersoncountypa.com/register-recorder/   Access to Recorder records/images for a fee at www.infoconcountyaccess.com/. Contact them at 814-472-6066 or icas@ic-access.com for subscription information.

Juniata County   *Recorded Documents*   www.co.juniata.pa.us/elected-officials/recorder-deeds/   Access to land records for a fee at www.landex.com/webstore/jsp/cart/DocumentSearch.jsp. Online for Recorder of Deeds from 1987 to present, images from 1980 to present. Also, access to Recorder records/images for a fee at www.infoconcountyaccess.com/. Contact them at 814-472-6066 or icas@ic-access.com for subscription information.

Lackawanna County   *Recorded Documents*   www.lackawannacounty.org/index.php/departmentsagencies/county-government/recorder-of-deeds   Access to Recorder of Deeds public records free at https://www.searchiqs.com/palac/Login.aspx. Must log in as a guest.
Property, Taxation Records   Access to Assessor's database free at www.lackawannacounty.org/index.php/lackawanna-county-assessors-office.

Lancaster County   *Recorded Documents*   www.lancasterdeeds.com/   Access to deeds, UCCs and other recordings is free after registration at https://searchdocs.lancasterdeeds.com/countyweb/login.do?countyname=Lancaster.

Lawrence County   *Recorded Documents*   http://co.lawrence.pa.us/gov/register-of-wills-and-recorder-of-deeds/   Access to Recorder of
Deeds records free at https://countyfusion1.propertyinfo.com/countyweb/login.do?countyname=Lawrence. This is the direct link site. Must log in with
username and password. Also, access to Recorder records/images for a fee at www.infoconcountyaccess.com/. Contact them at 814-472-6066 or icas@ic-access.com for subscription information.
Property, Taxation Records   Search property records after free registration at http://co.lawrence.pa.us/assessment-property-search/. Must register.
For detailed records must subscribe. There is an assessment list with owner names and by district at http://co.lawrence.pa.us/lawrence-county-assessments-by-district-lawrence_county/.

Lebanon County   *Recorded Documents*   www.lebcounty.org/Recorder_of_Deeds/Pages/home.aspx   Access to land records for a fee at
www.landex.com/webstore/jsp/cart/DocumentSearch.jsp. Online for Deeds from 1933 to present, mortgages from 1933 to present and misc from 1969 to
present; images of deeds from 1952 to present, mortgagews from 1990 to present, misc from 1969 to present.
Property, Taxation Records   Access property data by subscription at www.courthouseonline.com/MyProperty.asp. Sub fee $9.95 3-days, up to $275
per year. If customer has control number and password from tax notice or are registered, can view for free.

Lehigh County   *Recorded Documents*   https://www.lehighcounty.org/Departments/Clerk-of-Judicial-Records/Recorder-of-Deeds   Access
to the county's full-access internet pay system is $300.00 a year initial cost. Call Lehigh County Tax and Licensing Dept at 610-782-3112 x0 for signup or
info. Also, subscribe to view naturalization, property tax, assessment, tax records for a fee. See https://www.lehighcounty.org/Services/Online-Records-Access. Also, access to land records for a fee at www.landex.com/webstore/jsp/cart/DocumentSearch.jsp. Online and images for Recorder of Deeds from
1984 to present.
Property, Taxation Records   Access assessor property data free at https://www.lehighcounty.org/Departments/Assessment/Search-Records, but no
name searching. Also, view sheriff's tax sales lists free at https://www.lehighcounty.org/Departments/Sheriffs-Office/Sheriff-Sale. Also, access to parcel
viewer for free at https://lehighgis.maps.arcgis.com/apps/Viewer/index.html?appid=44c36d2a3ddf41e69e778113e35d2dbf.

Luzerne County   *Recorded Documents*   www.luzernecounty.org/county/row_offices/recorder_of_deeds   Access to land records for a fee at
www.landex.com/webstore/jsp/cart/DocumentSearch.jsp. Online for Recorder of Deeds from 9/1983 to present, images from 1963 to present.
Property, Taxation Records   Access data by subscription at www.courthouseonline.com/MyProperty.asp. $9.95 3-day, up to $275 per year. Get free
view with control number & password from tax notice-registration.

Lycoming County   *Recorded Documents*   www.lyco.org/ElectedOfficials/RegisterandRecordersOffice.aspx   Access to the land record
index for free at https://pa.uslandrecords.com/palr2/PalrApp/index.jsp. For detailed records, must subscribe. Fee is $.50 per page for the entire document.
Also, access to Recorder records/images for a fee at www.infoconcountyaccess.com/. Contact them at 814-472-6066 or icas@ic-access.com for
subscription information.
Property, Taxation Records   Access property data by subscription at www.courthouseonline.com/MyProperty.asp. Sub fee $9.95 3-days, up to $275
per year. If customer has control number and password from tax notice or are registered, can view for free.

McKean County   *Recorded Documents*   www.mckeancountypa.org/Departments/Recorder_Of_Deeds/Index.aspx   Access to land records
for a fee at www.landex.com/webstore/jsp/cart/DocumentSearch.jsp. Online and images for Deeds from 1929 to present, mortgages from 1972 to present.
Also, access to Recorder records/images for a fee at www.infoconcountyaccess.com/. Contact them at 814-472-6066 or icas@ic-access.com for
subscription information.

Mercer County   *Recorded Documents*   https://www.mcc.co.mercer.pa.us/Recorders/default.htm   Access to records for a fee at
https://recorder.mcc.co.mercer.pa.us/User/Login.aspx?ReturnUrl=%2fIndex.aspx. Can sign in as a guest or account sign-in. Also, access to Recorder
records/images for a fee at www.infoconcountyaccess.com/. Contact them at 814-472-6066 or icas@ic-access.com for subscription information.
Property, Taxation Records   Search dog ownership database for free at https://www.mcc.co.mercer.pa.us/DogOwnerSearch/default.htm but no
name search.

Mifflin County   *Recorded Documents*   www.co.mifflin.pa.us/dept/RegRec/Pages/default.aspx   Access to Recorder records/images for a fee at
www.infoconcountyaccess.com/. Contact them at 814-472-6066 or icas@ic-access.com for subscription information.
Property, Taxation Records   Access to GIS/mapping free at www.co.mifflin.pa.us/dept/GIS/Pages/GIS-Data-Agreement.aspx.

Monroe County   *Recorded Documents*   Access to land records for a fee at www.landex.com/webstore/jsp/cart/DocumentSearch.jsp. Online
for Recorder of Deeds from 1979 to present, images from 1958 to present. Also, access to Recorder records/images for a fee at
www.infoconcountyaccess.com/. Contact them at 814-472-6066 or icas@ic-access.com for subscription information.

Montgomery County   *Recorded Documents*   www.montcopa.org/353/Recorder-of-Deeds   Recorder of Deeds records are at
https://rodviewer.montcopa.org/countyweb/login.do?countyname=Montgomery. Login as Guest or subscribe. Records date back to 1972. Lending agency
and Prothonotary data on system. Certified online copies are $10.50. Subscription fee to see documents are $250.00 per month. Copy Fee $.50 per page.
Property, Taxation Records   Search property records free at http://propertyrecords.montcopa.org/Main/home.aspx. Also, search parcels and court
data at https://courtsapp.montcopa.org/psi/v/search/case.

Montour County   *Recorded Documents*   www.montourco.org/RegisterRecorder/Pages/RegisterRecorder.aspx   Access to the index of wills
free at www.montourco.org/RegisterRecorder/Lists/Index%20Of%20Wills/AllItems.aspx. Also, access to Recorder records/images for a fee at
www.infoconcountyaccess.com/. Contact them at 814-472-6066 or icas@ic-access.com for subscription information.

Northampton County *Recorded Documents* www.northamptoncounty.org/northampton/site/default.asp   Access to land records for a fee at www.landex.com/webstore/jsp/cart/DocumentSearch.jsp. Online for Recorder of Deeds from 5/19/1978 to present, mortgages from 12/1984 to present, misc from 12/1985 to present; images for deeds from 8/1947 to present, mortgages from 2/1951 to present and misc from 12/1947 to present.
Property, Taxation Records   Access to assessor's property records data is free at www.ncpub.org/_web/forms/htmlframe.aspx?mode=content/home.htm.

Northumberland County *Recorded Documents* www.northumberlandco.org/   Access to land records for a fee at www.landex.com/webstore/jsp/cart/DocumentSearch.jsp. Online for Recorder of Deeds from 1928 to present, images from 1903 to present.

Perry County *Recorded Documents* www.perryco.org/Dept/RegisterAndRecorder/Pages/RegisterAndRecorder.aspx   Access to land records for a fee at www.landex.com/webstore/jsp/cart/DocumentSearch.jsp. Online for Recorder of Deeds from 1855 to present, images from 1820 to present.
Property, Taxation Records   Access property data by subscription at www.courthouseonline.com/MyProperty.asp. Sub fee $9.95 3-days, up to $275 per year. If customer has control number and password from tax notice or are registered, can view for free.

Philadelphia County *Recorded Documents* www.phila.gov/Records/index.html   Name search recorder data for a fee at http://epay.phila-records.com/phillyepay/web/; registration required; $15.00 for 1 dayr, $60.00 for 1 week (7 days), $125.00 for 1 month. $750 for 1 year. Images and indexes go back to 1974.
Property, Taxation Records   Search property assessment data for free at http://property.phila.gov/.

Pike County *Recorded Documents* www.pikepa.org/recdeed.html   Access to the land record index for free at https://pa.uslandrecords.com/palr2/PalrApp/index.jsp. For detailed records, must subscribe. Also, access to Recorder records/images for a fee at www.infoconcountyaccess.com/. Contact them at 814-472-6066 or icas@ic-access.com for subscription information.
Property, Taxation Records   Access parcel data and GIS/mapping for free at www.pikegis.org/pike/disclaimer.htm.

Potter County *Recorded Documents* www.pottercountypa.net/post.php?pid=19   Access to land records for a fee at www.landex.com/webstore/jsp/cart/DocumentSearch.jsp. Online for Recorder of Deeds from 1997 to present, images from 2003 to present. Also, access to Recorder records/images for a fee at www.infoconcountyaccess.com/. Contact them at 814-472-6066 or icas@ic-access.com for subscription information.

Schuylkill County *Recorded Documents* www.co.schuylkill.pa.us/Offices/RecorderOfDeeds/RecorderOfDeeds.asp   Recorded civil judgments viewable at www.co.schuylkill.pa.us/info/Civil/Inquiry/Search.csp. Also, access to the land record index for a fee at https://pa.uslandrecords.com/palr2/PalrApp/index.jsp.

Snyder County *Recorded Documents* www.snydercounty.org/Depts/Register_and_Recorder/Pages/RegisterandRecorder.aspx   Access to land records for a fee at www.landex.com. Online for Recorder of Deeds from 1973 to present.
Property, Taxation Records   Access to GIS/mapping free at www.snydercounty.org/Depts/GIS/Pages/GIS.aspx.

Somerset County *Recorded Documents* www.co.somerset.pa.us   Access property records by monthly subscription; $35.00 start-up fee plus $10.00 per month. For info or signup, call Cindy or John at 814-445-1536. Provide email, company info and check. System to provide images and comparable sales. Also, access to land records for a fee at www.landex.com/webstore/jsp/cart/DocumentSearch.jsp. Online and images for Recorder of Deeds from 1985 to present. Access to real estate records at www.co.somerset.pa.us/pages/realestatehome.asp. Also, access to Recorder records/images for a fee at www.infoconcountyaccess.com/. Contact them at 814-472-6066 or icas@ic-access.com for subscription information.
Property, Taxation Records   Access property data for a fee at www.co.somerset.pa.us/department.asp?deptnum=110.

Sullivan County *Recorded Documents* www.sullivancounty-pa.us/offices/prothonotary/   Access to land records for a fee at www.landex.com/webstore/jsp/cart/DocumentSearch.jsp. Online for Recorder of Deeds from 1980 to present, images from 1847 to present.

Susquehanna County *Recorded Documents* http://susqco.com/county-government/register-recorder/   Access to land records for a fee at www.landex.com/webstore/jsp/cart/DocumentSearch.jsp. Online and images for Recorder of Deeds from 1974 to present. Also, access to Recorder records/images for a fee at www.infoconcountyaccess.com/. Contact them at 814-472-6066 or icas@ic-access.com for subscription information.
Property, Taxation Records   Access property data by subscription at www.courthouseonline.com/MyProperty.asp. Sub fee $9.95 3-days, up to $275 per year. If customer has control number and password from tax notice or are registered, can view for free.

Tioga County *Recorded Documents*
www.tiogacountypa.us/Departments/Register_Recorder/Pages/RegisterofWills_RecorderofDeeds_ClerkofOrphans%27Court.aspx   Access to land records for a fee at www.landex.com/webstore/jsp/cart/DocumentSearch.jsp. Online for Recorder of Deeds from 1977 to present, images from 1806 to present.
Property, Taxation Records   Access property data by subscription at www.courthouseonline.com/MyProperty.asp. Sub fee $9.95 3-days, up to $275 per year. If customer has control number and password from tax notice or are registered, can view for free. Access to the assessment database is free at http://gis.vgsi.com/tiogapa/. Sheriff sales lists free online at www.tiogacountypa.us/Departments/Sheriffs_Office/Pages/SheriffSales.aspx.

Union County *Recorded Documents* www.unioncountypa.org/departments/recorder-of-deeds/recorder-of-deeds/page.aspx?id=1403   Access to Recorder of Deeds land records for a fee at https://pa.uslandrecords.com/palr2/PalrApp/index.jsp.

Property, Taxation Records   Access to GIS/mapping free at www.unionco.org/unionbase/. Also, access to land records for a fee for the images at https://pa.uslandrecords.com/palr_new/PalrApp/index.jsp. Fees are $.50 per page with maximum charge of $5.00 per document.

Venango County   *Recorded Documents*   www.co.venango.pa.us/index.php?option=com_content&view=article&id=75&Itemid=119
Access to Recorder records/images for a fee at www.infoconcountyaccess.com/. Contact them at 814-472-6066 or icas@ic-access.com for subscription information.

Property, Taxation Records   Access property data by subscription at www.courthouseonline.com/MyProperty.asp. Subscription fee $9.95 3-days, up to $374.95 per year. If customer has control number and password from tax notice or are registered, can view for free. Also, access to GIS/mapping free at http://gis.venangopa.us/parcelviewer/default.aspx

Warren County   *Recorded Documents*   www.warrencountypa.net/current/depts.php?name=Register%20-%20Recorder   Access to Recorder records/images for a fee at www.infoconcountyaccess.com/. Contact them at 814-472-6066 or icas@ic-access.com for subscription information.

Washington County   *Recorded Documents*   www.co.washington.pa.us/index.aspx?nid=205   Access to land records for a fee at www.landex.com/webstore/jsp/cart/DocumentSearch.jsp. Online for Recorder of Deeds from 1952 to present, images of deeds from 1780 to present and mortgages from 1841 to present.

Property, Taxation Records   Access treasurer real estate tax data free at http://washcounty.info/wcmtp/tri_stringVar.asp.

Wayne County   *Property, Taxation Records*   Search assessor property data free at http://taxpub.co.wayne.pa.us/.

Westmoreland County   *Recorded Documents*   www.co.westmoreland.pa.us/index.aspx?nid=146   A free, searchable site is at www.wcdeeds.us/dts/default.asp. Choose simple, advanced, or instrument search. Documents prior to 1943 can be found using the Archive Search.

Property, Taxation Records   A links list to a variety of county records accessible online is at www.co.westmoreland.pa.us/index.aspx?NID=1572. Subscription services from http://pa-westmorelandcounty.civicplus.com/index.aspx?nid=1041. Property tax, estate search, and marriage license search from http://westmorelandweb400.us:8088/EGSPublicAccess.htm. Also, access to GIS/mapping for free at www.co.westmoreland.pa.us/index.aspx?NID=1980.

Wyoming County   *Recorded Documents*   www.wycopa.org/Offices/RegRec/Pages/default.aspx   Access to records for free at https://portal1.recordfusion.com/countyweb/login.do?countyname=Wyoming. For detailed information must subscribe.

York County   *Recorded Documents*   https://yorkcountypa.gov/property-taxes/recorder-of-deeds.html   Access to land records for a fee at www.landex.com/webstore/jsp/cart/DocumentSearch.jsp. Online and images for Recorder of Deeds from 1981 to present.

Property, Taxation Records   Access to GIS/mapping free at http://gis.york-county.org/Disclaimer.aspx.

Rhode Island

Capital: Providence
             Providence County
Time Zone: EST
Population: 1,056,298
# of Counties: 5

Useful State Links

Website: **www.ri.gov/**
Governor: **www.governor.state.ri.us**
Attorney General: **www.riag.ri.gov**
State Archives: **http://sos.ri.gov/divisions/Civics-And-Education/archives**
State Statutes and Codes: **http://webserver.rilin.state.ri.us/Statutes/Statutes.html**
Legislative Bill Search: **http://webserver.rilin.state.ri.us/legislation/**
Unclaimed Funds: **www.treasury.ri.gov/unclaimedproperty/**

State Public Record Agencies

Sexual Offender Registry

Sex Offender Community Notification Unit, Rhode Island Parole Board,   www.paroleboard.ri.gov/   Website information about a sex offender is available to the public only if the Sex Offender Board of Review has classified the offender as a Level 3, or as a Level 2 as of January 1, 2006. Per Rhode Island Law information pertaining to Level 1 sex offenders cannot be posted on the website. Go to www.paroleboard.ri.gov/sexoffender/agree.php. Also, search by town or ZIP.

Incarceration Records

Rhode Island Department of Corrections, Records,   www.doc.ri.gov/index.php   A free DOC search is available at www.doc.ri.gov/inmate_search/index.php. The database only has inmates currently incarcerated and there is a 24 hour lag time on updates.

Corporation, LLC, LP, LLP, Fictitious Name, Non-Profits

Secretary of State, Division of Business Services,   http://sos.ri.gov/divisions/Business-Portal/   At the web, search filings for active and inactive Rhode Island and foreign business corporations, corporations, limited partnerships, limited liability companies, limited liability partnerships, and the non-profits as well. Weekly listings of new corporations are also available. There is no fee. A variety of certifications can also be requested, fees involved. See http://sos.ri.gov/divisions/Business-Portal/databases. Online filing is available for corporations, LLCs and LPs. *Other Options:* Various databases may be downloaded or purchased on CD. Call for pricing.

Trademarks/Servicemarks

Secretary of State, Trademark Section,   http://sos.ri.gov/divisions/Business-Portal/Forms/trademark-servicemark   Search the trademark/servicemark database at http://ucc.state.ri.us/trademarks/trademarksearch.asp.   *Other Options:* For a fee of $100 per year, the agency will provide quarterly disks with all new filings processed in a quarter. Set dates are Jan 1, April 1, July 1, and Oct 1.

Uniform Commercial Code

Secretary of State, Div. of Business Srvs - UCC Section,   http://sos.ri.gov/divisions/Business-Portal/databases/ucc-database   View debtor names in the Pubic Search Index at http://ucc.state.ri.us/psearch/. One may also search by file number or business organization. Rhode Island's UCC Public Search Index allows its users to search using both Standard Search Logic and Non-Standard Search Logic.   *Other Options:* Bulk data can be purchased by request. Call for details.

Sales Tax Registrations

Taxation Division, Sales & Use Tax Office,   www.tax.state.ri.us   View administrative decisions by this office at www.tax.state.ri.us/AdministrativeDecisions/. Search by Tax Type or Decision Number.

Driver Records

Division of Motor Vehicles, Driving Record Clerk, Operator Control, www.dmv.ri.gov Driving records are available in two manners. From the home page above, anyone may request a record online, pay the $19.50 service fee with a credit card and the record will be mailed to the address shown on the DL. This record does not contain the driver's address or SSN. The driver name. DOB and license number must be submitted. Ongoing requesters who qualify to receive records with personal information may obtain a subscription account for interactive service. The same record fee applies. For more information about becoming a subscriber visit www.ri.gov/subscriber/.

Vehicle Ownership & Registration

Division of Motor Vehicles, Vehicle Records, www.dmv.ri.gov This application allows RI.gov subscribers to access title records currently on file with the Rhode Island Division of Motor Vehicles. The record presented is the most recent record on file with the Division of Motor Vehicles. Historical records must be obtained in person or by mail. The total fee for this service is $53.30. For more information on becoming a subscriber call 401-831-8099 x230 or visit www.ri.gov/subscriber. *Other Options:* Bulk retrieval of vehicle and ownership information is limited to statistical purposes.

Crash Reports

Rhode Island State Police, Accident Reports, www.risp.ri.gov/ The agency has outsourced online record requests to a vendor at www.getcrashreports.com/. Search by name or by any number of factors. Fee is $20.00. Records include reports from at least 32 cities/towns in Rhode Island. The site works well, provides detailed information, but lacks upfront details on costs and record throughput. One must basically to go through the order process to find these details. There is a subscription program for ongoing requesters, but no details given until the third step in the order process.

Voter Registration. Campaign Finance PACs

Secretary of State, Elections Division, www.sos.ri.gov A specific look-up or verification of voter registration is available at https://vote.sos.ri.gov/. The name, DOB and town is needed. The search shows voter preferences. Also, one may make requests by email at elections@sos.ri.gov. Form the Board of Elections, search candidate, PAC, and committee filed reports at www.elections.ri.gov/finance/publicinfo/. *Other Options:* The web offers voter lists sales statewide on paper ($700) or CD ($25). Customized lists are also available. Click on Voter Registration List at the home page.

Occupational Licensing Boards

These Health Care related licenses are all searchable at
http://209.222.157.144/RIDOH_Verification/Search.aspx?facility=N&SubmitComplaint=Y

Acupuncturist	Emergency Med Technician/Service	Outpatient Rehabilitation
Ambulatory Care Facility	Esthetician/Manicurist/Shop	Pharmacist/Pharmacy/Technician
Asbestos Worker	Funeral Director	Phlebotomy Station
Assisted Living Facility/Admin	Hearing Aid Dispenser	Physical Therapist/Assistant
Athletic Trainer	Histologic Technician, Clinical	Physician/Medical Doctor/Assistant
Audiologist	Home Nursing Care Provider	Physicians Controlled Substance
Barber/Barber Instructor/Ship	Hospice Provider	Podiatrist
Birth Center	Hospital	Prosthetist
Blood Test Screener	Hypodermic Dispenser	Psychologist
Chiropractor	Interpreter for the Deaf	Radiation Therapist
Clinical Lab Scientist/Technician/Cytogenetic	Laboratory/Medical	Radiographer
Controlled Substance Wholesaler	Marriage & Family Therapist	Residential Care Facility
Cosmetologist/Cosmetology Instructor	Massage Therapist	Respiratory Care Practitioner
Cytotechnologist	Midwife	Sanitarian
Dentist/Dental Hygienist	Nurse-LPN/Aide	Social Worker
Dietitian/Nutritionist	Nursing Home Administrator	Speech/Language Pathologist
Electrologist	Nursing Service	Tanning Facility
Electron Microscopy, Lab Scientist	Occupational Therapist	Tattoo Artist
Embalmer	Optician	Veterinarian
Emergency Care Facility	Optometrist	X-Ray Equipment (Portable)/Facility

The Rest:

Accountant Firm...www.dbr.state.ri.us/documents/divisions/accountancy/Licensed_Public_Accounting_Firms.pdf
Accountant-CPA, PA ....www.dbr.state.ri.us/documents/divisions/accountancy/LicensedCPAsandPAs.pdf
Alarm Agent/Company ....www.dlt.ri.gov/profregsonline/PROLentree.aspx
Architect...www.dbr.ri.gov/licenses/lookup.php
Attorney ....http://rijrs.courts.ri.gov/rijrs/attorney.do
Automobile Body Shop ....www.dbr.state.ri.us/divisions/commlicensing/autobody.php

Automobile Glass Installer	www.dbr.state.ri.us/divisions/commlicensing/autoglass.php
Automobile Wrecker	www.dbr.state.ri.us/divisions/commlicensing/autowrecking.php
Bank	www.dbr.ri.gov/licenses/lookup.php
Bank Holding Company	www.dbr.ri.gov/licenses/lookup.php
Boxer	www.dbr.state.ri.us/divisions/commlicensing/boxing.php
Business Filing/Annual Report	https://www.lobbytracker.sos.ri.gov/Public/LobbyingReports.aspx
Check Casher	www.dbr.ri.gov/licenses/lookup.php
Chemical Dependency Clinical Spvr/Prof/Adv	www.ricertboard.org/professionals.html
Contractor, Resid'l Building	www.crb.state.ri.us/search.php
Contractor, Watch List	www.crb.state.ri.us/watchlist.php
Counselor in Training	www.ricertboard.org/professionals.html
Credit Union	www.dbr.ri.gov/licenses/lookup.php
Criminal Justice Professional	www.ricertboard.org/professionals.html
Day Care, Provider	www.dcyf.state.ri.us/child_care_provider.php
Debt Pooler	www.dbr.ri.gov/licenses/lookup.php
Electrician	www.dlt.ri.gov/profregsonline/PROLentree.aspx
Elevator Inspector/Mechanic	www.dlt.ri.gov/profregs/
Family/Group Day Care Home Provider	www.dcyf.state.ri.us/child_care_provider.php
Financial Institution	www.dbr.ri.gov/licenses/lookup.php
Hazardous Waste Transporter	www.dem.ri.gov/onlineservices/
Hoisting Engineer	www.dlt.ri.gov/profregsonline/PROLentree.aspx
Home Inspector	www.crb.state.ri.us/search.php
Insurance Adjuster/Appraiser/Solicitor	www.dbr.ri.gov/divisions/insurance/licensed.php
Insurance Broker/Producer/Agent	www.dbr.ri.gov/divisions/insurance/licensed.php
Investment Advisor	www.adviserinfo.sec.gov/
Landscaper	www.dbr.ri.gov/licenses/lookup.php
Lender/Loan Broker	www.dbr.ri.gov/licenses/lookup.php
Liquor Control	www.dbr.ri.gov/licenses/lookup.php
Lobbyist Registration	https://www.lobbytracker.sos.ri.gov/Public/LobbyingReports.aspx
Medical Waste Transporter	www.dem.ri.gov/onlineservices/
Mobile Home Park	www.dbr.state.ri.us/divisions/commlicensing/mobile.php
Mobile/Manufact'd Home Mfg/Dealer	www.dbr.state.ri.us/divisions/commlicensing/mobile.php
Money Broker	www.dbr.ri.gov/licenses/lookup.php
Money Transferer	www.dbr.ri.gov/licenses/lookup.php
Mortgage Broker	www.dbr.state.ri.us/documents/divisions/banking/program_operations/List_of_Licensees.pdf
Notary Public	http://ucc.state.ri.us/notarysearch/onlinesearch.asp
Open Meeting	http://sos.ri.gov/openmeetings/
Pipefitter	www.dlt.ri.gov/profregsonline/PROLentree.aspx
Plumber/Master Plumber/Journey'n	www.dlt.ri.gov/profregsonline/PROLentree.aspx
Prevention Specialist/Supvr/Advanced	www.ricertboard.org/professionals.html
Real Estate Agent/Seller/Broker	www.dbr.state.ri.us/divisions/commlicensing/realestate.php
Real Estate Appraiser	www.dbr.state.ri.us/divisions/commlicensing/realestate.php
Refrigeration Technician	www.dlt.ri.gov/profregs/
Roofer, Commercial	www.crb.state.ri.us/search.php
Salvage Yard	www.dbr.state.ri.us/divisions/commlicensing/autosalvage.php
Securities Broker/Dealer/Seller	www.dbr.ri.gov/licenses/lookup.php
Septic Transporter	www.dem.ri.gov/onlineservices/
Sheet Metal Technician/Worker	www.dlt.ri.gov/profregs/
Student Assistance Counselor	www.ricertboard.org/professionals.html
Surveyor, Land	www.dbr.ri.gov/licenses/lookup.php
Telecommunications Technician	www.dlt.ri.gov/profregsonline/PROLentree.aspx
Upholstery/Bedding Mfg	www.dbr.state.ri.us/divisions/commlicensing/upholster.php
Vendor Employee	www.dbr.ri.gov/licenses/lookup.php
Waste Water Treatm't Plant System	https://www.ri.gov/DEM/isdssearch/
Wrestler	www.dbr.ri.gov/licenses/lookup.php

State and Local Courts

About Rhode Island Courts: The **Superior Court** has original jurisdiction in all felony proceedings, in civil cases where the amount in controversy exceeds $10,000, and in equity matters. The court has concurrent jurisdiction with the District Court in civil matters when the amount in controversy is between $5,000 and $10,000.

The **District Court** has exclusive jurisdiction of all civil actions at law wherein the amount in controversy is under $5,000. The District Court handles arraignments for felony and misdemeanor cases. Misdemeanor cases are punishable for up to one year in prison and fines are not to exceed $1,000. There are no jury trials heard in District Court.

Rhode Island has five counties but only four **Superior/District Court Locations**— 2nd-Newport, 3rd-Kent, 4th-Washington, and 6th-Providence/Bristol Districts. Bristol and Providence counties are completely merged at the Providence location. 26 of the 39 cities and towns in Rhode Island have **Municipal Courts**. In general, Municipal Courts oversee traffic, ordinance, housing and zoning violations, but not every court has authority in all areas. The Municipal Courts do not hear cases involving state criminal laws nor are they administrated by the State Court Administrator's Office. For more information on municipalities, see www.muni-info.ri.gov.

Probate is handled by the Town Clerk at the 39 cities and towns, not at the Superior or District courts. The contact information is shown herein.

Civil traffic violations are heard either at a Municipal Court or at the **Traffic Tribunal which** has original jurisdiction over civil traffic offenses committed in Rhode Island, including breathalyzer refusals. Reach the Traffic Tribunal at 401-275-2700.

The web page for the Judicial Branch is https://www.courts.ri.gov/Pages/default.aspx.

Appellate Courts: The Rhode Island Supreme Court is the court of last resort and has absolute appellate jurisdiction over questions of law and equity, supervisory powers over other state courts. The Supreme Court has its own web page with a case docket search, opinions and orders, and other content at https://www.courts.ri.gov/Courts/SupremeCourt/Pages/default.aspx.

Online Court Access

All courts participate in the system described below.

The Rhode Island Judiciary provides two online record search systems; however, one system is not open to everyone.

1. CourtConnect

The general public has free access to an index of county criminal cases statewide at http://courtconnect.courts.state.ri.us. Access to civil records is not available (regardless of what drop down box says).

There are several cautions regarding the use of this system:

- Only the year of birth is shown on results.

- There is a very strong disclaimer that specifically states this site cannot be used for background checks or employment screening.

- Comments from local record searchers indicate this site is known to show cases that were sealed or were supposed to be removed. It is suggested to confirm case existence before reporting to a client.

2. Public Access Portal

The Judiciary's Public Access Portal (https://www.courts.ri.gov/Pages/access-caseinfo.aspx) provides access to a database of court records displayed as a register of actions or docket sheet. This system only provides access to Civil, Family Court, and Workers' Compensation Court, and does not provide access to criminal case records. **Despite the name, this system is only open to attorneys, self-represented litigants and to state or federal agencies, but NOT to the public.** Registration and a subscription agreement are both required. This system can be accessed via the Web or from terminals located onsite at the courthouses. However, there are several limitations.

- For all other cases in which they are not directly involved, attorneys shall have remote access to the register of actions or docket but shall not have remote access to other electronic case information

- Self-represented litigants shall have no greater access than the public to information about cases in which they are not directly involved.

Note: No individual Rhode Island court offers online access, other than as described above.

Recorders, Assessors, and Other Sites of Note

About Rhode Island Recording Offices: There are 5 counties in Rhode Island, but there is no county recording of public records in this state. All recording is done at the town/city level at one of 39 locations. The recording officers are the town/city clerks and this job title is often referred to as the the Recorder of Deeds.

Be aware that three sites bear the same name as their respective counties - Bristol, Newport, and Providence

About Tax Liens: All federal and state tax liens on personal property and on real property are filed with the City or Town Clerk.

Online Access

Recorded Documents

At least 24 towns provide online access either direct from their site or via a vendor.

Assessor Records

All towns provide online access. 27 towns are affliated with www.vgsi.com/vision/Applications/ParcelData/RI/Home.aspx.

Town Sites:

Barrington Town in Bristol County *Recorded Documents* www.barrington.ri.gov/departments/clerk.php   View recorded documents for free at https://i2b.uslandrecords.com/RI/. Printing and/or downloading will incur charges.
Property, Taxation Records Access to GIS/mapping free at www.mainstreetmaps.com/RI/Barrington/public.asp. Also, access to the Assessor's database for free at www.nereval.com/Home.html?aspxerrorpath=/OnlineDatabases.aspx.

Bristol Town in Bristol County *Property, Taxation Records* Access property data on a private site at www.clipboardinc.com/bristolsearchpage.html.

Burrillville Town in Providence County *Recorded Documents* www.burrillville.org/town-clerk   Access to recorded documents free at www.crcpropertyinfo.com/crcdb/burrillville.htm. View recorded documents for free at https://i2b.uslandrecords.com/RI/. Printing and/or downloading will incur charges.
Property, Taxation Records Access to property records is free at www.crcpropertyinfo.com/crcdb/burrillville.htm. Also, access to the Assessor's database free at www.vgsi.com/vision/Applications/ParcelData/RI/Home.aspx.

Central Falls City in Providence County *Property, Taxation Records* Access to the Assessor's database free at www.nereval.com/Home.html?aspxerrorpath=/OnlineDatabases.aspx.

Charlestown Town in Washington County *Recorded Documents* www.charlestownri.org/   View recorded documents for free at https://i2b.uslandrecords.com/RI/. Printing and/or downloading will incur charges.
Property, Taxation Records Access to the Assessor's database free at www.vgsi.com/vision/Applications/ParcelData/RI/Home.aspx. Also, GIS/mapping for free at www.charlestownri.org/index.asp?Type=B_BASIC&SEC={707D6067-952E-4FDD-BBAF-1C0197B6ED04}&DE={78333F2B-3E2A-4D93-A5B0-6072B82B5838}.

Coventry Town in Kent County *Property, Taxation Records* Access to the Assessor's database free at www.nereval.com/Home.html?aspxerrorpath=/OnlineDatabases.aspx.

Cranston City in Providence County *Property, Taxation Records* Access to tax rolls and Assessor maps free at www.cranstonri.com/taxfiles2015.php. Also, access to the Assessor's database free at www.vgsi.com/vision/Applications/ParcelData/RI/Home.aspx. Also, access to GIS/mapping for free at http://gis.cranstonri.org/assessor/.

Cumberland Town in Providence County *Property, Taxation Records* Access to the Assessor's database free at www.vgsi.com/vision/Applications/ParcelData/RI/Home.aspx.

East Greenwich Town in Kent County *Voter Registration Records* www.eastgreenwichri.com   Access to voter registration free at https://sos.ri.gov/vic/index.php.
Property, Taxation Records Access to the Assessor's database free at www.nereval.com/Home.html?aspxerrorpath=/OnlineDatabases.aspx.

East Providence City in Providence County *Recorded Documents* www.eastprovidenceri.net/content/9457/9568/default.aspx View recorded documents for free at https://i2b.uslandrecords.com/RI/. Printing and/or downloading will incur charges.
Property, Taxation Records Access to the Assessor's database free at www.vgsi.com/vision/Applications/ParcelData/RI/Home.aspx.

Exeter Town in Washington County *Recorded Documents* www.town.exeter.ri.us/town-clerk.html   View recorded documents for free at https://i2b.uslandrecords.com/RI/. Printing and/or downloading will incur charges.

Property, Taxation Records   Access property data free at www.crcpropertyinfo.com/crcdb/exeter.htm. Access to real estate tax collection data is by subscription from a vendor at www.opaldata.net/OnlineTax/.

Foster Town in Providence County   *Property, Taxation Records*   Access property data free at
www.crcpropertyinfo.com/crcdb/foster.htm. Also, access to the Assessor's database free at www.vgsi.com/vision/Applications/ParcelData/RI/Home.aspx.

Glocester Town in Providence County   *Recorded Documents*   www.glocesterri.org/townclerk.htm   View recorded documents
for free at https://i2b.uslandrecords.com/RI/. Printing and/or downloading will incur charges. Indexes available from 8/1965 to present, images available from 9/2002 to present. members/search and search results printing.

Property, Taxation Records   Access property data free at www.glocesterri.org/taxassessor.htm. Also, access to the Assessor's database free at www.vgsi.com/vision/Applications/ParcelData/RI/Home.aspx. Also, access to Assessor's maps 1-20 for free at www.glocesterri.org/taxassessor.htm#gis.

Hopkinton Town in Washington County   *Property, Taxation Records*   Access to the Assessor's database free at
www.vgsi.com/vision/Applications/ParcelData/RI/Home.aspx. Also, access old property record cards free at
www.crcpropertyinfo.com/crcdb/hopkinton.htm. Also, access to tax maps for free at www.hopkintonri.org/tax-maps/.

Jamestown Town in Newport County   *Property, Taxation Records*   Plat Map data for free at www.jamestownri.gov/town-
departments/tax-assessor/tax-maps. Also, access to the Assessor's database free at www.vgsi.com/vision/Applications/ParcelData/RI/Home.aspx.

Johnston Town in Providence County   *Property, Taxation Records*   Also, access to the Assessor's database free at
www.vgsi.com/vision/Applications/ParcelData/RI/Home.aspx.

Lincoln Town in Providence County   *Property, Taxation Records*   Property data free at
www.crcpropertyinfo.com/crcdb/lincoln.htm. Also, access to the Assessor's database free at
www.vgsi.com/vision/Applications/ParcelData/RI/Home.aspx.

Little Compton Town in Newport County   *Property, Taxation Records*   Also, access to the Assessor's database free at
www.vgsi.com/vision/Applications/ParcelData/RI/Home.aspx.

Middletown Town in Newport County   *Recorded Documents*   www.middletownri.com/government/19/Town-Clerk-Voter-
Registration   View recorded documents for free at https://i2b.uslandrecords.com/RI/. Printing and/or downloading will incur charges.
Property, Taxation Records   Access to the Assessor's database free at www.vgsi.com/vision/Applications/ParcelData/RI/Home.aspx.

Narragansett Town in Washington County   *Recorded Documents*   www.narragansettri.gov/331/Town-Clerks-Office   View
recorded documents for free at https://i2b.uslandrecords.com/RI/. Printing and/or downloading will incur charges.
Property, Taxation Records   Access to the Assessor's database free at www.vgsi.com/vision/Applications/ParcelData/RI/Home.aspx.

New Shoreham Town in Washington County   *Property, Taxation Records*   Access to the Assessor's database free at
www.vgsi.com/vision/Applications/ParcelData/RI/Home.aspx.

Newport City in Newport County   *Recorded Documents*   www.cityofnewport.com/departments/finance/assessing-division/property-
records   View recorded documents for free at https://i2f.uslandrecords.com/RI/Newport/D/Default.aspx. Printing and/or downloading will incur charges.
Property, Taxation Records   Access to the Assessor's database free at www.vgsi.com/vision/Applications/ParcelData/RI/Home.aspx.

North Kingstown Town in Washington County   *Recorded Documents*   www.northkingstown.org/departments/town-clerk
View recorded documents for free at https://i2b.uslandrecords.com/RI/. Printing and/or downloading will incur charges.
Property, Taxation Records   Access to the Assessor's database free at www.vgsi.com/vision/Applications/ParcelData/RI/Home.aspx.

North Providence Town in Providence County   *Recorded Documents*   http://northprovidenceri.gov/town-clerk/   View
recorded documents for free at https://i2b.uslandrecords.com/RI/. Printing and/or downloading will incur charges.
Property, Taxation Records   Access to the Assessor's database free at www.nereval.com/Home.html?aspxerrorpath=/OnlineDatabases.aspx.

North Smithfield Town in Providence County   *Property, Taxation Records*   Access to the Assessor's database for free at
www.nereval.com/Home.html?aspxerrorpath=/OnlineDatabases.aspx.

Pawtucket City in Providence County   *Recorded Documents*   www.pawtucketri.com/city-clerks-office   Access real estate data
free at http://72.248.180.6/ALIS/WW400R.HTM?WSIQTP=SY00. Online indices go back to 1970.
Property, Taxation Records   Access to the Assessor's database free at www.vgsi.com/vision/Applications/ParcelData/RI/Home.aspx.

Portsmouth Town in Newport County   *Recorded Documents*   www.portsmouthri.com/154/Town-Clerk   View recorded
documents for free at https://i2b.uslandrecords.com/RI/. Printing and/or downloading will incur charges.
Property, Taxation Records   Access to the Assessor's database free at www.vgsi.com/vision/Applications/ParcelData/RI/Home.aspx.

Providence City in Providence County   *Recorded Documents*   www.providenceri.com/deeds/   View recorded documents for free
at https://i2b.uslandrecords.com/RI/. Printing and/or downloading will incur charges.

Property, Taxation Records   Access to the Assessor's database free at www.vgsi.com/vision/Applications/ParcelData/RI/Home.aspx.

Richmond Town in Washington County   *Property, Taxation Records*   Access to the Assessor's database free at
www.vgsi.com/vision/Applications/ParcelData/RI/Home.aspx.

Scituate Town in Providence County   *Property, Taxation Records*   Access to town property data is free at
www.crcpropertyinfo.com/crcdb/scituate.htm.

Smithfield Town in Providence County   *Recorded Documents*   http://smithfieldri.com/town-clerk/   View recorded documents for
free at https://i2b.uslandrecords.com/RI/. Printing and/or downloading will incur charges. Land records from 1/2/1965 to present; plans from 1/1871 to
present.
Property, Taxation Records   Access to the Assessor's database free at www.vgsi.com/vision/Applications/ParcelData/RI/Home.aspx.

South Kingstown Town in Washington County   *Recorded Documents*   www.southkingstownri.com/town-
government/municipal-departments/town-clerk   Access town real estate data free at http://70.168.204.238/ALIS/WW400R.HTM. Land indexes and
images go back to 1980 (excluding maps). More to be added. Registration required for full data.
Property, Taxation Records   Access to the tax maps for free at www.southkingstownri.com/town-government/tax-maps. Also, access to the
Assessor's database free at www.vgsi.com/vision/Applications/ParcelData/RI/Home.aspx.

Tiverton Town in Newport County   *Recorded Documents*   www.tiverton.ri.gov/departments/townclerk/index.php   View recorded
documents for free at https://i2b.uslandrecords.com/RI/. Printing and/or downloading will incur charges. Document index and images from 1/2/1969 to
present.
Property, Taxation Records   Access tax rolls free at www.tiverton.ri.gov/departments/taxassessor/taxrolls.php. Also, access to GIS/mapping for
free at www.tiverton.ri.gov/departments/taxassessor/gismaps.php. Also search Real Estate Data for free at www.crcpropertyinfo.com/crcdb/tiverton.htm.
Also, access to the Assessor's database free at www.vgsi.com/vision/Applications/ParcelData/RI/Home.aspx.

Warren Town in Bristol County   *Recorded Documents*   www.townofwarren-ri.gov/departmentsaz/townclerk.html   View recorded
documents for free at https://i2b.uslandrecords.com/RI/. Printing and/or downloading will incur charges.
Property, Taxation Records   Access to the Assessor's database free at www.nereval.com/Home.html?aspxerrorpath=/OnlineDatabases.aspx. Also,
plat records are available free at www.townofwarren-ri.gov/documentlibraries/platmaps.html.

Warwick City in Kent County   *Recorded Documents*   www.warwickri.gov/city-clerks-office   View recorded documents for free at
https://i2b.uslandrecords.com/RI/. Printing and/or downloading will incur charges.
Property, Taxation Records   Access to the Assessor's database free at www.vgsi.com/vision/Applications/ParcelData/RI/Home.aspx. Access to plat
maps for free at www.warwickri.gov/index.php?option=com_content&view=article&id=1353:warwick-assessor-plat-maps&catid=142:warwick-
maps&Itemid=209.

West Greenwich Town in Kent County   *Property, Taxation Records*   Access property data free at
www.crcpropertyinfo.com/crcdb/westgreenwich.htm. Also, access to the Assessor's database for free at
www.nereval.com/Home.html?aspxerrorpath=/OnlineDatabases.aspx.

West Warwick Town in Kent County   *Recorded Documents*   www.westwarwickri.org/index.asp?   View recorded documents for
free at https://i2b.uslandrecords.com/RI/. Printing and/or downloading will incur charges.
Property, Taxation Records   Access to the Assessor's database free at www.nereval.com/Home.html?aspxerrorpath=/OnlineDatabases.aspx.

Westerly Town in Washington County   *Recorded Documents*
www.westerly.govoffice.com/index.asp?Type=B_BASIC&SEC={66DF58E6-9381-4FD9-B6DB-6B7EE81794FD}   View recorded documents for free
at https://i2b.uslandrecords.com/RI/. Printing and/or downloading will incur charges.
Property, Taxation Records   Access to GIS/mapping is free at http://host.cdmsmithgis.com/WesterlyRI/. Also, access to the Assessor's database
free at www.vgsi.com/vision/Applications/ParcelData/RI/Home.aspx.

Woonsocket City in Providence County   *Recorded Documents*   www.ci.woonsocket.ri.us/   View recorded documents for free at
https://i2b.uslandrecords.com/RI/. Printing and/or downloading will incur charges.
Property, Taxation Records   Access to GIS/mapping free at www.mainstreetmaps.com/RI/Woonsocket/. Also, access to the Assessor's database
free at www.vgsi.com/vision/Applications/ParcelData/RI/Home.aspx.

South Carolina

Capital: Columbia
            Richland County
Time Zone: EST
Population: 4,896,146
# of Counties: 46

Useful State Links

Website: **www.sc.gov**
Governor: **www.governor.sc.gov/**
Attorney General: **www.scag.gov/**
State Archives: **http://scdah.sc.gov/**
State Statutes and Codes: **www.scstatehouse.gov/research.php**
Legislative Bill Search: **www.scstatehouse.gov**
Unclaimed Funds: **http://treasurer.sc.gov/unclaimed-property/**

State Public Record Agencies

Criminal Records

South Carolina Law Enforcement Division (SLED), Criminal Records Section, www.sled.sc.gov/ SLED CATCH offers access to criminal record history from 1960 forward at https://catch.sled.sc.gov/. Fees are $26.00 per screening or $8.00 if for a charitable organization. Credit card ordering accepted. Visit the website for details. Documentation of charitable status is required

Sexual Offender Registry

Sex Offender Registry, c/o SLED, http://scor.sled.sc.gov/ConditionsOfUse.Aspx See http://scor.sled.sc.gov/ConditionsOfUse.Aspx, this is the Law Enforcement Division of the Sex Offender Registry (SORT). Access to statewide offender database search is available at www.dppps.sc.gov/Offender-Supervision/Offender-Search.

Incarceration Records

Department of Corrections, Inmate Records Branch, www.doc.sc.gov/pubweb/ The Inmate Search on the Internet is found at www.doc.sc.gov/pubweb/InmateSearchDisclaimer.jsp, or click on Inmate search at the main website. The inmate search does not provide information for offenders released from SCDC, sentenced to county detention facilities, or those under parole, probation or other community supervision.

Corporation, LP, LLP, LLC, Trademarks/Servicemarks

Secretary of State, Division of Business Filings, www.sos.sc.gov/ One may search business filings and a database of registered charities from the home page. The database provides access to basic filing information about any entity filed with the office. Registered agents' names and addresses, dates of business filings and types of filings are all available. The database is updated every 24 hours.

Uniform Commercial Code

UCC Division, Secretary of State, www.scsos.com One may do a "free search" to find a filing number, but the fee kicks in to view the documents. A pay system to index of records is at https://ucconline.sc.gov/UCCFiling/UCCMainPage.aspx. Search by debtor name or number. Records are generally current within 48 hours. The fee is $10.00 per search using a credit card. Frequent requesters may obtain a subscription account and be billed. Transactions over $100, increase by $2.25 for each additional $100. Transactions over $100, increasing by $2.25 for each additional $100. There is a $75 annual fee. See https://ucconline.sc.gov/UCCFiling/SubscriptionServices.aspx.

Vital Records

South Carolina DHEC, Vital Records, www.scdhec.gov/VitalRecords/ Order from state-designated vendor - www.vitalchek.com. See expedited services.

Workers' Compensation Records

Workers Compensation Commission, Claims Dept,   www.wcc.sc.gov/Pages/default.aspx   ECase Status provides with electronic access to workers' compensation cases. Public information for cases on appeal is available to site visitors, and parties to a claim may register to access confidential case status information. See https://wccprogress.sc.gov/wccprod.wsc/onlinereports.html.

Driver Records

Department of Motor Vehicles, Driver Records Section,   www.scdmvonline.com/DMVNew/default.aspx   Commercial records are available from the portal https://dmvdhr.sc.gov/DriverHistoryRecords/Interactive/CDBLogin.aspx. Authorized businesses must establish an account through a formal approval and acceptance process. The fee is $7.25 per record and a $75.00 annual fee is required. Members have access to additional online services. For more information about setting up an account, call 803-771-0131 or email support@sc-egov.com. For no fee, at https://www.scdmvonline.com/DMVpublic/trans/DRecPoints.aspx one may view a driver license status. The status includes points history. The DL, SSN and DOB are needed. Also, SC drivers may purchase their own record after viewing at https://www.scdmvonline.com/dmvpublic/trans/DrvRecWarn.aspx. A certified copy is mailed for $6.00.

Voter Registration

State Election Commission, Records,   www.scvotes.org/   Intended to check your own registration, free verification is offered at https://info.scvotes.sc.gov/eng/voterinquiry/VoterInformationRequest.aspx?PageMode=VoterInfon. When checking information, must provide the name, county and date of birth exactly as registered. *Other Options:* Lists, labels, diskettes, and electronic media are available with a variety of sort features. The minimum charge varies from $75 to $160 depending on the media.

Campaign Finance, Lobbyists, Ethics Violations

State Ethics Commission, 5000 Thurmond Mall, Suite 250,   http://ethics.sc.gov/Pages/default.aspx   Search by candidate or by contributor at https://ssl.sc.gov/Ethics/. Search reports at http://apps.sc.gov/PublicReporting/Index.aspx?AspxAutoDetectCookieSupport=1. The State Ethics Commission levies late filing penalties, and enforcement fines against violators. A list is viewable at http://ethics.sc.gov/Debtors/Pages/index.aspx. Search lobbyists and reporting at http://apps.sc.gov/LobbyingActivity/LAIndex.aspx.

GED Certificates

Office of Adult Educations - GED Testing, 1429 Senate Street,   http://ed.sc.gov/instruction/adult-education/general-education-development-ged/   One may order an unofficial copy through GED Wizard at https://secure.gedwizard.com/. Students may order a copy of a GED transcript or diploma at www.ed.sc.gov/apps/ged/. The DOB and last four digits of SSN is required. Use of a credit card is required. Fee is $10.00 for document to be delivered by mail, $5.00 if by fax.

Occupational Licensing Boards

Accountant-CPA/PA	https://verify.llronline.com/LicLookup/(X(1)S(bdnelrgdbfce0gb0ik1g53ja))/Acct/Acct.aspx
Accounting Firm	https://verify.llronline.com/LicLookup/(X(1)S(bdnelrgdbfce0gb0ik1g53ja))/Acct/Acct.aspx
Acupuncturist	https://verify.llronline.com/LicLookup/Med/Med.aspx
Agricultural Dealer/Handler	www.kellysolutions.com/SC/handlers/showall.asp
Airport Professional/Contact	www.scaeronautics.com/directorySearch.asp
Alcoholic Beverage Sunday Seller	https://dor.sc.gov/tax/abl/licenses
Alcoholic Beverage Vendor/Mfg/Whlse	https://dor.sc.gov/tax/abl/licenses
Amusement Ride/Inspectors	www.llronline.com/elevators/index.asp
Animal Health Technician	https://verify.llronline.com/LicLookup/Vet/Vet.aspx
Architect/Architectural Partnership/Corp	https://verify.llronline.com/LicLookup/(X(1)S(vos4v00x0jilxdo12ivinr4s))/Arch/Arch.aspx
Athletic Event/Contest	https://verify.llronline.com/LicLookup/Athletic/Athletic.aspx
Athletic Trainer	https://verify.llronline.com/LicLookup/Athletic/Athletic.aspx
Attorney	www.scbar.org/Bar-Members
Auctioneer/Auctioneer Apprentice/Company	https://verify.llronline.com/LicLookup/Auctioneer/Auctioneer.aspx
Audiologist	https://verify.llronline.com/LicLookup/Speech/Speech.aspx
Aviation Facility	www.scaeronautics.com/AirportList.asp
Barber Instructor/School	https://verify.llronline.com/LicLookup/Barbers/Barbers.aspx
Barber/Barber Apprentice	https://verify.llronline.com/LicLookup/Barbers/Barbers.aspx
Bodywork Therapist	https://verify.llronline.com/LicLookup/Mass/Mass.aspx
Boxer/Boxing Professional	https://verify.llronline.com/LicLookup/Athletic/Athletic.aspx
Building Inspector/Official	https://verify.llronline.com/LicLookup/BCO/BCO.aspx
Chiropractor	https://verify.llronline.com/LicLookup/Chiro/Chiro.aspx
Contact Lens License	https://verify.llronline.com/LicLookup/Optometry/Optometry.aspx
Contractor, Specialty Resid'l	https://verify.llronline.com/LicLookup/Resbu/Resbu.aspx

Cosmetologist/Instructor/School	https://verify.llronline.com/LicLookup/Cosmo/Cosmo.aspx
Counselor, Professional/Intern	https://verify.llronline.com/LicLookup/Counselors/Counselors.aspx
Dental Hygienist/Specialist/Technician	https://verify.llronline.com/LicLookup/Dent/Dent.aspx
Dentist	https://verify.llronline.com/LicLookup/Dent/Dent.aspx
Elevator Service/Inspectors	www.llronline.com/elevators/index.asp
Embalmer	https://verify.llronline.com/LicLookup/Funeral/Funeral.aspx
Engineer	https://verify.llronline.com/LicLookup/Engineers/Engineer.aspx
Esthetician/Manicurist/Nail Technician	https://verify.llronline.com/LicLookup/Cosmo/Cosmo.aspx
Ethics Debtors	http://ethics.sc.gov/Debtors/Pages/index.aspx
Funeral Director/Home	https://verify.llronline.com/LicLookup/Funeral/Funeral.aspx
Geologist	https://verify.llronline.com/LicLookup/Geologist/Geologists.aspx
Hair Care Master Specialist	https://verify.llronline.com/LicLookup/Barbers/Barbers.aspx
Home Builder, Residential	https://verify.llronline.com/LicLookup/Resbu/Resbu.aspx
Home Inspector	https://verify.llronline.com/LicLookup/BCO/BCO.aspx
Inspector, Bldg/Housing/Mech/Elec/Plumb/Prov	https://verify.llronline.com/LicLookup/BCO/BCO.aspx
Insurance Agent/Agency/Company/Filing	https://online.doi.sc.gov/Eng/Public/Static/DBSearch.aspx
Landscape Architect	https://verify.llronline.com/LicLookup/(X(1)S(vos4v00x0jilxdo12ivinr4s))/Arch/Arch.aspx
Liquor Permit-Special Event	https://dor.sc.gov/tax/abl/licenses
Lobbyist/Principal	http://apps.sc.gov/LobbyingActivity/LAIndex.aspx
Manicure Assistant	https://verify.llronline.com/LicLookup/Barbers/Barbers.aspx
Manufact'd House Install/Repair	https://verify.llronline.com/LicLookup/MH/MH.aspx
Manufact'd House Mfg/Dealer/Rep	https://verify.llronline.com/LicLookup/MH/MH.aspx
Marriage & Family Therapist/Intern/Spvr	https://verify.llronline.com/LicLookup/Counselors/Counselors.aspx
Massage Therapist	https://verify.llronline.com/LicLookup/Mass/Mass.aspx
Notary Public	www.scsos.com/Notaries_and_Apostilles/Notary_Search
Nurse-RN/LPN	https://verify.llronline.com/LicLookup/Nurse/Nurse.aspx
Nursing Home Administrator	https://verify.llronline.com/LicLookup/LTC/LTC.aspx
Occupational Therapist/Assistant	https://verify.llronline.com/LicLookup/OT/OT.aspx
Optician/Apprentice	https://verify.llronline.com/LicLookup/Optometry/Optometry.aspx
Optometrist	https://verify.llronline.com/LicLookup/Optometry/Optometry.aspx
Osteopathic Physician	https://verify.llronline.com/LicLookup/Med/Med.aspx
Pesticide Registration	www.kellysolutions.com/clemson/pesticides/pesticideindex.asp
Pharmacist/Pharmacy Technician	https://verify.llronline.com/LicLookup/Pharmacy/Pharmacy.aspx
Pharmacy/Drug Outlet	https://verify.llronline.com/LicLookup/Pharmacy/Pharmacy.aspx
Physical Therapist/Therapist Asst	https://verify.llronline.com/LicLookup/PT/PT.aspx
Physician/Medical Doctor/Assistant	https://verify.llronline.com/LicLookup/Med/Med.aspx
Plans Examiner, Building	https://verify.llronline.com/LicLookup/BCO/BCO.aspx
Podiatrist	https://verify.llronline.com/LicLookup/Podiatry/Podiatry.aspx
Produce Whlse Dealer	www.kellysolutions.com/SC/handlers/showall.asp
Property Manager	https://verify.llronline.com/LicLookup/Rec/Rec.aspx
Psycho-Educational Specialist	https://verify.llronline.com/LicLookup/Counselors/Counselors.aspx
Psychologist	https://verify.llronline.com/LicLookup/Psyc/Psyc.aspx
Real Estate Appraiser	https://verify.llronline.com/LicLookup/Rec/Rec.aspx
Real Estate Broker	https://verify.llronline.com/LicLookup/Rec/Rec.aspx
Residential Care, Community	https://verify.llronline.com/LicLookup/LTC/LTC.aspx
Respiratory Care Practitioner	https://verify.llronline.com/LicLookup/Med/Med.aspx
Shampoo Assistant	https://verify.llronline.com/LicLookup/Barbers/Barbers.aspx
Social Worker	https://verify.llronline.com/LicLookup/SW/SW.aspx
Soil Classifier	www.llr.state.sc.us/POL/Soil/
Soil Classifier	https://verify.llronline.com/LicLookup/SoilClassify/SoilClassify.aspx
Speech-Language Pathologist	https://verify.llronline.com/LicLookup/Speech/Speech.aspx
Structural Pest Control Business	http://regfocus.clemson.edu/dpr/blicense.htm
Surveyor, Land	https://verify.llronline.com/LicLookup/Engineers/Engineer.aspx
Veterinarian/Intern	https://verify.llronline.com/LicLookup/Vet/Vet.aspx
Waste Water Plant Operator	https://verify.llronline.com/LicLookup/Environmental/Enviro.aspx

Water Treatment Registration .... https://verify.llronline.com/LicLookup/Environmental/Enviro.aspx
Well Driller .... https://verify.llronline.com/LicLookup/Environmental/Enviro.aspx
Wholesaler/Shipper (Food)....................................... www.kellysolutions.com/SC/handlers/showall.asp
Wrestler/Wrestling Professional .... https://verify.llronline.com/LicLookup/Athletic/Athletic.aspx

State and Local Courts

About South Carolina Courts: The **Circuit Court** is the state's court of general jurisdiction. It has a civil court called the **Court of Common Pleas** and a criminal court called the **Court of General Sessions**. In addition to its general trial jurisdiction, the Circuit Court has limited appellate jurisdiction over appeals from the Probate Court, Magistrate's Court, and Municipal Court. Masters-In-Equity have jurisdiction in matters referred to them by the Circuit Courts.

Magistrate Courts (also known as **Summary Courts**) generally have criminal trial jurisdiction over all offenses subject to the penalty of a fine, as set by statute, but generally, not exceeding $500.00 or imprisonment not exceeding 30 days, or both. In addition, they are responsible for setting bail, conducting preliminary hearings, and issuing arrest and search warrants. Magistrates have civil jurisdiction when the amount does not exceed $7,500.

Municipal Courts have jurisdiction over cases arising under ordinances of the municipality, and over all offenses which are subject to a fine not exceeding $500.00 or imprisonment not exceeding 30 days, or both, and which occur within the municipality. In addition, Municipal Courts may hear cases transferred from General Sessions when the penalty for which does not exceed one year imprisonment or a fine of $5,000, or both. However, a municipality may, establish an agreement to prosecute its cases in the Magistrate court, in lieu of establishing its own Municipal Court.

Probate Courts have jurisdiction over marriage licenses, estates, guardianships of incompetents, conservatorships of estates of minors and incompetents, minor settlements under $25,000 and involuntary commitments to institutions for mentally ill and/or chemically dependent persons.

The **Family Court** has exclusive jurisdiction over all matters involving domestic or family relationships.

The web page for the Judicial Branch is www.sccourts.org.

Appellate Courts: The Court of Appeals was created to hear most types of appeals from the circuit court and the family court. Exceptions are when the appeal falls within any of the seven classes of exclusive jurisdiction listed under the Supreme Court. Various Opinion searches of the Supreme Court and Court of Appeals are viewable from the web page above.

Online Court Access

All Counties Provide Online Access

The web page at www.sccourts.org/caseSearch/ provides individual county links for a case record search. All counties participate. But note the search is available only on a per-county look-up; there is no statewide single search.

Many of these county online search sites give users an initial choice between searching for records from a Circuit Court or Summary Court. Some counties include records from the magistrate Courts; some include state and federal tax liens. However per local record researchers, it is worth cautioning that although all Summary (Magistrate) Courts' records are online there are instances when Summary records may be missing cases, sentence details, and probation updates and violations.

The online Circuit Court search is essentially the same search viewable at each of the local court locations using the on-site public use terminal.

Ten Counties (Barnwell, Beaufort, Charleston Marriage & Probate, Colleton, Dorchester, Jasper, Marlboro, Newberry, Saluda, and York) provide a name search of probate docket data online at https://www.southcarolinaprobate.net/search/default.aspx

A Problem With identifiers

Per a 2014 amendment to the South Carolina Rules of Civil Procedure (SCRCP), personal identifying information is now redacted from the public. For example, the docket index will only include the year of birth if it was included in the original filing. Many records do not have any DOB. Most courts will give a Y/N response if a searcher has the case number and the full DOB and asks the clerk to verify the identity if there is a common name. But unfortunately but not all courts will do this.

View the Rule online at www.judicial.state.sc.us/courtOrders/displayOrder.cfm?orderNo=2014-01-15-03.

County Sites:

Circuit Court   www.abbevillecountysc.com/clerkcourt.aspx
Civil: Online access to the index for both the Circuit and Summary courts at http://publicindex.sccourts.org/abbeville/publicindex.   *Criminal:* same

Aiken County
Circuit Court   https://www.aikencountysc.gov/DspDept.php?qDeptID=COC
Civil: Access the record index at http://publicindex.sccourts.org/aiken/publicindex/.   *Criminal:* same

Allendale County
Circuit Court
Civil: Search the index at http://publicindex.sccourts.org/allendale/publicindex/.   *Criminal:* same

Anderson County
Circuit Court   www.judicial.state.sc.us/index.cfm
Civil: Access the record index at http://publicindex.sccourts.org/anderson/publicindex/.   *Criminal:* same

Bamberg County
Circuit Court
Civil: Free access to the Circuit and Summary Courts' record index at http://publicindex.sccourts.org/bamberg/publicindex/.   *Criminal:* same

Barnwell County
Circuit Court
Civil: Record docket online at http://publicindex.sccourts.org/barnwell/publicindex/. Includes General Sessions records.   *Criminal:* same

Beaufort County
Circuit Court   www.bcgov.net/
Civil: Access to public case index and court dockets for free go to http://publicindex.sccourts.org/beaufort/publicindex/.   *Criminal:* same

Berkeley County
Circuit Court   https://www.berkeleycountysc.gov/drupal/?q=clerkofcourts
Civil: A case index search is offered at http://publicindex.sccourts.org/berkeley/publicindex/.   *Criminal:* same

Calhoun County
Circuit Court
Civil: Search the index at http://publicindex.sccourts.org/calhoun/publicindex/.   *Criminal:* same

Charleston County
Circuit Court   www.charlestoncounty.org/departments/clerk-of-court/circuit-court.php#go
Civil: Civil case details 1988 forward, also judgments and lis pendens are free at http://jcmsweb.charlestoncounty.org/publicindex/. Online document images go back to 1/1/1999. Also accessible via www.sccourts.org/casesearch/.   *Criminal:* Access to criminal case details from 04/92 forward free at www3.charlestoncounty.org/connect. Search by name or case number. Also accessible via www.sccourts.org/casesearch/.

Cherokee County
Circuit Court
Civil: Civil case details online at http://publicindex.sccourts.org/cherokee/publicindex/.   *Criminal:* same

Chester County
Circuit Court   www.chestercounty.org/government/clerk-of-court.aspx
Civil: Search the index at http://publicindex.sccourts.org/chester/publicindex/.   *Criminal:* same

Chesterfield County
Circuit Court   www.chesterfieldcountysc.com/ClerkOfCourt
Civil: Access the docket index for free at http://publicindex.sccourts.org/chesterfield/publicindex/.   *Criminal:* same

Clarendon County
Circuit Court
Civil: Civil case details free on state system at http://publicindex.sccourts.org/clarendon/publicindex/.   *Criminal:* same

Colleton County
Circuit Court   www.colletoncounty.org/
Civil: Online access to the index is at http://publicindex.sccourts.org/colleton/publicindex/.   *Criminal:* same

Darlington County
Circuit Court   www.darcosc.com/government/clerk_of_the_court/index.php
Civil: Access the docket index at http://publicindex.sccourts.org/darlington/publicindex/.   *Criminal:* same

Dillon County
Circuit Court
Civil: Access online index at http://publicindex.sccourts.org/dillon/publicindex/.   *Criminal:* same

Dorchester County
Circuit Court   https://www.dorchestercounty.net/index.aspx?page=523
Civil: Access case index free at http://publicindex.sccourts.org/dorchester/publicindex/.   *Criminal:* same

Edgefield County
Circuit Court   www.edgefieldcounty.sc.gov/Pages/Home.aspx
Civil: Civil   case   details   free   at   http://publicindex.sccourts.org/edgefield/publicindex/.   Also   search   pending   cases   free   at
http://publicindex.sccourts.org/edgefield/courtrosters/PendingCases.aspx.   *Criminal:* same

Fairfield County
Circuit Court   www.fairfieldsc.com/secondary.aspx?pageID=123
Civil: A case index search if found at http://publicindex.sccourts.org/fairfield/publicindex/.   *Criminal:* same

Florence County
Circuit Court   http://florenceco.org/elected-offices/clerk-of-court/
Civil: Search judgments back to 1994 at http://publicindex.sccourts.org/florence/publicindex/.   *Criminal:* same

Georgetown County
Circuit Court   www.georgetowncountysc.org
Civil: Access   the   court   dockets   free   at   http://publicindex.sccourts.org/georgetown/publicindex/   Also,   access   court   rosters   at
http://publicindex.sccourts.org/georgetown/courtrosters/.   *Criminal:* same

Greenville County
Circuit Court   www.greenvillecounty.org
Civil: Family Court and civil index at https://www2.greenvillecounty.org/scjd/publicindex/?Aspx.   *Criminal:* same

Greenwood County
Circuit Court   www.greenwoodsc.gov/countywebsite/index.aspx?page=138
Civil: Online access to the docket index is at http://publicindex.sccourts.org/greenwood/publicindex/.   *Criminal:* same

Hampton County
Circuit Court   www.hamptoncountysc.org/11/Clerk-of-Court
Civil: Search the index free at http://publicindex.sccourts.org/hampton/publicindex/.   *Criminal:* same

Horry County
Circuit Court   www.horrycounty.org/Departments/ClerkOfCourt.aspx
Civil: A free search site of the docket index for all courts in the county is found at http://publicindex.sccourts.org/horry/publicindex/. Also, civil case
details free at http://publicindex.sccourts.org/horry/courtrosters/.   *Criminal:* A free search site of the docket index for all courts in the county is found at
http://publicindex.sccourts.org/horry/publicindex/. Also the criminal court roster is free at http://publicindex.sccourts.org/horry/courtrosters/. County
bookings are at http://sheriff.horrycounty.org/Detention/DailyBookingsandReleases.aspx.

Jasper County
Circuit Court   www.jaspercourt.org/
Civil: Civil case details and dockets free at http://publicindex.sccourts.org/Jasper/publicindex/.   *Criminal:* same

Kershaw County
Circuit Court   www.kershaw.sc.gov/Index.aspx?page=226
Civil: Online access to the docket index is at www.sccourts.org/caseSearch/.   *Criminal:* same

Lancaster County
Circuit Court
Civil: Online access to the docket index is at www.sccourts.org/caseSearch/.   *Criminal:* same

Laurens County
Circuit Court
Civil: Online access to the docket index for the Circuit and Summary Courts at http://publicindex.sccourts.org/laurens/publicindex/.   *Criminal:* same

Lee County
Circuit Court
Civil: Access to civil index for free at http://publicindex.sccourts.org/lee/publicindex/.   *Criminal:* same

Lexington County

Circuit Court   www.lex-co.sc.gov/departments/DeptAH/clerkofcourt/Pages/default.aspx
Civil: Search record index free at http://cms.lex-co.com/scjdweb/publicindex/.   *Criminal:* Search the record index at http://cms.lex-co.com/scjdweb/publicindex/. Note online records prior to 1994 may include missing/incorrect IDs, wrong charge codes, and be missing some cases, also sentence details, probation updates/violations.

Marion County

Circuit Court   www.marionsc.org/clerkofcourt
Civil: A free name index search is at http://publicindex.sccourts.org/marion/publicindex/.   *Criminal:* same

Marlboro County

Circuit Court   www.marlborocounty.sc.gov/departments/Pages/default.aspx
Civil: Free access to the docket index at http://publicindex.sccourts.org/marlboro/publicindex/. Includes search for civil judgments.   *Criminal:* same

McCormick County

Circuit Court   www.mccormickcountysc.org/mccormick_county_clerk.php
Civil: A free index search is at http://publicindex.sccourts.org/mccormick/publicindex/.   *Criminal:* same

Newberry County

Circuit Court   www.newberrycounty.net/departments/clerk
Civil: Access the docket index from the Circuit and Summary Courts at http://publicindex.sccourts.org/newberry/publicindex/.   *Criminal:* same

Oconee County

Circuit Court   www.judicial.state.sc.us/countyLookup.cfm
Civil: Search the index free at http://publicindex.sccourts.org/oconee/publicindex/.   *Criminal:* same

Walhalla Magistrate (Summary) Court   www.oconeesc.com/Departments/KZ/Magistrate.aspx
Civil: The index is searchable at http://publicindex.sccourts.org/oconee/publicindex/.   *Criminal:* same

Orangeburg County

Circuit Court   www.orangeburgcounty.org/
Civil: Online access to the docket index is at http://publicindex.sccourts.org/orangeburg/publicindex/.   *Criminal:* same

Pickens County

Circuit Court   www.co.pickens.sc.us
Civil: Civil case details free at http://publicindex.sccourts.org/pickens/publicindex/.   *Criminal:* same

Richland County

Circuit Court   www.richlandonline.com/Government/Courts/ClerkofCourt.aspx
Civil: Limited civil case details free at www5.rcgov.us/SCJDWeb/PublicIndex/disclaimer.aspx?AspxAutoDetectCookieSupport=1. Limited court rosters online at ww5.rcgov.us/scjdweb/courtrosters/disclaimer.aspx; search by date. Family court data is at www4.rcgov.us/familycourtPublicIndex/main.aspx. *Criminal:* same

Saluda County

Circuit Court   http://saludacounty.sc.gov/Government/CourtSystem/Clerk%20of%20Court/Pages/default.aspx
Civil: Search the case record index at http://publicindex.sccourts.org/saluda/publicindex/. Includes access to civil judgments.   *Criminal:* same

Spartanburg County

Circuit Court   www.spartanburgcounty.org/174/Clerk-of-Court
Civil: Civil case details free at http://publicindex.sccourts.org/spartanburg/publicindex/.   *Criminal:* same

Sumter County

Circuit Court   www.sumtercountysc.org
Civil: Civil record index is at www.sumtercountysc.org/?q=online-service/judicial-court-records-search. Family court case details online at the website. *Criminal:* Access criminal record index is at www.sumtercountysc.org/?q=online-service/judicial-court-records-search.

Union County

Circuit Court   www.countyofunion.org/default.asp?sec_id=180003405
Civil: Search the case index free at http://publicindex.sccourts.org/union/publicindex/. Also includes search of civil judgments.   *Criminal:* same

Williamsburg County

Circuit Court   www.williamsburgcounty.sc.gov
Civil: Search record index free at http://publicindex.sccourts.org/williamsburg/publicindex/.   *Criminal:* same

York County
General Sessions   www.yorkcountygov.com/departments/clerkCourt/COC-GeneralSessions
Criminal: Access case details free at http://publicindex.sccourts.org/york/publicindex/disclaimer.aspx Also. search current court dockets free at http://scsolicitor16.org/GeneralSessions/CourtDocket.
Circuit Court - Common Pleas   www.yorkcountygov.com/departments/clerkCourt/COC-CommonPleas
Civil: Access case details free at http://publicindex.sccourts.org/york/publicindex/disclaimer.aspx. Also. search current court dockets free at http://scsolicitor16.org/GeneralSessions/CourtDocket.

Recorders, Assessors, and Other Sites of Note

About South Carolina Recording Offices: South Carolina is divided into 46 recorder districts with an elected or appointed Recorder or Clerk responsible for each office. Documents related to the ownership of real estate within the county are recorded at either the Register of Deeds Office, or the Clerk of Courts Office depending on the county. In some counties this postion is known as the Register of Mense Conveyances. Note the Clerk of Court also serves as the Register of Deeds in smaller counties.

About Tax Liens: All federal and state tax liens on personal property and on real property are filed with the Register of Mesne Conveyances or Clerk of Court.

Online Access

Recorded Documents:
There is no statewide system. 35 county recorders offer free access to information via the web.

Assessor and Tax Records:
All but three counties provide online to assessor and tax related data.

County Sites:
Abbeville County   *Property, Taxation Records*   Assess to GIS/mapping for free at https://qpublic.schneidercorp.com/.

Aiken County   *Recorded Documents, Comparable Sale Records*   https://www.aikencountysc.gov/DspDept.php?qDeptID=RMC   Access to the county e-services are free at https://www.aikencountysc.gov/ but not all modules allow name searching. For full data and name searching, must register and currently no charge. Registration and password required for Property Cards and Comparable Sales. Also, access to property and deeds indexes and images is via a private company at www.titlesearcher.com/. Fee/registration required. Deeds and index goes back to 1/1982; images back to 6/13/2005.
Property, Taxation Records   Search Assessor land records at www.qpublic.net/sc/aiken/. Search by parcel information at https://cxap2.aikencountysc.gov/EGSV2Aiken/RPSearch.do. Search GIS at https://www.aikencountysc.gov/DspSvc.php?qSvcID=21.

Allendale County   *Real Estate, Grantor/Grantee, Deed, Mortgage, Lien Records*   http://allendalecounty.com/   Access to recorders data is free via a private firm at https://portal2.recordfusion.com/countyweb/login.do?countyname=Allendale. Logon as Guest to search free. Judgments found in the Clerk of Courts office.

Anderson County   *Recorded Documents*   www.andersoncountysc.org/Departments/Register-of-Deeds   Access to the county ACPASS super search site is free at http://acpass.andersoncountysc.org/index.htm.
Property, Taxation Records   Access to GIS/mapping for free at http://propertyviewer.andersoncountysc.org/mapsjs/. Access property tax and vehicle tax and other data free at http://acpass.andersoncountysc.org/index.htm.

Bamberg County   *Property, Taxation Records*   Access to property records and GIS/mapping for free at www.qpublic.net/sc/bamberg/.

Barnwell County   *Recorded Documents*   www.sccourts.org/clerks/barnwell/   Access to land records for free at https://www.sclandrecords.com/sclr/. Records from 1/3/1978 to present
Property, Taxation Records   Access to Assessor records is free at www.qpublic.net/sc/barnwell/.

Beaufort County   *Recorded Documents*   www.bcgov.net/departments/Real-Property-Services/register-of-deeds/index.php   Access to recorded documents form 1983 to present is free at http://rodweb.bcgov.net/searchng/.
Property, Taxation Records   Search assessor data free at http://sc-beaufort-county.governmax.com/svc/default.asp.

Berkeley County   *Recorded Documents*   https://www.berkeleycountysc.gov/drupal/?q=deeds   Access real estate data at http://search.berkeleydeeds.com/NameSearch.php?Accept=Accept. Images only. Must contact office for certified copies.
Property, Taxation Records   Access to property records for free at http://server1.berkeleycountysc.gov/EGSBKLY/RPSearch.do.

Calhoun County *Recorded Documents* www.judicial.state.sc.us/clerksCourt/clerkID.cfm?clerkID=93&countyNo=9   Access to property and deeds indexes and images is via a private company at www.titlesearcher.com/countyInfo.php?cnum=S1. Fee/registration required. Images and indices go back to 8/2004.
Property, Taxation Records   Access to sales lists for free at www.calhouncounty.sc.gov/departments/assessor/Pages/default.aspx.

Charleston County *Recorded Documents* www.charlestoncounty.org/elected/bio-rmc.php   Access RMC recording data free at www.charlestoncounty.org/departments/rmc/rmcsearch.php, land records/images go back to 2/1997. Marriages-www3.charlestoncounty.org/connect/LU_GROUP_2?ref=Marriage. Business licenses- www3.charlestoncounty.org/surfer/group3?s=b.
Property, Taxation Records   Access auditor & treasurer's tax system free at http://sc-charleston-county.governmax.com/svc/. Access the county's GIS mapping database of property records free at http://ccgisapps.charlestoncounty.org/public_search/.

Cherokee County *Recorded Documents* http://cherokeecountysc.gov/government-services/clerk-of-court   Access to land records for free at https://www.sclandrecords.com/sclr/. Indexes from 1/3/1995 to present; scanned images from 9/25/2002 to present.
Property, Taxation Records   Access to GIS/mapping for free at http://cherokeecountysc.gov/government-services/mapping-and-gis/acog-map.

Chester County *Property, Taxation Records*   Access to Assessor's database is free at www.chestercountysctax.com/.

Chesterfield County *Recorded Documents* www.chesterfieldcountysc.com/ClerkOfCourt   Access to land records for free at https://www.sclandrecords.com/sclr/.
Property, Taxation Records   Access to assessor data is free at www.chesterfieldcountysc.com/OnlineAssesor.

Clarendon County *Recorded Documents* http://clarendoncountygov.org/index.php/register-of-deeds   Access to records for free at http://oncore.clarendoncountygov.org/oncoreweb/.
Property, Taxation Records   Access to public records free at www.qpublic.net/sc/clarendon/search.html.

Colleton County *Recorded Documents* www.colletoncounty.org/register-of-deeds   Access to land records for free at https://www.sclandrecords.com/sclr/. Index from 8/1/1986 to present.
Property, Taxation Records   Access property and vehicle tax data free at http://sc-colleton-county.governmax.com/svc/default.asp?sid=53EB5F78D5044B628583D69CA6863444.

Darlington County *Recorded Documents* www.darcosc.com/government/clerk_of_the_court/index.php   Access to records free at http://rod.darcosc.com/external/LandRecords/protected/v4/SrchName.aspx.
Property, Taxation Records   Access property records free at www.qpublic.net/sc/darlington/search.html.

Dorchester County *Recorded Documents* https://www.dorchestercounty.net/index.aspx?page=955   Access to Register of Deeds real estate records is free at https://www.dorchestercounty.net/index.aspx?page=999.
Property, Taxation Records   Search tax and property records free on the GIS-mapping site at https://gisservices.dorchestercounty.net/imap/GISsplash.html.

Edgefield County *Recorded Documents* www.edgefieldcounty.sc.gov/Pages/Home.aspx   Access to land records for free at https://www.sclandrecords.com/sclr/. Certification starts at 7/1995 for deeds, mortgages, misc, plats; UCC at 1/2003 and tax liens and lis pendens at 12/2006.
Property, Taxation Records   Access property assessor data free at www.edgefieldcountysc.com/search.aspx. Also, access county land record index and images free at http://publicindex.sccourts.org/edgefield/PUBLICINDEX/%28X%281%29S%28ul5o2vymemklg1rhshqpo1ba%29%29/Disclaimer.aspx?AspxAutoDetect CookieSupport=1.

Fairfield County *Property, Taxation Records*   Access to records for free at http://qpublic.net/sc/fairfield/search.html.

Florence County *Recorded Documents* http://florenceco.org/elected-offices/clerk-of-court/   Access recorder data free at http://web.florenceco.org/cgi-bin/coc/coc.cgi.
Property, Taxation Records   Access property tax records free at http://web.florenceco.org/cgi-bin/ta/tax-inq.cgi.

Georgetown County *Recorded Documents* www.georgetowncountysc.org/Register_Deeds/   Access to land records for free at https://www.sclandrecords.com/sclr/. Certification start dates-- deeds-1/1/1997, mortgages-7/1/1986, misc liens-7/1/2002, plats-7/1/1988, tax liens-7/1/1989 and UCCs-1/1/1989.
Property, Taxation Records   Access to property data for free at www.qpublic.net/sc/georgetown/search.html.

Greenville County *Recorded Documents* www.greenvillecounty.org/rod/   Search the Register of Deeds database free at www.greenvillecounty.org/rod/searchrecords.asp. There are tow choices, a search for records prior to 1985 and a search records after 1985.
Property, Taxation Records   Search the property tax and vehicles data at www.greenvillecounty.org/appsas400/votaxqry/. Also, search real estate tax data by name or address at www.greenvillecounty.org/appsAS400/RealProperty/.

Greenwood County *Real Estate, Grantor/Grantee, Deed, Mortgage Federal & State Tax Liens, Judgment Records* www.greenwoodsc.gov/countywebsite/index.aspx?page=138   Document search for free at www.greenwoodsc.gov/docsearch/default.aspx.

Property, Taxation Records   Access to GIS/mapping free at www.greenwoodsc.gov/GreenwoodSL/.

Hampton County   *Recorded Documents*   www.hamptoncountysc.org/11/Clerk-of-Court   Access to land records for free at https://www.sclandrecords.com/sclr/. Recorded dates from 1/3/2000 to present.
Property, Taxation Records   Access to Appraiser property records (limited) for free at http://qpublic5.qpublic.net/sc_search.php?county=sc_hampton. For full detailed features, must subscribe.

Horry County   *Recorded Documents*   www.horrycounty.org/Departments/RegisterofDeeds.aspx   Access the recorded documents free at www.horrycounty.org/OnlineServices/searchdeeds.
Property, Taxation Records   Access to the delinquent tax files for free at www.horrycounty.org/OnlineServices/DelinquentTax.

Jasper County   *Recorded Documents*   www.jaspercountysc.org/secondary.aspx?pageID=62   Access to recorders data is free via a private firm at https://countyfusion1.propertyinfo.com/countyweb/login.do?countyname=Jasper. Logon as Guest to search free. Judgments found in the Clerk of Courts office.

Kershaw County   *Recorded Documents*   www.kershaw.sc.gov/Index.aspx?page=148   Access to land records for free at https://www.sclandrecords.com/sclr/.
Property, Taxation Records   Access to property/vehicle tax (Treasurer's) for free at www.kershawcountysctax.com/. Also, access to parcel records for free at http://scassessors.com/. Also, access to GIS/mapping for free at http://kershaw.sc.wthgis.com/.

Lancaster County   *Recorded Documents*   www.mylancastersc.org/index.asp?Type=B_BASIC&SEC={1AE29148-C09A-487D-983C-47A02BC9D737}   Access to property and deeds indexes and images is via a private company at www.titlesearcher.com/. Fee/registration required. Indices and images go back to 8/27/2002.
Property, Taxation Records   Access property records data free at www.qpublic.net/sc/lancaster/search.html. Also, access to property assessment data free at http://patriotproperties.com/.

Laurens County   *Recorded Documents*   www.laurenscountysc.org/secondary.aspx?pageID=150   Access to property and deeds indexes and images is via a private company at www.titlesearcher.com. Fee/registration required. Deed records go back to 7/1991; indices back to 6/1/1996; images to 8/26/2006.
Property, Taxation Records   Access to online tax search, view and pay for free at www.laurenscountysctaxes.com/secondary.aspx?pageID=146#/. Also, access to property tax searches free at www.laurenscountysc.org/secondary.aspx?pageID=175. Also, access to GIS/mapping for free at www.laurenscountygis.org/LaurensGIS/.

Lee County   *Property, Taxation Records*   Access to records for a fee at www.qpublic.net/sc/lee/gen-info.html. Must have email and password for login.

Lexington County   *Recorded Documents*   www.lex-co.sc.gov/onlineservices/Pages/RODOnlineServices.aspx   Access Register of Deeds records free at www.lex-co.sc.gov/onlineservices/Pages/RODOnlineServices.aspx.
Property, Taxation Records   Access to GIS/mapping for free at www.lex-co.sc.gov/departments/DeptAH/PGIS/Pages/default.aspx. Property tax, vehicle tax, etc is found at www.lex-co.com/PCSearch/TaxInfoPropertySearch.asp.

Marion County   *Property, Taxation Records*   A free search to the assessor data is rpovided at www.marionsc.org/taxes.html#/. This site is meant to be used to pay taxes, but is can also be used as a search site.

Marlboro County   *Property, Taxation Records*   Access to property tax information for free at www.marlborocountytax.com/taxes.aspx#/.

McCormick County   *Property, Taxation Records*   Access to GIS/mapping free at http://thinkopengis.mccormick.sc.wthtechnology.com/.

Newberry County   *Property, Taxation Records*   Access to assessor database is free at www.qpublic.net/sc/newberry/search.html.

Oconee County   *Recorded Documents*   www.oconeesc.com/Departments/KZ/RegisterofDeeds.aspx   Access recorder's index search free at http://deeds.oconeesc.com/External/LandRecords/protected/SrchQuickName.aspx.
Property, Taxation Records   Free access to property records at www.qpublic.net/sc/oconee/search2.html.

Orangeburg County   *Recorded Documents*   www.orangeburgscrod.org/Opening.asp   Access free deeds, mortgages and plat records back to 1989 at www.orangeburgscrod.org/Opening.asp.
Property, Taxation Records   Access to county property tax records is free at http://sc-orangeburg-assessor.governmax.com/propertymax/rover30.asp?sid=07544F662DD64AB49267AE2C4D48969E.

Pickens County   *Recorded Documents*   www.co.pickens.sc.us/deeds/default.aspx   Access the recorders database back to 12/1/1986 free at http://67.32.48.38/oncoreweb/.
Property, Taxation Records   A variety of search choices are offered at www.pickensassessor.org including owners name. parcel number, sales list and mailing addresses.

Richland County   *Recorded Documents*   www.richlandonline.com/Government/Departments/BusinessOperations/RegisterofDeeds.aspx   Subscription Management System available for a fee at https://www4.rcgov.us/SMS_External/Login.aspx?AspxAutoDetectCookieSupport=1.

Property, Taxation Records   Access to county property data is free at www.richlandmaps.com/.

Saluda County *Property, Taxation Records*   Access to tax parcel records for free at http://saludacounty.sc.gov/Government/TaxSystem/Assessor/Pages/AssessorData.aspx.

Spartanburg County *Recorded Documents* www.spartanburgcounty.org/160/Register-of-Deeds   Access recording data free at http://search.spartanburgdeeds.com/. Currently, the system has a limited number of images available; however, new images are being added daily.
Property, Taxation Records   Access property tax data free at http://qpublic.net/sc/spartanburg/search.html. GIS Mapping is offered at http://192.146.148.33/Freeance/Client/PublicAccess1/index.html?appconfig=DetailedWeb. Also, access to public document search www.spartanburgcounty.org/288/Assessor-Property-Records-Search (at bottom of legal disclaimer page).

Sumter County *Recorded Documents* www.sumtercountysc.org/?q=department/register-deeds-0   Search county data free at https://countyfusion2.propertyinfo.com/countyweb/login.do?countyname=SumterSC.
Property, Taxation Records   Search assessment data and property cards free at www.sumtercountysc.org:8080/EGSV2SMTR/PCSearch.do. Also, access to GIS/mapping free at http://svr4.sumtercountysc.org/publicsearch/.

Union County *Recorded Documents* www.countyofunion.org/site/cpage.asp?cpage_id=180008515&sec_id=180003405   Access to the records search for free at http://cotthosting.com/scunionexternal/LandRecords/protected/v4/SrchName.aspx.
Property, Taxation Records   Access to assessor records is free at http://qpublic.net/sc/union/.

Williamsburg County *Recorded Documents* www.williamsburgcounty.sc.gov/index.aspx?page=56   Access to land records for free at https://www.sclandrecords.com/sclr/. Indexes (only) from 1/3/1994 to present.
Property, Taxation Records   Access to GIS/mapping free at http://williamsburg.sc.wthgis.com/.

York County *Recorded Documents* www.yorkcountygov.com/departments/clerkCourt/default.aspx   Access to land records for free at https://www.sclandrecords.com/sclr/. Certification start dates--deeds and mortgages-7/1/1982, misc liens-1/1/1986, plats-7/1/1984, tax liens-1/1/1986 and UCCs-1/1/2001-9/24/2007.

Property, Taxation Records   Access to the county GIS/mapping for free at www.yorkcountygov.com/Business/GIS/OnlineMappingApplications. Also, the assessors sales report free at www.yorkcountygov.com/departments/assessor/AssessorsSalesReport. Also, search tax records free at http://onlinetaxes.yorkcountygov.com/taxes#/. Also, access to the Assessor's database for free at http://qpublic.net/sc/york/.

South Dakota

Capital: Pierre
             Hughes County

Time Zone: CST

South Dakota's eighteen western-most counties are MST:

They are: Bennett, Butte, Corson, Custer, Dewey, Fall River, Haakon,

Harding, Jackson, Lawrence, Meade, Mellette, Pennington, Perkins, Shannon, Stanley, Todd, and Ziebach

Population: 858,469

# of Counties: 66

Useful State Links

Website: **http://sd.gov/**

Governor: **http://sd.gov/governor**

Attorney General: **http://atg.sd.gov**

State Archives: **http://history.sd.gov**

State Statutes and Codes: **http://sdlegislature.gov/**

Legislative Bill Search: **http://legis.state.sd.us/statutes/index.aspx**

Unclaimed Funds: **https://southdakota.findyourunclaimedproperty.com/**

State Public Record Agencies

Sexual Offender Registry

Division of Criminal Investigation, Identification Section - SOR Unit,   http://sor.sd.gov/   Searching is available from the website. One may search by name, map, or neighborhood. There is a search option to include incarcerated offenders.

Incarceration Records

SD Department of Corrections, Central Records Office,   http://doc.sd.gov/   An Offendor Locator search is free at http://doc.sd.gov/adult/lookup/. Information on offenders sentenced to county jail, probation, or any other form of supervision is not included. A department most wanted list is available at http://doc.sd.gov/adult/wanted/.

Corporation, LP, LLC, Trademarks/Servicemarks

Corporation Division, Secretary of State,   http://sdsos.gov/business-services/default.aspx   Check an entity name for corporate status, file number, incorporation/formation date, registered agent name, address, phone number and residency from https://icis.corp.delaware.gov/Ecorp/EntitySearch/NameSearch.aspx. Search the Secretary of State Corporations Div. Database free at https://sos.sd.gov/business/search.aspx. One may also search commercial registered agents from this site. Trademark searches may be requested via e-mail at trademark@state.sd.us. The Secretary of State offers a Fictitious Name Registration search at https://apps.sd.gov/st08bnrs/secure/ASPX/BNRS_Search.aspx. *Other Options:* FTP downloads are available for purchase.

Uniform Commercial Code, Federal Tax Liens

UCC Division, Secretary of State,   http://sdsos.gov/business-services/uniform-commercial-code/ucc-efs-information/default.aspx   Dakota Fast File is the filing and searching service available from the home page. This commercial service requires registration and a $200.00 fee per year. Certified search and printing is offered. Also, other requesters may ask that a document be returned by email, there is an additional $5.00 fee. Search the Fictitious Name Registration at https://apps.sd.gov/st08bnrs/secure/ASPX/BNRS_Search.aspx. *Other Options:* FTP downloads are available for purchase.

Birth Certificates

South Dakota Department of Health, Vital Records,   https://doh.sd.gov/records/   Records may be ordered online at the website via a state supported vendor. You can order recent (less than 100 years) birth records at the website, for a fee. You can search free at http://apps.sd.gov/PH14Over100BirthRec/index.aspx for birth records over 100 years old.

Death, Marraige, Divorce Records

South Dakota Department of Health, Vital Records, https://doh.sd.gov/records/ Records may be ordered online at the website via a state supported vendor.

Driver Records

Dept of Public Safety, Driver Licensing Program, http://dps.sd.gov/licensing/driver_licensing/default.aspx The system is open for batch requests 24 hours a day. There is a minimum of 250 requests daily. It generally takes 10 minutes to process a batch. The current fee is $5.00 per records and there are some start-up costs. For more information, call 605-773-6883.

Crash Reports

Department of Public Safety, Office of Accident Records, http://dps.sd.gov/enforcement/accident_records/default.aspx Records may be purchased online for $10.00 per record. Use of a credit card is required. See http://safesd.gov/. Records prior to 2004 are not available for purchase.

Voter Registration, Campaign Finance, PACs

Secretary of State, Elections Division, http://sdsos.gov/elections-voting/default.aspx An advanced search for campaign finance matters is found at http://sdsos.gov/elections-voting/campaign-finance/default.aspx. This includes donations by PACs. *Other Options:* The webpage has a list of various files available for purchase on CD or paper. For example, statewide CD is $2,500, statewide printed list is $5,500. Data may be purchased by county or legislative district.

GED Certificates

SD Department of Labor, GED Program, http://dlr.sd.gov/workforce_training/ged.aspx Third parties are routed to set up an account at: http://exchange.parchment.com/ged-receiver-registration-page. Parchment verifies that they are who they say they are so that they can place orders on behalf of students Parchment contacts the third party and provides training on the site for ordering. During this training any orders they have are placed. After this the third party can order on behalf of students. They still must upload a consent form for each student during the process. GED test takers can order duplicate copies of official GED transcripts and duplicate diplomas online at: www.gedtestingservice.com/testers/gedrequest-a-transcript

Occupational Licensing Boards

Abstractor/Abstractor Company	http://dlr.sd.gov/bdcomm/abstracters/roster.aspx
Accountant-CPA/Firm	https://apps.sd.gov/ld01dol/template/main.aspx?templateid=22
Architect/Landscape	https://apps.sd.gov/LD17BTP/firmlist.aspx
Athletic Trainer	https://login.sdbmoe.gov/Public/Services/VerificationSearch
Attorney	http://www.statebarofsouthdakota.com/p/cm/ld/fid=54
Auctioneer	https://sdrec.sd.gov/registration/licenseelist.aspx
Audiologist	http://doh.sd.gov/boards/audiology/roster.aspx
Bail Bond Agent	http://dlr.sd.gov/insurance/license_inquiry_service_intro.aspx
Bank	http://dlr.sd.gov/banking/banks.aspx
Barber	http://dlr.sd.gov/bdcomm/barber/barberpdfs/rosterofbarbers.pdf
Barber Shop	http://dlr.sd.gov/bdcomm/barber/barberpdfs/rosterofbarbershops.pdf
Beauty Shop/Nail/Beauth Salon	https://apps.sd.gov/ld19cosmetology/licenseverification.aspx
Chiropractic Disciplinary Action Reports	http://doh.sd.gov/Boards/chiropractic/Discipline.aspx
Chiropractor	http://doh.sd.gov/boards/chiropractic/assets/roster.pdf
Clinical Nurse Specialist	https://www.sduap.org/verify/
Cosmetologist/Instructor/Salon	https://apps.sd.gov/ld19cosmetology/licenseverification.aspx
Cosmetology Schools	https://apps.sd.gov/ld19cosmetology/licenseverification.aspx
Counselor	http://dss.sd.gov/docs/licensing/soc-licensed-list.pdf
Crematory	http://doh.sd.gov/boards/funeral/roster.aspx
Dental Hygienist/Assistant	https://www.sdboardofdentistry.com/verify.asp
Dentist	https://www.sdboardofdentistry.com/verify.asp
Dietitian/Nutritionist	https://login.sdbmoe.gov/Public/Services/VerificationSearch
Driller, Oil and Gas Supervisor	http://denr.sd.gov/des/og/OilGasOperators.aspx
Drug Wholesaler	http://doh.sd.gov/boards/pharmacy/verification.aspx
Electrical Inspector	http://dlr.sd.gov/bdcomm/electric/ecinspections.aspx
Embalmer	http://doh.sd.gov/boards/funeral/roster.aspx
Emergency Medical Technician/Paramedic	https://login.sdbmoe.gov/Public/Services/VerificationSearch
Engineer/ Petroleum Environmental	https://apps.sd.gov/LD17BTP/firmlist.aspx
Esthetician/Manicurist/Nail Technician	https://apps.sd.gov/ld19cosmetology/licenseverification.aspx

Funeral Director/Establishment .... http://doh.sd.gov/boards/funeral/roster.aspx
Gaming Manufacturer .... http://dor.sd.gov/Gaming/Licensed_Manufacturers_Distributors/
Health Insurer .... http://dlr.sd.gov/insurance/license_inquiry_service_intro.aspx
Hearing Aid Dispenser .... http://doh.sd.gov/boards/audiology/roster.aspx
Home Inspector .... https://sdrec.sd.gov/registration/licenseelist.aspx
Insurance Agent .... http://dlr.sd.gov/insurance/license_inquiry_service_intro.aspx
Insurance Company .... http://dlr.sd.gov/insurance/license_inquiry_service_intro.aspx
Insurer of Health/Re-Insurer, Accredited/Qualified ...... http://dlr.sd.gov/insurance/license_inquiry_service_intro.aspx
Investment Advisor/Firm .... http://www.adviserinfo.sec.gov/
Landfill .... http://denr.sd.gov/des/wm/asb/asbhomepage.aspx
Lobbyist https://apps.sd.gov/ST12ODRS/LobbyistViewlist.asp
Marriage & Family Therapist .... http://dss.sd.gov/docs/licensing/soc-licensed-list.pdf
Marriage/Family Therapist Disciplinary Action ... http://dss.sd.gov/docs/licensing/soc-licensed-list.pdf
Midwife .... https://www.sduap.org/verify/
Money Lender .... http://dlr.sd.gov/banking/money_lenders/documents/money_lender_licensee_list.pdf
Money Order Business/Money Transmitters ...... http://dlr.sd.gov/banking/money_transmitters/documents/money_transmitter_licensee_list.pdf
Mortgage Broker/Lender .... http://www.nmlsconsumeraccess.org/
Notary https://apps.sd.gov/ST12ODRS/aspx/frmNotaryViewlist.aspx
Nurse-RN/LPN/Aide Certified/Anesthetist .... https://www.sduap.org/verify/
Nurses Aide/Applicant .... https://www.sduap.org/verify/
Nursing Facility Admin Disciplinary Actions .... http://doh.sd.gov/boards/nursingfacility/discipline.aspx
Nursing Facility Administrator .... http://doh.sd.gov/boards/nursingfacility/
Occupational Therapist/Assistant .... https://login.sdbmoe.gov/Public/Services/VerificationSearch
Oil & Gas Driller Senior Geologist .... http://denr.sd.gov/des/og/OilGasOperators.aspx
Optometrist .... http://doh.sd.gov/boards/optometry/verification.aspx
Optometrist Disciplinary Actions .... http://doh.sd.gov/boards/optometry/discipline.aspx
Osteopathic Physician .... https://login.sdbmoe.gov/Public/Services/VerificationSearch
Pet Health Insurer .... http://dlr.sd.gov/insurance/license_inquiry_service_intro.aspx
Petrol Release Assessor/Remediator https://apps.sd.gov/LD17BTP/firmlist.aspx
Pharmacist/Pharmacy .... http://doh.sd.gov/boards/pharmacy/verification.aspx
Physical Therapist/Assistant .... https://login.sdbmoe.gov/Public/Services/VerificationSearch
Physician/Medical Doctor/Assistant .... https://login.sdbmoe.gov/Public/Services/VerificationSearch
Podiatrist .... http://doh.sd.gov/boards/podiatry/assets/roster.pdf
Property Manager .... https://sdrec.sd.gov/registration/licenseelist.aspx
Radiology (Dental) .... https://www.sdboardofdentistry.com/verify.asp
Real Estate Agent/Seller/Broker/Firm .... https://sdrec.sd.gov/registration/licenseelist.aspx
Residential Rental Agent .... https://sdrec.sd.gov/registration/licenseelist.aspx
Respiratory Care Practitioner .... https://login.sdbmoe.gov/Public/Services/VerificationSearch
Septic Tank Installer .... http://denr.sd.gov/des/sw/SepticInstallers.aspx
Social Worker .... http://dss.sd.gov/docs/licensing/soc-licensed-list.pdf
Storage Tank, Above/Below Ground .... http://denr.sd.gov/des/gw/tanks/ust_ast_definition.aspx
Surveyor, Land https://apps.sd.gov/LD17BTP/firmlist.aspx
Timeshare Real Estate, Registered Project .... https://sdrec.sd.gov/registration/licenseelist.aspx
Tobacco Manufacturer Brands .... http://dor.sd.gov/Taxes/Special_Taxes/Tobacco/PDFs/Brands.pdf
Trust Company .... http://dlr.sd.gov/banking/trusts/documents/state_chartered_trust_companies.pdf
Veterinarian/Veterinary Technician .... http://sdda.sd.gov/boards-and-commissions/sd-board-of-veterinary-medical-
examiners/veterinary/licvet.aspx
Waste Water System Operator .... http://denr.sd.gov/des/dw/documents/operator.pdf
Waste Water Treatm't Plant Operator .... http://denr.sd.gov/des/wm/hw/hwcontractors.aspx
Water Distributor/Treatment Operator .... http://denr.sd.gov/des/wm/hw/hwcontractors.aspx
Weapon, Concealed .... https://sdsos.gov/services-for-individuals/concealed-pistol-permits/default.aspx
Well Driller .... http://denr.sd.gov/des/wr/dbdrillerlist.aspx

911 Telecommunicator	http://dci.sd.gov/LawEnforcementTraining/911BasicTelecommunicatorCertification.aspx
Abstractor/Abstractor Company	http://dlr.sd.gov/bdcomm/abstracters/roster.aspx
Accountant-CPA/Firm	http://apps.sd.gov/applications/ld01DOL/Template/main.aspx?templateid=15
Alcoholic Beverage Distributor	www.state.sd.us/drr2/propspectax/alcohol/licenses/licenses.htm
Ambulance Service	http://dps.sd.gov/emergency_services/emergency_medical_services/ambulance_service_directories.aspx
Animal Feed Seller/Producer	http://sdda.sd.gov/farming-ranching-agribusiness/feed-animal-remedy-program/default.aspx
Animal Remedy (medicine/drug)	http://sdda.sd.gov/farming-ranching-agribusiness/feed-animal-remedy-program/default.aspx
Architect/Landscape	https://apps.sd.gov/applications/ld17btp/takehomeexam/(S(dxrzmoyvdgpncaxn3t5znqog))/FirmRoster.aspx
Asbestos Service Company/Worker	http://denr.sd.gov/des/wm/asb/Documents/AsbestosServices.pdf
Athletic Trainer	https://login.sdbmoe.gov/Public/Services/VerificationSearch
Auctioneer	https://sdrec.sd.gov/registration/licenseelist.aspx
Audiologist	http://doh.sd.gov/boards/audiology/roster.aspx
Bail Bond Agent	http://dlr.sd.gov/insurance/license_inquiry_service_intro.aspx
Bank	http://dlr.sd.gov/banking/banks.aspx
Barber	http://dlr.sd.gov/bdcomm/barber/barberpdfs/rosterofbarbers.pdf
Barber Shop	http://dlr.sd.gov/bdcomm/barber/barberpdfs/rosterofbarbershops.pdf
Beauty Shop/Nail/Beauth Salon	http://dlr.sd.gov/bdcomm/cosmet/ccverification/
Canine Team	http://dci.sd.gov/LawEnforcementTraining/CanineTeamCertification.aspx
Chiropractor	www.sdchiropractors.com/search.php
Chiropractor Disciplinary Action Reports	http://doh.sd.gov/Boards/chiropractic/Discipline.aspx
Clinical Nurse Specialist	https://ifmc.sd.gov/lookup.php
Cosmetologist/Instructor/Salon	http://dlr.sd.gov/bdcomm/cosmet/ccverification/
Cosmetology Schools	http://dlr.sd.gov/bdcomm/cosmet/ccschools.aspx
Counselor	http://dss.sd.gov/behavioralhealthservices/docs/CounselorsMarriageFamily/BCEWEBLIST05.10.2013.pdf
Court/Shorthand Reporter	www.southdakotacourtreporters.org/2.html
Crematory	http://doh.sd.gov/Boards/FuneralBoard/Roster.aspx
Dentist, Dental Hygienist/Assistant	https://www.sdboardofdentistry.com/verify.asp
Dietitian/Nutritionist	https://login.sdbmoe.gov/Public/Services/VerificationSearch
Driller, Oil and Gas Supervisor	http://denr.sd.gov/des/og/welldata.aspx
Electrical Inspector	http://dlr.sd.gov/bdcomm/electric/ecinspections.aspx
Embalmer	http://doh.sd.gov/Boards/FuneralBoard/Roster.aspx
Emergency Medical Technician/Paramedic	https://login.sdbmoe.gov/Public/Services/VerificationSearch
Engineer/ Petroleum Environmen'l	https://apps.sd.gov/applications/ld17btp/takehomeexam/(S(dxrzmoyvdgpncaxn3t5znqog))/FirmRoster.aspx
Esthetician/Manicurist/Nail Technician	http://dlr.sd.gov/bdcomm/cosmet/ccverification/
Fertilizer	http://sdda.sd.gov/farming-ranching-agribusiness/fertilizer-program/default.aspx
Funeral Director/Establishment	http://doh.sd.gov/Boards/FuneralBoard/Roster.aspx
Gaming Manufacturer	http://gaming.sd.gov/LicensedMfgDistributors.aspx
Health Insurer	http://dlr.sd.gov/insurance/license_inquiry_service_intro.aspx
Hearing Aid Dispenser	http://doh.sd.gov/boards/audiology/roster.aspx
Home Inspector	https://sdrec.sd.gov/registration/licenseelist.aspx
Insurance Agent, Company	http://dlr.sd.gov/insurance/license_inquiry_service_intro.aspx
Insurer of Health/Re-Insurer, Accredited/Qualified	http://dlr.sd.gov/insurance/license_inquiry_service_intro.aspx
Investment Advisor/Firm	www.adviserinfo.sec.gov/(S(lto1ii0alerchaz455qv2mwt))/IAPD/Content/Search/iapd_Search.aspx
Landfill	http://denr.sd.gov/des/wm/asb/asbhomepage.aspx
Law Enforcement Officer	http://dci.sd.gov/LawEnforcementTraining/BasicOfficerCertification.aspx
Lobbyist	http://apps.sd.gov/applications/ST12ODRS/
Marriage & Family Therapist	http://dss.sd.gov/behavioralhealthservices/docs/CounselorsMarriageFamily/BCEWEBLIST05.10.2013.pdf
Midwife	https://ifmc.sd.gov/lookup.php
Money Lender	http://dlr.sd.gov/banking/money_lenders/documents/money_lender_licensee_list.pdf
Money Order BusinessMoney Transmitters	http://dlr.sd.gov/banking/money_transmitters/documents/money_transmitter_licensee_list.pdf
Mortgage Broker/Lender	www.nmlsconsumeraccess.org/
Notary	http://apps.sd.gov/applications/ST12ODRS/aspx/frmNotaryViewlist.aspx?cmd=resetall
Nurse-RN/LPN/Aide Certified/Anesthetist	https://ifmc.sd.gov/lookup.php
Nursing Facility Administrator	http://doh.sd.gov/Boards/NursingFacility/PDF/LicenseeList.pdf
Occupational Therapist/Assistant	https://login.sdbmoe.gov/Public/Services/VerificationSearch

Oil & Gas Driller Senior Geologist...............	http://denr.sd.gov/des/og/welldata.aspx
Optometrist...	http://doh.sd.gov/Boards/Optometry/PDF/LicenseVerification.pdf
Osteopathic Physician	https://login.sdbmoe.gov/Public/Services/VerificationSearch
Pesticide Applicator/Dealer........................	http://sdda.sd.gov/farming-ranching-agribusiness/pesticide-program/default.aspx
Pet Health Insurer	http://dlr.sd.gov/insurance/license_inquiry_service_intro.aspx
Petrol. Release Assessor/Remediator........	https://apps.sd.gov/applications/ld17btp/takehomeexam/(S(dxrzmoyvdgpncaxn3t5znqog))/FirmRoster.aspx
Physical Therapist/Assistant.......................	https://login.sdbmoe.gov/Public/Services/VerificationSearch
Physician/Medical Doctor/Assistant............	https://login.sdbmoe.gov/Public/Services/VerificationSearch
Podiatrist..	http://doh.sd.gov/boards/podiatry/PDF/roster.pdf
Polygraph Examiner....................................	http://dci.sd.gov/LawEnforcementTraining/PolygraphLicensingPage.aspx
Property Manager	https://sdrec.sd.gov/registration/licenseelist.aspx
Psychologist..	http://dss.sd.gov/behavioralhealthservices/docs/Psychologists/SDLicensedPsychologists4-2-13.pdf
Radiology (Dental)	https://www.sdboardofdentistry.com/verify.asp
Real Estate Agent/Seller/Broker/Firm.........	https://sdrec.sd.gov/registration/licenseelist.aspx
Respiratory Care Practitioner.....................	https://login.sdbmoe.gov/Public/Services/VerificationSearch
Securities Agent/Broker/Dealer..................	www.finra.org/Investors/ToolsCalculators/BrokerCheck/index.htm
Septic Tank Installer...................................	http://denr.sd.gov/des/sw/SepticInstallers.aspx
Social Worker..	http://dss.sd.gov/behavioralhealthservices/docs/SocialWorkers/SDLicensedSocialWorkers4-2-13.pdf
Storage Tank, Above/Below Ground	http://denr.sd.gov/des/gw/tanks/ust_ast_definition.aspx
Surveyor, Land..	https://apps.sd.gov/applications/ld17btp/takehomeexam/(S(dxrzmoyvdgpncaxn3t5znqog))/FirmRoster.aspx
Timeshare Real Estate, Registered Project.	https://sdrec.sd.gov/registration/licenseelist.aspx
Tobacco Wholesaler	www.state.sd.us/drr2/propspectax/tobacco/manufacturer.htm
Trust Company..	http://dlr.sd.gov/banking/trusts/documents/state_chartered_trust_companies.pdf
Waste Water System Operator	http://denr.sd.gov/des/dw/PDF/operator.pdf
Waste Water Treatm't Plant Operator..........	http://denr.sd.gov/des/wm/hw/hwcontractors.aspx
Water Distributor/Treatment Operator	http://denr.sd.gov/des/wm/hw/hwcontractors.aspx
Weapon, Concealed..............................	http://sdsos.gov/content/viewcontent.aspx?cat=adminservices&pg=/adminservices/concealedpistolpermits.shtm
Well Driller..	http://denr.sd.gov/des/wr/dbdrillerlist.aspx

State and Local Courts

About South Dakota Courts: The **Circuit Courts** are the general trial courts of the Unified Judicial System (UJS). These courts have original jurisdiction in all civil and criminal cases. **Magistrate Courts** operate under the authority and supervision of the Circuit Courts, and assist in processing preliminary hearings for felony cases, hear minor criminal cases, municipal ordinance violations, and hear uncontested civil and small claims cases under $12,000. Circuit Courts also have jurisdiction over appeals from **Magistrate Court** decisions.   There are 66 counties, but 63 courts. Circuit cases for Buffalo County are handled at the Brule County Circuit Court. Circuit cases for Shannon County are handled by the Fall River County Circuit Court. Circuit cases for Todd County are handled by the Tripp County Circuit Court. The state re-aligned their circuits from 8 to 7 effective June, 2000.

The web page for the Judicial System is http://ujs.sd.govwww.courts.maine.gov.

Appellate Courts: The Supreme Court has the responsibility of administering the statewide unified court system which includes the Circuit and Magistrate Courts. There is not a Court of Appeals in South Dakota. The Supreme Court calendar, opinions, rules and archived oral arguments may be searched from the judicial website.

Online Court Access

All Courts Participate in the Statewide System Described Below.

The Judiciary provides separate online portals for civil and criminal record searching.

Criminal Docket Online Access

Public information viewed on the Public Access Record System at https://ujspars.sd.gov reflects the docket entries for criminal cases as well as domestic protection orders, stalking protection orders and foreign protection orders. Note this is not an interactive system: results are emailed in PDF format within a few minutes. The search requires a name and DOB. The fee is $20.00 per search. If using a credit card, use the Search as Guest option. Ongoing searchers can set up a drawdown account. To establish an account, email UJS.HelpDesk.@UJS.state.sd.us or call the HelpDesk at 605-773-8000.

Civil Docket Online Access

A web search is offered by the UJS for all active money judgments and for all completed or inactive civil money judgments from 04/19/2004 forward. This service includes a search of both the Circuit and Magistrate Courts. Case document images are not provided. This online system does not provide probate or criminal information. Charges for searches are $4.00 per name or date range search. There is an additional $1.00 charge to access the judgment docket. The system works off a pre-paid deposit using a credit card, so the system deducts from your balance. Users may also obtain unlimited access to system, including bulk downloading of civil money judgment information, by subscribing on a monthly or yearly basis. To establish an account, email UJS.HelpDesk@UJS.state.sd.us, or call the HelpDesk at 605-773-8000. Case document images are not provided. See https://ujsjudgmentquery.sd.gov/login.aspx.

Historical bulk data on civil money judgments filed in South Dakota dating back twenty years on active judgments and back to April 19, 2004 on inactive judgments may be obtained by contacting the State Court Administrator's Office, 500 E. Capitol Avenue, Pierre, SD 57501 with a prepaid request. Pursuant to SDCL 16-2-29.6, the cost for accessing this historical database is $3,000. This data is provided on a DVD in XML format. **Reselling is Prohibited.** Use of SD court records, including the UJS's Electronic Civil Money Judgment System mentioned above, is governed by SDCL 1-27-1, South Dakota's open records law, and SDCL ch. 15-15A, South Dakota's Court Records law. **Pursuant to these statutes, reselling or redistributing lists of information from this database or from the paper court records is prohibited by law as a Class 2 misdemeanor. Thus be careful purchasing this information online direct from a private vendor.**

No individual South Dakota court offers online access, other than as described above.

Recorders, Assessors, and Other Sites of Note

Recording Office Organization: 66 counties, 66 recording offices. The recording officer is the Register of Deeds.

About Tax Liens: Federal tax liens on personal property of businesses are filed with the Secretary of State. Other federal and state tax liens are filed with the county Register of Deeds..

Online Access

Recorded Documents

Only Meade County offers access to recorded documents.

Tax Assessor Records

At least 22 counties offer access to assessor data or GIS/mapping. Many counties use https://beacon.schneidercorp.com, a vendor subscription service.

County Sites:

Brookings County   *Property, Taxation Records*   Access to GIS/mapping free at https://beacon.schneidercorp.com/.

Brown County   *Property, Taxation Records*   Search assessor property data for a fee on the GIS system at http://beacon.schneidercorp.com/?site=BrownCountySD. Registration and username required.

Brule County   *Property, Taxation Records*   Access to GIS/mapping free at http://ims.districtiii.org/brule/.

Charles Mix County   *Property, Taxation Records*   Access to GIS/mapping free at https://beacon.schneidercorp.com/.

Clay County   *Property, Taxation Records*   Search assessor property data for a fee on the GIS system at https://beacon.schneidercorp.com/.

Corson County   *Property, Taxation Records*   Access to real estate and sale records for free at http://corson.southdakotadirectors.com/.

Custer County   *Property, Taxation Records*   Search assessor property data for a fee on the GIS system at https://beacon.schneidercorp.com/. Registration and username required.

Davison County   *Property, Taxation Records*   Access to porperty searches for free at www.davison.gisworkshop.com/.

Fall River County   *Property, Taxation Records*   Access to GIS/mapping free at http://fallriver.sdcounties.org/gis-maps/online-map/.

Harding County   *Property, Taxation Records*   Access to records for free at https://beacon.schneidercorp.com/. For detailed records can purchase subscription.

Jackson County   *Property, Taxation Records*   Access to GIS/mapping free at https://beacon.schneidercorp.com/.

Lake County   *Property, Taxation Records*   Search assessor property data for a fee on the GIS system at https://beacon.schneidercorp.com/.

Lawrence County   *Property, Taxation Records*   Access to GIS/mapping free at http://lawrencecounty.connectgis.com/Disclaimer.aspx.

Lincoln County   *Property, Taxation Records*   Access to the AG, commercial and residential sales are at http://lincolncountysd.org/Page.cfm/Departments/1166/Sales.

McCook County   *Property, Taxation Records*   Access assessor property data for a fee on the GIS system athttps://beacon.schneidercorp.com/.

Meade County   *Recorded Documents*   www.meadecounty.org/register-of-deeds/   Access to recorded documents for a fee at https://www.idocmarket.com/sites. Must subscribe before use. Fees vary depending on plan picked. Images back to 10/1985.

Minnehaha County   *Property, Taxation Records*   Access to the county property tax database is free at www2.minnehahacounty.org/property_tax/index.aspx. No name searching at this time. Access to Commercial, Residential, Ag and Acreage Sales lists at www.minnehahacounty.org/dept/eq/eq.php.

Moody County   *Property, Taxation Records*   Search assessor property data for a fee on the GIS system at https://beacon.schneidercorp.com/.

Pennington County   *Property, Taxation Records*   Access to the county property tax database is free at http://209.159.193.156/appraisal/publicaccess/. Also, access to mapping for free at www.rcgov.org/departments/community-resources/geographic-information-system/rapidmap-214.html.

Perkins County   *Property, Taxation Records*   Basic access to GIS/mapping for free at https://beacon.schneidercorp.com/. For more detailed information, must subscribe-fees are $15.00 daily, $50.00 monthly and $575.00 for yearly.

Spink County   *Property, Taxation Records*   Search assessor property data for a fee on the GIS system at https://beacon.schneidercorp.com/.

Union County   *Property, Taxation Records*   Search assessor property data for a fee on the GIS system at https://beacon.schneidercorp.com/.

Yankton County   *Property, Taxation Records*   GIS information is available from a designated vendor at https://beacon.schneidercorp.com/.

Tennessee

Capital: Nashville
             Davidson County

Time Zone: CST

Tennessee's twenty-nine eastern-most counties are EST.

They are: Anderson, Blount, Bradley, Campbell, Carter, Claiborne, Cocke, Grainger, Greene, Hamilton, Hancock, Hawkins, Jefferson, Johnson, Knox, Loudon, McMinn, Meigs, Monroe, Morgan, Polk, Rhea, Roane, Scott, Sevier, Sullivan, Unicoi, Union, Washington.

Population: 6,600,299
# of Counties: 95

Useful State Links

Website: **www.tennessee.gov**
Governor: **www.tn.gov/governor**
Attorney General: **www.tn.gov/attorneygeneral**
State Archives: **http://sos.tn.gov/tsla**
State Statutes and Codes: **www.lexisnexis.com/hottopics/tncode**
Legislative Bill Search: **www.legislature.state.tn.us**
Unclaimed Funds: **www.treasury.state.tn.us/unclaim**

State Public Record Agencies

Criminal Records

Tennessee Bureau of Investigation, TN Open Records Information Svcs,   www.tn.gov/tbi/article/background-checks   Records may be requested at https://www.tbibackgrounds.com/toris/. The site does not have much information about the service other than the fee ($29.00). This is not an interactive service. Records are manually searched by the TBI and are returned in 2-3 days by email. The SSN is included.

Sexual Offender Registry

Tennessee Bureau of Investigation, Sexual Offender Registry,   www.tn.gov/tbi/topic/sex-offender-registry-search   Search sexual offenders at http://sor.tbi.tn.gov/SOMainpg.aspx by last name, city, county or ZIP Code. One may also search for missing children, and people placed on parole who reside in Tennessee. A search by map is offered at www.tn.gov/tbi/topic/map-offenders.

Incarceration Records

Dept of Correction-ATTN: PIO/FOIL, Rachel Jackson Building, Ground Fl,   www.tn.gov/correction/topic/tdoc-department-overview   The information is available online pertains to Tennessee felony offenders who are or who have been in the custody of the Tennessee Department of Correction or under the Supervision of the Tennessee Board of Probation and Parole. See https://apps.tn.gov/foil/. There is alos a Tennessee Felony Offender Search Mobile App on this page.   *Other Options:* A CD-Rom is available with public information from the current offender database. There is a nominal fee, contact the Planning & Research Division.

Corporation, LLC, LP, LLP, Fictitious Name, Assumed Name

TN Sec of State: Corporation Filing Unit, William R Snodgrass Tower,   http://sos.tn.gov/business-services   There is a free online search for business information at https://tnbear.tn.gov/ECommerce/FilingSearch.aspx for business records. This gives online access to over 4,000,000 records relating to corporations, limited liability companies, limited partnerships and limited liability partnerships formed or registered in Tennessee. A separate name availability search is at https://tnbear.tn.gov/Ecommerce/NameAvailability.aspx.   Also, search securities department enforcement actions at http://tn.gov/commerce/article/securities-enforcement-actions.   *Other Options:* Some data can be purchased in bulk or list format. Call 615-253-4015 for more details.

Trademarks/Servicemarks, Trade Names

Sec. of State - Trademarks Unit, Willima R Snodgrass Tower - 6th Fl,   www.tn.gov/sos/bus_svc/trademarks.htm   The Internet provides a record search of TN Trademarks, newest records are 3 days old. Search free at www.tn.gov/sos/bus_svc/TrademarkSearch.htm.   *Other Options:* The agency will provide a file update every three months for $1.00 per page. Requests must be in writing.

Uniform Commercial Code

Dept of State - UCC Division, William R Snodgrass Tower,   http://sos.tn.gov/business-services/ucc   Free access to general, limited information at https://tnbear.tn.gov/UCC/Ecommerce/UCCSearch.aspx. Search by debtor name or file number. Images are not available. A disclaimer mentions that this data may not be reflective of an official search per TN statutes. The UCC database is updated between 7:30AM and 11AM (CST). During the update process, secured party information may not be available and/or related UCC document information may not be accurately reflected for a UCC1 filing.

Birth, Marriage, Divorce Records

Tennessee Department of Health, Office of Vital Records,   www.tn.gov/health/section/vital-records   Records may be ordered from the designated vendor - www.vitalchek.com. Extra fees involved.

Death Records

Tennessee Department of Health, Office of Vital Records,   www.tn.gov/health/section/vital-records   Records may be ordered from the designated vendor - www.vitalchek.com. Extra fees involved. The Cleveland (Tennessee) Public Library staff and volunteers have published the 1914-1933 statewide death records at http://sos.tn.gov/products/tsla/statewide-index-tennessee-death-records-1914-1933. Note that the records of children under two years of age have been omitted from this project.

Driver Records

Dept. of Safety, Financial Responsibility Section, Attn: Driving Records,   www.tn.gov/safety/section/dlmain   Commercial online record service via the e-government services website at https://apps.tn.gov/imvr/ is available for a driving record and for a license status check. The program is called Interactive Moving Violation Record application (IMVR). Users must be authorized per DPPA and complete a Network Registration Agreement and be authorized per DPPA. The fee is $7.00 per three-year driving record or $1.25 for a DL Status Report which gives name, DOB, address and DL expire date. Companies retrieving more than 500 records per month can use a "batch" process in which multiple license numbers can be searched and the results are returned in one file. Call 1-866-886-3468 for more information. An annual $75.00 registration fee is charged. For more information, call 1-866-886-3468. *Other Options:* Bulk retrieval is available for high volume users. Purchase of the DL file is available for approved requesters. Call Information Systems at 615-251-5322.

Vehicle Ownership & Registration

Vehicle Services Division, Records,   www.tn.gov/revenue/section/title-and-registration   Tennessee offers commercial online inquires on the Interactive Vehicle, Title, and Registration (IVTR) system. Search by plate license number or VIN. Users must complete a Network Registration Agreement and be authorized per DPPA and state law. The cost for Vehicle, Title, and Registration Inquires (IVTR) is $2.00 per search, regardless of your search results. The $2.00 search fee allows you to view one "Details" page for free. Viewing more than one Details page is an additional $2.00 for each one selected. There is also a $75.00 annual registration fee. Records are available on an interactive basis only. For more information see https://apps.tn.gov/ivtr or call 866-886-3468.

Vessel Ownership & Registration

Wildlife Resources Agency, Boating Division,   www.tn.gov/twra/topic/boating-registration   One may request records via email to darren.rider@state.tn.us. The agency offers a "Check Hull ID" search page at https://twra.state.tn.us/boathullchecker/. This service is primarily a verification of Hull ID and year the boat was built, not a name search.

Campaign Finance, PACs, Lobbyists

Bureau of Ethics and Campaign Finance, 404 James Robertson Parkway, Suite 104,   www.tn.gov/tref   The web page at www.tn.gov/tref/article/tref-campaign-finance-disclosure-reports provides searches for campaign finance report and contributions. PAC information and searches are at www.tn.gov/tref/section/tref-pacs. Information on lobbyists is found at https://www.tn.gov/tec/section/tec-lobbyist.

GED Certificates

TN Dept of Labor & Workforce Development, Division of Adult Education,   www.tn.gov/workforce/article/ae-records   . Records may be requested from https://www.diplomasender.com. A credit card is needed. Request must be ordered by the test taker. Employers and third parties must receive an email and/or Authentication Code from the test taker to then access the authorized documents. Turnaround time is 1-3 days.

Occupational Licensing Boards

These licenses are all searchable at http://verify.tn.gov/

Accountant-CPA/Firm/Related	Barber/Shop/School/Related	Cosmetologist/Shop/School
Alarm Contractor/Related	Boxing/Racing Personnel	Electrician
Architect/Related	Collection Agent/Manager/Firm	Embalmer
Auctioneer/Auction-Firms/Related	Contractor	Engineer/Firm, Related

Fire Extinguisher Agents/Related
Fire Protect'n Sprinkler System Cont'r
Fireworks Display/Exhibit/Related
Fireworks/Display/Related
Funeral & Burial Director/Est/Related
Geologist
Home Inspector/Improvement
Insurance Agent/Firm/Education Provider
Interior Designer
Investment Advisor
Landscape Architect/Firm

Locksmith/Firm
LP Gas Dealer/Related
Manicurist/Shampoo Technician
MFGR/Housing/Modular/Related
Motor Vehicle Dealer/Auction-Related
Pharmacist/Pharmacy/Researcher
Plumber/Plumbing Company
Polygraph Examiner
Private Investigator/Agency-Related
Private Security Guard
Racetrack

Real Estate Agent/Firm-Related
Real Estate Appraiser
Refrigeration Installer/Contractor
Scrap Metal/Related
Securities Agent/Broker/Dealer
Security Guard/Company/Trainer
Soil Scientist
Surveyor, Land
Timeshare Agent

These health-related licenses are all searchable at https://apps.health.tn.gov/Licensure/

Acupuncturist
Athletic Trainer
Audiologist
Chiropractor/Chiropractic Assist
Clinical Lab Technician/Personnel
Counselor, Alcohol & Drug Abuse
Counselor, Associate/Professional
Dentist/Dental Hygienist/Assistant
Dietitian/Nutritionist
Electrologist/Instructor/School
Emergency Med Personnel/Dispatch/Service
Environmentalist
First Responder EMS
Genetic Counselor

Hearing Aid Dispenser
Laboratory Personnel, Medical
Marriage & Family Therapist
Massage Therapist/Establishment
Midwife
Nurse-RN/LPN/Aide
Nursing Home Administrator
Occupational Therapist/Assistant
Optician, Dispensing
Optometrist
Orthopedic Physician/ Assistant
Pastoral Therapist, Clinical
Pharmacist/Related
Physical Therapist/Assistant

Physician/Assistant-Related
Podiatrist
Psychologist/Psychological Examiner
Radiologic Assistant
Radiologic Tech/Assistant
Reflexologist
Respiratory Care Therapist/Tech/Asst
Social Worker, Master/Clinical
Speech Pathologist/Aide
Veterinarian/Animal Euthanasia Technician
X-Ray Technician/Firm
X-Ray Technologist-Podiatry

The Rest:

Attorney	www.tbpr.org/
Attorney - Disciplinary Actions	www.tbpr.org/news-publications/recent-disciplinary-actions
Boiler Inspector	http://tennessee.gov/assets/entities/labor/attachments/boiler_map.pdf
Elevator Inspector	http://tennessee.gov/workforce/article/workforce-elevator-inspectors
Lobbyist	https://apps.tn.gov/ilobbysearch-app/search.htm
Medical Disciplinary Tracking	http://tn.gov/health/article/boards-disciplinary-actions#dars
Notary Public	www.tn.gov/sos/bus_svc/NotarySearch.htm?
Pesticide Control Companies	https://agriculture.tn.gov/listcharter.asp

State and Local Courts

About Tennessee Courts: **Circuit Courts** hear civil and criminal cases and appeals of decisions from City, Juvenile, Municipal and General Sessions Courts. The jurisdiction of Circuit Courts often overlaps with that of the Chancery Courts.

Criminal cases are tried in Circuit Court except in districts with separate **Criminal Courts. These courts were established by the** General Assembly in counties with heavy caseloads. Criminal Courts exist in 13 of the 31 districts and hear felony cases and misdemeanor appeals from the lower courts.

Chancery Courts handle a variety of issues including lawsuits, contract disputes, application for injunctions and name changes. A number of matters, such as divorces, adoptions, and workers' compensation, can be heard in either Chancery or Circuit court.

General Sessions Court jurisdiction varies from county to county based on state laws and private acts. But every county is served by this court of limited jurisdiction. Civil jurisdiction is restricted to specific monetary limits and types of actions. Criminal jurisdiction is limited to preliminary hearings in felony cases and to most misdemeanor cases. Combining of Circuit Court and General Sessions Courts in smaller population counties often occurs.

Each **Juvenile & Family Court**, with the exception of Bristol and Johnson City, is county-based and administered with at least one juvenile court located in each of the state's 95 counties. There are 98 courts, but 17 are designated "Private Act" Juvenile Courts while the remaining 81 are General Sessions Courts with juvenile jurisdiction.
The web page for the Judicial Branch is www.tncourts.gov.

Appellate Courts: The Supreme Court is the court of last resort. The Court of Appeals hears appeals in civil—or non-criminal—cases from trial courts and certain state boards and commissions. The Court of Criminal Appeals hears trial court appeals in felony and misdemeanor cases, as well as post-conviction petitions.

Online Court Access

A limited number of counties offer online access to court records. There is no statewide access system other than the access to Supreme and Appellate Court mentioned above.

County Sites:
Anderson County
7th District Circuit Court   www.andersoncountycircuitcourtclerk.com/
Civil: A case search is offered at www.andersoncircuitcourt.com/search/webFormFrame.aspx?page=main. Search by case number or name. There is no indication of the throughput date. A current Docket Search is offered at www.andersoncountycircuitcourt.com/docket/.   *Criminal:* same

Chancery Court   http://andersoncountyclerkandmaster.com/
Civil: A case search is offered at www.andersoncircuitcourt.com/search/webFormFrame.aspx?page=main. Search by case number or name. There is no indication of the throughput date. A current Docket Search is offered at www.andersoncountycircuitcourt.com/docket/.
General Sessions Court - Clinton   www.andersoncountycircuitcourt.com/
Civil: A case search is offered at www.andersoncircuitcourt.com/search/webFormFrame.aspx?page=main. Search by case number or name. There is no indication of the throughput date. A current Docket Search is offered at www.andersoncountycircuitcourt.com/docket/.   *Criminal:* same

Blount County
Circuit Court   www.blountccc.com/circuitcourt.aspx
Civil: A subscription services allows users to view case information including; case filings, service of process, charges, court dockets, hearings, attorneys, fees, payment history, rule dockets, execution dockets and court dockets. Fee is $350 per year. Records are updated nightly. No information is given as to the throughput or if any identifiers are displayed. One must call the contact the Clerk to sign-up. *Criminal:* same
General Sessions Court   www.blountccc.com/generalsessions.aspx
Civil: A subscription services allows users to view case information including; case filings, service of process, charges, court dockets, hearings, attorneys, fees, payment history, rule dockets, execution dockets and court dockets. Fee is $350 per year. Records are updated nightly. No information is given as to the throughput or if any identifiers are displayed. One must call the contact the Clerk to sign-up. *Criminal:* same

Carter County
1st District Circuit Court   www.cartercountytn.gov/government/officials/circuitcourtclerk.html
Civil: Dockets are shown online at www.cartercountycircuitcourt.com/gensessions.asp. Data is shown by day in a PDF format.
Criminal Court   www.cartercountytn.gov/government/officials/circuit-court-clerk/
Criminal Court Dockets are shown online at www.cartercountycircuitcourt.com/circuitcriminal.asp. Data is shown by day in a PDF format.
General Sessions Court   www.cartercountytn.gov/government/officials/circuitcourtclerk.html
Civil: General Session Dockets are shown online at www.cartercountycircuitcourt.com/gensessions.asp. Data is shown by day in a PDF format.
Criminal: Dockets are shown online at www.cartercountycircuitcourt.com/circuitcriminal.asp. Data is shown by day in a PDF format.

Davidson County
General Sessions Court - Criminal Court   http://ccc.nashville.gov/
Access Davidson County Criminal Court Clerk database at hhttps://sci.ccc.nashville.gov/. The site also provides ability to search current session dockets.
Circuit Court   http://circuitclerk.nashville.gov/
Civil: Access filed cases online on CaseLink at http://circuitclerk.nashville.gov/caselink/; $35.00 per month fee required plus username, password. Email Caselink@Nashville.Gov for signup or add'l info. The type of case information accessible through CaseLink is: style of the case (plaintiff vs. defendant), pleadings filed, court dates, judgments, addresses, representing attorneys, service of process, and history of payments.
General Sessions Court   http://circuitclerk.nashville.gov/sessions/
Civil: Access filed cases online on CaseLink at http://caselink.nashville.gov/; $35.00 per month fee required, plus username and password. Email Caselink@Nashville.Gov for signup or add'l info. The type of case information accessible through CaseLink is: style of the case (plaintiff vs. defendant), pleadings filed, court dates, judgments, addresses, representing attorneys, service of process, and history of payments.   *Criminal:*

Franklin County
12th District Circuit Court   https://franklincountycircuitcourtclerk.org/

Civil: A subscription services allows users to view case information including; case filings, service of process, charges, court dockets, hearings, attorneys, fees, payment history, rule dockets, execution dockets and court dockets. Fee is $350 per year. Records are updated nightly. No information is given as to the throughput or if any identifiers are displayed. One must call the contact the Clerk to sign-up. *Criminal:* same

General Sessions Court   http://franklincountycircuitcourtclerk.org/

Civil: A subscription services allows users to view case information including; case filings, service of process, charges, court dockets, hearings, attorneys, fees, payment history, rule dockets, execution dockets and court dockets. Fee is $350 per year. Records are updated nightly. No information is given as to the throughput or if any identifiers are displayed. One must call the contact the Clerk to sign-up. *Criminal:* same

Greene County

3rd District Circuit Court   www.greenecountytngov.com/e_circuitcourtclerk.php

Civil: A subscription services allows users to view case information including; case filings, service of process, charges, court dockets, hearings, attorneys, fees, payment history, rule dockets, execution dockets and court dockets. Fee is $350 per year. Records are updated nightly. No information is given as to the throughput or if any identifiers are displayed. One must call the contact the Clerk to sign-up.

Criminal Court   www.greenecountytngov.com/e_circuitcourtclerk.php

A subscription services allows users to view case information including; case filings, service of process, charges, court dockets, hearings, attorneys, fees, payment history, rule dockets, execution dockets and court dockets. Fee is $350 per year. Records are updated nightly. No information is given as to the throughput or if any identifiers are displayed. One must call the contact the Clerk to sign-up.

General Sessions Court   www.greenecountytngov.com/e_circuitcourtclerk.php

Civil: A subscription services allows users to view case information including; case filings, service of process, charges, court dockets, hearings, attorneys, fees, payment history, rule dockets, execution dockets and court dockets. Fee is $350 per year. Records are updated nightly. No information is given as to the throughput or if any identifiers are displayed. One must call the contact the Clerk to sign-up. *Criminal:* same

Hamblen County

3rd District Circuit Court   www.hamblencountytn.gov/circuit-court-and-general-sessions-court/

Civil: A subscription services allows users to view case information including; case filings, service of process, charges, court dockets, hearings, attorneys, fees, payment history, rule dockets, execution dockets and court dockets. Fee is $350 per year. Records are updated nightly. No information is given as to the throughput or if any identifiers are displayed. One must call the contact the Clerk to sign-up. *Criminal:* same

General Sessions Court   www.hamblencountytn.gov/circuit-court-and-general-sessions-court/

Civil: A subscription services allows users to view case information including; case filings, service of process, charges, court dockets, hearings, attorneys, fees, payment history, rule dockets, execution dockets and court dockets. Fee is $350 per year. Records are updated nightly. No information is given as to the throughput or if any identifiers are displayed. One must call the contact the Clerk to sign-up. *Criminal:* same

Hamilton County

Criminal Court   www.hamiltontn.gov/courts/

Criminal: Search court's disposition records and court dates free at http://cjuscriminal.hamiltontn.gov/AppFolder/CC_Web_Calendar.aspx and records go back to 1989. Also, online access to current court dockets is free at www.hamiltontn.gov/courts/Criminal/CrimDisclaimer.aspx.

Circuit Court   www.hamiltontn.gov/courts/

Civil: A free search of the civil docket (Equity) is at https://hamilton.tncrtinfo.com/cvCaseList.aspx.

Chancery Court   www.hamiltontn.gov/courts/Default.aspx

Civil: A free search of the civil docket (Equity) and probate is at https://hamilton.tncrtinfo.com/cvCaseList.aspx. Chancery motion dockets are online at www.hamiltontn.gov/courts/Chancery/dockets/default.aspx

General Sessions Court   www.hamiltontn.gov/courts/sessions/

Civil: A free search of the civil docket (Equity) is at https://hamilton.tncrtinfo.com/cvCaseList.aspx. Online access to current (7 days) court dockets is free at http://cjusgeneralsessions.hamiltontn.gov/appfolder/GS_Web_Calendar.aspx.   *Criminal:*

Hawkins County

3rd District Circuit Court   www.hawkinscountytn.gov/index.php?option=com_content&view=article&id=22&Itemid=33

Civil: Online access to a name search of the dockets is at https://hawkins.tncrtinfo.com/?quick=444bf34b. There is no information provided about the throughput of the data.   *Criminal:* same

General Sessions Court   www.hawkinscountytn.gov/index.php?option=com_content&view=article&id=22&Itemid=33

Civil: Online access to a name search of the dockets is at https://hawkins.tncrtinfo.com/?quick=15a3bee1. There is no information provided about the throughput of the data.   *Criminal:* same

Jefferson County

4th District Circuit Court   www.jeffersoncountytn.gov/

Civil: Records are not online, but a PDF list of the daily docket schedule for at least 7 days appears at www.jeffersoncountytn.gov/law-justice/circuit-court-and-sessions-court-clerk-information/court-dockets/.   *Criminal:* same

General Sessions Court   www.jeffersoncountytn.gov/

Civil: Records are not online, but a PDF list of the daily docket schedule for at least 7 days appears at www.jeffersoncountytn.gov/law-justice/circuit-court-and-sessions-court-clerk-information/court-dockets/.   *Criminal:* same

Lawrence County

22nd District Circuit Court www.lawrencecountytn.gov/Departments/circuit-court-clerk
Civil: Online access to a name search of the dockets is at https://lawrence.tncrtinfo.com/?quick=5aba938e. There is no information provided about the throughput of the data. *Criminal:* same

General Sessions Court www.lawrencecountytn.gov/Departments/circuit-court-clerk
Civil: Online access to a name search of the dockets is at https://lawrence.tncrtinfo.com/?quick=e4a94d48. There is no information provided about the throughput of the data. *Criminal:* same

Macon County

Circuit Court Www.maconcircuitcourt.com
Civil: Online access to a name search of the dockets is at https://macon.tncrtinfo.com/?quick=91cf58da. There is no information provided about the throughput of the data. *Criminal:* same

General Sessions Court Www.maconcircuitcourt.com
Civil: Online access to a name search of the dockets is at https://macon.tncrtinfo.com/?quick=63b47d20. There is no information provided about the throughput of the data. *Criminal:* same

Monroe County

Circuit Court www.monroecircuitcourt.com/
Civil: A free search of the Circuit civil docket index is at www.monroecircuitcourt.com/Search/webFormFrame.aspx?page=main. View case dockets by entering the case number, party's name, and/or CSE number. *Criminal:* A free search of the Circuit criminal docket index is at www.monroecircuitcourt.com/Search/webFormFrame.aspx?page=main. View case dockets by entering the case number, party's name, and/or CSE number.

Montgomery County

Circuit Court https://mcgtn.org/circuit
Civil: Access the civil docket index free from May 1, 2006 at https://montgomery.tncrtinfo.com/Default.aspx. A username and password is supplied. *Criminal:* Access the criminal/traffic docket index free from November 1, 1999 at https://montgomery.tncrtinfo.com/Default.aspx. A username and password is supplied.

General Sessions Court www.mcgtn.org/circuit
Civil: Access the civil docket index free from May 1, 2006 at https://montgomery.tncrtinfo.com/Default.aspx. A username and password is supplied. *Criminal:* Access the criminal/traffic docket index free from November 1, 1999 at https://montgomery.tncrtinfo.com/Default.aspx. A username and password is supplied.

Putnam County

13th District Circuit Court www.putnamcountytn.gov/index.php?p=departments&s=circuitcourt
Civil: Online access to a name search of the dockets is at https://putnam.tncrtinfo.com/?quick=d7a0ff23. There is no information provided about the throughput of the data. *Criminal:* same

General Sessions Court www.dockets.putnamco.org
Civil: Online access to a name search of the dockets is at https://obion.tncrtinfo.com/?quick=db0e86d8. There is no information provided about the throughput of the data. *Criminal:* same

Roane County

Circuit Court www.roanecourts.com/
Civil: Online access to a name search of the dockets is at https://roane.tncrtinfo.com/?quick=7ffcb9a3. There is no information provided about the throughput of the data. *Criminal:* same

General Sessions Court www.roanecourts.com/
Civil: Online access to a name search of the dockets is at https://roane.tncrtinfo.com/?quick=4ccc8fd6. There is no information provided about the throughput of the data. *Criminal:* same

Robertson County

Circuit Court www.robertsoncountytn.org/node/13
Civil: Access civil online court records systems for free at https://robertson.tncrtinfo.com/?quick=76b80836. *Criminal:* Access criminal online court records systems for free at https://robertson.tncrtinfo.com/?quick=76b80836.

General Sessions Court www.robertsoncountytn.org/node/13
Civil: Online access to a name search of the dockets is at https://robertson.tncrtinfo.com/?quick=76b80836. There is no information provided about the throughput of the data. *Criminal:* same

Shelby County
30th District Criminal Court   www.shelbycountytn.gov/index.aspx?nid=224
Search the criminal court records for free at http://jssi.shelbycountytn.gov/.
Circuit Court   www.shelbycountytn.gov/index.aspx?nid=223
Civil: Search clerk's circuit court records for free at the website or at http://circuitdata.shelbycountytn.gov/crweb/ck_public_qry_main.cp_main_idx.
General Sessions Court - Criminal   http://gs4.shelbycountytn.gov/index.aspx?NID=31
Search criminal court records free at http://gs4.shelbycountytn.gov/index.aspx?NID=111 or http://jssi.shelbycountytn.gov/.
General Sessions Court - Civil   http://gs4.shelbycountytn.gov/
Search case history for free at http://gscivildata.shelbycountytn.gov/pls/gnweb/ck_public_qry_main.cp_main_idx.
Chancery Court   www.shelbycountytn.gov/index.aspx?nid=222
Civil: Search court records for free at http://chancerydata.shelbycountytn.gov/chweb/ck_public_qry_main.cp_main_idx. Note the disclaimer, the court will not guarantee or warrant the correctness, completeness, currency or utility for any general or specific purpose of the data made available through the access of this site.

Sullivan County
2nd District Circuit and Criminal Court - Blountville   www.sullivancountytn.gov/node/16
Criminal: Online access to a name search of the dockets is at https://sullivan.tncrtinfo.com/?quick=8b75b879. There is no information provided about the throughput of the data.
Bristol Circuit Court - Civil Division   www.sullivancountytn.gov/node/16
Civil: Online access to a name search of the dockets is at https://sullivan.tncrtinfo.com/?quick=8b75b879. There is no information provided about the throughput of the data.
Kingsport Circuit Court - Civil Division   www.sullivancountytn.gov/node/16
Civil: Online access to a name search of the dockets is at https://sullivan.tncrtinfo.com/?quick=8b75b879. There is no information provided about the throughput of the data.
Kingsport General Sessions   www.sullivancountytn.gov/node/16
Civil: Online access to a name search of the dockets is at https://sullivan.tncrtinfo.com/?quick=04ab43e0. There is no information provided about the throughput of the data. Current daily dockets are posted at http://sullivan.mytncourts.com/.   *Criminal:* same

Sumner County
18th District Circuit Court   www.sumnertn.org/offices/courts
Civil: Online access to a name search of the dockets is at https://sumner.tncrtinfo.com/?quick=34d8dd1f. There is no information provided about the throughput of the data.   *Criminal:* same

18th District General Sessions Court   www.sumnertn.org/offices/courts
Civil: Online access to a name search of the dockets is at https://sumner.tncrtinfo.com/?quick=957ea97e. There is no information provided about the throughput of the data.   *Criminal:* same

White County
Circuit Court   www.whiteccc.com/
Civil: Current case dockets available free at www.whiteccc.com/ but no historical data.
General Sessions Court   www.whiteccc.com/
Civil: Current case dockets available free at www.whiteccc.com/ but no historical data.   *Criminal:* same

Williamson County
Circuit Court   www.williamsoncounty-tn.gov/index.aspx?NID=221
Civil: Name search of the docket indexed is free at https://williamson.tncrtinfo.com/Default.aspx. There is a subscription product also offered, call for details. *Criminal:* same

Chancery Court   www.williamsonchancery.org/
Civil: Name search of the docket indexed is free at https://williamson.tncrtinfo.com/Default.aspx. Use the Clerk and Master search. There is a subscription product also offered, call for details.
General Sessions Court   www.williamsoncounty-tn.gov/index.aspx?NID=221
Civil: Name search of the docket indexed is free at https://williamson.tncrtinfo.com/Default.aspx. There is a subscription product also offered, call for details. *Criminal:* same

Recorders, Assessors, and Other Sites of Note

About Tennessee Recording Offices: 95 counties, 96 recording offices. Sullivan County has two recording offices. The recording officer is the Register of Deeds.

About Tax Liens: All state and federal tax liens are filed with the Register of Deeds.

Online Access

Recorded Documents

Online access to 52 county Register of Deeds data is available from a vendor at www.titlesearcher.com. Fees are based on the county tier and number of counties included in the subscription. Participating counties are: Anderson, Bedford, Bledsoe, Bradley, Campbell, Carter, Clairborne, Clay, Cocke, Coffee, Cumberland, Decatur, Fayette, Fentress, Franklin, Giles, Grainger, Greene, Hamblen, Hawkins, Hickman, Humphreys, Jackson, Jefferson, Johnson, Lawrence, Lincoln, Loudon, Macon, Madison, Marion, Maury, Monroe, Moore, Perry, Pickett, Polk, Rhea, Roane, Sequatchie, Sevier, Shelby, Smith, Sullivan, Unicoi, Union, Van Buren, Washington, Weakley, White, Williamson, and Wilson.

Online access 37 county Register of Deedsdata including judgment, liens, and UCCs is available from a vendor at www1.ustitlesearch.net/. Registration, login, and monthly $25 fee required, plus a $50 set up fee. Use DEMO as your username to sample the system. Participating counties are: Benton, Cannon, Carroll, Cheatham, Chester, Crockett, Dickson, Dyer, Gibson, Grundy, Hancock, Hardeman, Hardin, Haywood, Henderson, Henry, Houston, Lake, Lauderdale, Lewis, Marshall, McMinn, McNairy, Meigs, Montgomery, Morgan, Obion, Overton, Putnam, Robertson, Rutherford, Stewart, Sumner, Tipton, Trousdale, Warren, and Wayne.

Tax Assessment

State Site: Search the State Comptroller of the Treasury Real Estate Assessment Database free at www.assessment.cot.tn.gov/RE_Assessment/. Select a county then search by name, property address or parcel ID for real property information. All Tennessee counties available except Davidson, Hamilton, Knox, and Shelby.

Statewide Vendor Site: See www.tnrealestate.com for free and fee services for property assessor data, attribute data, real estate sales, MLS listings, property taxes, property owners, legal references, improvement and land descriptions, aerial photographs, tax and topographical maps from all Tennessee counties.

County Sites (The two sites for tax assessment are not displayed on each profile).

Anderson County *Recorded Documents* www.andersondeeds.com/   The county provides free access to records at http://search.andersondeeds.com/menu.php. Both indexes and images provided from 1/1/1990 to present. Access property and deeds indexes/images at www.titlesearcher.com/countyHomepages.php?state=TN. Must register with user name and password. See Pricing Tab for fees.
Property, Taxation Records   See www.tnrealestate.com for free and fee services for property assessor and ownership data. Also, access to GIS/mapping for free at http://tn.anderson.geopowered.com/.

Bedford County *Recorded Documents* www.bedfordcountytn.org/registerofdeeds.html   Access property and deeds indexes/images at www.titlesearcher.com/countyHomepages.php?state=TN. Must register with user name and password. See Pricing Tab for fees.
Property, Taxation Records   See www.tnrealestate.com for free and fee services for property assessor and ownership data.

Benton County *Recorded Documents* www.bentoncountytn.gov/   Access to indexes and images for a fee at www1.ustitlesearch.net/.
Property, Taxation Records   See www.tnrealestate.com for free and fee services for property assessor and ownership data.

Bledsoe County *Recorded Documents* https://www.deeds.com/recorder/tennessee/bledsoe/   Access property and deeds indexes/images at www.titlesearcher.com/countyHomepages.php?state=TN. Must register with user name and password. See Pricing Tab for fees.
Property, Taxation Records   See www.tnrealestate.com for free and fee services for property assessor and ownership data.

Blount County *Property, Taxation Records*   See www.tnrealestate.com for free and fee services for property assessor and ownership data.

Bradley County *Recorded Documents* www.bradleyco.net/registerofdeedshome.aspx   Access property and deeds indexes/images at www.titlesearcher.com/countyHomepages.php?state=TN. Must register with user name and password. See Pricing Tab for fees.
Property, Taxation Records   Access to property assessment data free at http://patriotproperties.com/. See www.tnrealestate.com for free and fee services for property assessor and ownership data. Also, access to tax maps for free at www.bradleyco.net/propassess_taxmap.aspx.

Campbell County *Recorded Documents* www.campbellcountytn.gov/elected_offices/register_of_deeds.aspx   Access property and deeds indexes/images at www.titlesearcher.com/countyHomepages.php?state=TN. Must register with user name and password. See Pricing Tab for fees.

Property, Taxation Records   See www.tnrealestate.com for free and fee services for property assessor and ownership data.

Cannon County   *Recorded Documents*   http://cannontn.com/county-office/   Access to indexes and images for a fee at www1.ustitlesearch.net/.
Property, Taxation Records   See www.tnrealestate.com for free and fee services for property assessor and ownership data.

Carroll County   *Recorded Documents*   https://www.deeds.com/recorder/tennessee/carroll/   Access to indexes and images for a fee at www1.ustitlesearch.net/.
Property, Taxation Records   See www.tnrealestate.com for free and fee services for property assessor and ownership data.

Carter County   *Recorded Documents*   www.cartercountytn.gov/government/officials/register-of-deeds/   Access property and deeds indexes/images at www.titlesearcher.com/countyHomepages.php?state=TN. Must register with user name and password. See Pricing Tab for fees.
Property, Taxation Records   See www.tnrealestate.com for free and fee services for property assessor and ownership data.

Cheatham County   *Recorded Documents*   http://cheathamcountytn.gov/government/register_of_deeds/   Access to indexes and images for a fee at www1.ustitlesearch.net/.
Property, Taxation Records   See www.tnrealestate.com for free and fee services for property assessor and ownership data.

Chester County   *Recorded Documents*   http://chestercountytn.org/county_offices/index.html#register   Access to indexes and images for a fee at www1.ustitlesearch.net/.
Property, Taxation Records   Access to property records for free at http://chester.capturecama.com/CAMA/CAPortal/CZ_MainPage.aspx. See www.tnrealestate.com for free and fee services for property assessor and ownership data.

Claiborne County   *Recorded Documents*   Access property and deeds indexes/images at www.titlesearcher.com/countyHomepages.php?state=TN. Must register with user name and password. See Pricing Tab for fees.
Property, Taxation Records   See www.tnrealestate.com for free and fee services for property assessor and ownership data.

Clay County   *Recorded Documents*   https://www.deeds.com/recorder/tennessee/clay/   Access property and deeds indexes/images at www.titlesearcher.com/countyHomepages.php?state=TN. Must register with user name and password. See Pricing Tab for fees.
Property, Taxation Records   See www.tnrealestate.com for free and fee services for property assessor and ownership data.

Cocke County   *Recorded Documents*   Access property and deeds indexes/images at www.titlesearcher.com/countyHomepages.php?state=TN. Must register with user name and password. See Pricing Tab for fees.
Property, Taxation Records   See www.tnrealestate.com for free and fee services for property assessor and ownership data.

Coffee County   *Recorded Documents*   www.coffeecountyregisterofdeeds.com/   Access property and deeds indexes/images at www.titlesearcher.com/countyHomepages.php?state=TN. Must register with user name and password. See Pricing Tab for fees.
Property, Taxation Records   See www.tnrealestate.com for free and fee services for property assessor and ownership data.

Crockett County   *Recorded Documents*   Access to indexes and images for a fee at www1.ustitlesearch.net/.
Property, Taxation Records   See www.tnrealestate.com for free and fee services for property assessor and ownership data.

Cumberland County   *Recorded Documents*   http://cumberlandcountytn.gov/register-of-deeds/   Access property and deeds indexes/images at www.titlesearcher.com/countyHomepages.php?state=TN. Must register with user name and password. See Pricing Tab for fees.
Property, Taxation Records   See www.tnrealestate.com for free and fee services for property assessor and ownership data.

Davidson County   *Property, Taxation Records*   Search county assessments free at www.padctn.org/real-property-search/. See www.tnrealestate.com for free and fee services for property assessor and ownership data. Also, access to GIS/mapping is free at http://maps.nashville.gov/HomePage/index.html.

Decatur County   *Recorded Documents*   www.decaturcountytn.org/contact_us.asp   Access property and deeds indexes/images at www.titlesearcher.com/countyHomepages.php?state=TN. Must register with user name and password. See Pricing Tab for fees.
Property, Taxation Records   See www.tnrealestate.com for free and fee services for property assessor and ownership data.

DeKalb County   *Property, Taxation Records*   See www.tnrealestate.com for free and fee services for property assessor and ownership data.

Dickson County   *Recorded Documents*   www.dicksoncountytn.gov/government/register_of_deeds/index.html   Access to indexes and images for a fee at www1.ustitlesearch.net/.
Property, Taxation Records   See www.tnrealestate.com for free and fee services for property assessor and ownership data.

Dyer County   *Recorded Documents*   Access to indexes and images for a fee at www1.ustitlesearch.net/.
Property, Taxation Records   See www.tnrealestate.com for free and fee services for property assessor and ownership data.

Fayette County   *Recorded Documents*   www.fayettetn.us/CountyDepts/Register.htm   Access property and deeds indexes/images at www.titlesearcher.com/countyHomepages.php?state=TN. Must register with user name and password. See Pricing Tab for fees.
Property, Taxation Records   See www.tnrealestate.com for free and fee services for property assessor and ownership data.

Fentress County *Recorded Documents*   Access property and deeds indexes/images at www.titlesearcher.com/countyHomepages.php?state=TN. Must register with user name and password. See Pricing Tab for fees.
Property, Taxation Records   See www.tnrealestate.com for free and fee services for property assessor and ownership data.

Franklin County *Recorded Documents*   www.franklincountyregister.com/   Access property and deeds indexes/images at www.titlesearcher.com/countyHomepages.php?state=TN. Must register with user name and password. See Pricing Tab for fees.
Property, Taxation Records   See www.tnrealestate.com for free and fee services for property assessor and ownership data.

Gibson County *Recorded Documents*   Access to indexes and images for a fee at www1.ustitlesearch.net/.
Property, Taxation Records   See www.tnrealestate.com for free and fee services for property assessor and ownership data. Also, access to a tax search for free at www.tennesseetrustee.com/node/20.

Giles County *Recorded Documents*   www.gilescounty-tn.us/CountyOfficials.aspx   Access property and deeds indexes/images at www.titlesearcher.com/countyHomepages.php?state=TN. Must register with user name and password. See Pricing Tab for fees.
Property, Taxation Records   See www.tnrealestate.com for free and fee services for property assessor and ownership data.

Grainger County *Recorded Documents*   www.graingertn.com/   Access property and deeds indexes/images at www.titlesearcher.com/countyHomepages.php?state=TN. Must register with user name and password. See Pricing Tab for fees.
Property, Taxation Records   See www.tnrealestate.com for free and fee services for property assessor and ownership data.

Greene County *Recorded Documents*   www.greenecountytngov.com/e_registerofdeeds.php   Access property and deeds indexes/images at www.titlesearcher.com/countyHomepages.php?state=TN. Must register with user name and password. See Pricing Tab for fees. In 1999 the Register's office implemented a computer imaging system. Once documents are saved into the data base they can be viewed by the public in deed room or via the web.
Property, Taxation Records   See www.tnrealestate.com for free and fee services for property assessor and ownership data.

Grundy County *Recorded Documents*   www.grundycountytn.net/officials/index.html#register   Access to indexes and images for a fee at www1.ustitlesearch.net/.
Property, Taxation Records   See www.tnrealestate.com for free and fee services for property assessor and ownership data.

Hamblen County *Recorded Documents*   www.hamblencountytn.gov/register-of-deeds/   Access property and deeds indexes/images at www.titlesearcher.com/countyHomepages.php?state=TN. Must register with user name and password. See Pricing Tab for fees.
Property, Taxation Records   See www.tnrealestate.com for free and fee services for property assessor and ownership data.

Hamilton County *Recorded Documents*   www.hamiltontn.gov/register/   County Register of Deeds subscription service is $50 per month and $1.00 per fax page. Search by name, address, or book & page. For info, call 423-209-6560; or visit www.hamiltontn.gov/Register/. Credit cards accepted.
Property, Taxation Records   Property assessor records are free at http://tpti.hamiltontn.gov/AppFolder/Trustee_PropertySearch.aspx. Also, access to property assessment data free at http://patriotproperties.com/. See www.tnrealestate.com for free and fee services for property assessor and ownership data. Also, search City of Chattanooga property tax database at www.chattanooga.gov/index.php/component/ptaxweb/searchpage.

Hancock County *Recorded Documents*   www.hancockcountytn.com/Register-of-Deeds.php   Access to indexes and images for a fee at www1.ustitlesearch.net/.
Property, Taxation Records   See www.tnrealestate.com for free and fee services for property assessor and ownership data. Also, access to a property viewer for free at http://tnmap.tn.gov/assessment/.

Hardeman County *Recorded Documents*   http://hardemancountytn.com/government/hardeman-county/registers-office.php   Access to indexes and images for a fee at www1.ustitlesearch.net/.
Property, Taxation Records   See www.tnrealestate.com for free and fee services for property assessor and ownership data.

Hardin County *Recorded Documents*   http://gml.ctas.tennessee.edu/official/62730   Access to indexes and images for a fee at www1.ustitlesearch.net/.
Property, Taxation Records   See www.tnrealestate.com for free and fee services for property assessor and ownership data.

Hawkins County *Recorded Documents*   www.hawkinscountytn.gov/index.php?option=com_content&view=article&id=26&Itemid=38   Access property and deeds indexes/images at www.titlesearcher.com/countyHomepages.php?state=TN. Must register with user name and password. See Pricing Tab for fees.
Property, Taxation Records   See www.tnrealestate.com for free and fee services for property assessor and ownership data.

Haywood County *Recorded Documents*   http://haywoodcountybrownsville.com/haywood-county/departments-services/register-of-deeds/   Access to indexes and images for a fee at www1.ustitlesearch.net/.
Property, Taxation Records   See www.tnrealestate.com for free and fee services for property assessor and ownership data.

Henderson County *Recorded Documents* www.hendersoncountytn.gov/index.aspx?nid=894 Access to indexes and images for a fee at www1.ustitlesearch.net/.
Property, Taxation Records See www.tnrealestate.com for free and fee services for property assessor and ownership data.

Henry County *Recorded Documents* http://henrycountytn.org/register-of-deeds-2/ Access to indexes and images for a fee at www1.ustitlesearch.net/.
Property, Taxation Records See www.tnrealestate.com for free and fee services for property assessor and ownership data.

Hickman County *Recorded Documents* www.hickmancountytn.com/directory/county-offices/land-and-property-records/register-of-deeds
Access property and deeds indexes/images at www.titlesearcher.com/countyHomepages.php?state=TN. Must register with user name and password. See Pricing Tab for fees.
Property, Taxation Records Access to assessment records for free at http://hickman.capturecama.com/CAMA/CAPortal/CZ_MainPage.aspx. See www.tnrealestate.com for free and fee services for property assessor and ownership data.

Houston County *Recorded Documents* Access to indexes and images for a fee at www1.ustitlesearch.net/.
Property, Taxation Records See www.tnrealestate.com for free and fee services for property assessor and ownership data.

Humphreys County *Recorded Documents* www.humphreystn.com/register_of_deeds/index.html Access property and deeds indexes/images at www.titlesearcher.com/countyHomepages.php?state=TN. Must register with user name and password. See Pricing Tab for fees.
Property, Taxation Records See www.tnrealestate.com for free and fee services for property assessor and ownership data.

Jackson County *Recorded Documents* www.jacksoncotn.com/countydepartments.php# Access property and deeds indexes/images at www.titlesearcher.com/countyHomepages.php?state=TN. Must register with user name and password. See Pricing Tab for fees.
Property, Taxation Records See www.tnrealestate.com for free and fee services for property assessor and ownership data.

Jefferson County *Recorded Documents* www.jeffersoncountytn.gov/businesses/register-of-deeds/ Access property and deeds indexes/images at www.titlesearcher.com/countyHomepages.php?state=TN. Must register with user name and password. See Pricing Tab for fees.
Property, Taxation Records See www.tnrealestate.com for free and fee services for property assessor and ownership data.

Johnson County *Recorded Documents* Access property and deeds indexes/images at www.titlesearcher.com/countyHomepages.php?state=TN. Must register with user name and password. See Pricing Tab for fees.
Property, Taxation Records See www.tnrealestate.com for free and fee services for property assessor and ownership data.

Knox County *Recorded Documents* www.knoxcounty.org/register/ Access to property record indexes for free go to http://tn-knox-assessor.publicaccessnow.com/PropertyLookup.aspx. For online subscription for recorded document records call Rose Browing at 865-215-3535. Reportedly the online index of recorded documents may be missing information on older records.
Property, Taxation Records Search the property tax rolls for free at https://www.knoxcounty.org/apps/tax_search/index.php. Search assessor records at http://tn-knox-assessor.publicaccessnow.com/Welcome.aspx. See www.tnrealestate.com for free and fee services for property assessor and ownership data.

Lake County *Recorded Documents* http://gml.ctas.tennessee.edu/official/62929 Access to indexes and images for a fee at www1.ustitlesearch.net/.
Property, Taxation Records See www.tnrealestate.com for free and fee services for property assessor and ownership data.

Lauderdale County *Recorded Documents* Access to indexes and images for a fee at www1.ustitlesearch.net/.
Property, Taxation Records See www.tnrealestate.com for free and fee services for property assessor and ownership data.

Lawrence County *Recorded Documents* www.lawrencecountytn.gov/Departments/register-of-deeds Access property and deeds indexes/images at www.titlesearcher.com/countyHomepages.php?state=TN. Must register with user name and password. See Pricing Tab for fees.
Property, Taxation Records See www.tnrealestate.com for free and fee services for property assessor and ownership data.

Lewis County *Recorded Documents* http://lewiscountytn.com/Register%20of%20Deeds.html Access to indexes and images for a fee at www1.ustitlesearch.net/.
Property, Taxation Records See www.tnrealestate.com for free and fee services for property assessor and ownership data.

Lincoln County *Recorded Documents* www.lincolncountytngov.com/county-offices Access property and deeds indexes/images at www.titlesearcher.com/countyHomepages.php?state=TN. Must register with user name and password. See Pricing Tab for fees.
Property, Taxation Records See www.tnrealestate.com for free and fee services for property assessor and ownership data.

Loudon County *Recorded Documents* Access property and deeds indexes/images at www.titlesearcher.com/countyHomepages.php?state=TN. Must register with user name and password. See Pricing Tab for fees.
Property, Taxation Records See www.tnrealestate.com for free and fee services for property assessor and ownership data.

Macon County *Recorded Documents* www.maconcountytn.com/register_of_deeds.htm Access property and deeds indexes/images at www.titlesearcher.com/countyHomepages.php?state=TN. Must register with user name and password. See Pricing Tab for fees.

Property, Taxation Records   See www.tnrealestate.com for free and fee services for property assessor and ownership data.

Madison County   *Recorded Documents*   www.co.madison.tn.us/index.aspx?nid=118   Access property and deeds indexes/images at www.titlesearcher.com/countyHomepages.php?state=TN. Must register with user name and password. See Pricing Tab for fees.
Property, Taxation Records   See www.tnrealestate.com for free and fee services for property assessor and ownership data.

Marion County   *Recorded Documents*   Access property and deeds indexes/images at www.titlesearcher.com/countyHomepages.php?state=TN. Must register with user name and password. See Pricing Tab for fees.
Property, Taxation Records   See www.tnrealestate.com for free and fee services for property assessor and ownership data.

Marshall County   *Recorded Documents*   www.marshallcountytn.com/register-of-deeds.html   Access to indexes and images for a fee at www1.ustitlesearch.net/.
Property, Taxation Records   See www.tnrealestate.com for free and fee services for property assessor and ownership data.

Maury County   *Recorded Documents*   www.maurycounty-tn.gov/index.aspx?page=103   Access property and deeds indexes/images at www.titlesearcher.com/countyHomepages.php?state=TN. Must register with user name and password. See Pricing Tab for fees.
Property, Taxation Records   Assessment data on state comptroller system is free at www.assessment.cot.tn.gov/RE_Assessment/ See www.tnrealestate.com for free and fee services for property assessor and ownership data.

McMinn County   *Recorded Documents*   http://mcminncountytn.gov/register_of_deeds/register_of_deeds.html   Access to indexes and images for a fee at www1.ustitlesearch.net/.
Property, Taxation Records   See www.tnrealestate.com for free and fee services for property assessor and ownership data. Also, access to parcel and maps data free at http://tn.mcminn.geopowered.com/.

McNairy County   *Recorded Documents*   www.mcnairycountytn.com/register_of_deeds.htm   Access to indexes and images for a fee at www1.ustitlesearch.net/.
Property, Taxation Records   See www.tnrealestate.com for free and fee services for property assessor and ownership data.

Meigs County   *Recorded Documents*   Access to indexes and images for a fee at www1.ustitlesearch.net/.
Property, Taxation Records   See www.tnrealestate.com for free and fee services for property assessor and ownership data.

Monroe County   *Recorded Documents*   Access property and deeds indexes/images at www.titlesearcher.com/countyHomepages.php?state=TN. Must register with user name and password. See Pricing Tab for fees.
Property, Taxation Records   See www.tnrealestate.com for free and fee services for property assessor and ownership data.

Montgomery County   *Recorded Documents*   https://mcgtn.org/deeds   Access to indexes and images for a fee at www1.ustitlesearch.net/.
Property, Taxation Records   Access to sales data for free at www.mcgtn.org:8080/County/assessor/webpro/disclaimer.aspx. See www.tnrealestate.com for free and fee services for property assessor and ownership data.

Moore County   *Recorded Documents*   http://gml.ctas.tennessee.edu/official/61883   Access property and deeds indexes/images at www.titlesearcher.com/countyHomepages.php?state=TN. Must register with user name and password. See Pricing Tab for fees.
Property, Taxation Records   See www.tnrealestate.com for free and fee services for property assessor and ownership data.

Morgan County   *Recorded Documents*   www.morgancountytn.org/deeds.htm   Access to indexes and images for a fee at www1.ustitlesearch.net/.
Property, Taxation Records   See www.tnrealestate.com for free and fee services for property assessor and ownership data.

Obion County   *Recorded Documents*   Access to indexes and images for a fee at www1.ustitlesearch.net/.
Property, Taxation Records   See www.tnrealestate.com for free and fee services for property assessor and ownership data.

Overton County   *Recorded Documents*   www.overtoncountytn.com/index.php?option=com_content&task=view&id=11&Itemid=16 Access to indexes and images for a fee at www1.ustitlesearch.net/.
Property, Taxation Records   See www.tnrealestate.com for free and fee services for property assessor and ownership data.

Perry County   *Recorded Documents*   Access property and deeds indexes/images at www.titlesearcher.com/countyHomepages.php?state=TN. Must register with user name and password. See Pricing Tab for fees.
Property, Taxation Records   See www.tnrealestate.com for free and fee services for property assessor and ownership data.

Pickett County   *Recorded Documents*   Access property and deeds indexes/images at www.titlesearcher.com/countyHomepages.php?state=TN. Must register with user name and password. See Pricing Tab for fees.
Property, Taxation Records   See www.tnrealestate.com for free and fee services for property assessor and ownership data.

Polk County   *Recorded Documents*   www.polkgovernment.com/register-deeds.php   Access property and deeds indexes/images at www.titlesearcher.com/countyHomepages.php?state=TN. Must register with user name and password. See Pricing Tab for fees.
Property, Taxation Records   See www.tnrealestate.com for free and fee services for property assessor and ownership data.

Putnam County   *Recorded Documents*   www.putnamcountytn.gov/index.php?p=departments&s=register   Access to indexes and images for a fee at www1.ustitlesearch.net/.
Property, Taxation Records   Also see state introduction. See www.tnrealestate.com for free and fee services for property assessor and ownership data. Also, access to property search for free at http://maps.putnamco.org/apps/taxparcelviewer/.

Rhea County   *Recorded Documents*   http://rheacountytn.com/   Access property and deeds indexes/images at www.titlesearcher.com/countyHomepages.php?state=TN. Must register with user name and password. See Pricing Tab for fees.
Property, Taxation Records   See www.tnrealestate.com for free and fee services for property assessor and ownership data.

Roane County   *Recorded Documents*   http://roanecountytn.gov/officialsdepartments/register-of-deeds/   Access property and deeds indexes/images at www.titlesearcher.com/countyHomepages.php?state=TN. Must register with user name and password. See Pricing Tab for fees.
Property, Taxation Records   See www.tnrealestate.com for free and fee services for property assessor and ownership data. Access to parcel search and maps free at http://tn.roane.geopowered.com/. Also, access to property assessment data free at http://patriotproperties.com/.

Robertson County   *Recorded Documents*   Access to indexes and images for a fee at www1.ustitlesearch.net/.
Property, Taxation Records   See www.tnrealestate.com for free and fee services for property assessor and ownership data.

Rutherford County   *Recorded Documents*   http://rutherfordcountytn.gov/registerofdeeds/   Access to indexes and images for a fee at www1.ustitlesearch.net/.
Property, Taxation Records   Access to property data for free at www.rutherfordcountytn.gov/apps/propertydata/. See www.tnrealestate.com for free and fee services for property assessor and ownership data. Also, access to GIS/mapping free at http://maps.rutherfordcountytn.gov/Rutherford/.

Scott County   *Property, Taxation Records*   See www.tnrealestate.com for free and fee services for property assessor and ownership data.

Sequatchie County   *Recorded Documents*   Access property and deeds indexes/images at www.titlesearcher.com/countyHomepages.php?state=TN. Must register with user name and password. See Pricing Tab for fees.
Property, Taxation Records   See www.tnrealestate.com for free and fee services for property assessor and ownership data.

Sevier County   *Recorded Documents*   www.seviercountytn.gov/index.php?option=com_content&view=article&id=293&Itemid=257   Access property and deeds indexes/images at www.titlesearcher.com/countyHomepages.php?state=TN. Must register with user name and password. See Pricing Tab for fees.
Property, Taxation Records   See www.tnrealestate.com for free and fee services for property assessor and ownership data.

Shelby County   *Recorded Documents*   http://register.shelby.tn.us/   Access the Register of Deeds databases free at http://register.shelby.tn.us/index.php. Partial indexes and images go back to 1812; full to 2014-current. Also, access property and deeds indexes/images at www.titlesearcher.com/countyHomepages.php?state=TN. Must register with user name and password. Fees vary from county to county.
Property, Taxation Records   Access property assessor data free at www.assessor.shelby.tn.us/content.aspx. Also, Access to GIS/mapping free at http://gis.assessor.shelby.tn.us/. See www.tnrealestate.com for free and fee services for property assessor and ownership data. Also, access to personal property search free at www.assessor.shelby.tn.us/Accept.aspx.

Smith County   *Recorded Documents*   http://gml.ctas.tennessee.edu/official/61916   Access property and deeds indexes/images at www.titlesearcher.com/countyHomepages.php?state=TN. Must register with user name and password. See Pricing Tab for fees.
Property, Taxation Records   See www.tnrealestate.com for free and fee services for property assessor and ownership data.

Stewart County   *Recorded Documents*   www.stewartcogov.com/elected_officials/elected_officials.html   Access to indexes and images for a fee at www1.ustitlesearch.net/.
Property, Taxation Records   See www.tnrealestate.com for free and fee services for property assessor and ownership data.

Sullivan County (Blountville Office)   *Recorded Documents*   www.sullivancountytn.gov/node/19   Access property and deeds indexes/images at www.titlesearcher.com/countyHomepages.php?state=TN. Must register with user name and password. See Pricing Tab for fees.
Property, Taxation Records   Assessment data on state comptroller system is free at http://assessorsullivantn.com/CAMA/CAPortal/CZ_MainPage.aspx. See www.tnrealestate.com for free and fee services for property assessor and ownership data.

Sumner County   *Recorded Documents*   www.deeds.sumnercounty.org   Access to indexes and images for a fee at www1.ustitlesearch.net/.
Property, Taxation Records   Search property data free on the GIS site at http://tn.sumner.geopowered.com/. See www.tnrealestate.com for free and fee services for property assessor and ownership data. Also, access to property assessment data free at http://patriotproperties.com/.

Tipton County   *Recorded Documents*   www.tiptonco.com/government/register_of_deeds/index.php   Access to indexes and images for a fee at www1.ustitlesearch.net/.
Property, Taxation Records   See www.tnrealestate.com for free and fee services for property assessor and ownership data.

Trousdale County   *Recorded Documents*   www.trousdalecountytn.gov/node/21   Access to indexes and images for a fee at www1.ustitlesearch.net/.
Property, Taxation Records   See www.tnrealestate.com for free and fee services for property assessor and ownership data.

Unicoi County *Recorded Documents* www.unicoicountytn.gov/index.php?option=com_content&view=article&id=203&Itemid=198
Access property and deeds indexes/images at www.titlesearcher.com/countyInfo.php?cnum=56. Must register with user name and password. See Pricing Tab for fees.
Property, Taxation Records Access to property tax search or payment for free at www.unicoi.tennesseetrustee.org/. See www.tnrealestate.com for free and fee services for property assessor and ownership data. Also, assessment data on state comptroller system is free at www.assessment.cot.tn.gov/RE_Assessment/.

Union County *Recorded Documents* www.unioncountytn.com Access property and deeds indexes/images at www.titlesearcher.com/countyHomepages.php?state=TN. Must register with user name and password. See Pricing Tab for fees.
Property, Taxation Records See www.tnrealestate.com for free and fee services for property assessor and ownership data.

Van Buren County *Recorded Documents* http://gml.ctas.tennessee.edu/official/64446 Access property and deeds indexes/images at www.titlesearcher.com/countyHomepages.php?state=TN. Must register with user name and password. See Pricing Tab for fees.
Property, Taxation Records See www.tnrealestate.com for free and fee services for property assessor and ownership data.

Warren County *Recorded Documents* www.warrencountytn.gov/deeds.asp Access to indexes and images for a fee at www1.ustitlesearch.net/.
Property, Taxation Records See www.tnrealestate.com for free and fee services for property assessor and ownership data.

Washington County *Recorded Documents* www.washingtoncountytn.org/government/register_of_deeds Access property and deeds indexes/images at www.titlesearcher.com/countyHomepages.php?state=TN. Must register with user name and password. See Pricing Tab for fees.
Property, Taxation Records See www.tnrealestate.com for free and fee services for property assessor and ownership data.

Wayne County *Recorded Documents* Access to indexes and images for a fee at www1.ustitlesearch.net/.
Property, Taxation Records See www.tnrealestate.com for free and fee services for property assessor and ownership data.

Weakley County *Recorded Documents* www.weakleycountytn.gov/registerofdeeds.html Access property and deeds indexes/images at www.titlesearcher.com/countyHomepages.php?state=TN. Must register with user name and password. See Pricing Tab for fees.
Property, Taxation Records See www.tnrealestate.com for free and fee services for property assessor and ownership data.

White County *Recorded Documents* http://whitecountytn.gov/government/county-offices/register-deeds Access property and deeds indexes/images at www.titlesearcher.com/countyHomepages.php?state=TN. Must register with user name and password. See Pricing Tab for fees.
Property, Taxation Records See www.tnrealestate.com for free and fee services for property assessor and ownership data.

Williamson County *Recorded Documents* www.williamsoncounty-tn.gov/index.aspx?nid=61 Access to the Professional Access database by subscription is a $50 per month fee. Info and sign-up at http://williamson-tn.org/co_gov/profacc.htm. Also, access property and deeds indexes/images at www.titlesearcher.com/countyHomepages.php?state=TN. Must register with user name and password. Fees vary from county to county.
Property, Taxation Records Access to property search data free go to http://inigo.williamson-tn.org/assessor/. See www.tnrealestate.com for free and fee services for property assessor and ownership data.

Wilson County *Recorded Documents* www.wilsondeeds.com Access to the Register of Deeds database requires a $35 1st month registration fee and $25.00 per month usage fee at www.wilsondeeds.com/. Includes indices back to 1989; images back to 191954. Also, access property and deeds indexes/images at www.titlesearcher.com/countyHomepages.php?state=TN. Must register with user name and password. Fees vary from county to county.
Property, Taxation Records See www.tnrealestate.com for free and fee services for property assessor and ownership data. Also, access to GIS/mapping for free at http://geopowered.wilson.wilsontngis.com/.

Reminder - These Sites are not Shown in the Profiles

Tax Assessment

State Site: Search the State Comptroller of the Treasury Real Estate Assessment Database free at www.assessment.cot.tn.gov/RE_Assessment/. Select a county then search by name, property address or parcel ID for real property information. All Tennessee counties available except Davidson, Hamilton, Knox, and Shelby.

Statewide Vendor Site: See www.tnrealestate.com for free and fee services for property assessor data, attribute data, real estate sales, MLS listings, property taxes, property owners, legal references, improvement and land descriptions, aerial photographs, tax and topographical maps from all Tennessee counties.

Texas

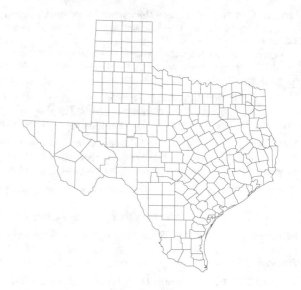

Capital: Austin
           Travis County

Time Zone: CST

    Texas' two most western ounties are in MST:
    They are El paso and Hudspeth.

Population: 27,469,114

# of Counties: 254

Useful State Links

Website: **www.texas.gov**
Governor: **http://gov.texas.gov**
Attorney General: **www.tn.gov/attorneygeneral/**
State Archives: **https://www.tsl.state.tx.us/**
State Statutes and Codes: **www.capitol.state.tx.us/**
    or search at **www.statutes.legis.state.tx.us/**
Legislative Bill Search and Monitoring: **www.legis.state.tx.us/Search/BillSearch.aspx**
    or if you know the number **www.legis.state.tx.us/BillLookup/BillNumber.aspx**
Unclaimed Funds: **https://mycpa.cpa.state.tx.us/up/Search.jsp**

State Public Record Agencies

Criminal Records

DPS - Access & Dissemination Bureau, Crime Records Service, https://records.txdps.state.tx.us/DpsWebsite/index.aspx   The Texas DPS offers two websites for accessing criminal records. The Public site is at https://records.txdps.state.tx.us/DpsWebsite/index.aspx. Public requesters may use a credit card or establish an account to pre-purchase credits. The fee is $3.00 per request plus a $2.25% handling fee if paying by credit card. Users may purchase credits by check. The 2nd site is strictly for eligible entities authorized by law. See https://secure.txdps.state.tx.us/DpsWebsite/Index.aspx. Fee is $1.00 per search. Searches submitted by batch are available from the Search History page for 7-days from the date searched and available for download from the message center for 30-days To determine eligibility call 512-241-2474. Checks from either site are instantaneous and provide convictions and deferred adjudications only.   *Other Options:* Conviction data may be purchased in bulk. See a list of purchasers and the last ypdate purchased at https://records.txdps.state.tx.us/DpsWebsite/CriminalHistory/Purchases.aspx.

Sexual Offender Registry

Dept of Public Safety, Sex Offender Registration, https://records.txdps.state.tx.us/SexOffender/PublicSite/Index.aspx   Sex offender data is available at the web page. There is no charge for a sex offender search. Search by name or city/ZIP/county or by map. The Department of Public Safety has a notification system that allows the public to subscribe to e-mail notifications regarding database changes relating to registered sex offenders. The signup is available at this site. Also, one may download the offender database from the web page. The data is updated twice a week and is available at no charge to users.

Incarceration Records

Texas Department of Criminal Justice, Bureau of Classification and Records, www.tdcj.state.tx.us/   Name searching is available from this agency at https://offender.tdcj.texas.gov/OffenderSearch/index.jsp. You may also send an email search request to exec.services@tdcj.state.tx.us.

Corporation, LLC, LP, Fictitious/Assumed Name, Trademarks/Servicemarks

Secretary of State, Corporation Section, www.sos.state.tx.us   Corporate and other TX Sec of State data is available via SOSDirect on the Web; visit www.sos.state.tx.us/corp/sosda/index.shtml. Printing and certifying capabilities available. Web access is available 24 hours daily. There is a $1.00 fee for each record searched. Filing procedures and forms are available from the website. Also, of note (but from another agency) one may search securities dept enforcement actions- www.ssb.state.tx.us/Enforcement/Recent_Enforcement_Actions.php. *Other Options:* The agency makes portions of its database available for purchase. Call 512-463-5589 for more information.

Uniform Commercial Code, Federal Tax Liens

UCC Section, Secretary of State, www.sos.state.tx.us/ucc/index.shtml   UCC and other Texas Secretary of State data is available via SOSDirect on the Web at www.sos.state.tx.us/corp/sosda/index.shtml. UCC records are $1.00 per search, with printing $1.00 per page and certifying $15.00. XML certified search report per debtor is $3.00. Note general information and forms can also be found at the website. *Other Options:* This agency offers the database for sale or as an upload with daily updates. See www.sos.state.tx.us/ucc/formfees.shtml or contact the Information Services Dept at 512-463-5609 for further details.

Sales Tax Registrations

Comptroller of Public Accounts, Sales Tax Permits,   http://comptroller.texas.gov/taxinfo/sales/   This office provides a taxable entity search at https://mycpa.cpa.state.tx.us/coa/Index.html. There is no fee. Send email requests to open.records@cpa.state.tx.us. *Other Options:* Sales tax registration lists are available to download as ftp files.

Birth Certificates

Department of State Health Svcs, Bureau of Vital Statistics,   www.dshs.state.tx.us/vs/birth-cert.shtm   Records may be ordered online at https://txapps.texas.gov/tolapp/ovra/index.htm. *Other Options:* Birth Indexes from 1926-1995 are available on CD-Rom and microfiche.

Death Records

Department of State Health Svcs, Bureau of Vital Statistics,   www.dshs.state.tx.us/vs/death-cert.shtm   Records may be ordered online at https://txapps.texas.gov/tolapp/ovra/index.htm.   Death   records   from   1964   thru   1998   may   be   viewed   at http://vitals.rootsweb.ancestry.com/tx/death/search.cgi. *Other Options:* Death indices from 1964-1998 are available on CD-Rom and microfiche.

Marriage Certificates

Department of State Health Svcs, Bureau of Vital Statistics,   www.dshs.state.tx.us/vs/default.shtm   Records may be ordered online at https://txapps.texas.gov/tolapp/ovra/index.htm.   The   department   provides   marriage   data   commercially   on   CD-Rom   at www.dshs.state.tx.us/vs/marriagedivorce/mindex.shtm, or you may download each year of the marriage index for free, from 1966 to 2008. Also, marriage records for 1966 to 20012 are available through a private company website at www.genlookups.com/texas_marriages/.

Divorce Records

Department of State Health Svcs, Bureau of Vital Statistics,   www.dshs.state.tx.us/vs/marriagedivorce/default.shtm   Records may be ordered online at www.dshs.state.tx.us/vs/default.shtm.   The   department   provides   divorce   data   commercially   on   CD-Rom   at www.dshs.state.tx.us/vs/marriagedivorce/dindex.shtm, or you may download each year of the divorce index for free, from 1968 to 2008. Also, a private company website at www.genlookups.com/texas_divorces/ offers records from 1968 to 2008.

Workers' Compensation Records

Texas Department of Insurance - Worker's Comp, 7551 Metro Center Dr, #100,   www.tdi.texas.gov/wc/indexwc.html   The website gives administrative decisions for cases back to 1991and also permits searching for employers with coverage. The company look-up is at https://apps.tdi.state.tx.us/pcci/pcci_search.jsp or at www.tdi.texas.gov/wc/employer/coverage.html. Also, the agency provides a list of Disiplinary orders posted for 2015 at https://wwwapps.tdi.state.tx.us/inter/asproot/commish/da/dwcclips2015.asp.

Driver Records

Department of Public Safety, License and Records Service,   www.dps.texas.gov/DriverLicense/   Status records and Types 1 ($4.50), 2 ($6.50), 2A ($10.00), 3 ($7.50), and Type 3A ($12.00) can be obtained online at www.dps.texas.gov for the price mentioned. Both batch and interactive modes are available. Call 512-424-5967 to receive a copy of the license agreement. An online service is also offered to eligible license holders (perosn of record). *Other Options:* Bulk data is available in electronic format for approved requesters. Weekly updates are available. The file does not include driver history data.

Vehicle Ownership & Registration

TX Department of Motor Vehicles, Titles and Registration,   www.txdmv.gov   The Technology Support Branch offers a web inquiry system for immediate VIN and plate look ups. A $200 deposit is required, there is a $23.00 charge per month and $.12 fee per inquiry. Searching by name or owner is not permitted. For more information, contact Technology Support. Also, the TxDMV provides access to various databases for use by the public to search for Motor Carrier records, such as registration, complaints, safety, and DPS records. See http://txdmv.gov/open-records. Special use systems include TexasSure is a vehicle insurance verification system, Weekly Dealer Supplemental Files, and eTag (Buyer's Tag) files. *Other Options:* The TxDMV Technology Support Branch offers CD and FTP retrieval of VIN and plate numbers (but not by name) to eligible organizations under signed contract. Fees are based on the cost of a "computer run" and on a small fee per record.

Crash Reports

Texas Department of Transportation, Crash Data and Analysis,   www.txdot.gov/inside-txdot/division/traffic/law-enforcement/crash-reports.html   The Crash Report Online Purchase System is designed for users to purchase a copy of the Texas Peace Officer's Crash Report (CR-3) filed with TxDOT. See https://cris.dot.state.tx.us/public/Purchase/. There is no fee to verify the existence of a record. The same fees ($6.00 uncertified or $8.00 certified) are charged to download the report. Credit cards are accepted. While not associated with this agency, quite a number of city and town police departments are hooked up with a vendor who supplies online ordering. See www.buycrash.com.

Vessel Ownership & Registration

Parks & Wildlife Dept, http://tpwd.texas.gov/fishboat/boat/owner/ Online search of current ownership information is offered at https://apps.tpwd.state.tx.us/tora/jump.jsf. Requester must certify that the Texas Parks Wildlife vessel/boat and/or outboard motor record information obtained will be used for lawful purposes. This inquiry provides the current owner/lienholder name(s), address(es), vessel/boat, and/or outboard motor description. This data is updated daily. *Other Options:* Records are released in bulk format; however, requesters are screened for lawful purpose. The agency requires a copy of any item mailed or distributed as a result of purchase. Media includes tape, labels, and printed lists.

Campaign Finance, PACs, Lobbyists

Texas Ethics Commission, P. O. Box 12070, https://www.ethics.state.tx.us/ Filing information is offered for candidates, lobbyists, PACs, political parties at home page https://www.ethics.state.tx.us/. Delinquent filer lists are at hhttps://www.ethics.state.tx.us/dfs/delinquent/. Search campaign finance reports and lobby reports at https://www.ethics.state.tx.us/main/search.htm.

GED Certificates

Texas Education Agency, Fedrerla and State Eductaion Policy, http://tea.texas.gov/TxCHSE.html All verifications and certificates purchases are made online at https://tea4avtuna.tea.state.tx.us/Tea.Gedi.Web/Forms/CertificateSearch.aspx. The DOB and File ID are requested. The resulting data may be printed. If the system states "No Records Found", then send email to ged@tea.staate.tx.us.

Occupational Licensing Boards

These licenses are all searchable at https://www.tdlr.texas.gov/LicenseSearch/

Air Condition'g/Refrigeration Contr	Elevator/Escalator	Temporary Common Worker
Auctioneer/Associate	Industrialized Housing	Tow Truck Operator/Company
Barber Student/School/Shop	Manicurist/Manicurist Shop	Vehicle Protection Provider
Boiler Inspector/Installer	Personal Employment Service	Vehicle Storage Facility/Employee
Boxing/Combative Sports Event	Property Tax Consultant	Water Well & Pump Installer
Career Counselor	Service Contract Provider	
Electrician	Staff Leasing	

The Rest:

Academic Alternative Program Providers	www.tcole.texas.gov/academic-alternative-programs
Academy Training Providers	www.tcole.texas.gov/contract-training-providers
Accountant-CPA/Firm	www.tsbpa.state.tx.us/general/database-search.html
Acupuncturist	https://public.tmb.state.tx.us/HCP_Search/searchinput.aspx
Alarm Installer/Firm/Seller/Security Instructor	https://www.dps.texas.gov/rsd/psb/psbSearch/company_search.aspx
Alcoholic Beverage Dist/Mfg/Retailer	www.tabc.state.tx.us/public_inquiry/index.asp
Alcoholic Beverage Permit	www.tabc.state.tx.us/public_inquiry/index.asp
Architect	www.tbae.state.tx.us/PublicInformation/SearchIndividual
Asbestos Consultant/Inspector	www.dshs.texas.gov/asbestos/locate.shtm
Asbestos Contractor/Worker	www.dshs.texas.gov/asbestos/locate.shtm
Asbestos Mgmt Planner/Air Monitor Tech	www.dshs.texas.gov/asbestos/locate.shtm
Athletic Agent	www.sos.state.tx.us/statdoc/index.shtml
Athletic Trainer	www.dshs.texas.gov/at/at_roster.shtm
Attorney	https://www.texasbar.com/AM/template.cfm?section=Public_Home
Audiologist/Assistant	https://vo.ras.dshs.state.tx.us/datamart/selSearchTypeTXRAS.do
Automobile Club	www.sos.state.tx.us/statdoc/index.shtml
Bank Agency, Foreign	www.dob.texas.gov/
Bank, State Chartered	www.dob.texas.gov/
Business Opportunity Offering	www.sos.state.tx.us/statdoc/index.shtml
Chemical Dependency Counselor	www.dshs.texas.gov/lcdc/lcdc_search.shtm
Child Care Facility/Admin	https://www.dfps.state.tx.us/Child_Care/Search_Texas_Child_Care/ppFacilitySearchDayCare.asp
Child Care Operation	https://www.dfps.state.tx.us/Child_Care/Search_Texas_Child_Care/ppFacilitySearchDayCare.asp
Child Support Agency, Private	www.dob.texas.gov/
Chiropractic Radiologic Technologist	https://www.tbce.state.tx.us/default.html

Chiropractor Disciplinary Action	https://www.tbce.state.tx.us/default.html
Chiropractor/Facility	https://www.tbce.state.tx.us/default.html
Code Enforcement Officer	www.dshs.texas.gov/op/op_roster.shtm
Contact Lens Dispenser	www.dshs.texas.gov/contactlens/cl_roster.shtm
Cosmetologist/Shop/Salon/Schools	https://www.license.state.tx.us/LicenseSearch/LicenseSearch.asp
Counselor, Professional/Supervisor	www.dshs.texas.gov/counselor/lpc_rosters.shtm
Courier Company	www.txdps.state.tx.us/RSD/PSB/Reports/searchOptions.htm
Court Reporting Firm	www.txcourts.gov/jbcc/court-reporters-certification/list-of-csrs-crfs.aspx
Court Reporting Schools	www.txcourts.gov/jbcc/court-reporters-certification/court-reporting-schools.aspx
Court/Shorthand Reporter	www.txcourts.gov/jbcc/court-reporters-certification/list-of-csrs-crfs.aspx
Credit Service Organization	www.sos.state.tx.us/statdoc/index.shtml
Crematory/Cemetery	https://vo.licensing.hpc.texas.gov/datamart/mainMenu.doCurrency Exchange
	www.dob.texas.gov/
Day Care Center/Residential	https://www.dfps.state.tx.us/Child_Care/Search_Texas_Child_Care/ppFacilitySearchDayCare.asp
Deaf Service Provider	www.dars.state.tx.us/dhhs/list.shtml
Dental Assistant/Hygienist/Laboratory	http://ls.tsbde.texas.gov/index.php
Dentist	http://ls.tsbde.texas.gov/index.php
Dietitian	https://vo.ras.dshs.state.tx.us/datamart/selSearchTypeTXRAS.do
Engineer/Firm	http://engineers.texas.gov/downloads.htm
Family Home Day Care	https://www.dfps.state.tx.us/Child_Care/Search_Texas_Child_Care/ppFacilitySearchDayCare.asp
Fire Alarm System Contractor	www.tdi.texas.gov/fire/fmli.html
Fire Extinguisher Contractor	www.tdi.texas.gov/fire/fmli.html
Fire Inspector/Investigator	www.tcfp.texas.gov/certification/certification_verification.asp
Fire Protection Sprinkler Contr	www.tdi.texas.gov/fire/fmli.html
Fire Suppression Specialist	www.tcfp.texas.gov/certification/certification_verification.asp
Firearm Instructor	www.txdps.state.tx.us/RSD/PSB/Reports/searchOptions.htm
Firefighter	www.tcfp.texas.gov/certification/certification_verification.asp
Fireworks Display	www.tdi.texas.gov/fire/fmli.html
Funeral Director/Embalmer/Related	https://vo.licensing.hpc.texas.gov/datamart/mainMenu.do
Funeral Prepaid Permit Holder	www.dob.texas.gov/
Guard Dog Company	www.txdps.state.tx.us/RSD/PSB/Reports/searchOptions.htm
Health Spa	www.sos.state.tx.us/statdoc/index.shtml
Hearing Instrument Dispenser/Fitter	https://vo.ras.dshs.state.tx.us/datamart/selSearchTypeTXRAS.do
Home Inspector	www.trec.state.tx.us/newsandpublic/licenseeLookup/
Incident/Complaint Summaries	http://dshs.texas.gov/radiation/incidents.aspx
Insurance Adjuster	https://txapps.texas.gov/NASApp/tdi/TdiARManager
Insurance Agency/Agent/Company	https://txapps.texas.gov/NASApp/tdi/TdiARManager
Interior Designer	www.tbae.state.tx.us/PublicInformation/SearchIndividual
Investment Advisor	https://www.ssb.texas.gov/securities-professionals/certificate-search
Irrigator/Installer	www2.tceq.texas.gov/lic_dpa/index.cfm
Landscape Architect	www.tbae.state.tx.us/PublicInformation/SearchIndividual
Lead Abatement Project Designer	www.dshs.texas.gov/elp/locate.shtm
Lead Abatement Worker/Supervisor	www.dshs.texas.gov/elp/locate.shtm
Lead Firm	www.dshs.texas.gov/elp/locate.shtm
Lead Risk Assessor/Inspector	www.dshs.texas.gov/elp/locate.shtm
Lead Training Program Provider	www.dshs.texas.gov/elp/locate.shtm
Loan Officer	www.sml.texas.gov:8080/licenseeDownload/
Lobbyist	https://www.ethics.state.tx.us/main/search.htm
Locksmith/School	www.txdps.state.tx.us/RSD/PSB/Reports/searchOptions.htm
Marriage & Family Therapist	www.dshs.texas.gov/mft/mft_search.shtm
Massage Therapist	www.dshs.texas.gov/massage/mt_rosters.shtm
Massage Therapy School/Instructor/Entity	www.dshs.texas.gov/massage/mt_rosters.shtm
Medical Physicist	www.dshs.texas.gov/mp/default.shtm
Medical Specialty (Doctor)	https://public.tmb.state.tx.us/HCP_Search/searchinput.aspx
Medication Aide	www.dads.state.tx.us/providers/NF/credentialing/sanctions/index.cfm

Money Service Business	www.dob.texas.gov/
Mortgage Banker/Broker	www.sml.texas.gov:8080/licenseeDownload/
Notary Public	https://direct.sos.state.tx.us/notaries/NotarySearch.asp
Nurse/Advanced Practice	www.bon.state.tx.us/licensure_verification.asp
Nurse/RN/Vocational	www.bon.state.tx.us/licensure_verification.asp
Nurses Aide	www.dads.state.tx.us/providers/NF/credentialing/sanctions/index.cfm
Nursing Home Administrator/Facility	www.dads.state.tx.us/providers/NF/credentialing/sanctions/index.cfm
Occupational Therapist/Assistant	www.ptot.texas.gov/page/look-up-a-license
Occupation'l/Physical Therapy Facility	www.ptot.texas.gov/page/look-up-a-license
Optician	www.dshs.texas.gov/optician/opt_roster.shtm
Optometrist	www.tob.state.tx.us/varifyinfo.htm
Optometrist Disciplinary Action	www.tob.state.tx.us/varifyinfo.htm
Orthotics & Prosthetics Facility	www.dshs.texas.gov/op/op_roster.shtm
Orthotist/Prosthetist	www.dshs.texas.gov/op/op_roster.shtm
Pawnshop/Employee Licensing Actions	http://occc.texas.gov/sites/default/files/uploads/licensing/pawn_admin_rept_16.pdf
Perfusionist	www.dshs.texas.gov/perfusionist/default.shtm
Perpetual Care Cemetery	www.dob.texas.gov/
Pharmacist/Intern	www.pharmacy.texas.gov/dbsearch/default.asp
Pharmacy/Technician	www.pharmacy.texas.gov/dbsearch/default.asp
Physical Therapist/Assistant	www.ptot.texas.gov/page/look-up-a-license
Physician/Medical Doctor/Assistant	https://public.tmb.state.tx.us/HCP_Search/searchinput.aspx
Plumber Master/Journeyman/Inspector	https://vo.licensing.hpc.texas.gov/datamart/mainMenu.do
Podiatrist	www.foot.state.tx.us/verifications.htm
Political Action Committee List	https://www.ethics.state.tx.us/dfs/paclists.htm
Political Contributor	https://www.ethics.state.tx.us/main/search.htm
Polygraph Examiner/School	www.tdlr.texas.gov/LicenseSearch/
Private Business Letter of Authority	www.txdps.state.tx.us/RSD/PSB/Reports/searchOptions.htm
Private Investigator	www.txdps.state.tx.us/RSD/PSB/Reports/searchOptions.htm
Professional Engineers Disciplinary Actions	http://engineers.texas.gov/disciplinary.htm
Psychologist, Provisional	https://vo.licensing.hpc.texas.gov/datamart/mainMenu.do
Psychologist/Associate/Related	https://vo.licensing.hpc.texas.gov/datamart/mainMenu.do
Public Safety Org, Promoter Solicitat'n	www.sos.state.tx.us/statdoc/index.shtml
Radiology Technician	https://public.tmb.state.tx.us/HCP_Search/SearchNotice.aspx
Real Estate Agent/Broker/Sales/Inspector	www.trec.state.tx.us/newsandpublic/licenseeLookup/
Real Estate Appraiser	https://www.talcb.texas.gov/apps/license-holder-search/
Representative Office-Foreign Bank	www.dob.texas.gov/
Respiratory Care Practitioner	www.dshs.texas.gov/respiratory/default.shtm
Sanitarian	https://vo.ras.dshs.state.tx.us/datamart/selSearchTypeTXRAS.do
Savings & Loan Association	www.sml.texas.gov:8080/licenseeDownload/
Savings Bank	www.sml.texas.gov:8080/licenseeDownload/
School Psychology Specialist	https://vo.licensing.hpc.texas.gov/datamart/mainMenu.do
Securities Agent/Seller	https://www.ssb.texas.gov/securities-professionals/securities-search
Securities Broker/Dealer	https://www.ssb.texas.gov/securities-professionals/certificate-search
Security Agency, Private	www.txdps.state.tx.us/RSD/PSB/Reports/searchOptions.htm
Security Agent/Service/Seller	www.txdps.state.tx.us/RSD/PSB/Reports/searchOptions.htm
Social Worker	www.dshs.texas.gov/socialwork/sw_rosters.shtm
Speech-Language Pathologist/Assistant	https://vo.ras.dshs.state.tx.us/datamart/selSearchTypeTXRAS.do
STAP Vendor	https://www.staptexas.org/Login/vendorsearchrpt.aspx
Surveyor, Land	http://txls.texas.gov/education/
Surveyor, State Land/Out-of-Texas	http://txls.texas.gov/education/
Tax Appraisal Professional	https://www.license.state.tx.us/LicenseSearch/LicenseSearch.asp
Teacher	https://secure.sbec.state.tx.us/SBECONLINE/virtcert.asp
Telephone Solicitation	www.sos.state.tx.us/statdoc/index.shtml
Training Providers	www.tcole.texas.gov/contract-training-providers
Transportation Service Provider	https://www.license.state.tx.us/LicenseSearch/LicenseSearch.asp

Trust Company .... www.dob.texas.gov/
Veterans Organization Solicitation .... www.sos.state.tx.us/statdoc/index.shtml
Veterinarian .... www.veterinary.texas.gov/Search/
Wig Specialist .... https://www.license.state.tx.us/LicenseSearch/LicenseSearch.asp

State and Local Courts

About Texas Courts: In general, Texas **District Courts** have general civil jurisdiction and exclusive felony jurisdiction, along with typical variations such as contested probate and divorce. There are 359 Districts fully within one county and 98 Districts contain more than one county. Plus, there can be multiple Districts and multiple District Courts in one courthouse. But the record keeping is organized by county and there is only one searchable database per courthouse. Therefore the profiles of the District Courts are herein organized by county.

The **County Court** structure consists of two forms of courts - **Constitutional** and **Statutory** (commonly called **At Law**). The Constitutional upper civil claim limit is $10,000. These courts are generally found in small populated counties and the judge is not required to be a licensed attorney. The At Law upper limit is $200,000, with some jurisdictions are higher. County Courts have original jurisdiction for misdemeanors with fines greater than $500 or jail sentences. Either the District Court or County Court can handle **evictions.** In approx. 69 counties, one individual serves as both the District Clerk and County Clerk.

The two **local courts** are the **Justice Courts** and **Municipal Courts**. Justice Courts handle small claims and civil actions of not more than $10,000 and eviction cases. They can also handle traffic cases outside a municipality's territorial limits plus Class C Misdemeanor cases - where the fine does not exceed $500. Municipal courts handle limited civil matters, municipal ordinance cases, traffic cases, and also Class C Misdemeanor cases - where the fine does not exceed $500.

Probate is handled in **Probate Court** in the ten largest counties and in the County Court elsewhere. The County Clerk is responsible for these records in every county.

A PDF file of the addresses and phone numbers of all the **Municipal Courts** is found on the OCA web page. However, this list is in *City Order* and does not present the county where located.
The web page for the Judicial Branch is www.txcourts.gov.

Appellate Courts: The Supreme Court has the final appellate jurisdiction in civil cases and juvenile cases. The Court of Criminal Appeals has the final appellate jurisdiction in criminal cases. The 14 Courts of Appeals hear intermediate appeals from trial courts with their respective districts.

Case records of the Supreme Court as well as the Appellate courts can be searched at www.txcourts.gov/supreme. The opinions from the Court of Criminal Appeals are found at www.txcourts.gov/cca.aspx.

Online Court Access

There is no statewide portal of case records. However many counties offer online access to court docket information. At least 195 individual local courts provide online access to civil records and at least 200 to criminal records.

The majority of the online courts use the iDocket's online system at http://idocket.com/homepage2.htm. There is one free name search permitted a day, otherwise a subscription required. The Table below indicates the counties, types of court, records, and data throughput. many courts also provide Fa,ily Law and Probate searches as well.

iDocket Table: (Cty = County Court: Dist = District Court)

County & Court	Misd.	Felony	Civil	County & Court	Misd.	Felony	Civil
Angelina - Cty	12/31/1983	N/A	11/30/1996	Briscoe - Cty	N/A	N/A	3/1/2001
Aransas - Cty	1/1/1992	N/A	1/1/1995	Briscoe - Dist	N/A	3/1/2001	3/1/2001
Aransas - Dist	N/A	1/1/1960	1/1/2001	Brown - Cty	1/1/1987	N/A	1/1/1987
Bandera - Cty	1/1/1992	N/A	1/1/1994	Calhoun - Cty	1/1/1992	N/A	1/1/2006
Bandera - Dist	N/A	12/31/1990	12/31/1990	Calhoun - Dist	N/A	1/1/1999	1/1/1998
Bee - Dist	N/A	12/31/1994	12/31/1987	Callahan - Dist	N/A	12/31/2001	12/31/2001
Bell - Cty	1/1/1986	N/A	N/A	Cameron - Cty	4/1/1984	N/A	12/1/1993
Bell - Dist	N/A	1/1/1987	N/A	Cameron - Dist	N/A	12/31/1988	12/31/1988
Bexar - Dist	N/A	1/1/1980	1/1/1980	Chambers - Cty	1/1/1990	N/A	1/1/1987
Brazoria - Cty	1/1/1986	N/A	1/1/1986	Chambers - Dist	N/A	12/31/1870	1/1/1900
Brazoria - Dist	N/A	6/1/1987	6/1/1987	Cherokee - Dist	N/A	1/1/1992	1/1/1992

County-& Court	Misd.	Felony	Civil	County-& Court	Misd.	Felony	Civil
Clay - Cty	3/1/2003	N/A	1/1/2007	McLennan - Dist	N/A	1/1/1981	1/1/1955
Coleman - Cty	4/1/2011	N/A	4/1/2011	Montgomery - Cty	12/31/1989	N/A	N/A
Collin - Cty	1/1/1988	N/A	1/1/1988	Motley - Cty	5/1/2008	5/1/2008	5/1/2004
Collin - Dist	N/A	1/1/1988	1/1/1986	Motley - Dist	5/1/2008	N/A	N/A
Coryell - Cty	1/1/1994	N/A	1/1/1994	Nacogdoches- Cty	12/31/1986	N/A	12/31/1986
Dallam - Cty	N/A	N/A	N/A	Nacogdoches Dist	N/A	12/31/1986	12/31/1986
Dallam - Dist	N/A	N/A	N/A	Navarro - Dist	N/A	12/31/1990	12/31/1990
Dallas - Cty	N/A	N/A	1/1/1963	Navarro - Cty	N/A	N/A	N/A
Dallas - Dist	N/A	N/A	N/A	Ochiltree - Cty	1/1/1983	N/A	1/1/1992
Duval - Dist	N/A	1/1/2015	1/1/2015	Ochiltree - Dist	N/A	1/1/2002	1/1/1948
Eastland - Cty	5/1/1987	N/A	N/A	Oldham - Cty	1/1/1993	N/A	3/1/1998
Ector - Dist	N/A	12/31/1994	N/A	Oldham - Dist	N/A	1/1/1992	3/1/1994
El Paso - Cty	N/A	N/A	N/A	Orange - Cty	01/01/1897	N/A	3/1/1982
Floyd - Cty	1/1/2003	N/A	1/1/2010	Parmer - Dist	N/A	12/31/1995	12/31/1995
Floyd - Dist	N/A	10/1/2005	10/1/2005	Polk - Cty	1/1/1990	N/A	1/1/1997
Freestone - Cty	12/31/2000	N/A	12/31/2000	Polk - Dist	N/A	1/1/2016	1/1/2016
Galveston - Cty	1/1/1984	N/A	1/1/1984	Potter - Cty	12/31/1990	N/A	9/1/1987
Galveston - Dist	N/A	09/00/2012	7/1/2010	Potter - Dist	N/A	12/31/1988	12/31/1988
Goliad - Cty	1/1/1997	N/A	1/1/1997	Presidio - Cty	2/1/2005	N/A	1/1/2010
Goliad - Dist	N/A	1/1/1997	1/1/1997	Presidio - Dist	N/A	1/1/2011	1/1/2011
Harris - Cty	N/A	N/A	12/31/1997	San Patricio - Cty	1/1/1997	N/A	1/1/1997
Hays - Cty	12/31/1987	N/A	12/31/1987	San Patricio - Dist	N/A	1/1/1994	11/1/1992
Hays - Dist	N/A	12/31/1986	12/31/1986	Schleicher - Cty	2/1/1979	N/A	N/A
Hidalgo - Cty	12/31/1991	N/A	12/31/1986	Schleicher - Dist	N/A	1/1/1996	1/1/1998
Hidalgo - Dist	N/A	12/31/1986	12/31/1986	Starr - Cty	12/31/1996	N/A	N/A
Hill - Dist	12/31/1990	12/31/1990	12/31/1990	Starr - Dist	N/A	1/1/2003	1/1/2003
Hopkins - Cty	1/1/1985	N/A	5/1/1989	Titus - Dist	N/A	12/1/1965	12/1/1955
Hopkins - Dist	N/A	5/1/1967	5/1/1921	Travis - Dist	N/A	11/1/2004	12/1/2005
Houston - Cty	1/1/1999	N/A	1/1/1999	Trinity - Cty	1/1/1990	1/1/1990	N/A
Houston - Dist	N/A	1/1/1997	1/1/1996	Tyler - Cty	12/31/1990	N/A	12/31/1990
Hudspeth - Cty	1/1/2005	N/A	1/1/2005	Upton - Cty	N/A	N/A	N/A
Hudspeth - Dist	N/A	1/1/2005	1/1/2005	Upton - Dist	N/A	N/A	N/A
Hunt - Cty	1/1/1987	1/1/2011	1/1/1986	Val Verde - Dist	N/A	12/31/1993	12/31/1989
Jack - Cty	1/1/1999	N/A	1/1/2000	Victoria - Cty	12/31/1989	N/A	12/31/1991
Jack - Dist	N/A	1/1/1958	1/1/1995	Victoria - Dist	N/A	12/31/1993	12/31/1993
Jefferson - Dist	N/A	N/A	1/1/1987	Washington - Cty	12/31/1985	N/A	12/31/1985
Jim Wells - Dist	N/A	5/5/1982	N/A	Washington - Dist	N/A	12/30/1988	12/30/1988
Johnson - Cty	12/31/1988	N/A	12/31/1985	Webb - Cty	12/31/1989	N/A	12/31/1989
Johnson - Dist	N/A	11/1/1989	11/1/1989	Webb - Dist	N/A	12/31/1988	12/31/1988
Kleberg - Cty	1/1/1983	N/A	1/1/1997	Wharton - Cty	1/1/1991	N/A	1/1/1991
Kleberg - Dist	1/1/2002	N/A	1/1/2002	Wharton - Dist	N/A	1/1/1990	1/1/1990
Liberty - Cty	N/A	N/A	N/A	Willacy - Cty	1/1/1990	N/A	1/1/2010
Liberty - Dist	N/A	10/1/1997	10/1/1997	Willacy - Dist	N/A	1/1/1989	1/1/1990
Maverick - Cty	1/1/1999	N/A	1/1/2006	Young - Cty	1/1/1992	N/A	1/1/1992
Maverick - Dist	N/A	8/1/1995	11/1/1994	Young - Dist	N/A	3/1/1998	3/1/1998
				Zapata - Cty	N/A	N/A	N/A

County Sites Not on iDocket: (To avoid redundancy, iDocket courts are not displayed below.)

Angelina County

District Court   www.angelinacounty.net/departments/dc

Civil: A free search of the docket is at http://public.angelinacounty.net/default.aspx. Records go back to 1996. If you are not sure of the spelling of the name, enter at least 3 initials and an asterisk. The site includes all civil, family and probate records in the county, including the County Court and JP. *Criminal:* Same. The site includes all criminal, jail and law enforcement records in the county, including the County Court and JP.

County Court at Law   www.angelinacounty.net/departments/cc

Civil: A free search of the docket is at http://public.angelinacounty.net/default.aspx. Records go back to 1996. If you are not sure of the spelling of the name, enter at least 3 initials and an asterisk. The site includes all civil, family and probate records in the county, including the County Court and JP. *Criminal:* Same. The site includes all criminal, jail and law enforcement records in the county, including the County Court and JP.

Bell County
District Court   www.bellcountytx.com/county_government/district_courts/index.php
Civil: Access the current civil docket data at www.bellcountytx.com/county_government/district_courts/27th_district_court/court_dockets.php. The data is in PDF format.
County Court   www.bellcountytx.com/county_government/county_courts/index.php
Civil: Historical docket information is not available, but current or recent dockets are shown at www.co.bell.tx.us/Countycoor/CSTMR/crt080c.pdf.

Bexar County
District Court - Records Division   http://gov.bexar.org/dc/
Civil: Access to the remote online system back to 1982 requires $100 setup fee, plus a $25 monthly fee, plus inquiry fees. Call BCIT for info at 210-335-0202. Also, search civil litigants free at https://apps.bexar.org/dklitsearch/search.aspx.   *Criminal:* A free search is offered at http://gov.bexar.org/dc/dcrecords.html. Data is in Excel sheet, updated first Fri of month.

Brazoria County
District Court   http://brazoriacountytx.gov/departments/district-clerk
Civil: Access civil record docket free at their Judicial Record Search site at www.brazoria-county.com/dclerk/.   *Criminal:* Same

Brazos County
District Court   www.brazoscountytx.gov/index.aspx?nid=135
Civil: Dockets available at http://justiceweb.co.brazos.tx.us/. The online site if very uninformative on the thruput dates and formatting issues (such as on or before dates and if wildcards are used. Proceed with caution.   *Criminal:* same
County Court   www.brazoscountytx.gov/index.aspx?nid=126
Civil: Dockets available at http://justiceweb.co.brazos.tx.us/. The online site if very uninformative on the thruput dates and formatting issues (such as on or before dates and if wildcards are used. Proceed with caution.   *Criminal:* same

Brooks County
District Court - 79th District   www.co.brooks.tx.us/default.aspx?Brooks_County/District.Clerk
Civil: Search civil case index free at http://eservices.brooks-county.com/eservices/home.page.2.   *Criminal:* same.
County Court   www.co.brooks.tx.us/default.aspx?Brooks_County/County.Clerk
Civil: Search civil case index free at http://eservices.brooks-county.com/eservices/home.page.2.   *Criminal:* same.

Burnet County
District Court   www.burnetcountytexas.org/default.aspx?name=dclerk.home
Civil: Search civil, family and probate cases at http://txburnetodyprod.tylerhost.net/PublicAccess/Login.aspx. Use visitor as both user ID and password. Current dockets are shown at www.dcourttexas.org/ (for the 33rd and 424th District Court).   *Criminal:* Search criminal cases free at http://txburnetodyprod.tylerhost.net/PublicAccess/Login.aspx. Use visitor as both user ID and password. The site also offers Law Enforcement records which includes a wide variety of incident types. The site also offers Law Enforcement records which includes a variety of incident types.
County Court   www.burnetcountytexas.org/default.aspx?name=cclerk.home
Civil: Search civil, family and probate cases at http://txburnetodyprod.tylerhost.net/PublicAccess/Login.aspx. Use visitor as both user ID and password. *Criminal:* same.   The site also offers Law Enforcement records which includes a variety of incident types.

Cameron County
County Court   www.co.cameron.tx.us/judicial_courts/index.php
Civil: Public access to the docket index is at www.co.cameron.tx.us/publicaccess/default.aspx. This includes Civil, Family and Probate.

Chambers County
District Clerk   www.co.chambers.tx.us/default.aspx?name=district.clerk
Civil: Search online after registering free for login and password at www.texasonlinerecords.com/clerk/index?office_id=7.

Collin County
District Clerk   www.collincountytx.gov/district_clerk/Pages/default.aspx
Civil: Name and case look up is at http://cijspub.co.collin.tx.us/ or at https://apps.collincountytx.gov/judicialrecords/case/.   From this site one can also search criminal, probate and family cases, and Justice of the Peace cases. A court calendar is also available. There is also a commercial system. Call Lisa Zoski at 972-548-4503 for subscription info.
County Court At Law   www.collincountytexas.gov/county_court_law/Pages/default.aspx
Civil: Name and case look up is at http://cijspub.co.collin.tx.us or at https://apps.collincountytx.gov/judicialrecords/case/.   From this site one can also search criminal, probate and family cases, and Justice of the Peace cases. A court calendar is also available.

Comal County
County Court at Law   www.co.comal.tx.us/CCL.htm
Civil: Online access county judicial records free at www.co.comal.tx.us/recordsearch.htm. Search by either party name. There are limited identifiers and no images are shown.   *Criminal:* same.
District Court   www.co.comal.tx.us/DC.htm

Civil: Online access county judicial records free at http://public.co.comal.tx.us/default.aspx. Search by either party name.   *Criminal:* Online access county criminal judicial records free at http://public.co.comal.tx.us/default.aspx. Data includes date filed, disposed, offense, warrant status and attorney.

Dallas County

District Court - Criminal   www.dallascounty.org

Search is at www.dallascounty.org/criminalBackgroundSearch/. Criminal index includes DOB. There is no fee unless a record is viewed, but many records can be viewed for free. Court Disposition Codes and Identification codes are displayed at www.dallascounty.org/criminalBackgroundSearch/disp_codes.jsp. There is another active site at www.dallascounty.org/public_access.php. Dallas County Jail look-up is free at www.dallascounty.org/jaillookup.

District Court - Civil   www.dallascounty.org/department/courts/courts_index.php

Search district civil and family case index free at https://courtsportal.dallascounty.org/DALLASPRODx. Cases go back to early 1960s.

County Court at Law - Civil   www.dallascounty.org/department/courts/county_court_at_law.php

Search civil judgment index at https://courtsportal.dallascounty.org/DALLASPROD. One may also search for probate and Family District Case information.

County Court - Misdemeanor   www.dallascounty.org

www.dallascounty.org/criminalBackgroundSearch/. Criminal index includes DOB. There is no fee unless a record is viewed but most records viewed for free. Court Disposition Codes and Identification codes are displayed at www.dallascounty.org/criminalBackgroundSearch/disp_codes.jsp. There is another active site at www.dallascounty.org/public_access.php. Email questions to DCRecordscriminal@dallascounty.org. Dallas County Jail look-up is free at www.dallascounty.org/jaillookup/.

Denton County

District Court   http://dentoncounty.com/Departments/District-Courts.aspx

Civil: Search civil and family records free at http://justice1.dentoncounty.com/PublicAccess/default.aspx. Search by name or cause number. For information about bulk data visit http://dentoncounty.com/Departments/Judicial-Record-Search/Records.aspx.   *Criminal:* Criminal searches are free at http://justice1.dentoncounty.com/PublicAccess/default.aspx. Records go back to 1990 forward. Access also includes sheriff bond and jail records.

County Court   http://dentoncounty.com/Departments/County-Courts.aspx

Civil: Search civil and probate records free at http://justice1.dentoncounty.com/PublicAccess/default.aspx. Search by name or cause number. For information about bulk data visit http://dentoncounty.com/Departments/Judicial-Record-Search/Records.aspx.   *Criminal:* Online access county criminal records free at http://justice.dentoncounty.com/CrimSearch/crimfrmd.htm.   Jail, bond, and parole records are also available at http://justice.dentoncounty.com. For information about bulk data visit http://dentoncounty.com/Departments/Judicial-Record-Search/Records.aspx. Search for registered sex offenders by ZIP Code at http://sheriff.dentoncounty.com/sex_offenders/default.htm.

El Paso County

District Court   www.epcounty.com/districtclerk/

Civil: Online access to civil case is free at http://casesearch.epcounty.com/PublicAccess/default.aspx. A Court Data Download is also offered. Family and Probate case records are also searchable.   *Criminal:* same.

County Court   www.epcounty.com/

Civil: Online access to civil court records is free at http://casesearch.epcounty.com/PublicAccess/default.aspx. Search includes Family and Probate. A Court Data Download is also offered.

Ellis County

District Courts - 40, 378, 443   www.co.ellis.tx.us/index.aspx?nid=79

Civil: A free name search is at www.lgs-hosted.com/rmtellcck.html. Use CAPS. No thruput dates given, but appears to go back to at least 1993. Includes search of probate records.   *Criminal:* same.

County Courts at Law   www.co.ellis.tx.us

Civil: A free name search is at www.lgs-hosted.com/rmtellcck.html. Use CAPS. No thruput dates given, but appears to go back to at least 1993. Includes search of probate records.   *Criminal:* same.

Erath County

District Court   http://co.erath.tx.us/districtclerk.html

Civil: Access to District Clerk records requires registration, login and password; signup online at www.texasonlinerecords.com/clerk/?office_id=22.   *Criminal:* same

County Court at law   http://co.erath.tx.us/countyclerk.html

Civil: Access to County Court records requires registration, login and password; signup online at www.texasonlinerecords.com/clerk/?office_id=21.   *Criminal:* same

Fannin County

District Court   www.co.fannin.tx.us/default.aspx?Fannin_County/District.Court

Civil: Access to civil, probate and family court dockets at http://txfanninodyprod.tylerhost.net/PublicAccess/default.aspx.   *Criminal:* same.

County Court   www.co.fannin.tx.us/default.aspx?Fannin_County/County.Clerk

Civil: Access to civil, probate and family court dockets at http://txfanninodyprod.tylerhost.net/PublicAccess/default.aspx.   *Criminal:* same.

Fort Bend County
District Court www.fortbendcountytx.gov/index.aspx?page=176
Civil: Search civil, probate and divorce index at http://tylerpaw.co.fort-bend.tx.us/default.aspx. Partial DOBs shown.   *Criminal:* same.
County Court www.fortbendcountytx.gov/index.aspx?page=147
Civil: Search civil, probate and divorce index at http://tylerpaw.co.fort-bend.tx.us/default.aspx. Partial DOBs shown.   *Criminal:* same. Searches records from 1982 forward.

Galveston County
District Court www.galvestoncountytx.gov/dc/Pages/default.aspx
Civil: Online access is at http://public1.co.galveston.tx.us/default.aspx. Generally records go back to 1995. Online access to judge's daily calendars is free at www2.co.galveston.tx.us/District_Clerk/courts.htm. *Criminal:* Online access is at http://public1.co.galveston.tx.us/default.aspx. Generally records go back to 1995. Online access to Judge's daily calendars is free at www2.co.galveston.tx.us/District_Clerk/courts.htm.
County Court www.galvestoncountytx.gov/cc/Pages/default.aspx
Civil: Online access is at http://public1.co.galveston.tx.us/default.aspx. Generally records go back to 1995. *Criminal:* Online access is at http://public1.co.galveston.tx.us/default.aspx. Index search is free. Generally records go back to 1995.

Gillespie County
District Court www.gillespiecounty.org/default.aspx?name=district_clerk
Civil: Online access to the docket index for Civil, Family, and Probate records county wide is at https://odysseypa.tylerhost.net/Gillespie/default.aspx. No indication is given on thruput dates. The site is fairly new, the number of years included in a search is not many. *Criminal:* same.
County Court www.gillespiecounty.org/
Civil: Online access to the docket index for Civil, Family, and Probate records county wide is at https://odysseypa.tylerhost.net/Gillespie/default.aspx. No indication is given on thruput dates. The site is fairly new, the number of years included in a search is not many. *Criminal:* same.

Grayson County
County Court www.co.grayson.tx.us/default.aspx?name=courts.home
Civil: The docket index is searchable at http://24.117.89.66/default.aspx. *Criminal:* same.. Includes traffic.

Gregg County
District Court www.co.gregg.tx.us/district-courts
Civil: Online access to county judicial records is free at http://beta.co.gregg.tx.us/OdysseyPA/default.aspx. Search by name, cause number, status. *Criminal:* same
County Court www.co.gregg.tx.us/county-clerk
Civil: Online access to county judicial records is free at http://beta.co.gregg.tx.us/OdysseyPA/default.aspx. Search by name, cause number, or status. *Criminal:* same

Guadalupe County
District Court www.co.guadalupe.tx.us/d_clerk/dclerk.php
Civil: Access to court records and hearings is available free at http://judicial.co.guadalupe.tx.us/default.aspx. The calendar is searchable from the home page. *Criminal:* Access to court records and hearings is available free at http://judicial.co.guadalupe.tx.us/default.aspx. Search sheriff's jail and bond records also. Dockets go back to 01/1970.
County Court www.co.guadalupe.tx.us/co_clerk/coclerk.php
Civil: Access to court records and hearings is available free at http://judicial.co.guadalupe.tx.us/default.aspx. *Criminal:* same. Also search sheriff's jail and bond records.

Hale County
District Court www.halecounty.org/district_offices/district_clerk.php
Civil: Docket access is free at http://txhaleodyprod.tylerhost.net/PublicAccess/default.aspx. Includes probate. *Criminal:* same. Jail records also available.
County Court www.halecounty.org/hale_co_courts/county_court/index.php
Civil: Docket access is free at http://txhaleodyprod.tylerhost.net/PublicAccess/default.aspx. Includes probate. *Criminal:* same. Jail records also available.

Harris County
District Court - Criminal www.hcdistrictclerk.com/Common/Default.aspx
Online criminal index case lookup is at www.hcdistrictclerk.com/Edocs/Public/Search.aspx?BGCheckTab=1. No county's records, or Justice of the Peace or other Municipalities Class C Misdemeanors are included. Also a separate general docket search is at www.hcdistrictclerk.com/Edocs/Public/Search.aspx?dockettab=1. Qualified subscribers may access records for a fee at http://home.jims.hctx.net/WebServices.aspx.
District Court - Civil Courthouse www.hcdistrictclerk.com/Common/Default.aspx
Civil: First, an online county case lookup service is free at www.cclerk.hctx.net/applications/websearch/Civil.aspx or http://apps.jims.hctx.net/courts/. Online records go back to 10/1989. A docket search is at www.hcdistrictclerk.com/eDocs/Public/Search.aspx. Purchase certified copies of civil orders and judgments. Qualified subscribers may access records for a fee at http://home.jims.hctx.net/WebServices.aspx. Search civil dockets free at http://apps.jims.hctx.net/courts/.

County Civil Court   www.cclerk.hctx.net
Civil: Online access is free at www.cclerk.hctx.net. Registration required to view documents. Watermarked documents can be printed free of charge. System includes civil index search, documents, and county civil settings inquiry and other county clerk functions. For further information, visit the website or call 713-755-6421.

Hays County
District Court   www.co.hays.tx.us/district-courts.aspx
Civil: Search by name, case number or attorney from http://public.co.hays.tx.us/default.aspx. One free name search permitted a day, otherwise subscription required. *Criminal:* same.
County Courts at Law   www.co.hays.tx.us/county-courts-at-law.aspx
Civil: Search the docket index free at http://public.co.hays.tx.us/default.aspx. Search by name or case number. Includes civil, family and probate cases. Index includes DOB, address on docket. *Criminal:* same.

Henderson County
District Court   www.henderson-county.com/departments/courts
Civil: Search the index at http://txhendersonodyprod.tylerhost.net/PublicAccess/default.aspx.   *Criminal:* Search the index at http://txhendersonodyprod.tylerhost.net/PublicAccess/default.aspx. Includes separate search of jail records and bond records.
County Court   www.henderson-county.com/departments/courts
Civil: Search the index at http://txhendersonodyprod.tylerhost.net/PublicAccess/default.aspx.   *Criminal:* same.

Hockley County
District Court   www.co.hockley.tx.us/
Civil: One may search the docket index online at www.texasonlinerecords.com/clerk/?office_id=9. There is no fee, but access requires a password. Search civil or probate by name or case number. Online results do not give identifiers.   *Criminal:* One may search the criminal docket index online at www.texasonlinerecords.com/clerk/?office_id=9. There is no fee, but access requires a password. Online results give DOB.

Hood County
District Court   www.co.hood.tx.us/index.aspx?nid=205
Civil: Online access to the court's dockets is free at http://txhoododyprod.tylerhost.net/PublicAccess/default.aspx.   *Criminal:* same
County Court   http://tx-hoodcounty.civicplus.com/index.aspx?NID=211
Civil: The civil index is found at www.texasonlinerecords.com/clerk/?office_id=24. Records go back to 1995. Search by name and by either plaintiff or defendant..   *Criminal:* Search the criminal index by year at www.texasonlinerecords.com/clerk/?office_id=24.

Hopkins County
County Court   www.hopkinscountytx.org/
Civil: Search county court index free after registering for login and password at www.hopkinscountyonline.net/countyclerk/. *Criminal:* same.

Houston County
County Court at Law   www.co.houston.tx.us/default.aspx?Houston_County/County.Court
Access to Judicial and Jail records for free at http://txhowardodyprod.tylerhost.net/PublicAccess/default.aspx. *Criminal Criminal:* same.

Howard County
District Court   www.co.howard.tx.us/default.aspx?Howard_County/District.Clerk
Civil: Online case access is available at http://txhowardodyprod.tylerhost.net/PublicAccess/default.aspx.   *Criminal:* Online case to Jail Records Only is available at http://txhowardodyprod.tylerhost.net/PublicAccess/default.aspx...

Hutchinson County
District Court   www.co.hutchinson.tx.us/default.aspx?Hutchinson_County/District.Clerk
Civil: Online case access is available for free at https://txhutchinsonodyprod.tylerhost.net/OdysseyPA/Login.aspx. Use Public for both the User ID and Password. The site does not indicate how far back records go. Nor does it tell you the free login! *Criminal:* same.
County Court   www.co.hutchinson.tx.us/default.aspx?Hutchinson_County/County.Clerk
Civil: Online case access is available for free at https://txhutchinsonodyprod.tylerhost.net/OdysseyPA/Login.aspx. Use Public for both the User ID and Password. The site does not indicate how far back records go. Nor does it tell you the free login!   *Criminal:* same

Jefferson County
District Court   www.co.jefferson.tx.us/dclerk/dc_home.htm
Civil: Online access to the civil records at www.co.jefferson.tx.us/dclerk/civil_index/main.htm. Search by year by defendant or plaintiff by year 1985 to present. Index goes back to 1995; images back to 12/1998. There is also a Domestic Index. *Criminal:* Online access to criminal records index is at www.co.jefferson.tx.us/dclerk/criminal_index/main.htm. Search by name by year 1981 to present.
County Court   www.co.jefferson.tx.us/cclerk/clerk.htm
Civil: Search county clerk's civil index free at http://jeffersontxclerk.manatron.com. Index goes back to 1995. Images are no longer available.   *Criminal:* Access to Class A&B and C Misdemeanor that are appealed indexes back to 1982 are free at http://jeffersontxclerk.manatron.com/. Images are no longer available.

Johnson County
District Court   www.johnsoncountytx.org
Search at http://ira.johnsoncountytx.org/. *Criminal:* same.
County Court   www.johnsoncountytx.org
Civil: Search at http://ira.johnsoncountytx.org/. *Criminal:* same.

Kaufman County
District Court   www.kaufmancounty.net/dc.html
Civil: Access court record index for civil and family free at http://12.14.175.53/default.aspx. Online court records do not always show all identifiers. *Criminal:* Access criminal court record index free at http://12.14.175.53/default.aspx. Online court records do not always show complete dispositions.
County Court   www.kaufmancountyclerk.com/
Civil: Access court record index for civil and probate free at http://12.14.175.23/default.aspx or use link from home page. Online court records do not always show all identifiers.   *Criminal:* Access criminal court record index free at http://12.14.175.23/default.aspx or use link from home page. Online court records do not always show complete dispositions.

Kerr County
District Court   www.co.kerr.tx.us/courts/
Civil: Search all court indexes also jail and bond indexes free at http://public.co.kerr.tx.us/CaseManagement/PublicAccess/default.aspx.   *Criminal:* same
County Court at Law   www.co.kerr.tx.us/ccourt/
Civil: Search docket index for all court records free at http://public.co.kerr.tx.us/CaseManagement/PublicAccess/default.aspx. The court also has a subscription product for the complete record. Contact the court for details.   *Criminal:* same.

Lamar County
District Court   www.co.lamar.tx.us/default.aspx?Lamar_County/District.Clerk
Civil: Access to county judicial records is free at www.co.lamar.tx.us/. Search by either party name.   *Criminal:* same. Search by defendant name.

County Court at Law   www.co.lamar.tx.us/default.aspx?Lamar_County/County.Court
Civil: Access to county judicial records is free at www.co.lamar.tx.us. Search by either party name.   *Criminal:* same. Search by defendant name.

Lee County
District Court   www.co.lee.tx.us/default.aspx?Lee_County/District.Clerk
Civil: A free name search is at www.lgs-hosted.com/rmtleecck.html. Use CAPS. No thru put dates given, but appears to go back to at least 1993. *Criminal:* A free name search of index is at www.lgs-hosted.com/rmtleecck.html. Use CAPS. No throughput dates given, but appears to go back to 1988.
County Court   www.co.lee.tx.us/default.aspx?Lee_County/County.Clerk
Civil: A free name search is at www.lgs-hosted.com/rmtleecck.html. Use CAPS. No thruput dates given, but appears to go back to at least 1993. Includes search of probate records.   *Criminal:* same. No throughput dates given, but appears to go back to 1988.

Liberty County
District Court   www.co.liberty.tx.us
Civil: A docket name search is offered at www.texasonlinerecords.com/clerk/?office_id=10. Must register before usage.*Criminal:* same.

Limestone County
County Court   www.co.limestone.tx.us/default.aspx?Limestone_County/County.Clerk
Civil: Online searching is not offered, but a daily list of dockets (back to Jan 2, 2014) is provided at www.co.limestone.tx.us/default.aspx?Limestone_County/CountyCourtDockets.   *Criminal:* same

Lubbock County
District Court   www.co.lubbock.tx.us/department/?fDD=11-0
Civil: A subscription service to records with an annual fee is offered, application is at www.co.lubbock.tx.us/egov/docs/1294749845_585784.pdf. Access includes images except files prior to May 2007. *Criminal:* same
County Courts   www.co.lubbock.tx.us/judiciary/
Civil: The court offers a subscription service to records. The application is found at www.co.lubbock.tx.us/egov/docs/1294749845_585784.pdf. Case file documents are available. *Criminal:* same

Matagorda County
County Court   www.co.matagorda.tx.us
Civil: The current dockets only are online, as a viewable PDF file.   *Criminal:* same

McLennan County
County Court - Clerk's Office   www.co.mclennan.tx.us/166/County-Clerk
Civil: Free access to the docket index is at http://24.173.220.139/McLennancc/start.aspx. Records go back to 2000.   *Criminal:* same

Medina County
District Court   www.medinacountytexas.org/default.aspx?Medina_County/District.Clerk

Civil: A free search site is at http://odysseypa.tylerhost.net/Medina/default.aspx. This includes Civil, Family and Probate. *Criminal:* A free search site of the criminal docket is at http://odysseypa.tylerhost.net/Medina/default.aspx. Some case dockets are displayed back to 1984.

County Court at Law   www.medinacountytexas.org/default.aspx?Medina_County/County.Court

Civil: Access to the civil and probate docket is free at http://odysseypa.tylerhost.net/Medina/default.aspx.   *Criminal:* same.

Midland County

District Court   www.co.midland.tx.us/departments/dc/Pages/default.aspx

Civil: Online access to district clerk database is by subscription. Registration and password required; Fee is $120 per year plus may be extra fees to view and print. Contact the clerk for access instructions. *Criminal:* same

Mitchell County

County Court

Civil: Access to dockets is free at www.edoctecinc.com, data is within 24 hours of being current.   *Criminal:* same

Montgomery County

County Court   www.mctx.org/dept/--county_courts/index.html

Civil: Search the civil docket and probate docket online at http://ccinternet.mctx.org/php/menu/menu-public.php. 14-day daily dockets free at the main website.   *Criminal:* Search the county clerk's misdemeanor records free at http://ccinternet.mctx.org/php/menu/menu-public.php. Online search results also give physical features. Also, 14-day daily dockets free at the main website.

Nueces County

District Court   www.co.nueces.tx.us/districtclerk/

Civil: Online access to civil District & County Court record indices is free www.co.nueces.tx.us/odyssey/PublicAccess/default.aspx. Includes access to Probate and Family records.   *Criminal:* There are two online access systems. The search at www.co.nueces.tx.us/districtclerk/login.asp is free, but does require the users to establish a login with password. There is also a free search at www.co.nueces.tx.us/odyssey/PublicAccess/default.aspx. This site includes traffic.

County Court at Law   www.co.nueces.tx.us/districtclerk/

Civil: Online access to civil District & County Court record indices is free www.co.nueces.tx.us/odyssey/PublicAccess/default.aspx. Includes access to Probate and Family records.   *Criminal:* There are two online access systems. The search at www.co.nueces.tx.us/districtclerk/login.asp is free, but does require the users to establish a login with password. There is also a free search at www.co.nueces.tx.us/odyssey/PublicAccess/default.aspx. This site includes traffic.

Orange County

County Court at Law   www.co.orange.tx.us

Criminal: Search misdemeanor warrants free at www.co.orange.tx.us/County_Courts_At_Law_Warrants.html.

Panola County

District Court   www.co.panola.tx.us/default.aspx?Panola_County/District.Clerk

Civil: Access to civil records is free at http://odysseypa.tylerhost.net/Panola/default.aspx.   *Criminal:* same.

County Court at Law   www.co.panola.tx.us/default.aspx?Panola_County/County.Court

Civil: Online access to the docket index for civil, family, and probate is offered at http://odysseypa.tylerhost.net/Panola/default.aspx.   *Criminal:* same.

Parker County

District Court   www.parkercountytx.com/Index.aspx?NID=182

Civil: Access to court records is free at http://txparkerodyprod.tylerhost.net/PublicAccess/default.aspx. Online civil records go back to 1/2003. Civil results include party names, case type, atty.   *Criminal:* Access to criminal records and sheriff inmates and bonds search is free at http://txparkerodyprod.tylerhost.net/PublicAccess/default.aspx. Online criminal records go back to 7/88. Online results include atty, offense, disposition.

County Court at Law 1   www.parkercountytx.com/index.aspx?nid=167

Civil: Access to court records is free at http://txparkerodyprod.tylerhost.net/PublicAccess/default.aspx. Online civil records go back to 1/2003. Civil results include party names, case type, atty.   *Criminal:* Access to court records is free at http://txparkerodyprod.tylerhost.net/PublicAccess/default.aspx. Online records go back to 1/2004.

County Court   www.co.polk.tx.us/default.aspx?Polk_County/County.Court

Civil: Current dockets can be viewed at www.polkcountytx.net/cas/cgicas103dp.html.

Rains County

District Court   www.co.rains.tx.us

Civil: Civil index at www.co.rains.tx.us/default.aspx?Rains_County/District.Clerk. Records from 1/1/03-3/31/13.   *Criminal:* same.

Randall County

District Courts   http://randallcounty.com/dclerk/default.htm

Civil: Civil and Family Law record index is searchable at http://odysseypa.tylerhost.net/Randall/default.aspx. This is a free search. *Criminal:* Felony record index is searchable at http://odysseypa.tylerhost.net/Randall/default.aspx. This is a free search.

County Court   http://randallcounty.com/cclerk/

Civil: Civil and Probate record index is searchable at http://odysseypa.tylerhost.net/Randall/default.aspx. This is a free search. *Criminal:* same.

Rockwall County
District Court   www.rockwallcountytexas.com/570/District-Court
Civil: Online access is free at https://portal.rockwallcountytexas.com/Portal/Home/Dashboard/29.   *Criminal:* same Search Sheriff records at http://southern.rockwallcountytexas.com/dcn/.
County Court at Law   www.rockwallcountytexas.com/77/County-Court-at-Law
Civil: Online access is same as criminal, see below.   *Criminal:* Online access is free at http://trueauto.rockwallcountytexas.com/judicialsearch/. Search sheriff bond and jail lists too. Online court records only go back 7 years; some dismissals/deferred cases are not online.

Shelby County
District Court   www.co.shelby.tx.us
Civil: Access public court records from www1.odcr.com/. Even though this court is listed as being in Oklahoma, this choice is really for this court in TX. There is no Shelby District Court in OK.   *Criminal:* same
County Court   www.co.shelby.tx.us/default.aspx?Shelby_County/County.Clerk
Civil: Access court index free at http://cc.co.shelby.tx.us/. Note that online may be temporarily unavailable at times.   *Criminal:* same.

Smith County
District Court   www.smith-county.com/Courts/DistrictCourt/Default.aspx
Civil: Access court indexes and sheriff's jail and bond data free at http://judicial.smith-county.com/judsrch.asp. This is a vendor site, Access current docket information - by the District Court - at www.smith-county.com/Courts/DistrictCourt/Default.aspx.   *Criminal:* Historical court record data is found at http://judicial.smith-county.com/judsrch.asp. This is a vendor site.
County Court at Law 1, 2, 3   www.smith-county.com/Courts/CountyCourt/Default.aspx
Civil: Access court and probate indexes and sheriff's jail and bond data free at http://judicial.smith-county.com/judsrch.asp.   *Criminal:* same

Swisher County
District Court   www.swisherclerk.com/
Civil: Only daily docket and monthly calendar for 242nd Court are online at www.242ndcourt.com/ and for the 64th District at www.halecountysheriff.org/64th/index.jsp. Note the 64th District is in Hale and Swisher counties.   *Criminal:* same
County Court at Law   www.swisherclerk.com/
Civil: Only daily docket and monthly calendar for 242nd Court are online at www.242ndcourt.com/ and for the 64th District at www.halecountysheriff.org/64th/index.jsp. Note the 64th District is in Hale and Swisher counties.   *Criminal:* same

Tarrant County
District Court   http://access.tarrantcounty.com/en/courts.html
Civil: Access to the remote online system requires $50 setup fee and $35.00 monthly with add'l month prepaid; for 1 to 5 users; fees increase with more users. Call 817-884-1345 for info and signup. Access a free search site at https://odyssey.tarrantcounty.com/PublicAccess/default.aspx.   *Criminal:* Access to the remote online system requires $50 setup fee and $35.00 monthly with add'l month prepaid; for 1 to 5 users; fees increase with more users. Call 817-884-1345 for info and signup. For felony only (not misdemeanor).
County Court - Criminal   http://access.tarrantcounty.com/en/courts.html
Criminal: Access a free search site at https://odyssey.tarrantcounty.com/PublicAccess/default.aspx.

Taylor County
District Court   www.taylorcountytexas.org/131/District-Clerk
Civil: Search Taylor County Case/Court records free online at http://publicaccess.taylorcountytexas.org/PublicAccess/default.aspx.   *Criminal:* same
County Court at Law - One & Two   www.taylorcountytexas.org/205/CCL1
Civil: Search Taylor County Case/Court records free online at http://publicaccess.taylorcountytexas.org/PublicAccess/default.aspx.   *Criminal:* same

Titus County
County Court   www.co.titus.tx.us/
Civil: Access to court records from www.tituscountyonline.net/clerk/. Must be registered. Also gives vital record index from home page, click on County Clerk then Index Search.   *Criminal:* Access to court records from www.tituscountyonline.net/clerk/. Must be registered.

Tom Green County
District Court   www.co.tom-green.tx.us/default.aspx?name=dc.DistrictCourtHome
Civil: Online access to civil case records back to 1994 is online at http://odysseypa.co.tom-green.tx.us/default.aspx. Search by name, case number.   *Criminal:* Online access to criminal case records back to 1994 at http://odysseypa.co.tom-green.tx.us/default.aspx. Search by name, case number.
County Court   www.co.tom-green.tx.us/default.aspx?name=ccl.Homepage
Civil: Online access to civil records from1994 is free at http://odysseypa.co.tom-green.tx.us/.   *Criminal:* Online access to criminal records from 1994 is free at http://odysseypa.co.tom-green.tx.us/.

Travis County
District Court - Criminal   https://www.traviscountytx.gov/courts/criminal/district

A free search site for misdemeanors 1981 forward is at http://deed.co.travis.tx.us/ords/f?p=105:1:0::NO. DOBs are shown. Current (up to one month) docket information is available at https://publiccourts.co.travis.tx.us/dsa/. A limited search site from the District Court is at https://www.traviscountytx.gov/district-clerk/online-case-information.Email requests to district.criminalrecords@co.travis.tx.us.

District Court - Civil   https://www.traviscountytx.gov/courts/civil/district
A limited search site from the District Court is at https://www.traviscountytx.gov/district-clerk/online-case-information.

County Court - Criminal   www.traviscountyclerk.org/eclerk/Content.do?code=Misdemeanor
A free search site for misdemeanors 1981 forward is at http://deed.co.travis.tx.us/ords/f?p=105:1:0::NO. DOBs are shown. Current (up to one month) docket information is available at https://publiccourts.co.travis.tx.us/dsa/. Email requests to district.criminalrecords@co.travis.tx.us.

County Court - Civil   www.traviscountyclerk.org/eclerk/Content.do?code=Civil
Two online systems (docket data from June 1986 forward) and images (2005 forward) are at www.traviscountyclerk.org/eclerk/Content.do?code=C.10. One search a day is free, otherwise fees involved. Fees involved to print copies.

Upshur County

District Court   www.countyofupshur.com
Civil: Access court records and hearings free at www.countyofupshur.com/judicialsearch/.   *Criminal:* same

County Court   www.countyofupshur.com/
Civil: Access court records and hearings free at www.countyofupshur.com/judicialsearch/. 4 months of dockets are shown at www.countyofupshur.com/Dockets/Dockets.htm.   *Criminal:* same

Victoria County

District Court   www.vctx.org/index.php/en/county-departments?id=97
Civil: Search the docket index free at http://odyssey.vctx.org/default.aspx. Includes family and probate. *Criminal:* Search the docket index free at http://odyssey.vctx.org/default.aspx.

County Court at Law   www.vctx.org/index.php/en/county-departments?id=30
Civil: Search the docket index free at http://odyssey.vctx.org/default.aspx. Includes family and probate. *Criminal:* Search the docket index free at http://odyssey.vctx.org/default.aspx.

Walker County

District Court   www.co.walker.tx.us/department/?fDD=9-0
Civil: Online access to case summary data at http://odysseypa.tylerhost.net/Walker/default.aspx. Includes civil, family, and probate.   *Criminal:* Online access to case summary data at http://odysseypa.tylerhost.net/Walker/default.aspx.

County Court at Law   www.co.walker.tx.us/department/index.php?fDD=5-0
Civil: Online access to case summary data at http://odysseypa.tylerhost.net/Walker/default.aspx. Includes civil, family, and probate.   *Criminal:* same.The site also provides access to jail records, jail bond records, and law enforcement incident records.

Waller County

District Court   www.co.waller.tx.us/default.aspx?Waller_County/District.Clerk
Civil: Free access to docket data at http://odysseypa.tylerhost.net/Waller/default.aspx. Includes Family Court records. *Criminal:* same.

County Court   www.co.waller.tx.us/default.aspx?Waller_County/County.Court
Civil: Access to civil records at http://odysseypa.tylerhost.net/Waller/default.aspx.   *Criminal:* same.

Webb County

County Court   www.webbcountytx.gov/
Criminal: An online search is for traffic warrants is at www.webbcountytx.gov/warrant-lookup/Search.aspx.

Williamson County

District Court   www.wilco.org/default.aspx?tabid=448
Civil: Search the civil docket index at http://judicialrecords.wilco.org/default.aspx. Search by case number, party, or attorney.   *Criminal:* same.

County Court   www.wilco.org/CountyDepartments/CountyCourts/tabid/235/language/en-US/Default.aspx
Civil: Access to civil and probate court records countywide available for free at http://judicialrecords.wilco.org/default.aspx.   *Criminal:* same. Jail and jail bond records also available.

Wise County

District Court   www.co.wise.tx.us/DC/
Civil: A case docket look-up is found at www.co.wise.tx.us:81/default.aspx. One may alos search Probate and Family Court records as well as the case calendar.   *Criminal:* same. Searches of jail records and law enforcement records are also available.

County Court at Law #1   www.co.wise.tx.us/cc/
Civil: A case docket look-up for civil and probate is found at www.co.wise.tx.us:81/default.aspx.   *Criminal:* same.Searches of jail records and law enforcement records are also available.

County Court at Law #2   www.co.wise.tx.us/CCL2/
Civil: A case docket look-up for civil and probate is found at www.co.wise.tx.us:81/default.aspx.   *Criminal:* same.Searches of jail records and law enforcement records are also available.

Wood County

District Court   www.mywoodcounty.com/default.aspx?name=distclerk
Civil: Search civil case index at http://txwoododyprod.tylerhost.net/PublicAccess/default.aspx.   *Criminal:* same.
County Court   www.mywoodcounty.com/default.aspx?name=cc_home
Civil: Search all courts free at http://txwoododyprod.tylerhost.net/PublicAccess/default.aspx.   *Criminal:* same.

Young County

County Court   http://co.young.tx.us/default.aspx?Young_County/County.Clerk
Civil: Access online site, which requires registration, at www.texasonlinerecords.com/clerk/index?office_id=11.

Recorders, Assessors, and Other Sites of Note

About Texas Recording Offices: 254 counties, 254 recording offices. The recording officer is the County Clerk. Federal tax liens on personal property of businesses are filed with the Secretary of State. Other federal and all state tax liens are filed with the County Clerk.

About Tax Liens: Federal tax liens on personal property of businesses are filed with the Secretary of State. Other federal and all state tax liens are filed with the County Clerk.

Online Access

Numerous counties offer online access to recorded document and Assessor data. Many use vendors. Selected vendors with the widest coverage are listed below with participating counties.

Recorded Documents

- The site at https://www.texasfile.com/search/texas offers limited Grantor/Grantee records for **all counties except Armstrong, Collingsworth, Concho, Cottle, Hidalgo, Jeff Davis, Lampasas, Red River, Sherman:** Search for free, purchase images for $1.00 per page after registration.

- The site at www.titlex.com offers access to the Recorders' Office county grantor/grantee indices - including real estate, deeds, liens, judgments records and more - for 103 Texas counties. In order to search, view, and print records you must first purchase Tokens for $.25 each. The number of tokens needed to search or view varies by county. The norm is 4 to search, 4 to view, 4 to print, and an advanced search is usually 20. You may pay by credit card and open or add to your account.

- **Titlex.com counties:**

Anderson	Cochran	Harrison	Knox	Palo Pinto	Uvalde
Angelina	Collin	Hays	Lavaca	Panola	Van Zandt
Atascosa	Colorado	Henderson	Leon	Parker	Victoria
Austin	Comanche	Hill	Liberty	Potter	Waller
Bailey	Dewitt	Hood	Limestone	Real	Washington
Bandera	Eastland	Hopkins	Live Oak	Refugio	Webb
Bastrop	Ector	Houston	Lubbock	Robertson	Wharton
Bee	El Paso	Hutchinson	Madison	Rockwall	Wichita
Bell	Erath	Jack	Marion	Rusk	Willacy
Bosque	Fayette	Jackson	Mc Lennan	San Patricio	Williamson
Brazoria	Freestone	Jasper	Midland	Shelby	Wilson
Brazos	Ft Bend	Jefferson	Milam	Smith	Wise
Burleson	Galveston	Jim Wells	Montague	Somervell	Wood
Burnet	Goliad	Johnson	Montgomery	Tarrant	
Calhoun	Grayson	Karnes	Nacogdoches	Taylor	
Carson	Gregg	Kaufman	Navarro	Tom Green	
Castro	Hale	Kendall	Nueces	Upshur	
Cherokee	Harris	Kleberg	Orange	Upton	

Property Taxes & Assessor Sites

- www.taxnetusa.com - offers appraisal district and property appraisal records **for all Texas counties.** Also, delinquent tax data is available for about half of the participating counties. Free searches as well as online subscriptions services using a sliding fee scale, or purchase bulk data download, are available. Visit the website or call 877-652-2707. To search free at the TaxNetUSA site, click on the "county" and fill out the top portion.

- View property tax data free on the True Automation site for these 90 Texas counties at http://trueautomation.com/.

Andrews	Caldwell	Falls	Kerr	Newton	Travis
Angelina	Calhoun	Gillespie	Kimble	Nueces	Upshur
Aransas	Cameron	Goliad	Kinney	Polk	Upton
Atascosa	Cass	Gregg	Kleberg	Real	Val Verde
Bailey	Cherokee	Guadalupe	Lamar	Rockwall	Victoria
Bandera	Cochran	Hale	Lamb	San Jacinto	Waller
Bell	Comal	Hamilton	Lavaca	San Patricio	Webb
Bexar	Cooke	Hidalgo	Lee Tax	Schleicher	Wichita
Blanco	Cotulla	Hill	Lyford	Scurry	Willacy
Brazoria	Dayton	Hockley	Madison	Shelby	Wilson
Brazos	Deaf Smith	Hudspeth	Matagorda	Sutton	Winkler
Brewster	Delta	Iowa Park	McLennan	Swisher	Wink-Loving
Brooks	Dimmit	Jefferson	Mitchell	Taylor	Yoakum
Brown	Edwards	Kendall	Moore	Terrell	Zapata
Burnet	Ellis	Kerr	Navarro	Titus	Zavala

Reference Site

A good place to find contact info and the web pages to County Appraisal Districts is http://appraisaldistrict.net/.

County Sites: (To avoid redundancy, these profiles do NOT include the 4 Bulleted Sites mentioned above.)

Anderson County
Recorded Documents, Marriage Records www.co.anderson.tx.us/default.aspx?Anderson_County/County.Clerk   Access to a county records search for free at www.countyinfosearch.com/. Must register for a username and login before use.
Property, Taxation Records   Access to property tax data for free at http://184.7.206.194/Appraisal/PublicAccess/.

Andrews County   *Recorded Documents* www.co.andrews.tx.us/departments/county_clerk.php   Access to index and summary required registration at https://tx.countygovernmentrecords.com/texas/web/. There is a fee charged to view a document image. After you log in, you may purchase images on a document by document basis or you may pruchase a monthly subscriptin that allows you ro view, download and print unlimited document images.
Property, Taxation Records   Access to property search options for free at www.andrewscountytax.com/taxSearch.

Angelina County   *Recorded Documents, Probate Records*   www.angelinacounty.net/departments/cc   Search grantor/grantee index free at https://www.texaslandrecords.com/txlr/TxlrApp/index.jsp. Registration and fees required for full data. Probate records are at the County Court but accessible through the County Clerks Office. Also see note at beginning of section for add'l property data
Property, Taxation Records   Access to property search for free at www.angelinacad.org/property-search.

Aransas County   *Property, Taxation Records*   Access dated appraiser and property tax data at www.aransascad.org/. Also, access to the resale property list for free at www.aransascountytx.gov/taxac/e-docs/OCT.2014_RESALE_LIST.pdf.

Austin County   *Recorded Documents Property, Taxation Records*   Search property records for free at http://search.austin.manatron.com/search.php?searchType=name. Also, property tax inquiries can be made via http://austincad.org/tax/accountSearch.asp.

Bandera County   *Recorded Documents, Probate Records*   www.banderacounty.org   Search grantor/grantee index free at https://www.texaslandrecords.com/txlr/TxlrApp/index.jsp. Registration and fees required for full data. Probate records are accessible through the County Clerks Office. *Property, Taxation Records*   Access to Appraisal District records is free at http://propaccess.banderaproptax.org/clientdb/?cid=1.

Bastrop County   *Recorded Documents* www.co.bastrop.tx.us/default.aspx?name=co.county_clerk   Access to real estate, vital records, UCC records for free at www.cc.co.bastrop.tx.us/.
Property, Taxation Records   Access to tax office records is free at www.bastroptac.com/Appraisal/PublicAccess/.

Bee County   *Recorded Documents*   www.co.bee.tx.us/default.aspx?Bee_County/County.Clerk   Search grantor/grantee index free at
https://www.texaslandrecords.com/txlr/TxlrApp/index.jsp. Registration and fees required for full data.
Property, Taxation Records   Access property records free at www.beecad.org/.

Bell County   *Recorded Documents*   www.bellcountytx.com/county_government/county_clerk/index.php   Search grantor/grantee index at
https://www.texaslandrecords.com/txlr/TxlrApp/index.jsp. Registration and fees required for full data.
Property, Taxation Records   Search property and parcel data free at http://propaccess.bellcad.org/clientdb/?cid=1.

Bexar County   *Recorded Documents*   https://gov.propertyinfo.com/TX-Bexar/   Access to the County Clerk database is free after free
registration at https://gov.propertyinfo.com/TX-Bexar/. Includes land records, deeds, UCCs, assumed names and foreclosure notices, and more.
Property, Taxation Records   Access the county Central Appraisal District database free at www.bcad.org/ClientDB/PropertySearch.aspx?cid=1.

Bosque County   *Recorded Documents*   www.bosquecounty.us/bosque-county-clerk/   Search grantor/grantee index free at
https://www.texaslandrecords.com/txlr/TxlrApp/index.jsp. Registration and fees required for full data. Also, access to recorded documents for a fee at
https://www.idocmarket.com/sites. Must subscribe before use. Fees vary depending on plan picked. Inages back to 1/19/1984.
Property, Taxation Records   Search online tax records for free at www.bosquecountytaxoffice.com/accountSearch.asp.

Bowie County   *Recorded Documents*   www.co.bowie.tx.us/default.aspx?Bowie_County/County.Clerk   Search grantor/grantee index free at
https://www.texaslandrecords.com/txlr/TxlrApp/index.jsp. Registration and fees required for full data.

Brazoria County   *Property, Taxation Records*   Access to the county Central Appraisal District database is free at www.brazoriacad.org/.
Also, access to property tax or delinquentcy roll for free at https://actweb.acttax.com/act_webdev/brazoria/index.jsp.

Brazos County   *Recorded Documents*   www.brazoscountytx.gov/index.aspx?nid=114   Search grantor/grantee index free at
https://texaslandrecords.com/txlr/TxlrApp/index.jsp. Registration and fees required for full data.
Property, Taxation Records   Property tax inquiries can be made via www.brazostax.org/. Also, see notes at beginning of section.

Brewster County   *Recorded Documents*   www.brewstercountytx.com/offices/brewster-county-offices/county-clerk/   Access to document
images and index information for a fee at https://gov.propertyinfo.com/TX-Brewster/.

Brooks County   *Recorded Documents*   www.co.brooks.tx.us/default.aspx?Brooks_County/County.Clerk   Access recording office land data
at www.etitlesearch.com/; registration required, fee based on usage. Probate records are at the County Court but accessible through the County Clerks
Office. *Property, Taxation Records*   Access to property searches for a fee at https://actweb.acttax.com/act_webdev/brooks/index.jsp. Fee is- For
transactions between $100.01 and $500.00, the fee ranges from 3% to 6%. Above $500.00, the fee is 3%.

Brown County   *Probate Records*   www.browncountytx.org/default.aspx?Brown_County/County.Clerk   Probate records are at the County
Court but accessible through the County Clerks Office. Also, access to real property records for a fee at
www.browncountytx.org/default.aspx?Brown_County/RealProperty. $5.00 per document plus $1.00 per page copy fee.

Burleson County   *Recorded Documents*   http://co.burleson.tx.us/government/county-clerk/   Search grantor/grantee index free at
https://texaslandrecords.com/txlr/TxlrApp/index.jsp. Registration and fees required for full data. Records from 1975 to present.

Burnet County   *Recorded Documents*   www.burnetcountytexas.org/default.aspx?name=cclerk.home   Also, access to records for free at
http://countyclerk.burnetcountytexas.org/.

Caldwell County   *Recorded Documents*   www.co.caldwell.tx.us/default.aspx?Caldwell_County/County.Clerk   Access to records for free at
http://edoctecinc.com/. Also, access to records for a fee at https://tx.countygovernmentrecords.com/texas/web/. Must register (for free).

Calhoun County   *Property, Taxation Records*   Access to GIS/mapping for free at http://calhouncad.org/PDFs/GISMaps.pdf.

Callahan County   *Property, Taxation Records*   Access to records from the appraisal district and the collections offices free at
http://iswdatacorp.azurewebsites.net/.

Cameron County   *Recorded Documents, Probate Records*   www.co.cameron.tx.us/administration/county_clerk/index.php   Search
grantor/grantee index free at https://texaslandrecords.com/txlr/TxlrApp/index.jsp. Registration and fees required for full data. Probate records are at the
County Court but accessible through the County Clerks Office. Also, see note at beginning of section for add'l property data.
Property, Taxation Records   Access to property taxes for free at www.cameroncountytax.org/faces/search.jsp.

Carson County   *Recorded Documents*   www.co.carson.tx.us/default.aspx?Carson_County/County.Clerk   Search official record index at
https://tx.countygovernmentrecords.com/texas/web/ for free. Registration is required. Fees charged for viewing and printing document copies.

Castro County   *Recorded Documents*   www.co.castro.tx.us/default.aspx?Castro_County/County.Clerk   Search grantor/grantee index free at
https://www.texaslandrecords.com/txlr/TxlrApp/index.jsp. Registration and fees required for full data.

Chambers County   *Recorded Documents*   www.co.chambers.tx.us/default.aspx?name=county.clerk   Access county clerk's real property
records free after registering for a login name and password at www.chambersonline.net/.

Property, Taxation Records   Search the appraiser property tax database free at www.chamberscad.org/. Click on 'Search Our Data'. Also, see note at beginning of section.

Cherokee County   *Recorded Documents*   www.co.cherokee.tx.us/ips/cms/countyoffices/countyClerk.html   Search grantor/grantee index free at https://texaslandrecords.com/txlr/TxlrApp/index.jsp. Registration and fees required for full data. Also, access to foreclosure listings for free at https://foreclosures.uslandrecords.com/FAM/TX/Cherokee/Foreclosures.aspx.

Childress County   *Property, Taxation Records*   Access to record data for free at www.childresscad.org/.

Clay County   *Probate, Criminal Records*   www.co.clay.tx.us/#!county-clerk/c1frm   Probate records are at the County Court but accessible through the County Clerks Office.
Property, Taxation Records   Access property tax records free at www.claycad.org/. Also, see note at beginning of section.

Cochran County   *Recorded Documents*   http://co.cochran.tx.us/default.aspx?Cochran_County/County.Clerk   Search grantor/grantee index free at https://texaslandrecords.com/txlr/TxlrApp/index.jsp. Registration and fees required for full data.

Coleman County   *Recorded Documents*   www.co.coleman.tx.us/default.aspx?Coleman_County/County.Clerk   Search grantor/grantee index free at https://texaslandrecords.com/txlr/TxlrApp/index.jsp. Registration and fees required for full data. Probate records are at the County Court but accessible through the County Clerks Office.

Collin County   *Recorded Documents, Vital Records Records*   www.co.collin.tx.us/county_clerk/Pages/default.aspx   Access to the county clerk Deeds database is free at http://countyclerkrecords.co.collin.tx.us/webinquiry/. Also, see note at beginning of section for more property data.
Property, Taxation Records   Search the Appraiser's property tax and business property database free at www.collincad.org/propertysearch. Also, search the tax assessor and collector look up free at http://taxpublic.collincountytx.gov/webcollincounty/accountsearch.htm.

Colorado County   *Recorded Documents*   www.co.colorado.tx.us/default.aspx?Colorado_County/County.Clerk   Access to public records (includes land, deeds, vital records) for free at http://24.173.220.138/colorado/HomePage.aspx?ID=Colorado.
Property, Taxation Records   For property search go to www.coloradocad.org/ and click on property search. Also, see note at beginning of section.

Comal County   *Property, Taxation Records*   Search property tax data free at http://taxweb.co.comal.tx.us/clientdb/?cid=1.

Cooke County   *Recorded Documents*   www.co.cooke.tx.us/default.aspx?Cooke_County/County.Clerk   Search grantor/grantee index free at https://texaslandrecords.com/txlr/TxlrApp/index.jsp. Registration and fees required for full data.

Crane County   *Recorded Documents*   www.co.crane.tx.us/default.aspx?Crane_County/County.Clerk   Search official record index at https://tx.countygovernmentrecords.com/texas/web/ for free. Registration is required. Fees charged for printing document copies.
Property, Taxation Records   Access to property search and tax payment for free at http://iswdatacorp.azurewebsites.net/.

Dallas County   *Recorded Documents, Marriage, Assumed Name Records*
www.dallascounty.org/department/countyclerk/countyclerk.php   Search most records for a fee at https://roamdallaspropertyrecords.com/. Must register for subscription. Name search recorded documents for deeds, marriages, assumed names, and UCCs back to 1964. Viewing and printing documents with watermarks are $1.00 1st page, $.50 each add'l page. With monthly subscription fee, copies can be obtained without the watermark. Also, access County Voter Registration Records free at https://www.dallascountyvotes.org/voter-lookup/.
Property, Taxation Records   Access Central Appraisal District data free at www.dallascad.org/SearchOwner.aspx.

Dawson County   *Property, Taxation Records*   Access to real estate roll, mineral roll and property taxes for free at www.dawsoncad.org/(S(dj2nux45ntf5skam4jc3zlyb))/search.aspx?clientid=dawsoncad.

De Witt County   *Property, Taxation Records*   Access appraisal district property data free at www.dewittcad.org/ and click on Search our data. Also, access assessor tax payment data free at www.texasonlinerecords.com/tax/?office_id=5.

Denton County   *Recorded Documents*   http://dentoncounty.com/Departments/County-Clerk.aspx   Search grantor/grantee index free at https://texaslandrecords.com/txlr/TxlrApp/index.jsp. Registration and fees required for full data. Also, search voter registration rolls free at https://www.votedenton.com/voter-lookup/#VoterEligibilitySearch.
Property, Taxation Records   Property tax inquiries and property searches for free can be made at http://dentoncounty.com/Departments/Tax-Assessor-Collector/Property-Tax/Search-Property-Tax-Records.aspx.

Duval County   *Recorded Documents*   Search grantor/grantee index free at https://texaslandrecords.com/txlr/TxlrApp/index.jsp. Registration and fees required for full data.

Eastland County   *Recorded Documents*   www.eastlandcountytexas.com/default.aspx?Eastland_County/County.Clerk   Search official record index at https://tx.countygovernmentrecords.com/texas/web/ for free. Registration is required. Fees charged for viewing and printing document copies. Probate records are at the County Court but accessible through the County Clerks Office.

Ector County   *Recorded Documents*   www.co.ector.tx.us/default.aspx?Ector_County/County.Clerk   Search official record index at https://tx.countygovernmentrecords.com/texas/web/ for free. Registration is required. Fees charged for viewing and printing document copies.
Property, Taxation Records   Search appraisal district property data and personal property free at www.ectorcad.org/.

Edwards County   *Recorded Documents*   www.edwardscountytexas.us/officials/clerk.htm   Search grantor/grantee index free at https://texaslandrecords.com/txlr/TxlrApp/index.jsp. Registration and fees required for full data.

El Paso County   *Recorded Documents, Probate Records*   www.epcounty.com/clerk/   Search official records free at www.epcounty.com/publicrecords/officialpublicrecords/OfficialPublicRecordSearch.aspx, also marriages at www.epcounty.com/publicrecords/marriagerecords/MarriageRecordSearch.aspx. Search assumed names free at www.epcounty.com/publicrecords/assumednames/AssumedNameRecordSearch.aspx. For county birth/deaths search www.epcounty.com/publicrecords/birthrecords/BirthRecordSearch.aspx; OR www.epcounty.com/publicrecords/deathrecords/DeathRecordSearch.aspx. *Property, Taxation Records*   Search property tax data free at www.epcad.org/Search.

Ellis County   *Reorded Documents, Marriage Records*   www.co.ellis.tx.us/index.aspx?nid=74   See www.lgs-hosted.com/rmtellcck.html for a public data inquiries. *Property, Taxation Records*   Access to property tax information for a fee at https://actweb.acttax.com/act_webdev/ellis/index.jsp. Various map choices for free at www.co.ellis.tx.us/index.aspx?nid=65.

Erath County   *Recorded Documents*   http://co.erath.tx.us/countyclerk.html   Search official record index at https://tx.countygovernmentrecords.com/texas/web/ for free. Registration is required. Fees charged for viewing and printing document copies. *Property, Taxation Records*   Find appraisal district data free at http://iswdatacorp.azurewebsites.net/. Also, search tax office records free at www.texaspayments.com/072000/. Also, see note at beginning of section.

Fannin County   *Recorded Documents*   www.co.fannin.tx.us/default.aspx?Fannin_County/County.Clerk   Search grantor/grantee index free at https://texaslandrecords.com/txlr/TxlrApp/index.jsp. Registration and fees required for full data.

Floyd County   *Probate Records*   www.floydcountytexas.us/   Probate records are at the County Court but accessible through the County Clerks Office. *Property, Taxation Records*   Find appraisal district data free at http://iswdatacorp.azurewebsites.net/.

Fort Bend County   *Recorded Documents*   www.fortbendcountytx.gov/index.aspx?page=107   Recorded records, property records, marriage, and divorce can be searched for free at www.fortbendcountytx.gov/index.aspx?page=122. Also, see note at beginning of section. *Property, Taxation Records*   Access appraisal records for the Ft Bend Central Appraisal Districe for free at www.fbcad.org/Appraisal/PublicAccess/. Also, property tax inquiries can be made free at https://actweb.acttax.com/act_webdev/fbc/index.jsp.

Franklin County   *Recorded Documents*   www.franklincountyclerk.net/   Search official record index at www.countygovernmentrecords.com/ for free. Registration is required. Fees charged for viewing and printing document copies. *Property, Taxation Records*   Access to property data is free at www.franklincad.com/. Click on Property Search. Also, see note at beginning of section. Also, access to tax records for free at www.franklincountytaxoffice.com/appraisal/publicaccess/.

Freestone County   *Recorded Documents, Probate Records*   www.co.freestone.tx.us/default.aspx?Freestone_County/County.Clerk   Search grantor/grantee index free at https://texaslandrecords.com/txlr/TxlrApp/index.jsp. Registration and fees required for full data. Probate records are at the County Court but accessible through the County Clerks Office. *Property, Taxation Records*   Access to Appraiser's property data is free at www.freestonecad.org/. Click on Search Our Data.

Galveston County   *Recorded Documents*   www.galvestoncountytx.gov/cc/Pages/default.aspx   Access the county online official records index free at http://public1.co.galveston.tx.us/default.aspx. *Property, Taxation Records*   Search Central Appraisal Dist. database free at www.galvestoncad.org/Appraisal/PublicAccess/. For info, call 409-766-5115.

Gillespie County   *Recorded Documents, Birth, Death, Marriage Records*   www.gillespiecounty.org/default.aspx?name=county_clerk   Free access to public records found at www.gillespiecounty.org/default.aspx?name=records_search.

Glasscock County   *Recorded Documents*   www.co.glasscock.tx.us/default.aspx?Glasscock_County/County.Clerk   Access to recorded documents for a fee at https://www.idocmarket.com/sites. Must subscribe before use. Fees vary depending on plan picked. Indexing and imaging back to 7/2/2015.

Goliad County   *Recorded Documents*   www.co.goliad.tx.us/default.aspx?Goliad_County/County.Clerk   Search grantor/grantee index free at https://texaslandrecords.com/txlr/TxlrApp/index.jsp. Registration and fees required for full data.

Gonzales County   *Property, Taxation Records*   Access to Assessor's database for free at http://tax.co.gonzales.tx.us/Appraisal/PublicAccess/.

Grayson County   *Recorded Documents*   www.co.grayson.tx.us/default.aspx?name=cclk.home   Search grantor/grantee index free at https://texaslandrecords.com/txlr/TxlrApp/index.jsp. Registration and fees required for full data.

Gregg County   *Recorded Documents, Vital Statistic Records*   www.co.gregg.tx.us/county-clerk   Access to the County Clerk's Official Public Records database is free to view at http://beta.co.gregg.tx.us/A2WebUI/. Fee to copy documents. *Property, Taxation Records*   Search property tax records for a fee at https://actweb.acttax.com/act_webdev/gregg/index.jsp. Credit cards accepted.

Grimes County *Recorded Documents* www.co.grimes.tx.us/default.aspx?Grimes_County/County.Clerk   Search grantor/grantee index free at https://texaslandrecords.com/txlr/TxlrApp/index.jsp. Registration and fees required for full data.

Guadalupe County *Property, Taxation Records*   Search appraisal roll, parcel tax data free at http://property.co.guadalupe.tx.us/Appraisal/PublicAccess/.

Hale County *Recorded Documents* www.halecounty.org/county_offices/county_clerk.php   Search official record index at https://tx.countygovernmentrecords.com/texas/web/ for free. Registration is required. Fees charged for viewing and printing document copies.

Hardin County *Property, Taxation Records*   Access to tax/property records for free at www.tax.cagi.com/#/TaxOfficeSearch?cc=C100.

Harris County *Recorded Documents* www.cclerk.hctx.net   Access to Assumed Name records, UCC filings, vital statistic, and Real Property are at www.cclerk.hctx.net/applications/websearch/. County Court Civil, marriage and informal marriage records also available. Search voter registrations free at www.tax.co.harris.tx.us/Voter/Search.
Property, Taxation Records   Appraiser records are at www.hcad.org/Records/. Search tax assessor data free at www.tax.co.harris.tx.us/Property/PropertyTax.

Harrison County *Recorded Documents* http://harrisoncountytexas.org/?page_id=174   Search official record index at https://tx.countygovernmentrecords.com/texas/web/ for free. Registration is required. Fees charged for printing document copies only.
Property, Taxation Records   Access to appraisal district data and tax collection office data free at http://iswdatacorp.azurewebsites.net/.

Hartley County *Recorded Documents* www.co.hartley.tx.us/default.aspx?Hartley_County/County.Clerk   Access to recorded documents for a fee at https://www.idocmarket.com/sites. Must subscribe before use. Fees vary depending on plan picked. Computer indexing back to 6/1/1994, imaging back to 10/24/2005.
Property, Taxation Records   Find appraisal district data and collection office data free at http://iswdatacorp.azurewebsites.net/.

Hays County *Recorded Documents, Probate Records* www.co.hays.tx.us/county-clerk.aspx   Search grantor/grantee index free at https://texaslandrecords.com/txlr/TxlrApp/index.jsp. Registration and fees required for full data. Probate records are at the County Court but accessible through the County Clerks Office. *Property, Taxation Records*   Access tax collector property data free at http://hayscountytax.com/taxes. Also, see notes at beginning of section for add'l property data.

Henderson County *Recorded Documents* www.henderson-county.com/departments/county-clerk   Search official record index at https://tx.countygovernmentrecords.com/texas/web/ and view for free. Registration is required. Fees charged for printing document copies.
Property, Taxation Records   Access to the appraisal district records free at http://iswdatacorp.azurewebsites.net/.

Hidalgo County *Recorded Documents* https://tx-hidalgocounty.civicplus.com/index.aspx?NID=161   Search grantor/grantee index free at https://www.texaslandrecords.com/txlr/TXHID/index.jsp. Registration and fees required for full data. Probate records are at the County Court but accessible through the County Clerks Office.
Property, Taxation Records   Search appraiser property records free at https://actweb.acttax.com/act_webdev/hidalgo/index.jsp.

Hill County *Recorded Documents* www.co.hill.tx.us/default.aspx?Hill_County/County.Clerk   Search official record index at https://tx.countygovernmentrecords.com/texas/web/ for free. Registration is required. Fees charged for viewing and printing document copies. Also, see note at beginning of section.

Hockley County *Recorded Documents* www.co.hockley.tx.us/default.aspx?Hockley_County/County.Clerk   Search grantor/grantee index free at https://texaslandrecords.com/txlr/TxlrApp/index.jsp. Registration and fees required for full data.

Hood County *Recorded Documents* www.co.hood.tx.us/index.aspx?nid=211   Search official record index at https://tx.countygovernmentrecords.com/texas/web/ for free. Registration is required. Fees charged for viewing and printing document copies.
Property, Taxation Records   Access to appraisal district data and collection office data for free at http://iswdatacorp.azurewebsites.net/. Add'l online access through private companies.

Hopkins County *Recorded Documents, Probate Records* www.hopkinscountytx.org/default.aspx?Hopkins_County/County.Clerk   Access real property records free after registering for login and password at www.texasonlinerecords.com/clerk/index?office_id=1. Probate records are at the County Court but accessible through the County Clerks Office.
Property, Taxation Records   Access to appraisal district data free at http://iswdatacorp.azurewebsites.net/. Also, access to tax records/tax payments online for free at www.hopkinscountyonline.net/.

Houston County *Recorded Documents* www.co.houston.tx.us/default.aspx?Houston_County/County.Clerk   Search official records after choosing county at www.edoctecinc.com/. All records are unofficial, can search freely; $1.00 per page fee applies for copies. For details and signup, contact clerk at 800-578-7746. *Property, Taxation Records*   Access to property tax records is free at www.houstoncad.org/.

Howard County *Recorded Documents* www.co.howard.tx.us/default.aspx?Howard_County/County.Clerk   Search official record index at https://tx.countygovernmentrecords.com/texas/web/ and view for free. Registration is required. Fees charged for printing document copies.
Property, Taxation Records   Access to tax records for free at http://tax.cagi.com/#/TaxOfficeSearch?cc=A114. Also, access to the appraisal district records free at http://iswdatacorp.azurewebsites.net/.

Hunt County *Recorded Documents* www.huntcounty.net   Probate records are at the County Court but accessible through the County Clerks Office. Also, access to real property records for free at https://search.kofile.com/48231/Home/Index/1.

Hutchinson County *Recorded Documents* www.co.hutchinson.tx.us/default.aspx?Hutchinson_County/County.Clerk   Search grantor/grantee index free at https://texaslandrecords.com/txlr/TxlrApp/index.jsp. Registration and fees required for full data.
Property, Taxation Records   Access to property tax data is free at www.hutchinsoncad.org/. Access to property appraisal and assessment searches free at www.hutchinsoncountytax.com/Appraisal/PublicAccess/.

Jackson County *Property, Taxation Records*   Access appraiser property records free at www.jacksoncad.org/#!__recordsearch.

Jasper County *Recorded Documents* www.co.jasper.tx.us/default.aspx?Jasper_County/County.Clerk   Search official record index at https://tx.countygovernmentrecords.com/texas/web/ for free. Registration is required. Fees charged for viewing and printing document copies.
Property, Taxation Records   Access to property tax free at www.jaspercotxtax.com/Appraisal/PublicAccess/.

Jefferson County *Recorded Documents* www.co.jefferson.tx.us/cclerk/clerk.htm   Access the recorder database free at http://jeffersontxclerk.manatron.com/. Recording index goes back to 1983; images to 1983. Marriages go back to 1995; UCCs to 7/2001. Also, see note at beginning of section. *Property, Taxation Records*   Access property tax records free at http://propaccess.jcad.org/clientdb/?cid=1.

Jim Hogg County *Recorded Documents* www.jimhoggcounty.net/index.php/departments/county-clerk-s-office   Access recording office land data at www.etitlesearch.com; registration required, fee based on usage.

Jim Wells County *Recorded Documents* www.co.jim-wells.tx.us/default.aspx?name=co.county.clerk   Access recording office land data at www.etitlesearch.com/; registration required, fee based on usage. Also, search grantor/grantee index free at https://texaslandrecords.com/txlr/TxlrApp/index.jsp. Registration and fees required for full data.

Johnson County *Recorded Documents* www.johnsoncountytx.org/government/county-clerk   Access to real property records (limited) for free at https://www.texaslandrecords.com/txlr/TxlrApp/index.jsp. For detailed records, must subscribe.
Property, Taxation Records   Records from the County Appraiser are free at www.johnsoncountytaxoffice.org/accountSearch.asp.

Jones County *Property, Taxation Records*   Access property tax records free at www.jonescad.org/ and click on Search Our Data.

Karnes County *Recorded Documents* www.co.karnes.tx.us/default.aspx?Karnes_County/County.Clerk   Search official record index at https://tx.countygovernmentrecords.com/texas/web/ and view for free. Registration is required. Fees charged for printing document copies

Kaufman County *Recorded Documents* www.kaufmancountyclerk.com   Search official record index at https://tx.countygovernmentrecords.com/texas/web/ for free. Registration is required. Fees charged for printing document copies. Also, see note at beginning of section.
Property, Taxation Records   Access to tax resale property list for free at www.kaufmancounty.net/ta.html. Click on County Resale Property.

Kendall County *Recorded Documents* www.co.kendall.tx.us/   Access to land records (index only) free at https://gov.propertyinfo.com/TX-Kendall/. Must register before being allowed to search. Also see note at beginning of section.

Kent County *Property, Taxation Records*   Access to the property data search for free at www.kentcad.org/%28S%28ejsk5tza5tobmyzazraknuzf%29%29/search.aspx?clientid=kentcad.

Kerr County *Recorded Documents, Marriage Records* www.co.kerr.tx.us/   Access to recorder land data at www.edoctecinc.com/. Registration and login required. *Property, Taxation Records*   Access to property records free at http://propaccess.kerrcad.org/clientdb/?cid=0.

Kinney County *Recorded Documents* www.co.kinney.tx.us/default.aspx?Kinney_County/County.Clerk   Access to records for free at http://gov.propertyinfo.com/tx-kinney/. Must register. Non subscribers receive unlimited view of index data and can purchase document images, subscribers get the same plus a history of all purchased document images maintained and available for subsequent view/print/save when available.

Kleberg County *Property, Taxation Records*   Access to county appraisal rolls and property data is free at www.klebergcad.org/search_appr.php. Also, access to tax records/payment online for free at www.texasonlinerecords.com/tax/?office_id=8. No name searching.

Knox County *Property, Taxation Records*   Access to the appraisal district records free at http://iswdatacorp.azurewebsites.net/.

La Salle County *Property, Taxation Records*   Access property tax data free at http://esearch.lasallecad.com/. Search tax sales lists free at http://tax.acttax.com/pls/sales/property_taxsales_pkg.search_page?PI_STATE=TX and chose Struck Off as sales type.

Lamar County *Recorded Documents* www.co.lamar.tx.us/default.aspx?Lamar_County/County.Clerk   Search official record index at https://tx.countygovernmentrecords.com/texas/web/ for free. Registration is required. Fees charged for printing document copies.

Lamb County *Recorded Documents* www.co.lamb.tx.us/default.aspx?Lamb_County/County.Clerk   Search grantor/grantee index free at https://texaslandrecords.com/txlr/TxlrApp/index.jsp. Registration and fees required for full data.

Lampasas County *Foreclosures Records* www.co.lampasas.tx.us/default.aspx?Lampasas_County/County.Clerk   Access to foreclosures & trustee sales for free at http://tools.cira.state.tx.us/default.aspx?Lampasas_County/ForeclosureSaleSite.

Lavaca County *Property, Taxation Records*   Access to property tax search for free at www.lavacacountytax.com/Appraisal/PublicAccess/.

Lee County *Recorded Documents, Marriage, Birth Records* www.co.lee.tx.us/default.aspx?Lee_County/County.Clerk   Access indexes free at www.lgs-hosted.com/rmtleecck.html.
Property, Taxation Records   Access to Plat maps at www.lgs-hosted.com/rmtleecck.html.

Leon County *Recorded Documents* www.co.leon.tx.us/default.aspx?Leon_County/County.Clerk   Search grantor/grantee index free at https://texaslandrecords.com/txlr/TxlrApp/index.jsp. Registration and fees required for full data.

Liberty County *Recorded Documents* www.co.liberty.tx.us/default.aspx?Liberty_County/County.Clerk   Access to record lists free at http://countyclerk.co.liberty.tx.us/. *Property, Taxation Records*   Access to property tax sales for free at http://tax.acttax.com/pls/sales/property_taxsales_pkg.search_page?PI_STATE=TX. Also, access to online taxes for free at www.libertycountytax.com/taxweb/.

Limestone County *Recorded Documents* www.co.limestone.tx.us/default.aspx?Limestone_County/County.Clerk   Search grantor/grantee index free at https://texaslandrecords.com/txlr/TxlrApp/index.jsp. Registration and fees required for full data. Fee is $1.00 per record to print.
Property, Taxation Records   Access appraiser's property data free at www.limestonetexas-tax.com/Appraisal/PublicAccess/.

Lipscomb County *Recorded Documents* www.co.lipscomb.tx.us/default.aspx?Lipscomb_County/County.Clerk   A subscription called Exavault is available for $50.00 per month. Contact County Clerk's office for details.
Property, Taxation Records   Find appraisal district and collection offices data for free at http://iswdatacorp.azurewebsites.net//.

Live Oak County *Recorded Documents* www.co.live-oak.tx.us/   Search grantor/grantee index free at https://texaslandrecords.com/txlr/TxlrApp/index.jsp. Registration and fees required for full data.

Llano County *Property, Taxation Records*   Find appraisal district and collection offices data free at http://http://iswdatacorp.azurewebsites.net/estdata.com/corp/.

Lubbock County *Recorded Documents* www.co.lubbock.tx.us/department/?fDD=2-0   Access to index only of records free at https://erecord.co.lubbock.tx.us/recorder/web/.
Property, Taxation Records   Search the property appraiser database free at www.lubbockcad.org/Appraisal/PublicAccess/.

Madison County *Recorded Documents* www.co.madison.tx.us/default.aspx?Madison_County/County.Clerk   Search grantor/grantee index free at https://www.texaslandrecords.com/txlr/TxlrApp/index.jsp. Registration and fees required for full data.

Marion County *Recorded Documents* www.co.marion.tx.us/default.aspx?Marion_County/County.Clerk   Search grantor/grantee index free at https://texaslandrecords.com/txlr/TxlrApp/index.jsp. Registration and fees required for full data.
Property, Taxation Records   Access property tax records free at www.marioncad.org/. Click on Search Our Data. Also, access to search and pay taxes site for free at www.marioncountytaxoffice.com/taxes.

Martin County *Property, Taxation Records*   Access to property data is free at www.martincad.org/.

Mason County *Property, Taxation Records*   Access to property data searches free at www.masoncad.org/, click on 'Search Our Data.'

Matagorda County *Recorded Documents* www.co.matagorda.tx.us/default.aspx?Matagorda_County/County.Clerk   Search grantor/grantee index free at https://texaslandrecords.com/txlr/TxlrApp/index.jsp. Registration and fees required for full data.

Maverick County *Recorded Documents* www.co.maverick.tx.us/default.aspx?Maverick_County/County.Clerk   Access to land record indexes free at https://gov.propertyinfo.com/tx-maverick/#. Must register first. Also available for a fee are the images.

McLennan County *Recorded Documents* www.co.mclennan.tx.us/166/County-Clerk   Access land records at http://etitlesearch.com. Can do a name search; choose from $50.00 monthly subscription or per-click account.
Property, Taxation Records   Search real estate appraisal records at www.mclennancad.org/. Property Tax balance information free at https://actweb.acttax.com/act_webdev/mclennan/index.jsp.

Medina County *Recorded Documents* www.medinacountytexas.org/default.aspx?Medina_County/County.Clerk   Search official record index at https://tx.countygovernmentrecords.com/texas/web/ for free. Registration is required. Fees charged for viewing and printing document copies.
Property, Taxation Records   Access to tax rolls for free at www.medinacountytx.org/Appraisal/PublicAccess/.

Midland County *Recorded Documents* www.co.midland.tx.us/departments/cc/Pages/default.aspx   Access grantor/grantee index free at https://texaslandrecords.com/txlr/TxlrApp/index.jsp. Registration and fees required for full data. Any judgment, lien records, etc, that contain SSNs will not be online; search at office. They redact SSN by request only.
Property, Taxation Records   Access property tax data free at http://iswdatacorp.azurewebsites.net/.

Milam County *Recorded Documents* www.milamcounty.net/countyclerk.html   Search grantor/grantee index free at
https://texaslandrecords.com/txlr/TxlrApp/index.jsp. Registration and fees required for full data.
Property, Taxation Records   Access to property search options free at http://esearch.milamad.org/. Also see note at beginning of section.

Mills County *Property, Taxation Records*   Find appraisal district and collection offices data free at
http://http://iswdatacorp.azurewebsites.net/estdata.com/corp/.

Mitchell County *Recorded Documents* www.mitchellcountytexas.us/   Search official records free after choosing county at
www.edoctecinc.com/. If records are stamped Unofficial, you copy them freely; Official, a $1.00 per page fee applies. For details and signup, contact Edoc
Tec at 800-578-7746. *Property, Taxation Records*   Access to real property searches for free found at www.mitchellcad.org/.

Montague County *Property, Taxation Records*   Find appraisal district and collection offices data free at
http://http://iswdatacorp.azurewebsites.net/estdata.com/corp/.

Montgomery County *Recorded Documents, Probate Records* www.co.montgomery.tx.us/dept/departments_c/county_clerk/index.html
Index search may also be performed free at www.courthousedirect.com/IndexSearches.aspx. Registration & password required for rull data. Probate
records are at the County Court but accessible through the County Clerks Office. Also, access to the county online records for free at
https://gov.propertyinfo.com/TX-Montgomery/. Registration & login required. Images from 1980 to present.
Property, Taxation Records   Access property appraiser data free at www.mcad-tx.org/html/records.html.

Morris County *Recorded Documents* www.co.morris.tx.us/default.aspx?Morris_County/County.Clerk   Search official record index at
https://tx.countygovernmentrecords.com/texas/web/ for free. Registration is required. Fees charged for viewing and printing document copies.

Motley County *Property, Taxation Records*   Access to the appraisal district records free at http://iswdatacorp.azurewebsites.net/.

Nacogdoches County *Recorded Documents, Probate Records* www.co.nacogdoches.tx.us/countyoffices/countyclerk.asp   Search
grantor/grantee index free at https://texaslandrecords.com/txlr/TxlrApp/index.jsp. Registration and fees required for full data. Probate records are at the
County Court but accessible through the County Clerks Office.
Property, Taxation Records   Access property tax data free at www.nacocad.org/. Click on Search Our Data.

Navarro County *Recorded Documents* www.co.navarro.tx.us/default.aspx?Navarro_County/County.Clerk   Search grantor/grantee index
free at https://texaslandrecords.com/txlr/TxlrApp/index.jsp. Land records from 1985 to present. Registration and fees required for full data. Must register.

Nueces County *Recorded Documents* www.co.nueces.tx.us/countyclerk/   Access to county clerk recording records (indexes for free) is
free after registration at https://gov.propertyinfo.com/tx-nueces/; subscription service (gives unlimited view of index data) also available, $50 monthly.
Property, Taxation Records   Access County Appraiser records free at www.ncadistrict.com/ and click on Search Property to choose search mode.
Also, see notes at beginning of section. Also, access to property tax balances for free at https://actweb.acttax.com/act_webdev/nueces/index.jsp.

Ochiltree County *Recorded Documents* www.co.ochiltree.tx.us/default.aspx?Ochiltree_County/County.Clerk   Search official record
index at https://tx.countygovernmentrecords.com/texas/web/ and view for free. Registration is required. Fees charged for printing document copies.

Oldham County *Probate Records* www.co.oldham.tx.us/default.aspx?Oldham_County/County.Clerk   Probate records are at the County
Court but accessible through the County Clerks Office.

Orange County *Property, Taxation Records*   Access to tax statements and payment for free at
www.texasonlinerecords.com/tax/?office_id=6.

Palo Pinto County *Recorded Documents* www.co.palo-pinto.tx.us/default.aspx?Palo-Pinto_County/County.Clerk   Search official record
index at https://tx.countygovernmentrecords.com/texas/web/ for free. Registration is required. Fees charged for printing document copies.
Property, Taxation Records   Access to appraisers property and collection offices data free at http://iswdatacorp.azurewebsites.net//.

Panola County *Recorded Documents* www.co.panola.tx.us/default.aspx?Panola_County/County.Clerk   Search grantor/grantee index free
at https://texaslandrecords.com/txlr/TxlrApp/index.jsp. Registration and fees required for full data. Also, access to land records for free at
https://www.texaslandrecords.com/txlr/TxlrApp/index.jsp.

Parker County *Recorded Documents* www.parkercountytx.com/Index.aspx?NID=105   Search official record index at
https://tx.countygovernmentrecords.com/texas/web/ for free. Registration is required. Fees charged for viewing and printing document copies.
Property, Taxation Records   Find appraisal district and collecting offices data free at http://http://iswdatacorp.azurewebsites.net/estdata.com/corp/.

Pecos County *Recorded Documents* http://12.227.48.139/member/countyclerk/   Search official record index for a fee at
https://tx.countygovernmentrecords.com/texas/web/. Registration is free. Fees charged for viewing and printing document copies.
Property, Taxation Records   Access to property data is free at www.pecoscad.org/. Click on Search Our Data.

Polk County *Recorded Documents, Probate Records* www.co.polk.tx.us/default.aspx?Polk_County/County.Clerk   Access to County
Clerk's data is by subscription at www.co.polk.tx.us/default.aspx?Polk_County/County.Clerk. Probate records are at the County Court but accessible
through the County Clerks Office.

Potter County *Recorded Documents, Probate Records* www.co.potter.tx.us/default.aspx?Potter_County/County.Clerk Probate records are at the County Court but accessible through the County Clerks Office. Also, search official record index at https://tx.countygovernmentrecords.com/texas/web/ and view for free. Registration is required. Fees charged for printing document copies.
Property, Taxation Records Records on the Potter-Randall Appraisal District database are free at www.prad.org/. Records periodically updated; for current tax info call Potter- 806-342-2600 or Randall- 806-665-6287.

Randall County *Recorded Documents* http://randallcounty.com/cclerk/default.htm Access to recorded documents for a fee at https://tx.countygovernmentrecords.com/texas/web/. Must register.
Property, Taxation Records Randall County appraisal and personal property records are combined online with Potter County; see Potter County for access info or visit www.prad.org/. Randall County sheriff sales records are combined online with Potter County; see Potter County for access info or www.prad.org/

Reagan County *Recorded Documents* Access to recorded documents for a fee at https://www.idocmarket.com/sites. Must subscribe before use. Fees vary depending on plan picked. Computer indexing and images back to 1876.
Property, Taxation Records Access records for free at www.reagancad.org/contact.htm. Click 'Search Our Data'.

Reeves County *Property, Taxation Records* Access to appraisal districts and collection offices data free at http://iswdatacorp.azurewebsites.net//.

Refugio County *Recorded Documents* www.co.refugio.tx.us/default.aspx?Refugio_County/County.Clerk Access online records for free at https://countyfusion5.propertyinfo.com/countyweb/login.do?countyname=Refugio. For further details, must subscribe.
Property, Taxation Records Access property data free at www.refugiocad.org/.

Robertson County *Recorded Documents* www.co.robertson.tx.us/default.aspx?Robertson_County/County.Clerk Search grantor/grantee index free at https://texaslandrecords.com/txlr/TxlrApp/index.jsp. Registration and fees required for full data.

Rockwall County *Recorded Documents* www.rockwallcountytexas.com/108/County-Clerk Access to records for a fee at https://countyclerk.rockwallcountytexas.com/.
Property, Taxation Records Access to property tax records for free at www.rockwallcountytexas.com/index.aspx?nid=205.

Runnels County *Property, Taxation Records* Find appraisal district and collection offices data free at http://http://iswdatacorp.azurewebsites.net/estdata.com/corp/.

Rusk County *Recorded Documents* www.co.rusk.tx.us/default.aspx?Rusk_County/County.Clerk Search grantor/grantee index free at https://texaslandrecords.com/txlr/TxlrApp/index.jsp. Registration and fees required for full data.
Property, Taxation Records Access property data free at www.ruskcad.org/. Click on Property Search.

San Augustine County *Recorded Documents* www.co.san-augustine.tx.us/countyClerk.html Search grantor/grantee index free at https://www.texaslandrecords.com/txlr/TxlrApp/index.jsp. Registration and fees required for full data.

San Jacinto County *Recorded Documents* www.co.san-jacinto.tx.us/default.aspx?San-Jacinto_County/County.Clerk Access to indexed real property records for free at https://www.texaslandrecords.com/txlr/TxlrApp/index.jsp. There is a charge to view or print the documents on-line.
Property, Taxation Records Access assessment records for free at www.sjc-tax.com/Appraisal/PublicAccess/.

San Patricio County *Probate Records* www.co.san-patricio.tx.us/default.aspx?San-Patricio_County/County.Clerk Probate records are at the County Court but accessible through the County Clerks Office.
Property, Taxation Records Access to property tax balance for a fee at https://actweb.acttax.com/act_webdev/sanpatricio/index.jsp.

Scurry County *Recorded Documents* www.co.scurry.tx.us/default.aspx?Scurry_County/County.Clerk Search grantor/grantee index free at https://texaslandrecords.com/txlr/TxlrApp/index.jsp. Registration and fees required for full data.

Shelby County *Recorded Documents, Marriage, Probate Records* http://cc.co.shelby.tx.us/ Access to record indexes free at http://cc.co.shelby.tx.us/. Probate index on this URL.
Property, Taxation Records Access to property data and the Appraisal District records for free at www.shelbycad.com/.

Smith County *Recorded Documents* www.smith-county.com/Government/ElectedOfficials/CountyClerk/Default.aspx Search grantor/grantee index free at https://texaslandrecords.com/txlr/TxlrApp/index.jsp. Registration and fees required for full data.
Property, Taxation Records Access to county appraisal district records is free at https://www.smithcountymapsite.org/. Also, access property searches free at https://www.smithcad.org/Search/PropertySearch.html. Also, see note at beginning of section.

Somervell County *Recorded Documents* www.co.somervell.tx.us/index.php/county-offices/county-a-district-clerk Access to public records for free at http://pa.co.somervell.tx.us/. Documents can be purchased for $1.00 per page for copies and $5.00 per document for certification.
Property, Taxation Records Access to appraisal district and collection offices data free at http://iswdatacorp.azurewebsites.net/.

Stephens County *Recorded Documents* www.co.stephens.tx.us/default.aspx?Stephens_County/County.Clerk Search official record index at https://tx.countygovernmentrecords.com/texas/web/ and view for free. Registration is required. Fees charged for printing document copies.

Property, Taxation Records   Find appraisal district and collection offices data free at http://iswdatacorp.azurewebsites.net//.

Sutton County   *Recorded Documents*   www.suttoncounty.org/   Access to recorded documents for a fee at https://www.idocmarket.com/sites. Must subscribe before use. Fees vary depending on plan picked. Computer indexing back to 6/1/1992, imaging back to 11/1/2003.

Tarrant County   *Recorded Documents*   http://access.tarrantcounty.com/en/county-clerk.html   Search records for free at http://access.tarrantcounty.com/en/county-clerk.html. Includes assumed names, marriage license, real property and UCC searches. But direct to recorded docs is https://tcrecordsonline.com/?linklocation=Iwantto&linkname=Real%20Estate%20Records
Property, Taxation Records   Access Tax Assessor/Collector database for free at data free at http://access.tarrantcounty.com/en/tax.html. Click on "Online Services" for choices.

Taylor County   *Recorded Documents*   http://taylorcountytexas.org/120/County-Clerk   Search grantor/grantee index free at https://texaslandrecords.com/txlr/TxlrApp/index.jsp. Registration and fees required for full data.

Titus County   *Recorded Documents*   www.co.titus.tx.us/   Access to real property records at www.texasonlinerecords.com/clerk/index?office_id=2. Must register before using. Also, access to public records go go to www.tituscountyonline.net/clerk/. Must also register before using. Search official record index at https://tx.countygovernmentrecords.com/texas/web/ and view for free. Registration is required. Fees charged for printing document copies.

Tom Green County   *Recorded Documents*   www.co.tom-green.tx.us/default.aspx?name=cck.CountyClerkHome   Access official public records including vital stats and fictitious names free at https://tomgreentx.countygovernmentrecords.com/TomGreenTXRecorder/eagleweb/. Records from 1/1/1982 to present. *Property, Taxation Records*   Access to appraisal district and collection offices data for free at http://http://iswdatacorp.azurewebsites.net/estdata.com/corp/.

Travis County   *Recorded Documents*   www.traviscountyclerk.org/eclerk/Content.do?code=Home   Access to recorders official records is free at http://deed.co.travis.tx.us/ords/f?p=105:3:0::NO:::
Property, Taxation Records   Access the Central Appraisal District database free at www.traviscad.org/property_search.html. Also search business personal property. Also, can search on the county tax payment system at https://tax-office.traviscountytx.gov/properties/account-search.

Upshur County   *Recorded Documents*   www.countyofupshur.com/Departments/County%20Clerk.htm   Access records free at www.countyofupshur.com/CC%20Notice%200022607.htm. Can view records only, cannot print from computer.

Upton County   *Recorded Documents*   www.co.upton.tx.us/default.aspx?Upton_County/County.Clerk   Search grantor/grantee index free at https://texaslandrecords.com/txlr/TxlrApp/index.jsp. Registration and fees required for full data.

Uvalde County   *Property, Taxation Records*   Access CAD eSearch data for free at http://esearch.uvaldecad.org/.

Val Verde County   *Recorded Documents*   http://valverdecounty.texas.gov/153/County-Clerk   Search grantor/grantee index free at https://texaslandrecords.com/txlr/TxlrApp/index.jsp. Registration and fees required for full data.

Van Zandt County   *Recorded Documents*   www.vanzandtcounty.org/default.aspx?Van-Zandt_County/County.Clerk   Search official record index at https://tx.countygovernmentrecords.com/texas/web/ and view for free. Registration is required. Fees charged for printing document copies.
Property, Taxation Records   Find appraisal district and collection offices data free at http://http://iswdatacorp.azurewebsites.net/estdata.com/corp/.

Victoria County   *Recorded Documents, Probate Records*   www.vctx.org/index.php/en/county-departments?id=30   County clerk web assess for free at https://manatron.vctx.org/.
Property, Taxation Records   Access to property assessment and tax information free at http://orion.vctx.org/appraisal/publicaccess/. Also, access to GIS/mapping for free at http://maps.victoriatx.org/MapViewer/PublicMap.html. Access to appraisal district records is free at www.victoriacad.org/.

Walker County   *Recorded Documents*   www.co.walker.tx.us/department/index.php?fDD=5-0   Search grantor/grantee index free at https://texaslandrecords.com/txlr/TxlrApp/index.jsp. Registration and fees required for full data.

Waller County   *Recorded Documents*   http://ww2.co.waller.tx.us/   Search official record index at https://tx.countygovernmentrecords.com/texas/web/ and view for free. Registration is required. Fees charged for printing document copies.
Property, Taxation Records   Access to tax record information for free at http://tax.co.waller.tx.us/Appraisal/PublicAccess/.

Ward County   *Recorded Documents*   www.co.ward.tx.us/default.aspx?Ward_County/County.Clerk   Search official record index at https://tx.countygovernmentrecords.com/texas/web/ for free. Registration is required. Fees charged for viewing and printing document copies.
Property, Taxation Records   Access to tax records for free at www.wardcountytax.org/.

Washington County   *Recorded Documents, Probate, Vital Records, Military Discharge Records*
www.co.washington.tx.us/default.aspx?Washington_County/County.Clerk   Probate records are at the County Court accessible through throught the County Clerks office. Also, search official records after choosing county at www.edoctecinc.com/. If records are Unofficial, search or copy them free; if Official, a $1.00 per page fee applies.
Property, Taxation Records   Access appraisal district property records free at www.washingtoncad.org/Appraisal/PublicAccess/.

Webb County *Recorded Documents, Probate Records* www.webbcounty.com/CountyClerk/ Access recorded documents for a fee at http://acclaimweb.webbcountytx.gov/county/webbportal. Probate records are at the County Court but accessible through the County Clerks Office.
Property, Taxation Records Search the county Central Appraisal District database at www.webbcountytax.com/faces/search.jsp.

Wharton County *Recorded Documents, Probate Records* www.co.wharton.tx.us/default.aspx?Wharton_County/County.Clerk Access to the county eSearch website at www.co.wharton.tx.us, click on county offices, then county clerk, then real properties records. There is a fee for this subscription, must have a user ID and password. Probate records are at the County Court but accessible through the County Clerks office.
Property, Taxation Records Access to tax roll and payments for free at www.whartoncountytaxoffice.com/.

Wheeler County *Property, Taxation Records* Find appraisal district and collection offices data free at http://http://iswdatacorp.azurewebsites.net/estdata.com/corp/.

Wichita County *Recorded Documents* www.co.wichita.tx.us/county.html Search grantor/grantee index free at https://texaslandrecords.com/txlr/TxlrApp/index.jsp. Registration and fees required for full data.
Property, Taxation Records Access to county appraisal district records is free at http://propaccess.wadtx.com/clientdb/?cid=1. Also, access to the Tax Office website for free at www.wichitatax.com/.

Wilbarger County *Recorded Documents* www.co.wilbarger.tx.us/default.aspx?Wilbarger_County/County.Clerk Search grantor/grantee index free at https://www.uslandrecords.com/uslr/UslrApp/index.jsp. Registration and fees required for full data. Also, access to the foreclosure listings for free at https://foreclosures.uslandrecords.com/FAM/TX/Wilbarger/Foreclosures.aspx.
Property, Taxation Records Access to property data is free at www.wilbargertax.org/. Click on Search Our Data.

Williamson County *Recorded Documents* www.wilco.org/CountyDepartments/CountyClerk/tabid/230/language/en-US/Default.aspx Access to recorded documents, liens, certain vital records for free at https://deed.wilco.org/. Records go back to 1838.
Property, Taxation Records Access the appraiser database free at http://orionpa.tylerhost.net/. Also, see note in the state summary section.

Wilson County *Recorded Documents* www.co.wilson.tx.us/default.aspx?Wilson_County/County.Clerk Search grantor/grantee index free at https://texaslandrecords.com/txlr/TxlrApp/index.jsp. Registration and fees required for full data.

Winkler County *Recorded Documents* www.co.winkler.tx.us/default.aspx?Winkler_County/County.Clerk Search official record index at https://tx.countygovernmentrecords.com/texas/web/ and view for free. Registration is required. Fees charged for printing document copies.

Wise County *Recorded Documents* www.co.wise.tx.us/CC/ Search official record index at https://tx.countygovernmentrecords.com/texas/web/ and view for free. Registration is required. Fees charged for printing document copies.
Property, Taxation Records Find appraisal district and collection offices data free at http://http://iswdatacorp.azurewebsites.net/estdata.com/corp/. Also, access to tax records for a fee at www.texasonlinerecords.com/tax/?office_id=10.

Wood County *Foreclosures Records* www.mywoodcounty.com/default.aspx?name=countyclerk Foreclosure information for free at www.mywoodcounty.com/users/0004/Foreclosure/Aug2015Foreclosure1.pdf. Also, search official record index at https://tx.countygovernmentrecords.com/texas/web/ and view for free. Registration is required. Fees charged for printing document copies.
Property, Taxation Records Search property tax records free at www.woodcountytax.com/taxSearch.

Yoakum County *Recorded Documents* www.co.yoakum.tx.us/default.aspx?Yoakum_County/County.Clerk Access to county records for a fee at https://www.texaslandrecords.com/txlr/TxlrApp/index.jsp. Must register. Search official record index at https://tx.countygovernmentrecords.com/texas/web/ and view for free. Registration is required. Fees charged for printing document copies.

Young County *Recorded Documents, Probate Records* www.co.young.tx.us/default.aspx?Young_County/County.Clerk Indexes available at www.texasonlinerecords.com/clerk/?office_id=11. Must register. Probate records are at the County Court but accessible through the County Clerks Office. *Property, Taxation Records* Access to property data is free at www.youngcad.org/. Click on Search Our Data.

Zapata County *Recorded Documents* www.co.zapata.tx.us/default.aspx?Zapata_County/County.Clerk Access recording office land data at www.etitlesearch.com/; registration required, fee based on usage. Also, search grantor/grantee index free at https://texaslandrecords.com/txlr/TxlrApp/index.jsp. Registration and fees required for full data.

Reminder:
To avoid redundancy, these profiles do NOT include the 4 Bulleted Sites mentioned at the beginning of this section.

Utah

Capital: Salt Lake City
           Salt Lake County
Time Zone: MST
Population: 2,995,919
# of Counties: 29

Useful State Links

Website: **www.utah.gov**
Governor: **www.utah.gov/governor/index.html**
Attorney General: **http://attorneygeneral.utah.gov**
State Archives: **http://archives.utah.gov/index.html**
State Statutes and Codes: **www.rules.utah.gov/publicat/code.htm**
Legislative Bill Search: **http://le.utah.gov/Documents/bills.htm**
Unclaimed Funds: **https://mycash.utah.gov/UP_Start.asp**

State Public Record Agencies

Sexual Offender Registry
Sex Offenders Registration Program, http://corrections.utah.gov/index.php?option=com_content&view=article&id=906&Itemid=191   The Registry may be searched from www.communitynotification.com/cap_office_disclaimer.php?office=54438 Records are searchable by name, city or geographic area, county, or ZIP Code. One can also search by specific area, please register for email alerts.

Incarceration Records
Utah Department of Corrections, Records Bureau, http://corrections.utah.gov   An offender search is provided at http://corrections.utah.gov/index.php?option=com_content&view=article&id=813&Itemid=107. Search by name or offender number. The site includes information on only current inmates; historical data is not available.

Corporation, LLC, LP, Fictitious/Assumed Name, Trademarks/Servicemarks
Commerce Department, Division of Corporations and Commercial Code, www.corporations.utah.gov/ A number of search options, including business entity, principle, Certificate of Existence is available at www.utah.gov/services/business.html?type=citizen. Basic information (name, address, agent) is free. Also a subscription service is offered with expanded data. The website also offers an Unclaimed Property search page. Also, search securities professions database free at www.securities.utah.gov/investors/before_verify.html. *Other Options:* State allows e-mail access for orders of Certification of Existence at orders@utah.gov

Uniform Commercial Code
Department of Commerce, UCC Division, https://secure.utah.gov/uccsearch/uccs   UCC uncertified records are available free online at https://secure.utah.gov/uccsearch/uccs. Search by debtor individual name or organization, or by filing number. Certified searches may also be ordered for $12.00 per search. To receive certified searches, you may be a registered user or use a credit card. The website gives details. Note for subscribers there is a $70 annual registration fee which includes 10 user logins. Email requests are accepted at orders@br.state.ut.us. *Other Options:* The agency has indicated that records are available in bulk from Utah Interactive. Call 801-983-0275.

Birth Certificates
Department of Health, Office of Vital Records & Statistics, http://health.utah.gov/vitalrecords/   Orders can be placed online via the agency's Silver system. See https://silver.health.utah.gov/birthinfo.html. Fee is $18.00, certificate is mailed is 7-10 days. Orders can also be placed via a state approved vendor. Go to www.vitalchek.com. Extra fees are involved. See expedited service.

Death Records

Department of Health, Office of Vital Records & Statistics, http://health.utah.gov/vitalrecords/ A Death Certificate index search for records 1904-1960 is found at http://archives.utah.gov/research/indexes/20842.htm. Orders can be placed online via the agency's Silver system. See https://silver.health.utah.gov/birthinfo.html. Fee is $18.00, certificate is mailed is 7-10 days. Orders can also be placed via a state approved vendor. Go to www.vitalchek.com. Extra fees are involved. See expedited service. There is a Utah - State Cemetery and Burial Database search at https://heritage.utah.gov/history/cemeteries. *Other Options:* Search the state's Cemetery and Burials database for free at http://heritage.utah.gov/history/cemeteries.

Marriage, Divorce Certificates

Department of Health, Office of Vital Records & Statistics, http://health.utah.gov/vitalrecords/ Orders can be placed online via the agency's Silver system. See https://silver.health.utah.gov/birthinfo.html. Fee is $18.00, certificate is mailed is 7-10 days. Orders can also be placed via a state approved vendor. Go to www.vitalchek.com. Extra fees are involved. See expedited service.

Driver Records

Department of Public Safety, Driver License Division, Customer Service Section, http://dld.utah.gov/ Driving records are available to eligible organizations through the eUtah. The system is available 24 hours daily. The fee per driving record is $9.00. There is an annual $95.00 subscription fee which includes access for 10 users. Eligible organizations may subscribe by visiting www.utah.gov/registration/ or call 801-983-0275. Subscribers can use a DL# verification service for $1.50 per check. Subscribers who are insurance organizations may also use the Address Verification service to check for uninsured drivers residing at the same address as current policyholders. Fee is $5.00. Also, drivers may secure their own record online at https://secure.utah.gov/mvr-personal/public/index.html. Use of a credit card is required AND the billing address of the credit card must match the address the Division has on file for the driver. *Other Options:* Utah offers a monitoring notification program to insurance firms. Fee is $.12 per driver plus if activity, an MVR is automatically generate and must be purchased. Also, must be a subscriber - see www.utah.gov/registration.

Vehicle, Vessel Ownership & Registration

State Tax Commission, Motor Vehicle Division Records Section, http://dmv.utah.gov The "Title, Lien and Motor Vehicle Information Service (TLRIS) is offered to qualified requesters. There is a $95 annual fee to be a subscriber to the online system at www.utah.gov/registration/. The record search fee is $2.00 per record. *Other Options:* Bulk requests are available for approved entities. Submit all requests in writing.

Crash Reports

Highway Patrol, Accident Reports Section, http://highwaypatrol.utah.gov/online-accident-reports/ Eligible requesters may order the electronically and instantly receive it at https://secure.utah.gov/accidentreport/index.html. The fee is $7.00 *Other Options:* The Utah Highway patrol will sell the complete accident file to qualified parties. Visit http://publicsafety.utah.gov/highwaypatrol/index.html. The fee is $5.00 for 1 to 10 pages and $25.00 for 11 to 50 pages.

Voter Registration, Campaign Finance, Lobbyists

Elections - Office of Lt Governor, PO Box 142325, https://elections.utah.gov/ Campaign finance repots and PAC disclosures are searchable from https://elections.utah.gov/campaign-finance. Also lobbyists data is shown at https://lobbyist.utah.gov/. Overall financial disclosures are shown at https://disclosures.utah.gov/. This includes those of lobbyists.

GED Certificates

Utah State Office of Education, GED Testing Records, www.schools.utah.gov/ged/ Third parties are routed to set up an account at: http://exchange.parchment.com/ged-receiver-registration-page. Parchment verifies that they are who they say they are so that they can place orders on behalf of students. Parchment contacts the third party and provides training on the site for ordering. During this training any orders they have are placed. After this the third party can order on behalf of students. They still must upload a consent form for each student during the process.

Occupational Licensing Boards

These licenses are all searchable at https://secure.utah.gov/llv/search/index.html

Accountant, Firm	Court Reporter, Shorthand/Voice	Factory Built Housing Dealer
Acupuncturist	Deception Detection Examiner/Intern	Funeral Service
ADRP/Arbitrator/Negotiator	Dental Hygienist/Local Anesthesia	Director/Apprentice/Establishment
Architect	Dentist	Genetic Counselor/Temp Counselor
Athletic Agent	Dentist w/ Anesthesia Class I-IV	Geologist
Building Inspector, Combo or Ltd	Dietitian, Certified or Temporary	Health Facility Administrator/Temp
Burglar Alarm Firm/Agent/Temp	Electrician, Appren/Journey'n/Master	Hearing Instrument Specialist/Intern
Chiropractic Physician/or/Temp	Electrician, Resid'l/Journeym'n/Master	Landscape Architect
Contractor-All	Electrologist Instructor/School	Marriage/Family Therapist/Temporary
Control'd Substance Precurs'r Dist/Prch	Engineer/Land Surveyor/Structural Professional	Massage Therapist/Apprentice
Cosmetology/Barber/School/Instruct	Enviro'l Health Scientist/or/in-training	Midwife
Counselor, Professional/Trainee/Intern	Esthetician Master/Instructor/School	Nail Technician/Instructor/School

Naturopath
Naturopathic Physician
Nurse/Controlled Substance
Nurse/LPN/RN/Practical
Occupational Therapist/Assist Temp
Optometrist/Cont'd Subst/Diagnostic
Osteo Phys'n/Surg'n/Cont'd Substance
Pharmac't/Intern/Tech/Contr'd Substance
Pharmacy Class A-E

Physical Therapist
Physician/Surgeon, Cont'd Substance/Assistant
Plumber Apprentice/Journeyman
Podiatric Physic'n/Control'd Substance
Pre-Need Provider/Sales Agent
Probation Provider/Private
Psychologist/Resident/Temporary
Radiology Practical Technician
Radiology Technologist/or/Temp

Recreational Therapist/master/Spec'l'st
Respiratory Care Practitioner
Security Company/Officer, Private
Social Worker-Clinical/Certified
Speech Pathologist/Audiologist
Substance Abuse Counselor/Temp
Veterinarian/Vet Intern/cont'l substance

The Rest:

Bank	www.utah.gov/dfi/FinancialInstitutions.html
Beekeeping Inspector	http://ag.utah.gov/plants-pests/beekeeping/37-plants-and-pests/259-beekeeping-county-inspectors.html
Brand Inspector	http://ag.utah.gov/licenses-registrations/36-animals/291-utah-brand-inspectors.html
Consumer Lender	www.utah.gov/dfi/ConsumerLending.html
Credit Union	www.utah.gov/dfi/FinancialInstitutions.html
Escrow Agent	http://dfi.utah.gov/money-services/escrow-agents/
Holding Company	http://dfi.utah.gov/non-depository/holding-companies/
Industrial Banks	www.utah.gov/dfi/FinancialInstitutions.html
Insurance Agent/Broker/Adjust./Consultants	www.utah.gov/agent-search/search.html;jsessionid=31bc93431198fd9a759062cb9898#
Insurance Establishment	www.utah.gov/agent-search/search.html;jsessionid=31bc93431198fd9a759062cb9898#
Interpreter Agency	www.utahinterpreterprogram.org/
Interpreter for the Deaf	www.utahinterpreterprogram.org/
Liquor Store/Package Agency	http://abc.utah.gov/stores/index.html
Lobbyist/Lobbyist Report	https://lobbyist.utah.gov/Search/PublicSearch
Mortgage Broker, Residential	https://secure.utah.gov/rer/relv/search.html
Mortgage Loan Service	www.utah.gov/dfi/MortgageLending.html
Notary Public	https://secure.utah.gov/notary/search.html
Political Candidate	https://elections.utah.gov/campaign-finance
Polygraph Association Members	www.utahpolygraph.org/membership.asp
Polygraph Examiner/Intern	www.polygraphplace.com/docs/c-15-s-Utah-examiners.html
Polygraph Schools	http://polygraphplace.com/docs/schools.htm
Real Estate Agent/Broker/Company	https://secure.utah.gov/rer/relv/search.html
Real Estate Appraiser	https://secure.utah.gov/rer/relv/search.html
Savings & Loan	www.utah.gov/dfi/FinancialInstitutions.html
Trust Company	http://dfi.utah.gov/non-depository/trust-companies/

State and Local Courts

About Utah Courts: The **District Court** has original jurisdiction for all civil cases, all criminal felonies, certain misdemeanors, domestic relations cases such as divorces, child custody and support, adoption, and probate.

At one time Utah had Circuit Courts (lower courts). Effective July 1, 1996 all Circuit Courts were combined with the District Courts.

Justice Courts, established by counties and municipalities, deal with class B and C misdemeanors, violations of ordinances, small claims, and infractions committed within their territorial jurisdiction.

The web page for the Judicial Branch is https://www.utcourts.gov/index.html.

Appellate Courts: The Court has appellate jurisdiction to hear first degree and capital felony convictions from the District Court and civil judgments other than domestic cases. The Court of Appeals hears all appeals from the Juvenile and District Courts, except those from the small claims department of a District Court and those mentioned above. Opinions, dockets and calendars are viewable at www.utcourts.gov/courts/sup/

Online Court Access

There is a Statewide Court Online Access Program

Case information from all Utah District Court locations and all Justice Courts is available online through XChange. The case information from Justice Courts became available recently on this system, thus the data throughout may vary. Fees include a $25.00 registration fee and $30.00 per month fee which includes 200 searches. Each additional search is billed at $.10 per search. The search provides a summary of the docket index; case files and copies are not available. Information about XChange and the subscription agreement can be found at https://www.utcourts.gov/xchange/ or call 801-578-3850.

To see the throughput dates see https://www.utcourts.gov/xchange/?content=coverage.

A name search on XChange is considered to be equivalent to an on-site name search using public access terminals in those courts which provide the terminals. Always use the asterisk wildcard * feature to keep your search broad enough to pull in any middle names or initials that may have been entered at the court.

No individual Utah courts offer online access, other than as described above.

Recorders, Assessors, and Other Sites of Note

About Utah Recording Offices: 29 counties, 29 recording offices. The recording officers are the County Recorder for real estate and the Clerk of District Court for state tax liens.

About Tax Liens: All federal tax liens are filed with the County Recorder. All state tax liens are filed with Clerk of District Court.

Online Access

Statewide Recorded Documents & Property Data

An excellent statewide search site for real estate records, provided by the Utah County Government, is found at www.utahcounty.gov/LandRecords/Index.asp. Search for many types of records, including recorded documents, property evaluations, by name, property address or parcel. There is also a delinquent tax search. One may also pull document images of recorded documents if the document number is given.

Individual County Recorder and Tax Assessor Data

Many Utah counites provide their own online access, as shown below.

Individual County Sites (The Statewide Site Above is Not Shown on Profiles):

Box Elder County *Recorded Documents* www.boxeldercounty.org/recorder.htm   Access to county recordings data is available free for indexed data only at http://erecord.boxeldercounty.org/eaglesoftware/taxweb/. Click on Public Login. Can purchase single documents by credit card for $1.50 per document or have the option to purchase a one or three month subscription. Must register first.
Property, Taxation Records   Access to GIS/mapping free at http://gis.vgsi.com/bownh/.

Cache County *Recorded Documents* https://www.cachecounty.org/recorder/   Access to recording records is via subscription at www.landlight.com/. Choose from 3 subscription plans; short free trial is offered. Grantor/Grantee Index goes back to 10/1980; Abstracts to 7/1984; images to 12/1992. Call 435-787-9003 for more info on online access.
Property, Taxation Records   Access to GIS/mapping free at https://www.cachecounty.org/gis/gis-data-downloads.html.

Carbon County *Recorded Documents* https://www.carbon.utah.gov/Administration   Access to images of recorded documents and plats free at www.carbon.utah.gov/sirepub/docs.aspx. *Property, Taxation Records*   Access to GIS/mapping and tax notices for free at www.carbon.utah.gov/sirepub/docs.aspx.

Davis County *Recorded Documents* www.co.davis.ut.us/recorder/home   Access (no name searches) to data for free at www.co.davis.ut.us/recorder/property-search.. *Property, Taxation Records*   A property search by address or parcel number is free at www.co.davis.ut.us/assessor/property-search. View tax records at www.co.davis.ut.us/treasurer/taxinfo, but the 9-digit Parcel Serial Number is required.

Duchesne County *Property, Taxation Records*   Access to GIS/mapping for free at http://maps.duchesne.utah.gov/flexviewers/Parcels/default.htm.

Emery County *Property, Taxation Records*   Access plat map data by parcel ID number or location on county map free at www.emerycounty.com/recorder/needa_plat.htm. Find a parcle number at www.emerycounty.com/maps/index.htm.

Iron County *Recorded Documents* https://www.ironcounty.net/department/recorder/ Access to online search database free at http://eagleweb.ironcounty.net/eaglesoftware/web/. See index of documents recorded not images.

Juab County *Property, Taxation Records* Access to the delinquent tax payment list for free at www.co.juab.ut.us/Files/Notice%20for%20Delinquent%20in%20paper.pdf.

Kane County *Recorded Documents* http://kane.utah.gov/deptinfo.cfm?ID=2 Access county property records (indexes only) free at http://eagleweb.kane.utah.gov/eaglesoftware/web/login.jsp.
Property, Taxation Records Access property data free at http://eagleweb.kane.utah.gov/eaglesoftware/taxweb/search.jsp but no name searching.

Millard County *Recorded Documents* www.millardcounty.org/your-government/elected-officials/recorder/

Morgan County *Recorded Documents* www.morgan-county.net/Departments/Recorder.aspx Access to records for a fee-$1,000 Item fee, $250.00 per 1/4 plus cost for copies. Contact office for information.
Property, Taxation Records Access to tax roll records for free at www.morgan-county.net/MCTaxRoll.aspx.

Rich County *Plats, Subdivision Plats Records* www.richcountyut.org/recorder.html Access to ownership plats and final subdivision plats free at www.richcountyut.org/property.html.
Property, Taxation Records Access to plats/subdivisions free at www.richcountyut.org/property.html.

Salt Lake County *Recorded Documents* www.slcorecorder.org/SLCR/Home.aspx Access to recording office records is by subscription at www.slcorecorder.org/SLCR/SLCRecLogin.aspx?ReturnUrl=%2fSLCR%2fSearch%2fDataSearches.aspx. Check an address on voter registration rolls free at https://slco.org/clerk/elections/?CFID=55602617&CFTOKEN=37345273&jsessionid=4a302559673d3364eaee1b38772574a79315.
Property, Taxation Records Name search assessor records free at http://slco.org/assessor/new/query.cfm. Also, search parcel data at http://slco.org/maps/.

Sanpete County *Recorded Documents* http://sanpete.com/pages/recorder

Sevier County *Recorded Documents* www.sevierutah.net/index.aspx?nid=102 Access to recorder's database index of data is available with free login at https://qdocs.sevierutah.net/recorder/web/. No images available.
Property, Taxation Records Assessor data and sales included in recorder document search lookup with free login at https://qdocs.sevierutah.net/recorder/web/.

Summit County *Recorded Documents* www.summitcounty.org/243/Recorder-Surveyor Access the county Document search page free at http://property.summitcounty.org/eaglesoftware/web/login.jsp?submit=Enter. For free search use username public and password public.
Property, Taxation Records Access property data free at http://property.summitcounty.org/eaglesoftware/web/.

Tooele County *Recorded Documents* www.co.tooele.ut.us/recorder.htm Access to a free basic search of public records at https://geodata.tooelecountyonline.org/. For detailed information must subscribe.
Property, Taxation Records Access the property information database free at www.co.tooele.ut.us/taxinfo.html.

Uintah County *Recorded Documents* www.co.uintah.ut.us/departments/q_-_z_departments/recorder/index.php Access to property searches free at www.co.uintah.ut.us/departments/q_-_z_departments/recorder/index.php. Also subscription access information available for more in-depth searches. *Property, Taxation Records* Access assessor property data free by name, address or serial # at http://co.uintah.ut.us/departments/a_-_e_departments/assessor/online_search_forms.php.

Utah County *Recorded Documents* www.utahcountyonline.org/Dept/Record/index.asp Also, access statewide records for free at www.utahcounty.gov/LandRecords/Index.asp.
Property, Taxation Records Access statewide tax records and GIS/mapping free at www.utahcounty.gov/LandRecords/Index.asp.

Wasatch County *Recorded Documents* www.wasatch.utah.gov/Recorder Access to a limited grantor/grantee index (entry#, book & page/date/KOI). Also, surveys & subdivisions https://beta.co.wasatch.ut.us/sirepub/docs.aspx. Documents from 1966 to present are accessible. Grantor/Grantee data back to 5/20/1994.
Property, Taxation Records Access to property tax look-up at http://maps.co.wasatch.ut.us/ROS_Map.html.

Washington County *Recorded Documents* https://www.washco.utah.gov/departments/recorder/ Access recorder data free at http://eweb.washco.utah.gov:8080/recorder/web/login.jsp.
Property, Taxation Records Search GIS property data free at https://www.washco.utah.gov/forms/assessor/search/, but no name searching.

Weber County *Recorded Documents* www.webercountyutah.gov/recorder_surveyor/ Access recorder's ownership and dedicated plats data free at www3.co.weber.ut.us/ded_plats.php.
Property, Taxation Records Property records on the County Parcel Search site are free at www3.co.weber.ut.us/psearch/. Also, access Abstract Title Registrations for a monthly fee at www.co.weber.ut.us/recorder/abstract_title_reg.php. Multiple GIS-mapping aps available free at www.co.weber.ut.us/gis/?content=interactive.

Vermont

Capital: Montpelier
                Washington County
Time Zone: EST
Population: 626,042
# of Counties: 14

Useful State Links

Website: **http://vermont.gov/portal**
Governor: **http://governor.vermont.gov**
Attorney General: **www.atg.state.vt.us**
State Archives: **https://www.sec.state.vt.us/archives-records.aspx**
State Statutes and Codes: **http://legislature.vermont.gov/**
Legislative Bill Search: **http://legislature.vermont.gov/**
Unclaimed Funds: **www.vermonttreasurer.gov/unclaimed-property**

State Public Record Agencies

Criminal Records

Criminal Record Check Section, Vermont Criminal Information Center,   http://vcic.vermont.gov/   The VCCRIS is available online at https://secure.vermont.gov/DPS/criminalrecords/. Search by name and DOB. One may use a credit or billing is available to subscribers to Vermont.gov. Results are immediate and can be printed. A validation service is also offered, but records are not certified. The fee is $30.00 per record. Search results report the date of conviction, charge, sentence and venue. It won't show the original charge filed, or give information about the circumstances of the crime. A free online validation service is offered. Disclosure of the contents of the conviction report to anyone other than the subject of the record or properly designated employees of any agency with a documented need to know the contents of the record is prohibited. *Other Options:* Any Criminal Conviction Record purchased through this service can be verified through the Vermont Criminal Information Center at no cost by entering the validation code through the Online Validation Service.

Sexual Offender Registry

State Repository, Vermont Criminal Information Center,   http://vcic.vermont.gov/sor   Search free online at www.communitynotification.com/cap_office_disclaimer.php?office=55275. There is a disclaimer:"This service does not contain the names of all the registered sex offenders in Vermont." but no indication who is not listed. The requestor must also acknowledge a statement which specifies the conditions under which the registry information is being released.

Incarceration Records

Vermont Department of Corrections, Inmate Information Request,   www.doc.state.vt.us   The website provides an Incarcerated Offender Locator to ascertain where an inmate is located. Click at the top of main page, or go directly to http://doc.vermont.gov/offender-locator/ Search results give name, DOB, location and case worker. This is not designed to provide complete inmate records nor is it a database of all inmates past and present in the system. The site actually links to a vendor site called JailTracker which manages a software platform for this agency.

Corporation, LLC, LLP, LP, L3C, Trade Name, Trademarks/Servicemarks

Secretary of State, Corporation Division,   https://www.sec.state.vt.us/corporationsbusiness-services.aspx   Information on Corporate and trademark records can be accessed from the Internet for no fee. For the corporation name search, go to https://www.vtsosonline.com/online. Many records are included including corporation, UCC, trademark, trade name, and name look-ups are available. Verify the validity of a Good Standing at https://www.vtsosonline.com/online/Certificate. *Other Options:* There is an option on the web to download the entire corporation (and trade name) database.

Uniform Commercial Code

UCC Division, Secretary of State,   https://www.sec.state.vt.us/corporationsbusiness-services/ucc-lien-services.aspx   A basic UCC search is free at the home page https://www.sec.state.vt.us/corporations/ucc-lien-services.aspx. One may order an Uncertified Debtor Report for $5.00. One may create a User Account and view/order uncertified reports, certified search reports, and certified copies.   *Other Options:* With a log-in, the database may be downloaded from the web. The data file is in a self extracting, IBM compatible, generic dbf format. Also the last 30 days of images may be downloaded in a ZIP format.

Workers' Compensation Records

VT Department of Labor, Workers' Compensation and Safety Division,   http://labor.vermont.gov/workers-compensation/   Hearing decisions, by year, are found at http://labor.vermont.gov/legal-information/

Driver Records

Department of Motor Vehicles, DI - Records Unit,   http://dmv.vermont.gov/   Record access is available to approved requesters as a premium service from Vermont.gov. The fee is $15.00 per record; a $75.00 annual subscription fee is also required. Single inquiry and batch mode are both available. The system is open 24 hours a day, 7 days a week (except for file maintenance periods). Only the license number is needed when ordering, the system does not ask for the name and DOB. All information concerning the forms and how to become a subscriber is found at https://secure.vermont.gov/DMV/mvr/help/. Contact Vermont Information Consortium directly at 802-229-4171.   *Other Options:* This agency will sell its license file to approved requesters for non-commercial use, but customization is not available.

Voter Registration, Campaign Finance, PACs, Lobbyists

Secretary of State, Election Division,   https://www.sec.state.vt.us/elections.aspx   View campaign finance reports at https://www.sec.state.vt.us/elections/campaign-finance.aspx. Search lobbyist data at https://www.sec.state.vt.us/elections/lobbying.aspx. This page includes listings of lobbyist employers.

Occupational Licensing Boards

These licenses are all searchable at https://secure.vtprofessionals.org/Lookup/LicenseLookup.aspx

Accountant Firm	Embalmer	Optician
Acupuncturist	Engineer	Optometrist
Architect	Esthetician	Osteopathic Physician
Athlete Agents	Funeral Director	Pharmacist/Pharmacy
Athletic Trainer	Hearing Aid Dispenser	Physical Therapist/Assistant
Auctioneer	Land Surveyor	Private Investigator
Barber	Landscape Architect	Psychoanalyst
Body Piercer/Tattooist	Manicurist	Psychologist/Psychotherapist
Boxing Manager/Promoter	Marriage & Family Therapist	Radiation Tech
Boxing Professional	Mental Health Counselor, Clinical	Real Estate Agent/Broker/Seller
Chiropractor	Midwife	Real Estate Appraiser
Cosmetologist	Motor Vehicle Racing	Respiratory Therapy
Crematory	Naturopath	Security Guard
Dental Assistant/Hygienist	Notary Public	Social Worker
Dentist	Nurse/Nurse Practitioner/LNA	Tattooist
Dietitian	Nursing Home Administrator	Veterinarian
Electrologist	Occupational Therapist	

The Rest:

Anesthesiologist Assistant	https://webmail.vdh.state.vt.us/CAVU/Lookup/LicenseLookup.aspx
Asbestos Contractor/Worker/Labs/Company	http://healthvermont.gov/enviro/asbestos/documents/asbestos_consult_contractor_list.pdf
Attorney	www.utahbar.org/public-services/i-need-a-lawyer/enhanced-attorney-listings/
Bank	www.dfr.vermont.gov/banking/depository-trusts/depository-trusts
Boiler & Pressure Vessel Inspectors	http://firesafety.vermont.gov/licensing
Caterers	http://liquorcontrol.vermont.gov/downloads
Chemical Suppression TQP Cert	http://firesafety.vermont.gov/licensing
Chimney Sweep TQP Cert	http://firesafety.vermont.gov/licensing
Credit Union	www.dfr.vermont.gov/banking/depository-trusts/depository-trusts
Driving Instructor/School, Commerc'l	http://dmv.vermont.gov/safety/training/commercial

Driving Instructor/School, Non-Commerc'l	http://dmv.vermont.gov/safety/training/drivers
Education Professionals Disciplinary Actions	http://education.vermont.gov/licensing/disciplinary-actions
Electrician	http://firesafety.vermont.gov/licensing
Elevator Inspector/Mechanic	http://firesafety.vermont.gov/licensing
Fire Alarm System Instal'r/Dealer	http://firesafety.vermont.gov/licensing
Fire Sprinkler System Design/Installer	http://firesafety.vermont.gov/licensing
Investment Advisor	www.dfr.vermont.gov/securities/investor/find-registered-professional
Lead Abatement Contractor/Worker/Labs/Company	http://healthvermont.gov/enviro/lead/documents/lead_consult_contractor_list.pdf
Lift Mechanic	http://firesafety.vermont.gov/licensing
Liquor, Retail/Wholesale	http://liquorcontrol.vermont.gov/downloads
Lobbyist Gift	https://www.sec.state.vt.us/elections/lobbying.aspx
Lobbyist/Employer/Firm	https://www.sec.state.vt.us/elections/lobbying.aspx
LPG/Propane Installer	http://firesafety.vermont.gov/licensing
Mortgage Company/Professional	www.dfr.vermont.gov/banking/licensees/mortgage-loan-originator-0
Natural Gas System Installer	http://firesafety.vermont.gov/licensing
Notary Public	https://www.sec.state.vt.us/archives-records/statutory-filings/notaries-public/find-a-notary.aspx
Oil Burning Equipment Installer	http://firesafety.vermont.gov/licensing
Physician/Medical Doctor/Surgeon/Assistant	https://webmail.vdh.state.vt.us/CAVU/Lookup/LicenseLookup.aspx
Plumber	http://firesafety.vermont.gov/licensing
Podiatrist	https://webmail.vdh.state.vt.us/CAVU/Lookup/LicenseLookup.aspx
Teacher	https://alis.edlicensing.vermont.gov/login.aspx

State and Local Courts

About Vermont Courts: The Superior Court has five Divisions: **Criminal, Civil, Family, Probate**, and **Environmental**. The Civil Division of the Superior Court hears predominantly civil, tort, real estate, and small claims cases. On rare occasion it hears criminal cases, but the Criminal Division of the Superior Court hears predominantly criminal cases, but will also hear some civil suspension cases, fish and wildlife violations, and appeals from the Judicial Bureau. Specialty courts include Probate Division Courts and Family Division Courts. The Environmental Division hears municipal land use enforcement cases and enforcement actions brought by states natural resources agencies.

In Vermont, the **Judicial Bureau** has jurisdiction over traffic, municipal ordinances, and Fish and Game violations, minors in possession, and hazing.

The web page for the Judicial Branch is https://www.vermontjudiciary.org/default.aspx.

Appellate Courts: The Supreme Court is the court of last resort and has appellate jurisdiction. Opinions from the Supreme Court are viewable from the web page, click on *Legal Information*.

Online Court Access

Statewide Access Provided to Civil and Small Claims Actions, Calendars

Vermont Courts Online provides access to civil and small claim cases and court calendar information from all county Superior Courts at a state judicial site. However, there is limited access for cases available from Chittenden (from 10/1/2012 for civil and 6/1/2012 for small claims) and from Franklin (from 1/1/2012 for civil and small claims). Go to https://secure.vermont.gov/vtcdas/user. Records are in real-time mode. There is a $12.50 activation fee plus a fee of $.50 per case for look-up after the 1st 5 cases. A disclaimer states "The information obtained from *VTCourtsOnLine* is not guaranteed to be complete or accurate."

Detailed case information about Criminal and Family Division cases is currently NOT accessible through VTCourtsOnline.

A great source of Vermont legal decisions including those made by Judiciary Boards is found at http://libraries.vermont.gov/law.

See Probate locations at https://www.vermontjudiciary.org/GTC/Probate/default.aspx.

There is NO online access to Courts other than as described above.

Recorders, Assessors, and Other Sites of Note

About Vermont Recording Offices: Vermont has 14 counties and 246 towns/cities. There is **no county recording** in this state. **All recording is done at the city/town level in the 246 locations.** Many towns are so small that their mailing addresses are in different towns. 4 towns had the same names as cities - Barre, Newport, Rutland, and St. Albans. 11 cities or towns bear the same name as a Vermont county - Addison, Bennington, Chittenden, Essex, Franklin, Grand Isle, Orange, Rutland, Washington, Windham, and Windsor.

About Tax Liens: All federal and state tax liens on personal property and on real property are filed with the Town/City Clerk in the lien/attachment book and indexed with real estate records.

Online Access

Town and City Sites:
Barnet Town in Caledonia County *Property, Taxation Records*   Access to the Grand List for free at http://barnetvt.org/?page_id=46.

Barre City in Washington County *Recorded Documents* www.barrecity.org/index.asp?Type=B_BASIC&SEC={30739B2F-F67C-44EF-B4F2-CAE6D9C2E652}   Access to land records for free at https://i2d.uslandrecords.com/VT/BarreCity_Public/D/Default.aspx. Printing or downloading fees are $3.00 per page. Online index back to 1989, online documents back to 6/9/2010.

Bennington Town in Bennington County *Property, Taxation Records*   Access to the Grand List search program is free at http://benningtonvt.org/departments/assessors-listers-office/grand-list-2/.

Brandon Town in Rutland County *Recorded Dcouments Records* http://townofbrandon.com/departments/town-clerk/   Access to land records for a fee at http://cotthosting.com/vtportal/User/Login.aspx?ReturnUrl=%2fvtportal%2f. Must subscribe. Indexes available from 1/1/2006 to present; images available from Volume 518 to present.

Brattleboro Town in Windham County *Recorded Documents* www.brattleboro.org/index.asp?SEC=D2B84780-DAA5-440E-A75D-65C89670222C&Type=B_BASIC   Access to land records for free at https://i2d.uslandrecords.com/VT/Brattleboro/D/Default.aspx. Printing and/or downloading will incur a $3.00 per page charge. Records available from 5/1962 to present and maps from 6/1857 to present.
Property, Taxation Records   Access to Grand List by Owner or Location for free at www.brattleboro.org/index.asp?SEC=034F3706-09C4-4E46-AA89-1FF70573060B&DE=361FA9C8-08F1-4DF1-9561-6E284AA54D8A&Type=B_BASIC. Also, access to maps for free at www.mapsonline.net/brattleborovt/index.html.

Bridgewater Town in Windsor County *Property, Taxation Records*   Access to appraisal data and GIS/mapping for free at http://gis.vgsi.com/bridgewatervt/.

Burke Town in Caledonia County *Property, Taxation Records*   Access to property assessment data free at http://patriotproperties.com/.

Burlington City in Chittenden County *Recorded Documents* https://www.burlingtonvt.gov/CT   Free access to town's index of recorded documents at http://cotthosting.com/vtportal/User/Login.aspx. For images must subscribe with a fee.
Property, Taxation Records   Access to city property tax indexes free at http://cotthosting.com/vtportal/User/Login.aspx?ReturnUrl=%2fvtportal%2f. For unlimited access to all indexes and images, must subscibe. Also, access to the Grand Lists for free at https://www.burlingtonvt.gov/Assessor/Grand-List.

Calais Town in Washington County *Recorded Documents* www.calaisvermont.gov/index.asp?SEC=B3172BA1-6AB3-4B7A-9F5E-7FCF7BC85C59&Type=B_BASIC   Free access to town's index of recorded documents at http://cotthosting.com/vtportal/User/Login.aspx. For images must subscribe with a fee.

Canaan Town in Essex County *Property, Taxation Records*   Access to the Grand List for free at www.canaan-vt.org/lister.html.

Castleton Town in Rutland County *Property, Taxation Records*   Access to the Grand List free at www.castletonvermont.org/assessor-department/pages/assessor-documents. Also, access to property assessment data free at http://patriotproperties.com/.

Clarendon Town in Rutland County *Recorded Documents* www.clarendonvt.org/index.html   Free access to town's index of recorded documents at http://cotthosting.com/vtportal/User/Login.aspx. For images must subscribe with a fee.

Colchester Town in Chittenden County *Recorded Documents* www.colchestervt.gov/322/Town-Clerk   Access to real estate records for free at https://i2d.uslandrecords.com/VT/Colchester/D/Default.aspx. Printing and/or downloading will incur $3.00 per page charges.
Property, Taxation Records   Access to appraisal data and GIS/mapping for free at www.axisgis.com/ColchesterVT/.

Corinth Town in Orange County   *Property, Taxation Records*   Access to the Grand Lists for free at http://corinthvt.org/town-govt/listers/.

Craftsbury Town in Orleans County   *Property, Taxation Records*   Access to Grand List or mappings free at www.townofcraftsbury.com/listers/.

Derby Town in Orleans County   *Property, Taxation Records*   Access to property assessment data free at http://derbyvt.patriotproperties.com/default.asp.

Dorset Town in Bennington County   *Recorded Documents*   www.dorsetvt.org/clerk.php   Free access to town's index of recorded documents at http://cotthosting.com/vtportal/User/Login.aspx. For images must subscribe with a fee.

East Montpelier Town in Washington County   *Property, Taxation Records*   Access to the Grand List, tax exempt properties and state-owned properties for free at http://eastmontpeliervt.org/administration/listers/

Elmore Town in Lamoille County   *Property, Taxation Records*   Access to the Grand List for free at www.elmorevt.org/town/listers.

Enosburgh Town in Franklin County   *Property, Taxation Records*   Access to GIS/mapping free at http://enosburghvermont.org/Maps/TownMap.php.

Essex Town in Chittenden County   *Property, Taxation Records*   Access to tax/parcel maps for free at www.essex.org/index.asp?Type=B_LIST&SEC={B8AF3EEC-F98B-4423-9C11-FC7E889BEF3B}.

Fairfax Town in Franklin County   *Recorded Records Records*   www.fairfax-vt.gov/index.asp?SEC=9DDD12B1-8F1C-4419-A093-BA498F954070&Type=B_BASIC   This is an individual site for property transfers, births, deaths and marriages for free at www.vtgrandpa.com/fhs/fxtwnhap.html.

Fairfield Town in Franklin County   *Recorded Documents*   www.fairfieldvermont.us/wordpress/   Access to land records for a fee at https://i2d.uslandrecords.com/VT/FairField_public/D/Default.aspx. Index and images are available from 3/1998 to present.
Property, Taxation Records   Access to GIS/Mapping for free at www.axisgis.com/FairfieldVT/.

Fairlee Town in Orange County   *Recorded Documents*   http://fairleevt.org/town-offices/town-clerk/   Free access to town's index of recorded documents at http://cotthosting.com/vtportal/User/Login.aspx. For images must subscribe with a fee.

Ferrisburgh Town in Addison County   *Property, Taxation Records*   Access to parcel listing for free at www.ferrisburghvt.org/index.asp?Type=B_BASIC&SEC={F73BEED9-246C-44F8-ABE5-DF6ED550EAD7}. Also, access to the Grant List (2013 thru 2015) at www.ferrisburghvt.org/index.asp?Type=B_BASIC&SEC={80CEA390-E14B-4D08-B242-C727D05E76AF}.

Guildhall Town in Essex County   *Property, Taxation Records*   Access to GIS/mapping free at www.guildhallvt.org/tax-map.html.

Hartford Town in Windsor County   *Property, Taxation Records*   Access to appraisal data and GIS/mapping for free at http://gis.vgsi.com/hartfordvt/.

Jay Town in Orleans County   *Property, Taxation Records*   Access to property assessment data free at http://patriotproperties.com/.

Killington Town in Rutland County   *Recorded Documents*   www.killingtontown.com/index.asp?Type=B_BASIC&SEC={CDDD41E8-D7DF-4229-ABFC-206C0F335173}   Free access to town's index of recorded documents at http://cotthosting.com/vtportal/User/Login.aspx. For images must subscribe with a fee.
Property, Taxation Records   A list of names, addresses and current property taxes may be viewed from the home page. Click on Grand List.

Ludlow Town in Windsor County   *Property, Taxation Records*   One may search property cards and taxes at www.caigisonline.com/LudlowVT/Default.aspx?Splash=True. Note you must have an updated browser and Chrome may not work.

Manchester Town in Bennington County   *Recorded Documents*   http://manchester-vt.gov/departments/   Free access to town's index of recorded documents at http://cotthosting.com/vtportal/User/Login.aspx.
Property, Taxation Records   Access to property records and GIS/mapping for free at www.mainstreetmaps.com/VT/Manchester/.

Marlboro Town in Windham County   *Property, Taxation Records*   Access to maps for free at http://marlborovt.us/government/listers/.

Marshfield Town in Washington County   *Recorded Documents (Indexes Only) Records*   www.town.marshfield.vt.us/index.asp?Type=B_BASIC&SEC={3F2E8902-9DD3-4DA0-99BD-2D9FA8315BBB}   Free access to town's index of recorded documents at http://cotthosting.com/vtportal/User/Login.aspx. For images must subscribe with a fee..

Middlebury Town in Addison County   *Recorded Documents*   www.townofmiddlebury.org/index.asp?Type=B_BASIC&SEC={6D985D33-06BE-4C3B-9096-76C03E6E2A10}&DE={88CF9FBE-6498-4849-B8CF-C8FFA8274988}   Free access to town's index of recorded documents at http://cotthosting.com/vtportal/User/Login.aspx. For images must subscribe with a fee.

Montpelier City in Washington County   *Recorded Documents*   www.montpelier-vt.org/162/City-Clerk   Free access to town's index of recorded documents at http://cotthosting.com/vtportal/User/Login.aspx. For images must subscribe with a fee.
Property, Taxation Records   Access to property sales for free at www.montpelier-vt.org/Archive.aspx?AMID=37. Also, access to property assessment data free at http://patriotproperties.com/. Also, access to the Grand Lists for free at www.montpelier-vt.org/Archive.aspx?AMID=36.

Morgan Town in Orleans County   *Property, Taxation Records*   Access to property maps for free at http://townofmorgan.com/wp-content/uploads/2015/11/MPM15.pdf.

Morristown Town in Lamoille County   *Recorded Documents*   www.morristownvt.org/towndepartments/townclerk.html   Access to land records for free at https://i2d.uslandrecords.com/VT/Morristown/D/Default.aspx. Printing and/or downloading will incur $3.00 per page charges.
Property, Taxation Records   Access to GIS/mapping free at www.axisgis.com/MorristownVT/.

Newfane Town in Windham County   *Recorded Documents*   http://newfanevt.com/   Free access to town's index of recorded documents at http://cotthosting.com/vtportal/User/Login.aspx?ReturnUrl=%2fvtportal%2f. For images must subscribe with a fee.

Newport City in Orleans County   *Property, Taxation Records*   Access is free at http://gis.vgsi.com/newportvt/.

Newport Town in Orleans County   *Property, Taxation Records*   Access to appraisal data and GIS/mapping for free at http://gis.vgsi.com/newportvt/.

North Hero Town in Grand Isle County   *Recorded Documents*   www.northherovt.com/faces/tclerk.xhtml   Access to land records for free at https://i2d.uslandrecords.com/VT/NorthHero_public/D/Default.aspx. Printing and/or downloading will incur a $3.00 per page charge. Search results may be printed for $1.50 per page.

Norwich Town in Windsor County   *Recorded Documents*   http://norwich.vt.us/town-clerk/   Free access to town's index of recorded documents at http://cotthosting.com/vtportal/User/Login.aspx. For images must subscribe with a fee.
Property, Taxation Records   Access to property assessment data free at http://patriotproperties.com/.

Pawlet Town in Rutland County   *Recorded Documents*   http://pawlet.vt.gov/town-offices/town-clerk/   Free access at http://cotthosting.com/vtportal/User/Login.aspx. For images must subscribe with a fee.
Property, Taxation Records   Access to GIS/mapping for free at www.axisgis.com/PawletVT/.

Pittsford Town in Rutland County   *Recorded Documents*   http://pittsfordvermont.com/departments/town-clerk/   Free access to town's index of recorded documents at http://cotthosting.com/vtportal/User/Login.aspx. For images must subscribe with a fee.
Property, Taxation Records   Access to the Grand List free from home page.

Poultney Town in Rutland County   *Recorded Documents*   www.vermont.gov/portal/government/towns.php?town=159   Free access to town's index of recorded documents at http://cotthosting.com/vtportal/User/Login.aspx. For images must subscribe with a fee.
Property, Taxation Records   Access to the Grand Lists for free at http://vermontassessor.com/GrandList.htm. Lists are for Hubbardton, Mendon, Newport City and Waitsfield.

Putney Town in Windham County   *Property, Taxation Records*   Access to town maps for free at www.putneyvt.org/map.php.

Randolph Town in Orange County   *Recorded Documents*   http://randolphvt.org/index.asp?Type=B_BASIC&SEC={C5BB9C85-ACEE-48F8-B611-B83D5247EDBC}   Free access to town's index of recorded documents at http://cotthosting.com/vtportal/User/Login.aspx. For images must subscribe with a fee.

Readsboro Town in Bennington County   *Property, Taxation Records*   Free access at https://readsborovt.org/Listers.html

Rockingham Town in Windham County   *Property, Taxation Records*   Access to GIS/mapping free at www.mainstreetmaps.com/VT/Rockingham/.

Rutland City in Rutland County   *Recorded Documents*   www.rutlandcity.org/index.asp?SEC=D0A4D01D-5919-4903-AAE4-0CC130FF2E49&Type=B_BASIC   Free access to town's index of recorded documents at http://cotthosting.com/vtportal/User/Login.aspx. For images must subscribe with a fee.

Rutland Town in Rutland County   *Property, Taxation Records*   Access town maps free at http://rutlandtown.com/?page_id=23.

Ryegate Town in Caledonia County   *Property, Taxation Records*   Free access at www.ryegatevt.org/listers-office.html.

Searsburg Town in Bennington County   *Property, Taxation Records*   Access to tax maps and Grand Lists for free at http://wilmingtonvermont.us/departments/board-of-listers-listers-office2013-wilmington-tax-maps/.

Sharon Town in Windsor County   *Property, Taxation Records*   Access to the Grand List for free at www.sharonvt.net/government/listers.html.

Shelburne Town in Chittenden County   *Property, Taxation Records*   The Grand List is free at www.shelburnevt.org/DocumentCenter/View/79.

South Burlington City in Chittenden County *Property, Taxation Records*   Access to the Grand List for free at www.sburl.com/index.asp?Type=B_BASIC&SEC={9F3596E0-9721-430E-9F6D-F2C28AAE6721}.

St. Albans City in Franklin County *Recorded Documents* www.stalbansvt.com   Free access to town's index of recorded documents at http://cotthosting.com/vtportal/User/Login.aspx. For images must subscribe with a fee.
Property, Taxation Records   Access to City maps for free at www.stalbansvt.com/index.asp (click on city department, then assessing/lister's office).

Stowe Town in Lamoille County *Property, Taxation Records*   Access to the Grand List for free at www.townofstowevt.org/index.asp?SEC=EEE0B312-D15A-4BBB-A248-63D02B6D82D6&Type=B_BASIC. Click on Grand List. Also, accesst to tax maps for free at www.townofstowevt.org/index.asp?SEC={D930020B-672F-42EC-A3DF-07F4B098D696}&Type=B_BASIC&persistdesign=none.

Stratton Town in Windham County *Property, Taxation Records*   Access to online database free at http://gis.vgsi.com/StrattonVT/Default.aspx. Also, access to the Grand List for free at www.townofstrattonvt.com/assessors--office.html. Click on 2015 Grand List with taxes.

Sunderland Town in Bennington County *Property, Taxation Records*   Access to the Grand List free at www.sunderlandvt.org/taxes/grand-list/.

Swanton Town in Franklin County *Property, Taxation Records*   Access to GIS/mapping for free at www.axisgis.com/SwantonVT/.

Thetford Town in Orange County *Recorded Documents* www.thetfordvermont.us/departments/clerk-office/   Free access to town's index of recorded documents at http://cotthosting.com/vtportal/User/Login.aspx. For images must subscribe with a fee.
Property, Taxation Records   Access to GIS/mapping free at www.axisgis.com/ThetfordVT/.

Townshend Town in Windham County *Property, Taxation Records*   Access to the Assessor's database search for free at http://realprop.townsend.ma.us/cgi-bin/assessor?get_strtform.htm?ticks=1465317137.

Warren Town in Washington County *Property, Taxation Records*   Access to property transfer tax returns for free at www.warrenvt.org/depts/clerk.htm. Click on 2008-Present or 2007-2002, 2001-1998 at bottom of page.

Waterbury Town in Washington County *Property, Taxation Records*   Access tp property/parcel mapping system for free at www.axisgis.com/WaterburyVT/.

Weathersfield Town in Windsor County *Recorded Documents* www.weathersfieldvt.org/portal/index.php/town-government/town-office/town-clerk   Free access to recorded documents at http://cotthosting.com/vtportal/User/Login.aspx. For images must subscribe with a fee.

West Fairlee Town in Orange County *Recorded Documents*
www.westfairleevt.com/index.asp?Type=B_BASIC&SEC={1DE1A4F7-D9D1-47EC-ABD4-2295797C416D}   Free access to town's index of recorded documents at http://cotthosting.com/vtportal/User/Login.aspx. For images must subscribe with a fee.
Property, Taxation Records   Access to assessment cards and tax maps for free at www.axisgis.com/West_FairleeVT/.

West Rutland Town in Rutland County *Recorded Documents* www.westrutlandtown.com/town-departments/town-clerk/   Free access to town's index of recorded documents at http://cotthosting.com/vtportal/User/Login.aspx. For images must subscribe with a fee.

Westford Town in Chittenden County *Property, Taxation Records*   Access to GIS/mapping free at http://map.ccrpcvt.org/westfordmapviewer/.

Westminster Town in Windham County *Property, Taxation Records*   Access to GIS/mapping free at www.westminstervt.org/index.asp?Type=B_BASIC&SEC={46765053-9BEE-4DD0-8A28-01AF3752806B}. Also, access to the Grand List free at www.westminstervt.org/index.asp?SEC=1010BD47-3E25-44BD-B788-8F1045E09D35&Type=B_BASIC.

Williamstown Town in Orange County *Property, Taxation Records*   Property maps at www.williamstownvt.org/board-of-listers.

Williston Town in Chittenden County *Property, Taxation Records*   Access to the Grand List Property Info free at www.town.williston.vt.us/index.asp?Type=B_DIR&SEC={55D445CF-5424-4797-A39D-324EFEC3A75E}.

Wilmington Town in Windham County *Recorded Documents* http://wilmingtonvermont.us/government/town-clerk/   Free access to town's index of recorded documents at http://cotthosting.com/vtportal/User/Login.aspx. For images must subscribe with a fee. Land records from 1797 to current.
Property, Taxation Records   Tax maps and the Grand List free at http://wilmingtonvermont.us/departments/board-of-listers-listers-office2013-wilmington-tax-maps/.

Windsor Town in Windsor County *Property, Taxation Records*   Access to tax maps for free at www.windsorvt.org/town-lister.

Woodstock Town in Windsor County *Property, Taxation Records*   Access to the Grand Lists free at home page.

Virginia

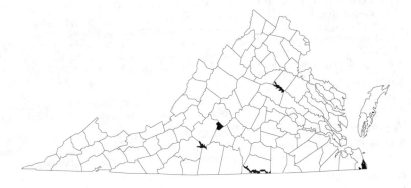

Capital: Richmond
        Richmond City County
Time Zone: EST
Population: 8,382,993
# of Counties: 95

Useful State Links

Website: **www.virginia.gov**
Governor: **https://governor.virginia.gov/**
Attorney General: **www.oag.state.va.us**
State Archives: **www.lva.virginia.gov/**
State Statutes and Codes: **http://leg1.state.va.us/000/src.htm**
Legislative Bill Search: **http://virginiageneralassembly.gov/**
Unclaimed Funds: **https://www.trs.virginia.gov/**

State Public Record Agencies

Criminal Records

Virginia State Police, CCRE, www.vsp.state.va.us   Certain entities, including screening companies, can apply for online access via the NCJI System, but it is ONLY available to IN-STATE accounts. NCJI allows requesters to receive notice of clean records faster (48 hours). If hits, record is mailed. The SP-167 release form must be kept on file and showable if audited. Fees are same as manual submission-$15.00 per record or $20.00 SOR record search. Username and password required. There is a minimum usage requirement of 10 requests per month. Turnaround time is 24-72 hours. See www.vsp.state.va.us/CJIS_NCJI.shtm.

Sexual Offender Registry

Virginia State Police, Sex Offender and Crimes Against Minors Registry,   http://sex-offender.vsp.virginia.gov/sor/index.html   Click on the Search the Sex Offender Registry tab on the left side of the home page. From there one may search by name, city, county or ZIP Code, or from a map. There is also a search for Wanted Sex Offenders, using a tab on the left side.

Incarceration Records

Virginia Department of Corrections, Records Unit, http://vadoc.virginia.gov/   Visit http://vadoc.virginia.gov/offenders/locator/index.aspx to locate a current offender by name or Offender ID Number. To search by name requires exact last name and at least the first 2 initials of the first name. To search by number requires to have either the inmates' Department of Corrections' seven digit (new) or six digit (old) identification number. Note this disclaimer: "This system is not designed to provide complete offender records nor is it a database of all offenders past and present in our system." A DOC wanted/fugitives list is found at www.vadoc.virginia.gov/offenders/wanted/fugitive.shtm.

Corporation, LLC, LP, Fictitious Name, Business Trust Records

State Corporation Commission, Clerks Office,   www.scc.virginia.gov/clk/bussrch.aspx   A business entity search is at www.scc.virginia.gov/clk/bussrch.aspx. The Clerk's Information System (CIS, also at this page, contains general information on file for Virginia and foreign corporations, limited liability companies, limited partnerships, and business trusts, but not as robust as the above. Visit www.scc.virginia.gov/docketsearch for SCC Case File Docket Search to review status of cases and public filings. Also, search securities companies, agents, and franchises registered with the state at www.scc.virginia.gov/srf/index.aspx.   *Other Options:* The database is available for bulk purchase. Monthly downloads are available with a signed agreement. Monthly fees are generally $150. Call for details.

Trademarks, Service Marks

State Corporation Commission, Virginia Securities Division,   https://www.scc.virginia.gov/srf/bus/tmsm_regis.aspx   Searching Trademarks and Service Marks are available at https://www.scc.virginia.gov/srf/SERFWEB/RegistrationSearches/WebForms/Search.aspx?SearchType=TMSM. Search criteria is not case sensitive.

Uniform Commercial Code, Federal Tax Liens

UCC Division, State Corporation Commission, www.scc.virginia.gov/clk/uccsrch.aspx The electronic access system, called the Clerk's Information System (CIS) , is available free at www.scc.virginia.gov/clk/uccsrch.aspx. Search by the name of the debtor or taxpayer, or by the file number/document control number (DCN). Images of UCC filings and tax liens are not available for online viewing. Collateral information is not available in CIS but can be obtained if a search is ordered and the associated fee paid. *Other Options:* The database is available for bulk purchase. Monthly downloads are available with a signed agreement. Monthly fee is $150 for UCC and federal lien data or $300 for the lien data plus business entity data. Call for details.

Vital Records

State Health Department, Office of Vital Records, www.vdh.virginia.gov/vital_Records/index.htm One may process a request online through an independent company that the Virginia Division of Vital Records has partnered with: VitalChek.com. Additional fee apply.

Workers' Compensation Records

Workers' Compensation Commission, Clerk's Office, www.workcomp.virginia.gov/ Some records, including Judicial Opinions, can be obtained online. There is no name searching option. The Opinions link is www.workcomp.virginia.gov/portal/vwc-website/OnlineServices/JudicialOpinions.

Driver Records

Department of Motor Vehicles, Customer Records Work Center, Rm 514, www.dmvnow.com/#/Locations The DMV must approve all customers. There are two forms required: Information Use Agreement Application (US-531A) and an Application for Extranet Transaction Access (US-531E), plus each user in 531E must be listed and issued an RSA SecurID token. There is a $25.00 application fee plus a $65 fee for each RSA SecureID token. Either a five year insurance record or seven year employment record can be ordered for the $7.00 fee. Certain non-profit entities are given free or 50% discount records. he system is open 24/7. The driver's address is provided as part of the record. The driver license number or name, date of birth and sex are needed to search. Billing is monthly. Drivers may use Record at a Glance to take a free look at limited information. Registration is required. See www.dmv.virginia.gov/general/#record_glance.asp. *Other Options:* The agency offers a Voluntary Monitoring program and a mandatory Driving Record Monitoring Programs for employers of commercial drivers. Call 804-497-7155 for details.

Vehicle Ownership & Registration

Department of Motor Vehicles, Vehicle Records, Cust Work Center, Rm 514, www.dmvnow.com/#/Locations The DMV must approve all customers. There are two forms required: Information Use Agreement Application (US-531A) and an Application for Extranet Transaction Access (US-531E), plus each user in 531E must be listed and issued an RSA SecurID token. here is a $25.00 application fee plus a $65 fee for each RSA SecureID token. The fee is $7.00 per record. t record can be ordered for the $7.00 fee. The system is open 24/7. Billing is monthly. Submitting the license plate number, VIN or title number is required for vehicle information. Also, a $12.00 vehicle verification search for prospective vehicle buyers is free at https://www.dmv.virginia.gov/dmvnet/ppi/intro.asp. Drivers may use Record at a Glance to take a free look at limited information. Registration is required. See www.dmv.virginia.gov/general/#record_glance.asp. *Other Options:* Insurance Verifictaion is free at https://www.dmv.virginia.gov/dmvnet/ins_mon/entry.asp.

Vessel Ownership & Registration

Dept of Game & Inland Fisheries, Boat Registration and Titling, www.dgif.virginia.gov The VA boat registration database may be searched on the web at https://vi.virginiainteractive.org/vi/premium-dgif.shtml. A subscription is required; there is a $95.00 annual fee. There are two options, one for commercial use, and for non commercial use. Fees of Individual Account: $1.00 per record for 1 to 50 record requests with a $25.00 minimum purchase. For Packet Request: $50.00 for a batch record query of 50 to 2500 record requests. *Other Options:* The entire database is available to subscribers for $3,000 for the initial access and $500 for each request thereafter.

Voter Registration, Campaign Finance, PACs

State Board of Elections, http://elections.virginia.gov View campaign finance reports for free at http://cfreports.sbe.virginia.gov/. This includes PACs. Contribution tracking is offered to registered users, see https://cf.sbe.virginia.gov/Account/LogOn?ReturnUrl=%2f. One may verify registration status at https://vote.elections.virginia.gov/VoterInformation, but site say one cannot search for another's status. *Other Options:* Voter data output is available on CD (CSV files), computer printout or on ready made labels.

GED Certificates

Virginia Dept of Education, GED Office, www.vaged.vcu.edu/ Third parties will set up an account at: http://exchange.parchment.com/ged-receiver-registration-page. Parchment verifies that they are who they say they are so that they can place orders on behalf of students. Parchment contacts the third party and provides training on the site for ordering. During this training any orders they have are placed. After this the third party can order on behalf of students. They still must upload a consent form for each student during the process. GED test takers can order duplicate copies of official GED transcripts and duplicate diplomas online at: www.gedtestingservice.com/testers/gedrequest-a-transcript

Occupational Licensing Boards

These licenses are all searchable at www.dpor.virginia.gov/LicenseLookup/

Architect	Barber/Barber School/Business	Carpenter
Asbestos-related Occupation	Boxer	Cemetery Company/Seller
Auctioneer/Auction Firm	Boxing/Wresting Occupation	Contractor

Cosmetologist/Cosmo School/Firm
Engineer
Fair Housing
Gas Fitter
Geologist
Hair Braider
Hearing Aid Specialist
Home Inspector
Interior Designer

Landscape Architect
Lead-Related Occupation
Nail Technician
Optician
Pilot, Branch
Polygraph Examiner
Property Association
Real Estate Agent/Business/School
Real Estate Appraiser/Appraiser Firm

Soil Scientist
Surveyor, Land
Tattoo Artist/Body Piercing
Tradesman
Waste Management Facility Operator
Waste Water Plant Operator
Wax Technician
Wetlands Delineator
Wrestler

These licenses are all searchable at https://dhp.virginiainteractive.org/Lookup/Index

Acupuncturist
Athletic Trainer
Audiologist
Chiropractor
Clinical Nurse Specialist
Cosmetic Procedure Certification
Counselor, Professional
Crematory
Dental Hygienist
Dentist
Embalmer
Funeral Director/Establ/Trainee/Service
Provider
Humane Society
Marriage & Family Therapist

Massage Therapist
Medical Equipment Supplier
Medical Wholesaler/Mfg
Nurse-LPN/RN/Aide
Nursing Home Administrator
Occupational Therapist
Optometrist
Oral/Maxillofacial Surgeon
Osteopathic Physician
Pharmacist/Pharmacy
Physical Therapist
Physician/Medical Doctor/Assistant
Podiatrist
Prescriptive Authorization
Psychologist at School

Psychologist, Clinical/Applied
Psychology School
Radiologic Technologist-limited
Rehabilitation Provider
Respiratory Care Practitioner
Social Worker, Clinical/Registered
Speech Pathologist at School
Speech Pathologist/Audiologist
Substance Abuse Counselor
Substance Abuse Treatm't Practitioner
University Limited Medical License
Veterinarian/Veterinary Technician/Facility
Warehouser, Medical

These licenses are all searchable at
https://www.cms.dcjs.virginia.gov/GLSuiteWeb/Clients/VADCJS/Public/Verification/Business/Search.aspx

Alarm Respondent
Armored Car Personnel
Central Station Dispatcher/Out of State
Electr'c Security Sales Rep/Tech/Asst
Locksmith

Personal Protection Specialist
Private Investigator
Security Business Services
Security Canine Handler
Security Officer, Unarmed/Armed

Security Technic'n (electronic security)
Special Conservator of the Peace
Training Schools/Instructor
Unarmed Security Officer/Courier

The Rest:

Accountant-CPA	https://secure1.boa.virginia.gov/Verification/
Accountant-CPA Firm	https://secure1.boa.virginia.gov/Verification/Search.aspx?facility=Y
Alcoholic Beverage Distributor	https://www.abc.virginia.gov/licenseesearch/welcome.do
Attorney/Attorney Assoc	www.vsb.org/attorney/attSearch.asp?S=D
Bank	www.scc.virginia.gov/bfi/reg_inst/banks.pdf
Check Casher	www.scc.virginia.gov/bfi/reg_inst/check.pdf
Consumer Finance Companys	www.scc.virginia.gov/bfi/reg_inst/sav.pdf
Credit Counseling Agencies	www.scc.virginia.gov/bfi/reg_inst/credit.pdf
Credit Union	www.scc.virginia.gov/bfi/reg_inst/check.pdf
EMS Provider	https://vdhems.vdh.virginia.gov/emsapps/f?p=200:3
Insurance Agent/Agency/Company	www.scc.virginia.gov/boi/ConsumerInquiry/default.aspx
Investment Advisor/Advisor Agency	www.scc.virginia.gov/srf/index.aspx
Lobbyist	https://solutions.virginia.gov/Lobbyist/Reports/Database
Money Transmitter	www.scc.virginia.gov/bfi/reg_inst/trans.pdf
Mortgage Lender/Broker	www.scc.virginia.gov/bfi/reg_inst/mort.pdf
Mortgage Loan Originators	www.nmlsconsumeraccess.org/
Motor VehicleTitle Lenders	www.scc.virginia.gov/bfi/reg_inst/title.pdf
Notary Public	https://solutions.virginia.gov/Notary/Search/Search

Payday Lender.. www.scc.virginia.gov/bfi/reg_inst/pay.aspx
Pesticide Applicator (Private) .... www.vdacs.virginia.gov/pesticide-applicator-certification.shtml
Pesticide Applicat'r/Firm (Commercial) .... www.vdacs.virginia.gov/pesticide-applicator-certification.shtml
Savings Institution... www.scc.virginia.gov/bfi/reg_inst/sav.pdf
School Guidance Counselor................................... https://p1pe.doe.virginia.gov/tinfo/
School Library Media Specialist https://p1pe.doe.virginia.gov/tinfo/
School Principal/Superintendent https://p1pe.doe.virginia.gov/tinfo/
Securities Broker/Brokerage/Dealer/Dealer Agent...... www.scc.virginia.gov/srf/index.aspx
Teacher.. https://p1pe.doe.virginia.gov/tinfo/
Trust Companies .... www.scc.virginia.gov/bfi/reg_inst/trust.aspx

State and Local Courts

About Virginia Courts: The **Circuit Court** handles felonies, all civil cases with claims of more than $25,000 but it shares authority with the General District court to hear matters involving claims between $4,500 and $25,000. The Circuit Court also handles family matters including divorce. There is a Circuit Court in each county and in each city that is county equivalent.

The **General District Court** decides all offenses involving ordinances laws, and by-laws of the county or city where it is located and all misdemeanors under state law, and small claims ($4,500 or less). A misdemeanor is any charge that carries a penalty of no more than one year in jail or a fine of up to $2,500, or both. Please note that a District can comprise a county or a city.

As stated, records of civil action from $4,500 to $25,000 can be at either the Circuit Court or District Court as either can have jurisdiction. Thus it is necessary to check both record locations as there is no concurrent database or index.

Fifteen independent cities share the Clerk of Circuit Court with the county (but have separate District Courts) - Bedford, Covington (Alleghany County), Emporia (Greenville County), Fairfax, Falls Church (Arlington or Fairfax County), Franklin (Southhampton County), Galax (Carroll County), Harrisonburg (Rockingham County), Lexington (Rockbridge County), Manassas and Manassas Park (Prince William County), Norton (Wise County), Poquoson (York County), South Boston (Halifax County), and Williamsburg (James City County).

Magistrate Offices issue various types of processes such as arrest warrants, summonses, bonds, search warrants, subpoenas, and certain civil warrants. Magistrates may also conduct bail hearings.

The web page for the Judicial Branch is www.courts.state.va.us.

Appellate Courts: The Supreme Court reviews decisions of the Circuit Courts, the Court of Appeals when such appeals have been allowed, decisions from the State Corporation Commission, and certain disciplinary actions of the Virginia State Bar regarding attorneys. Virginia's intermediate appellate court, the Court of Appeals, reviews decisions of the Circuit Courts in domestic relations matters, traffic infractions and criminal cases (except death penalty cases), appeals from administrative agencies, and decisions of the Virginia Workers' Compensation Commission. Opinions are available from the home page.

Online Court Access

How to Search Online for Circuit Court Records

For **criminal** case information, go to www.courts.state.va.us/caseinfo/home.html#cc and click on the "Case Information" link. One may search historical case information by name, case number, or hearing date. Results show address of subject and the day and month of birth, but not year. The Circuit Courts of Alexandria and Fairfax do not use the statewide system. Virginia Beach does use the system; civil and criminal cases filed from 7/31/2009 thru 10/1/2014 must be searched on their county sites.

For **civil** case searching, two possible civil searches are accessible from www.courts.state.va.us/caseinfo/home.html#cc. The **Case Information link** provides historical case information searchable by name, case number, or hearing date. Results show address of subject and the day and month of birth, but not year. The **Records Information link** provides access to certain judgments and recorded documents. However, each local Circuit Court Clerk's office must be contacted for requirements, fees, and log-in. Same as criminal, the Virginia Beach Circuit Court does use the above system for civil records; however cases filed from 7/31/2009 thru 10/1/2014 must be searched on their county site for both civil and criminal cases.

How to Search Online for District Court Records

All District Courts participate in a free online search by name or case number. Available records include Criminal, Civil, and Traffic. See https://eapps.courts.state.va.us/gdcourts/captchaVerification.do?landing=landing. Results go back 10 years and show address of subject and the day and month of birth, but not year.

Other County or City Sites - These profiles do not include the statewide sites mentioned above

Alexandria City

18th Circuit Court   https://www.alexandriava.gov/clerkofcourt/
Civil: There is limited free online access to civil docket information from 1/01/1983, and a subscription service ($500 per year or $50 per month) to full data including images since 6/2003. Visit https://secure.alexandriava.gov/ajis/index.php. *Criminal:* Online access to criminal record index is free, access to images require a subscription (either $500 a year or $0 a month). Data available back to 7/01/1987, images since 6/2003.

Carroll County

27th Circuit Court   http://www.courts.state.va.us/courts/circuit.html
Civil: Certified or non-certified documents may be ordered online at https://www.clerkepass.com/Carroll/. There are added fees which depend on the type of document ordered. *Criminal:* same

Fairfax County

19th Circuit Court   http://www.fairfaxcounty.gov/courts/circuit/
Civil: Also, access to current court case indexes is via CPAN subscription; call 703-246-2366 IT Dept. or see www.fairfaxcounty.gov/courts/circuit/cpan.htm to apply. Fee is $50.00 per month per user. Also, daily and Friday's Motion dockets are available free at www.fairfaxcounty.gov/circuitcourtdocket/. *Criminal:* same

Hanover County

15th Circuit Court   http://www.hanovercounty.gov/Courts/Courts/
Civil: Certified documents may be ordered online at https://www.clerkepass.com/hanover/. There are additional fees imposed. *Criminal:* same.

King George County

15th Circuit Court   http://www.courts.state.va.us/courts/circuit/King_George/home.html
Civil: Certified documents may be ordered online at https://www.clerkepass.com/KingGeorge/. There is a total fee of $1.00 per document Plus $.50 a page, plus shipping. *Criminal:* same.

Loudoun County

20th Circuit Court   http://www.loudoun.gov/index.aspx?nid=97
Civil: Also, docket lists are free at https://www.loudoun.gov/DocumentCenter/Index/3363.   *Criminal:* same.

Martinsville City

21st Circuit Court   http://www.martinsville-va.gov/Circuit-Court-Clerk.html
Civil: Also, with subscription and password, access judgments at https://www.ci.martinsville.va.us/crms/.

Montgomery County

27th Circuit Court   http://www.courts.state.va.us/courts/circuit.html
Civil: Certified documents may be ordered online at https://www.clerkepass.com/montgomery/. There are additional fees imposed.   *Criminal:* Same.

Norfolk City

4th Circuit Court   http://www.norfolkcircuitcourt.us/
Civil: Also, the Clerk of Circuit court subscription online system contains judgment records, wills, marriages, recorded documents etc at www.norfolk.gov/Circuit_Court/remoteaccess.asp. Fee is $50 per month. Judgments, Wills, Marriages, etc. back to 1993.

Portsmouth City

Circuit Court   http://www.courts.state.va.us/courts/circuit.html
Civil: Certified documents may be ordered online at https://www.clerkepass.com/portsmouth/. There are additional fees imposed.   *Criminal:* Same

Pulaski County

Circuit Court   http://www.courts.state.va.us/courts/circuit/pulaski/home.html
Civil: See above for the state sites.Certified or non-certified documents may be ordered online at http://clerkepass.com/pulaski/. There are added fees which depend on the type of document ordered. *Criminal:* same

Rockingham County

26th Circuit Court   http://www.courts.state.va.us/courts/circuit.html
Civil: Certified or non-certified documents may be ordered online at https://www.clerkepass.com/rockingham/. There are added fees which depend on the type of document ordered. *Criminal:* Same

Scott County

30th Circuit Court   http://www.courts.state.va.us/courts/circuit.html

Civil: Certified or non-certified documents may be ordered online at https://www.clerkepass.com/scott/. There are added fees which depend on the type of document ordered. *Criminal:* same

Smyth County
28th Circuit Court   http://www.courts.state.va.us/courts/circuit/smyth/home.html
Civil: Certified or non-certified documents may be ordered online at https://www.clerkepass.com/Smyth/. There are added fees which depend on the type of document ordered. *Criminal:* same

Suffolk City
Suffolk 5th Circuit Court   http://www.courts.state.va.us/courts/circuit.html
Civil: Certified or non-certified documents may be ordered online at https://www.clerkepass.com/suffolk/. There are added fees which depend on the type of document ordered. *Criminal:* same

Surry County
Circuit Court   http://www.courts.state.va.us/courts/circuit.html
Civil: There is a subscription service for access to lien judgment documents at http://www.surryvacocc.org/Opening.asp. The fee is $50 per month paid quarterly.

Washington County
Circuit Court   http://www.courts.state.va.us/courts/circuit/Washington/home.html
Civil: Certified or non-certified documents may be ordered online at https://www.clerkepass.com/WashingtonCircuit/. There are added fees which depend on the type of document ordered. *Criminal:* same

Wise County
30th Circuit Court   http://www.courts.state.va.us/courts/circuit/wise/home.html
Civil: Also, access court indexes and images via www.courtbar.org. Records go back to June, 2000. Certified or non-certified documents may be ordered online at https://www.clerkepass.com/wise/. There are added fees which depend on the type of document ordered.   *Criminal:* Certified or non-certified documents may be ordered online at https://www.clerkepass.com/wise/. There are added fees which depend on the type of document ordered.

Recorders, Assessors, and Other Sites of Note

About Virginia Recording Offices: 95 counties and 41 independent cities; 123 recording offices. The recording officer is the Clerk of Circuit Court. Sixteen independent cities share the Clerk of Circuit Court with the county – Bedford; Covington and Clifton Forge (Alleghany County); Emporia (Greenville County); Fairfax; Falls Church (Arlington or Fairfax County); Franklin (Southhampton County); Galax (Carroll County); Harrisonburg (Rockingham County); Lexington (Rockbridge County); Manassas and Manassas Park (Prince William County); Norton (Wise County); Poquoson (York County); South Boston (Halifax County); and Williamsburg (James City County).

Charles City and James City are counties, not cities. The City of Franklin is not in Franklin County. The City of Richmond is not in Richmond County. The City of Roanoke is not in Roanoke County.

About Tax Liens: Federal tax liens on personal property of businesses are filed with the State Corporation Commission. Other federal and all state tax liens are filed with the county Clerk of Circuit Court and are usually filed in a "Judgment Lien Book."

Online Access

Recorded Documents
At least 88 Virginia jurisdictions provide online access to recorded documents and/or land records.

Tax Assessor Records
At least 110 Virginian jurisdictions offer online access to assessor data online. There is a vendor offering tax assessor data with free online access to 14 juriisdictions plus provides a subscription service to 40 jurisdictions. See www.vamanet.com/cgi-bin/HOME.

County and City Sites:

Accomack County *Recorded Documents* www.co.accomack.va.us/departments/clerk-of-circuit-court   Access recorder's index by subscription service www.co.accomack.va.us/government/constitutional-officers/clerk-of-circuit-court/land-records to apply. There is a $50 monthly fee. *Property, Taxation Records*   Access parcel assessment value data free at www.co.accomack.va.us/departments/real-estate-assessment/real-estate-land-book-2015.

Albemarle County *Real Estate, Deed, Lien, Judgment, UCC Records* www.courts.state.va.us/courts/circuit/Albemarle/home.html Access to clerk's recorded index available by subscription; fee- $600 per year per user or $1200 for corporate 4-user sub. Does not include vital records. Land records go back to 1957. Contact clerk Debra Shipp at 434-972-4083.

Property, Taxation Records   Access to tax map grid searches for free at www.albemarle.org/department.asp?department=cdd&relpage=2771#MAP. Also, search parcel data on GIS-mapping site free at http://gisweb.albemarle.org/GISWeb/Welcome.aspx. Also, search zoning notices free at www.albemarle.org/upload/images/webapps/zoning/.

Alexandria City   ***Recorded Documents***   https://www.alexandriava.gov/clerkofcourt/   Land Records (Deeds) with images, since Jan. 2, 1970 is available for $500 per year or $50 per month. See https://secure.alexandriava.gov/ajis/index.php. At this site the free case information does not include images.   ***Property, Taxation Records***   Access to city real estate assessments is free at http://realestate.alexandriava.gov/ but no name searching. Search property free at the GIS-mapping site at http://alexandriava.gov/realestate/default.aspx.

Alleghany County   ***Recorded Documents***   www.courts.state.va.us/courts/circuit/Alleghany/home.html   Subscription available for $50.00 per month. Contact Carol Davis.
Property, Taxation Records   Access City of Covington property data free at www.vamanet.com/cgi-bin/HOME. Access Alleghany County data free also at www.vamanet.com/cgi-bin/HOME. Also, access to GIS/mapping free at http://alleghany.mapsdirect.net/default.aspx.

Amelia County   ***Recorded Documents***   www.ameliacova.com/your_government/circuit_court.php   Access real estate recording records by subscription only, contact Clerk of Circuit Court for information.
Property, Taxation Records   Search for property card and assessment data free at www.ameliacountyrealestate.com/.

Amherst County   ***Recorded Documents***   www.courts.state.va.us/courts/circuit/amherst/   Access to clerks records free at https://cotthosting.com/VAAmherst/User/Login.aspx?ReturnUrl=%2fvaamherst%2fIndex.aspx. Must have UserID and Password.
Property, Taxation Records   Access subscription data for a fee at www.vamanet.com/cgi-bin/HOME.

Appomattox County   ***Recorded Documents***   www.courts.state.va.us/courts/circuit/Appomattox/home.html   Access to land records for a fee at https://lto.landsystems.com/LTOonline/logon.aspx?ReturnUrl=%2fLTOOnline%2fdefault.aspx. An application must be completed and approval granted to receive access. Also, access to the Opinions Search for free at www.courts.state.va.us/search/textopinions.html.
Property, Taxation Records   Access to GIS/mapping free at http://appomattoxgis.timmons.com/.

Arlington County   ***Recorded Documents***   https://courts.arlingtonva.us/circuit-court/   Access to land records for a fee at https://landrec.arlingtonva.us/public/. Must have email and password access.
Property, Taxation Records   Property records on the County assessor database are free at https://propertysearch.arlingtonva.us/.

Augusta County   ***Real Estate Records***   www.courts.state.va.us/courts/circuit/Augusta/home.html   For subscription service information contact Gina Coffey at 540-245-5321.   ***Property, Taxation Records***   Click on Augusta County to search property data for free at www.vamanet.com/cgi-bin/MAPSRCHPGM?LOCAL=AUG.

Bath County   ***Recorded Documents***   www.courts.state.va.us/courts/circuit/Bath/home.html   A subscription is available, contact Clerk for information and application.   ***Property, Taxation Records***   Access current assessment info and sales by VamaNet subscription at www.vamanet.com/cgi-bin/HOME. Fee is $35 per month or $300 per year with discounts for multiple localities, regions.

Bedford County   ***Recorded Documents***   www.courts.state.va.us/courts/circuit/bedford/home.html   Access to real estate records free at www.co.bedford.va.us/Realestate/default.asp.
Property, Taxation Records   Real estate records on the Bedford County GIS site are free at http://webgis.bedfordcountyva.gov/Bedford/Account/Logon; however, no name searching at this time.

Bland County   ***Property, Taxation Records***   Access current assessment info and sales by VamaNet subscription at www.vamanet.com/cgi-bin/HOME. Fee is $35 per month or $300 per year with discounts for multiple localities, regions.

Botetourt County   ***Property, Taxation Records***   Access property data free at http://botetourtbillpay.com/secondary.aspx?pageID=117.

Bristol City   ***Recorded Records Records***   www.courts.state.va.us/courts/circuit/Bristol/home.html   For remote access, contact Clerk Kelly F Duffyr at 276-645-7348. Images available back to 1994.
Property, Taxation Records   Access to City of Bristol Tax e-search for free at https://eservices.bristolva.org/applications/trapps/default.htm. Images only. Also, access to GIS/mapping for free at http://geo.alexandriava.gov/Html5Viewer/Index.html?viewer=parcelviewer&run=initialSettings.

Brunswick County   ***Recorded Documents***   www.brunswickco.com/co_clerk.asp   Access to Circuit Court Records Search System is by subscription at www.courts.state.va.us/rmsweb/. $300 per year, username and password required, signup with local Circuit Court Clerk.

Buchanan County   ***Recorded Documents***   www.courts.state.va.us/courts/circuit/Buchanan/home.html   Access to the recorder's database is available by subscription, registration and password required; $50.00 per month. Contact clerk's office for signup and info. Data goes back to 1991. Deeds index will go back to 1976.

Buckingham County   ***Recorded Documents***   www.buckinghamcountyva.org/ccclerk.html   Access to land titles office records for a fee at https://lto.landsystems.com. Must get a login and password.

Buena Vista City   *Recorded Documents*   www.courts.state.va.us/courts/circuit/buena_vista/home.html   Access to subscription database for a fee contact Clerk at above number.   *Property, Taxation Records*   Access current assessment info and sales by VamaNet subscription at www.vamanet.com/cgi-bin/HOME. Fee is $35 per month or $300 per year with discounts for multiple localities, regions.

Campbell County   *Property, Taxation Records*   Access county property data from Dept of Real Estate and Mapping free at http://campbellvapropertymax.governmaxa.com/propertymax/rover30.asp?. Also, search property by name on the county GIS-mapping site at http://gis.worldviewsolutions.com/campbell/account/logon.

Caroline County   *Recorded Documents*   www.courts.state.va.us/courts/circuit/caroline/home.html   Access to land records and other related records for a fee at http://carolinevacocc.org/.
Property, Taxation Records   Click on Caroline County to search property records for free at www.vamanet.com/cgi-bin/HOME.

Carroll County   *Recorded Documents*   www.courts.state.va.us/courts/circuit/carroll/home.html   Access to Carroll county property data indexes and images requires a $25 monthly fee. Username and password required; signup through Clerk of Circuit Court, 276-730-3070. Land index and images go back to 1842.   *Property, Taxation Records*   There is no countywide site, but access Town of Hillsville property tax maps at http://carrollcountyva.org/docs/maps/Hillsville_Map_Set.pdf.

Charlotte County   *Property, Taxation Records*   Access to property cards for free at www.charlottecountypropertycards.com/.

Charlottesville City   *Recorded Dcouments Records*   www.courts.state.va.us/courts/circuit/charlottesville/home.html   Access to real estate records for a fee at https://www.uslandrecords.com/valr/.
Property, Taxation Records   Access to Assessor data and GIS/mapping is free at http://gisweb.charlottesville.org/GISViewer/.

Chesapeake City   *Recorded Documents*   www.cityofchesapeake.net/Government/City-Departments/courts-judicial-offices/circuit-court-clerk.htm   Access to records for a fee at www.chesapeakeccland.org/. Yearly subscription is $600.00 per subscriber.
Property, Taxation Records   Access to property data for free at www.cityofchesapeake.net/Government/City-Departments/Departments/Real-Estate-Assessor/app.htm.

Chesterfield County   *Recorded Documents*   www.chesterfield.gov/circuitclerk/   Access to land records for a fee at https://www.ccclandrecords.org/Opening.asp. Must have a user name and password for this subscription service. Records are available from 1749 to present.   *Property, Taxation Records*   Search the real estate assessment data free at www.chesterfield.gov/eServices/RealEstateAssessments/RealEstate.aspx?id=11063.

Clarke County   *Recorded Documents*   www.courts.state.va.us/courts/circuit/Clarke/home.html   With username and password (application obtained by contacting the Clerk's Office), can access recorder's land records at www.clarkevacocc.org/. Includes deed books back to 1836. Set up account online; fee is $25.00 per month.
Property, Taxation Records   Access current assessment info and sales by VamaNet subscription at www.vamanet.com/cgi-bin/HOME. Fee is $35 per month or $300 per year with discounts for multiple localities, regions. Also, access to MapsOnline for free at https://www.mapsonline.net/clarkecounty/index.html.

Colonial Heights City   *Recorded Documents*   www.colonialheightsva.gov/index.aspx?nid=86   Access to a subscription service for records contact Nancy Wood at 520-9364.
Property, Taxation Records   Access real estate property and assessor records for free at www.colonialheightsva.gov/index.aspx?NID=88.

Craig County   *Recorded Documents*   www.courts.state.va.us/courts/circuit/craig/home.html   Access to online services for a fee ($50.00 a month). Contact the office to get application.

Culpeper County   *Recorded Documents*   http://web.culpepercounty.gov/Government/Constitutional-Officers/Clerk-of-the-Court   Access to subscription records for a fee of $600.00 per year available. Contact Janice J Corbin, Clerk at 540-727-3438.
Property, Taxation Records   View property tax estimator free at http://web.culpepercounty.gov/eServices/TaxEstimator. Also via a vendor access property data free at www.onlinegis.net/newversion.html. No name searching. Also, access current assessment info and sales by VamaNet subscription at www.vamanet.com/cgi-bin/HOME. Fee is $35 per month or $300 per year with discounts for multiple localities, regions.

Cumberland County   *Recorded Documents*   www.courts.state.va.us/courts/circuit/cumberland/home.html   County deed and land records available by subscription to the Records Management System at https://risweb.courts.state.va.us/.
Property, Taxation Records   Access to property values data for free at www.cumberland.interactivegis.com/index.php.

Danville City   *Recorded Documents*   www.danville-va.gov/496/Clerk-of-Circuit-Court   Access to internet excess to records management contact-Clerk's office. Fee is $150.00 quarterly and an application is required.
Property, Taxation Records   Access to Danville City assessor online records is free at http://gis.danville-va.gov/GISPortal/. Also, access to GIS/mapping free at www.discoverdanvillesites.com/.

Dickenson County   *Recorded Documents*   www.dickensonva.org/index.aspx?nid=112   Access to real estate records free at www.dickensonva.org/index.aspx?NID=289.
Property, Taxation Records   Access to county tax maps for free at www.dickensonva.org/index.aspx?NID=289.

Dinwiddie County *Recorded Documents* www.dinwiddieva.us/index.aspx?nid=153   Online Index/Images from 1833 to present in subscription service. Contact www.dinwiddieva.us/index.aspx?nid=739 for further information. Also, access to parcel viewer free at http://dinwiddie.mapsdirect.net/.
Property, Taxation Records   Access current assessment info and sales by VamaNet subscription at www.vamanet.com/cgi-bin/HOME. Fee is $35 per month or $300 per year with discounts for multiple localities, regions.

Essex County *Recorder Documents Records* www.courts.state.va.us/courts/circuit/essex/home.html   Subscription service available. Records go back to 2006 only. $50.00 per month, must be paid 6 months at a time. Contact Clerk for more information.
Property, Taxation Records   Access to property identification card searches for free at https://county.essex-va.org/applications/txapps/PropCardsIndex.htm. RE taxes free at https://county.essex-va.org/applications/trapps/REIindex.htm. Also, access assessment info and sales by VamaNet subscription at www.vamanet.com/cgi-bin/HOME. Fee- $35/month or $300/year with discounts for multiple localities.

Fairfax County *Recorded Documents* www.fairfaxcounty.gov/courts/circuit/   A subscriber-based internet service that allows users to access recorded documents found at www.fairfaxcounty.gov/courts/circuit/cpan.htm (known as CPAN).
Property, Taxation Records   Records on the Dept. of Tax Administration RE Assessment database are free at http://icare.fairfaxcounty.gov/ffxcare/search/commonsearch.aspx?mode=address. Also, the list of auction properties is free at www.fairfaxcounty.gov/dta/auction.htm. Also, access to property assessment data free at http://patriotproperties.com/.

Fauquier County *Recorded Documents* www.fauquiercounty.gov/government/departments-a-g/circuit-court-clerk   Real estate data is available by subscription, $600.00 annual only fee; visit website www.fauquiercounty.gov/government/departments-a-g/circuit-court-clerk then click on Subscriptin information.
Property, Taxation Records   Search Town of Warrenton property index free at http://quicksearch.webgis.net/search.php?site=va_warrenton. Also, access to real estate online searches for free at http://reo.fauquiercounty.gov/.

Floyd County *Property, Taxation Records*   Access the property assessment and GIS/mapping search page free at http://floyd.interactivegis.com/.

Fluvanna County *Property, Taxation Records*   Click on Fluvanna County to search property data for free at www.vamanet.com/cgi-bin/HOME. Also, access to the Tax Map Book for free at http://fluvannacounty.org/services/commissioner/tax-map-book.

Franklin County *Recorded Documents* www.franklincountyva.gov/courts   Online subscription service available by contacting Teresa J Brown, Clerk and 540-483-3065. Records available through secure remote assess.
Property, Taxation Records   Access property data free at http://arcgis.webgis.net/va/Franklin/. Also, access current assessment info and sales by VamaNet subscription at www.vamanet.com/cgi-bin/HOME. Fee is $35 per month or $300 per year with discounts for multiple localities, regions.

Frederick County *Recorded Documents* www.winfredclerk.com/   Access to the County Records management System is by subscription; base fee is $500 per year for 3 users. Contact Elizabeth Ann Smith in the Circuit Court Clerk's office or website for info.
Property, Taxation Records   Access current assessment info and sales by VamaNet subscription at www.vamanet.com/cgi-bin/HOME. Fee is $35 per month or $300 per year with discounts for multiple localities, regions.

Fredericksburg City *Recorded Documents* http://fredericksburgva.gov/index.aspx?NID=548   Access to Circuit Court Records Search System is by subscription at www.fredericksburgva.gov/index.aspx?NID=649. Includes images for other selected jurisdictions; username and password required, signup with local Circuit Ct Clerk. Access to real estate inquiry options for free at https://apps.fredericksburgva.gov/applications/trapps/index.htm.
Property, Taxation Records   Access current assessment info and sales by VamaNet subscription at www.vamanet.com/cgi-bin/HOME. Contact for fees. Also, access to GIS/mapping free at http://gis.fredericksburgva.gov/ParcelViewer/Account/Logon.

Giles County *Recorded Documents, Marriage Records* www.gilescounty.org/clerk-of-court/index.htm   Access land records and deeds on subscription service ILS; call 804-786-5511 to apply; $50 monthly fee.
Property, Taxation Records   Click on Giles County to search for property records for free at www.vamanet.com/cgi-bin/HOME. Search property info on the county GIS site for free at http://arcgis.webgis.net/va/Giles/.

Gloucester County *Recorded Documents* www.gloucesterva.info/CircuitCourtClerksOffice/tabid/926/Default.aspx   The Clerk's Office offers remote access to land records management system via the internet through paid subscription only & subject to approval of the Clerk. The prepaid fee for this service is $150.00 per user, per quarter. To obtain a subscription, complete the Secured Remote Access User's Agreement found at www.gloucesterva.info/Portals/0/clerk/documents/SUBSCRIBERAGREEMENT-REMOTEACCESS.pdf, mail it with the fee to the Clerk of Circuit Court. Deeds, land records & financing statements from 9/1/19 to present, general misc from 8/5/19 to present and judgments from 10/18/19 to present.
Property, Taxation Records   Access to Real Estate assessment data for free at www.gloucesterva.info/RealEstateAssessment/tabid/623/Default.aspx Also, access current assessment info and sales by VamaNet subscription at www.vamanet.com/cgi-bin/HOME. Fee is $35 per month or $300 per year with discounts for multiple localities, regions.

Goochland County *Property, Taxation Records*   Click on Goochland County to search property data for a fee at www.vamanet.com/cgi-bin/HOME. Must subscribe. Also, access to GIS/mapping free at http://gis.co.goochland.va.us/GoochlandPV/Account/Logon.

Grayson County *Recorded Documents* www.graysoncountyva.gov/grayson-county-clerk-of-circuit-court/   Online access is available for a monthly fee of $25.00 per month. Contact--Susan M Herrington, Clerk or Debbie Hensley, DC.
Property, Taxation Records   Access property data free at http://arcgis.webgis.net/va/Grayson/. Also, access current assessment info and sales by VamaNet subscription at www.vamanet.com/cgi-bin/HOME. Fee is $35 per month or $300 per year with discounts for multiple localities, regions.

Greene County *Recorded Documents* www.greenecountyva.gov/government/local/clerk-court   Can subscribe for a fee of $600.00 per year for internet access to indexes-Deed 1/1/86 to present, Images 9/1/2006 to present, and Judgments 9/1/06 to present. Contact Brenda M Compton, Clerk at 434-985-5208.
Property, Taxation Records   Access to the property cards for free at https://treasurer.gcva.us/applications/txapps/PropCardsIndex.htm.

Greensville County *Property, Taxation Records*   Access current assessment info and sales by VamaNet subscription at www.vamanet.com/cgi-bin/HOME. Fee is $35 per month or $300 per year with discounts for multiple localities, regions.

Halifax County *Recorded Documents* www.courts.state.va.us/courts/circuit/Halifax/home.html   Access to online records is $50.00 a month with a contract. Contact Clerk's Office for more information.

Hampton City *Recorded Documents*   Access to the State Records Management System for a fee at www.courts.state.va.us/rmsweb/. Must read the terms and conditions of the Subscriber Agreement, then return the completed notarized application along with subscription fees, before use.

Hanover County *Recorded Documents* www.courts.state.va.us/courts/circuit/Hanover/home.html   Access to Secure Remote Assess records for a fee at https://hanover.landrecordsonline.com/. Must apply for subscription.
Property, Taxation Records   Access the parcel search function of the GIS site free at www.hanovercountygis.org/.

Henrico County *Recorded Documents* http://henrico.us/clerk/   Access to records can be obtained through a subscription. For information regarding subscription go to www.henricovalandrecords.org/Opening.asp.
Property, Taxation Records   Access to GIS/mapping free at http://gis.co.henrico.va.us/ExternalViewer/Account/Logon. Also, access to real estate data for free at http://henrico.us/finance/disclaimer/.

Henry County *Recorded Documents* www.courts.state.va.us/courts/circuit/henry/home.html   Online access available via secure remote access with paid subscription for $50.00 per month or $500.00 per year.. Contact the Clerks office at above phone number.
Property, Taxation Records   The Henry County and Martinsville GIS site has many searching capabilities at http://gis.co.henry.va.us/.

Highland County *Recorded Documents* www.courts.state.va.us/courts/circuit/highland/home.html   For subscription information contact Judy W Hupman, Clerk at 540-468-2447.

Hopewell City *Recorded Documents* www.hopewellva.gov/government/constitutional-officers/clerk-of-the-circuit-court/   A subscription service is available to in-state users only. The fee is $600 per year per a signed contractual agreement. Contact the Clerk's Office for details.
Property, Taxation Records   Access to Real Estate tax records for free at www.hopewellva.gov/real-estate/.

Isle of Wight County *Recorded Documents* www.co.isle-of-wight.va.us/clerk-of-the-circuit-court/   Access to recorder land records is by subscription; fee is $600.00 for 6 months or $500 per year; online deed records go back to 1914, judgments to 1991. Contact Wanda Wills at 757-365-6233 for registration and info.
Property, Taxation Records   Access property data via the GIS-mapping site free at http://iowgis.maps.arcgis.com/apps/webappviewer/index.html?id=4889333b70534c018c2c723b4d953f51. Also, access current assessment info and sales by VamaNet subscription at www.vamanet.com/cgi-bin/HOME. Fee is $35 per month or $300 per year with discounts for multiple localities, regions.

James City County *Recorded Documents* www.jamescitycountyva.gov/150/Clerk-of-the-Circuit-Court   Access to records for a fee - contact 757-564-2242 for forms to fill out.
Property, Taxation Records   Access assessment data free at http://property.jamescitycountyva.gov/JamesCity/. Search City of Williamsburg property assessor data free at http://williamsburg.timmons.com/flex/index.html.

King and Queen County *Land Records Records* www.kingandqueenco.net/html/Govt/circct.html   Secure remote access to land records available by subscription. Contact Vanessa D Porter, Clerk for details.
Property, Taxation Records   Access property cards for free at https://eservices.kingandqueenco.net/applications/txapps/default.htm.

King George County *Recorded Documents* www.king-george.va.us/county-offices/circuit-court/circuit-court.php   Subscription available-contact Janine McCarty, Deputy Clerk at 540-775-3322.
Property, Taxation Records   Access current assessment info and sales by VamaNet subscription at www.vamanet.com/cgi-bin/HOME. Fee is $35 per month or $300 per year with discounts for multiple localities, regions.

King William County *Recorded Documents*   Access to online search subscription (SRA) available for $600.00 per year. Contact office for details.
Property, Taxation Records   Access to property cards for free at https://e-services.kingwilliamcounty.us/applications/txapps/index.htm.

Lancaster County *Property, Taxation Records*   Click on Lancaster County to search property data for a fee at www.vamanet.com/cgi-bin/HOME. Must subscribe. Also, access parcel data free on the GIS-mapping site free at http://gis.lancova.com/.

Lee County *Recorded Documents* www.leeccc.com/   Access to the recorder's database is available by subscription, registration and password required; $50 per month or $500 per year. Contact clerk's office for registration form. Deeds go back to 2/1939, judgments and wills from 3/3/1794 to present, marriages from 1/5/1933 to present, financing statements to 1/1995.
Property, Taxation Records   Access to property cards for free at http://corpac.leecova.org/Applications/TXAPPS/VPCindex.htm.

Loudoun County *Property, Taxation Records*   Search the property assessor data for free at http://reparcelasmt.loudoun.gov/pt/search/commonsearch.aspx?mode=address. No name searching; search by address, number, or ID only. Access property data on the GIS-mapping site free at https://logis.loudoun.gov/weblogis/ but no name searching.

Louisa County *Recorded Documents* www.courts.state.va.us/courts/circuit/Louisa/home.html   Online access is available for a fee of $600 per year. Contact the Clerk for more information.
Property, Taxation Records   Search property and person property tax data for free at https://louweb.louisa.org/Applications/web/default.htm. Also, search property on the GIS-mapping site free at http://louisagis.timmons.com/#/. Also, access data for a fee at www.vamanet.com/cgi-bin/HOME.

Lynchburg City *Recorded Documents* www.courts.state.va.us/courts/circuit/Lynchburg/home.html   The Clerks states thatere is online access to recorded documents by subscription only and one must call the offcie to set-up. No informtaion about the service is provided on the web.
Property, Taxation Records   Access to parcel searches free at http://mapviewer.lynchburgva.gov/ParcelViewer/Account/Logon.

Madison County *Recorded Documents* www.madisonco.virginia.gov/clerkofcircuitcourt.php   Contact for Remote Access Service - Liz Smith at 540-948-6888.
Property, Taxation Records   Access data free at www.vamanet.com/cgi-bin/HOME. Also, access to GIS/mapping for free at http://arcgis.webgis.net/va/Madison/.

Martinsville City *Recorded Documents* www.martinsville-va.gov/Circuit-Court-Clerk.html   Access to Circuit clerk records is at www.ci.martinsville.va.us/Circuitclerk/subscription_page.htm. Fee is $50.00 per month, or one can search at a rate of $1.00 per doc. For info, call office of Ashby Pritchett at 276-403-5106 or visit website.
Property, Taxation Records   Access to GIS/mapping free at http://gis.co.henry.va.us/.

Mathews County *Property, Taxation Records*   Access to land records for free at http://emaps.emapsplus.com/standard/mathewscova.html.

Mecklenburg County *Recorded Documents* www.mecklenburgva.com/circuit-court.aspx   The clerk provides
Property, Taxation Records   Access to land files for free at www.mecklenburgva.com/govt/LB_DL.html.

Middlesex County *Property, Taxation Records*   Access current assessment info and sales by VamaNet subscription at www.vamanet.com/cgi-bin/HOME. Fee is $35 per month or $300 per year with discounts for multiple localities, regions. Also, access to property record card search free at https://websrv-vmw.dmz.co.middlesex.va.us/applications/TXApps/PropCardsIndex.htm.

Montgomery County *Recorded Documents* www.montgomerycountyva.gov/content/15987/16001/default.aspx   Access to land records (deeds, deeds of trust, refinanced deeds of trust, credit line deeds of trust, assignments, plate, deeds of easement, etc) available for a fee at www.montgomeryvalandrecords.org/. Deeds scanned for online assess date back to 1967.
Property, Taxation Records   Search county property index free at http://quicksearch.webgis.net/search.php?site=va_montgomery. Also, access to property records and view reassessment values search for free at http://realestate.montva.com/search/commonsearch.aspx?mode=owner. Records on the Town of Blacksburg GIS site are free at http://arcgis.webgis.net/va/blacksburg/.

Nelson County *Recorded Documents* www.courts.state.va.us/courts/circuit/nelson/home.html   Access to secure remote access for a fee, contact Clerks office for details.
Property, Taxation Records   Access to GIS/mapping free at www.nelsoncountygis.org/.

New Kent County *Property, Taxation Records*   Access to New Kent county assessor records is free at http://gis.vgsi.com/NewKentCountyVA/. Register free for full data.

Newport News City *Real Estate Recordings Records* www.courts.state.va.us/courts/circuit/Newport_News/home.html   Visit www.courts.state.va.us/rmsweb/ for remote access to land records including both indices and images. This is a subscription based service that runs $500 per year.
Property, Taxation Records   Access to property address search for free at http://assessment.nnva.gov/PT/Search/Disclaimer.aspx. Search for property data free on the GIS/mapping site at http://gis2.nngov.com/gis/. No name searching.

Norfolk City *Property, Taxation Records*   The City of Norfolk Real Estate Property Assessment database data is free at http://norfolkair.norfolk.gov/norfolkair/.

Northampton County *Real Estate, Deeds Records* www.co.northampton.va.us/gov/clerkofcourt.html   Access to land records for a fee at www.courts.state.va.us/rmsweb/.

Northumberland County *Recorded Documents* www.co.northumberland.va.us/   Access to land title, wills, judgments, UCC and marriage records for a fee at https://risweb.courts.state.va.us/. Must register before using.
Property, Taxation Records   Access Land Book data free at www.co.northumberland.va.us/NH-land-book.htm.

Orange County *Property, Taxation Records*   Access property data free at www.onlinegis.net/newversion.html. Also, access current assessment info and sales by VamaNet subscription at http://vamanet.com/cgi-bin/MAPSRCHPGM?LOCAL=ORA. Fee is $35 per month or $300 per year with discounts for multiple localities, regions.

Page County *Property, Taxation Records*   Access current assessment info and sales by VamaNet subscription at www.vamanet.com/cgi-bin/HOME. Fee is $35 per month or $300 per year with discounts for multiple localities, regions. Also, access the GIS/mapping for free at www.pagecountygis.com/Account/Logon.

Patrick County *Recorded Documents* http://co.patrick.va.us/clerk-of-court   Access to land records by subscription. Contact the office at 276-694-7213 for an application and add'l information. Fee of $40.00 per month is charged.
Property, Taxation Records   Access property data free at www.patrick.interactivegis.com/. Must register.

Pittsylvania County *Property, Taxation Records*   Search parcel information free at http://pittsylvaniacountyva.gov/247/Real-Estate-GIS.

Portsmouth City *Real Estate Records* www.portsmouthva.gov/651/Circuit-Court   Subscription service at $600.00 per year. Contact Cynthia Morrison at 757-393-8160.
Property, Taxation Records   Access to property records/tax maps are free at http://data.portsmouthva.gov/assessor/data/realestatesearch.aspx. No name searching. Access the treasurer's Real Estate Receivable Data free at http://data.portsmouthva.gov/treasurer/data/. Also, search GIS-mapping site for parcel data free at www2.portsmouthva.gov/portsmap/. Use map tools to identify parcel data.

Powhatan County *Recorded Documents* www.powhatanva.gov/223/Circuit-Court   Access recorder's index by subscription service. Contact the clerk's office for additional information.
Property, Taxation Records   Access current assessment info and sales by VamaNet subscription at www.vamanet.com/cgi-bin/HOME. Fee is $35 per month or $300 per year with discounts for multiple localities, regions. Also, access to the parcel viewer site for free at http://powhatanvarealestate.org/parcelviewer/.

Prince Edward County *Property, Taxation Records*   Access to property cards for free at https://epayments.co.prince-edward.va.us/applications/txapps/VPCindex.htm.

Prince William County *Recorded Documents, Marriage Records* www.pwcgov.org/government/courts/circuit/Pages/default.aspx Access to the records index for free at www.pwcgov.org/government/courts/circuit/Pages/Records-for-Occasional-User.aspx. To view or print documents, fee is $.50 per image. In addition, to offset the costs of providing this service, an Internet Convenience Fee of $2.00 will be added and displayed at the time of purchase.
Property, Taxation Records   Records on the county Property Assessment Information database are free at http://pwc.publicaccessnow.com/.

Pulaski County *Recorded Documents* www.courts.state.va.us/courts/circuit/Pulaski/home.html   The county participates in a subscription service offered at https://risweb.courts.state.va.us/. The Clerk prefers that all interested parties contact the office for an account name and password.
Property, Taxation Records   Access to the county GIS mapping info for a fee at www.pulaski.interactivegis.com/. Annual fee of $250.00 to access the netGIS information containing parcel owner names and addresses.

Radford City *Property, Taxation Records*   Access City property card info for a fee at http://208.88.162.36/inVizeDA/login.aspx?ReturnUrl=%2finVizeDA%2finVizeDA.aspx. Must have username and password. Also, access to the City of Radford's GIS/mapping for free at http://radfordgis.radford.va.us/flexviewer3.1/Radford_City_Map/.

Rappahannock County *Recorded Documents* www.courts.state.va.us/courts/circuit/rappahannock/home.html   Record access is by subscription through Clerk's Office. Fee-$600.00 per year.
Property, Taxation Records   Access current assessment info and sales by VamaNet subscription at www.vamanet.com/cgi-bin/HOME. Fee is $35 per month or $300 per year with discounts for multiple localities, regions.

Richmond City *Property, Taxation Records*   Search the city's Property & Real Estate Assessment data for free at http://eservices.ci.richmond.va.us/applications/propertysearch/. Also, access to GIS, mapping and links for free at www.richmondgov.com/Assessor/Mapping.aspx. City's Property & Real Estate Assessment data for free at http://map.richmondgov.com/parcel/.

Richmond County *Recorded Documents* www.co.richmond.va.us/departments/circuit-court-clerk-s-office   Access recorders land data by subscription at https://lto.landsystems.com/LTOOnline/logon.aspx?ReturnUrl=%2fLTOOnline%2fdefault.aspx. Individual account- $50.00 per month; 5-user business account- $200 per month.
Property, Taxation Records   Search county parcel data on the GIS-mapping site free at www.onlinegis.net/RichmondCountyVA/Map.html. Also, access to property cards for free at www.richmondcountypropertycards.com/.

Roanoke City *Deeds, Marriage, Judgment Records* www.roanokeva.gov/746/Clerk-of-Circuit-Court   Access to certain land records available by subscription only. Contact Clerk of Circuit court. Minimum subscription of 1 year at $50 per month ($600) required.

Property, Taxation Records   Access to property data is free on the City GIS website at http://gisre.roanokeva.gov/.

Roanoke County   *Recorded Documents*   www.roanokecountyva.gov/index.aspx?nid=26   The Roanoke County Circuit Court Clerk's office now has Real Estate Records online, along with other real estate related documents, via Secure Remote Access (SRA). To access these records online via SRA, one must submit a SRA Application & SRA Agreement for approval by the Clerk along with the a fee of $50.00 per month with a minimum 3 month subscription for $150.00. For a list of the record types available, including those with images, and how far back records are kept see www.roanokecountyva.gov/index.aspx?NID=425.   *Property, Taxation Records*   Access to property data is free on the county GIS mapping site at http://roanokecountyva.gov/index.aspx?NID=76. Property Assessment Data is available at http://webpro.roanokecountyva.gov/.

Rockbridge County   *Recorded Documents*   www.courts.state.va.us/courts/circuit/Rockbridge/home.html   Access by paid subscription only. $50.00 per month subscription fee payable 6 months in advance. Contact Clerk for more information.
Property, Taxation Records   Access county records on the GIS/mapping site free at http://quicksearch.webgis.net/search.php?site=va_rockbridge. Also, access City of Lexington property data free at www.vamanet.com/cgi-bin/MAPSRCHPGM?LOCAL=LEX. Also, access county current assessment info and sales by VamaNet subscription at www.vamanet.com/cgi-bin/HOME. Fee is $35 per month or $300 per year with discounts for multiple localities, regions.

Rockingham County   *Recorded Documents*   www.rockinghamcountyva.gov/index.aspx?nid=173   Access to real property by subscription at https://www.uslandrecords.com/valr/.   *Property, Taxation Records*   Access to Tax records and payment site at http://eservicesrc.com/taxes. Access to GIS/mapping for free at http://rockingham.interactivegis.com/. For more detailed information must register for a fee.

Russell County   *Property, Taxation Records*   Access current assessment info and sales by VamaNet subscription at www.vamanet.com/cgi-bin/HOME. Fee is $35 per month or $300 per year with discounts for multiple localities, regions.

Salem City   *Property, Taxation Records*   Access to GIS/mapping free at http://gis.salemva.gov/.

Scott County   *Recorded Documents*   www.courts.state.va.us/courts/circuit/scott/home.html   Access recorder's data by subscription; signup at clerk's office. Instruments scanned into system, with the old indexes.
Property, Taxation Records   Access current assessment info and sales by VamaNet subscription at www.vamanet.com/cgi-bin/HOME. Fee is $35 per month or $300 per year with discounts for multiple localities, regions.

Shenandoah County   *Recorded Documents*   www.courts.state.va.us/courts/circuit/shenandoah/home.html   Recorded data available by subscription with images back to 1999 and earlier being added. Fee is $50.00 per month or $500.00 per year, contact Sarona Irvin 540-459-6153 in clerk's office.   *Property, Taxation Records*   Access current assessment info and sales by VamaNet subscription at www.vamanet.com/cgi-bin/HOME. Fee is $35 per month or $300 per year with discounts for multiple localities, regions. Also, access tax payment histories free at http://shenandoahcountyva.us/revenue/tax_books/. Also, access parcel data on the GIS-mapping site free at www.shenandoahgis.org/ and click on Find to name search.

Smyth County   *Recorded Documents*   www.courts.state.va.us/courts/circuit/smyth/home.html   For subscription service contact Shirley Blevins.   *Property, Taxation Records*   Access current assessment info and sales by VamaNet subscription at www.vamanet.com/cgi-bin/HOME. Fee is $35 per month or $300 per year with discounts for multiple localities, regions. Also, search county property index free at http://quicksearch.webgis.net/search.php?site=va_smyth.

Southampton County   *Recorded Records Records*   www.southamptoncounty.org/Clerk-of-the-Circuit-Court.aspx   For subscription service contact Richard Francis, Clerk or Heather Simmons, DC
Property, Taxation Records   Click on Southampton County to search property data for free at www.vamanet.com/cgi-bin/HOME.

Spotsylvania County   *Recorded Documents*   www.spotsylvania.va.us/content/20925/20945/default.aspx   Access the recorder's recording index and images by subscription; fee is $150.00 per quarter; contact Land Recording Desk at 540-507-7615 at the clerk's office or go to http://spotsylandrecords.org/ for instructions.   *Property, Taxation Records*   Access to property assessment found at www.spotsylvania.va.us/cor/realestate/assessmentsearch, GIS/mapping for free at http://gis.spotsylvania.va.us/Spotsylvania/Account/Logon.

Stafford County   *Recorded Documents*   http://co.stafford.va.us/index.aspx?NID=760   Access to remote access site for a fee at www.staffordcocc.org/. Must have username and password. Contact Clerk's office for information. Judgments available in imaged index from 9/1/1987 to 6/30/1994. This is both indexing and imaging data. Add'l judgment images in instrument number format from 7/1/1994 to 12/31/1995.
Property, Taxation Records   Access taxes paid free at http://staffordcountyva.gov/index.aspx?NID=1174. Must register for username and password.

Staunton City   *Property, Taxation Records*   Access property tax data on the City GIS site free at http://gis.ci.staunton.va.us:8087/mapsandapps/.

Suffolk City   *Recorded Documents*   www.suffolkva.us/citygovt/co/clerk-of-the-circuit-court   Access to land record indexes for free to go www.suffolkvaland.org/. Get indexes for free, for images must register and pay a fee.   *Property, Taxation Records*   Access property assessment data free at http://apps.suffolkva.us/realest/Search_Real_Estate_3.html, but no name searching.

Surry County *Recorded Documents* www.surryvacocc.org/Opening.asp   Access to Circuit Court Records Search System is by subscription at www.surryvacocc.org/Opening.asp. $600.00 per year payable $50 per month, username and password required.
Property, Taxation Records   Access to GIS/mapping free at http://surry.mapsdirect.net/Account/Logon.

Sussex County *Property, Taxation Records*   Access to assessor property records is free at https://eservices.sussexcountyva.gov/applications/txapps/.

Tazewell County *Recorded Documents* http://tazewellcountyva.org/government/clerk-of-the-circuit-court/   Access to online records by subscription contact--Tammy Allison, Chief Deputy Clerk at 276-988-1221 or tallison@courts.state.va.us.
Property, Taxation Records   Click on Tazewell County to search property data for free at www.vamanet.com/cgi-bin/MAPSRCHPGM?LOCAL=TAZ.

Virginia Beach City *Recorded Documents, Marriage Records* https://www.vbgov.com/government/departments/courts/circuit-court-clerks-office/Pages/default.aspx   Access the database free at www.vbcircuitcourt.com/public/search.do. The second method of access will be via a $50 per month Monthly Subscription using credit card. Direct general questions to Emillie Inman at 757-385-4462. Also, browse city document archives free at http://edocs.vbgov.com/weblink/Browse.aspx. Free access is no image access, subscription fee is $50 per month (full image access); pay as you go access is $2.00 per doc plus $.50 per page (first page doc preview) at https://vblandrecords.com/subscriptions.html.
Property, Taxation Records   Search the assessor database free at http://va-virginiabeach-realestate.governmax.com/ but no name searching. This will lead to several search sites/choices.

Warren County *Recorded Documents* www.warrencountyva.net/index.php?option=com_workforce&view=department&id=3&Itemid=70   Access the Clerk's data on the web for a fee; username and password required. For a fee username and password contact Jennifer Sims at 540-635-2435 or at jsims@courts.state.va.us. Images go back to 1994. *Property, Taxation Records*   Access current assessment info and sales by VamaNet subscription at www.vamanet.com/cgi-bin/HOME. Fee is $35 per month or $300 per year with discounts for multiple localities, regions.

Washington County *Property, Taxation Records*   Access current assessment info and sales by VamaNet subscription at www.vamanet.com/cgi-bin/HOME. Fee is $35 per month or $300 per year with discounts for multiple localities, regions.

Waynesboro City *Recorded Documents* www.waynesboro.va.us/708/Circuit-Court   To access paid subscription, contact Clerk of Court for inquires to remote access to land records.

Westmoreland County *Recorded Documents* www.westmoreland-county.org/index.php?p=govt&c=countyCourts   Access to subscription records for a fee of $600.00 per year available. Contact G J Chatham at 804-493-0108. Must come to the office to receive a password.
Property, Taxation Records   Access real estate tax payment database free at https://eservices.westmoreland-county.org/applications/trapps/REIindex.htm. Also, search property card records free at https://eservices.westmoreland-county.org/applications/txapps/index.htm. Also, search utility payment records free at https://eservices.westmoreland-county.org/applications/trapps/UTIindex.htm.

Winchester City *Recorded Documents* www.winfredclerk.com   Access to the County Records management System is by subscription; base fee is $500 per year for 3 users. Contact the Winchester County Circuit Court Clerk's office for info.
Property, Taxation Records   Access current assessment info and sales by VamaNet subscription at www.vamanet.com/cgi-bin/HOME. Fee is $35 per month or $300 per year with discounts for multiple localities, regions. Also, access surrounding Frederick County parcel data on the GIS-mapping site free at http://gis.co.frederick.va.us/Freeance/Client/PublicAccess1/index.html?appconfig=FCMap.

Wise County (City of Norton) *Property, Taxation Records*   Property data is at www.wise-assessor.org/assessor/web/. Must register to login. Also, search county parcel data free at http://quicksearch.webgis.net/search.php?site=va_wise. Also, access to GIS/mapping for free at http://arcgis.webgis.net/va/Wise/.

Wythe County *Recorded Documents* www.wytheco.org/index.php/departments/clerk-of-circuit-court.html   Access to recording index and judgments records is by subscription; $25.00 per month for username and password, Contact the clerk office for signup.
Property, Taxation Records   Access current assessment info and sales by VamaNet subscription at www.vamanet.com/cgi-bin/HOME. Fee is $35 per month or $300 per year with discounts for multiple localities, regions. Also, search the GIS site free at http://wythe.interactivegis.com/index.php but no name searching.

York County-Poquoson *Recorded Documents* www.yorkcounty.gov/Default.aspx?alias=www.yorkcounty.gov/circuitcourt   Subscription information found at www.yorkcounty.gov/CountyGovernment/Courts-Circuit/LandRecords.aspx. Must apply and sign subscriber agreement. Fee is $150.00 per quarter.
Property, Taxation Records   Access to property search and GIS/mapping for free at http://maps.yorkcounty.gov/York/Account/Logon.

Washington

Capital: Olympia
          Thurston County
Time Zone: PST
Population: 7,170,351
# of Counties: 39

Useful State Links

Website: http://access.wa.gov
Governor: www.governor.wa.gov
Attorney General: www.atg.wa.gov
State Archives: www.digitalarchives.wa.gov
State Statutes and Codes: www.leg.wa.gov/LawsAndAgencyRules/Pages/default.aspx
Legislative Bill Search: http://apps.leg.wa.gov/billinfo/
Bill Monitoring: www.leg.wa.gov/pages/home.aspx
Unclaimed Funds: http://ucp.dor.wa.gov/

State Public Record Agencies

Criminal Records

Washington State Patrol, Identification and Criminal History Section,   www.wsp.wa.gov/crime/crimhist.htm   WSP offers access through a system called WATCH, which can be accessed from their website. The fee per name search is $10.00. The exact DOB and exact spelling of the name are required. Credit cards are accepted online. Add $10.00 for notarize seal (fax requests accepted for these). To set up a WATCH account, call 360-534-2000 or email watch.help@wsp.wa.gov. Non-profits (for Washington State Only) can request a fee-exempt account. WATCH stands for Washington Access To Criminal History. *Other Options:* See the State Court Administrator's office for information about their criminal records database (JIS-Link).

Sexual Offender Registry

Washington State Patrol, SOR,   www.wsp.wa.gov/   In cooperation with the Washington Assoc. of Sheriffs and Police Chiefs, free online access to Level II and Level III sexual offenders is available at www.icrimewatch.net/index.php?AgencyID=54528. Also shown to the public are non-compliant Level I offenders. *Other Options:* The website provides a printable list of all offenders, but on a page by page basis.

Incarceration Records

Washington Department of Corrections, Public Disclosure Unirt,   www.doc.wa.gov   "Find an Offender" is free at www.doc.wa.gov/offenderinfo/default.aspx. Search by name or DOC number. *Other Options:* Data is available by subscription for bulk users; for information, contact the Contracts Office at 360-725-8363.

Corporation, Trademarks, Charities, LP, LLC Records

Secretary of State, Corporations Division,   www.sos.wa.gov/corps/   There are two main ways to search for corporations registered in Washington; by name or by UBI number. A free search is at the home page as well as at www.sos.wa.gov/corps/corps_search.aspx. Information is updated daily. While not part of this agency, there is a free search of securities companies and other financial institutions registered with the state at http://dfi.wa.gov/public-records-index.   *Other Options:* One may download an entire extract of the corporations search database in Text or XML format at www.sos.wa.gov/corps/AllData.aspx. The data cannot be used for commercial purposes.

Trade Names

Master License Service, Department of Licensing,   www.dol.wa.gov   The web page give the ability to check trade name ability, assuming the business name listed is the trade name. *Other Options:* Records can be purchased on cartridges or 9 track tapes. Information includes date of registration, owner name, state ID numbers, and cancel date if cancelled. Call same number and ask for Jody Miller.

Uniform Commercial Code, Federal Tax Liens

Department of Licensing, UCC Records, www.dol.wa.gov/business/UCC/ For online access, go to https://fortress.wa.gov/dol/ucc. There is no search fee for name search or by file number. One may view collateral documents if the document was filed online. However to view documents filed by paper, they can be mailed or picked up (or picked up) for a fee of $15.00. *Other Options:* The database may be purchased via FTP.

Sales Tax Registrations

Department of Revenue, Public Records Officer, http://dor.wa.gov/Content/Home/Default.aspx The agency provides a state business records database with free access on the Internet at http://dor.wa.gov/content/doingbusiness/registermybusiness/brd/. Look-ups are by owner names, DBAs, tax reporting numbers, and reseller permit numbers. Results show a myriad of data.

Vital Certificates

Department of Health, Center for Health Statistics, www.doh.wa.gov/LicensesPermitsandCertificates/BirthDeathMarriageandDivorce Access death records 1940 thru 1997 at http://vitals.rootsweb.ancestry.com/ca/death/search.cgi. Records may requested from www.Vitalchek.com, a state-endorsed vendor. *Other Options:* The Digital Archives, launched in 2004, contains various periods for marriages, death, birth, military, naturalization, institution, and various historical records at www.digitalarchives.wa.gov/default.aspx.

Workers' Compensation Records

Labor and Industries, Public Records Unit, www.lni.wa.gov/ClaimsIns/default.asp Claim information is accessible to authorized users at www.lni.wa.gov/orli/logon.asp. Claims inactive for 18+ months or crime victims claims are not in the Claim & Account Center. *Other Options:* Many claim files are available on CD. Records may not be available include file records received before June 16, 1994. For more info call 360-902-5556.

Driver Records

Department of Licensing, Driver Record Section, www.dol.wa.gov FTP retrieval is offered for high volume requesters, minimum of 2,000 requests per month. Requesters must be approved and sign a contract. Call Data Sales Management at 360-902-3851. Contract holders may also participate in a notification program (monitoring and notification of activity on a record), but strictly used for only insurance company needs. There is a secondary online check for status of a driver license, permit or ID card free at https://fortress.wa.gov/dol/dolprod/dsdDriverStatusDisplay/. Online access is available for drivers to obtain their own driving records at https://fortress.wa.gov/dol/dolprod/dsdiadr/. Use of a credit card is required. Record is shown as PDF.

Vehicle, Vessel Ownership & Registration

Department of Licensing, Public Disclosure Unit, www.dol.wa.gov/vehicleregistration/ Pre-approved users may search for and access vehicle and boat records using a web-based system known as IVIPS (Internet Vehicle/Vessel Information Processing System). With an IVIPS account, one may obtain lien holder name(s). There is a charge of $2.00 per vehicle record accessed through IVIPS and a charge of $.04 per search performed. Contact the Public Disclosure Section at 360-359-4001 during normal business hours for more information about applying for IVIPS access. Or see application at www.dol.wa.gov/forms/224002.pdf. *Other Options:* Large bulk lists cannot be released for any commercial purposes. Lists are released to non-profit entities and for statistical purposes.

Crash Reports

State Patrol, Collision Records Section, www.wsp.wa.gov/publications/collision.htm Purchase a collision report online at https://fortress.wa.gov/wsp/wrecr/WSPCRS/Search.aspx. The fee is $9.50 per record.

Campaign Finance

Public Disclosure Commission, 711 Capitol WAY #206, https://www.pdc.wa.gov/ All searches can be made at http://web.pdc.wa.gov/MvcQuerySystem. This includes campaign finance, lobbyists, and PACs. Email questions to pdc@pdc.wa.gov.

GED Certificates

State Board for Community & Technical Colleges, GED Transcripts, www.sbctc.edu/becoming-a-student/basic-education/ged-students.aspx SE completed prior to December 31, 2001: Submit requests for official Washington State GED® verification through Washington GED® Test Verify at https://gedverify.org/default.aspx?ReturnUrl=/. You will be asked to create an account in order to verify the completion status of a Washington State GED® examinee. Verification and transcript information for GED® tests taken after January 1, 2002 is available at www.gedtestingservice.com/testers/gedrequest-a-transcript. This is a designated vendor. Third parties are routed to set up an account at: http://exchange.parchment.com/ged-receiver-registration-page. Service fees apply for both vendors.

Occupational Licensing Boards

These licenses are all searchable at https://fortress.wa.gov/doh/providercredentialsearch/

Acupuncturist	Dentist	Marriage & Family Therapist
Animal Technician	Dietitian	Massage Therapist
Audiologist	Emergency Medical Technician	Mental Health Counselor
Chiropractor	Hearing Instrument Fitter/Dispenser	Midwife
Counselor	Home Health Care Agency	Naturopathic Physician
Dental Hygienist	Hypnotherapist	Nurse-LPN/Aide

Nursing Home Administrator
Occupational Therapist
Ocularist
Optician
Optometrist
Osteopathic Physician

Pharmacist/Pharmacy Technician
Physical Therapist
Physician/Medical Doctor/Assistant
Podiatrist
Psychologist
Radiologic Technologist

Respiratory Therapist
Sex Offender Treatment Provider
Social Worker
Speech-Language Pathologist
Veterinarian/Veterinary Medical Clerk
X-Ray Technician

These licenses are all searchable at https://fortress.wa.gov/dol/dolprod/bpdLicenseQuery/

Announcer, Athletic Event/Ring
Architect/Architectural Corp
Athl' Judge/Timekeeper/Physician
Athlete, Professional/Inspector
Athletic Mgr/Promot'r/Matchmaker
Bail Bond Agent/Agency
Barber
Barber Instructor/School/Shop/Mobile
Boxer
Cemetery
Cemetery Certificate of Authority
Cemetery Prearrangem't Seller
Collection Agency
Cosmetologist

Cosmetology Instructor/School/Shop/Mobile
Cremated Remains Dispositor
Crematory
Embalmer/Intern
Employment Agency
Engineer
Engineering Geologist
Engineering/Land Surveying Firm
Esthetician/Esthetician Instructor/Salon/Mobile
Funeral Director/Intern
Funeral Establishment/Branch
Funeral Prearrangement Contract
Geologist
Hydrogeologist

Kickboxer
Land Surveyor/Surveyor-in-Training
Landscape Architect
Manicurist/Manicurist Instructor/Salon/Mobile
Private Investigator/Agency/Trainer
Real Estate Agent/Seller/Broker
Real Estate Appraiser
Referee (Athletic)
Security Guard, Private/Agency
Wastewater System Designer/Inspect
Whitewater River Outfitter
Wrestler

The Rest:

Accountant Firm	http://apps.cpaboard.wa.gov/Default.aspx?querytype=Firm
Accountant-CPA	http://apps.cpaboard.wa.gov/
Adult Family Home	https://fortress.wa.gov/dshs/adsaapps/lookup/AFHPubLookup.aspx
Applicator, Pesticide, Private/Commercial	http://agr.wa.gov/PestFert/LicensingEd/Search/
Attorney	https://www.mywsba.org/LawyerDirectory.aspx
Bank	www.dfi.wa.gov/banks/who-we-regulate/commercial
Boarding Home	https://fortress.wa.gov/dshs/adsaapps/lookup/BHPubLookup.aspx
Boiler Inspector	www.lni.wa.gov/TradesLicensing/Boilers/Inspectors/default.asp
Business Opportunity Offering	www.dfi.wa.gov/consumers/verify-license
Charitable Gift Annuity	https://www.insurance.wa.gov/consumertoolkit/search.aspx
Check Casher/Seller	www.dfi.wa.gov/consumers/verify-license
Child Care Provider/Facility	www.childcarenet.org/acl_users/credentials_cookie_auth/require_login
Consumer Loan Company	www.dfi.wa.gov/consumers/verify-license
Contractor, Construction	https://secure.lni.wa.gov/verify/
Contractor, General, Company	https://secure.lni.wa.gov/verify/
Contractor, General, Individual	www.dol.wa.gov/listoflicenses.html
Contributor, Political	http://web.pdc.wa.gov/MvcQuerySystem
Currency Exchange	www.dfi.wa.gov/consumers/verify-license
Domestic Insurance Carrier	https://www.insurance.wa.gov/consumertoolkit/search.aspx
Electrical Contractor/Administrator	https://secure.lni.wa.gov/verify/
Electrician	https://secure.lni.wa.gov/verify/
Elevator Contractor/Mechanic	https://secure.lni.wa.gov/verify/
Escrow Company/Officer	www.dfi.wa.gov/consumers/verify-license
Feedlot	http://agr.wa.gov/FoodAnimal/Livestock/LicensedCertifiedFeedlotsPublicMarkets.aspx
Fishing/Hunting License Dealer	http://wdfw.wa.gov/licensing/vendors/
Franchise	www.dfi.wa.gov/consumers/verify-license
Healthcare Service Company	https://www.insurance.wa.gov/consumertoolkit/search.aspx
HMO	https://www.insurance.wa.gov/consumertoolkit/search.aspx
Hospital	https://fortress.wa.gov/doh/facilitysearch/
Insurance Agent/Broker	https://www.insurance.wa.gov/consumertoolkit/search.aspx

Insurance Broker, Resident/Non-Resi .... https://www.insurance.wa.gov/consumertoolkit/search.aspx
Insurance Company .... https://www.insurance.wa.gov/consumertoolkit/search.aspx
Insurance Corporation, Resident .... https://www.insurance.wa.gov/consumertoolkit/search.aspx
Investment Advisor .... www.dfi.wa.gov/consumers/verify-license
Livestock Market .... http://agr.wa.gov/FoodAnimal/Livestock/LicensedCertifiedFeedlotsPublicMarkets.aspx
Lobbyist/Lobbyist Report .... http://web.pdc.wa.gov/MvcQuerySystem
Medical Gas Plumber .... https://secure.lni.wa.gov/verify/
Money Transmitter .... www.dfi.wa.gov/consumers/verify-license
Mortgage Broker .... http://brokercheck.finra.org/
Nursing Home .... https://fortress.wa.gov/dshs/adsaapps/lookup/NHPubLookup.aspx
Payday Lender .... www.dfi.wa.gov/consumers/verify-license
Pest Control Operator/Consul't, Public ..... http://agr.wa.gov/PestFert/LicensingEd/Search/
Pesticide Dealer/Manager .... http://agr.wa.gov/PestFert/LicensingEd/Search/
Pesticide Demo & Research Applicator .... http://agr.wa.gov/PestFert/LicensingEd/Search/
Pesticide Operator/Applicator .... http://agr.wa.gov/PestFert/LicensingEd/Search/
Pesticide Private Application .... http://agr.wa.gov/PestFert/LicensingEd/Search/
Pilot, Marine, Commercial .... https://pilotagewa-public.sharepoint.com/Documents/Directories/Pilotsandtraineeslist.pdf
Plumber .... https://secure.lni.wa.gov/verify/
Political Candidate .... http://web.pdc.wa.gov/MvcQuerySystem
Political Committee .... http://web.pdc.wa.gov/MvcQuerySystem
Purchasing Group (Insurance) .... https://www.insurance.wa.gov/consumertoolkit/search.aspx
Real Estate LLC, LLP, Corp, etc .... www.dol.wa.gov/listoflicenses.html
Recreational Hunting .... http://wdfw.wa.gov/licensing/vendors/
Risk Retention Group .... https://www.insurance.wa.gov/consumertoolkit/search.aspx
Savings & Loan/Savings Bank .... www.dfi.wa.gov/banks/who-we-regulate/commercial
Service Contract Provider (Ins) .... https://www.insurance.wa.gov/consumertoolkit/search.aspx
Structural Pest Inspector .... http://agr.wa.gov/PestFert/LicensingEd/Search/
Trust Company .... www.dfi.wa.gov/banks/who-we-regulate/trusts
Viatical Settlement Provider .... https://www.insurance.wa.gov/consumertoolkit/search.aspx

State and Local Courts

About Washington Courts: **Superior Court** is the court of general jurisdiction, and has exclusive jurisdiction for felony matters, real property rights, domestic relations, estate, mental illness, juvenile, and civil cases over $50,000. The Superior Courts also hear appeals from courts of limited jurisdiction.

District Courts have concurrent jurisdiction with superior courts over misdemeanor and gross misdemeanor violations, and civil cases under $75,000. District Courts have exclusive jurisdiction over small claims and infractions. Criminal jurisdiction over misdemeanors, gross misdemeanors, and criminal traffic cases. The maximum penalty for gross misdemeanors is one year in jail and a $5,000 fine. The maximum penalty for misdemeanors is 90 days in jail and a $1,000 fine.

Municipal Courts have concurrent jurisdiction with Superior Courts over misdemeanor and gross misdemeanor violations and have exclusive jurisdiction over infractions. Cities electing not to establish a Municipal Court may contract with the District Court for services. Many Municipal Courts combine their record keeping with a District Court housed in the same building.
The web page for the Judicial Branch is www.courts.wa.gov.

Appellate Courts: The Supreme Court is the state's court of last resort. Most cases come from the state Court of Appeals, though certain cases can be appealed directly from Superior Court. Supreme and Appellate opinions are at www.courts.wa.gov/appellate_trial_courts.

Online Court Access
All Courts Participate in the Statewide System Described Below.

For **detailed case docket data**, the AOC provides the Judicial Information System's subscription service called **JIS-Link** which provides access to all counties and court levels. One may search a single county or statewide for criminal searches; however, searching for civil records is by single county only. Civil cases include small claims, domestic violence, vehicle impounds, name changes, anti-harassment petitions, and lien foreclosures vehicle impounds, and property damages.

The state is in the midst of replacing the JIS-Link system software the software supplied by Tyler technologies - called Odyssey. See the section to follow for details.

The JIS subscription includes access to SCOMIS (the case management system) and ACORDS (appellate courts data). SCOMIS enables the superior court to record parties and legal instruments filed in superior court cases, to set cases on court calendars, and to enter case judgments and final dispositions. It is important to note that when a SCOMIS case number is found in the JIS application, detail level of the case may need to be viewed within the appropriate SCOMIS court display.

The throughput date for JIS is normally back to 1994 or 1995 and the dates vary from 1979 to 1993 for SCOMIS. The subscription fees include a one-time $100.00 per site, a transaction fee of $.065. There is a $6.00 per month minimum charge. Visit www.courts.wa.gov/jislink or call 360-357-3365.

A **limited, free look-up of docket information** is at http://dw.courts.wa.gov/. Search by name or case number. The index is of cases filed in the municipal, district, superior, and appellate courts of the state of Washington. The purpose of this site is to point where the official or complete court record is housed. As such, the outcome is not shown, but a link to a summary of the judgment does appear. No identifiers are shown. The search is by Municipal and District cases or by Superior cases or by Appellate cases.

About the Move to Odyssey

AOC implemented the Odyssey system in the SC-CMS Pilot site – Lewis County – in June 2015. Three early adopter sites (Thurston, Yakima, and Franklin counties) have also gone live with Odyssey in November 2015. Snohomish County followed in May 2016. The remaining counties will go live in groups approximately every 6 months beginning in November 2016. The statewide rollout is expected to be complete by 2018.

An unregistered public user will be able to access Odyssey Portal online at https://odysseyportal.courts.wa.gov/odyportal. This access will not require any credentials and will provide information similar to what is available to public users on the Washington Courts website. Public users will have more access to case information, as well as publically available documents, at the Clerk's Office lobby terminal. Access and fees will be administered by each County Clerk.

Courts with Online Sites Other Than the Statewide Systems Profiled Above

Chelan County
Superior Court   www.co.chelan.wa.us/superior-court
Civil & Criminal: Certified or non-certified documents may be ordered online at https://www.clerkepass.com/Chelan/. There are added fees which depend on the type of document ordered. No name searching here.

Clark County
Superior Court   https://www.clark.wa.gov/superior-court
Civi & Criminal: Daily dockets are at www.clark.wa.gov/courts/superior/docket.html. Search by name or case number. Also, certified or non-certified documents may be ordered online at https://www.clerkepass.com/Clark/. There are added fees which depend on the type of document ordered. No name searching here.
District Court   https://www.clark.wa.gov/district-court
Civil & Criminal: Daily dockets are at www.clark.wa.gov/courts/district/docket.html

Douglas County
Superior Court   www.douglascountywa.net
Civil & Criminal: Certified or non-certified documents may be ordered online at https://www.clerkepass.com/Douglas/. There are added fees which depend on the type of document ordered. No name searching here.

Grant County
Superior Court   www.grantcountywa.gov/Clerk
Civil & Criminal: Certified or non-certified documents may be ordered online at https://www.clerkepass.com/Grant/. There are added fees which depend on the type of document ordered. No name searching here.

Island County
Superior Court   https://www.islandcountywa.gov/clerk/Pages/Home.aspx
Civil & Criminal: Certified or non-certified documents may be ordered online at https://www.clerkepass.com/Island/. There are added fees which depend on the type of document ordered. No name searching here.

Jefferson County
Superior Court   www.co.jefferson.wa.us/supcourt/
Civil & Criminal: Certified or non-certified documents may be ordered online at https://www.clerkepass.com/jefferson/. There are added fees which depend on the type of document ordered. No name searching here.

King County

All Superior Courts   www.kingcounty.gov/courts/Clerk.aspx
Civl & Criminal: Order court documents online at http://dja-eweb.kingcounty.gov/records/. Registration and copy fees involved.

Kitsap County

Superior Court   www.kitsapgov.com/clerk/
Civil & Criminal: Certified or non-certified documents may be ordered online at https://www.clerkepass.com/kitsap/. There are added fees which depend on the type of document ordered. No name searching here.

Kittitas County

Superior Court   www.co.kittitas.wa.us/clerk/
Civil & Criminal: Certified or non-certified documents may be ordered online at https://www.clerkepass.com/kittitas/. There are added fees which depend on the type of document ordered. No name searching here.

Klickitat County

Superior Court   www.klickitatcounty.org/
Civil & Criminal: Certified or non-certified documents may be ordered online at https://www.clerkepass.com/Klickitat/. There are added fees which depend on the type of document ordered. No name searching here.

Mason County

Superior Court   www.co.mason.wa.us/clerk/index.php
Civil & Criminal: Certified or non-certified documents may be ordered online at https://www.clerkepass.com/mason/. There are added fees which depend on the type of document ordered. No name searching here.

Okanogan County

Superior Court   http://okanogancounty.org/superiorcourt/
Civil & Criminal: Certified or non-certified documents may be ordered online at https://www.clerkepass.com/Okanogan/. There are added fees which depend on the type of document ordered. No name searching here.

Pend Oreille County

Superior Court   http://pendoreilleco.org/your-government/county-clerk/superior-court-calendar-and-docket
Civil & Criminal: Certified or non-certified documents may be ordered online at https://www.clerkepass.com/PendOreille/. There are added fees which depend on the type of document ordered. No name searching here.

Skagit County

Superior Court   www.skagitcounty.net/Departments/SuperiorCourt/main.htm
Civil & Criminal: Certified or non-certified documents may be ordered online at https://www.clerkepass.com/Skagit/. There are added fees which depend on the type of document ordered. No name searching here.

Skamania County

Superior Court   www.courts.wa.gov/court_dir/orgs/289.html
Civil & Criminal: Certified or non-certified documents may be ordered online at https://www.clerkepass.com/Skamania/. There are added fees which depend on the type of document ordered. No name searching here.

Stevens County

Superior Court
Civil & Criminal: Certified or non-certified documents may be ordered online at https://www.clerkepass.com/Stephens/. There are added fees which depend on the type of document ordered. No name searching here.

Walla Walla County

Superior Court   www.co.walla-walla.wa.us/
Civil & Criminal: Certified or non-certified documents may be ordered online at https://www.clerkepass.com/WallaWalla/. There are added fees which depend on the type of document ordered. No name searching here. *Criminal:* same

Recorders, Assessors, and Other Sites of Note

About Washington Recording Offices: 39 counties, 39 recording offices. The recording officer is the County Auditor. County records are usually combined in a Grantor/Grantee index. All federal tax liens are filed with the Department of Licensing.

About Tax Liens: All federal tax liens are filed with the State Department of Licensing. All state tax liens are filed with the County Auditor..

Online Access

There is no statewide access to recorded documents or assesor data. 26 counties offer online access to recorded documents and all but 2 counties (Asotin and Garfield) offer online access to assessor data.

County Sites:

Adams County *Property, Taxation Records*   Access to county property tax and sales records, and inmate records is free at http://adamswa.taxsifter.com/Disclaimer.aspx.

Benton County *Recorded Documents* www.bentonauditor.com/benton   Access to index for free at http://64.146.238.12/recorder/web/. Access by subscription to grantor/grantee index, parcels and recordings back to 1/1/85.
Property, Taxation Records   Access to Benton County assessor data is free at http://bentonpropertymax.governmaxa.com/propertymax/rover30.asp. Search by parcel ID#, address or map; no name searching.

Chelan County *Recorded Documents, Marriage Records* www.co.chelan.wa.us/auditor   Access to Oncore Web searches free at http://63.135.55.89/oncoreweb/Search.aspx. Index from 1974 forward. All images available back to county inception.
Property, Taxation Records   Access the parcel and sale search and the GIS/mapping free at www.co.chelan.wa.us/assessor/.

Clallam County *Recorded Documents* https://wei.sos.wa.gov/county/clallam/en/pages/default.aspx   Access to recording records free at http://vpn.clallam.net:8080/recorder/web/.
Property, Taxation Records   Access to assessor property data is free at http://websrv8.clallam.net/propertyaccess/?cid=0. Auditor property maps are also downloadable at www.clallam.net/RealEstate/html/recorded_maps.htm. Add'l property maps at www.clallam.net/Maps/index.html.

Clark County *Recorded Documents* https://www.clark.wa.gov/auditor   Access to Auditor's documents for free at www.clark.wa.gov/auditor/.
Property, Taxation Records   Search property tax sales data free at http://gis.clark.wa.gov/gishome/property/. GIS database searchable free at http://gis.clark.wa.gov/applications/gishome/auditor/index.cfm.

Columbia County *Property, Taxation Records*   Access to property search data for free at http://64.184.153.98/PropertyAccess/PropertySearch.aspx?cid=0.

Cowlitz County *Recorded Documents, Marriage Records* www.co.cowlitz.wa.us/Index.aspx?NID=126   Access Auditor and recorded documents free at http://apps.co.cowlitz.wa.us/cowlitzapps/cowlitzauditorpublicrecords/%28S%280qoaqg450htoadvanrnkkgfx%29%29/default.aspx.
Property, Taxation Records   Access Assessor property records free at www.cowlitzinfo.net/applications/cowlitzassessorparcelsearch/(S(b4whnpqppwwhvh55p323e455))/Default.aspx.

Douglas County *Recorded Documents* www.douglascountywa.net/elected-offices/auditor   Access to records free at https://edocs.douglascountywa.net/. Records go back to 1972.
Property, Taxation Records   Access to the County Parcel Search including taxes, plats and parcels is free at http://douglaswa.taxsifter.com/Disclaimer.aspx.

Ferry County *Property, Taxation Records*   Access property data on the TaxSifter database free at http://ferrywa.taxsifter.com/Disclaimer.aspx.

Franklin County *Recorded Documents* www.co.franklin.wa.us/auditor/   Access to records free at http://auditor.co.franklin.wa.us/oncoreweb/.
Property, Taxation Records   Search for assessor property data and map search for free at www.co.franklin.wa.us/assessor/.

Grant County *Recorded Documents* www.grantcountywa.gov/Auditor/   Access to document index only free at http://eagleweb.grantcountywa.gov:8080/grantrecorder/eagleweb/.
Property, Taxation Records   Access MapSifter and TaxSifter for free at www.grantcountywa.gov/Assessor/index.htm.

Grays Harbor County *Property, Taxation Records*   Access to online parcel database and sales searches for free at www.co.grays-harbor.wa.us/info/assessor/AppraisalDept.asp.

Island County *Recorded Documents* https://www.islandcountywa.gov/auditor/pages/home.aspx   Recorded index search free at http://auditor.islandcounty.net/recorder/web/. The images are not free-$100.00 per month.
Property, Taxation Records   Access county property tax data free at www.islandcountyassessor.com/parcel-sales-search/parcel-search/. Also, access to GIS/mapping for free at www.islandcountyassessor.com/about-us/gis-mapping/.

Jefferson County *Recorded Documents* www.co.jefferson.wa.us/auditor/Default.asp   Access the Recorded Document Search database at https://er-web.co.jefferson.wa.us/recorder/web/. Includes grantor/grantee index and records on the County Property (Tax Parcel) Database Tool, also plats and survey images. Search documents from 8/3/1981 to present.
Property, Taxation Records   Search assessor data free at www.co.jefferson.wa.us/assessors/parcel/ParcelSearch.asp, but no names searching.

King County *Recorded Documents* www.kingcounty.gov/depts/records-licensing/recorders-office.aspx   Access is free at http://146.129.54.93:8193/legalacceptance.asp?.
Property, Taxation Records   Access property records, sales, listings and maps free at www.kingcounty.gov/depts/assessor.aspx.

Kitsap County *Recorded Documents* www.kitsapgov.com/aud/default.htm   Search property data free on the land information system site at http://kcwaimg.co.kitsap.wa.us/recorder/web/. Click on Public Login. . Fee to print official documents.
Property, Taxation Records   Search property and tax data free on the land information system site at www.kitsapgov.com/assr/main/public_records.htm/. No name searching. Fee to print official documents. Also, access to GIS/mapping for free at http://kcwppub3.co.kitsap.wa.us/SectionDownloads/ and at https://psearch.kitsapgov.com/webappa/ are parcel searches.

Kittitas County *Property, Taxation Records*   Access property data free at http://gis.co.kittitas.wa.us/compas/default.aspx.

Klickitat County *Archived Documents Records* https://wei.sos.wa.gov/county/klickitat/Pages/default.aspx   Access to archived records for free at www.digitalarchives.wa.gov.
Property, Taxation Records   Access GIS/mapping site free at www.klickitatcounty.org/road// but no name searching.

Lewis County *Grantor/Grantee, all Recorded Documents* http://lewiscountywa.gov/auditor   Search the index online at https://quickdocs.lewiscountywa.gov/recorder/web/. Both a basic and advanced search are offered. Documents from 7/4/1848 to present.
Property, Taxation Records   Access property data free at http://parcels.lewiscountywa.gov/. Search by parcel number at https://quickdocs.lewiscountywa.gov/recorder/web/. The GIS/Mapping data found for free at http://maps.lewiscountywa.gov/.

Lincoln County *Property, Taxation Records*   Access to property search for free at http://lincolnwa.taxsifter.com/Disclaimer.aspx.

Mason County *Recorded Documents* https://wei.sos.wa.gov/county/mason/en/Pages/default.aspx   Access to records for free at http://216.235.102.169/masonrecorder/web/.
Property, Taxation Records   Access to Assessor data is free at http://property.co.mason.wa.us/Taxsifter/Disclaimer.aspx. Permit information is dipslayed at www.co.mason.wa.us/permits/index.php. Access the GIS-mapping site at www.co.mason.wa.us/gis/index.php.

Okanogan County *Property, Taxation Records*   Access to county property search is free at www.okanogancounty.org/Assessor/map.htm.

Pacific County *Recorded Documents* https://wei.sos.wa.gov/county/pacific/en/pages/auditorhome.aspx   Access to recorded documents free at http://pacificwa.countygovernmentrecords.com/pacificwa/web/.
Property, Taxation Records   Access County Auditor property data free on the TaxSifter system at www.co.pacific.wa.us/assessor/TaxSifter.htm.

Pend Oreille County *Property, Taxation Records*   Access property records free at https://gis.pendoreilleco.org/POCGISWeb/. Also, access to property sales for free at http://taweb.pendoreille.org/PropertyAccess/SaleSearch.aspx?cid=0.

Pierce County *Recorded Documents* www.co.pierce.wa.us/index.aspx?nid=93   Search index and images back to 1984 on the auditor's recording database for free at https://armsweb.co.pierce.wa.us/. Marriage index search for free at https://armsweb.co.pierce.wa.us/Marriage/SearchEntry.aspx.
Property, Taxation Records   Property records on County Assessor-Treasurer database are free at https://epip.co.pierce.wa.us/CFApps/atr/ePIP/search.cfm.

San Juan County *Recorded Documents* www.sanjuanco.com/165/Auditor   Free access to the auditor database of real estate recording records found at www.sanjuanco.com/171/Recorded-Document-Search.
Property, Taxation Records   Access to GIS/mapping free at http://sjcgis.maps.arcgis.com/home/index.html. Access to parcel search info free at http://parcel.sanjuanco.com/PropertyAccess/?cid=0.

Skagit County *Recorded Documents* www.skagitcounty.net/Departments/Auditor/main.htm#   Access auditor's recorded documents for free at www.skagitcounty.net/Search/Recording/default.aspx.
Property, Taxation Records   Search assessor data free at www.skagitcounty.net/Search/Property/, but no name searching. Also, access to GIS/mapping for free at www.skagitcounty.net/Maps/iMap/.

Skamania County *Property, Taxation Records*   Access to parcel information for free at http://skamaniawa.taxsifter.com/Disclaimer.aspx. Also, access to GIS/mapping free at http://skamaniawa.mapsifter.com/Disclaimer.aspx?ReturnUrl=%2fdefault.aspx.

Snohomish County *Recorded Documents* www.snohomishcountywa.gov/176/Auditor   Access to the Auditor's office database back to 1997 is free at www.snoco.org/RecordedDocuments/.
Property, Taxation Records   Search the assessor property data for free at http://assessor.snoco.org/propertysearch.aspx, but no name searching. Also, access to GIS/mapping for free at www.snohomishcountywa.gov/332/GIS-Mapping.

Spokane County *Recorded Documents (Index Only) Records* www.spokanecounty.org/237/Auditor   Indexes of certain records available at https://recording.spokanecounty.org/recorder/web/. Must register for a subscription to view images.
Property, Taxation Records   Search the County Parcel Locator database free at http://cp.spokanecounty.org/scout/SCOUTDashboard/. No name searching. Search GIS at www.spokanecounty.org/222/Geographic-Information-Systems.

Stevens County *Property, Taxation Records*   Access to property search/tax search for free at http://propertysearch.trueautomation.com/PropertyAccess/?cid=0.

Thurston County *Recorded Documents* www.co.thurston.wa.us/auditor/   Access the Auditor Recording data at www.co.thurston.wa.us/auditor/pub_rec_info.htm.
Property, Taxation Records   Assessor and property data on Thurston GeoData database is free at www.geodata.org/parcelsrch.asp. No name searching.

Wahkiakum County *Property, Taxation Records*   Access the yearly property sales list for free at www.co.wahkiakum.wa.us/agreement.html.

Walla Walla County *Recorded Documents* https://wei.sos.wa.gov/county/wallawalla/en/pages/default.aspx   Access to records found at http://recorder.co.walla-walla.wa.us/recorder/web/. Unofficial copies printed from images for free. Official copies must be requested at the office or by mail and fee is $3.00 for 1st page, $1.00 for each add'l page.
Property, Taxation Records   Access to property search for free at http://propertysearch.co.walla-walla.wa.us/PropertyAccess/propertysearch.aspx?cid=0.

Whatcom County *Recorded Documents* www.whatcomcounty.us/199/Auditor   Access to recorded records free at http://recording.whatcomcounty.us/search.asp. Records are from 1988 forward.
Property, Taxation Records   Access to property records for free at http://property.whatcomcounty.us/.

Whitman County *Property, Taxation Records*   Access to tax and property records for free at http://terrascan.whitmancounty.net/Taxsifter/Disclaimer.aspx.

Yakima County *Recorded Documents* www.yakimacounty.us/160/Auditor   Access to records for a fee at https://tapestry.fidlar.com/Tapestry2/Default.aspx. Contact 563-345-1283 or kylec@fidlar.com for subscription information. Search fee is $5.95 each, printed images $.50 each unless otherwise noted. Also, access to land records index for free at http://recording.yakimacounty.us/DirectSearch/Default.aspx.
Property, Taxation Records   Assessor and property data on County Assessor database are free at www.yakimacounty.us/627/Parcel-Search. Access to the treasurer parcel database is free at https://yes.co.yakima.wa.us/ascend/%28zjwf1z22ajfm3d550apmyhb2%29/search.aspx. No name searching.

West Virginia

Capital: Charleston
          Kanawha County
Time Zone: EST
Population: 1,844,128
# of Counties: 55

Useful State Links

Website: **www.wv.gov**
Governor: **www.governor.wv.gov**
Attorney General: **www.ago.wv.gov**
State Archives: **www.wvculture.org/history/archivesindex.aspx**
State Statutes and Codes: **www.legis.state.wv.us/WVCODE/Code.cfm**
Legislative Bill Search: **www.legis.state.wv.us/Bill_Status/bill_status.cfm**
Bill Monitoring: **www.legis.state.wv.us/billstatus_personalized/persbills_login.cfm**
Unclaimed Funds: **www.wvtreasury.com/Unclaimed-Property/Search-Claim**

State Public Record Agencies

Sexual Offender Registry

State Police Headquarters, Sexual Offender Registry, www.wvsp.gov/Pages/default.aspx   Online searching is available from website, search by county or name, or by most wanted. Email questions to registry@wvsp.state.wv.us. Direct link is https://apps.wv.gov/StatePolice/SexOffender. Search the offender database to determine if a specific email address or username used on the internet belongs to a registered sex offender and has been reported.

Incarceration Records

West Virginia Division of Corrections, Records Room, www.wvdoc.com/wvdoc/   This agency offers a free search for active inmates and parolees at www.wvdoc.com/wvdoc/OISOffenderSearch/tabid/200/Default.aspx. This site shows offenders who are under active supervision, in prison or on parole status only, with WVDOC. Those that have discharged or have moved from the custody of the WVDOC will NOT appear in the search.

Corporation, LLC, LP, LLP, Trademarks/Servicemarks

Sec. of State - Business Organizations Division, 1900 Kanawha Blvd E, www.sos.wv.gov/business-licensing/Pages/default.aspx   Corporation and business types records on the Secretary of State Business Organization Information System are available free online at http://apps.sos.wv.gov/business/corporations/. Search by organization name.   *Other Options:* Bulk sale of records is available in CD or DVD format, retrievable in CSV, Access or XML. Monthly or weekly updates are offered. Call 304-414-0265 for further details or visit https://apps.wv.gov/sos/bulkdata/Help/Default.aspx.

Uniform Commercial Code

Sec. of State - UCC Division, Bldg 1, Suite 157-K, www.sos.wv.gov/business-licensing/uniformcommercialcode/Pages/default.aspx   There is a free service to search, and the website also gives the ability to order copies. Search the database free at https://apps.wv.gov/sos/ucc/ to determine if a specific individual/organization has active, expired or terminated liens filed. Results give UCC number, secured party, debtor and status. Online record requesters can be ordered by email - E-mail to ucc@wvsos.com.   *Other Options:* Bulk sale of records is available in CD or DVD format, retrievable in CSV, Access or XML. Monthly or weekly updates are offered. Call 304-414-0265 for further details or visit https://apps.wv.gov/sos/bulkdata/RegistrationInformation.aspx.

Driver Records

Division of Motor Vehicles, Driving Records, www.transportation.wv.gov/DMV/Drivers/Pages/default.aspx   The designated service manager for online access to WV driving records is at WV.gov (handled by WV Interactive, an NIC affiliate). All requesters must complete three agreement documents necessary for account approval. The system processes requests on an interactive basis. The fee is $9.00 per record; there is a $100.00 subscription fee that permits 10 users. Subscribers have access to other information services. For more info call WV.gov at 304-414-0265. West Virginia offers a free Driver's License Status Check at https://apps.wv.gov/DMV/SelfService/DrivingRecord or at https://apps.wv.gov/dmv/selfservice/dl. *Other Options:* West Virginia offers a unique way for someone who does not have a permissible use to request the DMV to contact the person of record and forward a specific message. This is via Message Forwarding Service Form DMV 102-DL. Fee is $5.00.

Voter Registration, Campaign Finance Reports, PACs

Sec of State - Election Division, Bldg 1 #157-K, www.sos.wv.gov/elections/Pages/default.aspx Search to see if someone is registered to vote at https://services.sos.wv.gov/Elections/Voter/AmIRegisteredToVote. Must know DOB. This shows the voter's polling place. Access campaign finance reports, including those for PACs, at www.sos.wv.gov/elections/campaignfinance/Pages/default.aspx. *Other Options:* Voter lists are available for political purposes. A complete statewide list is approx. $500. Turnaround time is generally 48 hours. Call for further information.

GED Certificates

WV Dept of Education, High School Equivalency Office, http://wvde.state.wv.us/tasc/ Records may be requested from https://www.diplomasender.com. A credit card is needed. Request must be ordered by the test taker. Employers and third parties must receive an email and/or Authentication Code from the test taker to then access the authorized documents. Turnaround time is 1-3 days.

Occupational Licensing Boards

Accountant Revocations/Suspensions	www.boa.wv.gov/disciplinary/Pages/RevocationsandSuspensions.aspx
Accountant-CPA/Firm	https://apps.wv.gov/accountancy/licensure/LicenseVerification/Default.aspx
Aesthetician	www.wvbbc.com/Home/LicenseeLookup/tabid/1856/Default.aspx
Amusement Ride Inspections	www.wvlabor.com/newwebsite/Pages/Amusement_ride_inspectionsNEW.cfm
Amusement Ride Inspector	www.wvlabor.com/newwebsite/Pages/Amusement_ride_inspectorNEW.cfm
Animal Technician	https://www.wvbvm.org/public/verify/index.asp
Architect	http://wvbrdarch.org/findarchitect.html
Asbestos Air Monitor-Clearance	www.wvdhhr.org/rtia/licensing.asp
Asbestos Contractor	www.wvdhhr.org/rtia/licensing.asp
Asbestos Inspector	www.wvdhhr.org/rtia/licensing.asp
Asbestos Laboratory	www.wvdhhr.org/rtia/licensing.asp
Asbestos Project Designer/Planner	www.wvdhhr.org/rtia/licensing.asp
Asbestos Supervisor	www.wvdhhr.org/rtia/licensing.asp
Asbestos Worker	www.wvdhhr.org/rtia/licensing.asp
Athlete Agent	http://apps.sos.wv.gov/business/licensing/
Athletic Trainers-BOC	www.wvbopt.com/documents/BOC%20listing%20-%20WV%20residents%20only4.pdf
Attorney - Disciplinary Decisions	www.wvodc.org/decisionslist.htm
Barber	www.wvbbc.com/Home/LicenseeLookup/tabid/1856/Default.aspx
Barber/Beauty Culture School	www.wvbbc.org/MenuStructure/SchoolStudentInformation/SchoolStudentInformation/ListofSchools/tabid/1546/Default.aspx
Charitable Organization	http://apps.sos.wv.gov/business/charities/help.html
Chiropractor	www.boc.wv.gov/Pages/License-Search.aspx
Contractor, General	www.wvlabor.com/newwebsite/Pages/contractor_searchNEW.cfm
Cosmetologist	www.wvbbc.com/Home/LicenseeLookup/tabid/1856/Default.aspx
Counselor LPC, Professional	www.wvbec.org/verificationoflicensure.html
Counselor, Professional	www.wvbec.org/verificationoflicensure.html
Crane Operator	www.wvlabor.com/newwebsite/Pages/crane_searchNEW.cfm
Cremation Education Providers	www.wvfuneralboard.com/LinkClick.aspx?fileticket=cWNPacHMLk4%3d&tabid=652
Dental Hygienist	www.wvdentalboard.org/verification%20instructions.htm
Dentist	www.wvdentalboard.org/verification%20instructions.htm
Educational Audiologist	https://wveis.k12.wv.us/certcheck/
Elevator Inspectors	www.wvlabor.com/newwebsite/Pages/Safety_elevators_private_inspectorsRESULTS1.cfm
Engineer	https://services.wvpebd.org/verification/
Engineer, Retired	https://services.wvpebd.org/verification/
Engineering Authorized Co	https://services.wvpebd.org/verification/
Forester/Forestry Technician	www.wvlicensingboards.com/foresters/roster.cfm
Insurance Adjuster	https://sbs-wv.naic.org/Lion-Web/jsp/sbsreports/AgentLookup.jsp
Insurance Agent/Agency	https://sbs-wv.naic.org/Lion-Web/jsp/sbsreports/AgentLookup.jsp
Landscape Architect	www.wvlaboard.org/

Lead Abatement Contractor .... www.wvdhhr.org/rtia/licensing.asp
Lobbyist/Lobbying Employer .... www.ethics.wv.gov/lobbyist/Pages/ListsandForms.aspx
Manicurist www.wvbbc.com/Home/LicenseeLookup/tabid/1856/Default.aspx
Manufactured Housing...................................... www.wvlabor.com/newwebsite/Pages/MH_contractor_license_search_NEW.cfm
Medical Corporation.. https://wvbom.wv.gov/public/search/index.asp
Medical License, Special Volunteer................. https://wvbom.wv.gov/public/search/index.asp
Medical Professional LLC/Company .... https://wvbom.wv.gov/public/search/index.asp
Milk Shipper... www.wvdhhr.org/phs/milk/records.asp
Mine Electrician www.wvminesafety.org/PDFs/CERTS%20ELECTRICAL.pdf
Mine Surveyor/Foreman .... www.wvminesafety.org/PDFs/SUPERCERTS.pdf
Miner, Underground/Surface .... www.wvminesafety.org/certificationlists.htm
Minister License... http://apps.sos.wv.gov/business/licensing/
Notary Public .... http://apps.sos.wv.gov/business/notary/
Nurse-LPN... https://apps.wv.gov/Nursing/RNSearch/
Occupation'l Therapist/Asst/Practit'n'r .... http://wvbot.org/dharris/members.pdf
Optometrist .... www.wvbo.org/verify-license.php
Osteopathic Corporation.................................. https://www.wvbdosteo.org/verify/
Osteopathic Physician/Phys'c'n Assist .... https://www.wvbdosteo.org/verify/
Pharmacies/Businesses .... www.state.wv.us/pharmacy/index.cfm?fuseaction=Home.main
Pharmacist... www.state.wv.us/pharmacy/index.cfm?fuseaction=Home.main
Physical Therapist/Assistant............................ www.wvbopt.com/licensesearch.cfm
Physician/Medical Doctor/Assistant................. https://wvbom.wv.gov/public/search/index.asp
Plumbers.. www.wvlabor.com/newwebsite/Pages/plumber_searchNEW.cfm
Podiatrist.. https://wvbom.wv.gov/public/search/index.asp
Private Investigator/Agency .... http://apps.sos.wv.gov/business/licensing/
Psychologist... www.wvpsychbd.org/license_verification.htm
Radiologic Technologist/Accredited Schools...... www.wvrtboard.org/LICENSESEARCH/tabid/358/Default.aspx
Radon Contractor/Trainer................................. www.wvdhhr.org/rtia/licensing.asp
Real Estate Appraisal Management Company... www.appraiserboard.wv.gov/Roster/Pages/default.aspx
Real Estate Appraiser (WV list) .... www.appraiserboard.wv.gov/Roster/Pages/default.aspx
Respiratory Care Practitioner www.wvborc.org/Home/LicenseVerifications/tabid/1117/Default.aspx
School Athletic Trainer..................................... https://wveis.k12.wv.us/certcheck/
School Principal/CounselorSuperintendent........ https://wveis.k12.wv.us/certcheck/
School Psychologist.. www.wvpsychbd.org/license_verification.htm
School Psychologist/Nurse https://wveis.k12.wv.us/certcheck/
School Social Svcs/attendance Invest'r............. https://wveis.k12.wv.us/certcheck/
Security Guard.. http://apps.sos.wv.gov/business/licensing/
Service of Process... http://apps.sos.wv.gov/business/service-of-process/
Shot Firer... www.wvminesafety.org/PDFs/CERTS%20TASK.pdf
Social Worker .... www.wvsocialworkboard.org/Licensure/LicenseVerification.aspx#.Vssyqk9Nrkd
Speech/Language Pathologist.......................... https://wveis.k12.wv.us/certcheck/
Supervisor of Instruction.................................. https://wveis.k12.wv.us/certcheck/
Surveyor Business... www.wvbps.wv.gov/Pages/SurveyingBusinessSearch.aspx
Surveyor, Land .... www.wvbps.wv.gov/Pages/SurveyorSearch.aspx
Teacher.. https://wveis.k12.wv.us/certcheck/
Veterinarian .... https://www.wvbvm.org/public/verify/index.asp
Veterinary Medicine Desciplinary Actions .... https://www.wvbvm.org/public/Disciplinary.asp
Water Brands, Bottled...................................... www.wvdhhr.org/phs/bottledwater/records3.asp

State and Local Courts

About West Virginia Courts: The trial courts of general jurisdiction are the Circuit Courts which handle civil cases at law over $300 or more or in equity, felonies and misdemeanor and appeals from the Family Courts. The Magistrate Courts, which are akin to small claims courts, issue arrest and search warrants, hear misdemeanor cases, conduct preliminary examinations in felony cases, and hear civil cases with $5,000 or less in dispute. Magistrates also issue emergency protective orders in cases involving domestic violence.

The Circuit Courts hear appeals of Magistrate Court cases.   Probate is handled by the Circuit Court. The highest court is the Supreme Court of Appeals of West Virginia.

Family Courts were created by constitutional amendment of January 1, 2002. Family Courts hear cases involving divorce, annulment, separate maintenance, family support, paternity, child custody, and visitation. Family Court judges also conduct final hearings in domestic violence cases. For further court details, see www.wvlrc.org/westvirginiacourtsystem2.htm.
The web page for the Judicial Branch is www.courtswv.gov.

Appellate Courts: The Supreme Court of Appeals is West Virginia's highest court and the court of last resort. West Virginia is one of only 11 states with a single appellate court. Supreme Court of Appeals Opinions and Calendar are available at the web page.

Online Court Access

There is no statewide access, a designated vendors has relationships in many courts as described below.
A vendor - **Circuit Express** (https://www.wvcircuitexpress.com/Default.aspx.) - is widely used in WV with 38 Circuit Courts providing data from the civil and criminal record dockets. Scanned images are available for viewing and printing to a local printer. There is a $125 sign-up fee and a monthly flat fee of $ 38.00 plus connect charge of $ 1.00 a minute. Records are available from 02/1997. A person may also pay $125 for a single day use. Subscribers can locate cases by last name, first name, middle initial or partial name. Sensitive court cases such as Juvenile, Mental Hygiene, Divorces and some others are not available. The docket entries with the scanned images are updated nightly from each Circuit Court. Search by name or case number. Note **Kanawha County images are NOT available to the public per judicial order.**

While a number of details are provided, **no identifiers are provided beyond the name**. This is because the WV Supreme Court prohibits court-related websites from displaying personal identifiers, so no identifiers are shown on Circuit Express.

The 38 Counties on Circuit Court Express are:

Barbour	Grant	Mason	Pendleton	Taylor
Boone	Hampshire	McDowell	Pocahontas	Webster
Brooke	Hancock	Mercer	Preston	Wetzel
Calhoun	Hardy	Mineral	Putnam	Wirt
Clay	Jackson	Mingo	Raleigh	Wood
Doddridge	Kanawha	Monroe	Ritchie	Wyoming
Fayette	Logan	Nicholas	Roane	
Gilmer	Marshall	Ohio	Summers	

Other Online Access (Sites mentioned above are not included on the profiles below.):

Jefferson County
Circuit Court   http://www.jeffcowvcircuitclerk.com/index.html
Civi & Criminal: Daily Circuit Ct dockets free at www.jeffcowvcircuitclerk.com/Circuit_Court_Docket.pdf. Also, certified or non-certified documents may be ordered online at https://www.clerkepass.com/FormsePass/Jefferson/. This is not a name search - the document number must be provided.

Kanawha County
Circuit Court   www.courtswv.gov/lower-courts/circuit-courts.html
Civi & Criminal: Certified or non-certified documents may be ordered online at https://www.clerkepass.com/FormsePass/Kanawha/. There are added fees which depend on the type of document ordered. Per state law no identifiers shown. T This is not a name search - the document number must be provided.

Monongalia County
Circuit Court   http://www.monongaliacircuitclerk.com/
Civil: There is an online access to case information, but one must be registered first. The site gives no particulars regarding what types of cases are included, the depth of information is provided, or the throughput dates. See http://129.71.117.92/CIRCUITCLERKS/signon.aspx.   *Criminal:* There is an online access to case information, but one must be registered first. The site gives no particulars regarding what types of cases are included, the depth of information is provided. or the throughput dates.

Recorders, Assessors, and Other Sites of Note

About West Virginia Recording Offices: 55 counties, 55 recording offices. The recording officer is the County Clerk.

About Tax Liens: All federal and state tax liens are filed with the County Clerk.

Online Access

Recorded Documents

There is no statewide service for access to recorded documents or assessor data. However at least 24 counties offer online access and usually via a vendor.

Property Tax Data

Over 50% of the counties have some type of online access to property tax assessor data.

A Statewide Site: Private company Digital Software offers subscription access to a searchable database of property owner and assessment information for all counties at http://digitalcourthouse.com. Data provided includes legal property descriptions, owner names; appraised land, building, and mineral values; building assessment info (CAMA data); and tax maps. An interactive GIS viewer for 48 counties is available A user agreement is required. Subscriptions range from $19 for two days to $303 annually.

County Sites (To avoid redundancy, the Statewide Site is not shown in each profile below.):

Barbour County *Recorded Documents* www.barbourcounty.wv.gov/countygovernmentagencies/Pages/countyclerk.aspx Access records (document or tax inquiry) for free at http://129.71.117.241/.
Property, Taxation Records Access tax records for free at http://129.71.117.241/.

Berkeley County *Recorded Documents* http://countyclerk.berkeleywv.org/countyclerk/ Subscription is available online for $15.00 per month plus $.50 per printed copy. Contact Ms Brooks at 304-264-1927 or jbrooks@berkeleywv.org for details. Deeds from 1970 to present, trusts from 1994 to present and liens/judgments & releases from 1998 to present. Vital records also available.
Property, Taxation Records Access to GIS/mapping free at http://maps.berkeleywv.org/berkeleyonline/. Access sheriff tax office record search for free at http://taxinq.berkeleywv.org/index.html.

Boone County *Recorded Documents* Access to land records for free at https://cotthosting.com/WVPortal/User/Login.aspx. For detailed records, must subscribe.
Property, Taxation Records Access property tax data free at http://boone.softwaresystems.com:8003/index.html.

Brooke County *Property, Taxation Records* Access to tax records for free at www.brookecountysheriff.com/tax/Search.aspx.

Cabell County *Property, Taxation Records* Access GIS/mapping for free at http://maps.cabellassessor.com/gis/. Also, access to online tax record search for free at http://66.208.230.116:8003/index.html.

Calhoun County *Recorded Documents* www.calhouncounty.wv.gov/countygovernmentagencies/Pages/countyclerk.aspx Access to land records for free at http://129.71.205.140/.
Property, Taxation Records Access to tax inquirys for free at http://129.71.205.140/.

Doddridge County *Recorded Documents* www.doddridgecounty.wv.gov/countygovernmentagencies/Pages/countyclerk.aspx Access to recorded records for free at http://129.71.205.241/. To print copies must obtain code from the Clerk's office.

Fayette County *Property, Taxation Records* Access to property record data and GIS/mapping for free at www.fayettecounty.wv.gov/assessor/Pages/Disclaimer.aspx. Also, access property tax data free at www.softwaresystems.com/ssi/taxinquiry/.

Hampshire County *Property, Taxation Records* Access to GIS/mapping free at www.hampshireassessor.com/searchclause.html. Also, access to property owner information for free at http://ias.hampshirewv.com/.

Hancock County *Property, Taxation Records* Access property and sales records for free at http://hancock.wvassessor.com/assrweb/Default.aspx.

Hardy County *Recorded Documents* www.hardycounty.com/hardy-county-clerk Access recorded index free at http://72.15.246.183/hardywv/.
Property, Taxation Records Access to GIS/mapping for free at http://map.hardy-wv.com/wv/hardy/.

Harrison County *Recorded Documents* http://countyclerk.harrisoncountywv.com/office/2015%20Susan/default.aspx Access to records free at www.harrisoncountywv.com/warning.aspx.

Property, Taxation Records   Access to Assessor's parcel ownership/GIS/mapping for free at www.harrisoncountyassessor.com/searchdisclaimer.aspx. Also, access to online tax record search for free at http://harrison.softwaresystems.com:8383/index.html?sm=ee.

Jackson County *Property, Taxation Records*   Access to Assessor's database free at http://portal.jacksonwvassessor.com/portal/.

Jefferson County *Recorded Documents* http://jeffersoncountywv.org/county-government/elected-officials/county-clerk/   Access to county records free at http://documents.jeffersoncountywv.org/.

Kanawha County *Recorded Documents* http://kanawha.us/county-agencies/county-clerks-office/   Access to records for free at https://www.clerkepass.com/FormsePass/Kanawha/. Copy and certification fees involved.

Lewis County *Recorded Documents* http://lewiscountywv.net/ccindex.html   Access to online land records at http://inquiry.lewiscountywv.org/. Deeds are indexed from 2003 to present, all other records are indexed from 7/1/2011.

Lincoln County *Property, Taxation Records*   Access to tax records for free at www.lincolncountywv.org/Assessor/IASSearch/tabid/187/Default.aspx.

Logan County *Recorded Documents* www.logancounty.wv.gov/countygovernmentagencies/Pages/countyclerk.aspx   Access to land records for free at https://cotthosting.com/WVPortal/User/Login.aspx. For detailed records, must subscribe.

Marion County *Property, Taxation Records*   Access property tax data free at http://marion.softwaresystems.com/index.html.

Marshall County *Recorded Documents* www.marshallcountywv.org/county.asp   Access to records for free at http://129.71.117.225/. *Property, Taxation Records*   Access to GIS/mapping for free at http://map.marshallwv.com/wv/marshall/.

Mercer County *Property, Taxation Records*   Access to assessor web portal for free at http://portal.mercerassessor.com/portal/.

Mingo County *Property, Taxation Records*   Access property tax data free at http://mingo.softwaresystems.com/index.html.

Monongalia County *Recorded Documents* www.monongaliacountyclerk.com/   Access to county records free at http://searchrecords.monongaliacountyclerk.com/. *Property, Taxation Records*   Access the County Parcel Search database free at www.assessor.org/parcelweb/.

Morgan County *Recorded Documents* http://morgancountywv.gov/CountyClerk/index.html   Access to Morgan County database free at http://129.71.205.187/.

Nicholas County *Recorded Documents* www.nicholascountywv.org/county-offices/countyclerk.aspx   Access to records free at https://cotthosting.com/wvnicholas/User/Login.aspx. For detailed records, must subscribe. Also, copies can only be made from a pre-payment account.

Pocahontas County *Property, Taxation Records*   Access to property database free at http://pocahontascountyassessor.com/property-records/. GIS and mapping is free at http://pocahontascountyassessor.com/maps/. This provides appraised values.

Preston County *Recorded Documents* www.prestoncountywv.gov/   Access to records free at www.prestoncountywv.gov/disclaimer.php. Records from 1/1/1900 to present. *Property, Taxation Records*   Access to the Assessor Land Book Viewer for free at http://129.71.117.27/landbook/.

Putnam County *Recorded Documents* http://putnamcoclerk.com/   Access to land records for free at https://cotthosting.com/WVPortal/User/Login.aspx. For detailed records. *Property, Taxation Records*   Access property tax data free at www.softwaresystems.com/ssi/taxinquiry/. Also, access to GIS/mapping for free at www.landmarkgeospatial.com/putnam/.

Raleigh County *Property, Taxation Records*   Access to records free at http://mapping.raleighcountyassessor.com/portal/search_all.php.

Randolph County *Recorded Documents*   Access records free at http://129.71.117.90/. Can view records only, no copies to be made. *Property, Taxation Records*   Search County Assessor tax information and GIS/mapping for free at www.randolphassessorwv.com/.

Summers County *Property, Taxation Records*   Access the tax inquiry database free at http://summerscountywv.org/index.php?page=online-tax-inquiry.

Taylor County *Property, Taxation Records*   GIS mapping info is at www.landmarkgeospatial.com/taylorgis/.

Tucker County *Recorded Documents* http://tuckercountycommission.com/county-government/county-offices/county-clerk/   Access to records free at www.tuckerwv.net/. Use -user- for username and -welcome- for password.

Tyler County *Recorded Documents* http://tylercountywv.com/admin/countyclerk.htm   Access to records for free at http://129.71.117.165/. *Property, Taxation Records*   Access to mapping for free at www.mapwv.gov/flood/.

Wayne County *Recorded Documents* www.waynecountywv.org/countyclerk.php   Access recorded document index back to 4/1/1989 free at www.waynecountywv.us/WEBInquiry/.
Property, Taxation Records   Access property tax data free at www.waynecountywv.us/WEBTax/Default.aspx.

Wetzel County *Recorded Documents* www.wetzelcountycommission.com/county_clerk.htm   Access to deeds, liens, etc records for free at www.wetzelcountycommission.com/records-acknowledgement.

Wood County *Recorded Documents* www.woodcountywv.com/page/page14.php   Access at http://129.71.205.120/webinquiry/. Some records go back to the 1800's.
Property, Taxation Records   Access to the tax inquiry for free at http://129.71.205.120/webtax/. Also, access property data on the GIS-mapping site free at www.onlinegis.net/WoodCountyWV/Map.html.

Wyoming County *Recorded Documents* www.wyomingcounty.com/   Access to real estate records for free at http://129.71.205.79/.

Reminder: This Statewide Site is Not Shown on the Profiles

A Statewide Site: Private company Digital Software offers subscription access to a searchable database of property owner and assessment information for all counties at http://digitalcourthouse.com. Data provided includes legal property descriptions, owner names; appraised land, building, and mineral values; building assessment info (CAMA data); and tax maps. An interactive GIS viewer for 48 counties is available A user agreement is required. Subscriptions range from $19 for two days to $303 annually.

Wisconsin

Capital: Madison
            Dane County
Time Zone: CST
Population: 5,771,337
# of Counties: 72

Useful State Links

Website: **www.wisconsin.gov**
Governor: **www.wisgov.state.wi.us**
Attorney General: **www.doj.state.wi.us**
State Archives: **http://www.wisconsinhistory.org/**
State Statutes and Codes: **http://docs.legis.wisconsin.gov/statutes/prefaces/toc**
Legislative Bill Search: **http://legis.wisconsin.gov**
Unclaimed Funds: **https://www.revenue.wi.gov/ucp/index.html**

State Public Record Agencies

Criminal Records

Wisconsin Department of Justice, Crime Information Bureau, Record Check Unit, https://www.doj.state.wi.us/dles/cib/crime-information-bureau The agency offers Internet access at http://wi-recordcheck.org. Access 1) with an account with PIN is required, or 2) pay as you go with Visa/MC credit card. Records must be "picked up" at the website within 10 days. They are not returned by mail. Fee is $7.00 per request.

Sexual Offender Registry

Department of Corrections, Sex Offender Registry Program, http://offender.doc.state.wi.us/public/ There are three separate searches available form the home page - by either name, ZIP Code or by mapping location. Exact address of residence is available.

Incarceration Records

Wisconsin Department of Corrections, Attn: Public Records Request, http://doc.wi.gov/Home An offender locator is available at http://offender.doc.state.wi.us/lop/. The site does not provide information on offenders sentenced to county jail, nor does it provide information on adjudicated (juvenile) offenders or those of interest to the Department of Justice. *Other Options:* Bulk lists or information is no longer available in electronic (CD) format.

Corporation, LP, LLC, LLP

Division of Corporate & Consumer Services, Corporation Record Requests, www.wdfi.org/corporations/ Selected elements of the database ("CRIS" Corporate Registration Information System) are available online on the department's website at https://www.wdfi.org/apps/CorpSearch/Search.aspx?. A Certificate of Status can be ordered online for $10.00 at https://www.wdfi.org/apps/ccs/directions.asp. To place orders for status, copy work, or ID Reports go to https://www.wdfi.org/apps/oos/. *Other Options:* Some data is released in database format and is available electronically via email or on CD.

Trademarks, Trade Names

Dept of Financial Institutions, Tradenames/Trademarks, https://www.wdfi.org/Apostilles_Notary_Public_and_Trademarks/defaultTrademark.htm Search by trademark description or trade name at https://www.wdfi.org/apps/TrademarkSearch/Search.aspx. One may also request information by email. *Other Options:* CD and paper bulk access is available. A CD with pubic trademark data (inlcuding name, address, and expiration date is $200. A Trademark Journal paper copy of $25.00 a month.

Uniform Commercial Code, Federal & State Tax Liens

Department of Financial Institutions, CCS/UCC, www.wdfi.org/ucc/ The URL at https://www.wdfi.org/apps/uccsearch provides free search for most records. You may search by filing number or debtor name. Filing submitted online are available immediately, otherwise there is a 3-5 day delay. The search includes federal tax liens. FYI there is a statewide real estate search at:

https://propertyinfo.revenue.wi.gov/WisconsinProd/forms/htmlframe.aspx?mode=content/home.htm. *Other Options:* Bulk Index data is available on CD. The initial subscription is $3,000, monthly updates of images are $250.00 per month.

Sales Tax Registrations

WI Department of Revenue, Sales & Use Tax Division,   https://www.revenue.wi.gov/salesanduse/   One may look-up an account number at https://tap.revenue.wi.gov/services/_/#3. One may find delinquent taxpayers at https://www.revenue.wi.gov/html/delqlist.html.

Vital Records

WI Deprtment of Health Services, Vital Records,   https://www.dhs.wisconsin.gov/vitalrecords/index.htm   Records may be ordered online via www.vitalchek.com, a state approved vendor.

Workers' Compensation Records

Dept of Workforce Development, Worker's Compensation Division,   http://dwd.wisconsin.gov/wc/   See if an employer has worker;s comp coverage at https://www.wcrb.org/WCRB/CoverageLookup/CoverageLookupSearch.aspx

Driver Records

Division of Motor Vehicles, Driver Records,   http://wisconsindot.gov/Pages/home.aspx   Interactive service is available for approved requesters. Records are provided in PDF format for $5.00 each. The program is called PARS. Call 608-266-0928 or email pars@dot.wi.govfor more information. PARS participants can also participate in an employer notification program. Employers can enroll CDL drivers and will be notified when activity occurs on the employees record. The fee is also $5.00 per record when accessed. Also, a free status check of a DL is at http://wisconsindot.gov/Pages/online-srvcs/online.aspx. Must submit either DL, SSN, and DOB, or submit full name and DOB. The DMV also offers an electronic program, known as Broker Volume, for batch processing using a data file application. The fee is $7.00. For more information, call (608) 250-4606 or email to helpdesk@egov.com. *Other Options:* The entire DL of the license file (without convictions, accidents, withdrawals, etc.) is available for $250. The file does not include those who have opted out or who hold merely an ID Card. Purchase of data cannot be used for marketing or solicitations.

Vehicle Ownership & Registration

Department of Transportation, Vehicle Records Section,   http://wisconsindot.gov/Pages/home.aspx   Wisconsin offers a free license plate check and free lien look-up at http://wisconsindot.gov/Pages/online-srvcs/online.aspx. Another free service exists at http://wisconsindot.gov/Pages/online-srvcs/other-servs/incidents.aspx. At this site one may check if a driver has any restrictions (incidents) that would restrict the driver from obtaining a vehicle product (such as a title, registration, etc.). There is an Interactive online inquiry for ongoing, approved requestors. Ongoing requesters use the PARS program at http://portal.wisconsin.gov/register/index.html#pars. Records include name and address of titled owners or lessees, plate info, vehicle information, and lien data. Fee is $5.00. Also WI drivers may order their own vehicle record abstract online at www.dot.wisconsin.gov/drivers/vehicles/request-record.htm.. The fee is $5.50 per record, use of a credit card is required. *Other Options:* .

Crash Reports

WI DOT- Qualifications and Issuance Sect., Crash Records Unit,   http://wisconsindot.gov/Pages/dmv/license-drvs/rcd-crsh-rpt/crashreporting.aspx Requests of Crash Reports are available online at https://app.wi.gov/crashreports. The same $6.00 fee applies. One may order up to 50 crash reports at a time. Crash reports are only available after law enforcement submits reports to DOT, which may take up to two weeks. *Other Options:* Bulk lists are available.

Voter Registration, Campaign Finance, Lobbyists

Government Accountability Board, Elections and Ethics,   www.gab.wi.gov   The search page for the campaign finance system is at https://cfis.wi.gov/. Much data including filed reports, expenses, registrants and conduit contributions may be viewed.

Occupational Licensing Boards

These licenses are all searchable at https://app.wi.gov/licensesearch

Accountant Firm	Audiologist	Cosmetologist
Accountant-CPA	Barber School	Cosmetology Instr/Mgr/Apprentice
Acupuncturist	Barber/Appren/Instruct/Mgr	Cosmetology School
Aesthetics Establishm't/School	Behavior Analyst	Counselor, Professional
Aesthetician/Aesthetics Instructor	Boxer/Judge/Timekeeper	Dance Therapist
Appraiser, Real Estate/Gen/Residential	Boxing Club, Amateur/Prof	Dental Hygienist
Architect	Boxing Show	Dentist
Architectural Corporation	Cemetery Authority/Warehouse	Designer, Engineering Systems
Art Therapist	Cemetery Pre-Need Seller	Dietitian
Athlete Agent/Trainer	Cemetery Salesperson	Drug Distributor/Mfg
Auction Company	Charitable Organization	Electrologist/Electrology Instructor
Auctioneer	Chiropractor	Electrology Establishment/School

Engineer/Engineer in Training
Engineering Corporation
Firearms Certifier
Firearms Permit
Fund Raiser, Professional
Fund Raising Counsel
Funeral Director/Director Apprentice
Funeral Establishment
Funeral Pre-Need Seller
Geologist
Geology Firm
Hearing Instrument Specialist
Home Inspector
Hydrologist
Hydrology Firm
Interior Designer
Land Surveyor
Landscape Architect

Manicurist Establ/Specialty School
Manicurist/Manicurist Instructor
Marriage & Family Therapist
Massage Therapist/Bodyworker
Matchmaker
Midwife
Mixed Artial Arts Contest
Music Therapist
Nurse-RN/LPN
Nursing Home Administrator
Occupational Therapist/Assistant
Optometrist
Osteopathic Physician
Pharmacy (instate/out of state)
Pharmacy/Pharmacist
Physical Therapist
Physician/Medical Doctor/Surgeon/Assistant
Podiatrist

Private Detective Agency
Private Investigator
Psychologist
Radiographer/X-Ray Machine Operator
Real Estate Agent/Broker/Sales
Real Estate Appraiser
Real Estate Business Entity
Respiratory Care Practitioner
School Psychology Private Practice
Security Guard
Sign Language Interpreter
Social Worker
Soil Science Firm
Soil Scientist
Speech Pathologist/Audiologist
Timeshare Salesperson
Veterinarian/Veterinary Technician

The Rest:

Adjustment Service Company .... www.wdfi.org/fi/lfs/licensee_lists/
Ambulance Service.......... https://www.dhs.wisconsin.gov/ems/provider/wicounties.htm
Asbestos Exterior Abatement Services .... https://www.dhs.wisconsin.gov/asbestos/contractors.htm
Asbestos Worker/Investigators/Contractors .... https://www.dhs.wisconsin.gov/asbestos/contractors.htm
Attorney .... www.wisbar.org/Pages/BasicLawyerSearch.aspx
Bank.......... www.wdfi.org/fi/banks/licensee_lists/default.asp?Browse=Banks
Boiler Repairer.......... http://apps.commerce.state.wi.us/SB_ServiceAgent/SB_RegObjMain.jsp
Building Inspector .... http://apps.commerce.state.wi.us/SB_ServiceAgent/SB_RegObjMain.jsp
Check Seller .... www.wdfi.org/fi/lfs/licensee_lists/
Collection Agency .... www.wdfi.org/fi/lfs/licensee_lists/
Credit Service Organization............ https://www.wdfi.org/apps/CorpSearch/Search.aspx?
Credit Union.......... http://mapping.ncua.gov/ResearchCreditUnion.aspx
Currency Exchange .... www.wdfi.org/fi/lfs/licensee_lists/Default.asp?Browse=CE
Debt Collector.......... www.wdfi.org/fi/lfs/licensee_lists/
Electrical Inspector .... http://apps.commerce.state.wi.us/SB_ServiceAgent/SB_RegObjMain.jsp
Electrician .... http://apps.commerce.state.wi.us/SB_ServiceAgent/SB_RegObjMain.jsp
Employee Benefits Plan Administrator .... https://sbs-wi.naic.org/Lion-Web/jsp/sbsreports/AgentLookup.jsp
EMT/Paramedic.......... https://www.wi-emss.org/public/wisconsin/lookup/
Fertilizer Dealers.......... https://datcp.wi.gov/Documents/FertilizerLicenseList.xls
Fireworks Manufacturer .... http://apps.commerce.state.wi.us/SB_ServiceAgent/SB_RegObjMain.jsp
HVAC Contractor .... http://apps.commerce.state.wi.us/SB_ServiceAgent/SB_RegObjMain.jsp
Indian Gaming Vendor.......... www.doa.state.wi.us/Documents/DOG/Indian%20Gaming/CertifiedVendorList.pdf
Insurance Company.......... https://sbs-wi.naic.org/Lion-Web/jsp/sbsreports/AgentLookup.jsp
Insurance Intermediary.......... https://sbs-wi.naic.org/Lion-Web/jsp/sbsreports/AgentLookup.jsp
Insurance Premium Financier.......... www.wdfi.org/fi/lfs/licensee_lists/
Insurance Producer .... https://sbs-wi.naic.org/Lion-Web/jsp/sbsreports/AgentLookup.jsp
Investment Advisor/Advisor Rep .... www.wdfi.org/fi/securities/registration/licensee_lists/default.asp
Loan Company .... www.wdfi.org/fi/lfs/licensee_lists/
Loan Solicitor/Originator .... www.wdfi.org/fi/lfs/licensee_lists/default.asp
Lobbying Organization, Principal......... https://lobbying.wi.gov/Directories/DirectoryOfRegisteredLobbyingOrganizations/2015REG
Lobbyist https://lobbying.wi.gov/Directories/DirectoryOfLicensedLobbyists/2015REG
Mobile Home & RV Dealer .... www.wdfi.org/fi/lfs/licensee_lists/
Mortgage Banker/Broker .... www.wdfi.org/fi/lfs/licensee_lists/default.asp
Motorcycle Dealer.......... www.wdfi.org/fi/lfs/licensee_lists/

Notary Public	https://www.wdfi.org/apps/NotarySearch/SearchCriteria.aspx
Payday Lender	www.wdfi.org/fi/lfs/licensee_lists/
Pesticide Applicator	www.kellysolutions.com/WI/Applicators/index.asp
Pesticide Applicator Business	www.kellysolutions.com/WI/Business/index.asp
Pesticide Dealer	www.kellysolutions.com/WI/Dealers/index.asp
Pesticide Manufacturer/Labeler	www.kellysolutions.com/wi/pesticideindex.asp
Plumber	http://apps.commerce.state.wi.us/SB_ServiceAgent/SB_RegObjMain.jsp
Sales Finance/Loan Company	www.wdfi.org/fi/lfs/licensee_lists/
Savings & Loan Financer	www.wdfi.org/fi/lfs/licensee_lists/
Savings Institution	www.wdfi.org/fi/lfs/licensee_lists/
School Librarian/Media Specialist	https://elo.wieducatorlicensing.org/datamart/publicSearchMenu.do
Securities Broker/Dealer/Agent	www.wdfi.org/fi/securities/registration/licensee_lists/default.asp
Soil Tester	http://apps.commerce.state.wi.us/SB_ServiceAgent/SB_RegObjMain.jsp
Teacher	https://elo.wieducatorlicensing.org/datamart/publicSearchMenu.do
Viatical Settlement Broker	https://sbs-wi.naic.org/Lion-Web/jsp/sbsreports/AgentLookup.jsp
Welder	http://apps.commerce.state.wi.us/SB_ServiceAgent/SB_RegObjMain.jsp

State and Local Courts

About Wisconsin Courts: **Circuit Courts** have original jurisdiction in all civil and criminal matters within the state, including juvenile, and some traffic matters, as well as civil and criminal jury trials. The Small Claims limit is $5,000. The Clerk of Court is the record custodian.

The majority of **Municipal Court** cases involve traffic and ordinance matters. **Probate filing** is a function of the Circuit Court; however, each county has a **Register in Probate** who maintains and manages the probate records, guardianship, and mental health records.

The web page for the Judicial Branch is https://wicourts.gov/.

Appellate Courts: The Supreme Court is the court of last resort. The Court of Appeals had four districts and hears appealed cases from the Circuit Courts. Appellate and Supreme Court opinions are available online from the court web page.

Online Court Access

All Counties Participate in the Statewide System as Described Below.

The Wisconsin Circuit Court Access (WCCA) is a public access website that provides open record information per state law §§ 19.21-.39. Users may view **Circuit Court** case information at https://wcca.wicourts.gov/index.xsl. Access is free; data is available from all counties.

Searches can be conducted either statewide or by a specific county. WCCA provides detailed information about circuit cases including criminal, civil and traffic. A docketed civil judgment search is also offered. Data throughput dates vary by county, but in general most counties have participated since the early 1990s.

Confidential court records not displayed include adoptions, juvenile delinquency, child protection, termination of parental rights, guardianship, and civil commitments.

The search allows a search by name, but if searching civil records, you cannot designate in the search if the subject is a plaintiff or a defendant. Also, the search result page may not reveal multiple defendant parties: the entire case must be reviewed. As a result, this can be quite cumbersome. Search results generally include the middle initial. The DOB is shown some of the time, and sometimes the DOB is only the month and year.

WCCA also offers the ability to generate reports. The probate records are included for all counties. Confidential court records not included are adoptions, juvenile delinquency, child protection, termination of parental rights, guardianship, restricted cases, and civil commitments.

Certain data on the WCCA site is available through **RSS feeds** and also a **data extraction** program. See the description located on the web page.

A Cautionary Note - In general, the online system provides the same access as the public terminals in the courthouse, except online access does not provide scanned document images. Also, while the information contained on the WCCA Web site has been entered by the official record-keepers in each county, it is voluntarily provided by county court staff. There is no mandate that all information must be reported. Note that WI has legislated that the WI Department of Justice to be the official record holder of criminal record information. So it is advised to check with an attorney if using the WCCA as the sole resources for pre-employment screening purposes.

Other County Sites Not Mentioned Above:

Dane County
The Dane County Sheriff's Office provides an online request only site for accident reports, incident reports, and other records. See www.danesheriff.com/records.aspx.

Milwaukee County
Municipal Court
Criminal: Criminal case records on Milwaukee Municipal Court Case Information System database are free at https://query.municourt.milwaukee.gov. Search ordinace and traffic violations by case or citation number, or by name..

Recorders, Assessors, and Other Sites of Note

About Wisconsin Recording Offices: 72 counties, 72 recording offices. The recording officers are the Register of Deeds for real estate and Clerk of Court for state tax liens. County Clerks hold marriage records and state tax liens.

About Tax Liens: Federal tax liens on personal property of businesses are filed with the Secretary of State. Only federal tax liens on real estate are filed with the county Register of Deeds. State tax liens are filed with the Clerk of Court, and at the State Treasurer at the State Department of Revenue.

Online Access

Recorded Documents

Most counties provide online access. There is no statewide system, but there is an agency-supported vendor for record access in 29 counties. See https://tapestry.fidlar.com/Tapestry2/Default.aspx. The base fee is $5.95 per search and $.50 per print image, but the county may set their own pricing. You can pay as you go using a credit or pre-pay using a subscription. Also, per the same vendor one may purchase a software program called Laredo (www.fidlar.com/laredo.aspx) with extensive search features. Contact the county for details and pricing.

A statewide search of the Real Estate Transfer Return (RETR) database to locate information on property sales going back five years is at https://propertyinfo.revenue.wi.gov/WisconsinProd/forms/htmlframe.aspx?mode=content/home.htm

The Wisconsin Register of Deeds Association website at www.wrdaonline.org/RealEstateRecords/WebRealEstateRecords.htm offers helpful guidance and links list to 68 counties with online access. However, this list has not been kept up-to-date and some the links no longer work.

Assessor & Treasurer Records

The agency handling property assessment records is generally known as the Treasurer or Real Property Lister. All but seven counties provde online access to record data.

County Sites:

Adams County *Recorded Documents* www.co.adams.wi.gov/Departments/RegisterofDeeds/tabid/82/Default.aspx   Access Register of Deeds data for a fee at www.adamscountylandrecords.com/. Access to records for a fee at https://tapestry.fidlar.com/Tapestry2/Default.aspx. Contact 563-345-1283 or kylec@fidlar.com for subscription information. Search fee is $5.95 each, printed images $.50 each unless otherwise noted.
Property, Taxation Records   Access tax parcel information and GIS/mapping free at www.adamscountylandrecords.com/.

Ashland County *Recorded Documents* www.co.ashland.wi.us/departments/register-of-deeds   Access to a general index to land related information free at https://landshark.co.ashland.wi.us/LandShark/login. Document images may be purchased using a credit card, establishing an escrow account or by paying a monthly fee for a subscription.

Barron County *Recorded Documents* www.barroncountywi.gov/index.asp?Type=B_BASIC&SEC={4E43BDA8-057A-4774-A3AA-FB80457689E9}   Access to records for a fee at https://tapestry.fidlar.com/Tapestry2/Default.aspx. Contact 563-345-1283 or kylec@fidlar.com for subscription information. Search fee is $5.95 each, printed images $.50 each unless otherwise noted.

Property, Taxation Records   Access to GIS/mapping for free at http://barroncowi.wgxtreme.com/.

Bayfield County   *Recorded Documents*   www.bayfieldcounty.org/148/Register-of-Deeds   Access to records for a fee at https://tapestry.fidlar.com/Tapestry2/Default.aspx. Contact 563-345-1283 or kylec@fidlar.com for subscription information. Search fee is $5.95 each, printed images $.50 each unless otherwise noted.

Property, Taxation Records   Access to property tax and land record information free at http://novus.bayfieldcounty.org:8081/.

Brown County   *Recorded Documents*   www.co.brown.wi.us/departments/?department=e7fb85d94ba9   Access to records for a fee at https://tapestry.fidlar.com/Tapestry2/Default.aspx. Contact 563-345-1283 or kylec@fidlar.com for subscription information. Search fee is $5.95 each, printed images $.50 each unless otherwise noted.

Property, Taxation Records   Access to land records at www.co.brown.wi.us/departments/?department=133c6a3594a2. Also, land records can be downloaded from an ftp site; contact the Land Information office at 920-448-6295 to register and user information. Also, GIS/mapping site at http://maps.gis.co.brown.wi.us/geoprime

Buffalo County   *Recorded Records Records*   www.buffalocounty.com/190/Register-of-Deeds   Access to recorded records free at http://gcs.co.buffalo.wi.us/GCSWebPortal/Search.aspx. Fees charged for copies.

Property, Taxation Records   Access to parcel data and mapping for free at http://gcs.co.buffalo.wi.us/GCSWebPortal/Search.aspx.

Burnett County   *Recorded Documents*   www.burnettcounty.com/index.aspx?nid=100   Access to records for a fee at https://tapestry.fidlar.com/Tapestry2/Default.aspx. Contact 563-345-1283 or kylec@fidlar.com for subscription information. Search fee is $5.95 each, printed images $.50 each unless otherwise noted.

Property, Taxation Records   Access to GIS/mapping free at http://burnettcowi.wgxtreme.com/.

Calumet County   *Property, Taxation Records*   Access to property tax data is free at http://calum400.co.calumet.wi.us/nsccalo/nsclndrec.

Chippewa County   *Recorded Documents*   www.co.chippewa.wi.us/government/register-of-deeds   Access to records for a fee at https://tapestry.fidlar.com/Tapestry2/Default.aspx. Contact 563-345-1283 or kylec@fidlar.com for subscription information. Search fee is $5.95 each, printed images $.50 each unless otherwise noted. Also, access to land records search for free at http://205.213.167.206/directsearch/default.aspx. Also, access to the sheriff sales for free at www.co.chippewa.wi.us/government/sheriff/sheriff-sales.

Property, Taxation Records   Access to GIS/mapping for free at http://mapping.co.chippewa.wi.us/. Also, access to real property data free at www.assessordata.org/.

Clark County   *Recorded Documents*   www.co.clark.wi.us/index.aspx?nid=397   Real estate recording, property data, and delinquent tax info is available by subscription, see the above website for information on Acciss Landshark (their online system). Credit card or escrow accounts used for fee to view documents ($2.00 + $1.00 per doc. No transaction fee.

Property, Taxation Records   GIS/mapping for free at http://clarkcowi.wgxtreme.com/.

Columbia County   *Recorded Documents*
www.co.columbia.wi.us/ColumbiaCounty/registerofdeeds/RegisterofDeedsHomePage/tabid/52/Default.aspx   Access to records for a fee at https://tapestry.fidlar.com/Tapestry2/Default.aspx. Contact 563-345-1283 or kylec@fidlar.com for subscription information. Search fee is $5.95 each, printed images $.50 each unless otherwise noted.

Property, Taxation Records   Search property info free at http://ascent.co.columbia.wi.us/LandRecords/PropertyListing/RealEstateTaxParcel. Also, access to the Sheriff foreclosure listing for free at www.co.columbia.wi.us/ColumbiaCounty/sheriff/SheriffForeclosureListing/tabid/1016/Default.aspx.

Crawford County   *Recorded Documents*   www.crawfordcountywi.org/register-of-deeds.html   Access to records for a fee at https://tapestry.fidlar.com/Tapestry2/Default.aspx. Contact 563-345-1283 or kylec@fidlar.com for subscription information. Search fee is $5.95 each, printed images $.50 each unless otherwise noted.

Property, Taxation Records   Access to GIS/mapping free at http://crawfordcowi.wgxtreme.com/.

Dane County   *Recorded Documents*   https://rod.countyofdane.com/realEstate/online.aspx   Access to records for a fee at https://tapestry.fidlar.com/Tapestry2/Default.aspx. Contact 563-345-1283 or kylec@fidlar.com for subscription information. Search fee is $5.95 each, printed images $.50 each unless otherwise noted.

Property, Taxation Records   Access parcel search for free at https://accessdane.countyofdane.com/. Also, City of Madison tax assessor data is at www.cityofmadison.com/assessor/property/index.cfm. Also, search property info for Village of Plain & Village of Spring Green at www.wendorffassessing.com/municipalities.htm.

Dodge County   *Recorded Documents*   www.co.dodge.wi.us/index.aspx?page=65   Search Register of Deeds data at http://landshark.co.dodge.wi.us/LandShark/login.jsp?url=http%3A%2F%2Flandshark.co.dodge.wi.us%2FLandShark%2Fsearchname.jsp, index search is free, but fees apply for images and copies, $2.00 1st page, $1.00 2nd page. Also, access to parcel data for free at http://list.co.dodge.wi.us/GCSWebPortal/Search.aspx.

Property, Taxation Records   Access to parcel data for free at http://list.co.dodge.wi.us/GCSWebPortal/Search.aspx. Also, GIS/mapping for free at http://dodgecowi.wgxtreme.com/.

Door County *Recorded Documents* www.co.door.wi.gov/localgov_departments_details.asp?deptid=48&locid=137   Access to property transfers from 7/1/2009 forward for free at www.co.door.wi.gov/docview.asp?docid=10044&locid=137.
Property, Taxation Records   Access to GIS/mapping free at http://map.co.door.wi.us/gis-lio/home.htm.

Douglas County *Recorded Documents* www.douglascountywi.org/index.aspx?nid=379   Access to the county Landshark system is at https://rdlandshark.douglascountywi.org/LandShark/login.jsp?logout=1&url=https%3A%2F%2Frdlandshark.douglascountywi.org%2FLandShark%2Fsearchname.jsp. Free registration is required.
Property, Taxation Records   Land and property tax records searches free at www.gcssoftware.com/douglas/search.aspx. Also, access to GIS/mapping for free at http://douglascowi.wgxtreme.com/.

Dunn County *Recorded Documents* www.co.dunn.wi.us/index.asp?SEC=3AB04401-7C0E-45DF-9F34-D31B3D978AB5&Type=B_BASIC
Access to records for a fee at https://tapestry.fidlar.com/Tapestry2/Default.aspx. Contact 309-794-3283 or kylec@fidlar.com for subscription information. Search fee is $5.95 each, printed images $.50 each unless otherwise noted.
Property, Taxation Records   Access to GIS/mapping data for free at http://216.222.161.54/DunnCoGIS/default.aspx. Also, access to tax-foreclosed property sales for free at www.co.dunn.wi.us/index.asp?SEC={12539C4A-082C-45AF-ADB1-2D3A9B2FF024}&Type=B_BASIC&persistdesign=none.

Eau Claire County *Recorded Documents* www.wrdaonline.org/biography/EauClaire.htm   Access to records for a fee at https://tapestry.fidlar.com/Tapestry2/Default.aspx. Contact 563-345-1283 or kylec@fidlar.com for subscription information. Search fee is $5.95 each, printed images $.50 each unless otherwise noted.
Property, Taxation Records   Access to GIS/mapping free at http://eauclairecowi.wgxtreme.com/. Also, access to property records for a fee at www.eauclairewi.gov/departments/assessing/property-and-assessment-information.

Fond du Lac County *Recorded Documents* www.fdlco.wi.gov/departments/departments-n-z/register-of-deeds   Subscription service is available; contact Jim Krebs at jim.krebs@fdlco.wi.gov for more information.
Property, Taxation Records   Access to GIS/mapping free at http://gisweb.fdlco.wi.gov/fonddulacsl/.

Forest County *Recorded Documents* www.co.forest.wi.gov/localgov_departments_details.asp?deptid=392&locid=145   Access to real estate and grantor/grantee information free at https://propertyinfo.revenue.wi.gov/WisconsinProd/forms/htmlframe.aspx?mode=content/home.htm.

Grant County *Recorded Documents* www.co.grant.wi.gov/localgov_departments_details.asp?deptid=524&locid=147   Access to real estate records for free at http://grantcountylandrecords.com/GCSWebPortal/Login.aspx?ReturnUrl=%2fGCSWebPortal%2fSearch.aspx. Fees for copies of images only.

Green County *Recorded Documents* www.co.green.wi.gov/localgov_departments_details.asp?deptid=119&locid=148   Access to records for a fee at https://tapestry.fidlar.com/Tapestry2/Default.aspx. Contact 563-345-1283 or kylec@fidlar.com for subscription information. Search fee is $5.95 each, printed images $.50 each unless otherwise noted.
Property, Taxation Records   Access to parcel data is free on the GIS-mapping site at www.co.green.wi.gov/localgov_departments_details.asp?deptid=122&locid=148. Click on choice.

Green Lake County *Recorded Documents* www.co.green-lake.wi.us/departments.html?Department=18   Access to records for a fee at https://tapestry.fidlar.com/Tapestry2/Default.aspx. Contact 563-345-1283 or kylec@fidlar.com for subscription information. Search fee is $5.95 each, printed images $.50 each unless otherwise noted.
Property, Taxation Records   Search GIS-mapping site for property data free at http://gis.co.green-lake.wi.us/gisweb/GIS_Viewer/ but no name searching.

Iowa County *Recorded Documents* www.iowacounty.org/departments/registerofdeeds/registerofdeeds.shtml   Access records for a fee at https://landshark.iowacounty.org/LandShark/login.jsp?url=https%3A%2F%2Flandshark.iowacounty.org%2FLandShark%2Fsearchname.jsp.
Property, Taxation Records   Access to TriCounty GIS/mapping for free at https://swwigis.ags.ruekert-mielke.com/. This covers Grant and Iowa counties. Free registration required.

Iron County *Recorded Documents* www.co.iron.wi.gov/localgov_departments_details.asp?deptid=243&locid=180   Land records available at http://69.179.87.74/LandShark/login.jsp?logout=1&url=http%3A%2F%2F69.179.87.74%2FLandShark%2Fsearchlegal.jsp. Registration is required. No fee to search, but fee for images. Records go back to 1994.
Property, Taxation Records   Access to the foreclosure sales for free at www.co.iron.wi.gov/section.asp?linkid=1750&locid=180.

Jackson County *Recorded Documents* www.co.jackson.wi.us/index.asp?Type=B_BASIC&SEC={EBDF6BC5-8296-4082-86C7-1F77C1F49B1D}   Access to document search (images only) free at http://jacksonwi.roddirect.com/. Copies may be purchased.
Property, Taxation Records   Access to property records are available online for free at http://jacksoncowi.wgxtreme.com/.

Jefferson County *Recorded Documents* www.jeffersoncountywi.gov/departments/departments_f-r/departments/register_of_deeds.php   Access parcel data free at http://jeffersoncountyapps.jeffersoncountywi.gov/jclrs/LIO/LIO_Search.php, but no name searching. Also, access to records for a fee at https://tapestry.fidlar.com/Tapestry2/Default.aspx. Contact 563-345-1283 or kylec@fidlar.com for subscription information. Search fee is $5.95 each, printed images $.50 each unless otherwise noted.

Property, Taxation Records Search records free at www.jeffersoncountywi.gov/departments/departments_f-r/land_records_online.php. Property data free on the GIS-mapping site at www.jeffersoncountywi.gov/departments/departments_f-r/interactive_gis_maps.php but no name searching.

Juneau County *Recorded Documents* www.co.juneau.wi.gov/register-of-deeds1.html
The ROD offers subscription, escrow and credit card services for Real Estate access; online docs go back to 01/01/1999 (as time allows, back indexing and tracting continues being done) at https://landshark.co.juneau.wi.us/LandShark/login.jsp?url=https%3A%2F%2Flandshark.co.juneau.wi.us%2FLandShark%2Fsearchtaxliens.jsp.
Property, Taxation Records Search the GIS-mapping site for property and assessment data free at http://gismap.co.juneau.wi.us/JuneauCoGIS/. To search land sales by town, click on Land Sales at www.co.juneau.wi.gov/land-sales.html.

Kenosha County *Recorded Documents* www.kenoshacounty.org/522/Register-of-Deeds
Access to land records is available from a vendor at https://landshark.co.kenosha.wi.us/LandShark/login.jsp, registration is required. Fees to search. Records go back to 1994.
Property, Taxation Records Search the Kenosha City Assessor's property database free at www.kenosha.org/departments/assessor/search.html. No name searching. Access real estate records free at www.co.kenosha.wi.us/864/Property-Inquiry-Application; interactive mapping at www.co.kenosha.wi.us/673/Interactive-Mapping.

Kewaunee County *Recorded Documents* www.co.kewaunee.wi.gov/localgov_departments_details.asp?deptid=670&locid=192
Access to the Register of Deeds CherryLAN Indexing and Imaging System is available. Escrow subscription with an initial $100 deposit plus signed contract. Fifty cents ($.50) comes off escrow for viewing details of index above copy fees to view and/or print documents. Index back to 3/12/1987.
Property, Taxation Records Access to assessment/property tax records for free at http://24.159.234.196/GCSWebPortal/Search.aspx. Search land/tax records free at https://kewauneeco.ags.ruekert-mielke.com/. Subscription required for full data.

La Crosse County *Recorded Documents* www.co.la-crosse.wi.us/registerofdeeds/
Access to records for a fee at https://tapestry.fidlar.com/Tapestry2/Default.aspx. Contact 563-345-1283 or kylec@fidlar.com for subscription information. Search fee is $5.95 each, printed images $.50 each unless otherwise noted.
Property, Taxation Records Search for property owner and land data for free at http://lacrossecounty.maps.arcgis.com/home/index.html. Also, access to GIS/mapping for free at http://lacrossecounty.maps.arcgis.com/home/index.html.

Lafayette County *Recorded Documents* www.co.lafayette.wi.gov/localgov_departments_details.asp?deptid=315&locid=152
Access to records for a fee at https://tapestry.fidlar.com/Tapestry2/Default.aspx. Contact 563-345-1283 or kylec@fidlar.com for subscription information. Search fee is $5.95 each, printed images $.50 each unless otherwise noted.
Property, Taxation Records Access to GIS/mapping free at www.co.lafayette.wi.gov/section.asp?linkid=2052&locid=152.

Langlade County *Recorded Documents, Birth Records* www.co.langlade.wi.us/registerofdeeds.htm
Access county birth index free at www.co.langlade.wi.us/Births/, from 1882 to 1909 Also, access to grantor/grantee records for free at http://langladewi.roddirect.com/.
Property, Taxation Records Access property data free at http://langladecowi.wgxtreme.com/.

Lincoln County *Recorded Documents* www.co.lincoln.wi.us/departments/?department=aa384fe82c0c
Access to records for a fee at https://tapestry.fidlar.com/Tapestry2/Default.aspx. Contact 563-345-1283 or kylec@fidlar.com for subscription information. Search fee is $5.95 each, printed images $.50 each unless otherwise noted.
Property, Taxation Records GIS/mapping for free at http://maps.co.lincoln.wi.us/publicaccess/.

Manitowoc County *Recorded Documents* www.co.manitowoc.wi.us/departments/q-z/register-of-deeds/
Access to Register of Deeds recorded land records system requires username and password at http://rod.manitowoc-county.com/landweb.dll/$/; contact Register of Deeds office for sign-up. Indexes available from 2/4/1987 to present. Can also sign-in as guest user-print copies and $5.00 service charged to a credit card.
Property, Taxation Records Search on GIS-map site at www.manitowocmaps.info/gisportal/index.html. Foreclosures- www.co.manitowoc.wi.us/departments/i-p/public-works/foreclosed-property/. Manitowoc City Assessor database free at http://assessor.manitowoc.org/CityAssessor/search.aspx. No name searching.

Marathon County *Property, Taxation Records* Access to county property records is free at http://online.co.marathon.wi.us/. No name
searching. Access by subscription is also available for full data. Also, access to GIS-mapping for free at www.co.marathon.wi.us/Departments/ConservationPlanningZoning/GEOServices/GeographicInformationSystem%28GIS%29/OnLineMaps.aspx.

Marinette County *Recorded Documents* www.marinettecounty.com/departments/?department=2ce81d5e7364
Access to real estate index at http://landshark.marinettecounty.com/LandShark/registration.jsp. Requires account. Search index free but $2.00 fee (plus $1.00 each add'l.) to view document. Registration and escrow account required.
Property, Taxation Records Access to GIS/mapping free at http://webgis.marinettecounty.com/.

Marquette County *Recorded Documents* www.co.marquette.wi.us/departments/register-of-deeds
Access to records for free at https://host.gcssoftware.com/marquette/search.aspx. Must pay for copies.

Milwaukee County *Recorded Documents* http://county.milwaukee.gov/RegisterofDeeds7722.htm
Access to records for a fee at https://tapestry.fidlar.com/Tapestry2/Default.aspx. Contact 563-345-1283 or kylec@fidlar.com for subscription information. Search fee is $5.95 each, printed images $.50 each unless otherwise noted.

Property, Taxation Records   Assessment data & sales data on Milwaukee City (not county) database at http://city.milwaukee.gov/assessor#.VqAKcV5Nrke. Search Franklin- at http://taxassessment.franklinwi.gov/assessmentsearch.cfm. West Allis-http://apps.westalliswi.gov/property_search/search.aspx.

Monroe County *Recorded Documents* www.co.monroe.wi.us/departments/register-of-deeds/   Land records search free at http://monroerodweb.co.monroe.wi.us/gcswebportal/search.aspx.
Property, Taxation Records   GIS/mapping site free at http://monroecowi.wgxtreme.com/.

Oconto County *Recorded Documents* www.co.oconto.wi.us/departments/?department=13771fafd73f   Access to Registrar of Deeds available by subscription or escrow account at https://landshark.co.oconto.wi.us/LandShark/. May also purchase a document with a credit card (convenience fee-$5.00 per session). Images available from 9/1978 to present. Images are available by document number or volume and page only.
Property, Taxation Records   Access to the county SOLO tax parcel search is free or by subscription at http://ocmaps.co.oconto.wi.us/SOLO/. The free service does not include name searching. Subscription fee for full data is $300 per calendar year. Phone 920-834-6800 for more info.

Oneida County *Recorded Documents* www.co.oneida.wi.gov/localgov_departments_details.asp?deptid=21&locid=135   Access to land records for a fee at http://landshark.co.oneida.wi.us/LandShark/login.jsp?url=http%3A%2F%2Flandshark.co.oneida.wi.us%2FLandShark%2Fsearchname.jsp.
Property, Taxation Records   Property tax data free at http://octax.co.oneida.wi.us/ONCTax/Taxrtr. Search land records by name on the GIS mapping site at http://ocgis.co.oneida.wi.us/oneida/index.htm.

Outagamie County *Recorded Documents* www.outagamie.org/index.aspx?page=72   Access recorded documents data at https://landshark.co.outagamie.wi.us/LandShark/login. Registration and fees required for full data. Also, access to real estate taxes and maps free at www.outagamie.org/. Click on GIS/Maps & Taxes/Deeds.
Property, Taxation Records   Property data free at http://outagamiecowi.wgxtreme.com/property, no name searching. Also, access a variety of property records at www.outagamie.org/index.aspx?page=76.

Ozaukee County *Recorded Documents* www.co.ozaukee.wi.us/199/Register-of-Deeds   Access to records for a fee at https://tapestry.fidlar.com/Tapestry2/Default.aspx. Contact 563-345-1283 or kylec@fidlar.com for subscription information. Search fee is $5.95 each, printed images $.50 each unless otherwise noted.
Property, Taxation Records   Access to property and tax records for free at www.ascent.co.ozaukee.wi.us/LandRecords/AccessManagement/Account/Login. Must register.

Pepin County *Recorded Documents* www.wrdaonline.org/Biography/pepin.htm   Access to records free at https://host.gcssoftware.com/pepin/search.aspx. Records available from 1/1/2010 to present.
Property, Taxation Records   Acess to property search for free at http://pepincowi.wgxtreme.com/.

Pierce County *Recorded Documents* www.co.pierce.wi.us/Register%20of%20Deeds/Register_Deeds_Main.php   Access to records for a fee at https://tapestry.fidlar.com/Tapestry2/Default.aspx. Contact 563-345-1283 or kylec@fidlar.com for subscription information. Search fee is $5.95 each, printed images $.50 each unless otherwise noted.
Property, Taxation Records   Property data search, municipal assessor list and municipal treasurer's list at www.co.pierce.wi.us/Land%20Information/Land_Information.html.

Polk County *Recorded Documents* www.co.polk.wi.us/index.asp?SEC=5E3D05B7-5254-4276-BEFA-98ADE1724243&Type=B_BASIC   Access to records information free at www2.co.polk.wi.us/GCSWebPortal/search.aspx/. Must purchase documents.
Property, Taxation Records   Access to GIS-mapping records free at http://polkcowi.wgxtreme.com/.

Portage County *Recorded Documents* www.co.portage.wi.us/rod/   Access to records for a fee at https://tapestry.fidlar.com/Tapestry2/Default.aspx. Contact 563-345-1283 or kylec@fidlar.com for subscription information. Search fee is $5.95 each, printed images $.50 each unless otherwise noted.
Property, Taxation Records   Search the county tax application database free at http://pctax.co.portage.wi.us/PCTax/Taxrtr?action=taxdefault but no name searching. GIS mapping site free at http://gisinfo.co.portage.wi.us/realestate/.

Price County *Recorded Documents* www.co.price.wi.us/270/Register-of-Deeds   Access to public records for free at www.co.price.wi.us/154/Property-Taxes.
Property, Taxation Records   Access to land record/GIS for free at http://pricecowi.wgxtreme.com/. Also, access to property tax information for free at http://records.co.price.wi.us/Access/master.asp.

Racine County *Recorded Documents* http://racinecounty.com/government/register-of-deeds   Access to land records for a fee at https://landshark.racinecounty.com/LandShark/login.
Property, Taxation Records   Tax inquiry is available free at http://racinecounty.com/government/county-treasurer/tax-inquiry. Also, access to property assessment data free at http://patriotproperties.com/.

Richland County *Recorded Documents* www.rclrs.net/rod/   Search recorded land index for free at https://host.gcssoftware.com/richland/search.aspx but fees apply to print images. Records go back to 9/1/1984.

Property, Taxation Records   Access property data free at https://rcz.maps.arcgis.com/home/index.html.

Rock County   *Recorded Documents*   www.co.rock.wi.us/registerofdeeds   Access to records for a fee at
https://tapestry.fidlar.com/Tapestry2/Default.aspx. Contact 563-345-1283 or kylec@fidlar.com for subscription information. Search fee is $5.95 each, printed images $.50 each unless otherwise noted.
Property, Taxation Records   GIS/mapping free at www.co.rock.wi.us/land-records. Also at www.co.rock.wi.us:8080/servlet/AttributeServletRock.

Rusk County   *Recorded Documents*   www.ruskcounty.org/departments/register-of-deeds/   To access the document database free at
https://host.gcssoftware.com/rusk/Search.aspx.
Property, Taxation Records   Access assessment land data free at http://ruskcowi.wgxtreme.com/.

Sauk County   *Recorded Documents*   https://www.co.sauk.wi.us/registerofdeeds   Access to recorder's land records is available by subscription
at https://www.co.sauk.wi.us/registerofdeedspage/register-deeds-property-information-land-shark. Registration required; setup account through Recorders Office. Occasional users search free, but view documents for $2 first page, $1 each add'l.
Property, Taxation Records   Access to GIS/mapping free at http://gis.co.sauk.wi.us:3344/webappbuilder/apps/8/.

Sawyer County   *Recorded Documents*   www.sawyercountygov.org/CountyDepartments/RegisterofDeeds/tabid/110/Default.aspx   Access to
records for a fee at https://tapestry.fidlar.com/Tapestry2/Default.aspx. Contact 563-345-1283 or kylec@fidlar.com for subscription information. Search fee is $5.95 each, printed images $.50 each unless otherwise noted.
Property, Taxation Records   Access to the land records portal for free at
www.sawyercountygov.org/CountyDepartments/LandRecords/LandRecordsPortal/tabid/117/Default.aspx.

Shawano County   *Recorded Documents*   www.co.shawano.wi.us/departments/?department=06ac28fbc5c4   Access to recorder's land
records is available free or by escrow for full-time access at http://landshark.co.shawano.wi.us/LandShark/about.jsp?aboutKey=LandShark. Registration required; setup account thru Recorder office. Occasional users search free, but view documents for $2 first page, $1 each add'l.
Property, Taxation Records   Access parcel data free at http://gis.co.shawano.wi.us/portal/default.aspx but no name searching. For more detailed information must subscribe for a fee.

Sheboygan County   *Recorded Documents*   www.sheboygancounty.com/government/departments-r-z/register-of-deeds   Access to records
for a fee at https://tapestry.fidlar.com/Tapestry2/Default.aspx. Contact 563-345-1283 or kylec@fidlar.com for subscription information. Search fee is $5.95 each, printed images $.50 each unless otherwise noted.
Property, Taxation Records   Lookup parcel and property tax data and GIS/mapping and surveys free at
www.co.sheboygan.wi.us/taxonline/RealEstateLookuppublic.aspx, but no name searching.

St. Croix County   *Recorded Documents*   www.co.saint-croix.wi.us/index.asp   Access to records for a fee at
https://tapestry.fidlar.com/Tapestry2/Default.aspx. Contact 563-345-1283 or kylec@fidlar.com for subscription information. Search fee is $5.95 each, printed images $.50 each unless otherwise noted.
Property, Taxation Records   GIS/mapping for free at http://stcroixcowi.wgxtreme.com/.

Taylor County   *Recorded Documents*   www.co.taylor.wi.us/departments/n-z/register-of-deeds/   Access county land records back to 1/1998
with subscription to Landshark at
https://landshark.co.taylor.wi.us/LandShark/login.jsp?url=https%3A%2F%2Flandshark.co.taylor.wi.us%2FLandShark%2Fsearchname.jsp. Index search is free; images are $2.00 1st page, $1.00 each add'l.
Property, Taxation Records   Search property and tax data free at http://taylorcowi.wgxtreme.com/.

Trempealeau County   *Recorded Documents*   www.tremplocounty.com/tchome/register_of_deeds/   Access to records for a fee at
https://tapestry.fidlar.com/Tapestry2/Default.aspx. Contact 563-345-1283 or kylec@fidlar.com for subscription information. Search fee is $5.95 each, printed images $.50 each unless otherwise noted.
Property, Taxation Records   Access to the county assessment database is free at www.tremplocounty.com/Search/Search.asp. GIS/mapping found at www.tremplocounty.com/tchome/landrecords/map_gallery.aspx.

Vernon County   *Recorded Documents*   www.vernoncounty.org/ROD/index.htm   Access to a document search is free at
www.vernoncounty.org/GCSWebPortal/Search.aspx. Use the Document tab.
Property, Taxation Records   The parcel tab search at www.vernoncounty.org/GCSWebPortal/Search.aspx provides a search of real estate address and ownership information.

Vilas County   *Recorded Documents*   www.co.vilas.wi.us/index.php?page=Register-of-Deeds   Access to land records data only for free at
https://landshark.co.vilas.wi.us/LandShark/login. The search and tract information is available at no cost, but there will be a statutory fee of $2.00 1st page, $1.00 each add'l page when you view an image. Also, access to properties for sale for free at www.vilascountyland.com/index.php?page=properties.
Property, Taxation Records   Access property data free by municipality name at http://webtax.co.vilas.wi.us/search.cfm.

Walworth County   *Recorded Documents*   www.co.walworth.wi.us   Search the Register of Deeds index for free on the county e-government
public search page at www.co.walworth.wi.us/contact/OnlineServices.aspx. Online records go back to 1969. Also, access to parcel index free at https://rodapps.co.walworth.wi.us/LandShark/login.jsp. Click on the ABOUT tab to learn how to set up a subscription.

Property, Taxation Records   Search the treasurer's tax list and GIS at www.co.walworth.wi.us/contact/OnlineServices.aspx. Eamil questions to treasurer@co.walworth.wi.us.

Washburn County   ***Property, Taxation Records***   Access to property tax records public access for free at
http://tax.co.washburn.wi.us/access/master.asp.

Washington County   ***Recorded Documents***   www.co.washington.wi.us/   Access to Landshark for real estate records available for a fee at
https://landshark.co.washington.wi.us/LandShark/login.jsp. Grantor/ee indexes from 1945 to present. Commuter legal description start 1/97. See TRACT to search paper subdivision/condo tract books prior to 1997. Volume/Page & Document images are accessible from 1830's forward for a fee of $2.00 for 1st page, $1.00 each add'l page plus $3.00 convenience fee.

Waukesha County   ***Recorded Documents***   https://www.waukeshacounty.gov/rod/   Also, access to deed records for a fee at
https://landrecordspublicaccess.waukeshacounty.gov/.
Property, Taxation Records   Search county tax listings and property sales for free at www.waukeshacounty.gov/Treasurer/. Also, access to the city assessment rolls for free at www.waukesha-wi.gov/206/Assessment-Roll.

Waupaca County   ***Recorded Documents***   www.co.waupaca.wi.us/departments/government_departments/register_of_deeds/index.php
Access county land records back to 7/1966 with subscription to Landshark at
www.co.waupaca.wi.us/departments/government_departments/register_of_deeds/index.php#. Click on Land Shark. Index search is free; images are $2.00 1st page, $1.00 each add'l plus credit card fee of $4.00..
Property, Taxation Records   Access land information office data free at
http://public1.co.waupaca.wi.us/GISviewer/index.html?config=config_parcel.xml. Also, access to GIS/mapping free at
http://public1.co.waupaca.wi.us/PublicGallery/. Also, access to tax records for free at
www.co.waupaca.wi.us/departments/government_departments/county_treasurer/tax_information_search.php.

Waushara County   ***Recorded Documents***   www.co.waushara.wi.us/pView.aspx?id=12726&catid=636   Access to records for a fee at
https://tapestry.fidlar.com/Tapestry2/Default.aspx. Contact 563-345-1283 or kylec@fidlar.com for subscription information. Search fee is $5.95 each, printed images $.50 each unless otherwise noted. Also, search property data free on the county land information system at
http://71.87.7.220/GCSWebPortal/Search.aspx.
Property, Taxation Records   Access to land records for free at http://gis.co.waushara.wi.us/GCSWebPortal/Search.aspx.

Winnebago County   ***Recorded Documents***   https://www.co.winnebago.wi.us/register-deeds   Access to records for a fee at
https://tapestry.fidlar.com/Tapestry2/Default.aspx. Contact 563-345-1283 or kylec@fidlar.com for subscription information. Search fee is $5.95 each, printed images $.50 each unless otherwise noted.
Property, Taxation Records   Property information look-up for free at
https://wcws10.co.winnebago.wi.us/LandRecords/AccessManagement/Account/Login. Property records on the City of Oshkosh assessor database are free at www.ci.oshkosh.wi.us/webinfo/Real_Estate/index.asp.

Wood County   ***Recorded Documents***   www.co.wood.wi.us/Departments/ROD/   Access to records for a fee at
https://tapestry.fidlar.com/Tapestry2/Default.aspx. Contact 563-345-1283 or kylec@fidlar.com for subscription information. Search fee is $5.95 each, printed images $.50 each unless otherwise noted.
Property, Taxation Records   A property tax search by parcel ID or name is at
www.co.wood.wi.us/Departments/Treasurer/TaxPublic/SearchTaxBill.aspx. Land maps/records also free at http://gis.co.wood.wi.us/FlexGIS/index.html.

Wyoming

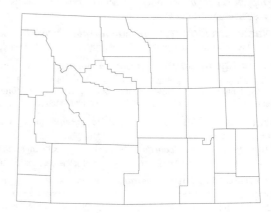

Capital: Cheyenne
       Laramie County
Time Zone: MST
Population: 586,107
# of Counties: 23

Useful State Links

Website: **www.wyo.gov/**
Governor: **http://governor.wyo.gov/**
Attorney General: **http://ag.wyo.gov/**
State Archives: **http://wyoarchives.state.wy.us/**
State Statutes and Codes: **http://legisweb.state.wy.us/LSOWEB/wyStatutes.aspx**
Legislative Bill Search: **http://legisweb.state.wy.us/LSOWEB/GeneralInfo.aspx**
Unclaimed Funds: **https://statetreasurer.wyo.gov/UnclaimedProperty.aspx**

State Public Record Agencies

Sexual Offender Registry

Division of Criminal Investigation, Division of Criminal Investigation,   http://wyomingdci.wyo.gov/dci-criminal-justice-information-systems-section/sex-offender-registry-section   The Sex Offender Registry is at http://wyomingdci.wyo.gov/dci-criminal-justice-information-systems-section/sex-offender-registry-section. See http://sheriffalerts.com/counties.php?state=wy for the county listings for community notifications. Data includes name including AKA, physical address, date and place of birth, date and place of conviction, crime for which convicted, photograph and physical description. Email questions to wysors@wyo.gov.

Corporation, LLC, LP, LLLP, GP, Fictitious Name, Trademarks/Servicemarks, Trade Names

Business Division, Attn: Records,   http://soswy.state.wy.us/Business/BusEntOverview.aspx   Information is available at https://wyobiz.wy.gov/Business/FilingSearch.aspx. You can search by corporate name or registered filing ID. Validate or generate a Certificate of Good Standing at https://wyobiz.wy.gov/Business/ViewCertificate.aspx, this is free. Search trademarks at http://will.state.wy.us/trademarks/.

Uniform Commercial Code, Federal Tax Liens

Secretary of State, UCC Division - Records,   http://soswy.state.wy.us/Business/UCCHome.aspx   One may email requests to SOSRequest@wyo.gov. The online filing system permits unlimited record searching, see https://ucc.state.wy.us/ExLogin.asp. Subscribers are entitled to do filings at a 50% discount. There is a $150 annual fee, with no additional fees charged for searches. Visit the webpage for more information.   *Other Options:* Lists of filings on CD or diskette are available for purchase. Download the database for $2,000 per year.

Driver Records

Wyoming Department of Transportation, Driver Services,   www.dot.state.wy.us/home/driver_license_records.html   Electronic access is available using Web service, fee is $5.00 per record. Only approved vendors and permissible users are supported. Call Marianne Bixler at 307-777-4830 or write to the above address for details.   *Other Options:* The entire driver license file may be purchased for $2,500 with an additional fee for monthly updates. This is only available with a signed contract and compliance with the DPPA.

Crash Reports

Highway Safety Program, Accident Records Section,   www.dot.state.wy.us/home/dot_safety.html   Online access to records is not offered, but records may be requested by email - Yolanda.pacheco@wyo.gov.

Voter Registration, Campaign Finance

Secretary of State - Election Division, 200 W 24th Street,   http://soswy.state.wy.us/Elections/Default.aspx   The agency provides a number of reports and searches at https://www.wycampaignfinance.gov/WYCFWebApplication/Reports/ResearchToolsAndLists.aspx for campaign finances, PACs, and

donations. Lobbying lists are at http://soswy.state.wy.us/Elections/Lobbying.aspx.   *Other Options:* An order form for bulk purchase is found at
http://soswy.state.wy.us/Forms/Elections/General/VoterProductOrderForm.pdf.

GED (HSED) Certificates
Wyoming Community College Commission, HSEC Program,   www.communitycolleges.wy.edu/hs-equivalency-program.aspx   Records may be
requested from https://www.diplomasender.com. A credit card is needed. Request must be ordered by the test taker. Employers and third parties must
receive an email and/or Authentication Code from the test taker to then access the authorized documents. Turnaround time is 1-3 days.

Occupational Licensing Boards

Accountant Firm	http://cpaboard.state.wy.us/firm.aspx
Accountant-CPA	http://cpaboard.state.wy.us/holder.aspx
Addiction Therapist/Practitioner/Assistant	https://sites.google.com/a/wyo.gov/wyoming-mental-health-professions-licensing-board/license-verification
Architect	https://sites.google.com/a/wyo.gov/architects/verification
Athletic Trainer	https://sites.google.com/a/wyo.gov/wyoming-board-of-athletic-training/public/license-verification
Attorney	https://www.wyomingbar.org/
Barber School/Shop, Instructors	https://wyboc.glsuite.us/glsuiteweb/clients/wyboc/public/verificationsearch.aspx
Barber, Stylist	https://wyboc.glsuite.us/glsuiteweb/clients/wyboc/public/verificationsearch.aspx
Chiropractor	http://chiropractic.wyo.gov/license-lookup
Clinical/Certified Social Worker	https://sites.google.com/a/wyo.gov/wyoming-mental-health-professions-licensing-board/license-verification
Collection Agency	http://wyomingbankingdivision.wyo.gov/home/collection-agency-board
Controlled Substance Registrants	https://wybop.glsuite.us/GLSuiteweb/clients/wybop/public/verification/search.aspx
Cosmetologist	https://wyboc.glsuite.us/glsuiteweb/clients/wyboc/public/verificationsearch.aspx
Cosmetology Instructor/School	https://wyboc.glsuite.us/glsuiteweb/clients/wyboc/public/verificationsearch.aspx
Counselor, Professional	https://sites.google.com/a/wyo.gov/wyoming-mental-health-professions-licensing-board/license-verification
Crematory Operator	https://sites.google.com/a/wyo.gov/board-of-funeral-service-practitioners/public/verification
Dental Assistant/Hygienist	http://dental.wyo.gov/public/verification
Dentist	http://dental.wyo.gov/public/verification
Electrical Inspectors	http://wsfm.wyo.gov/electrical-safety/personnel-and-inspectors
Embalmer	https://sites.google.com/a/wyo.gov/board-of-funeral-service-practitioners/public/verification
Engineer, Professional	http://engineersroster.wyo.gov/
Esthetician	https://wyboc.glsuite.us/glsuiteweb/clients/wyboc/public/verificationsearch.aspx
Funeral Director	https://sites.google.com/a/wyo.gov/board-of-funeral-service-practitioners/public/verification
Funeral Pre-Need Agent	https://www.sircon.com/ComplianceExpress/Inquiry/consumerInquiry.do
Geologist/Geologist-in-training	http://wbpg.wy.gov/RosterSearch.aspx
Hearing Aid Specialist	http://hearingaid.wyo.gov/public/license-verification
Insurance Claims Adjuster	https://www.sircon.com/ComplianceExpress/Inquiry/consumerInquiry.do
Insurance Consultant/Producer/Service Rep	https://www.sircon.com/ComplianceExpress/Inquiry/consumerInquiry.do
Landscape Architect	https://sites.google.com/a/wyo.gov/architects/verification
Lobbyist	http://soswy.state.wy.us/Elections/Lobbying.aspx
Manicurist/Nail Technician	https://wyboc.glsuite.us/glsuiteweb/clients/wyboc/public/verificationsearch.aspx
Marriage & Family Therapist	https://sites.google.com/a/wyo.gov/wyoming-mental-health-professions-licensing-board/license-verification
Mental Health Worker	https://sites.google.com/a/wyo.gov/wyoming-mental-health-professions-licensing-board/license-verification
Midwife	https://sites.google.com/a/wyo.gov/wyoming-midwifery-board/public/license-verification
Motor Club Agent	https://www.sircon.com/ComplianceExpress/Inquiry/consumerInquiry.do
Nurse-LPN/RN/Aide/CAN-Discipline	https://nursing-online.state.wy.us/Verifications.aspx
Nurse-LPN/RN/Aide/CAN-List	https://nursing-online.state.wy.us/Verifications.aspx
Occupational Therapist/Assistant	http://ot.state.wy.us/search.aspx
Optometrist	http://optometry.wyo.gov/public/license-verification
Outfitter	http://outfitters.state.wy.us/PDF%5Cdirectory%5COutfitterDirectory.pdf

Pharmacist/Pharmacy Technician .... https://wybop.glsuite.us/GLSuiteweb/clients/wybop/public/verification/search.aspx
Pharmacy, Institutional .... https://wybop.glsuite.us/GLSuiteweb/clients/wybop/public/verification/search.aspx
Physical Therapist/Assistant................................ https://sites.google.com/a/wyo.gov/wyoming-board-of-physical-therapy/public/verification
Physician Assistant.. https://wybom.glsuite.us/GLSuiteWeb/Clients/WYBOM/Public/LicenseeSearch.aspx?SearchType=PA
Physician/Medical Doctor/Psychiatrist.............. https://wybom.glsuite.us/GLSuiteWeb/Clients/WYBOM/Public/LicenseeSearch.aspx
Physicians - Disciplinary Actions .... http://wyomedboard.wyo.gov/consumers/alphabetical-disciplinary-action-list
Podiatrist... https://sites.google.com/a/wyo.gov/wyoming-board-of-podiatry/public/license-verification
Prescription Drugs/Substances Mfg/Seller .... https://wybop.glsuite.us/GLSuiteweb/clients/wybop/public/verification/search.aspx
Property Appraiser.. https://wyrec.glsuite.us/glsuiteweb/Clients/WYREC/public/verification/search.aspx
Psychologist/Psychological Practitioner .... https://sites.google.com/a/wyo.gov/psychology/public/verification
Radiologic Technologist/Technician .... https://sites.google.com/a/wyo.gov/rad-tech/public/verification
Real Estate Agent... https://wyrec.glsuite.us/glsuiteweb/Clients/WYREC/public/verification/search.aspx
Real Estate Appraiser... https://wyrec.glsuite.us/glsuiteweb/Clients/WYREC/public/verification/search.aspx
Reinsurance Intermediary..................................... https://www.sircon.com/ComplianceExpress/Inquiry/consumerInquiry.do
Rental Car Agents .... https://www.sircon.com/ComplianceExpress/Inquiry/consumerInquiry.do
Retail Pharmacy .... https://wybop.glsuite.us/GLSuiteWeb/clients/wybop/public/verification/search.aspx
Risk Retention .... https://www.sircon.com/ComplianceExpress/Inquiry/consumerInquiry.do
School Psychologist/Specialist............................ https://sites.google.com/a/wyo.gov/psychology/public/verification
Social Worker ....https://sites.google.com/a/wyo.gov/wyoming-mental-health-professions-licensing-board/license-verification
Speech Pathologist/Audiologist .... http://speech.wyo.gov/public/license-verification
Surplus Line Broker, Resident............................. https://www.sircon.com/ComplianceExpress/Inquiry/consumerInquiry.do
Surveyor, Land .... http://engineersroster.wyo.gov/
Third Party Administrator..................................... https://www.sircon.com/ComplianceExpress/Inquiry/consumerInquiry.do
Travel & Baggage Agent....................................... https://www.sircon.com/ComplianceExpress/Inquiry/consumerInquiry.do
Veterinarian .... https://sites.google.com/a/wyo.gov/veterinary-medicine-board/public/verification
Water Dist/Collection Operator............................ https://opcert.wqd.apps.deq.wyoming.gov/Login.aspx
Water/Waste Treatm't Plant Operator .... https://opcert.wqd.apps.deq.wyoming.gov/Login.aspx

State and Local Courts

About Wyoming Courts: Each county has a **District Court** which oversees felony criminal cases, large civil cases, and juvenile and probate matters.

The **Circuit Court** is of limited jurisdiction and oversee civil cases when the amount sought does not exceed $50,000 (raised from $7,000 effective 07/2011) and small claims to $5,000. Circuit Courts also hear family violence cases and all misdemeanors. Three counties have two Circuit Courts each: Fremont, Park, and Sweetwater. Cases may be filed in either of the two court offices in those counties, and records requests are referred between the two courts. At one time the Circuit Courts were known as Justice Courts. Effective January 1, 2003, all Justice Courts became Circuit Courts and follow Circuit Court rules. A circuit court may also have the jurisdiction of a municipal court over ordinance violations if requested by a municipality.

Municipal Courts operate in all incorporated cities and towns; their jurisdiction covers all ordinance violations and has no civil jurisdiction. The Municipal Court judge may assess penalties of up to $750 and/or six months in jail.

The web page for the Judicial Branch is www.courts.state.wy.us.

Appellate Courts: The Supreme Court is the court of last resort. There is no intermediate court of appeals. Most cases docketed in the Supreme Court are appeals from District courts. The docket is searchable from the web page.

Online Court Access

Wyoming's statewide case management system is for internal use only. Planning is underway for a new case management system that will ultimately allow public access.

But at this time there is no online access to civil, criminal, or other court case files or dockets.

Recorders, Assessors, and Other Sites of Note

About Wyoming Recording Offices: 23 counties, 23 recording offices. The recording officer is the County Clerk.

About Tax Liens: Federal tax liens on personal property of businesses are filed with the Secretary of State. Other federal and all state tax liens are filed with the County Clerk..

Online Access

There is no statewide database of county recorder or assessor data. However, 12 counties offer online access to recorded documents and 19 counties provide online access to property or assessor records.

Albany County   *Recorded Documents*   www.co.albany.wy.us/Clerk.aspx   For subscription services contact IT Department at 307-721-5500.
Property, Taxation Records   Search the county assessor database free at http://assessor.co.albany.wy.us. Also, access to GIS/mapping for free at www.co.albany.wy.us/map/.

Campbell County   *Property, Taxation Records*   Search property records free at https://www.ccgov.net/131/Property-Search.

Carbon County   *Recorded Documents*   www.carbonwy.com/index.aspx?nid=938   The county site is at http://gov.arcasearchdev.com/uswycb/.
Property, Taxation Records   Access to GIS/mapping free at http://gis.carbonwy.com/. Also, access to property data free at http://assessor.carbonwy.com/.

Converse County   *Recorded Documents*   http://conversecounty.org/gov-admin/county-clerk   Access to recorded documents for a fee at https://www.idocmarket.com/. Free registration.
Property, Taxation Records   Access to Assessor's maps for free at http://conversecounty.org/gov-admin/county-assessor/maps.

Crook County   *Recorded Documents*   www.crookcounty.wy.gov/elected_officials/clerk/index.php   Access to records for a fee at www.crookcounty.wy.gov/elected_officials/clerk/online_land_records.php. Fee is $250.00 annually or $25.00 per month. Must have a valid username and password to access the site.
Property, Taxation Records   Access to property ownership maps for free at www.crookcounty.wy.gov/elected_officials/assessor/property_ownership_maps/index.php.

Fremont County   *Recorded Documents*   http://fremontcountywy.org/county-clerk/   Access to records database (basic) for free at http://216.67.176.27/recorder/web/. Documents from 9/1/88 to present. For detailed records must subscribe. Some older documents are available by accessing ArcaSearch at http://news2.arcasearch.com/uswyfr/.
Property, Taxation Records   Access to GIS/mapping for free at http://maps.greenwoodmap.com/fremontwy/.

Goshen County   *Recorded Documents*   www.goshencounty.org/index.php/clerk   Access to records for a fee at http://idoc.goshencounty.org/. Must subscribe before use. Contact the County Clerk's office at 307-532-4051 and ask for Donna or Julie for pro-rated fee.
Property, Taxation Records   Access to property details search for free at www.goshencounty.org/assessor/property_detail/basicsearch.php.

Hot Springs County   *Property, Taxation Records*   Access GIS/mapping data for free at http://cama.state.wy.us/DISTRICTS/MAPS_ONLINEDOCUMENTS/ShowMAPS_ONLINEDOCUMENTSTable.aspx. Also, access to MapServer for free at http://maps.hscounty.com/mapserver/.

Johnson County   *Recorded Documents*   www.johnsoncountywyoming.org/government/clerk/   Access to recorded documents for a fee at https://www.idocmarket.com/. Free registration.
Property, Taxation Records   Access to GIS/mapping free at http://maps.greenwoodmap.com/johnson/.

Laramie County   *Recorded Documents, Marriage Indices Records*   www.laramiecountyclerk.com/   Indices from 1985 back to patent are available at http://gov.arcasearchdev.com/uswylar/. Access to recorded documents for a fee at https://www.idocmarket.com/. Free registration.
Property, Taxation Records   Search property data free at http://arcims.laramiecounty.com/ but no name searching.

Natrona County   *Recorded Documents*   www.natronacounty-wy.gov/index.aspx?nid=18   Access to recorded documents for a fee at https://www.idocmarket.com/. Free registration.
Property, Taxation Records   Access to property search information for free at www.natronacounty-wy.gov/index.aspx?NID=311.

Niobrara County   *Property, Taxation Records*   Access to Parcel Viewer for free at www.niobraracounty.org/_departments/_assessor/parcel_viewer.asp.

Park County   *Property, Taxation Records*   Search the county tax database by property owner or by address or by property Tax ID at http://itax.parkcounty.us/. Also, access to GIS/mapping and property search for free at http://mapserver.parkcounty.us/.

Sheridan County   *Property, Taxation Records*   Access county property tax records free at https://itax.tylertech.com/SheridanWY/. Also, a GIS-mapping site provides parcel data free at www.sheridancounty.com/depts/information-technology/gis-and-interactive-mapping/.

Sublette County *Property, Taxation Records*   Access property data and GIS-mapping free at www.sublettewyo.com/index.aspx?NID=35. Also, access to county land records search for free at http://maps.greenwoodmap.com/sublette/clerk/query/.

Sweetwater County *Recorded Documents* https://www.sweet.wy.us/index.aspx?nid=65   There is both a free and subscription service at http://idoc.sweet.wy.us/. Online land records available from 9/85 to present. Online UCC records available from 10/11 to current.
Property, Taxation Records   Search property tax and assessements at https://www.sweet.wy.us/index.aspx?NID=210.

Teton County *Recorded Documents* www.tetonwyo.org/cc   Access to the Clerk's database of scanned images is free at http://maps.greenwoodmap.com/tetonwy/clerk/query/. Search for complete documents back to 7/1996; partial documents back to 4/1991.
Property, Taxation Records   Access to Assessor's Tax Roll and GIS system is free at http://tetonwy.greenwoodmap.com/gis/download/. Must register first time. The Assessor's Tax Roll is downloadable at www.tetonwyo.org/assess/topics/assessor-list/100084/.

Uinta County *Recorded Documents* www.uintacounty.com/16/County-Clerk-Recorder   Access to records for free at http://property.uintacounty.com/RecordingsSearch.aspx.
Property, Taxation Records   Access to property tax listing search for free at http://property.uintacounty.com/propertylistingsearch.aspx.

Washakie County *Property, Taxation Records*   Access to MapServer for free at http://maps.greenwoodmap.com/washakie/map.

Chapter 7

Searching Federal Court Records

Searching records at the federal court system can be one of the easiest or one of the most frustrating experiences that public record searchers may encounter. Although the federal court system offers advanced electronic search capabilities, at times it is practically impossible to properly identify a subject when searching civil or criminal records. Before reviewing searching procedures, a brief overview is in order.

Federal Court Structure

At the federal level, all cases involve federal or U.S. constitutional law or interstate commerce. The federal court system includes three levels of courts, plus several specialty courts. The home page for the U.S. Courts is www.uscourts.gov.

U. S. District Courts

The United States District Courts are the **trial courts** of the federal court system. District Courts have jurisdiction over civil and criminal matters.

Overall, there are 94 federal judicial districts, with at least one district in each state, the District of Columbia and Puerto Rico. The three territories of the United States (the Virgin Islands, Guam, and the Northern Mariana Islands) also have District Courts that hear federal cases.

Technically, Bankruptcy Courts are actually units of the U.S. District Courts.

U. S. Bankruptcy Courts

Each of the 94 federal judicial districts handles bankruptcy matters through the U.S. Bankruptcy Courts. The Bankruptcy Courts often use the same hearing locations (building) as the District Courts. If court locations differ, the usual variance is to have fewer Bankruptcy Court locations.

In some states, such as Colorado, the U.S. District Court or the Bankruptcy Court is comprised of a single judicial district. Others states, such as California, are composed of multiple judicial districts – Central, Eastern, Northern, and Southern. Also, within each judicial district there can be multiple divisions. Counting all the divisions and districts, there are actually over 280 U.S. District Court locations and nearly 195 U.S. Bankruptcy Court locations.

United States Court of Appeals

The 94 judicial districts are organized into 12 regional circuits, each of which has a United States Court of Appeals. A Court of Appeals hears appeals from the district courts located within its circuit, as well as appeals from decisions of federal administrative agencies.

In addition, the Court of Appeals for the Federal Circuit has nationwide jurisdiction to hear appeals in specialized cases, such as those involving patent laws and cases decided by the Court of International Trade and the Court of Federal Claims.

Supreme Court of the United States

The Supreme Court of the United States is the court of last resort in the United States. The Supreme Court is located in Washington, DC and it hears appeals from the United States Courts of Appeals and from the highest courts of each state.

How Federal Trial Court Case Records are Organized

Indexing and Case Numbering

Federal court cases are organized very similar to the state courts. When a case is filed with a federal court, a case number is assigned and dockets are used. District courts index by defendant and plaintiff as well as by case number. Bankruptcy courts usually index by debtor and case number. Therefore, when you search by name you will first receive a listing of all cases where the name appears, both as plaintiff and defendant.

To view case records you will need to know, or find, the applicable case number. Case numbering procedures are not consistent throughout the federal court system. One judicial district may assign numbers by district while another may assign numbers by location (division) within that judicial district, or by judge within the division. Remember that case numbers appearing in legal text citations may not be adequate for searching unless they appear in the proper form for that particular court.

Case Assignments and Court Locations

At one time, all cases were assigned to a specific district or division based on the county of origination. Although this is still true in most states, computerized tracking of dockets has led to a more flexible approach to case assignment. For example, rather than blindly assigning all cases originating from one county to designated court location, some Districts use random numbers and other methods to logically balance caseloads among their judges, regardless of the location. This trend seemingly confuses the case search process. But finding cases has become significantly easier with the availability of Case Management/ Electronic Case Files (CM/ECF) and the PACER Case Locator (see descriptions to follow). Most case files created prior to 1999 were maintained in paper format only. Since 2006, all cases are filed electronically through CM/ECF.

Case information and images of documents are available the individual federal courts for a timeframe determined by that court and then are forwarded to a designated Federal Records Center (FRC), found at archives.gov/frc. Older case files may be ordered from the court which in turn obtains the needed documents directly from the FRC.

Electronic Access - CM/ECF and PACER

The two important acronyms associated with federal court case information are CM/ECF and PACER.

Case Management/Electronic Case Files (CM/ECF)

CM/ECF is the case management system for the Federal Judiciary used by all Bankruptcy, District, and Appellate courts. The CM/ECF system allows attorneys to file and manage cases documents electronically and offers expanded search and reporting capabilities.

A significant fact affecting record researchers is the CM/ECF Rules of Procedure that require filers redact certain personal identifying information. This means filings cannot include the full Social Security or taxpayer-identification numbers, full dates of birth, names of minor children, financial account numbers, and in criminal cases, home addresses, from their filings.

For further information on CM/ECF, visit pacer.gov/cmecf/index.html.

PACER and the PACER Case Locator

PACER, an acronym for Public Access to Electronic Court Records, is the electronic subscription service that allows the public to obtain case and docket information from the U.S. District, Bankruptcy, and Appellate courts. The site is pacer.gov.

To search for records, you must know the individual court where the case was filed or held. Therefore, a researcher will likely need to use the PACER Case Locator – a national index for U.S. District, Bankruptcy, and Appellate courts. Using the Case Locator, a researcher can determine whether or not a party is involved in federal litigation and, if so, the court location.

The information gathered from the PACER system is a matter of public record and may be reproduced without permission. Essentially each court maintains its own database of case information and decides what to make available on PACER. PACER normally provides the following information:

- A listing of all parties and participants including judges, attorneys, trustees
- A compilation of case related information such as cause of action, nature of suit, dollar demand
- A chronology of dates of case events entered in the case record
- A claims registry
- A listing of new cases each day in the bankruptcy courts
- Appellate court opinions
- Judgments or case status
- Types of case documents filed for certain districts.

PACER Fees

Registration and fees are required to use PACER. Electronic access to any case document, docket sheet, or case specific report is $0.10 per page, not to exceed the fee for thirty pages. The fee to access an audio file of a court hearing via PACER is $2.40 per audio file. If an account holder does not accrue charges of more than $15.00 in a quarterly billing cycle there is no fee charged.

Bankruptcy Records and the Multi-Court Voice Case Information System (McVCIS)

McVCIS (Multi-Court Voice Case Information System) is a another means of accessing information regarding open bankruptcy cases. Information is available 24/7 by using a touch-tone telephone. An automated voice response system will read a limited amount of bankruptcy case information directly from the court's database in response to touch-tone telephone inquiries. The advantage? There is no charge. Individual names are entered last name first with as much of the first name as you wish to include. For example, Joe B. Cool could be entered as COOLJ or COOLJOE. Do not enter the middle initial. Business names are entered as they are written, without blanks.

At one time each Bankruptcy Court had its own telephone number (VCIS) associated with this service. But now all Bankruptcy Courts provide access through one centralized phone number at 866-222-8019 and the service is now referred to as McVCIS, which stands for Multi-Court Voice Case Information System. But some courts still refer to the service as VCIS on their Web page.

Federal Court Record Searching Hints

The best way to search federal court records is to make use of CM/ECF, PACER, and McVCIS. If you have trouble finding the location of a current case (there can be multiple Divisions within a District), then also check the Web page of the court for the assigned counties for each Division. A Federal Court Locator is at www.uscourts.gov/court_locator.aspx.

As mentioned, one of the biggest problems when searching federal court records is the lack of identifiers. As mentioned, very few identifiers are entered in the CM/ECF system. See below. Federal courts have a well deserved reputation of no longer providing the means to accurately identify a subject of a search.

The Issue of Few Identifiers on Federal Court Records

However, you cannot search civil or criminal litigation at the District Courts by the Social Security Number. Those searches can only be conducted by name. According to public record search expert Lynn Peterson, you might be able to find SSNs buried in some older case files, but now they are truncated.

There are three ways to search for records at the District & Bankruptcy Courts:

1. By name
2. By last 4 digits of the SSN plus the name.
3. By full SSN.

What to Do When Record Search Results Do Not Include Identifiers

This is a struggle and a tough problem to solve, especially if a researcher is dealing with a common name and trying to match a court case to a specific subject (perosn). Below are several ideas to help verify a subject's identity.

- **View Case Files** - Review the documents found in the case files for any hints of identification.
- **Call an Attorney Involved in the Case** - The docket will list the attorney (or prosecuting attorney) involved in a case. Sometime the people will help you determine the identity of a subject.
- **Check Incarceration Records** - Searching prison records is an alternative means for identity verification. Search the Bureau of Prisons at bop.gov.
- **Check the News Media** - Some record searchers have been successful in confirming an identity by using news media sources such as newspapers and the Web. Even blogs may help.

Obtaining Closed Case Files and the Federal Records Centers

After a federal case is closed, the documents are held by the federal courts location for a predetermined time. This can be as little as immediately or as long as 15 years. The closed cases are then sent to and stored at a designated Federal Records Center (FRC). These offices are administered by the National Archives and Records Administration (NARA). See www.archives.gov/research. This procedure applies to all closed bankruptcy, civil, criminal, and court of appeals case files

The National Archives and Records Administration (NARA) provides access to archived court records exclusively by online ordering or by mail or fax. NARA once provided on-site court case review services to the public at its Federal Records Centers. But now access to court cases is available only via online ordering at www.archives.gov/research/court-records or by mail or fax at these facilities.

A list of Federal Record Centers with phone numbers, web pages, and list of the federal courts serviced at each FRC is found at www.brbpublications.com/documents/federal.records.centers.pdf

Other Federal Courts

Three significant additional courts were created to hear cases or appeals for certain areas of litigation that demand special expertise. These courts are the U.S. Tax Court, the Court of International Trade, and the U.S. Court of Federal Claims.

U.S. Court of Federal Claims

The Court of Federal Claims is authorized to primarily hear money claims in regard to federal statutes, executive regulations, the Constitution, or contracts, expressed- or implied-in-fact, with the United States. Approximately a quarter of the cases involve complex factual and statutory construction issues in tax law. About a third of the cases involve government contracts. Cases involving environmental and natural resource issues make up about ten percent of the caseload. Another significant category of cases involve civilian and military pay questions. In addition, the Court hears intellectual property, Indian Tribe, and various statutory claims against the United States by individuals, domestic and foreign corporations, states and localities, Indian Tribes and Nations, and foreign nationals and governments.

Direct questions to the U.S. Court of Federal Claims, Attention: Clerks Office, 717 Madison Place, NW, Washington, DC 20005, or call 202-357-6400. See www.uscfc.uscourts.gov.

U.S. Tax Court

The jurisdiction of the U.S. Tax Court includes the authority to hear tax disputes concerning notices of deficiency, notices of transferee liability, certain types of declaratory judgment, readjustment and adjustment of partnership items, review of the failure to abate interest, administrative costs, worker classification, relief from joint and several liability on a joint return, and review of certain collection actions.

Docket information is available for cases filed on or after May 1, 1986. Call Docket Information at 202-521-4650. For case records, call Records and Reproduction at 202-521-4688. Direct questions to the U.S. Tax Court at 400 Second Street, NW, Washington, DC 20217. The main number is 202-521-0700. Dockets and opinions also may be searched from the home page at www.ustaxcourt.gov.

U.S. Court of International Trade

The U.S. Court of International Trade oversees disputes within the international trade community for individuals, foreign and domestic manufacturers, consumer groups, trade associations, labor unions, concerned citizens, and other nations.

The geographical jurisdiction of the United States Court of International Trade extends throughout the U.S. The court is also authorized to hold hearings in foreign countries. Appeals from final decisions of the court may be taken to the United States Court of Appeals for the Federal Circuit and, ultimately, to the Supreme Court of the United States.

The court provides online access to opinions and judgments. From 1999-2006, the Court published only the slip opinions online. Since January 1, 2007, the online postings contain both the slip opinion and judgment in each case. Registered users of the CM/ECF system have the ability to open a case as of October 11, 2006.

The Court's Administrative Office is located at One Federal Plaza, New York, New York 10278-0001, or call 212-264-2800. See www.cit.uscourts.gov

Meet the Authors

Cynthia Hetherington, CFE has more than 20 years of experience in research, investigations, and corporate intelligence. She is the founder of Hetherington Group, a consulting, publishing, and training firm focusing on intelligence, security, and investigations. Cynthia was the leader of Aon Consulting's Corporate Strategic Intelligence group. She was also named the 2012 James Baker Speaker of the Year for the Association of Certified Fraud Examiners.

A widely-published author, Cynthia authored *The Guide to Due Diligence Online* (2015), Business Background Investigations (2007), and co-authored The Manual to Online Public Records, 3rd Ed. (2013), published by Facts on Demand Press. She is the publisher of Data2know.com: Internet & Online Intelligence Newsletter and has co-authored articles on steganography, computer forensics, Internet investigations, and other security-focused monographs.

She is also recognized for providing corporate security officials, military intelligence units, and federal, state, and local agencies with training on online intelligence practices. In addition, Cynthia is also a faculty member at the Association of Certified Fraud Examiners, where she teaches a program on advanced Internet fraud investigations.

To contact Ms. Hetherington, please email her at ch@hetheringtongroup.com.

Michael Sankey is founder and CEO of BRB Publications, Inc. and is Director of the Public Record Retriever Network, one of the nation's largest membership organizations of professionals in the public record industry. Michael has more than 30 years of experience in research and public record access. He has authored or edited over 75 publications and editions including *The Sourcebook to Public Record Information, The Public Record Research TIPS Book*, and *The MVR Access and Decoder Digest*.

In the 1980s, he was president and CEO of Rapid Info Services, a national vendor of electronic-processed driving records.

Michael was a member of the Steering Committee that founded the National Association of Professional Background Screeners (NAPBS), a professional trade association for the screening industry. He was also elected to the first Board of Directors in 2004 and served two years.

He is regarded as a leading industry expert in public records, criminal record access, state DMV policies and procedures, as well as knowing who's who in the commercial arena of public information vendors.

To contact Michael, please email him at mike@brbpublications.com.